CRIMINAL LAW AND PROCEDURE FOR THE PARALEGAL
A SYSTEMS APPROACH
Second Edition

The West Legal Studies Series

Your options keep growing with West Legal Studies

Each year our list continues to offer you more options for every area of the law to meet your course or on-the-job reference requirements. We now have over 140 titles from which to choose in the following areas:

Administrative Law	Family Law
Alternative Dispute Resolution	Federal Taxation
Bankruptcy	Intellectual Property
Business Organizations/Corporations	Introduction to Law
Civil Litigation and Procedure	Introduction to Paralegalism
CLA Exam Preparation	Law Office Management
Client Accounting	Law Office Procedures
Computer in the Law Office	Legal Research, Writing, and Analysis
Constitutional Law	Legal Terminology
Contract Law	Paralegal Employment
Criminal Law and Procedure	Real Estate Law
Document Preparation	Reference Materials
Environmental Law	Torts and Personal Injury Law
Ethics	Will, Trusts, and Estate Administration

You will find unparalleled, practical support

Each book is augmented by instructor and student supplements to ensure the best learning experience possible. We also offer custom publishing and other benefits such as West's Student Achievement Award. In addition, our sales representatives are ready to provide you with dependable service.

We want to hear from you

Our best contributions for improving the quality of our books and instructional materials are feedback from the people who use them. If you have a question, concern, or observation about any of our materials, or you have a product proposal or manuscript, we want to hear from you. Please contact your local representative or write us at the following address:

West Legal Studies, 3 Columbia Circle, P.O. Box 15015, Albany, NY 12212-5015

For additional information point your browser at

www.westlegalstudies.com

WEST
™
THOMSON LEARNING

CRIMINAL LAW AND PROCEDURE FOR THE PARALEGAL

A SYSTEMS APPROACH

Second Edition

James W. H. McCord, J. D.

Eastern Kentucky University

Sandra L. McCord, M. A.

WEST

THOMSON LEARNING™

Australia Canada Mexico Singapore Spain United Kingdom United States

WEST

™

THOMSON LEARNING

WEST LEGAL STUDIES

Criminal Law and Procedure for the Paralegal A Systems Approach
Second Edition
by James W.H. McCord and Sandra L. McCord

Business Unit Director:
Susan L. Simpfenderfer

Executive Editor:
Marlene McHugh Pratt

Acquisitions Editor:
Joan M. Gill

Developmental Editor:
Rhonda Dearborn

Editorial Assistant:
Lisa Flatley

Executive Production Manager:
Wendy A. Troeger

Production Editor:
Betty L. Dickson

Cover Design:
McKinley Griffen Design

Cover Image:
Photo: www.comstock.com

Executive Marketing Manager:
Donna J. Lewis

Channel Manager:
Nigar Hale

For permission to use material from this text or product, contact us by
Tel   (800) 730-2214
Fax   (800) 730-2215
www.thomsonrights.com

Library of Congress Cataloging-in-Publication Data

McCord, James W. H.
    Criminal law and procedure for the paralegal a systems approach/James W. H. McCord and Sandra L. McCord— 2nd ed.
        p. cm.
    "West Legal Studies series."
    ISBN 0-7668-1965-5
    1. Criminal law—United States. 2. Criminal procedure— United States. 3. Legal assistants—United States—Handbooks, manuals, etc. I. McCord, Sandra L. II. Title.
    KF9219.3 .M33 2000
    345.73—dc21   00-043756

NOTICE TO THE READER

Publisher does not warrant or guarantee any of the products described herein or perform any independent analysis in connection with any of the product information contained herein. Publisher does not assume, and expressly disclaims, any obligation to obtain and include information other than that provided to it by the manufacturer.

The reader is notified that this text is an educational tool, not a practice book. Since the law is in constant change, no rule or statement of law in this book should be relied upon for any service to any client. The reader should always refer to standard legal sources for the current rule or law. If legal advice or other expert assistance is required, the services of the appropriate professional should be sought.

The Publisher makes no representation or warranties of any kind, including but not limited to, the warranties of fitness for particular purpose or merchantability, nor are any such representations implied with respect to the material set forth herein, and the publisher takes no responsibility with respect to such material. The publisher shall not be liable for any special, consequential, or exemplary damages resulting, in whole or part, from the readers' use of, or reliance upon, this material.

To our son
Quinten James McCord
with love

Contents

4   CRIMES AGAINST PERSONS AND CRIMES AGAINST HABITATION   77

5   CRIMES AGAINST PROPERTY, PUBLIC ORDER AND SAFETY, PUBLIC MORALS, AND JUSTICE AND PUBLIC ADMINISTRATION   139

6   INCHOATE AND ORGANIZED CRIMES   185

7   DEFENSES   223

8   INTAKE AND DRAFTING THE COMPLAINT   263

11   PRETRIAL: INITIAL APPEARANCE TO PRELIMINARY HEARING   409

12   PRETRIAL: GRAND JURY TO PRETRIAL CONFERENCE   443

TABLE OF EXHIBITS

TABLE OF CASES

PREFACE

This thoroughly revised and completely updated second edition of *Criminal Law and Procedure for the Paralegal A Systems Approach* provides more practice skills and competencies for paralegal majors studying criminal law than any similar text. It helps to prepare students for that first day on the job, while providing the skills and knowledge to adapt to the demands of a dynamic area of employment. The text is not limited to study by paralegal students, however. Its clear organization and presentation of the law make it appropriate for all types of undergraduate courses on criminal law and procedure. In addition, practicing paralegals and other persons on the legal team will find that the step-by-step coverage of each stage of the criminal process and the related checklists, forms, Web sites, practice tips, and ethical standards comprise a valuable office resource.

The text is comprehensive and generously complemented with examples of actual cases, which make concepts easy to grasp and make learning more interesting. Its relevancy is based not only on our own research and experience, but also on the advice and experience of a number of paralegals working in the field, as well as colleagues in education and criminal law. For professors, the text provides the opportunity for a variety of teaching approaches—traditional reading and lecture, discussion, critical thinking and analysis, problem solving, group work, research, self-directed study, law office simulation, role playing, and others.

ORGANIZATION OF TEXT

The text has two main sections; one on substantive criminal law and one on criminal procedure. The substantive section emphasizes the foundations of law and its institutions, and the elements and rationale for each class of crimes. On completion of this section, students should not only know the principles of law and their sources, but also how to apply that law to factual situations to determine what crimes have been committed.

Chapter 8, "Intake and Drafting the Complaint," is placed at the end of this first section to immediately apply the knowledge gained in the substantive chapters, and to bring some practical hands-on skills into this first section. Instructors may decide to teach this chapter later in the second section on procedure.

The second section on procedure emphasizes the legal principles, rules, and step-by-step practice skills needed for a paralegal involved in criminal litigation from the perspective of both prosecution and defense.

In general, the text introduces a concept, crime, or procedure as it most commonly occurs. Then examples further explain the scope and possible variations on the topic.

It is the aim of the text for students to become knowledgeable about their state law and practice as well as federal law and practice. Sample cases and forms use the state of Columbia as a stand-in for your state. Use every opportunity that time permits to apply the law, cases, and rules of procedure of your state to the issues, problems, and assignments in this text. Space is provided in the text's tables for you to add state-specific information.

FEATURES OF THE TEXT

- **Case Law** Precedent and illustrative cases are quoted in the text to emphasize key principles of law and enhance legal reasoning. Numerous other cases are cited as examples to reinforce key concepts, illustrate variations in statutes and court interpretations, and stimulate inquiry and problem solving. Case citations are not included in the text but are compiled in the Table of Cases in the front of the text.

- **Sample Practice Forms and Checklists** Many practice forms, pleadings, motions, and other documents are included to provide familiarity with forms and to give a basis from which to work with state forms or to draft forms. Checklists give step-by-step guidance in specific practice situations and provide examples for developing additional checklists as needed.

- **Graphs, Diagrams, Tables, and Charts** Visual aids facilitate learning, stimulate interest, and summarize and organize important information. Space is provided in exhibits for the addition of state-specific information.

- **Sample Jury Instructions** Jury instructions are an excellent resource for legal definitions and elements of crimes. Samples are included throughout the text to illustrate elements of crimes, for comparisons with your state instructions, and as a resource in research and drafting assignments.

- **Legal Terminology and Notable Quotations** Key legal terms are highlighted in bold and defined in the text as well as in the margins for quick access. They also are listed at the end of each chapter and in the Glossary at the end of the text. Appendix A is a glossary of Spanish equivalents for important legal terms in English. Quotations related to criminal law appear in the text and in the margins to emphasize ideas and provoke thought and discussion (and maybe a smile) about the subject matter.

- **Application of Knowledge** Each chapter, according to its focus, contains a varying balance of exercises for in-class or out-of-class assignments and discussions.

  Analysis problems throughout the chapters present legal issues, social concerns, or other problems to stimulate critical thinking and analysis.

  System folder assignments structure the building of an impressive practice system of topically arranged forms, legal principles, rules, checklists, and other material. An outline of the system folder contents is in Appendix B. Practical time restraints may dictate that some or all of the summaries or outlines of the law and rules referred to in the system folder assignments be reduced to short lists of citations to applicable statues, rules, and cases. References to pertinent pages in the text can be a useful time-saver for students intending to keep the text.

  Application assignments require the application of legal principles to new fact situations or to practice skills in research and writing.

  Helpful Web sites provide useful electronic resources.

  Internet exercises encourage familiarity with electronic research.

  Study and review questions are deliberately comprehensive to provide a method of learning and reviewing important material for the student. Instructors can use the study questions as a pre- or posttest, and students can use them as a study guide for exams.

NEW THROUGHOUT THE SECOND EDITION

New Analysis Problems, Questions for Study and Review, and Application Assignments have been added throughout to correspond to new text material.

■ **New Feature: Helpful Web Sites**
At the end of Chapter 1 is a list of general law research Web sites. Subsequent chapters each include a list of Web sites that pertain to that chapter's subject matter. These Web sites can be used for research, assignments, and general interest. Chapter 3 includes a site that follows a murder case from beginning to end, which might be the focus of a course-long assignment.

■ **New Feature: Internet Exercises**
The Internet exercises have two purposes: to help students become familiar with some of the law-related sites available and to provide substantive research assignments.

■ **Edited text of many new cases**
Both landmark decisions and cases illustrating the scope of a particular crime or issue are included.

■ **Updated and numerous illustrative case examples**
Case references demonstrate how issues have been decided in various jurisdictions.

■ **Repositioned exhibits to enhance the flow of text**
Long exhibits and exhibits that are concentrated in one area of the text have been moved to the ends of the chapters where they can be easily found, and where they do not interrupt the text or force readers to hopscotch through pages of exhibits to follow the thread of the narrative.

■ **Appendix B, "System Folder Contents"**
The system folder contents can help organize assignments and serve as a table of contents for the completed system folder.

■ **Appendix C, "Excerpts from the Constitution of the United States of America"**
Sections of the Constitution pertinent to text materials are included.

CHANGES BY CHAPTER

Chapter 1

- Foundations of criminal law is moved from Chapter 2 and expanded to include federalism and police power
- Updated current crime trends
- Revisions in punishment and classification of crimes sections

Chapter 2

- Updated and streamlined

Chapter 3

- New section on corporate crimes, including the text of a corporate negligence case
- Significant revision of mens rea, strict liability, and supervening and superseding causes sections
- New section on concurrence
- Revisions in complicity and vicarious liability sections

Chapter 4

- First edition Chapter 4 is split into Chapters 4 and 5 and expanded
- New sections on lesser included offenses, reckless endangerment, terroristic threatening, stalking, hate crimes, civil rights violations, and Megan's Law and sexually violent predator acts

- Substantially revised and expanded section on criminal abuse, including provisions of the Violence Against Women Act and elder abuse
- Text of the Tennessee sexual battery statutes and two cases based on those statutes
- Edited texts of cases on elements of manslaughter, assault and battery, and custodial interference
- Revised and expanded sections on homicide, false imprisonment, and custodial interference

Chapter 5

- New sections on bad checks, cybercrimes, white-collar crime, health care fraud, trademark infringement, economic espionage, money laundering, securities fraud, endangering public health and environment, use and distribution of firearms, new Internet obscenity laws, child pornography and exploitation, and gambling
- Substantially revised and expanded sections on larceny, fraud, and disorderly conduct
- Edited text of cases dealing with issues of use of force after robbery, larceny involving mistakenly honored bank overdrafts, insider trading, and standards for determining child pornography
- Revisions of sections on embezzlement, receiving stolen property, robbery, drug offenses, crimes against justice and public administration

Chapter 6

- New sections on hearsay exception in conspiracy, RICO, continuing criminal enterprise, and criminal gang control
- Edited text of cases involving issues of substantial step in attempt, unilateral conspiracy, hearsay exception in conspiracy, and meaning of "organizer" in continuing criminal enterprise (CCE)
- Revision of conspiracy section to include "wheel" and "chain" conspiracies and an update on the last conspirator defense

Chapter 7

- Substantially expanded sections on burden of proof, necessity, entrapment, and syndromes
- Edited text of cases involving issues of subjective and objective entrapment standards and requirements of the M'Naghten insanity defense

Chapter 8

- Updates and clarifications

Chapter 9

- New or expanded discussions on state action, computer searches, anticipatory search warrants, sufficient suspicion for stop and frisk, vehicle searches, suspicionless drug tests and student searches, community caretaking function exception, and electronic surveillance
- Edited text of Supreme Court cases updating search and seizure issues: *Minnesota v. Carter, Whren v. U.S.,* and *Wyoming v. Houghten*

Chapter 10

- Recent cases on *Miranda*
- Impeachment exception to *Miranda*

Chapter 11

- Updates and clarifications
- Expanded section on extradition

Chapter 12

- New rules of criminal procedure
- New sections on motion to obtain funds for expert and notice of defenses
- Expanded sections on motion in limine and plea bargains

Chapter 13

- New rules of evidence
- Updates on racially motivated peremptory challenges
- Study of jury attitudes
- Updated section on scientific evidence

Chapter 14

- Updated sections on new limits on prisoners' suits and new habeas corpus restrictions
- Expanded section on sentencing guidelines and presentence report procedure
- New section on three strikes laws

ANCILLARY MATERIALS

TEACHING AIDS AND SUPPLEMENTS

Instructor's Manual with Test Bank The *Instructor's Manual* for this text is designed to save the instructor's time in organizing and preparing for class. Written by the authors of the text the *Instructor's Manual* contains the chapter objectives, lecture outlines, suggestions for supplementing class material, ideas for class activities, assignments and prepared solutions for application assignments, chapter test questions and answers.

Computerized Test Bank (Thomson Testing Tools) The Test Bank found in the *Instructor's Manual* is also available in a computerized format on CD-ROM. The platforms supported include Windows™ 3.1 and 95, Windows™ NT, and Macintosh. Features include:

- Multiple methods of question selection
- Multiple outputs—that is, print, ASCII, and RTF
- Graphic support (black and white)
- Random questioning output
- Special character support

Web Page Come visit our Web site at www.westlegalstudies.com, where you will find valuable information specific to this book such as hot links and sample materials to download, as well as other West Legal Studies products.

Survival Manual for Paralegal Students written by Bradene Moore and Kathleen Reed of the University of Toledo, covers practical and basic information to help students make the most of their paralegal courses. Topics covered include choosing courses of study and note-taking skills. ISBN 0-314-22111-5

Strategies and Tips for Paralegal Educators written by Anita Tebbe of Johnson County Community College, provides teaching strategies specifically designed for paralegal educators. A copy of this pamphlet is available to each adopter. Quantities for distribution to adjunct instructors are available for purchase at a minimal price. A coupon in the pamphlet provides ordering information. ISBN 0-314-04971-1

WESTLAW® West's on-line computerized legal research system offers students "hands-on" experience with a system commonly used in law offices. Qualified adopters can receive ten free hours of WESTLAW®. WESTLAW® can be accessed with Macintosh and IBM PC and compatibles. A modem is required.

Court TV Videos West Legal Studies is pleased to offer the following videos from Court TV. Available for a minimal fee:

Fentress v. Eli Lilly & Co., et al—Prozac on Trial
ISBN 0-7668-1095-X
Ohio v. Alfieri—Road Rage
ISBN 0-7668-1099-2
New York v. Ferguson—Murder on the 5:33: The Trial of Colin Ferguson
ISBN 0-7668-1098-4

West's Paralegal Video Library includes:

The Drama of the Law II: Paralegal Issues Video
ISBN 0-314-07088-5
I Never Said I Was a Lawyer Paralegal Ethics Video
ISBN 0-314-08049-X

These videos are available at no charge to qualified adopters.

> Please note the Internet resources are of a time sensitive nature and URL addresses may often change or be deleted.

Contact us at www.westlegalstudies@delmar.com

ABOUT THE AUTHORS

James W. H. McCord earned his law degree at the University of Wisconsin-Madison and practiced criminal and civil law for six years before becoming the first director of the paralegal program at Eastern Kentucky University, where he continues to serve both as an administrator and professor. He has served as president of the American Association for Paralegal Education, as a member of the American Bar Association Commission on Approval of Legal Assistant Programs, and he continues to be prominent in the field of paralegal education.

Sandra L. McCord earned her M.A. in comparative literature at the University of Wisconsin-Madison, has taught English composition at Eastern Kentucky University, and has published work in more than twenty-five literary journals.

The authors' experience with criminal law, teaching, and writing combine to make this a particularly clear and readable textbook. Whereas most criminal law texts are general in focus, this one was written specifically to prepare paralegals to work in the field of criminal law.

ACKNOWLEDGMENTS

A text such as this is a major undertaking, and its ultimate publication involves the work of more people than the authors. We acknowledge the special contributions of the following persons. Loving thanks go to Quinten McCord, our son, for his willingness to pitch in when needed and for his work on the case list, glossary, and other items. We are grateful to Marjorie Farris for her assistance in proofreading galleys and page proofs; to graduate assistants Jeff Forsell for some troubleshooting research and Thomas R. Brown for research on resources for victims of crimes; to Jim McCord's LAS 340 Criminal Law class at EKU for testing materials and providing comments; to Mark A. Evans, Law Library Assistant at Eastern Kentucky University, for tracking down citation problems; to Pamela Cox, Paralegal Program Secretary for her assistance on a variety of tasks; to David Grise, Assistant U.S. Attorney in Lexington, Kentucky, for his expertise and the sharing of numerous federal forms; and to the attorneys in the Department of Public Advocacy in Richmond, Kentucky, for their assistance.

The unique focus of the text on the tasks of the paralegal was greatly enhanced by the contributions of numerous paralegals. These persons include Chris Brown of Kentucky's Department of Public Advocacy in Frankfort, Kentucky, who provided us with a wealth of information and resources; Vicki Doolin Mills, Commonwealth Detective for Madison and Clark counties in Kentucky, who provided us with valuable insight and material on the role of the prosecution paralegal; Sarah J. Farris of the Madison County Attorney's Office; Denise M. Cunningham of the M. Lynne Osterholt Law Office in Louisville, Kentucky; and all of the other criminal law paralegals across the nation who have responded to our questions and provided valuable information.

Special thanks to Eastern Kentucky University for the use of its legal research and other resources.

Further, we thank the editors from West Legal Studies for all of their encouragement, suggestions, and outstanding help in bringing this book to publication. For the first edition, we thank Elizabeth Hannan, Acquisitions Editor; Patty Bryant, Developmental Editor; Peter Krall, Production Editor; and Amelia Jacobsen, Promotion Manager. For the second edition, we thank Joan Gill, Acquisitions Editor; Rhonda Dearborn, Developmental Editor; Betty Dickson, Production Editor; and Nigar Hale, Channel Manager. Our appreciation also goes to all who provided us with forms, exhibits, graphs, and cartoons, and the permission to reprint them.

Finally, we are deeply indebted for the many hours spent by our colleagues in reviewing drafts of the manuscript and giving us valuable encouragement and suggestions for improvement in the second edition. These reviewers include Chana Barron, Auburn University–Montgomery, Alabama; John Hinds, Draughons Junior College, Tennessee; Kathryn Myers, St. Mary of the Woods, Indiana; Lisa Rieger, University of Alaska; Gerald Rogers, Front Range Community College, Colorado; Kay Rute, Washburn University, Kansas; Joy Smucker, Highline Community College, Washington; and John O. Woodruff, Bay Path College, Massachusetts.

Jim and Sandy McCord
Richmond, Kentucky

FOUNDATIONS OF CRIMINAL LAW

I. INTRODUCTION

criminal law:
the branch of law that identifies conduct subject to prosecution and penalty by the state, and the procedure by which it is carried out.

Criminal law is the branch of law that identifies conduct subject to prosecution and penalty by the state, and the procedure by which it is carried out. Its purpose, broadly speaking, is to protect individuals and society from harmful conduct by punishing those who engage in it. An entire system has been established to implement criminal law. Paralegals are employed throughout that system, primarily by prosecutors, defense attorneys, judges, juvenile services offices, prisons, investigative services, a variety of police and law enforcement agencies, environmental enforcement, and other administrative agencies.

II. OVERVIEW OF THE LEGAL SYSTEM

A. RULE OF LAW

rule of law:
the principle that all people and organizations, both governmental and private, in a nation or state must obey the established laws rather than be above the law or conduct their lives and business any way they choose.

Criminal law is one component of a larger legal system: the system of the federal government, its territories, and the governments of each of the fifty states and their subdivisions (counties, parishes, townships, and municipal corporations). Underlying the formation of the legal system is the belief that society works best when citizens are subject to the **rule of law,** the principle that all people and organizations, both governmental and private, in a nation or state must obey the established laws rather than be above the law or conduct their lives and business any way they choose. This preeminence of law is expressed in the phrase, "a government of laws and not men." Pursuant to this most fundamental of principles of government, the founders of our nation established the Constitution of the United States.

B. THE CONSTITUTION

The Constitution and laws of the United States comprise the "supreme Law of the Land; and the judges in every State shall be bound thereby, any thing in the Constitution or Laws of any State to the Contrary notwithstanding" [Article VI, clause 2, United States Constitution]. Clause 3 of Article VI requires all government officials, state and federal, to be bound "by oath or affirmation" to support the Constitution.

federalism:
is the relationship between the national government and each state, and the relationship among states.

The governmental structure of the United States as set out in the Constitution, **federalism,** is the relationship between the national government and each state, and the relationship among states. In this legal network, the United States Constitution and laws reign supreme. The constitutions, laws, and conduct of state officials must comply with the Constitution. The federal government is limited by the Constitution to certain, significant powers (authority). Those powers relevant to criminal law include the power to punish counterfeiters, to punish piracy and crimes on the high seas, to regulate interstate and foreign commerce, and to make all laws necessary and proper for the federal government to exercise the powers specified in the Constitution. The last two broad powers, the regulation of interstate commerce and the enactment of laws necessary and proper, impact most importantly on the creation of a body of federal criminal law. Other federal crimes extend to violations related to civil rights, the military, the mail, and immigration and naturalization.

All powers not specifically vested in the federal government or prohibited to the states by the Constitution "are reserved to the States . . . or to the people" by the Tenth Amendment. Subject to the Constitution, each state is a sovereign entity with its own constitution, its own governmental bodies, and its own laws. Because the federal government enacts laws pursuant only to the powers specifically enumerated, most criminal law and the execution of it exists at the state level. Should there be a conflict between a federal and state law, the federal law prevails. If a specific federal law, however, is the same as a specific state law, then both laws are in effect and a person can be prosecuted under each respective law by the enacting governmental entity. A considerable body of law has evolved to define where federal authority ends and states rights begin.

Federalism also encompasses the relationship among states. Article IV of the Constitution dictates that each state, under the full faith and credit doctrine, shall recognize the acts, records, and judicial proceedings of another state. More specifically, a person accused of a crime in one state and captured in another state shall, on proper request, be returned to the state where the crime was committed.

In 1868, in the aftermath of the Civil War and slavery, the Fourteenth Amendment was added to the United States Constitution.

AMENDMENT XIV
Section 1. All persons born or naturalized in the United States, and subject to the jurisdiction thereof, are citizens of the United States and of the State wherein they reside. No State *shall make or enforce any law which shall abridge the privileges or immunities of citizens of the United States; nor shall any State deprive any person of life, liberty, or property, without due process of law; nor deny to any person within its jurisdiction the equal protection of the laws.* [Emphasis added]

As a general principle, this amendment ensured that the constitutional rights and liberties of all citizens could not be violated by the states. In the 1960s and 1970s nearly every right or protection enumerated in the Bill of Rights was "selectively incorporated" as a "fundamental right" into the Fourteenth Amendment by Supreme Court decisions.

C.   SEPARATION OF POWERS

The federal government and each state government is divided into three branches: the legislative, executive, and judicial. The doctrine of separation of powers delineates and limits these branches so that they can act as checks and balances to each other. In the criminal law context, the legislative branch enacts laws, the executive branch administers and executes the law, and the judicial branch decides disputes about the law and in that process interprets the law. Checks and balances keep one branch from encroaching on the others or becoming too powerful. Thus, the executive branch (president or governor) has the power to veto laws; the legislature has the power to allocate money for the operation of the executive and judicial branches and to appoint some officials in the other two branches; and the judicial branch has the power to strike down unconstitutional laws and acts of the other two branches.

Since *Marbury v. Madison* (1803) any law passed by the Congress of the United States must be fair and not abridge any provision of the Constitution (including the Bill of Rights). This landmark case established the concept of judicial review, the intention of the drafters of the Constitution that all statutes must fall within constitutional standards and if they did not, the courts of the United States had the right and obligation to declare the law unconstitutional. Thus, all laws, including criminal statutes, are subject to legal challenges and judicial review.

D.   POLICE POWER

Police power is the government's authority to enact laws to promote the public health, safety, morals, and welfare and, pursuant thereto, to establish police departments and prevent crimes. Police power stems from the purposes stated in the Preamble of the Constitution: "To . . . establish justice, insure domestic tranquility, . . . promote the general Welfare, and secure the Blessings of Liberty . . . ." The Constitution, as previously mentioned, gives Congress authority to address crime in specifically enumerated areas.

police power:
the government's authority to enact laws to promote the public health, safety, morals, and welfare and, pursuant thereto, to establish police departments and prevent crimes.

The states, however, have broad police power that is preserved by the Tenth Amendment. This power goes beyond establishing well-recognized crimes such as murder, assault, and theft to encompass criminal penalties for violating health and safety laws such as those regulating the work place, the environment, and housing codes. Police power also extends to morals and the protection of privacy.

The police power of the states to regulate conduct is not unlimited. It is subject to the restraint imposed by the Constitution of the United States, which includes the requirement that there be a compelling need to regulate the conduct, that the law not impinge on specific rights and liberties, and that the prohibited conduct be clearly defined for the public. One role of the defense is to examine the criminal statute being applied to the accused to see that it does not violate any of these limitations. The limits of police power are discussed in more detail in Chapter 7 defenses to criminal charges.

ANALYSIS PROBLEM

1–1. Concern has been voiced over the increased federalization of criminal law (passage of federal laws that parallel state crimes). Considering federalism and states rights issues, under what circumstances should the federal government add—or not add—new crime laws?

III. CRIMINAL LAW

A. PURPOSE OF CRIMINAL LAW

law:
a set of formal rules enacted by government officials that governs the relationships among citizens, businesses, government, and nations for the purpose of maintaining society and preventing chaos.

Civilization has given us the benefits of peace, order, safety, and freedom in varying degrees. One of the cornerstones in securing those benefits is law. **Law** is a dynamic force consisting of a set of formal rules enacted by government officials that governs the relationships among citizens, businesses, government, and nations for the purpose of maintaining society and preventing chaos. We might ask what life would be like without law. Hobbes answered in the *Leviathan*.

> [Without law] there is no place for industry; because the fruit thereof is uncertain; and consequently no Culture of the Earth, no Navigation, nor use of the commodities that may be imported by Sea; no commodious Building; no Instruments of moving, and removing such things as require much force; no Knowledge of the face of Earth; no account of Time; no Arts; no Letters; no Society; and which is worst of all, continuall feare, and danger of violent death; And the life of man, solitary, poore, nasty, brutish, and short.

The wisest legislators base the laws they write on the culmination of human experience. When law accomplishes its purpose to keep society in existence, functioning, and as free of chaos as possible, it gives us security, predictability, and efficiency; it allows us to use our time to be productive, creative, fulfilled human beings. Our own society has additional goals—goals that we believe are born of the highest expression of civilized human progress. These are freedom, equality, and the preservation of human dignity.

civil law:
law that defines the rights of individuals in their relationships with other individuals and establishes a process for righting wrongs, mainly through monetary reimbursement.

The system of law that aids us in our efforts to achieve these societal goals is divided into two main branches, civil law and criminal law. **Civil law** defines the rights of individuals in their relationships with other individuals. It defines our obligations and duties to each other and establishes a process for righting wrongs, mainly through monetary reimbursement. The major areas of civil law are contracts, real estate, probate, and personal injury.

Criminal law identifies conduct subject to prosecution and penalty by the state, and the procedure by which it is carried out. Common crimes include homicide, burglary, rape, battery, theft, treason, and others. Civil and criminal law overlap somewhat. Consider a person who wrongfully takes the property of another. The victim can sue that person to recover the property or to be paid for its loss. The state can prosecute the same person for theft and, if a conviction is reached, administer punishment of fines or imprisonment.

Civil law is designed to provide fair compensation for injured persons. Criminal law is designed to punish bad or immoral acts that carry a more serious social stigma than civil wrongs. Procedural rules in both areas are similar.

B. SOURCES OF CRIMINAL LAW

Our criminal law has evolved from the laws of previous civilizations: The Hebrews codified a strongly moral law based on the Mosaic Code (law of Moses) including the Ten Commandments; the Greeks used large citizen juries, defined the rights of citizens in a democracy, and were the first to believe laws were made by people and not by gods; the Romans built on Greek law and expanded it to include a reasonably complete body of criminal law that is the basis for much criminal law today; and the Roman Catholic Middle Ages preserved significant aspects of Roman and other law through the **canon law** of the church.

It was the English, however, who contributed the most to our current criminal law. Influenced by previous civilizations and institutions, the English went on to develop their own **common law** originating in the customs and traditions of a rural economy. As it was passed from generation to generation and applied by magistrates and judges, the common law was eventually recorded in thousands of judicial opinions. Each new generation of judges consulted previous opinions and became bound, more or less, to follow them. Thus was established the principle of **legal precedent—** *stare decisis*—that governs much of our legal decision-making process and assures us of a degree of certainty and predictability in our law. Read the decision and dissent in *Payne v. Tennessee* (1991) in Chapter 14 for a lively argument on the application of *stare decisis*—letting the decision stand.

Some of our important legal rights evolved with the common law of England. Trial by battle and trial by ordeal succumbed to the use of juries by the thirteenth century. The responsibility for the prosecution of crimes was shifted from the victim, including the powerless poor, to the state. Thus, crimes are said to be against the state, and prosecutions pit the United States, the state, or the people against the alleged offender. Most defendants, however, are no match for a powerful government. The signing of the **Magna Carta** in 1215 improved the likelihood of justice by establishing principles of fair procedure and protections for the accused. This important document and subsequent developments gave us the writ of habeas corpus that prevents incarceration without justification; the right to trial by jury; the right against unreasonable searches and seizures; the right against conviction by *ex post facto* **laws** that are passed after the act is committed; the freedom of religion, speech, and press; the right to representation; the right to confront one's accusers; the right against self-incrimination; the presumption of innocence; and the right to proof beyond a reasonable doubt.

These cornerstones of criminal law literally sailed to the New World in copies of Blackstone's *Commentaries on the Common Law,* a written record and analysis of the English common law. Despite some aversion to English traditions following the Revolutionary War, common law, and specifically its criminal components, became the basis of law in the United States.

The common law is both preserved and rejected in our modern criminal statutes. Though most states and the federal courts rely entirely on codified criminal law, Florida, Rhode Island, and a few other states allow the courts to rule according to common law.

canon law:
law of the church that preserved significant aspects of Roman and other law through the Middle Ages.

common law:
traditional law originating in England, recorded in judicial opinions rather than legislative statutes.

legal precedent *(stare decisis):*
a previous court decision that serves as an authority in a subsequent case with similar issues in question.

stare decisis:
let the decision stand, precedent.

Magna Carta:
English document signed in 1215 that established the principles of fair procedure and protections for the accused that are still cornerstones in our criminal justice system.

ex post facto **laws:**
laws that are passed after the act is committed.

"[Common law] stands as a monument slowly raised, like a coral reef, from the minute accretions of past individuals of whom each built upon the relics which his predecessors left, and in his turn left a foundation upon which his successors might work."

—Learned Hand, "Review of Judge Cardozo's *The Nature of the Judicial Process*," 35 *Harvard Law Review* 481 (1922)

Even those states that have abolished common law crimes (called code jurisdiction states) join the other states in employing common law defenses such as self-defense, incapacity, and insanity. In some states even codified crimes such as murder, rape, and others may be defined by referring to the common law. In common law states, some crimes may exist only in the common law: "burning a body in a furnace, keeping a house of prostitution . . . discharging a gun near a sick person; drunkenness . . . and eavesdropping."[1]

Keep in mind that the federal government, because its power in establishing crimes is limited, never adopted common law. Because the federal government must exercise broad police power similar to that of the states in Washington, DC, and United States territories, common law is applied in those areas.

The sources of criminal law include contributions of ancient societies; Roman/French law; federal and state constitutions; English common law as adapted to the states and territories; bodies of criminal statutes called codes, ordinances, administrative law, treaties, and international law; and court decisions interpreting the law and establishing rules and principles.

Our common law heritage is important. When you research the law, pay attention to whether the jurisdiction in which you are working uses the common law to define crimes or to interpret statutory crimes. An understanding that our law is based on centuries of experience and trial and error should instill a proper skepticism of proposed changes in law that fail to take into account this legal heritage and tradition.

C. MODEL PENAL CODE

Model Penal Code and Commentaries:
a guide by the American Law Institute to reform and unify criminal law in the United States.

The **Model Penal Code and Commentaries** is another source of modern criminal law. First published in 1961, the Model Penal Code reduces the many and often conflicting traditional sources of criminal law into a concise statement of criminal law. Not a law itself, it is a model that serves as a guide to legislators, judges, and students of the law. Many jurisdictions have clarified their criminal law by enacting substantial portions of the Model Penal Code or adapting portions of it in court opinions. We refer to this code as a benchmark for purposes of comparison and analysis.

D. ADMINISTRATIVE CRIME

"Fred Rodell . . . once compared the law to the Killyloo bird, a creature that he said insisted on flying backward because it didn't care where it was going but was mightily interested in where it had been."

—Fred Rodell, American educator; professor, Yale Law School Paraphrase in the *New York Times*, June 27, 1984

In addition to statutes that set out crimes, administrative rules and regulations also criminalize the violation of these rules and regulations. People may be prosecuted and penalized, for example, for violating health and safety standards, toxic waste provisions, building codes, securities regulations, and for a variety of other offenses not found in the criminal statutes. Legislatures may delegate some of their law-making authority to agencies, but only through an enabling law that provides clear guidelines for the agency to follow. Legislatures, however, not agencies, must set the extent of the penalties for violation of administrative crimes.

E. INTERNATIONAL CRIME

Citizens of a country may be subject to prosecution not only under their own nation's criminal law, but also for violations of international criminal law. Most often, these are matters agreed to in international treaties. Recently individuals in Africa and the Balkans have been indicted for horrendous acts prohibited by international war crimes laws.

"That man is a creature who needs order yet yearns for change is the creative contradiction at the heart of the laws which structure his conformity and define his deviancy."

—Freda Adler, American educator, *Sisters in Crime*, 1975

F. CHANGE IN THE CRIMINAL LAW

Statutory laws change when legislatures pass new laws and repeal others, and when courts declare laws unconstitutional. Legal precedent evolves as courts interpret statutes and further define, and occasionally overturn, precedents. Though remaining relatively constant, criminal law is dynamic, changing to meet new demands and new circumstances. For example, the following laws are no longer on the books.

> *No female shall appear in a bathing suit on any highway within this state unless she is escorted by at least two officers or unless she be armed with a club. (Kentucky)*
> *It is illegal to place slot machines or other gambling devices in an outhouse. (Ohio)*
> *It shall be unlawful to put any hypnotized person in a display window. (Oklahoma)*[2]

New laws now include computer theft in the definition of theft, establish controls on the sale of certain firearms, determine whether a fetus is a person within the meaning of murder and neglect statutes, and outlaw smoking in many public places.

The criminal law also hangs on to the old. Laws still on the books in some jurisdictions, though rarely enforced, prohibit hunting on Sunday, buying a domestic animal between sunset and sunrise, fornication, and profanity.[3]

G.   DIVISIONS OF CRIMINAL LAW

Criminal law has two divisions or subfields. **Substantive criminal law** comprises definitions of crimes and principles governing punishment. **Procedural criminal law** comprises the rules that the prosecution, the defense, and the courts must follow for the step by step processing of a person from accusation to sentencing and appeal.

H.   DUE PROCESS

The Fifth and Fourteenth Amendments of the Constitution state that a person may not be deprived of life, liberty, or property without **due process** of law. Both substantive and procedural criminal law are subject to this significant, fundamental principle. **Substantive due process** prohibits laws that are too vague, overbroad, unreasonable, arbitrary, or capricious. **Procedural due process** requires the steps in a criminal proceeding to be fundamentally fair, assuring to some degree of certitude that justification exists for arrest, prosecution, and punishment. The right to trial by jury, to an attorney, against self-incrimination, and other constitutional guarantees are specific due process requirements. Due process serves as a significant restraint on the power of government.

Related, if not an integral part of due process, is the principle expressed by the Latin maxim *nullem crimen, nulla poena sine lege,* there can be no crime and no punishment without law. That is, the crime must be a previously stated part of the law. This provides citizens with a fundamental of fairness, included in due process, called **notice,** meaning a person cannot be convicted of a crime unless that person was given prior warning (notice) that the conduct was prohibited. Unless conduct has been written into our criminal code or established in common law (recorded in judicial opinions), that conduct is not criminal and no charges can legally be brought against a person for engaging in it. Federal crimes, therefore, are published in the United States Code and state crimes in the codes of the respective states. Federal administrative crimes are published in the Code of Federal Regulations (CFR), and state administrative crimes in parallel publications of state administrative rules and regulations.

I.   CLASSIFICATION OF CRIMES

Historically, crimes have been identified as *mala in se,* inherently evil or obvious wrongs generally accepted by most societies through time as serious crimes: murder, rape, robbery, and arson; or *mala prohibita,* crimes not inherently evil but sufficiently bad to have been prohibited by law, such as speeding, gambling, the sale of intoxicating beverages, and possession of illegal drugs. Although some judicial opinions still refer to these terms when deciding, for example, whether a specific crime requires proof of intent or a jury trial, they are of relatively little value in classifying crimes.

substantive criminal law: definitions of crimes and principles governing punishment.

procedural criminal law: the rules that the prosecution, the defense, and the courts must follow for the step by step processing of a person from accusation to sentencing and appeal.

due process: Fifth and Fourteenth Amendment right not to be deprived of life, liberty, or property without a process that is fundamentally fair and just.

substantive due process: a restraint on government prohibiting laws that are too vague, overbroad, unreasonable, arbitrary, or capricious.

procedural due process: requirement that the steps in a criminal proceeding be fundamentally fair, assuring to some degree of certitude that justification exists for arrest, prosecution, and punishment.

notice: prior warning that specified conduct is prohibited.

mala in se: inherently evil or obvious wrongs generally accepted by most societies through time as serious crimes.

mala prohibita: crimes not inherently evil but sufficiently bad to have been prohibited by law.

Today crimes are classified primarily by the seriousness of the resulting or intended harm. Therefore, crimes that harm people are separated from crimes that harm property, an intentional killing is separated from a negligent one, embezzlement of $20,000 is separated from theft of $20. The more serious the harm of the crime, the more serious the punishment that is assigned to it. **Felonies** are the most serious crimes and require a minimum of one year in a state or federal prison (not a county jail). A **capital crime** is a crime for which a person can receive the death penalty. Today capital offenses are limited to murder and treason. **Misdemeanors** are lesser crimes than felonies and have penalties that include fines and up to one year in a county jail (as opposed to prison). **Violations** are noncriminal offenses, such as traffic violations and public drunkenness, for which the city, county, or state may only fine the offender. Classes of crimes are discussed in more detail in Chapter 3.

IV. PUNISHMENT AND CRIMINAL LAW

A. INTRODUCTION

The purpose of criminal law is to prevent individual harm, but more importantly it is to protect society, the always-vulnerable state of civilization, from those forces that most threaten the peace, harmony, security, integrity, and stability of each citizen and of society as a whole. It is to protect us from a life that is "nasty, brutish, and short." You could say that criminal law is social self-defense.

Acts that threaten or harm individuals and, thus, society, are sufficiently serious that they require punishment. Punishment for the wrongdoer is more than physical or monetary punishment; it encompasses the formal, moral condemnation of the community.[4] Authorities argue that the most commonly voiced objectives of punishment are retribution, deterrence, and rehabilitation. They cannot agree, however, on which of these objectives is most important or whether each one is appropriate. The crimes defined in the criminal law, the penalties assessed, and the condition of punishment imposed stem from an application of retribution, deterrence, and rehabilitation in varying combinations and degrees.

B. RETRIBUTION

Retribution is an expressed purpose of punishment reflecting the concept of just desserts—if a person elects to commit a crime, that person deserves to be punished and to the degree warranted by the seriousness of the crime. Dating back at least as far as the Code of Hammurabi (2100 B.C.), retribution also has been expressed as "an eye for an eye" and the "law of equivalent retaliation." If one knocked out the eye or tooth of another, the same was to be done to the assailant; if a son struck his father, the son's hand was cut off; and if a physician caused a patient to lose an eye or to die, the physician's fingers were cut off.[5]

More recently, however, the focus has been on the idea of just desserts—wrongful acts deserve punishment. In addition, proponents argue that retribution has the value of expiation: cleansing the community and offering the offender a chance to rejoin society by atoning for the sin and paying a prescribed debt to society. The seventeenth-century Salem witchcraft trials were heavily justified on the basis of cleansing the community of the devil and his helpers by hanging those that held fast to their innocence and refused to repent.

Another justification given for retribution is that if the government takes action against the criminal, then individuals will be less inclined to do so. Thus, the goals of social order and peace are better preserved.

On that score, I would say only that I cannot agree that retribution is a constitutionally impermissible ingredient in the imposition of punishment. The instinct for retribution is part of the nature of man, and channeling that instinct in the administration of

felony:
the most serious crime; requires a minimum of one year in a state or federal prison (not a county jail).

capital crime:
a crime for which a person can receive the death penalty.

misdemeanor:
lesser crime than a felony; penalties include fines and up to one year in a county jail (as opposed to prison).

violation:
noncriminal offense, such as traffic violations and public drunkenness, for which the city, county, or state may only fine the offender.

retribution:
an expressed purpose of punishment reflecting the concept of just desserts.

criminal justice serves an important purpose in promoting the stability of a society governed by law. When people begin to believe that organized society is unwilling or unable to impose upon criminal offenders the punishment they "deserve," then there are sown the seeds of anarchy—of self-help, vigilante justice and lynch law.

—Furman v. Georgia (1972)

Critics of retribution attack its validity on the basis that human civilization has advanced beyond the idea of equivalent retaliation. Opponents further argue that its premise, that criminals elect to commit crimes, ignores all of the other factors that may cause a person to commit crime. Factors such as ignorance, fear, and desperation brought on by poverty, as well as dysfunctional families, child abuse, and other physical and emotional trauma raise serious questions about the degree of choice involved in criminal conduct.

C.   DETERRENCE

Deterrence, the prevention of crime, is widely accepted as a goal of punishment. The premise is that individuals will be dissuaded from committing crimes if the pain of punishment outweighs the benefits derived from committing the crime. Legal history is replete with punishments that run the entire scale of human imagination: banishment, dismemberment, crucifixion, branding, hanging, electrocution, imprisonment, fines, and public dunking.

deterrence: the prevention of crime as a goal of punishment.

General deterrence is aimed at most of society—those who have not yet committed a crime. One of its purposes is to bring about conformity with society's norms by identifying bad conduct. The fear of being labeled a criminal—an undesirable, an unworthy member of society—with all the social and economic stigmas that are attached is enough to keep most people on the straight and narrow. The fear of condemnation by family, peers, religious establishments, and the community has long been an effective deterrent for even the most primitive of societies.

general deterrence: prevention of crime in society as a whole; to bring about conformity with society's norms by identifying bad conduct.

Proponents of deterrence argue that another benefit is that the threat of punishment leads to habitual and subconscious conformity that, over time and from generation to generation, achieves a high degree of socialization without any eventual awareness of or fear of punishment. It simply becomes the way things are done.[6]

Opponents argue that punishment as a deterrent has not been substantiated. Ambitious studies on deterrence, especially in the area of capital punishment as a means of preventing murder, have been largely inconclusive. It is argued that most criminals do not believe that they will get caught, and few have much conception of what their punishment is likely to be if they do get caught. Studies show no scientific proof that criminals fear punishment, citing how French pickpockets fleeced spectators watching the execution by hanging of their fellow pickpockets. There seems to be evidence that some criminals hope to get caught and use crime as their only hope to become "somebody." Further, opponents contend that punishment has absolutely no effect on criminals who are insane, psychologically compulsive such as kleptomaniacs, highly distraught as in some murders or suicide, incapacitated as by retardation or intoxication, and those that commit crimes in the heat of passion.

Individual (specific) deterrence focuses on the person who has been convicted of a crime. The premise here is that if criminals are punished severely enough, they will not want to experience the same or a similar punishment again and, therefore, will conform. The degree of **recidivism** (repeat offenses) that now exists, however, suggests that this premise is questionable.

individual (specific) deterrence: incapacitation or punishment to prevent criminals from repeating as offenders.

recidivism: repeat offenses.

Another basis of specific deterrence is incapacitation. This has the appeal of inescapable logic: identify those who commit crimes, especially those who are likely to repeat as offenders, and place them where they will not cause crime, thus ridding society of its criminal element. No matter what the arguments are against it, it must work at least to some degree.

Unfortunately, there are weaknesses in this argument, not in its logic but in its simplicity. One serious problem is predicting who will be a repeat offender. Psychologists have studied that issue for years and have been asked by the courts to give their opinions about who is dangerous and who is not, but they pretty much agree today that they may be no better equipped to make such predictions than anyone else.[7]

Further, can we prevent criminals from being repeat offenders through punishment when our prisons and jails are admittedly "schools for crime"? Recidivists admit to learning new sophisticated methods to carry out their crimes, making good criminal contacts, and discovering better means to avoid detection. Sociologists tell us that people learn to identify with the society or subculture in which they associate. If that is so, then our prisons do more to reinforce a criminal subculture than they do to prevent the repetition of crime.

Opponents of the idea of deterrence through incapacitation (imprisonment) say that most citizens want longer prison terms assessed. Yet, our prisons are already antiquated and bursting at the seams, and tax-paying citizens are unwilling to pay for the space needed to accommodate longer prison sentences.

D.   REHABILITATION

rehabilitation:
the objective of criminal law to reform criminals and give them the ability to compete in society.

Rehabilitation (reformation) is the third factor long argued to be an objective of punishment. Logically it might be considered as part of deterrence, because part of the justification for rehabilitation is that the reformed criminal will not be a repeat offender. Rehabilitation aims to treat criminal behavior as a disease by replacing ignorance with education, lack of job skills with job training, dependence on alcohol and drugs with abstinence and discipline, and by treating emotional and psychological disturbances with therapy. Its design is to take persons who have previously been unable to compete in a highly competitive society and give them the ability to compete and the ability to become contributing citizens with appropriate doses of self-esteem.

During the 1960s and 1970s rehabilitation programs directed thousands of offenders from jails and prisons into community health and education programs. Early release from prison was often based on successful completion of such programs.

Though it was seen as an enlightened approach to penology and greeted with considerable enthusiasm at first, rehabilitation lost favor by the 1980s for several reasons. Statistics reflected little change in recidivism rates. Society and political officials wanted quick, verifiable results for their tax dollars. The children of the post–World War II baby boom came of age for crime (fifteen to twenty-four years old). The Vietnam War and the drug culture of the 1960s led to a disruption of accepted behavior, and a related expansion of crime even to rural areas to support drug habits. Exacerbating that scenario was the fact that government revenues were drying up.

The fruits born of this shift in focus include longer and determinate (certain length) prison sentences, fewer rehabilitation programs, increased penalties for repeat felons, the reestablishment of executions for murder, more attention on the victim of crime than on the perpetrator, pressure on parole boards to keep prisoners longer, an expensive war on drugs, and terribly crowded prisons. The United States is approaching the highest imprisonment rate of all modern nations.[8] Another study indicates that prisoner work and training programs produce lower recidivism rates.[9] Whether general rehabilitation was ever given a fair shake as a deserving aim for criminal law remains an issue.

So, the classic debate on rehabilitation continues. Proponents argue that there was enough success in the 1960s and 1970s to warrant rehabilitation efforts for those offenders most likely to benefit from them, and that punishment still should be individualized. Opponents argue that the emphasis must be on swift and stern deterrence, and that rehabilitation can actually be more cruel and result in longer sentences than those under a determinate system. One interesting justification for this position is captured by the writer C. S. Lewis:

Of all tyrannies a tyranny sincerely exercised for the good of its victims may be the most oppressive. . . . Those who torment us for our own good will torment us without end for they do so with the approval of their own conscience. . . . To be "cured" against one's will and cured of states which we may not regard as disease is to be put on a level with . . . the infants, imbeciles, and domestic animals.[10]

In the twenty-first century our society must continue to reexamine to what extent our criminal justice system will be motivated by retribution, deterrence, and rehabilitation. More immediately, paralegals and attorneys need to be aware of their motivations in each charge they bring, each case they try, and each sentence they recommend. As a citizen of this country, which of these three concepts do you believe deserves the most attention? Should any be completely excluded? Are there other solutions? Think about that in terms of the mass murderer, the retarded murderer, the facilitator of euthanasia, the uneducated thief, the Wall Street broker who benefits from insider trading, the people who cheat on their income tax reports, and others. Does your perspective change at all if you are the offender, or if a parent or a sibling is the offender? What if you or someone close to you is the victim?

Look at the decisions and dissents in *Gregg v. Georgia* (1976) and *Payne v. Tennessee* (1991) in Chapter 14 for an idea about the ongoing debate on the proper objectives of punishment.

ANALYSIS PROBLEM

1–2.   Assume that each of the defendants in the sample cases at the end of this chapter has been convicted. For each case, decide whether retribution, deterrence, or rehabilitation is most appropriate in sentencing.

V.   CRITICAL REASON AND CRIMINAL LAW

Law is based on reason, which in turn is based on knowledge and human experience. Persons working with criminal law, or those simply wishing to understand it, will better succeed if they delve into the reasoning or rationale behind a specific statute or judicial opinion. Some citizens accept a statute as valid simply because it is a product of a representative legislative process and on its face appears beneficial, or at least does not directly impact on them. Others argue that each statute, each new judicial opinion, should be seriously scrutinized, because the law defines crimes and crimes create criminals.

Prisons are built with stones of Law . . . .
                 —William Blake

Men are not hanged for stealing horses, but that horses may not be stolen.
                 —George Savile

If the legislature enacts a criminal statute and the ramifications it will have on the public are thoroughly considered from all important perspectives, there should be no serious problem. Unfortunately, the same historical experience that tells us what is good law also tells us that criminal statutes are enacted for other, not so altruistic reasons. Law reflects the values and morals of a society, but it can be argued that too often the society reflected by law is that of the rich and the powerful, including special interest groups. As the theory goes, the powerful enact laws to help them make and protect wealth, and then use the criminal law to coerce others into helping them in the process. Crimes once prohibiting the organization of unions helped to protect the powerful owners of industry, laws prohibiting African Americans from sitting in the front of a bus or eating at certain diners helped preserve the power and social status of whites, laws requiring young people to serve in the military can be viewed as laws protecting the wealth and property of the nation's most powerful, and laws prohibiting vagrancy or sleeping on park benches facilitate the middle class in controlling the homeless. Those who believe that crimes are defined by the most influential see criminal law as a net that allows the rich and powerful to swim free while smaller fry are ensnared.

Sometimes the power to change criminal law comes from panic or simply a wave of strong public sentiment that drowns the voices of reason and caution.

Necessity is the plea for every infringement of human freedom. It is the argument of tyrants; it is the creed of slaves.

—William Pitt, House of Commons, Nov. 18, 1783

Thus our society has borne witness to laws that have imprisoned thousands of Japanese Americans during World War II, laws that prohibited peaceful protest marches, and, increasingly, laws that inhibit individual freedom in the attempt to contain the spread of illegal drugs.

Another danger in the relationship between power and criminal law is that once a crime is defined, characteristics of those likely to commit the crime are also defined. For example, in the seventeenth-century witchcraft trials, witches were defined according to what people in power disliked or distrusted. Thus, those who were poor, crotchety, alone, old, and female became prototypes of suspected, and eventually executed, witches. A similar principle of defining crime seems to be used by city councils when they define vagrants.

Rogues and vagabonds, or dissolute persons who go about begging, common gamblers, persons who use juggling or unlawful games or plays, common drunkards, common night walkers, thieves, pilferers or pickpockets, traders in stolen property, lewd, wanton and lascivious persons, keepers of gambling places, common railers and brawlers, persons wandering or strolling around from place to place without any lawful purpose or object, habitual loafers, disorderly persons, persons neglecting all lawful business and habitually spending their time by frequenting houses of ill fame, gaming houses, or places where alcoholic beverages are sold or served, persons able to work but habitually living upon the earnings of their wives or minor children shall be deemed vagrants and, upon conviction in the Municipal Court shall be punished as provided for Class D offenses [90 days' imprisonment, $500 fine, or both].

—Papachristou et al. v. City of Jacksonville (1972)

"Hungry people cannot be good at learning or producing anything, except perhaps violence."

—Pearl Bailey, *Pearl's Kitchen*, 1973

Imagine the potential abuse if such statutes were allowed to stand. A number of theories are often at work in criminal law, so it is important that each crime, each definition of crime, and each procedure be critically examined to see that it is fair to all and truly in the (admittedly elusive) "best interest of society."

VI.   THE DILEMMA OF CRIME IN A FREE SOCIETY

This nation, by its origin and Constitution, strives to foster and preserve individual liberty and dignity. Freedom of speech, mobility, association, religion, and press, and freedom from governmental intrusion into our private lives are all cornerstones of our right to think what we want, go where we want, do what we want to do in the privacy of our own dwellings—to fully enjoy the right to life, liberty, and property.

Yet, to fully enjoy these freedoms we turn to government to protect us from those who abuse their freedoms to carry out murder, burglary, fraud, kidnapping, drug dealing, toxic dumping, and a host of other crimes. The dilemma is in how much power to give the government and its law enforcement agencies in trade for our liberty. Where is the line between protection and freedom in respect to searches of our homes and vehicles, to extraction of a confession, to seizure or destruction of the property of suspected criminals, to the privacy of family relationships in investigations of spouse or child abuse, to records kept on each one of us or in the monitoring of our movements or our phone conversations? How much are we as a free people willing to give up to have order?

Ben Franklin said something to the effect that the society that favors order over liberty shall be a society of slaves. What price are we willing to pay in tolerating crimes so that our liberty will remain inviolate? This issue is played out constantly on our streets, in our legislatures, and in our courtrooms. Whether you work in criminal law or become an interested observer, be acutely aware of this dilemma, because the preservation of individual liberty and, yes, even of this nation as we know it rests in how we decide, or demand, that this issue be resolved.

 ANALYSIS PROBLEM

1–3.   In what ways does the Internet enhance our liberty? Should the government be allowed to limit that liberty?

VII.   CRIME IN THE UNITED STATES

A.   CURRENT STATE OF CRIME

Public polls indicated that crime should be a top concern addressed by politicians in the national elections in 1992, 1994, and 1996. Crime rates had ballooned in the 1980s, spurred largely by drug market warfare, especially for control of the sale of crack cocaine. Growing crime rates were fed by a large population of crime-prone young people, use of drugs and alcohol, gangs, poverty, mental illness, deterioration of the nuclear family, increasing numbers of female criminals, and other complex reasons. Some recent studies tie criminal inclination to children whose mothers smoke[11] and for those exposed to excessive quantities of lead.[12] Crime rates peaked, however, in 1993 and have dropped steadily since then. The rate of juvenile crime has fallen twice as fast as that for adult crime.[13] Other factors mentioned have been a strong economy, creating the lowest unemployment rate in decades, and higher literacy and school graduation rates. The reduction in the crime rate has also given police agencies a chance to solve old crimes.[14]

Rates of violent crime have fallen nearly 30 percent since 1993 and are the lowest since the Justice Department started reporting data in 1973.[15] Murder rates in some major cities, especially New York, have declined even more. "The most populated Southern states accounted for 40 percent of the total volume of criminal index offenses."[16] Exhibit 1–1 displays the comparative crime rates for the four regions of the United States.[17]

"If poverty is the mother of crime, then want of sense is its father."

—Jean de La Bruyere,
   Caracteres, 1688

B.   REASONS FOR DROP IN CRIME[18]

It is difficult to pinpoint any one reason for the drop in crime because several important factors exist simultaneously that may bear on the decline in crime. Demographically, the crime-prone age group (fifteen to twenty-nine year olds) was the smallest in decades, bottoming out in 1994. The drug markets seem to have stabilized, bringing a reduction in related crimes. Police have instituted new and more aggressive strategies to stop crime. These include more foot patrols, sponsorship and involvement in after-school programs for children, support for neighborhood "take back the

EXHIBIT 1–1
Regional Violent and
Property Crime Rates,
1993 and 1997
(per 100,000
inhabitants)

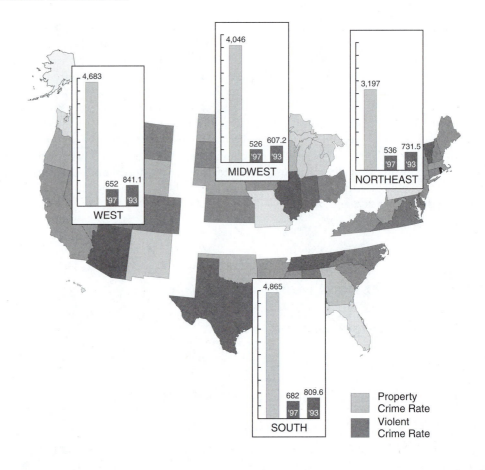

night" programs, aggressive enforcement of petty crimes (which seems to reduce more serious crimes), interception of the flow of illegal handguns, and the use of technology to rapidly pinpoint "hot spots" of crime so resources can be deployed to those areas. More people are in prisons and jails than at any time in our history. Incarceration rates remained flat from 1925 to 1975, but have quadrupled in the past twenty-five years.

C. SPECIAL CONCERNS: PRESENT AND FUTURE

Although the drop in the crime rate is encouraging, there are some special areas of concern. Although teen crime rates are declining, school shootings continue to rock the nation, and this crime-prone age group will grow in population considerably until it peaks in about 2020.[19] Workplace shootings continue to alarm the public, and the availability of cheap handguns and automatic weapons fuels debate. Not only are guns available on the market, but they are also found in 40 percent of households with children ages three to seventeen.[20] More persons are killed by guns every two years in the United States than were United States soldiers killed in the entire Vietnam War.[21] More than half the states permit the carrying of concealed weapons. Our legislators will weigh the role of guns in juvenile and other crime and the need for self protection from criminals in the polarized debate over legislation for gun control.

Another area of concern is minorities' growing lack of faith in the criminal justice system. Years of discrimination in arrests, sentencing, and the death penalty have recently been aggravated by racial profiling in traffic arrests, some horrendous hate crimes, and the low number of minorities in criminal justice jobs.

As aggressive police tactics have resulted in a rise in arrests, they have also resulted in a rise in complaints about police use of excessive force, overzealousness in general, and the violation of civil liberties.

People crushed by law have no hope but from power. If laws are their enemies, they will be enemies to the laws; and those, who have much to hope and nothing to lose, will always be dangerous, more or less.

—Edmund Burke, October 1777

Finally, although many take comfort in the fact that more criminals have received longer sentences and are incarcerated in our jails and prisons, few people have given thought to what will happen when this large volume of convicts is released. The strained prison system has not had the resources for effective rehabilitation programs, and an increasingly significant number of inmates have severe mental illnesses for which little, if any, treatment is available.[22]

 ANALYSIS PROBLEM

1–4. Of the concerns about crime presented in this section, which deserve the most resources and why?

VIII. PRACTICAL CONSIDERATIONS FOR THE STUDY OF CRIMINAL LAW

A. THE SIGNIFICANCE OF STUDYING CRIMINAL LAW

Paralegals who choose to work in criminal law not only will see the intrusion of crime into neighborhoods and lives, but also will realize that the protection of society and the preservation of the freedom—and occasionally the safety—of real people depends on the quality of work that they perform. Your study of this text is an important step toward that work. For those who choose another field, the materials in this text should help you better understand the scope and importance of criminal law, how the system works, and how it can be a snare for the unwary in nearly every other field of law. In other words, a good foundation in criminal law will help you become a more astute citizen and a better paralegal regardless of what field you will work in.

B. ABOUT THIS TEXT: APPLYING STATE LAW

This text is divided into two main sections: substantive criminal law and procedural criminal law. It presents prevailing trends and practices in the law, often in the context of the fictional state of Columbia. For the necessary knowledge about your state law and practice, use the references to the state of Columbia to stand for your state, and use every opportunity that time permits to apply the law, cases, and rules of procedure of your state to the issues, problems, and assignments in this text. In this regard, space is provided in the text's tables for you to add state-specific information.

C. THE SYSTEM FOLDER

The list of system folder assignments at the end of each chapter, when completed, will help you create a paralegal's system folder for criminal law. A system folder is a collection of forms, documents, checklists, procedural rules, and principles of law, including case law and statutes and the rationale behind them. Once organized, the system folder will provide you with a valuable reference for quickly and accurately completing the most important and commonly repeated tasks performed by the paralegal in the criminal law context. The system folder can be carried from the classroom to the office, it can be used as a portfolio to demonstrate your acquired skills to a potential employer, and it easily can be adapted and modified to accommodate different styles and areas of practice. In short, a criminal law system, when created with care and diligence, can greatly assist you in becoming an efficient, accurate, and valuable paralegal.

The assignments in this course program and the outline in Appendix B at the end of this text will guide you in developing your system. A two-inch, three-ring binder provides the room and flexibility for your first criminal litigation system.

As you complete each assignment, place the information needed to perform it, including pertinent sample documents, into the corresponding section of the system folder. Because some instructors will assign more of the tasks set out in this text than others, consider building your system to be as complete as possible by going beyond what you might be assigned.

If you have had a litigation course or after you read Chapter 13, you will note the similarity between organizing a system folder and organizing a trial notebook. Whereas a trial notebook is specific to a particular case in preparation for trial, a system folder is a general collection of resources that can be adapted to the needs of a wide range of cases.

IX.   SAMPLE CASES

In the chapters that follow, criminal law and procedure and relevant paralegal tasks are presented in the context of one or more of the following cases. Case I, the sexual assault case, serves as our main reference. The other cases are used for examples, assignments, and to provide your instructor with some flexibility in choosing a case for instructional purposes. The cases help place you in as realistic a criminal law office environment as a textbook and classroom can create. Please take the time to read these cases now so the situations will be familiar to you when they come up in the text.

A.   CASE I

Kate Lamb slung her bookpack over her shoulder and left the lecture hall, letting the echoes of her professor's voice give way to the nighttime beauty of Legalville State College's campus. Enormous old trees lined the hushed path and the scent of crab apple blossoms hung in the air. Still, the late evening class did not give her much time to prepare for tomorrow's classes, so she hurried on across the high footbridge over Smiley Creek to the parking lot beyond. Her car was at the back of the now-empty lot, and she approached it on the path between a dense stand of pines and the marked parking stalls.

Suddenly there was a rush and strong arms around her dragging her toward the trees. Kate screamed, twisted, struggled. The hands began tearing her clothes, the low voice grunted that she would get what all pretty little college girls asked for. Kate's efforts finally freed one arm and allowed her to face her attacker. With all the strength of her free arm she swung her heavy bookbag at his head. He fell into the darkness under the pines. Hesitating, in shock, she heard him scramble to his feet. His footsteps echoed hers as she tried desperately to run.

Sobbing and shaking, Kate stumbled back to the bridge. She could hear her assailant begin to pursue. When she was halfway across the bridge she saw several dark forms, men, emerge from the trees on the other side. Kate panicked and felt trapped between them and the man behind her in the pine trees. Twenty feet below were the rocky banks and spring-swollen waters of Smiley Creek. Crying frantic words of prayer, she clambered over the railing and jumped, not landing in the safe water but on the rocks.

Five days later Kate regained consciousness in the intensive care unit of a hospital. She was able to make a statement to police and described the assailant the best she could. Shortly thereafter she lapsed into a coma and in August, four months later, she died.

In October, police arrested a suspect, Eldon Spiers.

B. CASE II

Miguel and Carmen Cordoba celebrated the first anniversary of their marriage with a candlelight dinner at the romantic restaurant where Miguel had proposed. After the waiter had taken their order, Miguel gave Carmen her gift, an heirloom ring. The diamond ring, recently appraised at $10,000, had been in his family for four generations, and was always given as a gift of great love. The last to wear it had been Miguel's Aunt Rosa, the dear lady who had been like a second mother to him. Now it was to be worn by Carmen, as a token of his love for her.

The ring had no magic, however, and the Cordoba's marriage deteriorated quickly. After a couple of years of stability, they went through five years of ever more frequent separations and unsuccessful visits to counselors. Finally, Miguel asked Carmen for a divorce and left their home.

Before the divorce was filed, Miguel returned to the house to get his clothes and other personal belongings. While there, he went to his wife's jewelry box and removed the heirloom ring. Soon it was being worn by Estella Anza, his new girlfriend.

Carmen Cordoba asked Miguel to return the ring and, when he did not, swore out a complaint against him for theft.

C. CASE III

Mayor Chen cradled the small cardboard box in his arms all the way home. This little jewel would make history in Legalville. Not only that, it would also clinch his re-election. He had promised to make Legalville a cultural center in spite of other cities in the state that bragged about their fine concert halls and art galleries. The museum had been set up in an unused upper floor of the library and was starting to look convincing with the donated artifacts and paintings that he had begged from a few local professors and businesspeople who were travelers and collectors. But the object in the box, this priceless pre-Columbian sun god of hammered gold, would authenticate the whole project. Mayor Chen chuckled to himself as he thought how he had cajoled a major insurance company into making the donation, how foxy he had been to have them send it from their headquarters by regular parcel post so as not to draw attention to it, and how he would shine beside it at the unveiling party tonight at his home.

Max Legrise sat at a polished teak desk making final assignments. Eddie Corr would drive the van, Henry Pogue would stand lookout, and Cat Bermuda would slip into the mayor's drawing room and remove the idol while it lay unattended as the mayor received guests in the front hall. He thanked Imp Satterfield for her impeccable research into the job and Barney Dobson for weapons procurement, then adjourned to the work of the evening.

Lacey Rude smoothed the apron of her maid's uniform and peeked at the crowd gathering in the front hall. There was still time before she would be required to arrange trays of refreshments in the dining room. On quiet rubber soles she was soon in the empty drawing room. She hid the idol under her apron and was halfway to the kitchen when a heavy object struck the back of her head.

Pandemonium reigned around the empty pedestal in the drawing room. Mayor Chen fought to keep from sobbing as he told all he knew to the police.

There was quiet exultation around the teak desk as Cat told of success in spite of unexpected difficulties.

A year later the Legrise gang was reassembled in the custody of police.

D. CASE IV

Billy McIntire let out a slow breath. Tomorrow was a day off and he planned to sleep through it, but not before he unwound a little. The months of overtime at the factory were getting to him but as the kids grew, so did the bills. He would not be running a drill press forever, though. If he could stick with these night classes he would get a better paying job that required a lot less sweat. The classes were taking their toll too. Studying for this examination had kept him up with his nose in a book, then just up, pacing, worrying. Now, after twelve hours on the job, an hour of lecture, and two hours writing the examination, it was up to the professor. Now Billy could relax.

Several people from the class had invited him to join them at The Zero Zone after the test. Billy was tired but pleased to be included. He drank beer and played pool with his new friends. Around 2:00 A.M. he headed home.

Flashing lights ahead, police cars. Uh-oh, a DUI roadblock.

Billy was asked to get out of his car and perform coordination tests. It seemed to him that he had done ok, but the police officers were frowning and mumbling. While he was out of the car, one officer looked through it, emerging with Billy's book bag. When the officer unzipped the pencil pocket, several marijuana cigarettes fell out.

Billy McIntire was taken to the police station.

E. CASE V

This was going to be the best Great Groundhog Day bash ever, and Nancy Stroud was glad to see her friends having a good time. It meant a lot to have this apartment where they could gather for parties. She had been lucky to find a roommate like Lisa Munden with her beautician's income to help with rent. Nancy's student loan certainly would not have been enough. Now Nancy's friends from college and Lisa's friends from work and town mingled at the party. Neither Nancy nor Lisa knew all the guests. Each assumed the unknowns were friends of her roommate.

As Nancy circulated among the guests she thought she saw indications that some of them were using cocaine there in the apartment. Because she did not use drugs herself, she was not sure about her suspicions.

After most of the guests had gone, there was a knock at the door and police officers were admitted to the apartment. They found residues of cocaine in several places. Nancy and Lisa were arrested.

F. CASE VI

Haden Hills Estates Homeowners Association met at the Craig residence to discuss the new developments in their subdivision. The Harveys and Wescotts had been concerned enough to join with the Craigs in calling the special meeting.

No time was wasted. The issue of two known homosexuals who had moved into the blue saltbox at the end of Meadow Drive had already inflamed the neighborhood and was now discussed in alarmed voices. "What is to be done about Mason Trew and Loren Jackson?" "Property values will surely drop." "Other gays will be attracted to Haden Hills Estates." "The neighborhood children will be in danger." The twenty people in the Craigs' living room grew more passionate in their condemnation of their new neighbors as concerns were aired. Something must be done, they all agreed.

Another quiet day and evening passed in Haden Hills, then at 1:00 A.M. a faded grey van pulled up a half block away from the blue saltbox on Meadow Drive. Three figures wearing sheets and hoods left the van. Soon a large wooden cross was burning on the front lawn of the Trew and Jackson residence. Signs with slogans "We don't want no fags here" and "Get out or die" were stuck in the yard. Gunshots broke windows in the house.

Three days later Richard Craig, John Harvey, and Mike Wescott were arrested.

X. CONCLUSION

The purpose of this chapter is to provide you with an understanding of the purpose, legal basis, scope and limits, origins, current sources, fundamental issues in, and the state of criminal law. It also introduces you to this textbook and the resources available in it. Your understanding of these foundations is fundamental to your work in coming chapters and gives you a context for focusing your thinking, writing, and other tasks in preparation for the law office.

SYSTEM FOLDER ASSIGNMENTS

Set up your system folder as follows. Arrange the tabs in a two-inch binder as needed and as indicated by the system folder assignments located at the end of each chapter and by the outline in Appendix B. Add to the table of contents as needed throughout the course. At the end of each chapter you will find a list of items to add to your folder.

HELPFUL WEB SITES

www.ncjrs.org
    National Criminal Justice Reference Service, links to statistics, victims services, courts, practice areas, and specific crimes
www.findlaw.com
    Federal and state resources, statutes and cases, articles
www.mother.com/~randy/law.html
    Clearly organized links to federal and state statutes and cases, municipal codes, practice areas
www.law.com
    Latest legal developments, updated daily; practice area sections
www.ilrg.com
    Internet Legal Resource Guide, forms, outlines, legal associations, practice areas, Supreme Court decisions
www.abanet.org
    American Bar Association, current information on areas of law practice
www.state.KY.us
    Substitute your state's abbreviation for KY in the address;
    state government Web sites, state statutes and cases
www.llrx.com
    Litigators Internet Resource Guide, links to federal, state, and local court rules
www.ojp.usdoj.gov/bjs
    Bureau of Justice Statistics, information on prisons, victims, crime rates, and so forth (phone 800-732-3277)
www.fedstats.gov
    Federal statistics
www.fbi.gov
    Federal Bureau of Investigation, uniform crime reports, Freedom of Information Act link

INTERNET EXERCISES

1. Visit the Web sites listed in the previous section and in chapters that follow. Make notes as to the information available in each, ease of use, helpful links, and so forth. Put the information in your system folder.
2. Go to the Bureau of Justice Statistics site. Find the section on courts and sentencing: court organization. What are the exceptions to twelve-member juries with a unanimous verdict?

QUESTIONS FOR STUDY AND REVIEW

1. Define law and explain its general purpose.
2. What is the rule of law and why is it so important?
3. What is federalism? What are the primary powers granted to the federal government? The states?
4. What is meant by the broad term *police power*?
5. What is the purpose of criminal law? How is it different from civil law?
6. Why is it important for a paralegal to understand our legal heritage?
7. Discuss some of the significant historical contributions to our criminal law and state why they are important.
8. Define common law and describe some of its characteristics.
9. What are the sources of criminal law?
10. What is the Model Penal Code and why is it important? Has it been adopted in your state?
11. What is the Code of Federal Regulations (CFR)?
12. What processes do we use to change our law?
13. Explain the difference between the two main divisions of criminal law.
14. What is due process? Substantive due process? Why is due process important to you as a citizen?
15. How are crimes classified?
16. What is a felony? A misdemeanor? A capital felony?
17. What does the Latin maxim *nullum crimen, nulla poena sine lege* mean and why is it important?
18. What is the difference between a *mala in se* crime and a *mala prohibita* crime?
19. Define retribution, deterrence, and rehabilitation. Briefly explain the benefits and problems of each.
20. What is the difference between general and specific deterrence?
21. Why should new criminal laws undergo the strictest scrutiny?
22. What do you believe are the primary reasons for crime in our society? Explain the decline in crime rates. What concerns remain and how should they be addressed?
23. What is the dilemma caused by crime in a free society? Should the police be permitted to stop all cars at a temporary roadblock to find drunk drivers? Or those possessing illegal drugs?

KEY TERMS LIST

Canon law
Capital crime
Civil law
Common law
Criminal law
Deterrence
  General deterrence
  Individual (specific) deterrence
Due process
  Substantive due process
  Procedural due process

Ex post facto laws
Federalism
Felony
Law
Legal precedent (*stare decisis*)
Magna Carta
Mala in se
Mala prohibita
Misdemeanor
Model Penal Code and Commentaries

Notice
Police power
Procedural criminal law
Recidivism
Rehabilitation
Retribution
Rule of law
Stare decisis
Substantive criminal law
Violation

ENDNOTES

1. WAYNE R. LAFAVE AND AUSTIN W. SCOTT, JR., SUBSTANTIVE CRIMINAL LAW, § 2.1, 94–95, West Group, 1986.
2. Dick Hyman, *Silly Statutes,* PHILIP MORRIS MAGAZINE, Jan.–Feb. 1989, 12–13.
3. NATIONAL LAW JOURNAL, Mar. 16, 1998, P. A23.
4. HENRY M. HART, *The Aims of the Criminal Law,* 23 LAW AND CONTEMPORARY PROBLEMS, 401, 402–406 (1958).
5. WILL DURANT, THE STORY OF CIVILIZATION: OUR ORIENTAL HERITAGE, 231 Vol. 1, Simon and Schuster, New York, 1954.
6. Johannes Andenaes, *General Prevention—Illusion or Reality,* 43 JOURNAL OF CRIMINAL LAW AND CRIMINOLOGY 180 (1952).
7. REPORT OF THE AMERICAN PSYCHOLOGICAL ASSOCIATION, 33 AM PSYCHOLOGIST 1099, 1100 (1978).
8. Anne Gearan, *U.S. Prison Population Doubles in 12 Years,* LEXINGTON HERALD-LEADER, Mar. 25, 1999, at A3.
9. A study by the Federal Bureau of Prisons of inmates released from 1984 through 1986, reported in *Inmates Who Work Less Likely to Repeat Crime, Study Shows,* LEXINGTON HERALD-LEADER, Dec. 20, 1991, at A12.
10. *The Humanitarian Theory of Punishment,* 6 RES JUDICATA 224 (1953).
11. *Moms Who Smoke May Produce Criminal Sons,* LEXINGTON HERALD-LEADER, June 15, 1999, P. A8, reporting on a study published in the AMERICAN JOURNAL OF PSYCHIATRY.
12. *Study Links Boys' Lead Exposure to Crime Rate,* LEXINGTON HERALD-LEADER, Feb. 7, 1996, at A8, reporting study done at the University of Pittsburgh School of Medicine.
13. *Juvenile Crime Rate Plummets Nationally,* LEXINGTON HERALD-LEADER, Oct. 18, 1999, at A1, A4.
14. *Cold Crime Squads,* NATIONAL LAW JOURNAL, Mar. 8, 1999, at A1.
15. NATIONAL CRIME VICTIMIZATION SURVEY, 1998, Bureau of Justice Statistics, U.S. Department of Justice, 1999.
16. UNIFORM CRIME REPORTS FOR THE UNITED STATES, 1997, Federal Bureau of Investigation, U.S. Department of Justice, 7, 1998.
17. *Id.* Chart 2.4, 10.
18. See LEGISLATIVE UPDATE, Kentucky Dept. of Public Advocacy, Feb. 1999, at 2, and Richard Lacayo, *Law and Order,* TIME, Jan. 15, 1996, at 48–53.
19. Lacayo, *Id.* p. 52.
20. *Forty Percent of Homes with Kids Have Guns,* LEXINGTON HERALD-LEADER, Nov. 14, 1998, at A3
21. ABC NEWS, July 15, 1999.
22. *Report Indicates Jails, Prisons Are Nation's New Mental Hospitals,* LEXINGTON HERALD-LEADER, July 12, 1999, at A1, quoting a Dept. of Justice report.

ADMINISTRATION OF CRIMINAL JUSTICE AND THE ROLE OF THE PARALEGAL

CHAPTER

2

I. INTRODUCTION

To implement the objectives of criminal law presented in Chapter 1, a system of agencies and offices, public and private, come together to provide the structure of the criminal justice system. Law enforcement agencies (police), prosecution and defense attorneys, corrections agencies (prison and parole), and courts each work to move a case from the commission of the crime itself to its legal resolution. From the adversary system come the responsibilities of prosecutors, defenders, and judges who use the competitive nature of the courts to seek the truth in a process that is fair.

In each of these components, paralegals work within prescribed limits to fulfill a broad variety of responsibilities to employers, clients, the paralegal profession, and the criminal justice system.

II. LAW ENFORCEMENT AGENCIES

Law enforcement agencies are a part of the executive branch of government. They are the police agencies charged with the responsibility of preventing and investigating crime. They have the authority within constitutional limits to seize property, detain suspicious individuals for questioning, and, where the facts and evidence warrant it, arrest the suspected perpetrators. Nearly 40,000 such agencies operate at the federal, state, and local levels. The largest law enforcement agency at the federal level is the Federal Bureau of Investigation (FBI). It is an arm of the Department of Justice and is responsible for the enforcement of the federal criminal laws. The bureau's 56 field offices, 400 satellite offices, 34 foreign liaison posts, and 11,400 special agents operate under a $3 billion annual budget and have jurisdiction over 200 categories of federal crimes.[1] It investigates crimes such as murder, rape, and burglary, and also covers internal security involving espionage and counterespionage activities. The FBI's centralized records on persons committing felonies; fingerprint, DNA, and other identification detection banks; highly trained agents; and some of the most advanced criminal detection technology available in the world offer a valuable resource for state law enforcement agencies.

A number of other federal agencies also enforce the law. The Bureau of Alcohol, Tobacco and Firearms enforces laws related to sale, possession, manufacture, and shipping of those items. The Drug Enforcement Administration covers the illegal production, sale, and possession of prescription drugs, as well as drugs such as cocaine, heroin, and methamphetamines. The Customs Service enforces statutes dealing with the illegal importation and exportation of goods (smuggling). The Immigration and Naturalization Service investigates crimes relating to persons' unauthorized entry through United States borders, their employment, and possible deportation. The Bureau of Postal Inspection investigates the violation of postal regulations, including use of the mails to defraud others and theft of checks and other property in the mail. The Secret Service, a branch of the United States Treasury, investigates offenses covering credit and debit card fraud, computer fraud, counterfeiting, and forgery of United States checks and bonds, and prevents and investigates attacks and threats on the lives of government officials. The Bureau of Indian Affairs is responsible for law enforcement on Native American reservations. Numerous divisions in other federal agencies are responsible for investigating violations of law concerning labor practices, toxic waste, mining, transportation, communication, and many others.

A variety of agencies enforce the law on the state level, as well. The most notable is the state police, whose responsibilities range from public education and protection of public officials to traffic enforcement and the prevention and investigation of all crimes covered by state law. Police agencies at the county level are most commonly sheriffs' departments. A vestige of our common law heritage, the sheriff is an elected official who oversees the law enforcement activities of civil service employees. Within a county there are usually several city or municipal police departments headed by appointed or civil service officials. Increasingly common are unified police departments that are a product of merged city and county governments.

State and local governments normally have divisions of agencies responsible for the investigation of crimes related to the jurisdiction of that agency. These often enforce child welfare, agricultural production and transportation, mining and occupational safety, insurance, banking, consumer fraud, and conservation and wildlife laws. Because of the broad nature of police responsibilities and limits in government funding, police exercise considerable discretion, ranging from who to stop for questioning to broad policy decisions such as what types of crimes will be allotted the greatest portion of the agency's resources.

One aspect of the law that is explored later is the need for criminal laws to provide sufficiently clear guidelines for police to avoid uneven and unfair enforcement of the law. One of the difficulties in law is balancing the need for flexibility in decision making with the need for limits to prevent police abuse of the decision-making process.

Law enforcement is an exceptionally demanding occupation, often requiring split-second decisions with potentially deadly consequences. Because of some high-profile cases involving abuse by officers, some departments have instituted citizen boards to review the policies and practices of the departments. Higher standards of training for police and education for law enforcement officials have resulted in increased professionalism among law enforcement agencies.

III. PROSECUTORIAL AGENCIES

Attorneys in prosecutorial agencies are responsible for using the information gathered by police agencies to determine what crime was committed and who should be prosecuted for it. They represent the government (the people) before and at trial and usually make recommendations on the sentencing of offenders.

Prosecutors exercise considerable discretion. Besides deciding criminal charges and against whom to file them, they recommend who should be permitted to go into a community service diversion program rather than receive a felony record, decide who should be offered plea bargains and the extent of the bargain, and, possibly because of community pressure, determine when there will be no plea bargaining, such as in driving while under the influence cases.

At the federal level the chief prosecutor is the attorney general of the United States, appointed by the president and subject to confirmation by the Senate. The attorney general serves as head of the Department of Justice and works closely with the executive branch of government to carry out its policies in federal law enforcement. The prosecutorial arm of the Department of Justice also includes the United States attorneys and assistant U.S. attorneys. The former are appointed by the president and the latter are civil service positions. Both handle cases in the federal district courts from offices distributed geographically throughout the country. Their primary function is to prosecute individuals and corporations for violations of federal criminal statutes. Occasionally special prosecutors are appointed to direct the prosecution of high government officials in order to avoid obvious conflicts of interest for the attorney general. Gaining unfavorable national attention recently in the unsuccessful impeachment trial of President Clinton, the independent counsel law was allowed to expire in 1999. For the near future, at least, the attorney general will appoint special prosecutors.

State prosecutorial agencies are similar to those at the federal level. The highest ranking state prosecutor is the state attorney general, usually an elected official responsible for running the office of attorney general and supervising assistant attorneys general and a large support staff divided into civil, criminal, appellate, consumer

Attorney General Opinions:

a set of formal opinions used as persuasive authority in the argument of criminal cases in that state.

fraud, legal education, and other sections. The attorney general's office handles most of the significant criminal appeals on behalf of the people or the state and may be responsible for prosecuting certain kinds of crimes. It also serves as a resource for other state and local prosecutors. The **Attorney General Opinions,** a set of formal opinions, are used as persuasive authority in the argument of criminal cases in that state.

Titles of prosecutors vary by state and include district attorney, county attorney, prosecuting attorney, commonwealth attorney, and state's attorney. These officials are usually elected in judicial districts that normally follow county or multiple county lines. They are responsible for prosecuting violators of state criminal law. Some of these offices—particularly those in urban counties—may be divided into a number of divisions according to felonies, misdemeanors, and juvenile matters. Assistant prosecutors are common.

Local governments elect or hire county attorneys and city attorneys to prosecute lesser state offenses (misdemeanors) and ordinance (noncriminal) violations. Many of these offices also handle civil cases for the local government and advise local officials on an array of matters.

IV.　DEFENSE BAR

Criminal defense lawyers can work for a public agency, like prosecutors, or for a private law firm (the private defense bar). Many members of the private defense bar specialize in criminal law, others take criminal cases as part of a general practice. Unless appointed to a case by the court, private defense attorneys are retained and paid by the defendant/client like any attorney in a civil case.

Many criminal defendants, however, cannot afford to hire an attorney. In 1963 the Supreme Court of the United States in the case of *Gideon v. Wainwright* stated that the Sixth Amendment to the Constitution of the United States guaranteeing the right to an attorney required the federal government and the states to appoint attorneys at public expense for indigent defendants in felony cases. This ruling was expanded to include misdemeanor cases in *Argersinger v. Hamlin* (1972). The initial attempts to appoint private attorneys to handle these cases met with mixed success, so most states, some with federal aid, established public defender agencies.

Public defender agencies normally are headed by a chief public defender appointed by the governor of the state or hired through state civil service and staffed by salaried attorneys assigned to represent indigent defendants in appellate, trial, and prisoners' rights divisions. On the determination that an accused is indigent, the judge appoints the public defender office to represent that person. Because public defender offices are often understaffed, a number of cases are still assigned to private counsel through the public defender agency or directly by the court.

V.　CORRECTIONS AGENCIES

Corrections agencies are responsible for jails and prisons. If a person is convicted of a misdemeanor, that person may be jailed in the county or municipal jail. Jails are operated under state guidelines but are the responsibility of the county or city government. Some jails are operated by the sheriff's department, others by the police department, and still others by a staff of jail employees. Jailers are still elected in some states, but most states use staff appointed by a county board or local police agency or hired through civil service. Jails, of course, also are used to retain arrested suspects pending court appearances. Many of our nation's local jails are seriously overcrowded and outmoded.

Most states and the federal government have a bureau of prisons or a department of corrections responsible for operating the prisons within the standards established by law. Prisons house the nation's incarcerated felons and range from high-security prisons for hard core, violent criminals to minimum-security prisons for nonviolent, minimum risk criminals. Prison officials are usually civil service employees, but some corrections heads are appointed.

Both the federal and state corrections systems have civil service probation and parole supervisors to assist and supervise offenders placed on probation or parole. **Probation** is a judicial sentence that permits a convicted person to remain free as long as that person meets the conditions imposed by the court.

Parole may be awarded to prison inmates after they serve some of their prison sentence. Parole release is usually reviewed and determined by an independent parole board whose members normally are appointed by the executive office. The board makes its decisions according to established guidelines for release. Parole has been eliminated in the federal correctional system for all crimes committed after November 1, 1987.

probation:
a judicial sentence that permits a convicted person to remain free as long as that person meets the conditions imposed by the court.

parole:
release awarded to prison inmates after they serve some of their prison sentence.

VI. CRIMINAL COURT SYSTEM

A. COURT STRUCTURE

The state and federal court systems most often use the same courts and the same judges for criminal matters as they do for civil matters, although some jurisdictions have established a branch or division specializing in criminal cases. Drug courts are one of the most recent developments in specialized courts. They are designed to help drug addicts (not dealers) break the cycle of dependency through treatment methods proven more effective than jail or prison. Drug courts are demonstrating considerable success both in human terms and in costs to the taxpayer. Some states have a specialized appellate court for criminal cases. A criminal case enters at the trial court level and, if appealed, goes on to the intermediate or final appeals court. If the case is decided by the high court of the state and if there are questions about federal law, including constitutional issues, it may be accepted for appeal by the Supreme Court of the United States. Exhibit 2–1 presents a diagram of the federal criminal court system.

B. JURISDICTION

State courts have jurisdiction over violations of their state criminal law that occur within the boundaries of the state. These courts are divided by counties, districts, or parishes and hear cases arising in those respective geographical areas. State courts also can consider state and federal constitutional questions.

The federal courts hear cases involving violations of federal criminal law and issues arising under the Constitution of the United States. Federal criminal laws cover crimes committed against federal officials, peace officers, foreign officials, and diplomats; crimes committed on federal property; crimes committed in interstate commerce; crimes committed on the high seas (maritime law); customs violations; and crimes related to federal regulatory laws, such as those involving federal banking regulations, securities laws, and others.

Military personnel are subject to the Uniform Code of Military Justice, and if they are accused of a crime, they are tried by military tribunals (courts-martial). Jurisdiction on Native American reservations is divided among tribal, state, and federal courts according to the nature of the offense and the parties involved.

The Internet raises new issues regarding what government, state or federal, has jurisdiction in particular circumstances. For example, does the federal government have jurisdiction over an e-mail transmitted from one resident of Utah to another? Because the transmission had to go from Utah to America OnLine facilities in Virginia and then back to the victim in Utah, the court ruled that the transmission was

EXHIBIT 2–1
Federal Criminal
Courts

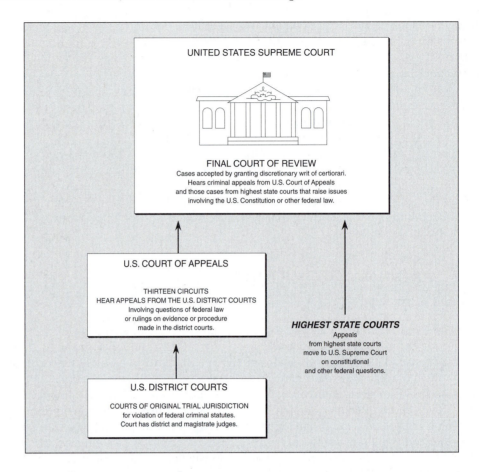

in interstate commerce, and the threat that was transmitted was a violation subject to federal jurisdiction [*U.S. v. Kammersell* (D. Utah, 1998)].

C. CRIMINAL PROCEDURE

In later chapters you will follow the step-by-step procedure of moving a case from complaint through appellate review. For now, however, an overview of what happens to cases as they progress through the system is shown in Exhibit 2–2, Tracking a Case Through the Criminal Justice System.

Many crimes go unreported or undetected and never enter the system. Cases that enter the system are observed by the police or reported to the police, who investigate the matter. As the diagram indicates, several things can happen from that point.

On investigation, (1) the police are unable to solve the crime or decide not to arrest the alleged perpetrator, (2) the perpetrator of the crime is a juvenile and enters the juvenile justice system (a separate arm of the criminal justice system), or (3) the police make an arrest. An **arrest** is the physical or implied seizure or taking into custody of a person by police, significantly restricting a person's freedom of movement and subjecting him or her to the authority of the officer. After arrest and some additional investigation or interrogation, the suspect may be either booked or released.

If the suspect is **booked,** basic information, possibly including fingerprints, is taken and personal property of the accused is inventoried and taken for safekeeping. Here, exculpatory information may be disclosed that leads to the individual's release without further prosecution. It is also at this time that an individual may be released with some preliminary bail deposit or on his or her own recognizance with a request to report back to court for an initial appearance.

arrest:
the physical or implied seizure or taking into custody of a person by police, significantly restricting a person's freedom of movement and subjecting him or her to the authority of the officer.

book:
to record basic information, possibly including fingerprints, from a suspect.

EXHIBIT 2–2
Tracking a Case
Through the Criminal
Justice System

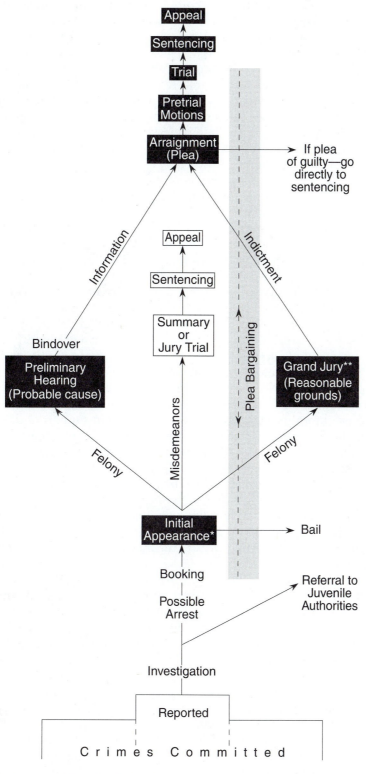

*Some jurisdictions have both preliminary hearings and grand jury, some have one or the other.
** A grand jury proceeding may begin without an arrest or an initial appearance.

initial appearance:
first court appearance where the judge informs the accused of the charges and basic rights to an attorney and to remain silent, and sets bail.

bail:
the amount of money or property that a defendant must post to be released; assurance to the court that the defendant will return to court when required to do so.

summary trial:
for minor charges, a brief judicial inquiry of the suspect and the police to determine guilt.

preliminary hearing:
court appearance to determine if there is probable cause to believe that the defendant has committed the crime as charged.

probable cause:
reasonable grounds for belief; "more than a bare suspicion" and "less than evidence that would justify . . . conviction."

grand jury:
a body of citizens that hears evidence regarding possible criminal activity and decides whether that evidence is sufficient to bring an accused to trial; serves the same function as the preliminary hearing.

arraignment:
an appearance before the judge where the charges, as they stand after the preliminary hearing or the grand jury, are read and a plea is entered.

information:
criminal charging document produced by a preliminary hearing.

indictment:
criminal charging document produced by the grand jury.

plea bargain:
negotiated settlement where the prosecutor reduces the charge, number of charges, or the recommended sentence in return for the defendant's plea of guilty.

Whether the defendant has been released on bail or has been retained in jail, he or she appears before a magistrate or a judge within a reasonable period of time for the **initial appearance.** The prosecutor's office must file charges before the initial appearance. There, the judge informs the accused of those charges and also of his or her basic rights to an attorney and to remain silent. The judge sets bail. **Bail** is the amount of money or property that a defendant must post to be released while assuring the court that the defendant will return to court when required to do so. If the defendant fails to appear as required, the bail money is forfeited. Bail is set according to the seriousness of the crime and the likelihood of the individual's return at the next scheduled court appearance. In relatively minor charges, a **summary trial** involving brief judicial inquiry of the suspect and the police officers may be conducted to determine guilt. If guilt is found, the matter moves immediately to sentencing. Some charges may be dropped or dismissed at the initial appearance after further review by the prosecutor's office. It is also at the initial appearance that the court may determine that the individual is indigent and will appoint counsel.

If the matter is a misdemeanor, it is scheduled for trial. If the crime is a felony, the defendant normally has the right to a **preliminary hearing** to determine whether the state can show that there is **probable cause** to believe that the defendant has committed the crime as charged. If the state fails to meet its burden at this stage, the charges are dismissed but may be reinstated later based on additional evidence. If the state meets its burden at the preliminary hearing, then the matter is moved forward to an arraignment, then to trial, and, if necessary, sentencing.

In other jurisdictions, felony matters are referred to a grand jury as well as, or in place of, the preliminary hearing. A **grand jury** is a body of citizens chosen from the community at large that hears evidence regarding possible criminal activity and decides whether that evidence is sufficient to bring an accused to trial. The grand jury proceeding serves the same function as the preliminary hearing. At the grand jury the prosecutor presents witnesses and evidence in support of the allegations. The defendant does not have the right to be present at the grand jury or to testify. If the grand jury determines that there are reasonable grounds to believe that the individual committed the crime, it indicts the accused, and the matter is referred to the next stage of the process. If the grand jury believes that there is not sufficient evidence to charge the individual, the matter may be dismissed at this point on a refusal to indict. After the grand jury has heard the case or after the court has held a preliminary hearing, charges may be amended from a felony to a misdemeanor. If so, the matter usually is referred back to the misdemeanor division of the criminal court system.

If the judge at the preliminary hearing or the grand jury finds that sufficient evidence exists to believe that the defendant committed the crime, then the defendant is arraigned. An **arraignment** is an appearance before the judge where the charges, as they stand after the preliminary hearing or the grand jury, are read. If the charges come out of the preliminary hearing process, the charging document is an **information.** If they are the product of the grand jury, the charging document is an **indictment.** In addition to reading the charges, the judge asks the defendant to enter a plea to the charge. If the plea is guilty, there is no trial and the matter immediately moves to sentencing. If the plea is not guilty, the defendant is informed of the right to a trial by jury and can elect whether to exercise that right or waive the trial by jury and have the matter tried by a judge. At the arraignment the judge also reconsiders any issue of bail and appoints an attorney for the defendant if necessary. A date for trial is then set.

Prior to trial the case may end as a result of a plea bargain. A **plea bargain** is a form of negotiated settlement where the prosecutor reduces the charge, number of charges, or the recommended sentence in return for the defendant's plea of guilty. If the plea bargain is accepted by the court, a plea is entered and the case goes to sentencing.

If it is necessary to go to trial, the state's duty is to present witnesses and evidence to prove that the defendant is guilty **beyond a reasonable doubt** of the crime charged (See Exhibit 2–3). If during the course of the trial it becomes obvious that the state cannot meet its burden of proof, the charges are dismissed. On completion of the trial, if the judge or jury finds insufficient evidence to convict, the defendant is **acquitted,** found not guilty of the crime. If the jury or the judge finds that the state has met its burden of proof, the defendant is found guilty and the matter moves to sentencing.

At **sentencing** the court considers information relevant to the possible penalty and then assesses the penalty. After sentencing, a **judgment of guilt and sentence** is entered by the court. It is from this judgment that the defendant may appeal. On some issues concerning procedure or other court error, it is possible that either side may appeal the case, depending on which one is dissatisfied with the judgment. The appeal is processed through the appellate court system.

Following sentencing, individuals enter the corrections phase of the system. They may be placed on probation, fined, required to perform community service, or incarcerated in a county jail or in a penitentiary. If a prisoner feels that the case has been mishandled or that an injustice has occurred, the prisoner may file for a **writ of habeas corpus.** This is a writ that requires law enforcement to present the individual

beyond a reasonable doubt:
the burden of proof borne by the state in a criminal trial; proof of sufficient weight to exclude any other reasonable explanation than the defendant's guilt.

acquit:
to find not guilty of a crime.

sentence:
assessment of penalty for a crime.

judgment of guilt and sentence:
the document entered by the court after sentencing from which the defendant may appeal.

habeas corpus, writ of:
prevents incarceration without justification; requires law enforcement to present the individual before a judge to determine whether the person has been fairly convicted and incarcerated.

EXHIBIT 2–3
Sample Jury Instructions

PRESUMPTION OF INNOCENCE—BURDEN OF PROOF— REASONABLE DOUBT

"(1) As you know, the defendant has pleaded not guilty to the crime charged in the indictment. The indictment is not any evidence at all of guilt. It is just the formal way that the government tells the defendant what crime he is accused of committing. It does not even raise any suspicion of guilt.

(2) Instead, the defendant starts the trial with a clean slate, with no evidence at all against him, and the law presumes that he is innocent. This presumption of innocence stays with him unless the government presents evidence here in court that overcomes the presumption, and convinces you beyond a reasonable doubt that he is guilty.

(3) This means that the defendant has no obligation to present any evidence at all, or to prove to you in any way that he is innocent. It is up to the government to prove that he is guilty, and this burden stays on the government from start to finish. You must find the defendant not guilty unless the government convinces you beyond a reasonable doubt that he is guilty.

(4) The government must prove every element of the crime charged beyond a reasonable doubt. Proof beyond a reasonable doubt does not mean proof beyond all possible doubt. Possible doubts or doubts based purely on speculation are not reasonable doubts. A reasonable doubt is a doubt based on reason and common sense. It may arise from the evidence, the lack of evidence, or the nature of the evidence.

(5) Proof beyond a reasonable doubt means proof which is so convincing that you would not hesitate to rely and act on it in making the most important decisions in your own lives. If you are convinced that the government has proved the defendant guilty beyond a reasonable doubt, say so by returning a guilty verdict. If you are not convinced, say so by returning a not guilty verdict."

Pattern Criminal Jury Instructions of the District Judges Association of the Sixth Circuit, Instruction No. 1.03 (1991).

See *United States v. Kirby,* 838 F.2d 189, 191–192 (6th Cir.1988).

Edward J. De Vitt, Charles B. Blackmar, Michael A. Wolff, and Kevin O'Malley, *Federal Jury Practice and Instructions,* vol. 1 (St. Paul: West Group, 1992), 365, with permission.

before a judge to determine whether the person has been fairly convicted and incarcerated. The prisoner may be released as a result of this habeas corpus petition. If a person on probation or parole violates its conditions, the probation or parole is revoked and the person is incarcerated. After completing the sentence, the individual is released.

VII. PROFESSIONAL ETHICS IN CRIMINAL LAW PRACTICE

A. INTRODUCTION

Surveys show that of the three branches of government, our judicial branch remains the most arcane and misunderstood. The criminal justice system is no exception to that unpleasant reality, even though crime receives much attention in our popular media. The fact is that the members of the media largely misunderstand the system and, therefore, do a poor job of educating the public. For this reason, most citizens do not understand why "guilty" criminals deserve to be represented by an attorney, why an attorney with any morals represents a "guilty" criminal, why judges dismiss cases against "criminals" simply on "technicalities," why expensive and time-consuming juries are necessary, and why we go through so much trouble just to find someone guilty whom "everyone already knows" is guilty.

Citizens need to be reminded regularly that this society places paramount importance on preserving individual liberty. Any deprivation of that liberty through punishment must be based on a fair determination of the truth. In the effort to find that truth, we adopted the adversary system of justice.

B. ADVERSARY SYSTEM

adversary system:
a highly competitive issue-resolving process in which two opposing sides attempt to provide the best information they can to convince the neutral tribunal of judge or jury to decide the issue in their favor.

Both our civil and criminal systems rely heavily on the **adversary system,** a highly competitive issue-resolving process in which two opposing sides attempt to provide the best information they can to convince the neutral tribunal of judge or jury to decide the issue in their favor. The system's rationale stems from the belief that if two opposed sides have much at stake in the outcome of the case, that stake will provide them with motivation to research the law, find witnesses, and present the most persuasive information they can to the decision maker. The decision maker (judge or jury) then has the best possible information submitted by the two opponents on which to decide the matter. If only one side could present evidence or, even worse, if a judge were responsible for both investigating and deciding a case, there might be little motivation to find all the facts. Who is likely to be more motivated to do the needed work, the person facing five years in prison or the judge who has heard it all before? Also, is it not possible that the nonadversary judge might become more interested in getting information to support conviction than in being impartial?

The adversary system, therefore, pits the prosecution, who represents the people, against the defense, who represents the accused. In order for the system to work, ethical attorneys for both sides must represent their clients zealously. Both sides must be thoroughly prepared, follow every avenue that leads to information, and present the best case for the client so that an impartial decision maker can make a fair judgment.

Though the theoretical heart of the adversary system is finding the truth, the system in its quest for the truth is hardly free from criticism. Its extreme competitiveness creates considerable stress for all participants, it invites unpleasant and sometimes demeaning confrontation, its theoretical balance can be too easily tipped toward one side or the other, and it may not be best suited for all types of cases. Nevertheless, the adversary system has established a reasonably good record for fairness and justice.

C. ROLE OF THE PROSECUTOR

To many, the prosecutor should be the champion of the people and the victim, and must stop crime by getting every conviction possible. The prosecutor's role, however, is more complex than that. Standard 3-1.1(c) of the American Bar Association (ABA) Standards for Criminal Justice states

The duty of the prosecutor is to seek justice, not merely to convict.[2]

The Commentary to the standard elaborates

Although the prosecutor operates within the adversary system, it is fundamental that the prosecutor's obligation is to protect the innocent as well as to convict the guilty, to guard the rights of the accused as well as to enforce the rights of the public.[3]

Therefore, the adversarial duty of the prosecutor to pursue conviction zealously must be restrained by the superseding duty to preserve fairness and to protect innocence. In addition, the prosecutor is responsible for the prosecutorial arm of government and the weighty decisions regarding when charges should be brought and for what crime, and what degree of punishment should be recommended for the convicted. The prosecutor is charged with achieving a "fair, efficient, and effective enforcement of criminal law."[4] The duality of the prosecutor's role is reflected in the following ethical rules paraphrased from the ABA's Model Rules of Professional Conduct and related ABA Standards for Criminal Justice:

1. A prosecutor should not exploit the office to gain personal publicity. (Standard 3-1.3)
2. It is unethical intentionally to misrepresent facts or mislead the court. (Standard 3-2.9, Model Rule 3.3)
3. The prosecutor must strive to avoid undue influence on the grand jury. [Standard 3-3.5, Model Rule 3.3(d)]
4. The prosecutor may pay witness expenses only; expert witnesses may be paid expenses and fees. (Standard 3-3.2)
5. If the prosecutor believes a witness's conduct may be illegal, the witness should be warned of possible incrimination and the need for an attorney. (Standard 3-3.2)
6. The prosecutor should avoid relationships that cast doubt on the independence and integrity of the office. (Standard 3-2.8)
7. The prosecutor should not seek to influence opinion of an expert witness. (Standard 3-3.3)
8. The prosecutor should not knowingly use or instruct others to use illegal means to obtain evidence or obstruct communication between a potential witness and defense counsel. (Standards 3-3.1, Model Rule 4.4)
9. The prosecutor should recommend to a grand jury that they not indict if the grand jury believes the evidence does not warrant indictment. (Standard 3-3.6)
10. It is unethical to bring charges the prosecutor knows are without sufficient admissible evidence or to "seek charges greater in number or degree" than evidence will reasonably support. [Standard 3-3.9, Model Rule 3.8(a)]
11. The prosecutor shall not seek an unrepresented defendant's waiver of rights. [Model Rule 3.8(c)]
12. It is unethical to avoid investigating leads favorable to the accused. (Standard 3-3.11)
13. The prosecutor cannot obstruct an opponent's access to evidence. (Model Rule 3.4)
14. The prosecutor must reveal to the defense in a timely fashion all evidence tending to negate guilt or reduce punishment of the accused. [Standard 3-3.11, Model Rule 3.8(d)]

15. It is unethical "to knowingly offer false evidence" or not to seek its withdrawal once discovered. (Standard 3-5.6)
16. The prosecutor should not use the power of cross-examination to discredit a witness he or she knows is telling the truth. (Standard 3-5.7)
17. It is unethical when addressing a jury to express opinions on the "truth or falsity of evidence or guilt of defendant." (Standard 3-5.8, Model Rule 3.4)
18. The prosecutor should not always seek the severest penalty, but should seek a fair and informed judgment. [Standard 3-6.1, Model Rule 3.8(d)]

The proper role of the prosecutor goes well beyond our society's need for aggressive prosecution of crime to encompass responsibilities both to the accused and to a fair system of justice. These responsibilities reflect some of humanity's highest aspirations, but in practice they are difficult to balance and are often misunderstood by the public. Consequently, the prosecutor is at the same time honored and burdened by the expectation to be all things for all people while providing a vital service to the community. Your awareness of the dual nature of the prosecutor's job and its strict ethical standards are critical to the successful performance of your job.

D. ROLE OF THE DEFENSE ATTORNEY

In an adversary system that is deliberately weighted to protect the innocent by placing the obligation on the state to prove that the defendant is guilty, it is the role and ethical duty of the defense attorney to put the state to the test of its proof. Regardless of any admission of guilt on the part of the defendant or of how heinous the crime accused, defense counsel has the obligation to represent the client zealously and courageously and has the right to put the government to its proof. Without such a test for the benefit of each defendant, all of us would eventually lose our right to be presumed innocent; all of us would be vulnerable to a failing, one-sided system in which due process would be a farce.

Even though the prosecutor has a duty to see that justice is done, it is the defense attorney who is likely to raise issues such as illegal investigation methods, illegal searches and seizures, unfair lineups, unconstitutional criminal laws, improper judicial decisions and procedures, illegal incarceration, and others. These objections often address serious invasions of a citizen's right to privacy, freedom of religion or speech, the right to a fair trial, the right to freedom from cruel and unusual punishment, the right to equal protection under the laws, and other rights absolutely essential to the preservation of individual liberty and dignity. It is the defense counsel who has the duty to challenge any overreaching of police, prosecutor, judge, and system to prevent the erosion of the rights of all citizens. For this reason the defense lawyer needs to be ever vigilant and aggressive.

Advocacy is not for the timid, the meek, or the retiring. Our system of justice is inherently contentious, albeit bounded by the rules of professional ethics and decorum, and it demands that the lawyer be inclined toward vigorous advocacy.[5]

Few of us will ever be wrongfully accused of a crime, so it is difficult to take seriously the need for such defense safeguards, but innocent individuals accused of crimes exist in greater numbers than most people realize, and not just on television or in novels. One sobering statistic helps make the point. Because of wrongful convictions, seventy-seven inmates of death row have been freed since the death penalty was reinstated in 1976.[6]

The defense lawyer is not subject to every whim or direction of the client. The defense lawyer must exercise firm, independent, professional judgment in order to be an effective advisor and representative.[7]

Because the role of the defense counsel, like that of the prosecutor, is so crucial to a fair system of justice, and because inevitable conflicts arise, the ABA's Standards for Criminal Justice and the Model Rules address the conduct of the defense attorney. A paraphrase of some of the more significant standards and rules for defense counsel follows:

1. It is unethical to misrepresent matters of fact or law or assist a client in committing perjury. (Standard 4-1.1, Model Rules 3.3, 3.4, and 4.1)
2. Defense counsel should avoid unnecessary delay and be punctual in submitting all briefs, motions, and other papers. [Standard 4-1.2(a), Model Rule 3.2]
3. Defense counsel should not accept more cases than can be discharged giving each client effective representation. [Standard 4-1.2(d)]
4. It is unethical to make an agreement to have law enforcement or court personnel or bondsmen refer potential clients to the lawyer or to divide a fee with a nonlawyer, or to approach people with the purpose of having them employ the lawyer. [Standard 4-2.3, Model Rules 4-3.3(d), 5.4, and 7.3]
5. Defense counsel should try to develop a "relationship of trust and confidence with accused," explaining that the accused needs to disclose all facts and that the confidentiality of those facts will be held inviolate. (Standard 4-3.1, p. 4.28, Model Rule 1.6)
6. It is unethical in criminal cases to loan the fee to a client, charge a fee contingent on results, or charge a fee that is excessive. [Standard 4-3.3(c)]
7. It is unethical while representing the client in a particular case to enter into an agreement for publication rights with respect to the case or to speak to the media with the intention of materially prejudicing the proceeding. (Standard 4-3.4, Model Rule 3.6)
8. Defense counsel must refrain from conflicts of interest or inform the client of such conflicts and proceed only with the client's permission and the lawyer's belief that conflicts will not affect the lawyer's loyalty to the client. [Standard 4-3.5(a), Model Rule 1.7]
9. Defense counsel should not represent more than one defendant in the same criminal case unless it is clear that conflicts of interest between the defendants are unlikely, and each defendant gives permission to the joint representation. (Standard 4-3.5, Model Rule 1.7)
10. It is unethical to defend a criminal case in which the lawyer's partner or associate is or has been the prosecutor. [Standard 4-3.5(d)]
11. It is unethical "to counsel a client in or knowingly assist a client to engage in conduct which the lawyer knows to be illegal or fraudulent." [Standard 4.37(b)]
12. Defense counsel should keep the client informed of all developments in the case. (Standard 4-3.8)
13. It is unethical knowingly to use illegal means to investigate a case or to hire, instruct, or urge others to do so. (Standard 4-4.2, Model Rule 4.4)
14. It is not necessary for a defense attorney to inform a witness that counsel suspects is guilty of criminal activity of that witness's right against incrimination or the need for counsel. [Standard 4-4.3(b)]
15. It is unethical to obstruct communication between a witness and the prosecution or not to correct a witness's misunderstanding of what the lawyer represents. [Standard 4-4.3(c), Model Rules 3.4 and 4.3]
16. Defense counsel should comply in good faith with all discovery requests. (Standard 4-5.5, Model Rule 3.4)
17. "A lawyer's advice to a defendant to plead guilty merely because the defendant has admitted guilt to the lawyer, without exploring all of the relevant facts or attempting to determine whether the prosecution can establish guilt, is improper." (Standard 4-5.1)
18. It is unethical in plea bargaining to favor one client at the expense of another. (Standard 4-6.2)
19. It is not unethical at trial for defense counsel to attempt to undermine the testimony of a witness that the attorney believes is telling the truth if it is for the purpose of putting the state to its proof. (Standard 4-7.6, Model Rule 3.1)

20. It is unethical for a lawyer to falsify evidence, to counsel or assist a witness to lie, or to offer an illegal inducement to a witness. [Model Rule 3.4(b)]
21. It is unethical to advertise services in a manner that is misleading or "likely to create unjustified expectation." (Model Rule 7.1)

E. ROLE OF THE JUDGE

The judge's role in criminal matters is essential for the system to work with proper dignity, fairness, and efficiency.

Standard 6-1.1

(a) The trial judge has the responsibility for safeguarding both the rights of the accused and the interests of the public in the administration of justice. The advocacy nature of the proceedings does not relieve the trial judge of the obligation of raising on his or her initiative at all appropriate times and in an appropriate manner, matters which may significantly promote a just determination of the trial. The only purpose of a criminal trial is to determine whether the prosecution has established the guilt of the accused as required by law, and the trial judge should not allow the proceedings to be used for any other purpose.

(b) The trial judge should require that every proceeding before him or her be conducted with unhurried and quiet dignity and should aim to establish such physical surroundings as are appropriate to the administration of justice. The trial judge should give each case individual treatment and the judge's decisions should be based on the particular facts of that case. The trial judge should conduct the proceedings in clear language and easily understood language using an interpreter when necessary.

(c) The trial judge should be sensitive to the important roles of the prosecutor and defense counsel; and the judge's conduct toward them should manifest professional respect, courtesy, and fairness.[8]

A few of the more specific ABA Standards for Criminal Justice related to the judge's role are paraphrased here.

1. The judge's conduct should promote confidence in the impartiality of the court and avoid impropriety or its appearance. (Standard 6-6.5)
2. The judge should not permit outside influences such as family, friends, or other matters to influence judicial judgments. (Standard 6-1.5)
3. Judges should disqualify (recuse) themselves if in any matter they doubt their ability to be fair or whenever their "impartiality can reasonably be questioned." (Standard 6-1.7)
4. The judge should carefully review all warrants for search or arrest to see that they meet constitutional standards and prevent these matters from becoming perfunctory. (Standard 6-1.8)

VIII. ROLE OF THE PARALEGAL

A. PARALEGAL TASKS IN CRIMINAL LAW OFFICES

Paralegals can perform a variety of tasks in criminal law offices in both public (government offices) and private offices. In prosecutors' offices, paralegal duties include all or some of the following:

1. Intake
   a. interview persons reporting criminal behavior;
   b. interview police officers or read police reports.
2. Recommend preliminary charges
   a. research facts and determine what crime has been committed and what statutes or ordinances apply;
   b. make recommendations to prosecuting attorney.

  3. Draft criminal complaint and other charging documents.
  4. Attend court to record the defendant's plea.
  5. Investigate
     a. when police officers are not available;
     b. to clarify minor points in the investigation record.
  6. Prepare for grand jury
     a. prepare documents for the grand jury;
     b. assist witnesses who appear before grand jury or other court proceedings.
  7. Take notes and assist at hearings or trials.
  8. Serve as resource person for victims of crimes and their families.
  9. Do legal research and prepare responses to motions submitted by the defense counsel.
  10. Prepare trial notebooks.
  11. Design and prepare exhibits.
  12. Help prepare witnesses for trial.
  13. Assist at trial.
  14. Assist in posttrial and appellate process.

In public defender and private defense attorney offices, paralegals perform all or some of the following tasks.

  1. Do initial interview with client and follow-up interviews.
  2. Do legal research into charge, its adequacy and appropriateness.
  3. Draft legal memoranda and briefs.
  4. Investigate the case and interview witnesses.
  5. Draft motions
     a. to dismiss complaint;
     b. to challenge the legality of evidence;
     c. to raise other points before the court.
  6. Attend preliminary hearing and take notes.
  7. Assist in the preparation of the case for trial.
  8. Design and prepare exhibits.
  9. Prepare trial notebook.
  10. Assist in the preparation of client and witnesses for trial.
  11. Draft subpoenas, locate witnesses, and serve subpoenas.
  12. Assist at trial.
  13. Prepare response to presentence report, including response to alternative sentencing proposals.
  14. Draft posttrial motions.
  15. Assist at appellate level.
  16. Serve as resource person for defendant, family, and witnesses.

Paralegals may also perform miscellaneous administrative and related functions, as follows:

  1. Prepare office and procedural manuals.
  2. Design and prepare office practice systems manuals.
  3. Manage and supervise paralegals and other office personnel.
  4. Perform other duties involving legal administration.

Although these are the most common duties of criminal law paralegals, other offices may require other tasks. In the Attorney General's office paralegals help investigate cases, file criminal charges, and do research and drafting in support of the appellate process. Paralegals are working in *child support officer programs* associated with many prosecutors' offices. Their duties include office administration, drafting legal forms, finding parents who are delinquent in child support payments, and preparing documents necessary to prosecute those delinquent parents.

Paralegals also work as *pretrial release officers*, interviewing individuals who have been arrested and jailed to determine whether there are grounds to have them released on bail prior to their first appearance. On gathering information about the jailed individual, the pretrial officer makes a recommendation to the court regarding the amount of bail required for release of this individual.

Some paralegals are employed as *mediation officers* who take minor criminal matters and bring both parties together to determine whether there is some fair and reasonable resolution. For example, mediation of a dispute between neighbors leading to a disorderly conduct charge may be preferable to a full-fledged trial. Adversarial court battles often make matters worse, particularly for people who must return to the same neighborhood.

Paralegals working as *sentencing specialists* may work in defense offices or be called in to prepare a sentencing recommendation more favorable to the defendant than that recommended by the prosecution or probation officer. The recommendation is based on intensive investigation into the defendant's background and circumstances.

In addition, paralegals are employed in government agencies at all levels of both the state and federal government. These *administrative agencies* have rules and regulations that carry criminal or quasi-criminal penalties for violations of such things as fair labor standards, food and drug administration standards, or civil rights. In such offices, paralegals primarily perform investigations, gather information, and prepare documents in support of any action that might be taken against the offender. Paralegals also perform supportive functions for the Federal Bureau of Investigation, police agencies at both the state and federal level, and in the Department of Justice. More recently paralegals have been hired in juvenile support services and as *victim and spouse abuse advocates*.

B. PARALEGAL ETHICAL RESPONSIBILITIES[9]

1. Introduction

Soon you will be working with cases and the people involved in those cases. In dealing with others, be ever mindful of the high standard of professional ethics to which your actions must conform. **Professional ethics** as applied to attorneys are the rules of conduct that govern the practice of law. It is the responsibility of each person working in the law office to know what is expected and to act accordingly. A breach of ethical standards will reflect badly on the entire office and also may lead to the disbarment of one or more attorneys. It may cost you your job and subject you to prosecution for the unauthorized practice of law.

2. What a Paralegal May Not Do

Except as specifically permitted by law, paralegals *may not* perform any of the following functions:

1. Provide legal services directly to the public without the supervision of an attorney.
2. Give legal advice or counsel a client. **Legal advice** is independent professional judgment based on knowledge of the law and given for the benefit of a particular client. It may be offered only by an attorney.
3. Represent a client in court or other tribunal or otherwise act as an advocate for a client.
4. Accept or reject cases for the firm.
5. Set any fee for representation of a client.
6. Split legal fees with an attorney (bonuses and profit-sharing plans not tied to a specific case are permissible).
7. Be a partner with a lawyer when any of the activities of the partnership include the practice of law.

---

professional ethics: rules of conduct that govern the practice of that profession.

"A lawyer's advice is his stock in trade."

—Attributed to Abraham Lincoln, 1809–1865
M. Francis McNamara, *Ragbag of Legal Quotations,* 1960

legal advice: independent professional judgment based on knowledge of the law and given for the benefit of a particular client; may be offered only by an attorney.

8. Perform tasks that require legal judgment without the supervision of an attorney unless specifically permitted by law.
9. Solicit cases for a lawyer.

Giving legal advice, item 2, is a particularly dangerous pitfall for paralegals. The question as to which judge would be best to try a case calls for knowledge about how judges have applied the law in the past, and for judgment about how that impacts on a particular case. Thus, answering that question would be giving legal advice. If the case is already assigned to a judge, however, asking which judge has been assigned to the case calls for factual information that is a matter of public record and requires no exercise of legal judgment. Thus, this question does not call for legal advice. Can a paralegal answer a question, for example, as to whether a repeat offender (three strikes) law exists in a given state? This is less clear. The answer is a matter of public record (the statutes) and requires no exercise of judgment. Nevertheless, some members of the bar are uncomfortable with a paralegal answering such a question.

3.   What a Paralegal May Do

Legislation has been proposed in several states to permit paralegals to provide limited legal services directly to the public. Although all of these bills have failed, unmet legal needs will be the basis for a continuing debate as to whether paralegals should be permitted to do more. Currently paralegals may perform a wide array of tasks and be confident their work will not create a breach of ethics if it meets certain criteria. A paralegal may be designated to render service under the following conditions.

1. The task must be delegated by an attorney.
2. The task must be performed under an attorney's supervision.
3. Paralegals must clearly designate their status as a paralegal.
4. The lawyer must retain a direct relationship with the client (the attorney must retain control over the relationship).
5. The task must involve information gathering or be ministerial and cannot involve the rendering of legal advice or judgment (unless the legal advice or judgment is provided by the paralegal directly to the attorney).
6. The work must be given final approval or be examined by the attorney.
7. The work must not have a separate identity but must merge with the attorney's final work product.

In addition, a paralegal may have a business card with the firm's name on it as long as the paralegal is designated as such.

4.   Confidentiality, Honesty, and Conflict of Interest

Paralegal ethical standards, for all practical purposes, are the same as those for attorneys. Attorneys, not paralegals, are subject to discipline by the bar for ethical breaches. Paralegals, however, are bound by the nature of their work to uphold each rule as if they were the attorney.

Attorneys are bound by the ethical standards set by their state's highest court. Most states have adopted the ABA's Model Rules of Professional Conduct with some local amendments. Studying these rules provides a paralegal with an understanding of most of the ethical standards in effect in any particular state. Because some states have deleted or amended some of the ABA's rules, however, you should obtain a copy of your state's version of the ethical standards.

A paralegal shall hold inviolate the confidences of a client. Except with written permission by the client, nothing the client tells you or that you learn about the client may be revealed to anyone outside the office, not even to a spouse or parent. In addition, to preserve confidentiality, a client's statement to you or other employees of the firm should not be made in the presence of outsiders. Careless use of cell phones, fax machines, and e-mail has resulted in breaches of client confidentiality. In either a prosecutor's office or a defender's office, treat each case and its contents as confidential.

Under rule 1.6 of the ABA's Model Rules of Professional Conduct, an attorney may breach client confidentiality only to prevent an act of the client that is likely to cause substantial physical harm. Some states including Florida, Virginia, Pennsylvania, New Jersey, Wisconsin, Ohio, and Hawaii permit disclosure to prevent or rectify serious crime, including fraud. The ABA is considering a similar approach.[10]

A paralegal must maintain the highest standards of professional integrity and avoid any dishonesty, fraud, deceit, or misrepresentation. This rule applies to all dealings with clients, judges, court employees, opposing attorneys, and the public.

A paralegal should avoid and reveal any conflicts of interest. A lawyer is required to represent the client zealously and to avoid interests or conflicts that would dilute allegiance to the client. A paralegal also must be loyal to the client and avoid such conflicts. At the prosecutor's office, the public is the "client" and a conflict of interest would occur if a paralegal on a case was related to the defendant in that case.

A conflict of interest would occur if a private firm representing Lacey Rude (Case III) also accepted the assignment to defend Cat Bermuda. In this situation, Ms. Bermuda might get an offer for a reduced sentence if she testified that Rude had stolen the artifact before Bermuda did. The firm cannot do the best for both clients. Therefore, the second client should not be accepted.

Another conflict of interest would arise if a prosecution paralegal had a financial interest in a local business, and the principal owners were being prosecuted for criminal activity. It is obvious that the paralegal may hesitate to do the best job possible when the outcome of the case could have an adverse effect on the paralegal's income. In such a situation, the paralegal should inform the supervising attorney of the conflict. A remedy for the conflict would be to take the paralegal off that case.

A third type of conflict of interest can occur when a paralegal changes jobs from one law office to another. If the paralegal worked on behalf of Miguel Cordoba (Case II) at a private firm, but now must handle the case against Mr. Cordoba at the prosecutor's office, it is likely that confidential information gained from Mr. Cordoba while working for the first firm would be used against him at the second office. Again, the paralegal should inform the supervising attorney and be removed from any involvement in any cases against Mr. Cordoba. If at any time paralegals feel unable to give clients their best work, they should discuss it with the attorneys on the cases.

C. OTHER PROFESSIONAL CONSIDERATIONS

There are some professional ethics that are not found in the codes, but are nevertheless quite important. It is especially important in professional working relationships to have mutual respect and loyalty between employer and employees. Publicly criticizing one's fellow workers is not consistent with professional loyalty. That is also true regarding crime victims as well as defense clients who deserve the utmost courtesy, respect, and every effort on your part to preserve their dignity.

Professional loyalty to the office extends to the practice of law, which supersedes loyalty to any specific individual. Attorneys are expected to call attention to the unethical practices of other attorneys, or in some instances, of their own clients. Similarly, a paralegal must be prepared to report unethical behavior to the appropriate person within the office.

In addition, paralegals must strive to be competent and current in the field. Firms also appreciate assistance in efforts to provide free legal services to the poor, called **pro bono** cases.

pro bono:
provision of free legal services to the poor.

Study ethics in more detail as you learn other paralegal tasks. The more you know about the ethical responsibilities of the attorney and paralegal, the more likely you will spot and avoid trouble. The standards and ethical rules are covered only in part in this chapter for the prosecutor, the defense attorney, and the judge. These rules and the guidelines set out for the paralegal should become a part of your personal awareness of what is expected of both attorney and paralegal. For all practical purposes, what binds and limits the attorney, binds and limits the paralegal.

D. PROFESSIONAL DEVELOPMENT

Professionals, including paralegals, continually take steps to improve themselves and their professions. You are encouraged to actively pursue your own professional development. Be informed on the progress and issues concerning the paralegal profession; attend continuing education seminars; seek leadership and other service positions in paralegal associations; support progressive paralegal education of high quality; and subscribe to literature that is pertinent to and will benefit your career. A list of helpful organizations and literature follows:

- Your local paralegal association
- American Association for Paralegal Education
  2965 Flowers Road South, Suite 105
  Atlanta, GA 30341
  (770) 452-9877
  Fax: (770) 458-3314
  e-mail: assnhq@mindspring.com
  web: http://www.aafpe.org
  Publications: *The Paralegal Educator; The Journal of Paralegal Education and Practice*
- American Bar Association
  750 North Lake Shore Drive
  Chicago, IL 60611
  (312) 988-5000
  e-mail: info@abanet.org
  web: http://www.abanet.org
  ABA Standing Committee on Legal Assistants
  e-mail: legalassts@abanet.org
  web: http://www.abanet.org/legalassts/home
- Legal Assistant Management Association
  2965 Flowers Road South, Suite 105
  Atlanta, GA 30341
  (770) 457-7746
  Fax: (770) 458-3314
  e-mail: lamaoffice@aol.com
  web: http://www.lamanet.org
- National Association of Legal Assistants
  1516 South Boston, #200
  Tulsa, OK 74119
  (918) 587-6828
  Fax: (918) 582-6772
  web: http://www.nala.org
  Publication: *Facts and Findings*
- National Federation of Paralegal Associations
  P.O. Box 33108
  Kansas City, MO 64114
  (816) 941-4000
  Fax: (816) 941-2725
  e-mail: info@paralegals.org
  web: http://www.paralegals.org
  Publication: *National Paralegal Reporter*

■ *Legal Assistant Today*
James Publishing, Inc.
3520 Cadillac Avenue, Suite E
Costa Mesa, CA 92626
(714) 755-5450
Fax: Managing Editor (714) 751-5508
e-mail: rhughes@jamespublishing.com
web: www.jamespublishing.com

IX. CONCLUSION

As a paralegal working within the criminal justice system, you are likely to have contact with people from several branches of the system: law enforcement, prosecution, defense, corrections, and courts. Understanding each of these components will help you master your own part of the system. A grasp of the rationale behind the adversary system gives you a basis for some of the procedural and ethical demands of the field. The roles of the officers of the court follow from those demands. Finally, it comes down to where you, the paralegal, fit into the system and into the limits, responsibilities, and expectations of your profession.

As you learn more about criminal law and work on the cases that are assigned to you, keep in mind that you are an important component in the criminal justice system. Your understanding of the system and your approach to your work in it can make a difference in the lives of real people and in the success of the system in achieving justice.

SYSTEM FOLDER ASSIGNMENTS

Complete the following and place the documents in your system folder:

- Diagram of your state court structure, indicating the responsibility of each level of court for criminal matters and the general flow of criminal cases.
- Diagram of the federal courts.
- Diagram or outline showing the steps of a case through the criminal justice system.
- Names, mail and electronic addresses, and phone numbers of your local and state paralegal associations and information on state prosecutor or criminal defense associations. (If you need help obtaining this information, try the director of a local paralegal program or any experienced paralegal. The headquarters of the state bar association also might have such information.)
- Expanded list of sources for professional development.
- Lists of rules of ethics.

APPLICATION ASSIGNMENTS

1. Assume that you are a research assistant for your United States senator. Also assume that recent publicity about long jury trials and numerous habeas corpus filings has made clear the high expense of these processes to the government. As a result, a serious proposal is scheduled to come before the Senate to amend the Constitution to abolish both the right to a jury trial and the right to file the writ of habeas corpus. Your job is to research the rationale and history behind these two rights and make a recommendation to the senator regarding the constitutional amendment. Using material in Chapter 14 and outside reading, write a two-page summary of your findings for a memo to the senator.

HELPFUL WEB SITES

www.uscourts.gov
  Administrative Office of the United States Courts
www.ncsc.dni.us
  National Center for State Courts
www.ojp.usdoj.gov/dcpo
  Office of Justice Programs, Drug Courts Program Office, state by state list of program managers
www.naag.org
  National Association of Attorneys General
www.legalethics.com
  General ethics codes, state and professional codes, Internet ethics issues
www.lectlaw.com
  Sections on paralegals, ethics, expert witnesses, and consultants; humor
www.nalanet.org
  National Association of Legal Assistants
www.paralegals.org
  National Federation of Paralegal Associations
www.lamanet.org
  Legal Assistant Management Association
www.lawjobs.com
  Listings of employment opportunities in legal fields

INTERNET EXERCISES

1. Visit www.legalethics.com. Make note of your state's code of ethics, if listed, and the Model Code of Professional Responsibility for Paralegals. Place outlines in your system folder.
2. Visit the NALA and NFPA sites to find out the current number of members in each.

QUESTIONS FOR STUDY AND REVIEW

Study the terms, definitions, concepts, and procedures covered in this chapter.
Prepare for a test on the material in this chapter by using the following questions to guide your study:

1. List the various criminal law agencies and the titles and functions of their various officers as described in this chapter.
2. In detail, describe the federal and your state court systems as relevant to the processing of criminal cases.
3. What are the steps in criminal procedure? At which point can cases leave the system without a conviction?
4. What is the adversary system? What is its function?
5. What is the role of the prosecutor in the adversary system? What is unique about that role?
6. What is the role of defense counsel in the adversary system, and why is it important to every citizen?
7. What ethical expectations must a paralegal keep in mind when working for a prosecutor? A defense attorney? A judge?
8. Briefly describe the various kinds of tasks a paralegal is likely to perform in a criminal law office.
9. Beyond the specific standards and rules of ethics that govern prosecutors and defense attorneys, what additional significant rules of ethics apply to paralegals?

10. What loyalties are important to the paralegal when working in the criminal law office?
11. Identify one local or state paralegal association.

KEY TERMS LIST

Acquit	Habeas corpus, writ of	Preliminary hearing
Adversary system	Indictment	Probable cause
Arraignment	Information	Probation
Arrest	Initial appearance	Pro bono
Attorney General Opinions	Judgment of guilt and	Professional ethics
Bail	sentence	Sentence
Beyond a reasonable doubt	Legal advice	Summary trial
Book	Parole	
Grand jury	Plea bargain	

ENDNOTES

1. *Mission Statement*, Federal Bureau of Investigation, www.fbi.gov/yourfbi/facts/fbimission.htlm, March, 1999.
2. 1 ABA STANDARDS FOR CRIMINAL JUSTICE § 3.6 (1980), with permission of the American Bar Association.
3. *Id.* § 3.7, with permission.
4. *Id.* Standard 3-2.5, § 3.24, with permission.
5. *Id.* Commentary to Standard 4-1.1 on the Role of Defense Counsel, § 4.8, with permission.
6. Viveca Novak, *The Cost of Poor Advice*, TIME, JULY 5, 1999, AT 38.
7. 1 ABA STANDARDS FOR CRIMINAL JUSTICE, STANDARD 4-1.1(c) (1980), with permission of the American Bar Association.
8. *Id.*
9. Excerpted and adapted from JAMES MCCORD, THE LITIGATION PARALEGAL: A SYSTEMS APPROACH 16–20 (3rd ed. 1997) with permission of West Group, St. Paul, Minnesota.
10. M. Goldhaber, *Blowing a Whistle on Client Misdeeds*, NLJ, Oct. 25, 1999, A1, A4.

COMPONENTS OF A CRIME

I. INTRODUCTION

A. COMPONENTS

This chapter focuses on the substantive law principles that define criminal liability—the components of a crime. The components of a crime are

1. Harm or likely harm—an injury or likely injury.
2. Actus reus—a guilty act.
3. Mens rea—a guilty mind.
4. Causation—that the harm or likely harm is a direct result of the guilty act.

Harm is usually placed after actus reus and mens rea in the consideration of components of crimes, but it is placed first here for three reasons. A discussion of harm is basic to the classification of crimes, harm is often the first component that is apparent when a crime has been committed, and harm is the reason that specific conduct has been criminalized.

An understanding of any specific crime and the paralegal tasks related to it is based on a grasp of these components. From them are drawn the elements that must be proven beyond a reasonable doubt by the prosecution in court.

After the discussion of these four components, we look at the principles of complicity, and vicarious and corporate liability. The concepts presented in this chapter, taken together, provide the basic tools for assessing and assigning criminal liability.

II. HARM OR LIKELY HARM: THE CLASSIFICATION OF CRIMES

harm:
actual damage, injury, or loss that must occur as the result of an act for that act to be considered criminal.

Harm is the actual damage, injury, or loss that must occur as a result of an act for that act to be considered criminal. The one harmed can be as specific as an individual person or piece of property, or as general as society as a whole.

Harm plays a significant role in the orderly classification of crime and the resulting assessment of penalties. The harms caused by criminal acts are divided first into broad general categories according to the direct object of the crime—life, habitation, property, public order, and public morality—and then ranked in that descending order based on the perception, for example, that the permanent taking of a life is more serious than the temporary disruption of public order. The respective penalties decrease with the seriousness of the harm.

Each of these broad categories is further divided by the nature of the act—crimes against life are divided into murder, kidnapping, battery, and so on; and crimes against habitation are divided into burglary and arson. These crimes may then be subdivided further according to the seriousness of the degree of mens rea. Thus murder is usually subdivided into first degree (purposeful intent), second degree (knowing intent), third degree (reckless intent), and fourth degree (negligent intent). Alternatively, the various gradations may be stated as class A, B, C, or D felonies or A, B, C, or D misdemeanors. These crimes may be subdivided further into completed or attempted crimes, with attempted crimes in that class having lighter penalties than completed crimes based on the fact that less harm has occurred.

Attempted crimes and other "incomplete" crimes such as conspiracy or possession do not require that harm has occurred. In these cases, the potential for harm is considered serious enough to warrant intervention. Incomplete or inchoate crimes are covered in Chapter 6.

III.   ACTUS REUS

A.   INTRODUCTION

Actus reus means wrongful or guilty act. It has long been a requirement of the law that a crime must be manifested by some act: striking with a fist or a club, pulling the trigger of a gun, physically delivering cocaine to another. The rationale behind the requirement of an act has several components. The first is that mere thoughts are hard to determine and harder yet to prove. As a medieval judge said, "The thought of man is not triable, for the devil himself knoweth not the thought of man."[1] A physical act is overt; it can be seen, heard, and felt. It has obvious detectable consequences. It can be proved.

Second, thoughts do not cause harm and may be simply the product of day-dreaming or fantasy. Because we have been given minds and imaginations that entertain thoughts both good and bad, a law that punished for thoughts alone would or could ensnare us all. The act establishes the line of demarcation between mere thought and the physical steps toward causing actual harm.

Third, and very critical to a democratic society, is the fact that punishment for thought alone practically guarantees abusive power in the hands of police, law enforcement, and other governmental officials. The requirement that there be evidence beyond a reasonable doubt of some "guilty" *act* limits their discretion and, thus, their action and helps preserve the liberty and dignity of innocent people. Think of the thousands of people who have been executed or tortured for being witches, heretics, or political dissenters. In some societies thoughts free of actions are still subject to persecution and prosecution. The requirement of a criminal act prevents the law from harassing individuals based on their status (who they are), for example, alcoholics, drug addicts, or people of a specific race, sexual orientation, or religion.

Fourth, the act must be defined as wrongful or criminal in the context of the surrounding circumstances and consequences. For instance, pulling the trigger on a loaded gun is not criminal in itself, but pulling the trigger of a gun while aiming at a person strongly suggests the desire to kill that person. Harmful consequences are most apparent. Therefore, actus reus is determined not only by the physical act or omission, but also by the circumstances and the consequential harm.

B.   VOLUNTARY AND INVOLUNTARY ACTS

The criminal act must be voluntary, a product of free will, such as pulling a trigger on a gun or reaching into a cash drawer and grasping money. Where there is a duty to act, the failure to act also must be voluntary. In other words, the accused could have refrained from pulling the trigger or could have reported the accident but did not.

If an act is not voluntary, however, criminal liability may not attach. Circumstances when criminal liability does not attach include coerced action (A holds a pistol to the head of B and says, "You forge this check or die"), reflex action (while driving a car, A is attacked by bees and the car goes out of control and causes injury), muscle contraction or paralysis caused by disease, and unconsciousness or impaired consciousness. A sleep walker (somnambulist) who kills her daughter with an axe while dreaming a rapist was attacking her daughter is not liable, because the act occurred in a semiconscious (involuntary) state.[2] Other conditions such as comas, high fevers, hypoglycemia, or temporary brain damage (concussion) may result in involuntary but harmful actions or inactions. Expert witnesses who said a defendant could have killed in his sleep did not prevent his murder conviction, however, when he stabbed his wife forty-four times and held her head under the water in their swimming pool, then hid evidence and bandaged his cut finger.[3] Hypnosis in theory and in fiction can cause a person to do things they would not ordinarily do. Medical authorities, however, argue that a person cannot be hypnotically induced to do things that the person believes are wrong.[4]

One reason involuntary behavior is not punished is because it bears no relationship to the purposes of criminal law, especially deterrence. Nevertheless, a person who is semiconscious from voluntarily consuming excessive amounts of intoxicants is generally not free of criminal liability for acts committed while semiconscious. Similarly, a person who voluntarily drives a vehicle knowing he or she is subject to epileptic seizures is criminally responsible for harm created as a result of a seizure while operating the vehicle.

Some acts are less clearly "acts" than others. Words, for example, can be acts sufficient for criminal penalties to attach. Conspiracy and threats are just two examples of words as acts.

C. OMISSIONS

omission:
failure to act.

The main purpose of criminal law is to prevent harm. Because most harm is caused by overt physical action, **omission,** or the failure to act, is generally not a crime.[5] When there is a legal duty to act, however, omission of that act is the actus reus of the offense. Not paying taxes owed, for example, is as harmful as embezzling the same amount of money; allowing a child in one's care to starve is as harmful as beating it. The duty to act is required by the following factors.

- **By Statute** A duty to act can be imposed by both civil and criminal statutes. Most states require a person involved in an accident to stay at the scene of an accident and render aid to the other party. Good Samaritan laws in some states require people to act if they see someone in distress. Health and safety laws require employers to maintain safe working conditions. Failure to do so is a crime.
- **By Contract** Similarly, the law imposes criminal liability for failure to act where the duty to act is contracted. A lifeguard is hired and paid to protect others. Failure to go to the aid of a drowning person under the lifeguard's supervision is a crime, often punishable through homicide statutes, the degree depending on the intent of the guard. Another example is the failure of a ship captain to render necessary emergency assistance to the ship's passengers. Omission by a nurse or a doctor also may lead to criminal liability.
- **By Special Relationship** If one stands in a special relationship to another, such as parent to child, spouse to spouse, or guardian to ward, a duty of rendering assistance is imposed by law. Failure to feed, clothe, and otherwise care properly for a child constitutes the crime of neglect. If the child becomes ill and dies as a result of the neglect, the parent or guardian is guilty of some degree of criminal homicide. A mother who sat by while her husband beat her seven-year-old daughter to death was found guilty of first degree murder in Florida.[6]

Consider the following case. A seriously diabetic man is convinced by his wife that he does not need his regular shots of insulin because God will heal him. He agrees and stops taking the insulin. When he begins to show signs of diabetic shock, she and a friend restrain him from getting insulin. He calms and agrees to continue to seek spiritual healing. They pray, but eventually he goes into a coma and dies. The wife is charged with manslaughter. Should she be found guilty because of her omission to provide her husband with the insulin or to get medical aid when he could not? Should there be such duty between spouses? What do you think?

The court held in *Commonwealth v. Konz* (Pa. 1982) that there was no such duty, at least in this case, and noted the husband's willingness to seek spiritual healing. (Food for thought: Do you think the same decision would have been made if the sexes had been reversed?) If an invalid relied on the care of a spouse who knowingly failed to provide prompt medical care when needed to prevent death, most jurisdictions would prosecute the spouse.

- ■ **By Volunteering**   There are times when one can voluntarily assume a duty. For example, if a person agrees to watch a child and the child drowns, or if the child needs emergency medical attention and the person fails to render assistance, that person may be charged with criminal homicide. There does not need to be a contract or payment involved for liability to attach. Criminal liability also can attach when a person voluntarily goes to the rescue of another, then stops at a time that precludes others from rendering assistance. For example, a swimmer is drowning and a bystander takes the only available boat to the rescue, then three-quarters of the way stops and it is too late for anyone else to reach the swimmer. If the swimmer drowns, the bystander may be guilty of criminal homicide. In a similar situation, a woman who voluntarily cared for a child but isolated the child and seldom fed, bathed, or cared for it had a duty of care, and incurred criminal liability when the baby died [*Jones v. U.S.* (D.C. Cir. 1962)].
- ■ **By Placing the Victim in Peril**   Failure to render assistance can be criminal when a person's criminal or negligent act places the victim in peril and in need of assistance, and the perpetrator fails to render assistance. For example, A forces B to take hallucinogenic drugs, and in a state of incapacity B stumbles through a window and is severely cut. A leaves or watches B bleed to death. A has not met a duty to assist, an omission that can be criminal [*Jones v. State* (Ind. 1942)]. A man who accidentally set fire to his wife's building but did nothing to stop the fire, though he could have, was held to have a duty to do so and was convicted [*Commonwealth v. California* (Mass. 1923)].

 ANALYSIS PROBLEM

3–1.   Have we reached the time in our society when people say "I do not want to get involved" so often that we need to legislate a general duty to rescue? What are some difficulties? Does a poor person have the same duty to rescue a starving beggar as a rich person? Should a poor swimmer have as great a duty to rescue a drowning person as an excellent swimmer? What about a mediocre swimmer?

D.   POSSESSION

The law imposes criminal liability for the minimal act of **possession,** the acquisition of something and then the failure to get rid of it. Possession is an exception to the general rule that the law punishes for acts that cause harm, as well as the rule that the law punishes people for what they have done as opposed to what they might do. It is clear that possession of a concealed weapon is not harmful, and it is equally clear that it is conjecture that the weapon will be used to cause harm. Yet, most state legislatures have decided that the gain to society of easier law enforcement and the prevention of crime justify possession as a basis for criminal liability.

Criminal possession addresses the physical control of two classes of objects, one unlawful and the other lawful. Unlawful objects include various weapons, illegal drugs, wiretapping devices, stolen property, obscene materials, and others. Criminal liability attaches to possession of lawful items such as crowbars and wire cutters (burglary tools) or drug paraphernalia, only when combined with the intent to commit an unlawful act.[7]

possession:
the acquisition of something and then the failure to get rid of it.

actual possession:
the object is on the person, under direct physical control, or within reach.

Actual possession requires that the object be on the person, under direct physical control, or within reach. Usually the act of actual possession must be coupled with knowledge. For example, a postal delivery person who unwittingly possesses a mail bomb in the act of delivering it would not be guilty of criminal possession. Some statutes, however, do not require any knowledge. Possession alone is well accepted as a proper basis for criminal prosecution.

constructive possession:
knowledge of where an item is and control of that area.

Criminal liability is also assessed for **constructive possession,** knowledge of where an illegal item is and control of that area. Therefore, a person can be convicted for possession if illegal drugs are found in a closet in the person's house or in the glove compartment of the person's car.

Common problems raised in constructive possession occur when there is more than one person in the room or car. Who then should be charged? The law varies in these instances. Depending on circumstances, all those present may be charged, but more than likely the person in charge of the car or room will incur the liability. It gets more confusing when the room is jointly controlled, such as by spouses, or roommates. Possession, and especially constructive possession, creates the very real problem of potentially convicting innocent persons. People may possess illegal items for legitimate purposes or be charged with possession simply for being in control of a room where someone else has brought in the illegal substance.

Though convenient for law enforcement, possession laws reach back far earlier in the alleged criminal preparation process than most other crimes, to where harm has not yet occurred; thus, there is more potential for innocent conduct to be charged. For this reason some scholars argue that possession should be a crime only when it involves the most dangerous of items, explosives and weapons, for example, as opposed to the more innocuous burglary tools.

E. STATUS

In the past, some jurisdictions took things a step further by trying to make it unnecessary even to show possession. Laws created criminal liability for being an alcoholic, drug addict, or homosexual. All that was necessary for conviction was one's reputation or status. No immediate act of harm was required. This type of thinking has led to statutes that declare loitering, vagrancy, or the inability to identify oneself adequately to police as criminal. Fortunately, because such laws tend to encroach on legitimate freedoms and give the police too much discretion, they have been declared illegal. It is along this front that law-and-order proponents and civil libertarians have fought for decades. Battles also have involved the prosecution of drug-addicted women whose babies die or suffer severe withdrawal shortly after birth.

IV. MENS REA

A. INTRODUCTION

An act is not generally criminal unless it is accompanied by the state of mind necessary to separate that act from the realm of innocent conduct. This culpable mentality is the component of **mens rea,** a wrongful state of mind or the intent to commit a crime. The law has long recognized the difference between intentional wrongs and unavoidable ones. Oliver Wendell Holmes, Jr., said, "Even a dog distinguishes between being stumbled over and being kicked."[8]

mens rea:
a wrongful state of mind or the intent to commit a crime.

Since the workings of the mind are not obvious, the proof of mens rea depends on the circumstances surrounding the act. For example, in a trial for molestation of a juvenile, the defendant's prurient statement to a young girl, not the victim, was admissible to demonstrate the defendant's "lustful disposition toward young victims," showing intent, preparation, plan, or knowledge of the offense charged [*State v. Miller* (La. 1998)]. Although such evidence is being more widely allowed in abuse cases, the general rule is closer to that expressed by the opinion in *Wall v. State* (Ga. 1998) that prior acts must not be used simply to show "bad character," and in the concurring opinion that they must deal only with the relationship between the defendant and the victim. Proof of intent also lies in other behavior before and during the commission of the offense.

Motive, which figures so prominently in classic detective stories, is not the same as criminal intent, but the reason behind the intent. In Case VI in Chapter 1, the Craigs' religious beliefs may be a motive to force a homosexual couple from their neighborhood, but that does not mean that they actually formed the intent to do so. If they commit a criminal act toward that end, however, their beliefs may be an indication of the state of mind that gave rise to the act itself. A sociopath may act with no motive at all, however, but with intent to do harm. Though motive is not a component of the crime itself, it may be used in sentencing. Persons convicted of **hate crimes** receive enhanced sentences for choosing their victims because of bias against their race, religion, sexual orientation, or other status. Conversely, a good motive may serve as a mitigating circumstance to lower the sentence.

Statutes and jurisdictions vary in their use of mens rea terminology and its interpretation. In the wording of a statute, the phrase "with intent to" is a clear indication of the mens rea requirement for that crime. Some statutes simply imply intent in the verb describing the act itself: whoever forcibly assaults, resists, opposes, impedes, intimidates, or interferes with any person [(18 U.S.C. § 111 (a)(1)]. Other statutes indicate mens rea requirements through such adverbs as willfully, maliciously, wantonly, knowingly, recklessly, and negligently. These words have distinct meanings in some jurisdictions but are used interchangeably in others. Here are judicial interpretations of some common mens rea terms.

- *Willful* and *wanton* have the same meaning: wrongful doing of an act without justification or excuse; acting purposely and deliberately against the law [*State v. Davis* (N.C. App. 1987)].
- *Willful* means intentional, knowing, and purposeful. *Wanton* means with conscious and intentional indifference to consequences and with knowledge that damage is likely to be done to persons or property [*Lewek v. State* (Fla. App. 1997)].
- *Wanton* is more than ordinary negligence and less than willful injury [*Saunders v. Shaver* (Kans. 1963)].
- Willfully and maliciously interfering with instruments used in the extinguishment of fire do not mean that the defendant must harbor ill will toward the owner of the property, but rather that the defendant acted intentionally and without justification or excuse [*Robinson v. State* (Fla. App. 1997)].

B. MODEL PENAL CODE DEFINITIONS

The Model Penal Code § 2.02 clarifies mens rea classifications by designating four types of mental culpability: purposely, knowingly, recklessly, and negligently. Compare definitions in your state.

Purposely indicates an intention to accomplish a specific result. For example, if A purposely kills B, A intended B to die as a result of A's actions. In this instance the purpose is directly consistent with the result or intended result. (See Exhibit 3–1.)

Knowingly means knowing that a specific type of conduct will almost certainly bring about a particular result, but without necessarily intending that or a related result. For example, a person might blow up a safe at a bank knowing that bank employees are present, but not specifically intending that they get killed. Further, knowingly can be a state of awareness that a certain fact or circumstance exists, as in the knowing possession of cocaine. In this instance, one does not have to intend any harm or know that the drug is illegal. If a defendant knows that the conspiracy he or she is involved in is illegal but does not know that it involves drugs, the person cannot be convicted of conspiracy to sell drugs [*U.S. v. Idowu* (3rd Cir. 1998)].

motive:
the reason behind the intent.

hate crime:
a crime motivated by bias against the victim's race, religion, sexual orientation, or other status.

purposely:
intending to accomplish a specific result.

knowingly:
to know that a specific type of conduct will almost certainly bring about a particular result, but without necessarily intending that or a related result; a state of awareness that a certain fact or circumstance exists.

EXHIBIT 3–1
Sample Jury Instructions

KNOWINGLY—DEFINED

An act is done knowingly if the defendant is aware of the act and does not act [or fail to act] through ignorance, mistake, or accident. The government is not required to prove that the defendant knew that [his] [her] acts or omissions were unlawful. You may consider evidence of the defendant's words, acts, or omissions, along with all the other evidence, in deciding whether the defendant acted knowingly.

DELIBERATE IGNORANCE

You may find that the defendant acted knowingly if you find beyond a reasonable doubt that the defendant was aware of a high probability that [e.g., drugs were in his automobile] and deliberately avoided learning the truth.

You may not find such knowledge, however, if you find that the defendant actually believed that [e.g., no drugs were in his automobile], or if you find that the defendant was simply careless.

Ninth Circuit Criminal Jury Instructions (St. Paul, MN: West Group, 1992), §§ 5.06 and 5.07, with permission.

recklessly:
knowing that there is a substantial and unjustifiable risk that conduct might cause a particular result but not intending the harmful result.

wantonly:
maliciously or arrogantly disregarding the known risk to the rights or safety of others.

negligently:
thoughtlessly or carelessly creating a significant unjustifiable risk of harm without realizing the risk has been created or without the intent to create the risk, yet the act is such that a reasonable person would have known that the act created such a risk.

Recklessly is knowing that there is a substantial and unjustifiable risk that conduct might cause a particular result but not intending the harmful result. Reckless behavior is driving an automobile down a deserted sidewalk late at night knowing there is a risk that someone will step suddenly out of the shadows and could be seriously harmed or killed, yet proceeding to commit the act. Recent cases have involved drug companies continuing to market a product even though they are aware of evidence that the product might cause serious injury or death. Oil tanker spills may have resulted from reckless delegation of authority. In being reckless, the perpetrator does not knowingly or purposefully intend the harm, but purposefully or knowingly creates a substantial and unjustifiable risk that the harm may occur. **Wantonly** describes behavior that is the most serious form of recklessness, characterized by malicious or arrogant disregard of the known risk to the rights or safety of others, such as firing a gun into a crowd.

Negligently means thoughtlessly or carelessly creating a significant unjustifiable risk of harm without realizing the risk has been created or without the intent to create the risk, yet the act is such that a reasonable person would have known that the act created such a risk. A driver who sees a number of small children playing near a street but continues to drive at normal speed could be guilty of negligent homicide should one of the children dash out into the street and be killed. Or, a person who thoughtlessly tosses down a cigarette butt at a service station causing an explosion and death would be guilty of negligent homicide. There is no intent to harm or even a thought that the act will cause harm, but to a reasonable person the risk is apparent and should have been avoided.

Of the four levels of state of mind, negligence is the most troublesome from a viewpoint of moral wrongdoing. Questions arise as to whether accidental or careless behavior should be the subject of criminal penalties. For example, should a parent or babysitter be guilty of negligent homicide for giving a child sick with the flu regular doses of aspirin when scientific evidence shows a link between aspirin and development of the deadly Reyes syndrome if the child dies? Should a person be punished for lack of intelligence or certain kinds of knowledge? Traditionally our law says no, they should not, but legislatures are increasingly passing laws that punish negligent conduct. One of the purposes of criminal law, however, is to deter unwanted conduct. The more likely that great harm will result from negligence, the more likely it is to be criminalized.

What about persons who are judgment proof, who cannot be touched for all practical purposes by civil suits for damages, or those (including corporations) who are sufficiently rich and powerful that a $100,000 lawsuit means little more than a temporary inconvenience? Does possible criminal punishment for negligence seem appropriate here?[9] For these reasons, the drafters of the Model Penal Code suggested that negligent behavior be an exception to traditional definitions of criminal intent, and that criminal liability for such conduct be imposed only when the legislature has made it absolutely clear that it should be imposed.[10] Criminal negligence by a corporation is clearly defined in *State v. Steenberg Homes, Inc.* (Wis. App. 1998) following the discussion of corporate crime at the end of this chapter.

C. GENERAL, SPECIFIC, AND TRANSFERRED INTENT

Some statutes require only general intent, whereas others are more exacting and require specific intent. Note the distinction when you research the law. **General intent** refers only to the act itself and does not require that the results be intended. To be guilty of arson, a general intent crime, one only need have malicious intent to set the fire and not necessarily the intent to burn down the house. **Specific intent** refers to carrying out the act for the purpose of achieving the resulting harm. A conviction for premeditated murder requires not only the intent to fire the gun, but also the specific intent to kill the victim. Someone who causes danger but is unaware of it because of voluntary intoxication by alcohol or drugs usually can be charged with general intent offenses, but not with those that require specific intent.

general intent:
intent to commit the act itself, but not necessarily to cause the results.

specific intent:
carrying out an act for the purpose of achieving the resulting harm.

Besides determining the requisite state of mind, mens rea requires the proper focus of criminal intent. If Ann secretly poisons a drink and hands it to Joe, who generously shares it with Pat, where is the mens rea? Ann did not intend to harm Pat, but her guilty state of mind toward Joe is transferred along with the poisoned drink. She is guilty according to the principle of **transferred intent,** the culpable state of mind to commit one crime while accidentally committing another.

transferred intent:
a legal device that holds one criminally liable for the harm to a person other than the intended victim.

D. CONCURRENCE

Concurrence, in the context of the components of a crime, is the logical and consistent connection that must exist between the perpetrator's wrongful intent and the wrongful act, and between the wrongful intent and the resulting harm, for criminal liability to attach. Return to the transferred intent example of the poisoned drink passed from its intended victim to an unintended victim. Ann's intent to kill Joe transfers, so Pat's death is not simply accidental, and Ann is guilty of criminal homicide. Because the intent must concur with the harm, however, Ann is not guilty of the more serious mens rea level of premeditation in the death of Pat as she would have been in the case of Joe.

concurrence:
in the context of the components of a crime, the logical and consistent connection that must exist between the perpetrator's wrongful intent and the wrongful act, and between the wrongful intent and the resulting harm, for criminal liability to attach.

Mens rea must also concur with the actus reus of the offense. In Case V of Chapter 1, if Nancy Stroud intended to provide cocaine for her party guests but changed her mind before acquiring the drugs, her intent and the presence of drugs (from some other source) at the party do not concur, and she is not criminally liable for distribution of a controlled substance. Even if she still intended to provide drugs but the package did not arrive, that intent does not concur with the act of a guest who secretly brings cocaine to the party.

If the intent is formed after the fact, again there is no concurrence. When the elements of second degree burglary include unlawful entry in an occupied building with the intent to commit some other crime, such as battery, on the premises, the defendant must have that other crime in mind at the same time that he or she enters the building. If the intent to commit battery is formed any time after the illegal entry has taken place, the charge of burglary is inappropriate [*Cooper v. People* (Colo. 1999)].

It is important to note that concurrence does not depend on the components occurring at the same time, but rather that mens rea actuates actus reus and the harm done. In other words, the state of mind is responsible for the occurrence of both the act itself and its resulting harm.

E.   STRICT LIABILITY

strict liability:
requires a wrongful act only; the state of mind is irrelevant.

Strict liability laws require a wrongful act only; the state of mind is irrelevant. These laws are an exception to the rule that every crime must include a guilty state of mind. Examples of strict liability offenses include traffic offenses, sale of adulterated foods or drugs, and failure to report child abuse. These offenses have in common a high standard of care necessary for safety and difficulty in establishing criminal intent.

As the difficulty of proving the intent in such cases became clear, the law changed, and the need to prove intent was eliminated for certain relatively minor offenses with little social stigma and punished by no more than fines. Now strict liability has grown to include some offenses leading to prison sentences.

When a statute itself has no language about mens rea, several factors, taken together, can provide a general idea of whether mens rea is required or strict liability is indicated. One factor alone, such as a prison sentence, is not necessarily determinative [*State v. Keihn* (Ind. 1989)]. The following factors are indications of strict liability.

1. The history of a statute can indicate legislative intent that it create a strict liability offense [filing a false statement in *State v. Dobry* (Iowa 1933)].
2. Some states require strict liability to be clearly or "plainly" stated in the statute [welfare fraud in *State v. Rushing* (Haw. 1980)].
3. The severity of punishment for the offense may indicate whether fault (mens rea) is required; the more severe the sentence the greater the likelihood that the offense has a mens rea element [owning a dog that causes injury in *State v. Bash* (Wash. 1996)].
4. The greater harm the offense poses toward the public, the greater is the likelihood that the offense is strict liability. The possession of illegal drugs in a school zone is deemed sufficiently dangerous to children that penalties were enhanced even though the school zone was not the intended location for distribution in *U.S. v. Oritz* (1st. Cir. 1998). The defendant kept the drugs in his parents' home 150 feet from a school. See also *Walker v. State* (Ind. 1996).
5. The difficulty for the defendant to know the facts may indicate that fault is required. Ignorance is less of an excuse when knowledge is easily obtained [depositing a dangerous substance on a highway in *Krueger v. Noel* (Iowa 1982)]. Driving with a suspended license is not a strict liability offense, however, when the driver has not been notified of the restriction [*State v. McCallum* (Md. 1991)].
6. The difficulty in proving mens rea makes it more likely that it is not a required burden on the prosecution. In *U.S. v. Flum* (8th Cir. 1975), the court emphasized the difficulty of proving mens rea in attempting to board an aircraft while carrying a weapon, making that a strict liability offense.
7. The greater number of prosecutions expected increases the likelihood that the statute is for a strict liability offense [bigamy in *People v. Vogel* (Cal. 1956)].

In interpreting statutes where state of mind is not spelled out, some courts come down between the necessity for the prosecution to prove mens rea and strict liability that eliminates the use of state of mind as a defense. These courts do not require the prosecution to prove fault (mens rea), but allow the defense to present evidence of lack of fault. Strict liability statutes have been criticized for making conviction of innocent people easier, and praised for making prosecution of dangerous conduct easier.

ANALYSIS PROBLEM

3–2. What do you think about strict liability? Should the state have to prove intent in a speeding case? A failure to report child abuse?

EXHIBIT 3–2
Sample Jury Instructions

UNLAWFUL SALE OF ALCOHOLIC BEVERAGE

You will find the Defendant guilty of Unlawful Sale of Alcoholic Beverage under this Instruction if, and only if, you believe from the evidence beyond a reasonable doubt all of the following:

    A. That in this county on or about _____(date) and within 12 months before the [finding of the Indictment herein] [issuance of the warrant for his arrest], he [sold] [gave] [furnished] _____(ID alcoholic beverage) to _____(victim);

    B. That he did so in the course of his business as a retail liquor licensee;

    [AND]

    C. That _____(victim) was then less than 21 years of age.

    [AND]

    [D. That the Defendant was not induced to do so by the use of a false, fraudulent or altered identification, and the appearance and character of _____(victim) was such that his age could not have been ascertained by any other means, and that _____(victim)'s appearance and character strongly indicated that he was 21 years of age or older.]

    [AND]

    [E. That he was not induced to do so by entrapment.]

    If you find the Defendant guilty under this Instruction, you shall fix his punishment at confinement in the county jail for not more than six months, at a fine of not less than $100.00, nor more than $200.00, or at both confinement and fine, in your discretion.

    [Provided, however, if you believe from the evidence beyond a reasonable doubt that prior to _____(date), the Defendant was convicted of Unlawful Sale of Alcoholic Beverage by Judgment of the _____(ID court) entered on _____(date-2), you shall fix his punishment for this offense at confinement in the county jail for not more than six months, at a fine of not less than $200.00, nor more than $500.00, or at both confinement and fine, in your discretion.]

William S. Cooper, *Kentucky Instructions to Juries (Criminal)*, 4th ed. § 9.39 (© Anderson Publishing, 1999), with permission.

V. CAUSATION

A. INTRODUCTION

The fourth element of criminal liability, **causation,** is the link between the intent, the act, and the harm. In other words, the intended or criminally negligent act must have been the direct cause of the death or injury. If A points a loaded pistol at B and pulls the trigger with the intent to kill B and B is killed, there is little doubt that the firing of the gun was the direct cause of B's death. The key here is that without that critical link of direct cause, there is, generally speaking, no crime.

causation:
the link between the intent, the act, and the harm.

corpus delicti:
the "body of the crime";
proof that loss or injury occurred as the result of someone's criminal conduct.

Corpus delicti, literally the "body of the crime," is the proof that loss or injury oc-curred as the result of someone's criminal conduct. The identity of a body plus a med-ical examiner's testimony that death was caused by two gunshot wounds established the corpus delicti in *Hammond v. State* (Tex. App. 1997).

The inherent problem in causation cases, mainly homicide cases, is what in fact caused the death. A shoots B, and B is bleeding but could survive with reasonably prompt medical attention. Along comes C who stabs B in the heart, instantly killing B. Is A criminally liable for B's death? In Case I Chapter 1, is the attack on Kate Lamb the cause of her death? It is this dilemma that has made it necessary for the courts to define what circumstances are adequate to show a sufficient link between the wrong-ful act and the result. The "but for" test says that there is sufficient causation if the vic-tim would have been alive "but for" the defendant's act. Let us say, however, that A threatens B with a knife, B runs and hides from A in a building that is blown up by a bomb planted by C. B would be alive "but for" A's action, but should A be held liable for B's murder? Probably not. B's death was not a probable or foreseeable conse-quence of A's action.

The law goes beyond the "but for" concept and uses the term proximate cause to define the sufficient link between the intended act and the harm. The **proximate cause** of an injury is the act that is most closely and directly responsible for that injury. In a strong wind, A hits B and knocks him off the roof of a five-story building to his death. Although the wind was strong enough to affect B's balance, the strike would still be interpreted as the most direct cause of the fall and, therefore, the proximate cause of B's death.

proximate cause:
the act that is most closely and directly responsible for the injury.

B.   FORESEEABLE CONSEQUENCES

What if A shoots at B and kills C? The law holds A liable for the death. In such cir-cumstances, hitting someone other than the target is a probable and foreseeable con-sequence of the act. Also, if A shoots at B and misses, but B immediately drops dead of heart failure, A is liable. It is foreseeable that the pointing and firing of the gun would cause such intense anxiety that a person in good health—let alone a person with a weak heart—might have a heart attack. However, if an act is committed with no intent to harm, such as when A drives so fast that his anxious passenger, whom A does not know has a weak heart, dies of a heart attack, then A is not liable for causing the death. A recklessly drunken driver should have foreseen that some victims would not be using seat belts, so their contributory negligence was not a defense in *State v. Freeland* (Ariz. App. 1993). An arsonist should have foreseen that the fire started in an uninhabited building would spread to an adjacent inhabited building, upholding a conviction for second degree arson in *People v. Davis* (N.Y. 1977).

"I am by no means sure that if a man kept a tiger, and lightning broke his chain, and he got loose and did mischief, that the man who kept him would not be liable."

—Lord William Bramwell, English jurist *Nichols v. Marsland,* L.R. 10 Ex. 260 (1875)

C.   SUPERVENING OR SUPERSEDING CAUSES

Between the action and the harm, another event may intervene to become the actual cause of the harm. This event is called a **supervening or superseding cause,** defined in *State v. Bartlett* (Neb. App. 1994) as "a new and independent act of a third person or another force which breaks the causal connection between the original wrong and the injury, and is itself a proximate cause, and, indeed, 'the' proximate cause of the in-jury in question." Supervening causes are most often involved in criminal homicide cases.

A supervening cause overturned an involuntary manslaughter conviction in *Peo-ple v. Hebert* (Cal. App. 1964). During an argument the defendant struck the victim, knocking him off a bar stool. Police half lifted, half dragged the victim to a squad car, allegedly dropping him face down onto the sidewalk in the process. At the station the victim fell backward, causing his head to bounce twice on the concrete floor. He died

supervening or supersed-ing cause:
a new and independent act of a third person or another force that breaks the causal connection between the original wrong and the injury, and is the proximate cause of the injury.

VI. Complicity ■ 61

later. In its decision the court noted that, ". . . we think that in ordinary circumstances all the definitions [of intervening and supervening causes] have had their roots in the doctrine of foreseeability." Because the falls of the victim were unforeseeable to the defendant when he struck the victim, they were eligible as the supervening cause of the death.

Even grossly negligent medical treatment after a stabbing was not enough to break the chain of causation between the stabbing and the death of the victim in *State v. Shabazz* (Conn. 1998), however. Medical treatment could be considered only if it was the sole cause of the death. In *Weidler v. State* (Ala. Cr. App. 1993), a manslaughter conviction was upheld for a defendant who beat the victim and left him helpless on the ground behind the wheels of a car. As occupants of the car attempted to escape a crowd trying to pull them from the car, the victim was driven over and killed. The harm caused by the car did not furnish a supervening cause sufficient to break the chain of causation.

A victim's decision not to receive a blood transfusion because of her religious beliefs was not considered a supervening cause of her death [*People v. Cook* (Pomona Super. Ct. 1998)]. The drunk driver responsible for her injuries was convicted on the lesser charge of manslaughter rather than murder, however. "At least in jurors' minds, it is difficult to conceptualize prosecution arguments that the defendant is responsible for a death that the defendant did not intend but that his victim did."[12]

VI. COMPLICITY

A. INTRODUCTION

As we have just seen, mens rea, actus reus, harm, and causation define when a person is liable for criminal activity. Complicity is a concept that further defines criminal liability by extending it beyond one person and beyond the most direct criminal act. It is the participation, including assistance, in the commission of a crime. It is the concept needed to determine whether the getaway driver is as guilty as the shooter of the bank teller, and whether they should be punished equally. In most jurisdictions the answer to both questions is yes, conditioned on the fact that all elements of the crime are present for both.

B. COMMON LAW

In common law, the primary actors in a crime were called the **principals,** those having direct participation in and responsibility for the crime and bearing equal culpability. **Accomplices,** those who aid and abet, gave approval and help to the primary actor through encouragement or active involvement in the commission of the crime. **Accessories** were defined as those guilty of complicity either before or after the crime. Degrees of complicity fell into four classifications.

The **principal in the first degree** committed the crime directly or caused it through the manipulation of an innocent agent. This was the person who shot the gun, picked up the gold and walked away with it, struck the match.

The **principal in the second degree** was not directly involved in the crime itself, but was actually present or constructively present (close enough to give aid to the principal in the first degree). This person led the night watchman away, held the extra crowbar, checked the address.

The **accessory before the fact** was not present at the scene of the crime, but provided means or advice before its commission. This person bought the poison, planned the getaway, decided on the victim.

principal:
one having participation in and responsibility for a crime.

accomplice:
one who aids and abets the primary actor through encouragement or active involvement in the commission of a crime.

accessory:
one guilty of complicity either before or after the crime.

principal in the first degree:
one who committed the crime directly or caused it through the manipulation of an innocent agent (common law).

principal in the second degree:
one who was not directly involved in the crime itself but was present to give aid (common law).

accessory before the fact:
one not present at the scene of the crime, but provided means or advice before its commission (common law).

accessory after the fact:
one not present at the scene
of the crime, but knowingly
gave assistance to the criminal after the crime (common
law).

The **accessory after the fact** also was not present but, knowing that a person had performed a felony, gave assistance to that person after the crime. This accessory re-painted the getaway car, hid the principal in an attic, told police that the principal had been playing cards right here the whole evening of the crime.

Principals in both degrees were subject to the same punishment. Accessories were not believed to be as culpable as principals, so were punished less severely. They could not even be brought to trial unless the principals had been tried and convicted.

C. MODERN LAW

In modern law the distinction among principals, accomplices, and accessories before the fact has generally been dissolved.

> *Whoever commits an offense against the United States or aids, abets, counsels, commands, induces, or procures its commission, is punishable as a principal.*
>
> —18 U.S.C.A. § 2(a)

An accessory before the fact can be convicted without the conviction of the principal. The liability of an accessory after the fact, however, still depends on the conviction of a principal.

Use your state's statutes as a guide as you consider the following aspects of complicity.

D. ACTUS REUS IN COMPLICITY

Even though a principal need not be convicted before an accomplice can be tried, the state must show that some person other than the defendant is guilty as the principal [*People v. Vaughn* (Mich. App. 1990). An accomplice could not be convicted of a first degree murder, however, when the principal had been convicted of the less serious offense of second degree murder [*State v. Ward* (Md. 1978)].

The accomplice must have provided some form of affirmative assistance to the principal actor in the offense. One cannot be charged for merely being present at a crime scene. Affirmative assistance can be

1. A physical act that furthers the purpose of the crime. The procurer of weapons, the lookout, and the hotel owner who rents to prostitutes provide such aid. It is not necessary to show that "but for" the aid of the accomplice, the crime would not have been committed, but it is essential that the aid provided had the possibility of being effective. In Case VI, if a bystander handed the principal what he thought was a can of gasoline to help ignite the cross and the contents turned out to be water, the bystander would not be liable.

2. Encouragement to the principal in the undertaking of the crime. The one who says, "That ring really should belong to you; just go take it," has been judged culpable.

3. Failure to act, when action is required by duty. When a mother stands by as her child is beaten, she is culpable for the breach of duty to protect that child and is an accomplice to the offense [*State v. Walden* (N.C. 1982)].

4. The relationship of the accomplice to the principal. Despite identification of the hand that actually committed the criminal act, a hierarchy of power behind the act may be established. The primary actor might be an innocent instrument of the principal, or might be guilty of a lesser charge.

In Case III, if Cat Bermuda had tricked the maid Lacey Rude into believing that she should bring the gold idol to the kitchen for safekeeping, Ms. Rude would then be considered simply an instrument of Ms. Bermuda and would not be charged. If X in the passion of the moment kills W with a knife handed by calculating Y, then X, the

EXHIBIT 3–3
Sample Jury Instructions

AIDING AND ABETTING

A defendant may be found guilty of [*name principal offense*], even if the defendant personally did not commit the act or acts constituting the crime but aided and abetted in its commission. To prove a defendant guilty of aiding and abetting, the government must prove beyond a reasonable doubt:

First, the [e.g., armed robbery] was committed;

Second, the defendant knowingly and intentionally aided, counseled, commanded, induced or procured _____ to commit _____; and

Third, the defendant acted before the crime was completed.

It is not enough that the defendant merely associated with _____, or was present at the scene of the crime, or unknowingly or unintentionally did things that were helpful to the principal.

The evidence must show beyond a reasonable doubt that the defendant acted with the knowledge and intention of helping _____ commit _____ .

The government is not required to prove precisely which defendant actually committed the crime and which defendant aided and abetted.

Ninth Circuit Criminal Jury Instructions (St. Paul, MN: West Group, 1993), § 5.01, with permission.

principal, is guilty of manslaughter whereas Y, the aider and abettor, is guilty of murder [*Parker v. Commonwealth* (Ky. 1918)].

The action of principals and accomplices is seen as the result of teamwork and is taken as a whole to establish the elements of a crime. The actus reus may be provided by only one member of the team, but the others share that element through their relationship to that member. The mens rea of each accomplice must be determined individually.

E.   MENS REA IN COMPLICITY

An accomplice must have "concurrent, specific intent to promote or facilitate the commission of the offense," according to the decision in *People v. Curtis* (Ill. App. 1998). The defendant's presence during the crime, affiliation with the principal after the commission of the crime, and failure to report the crime all may be used to show the specific intent of the accomplice. There is no shared intent if the defendant did not know of the principal's offense; presence at the crime scene and close association are not enough to stand alone. In *U.S. v. Stewart,* (5th Cir. 1998), the defendant acted nervous during a traffic stop. The friend he was accompanying was discovered to be carrying crack cocaine and weapons. In the patrol car the two friends had a partially incriminating conversation, but it did not establish that the defendant knowingly and purposefully participated in the possession and intent to distribute the cocaine, so his conviction was reversed.

It would seem that the easiest proof of mens rea in aiding and abetting would involve showing the provision of aid in some physical form—procuring weapons, drawing maps—that demonstrates a purposive interest in the crime. Much more problematic, however, is the aid provided with knowledge but without any purpose in the success of the crime. What difference is there between the intention to promote an action and the knowing assistance of that action? How should the criminal justice system deal with the gun dealer who sells ammunition, knowing it will be used in an assassination? The blacksmith who forges special tools to be used in a burglary? What is Imp Satterfield's culpability in Case III if she is simply a librarian providing information about the potential market for pre–Columbian gold?

Except where the aider obtains some profit from the venture and thus has a clear purpose in the crime, these situations are slippery ones for the courts to consider. Two landmark cases provide some handles. *Backun v. U.S.* (4th Cir. 1940) upheld the conviction of the seller of stolen silverware to another who resold it in interstate commerce.

> *To say that the sale of goods is a normally lawful transaction is beside the point. The seller may not ignore the purpose for which the purchase is made if he is advised of that purpose, or wash his hands of the aid he has given the perpetrator of a felony by the plea that he has merely made a sale of merchandise. [Backun, 637.]*

In *U.S. v. Peoni* (2d Cir. 1938) Judge Learned Hand provides a different twist in overturning the conviction of Peoni who had sold counterfeit bills to Regno who in turn sold them to Dorsey, the one who finally passed them into circulation. Hand concedes that Peoni's involvement "was indeed a step in the causal chain which ended in Dorsey's possession, but that was all. . . ." The opinion continues in stronger language.

> *It will be observed that all these definitions [of complicity] have nothing whatever to do with the probability that the forbidden result would follow upon the accessory's conduct; and that they all demand that he in some sort associate himself with the venture, that he participate in it as in something that he wishes to bring about, that he seek by his action to make it succeed. All the words used—even the most colorless, "abet"—carry an implication of purposive attitude towards it. [Peoni, 401.]*

Although some jurisdictions favor *Backun*, the general tendency, including that of the Model Penal Code § 2.06(3)(a), is to conform more closely with *Peoni* in requiring a more substantial stake in the venture on the part of the defendant.

In some jurisdictions, an accomplice is also liable for crimes committed by the principal that are a foreseeable extension of the crime originally intended. Cat Bermuda's battery of Lacey Rude in Case III was not intended by the Legrise gang, but it could be argued that a violent confrontation was a foreseeable result of the planned burglary. In such jurisdictions, the rest of the gang would be accomplices to the attack on Ms. Rude.

The accomplice is "also guilty of any other crime the direct perpetrator actually commits that is a natural and probable consequence of the target offense" [*People v. Mendoza* (Cal. 1998)]. The defendant and friends had been drinking and tried to crash a party, but they were sent away. The defendant went to get another friend who had a gun. They returned, and the friend shot the gun into the building where the party was taking place, killing one person and wounding five others. The shooting was a natural and probable consequence of the defendant's action, sufficient to sustain the defendant's conviction for the shooting. Because evidence of the defendant's intoxication had not been admitted at trial, however, his conviction was reversed and remanded (sent back to the lower court for reconsideration). That evidence could have shown a lack of specific intent to further the principal's purpose.

A special case limits liability of those who are protected by the law. For example, a minor, even though she encourages the act, cannot be convicted of complicity in the carnal knowledge of herself because the law was written specifically to protect her from that act.

Others are legally incompetent to commit certain crimes. In some jurisdictions, husbands cannot be charged with rape of their wives, but a husband can be an accomplice to the rape of his wife by a third person. Women, incapable of rape by definition in some jurisdictions, may be accomplices to a rapist.

In illegal transactions—selling liquor without a license, prostitution—the purchaser is generally not punished as an accessory because the purchaser is involved with a smaller percentage of the crimes than the seller. Also the purchaser is valuable

ANALYSIS PROBLEM

3–3. If a principal breaks a strict liability law without knowing or intending to do so, is the unknowing accomplice also culpable? How does the First Amendment enter the question when a speaker urges young men not to register for the draft as an antiwar protest? Is that speaker guilty of aiding and abetting illegal activity? Is the undercover narcotics agent who purchases illegal substances to obtain evidence a participant in crime?

as a witness against the seller who is seen as the more culpable party, the more dangerous to society's standards.

F. ABANDONMENT

There are two situations in which abandonment of participation in criminal activity can negate liability for a would-be accomplice. If, after having given assistance to the primary actor, the accomplice changes course and either (1) withdraws the aid given or (2) goes to the police in time to halt the crime, the accomplice's part in the enterprise is negated. The aid withdrawn needs to be equal to the aid given. If vocal encouragement was given, it can be balanced by equally emphatic discouragement. If a weapon was procured, it must be taken back. If a law enforcement agency is contacted, it must be in time to facilitate effective countermeasures. In Case III, after lookout Henry Pogue saw Cat Bermuda safely into the van with the treasure, it would be too late for effective abandonment. If John Harvey in Case VI changed his mind after the vehemence of the group was evident and tried to convince them to calm down and give up any action, or if he went to the police with the fear that things might get out of hand, he would be exculpated. Chapter 5 includes a discussion of abandonment as a defense to attempt charges.

G. ACCESSORY AFTER THE FACT

The common law distinction of accessory after the fact, giving aid to a known felon after the commission of a crime, is retained in most jurisdictions but is usually defined as a separate offense. Rather than being named as a party to the original crime, the accessory is charged with harboring a felon; aiding in escape; providing a weapon, transportation, or disguise; tampering with evidence; giving false information—usually lumped under obstruction of justice. This is a separate, less serious crime than the original one. *Little v. U.S.* (D.C. 1998) defined accessory after the fact as having four components: (1) the completed felony was committed by another prior to accessoryship, (2) the accessory was not the principal in the felony, (3) the accessory had knowledge of the felony, and (4) the accessory acted personally to aid or assist the felon to avoid detection or apprehension for the crimes. Based on the first component, the defendant could not be convicted of accessory after the fact to second degree murder when the victims were dying but not yet dead at the time the defendant transported the killer from the scene. Conviction of the lesser included offense of accessory after the fact to assault with a deadly weapon was more proper. The defining lines are not always followed, however. A defendant in *People v. Cooper* (Cal. 1991) had no prior knowledge of a robbery, but when the robbers brought the loot to his car, he drove away with it, intending to help them. His conviction as a principal, not just an accessory after the fact, was upheld.

In most jurisdictions elements of the crime include knowing that the person given assistance had committed a felony, or was charged or sought in connection with such a crime. Federal law, however, leaves prosecution open for accessories to misdemeanants as well [18 U.S.C.A. § 3]. Also, some affirmative aid must be given. This requires the performance of an act by the accessory, or the offering of false statements to authorities. Simple withholding of information or refusal to cooperate are usually not sufficient. In addition, some states allow a spouse's common law duty, as well as other family ties, to override this offense and exempt culpability for being accessories after the fact to a spouse or other relative.

Two other postcrime laws remain from common law tradition, but are seldom enforced. Compounding a felony, and in some jurisdictions compounding a misdemeanor, is the acceptance of a bribe for not reporting or prosecuting a crime. If it is prosecuted, it is usually as obstruction of justice, such as in the case of bribed witnesses.

The second, misprision of a felony, is simply the failure to report a crime. It has become a textbook crime seldom seen in courts for the reason that Chief Justice Marshall gives in the 1822 decision in *Marbury v. Brooks*:

> *It may be the duty of a citizen to accuse every offender, and to proclaim every offense which comes to his knowledge; but the law which would punish him in every case for not performing this duty is too harsh for man. [Marbury.]*

VII. VICARIOUS AND CORPORATE LIABILITY

A. INTRODUCTION

vicarious liability: culpability of one person for the criminal act of another.

corporate liability: culpability of a corporation for the criminal act of one of its representatives.

Vicarious liability, the assigning of culpability to one person for the criminal act of another, and **corporate liability,** the assigning of culpability to a corporation for the criminal act of its representatives, are devices for dealing with criminal behavior in our complex society. In networks of people held together by ties of obligation, sometimes it seems that everyone has some authority, but no one has complete authority. Vicarious and corporate liability reach into the network to assign responsibility and impose criminal sanctions for business activities that place the public welfare in danger.

respondeat superior: the employer is responsible for the acts of the employee carrying out the employer's business.

Vicarious liability usually applies in a business setting where the conduct of an employee acting within the scope of employment is imputed to the employer. Corporate liability is similar, with the corporation standing as the employer. This concept of **respondeat superior,** that the employer is responsible for the acts of the employee carrying out the employer's business, comes from civil law. Liability does not completely shift from the employee to the employer, however, so both may be charged with criminal conduct.

B. VICARIOUS LIABILITY

Because the liquor business is so heavily regulated, it serves as a good example of the way vicarious liability works. The defendant in *Commonwealth v. Koczwara* (Pa. 1959), the operator of a tavern, was convicted of selling beer to minors. On a previous such violation, the defendant was fined in the range of $100 to $300, but for the repeat offense the sentence was a $500 fine and three months' imprisonment. On appeal, the opinion noted that sale of the beer was made by a bartender; in fact, there was no evidence that the defendant was present or had any personal knowledge of the sales. However,

> *[W]e find that the intent of the legislature in enacting this code was not only to eliminate the common-law requirement of mens rea, but also to place a very high degree*

of responsibility upon the holder of a liquor license to make certain that neither he nor anyone in his employ commit any of the prohibited acts upon the licensed premises. . . .

In spite of this legislated responsibility, the court found the sentence too harsh.

A man's liberty cannot rest on so frail a reed as whether his employee will commit a mistake in judgment. . . . We have found no case in any jurisdiction which has permitted a prison term for a vicarious offense. . . .

The conviction was upheld with the amended sentence allowing only the fine. The dissent stated

[The majority] speaks of "vicarious criminal liability." Such a concept is as alien to American soil as the upas tree. There was a time in China when a convicted felon sentenced to death could offer his brother or other close relative in his stead for decapitation. The Chinese law allowed such "vicarious criminal liability." I never thought that Pennsylvania would look with favor on anything approaching so revolting a barbarity. . . .

Employees acting only on their own behalf and outside the scope of their employment, however, do not pass on vicarious liability to their employers.

Vicarious liability reaches beyond business regulation violations into parental responsibility. All states, except Delaware and Vermont, and many cities have laws that impose sanctions on parents for the actions of their children. Not all of these are criminal sanctions or true vicarious liability offenses because they require some culpable act or state of mind by the parent, such as knowingly neglecting the child or encouraging a child to violate laws. Arkansas's truancy law, however, is a true vicarious liability law, imposing civil fines on parents for the child's actions only.[13]

Statutes containing wording such as "whoever, by himself or by his agent, . . ." or "act by an employee shall be deemed the act of the employer as well as the act of the employee . . ." clearly impose vicarious liability on the employer. Liability is not vicarious when the employer's or parent's involvement is implied by such words as *knowingly* or *with intent to.* Terms such as *allow* or *permit* have been interpreted inconsistently by the courts. The indications for strict liability—legislative history, severity of punishment, danger to the public, and so forth—are also good clues as to whether a statute allows vicarious liability.[14]

ANALYSIS PROBLEM

3–4. Do you find vicarious liability as in *Koczwara* "a barbarity"? How would you deal with the owner of an establishment where regulations are repeatedly violated?

Parental responsibility laws have been criticized as being too vague or overbroad, invasive of family privacy, and subject to abuse by children who intentionally cause trouble for their parents. Do you think parents should be vicariously responsible for their children's behavior? If so, under what circumstances?

C. CORPORATE LIABILITY

Compared with the crime of an individual, the harm that can be done by even one corporate offense may be vast. The loss to victims in one-third of corporate crime convictions amounts to $10 million or more per case.[15] According to the law, a corporation is a person and, therefore, is liable for its criminal activity. The acts of a

"A corporation cannot blush. It is a body, it is true; has certainly a head—a new one every year; arms it has and very long ones, for it can reach at anything; . . . a throat to swallow the rights of the community, and a stomach to digest them! But who ever yet discovered, in the anatomy of any corporation, either bowels or a heart?"

—Howell Walsh, Speech, Tralee assizes, c. 1825

corporation are those carried out by its agents or employees within the scope of their employment. When offenses require specific criminal intent, the corporation must appear to authorize or at least acquiesce in their commission. A repeated pattern of illegal acts may tend to show this acquiescence. The intent of the corporation's officers is assumed to be the intent of the corporation.

When specific intent is not required, the corporation still may be liable for employees' acts, even if they were not authorized, or even if they were forbidden. *State v. Steenberg Homes, Inc.* at the end of this chapter contains a good example of liability under such circumstances.

Besides ordinary criminal statutes, corporations are subject to many administrative regulations that are enforced with criminal penalties. A corporation cannot be imprisoned, of course, and fines that would be fitting for an individual's crime would be negligible to a large corporation, so huge fines have been used to control corporate behavior that is dangerous to individuals and to the public as a whole. Recent prosecutions of corporations have included the following cases.

From the 1996 ValuJet plane crash in the Everglades came state charges of 110 counts of third degree murder, 110 counts of manslaughter, and one count of unlawful transportation of hazardous materials against SabreTech, the company that sent improperly secured and labeled oxygen-generating canisters on that flight. Federal charges in the case included twenty-four counts of making false statements to the FAA, using falsified documents, and endangering public safety. SabreTech was convicted on nine federal criminal charges.[16] Royal Caribbean Cruises, Ltd., pleaded guilty to twenty-one felony counts of dumping oil and hazardous chemicals in United States water and lying about it to the Coast Guard. Their $18 million fine was in addition to a $9 million fine for a similar plea agreement the prior year. Since 1993, six other cruise lines have paid fines up to $1 million for illegal dumping.[17] For years agents for a subsidiary of Prudential Insurance Company influenced customers to turn in old policies, which then lost their value, for more expensive ones without explaining the loss. As a result, the company was fined $20 million for violating federal securities laws.[18]

Officers or agents of a corporation can be convicted of acts in which they participate, or direct or permit others to perform, whether the acts are for their own benefit or for the benefit of the corporation. A meat packing company was held criminally liable for shipping adulterated meat, misdating meat, evading federal inspection, and "reworking" and reselling returned meat. In addition to convictions of the corporation and the general sales manager who was directly involved in the infractions, the company president, who was in a "responsible relationship" to the activity but was not personally involved, received a four-year prison sentence [*U.S. v. Cattle King Packing Co., Inc.* (10th Cir. 1986). The case of *State v. Steenberg Homes, Inc.* (Wis. App. 1998) illustrates both negligence and corporate responsibility in a criminal offense.

STATE v. STEENBERG HOMES, INC
Court of Appeals of Wisconsin, 1998
589 N.W. 2d 668 Wis. App. 1988
[Citations omitted]

. . .

J. ROGGENSACK

Steenberg Homes, Inc. (Steenberg) appeals from a conviction of two counts of homicide by negligent operation of a vehicle pursuant to § 940.10, STATS., and one count of causing

great bodily harm by negligent operation of a vehicle pursuant to § 346.62(4), STATS.. . .

BACKGROUND

On August 8, 1995, Daniel Oliver, a Steenberg employee, was driving a Steenberg tractor-trailer when the trailer disengaged from the tractor and struck three bicyclists who were riding on the shoulder of the road. Two of the bicyclists were killed, and the third was seriously injured.

Oliver began his employment as a truck driver with Steenberg on July 31, 1995. During the week of July 31, 1995, Paul Cwikla, a Steenberg employee, trained Oliver. Cwikla showed Oliver the trailer hookup procedures. Under Cwikla's supervision, Oliver hooked and unhooked the coupling devices and safety chains, and he drove a tractor hauling a mobile home. He also drove with another driver and was involved with at least four other trailer hookups during his training period. Oliver understood that he was responsible for his tractor-trailer's equipment, safety, and operation. After Oliver completed his training, Cwikla gave a positive evaluation approving Oliver to drive on his own. On August 7, 1995, Oliver drove a tractor hauling a mobile home. He hooked and unhooked the coupling devices and safety chains between the tractor and trailer without any problems.

On August 8, 1995, the day of the accident, Oliver, Cwikla, and another employee loaded timbers onto the trailer. Oliver backed up his tractor to the loaded trailer, and Cwikla attached the coupler to the ball hitch between Oliver's tractor and the trailer. Neither Cwikla nor Oliver attached the safety chains.

After Oliver left the lot, he operated the truck in a safe and prudent manner, driving at an appropriate speed. When he reached a hill overlooking a bridge, he saw three bicyclists riding along the roadway. Before he passed them, he slowed, beeped his horn, and moved to the center of the road. As he drove past the bicyclists, the trailer disengaged from the tractor and hit the bicyclists. If either the ball hitch or the safety chains had been properly attached, the trailer would not have disengaged and struck the bicyclists.

On May 9 and 10, 1996, the State conducted an inquest to determine the cause of the accident. At the inquest, evidence was presented which showed that prior to this accident, no Steenberg tractor-trailer had ever disengaged causing injury, and there had never been any previous problem with the utility trailer or its hitch, although it was difficult to determine when the hitch was locked. However, Steenberg had not established a procedure to ensure that the ball hitch and safety chains were both secure before a tractor-trailer entered a public roadway. At the conclusion of the proceeding, the jury concluded that probable cause existed to charge Steenberg with two counts of second-degree reckless homicide, pursuant to § 940.06, STATS.

On September 11, 1996, the State filed an information charging Steenberg with two counts of homicide by the negligent operation of a vehicle, pursuant to § 940.10, STATS., and one count of causing great bodily harm by the negligent operation of a vehicle, pursuant to § 346.62(4), STATS. The circuit court found probable cause to believe that Steenberg committed the crimes in the information. Thereafter, Steenberg filed a motion to dismiss the information on the grounds that no probable cause existed to charge Steenberg with criminal negligence in the operation or handling of a vehicle. The circuit court denied the motion to dismiss.

On October 1, 1997, a trial was conducted before the circuit court on stipulated facts from the inquest. The court convicted Steenberg of all three offenses on the grounds that the Steenberg employees, acting within the scope of their employment, were negligent for failing to attach the safety chains; that Steenberg failed to ensure that necessary safety procedures were followed by employees in order to avoid a substantial risk of death or great bodily harm; and that the lack of the safety chains was a cause of the accident. This appeal followed.

DISCUSSION

. . .

Section 940.10, STATS.

Under Wisconsin's homicide by the negligent operation of a vehicle statute, "[w]hoever causes the death of another human being by the negligent operation or handling of a vehicle is guilty of a Class E felony." Section 940.10, STATS.

Steenberg claims that § 940.10, STATS., does not apply to it as a matter of law because: (1) corporations cannot be charged with negligent vehicular homicide; . . . and (3) Oliver was not acting within the scope of his employment when he failed to hookup the safety chains.

1. Corporations and negligent vehicular homicide.

Steenberg contends that § 940.10, STATS., does not apply to it because corporations cannot be charged with negligent vehicular homicide. We previously addressed this argument in *State v. Richard Knutson, Inc.,* 196 Wis.2d 86, 93–107, 537 N.W.2d 420, 422–427 (Ct. App. 1995), and we concluded that corporations may be charged with and convicted of homicide by the negligent operation of a vehicle in violation of § 940.10. We do not have the authority to overrule our own opinions. *Cook v. Cook,* 208 Wis.2d 166, 189–90, 560 N.W.2d 246, 256 (1997). Therefore, *Knutson* conclusively decides this question.

. . .

No Wisconsin case addresses the maintenance, loading or method of attaching a trailer to a tractor as a basis for criminal negligence; however, the statutory language is broad enough to encompass such a situation. Although the trailer itself was not a "self-propelled device," it was attached to a self-propelled device, the tractor, by the coupling. Once the tractor and trailer were connected, they became a tractor-trailer unit, and this unit was a "vehicle" for the purposes of § 940.10, STATS. The coupling device and the safety chains, which were supposed to connect the tractor and trailer, are the very mechanisms that Steenberg negligently controlled. Either Oliver or Cwikla, or both, failed to properly perform the functions of coupling the tractor to the trailer and attaching the safety chains; therefore, they were negligent in "handling" the vehicle.

3. Scope of employment.

Steenberg contends that it cannot be criminally liable for the conduct of its employee, Oliver, because Oliver knew that he was responsible for safely maintaining and coupling the tractor-trailer. Therefore, Steenberg argues that Oliver was not acting within the scope of his employment when he negligently coupled the tractor-trailer because Steenberg employees are instructed not to act negligently. Steenberg's argument is not supported by Wisconsin law.

A corporation can be held liable for the acts of its employees committed within the scope of employment. *Vulcan Last Co. v. State,* 194 Wis. 636, 643, 217 N.W. 412, 415 (1928); *State v. Dried Milk Prods. Co-op.,* 16 Wis.2d 357, 361, 114 N.W.2d 412, 415 (1962); *Knutson,* 196 Wis.2d at 101–107, 537 N.W.2d at 425–417. Employees act within the scope of employment when they perform acts which they have express or implied authority to perform and their actions benefit or are intended to benefit the employer.

An employer can be held responsible for the acts of an employee performed within the scope of employment, even though the conduct of the employee is contrary to the employer's instructions or stated policies. *Vulcan Last,* 194 Wis. at 643, 217 N.W. at 415. As the supreme court stated:

> Corporations must of necessity act through their agents. When these agents act within the scope of their authority their acts are the acts of the corporation, for which the corporation is liable both civilly and criminally. If the acts are within the scope of the authority of the agent, the corporation is liable criminally for the act although the act may not have been expressly authorized by the corporation, even if the corporation has expressly forbidden its agent to act in the manner that made it answerable to punishment under the criminal law.

The relationship described in *Vulcan Last* is precisely the relationship between Steenberg and Oliver and between Steenberg and Cwikla. Steenberg gave both Oliver and Cwikla express authority to drive, maintain, and couple tractor-trailers, and these acts were performed exclusively for the benefit of Steenberg. When Cwikla improperly coupled the tractor-trailer and when Oliver failed to check the hookup and attach the safety chains, each was acting within the scope of his employment. That Oliver and Cwikla did not heed Steenberg's warnings to use caution and that Oliver did not undertake responsibility for the safety and maintenance of his tractor-trailer does not place their negligent actions outside the scope of employment. Therefore, Steenberg may be liable for the acts of its employees, Oliver and Cwikla.

Sufficiency of the Evidence.

Homicide by the negligent use of a vehicle has three elements: (1) the defendant caused a death, (2) by criminal negligence, (3) in the operation or handling of a vehicle. *Knutson,* 196 Wis.2d at 109, 537 N.W.2d at 428. One cannot be held criminally liable for ordinary negligence under § 940.10, STATS. Rather, the negligent act must rise to the level of criminal negligence.

> Criminal negligence differs from ordinary negligence in two respects. First, the risk is more serious—death or great bodily harm as opposed to simple harm. Second, the risk must be more than an unreasonable risk—it must also be substantial. Criminal negligence involves the same degree of risk as criminal recklessness—an unreasonable and substantial risk of death or great bodily harm. The difference between the two is that recklessness requires that the actor be subjectively aware of the risk, while criminal negligence requires only that the actor should have been aware of the risk—an objective standard.

Id. at 110, 537 N.W.2d at 428 (citation omitted).

In *Knutson,* we concluded that evidence supported a corporation's conviction of negligent vehicular homicide pursuant to § 940.10, STATS., for an act of its backhoe operator whose vehicle touched a power line causing the electrocution of another worker. The corporation did not comply with written Occupational Safety and Health Act (OSHA) safety guidelines applying to the job, and failed to follow safety guidelines required by the job contract. Those guidelines put the corporation on notice that working in the vicinity of high voltage electrical lines posed a substantial risk to its employees. Even though the corporation knew or should have known of the danger, it took no precautions such as shutting down the electricity to the lines or erecting barriers. Instead, it merely warned its employees about the overhead lines. Therefore, we concluded that the jury could reasonably find that the corporation did not use due diligence to ensure the safety of its employees, and its conduct created a substantial and unreasonable risk of death or great bodily harm. Furthermore, had the corporation complied with the various safety requirements, the electrocution death would likely not have happened. Therefore, the jury could also reasonably find that the corporation's failure to take necessary precautions for the safety of its employees was a cause of the electrocution death.

In applying the rationale of *Knutson* to the case at hand, we note that both state and federal law require that safety chains be attached when a trailer is being pulled on a public highway. Section 347.47(3), STATS.; WIS. ADM.CODE § TRANS 308.12; 49 C.F.R. § 393.70(d). The potential for death or great bodily harm, if a tractor disengages from a trailer while driving on a public highway was not contested by Steenberg. In addition, Steenberg had an express policy of requiring its drivers to attach safety chains and to maintain their vehicles. Therefore, the circuit court's finding that Steenberg knew or should have known that not using safety chains posed a substantial risk of death or great bodily harm to people using public highways is well grounded in the record. However, even though Steenberg knew or should have known of the danger, it had no procedure which required a safety check, such as a form checklist the driver was required to complete, showing he had attached the safety chains, before he could begin his driving assignment. Steenberg did not use due diligence to ensure that its employees properly coupled the tractor-trailers and attached the safety chains. Therefore, we conclude that the evidence, viewed most favorably to the State and the convictions, supports the circuit court's finding that Steenberg's conduct was a cause of the bicyclists' deaths because had there been a checking procedure, established and enforced, the safety chains would have been attached; the trailer would not have detached from the tractor; and the accident would likely not have happened. Therefore, we affirm the judgment of the circuit court.

CONCLUSION

Sections 940.10 and 346.62(4), STATS., apply to Steenberg, a corporation, whose employees were acting within the scope of their employment when they negligently attached a tractor to a trailer. The evidence was sufficient to convict Steenberg of negligent vehicular homicide and causing great bodily harm by the negligent operation of a motor vehicle because Steenberg's failure to establish and enforce a procedure to ensure that its employees properly coupled the tractor-trailer and attached the safety chains created a substantial risk of death or great bodily harm which was a cause of the deaths and the injuries to the bicyclists.

Judgment affirmed.

VIII.   CONCLUSION

This chapter presents principles of criminal law that generally apply to any criminal statutes. Knowing these principles will help you assess culpability in each case with which you work.

A review of the components of crime—harm or likely harm, actus reus, mens rea, and causation—will help you understand the statutory elements that define each offense. Be alert to situations where those components drop or shift, as in strict liability, supervening causes, and vicarious liability.

Another factor bearing on the culpability of the accused is the level of that person's complicity in the crime. It is important to understand the actus reus and mens rea that define participation in a criminal act.

The special situations of vicarious and corporate liability allow for a person or entity to be punished for actions of their agents, even though those actions were not expressly condoned by that person or entity. Here again we see the law on the thin line between freedom and restraint, trying to act for the greater good of the people.

"Eight points of the law:

1. A good cause;

2. A good purse;

3. An honest and skillful attorney;

4. An upright judge;

5. Good evidence;

6. Able counsel;

7. An upright judge;

8. Good luck."

—Attributed to Charles James Fox, English statesman, John Campbell, *Lives of the Lord Chancellors,* 1845–1847

SYSTEM FOLDER ASSIGNMENTS

Complete the following and place the documents in your system folder:

- Summary of the categories of actus reus: acts, voluntary and involuntary; omissions; possession; and status.
- Your state's definitions and your own clear examples of transferred intent, general intent, specific intent, purposely, knowingly, recklessly, wantonly, negligently, strict liability, and lesser included offense.
- Definitions of principal, accomplice, and accessory used in your jurisdiction. Note whether your jurisdiction is consistent with *Peoni* or with *Backun*.
- Laws indicating whether and how vicarious liability applies in your state.

APPLICATION ASSIGNMENTS

1.   A man in his wife's absence entertains a woman. They drink heavily at the man's place. The woman also takes morphine and becomes quite ill. Knowing

that his wife is about to return, the man has a friend move the woman to another location. Shortly thereafter she dies. Did the man have a duty to seek emergency medical aid for the woman? See *People v. Beardsley* 113 N.W. 1128 (Mich. 1907).

2. Based on statutes and cases in your jurisdiction, could bookstore operators be punished for possessing obscene material in their bookstores without proof of intent? Why or why not? See *Smith v. California* (1959).

3. What if B is running and bumps into A, and B falls into a pool? A, an excellent swimmer, refuses to assist B. Does A have a duty to B on the theory that B would not have been in peril if not for the presence of A?

4. Should the following be charged with complicity: a guest of Mayor Chen in Case III who went to the kitchen for a drink of water just as Cat Bermuda dashed through with the idol under her arm, then returned to the hall without saying anything? A guest who helped Ms. Bermuda crawl through the kitchen window?

5. The owner of an automobile rides calmly in the back seat while a friend drives it recklessly. Is the owner an accomplice to the reckless driving? See *Story v. United States*, 16 F.2d 342 (D.C. Cir. 1926).

6. Who would receive the most severe punishment in the burglary case (Case III) under common law? Under modern law? If the principals are never found in the cross burning in Case VI, are Craig, Harvey, and Wescott criminally liable under modern law? Under common law?

7. Where is the liability in the following scenario?
   State law requires all taverns to close by 1:00 A.M. At 3:45 A.M., a bartender is caught standing behind the bar serving and drinking with two friends who had been there since before 1:00 A.M. The bartender had been instructed by the owner to abide by all liquor laws. No money was paid by the friends for liquor served after 1:00 A.M., so the owner did not benefit from the incident in any way. See *State v. Beaudry* 365 N.W.2d 593 (Wis. 1985).

HELPFUL WEB SITES

www.supremecourtus.gov
   U.S. Supreme Court, current opinions, docket, case handling guides
http://library.thinkquest.org/2760/
   Anatomy of a Murder: A Trip Through Our Nation's Legal Justice System, includes arrest forms, landmark Supreme Court cases

INTERNET EXERCISES

1. Using Web sites listed at the end of Chapter 1, compare your state's actus reus and mens rea requirements for the crime of criminal assault with those of another state.

2. Go to www.law.com. Check for news of current corporate crimes in the Corporate Law Center of the Practice Central section.

3. Explore the thinkquest site. Return to it to trace the steps of criminal justice procedures as you read about those steps in the following chapters.

QUESTIONS FOR STUDY AND REVIEW

1. Why is it imperative for a paralegal working in criminal law to know the principles of criminal law?

2. What are the components of a crime? Define each?

3. Explain how crimes are classified.
4. What are the reasons for requiring a criminal act in prosecuting crime?
5. What factors are considered in determining or proving actus reus?
6. Explain what is meant by the principle that a wrongful act must be voluntary. Define the types of conduct that are not voluntary and, therefore, not criminal. Give examples of involuntary conduct.
7. Explain the actus reus of omission. Give examples.
8. How is the crime of possession different from most crimes? On what basis is it justified?
9. What is the difference between crimes that punish for possession of unlawful objects and those that punish for possession of lawful objects?
10. What is the difference between actual and constructive possession? What is the danger of prosecuting for constructive possession?
11. What does it mean to be charged with crime based on status? What is the problem with such laws?
12. How does the Model Penal Code define actus reus?
13. Since courts cannot read a person's mind, what kind of proof is often used to prove criminal intent?
14. Identify and define the states of mind as classified in the Model Penal Code, ranking them from the most wrongful level of culpability to the least wrongful. Provide your own examples to illustrate each of the states of mind.
15. Explain the concurrence of mens rea with actus reus and harm.
16. Define strict liability and give examples of such offenses. How do you recognize a strict liability statute?
17. Define proximate cause and intervening or supervening causes.
18. Compare the levels of complicity in common law with those in modern law.
19. Define affirmative assistance and give examples of several types.
20. What factors must be considered to determine whether the aid an accomplice renders is sufficient for liability?
21. Compare the decisions rendered in *Backun* and in *Peoni*. What issues are involved?
22. What two forms of abandonment of a crime can free an accomplice from liability? To what extent must they be performed?
23. Define the three postcrime offenses that are discussed in this chapter and provide an example of each. Which is most likely to be prosecuted and why?
24. Explain respondeat superior.
25. What kinds of penalties are usually assessed for vicarious and corporate crimes?
26. What factors make the conduct of an employee the responsibility of a corporation?

KEY TERMS LIST

Accessory
  Accessory after the fact
  Accessory before the fact
Accomplice
Actus reus
Causation
Concurrence
Corporate liability
Corpus delicti
General intent
Harm
Hate crime
Knowingly

Mens rea
Motive
Negligently
Omission
Possession
Actual possession
Constructive
  possession
Principal
  Principal in the first
    degree
  Principal in the
    second degree

Proximate cause
Purposely
Recklessly
Respondeat superior
Specific intent
Strict liability
Supervening or
  superseding cause
Transferred intent
Vicarious liability
Wantonly

ENDNOTES

1. Quoted in G. WILLIAMS, CRIMINAL LAW (2d ed. rev. 1961).
2. See Morris, *Somnambulistic Homicide: Ghosts, Spiders, and North Koreans*, 5 RES JUDICATA 29 (1951).
3. *Sleepwalking Killer Convicted of Murder*, LEXINGTON HERALD-LEADER, June 26, 1999, at A3.
4. Confirmed by Robert Adams, PhD., Chair, Dep't of Psychology, Eastern Kentucky University, July 23, 1992.
5. For additional reading on omissions in general, see Kirchheimer, *Criminal Omission*, 55 Harv. L. REV. 615, 619–36 (1942), and Robinson, *Criminal Liability for Omission: A Brief Summary and Critique of the Law in the United States*, 29 N.Y.L. SCH. L. REV. 101 (1984); and on the duty to rescue, see Woozley, *A Duty to Rescue*, 69 VA. L. REV. 1273 (1983).
6. *Mother Convicted in Daughter's Death*, LEXINGTON HERALD-LEADER, April 12, 1995, at !3.
7. PETER W. LOW, JOHN CALVIN JEFFRIES, JR., AND RICHARD J. BONNIE, CRIMINAL LAW: CASES AND MATERIALS 144 (2d ed. 1986).
8. HOLMES, OLIVER WENDELL, JR., THE COMMON LAW 3 (1881).
9. For further discussion on this issue, see *Comment: Is Criminal Negligence a Defensible Basis for Penal Liability?*, 16 BUFFALO L. REV. 749, 750–52 (1967); Fletcher, *The Theory of Criminal Negligence: A Comparative Analysis*, 119 U. Pa. L. REV. 401 (1971).
10. *Model Penal Code*, Comments to § 2.02, at 127 (tent. draft no. 4, 1955).
11. WAYNE R. LaFAVE, AUSTIN W. SCOTT, JR., SUBSTANTIVE CRIMINAL LAW, VOL. 1, § 3.8, pp. 340–346. West Group, 1986, pocket part 1997.
12. LAURIE L. LEVENSON, *Criminal Law, The Causation Chain*, THE NATIONAL LAW JOURNAL, June 7, 1999, B21.
13. A. DALE IHRIE, III, *Parental Delinquency Laws*, 74 U. DET. MERCY LAW REVIEW 113 (1996).
14. LaFAVE, *supra* at § 3.9, 351–357.
15. *Corporate Crime in America: Strengthening the "Good Citizen" Corporation, Update on Cases*, Proceedings of the Second Symposium on Crime and Punishment in the United States, Sept., 1995.
16. Ina Paiva Cordle, *Murder Charges Filed in Air Crash*, LEXINGTON HERALD-LEADER, July 14, 1999, at A3; and Catherine Wilson, *SabreTech Convicted in '96 Crash*, LEXINGTON HERALD-LEADER, Dec. 7, 1999, at A9.
17. *Id*, July 22, 1999, at A3.
18. *Id*, July 9, 1999, at D1.

CRIMES AGAINST PERSONS AND CRIMES AGAINST HABITATION

CHAPTER

4

I. INTRODUCTION

A. ELEMENTS OF CRIMES

elements:
those specific requirements enumerated in statutes or common law that define a particular offense.

Elements of a crime are those specific requirements enumerated in statutes or common law that define a particular offense. Chapter 3 discussed actus reus, mens rea, and other general components of offenses; Chapter 4 narrows those components into the specific elements of individual crimes. For example, a statute specifies that one is guilty of arson who starts a fire with the purpose of (1) destroying an occupied structure of another or (2) damaging any property, his own or another's, to collect insurance. The actus reus element is that a fire is started. The mens rea element is that the act was done purposely. The harm elements are destroying and damaging, along with the specific types of structures targeted. The prosecution must carefully match each of these elements of the charge to the facts of the case so the burden of proof can be met on each element. The defense also matches elements to facts to see if lesser charges are appropriate or, when the match is less than perfect, to attack the charging document or to find defenses to the charge. To do your work accurately, you must know the difference between larceny and robbery, between arson and attempted arson, between first and second degree murder. In later chapters you will learn how to apply this knowledge toward procedures necessary to the prosecution or defense of a case.

In dealing with crimes against the person, you will be caught in the middle of change. Neither statutes nor court opinions change at an even rate across the country, or even within one state. New developments discussed here may soon be settled, only to make way for newer, more complex issues. Criminal law simply will not remain static in a dynamic society. You are best prepared if you stay aware of the first breaking of the ice in a new area and can see the coalescing of enough cases or statutes to constitute a trend. Most importantly, though, you must understand the legislative and judicial law in your own jurisdiction.

"Law has always been unintelligible, and I might say that perhaps it ought to be. And I will tell you why, because I don't want to deal in paradoxes. It ought to be unintelligible because it ought to be in words—and words are utterly inadequate to deal with the fantastically multiform occasions which come up in human life. . . ."

—Learned Hand "Thou Shalt Not Ration Justice," *Brief Case*, Nov. 4, 1951

These chapters cannot possibly give you all the legal variations of all the acts criminalized by our society. Their purpose is to lay the foundation of understanding so that you can do specific research efficiently as the need arises with each case. Chapter 6 covers inchoate, or incomplete, crimes. Chapters 4 and 5 are divided according to categories of crimes that share a common objective and, therefore, a common rationale for criminalization. Within these categories, the individual crimes are considered separately. Examples of pertinent cases, statutes, jury instructions, and Model Penal Code sections give you reference points for the cases that you will encounter in the office. The discussion of homicide illustrates the complexity of grading crimes. Use these examples, and check your state's statutes for the fine points marking the differences in elements and grading of each crime as you encounter it. For an overview of crimes, their classification and elements, see the charts at the end of this chapter and Chapters 5 and 6.

B. LESSER INCLUDED OFFENSE

lesser included offense (or necessarily included offense):
one whose elements are all included among the elements of the more serious crime that is being charged.

A **lesser included offense (or necessarily included offense)** is one whose elements are all included among the elements of the more serious crime that is being charged. For example, misdemeanor theft is a lesser included offense of felony theft when the act and intent are the same, with simply a lesser degree of harm. A lesser included offense may be joined in the charging document or be stated in instructions to the jury, who then decide not only whether to convict, but also on which charge to convict. The Model Penal Code §§ 1.07 (4) and (5) defines a lesser included offense as one that:

1. Is provable by the same or less than all the facts necessary to prove the charged offense.
2. Is the attempt or solicitation to commit the charged offense.

3. Is the same as the charged offense, except that it involves "less serious injury or risk of injury" to "the same person, property, or public interest" as that in the charged offense, or involves a "lesser kind of culpability" than that in the charged offense.

In *People v. Richmond* (Cal. 1991), assault with a deadly weapon was not allowed as a lesser included offense of attempted murder, because attempted murder can be committed without the use of a deadly weapon. Also, evidence showed that the defendant had the necessary specific intent to kill. In *State v. Stone* (Kan. 1993), a defendant who knew he was dragging his victim under the van he was driving during his flight from the scene of a theft was prevented from claiming vehicular homicide as a lesser included offense of second degree murder. The gross negligence involved in the murder was not an element of the lesser charge.

State v. Sage (Ohio 1987) ruled that when there is a complete defense to the crime charged, jury instructions on lesser included offenses will not be permitted, because they could lead to an unreasonable compromise by the trier.

At the end of the discussion of assault and battery in this chapter is the text of *Lamb v. State* (Md. App. 1992) that contains a consideration of lesser included offenses, as does *State v. Tutton* (Tenn. Cr. App. 1993) at the end of the sexual battery section. Read these cases to see the role lesser included charges can play at trial and appeal.

A few states allow jury instructions for **lesser related offenses,** offenses that do not meet the requirements of lesser included offenses, but bear a substantial relationship to the charged offense.[1]

A defendant found near a restaurant whose window had just been broken was convicted of second degree burglary, but jury instructions should have covered the lesser related offense of vandalism in *People v. Geiger* (Cal. 1984). Vandalism was considered to be sufficiently related to burglary, and the necessary proof of intent for burglary was defective.

lesser related offense: one that does not meet the requirements of lesser included offenses, but bears a substantial relationship to the charged offense.

II.   CRIMES AGAINST PERSONS

A.   INTRODUCTION

From Sherlock Holmes mysteries through television docudramas to the headlines of your local newspaper, the crimes that captivate us with shivers of horror are those that bring harm to life or limb. Homicide, assault, rape, and kidnapping, ancient common law crimes the perpetrators of which were punished for depriving the king of healthy subjects, have advanced into our times with a vengeance. A mere interest in macabre stories or the king's loss of the taxpaying ability of the victim seem quaint beside the physical and psychological toll to the lives of people we know and the social as well as economic damage to the communities where we live. It is no surprise that these are considered some of the most serious offenses in criminal law.

As these common law offenses became codified, they also gradually became more and more complex. Both the division of crimes into felony and misdemeanor levels and then their gradation into degrees of severity correspond to the complexity of circumstances in which these crimes occur. A simple "off with their heads," the ancient response to these crimes, has given way to an attempt at understanding differences in intent and damages, and to punish accordingly.

Along with this increased complexity in the grading of basic common law crimes, the past century has seen the kinds of changes that spawn entirely new crimes of violence. Vehicular homicide and "carjacking" did not exist a hundred years ago, nor did AIDS as an aggravating circumstance to rape. Recently, cyberspace has provided another avenue for stalking. Increasing emphasis on the rights of children and women has expanded rape into many levels of sex offenses, by and against both sexes, and has helped establish criminal abuse as a separate crime.

Advances in medicine have changed the very definitions of life and death, and homicide laws have been reinterpreted accordingly.

As with all the sections in Chapters 4 and 5, the following discussions of specific crimes against the person present the most usual elements and gradations, along with some possible variations for your general knowledge. You must accompany this background material with careful reading of your state's statutes.

B.   HOMICIDE

1.   Introduction

Common law homicide, the killing of one person by another, was divided into justifiable homicide such as that committed by police in the line of duty, excusable homicide such as that committed by one insane, and criminal homicide. The first two are discussed in Chapter 7 as defenses.

Historically, criminal homicide was always punishable by death, regardless of circumstances. In medieval England, however, offenses of clerics came under the jurisdiction of ecclesiastic courts (by "benefit of clergy") that did not impose the death penalty. Their greatest punishment was one year in prison, a brand on the thumb, and forfeiture of goods. By the fifteenth century, anyone who could read qualified as "clergy," so this "benefit" softened the harsh justice of common law, at least among the educated few. By the sixteenth century, premeditated murders, "wilful prepense murders" and "murder upon malice prepensed," were separated from those without such malice. These premeditated murders all were subject to capital punishment under common law, and the lesser "manslaughter" defendants were given "benefit of clergy."[2] Malice aforethought is still the line between murder and manslaughter.

The refinement of gradations in homicide statutes evolved, and now the death penalty may be imposed only when murders are committed under specified aggravating circumstances and with specified mitigating circumstances and procedural safeguards taken into account. Thirty-eight states use capital punishment.

Federal homicide laws include 18 U.S.C.A. § 351, which covers assassination of major governmental officers; 18 U.S.C.A. §§ 1111 and 1112, which define first degree murder, felony murder, and manslaughter; 18 U.S.C.A. § 1114, which gives federal courts jurisdiction over murders of specified United States officers such as federal judges, CIA agents, and national park rangers carrying out their duties; 18 U.S.C.A. § 1116, which includes the killing of foreign officials; and 18 U.S.C.A. § 2332, which includes killing United States citizens in international terrorism. The phrase "while engaged in, or on account of, performance of official duties" has been broadly interpreted. Most homicide cases, however, arise under state statute.

2.   Actus Reus in Homicide

Taking the life of another human being is the actus reus of homicide. Hidden in this definition is the assumption that the victim was alive before the act. That seems simple enough, but there are many cases where the cause and timing of death are less clear.

Statutes in some states still include the common law rule that death must occur within a year and a day from the time of the injury for criminal homicide to be charged. Because of medical advances, some states have extended the limit to three years and a day, and others have dropped the limitation altogether, either through judicial or legislative decision.

A man shot in the neck lived for six years, paralyzed and unable to breathe on his own for more than short periods. When he died, his attacker, already convicted on armed assault charges, was indicted for first degree murder. The defendant filed a motion to dismiss murder charges, claiming that Massachusetts's rejection of the year-and-a-day rule kept a potential prosecution hanging over his head and that a trial six years after the shooting would be a "costly and confusing battle of experts" over the cause of death. The court denied the motion, citing advances in medical science that render the year-and-a-day or any other time limitation obsolete [*Commonwealth v. Casanova* (Mass. 1999)].

Further complicating this question is the changing definition of "death." The once easy line between heartbeat and no heartbeat has given way to machines that sustain respiration and heartbeat, even if the brain is entirely nonfunctioning. When the brain stem still maintains heartbeat and breathing but there is no other brain activity, the patient is left in a deep coma and must be given food and water through tubes. Which is the actus reus of murder: the act that causes the injury, or the act that ends the "heroic medical measures"? Although the withdrawal of hydration and nourishment from a patient in a nonreversible coma remains controversial, some courts permit it free of criminal liability. In 1993 the Kentucky Supreme Court ruled that feeding tubes could be withdrawn from a woman who had been comatose for ten years after being beaten and burned.[3] In 1999 a Florida court allowed similar support to be removed at the victim's request after she had been shot and paralyzed by her mother. Although murder charges had been considered, the mother was tried for attempted murder and acquitted.[4] More commonly accepted than denying food and water is the termination of cardiopulmonary support by machines, although there may be resistance if the patient is a minor or incompetent, or if an adult's wishes in the matter are unknown. Generally, however, most legislatures and courts accept brain death as final. *In re Quinlan* (N.J. 1976) set a widely publicized precedent for ending life support that was carried into the criminal realm in *Commonwealth v. Golston* (Mass. 1977), where the victim had been brutally clubbed with a baseball bat. Golston's conviction for murder was upheld on the basis that the victim was already legally dead (brain dead) when the plug was pulled.

Also, it is not so simple to determine when "life" begins. Personal morals, religion, and philosophy join medicine and law in the search for an objective definition of that point. The contentions range all the way from conception to viability (capable of living normally outside the womb) to live birth. In cases involving fatal injury to a fetus, state courts are not unanimous. An Oklahoma court rejected the common law requirement of live birth and applied a viability standard when considering the "personhood" of the fetus in a vehicular manslaughter case [*Hughes v. State* (Okl. Crim. App. 1994)].[5]

Some states have passed laws that remove the ambiguity in fetal death cases. Missouri declares that life begins at conception, so the fetal death manslaughter charge in *State v. Knapp* (Mo. 1992) was affirmed. California law criminalizes the killing of any fetus beyond the embryonic stage of seven to eight weeks when the mother's privacy interests are not at stake, as in abortion [*West's* Ann. Cal. Penal Code § 187(a)]. Viability is not an element, so a murder charge was appropriate when an unviable fetus died after the mother was shot during a robbery [*People v. Davis* (Cal. 1994)]. Ohio includes "unlawful termination of another's pregnancy" in its murder statute (§ 2903.02). Another case upheld a criminal conviction only because the baby had been born alive after the in utero injury and before the resulting death [*Jones v. Commonwealth* (Ky. 1992)].

3. Causation in Homicide

One element of crime is the link of causation between the act of the accused and the harm to the victim, but that link is seldom at issue except in homicide. It may be difficult to determine which among several factors was the actual cause of death. When one act sets in motion other events that eventually result in death, courts are most likely to trace cause to the originating act. As seen in *Golston*, it was the act of the beating that caused death, not the intervening act of removing life support.

A man slashes his girlfriend's throat. In treatment for her wounds she receives blood transfusions contaminated with hepatitis. She dies six weeks later of hepatitis. Who is guilty? The boyfriend's conviction for first degree murder was upheld in *McKinnon v. U.S.* (D.C. App. 1988).

"Clarissa: Oh dear, I never realized what a terrible lot of explaining one has to do in a murder!"

—Agatha Christie, *Spider's Web,* 1956

A helplessly intoxicated man is offered a ride home. In the car the driver and his companions rob the man and leave him partially disrobed on a dark road. The temperature is near zero in heavy winds. Later, another car accidently hits and kills the man. Who is guilty? A homicide conviction of the robbers was upheld in *People v. Kibbe* (N.Y. 1974).

If an intervening cause of death is not part of a chain linked to the original act but is instead a separate, coincidental occurrence, it is the "superseding cause" bearing responsibility for the death. In *McKinnon,* for example, if the victim was recovering nicely from her wounds without the aid of transfusions but was discovered to have a chronic blood disorder requiring them, the slashing would not have been the reason the transfusions were given and, therefore, not the cause of death. Even if the original act is not linked to the death by cause, it may be chargeable as attempted homicide.

4. Mens Rea in Homicide

Because of the seriousness of taking a life, both as a crime and as a punishment, mens rea is analyzed more finely in homicide than in any other crime. For centuries the term *malice aforethought* has separated killings that were intentional and punishable from those that were accidental and not punished. Qualifications of the state of mind of the accused were further divided and subdivided until a thinly layered and not entirely universal nor objective scheme of culpability emerged. Not all of the points of grading homicide depend on mens rea; some are determined by the degree of harm in terms of cruelty, and others by circumstances such as accompanying crimes. Mens rea, however, forms the framework for the system.

The usual descending order of culpability in the breakdown of mens rea into purposeful, knowing, reckless, and negligent states of mind gets scrambled somewhat when at issue in homicide. Wanton recklessness can be more serious than an intentional killing in the heat of passion. Even the "malice aforethought" that so staunchly divides murder from lesser forms of killing has such a slippery meaning that it not only defies the common understanding of both "malice" and "aforethought," but also leaves its legal significance open to a wide range of interpretation. Sir James Stephen characterized the problem in the *Digest of the Criminal Law,* 1877.

> *The loose term "malice" was used, and then when a particular state of mind came under their notice the Judges called it "malice" or not according to their view of the propriety of hanging particular people. That is, in two words, the history of the definition of murder.*

Although definitions are often subjective and state variations are many, a general scheme of grading homicides starts at second degree murder as a baseline, with first degree murder being those killings aggravated by premeditation or other circumstances, and manslaughter being those mitigated by the victim's provocation or other circumstances.

Capital Murder

1. First degree murders that are aggravated by specified circumstances and lacking specified mitigating circumstances.

First Degree Murder

1. Killings that are purposeful, premeditated, deliberate.
2. Heinous or cruel killings.
3. Unintentional killings during the commission of a dangerous felony (felony murder).
4. Outrageously reckless acts creating a risk of death to a number of people (second degree in some jurisdictions).

Second Degree Murder

1. Intended but not premeditated killings evincing a "depraved heart" or wanton recklessness.
2. Killings resulting from a period of extreme emotional distress, not heat of passion.
3. Unintentional killings during the commission of a felony (less dangerous felonies than in first degree felony murder).

Voluntary Manslaughter

1. Killings on adequate provocation (heat of passion).
2. Killings when self-defense is not a complete excuse.

Involuntary Manslaughter

1. Reckless or grossly negligent conduct causing death.
2. Unintentional killing during the commission of a misdemeanor (misdemeanor manslaughter).

Reckless Homicide

1. Vehicular homicide (not intentional).
2. Negligent homicide.

Note the importance of mens rea in the grading of murder and manslaughter.

5. Murder

a. Introduction   The malice aforethought that separates murder from other killings is not hate or spite, nor must it necessarily be of a particular duration. It is a level of intent that is seen as being particularly dangerous to society. It can be observed in evidence of premeditation, inferred from cruelty or a disregard for human safety, or derived from the intent to commit a different felony.

b. Capital Murder   Federal law and statutes in thirty-eight states allow murderers to be put to death if the commission of their crimes includes certain aggravating factors such as previous convictions, special cruelty, vulnerability of the victim, and payment for the murder. These factors are to be weighed against mitigating factors such as impaired capacity of the defendant, relatively minor participation in the crime, and no previous history of crime. United States death penalty requirements are covered in 18 U.S.C.A. §§ 3591 and 3592. They include special aggravating factors for the death of a high public official or as the result of a continuing criminal enterprise involving drug sales, as well as factors involving espionage or treason.

c. Premeditation   Premeditation is the red flag of first degree murder. Any passage of time allows reservations against killing to surface. Then, the theory goes, if there are no reservations strong enough to prevent the act, the perpetrator is dangerous indeed. The Model Penal Code § 210.2 and some states reject the term "premeditation" and use "purposely," "knowingly," "with deliberation," or simply "with intent."

In *Willey v. State* (Md. 1992), deliberation meant that the defendant "thought about killing" and was "conscious of his intent to kill" in order for the first degree murder conviction rather than second degree to be affirmed. Even though the defendant testified that he had no intent to kill his former girlfriend when he shot her, he had threatened her and described exactly how he would kill her two weeks before he did so. The court in *State v. Guthrie* (W.Va. 1995) ruled that "any interval between forming intent and execution of intent allowing the accused to be fully conscious of the intent is sufficient" to differentiate it from a second degree murder by "spontaneous and nonreflective" action.

d. Heinous or Cruel The perpetrator's indifference to pain in an atrociously brutal killing is enough to aggravate charges to first degree murder in some states, even when premeditation or deliberation are not shown. *Golston,* where the definition of brain death was established, is an example of first degree murder based on the brutality of the attack. Golston's blow with a baseball bat opened a four-inch cut in his victim's skull. The victim fell, struggled to his feet, and fell again. Two days later his brain ceased functioning; a week after the attack, life support was withdrawn. Causing such suffering "for kicks," as the defendant admitted, constituted "extreme atrocity or cruelty."

e. Felony Murder Felony murder typically is an unintentional killing during the commission of a dangerous felony. The mens rea in the felony transfers to the killing to constitute first degree murder in most jurisdictions. When such a statute is unrestricted, any death related to a dangerous felony could be included.

A few states, including Hawaii and Kentucky, have abandoned the charge of felony murder. Other states have adopted one or more of the following restrictions: the underlying felony must be a cause of the murder; the risk of death must be foreseeable; death must be caused by the felon or accomplices, including using a victim as a shield; the felony must be among strictly enumerated crimes. The Model Penal Code section 210.2(b) and several states presume an indifference to life in the commission of certain dangerous felonies; it is the indifference to life rather than the felony that gives rise to the first degree culpability.

Read the decision for *State v. Houck* in Chapter 8 to see the ramifications of charging the wrong felony in a felony murder prosecution.

Check your state's statutes to see how the following cases would be decided in your jurisdiction.

People v. Bodely (Cal. 1995) ruled that felony murder included the death of a pedestrian who was struck when he attempted to stop the defendant's getaway car, even though the burglary committed by the defendant had come to an end. Flight to a place of safety was considered to be part of the felony transaction, with the felony and killing both part of one continuous occurrence.

Mens rea in killings by someone other than the defendant was based on acts in furtherance of the underlying crime in *People v. Hernandez* (N.Y. 1993). In this case it was ruled not simply coincidental that a police officer was shot by another police officer in a gunfight after the defendant's attempted robbery. Felony murder was not sustained against cofelons who were robbing a restaurant through one entrance while their accomplices at another entrance were being shot by a security guard, however. *State v. Bonner* (N.C. 1992) ruled that the killing must result directly from the act of the defendant or someone acting in concert with him.

f. Outrageous Recklessness A wanton disregard for human life, such as a person shooting into a crowd or randomly poisoning over-the-counter medicines on a store shelf is equated with intent in homicide. The general intent to perform an act placing people in risk of death is usually considered second degree murder but is sufficient to charge first degree murder in many jurisdictions, particularly when more than one person has been killed or placed at risk. In these cases the level of risk is an issue to be weighed. Outrageousness is judged either objectively against what a reasonably prudent person would do, regardless of knowing the risk, or subjectively by whether the defendant knew the risk and disregarded it.

Voluntary intoxication is not a defense to recklessness. An intoxicated man entered a bar and shot at his intended victim, missing him and wounding another person. He then shot and wounded the first man and proceeded to shoot randomly and kill a third person. The court in *People v. Register* (N.Y. 1983), upholding his conviction, ruled that "the risk of excessive drinking should be added to and not subtracted from the risks created by the conduct of the drunken defendant."

g. Second Degree Murder   Second degree murder, rather than being premeditated or deliberated, arises from the "wanton recklessness," "depraved heart," "depraved indifference," or "outrageous disregard for life" of the killer. For a street fight hail of bullets that killed a bystander, the court in *Alston v. State* (Md. 1995) ruled that "each participant has exhibited mens rea that qualifies him for depraved heart murder," as an aider and abettor of urban warfare. The defendant convicted of second degree murder had been fighting against the person whose bullet actually did the killing. A defendant who fired a pistol into a vehicle on an interstate highway, killing the occupant "without excuse of provocation," was judged to be aware of great risk of death and consciously disregarded it" [*King v. State* (Ala. Crim. App. 1987)].

Second degree murder also is charged when the defendant has suffered extreme emotional distress that accumulates and builds beyond sudden heat of passion, the usual mens rea element in manslaughter. A husband who killed his wife with thirty to forty blows from a sugar cane machete could not claim that the years of his wife's infidelity and their marital squabbles were a provocation to manslaughter. His second degree murder conviction was upheld in *Douglas v. State* (Fla. App. 1995).

Second degree murder also is charged in felony murder when the underlying felony is less dangerous than that for first degree felony murder. When the facts do not meet the requirements of first degree murder and exceed those of manslaughter, second degree murder serves as a catch-all charge.

A second degree murder charge was affirmed against a father who shook his four-month-old child so severely that the baby died from the resulting brain damage [*State v. Hemphill* (N.C. App. 1991)].

Second degree murder can be something of a jury pardon used when "the propriety of hanging" is lacking.

6. Manslaughter

a. Introduction   Manslaughter is a killing under circumstances deemed less dangerous to society than those required for the charge of murder. It is a separate crime from murder, not simply a different degree. Although some states do not make a distinction, manslaughter charges are usually divided between voluntary and involuntary offenses.

b. Voluntary Manslaughter   Malice aforethought is not an element of voluntary manslaughter, but a specific intent to kill is a requirement in most jurisdictions. Another dividing line between murder and voluntary manslaughter is the culpability of the victim. Generally, a murder victim is relatively innocent, but the victim of voluntary manslaughter has provoked the killing. In typical manslaughter cases, the defendant either defends self or family against the victim's threat with unreasonably deadly force or is provoked by the victim to a "heat of passion," to "extreme emotional disturbance," or by "sudden combat."

Unreasonable self-defense could be found if Eldon Spiers simply put his arm around Kate Lamb's shoulder and whispered an obscene suggestion in her ear, and she reacted by pulling a gun and shooting him dead.

For true self-defense, the defendant must subjectively believe that he or she is in danger and that force is necessary for self-protection. If either or both beliefs are objectively unreasonable, the defense is flawed, and a charge of voluntary manslaughter is warranted. In a basketball court dispute the defendant thought the victim was on the verge of drawing a gun, so the defendant drew first and shot him. The court in *Swann v. U.S.* (D.C. App. 1994) ruled that a jury instruction on imperfect self-defense, voluntary manslaughter, should have been given.

Provocation must be adequate to stir a reasonable person to passion. The traditional basis for this charge is the husband who finds his wife committing adultery with another man and shoots one or both of them. A defendant intended to secretly take pictures of his wife with her lover, but when he saw them engaged in sexual intercourse, he was so enraged that he shot the lover. The court in *State v. Thornton* (Tenn. 1987) reduced his first degree murder conviction to voluntary manslaughter. Adequate provocation can include adultery as well as serious mutual combat, serious battery or assault, trespass, gestures threatening deadly force, and informational words, such as those in *State v. Munoz* (N.M. App. 1992). In this case voluntary manslaughter was ruled the appropriate charge against a man who killed his wife's stepfather on receiving information that the stepfather allegedly sexually molested the defendant's wife years earlier.

To amount to adequate provocation, the gestures and words must go beyond insult. In refusing to reduce a second degree murder charge to voluntary manslaughter in *Girouard v. State* (Md. 1991), the Maryland Supreme Court ruled that the taunts of a wife during a domestic dispute did not constitute adequate provocation. "We perceive no reason for holding in favor of those who find the easiest way to end a domestic dispute is by killing the offending spouse."

As already seen in the case of *People v. Register* where intoxication did not mitigate a charge of outrageously reckless murder, diminished capacity such as partial insanity or intoxication does not usually mitigate murder to manslaughter. Extreme emotional disturbance or heat of passion must be externally provoked, not an internal condition of the defendant. The provocation must be adequate to move a reasonable person, not just to feed on the quirks of an individual personality, in most statutes. And, finally, the provocation must actually cause emotional disturbance in the defendant, without a "cooling off period" that allows the defendant to form a deliberate plan to murder. A wife's threat to find someone to have sex with was not immediate or certain enough to constitute provocation, and the time it took her husband to strangle her with a belt was sufficient for him to form intent, even though he claimed the killing was reckless and unintentional [*Speake v. State* (Ala. Cr. App. 1992)].

The traditional term *heat of passion* is replaced in the Model Penal Code and increasingly in state statutes by *extreme emotional disturbance*. The suddenness of passion that gives way to a cooling off period is replaced by an allowance for a time of brooding, of simmering emotion, and a broader interpretation of adequate provocation. To compensate for the inclusion of these circumstances more closely approaching the elements of murder, sentencing under statutes using "extreme emotional disturbance" tends to be more severe (twenty-five years in New York and twenty years in Oregon) than under those using "heat of passion" (ten years in Virginia).[6]

c. Involuntary Manslaughter One type of involuntary manslaughter, misdemeanor manslaughter, involves the same issues that arise in felony murder. It is an unintentional death accompanying an unlawful act (though not the serious felonies included in felony murder). The Model Penal Code and some jurisdictions reject it altogether, and it is restricted in some other jurisdictions by requirements of proximate cause or criminal negligence.

Poking a helpless, homeless victim with a stick, urinating on him, and kicking dirt and trash over him was a sufficient unlawful act for an involuntary manslaughter charge when the victim died of a fatal heart attack caused by the battery. [*Schlossman v. State* (Md. App. 1995)]. An involuntary manslaughter charge was upheld in *State v. Wassil* (Conn. 1995) for delivery of illegal narcotics to the victim who injected them, then died.

Other involuntary manslaughter is the result of criminal negligence or recklessness. No intent to harm is required, but a higher level of negligence or recklessness is required than that necessary in civil cases for wrongful death. That level of recklessness was not met when a witness to the theft of $110 from a church collection plate died of a heart attack while chasing the defendant [*Todd v. State* (Fla. App. 1992)], or when a wife bled to death after falling on a piece of glass from the lamp her husband had knocked to the floor during an argument [*State v. Torres* (Iowa 1993)]. In both cases the danger was not foreseeable, so manslaughter convictions were reversed.

A manslaughter charge is usually applied when gross negligence is proved in the handling of such things as explosives, vicious animals, medicines, or public transportation. Also, when there is a duty to act, such as to provide nourishment and medical care to children by parents, death caused by a failure to act often results in a manslaughter charge. A physician who delivered a premature baby at home without proper examination of the mother, ignoring obvious signs of respiratory distress syndrome in the baby even after the mother asked about them, was convicted of negligent homicide in *State v. Warden* (Utah 1991). When misread Pap smear tests led to the cervical cancer deaths of two women, the medical laboratory responsible pleaded no contest to charges of reckless homicide.[7]

d. Vehicular Homicide Because of the reluctance of juries to convict automobile drivers of murder or manslaughter, some states have separate statutes for vehicular homicide, those deaths caused by reckless or negligent driving. The standards of proof and those for sentencing are less stringent than for involuntary manslaughter. In some states it is a lesser included offense in manslaughter, and in others it is manslaughter. In some states it is part of the vehicle code rather than the criminal code, and in others drunken drivers can face murder charges. An Ohio man pleaded no contest to charges of running a red light and vehicular homicide when an airbag deployed in an accident and killed his infant son. Though there was no law requiring the airbag to be switched off, safety stickers in the vehicle and on the baby's car seat warned of the danger. The father was sentenced to spend the child's birthday and the anniversary of the accident in jail.[8]

7. Suicide

Under common law, a suicide victim forfeited his or her possessions to the king. Now suicide laws focus on those who aid another to commit suicide. A defendant who held a gun to the victim's head and pulled the trigger was guilty of second degree murder, even though the defendant and victim had agreed to a suicide pact [*State v. Sexson* (N.M. App. 1994)]. Directly causing the death was murder; providing the means for the victim to commit suicide would have been assisted suicide, a separate crime in New Mexico. Similarly, in California a defendant who strangled an AIDS patient in a suicide plan was convicted of second degree murder. The intentional, overt act of strangulation precluded manslaughter charges, *People v. Cleaves* (Cal. App. 1991).

Michigan passed a law effective March 1993 establishing criminal sanctions against assisting suicide. Previously, murder charges against Dr. Jack Kevorkian were dismissed there for helping several chronically ill patients commit suicide with a machine delivering carbon monoxide. The famous "Dr. Death" was charged with assisting subsequent suicides under the new law. He was finally convicted of second degree murder and sentenced to ten to twenty-five years in prison in 1999. Publicity surrounding his assisting 130 suicides since 1990 influenced some states to ban or increase penalties for assisted suicide, and some others to consider legalizing it. Two-thirds of Americans favor the legalization of assisted suicide, so further changes are likely.[9] It is banned by statute in thirty-eight states and by common law in seven others. Only Oregon explicitly allows a form of physician assistance in suicide.[10] Because Ohio does not have an assisted suicide statute, *State v. Sage* (Ohio 1987) ruled that a mutual suicide pact was a complete defense to any crime by the survivor to the pact. In upholding Florida's ban on assisted suicide in *Krischer v. McIver* (Fla. 1997), the court stated that a "well crafted statute" allowing assisted suicide could be held to be constitutional.

Extensive discussions of the principles involved with assisted suicide are found in the decisions of *Compassion in Dying v. Washington* (9th Cir. 1996), which overturned Washington's ban on assisted suicide, and the subsequent Supreme Court decision in

Washington v. Glucksberg (1997), which reinstated the ban. In October, 1999, the House of Representatives passed a bill that would make physician-assisted suicide a federal crime and nullify the Oregon law permitting it. Senate action was delayed. Watch for further action on this issue.

ANALYSIS PROBLEM

4–1.   The aim in homicide cases to weigh the preciousness of human life and to fathom the human mind has resulted in a complex, uneven network of standards and statutes. In your task of deciphering the law so you can work with it in your own jurisdiction, take some time out to consider it from your own perspective. Do you agree with the predominant grading scheme for homicide? Would you feel safer living next to the man who helped the AIDS patient die and was convicted of murder, or the man who shot his wife's stepfather and was convicted of manslaughter? Is the parent who starves her child to death less culpable than the one who drops hers off a building? Can a truly "reasonable person" be provoked to kill? If so, why do we punish such a killing?

Read *Comber v. U.S.* for a discussion of the elements of second degree murder, voluntary manslaughter, and manslaughter, and how they are applied in this case.

COMBER v. UNITED STATES
HAYWARD v. UNITED STATES
District of Columbia Court of Appeals, 1990
584 A.2d 26 D.C. App. 1990
[Citations omitted]

. . .

STEADMAN, Associate Judge

In these consolidated appeals, we are faced with the immediate question of what jury instructions for the crime of manslaughter are appropriate where a person dies as a result of bare-fisted blows to the face. Like an unraveling string, this inquiry has led to and necessitated a more general examination of the law of manslaughter and particularly its division in our jurisdiction into "voluntary" and "involuntary" components. . . . Both appellants challenge the voluntary manslaughter instructions upon which the juries based their verdicts. They also raise challenges pertaining to involuntary manslaughter instructions: appellant Hayward claims the trial court erred in refusing to give such an instruction, while appellant Comber claims the involuntary manslaughter in-

struction in his case was improper. Because we agree with these contentions of instructional error, we reverse and remand for new trials.

I.   THE HOMICIDES

A.   Appellant Comber

Gilbert Comber apparently did not approve of his sister Mary Comber's relationship with Joseph Pinkney. . . . A friend of the Combers mistakenly told appellant that Pinkney and Ms. Comber had secretly been married. Saying he was going to get his sister, appellant went out to the alley where Ms. Comber and Mr. Pinkney had parked their car. Witnesses differed as to what happened next. All agreed, however, that Comber, who was substantially smaller by weight than

Pinkney, punched Pinkney either once or twice in the face. Pinkney, who was extremely intoxicated at the time of death, fell down, and appellant returned to his house. Though Pinkney was still conscious after being knocked to the ground, he later lapsed into unconsciousness; by the time police arrived, he appeared to be dead. The medical examiner who performed an autopsy on Pinkney's body testified that the cause of death was one or more extremely forceful blows to the face which caused subarachnoid brain hemorrhaging, or bleeding in the part of the brain which controls the heartbeat and respiration. According to the medical examiner, there was no evidence that Pinkney's death resulted from his head striking the pavement when he fell. Appellant Comber testified that he struck Mr. Pinkney only once, and in self-defense. He stated that Pinkney took a swing at him when he tried to get his sister to return to the house with him, and that he never intended to kill Pinkney.

B. Appellant Hayward

In the early morning hours of November 27, 1987, appellant Hayward struck Geriel Butler in the jaw. Butler fell into the street, hit his head, and lost consciousness. He soon regained consciousness, stood up, and walked away. Witnesses disagreed about precisely what happened next, but they all agreed that appellant Hayward and Butler encountered one another again a short time later near a van from which a vendor sold clothes. Appellant Hayward again punched Butler in the jaw. As Butler fell to the ground, the back of his head struck the concrete. Butler lost consciousness and died later that morning at D.C. General Hospital. The medical examiner who performed an autopsy on Butler's body testified that the cause of death was swelling and herniation of the brain, caused by the impact to the back of Butler's head when he fell and hit the ground.

Appellant Hayward testified that he struck Butler in self-defense. He stated that Butler approached him and asked to purchase drugs. After being rebuffed, Butler hollered at appellant Hayward and approached him with his fist balled up. Thinking Butler was about to hit him, appellant Hayward struck Butler. Hayward stated that he then walked across the street to the clothes van, where a short time later Butler again approached, shaking his fist and seeking retribution for the earlier incident. Thinking that Butler would strike him, Hayward again hit Butler, who fell, hitting his head on the concrete.

II. THE INSTRUCTIONS

A. Appellant Comber

After extended discussions, the trial court in Comber's case decided to instruct the jury on both the lesser-included offenses of voluntary manslaughter and involuntary manslaughter. As to each offense, the judge modified the District's standard jury instructions. The court gave the following instructions on voluntary manslaughter:

Now, let me read to you the jury instructions on voluntary manslaughter. Manslaughter is the unlawful killing of a human being without malice. Manslaughter is committed when a human being is killed unlawfully in the sudden heat of passion caused by adequate provocation as the Court has already defined those terms for you. The elements of this offense, each of which the Government must prove beyond a reasonable doubt are as follows:

One: That the defendant inflicted an injury or injuries upon the deceased from which the deceased died.

Two: That the killing was committed without legal justification or excuse.

And three: That the defendant intended to commit the acts which inflicted the injury or injuries.

To establish the first essential element it is necessary that the defendant have inflicted an injury or injuries upon the deceased and that the deceased died as a result of such injury or injuries.

To establish the second essential element of the offense it is necessary that you find the defendant guilty beyond a reasonable doubt, *that the defendant did not act in self-defense.*

And to establish the third essential element it is necessary that you find that the defendant intended to commit the act which inflicted the injury or injuries upon the deceased. (Emphasis added)

On the crime of involuntary manslaughter, the trial court instructed the jury as follows:

[I]nvoluntary manslaughter is the unlawful killing of a human being without malice. It may be a killing committed without a specific intent to kill or even without the specific intent to inflict injury which causes death. One may be found guilty of involuntary manslaughter if you find that his conduct was so reckless that it involved extreme danger of death or serious bodily harm and was a gross deviation from the standard of conduct a reasonable person should have observed under the circumstances.

Now, the elements of this offense, each of which the Government must prove beyond a reasonable doubt, are as follows:

One: That the defendant inflicted an injury upon the deceased from which the deceased died.

Two: That the injury was a result of a course of conduct involving extreme danger of death or serious bodily injury.

Three: That *although the conduct was not intentional* it amounted to recklessness and was a gross deviation from the standard of conduct that a reasonable person should have observed.

And four: That the killing was committed without legal justification or excuse. (Emphasis added)

According to these instructions, the essential difference between voluntary and involuntary manslaughter lies in whether or not the defendant intentionally committed the act that caused death. In effect, the court instructed the jury that if Comber intentionally punched Pinkney in the face, the jury should find him guilty of voluntary manslaughter. On the other hand, if Comber punched Pinkney only accidentally, and the unintentional punch rose to the requisite level of recklessness, then the jury should find him guilty of involuntary manslaughter.

B. Appellant Hayward

Hayward requested instructions on both voluntary and involuntary manslaughter. The trial court agreed to instruct the jury on voluntary manslaughter, and gave the jury the following charge:

Voluntary manslaughter . . . is the unlawful killing of a human being without malice. The essential elements of the offense of voluntary manslaughter, each of which the Government must prove beyond a reasonable doubt are:

One, that the defendant inflicted an injury or injuries upon the deceased from which the deceased died;

[A]nd, two, that the killing was committed without legal justification or excuse.

To establish the first essential element of that offense, it is as I have told you necessary that the defendant . . . inflicted an injury or injuries. With regard to the second element of that offense, it is necessary that the killing or homicide [was] committed without legal justification or excuse.

Justifiable homicide is the necessary killing of another person in the performance of a legal duty or where the person who kills not being himself at fault has the legal right to kill. Excusable homicide occurs where the person who kills although himself at fault had the legal right so to kill or where the killing was the accidental result of a lawful act done in a lawful manner.

In response to the appellant's request for an involuntary manslaughter instruction, however, the trial court declared that Butler's killing "wasn't . . . a result of recklessness." Accordingly, the court refused to give such an instruction.

III. THE CRIME OF MANSLAUGHTER

A. Historical Background

Although D.C. Code § 22–2405 (1989) establishes the penalty for manslaughter, "there is no statutory definition of manslaughter in the District of Columbia." "[M]anslaughter is defined, rather, by reference to the common law." . . .

[E]arly statutory developments . . .

led to the division of criminal homicides into murder, which retained its status as a capital crime, and the lesser offense of manslaughter. The courts defined murder in terms of the evolving concept of "malice aforethought" and treated manslaughter as a residual category for all other criminal homicides.

Thus, manslaughter, "[i]n its classic formulation . . . consisted of homicide without malice aforethought on the one hand and without justification or excuse on the other." Model Penal Code, *supra*, § 210.3 comment 1, at 44.

This definition has been adopted in the District of Columbia. . . .

2. The division of manslaughter into voluntary and involuntary manslaughter

The broad and undifferentiated early definition of manslaughter created pressure for refinement. In the same way that the early common law concept of unlawful homicide had evolved into murder and manslaughter, so too did manslaughter divide into separate categories of voluntary and involuntary manslaughter, depending on the type of conduct involved. . . . Recognition of this distinction was based at least in part on the perception that voluntary manslaughters ordinarily involve more culpable behavior than involuntary manslaughters, and that voluntary manslaughter frequently warrants a more severe sentence than involuntary manslaughter. . . .

B. "Malice Aforethought" for Purposes of Second-Degree Murder

Because of the relationship between voluntary manslaughter and murder, an understanding of the scope of the offense of voluntary manslaughter requires an examination of the states of mind which would make an unlawful killing second-degree murder. At common law, an unjustified or unexcused homicide rose to the level of murder if it was committed with malice aforethought.

For purposes of second-degree murder, "malice aforethought" has evolved into "a term of art" embodying several distinct mental states. . . .

First, a killing is malicious where the perpetrator acts with the specific intent to kill. Second, a killing is malicious where the perpetrator has the specific intent to inflict serious bodily harm. Third, "an act may involve such a wanton and willful disregard of an unreasonable human risk as to constitute malice aforethought even if there is not actual intent to kill or injure." [W]e referred to this kind of malicious killing as "depraved heart" murder. . . .

Historically, a fourth kind of malice existed when a killing occurred in the course of the intentional commission of a felony. Under this "felony-murder" rule, "[m]alice, an essential element of murder, is implied from the intentional commission of the underlying felony even though the actual killing might be accidental." . . .

C. Justification, Excuse, and Mitigation

Even where an individual kills with one of the four states of mind described above, the killing is not malicious if it is justified, excused, or committed under recognized circumstances of mitigation. . . .

Unlike circumstances of justification or excuse, legally recognized mitigating factors do not constitute a total defense to a murder charge. Such circumstances may, however, serve to "reduc[e] the degree of criminality" of a homicide otherwise committed with an intent to kill, an intent to injure, or in conscious and wanton disregard of life. Though such mitigating circumstances most frequently arise "where the killer has been provoked or is acting in the heat of passion, with the latter including fear, resentment and terror, as well as rage and anger," mitigation may also be found in other circumstances, such as "when excessive force is used in self-defense or in defense of another and '[a] killing [is] committed in the mistaken belief that one may be in mortal danger.' " The mitigation principle is predicated on the legal system's recognition of the "weaknesses" or "infirmity" of human nature, . . . as well as a belief that those who kill under "extreme mental or emotional disturbance for which there is reasonable explanation or excuse" are less "morally blameworth[y]" than those who kill in the absence of such influences. . . .

D. Voluntary Manslaughter

In this jurisdiction, a homicide constitutes voluntary manslaughter where the perpetrator kills with a state of mind which, but for the presence of legally recognized mitigating circumstances, would render the killing murder. . . .

The government agrees. . . . However, the government contends that voluntary manslaughter also encompasses another distinct category of killings, namely, homicides resulting when a defendant acts with the intent to cause any injury to or apply any force against the victim. Since a killing occurring under mitigating circumstances would rise to the level of voluntary manslaughter if the perpetrator acted with specific intent to cause serious bodily injury, the only killings included in the government's proposed definition not already encompassed by the above-discussed definition are those resulting from an act committed with intent to cause non-serious injury but which result in death. For several reasons, we must disagree with the government's assertion. . . . We think that both common law and authority make a death-oriented mental state the determinative dividing line between the two forms of manslaughter, which should reflect their differing connotations of culpability. . . .

We must conclude, in conformity with the overwhelming weight of authority on the matter, that voluntary manslaughter involves only those homicides where the perpetrator's state of mind would constitute malice aforethought and the homicide murder, but for the presence of legally recognized mitigating circumstances. If the perpetrator's state of mind is not one which would constitute malice, the fact that he or she intends to inflict non-serious injury or otherwise direct force against the victim does not render a killing voluntary manslaughter. Thus, to the extent that a death resulting from conduct accompanied by an intent to cause something less than serious bodily injury rises to the level of an unlawful homicide, it is governed by the involuntary manslaughter doctrines to which we now turn.

E. Involuntary Manslaughter

As described in the preceding subsection, voluntary manslaughter is a killing committed with an intent to kill or do serious bodily injury, or with a conscious disregard of an extreme risk of death or serious bodily injury, where the presence of mitigating factors precludes a determination that the killing was malicious. The absence of malice under these circumstances thus reduces the offense to one form of manslaughter. In contrast, where a killing is not committed with a specific intent to kill or do serious bodily injury, or in conscious disregard of an extreme risk of death or serious bodily injury, there is no question that the killing was without malice. However, even such an unintentional or accidental killing is unlawful, and thus constitutes involuntary manslaughter, unless it is justifiable or excusable. Indeed, it is the absence of circumstances of justification or excuse which renders a non-malicious killing "unlawful." Accordingly, one key to distinguishing those unintentional killings which are unlawful, and hence manslaughter, from those to which no homicide liability attaches is determining the circumstances under which a killing will be legally excused.

Generally, at common law, where a person kills another in doing a "lawful act in a lawful manner," the homicide is excusable. As this phrase implies, two categories of unintentional killings were not excused and thus were manslaughter: killings in the course of lawful acts carried out in an unlawful, *i.e.*, criminally negligent, fashion, and killings in the course of unlawful, *i.e.*, criminal, acts.

1. Criminal-negligence involuntary manslaughter

. . .

Under current law in the District of Columbia, one who unintentionally causes the death of another as the result of non-criminal conduct is guilty of involuntary manslaughter only where that conduct both creates "extreme danger to life or of serious bodily injury," and amounts to "a gross deviation from a reasonable standard of care." Thus, provided it does not fall within the scope of the misdemeanor-manslaughter doctrine, conduct resulting in death is excused unless it creates an extreme risk of death or serious bodily injury. Indeed, in our jurisprudence the only difference between risk-creating activity sufficient to sustain a "depraved heart" murder conviction and an involuntary reckless manslaughter conviction "lies in the quality of [the actor's] awareness of the risk." "[I]f [the actor] is aware of the risk, the crime is murder and not involuntary manslaughter. If he is not aware . . . and he should have been aware, the crime is involuntary manslaughter"). The gravity of the risk of death or serious bodily injury required in each case is the same.

2. Misdemeanor involuntary manslaughter

The second category of unexcused unintentional homicides are those occurring in the course of certain unlawful acts. Centuries ago, the "unlawful act" category of involuntary manslaughter included all killings occurring in the course of a criminal act not amounting to a felony, *i.e.,* a misdemeanor. The doctrine became known as the "misdemeanor-manslaughter rule," something of an analogue to the felony-murder rule. As time passed, however, the misdemeanor-manslaughter rule "came to be considered too harsh," and "the courts began to place limitations upon it." Thus, in many jurisdictions, a homicide occurring in the course of a misdemeanor is involuntary manslaughter only if the offense is *malum in se,* rather than *malum prohibitum.*[1] Where the misdemeanor manslaughter doctrine applies, involuntary manslaughter liability attaches even where the defendant does not act with the degree of recklessness ordinarily required for involuntary manslaughter predicated on criminally negligent behavior. In effect, the defendant's intentional commission of a misdemeanor supplies the culpability required to impose homicide liability.

In the District of Columbia, the misdemeanor-manslaughter doctrine has developed along substantially similar lines. Although the doctrine is established in the law in this jurisdiction, we have been mindful of the danger that the traditional misdemeanor-manslaughter rule, imposing involuntary manslaughter liability whenever a killing occurs in the commission of a misdemeanor *malum in se,* might cast too wide a net. The risk of an unreasonable application of involuntary manslaughter liability is especially pronounced in view of the massive increase since the early common-law era in the number and forms of misdemeanors. In *Bradford v. United States, supra,* 344 A.2d at 215, we described as a variety of

involuntary manslaughter a killing occurring "as the result of an unlawful act which is a misdemeanor involving danger of injury.". . . We think that the category of misdemeanors dangerous in and of themselves encompasses misdemeanors which bear an inherent danger of physical injury, and includes simple assault, D.C.Code § 22–504 (1989), the misdemeanor at issue in this case.

This limitation, however, is incomplete. Although some misdemeanors, at least when viewed in the abstract, prohibit activity which seems inherently dangerous, they may also reach conduct which might not pose such danger. A special difficulty arises in the case of simple assault, as presented here, because that misdemeanor is designed to protect not only against physical *injury,* but against all forms of offensive touching. To hold a defendant liable for involuntary manslaughter where a death freakishly results from spitting at another, putting one's hand on another in a sexually offensive manner, or lightly tapping another on the face, would create too severe an attenuation of the link between the criminal sanction imposed and the defendant's culpability. In such circumstances, there is no foreseeable risk of bodily injury of any appreciable sort.

Accordingly, the fact that death results in the commission of what is classified as an inherently dangerous misdemeanor, is alone insufficient to establish guilt of misdemeanor involuntary manslaughter. Rather, the defendant must commit the misdemeanor in a way which is dangerous under the particular circumstances of the case. We think a misdemeanor will be dangerous under the circumstances if the manner of its commission entails a reasonably foreseeable risk of appreciable physical injury. If the manner in which an inherently dangerous misdemeanor is committed creates such a foreseeable risk of appreciable physical injury, the defendant should bear the consequences of criminal homicide if the result is not just bodily injury but death itself. A killing resulting from a misdemeanor which does not satisfy the standard just described will be excused.

In sum, it can be seen that as a whole, the law of homicide is broadly symmetrical. The four mental states recognized as malicious for purposes of second-degree murder exist in manslaughter, as well. One who acts with the specific intent to kill or to inflict serious bodily injury is guilty of murder. If those two states of mind are accompanied by recognized circumstances of mitigation, however, the crime is voluntary manslaughter. (It is conceivable that voluntary manslaughter liability might arise where one, acting under circumstances of mitigation, consciously disregards an extreme risk of death of serious bodily injury, but such scenarios seem highly improbable.) The other two malicious mental states also have corollaries in the involuntary manslaughter category. One who acts in conscious disregard of an extreme risk of death or serious bodily injury is guilty of murder, but if he or she is only unreasonably unaware of such a risk, the crime is involuntary manslaughter.

---

1. *Malum in se* is defined as "[a] wrong in itself. . . . An act is said to be *malum in se* when it is inherently and essentially evil, that is, immoral in its nature and injurious in its consequences, without any regard to the fact of its being noticed or punished by the law of the state." *Black's Law Dictionary* 865 (5th ed. 1979). *Malum prohibitum* is defined as "[a] wrong prohibited . . .; an act which is not inherently immoral, but becomes so because its commission is expressly forbidden by positive law. . . ." *Id.*

Finally, one who kills in the course of a felony enumerated in D.C.Code § 22–2401 is guilty of murder, but one who kills in the commission of a misdemeanor under the circumstances described above is guilty of involuntary manslaughter.

IV. THE INSTANT APPEALS

Guided by the foregoing discussion of the law of manslaughter, we turn now to an assessment of the manslaughter instructions in appellants' cases. We conclude that the jury instructions given in each case were erroneous.

A. Appellant Comber

Both the voluntary and involuntary manslaughter instructions given in appellant Comber's case misstated the law as above explicated in significant respects. With regard to voluntary manslaughter, the trial court's instruction erroneously defined the mental states required for the offense. The trial court instructed the jury that to prove voluntary manslaughter, the government had to prove that the defendant committed an unjustified or unexcused killing, and that the defendant intended to commit the acts which caused death. The trial court then explained that to prove a killing was without justification or excuse, the government had to prove that the defendant did not kill in self-defense. In effect, then, the trial court instructed the jury that as long as he was not acting in self-defense, appellant Comber was guilty of voluntary manslaughter if he intended to commit some act which in fact caused Joseph Pinkney's death, no matter how unexpectedly. As is plain from our discussion above, however, to be guilty of voluntary manslaughter, a person must intend to kill, intend to inflict serious bodily injury, or act in conscious disregard of an extreme risk of death or serious bodily injury. . . . The instruction thus allowed the jury to convict Comber of voluntary manslaughter where his mental state and conduct would not constitute that offense.

The involuntary manslaughter instruction given in Comber's case was also erroneous. The instruction described the criminal negligence variety of involuntary manslaughter, not the misdemeanor-manslaughter variety. . . . However, the addition that the jury could find appellant guilty of involuntary manslaughter only if it concluded that appellant Comber's conduct was not intentional was an incorrect statement of law. Although it is true that an involuntary manslaughter conviction is appropriate only where *death* is unintentional, the offense is not limited to killings resulting from death-producing *conduct* which is unintentional. In fact, many intentional acts, provided that they either involve the creation of the requisite risk of death or constitute inherently dangerous misdemeanors committed in such a way that appreciable bodily injury is a foreseeable result, may constitute involuntary manslaughter. The instructions given in appellant Comber's case thus precluded the jury from finding him guilty of involuntary manslaughter under circumstances where such a verdict might have been appropriate.

B. Appellant Hayward

Two types of instructional error similarly occurred at appellant Hayward's trial. First, the trial court gave the standard voluntary manslaughter instruction, which erroneously defines that offense. Second, the trial court refused to give an involuntary manslaughter instruction upon the defendant's request.

Unlike the voluntary manslaughter instruction given in appellant Comber's case, the voluntary manslaughter instruction in appellant Hayward's case contained no description of the mental state required for the offense but included a definition of justification and excuse. . . . The instruction makes voluntary manslaughter of all unexcused homicides, including involuntary manslaughter of both the criminal negligence and misdemeanor varieties. . . . Furthermore, under the instructions given by the trial court, the jury was authorized to find Hayward guilty of voluntary manslaughter without ever finding that he acted with the mental state required for that offense. . . .

Appellant Hayward was entitled to an involuntary manslaughter instruction which the trial court declined to give.

C. Disposition

At bottom, the key element of discussion in this case is not whether appellants were improperly convicted of manslaughter, but whether they were convicted of the proper type of manslaughter. Because the punishment for both forms of manslaughter is governed by a single statutory provision, at first blush it may seem that a proper disposition of these cases might simply be to remand for resentencing for involuntary, rather than voluntary, manslaughter. . . . We recognize, moreover, that to the extent appellants could have been convicted of involuntary, rather than voluntary, manslaughter, it might well have been on the basis of a misdemeanor-manslaughter theory. Just as the jury must decide in a felony-murder case that the defendant committed the underlying felony, so too should the jury decide in a misdemeanor-manslaughter case that the defendant committed the underlying misdemeanor and in such a manner that appreciable physical injury was reasonably foreseeable. Conversely, in both cases, the evidence could have supported a jury finding that appellants acted with a state of mind which would have amounted to malice, but that each appellant killed in the heat of passion so that the killing was mitigated to voluntary manslaughter. Because the evidence was sufficient to support such a conclusion, the government is entitled to retry both appellants on the charge of voluntary manslaughter. We conclude under all the circumstances that retrial is appropriate for both appellants.

Reversed and remanded.

C. ASSAULT AND BATTERY

1. Introduction

Some statutes separate the definitions of "assault," the threat or attempt to cause injury, and "battery," actual harmful contact between the perpetrator and victim. Others, including federal laws and the Model Penal Code § 211.1, include the definition of battery as one type of assault. Assault or battery can be simple, usually a misdemeanor, or aggravated by circumstances raising it to the level of a felony. Other charges, such as reckless or wanton endangerment, menacing, stalking, and terroristic threatening often are included in assault statutes.

Federal assault prosecutions, like federal homicide prosecutions, are rare because federal laws only establish jurisdiction over "forcible resistance or interference with, or assault upon" officers of the United States, 18 U.S.C.A. § 111; on foreign officers, 18 U.S.C.A. § 112; and within maritime and territorial areas, 18 U.S.C.A. § 113. The federal stalking statute, 18 U.S.C.A. § 2261A, however, covers crimes involving the crossing of state lines.

2. Battery

The actus reus of battery is physical injury or offensive touching of another person. The amount of harm varies, with some states including intimate fondling or a spit in the face. Others and the Model Penal Code require actual injury, leaving other offenses to criminal sexual conduct statutes and civil law. No actual injury to the victim was necessary, however, for an aggravated battery conviction in *State v. Townsend* (Ida. 1993). The defendant had intentionally struck his wife's car with his truck.

In all jurisdictions the mens rea element of battery can be intent to injure or offensively touch. In most jurisdictions negligence is sufficient to convict for battery when harm is caused "with a deadly weapon." As in felony murder, a few states allow intent to commit some other unlawful act to serve as the mens rea for battery when injury occurs as a result of the commission of that act.[11] In some cases, intent can be transferred. *People v. Psichalinos* (Ill. App. 1992) upheld the conviction of a defendant who aimed a swinging fist at another adult, knowing injury would be the result, and accidentally struck a child.

Battery mens rea is negated when there is justification for the intent to make harmful contact. In Chapter 1, Case I, someone who pushed Kate Lamb back from the bridge rail to prevent her from jumping off would not be guilty of battery.

Consent is assumed in contact sports where injury might occur in furtherance of the object of the game. A tackled football player cannot press charges for battery, for example, but a recreational basketball player who came off the bench and attacked an opposing player during a break in the game was guilty of battery, *State v. Floyd* (Iowa App. 1990). Likewise, there is an allowance for the reasonable discipline of a child by parents or other authorities, but excessive force amounts to battery, or the separate crime of child abuse.

3. Assault

Whereas battery may be committed recklessly, assault involves purposeful intent. One type of assault is attempted battery. Here, the intent is obviously to commit the battery. This is an inchoate crime, because the battery is not completed and there is no injury. The victim need not even be aware of the attempt. As in other attempt crimes, the assailant must take substantial steps toward completing the battery. In some states the "present ability" to commit the battery must exist; that is, the victim must be within reach, the gun must be loaded, and so forth.

Where "present ability" was not required, the defendant was convicted of aggravated assault for firing into the victim's home, not knowing that no one was there [*Commonwealth v. Lopez* (Pa. Super. 1995)]. The battery attempted may be extremely slight, and an assault (attempted battery) conviction may be affirmed even though the battery was actually completed. The assault conviction of a defendant who spat in a police officer's face during a narcotics arrest was affirmed in *Ray v. U.S.* (D.C. App. 1990).

Another type of assault is threatened battery, where the intent is to frighten the victim. Though no physical injury occurs, this is a complete rather than an inchoate crime. Generally, the victim knows of the threat and does, in fact, fear serious injury as a result of it. Because the harm done is the creation of an emotional state, the actual ability to commit battery is not usually necessary, only the perception by the victim that the assailant is able to carry out the threat. A homeless man in an alley held a paring knife while demanding of a passerby, "What are you looking at? Get out of here." The court in *Mihas v. U.S.* (D.C. App. 1992) ruled that when an item has a legitimate use, the purpose for which it is carried is the ultimate test for whether it is a deadly or dangerous weapon. Although the defendant claimed he was using the two-and-a-half-inch blade to clean his fingernails, his hostile words and approach within four feet of the victim constituted assault. The dissenting opinion noted that the mens rea of the defendant should have been taken into account along with the perceptions of the victim.

After a physical altercation with her husband, a woman locked herself in the bathroom and heard a clicking sound that she thought was her husband's loaded shotgun just outside the door. He said he was in the kitchen cleaning the gun. His conviction for assault was reversed for lack of proof of intent to cause fear [*Commonwealth v. Spencer* (Mass. App. 1996)].

Words alone do not form assault, particularly if they are conditional or if the threat is not immediate. Statements such as "I'd kick you if you weren't a girl" or "I'll be back tomorrow with a gun" are not assault. Positioning oneself for the kick or aiming a gun at the victim is assault.

Some states do not have assault statutes, but include these offenses in attempt, threatening, and menacing statutes. Some states use the term *assault* in place of battery to define actual contact causing injury or offensive touching.

4.   Aggravated Assault and Battery, Mayhem

Mutual consent, as in a fight willingly engaged in by both combatants, is a mitigating circumstance reducing battery to a petty misdemeanor in many jurisdictions. Several aggravating circumstances may elevate both assault and battery to the felony level, however: assault or battery of a police officer on duty or of a child or otherwise helpless or designated person, with a force likely to cause serious injury, with intent to commit a violent felony, or with a deadly weapon or dangerous instrument.

In determining what could be classified as a dangerous instrument in aggravated assault, the court in *U.S. v. Johnson* (4th Cir. 1963) held that, "Not the object's latent capability alone, but that, coupled with the manner of its use, is determinative." The instrument must not only be capable of use as a weapon, but also be used or intentionally displayed, not just rest in the possession of the assailant. Unconventional "weapons," including a tennis shoe in a kicking attack [*State v. Munoz* (La. App. 1991)], a bare hand [*Dixon v. State* (Fla. App. 1992)], and thrown fecal matter from an HIV and hepatitis B positive defendant [*Commonwealth v. Brown* (Pa. 1992)], have been accepted in aggravated assault and battery cases. A defendant who slammed his wife's head against a bathtub, sink, and toilet, however, was not "armed" with a dangerous weapon [*Edwards v. U.S.* (D.C. App. 1990)], nor was the man who threw a woman overboard five miles from shore [*Commonwealth v. Shea* (Mass. App. 1995)], because neither the bathroom fixtures nor the ocean were under the defendants' control. Codefendants in *People v. Aguilar* (Cal. 1996) were both convicted of aggravated assault for kicking and beating their victim, one under the "deadly weapon" clause, the other under the "force likely to produce great bodily injury" clause of the statute. The conviction of the first was reversed because only "objects extrinsic to the body" could be considered deadly weapons. The conviction of the second was affirmed.

EXHIBIT 4–1
Sample Jury Instructions

ASSAULT WITH DANGEROUS WEAPON [18 U.S.C. § 113(c)]

The defendant is charged in [Count _____ of] the indictment with assault with a dangerous weapon in violation of Section 113(c) of Title 18 of the United States Code. In order for the defendant to be found guilty of that charge, the government must prove each of the following elements beyond a reasonable doubt:

First, the defendant intentionally [struck or wounded _____] [or] [used a display of force that reasonably caused _____ to fear immediate bodily harm];

Second, the defendant acted with the specific intent to do bodily harm to _____; and

Third, the defendant used a [e.g., knife].

[A _____ is a dangerous weapon if it is used in a way that is capable of causing death or serious bodily injury.]

Ninth Circuit Criminal Jury Instructions (St. Paul, MN: West Group, 1992), § 8.02D, with permission.

Laws against mayhem, the permanent dismembering or disabling of another person, are still on the books in some states. Specific intent or the intent to do bodily injury is an element. Other states include mayhem in aggravated battery statutes.

An injury may be considered permanent for the purposes of a mayhem conviction even though cosmetic surgery is feasible [*People v. Hill* (Cal. 1994)]. The intoxicated defendant beat the victim after the victim's car bumped his while parking. The victim's injuries required metal plates and wires to hold his facial bones in place, left his eye sunken with double and triple vision, and impaired sensation in his upper lip.

Read the decision in *Lamb v. State* for a clear delineation of the elements in assault and battery.

LAMB v. STATE
Court of Special Appeals of Maryland, 1992.
613 A.2d 402 Md. App. 1992
[Citations omitted]

...

MOYLAN, Judge

The appellant, Todd William Lamb, was convicted by a Somerset County jury, presided over by Judge Daniel M. Long, of (1) breaking and entering, (2) assault, (3) battery, (4) false imprisonment, and (5) reckless endangerment. He received a sentence of two years for breaking and entering and that judgment is of no further concern to us. The conviction for reckless endangerment was merged into that for assault and is also of no further concern to us.

The appellant received a consecutive sentence of ten years for assault, a consecutive sentence of six years for bat-

tery, and a consecutive sentence of six years for false imprisonment for a total of twenty-four years. He now argues:

1. That his conviction for assault should, as a lesser included offense, have merged into his conviction for battery; and

2. That his conviction for battery, in turn, should also, as a lesser included offense, have merged into his conviction for false imprisonment.

With the three convictions thus merged in the fashion the appellant would have them merged, his total sentence of twenty-four years would be reduced to a sentence of but eight years. ...

THE RELATIONSHIPS AMONG ASSAULTS AND BATTERIES

We turn our attention initially to the arguable merger of assault into battery. It requires us to look at the crime (or crimes) of assault and the crime (or crimes) of battery generally and then to look at the particular assault in this case and the particular battery in this case specifically. Our general investigation will be doomed at the outset if we conceive of it as an exploration of *the* relationship between *assault* and *battery*. We must conceptualize it, rather, as an exploration of the multiple *relationships* among various *assaults* and various *batteries.* The key to avoiding the almost hopeless confusion clogging much of the case law is to think plural.

Ironically, it is sometimes these seemingly simplest of crimes that are the most difficult to master. . . . The elements of latter-day statutory crimes, no matter how intricate, have been hammered out on the legislative anvil with meticulous precision. The common law standbys, by contrast, have grown by gradual and random accretion. As with a coral reef, there is no perceptible change from year to year. Over centuries, however, there develop forms and shapes that bear but slight resemblance to the aboriginal prototype. Once reliable descriptions lose currency. Thus has it been with assault and battery.

THE VARIOUS FORMS OF ASSAULT

Today, the term of art "assault" may connote any of three distinct ideas:

1. A consummated battery or the combination of a consummated battery and its antecedent assault;
2. An attempted battery; and
3. A placing of a victim in reasonable apprehension of an imminent battery.

A. A Battery Itself or a Combined "Assault and Battery".

By way of informal (or sometimes even formal) shorthand, both the case law and the statutory law frequently use the simple noun "assault" to connote a consummated battery alone and at other times to connote the combination of the inchoate attempt to beat or to batter followed immediately by the consummation of that attempt. . . .

When the word "assault" is used in this comprehensive way exclusively to connote or inclusively to embrace a battery, one cannot, of course, speak of *a relationship between* assault and battery. The present problem before us, however, deals with a relationship. This broad meaning of the word "assault," therefore, will be used no further in this opinion and all subsequent discussion will deal only with those narrower and more precise connotations of "assault" that are distinct from any suggestion of a consummated battery.

B. An Attempted Battery:

One of the two more precise meanings of the term "assault" is that of an attempted battery. This was the only meaning of "assault" at the early criminal law. . . .

As an attempt, it is, of course, a specific intent crime. The specific object or purpose intended is the commission of a battery, the inflicting of physical injury upon the victim or some other offensive touching of the victim. As with all attempts, the assault of the attempted-battery variety is established regardless of whether the effort succeeds or fails to achieve its purpose. . . .

That original, criminal-law meaning of "assault" as an attempted battery has, to be sure, retained its full vitality. What it has lost is its exclusivity. For those who have not kept pace with the loss of exclusivity, the resultant narrow conceptualization of assault simply as an attempted battery, and nothing more, has given rise to such slippery and treacherous half-truths (to be more fully discussed hereinafter) as:

1. Assault is an inchoate crime;
2. Assault requires a specific intent to commit a battery;
3. Every battery includes an assault;
4. There can be no such crime as an attempted assault.

None of these familiar and oft-quoted "principles" is totally true. None of them, however, is totally false. They are all half-truths; and therein lurks their insidious capacity to lead the unwary astray.

C. A Threatening of an Imminent Battery:

The more recent accretion to the coral reef of criminal assault is the replication in that new environment of the familiar tort of assault. . . .

> "This action, which developed very early as a form of trespass, is the first recognition of a mental, as distinct from a physical, injury. There is 'a touching of the mind, if not of the body.'"

For this variety of assault, it is not necessary that the victim be actually frightened or placed in fear of an imminent battery at the hands of one with the apparent present ability to commit such a battery. The critical state of mind on the part of the victim is to be placed "in reasonable apprehension" of an impending battery. This distinction preserves the rights of the intrepid crime victim or intrepid plaintiff. . . .

The Maryland State Bar Association's *Maryland Criminal Pattern Jury Instructions* has handled the plural nature of common law assault by providing not one recommended instruction, but three. MPJI-CR 4:01.1 defines for the jury the necessary elements of assault of the "intent to frighten" variety. MPJI-CR 4:01.2 provides a different instruction, listing different elements, for assault of the "attempted battery" variety. MPJI-CR 4:01 provides an omnibus instruction for the situation where the evidence of assault supports either variety of the crime. It begins by informing the jury of the plural nature of the crime:

> "The defendant is charged with the crime of assault. There are two types of assault. The first type is committed by intentionally making another person fear immediate [offensive physical contact] [physical harm]. The second type is committed by actually attempting to cause [offensive physical contact] [physical harm]."

It then takes up each of the two varieties in turn, providing a separate list of required elements for each. It does not attempt to lump the two together under any sort of composite definition.

D. A Comparison of Attempted Battery and Intentional Frightening:

Leaving aside for the moment any connotation of "assault" as either (1) a consummated battery or (2) a combination of assault and battery, the remaining two connotations alone illustrate how dangerous it is to make any generalized statement about the "crime of assault." A perfectly correct, albeit incomplete, statement will frequently be made about one species of assault. The unwary auditor or reader, however, will unwittingly assume that the given description of one species of assault applies with equal validity to the entire genus "assault." That description may then, in turn, be erroneously misapplied to a different species of assault as to which is totally inappropriate.

Assault of the attempted battery variety, for instance, is an inchoate crime. It shares with all other attempts the general characteristics of that variety of inchoate crime. Assault of the intentional threatening variety, on the other hand, is not in any sense inchoate. It is a fully consummated crime once the victim is placed in reasonable apprehension of an imminent battery.

It is generally agreed that an assault of either variety requires only an *apparent* present ability rather than an *actual* present ability to consummate the battery. The apparency, however, is assessed from opposite perspectives. For an assault of the attempted battery variety, there must be an apparent present ability from the viewpoint of the would-be assailant. Unless he thinks he can execute the battery, he will lack the required specific intent to do so.

For an assault of the intentional frightening variety, on the other hand, the assailant may be guilty even though he knows full well that he lacks any ability to follow through on his threat. That he knows the gun he points is unloaded or defective or is no gun at all is of no consequence. . . . All that is required in terms of perception is an apparent present ability from the viewpoint of the threatened victim. If, on the other hand, the would-be victim of the threat is unaware of the threatening conduct, there can be no assault of this variety. If the would-be victim perceives the threatening conduct but knows, for instance, that the gun is defective, there is no ap-

prehension of an imminent battery and, therefore, no assault of the threatening variety.

In terms of whose perception matters, that aspect of assault which came originally from the criminal law, concerned as it is with blameworthiness, is primarily defendant-oriented. That aspect of criminal assault which appeared initially in tort law, concerned as it is with harm, is primarily victim-oriented.

Both varieties of assault are specific intent crimes. The specific intents, however, are not identical. An assault of the attempted battery variety requires a specific intent to perpetrate a battery. No design or purpose to threaten or to frighten the victim is in any way necessarily implicated, although it certainly is not precluded. An attempted battery can be perpetrated on a victim who is asleep, is facing in another direction or is otherwise oblivious of any danger. A truly deadly assailant may, indeed, prefer not to tip his hand with any antecedent threat.

An assault of the intentional frightening variety, on the other hand, requires a specific intent to place the victim in reasonable apprehension of an imminent battery. That the assailant definitely does *not* intend to carry through on the threat is of no consequence. If, however, the threatening assailant does intend to carry through on the threat and attempts to do so, then both varieties of assault have converged in a single criminal attack. The two forms of assault need not necessarily be in the alternative. They may combine and they frequently do.

In terms of specific intent, the attempted battery variety of assault requires that the assailant intend to punch, whether he intends to signal the punch or not. The threatening variety of assault, on the other hand, requires that the assailant intend to signal the punch, whether he intends to punch or not.

THE VARIOUS FORMS OF BATTERY

Today, the term of art "battery" may connote either of two forms of offensive touching or other application of force:

1. An intended battery; or
2. An unintended battery.

A. An Intended Battery

The definition of the physical component of the common law misdemeanor of battery is hornbook law. It is any unlawful application of force, direct or indirect, to the body of the victim. . . .

The overwhelming majority of the criminal batteries that are committed are intended and this has led to the mistaken belief that all criminal batteries are intended. An intended battery is, by definition, a specific intent crime. It embraces its inchoate antecedent of assault, attempted-battery variety, which involves, of course, precisely the same specific intent to perpetrate the battery. The combination of the attempt and its successful consummation is classic "assault and battery."

Almost all statements made about the relationship between an assault and a battery take for granted that the battery was intended.

B. An Unintended Battery

The field of criminal battery, however, is actually more complicated than many realize because of the less well-known inclusion in that field of unintended batteries. When the physical application of force is inflicted on the body of the victim, the specific intent to harm the victim is not the only *mens rea* that may give rise to the crime of battery. There are two separate forms of unintended battery. . . .

What we have in the case of the unintended batteries are two nonfatal, junior-varsity analogues to two similarly blameworthy states of mind in cases of unintended murders and involuntary manslaughters. When unintended harm results from the doing of an act *malum in se,* the resulting crime may be, if death results, unintended murder under the common law felony-murder doctrine or involuntary manslaughter under the analogous common law misdemeanor-manslaughter doctrine. If death does not result, there is an unintended battery.

The other set of unintended crimes arises out of criminal negligence. The unintended harm, if death results, may be unintended murder if the indifference to the consequences is sufficiently wanton and reckless to constitute depraved-heart murder. If the state of mind is less than depraved but still a case of gross criminal negligence, it is involuntary manslaughter. At the nonfatal level, it is unintended battery.

An intended battery is, by definition, a specific-intent crime. An unintended battery, on the other hand, requires only a general intent to do 1) the criminally negligent act or 2) the unlawful act, with no thought being necessary as to the consequences of such act.

* * *

These then are the various forms of common law assault and the various forms of common law battery with which the case law must contend. One may as well attempt to trisect an angle or to carry out Pi to the last decimal place as to provide a single definition for these plural phenomena. Attempts to do so have produced numerous misstatements and half-truths. Those misstatements and half-truths should be laid to rest.

HALF-TRUTH NO. 1: "ASSAULT IS AN INCHOATE CRIME"

The half-truth "assault is an inchoate crime" is frequently heard. . . .

When, as previously discussed, the word "assault" is used as a synonym for "battery" or as a synonym for the combination "assault and battery," it obviously is not an inchoate crime. It is or it includes a fully consummated battery.

. . . As an attempted battery, it is, of course, inchoate. All attempts are inchoate. It is, by definition, an inchoate battery. In its other manifestation, that of placing the victim in reasonable apprehension of an imminent battery, it is, however, in no sense inchoate. It is a fully consummated crime in its own right. . . .

HALF-TRUTH NO. 2: "ASSAULT REQUIRES A SPECIFIC INTENT TO COMMIT A BATTERY"

. . . An assault of the attempted-battery variety does indeed involve, by definition, a specific intent to commit the battery. An assault of the threatening variety, on the other hand, does not necessarily include any such intent. It is enough that the assailant intends to place the victim in reasonable apprehension of an imminent battery, even if the assailant possesses the diametric specific intent *not* to commit the threatened battery.

HALF-TRUTH NO. 3: "EVERY BATTERY INCLUDES AN ASSAULT"

. . . An *intended* battery includes, by its very nature, an antecedent attempt, which is a form of assault.

An unintended battery, on the other hand, does not include such an attempt (or assault) lest it lose its very character of being unintended. An unintended battery, moreover, normally will not include an assault of the intended frightening variety. . . .

HALF-TRUTH NO. 4: "THERE CANNOT BE AN ATTEMPTED ASSAULT"

The half-truth that "there cannot be an attempted assault" is deeply entrenched. . . .

Such a misconception obviously results from the misperception of the common law crime of assault as an attempted battery and nothing else. . . .

May there be an attempted assault? The answer is obviously both "no" and "yes." There may not, of course, be an attempted assault of the attempted-battery variety. That type of assault is already inchoate and there may not be an attempted attempt.

Where the assault, on the other hand, is of the intent-to-frighten variety, there is no reason whatsoever why there cannot be an attempt to commit it. One attempts to put a victim in reasonable apprehension of an imminent battery, but, for some reason, the victim (unconscious, blind, deaf) fails to apprehend the danger. The assault that was contemplated was not of an inchoate crime but of a fully consummated crime. It, therefore, like any other crime may be attempted as long as the normal prerequisites of attempt law are satisfied. It would not be an attempted attempt, which is the only thing that gave rise to the old cliche in the first place. . . .

* * *

As we turn to the case at hand, it is against the backdrop that Assault and Battery, Combined, are by no means the simple ABC's of criminal law.

THE BATTERY IN ISSUE:

The present case involves one of those paradoxical situations where the physical battery of the victim not only did not embrace but was actually far less serious than an assault upon that victim during the same time frame that did not involve any ultimate application of force. The battery conviction was under the sixth count. Upon that conviction, the appellant received a sentence of six years. We meticulously distinguish that conviction on the sixth count from the separate conviction on the fifth count, charging assault alone, for which the appellant received a consecutive sentence of ten years.

The sixth count itself literally charged the classic combination of "assault and battery" as it alleged that the appellant "did make an assault upon and did batter Sharon Lynn Herz." That is the garden variety assault and battery combination. The battery was of the ordinary intentional sort, involving a specifically intended and attempted application of physical force to the body of the victim. As such, it comprehended the inchoate attempt (assault) and the immediate consummation of that attempt (battery) in one intertwined totality. That assault, obviously of the attempted-battery variety, was, as a matter of course, subsumed within its complementary and consequential battery for purposes of pleading, verdict and sentencing. It is to be carefully distinguished from the separate charge of assault drawn under the fifth count.

The gravamen of that assault-and-battery conviction under the sixth count was the physical harm literally inflicted upon the body of Sharon Lynn Herz. It embraced no other variety of trauma, for battery never does. To analyze the extent of that battery, therefore, we must set out the full extent of all physical touching involved.

The entire criminal episode took place at Sharon Herz's apartment in Crisfield on May 13, 1990, between approximately 8:30 P.M. and 11:50 P.M. Ms. Herz had known the appellant for almost four years, since the summer of 1986. For a time, the two of them lived together in Baltimore City. Ms. Herz bore a daughter, Brittany, to the appellant. In May of 1988, two years before the crimes involved in this case, Ms. Herz and the appellant separated. Ms. Herz moved in initially with her sister on Maryland Avenue in Baltimore and subsequently moved to her apartment in Crisfield. . . .

On May 13, Ms. Herz . . . got off from work at approximately 7:30 P.M., picked up Brittany and the two of them returned home. Ms. Herz gave Brittany her bath and put her to bed. She then performed a few miscellaneous chores about the apartment and took a shower. As she walked downstairs from her shower, the time was about 8:30 P.M. As Sharon Herz turned the corner into her living room, she saw the ap-

pellant standing in front of her. In a subsequent statement to the police, the appellant stated that he had pried the door open with a knife. In his testimony, he claimed that he had climbed in through an open window. In either event, Sharon Herz was then required to remain in the apartment, under the appellant's compulsion, for approximately the next three-and-a-half hours.

Three times during that period—once early, once in the middle and once late—the appellant perpetrated a literal battery upon her. Neither the indictment nor the jury instructions nor the arguments of counsel nor the verdicts attempted to make any distinction on a time line between those three discrete applications of physical force. Neither do we. They occurred in the course of a single, albeit protracted, criminal episode and may well be treated as a single battery. The critical distinction is not on the time line but, rather, in the nature of the respective harms inflicted.

The first installment of the battery occurred as soon as Ms. Herz saw the appellant standing in her living room. She immediately screamed. As she went to scream a second time, he capped his hand over her mouth, pushed her against the wall, and ordered her "to stop screaming and to be quiet." Effectively gagging his victim with a hand over her mouth and pushing her against a wall was a quintessential battery. What then followed for the next few hours, to be more fully discussed hereinafter, constituted criminal conduct other than a battery.

The second installment of the battery occurred an hour or two later as Sharon Herz's brother-in-law, Jay Freeman, stood at the front door of the apartment. The appellant initially stood behind the door and, pointing a gun at Ms. Herz, directed her to get rid of her brother-in-law. In the course of the confrontation, however, the appellant moved into the open doorway to make his point more forcefully. As he did so, he pressed the barrel of the gun into the right side of Ms. Herz's body as he simultaneously placed his left arm around the upper part of her body. Jay Freeman then obeyed the appellant's direction to leave, asking the appellant, "Well, just don't hurt her. Calm down, don't hurt her." Putting Ms. Herz in a wrestler's hold with his left arm while pressing a gun barrel in her ribs was also a quintessential battery.

The third and final installment of the battery occurred near the end of the criminal episode, as the police arrived at the apartment and faced down the appellant. The appellant had already ordered Ms. Herz to the top of the stairs, where he and she sat on the top step facing the police in the doorway below. In the course of the standoff, the appellant with his left hand had pressed the barrel of the gun against Ms. Herz's temple and locked his right arm around her neck. That also constituted a classic battery. . . .

THE ASSAULT IN ISSUE:

The assault charged under the fifth count, by contrast, was no mere attempted or inchoate form of battery. That other (attempted-battery) variety of assault was alleged in the distinct sixth count and was properly subsumed in the battery conviction. The fifth count alleged a far more serious offense than that involved in the sixth count. It was the deliberate placing of Sharon Herz in reasonable apprehension of having a bullet fired into her head. . . .

As the sentencing reflected, the placing of Sharon Herz in literal fear of her life was unquestionably the most serious charge for which the appellant was convicted. The relative gravity of various charges is something that has to be determined on an *ad hoc* basis and does not lend itself to resolution in the abstract. Compared to the threat to her life, the breaking and entering by the former live-in boyfriend was secondary. Being confined for almost three-and-a-half hours was also, compared to the threat to life, relatively secondary. Clearly secondary as well was the physical touching actually suffered.

The evidence overwhelmingly demonstrated that the appellant deliberately placed Ms. Herz in fear of her life. Immediately after she confronted him in her living room, he pushed her against the wall and told her to stop screaming. As she started crying, he told her to sit down on the floor. It was then that he lifted up his shirt and revealed, stuck in the front of his pants, a .38 revolver. From that point on, the conversation between them continuously reverted to the question of what he was going to do with the gun and whether he was going to harm her. For most of the time, the appellant took the gun from his pants and held it in his hand. The first time he took the gun out, Ms. Herz asked him what he was going to do with it and "he kept saying he didn't know and he was holding it then.". . .

The appellant himself recognized that the trauma he inflicted on Sharon Herz was not so much physical as psychic. In the course of his statement to the police, he observed:

> "Sharon came out of the shower. Sharon got dressed for bed and also came downstairs where I scared the shit out of her."

At one point during the confinement, the telephone rang. Ms. Herz explained that if she didn't answer it, the caller would know that something was wrong. The appellant then let her answer but kept the gun pointed toward her while she was on the phone. When, shortly thereafter, Ms. Herz's brother-in-law showed up at the door, the appellant stood behind the door with the gun trained on her. A minute or so into that conversation, he moved into the doorway and held her with one arm, while pressing the gun barrel against her with his other hand. The appellant terminated this brief encounter with Jay Freeman with the conditional threat, "If you don't go to the police, I won't hurt her." Freeman assured him that he was only going to work. The appellant repeated, "Just don't go to the police and she won't get hurt."

Ms. Herz's apprehension grew as the appellant locked the door. "He started getting shaky and he was nervous and I was starting to cry." Ms. Herz warned him that this might be his last chance to leave and he replied, "I'm not leaving, they'll get me anyway." The picture created was of a desperate and emotionally-distraught man who thought he had nothing to lose by killing her.

When the police team arrived at the apartment at 11:50 P.M., a deadly facedown occurred, during every split-second of which Sharon Herz's life hung in the balance. When the first knock at the door occurred, the appellant ordered Ms. Herz upstairs. When she initially demurred, he cocked the gun and pointed it at her and reiterated, "Yes, we're going upstairs." At the top of the stairs, the appellant positioned her between himself and the police, using her as a human shield. As the police at the foot of the stairs trained their guns on him, he held his gun at Ms. Herz's temple.

The threatened and imminent battery that Sharon Herz feared, but which fortunately never came to pass, was not the appellant's shoving of her against a wall or his hand across her mouth or his arm about her neck and shoulder. It was the terrifying dread that in the next split-second, a bullet could implode into her skull. . . . The threatened killing that never took place was on a plane far transcending the relatively trivial wrestling that did take place and certainly was not subsumed within it. . . .

Assault under the fifth count will not merge, as a lesser included offense, into battery under the sixth count for either of two reasons. As an abstract proposition, assault of the threatening variety is not "the same offense" as the battery thus threatened, within the contemplation of *Blockburger v. United States,* 284 U.S. 299, 52 S.Ct. 180, 76 L.Ed. 306 (1932). Assault of the attempted-battery variety, of course, is a lesser included offense within its greater inclusive offense of intended battery, for it possesses no legal element of its own. Assault of the threatening variety, on the other hand, possesses a required element—the reasonable apprehension in the mind of the victim—not possessed by battery. Battery, for its part, possesses a required element—the offensive touching—not possessed by assault. Double jeopardy law according to *Blockburger* would never, therefore, mandate a merger of an assault into a battery when the assault is of the threatening variety.

Quite independently, the assault conviction will not merge into the battery conviction under the particular facts of this case because the battery that was threatened under the assault (fifth) count was not the same as the battery that was consummated under the sixth count. The threatened battery never took place and there was nothing, therefore, into which the antecedent threat might properly merge, even if merger were otherwise appropriate.

FALSE IMPRISONMENT

The assault conviction and the battery conviction are separate and distinct and will not be merged. Our attention now must turn to the third entrant in this merger/nonmerger sweepstakes—false imprisonment. The appellant was convicted of false imprisonment under the seventh count and sentenced to a term of six years, to be served consecutively with all other sentences. . . .

False imprisonment is, thus, an unlawful confinement or detention brought about by the instrumentality, *inter alia,* of either force or threat of force. Although there are other possible catalytic agents for the unlawful confinement, such as fraud or a false claim of legal authority, false imprisonment is most frequently the product of either an assault or a battery. Like the compound larceny we know as robbery, it may be accomplished by either of those instrumentalities.

On the issue of required merger, the analogy of false imprisonment to robbery is most helpful. Robbery, of course, is larceny accomplished by (1) force or (2) threat of force. False imprisonment is confinement accomplished by, *inter alia,* (1) force or (2) threat of force. The appellant is, therefore, quite correct that the false imprisonment for which he was convicted under the seventh count is a greater inclusive offense embracing within it either (1) the battery for which he was convicted under the sixth count or (2) the assault for which he was convicted under the fifth count. One of those two was, under the facts of this case, the necessary instrumentality for the false imprisonment. . . .

As we have already exhaustively discussed, using various clues and guidelines, it is clear that the assault and the battery are separate and distinct from each other and do not merge. Therefore, one of the two will merge into the conviction for false imprisonment but the other will not. It is a question of choosing the more likely candidate.

In terms of which of the two will merge, it is a matter of indifference both to double jeopardy law and to sub-constitutional merger law. Both of those legal doctrines are concerned with avoiding multiple punishment. Either possible merger adequately accomplishes that end. Merger is essentially a sentencing problem, not a verdict problem.

Every aspect of this trial—the evidence, the jury arguments, the judge's instructions, the presentence arguments, the judge's explanation of the sentences, the sentences themselves—combine to make it indisputably clear that the major crime for which the appellant was convicted was his deliberate placing of Sharon Herz in fear of losing her life. The jury instructions focused upon and highlighted the assault charge. . . .

The assault received the ten-year sentence, beside which the breaking and entering, the actual battery and the false imprisonment all paled into relative insignificance, as was apparent throughout the trial. The assault under the fifth count was obviously no mere instrumentality in bringing about an unlawful confinement. It was rather the case that the false imprisonment was a mere incident of it.

The battery, on the other hand, was nothing more than an instrumentality of the confinement. As we have discussed, the battery consisted of three discrete instances. Not one of them involved any effort to harm or to punish the victim as such. It was the necessary force employed to keep her from leaving the apartment. . . .

We hold that the conviction for battery should, as a lesser included offense, be merged into the conviction for false imprisonment and that the separate six-year sentence for battery should, therefore, be vacated.

JUDGMENT OF CONVICTION FOR BATTERY UNDER THE SIXTH COUNT MERGED INTO CONVICTION FOR FALSE IMPRISONMENT UNDER THE SEVENTH COUNT; SENTENCE OF SIX YEARS FOR BATTERY VACATED; ALL OTHER JUDGMENTS AFFIRMED; COSTS TO BE DIVIDED EQUALLY BETWEEN THE APPELLANT AND SOMERSET COUNTY.

5. Reckless Endangerment

Reckless endangerment requires no actual physical or emotional harm. There is no specific intent to harm, but rather general intent to commit the act that does, indeed, cause substantial risk of death or serious injury. A defendant who discussed Russian roulette with his brother, handed him a loaded shotgun, and dared him to pull the trigger was guilty of reckless endangerment, even though he did not believe his brother would pull the trigger [*Minor v. State* (Md. App. 1991)]. *Beach v. State* (Ind. App. 1987) affirmed the conviction for attempted battery and criminal recklessness of the defendant who twice drove his car at thirty to forty miles per hour on the sidewalk in a residential area, nearly striking people both times.

Reckless and wanton endangerment can include the transmission of disease. A man who did not believe the report that he was HIV-positive and continued having unprotected sex pleaded guilty to reckless endangerment in New York.[12] Some states have statutes specifically for criminal exposure to HIV.

6. Terroristic Threatening, Menacing

Terroristic threatening is recklessly or intentionally placing a person in fear for their own or another's safety, or causing the evacuation or disruption of a public space or facility. Menacing generally covers immediate threat of harm to individuals rather than groups or public areas. Threatening words alone can suffice, such as the defendant's saying "Do you want to live?" in an effort to keep his victim quiet during a rape [*Allen v. State* (Del. 1982)].

A threat can also be inferred from a physical act or innuendo of language. During a brawl among two officers and a burglary suspect, plus the suspect's aunt, a revolver belonging to one of the officers was pulled from its holster and turned on him by the defendant. As he tried to retreat, the defendant shot him several times. The second officer, still on the ground struggling with the defendant's aunt, turned at the sound of the shots and saw the defendant 3 to 4 feet away aiming the loaded gun at his chest. The defendant repeated, "Let her go." When the officer attempted to get up, the defendant quickly approached, then gradually backed off and ran. Besides the assault on the first officer, the defendant was guilty of terroristic threatening of the second officer, based on his physical acts and the implication of his words [*State v. Tillman* (Neb. App. 1993)].

Generally, a terroristic threatening charge does not require the defendant to mean what he or she says, nor to have the immediate ability to carry out the threat, and it is not necessary to show that the victim was actually afraid. Some statutes allow conditional threats, "you do this or I will harm you," and others include only unconditional threats. Threats against the president of the United States are a federal crime under 18 U.S.C.A. § 871(a), against other federal officers and their families under 18 U.S.C.A. § 115a(1)(B), and any threat to kidnap or injure that is transmitted in interstate or foreign commerce falls under 18 U.S.C.A. § 875(c).

Harassment statutes cover insults, taunts, or challenges made with specific intent and in a manner likely to provoke a violent response in a reasonable person. It has been called "disorderly conduct aimed at a single person rather than the public" [*In Interest of Doe* (Haw. 1994)].

7. Stalking

One who makes a credible threat to the safety of another person or a member of that person's family and willfully, maliciously, and repeatedly follows, places under surveillance, or harasses that person has committed the crime of stalking. Aggravated stalking occurs when the offender causes bodily harm; confines or restrains the victim; or violates a restraining order, protective order, or injunction. It is a federal crime to travel across a state line or within maritime and territorial jurisdiction with the intent to stalk, 18 U.S.C.A. § 2261A, or with intent to violate or in violation of a protective order, 18 U.S.C.A. § 2262.

A defendant who had threatened his brother by saying, "Maybe I'll just blow you and your whole family away," then parked across the street from his brother's home for five minutes and later closely followed his brother home from work at midnight was guilty of stalking [*People v. Bailey* (Ill. 1995)]. An attempted stalking conviction was affirmed in *State v. Rooks* (Ga. 1996). The defendant, under court order not to have contact with the victim or her family, called the victim's office and spoke with her co-worker, threatening both the victim and the co-worker. The defense argued that because there is no crime for attempted assault, there also could be no attempted stalking. The court, however, differentiated the immediate threat of assault from the less immediate threat of stalking, and pointed out that stalking includes actions such as following and contact that can be attempted. A concurring opinion added that "contact" within the meaning of the statute had been accomplished and stalking, not attempted stalking, was the appropriate charge.

"Virtual harassment" and "cyberstalking" through computer communications has increased 1,000 percent since 1996, according to the International Web Police, an agency that provides on-line law enforcement and crime prevention. States are beginning to respond with prosecutions and specific statutes. In 1999 California was the first state to include electronic communications in their stalking and harassment statutes.[13] Now almost a third of the states have cyberstalking laws. A 1998 federal law (18 U.S.C.A.

§ 2425) criminalizes the use of any form of interstate commerce, including telephone and Internet transmissions, to solicit or entice a child into unlawful sexual activity.

8. Hate Crimes

Nearly 60 percent of the 8,049 hate crimes reported to the FBI in 1997 were motivated by racial bias.[14] Those did not include, however, the terrorizing and shooting of a West African immigrant in Denver by a skinhead who hated the stranger's skin color or the torching of a church with an African American congregation after a Ku Klux Klan rally in Alabama. The report also is missing the neo-Nazi in Alabama who cut the throat, smashed the head, and burned the body of his victim because he made a homosexual pass at him weeks before, because Alabama reported no hate crimes. In spite of the prominence of particularly heinous hate crimes "from the dragging death of a black man in Texas to the bludgeoning of a gay student in Wyoming to the one-man riot of white racist Buford O. Furrow Jr.," the reporting of hate crimes is less than consistent, and state hate crime statutes vary in their coverage. "Twenty-one states exclude sexual orientation from their laws. Others add age or gender, while some stick to race, creed and color. Eight have no hate crime laws at all. Oregon protects people from prejudice based on political party, purchasing power, union membership, social standing or marital status. . . ."[15]

Some statutes specify terroristic threatening in the area of ethnic intimidation or hate crimes motivated by the offender's bias against a race, religion, disability, sexual orientation, or ethnicity. California prohibits malicious cross burning on the basis that the victim is subjected to fear and threat of future physical harm, separating the offense from First Amendment protections and bringing it into the criminal realm of "true threat" and "fighting words" [*In re Steven S.* (Cal. App. 1994)]. Other statutes that criminalize conduct that "produces or is capable of producing an effect tending to excite" [*State v. Ramsey* (S.C. 1993)] or "arouses anger, alarm, or resentment in others on the basis of race, color, creed, religion, or gender" [*R.A.V. v. City of St. Paul* (1992)] have been declared unconstitutional as being too broad and encroaching on First Amendment freedoms. Still other statutes that enhance punishment for "conduct that is already illegal, and thus unprotected by the First Amendment, which is seen as especially harmful because it is motivated by group hatred" have been upheld [*State v. Vanatter* (Mo. 1994) following *Wisconsin v. Mitchell* (1993)]. In *Vanatter*, a cross burned in front of a church damaged the front porch of the building, so the offense was based on conduct rather than speech.

In *Apprendi v. New Jersey* (2000), the Supreme court ruled unconstitutional the laws allowing a judge to enhance a sentence based on a preponderance of the evidence that the defendant was motivated by bias to commit the crime for which he or she was convicted. Instead, bias must be considered an element of the crime to be included in the charge and decided by the jury.

Wisconsin's hate crime enhancement law was reviewed by the Supreme Court in *Wisconsin v. Mitchell* (1993).

WISCONSIN v. MITCHELL
Supreme Court of the United States, 1993.
508 U.S. 476, 113 S. Ct. 2194.
[Citations omitted]

CHIEF JUSTICE REHNQUIST delivered the opinion of the Court.

Respondent Todd Mitchell's sentence for aggravated battery was enhanced because he intentionally selected his victim on account of the victim's race. The question presented in this case is whether this penalty enhancement is prohibited by the First and Fourteenth Amendments. We hold that it is not.

On the evening of October 7, 1989, a group of young black men and boys, including Mitchell, gathered at an apartment complex in Kenosha, Wisconsin. Several members of the group discussed a scene from the motion picture "Mississippi Burning," in which a white man beat a young black boy who was praying. The group moved outside and Mitchell asked them: "Do you all feel hyped up to move on some white people?" Shortly thereafter, a young white boy approached the group on the opposite side of the street where they were standing. As the boy walked by, Mitchell said: " 'You all want to fuck somebody up? There goes a white boy; go get him.' " Mitchell counted to three and pointed in the boy's direction. The group ran towards the boy, beat him severely, and stole his tennis shoes. The boy was rendered unconscious and remained in a coma for four days.

After a jury trial in the Circuit Court for Kenosha County, Mitchell was convicted of aggravated battery. Wis. Stat. §§ 939.05 and 940.19(1m) (1989–1990). That offense ordinarily carries a maximum sentence of two years' imprisonment. §§ 940.19(1m) and 939.50(3)(e). But because the jury found that Mitchell had intentionally selected his victim because of the boy's race, the maximum sentence for Mitchell's offense was increased to seven years under § 939.645. That provision enhances the maximum penalty for an offense whenever the defendant "[i]ntentionally selects the person against whom the crime . . . is committed . . . because of the race, religion, color, disability, sexual orientation, national origin or ancestry of that person. . . ." § 939.645(1)(b). The Circuit Court sentenced Mitchell to four years' imprisonment for the aggravated battery.

Mitchell . . . appealed his conviction and sentence, challenging the constitutionality of Wisconsin's penalty-enhancement provision on First Amendment grounds. . . . [T]he Wisconsin Supreme Court reversed [on grounds] that the statute "violates the First Amendment directly by punishing what the legislature has deemed to be offensive thought." . . .

The Supreme Court also held that the penalty-enhancement statute was unconstitutionally overbroad. . . . Finally, the court distinguished antidiscrimination laws, which have long been held constitutional, on the ground that the Wisconsin statute punishes the "subjective mental process" of selecting a victim because of his protected status, whereas antidiscrimination laws prohibit "objective acts of discrimination."

We granted certiorari because of the importance of the question presented and the existence of a conflict of authority among state high courts on the constitutionality of statutes similar to Wisconsin's penalty-enhancement provision. We reverse.

. . .

The State argues that the statute does not punish bigoted thought, as the Supreme Court of Wisconsin said, but instead punishes only conduct. While this argument is literally correct, it does not dispose of Mitchell's First Amendment challenge. To be sure, our cases reject the "view that an apparently limitless variety of conduct can be labeled 'speech' whenever the person engaging in the conduct intends thereby to express an idea." Thus, a physical assault is not by any stretch of the imagination expressive conduct protected by the First Amendment.

But the fact remains that under the Wisconsin statute the same criminal conduct may be more heavily punished if the victim is selected because of his race or other protected status than if no such motive obtained. Thus, although the statute punishes criminal conduct, it enhances the maximum penalty for conduct motivated by a discriminatory point of view more severely than the same conduct engaged in for some other reason or for no reason at all. Because the only reason for the enhancement is the defendant's discriminatory motive for selecting his victim, Mitchell argues (and the Wisconsin Supreme Court held) that the statute violates the First Amendment by punishing offenders' bigoted beliefs.

Traditionally, sentencing judges have considered a wide variety of factors in addition to evidence bearing on guilt in determining what sentence to impose on a convicted defendant. The defendant's motive for committing the offense is one important factor. . . .

But it is equally true that a defendant's abstract beliefs, however obnoxious to most people, may not be taken into consideration by a sentencing judge. *Dawson v. Delaware,* 503 U.S. _____ (1992). In *Dawson,* the State introduced evidence at a capital-sentencing hearing that the defendant was a member of a white supremacist prison gang. Because "the evidence proved nothing more than [the defendant's] abstract beliefs," we held that its admission violated the defendant's First Amendment rights. In so holding, however, we emphasized that "the Constitution does not erect a *per se* barrier to the admission of evidence concerning one's beliefs and associations at sentencing simply because those beliefs and associations are protected by the First Amendment." Thus, in *Barclay v. Florida,* 463 U.S. 939 (1983) (plurality opinion), we allowed the sentencing judge to take into account the defendant's racial animus towards his victim. The evidence in that case showed that the defendant's membership in the Black Liberation Army and desire to provoke a "race war" were related to the murder of a white man for which he was convicted. Because "the elements of racial hatred in [the] murder" were relevant to several aggravating factors, we held that the trial judge permissibly took this evidence into account in sentencing the defendant to death.

Mitchell suggests that *Dawson* and *Barclay* are inapposite because they did not involve application of a penalty-enhancement provision. But in *Barclay* we held that it was permissible for the sentencing court to consider the defendant's racial animus in determining whether he should be sentenced to death, surely the most severe "enhancement" of all. And the fact that the Wisconsin Legislature has decided, as a general matter, that bias-motivated offenses warrant greater maximum penalties across the board does not alter the result here. For the primary responsibility for fixing criminal penalties lies with the legislature.

. . .

[R. A. V. v. St. Paul, 505 U.S. _____ ,] involved a First Amendment challenge to a municipal ordinance prohibiting the use of " 'fighting words' that insult, or provoke violence, 'on the basis of race, color, creed, religion or gender.' ". . . (quoting St. Paul Bias-Motivated Crime Ordinance, St. Paul, Minn., Legis. Code § 292.02 (1990)). Because the ordinance only proscribed a class of "fighting words" deemed particularly offensive by the city—*i.e.,* those "that contain . . . messages of 'bias-motivated' hatred," . . . we held that it violated the rule against content-based discrimination. . . . But whereas the ordinance struck down in *R. A. V.* was explicitly directed at expression (*i.e.,* "speech" or "messages,") . . . the statute in this case is aimed at conduct unprotected by the First Amendment.

Moreover, the Wisconsin statute singles out for enhancement bias-inspired conduct because this conduct is thought to inflict greater individual and societal harm. For example, according to the State and its *amici,* bias-motivated crimes are more likely to provoke retaliatory crimes, inflict distinct emotional harms on their victims, and incite community unrest. . . . The State's desire to redress these perceived harms provides an adequate explanation for its penalty-enhancement provision over and above mere disagreement with offenders' beliefs or biases. As Blackstone said long ago, "it is but reasonable that among crimes of different natures those should be most severely punished, which are the most destructive of the public safety and happiness." 4 W. Blackstone, Commentaries.

Finally, there remains to be considered Mitchell's argument that the Wisconsin statute is unconstitutionally overbroad because of its "chilling effect" on free speech. Mitchell argues (and the Wisconsin Supreme Court agreed) that the statute is "overbroad" because evidence of the defendant's prior speech or associations may be used to prove that the defendant intentionally selected his victim on account of the victim's protected status. Consequently, the argument goes, the statute impermissibly chills free expression with respect to such matters by those concerned about the possibility of enhanced sentences if they should in the future commit a criminal offense covered by the statute. We find no merit in this contention.

The sort of chill envisioned here is far more attenuated and unlikely than that contemplated in traditional "overbreadth" cases. We must conjure up a vision of a Wisconsin citizen suppressing his unpopular bigoted opinions for fear that if he later commits an offense covered by the statute, these opinions will be offered at trial to establish that he selected his victim on account of the victim's protected status, thus qualifying him for penalty-enhancement. . . . This is simply too speculative a hypothesis to support Mitchell's overbreadth claim.

The First Amendment, moreover, does not prohibit the evidentiary use of speech to establish the elements of a crime or to prove motive or intent. Evidence of a defendant's previous declarations or statements is commonly admitted in criminal trials subject to evidentiary rules dealing with relevancy, reliability, and the like. . . .

For the foregoing reasons, we hold that Mitchell's First Amendment rights were not violated by the application of the Wisconsin penalty-enhancement provision in sentencing him. The judgment of the Supreme Court of Wisconsin is therefore reversed, and the case is remanded for further proceedings not inconsistent with this opinion.

It is so ordered.

Wisconsin's hate crime enhancement law was unanimously approved by the Supreme Court in *Wisconsin v. Mitchell* (1993), with all other states filing a joint brief in support of the law. This law requires the jury, after conviction of the defendant, to decide whether the crime was motivated by bias and, therefore, requires an enhanced sentence. Since the statute is aimed at conduct and not expression alone, it was held to comply with the First Amendment. Do you think it also complies with the *Apprendi* decision?

D.   CIVIL RIGHTS VIOLATIONS

Chapter 13 of the federal criminal code criminalizes a range of conduct that hinders the free exercise of rights and privileges of people living under the Constitution of the United States. Federal statute 18 U.S.C.A. § 241 criminalizes conspiracy by two or more persons to threaten or intimidate anyone in the exercise of constitutional rights or privileges. Section 242 criminalizes deprivation under color of law of those rights, privileges, or immunities, or subjection to different punishments because of race, color, or alien status. "Under color of law" refers to the conduct of government officials in carrying out their duties under the authority of the government.

Section 242 provided grounds for the famous federal trial and conviction of police officers for beating Rodney King while placing him under arrest for a traffic violation, depriving him of his right to be free from harm while in custody [*U.S. v. Koon* (9th Cir. 1994)]. The same law was used to convict a state judge for sexually assaulting female employees and litigants [*U.S. v. Lanier* (1997)]. *U.S. v. Epley* (6th Cir. 1995) affirmed the conviction under §§ 241 and 242 of police officers who had planted cocaine and an illegal gun in the vehicle of a man they wanted to silence, then arrested him and gave false testimony against him.

Chapter 13 of the federal code also covers exclusion of jurors on the basis of race or color, § 243; discrimination against a person wearing the uniform of the armed forces, § 244; protection of a wide range of activities from election rights to public school enrollment to interstate businesses during a riot, § 245; deprivation of relief benefits, § 246; damage to religious property or obstruction of the free exercise of religious beliefs, § 247; and obstruction of access to reproductive health services, § 248. Penalties are primarily fines, but also include up to life imprisonment and sentence of death for serious violations and inclusion of kidnapping, sexual abuse, or killing in the crime.

E. SEXUAL BATTERY

1. Reform

a. Introduction Rape, a type of aggravated battery, is so universally abhorrent that it has held its place as a separate and more serious crime. Unlawful sexual intercourse against the victim's will by force or threat of immediate force could be punished by death until *Coker v. Georgia* (1977) declared the death penalty for rape unconstitutional. The intimate nature that makes this offense so serious makes it difficult to discuss and evaluate. Rigid perceptions of gender roles also have hindered a willingness to be more open in discussing sex. Recently, however, reforms in social attitudes have reached the law, expanding protection against a greater variety of offenses and placing greater emphasis on harm to the victim. New statutes increasingly reflect the following changes.

b. Victim Testimony Sexual offense trials often pit the word of the victim against the word of the defendant. Traditionally, the victim's credibility had to be bolstered by evidence of her previous chastity and corroboration of witnesses. Her believability dwindled further with any delay in reporting the crime.

A defendant charged with rape claimed the victim's testimony was false based on differences between her testimony at the preliminary hearing and at trial. The differences concerned only her whereabouts before the incident and whether she viewed a photographic lineup alone or with her mother. She explained the differences as a result of being upset and confused by the questioning during the hearing. The jury found her testimony believable, however, and convicted the defendant [*State v. Embry* (Tenn. Crim. App. 1995)].

Now **rape shield laws** prevent evidence of the victim's prior sexual activity from being introduced in court, unless it is relevant to consent. Children can testify in some courts via videotape or with the aid of anatomically correct dolls to make the experience less traumatic. Sexual offenses against children have been reported and successfully prosecuted years later, after the victims became adults, although more timely reporting by adult victims may be required. Corroboration may be circumstantial.

These changes are not without problems. A defendant's Sixth Amendment right to confront the accuser may be diminished by videotaped testimony. Expert opinion that "rape trauma syndrome" may cause the victim to repress the experience, making difficult the identification of the offender and reporting of the crime, is not admissible in some courts as a still questionable and prejudicial theory. Such changes

rape shield law:
statute that prevents evidence of the victim's prior sexual activity from being introduced in court, unless it is relevant to consent.

may interfere with the defendant's right to a speedy trial, as well as with the timely gathering of evidence. FBI reports continue to show that rape has the highest rate of acquittal or dismissal among violent crimes.[16]

c. Definitions The old requirement of utmost resistance from the victim has given way to "reasonable resistance," taking into account the risk of death or serious injury against overwhelming force or threat as well as psychological factors [*State v. Studham* (Utah 1997)]. The expectation that all sexual offense victims are female and all offenders male is beginning to change because of the reality of homosexual rape and the involvement of women as accomplices in rape and aggressors in sexual contact cases. New gender neutral statutes attempt to cover all participants, and definitions have been expanded to include oral, anal, and vaginal penetration, as well as other forms of sexual contact.

marital exception: disallows prosecution of husbands for rape of their wives.

d. Marital Exception The **marital exception,** disallowing prosecution of husbands for rape of their wives, is based on the common law doctrine that a woman is her husband's property and the observation by seventeenth-century English jurist Sir Matthew Hale that by "mutual matrimonial consent and contract the wife hath given up herself in this kind to her husband, which she cannot retract."[17] Modern statutes and court decisions have chipped away at the marital exception. *People v. Liberta* (N.Y. 1984) found that the New York exception violated constitutional equal protection. The opinion rebuffed claims that the exception facilitates reconciliation and asserted that "if the marriage has already reached a point where intercourse is accomplished by violent assault it is doubtful that there is anything left to reconcile." A defendant convicted of aggravated criminal sexual assault against his wife argued that he was denied equal protection and due process. *People v. M.D.* (Ill. App. 1992) not only upheld his conviction, but also declared the marital exception to be unconstitutional and based on "archaic doctrines that have no place in modern society." The marital exception in some states includes only those partners who are living together, not those who are separated, and cases where weapons are used or serious injury results. Others consider spousal sexual assaults as crimes on a less serious level than the same conduct by nonspouses.

2. Mens Rea: Consent and Force

a. Statutory Rape State of mind is at issue in sexual assault cases primarily in determining whether the victim consented to the act and whether the defendant reasonably believed the victim consented. When the victim is under the "age of consent," which varies from state to state, or is mentally or physically incapacitated, a lack of consent to sexual conduct with older partners is presumed. **Statutory rape,** unforced sexual intercourse with an underage child, is a strict liability offense in some states. Other states allow a reasonable mistake about the victim's age as a defense. In *State v. Ealey,* (Tenn. Crim. App. 1997), the defendant, charged with rape of a child under thirteen years of age, said he believed the victim's statement that she was sixteen years old when she was actually eleven. Because of his belief, a jury instruction on statutory rape of a child between thirteen and eighteen was allowed, and he was convicted on that charge.

statutory rape: unforced sexual intercourse with an underage child.

Here again, social realities are seeping into the courtroom. In *State v. Bartlett* (Ariz. 1992), the court recognized that today's teenagers are frequently sexually active, and overturned as excessive the forty-year sentence of a twenty-three-year-old man for the statutory rape of consenting girls just under that state's age limit of fifteen years. Some states specify an age gap between offender and victim for statutory rape.

b. Consent and Force When victims are adults, however, rape cases frequently turn on the issue of consent; the state of mind of the victim seems to have been of greater interest to courts in the past than the state of mind of the defendant. The Model Penal Code § 213 and some modern state laws are now shifting the focus, not even mentioning consent but emphasizing the level of threat or force exerted by the defendant. Consent remains as an implied defense.

Helplessness of the victim as a result of intoxication, use of "date rape" drugs such as Rohypnol (roofies) and Gamma-hydrobutiric acid (GHB), or other causes is more frequently being allowed as an alternative to the element of physical force by the offender.

The overwhelming majority of rapes are committed by acquaintances of the victims, but juries are more reluctant to convict these offenders than to convict strangers. Therefore, the Model Penal Code and some states reduce the classification from first to second degree felony if the victim was a "voluntary social companion" of the accused.

 ANALYSIS PROBLEM

4–2. Do you think that decreasing the seriousness of "date rape" is properly offset by the probability of a higher rate of conviction? Do you think a spousal relationship is relevant in sexual assault cases?

3. Actus Reus in Sexual Battery

Rather than classifying sexual offenses according to mens rea as in homicide, harm and threat of harm are the criteria for grading the seriousness of sexual crimes. The victim's age and the relationship of the offender to the victim contribute to the evaluation of harm. Simple criminal penetration or rape is more serious than simple criminal sexual contact, which is sexual touching that the actor knows is offensive to the victim. Both are usually aggravated to more serious penalties if the victim sustains serious bodily injury, is a minor with an older assailant, is incompetent or helpless, is attacked by a stranger or one who has accomplices, is threatened with deadly weapons, or is assaulted in connection with another crime. Also, an aggravated charge is likely if the offender is a parent or otherwise in a position of trust or authority. Incest, sexual conduct between specified family members regardless of age, is an aggravating factor in some statutes and a separate crime in others.

The following cases illustrate some of the problems in sexual crimes. *State v. Ohrtman* (Minn. App. 1991) held that a hug by a pastor during a counseling session was not "sexual conduct." Evidence of physical force was not necessary to establish constructive "force" in the rape case of a defendant who falsely identified himself as a police officer to a female motorist and threatened to lock her up before having sexual intercourse with her [*Commonwealth v. Caracciola* (Mass. 1991)]. Transmitting HIV to a minor during anal intercourse [*Zule v. State* (Tex. App. 1990)] and intercourse by an HIV-positive man using a condom regardless of the consent of his female partner [*U.S. v. Joseph* (NMCMR 1991)] were both sufficient for aggravated sexual assault convictions.

4. Megan's Law and Sexually Violent Predator Acts

The 1994 rape and murder of seven-year-old Megan Kanka led to a new law in her home state of New Jersey. Outrage that the killer's previous record of sex offenses against children was unknown in the community shaped the "Megan's Law" requirement that convicted sex offenders who are released from prison must register their addresses and other identifying information with local law enforcement agencies. The agencies then release that information to the public in the hope that greater vigilance from informed neighbors will keep the offender from attacking again. Failure to register each new address within ten days of moving is a crime. After ten years without further offenses, the registrant may request release from the registration requirement.

In 1996 a federal version of Megan's Law was passed, 42 U.S.C.A. § 14071, along with a companion law that provides for a federal reporting system accessible to the states, 42 U.S.C.A. § 14072. Nearly all states have passed their own versions of Megan's Law. Some of those laws provide for prerelease psychological testing and a hearing to separate those who have been evaluated as high-risk offenders from those who pose a lower risk. Local law enforcement agencies, victims, and victims' advocacy groups are notified of the release of low-risk offenders. A high-risk offender's name, photograph, address, and criminal history are also released to news media. Massachusetts's law did not provide for hearings, but the Massachusetts Supreme Judicial Court ruled in 1999 that offenders were not required to register until a hearing was held.[18]

Megan's laws have survived constitutional challenges in several states because they are intended for community awareness, not punishment. Critics argue that negative public reaction to the registrants is indeed punitive, is based on status rather than conduct, and that the hearings violate the constitutional protection against being tried twice for the same crime (double jeopardy). Others believe the laws are ineffective and exaggerate public anxiety.[19]

Thirteen states have passed laws requiring sex offenders who have served their prison sentences to undergo civil trial to determine their further threat to society. If they are found to be violent sexual predators, offenders may be held at psychiatric hospitals involuntarily and indefinitely. The Supreme Court narrowly approved Kansas' Sexually Violent Predator Act in *Kansas v. Hendricks* (1997), allowing commitment based on mental abnormality rather than mental illness and rejecting the claim of double jeopardy, because the commitment trials are civil rather than criminal.

In spite of mental health experts' opinion that they cannot be "cured," more than 500 offenders had been committed to psychiatric hospitals by the end of 1998. The Criminal Justice Council of Kentucky called such laws dishonest. "At a criminal trial, the state says a sex offender must be punished for not controlling his behavior. Then, at a commitment hearing, the state would have to reverse itself and say the offender needs medical help because he cannot control his behavior."[20]

 ANALYSIS PROBLEM

4–3. Do you think the federal approach to Megan's Law is a good idea? Do you think psychiatrists and courts can predict criminal behavior? In your opinion, do the benefits of Megan's Law and sexually violent predator laws outweigh the problems? What if their provisions were extended to cover all violent criminals?

5. Sexual Battery and Rape Statutes

Compare the following set of sexual offenses statutes from Tennessee, or statutes from another state, with your state's statutes. Note gender neutral language; differences in elements and how elements are organized among the crimes; the use of nonconsent; the use of incapacitation, force, and age; and limitations on marital exception (spousal exclusion). Following the statutes are two cases showing the courts' interpretations of the statutes.

Other sexual offenses are covered under prostitution, obscenity, pornography, exploitation, and sodomy statutes. These are discussed in Chapter 5.

TENNESSEE CRIMINAL CODE: SEXUAL OFFENSES

39-13-501. Definitions

As used in §§ 39-13-501–39-13-511, except as specifically provided in § 39-13-505, unless the context otherwise requires:

(1) "Coercion" means threat of kidnapping, extortion, force or violence to be performed immediately or in the future or the use of parental, custodial, or official authority over a child less than fifteen years of age;

(2) "Intimate parts" includes the primary genital area, groin, inner thigh, buttock or breast of a human being;

(3) "Mentally defective" means that a person suffers from a mental disease or defect which renders that person temporarily or permanently incapable of appraising the nature of such person's conduct;

(4) "Mentally incapacitated" means that a person is rendered temporarily incapable of appraising or controlling the person's conduct due to the influence of a narcotic, anesthetic or other substance administered to that person without the person's consent, or due to any other act committed upon that person without the person's consent;

(5) "Physically helpless" means that a person is unconscious, asleep or for any other reason physically or verbally unable to communicate unwillingness to do an act;

(6) "Sexual contact" includes the intentional touching of the victim's, the defendant's, or any other person's intimate parts, or the intentional touching of the clothing covering the immediate area of the victim's, the defendant's, or any other person's intimate parts, if that intentional touching can be reasonably construed as being for the purpose of sexual arousal or gratification;

(7) "Sexual penetration" means sexual intercourse, cunnilingus, fellatio, anal intercourse, or any other intrusion, however slight, of any part of a person's body or of any object into the genital or anal openings of the victim's, the defendant's, or any other person's body, but emission of semen is not required; and

(8) "Victim" means the person alleged to have been subjected to criminal sexual conduct.

39-13-502. Aggravated rape

(a) Aggravated rape is unlawful sexual penetration of a victim by the defendant or the defendant by a victim accompanied by any of the following circumstances:

(1) Force or coercion is used to accomplish the act and the defendant is armed with a weapon or any article used or fashioned in a manner to lead the victim reasonably to believe it to be a weapon;

(2) The defendant causes bodily injury to the victim;

(3) The defendant is aided or abetted by one or more other persons; and

(A) Force or coercion is used to accomplish the act; or

(B) The defendant knows or has reason to know that the victim is mentally defective, mentally incapacitated or physically helpless.

(b) Aggravated rape is a Class A felony.

39-13-503. Rape

(a) Rape is unlawful sexual penetration of a victim by the defendant or of the defendant by a victim accompanied by any of the following circumstances:

(1) Force or coercion is used to accomplish the act;

(2) The sexual penetration is accomplished without the consent of the victim and the defendant knows or has reason to know at the time of the penetration that the victim did not consent;

(3) The defendant knows or has reason to know that the victim is mentally defective, mentally incapacitated or physically helpless; or

(4) The sexual penetration is accomplished by fraud.

(b) Rape is a Class B felony.

(c) When imposing sentence under the provisions of title 40, chapter 35, for a conviction under this section, the court shall consider as an enhancement factor that the defendant caused the victim to be mentally incapacitated or physically helpless by use of a controlled substance.

39-13-504. Aggravated sexual battery

(a) Aggravated sexual battery is unlawful sexual contact with a victim by the defendant or the defendant by a victim accompanied by any of the following circumstances:

(1) Force or coercion is used to accomplish the act and the defendant is armed with a weapon or any article used or fashioned in a manner to lead the victim reasonably to believe it to be a weapon;

(2) The defendant causes bodily injury to the victim;

(3) The defendant is aided or abetted by one or more other persons; and

  (A) Force or coercion is used to accomplish the act; or

  (B) The defendant knows or has reason to know that the victim is mentally defective, mentally incapacitated or physically helpless; or

(4) The victim is less than thirteen years of age.

(b) Aggravated sexual battery is a Class B felony.

39-13-505. Sexual battery

(a) Sexual battery is unlawful sexual contact with a victim by the defendant or the defendant by a victim accompanied by any of the following circumstances:

(1) Force or coercion is used to accomplish the act;

(2) The sexual contact is accomplished without the consent of the victim and the defendant knows or has reason to know at the time of the contact that the victim did not consent;

(3) The defendant knows or has reason to know that the victim is mentally defective, mentally incapacitated or physically helpless; or

(4) The sexual contact is accomplished by fraud.

(b) As used in this section, "coercion" means the threat of kidnapping, extortion, force or violence to be performed immediately or in the future.

(c) Sexual battery is a Class E felony.

(d) When imposing sentence under the provisions of title 40, chapter 35, for a conviction under this section, the court shall consider as an enhancement factor that the defendant caused the victim to be mentally incapacitated or physically helpless by use of a controlled substance.

39-13-506. Statutory rape

(a) Statutory rape is sexual penetration of a victim by the defendant or of the defendant by the victim when the victim is at least thirteen but less than eighteen years of age and the defendant is at least four years older than the victim.

(b) If the person accused of statutory rape is under eighteen years of age, such a defendant shall be tried as a juvenile and shall not be transferred for trial as an adult.

(c) Statutory rape is a Class E felony.

39-13-507. Limited spousal exclusion

(a) A person does not commit an offense under this part if the victim is the legal spouse of the perpetrator except as provided in subsections (b) and (c).

(b) (1) "Spousal rape" means the unlawful sexual penetration of one spouse by the other where:

    (A) The defendant is armed with a weapon or any article used or fashioned in a manner to lead the victim to reasonably believe it to be a weapon;

    (B) The defendant causes serious bodily injury to the victim; or

    (C) The spouses are living apart and one of them has filed for separate maintenance or divorce.

(2) (A) "Spousal rape," as defined in subdivision (b)(1)(A) or (B), is a Class C felony.

    (B) "Spousal rape," as defined in subdivision (b)(1)(C) shall be punished pursuant to § 39-13-502 or § 39-13-503.

(c) (1) "Aggravated spousal rape" is the unlawful sexual penetration of one spouse by the other where the defendant:

    (A) Knowingly engaged in conduct that was especially cruel, vile and inhumane to the victim during commission of the offense; and either;

    (B) Causes serious bodily injury to the victim; or

    (C) Is armed with a weapon or any article used or fashioned in a manner to lead the victim to reasonably believe it to be a weapon.

(2) Aggravated spousal rape is a Class B felony.

(d) (1) "Spousal sexual battery" means the unlawful sexual contact by one spouse of another where:

    (A) The defendant is armed with a weapon or any article used or fashioned in a manner to lead the victim to reasonably believe it to be a weapon;

    (B) The defendant causes serious bodily injury to the victim; or

    (C) The spouses are living apart and one of them has filed for separate maintenance or divorce.

(2) (A) "Spousal sexual battery," as defined in subdivision (c)(1)(A) or (B), is a Class D felony.

    (B) "Spousal sexual battery," as defined in subdivision (c)(1)(C) shall be punished pursuant to § 39-13-504 or § 39-13-505. [Acts 1989, ch. 591, § 1; 1990, ch. 980, § 5; 1997, ch. 480, § 1; 1998, ch. 1068, § 1.]

39-13-522. Rape of a child

(a) Rape of a child is the unlawful sexual penetration of a victim by the defendant or the defendant by a victim, if such victim is less than thirteen (13) years of age.

(b) Rape of a child is a Class A felony.

(c) When imposing sentence under the provisions of title 40, chapter 35, for a conviction under this section, the court shall consider as an enhancement factor that the defendant caused the victim to be mentally incapacitated or physically helpless by use of a controlled substance.

39-13-523. Multiple rapists—Child rapists—Definitions—Sentencing—Release and parole

(a) As used in this section, unless the context otherwise requires:

(1) "Child rapist" means a person convicted one (1) or more times of rape of a child as defined by § 39-13-522; and

(2) "Multiple rapist" means a person convicted two (2) or more times of violating the provisions of § 39-13-502 or § 39-13-503, or a person convicted at least one (1) time of violating § 39-13-502, and at least one (1) time of § 39-13-503.

(b) Notwithstanding any other provision of law to the contrary, a multiple rapist or a child rapist, as defined in subsection (a), shall be required to serve the entire sentence imposed by the court undiminished by any sentence reduction credits such person may be eligible for or earn. A multiple rapist or a child rapist shall be permitted to earn any credits for which such person is eligible and such credits may be used for the purpose of increased privileges, reduced security classification, or for any purpose other than the reduction of the sentence imposed by the court.

(c) The provisions of title 40, chapter 35, part 5, relative to release eligibility status and parole shall not apply to or authorize the release of a multiple rapist or child rapist, as defined in subsection (a), prior to service of the entire sentence imposed by the court.

(d) Nothing in the provisions of title 41, chapter 1, part 5, shall give either the governor or the board of probation and parole the authority to release or cause the release of a *multiple rapist or child rapist, as defined in subsection (a), prior to service of the entire sentence imposed by the court.*

(e) *The provisions of this section requiring multiple rapists to serve the entire sentence imposed by the court shall only apply if at least one (1) of the required offenses occurs on or after July 1, 1992.*

39-13-524. Sentence of community supervision for life

(a) *In addition to the punishment authorized by the specific statute prohibiting the conduct, any person who, on or after July 1, 1996, commits a violation of § 39-13-502, § 39-13-503, § 39-13-504, § 39-13-522, or attempts to commit a violation of any such section, shall receive a sentence of community supervision for life.*

(b) *The judgment of conviction for all persons to whom the provisions of subsection (a) apply shall include that such person is sentenced to community supervision for life.*

(c) *The sentence of community supervision for life shall commence immediately upon the expiration of the term of imprisonment imposed upon such person by the court or upon such person's release from regular parole supervision, whichever first occurs.*

(d)(1) *A person on community supervision shall be under the jurisdiction, supervision and control of the board of probation and parole in the same manner as a person under parole supervision. The board is authorized on an individual basis to establish such conditions of community supervision as are necessary to protect the public from such person committing a new sex offense as well as promoting the rehabilitation of the person.*

(2) *The board is authorized to impose and enforce a supervision and rehabilitation fee upon a person on community supervision similar to the fee imposed by § 40-28-201. To the extent possible, the board shall set such fee in an amount that will substantially defray the cost of the community supervision program. The board shall also establish a fee waiver procedure for hardship cases and indigency.*

39-13-525. Release from community supervision

(a) *After a person sentenced to community supervision pursuant to § 39-13-524 has been on such supervision for a period of fifteen (15) years, such person may petition the sentencing court for release from community supervision.*

(b) *Upon receiving such a petition, the court shall, at least thirty (30) days prior to a hearing on the petition, cause the office of the district attorney general responsible for prosecuting the person to be notified of the person's petition for release from supervision. Upon being notified, the district attorney general shall conduct a criminal history check on such person to determine if the person has been convicted of a criminal offense during the period of community supervision. The district attorney general shall report the results of such criminal history check to the court, together with any other comments the district attorney general may have concerning the person's petition for release. The district attorney general may also appear and testify at the hearing in lieu of or in addition to submitting written comments.*

(c) *Between the date the petition is filed with the court and the date established by the court for a hearing on the petition, if the person is entitled to a hearing, the person shall be examined and evaluated by a psychiatrist or licensed psychologist with health service designation approved by the board. The cost of such examination and evaluation shall be the sole responsibility of the person petitioning for release from supervision. No hearing on such petition may be conducted until such person has been examined and evaluated in accordance with this subsection.*

(d)(1) *If the report of the district attorney general indicates that the petitioner has been convicted of a criminal offense while under community supervision, the court shall deny the petition without conducting a hearing.*

(2) *If the report of the district attorney general indicates that the petitioner has not been convicted of a criminal offense while under community supervision, the court shall conduct a hearing on the petition. At the hearing, the court shall call such witnesses, including the examining psychiatrist or licensed psychologist with health service designation or the prosecuting district attorney general, as the court deems necessary to reach an informed and just decision on whether the petitioner should be released from community supervision. The petitioner may offer such witnesses and other proof at the hearing as is relevant to the petition.*

(3) *If a petition for release from supervision is denied by the court, such person may not file another such petition for a period of three (3) years.*

39-13-526. Violations of community supervision

(a) *It is an offense for a person to knowingly violate a condition of community supervision imposed upon such person pursuant to § 39-13-524.*

(b) (1) *If the conduct that is a violation of a condition of community supervision does not constitute a criminal offense, such violation is a Class A misdemeanor.*

(2) *If the conduct that is a violation of a condition of community supervision also constitutes a criminal offense that is classified as a misdemeanor, such violation is a Class A misdemeanor.*

(3) *If the conduct that is a violation of a condition of community supervision also constitutes a criminal offense that is classified as a felony, such violation is a Class E felony.*

(4) *Each violation of a condition of community supervision constitutes a separate offense.*

(c) *If the violation of community supervision involves the commission of a new offense, the sentence for a violation of this section shall be served consecutive to any sentence received for commission of the new offense.*

39-13-527. Sexual battery by an authority figure

(a) *Sexual battery by an authority figure is unlawful sexual contact with a victim by the defendant or the defendant by a victim accompanied by the following circumstances:*

(1) *The victim was, at the time of the offense, thirteen years of age or older but less than eighteen years of age; and either*

(A) *The defendant had, at the time of the offense, supervisory or disciplinary power over the victim by virtue of the defendant's legal, professional or occupational status and used such power to accomplish the sexual contact; or*

(B) *The defendant had, at the time of the offense, parental or custodial authority over the victim and used such authority to accomplish the sexual contact.*

(b) *Sexual battery by an authority figure is a Class C felony.*

39-13-528. Solicitation of a minor

(a) *It is an offense for a person eighteen years of age or older, by means of oral, written or electronic communication, directly or through another, to intentionally command, request or hire a person who the person making the solicitation knows or should know is less than eighteen years of age to engage in conduct that if completed would constitute a violation by the soliciting adult of one or more of the following offenses:*

(1) *Rape of a child pursuant to § 39-13-522;*

(2) *Aggravated rape pursuant to § 39-13-502;*

(3) *Rape pursuant to § 39-13-503;*

(4) *Aggravated sexual battery pursuant to § 39-13-504;*

(5) *Sexual battery pursuant to § 39-13-505;*

(6) *Statutory rape pursuant to § 39-13-506; and*

(7) *Especially aggravated sexual exploitation of a minor pursuant to § 39-17-1005.*

(b) It is no defense that the solicitation was unsuccessful and the conduct solicited was not engaged in. It is no defense that if the solicited conduct were engaged in the minor would not commit any of the listed offenses. It is no defense that the minor solicited was unaware of the criminal nature of the conduct solicited.

(c) A violation of this section is a Class E felony.

STATE v. TUTTON
Court of Criminal Appeals of Tennessee, at Jackson, 1993
875 S.W.2d 295 Tenn. Cr. App.
[Citations omitted]

. . .

OPINION

WADE, Judge

The defendant, Reginald D. Tutton, was convicted of aggravated rape and attempted first degree murder. A charge of kidnapping ended in a mistrial. The trial court sentenced the defendant as a Class A, multiple offender to consecutive prison sentences of 25 and 35 years, respectively.

The single issue presented for review relates to the aggravated rape conviction. The defendant contends the trial court erred by failing to instruct the jury on the lesser included offense of rape.

We find the aggravated rape conviction should be modified to simple rape. We remand to the trial court for a new sentencing hearing.

The defendant is the boyfriend of the victim's aunt. At approximately 11:30 P.M. on June 7, 1991, the victim, Valerie Walton, left a friend's home to walk home. The defendant, driving a brown, four-door car, resembling one owned by the victim's aunt, stopped to talk. After confirming the victim's identity and learning that she intended to go home, the defendant said, "[N]o, you're not, you're going to the park." The victim then attempted to flee, but was overcome by the defendant and led back to the car.

The defendant then told her that he was going to the store to buy beer but indicated that he would take the victim home. After purchasing the beer, defendant returned to his vehicle and instead of driving the victim home, he drove the victim to "the park," an isolated spot on the northern end of Mud Island in Memphis.

When the defendant stopped, the victim attempted to flee but was again subdued by the defendant. After returning her to the car, the defendant removed her clothes and raped the victim in the front seat of the car. Immediately afterward, the victim put her clothes back on and agreed to a walk with the defendant. He warned her to tell no one about the occurrence.

As the two returned to the car, the defendant suddenly struck the victim from behind several times with an object, causing her to fall to the ground. He then stabbed her repeatedly with some type of file. The defendant fled the scene and the victim found her way to the nearby Kimberly Clark guard station from where authorities were contacted.

Dorothy Clark, the guard on duty, testified that the victim was dazed and covered in blood. Initially, paramedics treated the victim. She was hospitalized three days for, among other things, stab wounds to her back, neck, and breast.

While the defendant did not testify, he presented three alibi witnesses. All testified that he was in a different part of Memphis at the time of the offenses.

Defense counsel requested that the trial court instruct the jury on rape, sexual battery, and assault, all lesser included offenses of aggravated rape. The trial court, however, charged the jury solely upon the offense of aggravated rape.

Pursuant to Tenn.Code Ann. § 39-13-502(a)(2), the state must prove that a rape is *accompanied by bodily injury* to the victim before the crime may be elevated to that of aggravated rape. In this appeal, the defendant claims an entitlement to a new trial because the trial court had a duty to instruct the jury on the lesser included offense of rape when the evidence did not show a temporal relationship between the rape and the subsequent stabbing. The state concedes that the record contains no proof that the rape itself was accompanied by bodily injury; it agrees that the defendant stabbed the victim only after the rape had been fully accomplished. The state, however, argues that the remedy is not a new trial; it contends that the defendant's conviction should be modified to simple rape. We agree.

We initially observe that the trial judge has the duty to give a complete charge of the law applicable to the facts of the case. It is settled law that when "there are any facts that are susceptible of inferring guilt on any lesser included offense or offenses, then there is a mandatory duty upon the trial judge to charge on such offense or offenses. Failure to do so denies a defendant his constitutional right of trial by a jury."

When there is a trial on a single charge of felony, there is also a trial on all lesser included offenses, "as the facts may be."

The record demonstrates that intervals of both time and distance separated the two offenses. The crime of rape, according to the account of the victim, had been fully accomplished well before the assault. That statute requires that the rape be "accompanied by" bodily injury to the victim. There was no proof of that here. The trial court's failure to charge the jury on the lesser included offense of rape was, therefore, error. . . .

This court recognizes that a new trial is generally the appropriate remedy where there is a failure to charge the jury on lesser included offenses. Under these circumstances, however, and where the evidence at trial was adequate to support the lesser included offense of rape, we elect to reduce the degree of the offense to simple rape and remand to the trial court for resentencing.

BIRCH, J., and F. LLOYD TATUM, Special Judge, concur.

STATE v. CLABO
Court of Criminal Appeals of Tennessee, at Knoxville, 1995
905 S.W.2d 197 Tenn. Cr. App.
[Citations omitted]

. . .

OPINION

PEAY, Judge

The defendant was convicted by a jury of two counts of aggravated sexual battery and one count of aggravated rape. For these convictions he received twelve years on each of the aggravated sexual battery convictions and twenty-five years on the aggravated rape conviction. The trial judge ordered all sentences to run consecutively, thereby resulting in an effective sentence of forty-nine years.

In this appeal as of right, the defendant presents five issues for review. . . .

4. Whether the trial court erred in admitting evidence of uncharged conduct and in failing to request an election of offenses. . . .

We find issues one, two, three, and five to be without merit. Therefore, we affirm the trial court on these issues. Regarding issue four, we reverse in part and affirm in part. On the sexual battery charges, we affirm the trial court. On the aggravated rape charge, we reverse and remand this case for a new trial.

The proof offered on behalf of the State established that on an evening in February of 1992, Wan Rayfield II (hereinafter, Junior) invited the defendant to Junior's home. The defendant and his wife stayed at Junior's home for three or four days. This period represents the only time that the defendant had ever been in the Rayfield home. On one of those evenings during the visit, Junior, Junior's wife, victim B, B's friend victim N, N's parents, B's sister, B's cousin, the defendant, and Teresa, the defendant's wife, were present at the Rayfield home. Late that evening, the defendant entered B's bedroom after B, age ten, had fallen asleep. After climbing into B's bed, the defendant fondled B's genitals. When B requested that the defendant stop these acts, the defendant ceased momentarily and then resumed the acts.

On a subsequent evening, while B and his friend N, also age ten, were playing Nintendo in his bedroom, the defendant entered and instructed B to accompany him to the bathroom. There the defendant offered B five dollars to buy his silence and keep him from reporting the prior sexual act to his mother and father. Upon returning from the bathroom, the defendant requested that N accompany him to the bathroom. In the bathroom, the defendant fondled N's genitals and performed oral sex on him. Then, forcibly pinning N against the sink, the defendant inserted his penis into N's anus. According to N, the defendant then started "hunching." After the defendant performed these sexual acts, N testified that the defendant had thrown a knife at him, cutting him on the leg; had kicked him out the door; and had thrown him twice. N also stated that he had thrown the knife back at the defendant and had struck him in the leg. According to B, N had returned from the bathroom after approximately ten minutes and had appeared mad and confused. N spoke to B about the events which had occurred in the bathroom, and B then alerted family members. In response, a mock trial was conducted with the defendant's wife presiding as "judge.". . .

For the jury to find the defendant guilty of aggravated sexual battery, the State must have proven beyond a reasonable doubt that there was unlawful sexual conduct with a victim by the defendant accompanied by any of the following circumstances:

(1) Force or coercion [was] used to accomplish the act and the defendant is armed with a weapon.

(2) The defendant [caused] bodily injury to the victim.

(3) The defendant [was] aided or abetted by one or more persons; and force [was] used to accomplish the act or the defendant [knew] or [had] reason to know the defendant [was] mentally defective, incapacitated or helpless.

(4) The victim [was] less than thirteen years of age.

For the jury to have found the defendant guilty of aggravated rape, the State must have proven one of the aforementioned circumstances enumerated in the preceding paragraph plus the element of unlawful sexual penetration of the victim by the defendant.

At trial, B testified that the defendant had come to his bedroom and played with his penis. N testified that the defendant had played with his penis, had "sucked" his penis, and had put his penis in N's "bottom."

The record reveals that the defendant articulated and signed a statement admitting to the commission of sexual offenses with both of these victims. Detective Harmon testified that the defendant had voluntarily waived his rights and confessed to these acts. The defendant reported details of the acts which had not been disclosed to him by the investigating officer and which were consistent with the victims' testimonies. The victims reported the acts of the defendant to family members, a medical doctor, an employee at the Department of Human Services, and a jury. Throughout this process, their account remained largely consistent and uncontradicted by any proof. Any minor discrepancies or lapses in memory may be attributed to the fact that these victims were nine [sic] years old at the time of the offense. Additionally, one of the victims suffers from a slight mental deficiency and experiences difficulty in recalling numbers or dates. The testimonies of the doctor and social worker largely corroborate the victims' testimonies. The jury has accredited the testimonies of the victims, Detective Harmon, Dr. St. Marie, and the social worker. A rational jury could conclude that any discrepancy in the victims' testimonies was minor and reasonable. In summary, a rational trier of fact could have convicted the defendant of two counts of aggravated sexual battery and one count of aggravated rape.

In his fourth issue the defendant contends that the trial court erred in admitting evidence of uncharged conduct and in failing to request an election of offenses. On this issue we affirm the trial court in part and reverse the trial court in part. . . .

In the case at bar, the trial court did not err in allowing admission of the evidence of uncharged conduct had the State elected as to the particular incident for which a conviction was being sought. The defendant was charged with cognate crimes. The victims were merely testifying about the circumstance surrounding the crimes which had been charged. Therefore, in strict accordance with the law in Tennessee, the trial judge properly allowed this evidence of uncharged, sexual conduct. This issue lacks merit.

As to the issue of election of offenses . . . [t]he law regarding election of offenses is expressed in *Burlison v. State,* 501 S.W.2d 801 (Tenn.1973). The *Burlison* rule applies to crimes of a sexual nature where there have been several separate incidents of sexual assault. *Burlison* states the following:

> We hold that it was the duty of the trial judge to require the State, at the close of its proof-in-chief, to elect the particular offense of carnal knowledge upon which it would rely for conviction, and to properly instruct the jury so that the verdict of every juror would be united on the one offense.

Burlison offers the following three fundamental reasons for the election requirement:

> First, to enable the defendant to prepare for and make his defense to the specific charge; second, to protect him from double jeopardy by individualization of the issue, and third, so that the jury's verdict may not be a matter of choice between offenses, some jurors convicting on one offense and others, another.

In the case at bar, the third justification addresses the gravest concern in that every defendant has "the well-established right under our state constitution to a unanimous jury verdict before a criminal conviction is imposed." The defendant has a constitutional right to a unanimous verdict on each offense. The defendant's "right to a unanimous jury before conviction requires the trial court to take precautions to ensure the jury deliberates over the particular charged offense, instead of creating a 'patchwork verdict' based on different offenses in evidence." Election ensures that each juror considers the same occurrence.

In the case at bar, the trial court did not err in failing to request the State to elect the offense for the first count of sexual battery on B. The defense counsel emphasizes the fact that B and the State referred to more than one episode of sexual contact, despite the fact that the defendant was only charged with one count of sexual battery against B. During testimony, B and the State, in an attempt to clarify, used phrases such as "the second time" or "the last time." In context, however, we do not find that the record indicates more than one incidence of sexual misconduct.

B testified in detail about one precise sexual incident in his bed. The State and defense counsel questioned B about that one precise incident. No details were provided about any other incident. The minor innuendos about another incident were harmless. In considering the entire record in this cause, we are satisfied that the judge did not err in failing to require that the State elect upon which offense it was seeking a verdict in that only one specific incident was alleged to have occurred.

We also find that the trial court did not err in failing to request the State to elect the offense for the second count of sexual battery on N. N testified to one incident of fondling which occurred in the bathroom. Questions presented by the State concerned only the one incident in the bathroom. No details were provided about any other incident.

We find, however, that the trial court did err in failing to request an election of offenses in connection with the charge of aggravated rape of N. The State provided proof that the defendant performed oral and anal sex on the victim. These are two separate acts, each constituting penetration under the charge of aggravated rape. Yet, the defendant was only charged with one count of aggravated rape. The court presented to the jury the proof and allegations of two acts and asked the jury if the defendant could be convicted of one count of this act. Therefore, some jurors could have concluded that the defendant was guilty based upon the proof of the oral sex and not the anal sex, and some jurors could have concluded that the defendant was guilty based upon the proof of the anal sex and not the oral sex. The defendant may have been convicted by a jury of less than twelve. Since all twelve members did not have to find the same facts or draw the same conclusions, we find that a grave constitutional error was committed in that the defendant may have been denied a unanimous jury verdict.

We cannot say that this error was harmless beyond a doubt. Prior to trial, the defendant moved to prevent the State from introducing proof concerning the oral sex incident. The State argued and the trial judge agreed that either the oral sex or the anal penetration constituted aggravated sexual rape. Further the State, in its summation to the jury, argued that the defendant had performed oral sex on the victim and had anally penetrated the victim. The trial judge expressly charged the jury to rely on the arguments of counsel for each side's theory of the case. The jury instructions defined sexual penetration as including fellatio and anal intercourse. Additionally, we note that nowhere in the record can we determine with certainty if the indictment was read to the members of the jury and/or was taken with them when they deliberated. Other than the indictment, we find nothing in the record to indicate that the jury was aware that the State was relying on the act of anal intercourse to support the aggravated rape count.

This case is unfortunate. The acts committed were egregious and disturbing. These acts grow more disturbing when we consider the victims. Two innocent boys suffered the immediate pain and tragedy of sexual abuse, and now they will suffer throughout their lives as victims of crimes of nature. We do not wish to cause these victims more harm. However, all defendants deserve a fair trial with a unanimous verdict. The trial court denied this defendant his right to a unanimous jury verdict, and we cannot, therefore, under the dictates of *Burlison,* affirm this conviction. In our legal system, we do not sacrifice the means by which we reach a conclusion in order to reach palatable ends. Therefore, we order a new trial on the aggravated rape charge.

F. CRIMINAL ABUSE

1. Introduction

Abuse crimes in general cover mistreatment and neglect; physical, sexual, and emotional damage; injury; exploitation; danger; and cruelty. These offenses are characterized by commission by a person in a position of trust or authority against someone in that person's care or influence or within the domestic circle. Besides ordinary criminal sanctions, abuse statutes also aim to prevent repeated abuse by enforcing protective orders and providing a cause of action for civil suits against abusers. Abuse of children and spouses or others in intimate partnerships is commonly covered, and abuse of the elderly in both private homes and group care facilities is sometimes included in abuse statutes. Illinois statutes include provisions against ritual mutilation and giving child athletes drugs for weight control in connection with participation in athletics.

2. Child Abuse

Nearly a million children were substantiated victims of child abuse in 1996, an 18 percent increase since 1990. Fifty-two percent of those children were victims of neglect, 24 percent of physical abuse, 12 percent of sexual abuse, 6 percent of emotional abuse, and 3 percent of medical neglect. More than 1,000 of those children died from their injuries. Parents were the abusers in 77 percent of the cases, and other relatives in 11 percent.[21]

Abusing or allowing someone else to abuse by causing injury, placing in risk of injury, confining or punishing cruelly, or torturing a child of a specified age, and sometimes a physically or mentally helpless person, in one's care generally constitutes child abuse. Offenses may be graded by degree of mens rea, from intentional as most serious, to wanton, then reckless as least serious. Another grading system uses degree of danger or injury and other evaluations of harm as aggravating factors.

The range of abuse offenses is suggested by the following cases. *Johnson v. State* (Fla. 1992), *People v. Morabito* (N.Y. City Ct. 1992), and *State v. Gray* (Ohio 1992) all refused to uphold convictions of mothers for "delivering" cocaine through the placenta to their babies shortly before birth. A mother's testimony that her thirteen-month-old daughter was "very bright" and "able to perceive everything" was not sufficient evidence that the baby was aware of her father's lewd conduct in her presence, so his conviction for child abuse was overturned in *Werner v. State* (Fla. App. 1991). The decision in *Nicholson v. State* (Fla. 1992) declared that "willful torture" in Florida's child abuse statute includes willful acts of omission such as the starvation of a child.

Proof of criminal negligence is required in omissions cases, but not when abuse is based on the direct infliction of injury, according to *People v. Sargent* (Cal. 1999). General intent was the element of mens rea when the act was shaking an infant until it fell into a coma. The defendant did not have to have knowledge of the danger of shaking.

The court in *Commonwealth v. Chandler* (Ky. 1987) ruled that abuse was not a lesser included offense of assault with a deadly weapon, and that injury from use of a deadly weapon is assault, regardless of whether the victim is related. Tying up children ages seven, six, and two years and forcing them to watch pornographic movies satisfied the element of cruel confinement in *Stokes v. Commonwealth* (Ky. 1992).

Investigation in child abuse cases, particularly in interviews of victims, needs to be conducted with great care. Some sexual abuse cases have turned into witch-hunts, such as the McMartin Day Care case in Los Angeles, underscoring the difficulties in dealing with highly emotional situations and suggestible children. A two-year investigation of a suspected child sex ring in Wenatchee, Washington, turned up more than 27,000 counts of sex abuse of sixty children by forty-three parents, foster parents, neighbors, and a pastor. Of twenty-eight people convicted, ten were sentenced to more than twenty years in prison. In 1999 pro bono attorneys appealed many of those convictions on grounds that coercive tactics were used to get statements from victims and defendants and that involvement of therapists tainted some evidence.[22]

Teachers, physicians, social workers, and others who observe children in the course of their work are required by state laws and 18 U.S.C.A. § 2258 to report suspected child abuse to law enforcement agencies.

Federal laws protecting children from sexual abuse and exploitation are located in 18 U.S.C.A. §§ 2241 through 2260 and §§ 2423 and 2425. Section 2423(b) is a 1994 sex-tourism law that provides up to fifteen years in prison and fines for Americans who travel to foreign countries to have sex with minors.[23]

3. Domestic Abuse

In domestic violence and spouse abuse, the offender and victim have an intimate relationship and share or have shared a residence, or have a child in common. The trauma and fear of the victim are exacerbated by continuing access and control by the offender. Such physical and psychological control, along with aspects of love, denial, and social and religious conventions, prevents many victims from reporting spouse abuse or from pressing charges. A Justice Department study showed that 21 percent of the violence against women from 1992 to 1996 came from a domestic partner; that was true of only 2 percent of the violence toward men.[24] "The single most dangerous place for a woman in our society is within the four walls of her home."[25]

Domestic abuse statutes encompass the standard assault, battery, and sexual offenses between domestic partners. They also provide criminal sanctions for violations of protective orders. Reforms bolstering those measures include emergency protective orders issued by judges to allow quick intervention by police and added penalties for violations. A Missouri court and several counties in Georgia allow battered women to e-mail requests for protective orders from their shelter house directly to the judge to speed approval time and avoid confronting their abusers.[26] Some prosecutors have adopted a "no drop" policy in spouse abuse cases, ensuring that charges will not be dropped even if the victim fails to cooperate with the prosecution. An Illinois law, the first of its kind in the nation, allows a death sentence when a murder victim had obtained a protective order against the murderer. Factors that more commonly raise murder to a capital offense include an elderly person or child as a victim. Opponents of the law argue that lack of a protective order does not make a murder less aggravated.[27]

A criminal conviction for a protective order violation was affirmed in *Lee v. State* (Tex. Cr. App. 1990). A lesbian partner's conviction of domestic violence was affirmed in *State v. Linner* (Ohio Mun. 1996). The defendant and victim were living and raising their children from previous relationships together, so their relationship qualified as "otherwise cohabiting" under the statute.

The Violence Against Women Act (VAWA) of 1994 makes it a federal crime to cross a state or Indian country line to commit a crime of violence against a spouse or intimate partner, 18 U.S.C.A. § 2262 (a)(1); or to force a partner to cross such a line and in the course or as a result of doing so commit a crime of violence, 18 U.S.C.A. § 2262 (a)(2). VAWA also criminalizes interstate stalking, § 2261A; crossing or causing to cross state lines in violation of a protective order, § 2262; and accords full faith and credit to protective orders so they can be enforced in all states and Indian lands, 18 U.S.C.A. § 2265.

A defendant's conviction under § 2261(a)(2) was upheld in *U.S. v. Page* (6th Cir. 1999). After severely beating his ex-girlfriend into near-unconsciousness, the defendant carried her to his car and drove for four hours across state lines, threatening her with more violence to keep her from seeking help while her injuries worsened. Aggravation of preexisting injuries while crossing state lines was held to be sufficient to prove a criminal violation of VAWA. Ironically, a woman was convicted under VAWA for driving from New Jersey to New York where she and an accomplice murdered her estranged husband with axes [*U.S. v. Gluzman* (2d Cir. 1998)].

Federal firearms restrictions also penalize domestic violence offenders. Those who are subject to a protective order and those who have been convicted of a misdemeanor crime of domestic violence are subject to further criminal sanctions for possession of a firearm or ammunition, 18 U.S.C.A. §§ 922 (g)(8) and (9).

4. Elder Abuse

Abuse of the elderly, as defined by a 1987 amendment to the Older Americans Act, comes from three sources: domestic abuse within the person's own home, institutional abuse from care providers, and self-neglect or abuse. Physical and sexual abuse and financial exploitation are criminalized in all states. Some states also recognize emotional abuse, neglect, abandonment, and self-neglect. Fifty-five percent of the cases of elder abuse are the result of neglect, and this percentage is growing. In all but eight states, certain professionals who provide services to the elderly are required to report suspected abuse. Those reports increased by more than 150 percent between 1986 and 1996, but it is still estimated that fewer than a tenth of the cases of abuse are reported.[28]

G. KIDNAPPING, FALSE IMPRISONMENT, AND CUSTODIAL INTERFERENCE

1. Federal Kidnapping Statutes

Kidnapping was not considered a serious crime in this country until the baby son of aviator Charles Lindburgh was kidnapped in 1932. The hysteria that followed spawned harsh new laws, including the death penalty in some jurisdictions. The death penalty has been dropped, but emotion continues to fuel reaction to any perceived threat of random kidnappings. Community programs to fingerprint, videotape, and get DNA samples from children for later identification in case they are abducted have been promoted, although most abductions are by parents who have lost custody through divorce proceedings.

The Federal Kidnapping Act, 18 U.S.C.A. § 1201, establishes federal jurisdiction if the victim is moved across state lines. It is not necessary for the defendant to know that lines have been crossed, simply that they have, in fact, been crossed. The 1932 law criminalized only kidnappings "for ransom or reward," but two years later "or otherwise" was added, which defined kidnapping as abduction for some benefit to the defendant. Besides financial return, this could include such "benefits" as revenge or silencing a witness.[29] The federal law covers kidnapping by deception, as well as by force. Receiving, possessing, or disposing of ransom is criminalized in 18 U.S.C.A. § 1202, and the taking of hostages by bank robbers in 18 U.S.C.A. § 2113(e). Threats to kidnap and ransom demands that are sent through interstate communications are prohibited by 18 U.S.C.A. § 875, and those sent through the mail are prohibited by §§ 876 and 877. The statute of limitations does not begin running as long as the victim is held.

2. Elements of Kidnapping

asportation:
the removal of the victim from a place of security to one of greater danger in kidnapping; removal of goods in theft.

Kidnapping usually includes the seizing, confining, and carrying away (asportation) of another by force, threat, or deception, and without consent. In some states kidnapping includes the elements of commission during a dangerous felony, for the purpose of obtaining a ransom, or for political aims; in others, these elements aggravate the crime to a more serious level. **Asportation,** the removal of the victim from a place of security to one of greater danger, is usually a key element, differentiating kidnapping from the less serious crime of false imprisonment. Risk rather than distance is the central issue. When a man dragged his victim thirty to forty feet from the street to a vacant lot to force her to perform fellatio, he was guilty of kidnapping [*State v. Dixon* (Tenn. 1997)]. The court ruled that the movement to avoid detection increased the risk of harm and was not merely incidental to the sexual assault. A defendant who took control of a victim's car by threatening the victim with a shotgun, drove to a bank, and forced the victim to withdraw funds was guilty of kidnapping, because Indiana law includes confinement of another while hijacking a vehicle as a possible element of kidnapping [*Wilson v. State* (Ind. 1984)].

The question of the degree of asportation remains a problem, and some states have dropped the element of asportation altogether, relying on other circumstances to establish the danger of confinement. A sleeping child who was not moved or even aware of being confined was still the victim of kidnapping in *Creek v. State* (Ind. App. 1992). The victim of a robbery who was restrained in a vacant apartment and tortured after his possessions were taken was also a victim of kidnapping, because the restraint was not simply incidental to the robbery but unnecessary and cruel in itself [*People v. Taylor* (N.Y. App. Div. 1992)].

Some kidnapping statutes include confinement for purposes of involuntary servitude, compelled labor against one's will, regardless of payment. Illegal aliens are particularly vulnerable victims of this offense, because their complaints would result in their deportation. Owners of garment workers' sweatshops in New York have forced illegal Chinese immigrants to work up to seventeen hours a day, seven days a week, with pay as low as a dollar an hour.[30]

Kidnapping statutes may also include such offenses as harboring a runaway and unlawful sale of a public conveyance travel ticket to a minor.

3. False Imprisonment

False imprisonment or criminal confinement is the restraining, and sometimes removal, of another without consent, but does not include the danger of injury, ransom, or other risk factors of kidnapping. Covering a victim's mouth to prevent her from screaming and wrapping an arm around her to prevent her from escaping were ruled criminal confinement [*Henley v. State* (Ind. 1988)]. Because Indiana law also includes removal (asportation) as an alternate element of criminal confinement, the same conviction was affirmed when the victims were taken upstairs in their home while the intruders ransacked the bedrooms, then back downstairs where they were tied with a vacuum cleaner cord [*Arnold v. State* (Ind. 1987)].

4. Custodial Interference

Parents or other relatives who take a child to another state with the intent of assuming or petitioning for custody from the legal guardian fall under child snatching or custodial interference statutes. States cooperate in the 1968 Uniform Child Custody Jurisdiction Act to keep jurisdiction of such cases in the home state. The Parental Kidnapping Prevention Act (PKPA), 28 U.S.C.A. § 1738, enforces "full faith and credit" of a state's child custody orders to be honored in all other states, thus removing an incentive for parental kidnapping. International parental kidnapping prosecutions fall under 18 U.S.C.A. § 1204.

People v. McDonald (N.Y. Co. Ct. 1990) and *State v. Butt* (Me. 1995) give two different answers to the same legal question in state custodial interference rulings.

ANALYSIS PROBLEM

4–4. Why does a request for ransom influence the seriousness of kidnapping? Why is custodial interference a separate offense from kidnapping?

PEOPLE v. MCDONALD
Fulton County Court, 1990
554 N.Y.S.2d 934 Co. Ct. 1990
[Citations omitted]

FINDINGS OF FACT

The defendant and his wife Heather were married on November 1, 1985. They are the parents of two children, Ian born November 7, 1985, and Kelly, born September 27, 1987. At the time of the incidents in question they were domiciled at 9 Orchard Street in the City of Gloversville. For reasons that are not relevant to this proceeding Heather McDonald left the marital residence with the two children of the parties on September 17, 1988. After September 17 Heather and the two children lived with her parents at 12 Wells Street in the City of Johnstown. Two days later she filed a petition in Fulton County Family Court seeking custody of the children.

The Order to Show Cause in the Family Court proceeding was evidently served on the defendant on September 24,

1988, and the matter was returnable on September 30, 1988. That Order to Show Cause did not contain a provision granting Heather McDonald custody pendente lite. On September 27, 1988, the defendant, under the pretense of visiting with the children, took them from their mother and took them to Buena Park, California, where his parents reside. On September 30 the Family Court granted Heather McDonald custody of the two McDonald children on the defendant's default.

It further appears that a felony complaint was filed against the defendant in the City of Johnstown and that the defendant was apprehended in Buena Park, California, on October 14, 1988. Defendant waived extradition and was returned to this State on November 1, 1988. The children were returned to their mother.

Defendant was indicted for Custodial Interference in the First Degree and makes this motion to dismiss the indictment.

CONCLUSIONS OF LAW

Custodial Interference in the Second Degree is a necessary subpart of Custodial Interference in the First Degree. PL 135.-50(1). Custodial Interference in the Second Degree occurs when a person ". . . being a relative of a child less than sixteen years old, intending to hold such child permanently or for a protracted period, and knowing that he has no legal right to do so . . . takes or entices such child from his lawful custodian. . . ." PL 135.45(1).

I begin my analysis of this statute by defining the *actus reus,* which is a taking or asportation. This is an act unitary in time, and cannot be the subject of a continuing offense.

Did the defendant have the legal right to remove the children at the time of the taking? Clearly he did not contravene any court order at the time of the taking. It is worth noting that the Order to Show Cause from the Family Court Judge did not contain an order granting the mother of the children temporary custody or prohibiting either party from removing the children from the jurisdiction of the court, until the first return date of the matter.

Therefore the issue around which this case revolves may be framed thus: Where there is no court order to the contrary may a parent remove the children from the residence of the other parent to some distant location? . . .

1) Would the meaning of the statute proposed by the People result in a significant expansion in activity defined as criminal, so that activity heretofore regarded as other than criminal would by my decision become criminal activity? and 2) Does the complainant have an adequate civil remedy and is her use of the criminal justice system in this instance inappropriate?

I find that to determine that the taking by a parent of a child or children from the home of another parent prior to the entry of any order on the issue of custody or visitation falls within the meaning of PL 135.45 would result in criminalizing a set of activities that is not currently regarded as criminal. For example the definition proposed by the People would mean that whenever a parent removed himself or herself from the marital residence, for whatever reason, and took the child or children along without the other parent's permission that activity would be custodial interference. I take cognizance of the fact that a large number of divorce cases and custody disputes start with this physical act. It may well be that to require one party or the other to obtain a court order before this step is taken would be in the best interests of all concerned. . . .

Finally it should be noted that in proceedings to determine custody the courts of this state take cognizance of the harmful effects on the welfare of children that result from acts like those alleged to have been committed by the defendant herein. Because of this I find that an adequate civil remedy exists for the mother of the children in this case and that use of the criminal justice system is inappropriate.

Accordingly the indictment herein is dismissed.

STATE v. BUTT
Supreme Judicial Court of Maine, 1995
656 A.2d 1225 Me 1995
[Citations omitted]

Butt was charged with committing two counts (one count for each of his two youngest children) of criminal restraint by a parent in violation of 17–A M.R.S.A. § 303(1)(A) during September 1992. In the same indictment, Merryanne Morningstar was charged with two counts of aiding Butt in committing criminal restraint by a parent. After the trial court granted Morningstar's motion to sever her trial, Butt was tried before a jury in April 1993, at which the following evidence was revealed:

At the time of trial, Butt had been married to Diane Butt for twenty-four years and they had four children, the two youngest being 12 and 7 years of age. Butt worked as a counselor helping people leave religious cults. He counseled Morningstar, and in May or June 1992, Morningstar moved in with the Butts. In early July, Butt told his wife that he and Morningstar had been married by God, that Diane would have to accept it, and that they all were going to live under the same roof as one family. Butt subsequently told Diane

that he had heard from God and she had to obey his decisions. Although Diane initially accepted the arrangement, she became troubled with the situation and expressed her concern to her husband. Butt told a friend that unless Diane accepted the situation, he was going to take the youngest children and not return. The friend warned Butt that there would be legal repercussions, but Butt "believed that God would take care of things."

On September 1, 1992, the situation came to a head. Butt and Diane had a physical struggle in their kitchen during which Butt pulled Diane to the floor and attempted to cast the "Jezebel spirit" out of her. Shortly after the struggle, Butt and Morningstar took the two youngest children and left.

Diane never consented to Butt and Morningstar taking the two children. Diane tried to get her children back and hired a private investigator. She learned that the children had been taken to Maryland. Diane received a letter from Butt telling her that she would not find the children and that he intended to keep the children and live elsewhere. Diane never spoke with Butt while he was away, but Butt did speak with his older son several times. Butt told his son that he would not bring the children back until Diane accepted Morningstar and that he could stay away without being found.

After an arrest warrant was issued, Butt was arrested in Waterville and the children were located at a mobile home in Canaan. In response to questioning by a detective, Butt said that his intention was to take the children to a place where Diane could not find them. He told the detective that he returned to Maine from Maryland because private detectives were looking for the children and he did not want them to be located.

At the close of the State's case, Butt moved for a judgment of acquittal. He contended that the State had presented insufficient evidence because it had not shown that he had violated a court order and, therefore, there was no evidence that he lacked the legal right to take the children. The trial court denied the motion. Butt then testified in his own defense.

The jury returned guilty verdicts on both counts, and the trial court accordingly entered judgments of convictions. Butt appealed.

17–A M.R.S.A. § 303(1) (1983) provides, in pertinent part:

1. A person is guilty of criminal restraint by parent if, being the parent of a child under the age of 16, and knowing he has no legal right to do so, he:

> A. Takes, retains or entices the child from the custody of his other parent, guardian or other lawful custodian with the intent to remove the child from the State or to secrete him and hold him in a place where he is not likely to be found; or
> B. Takes, retains or entices the child from the custody of his other parent, guardian or other lawful custodian, whose custodial authority was established by a court of this State, in the state in which the child is residing with his legal custodian with the intent to remove the child from that state or to secrete him and hold him in a place where he is not likely to be found.

Whether a violation of a custody decree is a prerequisite to prove a violation of section 303(1)(A) is a question of statutory interpretation, and thus a matter for this court. In interpreting a statute, we first examine the plain meaning of the statutory language. The fundamental rule in the interpretation of any statute is that the intent of the legislature, as divined from the statutory language itself, controls.

Section 303(1)(A) does not prohibit a parent from taking his or her child. Rather, it prohibits the taking of a child from the custody of the other parent with the purpose of secreting and holding the child in a place where the child is not likely to be found, with the knowledge that the parent has no legal right to do so. The plain language of section 303(1)(A) does not require a violation of a custody decree for there to be a violation of its provisions. In contrast, section 303(1)(B) provides explicitly that the custody of a parent or a lawful custodian must be "established by a court of this state" in order for there to be a violation of that section.

The State proved that Butt, as the parent, took his children from their home where their mother had equal legal custody and control over them, and that his purpose was to keep them away from their mother; to secrete them and hold them in a place where they were not likely to be found. Butt contends, however, that the State failed to prove that he knew he had no legal right to take the children and keep them from their mother. Relying on the legislative history of section 303, he points to the absence of a court order granting custody to the mother and contends that such an order is required in order for there to be a violation of section 303(1)(A). We disagree.

In the absence of a court order awarding custody of children, both parents are jointly entitled to their care, custody, and control. 19 M.R.S.A. § 211 (1981). Although as a parent, Butt had rights of custody in regard to his children, so too did his wife Diane, the mother of those children. Butt can point to no convincing reason or any authority why, absent a contrary court order, section 303(1)(A) does not prohibit one parent from depriving the other parent of their legal right to joint custody. Butt, after all, deprived Diane of any and all contact with the children. There is no requirement in the plain language of section 303(1)(A), as there is in section 303(1)(B), that those custody rights flow from a court order or decree. Moreover, Butt can point to no court order granting custody of his minor children to him. Accordingly, the jury was entitled to find that Butt knew that he had no legal right to take and secrete his children, and to keep them from their mother. . . .

Neither in the original comment to the statute, nor in its subsequent changes, has the Legislature ever stated that a person cannot violate section 303 unless he is in contravention of a court ordered custody decree.

The entry is judgments affirmed. All concurring.

ANALYSIS PROBLEM

4–5. In the decisions of *McDonald* and *Butt*, what are the factors you think were most influential in bringing the courts to opposite opinions? Do you think these factors were appropriate considerations in these cases?

III. CRIMES AGAINST HABITATION

A. INTRODUCTION

Offenses against habitation are a special type of property crime. Besides damage and potential damage to property, these crimes pose a threat to the security and privacy of people. Focusing on that right of security, common law burglary and arson included only offenses against dwellings and other buildings within the curtilage or walled area around the dwelling. The possible targets for these crimes have been widely expanded by modern statutes and decisions.

B. ARSON

1. Burning

All the actus reus elements of the common law offense have been broadened in at least some jurisdictions. "Burning" often includes "exploding" and requires that fire not only be started, but actually cause damage to the structure. Many states, however, now include "damage caused by fire" or "sets fire to" as part of the definition of arson, allowing for conviction where there is limited damage. There must be at least a perceptible change in composition or structure. In the case of *Lynch v. State* (Ind. App. 1977) the defendant's conviction for arson was upheld even though damage from a burning object thrown at a house was limited to blistering and discoloration of paint. Explosion is not technically "burning," but many states specifically include it in their arson statutes. Burning crimes also include setting fire to woods, prairies, and crops; and refusing to aid or obstructing extinguishment of fires.

2. Property

Property subject to arson now goes far beyond the "dwelling house" of common law to include commercial buildings, public buildings, and even bridges. Some statutes classify arson according to the value or use of property damaged. First degree arson usually involves occupied buildings, including homes, where fire presents a danger to life. Second degree arson includes unoccupied buildings and sometimes vehicles. There may be a third degree that refers to other types of property. Charges may be aggravated if a firefighter or police officer is injured in the line of duty relating to the crime.

A defendant convicted of felony murder based on arson had his conviction remanded (returned for further action) in *People v. Reeves* (Mich. 1995). The building he burned was a dilapidated, abandoned house not considered a dwelling. Because there was no arson, there also was no felony murder of the firefighter who was killed in the fire. In *Fox v. State* (Ind. App. 1979), the burning of a barn converted into a combination garage and recreation room about 100 feet from the house was considered arson. Its domestic use placed it within the curtilage of the dwelling.

3. Ownership

The element that the building must belong to another has been adhered to except where the owner intends to defraud an insurance company or lienholder, or if another person has an interest in the building. This led to an interesting technical problem in *State v. Houck* (Kan. 1986). Read the decision in this case in Chapter 8. A defendant and his wife were making payments toward ownership of a mobile home. The defendant had moved out, and the home was occupied by his wife, stepdaughter, and her family. When he burned the home he was guilty of arson, in spite of his co-ownership, because of his wife's possessory interest [*Livingston v. State* (Ala. Cr. App. 1979)].

4. Mens Rea

"Malicious" and "willful" are the usual mens rea requirements of arson. Intent is general with regard to setting the fire, not specific as to the damage caused by the fire. An intent to destroy, of course, raises the degree of the offense.

Some statutes require specific intent to burn a structure when that burning is caused by setting fire to a substance other than the structure, as shown in *People v. Fabris* (Cal. 1995). The defendant claimed that a neighbor's goats had gotten into his house through a door left ajar and either chewed through wiring or tipped over a gas can to start the fire that burned the home. Although the bodies of two goats were found in the house, other evidence showed that the doors had been locked, gasoline had been used to set fires to draperies in two areas of the house, and the defendant was desperate for the insurance money, so his conviction for arson was affirmed.

5. Federal Statutes

Federal arson statutes include 18 U.S.C.A. § 81, which covers arson within maritime and territorial jurisdiction, and 18 U.S.C.A. § 844, which covers use of explosives or fire while committing any other federal crime or to threaten persons or destroy property used in interstate commerce. A juvenile who burned papers in the principal's office of a school on Indian lands and caused more than $400,000 worth of damage was guilty of arson under § 81 [*U.S. v. M.W.* (10th Cir. 1989)]. The court found that the defendant had "practically certain" knowledge the papers would ignite the building and serious damage would result.

Even though a defendant had no knowledge that interstate commerce was involved at a tavern he set on fire, interstate shipments of liquor brought the tavern under the protection of § 844(i) for an arson conviction [*U.S. v. Muza* (8th Cir. 1986)]. Arson of a home used as a rental property also qualified for a federal charge under the interstate commerce clause [*Russell v. U.S.* (1985)]. In *Jones v. U.S.* (2000), the Supreme Court ruled that "use" in interstate commerce did not include the passive use of out-of-state providers of natural gas, a mortgage, and insurance for a private dwelling, but that the property itself must be actively used in commerce.

C. VANDALISM

Vandalism or malicious mischief is intentional or wanton damage done to real or personal property. Unlike arson, there is no limit on the means of causing the damage nor on the type of property targeted. Penalties usually depend on the amount of damage done.

D. BURGLARY

1. Common Law

In medieval Europe, intrusion into a secure place such as a dwelling, church, or even a walled town was considered burglary. By the seventeenth century the definition of a burglar was narrowed, according to English jurist Sir Edward Coke, to "a felon, that in the night breaketh and entereth into the mansion house of another, with the intent to kill some reasonable creature, or to commit some other felony within the same, whether his felonious intent be executed or not."[31] Modern statutes have modified each of the elements in Sir Coke's definition, moving toward the broader scope of medieval law.

2. Breaking

"Breaking" can mean anything from actually breaking down a door to pushing through an already unlatched door. If something is moved to gain entry, the element of breaking is satisfied. Constructive breaking goes even further to include tricking or threatening the owner to open the door. Entry through an unusual opening, such as a chimney, is also constructive breaking.

Under a statute that had been expanded to include "effective consent" for legal entry, a defendant who walked through an open door with the intent to commit rape and theft was guilty of burglary, because the building was not open to the public [*Clark v. State* (Tex. App. 1984)]. When a defendant took his victim to her home and made her open the door at gunpoint, the threat of force was enough to qualify as breaking in *Dew v. State* (Ind. 1982). The victim's consent to enter his home was nullified by the intent of the defendant to sell fraudulent securities [*People v. Salemme* (Cal. App. 1992)].

3. Entering

"Entry" is the process of going into the private area after access has been gained through "breaking." It can be ever so slight, including in one case a severed finger caught under a window. A defendant who presented a stolen and forged check to a teller at a check cashing business by placing the check in a chute at the walk-up window had not "entered" the building and so was not guilty of burglary [*People v. Davis* (Cal. 1998)].

surreptitious remaining: entering an area lawfully but staying beyond a lawful time without permission, such as in a store after closing hours.

A substitute for entry under some state statutes is **surreptitious remaining,** entering an area lawfully but staying beyond a lawful time without permission, such as in a store after closing hours. A defendant who simply entered a store during business hours with the intent to rob had committed burglary [*Clark v. Commonwealth* (Va. App. 1996)].

4. Structure

The type of structure that burglary applies to varies and is likely to affect the degree of the charge, so careful reading of the statute is especially necessary here. An attached garage has been construed as part of a dwelling, *People v. Jiminez* (Colo. 1982). Many states include any structure or building and even vehicles, and may allow more severe penalties for entering a car to steal a jacket from the seat than for stealing the entire car. *People v. Frey* (Ill. App. 1984) upheld a burglary conviction for stealing a hammer from the open back of a pickup. The court maintained that "unlawful entry may be accomplished by 'breaking the close' defined by the four sides, the bottom, and the imaginary plane extending atop the sides and parallel to the bottom." A similar burglary conviction occurred under a statute prohibiting "unauthorized entry of a motor vehicle" [*State v. Rodriquez* (N.M. App. 1984)]. In reaction to such convictions, some states have revised their laws to specify a "closed vehicle," so there was no burglary where the defendant reached through an open window to steal a stereo from a truck in *State v. Martinez* (Idaho App. 1995). A nondwelling was allowed in the burglary of an office [*State v. Sisneros* (Utah 1981)] and a fenced enclosure [*McCovens v. State* (Ind. 1989)].

The Model Penal Code § 221.0(1) deals with the problems inherent in these cases by limiting burglary to occupied structures, that is, "any structure, vehicle or place adapted for overnight accommodation of persons, or for carrying on business therein, whether or not a person is actually present." Some states have adopted this definition. An abandoned building is not subject to burglary, according to the code.

5. Ownership

The element requiring the burglarized structure to belong to another comes into dispute when the defendant may share the right to enter the structure. A defendant who owned a house jointly with his wife committed burglary when he entered it against an order of protection giving her exclusive possession of it, *People v. Williams* (Ill. App. 1991). When no such protective order had been issued, however, an estranged husband could legally enter his wife's residence [*Kennedy v. State* (Ga. App. 1994)]. A juvenile who entered his mother's home after she locked him out without care or other means for shelter or support was not guilty of burglary, because the parental duty of care was not met, *State v. Howe* (Wash. 1991).

6. Time of Day

Some jurisdictions eliminate the element of nighttime from burglary. Most retain it as an aggravating circumstance because darkness favors the stealth of the burglar, making identification more difficult and increasing the fear of the victim.

7. Mens Rea

The mens rea of burglary is the specific intent to commit a crime. Many jurisdictions require that crime to be a felony or any level of theft, but some allow the intent to commit any crime, no matter how petty, to suffice. Completion of the intended crime is not an element of burglary. Intent may be inferred from circumstances. In *Sisneros*, intent was evident from the act of breaking and entering without consent at night and by the disturbance of a desk drawer. In *McCovens*, intent could be inferred from the movement of items to the front gate. When the intended crime is a legal impossibility, however, burglary has not taken place. A defendant in custody fled into a nearby apartment with the intent to escape, but because the escape was already complete, intent was nullified and his burglary conviction was reversed [*Lawhorn v. State* (Tex. Cr. App. 1995)].

Entry for other purposes, such as to take shelter, is not burglary. Defendants who enter with intent but later change their minds are still guilty of burglary. Those who enter the premises without intent, such as a houseguest who is shown the host's coin collection and later decides to steal it, are not burglars. Some statutes incorporate mens rea into their grading system, placing a higher degree of severity on intent to commit a felony or larceny than on intent to commit other misdemeanors.

8. Breaking and Entering

Breaking and entering without intent to commit a crime is criminal trespass, a misdemeanor. Grading is more severe if entry is into a dwelling, involves a weapon, occurs at night, or is in defiance of notice not to trespass, such as posting or fencing. Severity of the crime usually depends on the probability of injury to persons rather than on the value of property.

9. Burglary as an Inchoate Crime

Burglary, as a preliminary step to another crime, can be seen as an inchoate, or incomplete, offense. As it disrupts the security of persons in their homes and in regard to their personal property, however, it is complete as soon as the intrusion is made. This dual nature is at the heart of a debate about whether the crime of burglary ought to be abolished, leaving its elements to be covered by attempt or as aggravating circumstances to other crimes, or retained and the grading schemes reformed to reflect the seriousness of the individual offense.

In effect piling an inchoate crime onto an inchoate crime, the possession of burglar's tools with the intent to use them in a burglary is a serious offense, a felony in some jurisdictions. Gloves that a defendant was trying to shake off as he ran from the site of a burglary were identified as burglar's tools in *Green v. State* (Fla. App. 1991). A discussion of inchoate crimes is in Chapter 6.

EXHIBIT 4–2
Sample Jury Instructions

SECOND-DEGREE BURGLARY

You will find the Defendant guilty of Second-Degree Burglary under this Instruction if, and only if, you believe from the evidence beyond a reasonable doubt all of the following:

A. That in this county on or about _____ (date) and before the finding of the Indictment herein, he entered or remained in the dwelling of _____ (victim) without the permission of _____ (victim) or any other person authorized to give such permission.

B. That in so doing, he knew he did not have such permission;

AND

C. That he did so with the intention of committing a crime therein.

William S. Cooper, *Kentucky Instructions to Juries (Criminal)*, 4th ed. § 5.08 (© Anderson Publishing, Cincinnati, Ohio, 1999), with permission.

IV. CONCLUSION

Chapter 4 covers crimes that result in death, injury, and fear to their victims. Crimes against persons attack the individual directly, as in murder, assault crimes, abuse crimes, and kidnapping. Crimes against habitation are indirect, destroying the security of the individual within the dwelling, as in arson and burglary.

Whether in common law or statute, each offense has specific elements that must be satisfied by the facts of the case. The most common elements have been discussed here, but your state's statutes and their interpretation in court decisions will form the bedrock of your work in criminal law. The chart in Exhibit 4-3 summarizes the elements of the crimes against persons and habitation.

The benefits of studying substantive law go beyond its strictly practical applications, beyond learning to use it as a tool, to an understanding of the development of our goals for a better society. What human values can you find in criminal statutes? Who or what is being protected, and why? Which laws are likely to endure, and which are ripe for change?

EXHIBIT 4–3
Common Elements of Crimes

CRIME	ACTUS REUS	MENS REA	GRADED BY	STATUTES
Homicide	Taking the life of another.		Mens rea.	
Capital murder	Aggravated first degree, continuing criminal enterprise.	With intent.	Aggravating and mitigating factors.	18 U.S.C.A. §§ 3591–3592
First degree Felony murder	Heinous or cruel during felony.	Premeditated; outrageously reckless; intention to commit felony.	Mens rea.	

EXHIBIT 4–3 *(Continued)*
Common Elements of Crimes

CRIME	ACTUS REUS	MENS REA	GRADED BY	STATUTES
Second degree	During less dangerous felony, resisting arrest.	Depraved heart; intent to cause great bodily harm; purposeful but not deliberate.	Mens rea.	
Voluntary manslaughter	Incomplete self-defense.	With intent on adequate provocation.	Mens rea.	
Involuntary manslaughter	During misdemeanor, traffic offense.	Reckless, grossly negligent.	Mens rea.	
Battery	Physical injury or offensive touching of another.	Purposeful, reckless, negligent.	Harm, aggravating factors.	18 U.S.C.A. §§ 111–113
Assault	Attempt to cause physical harm, threat of immediate physical harm creating fear.	Intent to commit battery, intent to frighten victim.	Aggravating factors.	
Reckless endangerment	Place another in risk of death or serious injury.	General intent.		
Terroristic threatening	Threat by language or action.	Recklessly, intentionally.		18 U.S.C.A. §§ 115(a), 871(a), 875(c)
Stalking	Threat and repeated surveillance or harassment.	Willful, malicious.	Harm, violation of restraining order.	18 U.S.C.A. §§ 2261A, 2262
Hate crimes	Threats, harassment, other crimes.	(Motivated by bias or group hatred.)		
Civil rights violations	Hinder exercise of rights, deprive of rights under color of law.	With intent, willfully.		18 U.S.C.A. §§ 241–248
Rape, sexual battery	Sexual intercourse or contact against victim's will by force or threat of force.	Knowledge, lack of consent.	Force, harm, circumstances.	
Statutory rape	Unforced sexual intercourse with one under age of consent.	Strict liability, knowledge of victim's age.		
Criminal sexual contact	Sexual touching offensive to victim.	Knowingly offensive.	Harm or force.	

Continued

EXHIBIT 4–3 (*Concluded*)
Common Elements of Crimes

CRIME	ACTUS REUS	MENS REA	GRADED BY	STATUTES
Criminal abuse	Commit or permit physical injury, placement in dangerous situation, torture, cruel confinement, cruel punishment to child or helpless person.	Intentionally, wantonly, recklessly.	Mens rea; harm or force; status of victim.	18 U.S.C.A. §§ 2241–2260, 2261A, 2262, 2265
Kidnapping	Seizing, confining, asportation (across state lines—federal) by force, threat, deception without consent.	For ransom, reward, or other benefit; specific intent; knowledge of state lines not necessary.	Danger, harm, ransom, servitude.	18 U.S.C.A. §§ 1201-1203.
False imprisonment	Restraint without consent. No danger.	Intentionally.		
Custodial interference	Parental violation of child custody orders.	With intent.		28 U.S.C.A. § 1738, 18 U.S.C.A. § 1204
Arson	Damage property of another by burning, explosion.	Malicious, willful intent to start fire.	Type of property, intent to do damage.	18 U.S.C.A. §§ 81, 844
Vandalism	Causing damage to real or personal property.	Intentional, wanton.	Amount of damage.	
Burglary	Breaking, entering, or surreptitious remaining in dwelling of another at night.	Intent to commit crime.	Type of building.	
Trespass	Breaking, entering property of another.	General intent.	Type of building, notice given.	

SYSTEM FOLDER ASSIGNMENTS

- Add your state's statutes to the chart in Exhibit 4–3.
- Revise the listing of elements to reflect the requirements in your state.
- Define lesser included charges

APPLICATION ASSIGNMENTS

1. In Case I, were the actions of Eldon Spiers the legally significant cause of Kate Lamb's death? What if she had died more than a year and a day after the incident, according to your state law? Explain.

2. Compare the following cases to examples of felony murder in the text. Could the defendants be convicted of felony murder based on those cases? How would they be decided based on statutes and cases in your jurisdiction?
   a. The defendant murdered a man, then raped the victim's wife. The felony murder charge was based on the felony of rape [*State v. Williams*, 660 N.E.2d 724 (Ohio 1996)].
   b. Accomplices armed with a BB gun, club, and pocket knife broke into a house to rob the owner. The victim, who had heard them coming and had his rifle ready, shot and killed one of them. The defendant had planned the robbery but remained outside in his truck while it was taking place [*State v. Oimen*, 516 N.W.2d 399 (Wis. 1994)].
   c. As two felons fled the scene of a drug deal, one was killed by pursuing police. The remaining defendant was charged with felony manslaughter [*State v. Kalathakis*, 563 So.2d 228 (La. 1990)].
   d. The driver of a stolen vehicle leads police on a high-speed chase. Two pursuing helicopters collide, killing officers riding in them [*People v. Acosta*, 284 Cal. Rptr. 117 (Cal. App. 1991)].
3. A fifteen-year-old boy loaded live and dummy shells into a shotgun, pointed it at the thirteen-year-old victim and said, "Let's play Polish roulette. Who is first?" then pulled the trigger [*People v. Roe*, 542 N.E.2d 610 (N.Y. 1989)]. What is the mens rea in this killing, and, therefore, what is the proper charge?
4. A man strangled his fiancee to death when she admitted to infidelity. What charge is appropriate [*State v. Shane*, 590 N.E.2d 272 (Ohio 1992)]?
5. A police officer heard gunshots and saw people running. At the scene he and the defendant moved back and forth between cars while the defendant pointed a gun at the officer, which indicated an intent to frighten. When the defendant eventually put the gun down, it was found to be loaded. A "present ability" to carry out a threat was required. The officer was not actually afraid. Should the defendant be charged with assault on the police officer [*Robinson v. U.S.*, 506 A.2d 572 (D.C. App. 1986)]?
6. Consistent with case examples of deadly weapons in assault, would you consider the teeth used to bite off a piece of a man's nose to be a deadly weapon in assault?
7. What is the appropriate charge against a defendant who knowingly has the AIDS virus and engages in unprotected, consensual sex?
8. A father who recklessly threw a hammer into the wall just above his baby son's crib was convicted of assault. The conviction was reversed because there was no intent and the baby was not aware of the danger [*Harrod v. State*, 499 A.2d 959 (Md. App. 1985)]. What criminal charge would have been more appropriate for the father's conduct?
9. A father began fondling his older daughter when she was six years old, then progressed to vaginal manipulation, then vaginal and anal penetration. This continued beyond the girl's thirteenth year, with oral sex being used as a punishment. The same conduct followed with the younger daughter from the age of five until seven, when the father stood trial for the offenses. Considering the Tennessee sexual offenses statutes in the text, for what crimes could the father be charged [*State v. Hallock*, 875 S.W.2d 285 (Tenn. Crim. App. 1993)]?
10. A rape victim suffered redness and swelling of the vagina and mental agitation after the attack. Would these factors qualify as "bodily injury" sufficient to raise charges to aggravated rape under Tennessee's statutes [*State v. Embry*, 915 S.W.2d 451 (Tenn. Crim. App. 1995)]?
11. When the actus reus of omission is not specifically stated in the statute, should a woman be charged with child abuse for watching her husband and another man engage in sexual intercourse with a twelve-year-old girl temporarily in her custody and replying to the girl that she "really didn't care" about it [*Degren v. State*, 722 A.2d 887 (Md. 1999)]?

12. If evidence shows that a defendant tied up a victim in his own home without moving the victim to another location or placing the victim in additional harm, can that defendant be convicted of kidnapping in your state? If the victim was moved to the basement before being tied, should the defendant be charged with kidnapping or false imprisonment in your state?

13. A defendant who set fire to an apartment building when he had been turned out by friends he had been staying with claimed that his intoxication and borderline mental retardation prevented intent for the crime of arson. Is this an effective defense [*State v. Doyon*, 416 A.2d 130 (R.I. 1980)]? Why or why not?

14. In Case III of Chapter 1, if Cat Bermuda had set fire to a pile of dry leaves to distract the mayor's guests as she made her entry into his house, and the leaves in turn set fire to the house, should she be charged with arson in your state?

15. Should burglary be charged in the following cases?
    a. A man knocks on the door, gives the name of the occupant's brother when asked who is there, and enters with the intent to commit armed robbery [*Commonwealth v. Labare*, 416 N.E.2d 534 (Mass. App. 1981)].
    b. A man walked into a bank and used another person's automatic teller card to receive cash [*State v. Hysell*, 569 So.2d 866 (Fla. App. 1990)].
    c. A man entered his own home in violation of a court order not to do so [*People v. Szpara*, 492 N.W.2d 804 (Mich. App. 1992)].
    d. Intending a felony, one man entered an apartment legally, then locked the occupant in the bathroom and opened the door to his partner. Did the partner commit burglary? What about another occasion when the partner gained entry by impersonating a police officer [*State v. Lozier*, 375 So.2d 1333 (La. 1979)]?
    e. Could requisite intent be inferred from the defendant's driving his truck near a home shortly before it was broken into and previously discussing stealing the victim's guns with a partner [*Hall v. State*, 293 S.E.2d 862 (Ga. App. 1982)]?

16. Should Miguel Cordoba be charged with burglary in Case II? Why or why not?

HELPFUL WEB SITES

www.splcenter.org
> Southern Poverty Law Center, legal action against hate groups

http://feminist.com/rainn.htm
> Rape, Abuse, and Incest National Network

www.calib.com/nccanch
> National Clearinghouse on Child Abuse and Neglect Information (phone: 800-FYI-3366, 703-385-7565)

www.gwjapan.com/ncea/
> National Center on Elder Abuse

www.usdoj.gov/vawa
> Violence Against Women Office

www.missingkid.com
> A global resource for parental abduction, legal section with laws and international conventions on custody disputes and international abduction

INTERNET EXERCISES

1. What method does the Southern Poverty Law Center use to fight hate crimes?
2. Go to www.usdoj.gov/vawa. How many states have enacted rape victim-counselor confidentiality statutes? What is their effect?

QUESTIONS FOR STUDY AND REVIEW

1. Know the basic elements of the crimes discussed in this chapter. Why is it important to know the elements of crimes?
2. What various definitions of the beginning and end of life affect homicide cases?
3. What is the dividing line between murder and manslaughter?
4. How are assault and battery related?
5. How does reckless endangerment differ from assault?
6. Compare and contrast terroristic threatening with stalking.
7. What elements of hate crimes are the deciding factors when these statutes come under constitutional scrutiny?
8. From whom do the federal civil rights statutes protect citizens?
9. How have social changes affected sex crimes?
10. What are the bases for classification of sex crimes in modern statutes?
11. What is Megan's Law?
12. How do abuse crimes differ from other assault crimes?
13. What crimes are covered by the Violence Against Women Act?
14. What landmark case changed kidnapping laws in the 1930s? What current phenomenon keeps the penalties stringent?
15. Why has asportation been considered an important element of kidnapping?
16. Are elements of involuntary servitude in kidnapping statutes outdated?
17. Why are federal custodial interference laws important?
18. Why are crimes against habitation more serious than most other property crimes?
19. What is the mens rea of arson? Of burglary?
20. How do modern burglary statutes compare to medieval law? To seventeenth-century law?

KEY TERMS LIST

Asportation
Elements
Lesser included offense
(or necessarily included
offense)

Lesser related
offense
Marital exception
Rape shield law

Statutory rape
Surreptitious remaining

ENDNOTES

1. Russell G. Donaldson, J.D., *Lesser-Related State Offense Instructions: Modern Statutes*, 50 ALR4th 1081, 1986.
2. J. STEPHEN, A HISTORY OF THE CRIMINAL LAW OF ENGLAND, 44 (1883), quoted in *Comber v. U.S.*, 584 A.2d 26 (D.C. App. 1990).
3. Andy Mead, *Supreme Court Says Family May End Life of Kentucky Woman*, LEXINGTON HERALD-LEADER, July 16, 1993, at A1.
4. Laurie L. Levenson, *Criminal Law, The Causation Chain*, NLJ, June 7, 1999, B21; Mike Schneider, *Paralyzed Florida Woman Taken Off Life Support*, LEXINGTON HERALD-LEADER, May 20, 1999, at A3; and picture caption, NLJ, Aug. 30, 1999, at A4.
5. See a discussion of beginning of life issues in FORSYTHE, *Homicide of the Unborn Child: The Born Alive Rule and Other Legal Anachronisms*, 21 VALPARAISO L.R. 563 (1987).
6. PETER W. LOW, JOHN CALVIN JEFFRIES, JR., & RICHARD J. BONNIE, CRIMINAL LAW, CASES AND MATERIALS 903 (2d ed. 1986).
7. The Associated Press, *Cancer Test Lab Pleads No Contest to Homicide*, LEXINGTON HERALD-LEADER, Dec. 5, 1995, at A3.
8. Associated Press, *Boy Killed by Airbag; Father Gets Two Jail Days*, LEXINGTON HERALD-LEADER, Dec. 15, 1998, at A6.

9. Michael Vitez, *Kevorkian's Influence Had Faded Long Before Judge Locked Him Up,* LEXINGTON HERALD-LEADER, April 18, 1999, at A8.

10. *Suicide Aid Is Curbed,* AARP BULLETIN, May 1999, at 12.

11. WAYNE R. LAFAVE and AUSTIN W. SCOTT, JR., SUBSTANTIVE CRIMINAL LAW, Vol. 2, 303–307 West Group 1986.

12. *Man Sentenced in AIDS Case,* LEXINGTON HERALD-LEADER, April 6, 1999, at A3.

13. Autumn De Leon, *You've Got Hell,* TIME DIGITAL, May 17, 1999, at 52.

14. Michael J. Sniffen, *Race Bias Behind More Than 50% of Hate Crimes, FBI Says,* LEXINGTON HERALD-LEADER, July 10, 1999, at A5.

15. Mark Fritz, *Hate Crime Punishment Inconsistent Across U.S.,* LEXINGTON HERALD-LEADER, Aug. 24, 1999, at A4.

16. JOHN M. SCHEB & JOHN M. SCHEB II, CRIMINAL LAW AND PROCEDURE 101 (1989).

17. WEST CRIMINAL LAW NEWS (No. 12), pp. 1–2.

18. *Court Gives Sex Offenders Hearing,* LEXINGTON HERALD-LEADER, Aug. 12, 1999, at A3.

19. John Curra, professor of criminology at Eastern Kentucky University, quoted by Scarlett Consalvi, *Some Think Megan's Law Won't Deliver,* RICHMOND REGISTER, Jan. 31, 1999, at A1.

20. John Cheves, *Damron Targets Repeat Sex Offenders,* LEXINGTON HERALD-LEADER, Aug. 16, 1999, at A1, A6.

21. U.S. Department of Health and Human Services, *Child Maltreatment 1996: Reports from the States to the National Child Abuse and Neglect Data System,* Washington, D.C., U.S. Government Printing Office, 1998.

22. Elizabeth Amon, *A White Knight's Tale,* NLJ, Aug. 23, 1999, A1, A8.

23. Timothy Roche, *Tourists Who Prey on Kids,* TIME, Feb. 15, 1999, at 58.

24. *Conference on Domestic Violence Kicks Off in Illinois,* THE RICHMOND REGISTER, Aug. 30, 1999, at A8.

25. Jerry J. Bowles, *Prosecution of Domestic Violence Offenders,* KATA Criminal Law Seminar, Oct. 16, 1992, Louisville, Kentucky.

26. *Justice at Light Speed,* USA WEEKEND, Aug. 27, 1999, at 12.

27. David Rovella, *Illinois Extends Reach of Death Penalty,* NLJ, Aug. 17, 1998, at A7.

28. National Center on Elder Abuse, www.gwjapan.com/NCEA/.

29. DEVITT, BLACKMAR, & O'MALLEY, FEDERAL JURY PRACTICE AND INSTRUCTIONS: CRIMINAL 468 (4th ed. 1990).

30. Edward Barnes, *Slaves of New York,* TIME, Nov. 2, 1998, at 72–75.

31. *Id.* at 436, quoting Sir Edward Coke, *The Third Part of the Institutes of the Laws of England* (London, 1797), p. 63.

CRIMES AGAINST PROPERTY, PUBLIC ORDER AND SAFETY, PUBLIC MORALS, AND JUSTICE AND PUBLIC ADMINISTRATION

CHAPTER

5

I. INTRODUCTION

Chapter 5 continues the study of elements of crimes, focusing on crimes against property (i.e., the ownership of property) and crimes against public rights to a decent, safe, and orderly society. You will see the marks of evolution in these areas of criminal law.

In crimes against property, element definitions got tangled as larceny broadened to include embezzlement and fraud. Elements of crimes against persons are carried into robbery and extortion. And change speeds up as criminal law tries to keep up with technological advancements.

In crimes against society, the law struggles to respond to public opinion as to the criminality of gun use, certain sexual acts, and drug use. Even crimes against justice and public administration, such as perjury, are the object of renewed scrutiny when a sitting President is charged.

This chapter presents an overview of elements of these crimes. Continue to refer to your state statutes and court opinions for concrete examples of the elements you need to know for work in your jurisdiction.

II. CRIMES AGAINST PROPERTY

A. INTRODUCTION

The variously detailed property crimes in modern statutes all grew out of the common law crime of larceny, a capital offense that served the needs of a simple, agrarian society. Taking animals or implements amounted to stealing one's means of livelihood and was punished severely. Stealing a harvested and stored crop was larceny, but unharvested crops were still part of the land and were covered by real estate law. Misappropriation by stealth or force was larceny, but cheating was a clever business angle.

tangible property: property that is valuable in itself, such as a cow or a coin.

intangible property: "choses in action"; property not valuable in itself but that conveys value, such as checks, bonds, and promissory notes.

Property accumulated and commerce increased, affording a wider variety of targets for the thief and means for obtaining them that outgrew the simple concept of larceny. **Tangible property** that was valuable in itself, such as a cow or a coin, was joined in importance by **intangible property,** or "choses in action," that was not valuable in itself but conveyed value, such as checks, bonds, and promissory notes. Property was frequently handled through intermediaries during the course of business transactions and banking processes, so trust and not trickery was essential to the growing commercial economy. In addition, judges were reluctant to expand the larceny death penalty to new forms of theft. One by one, statutes were written to deal with new circumstances as they arose. The resulting confusion gives us a picture of the development of history rather than of a logical body of law.

B. LARCENY

1. Introduction

Larceny elements include the wrongful taking and carrying away of another's property with intent to permanently deprive the owner of its possession. The value of the property taken is the element that usually determines the degree of the crime. The cutoff between misdemeanor (petit) and felony (grand) larceny can range as low as $20 to as much as $2,000, but usually falls between $100 and $400. Some jurisdictions include specific kinds of property that are locally significant and often specify value levels for that property. For example, grand larceny in California is the theft of property with a value of more than $400, or farm crops valued at more than $100. Texas specifically includes oil and natural gas in its larceny statute. It is not necessary that the defendant know the value of the property, or intend to steal only a certain amount; the grading is based on the actual value of the property. Problems arise in determining the value of a credit card, for example, or of trade secrets, or of the use of a computer.

The method of taking also can affect grading and even the definition of the crime committed. Because of potential harm to persons, pickpocketing and stealing from a dwelling are always felonies. If force is used, the crime is no longer larceny, but robbery.

2.   Actus Reus in Larceny

Taking or appropriating is the element of establishing control over the property, such as picking a wallet from a pocket or getting into a stranger's car and starting the engine. Wrongful or trespassory taking is taking from the possession of the owner without consent. The thief, in effect, "trespasses" on the possession of the owner in order to remove the property from him or her. Possession originally meant in the physical presence of the owner, but came to include constructive possession of goods not under physical control of the owner, such as goods in the custody of an employee, an item given over for repair while the owner waits, or a lost item. As you will see in the discussion of embezzlement, false pretenses, and extortion, consent and possession are difficult to define and have a great effect on the decision of what crime to charge.

Carrying away is the element of asportation that we saw in kidnapping. In larceny, however, the amount of movement required is only slight, such as the few inches it takes to begin to remove a wallet from a pocket. "Carrying" can be the driving away of a car, or may not involve touching the property at all. A student who finds an instructor's exam answer key on a table in the library and without touching it sells it to a second student who carries it off in a bookpack, is responsible for the wrongful taking and asportation of the key by use of an innocent agent. The transfer of funds by wire from a federally insured savings and loan bank to an account elsewhere fulfilled the element of asportation in *U.S. v. Morgan* (9th Cir. 1986).

Determining sufficient asportation is difficult when goods are taken from the shelf of a store and carried toward the exit, but the taker is apprehended before leaving the store. Usually some evidence to show intent is necessary, such as concealment of the goods in a pocket. The defendant in *Welch v. Commonwealth* (Va. App. 1992) was confronted by the store manager as he was pushing a shopping cart containing two television sets through an outdoor gardening department where there were no cash registers. The defendant fled, warning the pursuing manager, "Don't make me shoot you," which was enough to indicate intent to steal. *State v. Richard* (Neb. 1984) overturned the conviction of a defendant who was stopped as he approached the checkout, because intent was not sufficiently shown by the circumstances.

The property that is subject to larceny under common law is tangible personal property that can be physically moved. Although modern codes with consolidated theft statutes include intangible property and services, codes that rely on common law larceny do not. Use of a landfill without paying fees was not larceny in *Commonwealth v. Rivers* (Mass. App. 1991). A defendant who stole a credit card and made purchases with it could be convicted only of theft of the value of the card itself. The merchandise and credit line available through the card were not subject to larceny, so his conviction was reduced from grand to petit larceny [*Owolabi v. Commonwealth* (Va. App. 1993)].

It is the owners loss, other than sentimental value, rather than the thief's gain that determines valuation for grading purposes. Theft of unendorsed checks was graded according to their face value rather than that they were worthless to the thief [*Gallegos v. State* (N.M. 1992)].

As in crimes against habitation, the property must belong to "another." Some states and the Model Penal Code hold that the property of partners or spouses is subject to larceny, except when the property is held in common by spouses, such as household goods. In *State v. Kuntz* (Mont. 1994), the defendant was convicted of felony theft for diverting partnership funds to a personal bank account. He "exerted unauthorized control" over property with intent to deprive the owner, a consolidated theft crime rather than common law larceny. Following common law, however, *State v. Durant* (Or. App. 1993) reversed the conviction of a defendant who had taken property from a business where he had 40 percent ownership. Larceny charges were reinstated against a defendant who took his own car from a wrecking service where he owed towing and storage charges [*People v. Sheldon* (Mich. App. 1995)].

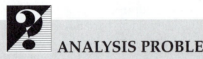

ANALYSIS PROBLEM

5–1. What guidelines would you offer in shoplifting cases such as *Welch* and *Richard?* What charges besides larceny could be brought?

3. Mens Rea in Larceny

Intent must be to permanently deprive the possessor of the property. Temporarily taking without permission, such as joyriding in another's car, is a less serious offense in most jurisdictions. Intent to pay the owner is not a defense, unless the property was for sale. An intent to return the property can be a defense if there is evidence of the intent along with a present ability to do so. As you can see in *State v. Langford* (La. 1986) at the end of the consolidated theft section, the fact that the money has already been spent and cannot be returned negates an intent to return it. The belief by the taker that he or she has a **claim of right** on the property, that is, that the property actually belongs to him or her, is a defense. Sally lends Joan her string of pearls for the holidays and Joan fails to return it. Later, if Sally takes a string of pearls that is lying on a table in Joan's house, believing it to be hers, she has a defense to the charge of larceny. A robber who said he was only recovering the money he loaned to the victim did not have a claim of right, however, according to the decision in *State v. Bull* (N.J. 1992). Under a New Jersey law that limits such claims to specific property, the money would have had to be the exact same bills that had been loaned to the victim for the claim to apply. The person leasing a piece of property to another would not have a claim of right on that property as long as the terms of the lease were in effect.

Larceny requires the concurrence of the taking and carrying away with an intent to steal. A defendant took clothes from a store rack, hid it on her person, and left the store without paying for it. When she saw a security officer following her, she ran back into the store and threw the clothing under a rack. *State v. Ellis* (La. App. 1993) affirmed her conviction, because her criminal intent was shown by circumstances to concur with the taking. Modern statutes, however, extend the definition of larceny to include criminal intent formed after an innocent taking.

4. Types of Larceny

Classic larceny is by stealth, where the thief sneaks behind the owner's back to steal the goods. Another type of larceny occurs when the defendant has innocent custody of property of another then decides to keep it, such as a finder taking lost property without an attempt to return it, a receiver keeping property that has been delivered by mistake, and a **bailee**—an employee or agent caring for the property of another— who converts the owner's property to the bailee's own use.

A defendant employed by a nonprofit organization conducted courses in basic trauma life support at a hospital and several mining companies. He took payment for the courses from the hospital and mines, deposited it in the organization's account, paid expenses from the account, then spent the rest as his own personal income. He was convicted of larceny by a bailee of the money received from the hospital that was

claim of right:
defense to theft; belief by the defendant that the property actually belongs to the defendant.

bailee:
an employee or agent caring for the property of another.

in excess of expenses. *Lahr v. State* (Wyo. 1992) reversed his conviction because the trauma education program was not owned by the hospital, and their payment to the defendant gave him "ownership" of the money. The court remarked that overbilling is a civil rather than criminal matter. Read *State v. Langford* (La. 1986) for an example of mistaken delivery larceny.

A third type of larceny is larceny by trick. It is the taking of custody but not title to property, using written or spoken misrepresentation of fact or false promises to achieve temporary custody (by borrowing or renting, for example) in order to remove the property from the owner. At this point the owner still has constructive possession of the property. The crime is completed when the thief takes the property under unauthorized control by selling it or keeping it for the thief's own use.

Larceny by trick was first defined by the English case of *Rex v. Pear* (Cr. Cas. Res. 1779). The defendant rented a horse to go to one town, intending instead to go to another town and sell the horse, which he did. The owner gave consent to take the horse, so the previous element of trespass on the possession of the owner had to be stretched to include the constructive possession that the owner retained throughout the rental. The trespassory taking occurred when the horse was sold. A larceny by trick conviction for obtaining credit cards by using false Social Security numbers was affirmed in *Owolabi v. Commonwealth* (Va. App. 1993). Likewise, in the previous example of the borrowing of the string of pearls, if Joan intended from the first to permanently deprive Sally of the pearls, she was guilty of larceny by trick.

Remember that the following crimes grew out of the common law offense of larceny, and that they share many of the same elements. We will concentrate on the ways they differ from larceny.

C. EMBEZZLEMENT

When a bank teller who stole money deposited by a customer was acquitted of larceny in *The King v. Bazeley* (K.B. 1799), it was clear that a new law was needed to cover theft without the element of trespass. In embezzlement, the offender has been given legal possession of goods or money by its owner. The larceny element of "taking" is replaced by **"conversion,"** or misappropriation, for one's own use of property in one's lawful possession. In some jurisdictions, this person must be an agent, fiduciary, public officer, or attorney. In others, anyone to whom property is entrusted, such as repairers, cleaners, or parking lot attendants, may be guilty of embezzlement. Where the latter group is excluded from prosecution for embezzlement, larceny by trick may be the appropriate charge.

conversion: misappropriation for one's own use, as in embezzlement.

The question is whether the agent has the greater authority of possession of the property and would be guilty of embezzlement with conversion, or has the lesser authority of custody (while the owner retains constructive possession) and would be guilty of larceny. Both possession and custody are covered by the terms *control* and *care* of property in some embezzlement statutes.

A contractor was paid in advance to do five remodeling jobs. For three of the jobs the prepayment was for materials needed to do the work. For the other two jobs, the prepayment was simply a part of the total cost of the job to the homeowner. In all cases, the contractor kept the money but did not do the work. He was convicted on five counts of embezzlement. *State v. Joy* (Wash. 1993) affirmed the three counts for money that was intended to purchase materials, because that was still "owned" by the homeowner. The other two counts were remanded for retrial on theft by deception, because the contractor had obtained "ownership" of the money when he was paid.

Intent to deprive, usually expressed by the term *fraudulently*, is the mens rea for embezzlement. A county sheriff who temporarily deposited in his own account and collected interest on funds intended for the purchase of food for prisoners was acquitted because neither the county nor the prisoners were deprived, *State v. Matthews*

(Okla. Cr. 1991). A chairman of the board of trustees who issued checks to himself from employee health and pension funds, however, was convicted on separate counts of embezzlement for each check, *U.S. v. Busacca* (6th Cir. 1991).

D. FALSE PRETENSES OR FRAUD

1. Transfer of Title

England closed another gap in the larceny law in 1757 by passing a statute criminalizing fraud. One who knowingly and intentionally makes a false representation of material past or present fact to cause the owner to give the offender title to the owner's property has committed the crime of obtaining property by false pretenses, or fraud. The difference from larceny by trick is the transfer not simply of possession but of the title, actual ownership. The permanence of the transfer is key. In larceny by trick, money or property is borrowed, leased, or otherwise temporarily in the possession of the defendant. An attorney who suggested the victim give him money to bribe the police, but kept the money for his own use, was guilty of larceny, because the money was to be in his possession only until it passed to the police [*Graham v. U.S* (D.C. Cir. 1950)]. False pretenses, however, involve a sale or otherwise permanent transfer of title to property or payment of money. Conviction for false pretenses was affirmed in *State v. Jones* (Utah 1982) against the representative of a company claiming to be a developer and marketer of inventions, when its only real function was to collect thousands of dollars from hopeful inventors.

2. False Representation of Fact

The representation of fact may be in words or in actions. A defendant's offering an ATM card for payment at a supermarket was a representation that the card was valid, even though it was not [*People v. Whight* (Cal. App. 1995)]. Hiding facts may be an alternate element in this crime, but mere silence is not sufficient.

Although traditional statutes limit the element of false representation to past or present fact, modern consolidated theft statutes may include false promises (future intentions). People who are unable to pay bills as promised lack fraudulent intent and are not culpable under these laws. Statements of value can constitute false pretenses, particularly when they are made by someone who is knowledgeable, such as a stockbroker who said certain stock was almost worthless so he could buy it from the owner for much less than its true value [*State v. Nash* (Kan. 1922)]. "Puffing" in advertising ("you won't find a better car on the market") is not taken literally by most shoppers, however.

3. Reliance

Causation is an important factor in false pretenses. The misrepresentation must be the cause of the transfer of title to the property or money. If the victim passes title to the defendant even though the victim knows the defendant is lying, does not believe the lies, or would have made the transaction regardless of the lies, then the defendant is not guilty of false pretenses. In these cases, however, the defendant is guilty of attempted false pretenses.[1]

In *People v. Whight,* when the defendant presented the invalid ATM card, the cashier tried to check it through a computer system but received no response. The cashier's reliance on the defendant's representation of the card as valid was the key element of the crime. If the computer had reported the card as valid and the cashier had relied on that report, the crime would not have been complete.

A fraudulent credit card transaction involves the reliance of the seller on a misrepresentation by the user of the card. It is the issuer of the card, however, who suffers the loss, so this type of fraud may slip through the cracks of false pretense laws. Some states have passed specific credit card statutes to fill the gap. The federal credit card fraud statute is 18 U.S.C.A. § 1029.

EXHIBIT 5–1
Levels of Possession in Theft

LARCENY BY TRICK	EMBEZZLEMENT	FALSE PRETENSES
Has temporary *custody*, then takes to permanently deprive.	Has authority of *possession*, then converts to permanently deprive.	Makes false statement to gain title of *ownership*.

4. Mens Rea

The false pretenses offender knowingly misrepresents fact, or at least "creates the impression that he believes something to be true when in fact he has no belief on the subject. . . ."[2] An honest and reasonable belief in their claim that the electronic machine they sold would cure almost any illness was a sufficient defense to reverse the defendants' false pretenses conviction in *People v. Marsh* (Cal. 1962). Besides knowingly making a false representation, the offender must also intend to defraud; that is, intend for the victim to rely on the misrepresentation to pass title to property or money to which the offender has no right.

5. Federal Fraud Crimes

Federal fraud and false statement crimes are enumerated in 18 U.S.C.A. §§ 1001 to 1035. These statutes include fraudulent bank entries and transactions (§ 1005), fraud in connection with access devices such as credit cards (§ 1029), fraud in connection with computers (§ 1030), and other fraudulent transactions with federal agencies. Fraudulent use of credit cards in interstate commerce is covered under 15 U.S.C.A. § 1644, and defrauding a bank under 18 U.S.C.A. §1344.

False impersonation as a citizen or United States officer to claim citizenship, obtain anything of value, or make an arrest or search is prohibited in 18 U.S.C.A. §§ 911 to 917. Fraudulent securities exchanges are prohibited in 15 U.S.C.A. § 78. Federal statutes also prohibit false claims (18 U.S.C.A. §§ 287 to 289), bankruptcy fraud (18 U.S.C.A. § 152), and tax fraud (26 U.S.C.A. §§ 7201 to 7217).

Mail fraud is covered in 18 U.S.C.A. §§ 1341 to 1347. These statutes prohibit use of the United States Postal Service; any interstate carrier; or wire, radio, or television transmission across state lines to send fraudulent communications. Under these laws, simply sending the communication with the intent to defraud is sufficient; the communication does not need to be relied on, or even to reach its target.

E.   BAD CHECKS

The use of bad checks presents difficulties in establishing the elements of false pretenses, so it has become the subject of separate statutes with lesser penalties. These statutes vary from state to state. Most do not require that the transaction be completed with the offender receiving something of value. Some require an intent to defraud, but in most only the knowledge that there are insufficient funds to cover the check is sufficient. Knowledge is shown when the bank refuses payment and the offender fails to make the check good within ten days of notice. A defendant who wrote twenty-two checks within seventeen days knowing there were no funds in the account and making no effort to make offsetting deposits was convicted on all but one count. One of the checks was postdated, so his conviction on that count was reversed because it did not misrepresent a present fact. Postdated checks are not payable until the stated date [*U.S. v. Aguilar* (5th Cir. 1992)]. Insufficient funds checks account for by far the greatest number of bad checks; no-account checks make up a small percentage; and forgeries are even less prevalent.[3]

F. RECEIVING STOLEN PROPERTY

The crime of receiving stolen property consists of knowingly or intentionally receiving, retaining, or disposing of property of another that has been the subject of theft. A defendant cannot be convicted of both stealing and receiving the same property. A defendant's conviction of receiving a stolen car was affirmed even though he admitted that he stole it, because he had not been charged with the theft [*Garcia v. State* (Wyo. 1989)]. Penalties for receiving are often as severe as for the larceny itself.

The receiver must assume control of the property from the thief for at least a short time. Evidence that a defendant placed his hands on a car knowing it was stolen and knowing the driver, and having intent "to drive around in it," was not enough to establish that he had exercised control over the stolen car, so he was allowed to withdraw his guilty plea [*State v. McCoy* (N.J. 1989)]. The case was remanded for trial on a possible attempt charge. The offender need not actually possess the property; buying and selling without touching is enough. Under some statutes, the receiver must benefit from the theft either financially or by use of the property.

Knowledge that the goods are stolen is often inferred from circumstances such as the furtiveness of the seller, unusually low price of the goods, or known character of the seller. A defendant arrested for attempted auto theft physically resisted a search that revealed a stolen wallet in his boot, enough to show that he knew the wallet was stolen [*Gibson v. State* (Ind. 1994)].

Stolen goods statutes are aimed at large-scale fencing operations, so in the case of likely fences such as pawn shops or secondhand dealers, negligence or recklessness may be enough to convict. Intent to deprive the owner is also part of the mens rea, so those who acquire stolen goods with the intent to return them to their rightful owner, such as police, are not guilty of receiving stolen goods.

G. FORGERY AND UTTERING A FORGED INSTRUMENT

Forgery and uttering, or issuing, a forged instrument are both felonies, usually regardless of the value, because they damage confidence in commercial and legal documents. Both the individual property owner and society are harmed. Forgery and uttering are completely separate crimes, so one who forges a document and then passes it into circulation is guilty of two separate felonies. Federal obligations or securities, such as currency, stamps, and public records, are protected under 18 U.S.C.A. §§ 471 to 510.

Making a false document or altering an authentic one is the actus reus of forgery. It is, essentially, false pretenses with regard to documents. In most jurisdictions, the document must have legal significance. Some statutes list included documents, and others refer to "any writing having legal efficacy." The Model Penal Code § 224, concerned with the theft of reputation as well as of property, broadens the definition to "symbols of value, right, privilege, or identification," which could include physicians' prescriptions, tokens, badges, diplomas, and so forth. Computer records pose another problem. In *People v. Avila* (Colo. App. 1988), the forgery conviction of a defendant who had deleted drivers' records from a state agency computer disk was upheld.

Changes must be to a material part of a document to constitute forgery. Cases vary about whether changing the amount on a check is forgery rather than false pretenses. Most often, if only the numbers and not the written amount is altered, the offense is not forgery. Signing the name of another to a check without authorization or writing a check on a nonexistent account is forgery.

The mens rea of forgery is the specific intent to defraud with the forged instrument, that is, acquire property or some other advantage, usually shown by circumstances. It is not necessary that the forger succeed in this aim; the crime is complete with the falsification of the document and the presence of intent. A parole officer who married a prison inmate, then forged a removal order with the intent to help him escape prison had her conviction affirmed in *People v. Gaul-Alexander* (Cal. App. 1995). The forgery was against the right of the state rather than for financial gain.

Uttering is passing or attempting to pass false documents on to others with intent to defraud. The offender may or may not be the one who falsified the document.

Federal obligations or securities such as currency and other financial and ownership documents including electronic fund transfers, stamps, and public records are protected from counterfeiting, forgery, and uttering under 18 U.S.C.A. §§ 470 to 514.

H. ROBBERY

Robbery includes all the elements of larceny—taking and carrying away the property of another with the intent to permanently deprive the other of ownership—with the addition of two more elements. Property must be taken from the person of the victim or in the victim's presence, and force or threat of immediate force must be used in the taking. These elements add a degree of danger to the victim that other theft crimes (except extortion, to be discussed next) do not have, so robbery is universally punished more severely than other kinds of theft.

Instead of grading on the basis of the value of goods stolen as in other theft offenses, robbery is graded on the amount of force used. Most serious is the use of deadly weapons or what appears to be deadly weapons, or severe injury to a victim. Presence of accomplices, even slight injury, or simply displaying a weapon might fall in the middle ground, whereas an unarmed attack or threat is considered least serious. The vulnerability of the victim may also be considered in the grading scheme, with robbery against the elderly or persons with disabilities punished more severely.

Any force greater than the effort used in taking and carrying away the property qualifies for robbery. The robbery conviction of a purse snatcher who had broken the strap of the purse without putting the victim in danger was upheld in *People v. Middleton* (N.Y. Sup. 1991). As in assault, the use of a deadly weapon is an aggravating factor. The definition of deadly weapon is broad. A plate glass window sufficed when the robber spun the victim into it in the course of a purse snatching, *People v. Coe* (N.Y. App. Div. 1990), and a glass soft drink bottle used in the robbery of a cab driver was considered capable of causing death or serious injury in *Enriquez v. State* (Tex. App. 1992).

The force or threat need not be against the possessor of the property, but can be against another person present. Although force may be minimal, a threat must be of severe consequence, death or great bodily harm, and usually has to instill such fear or apprehension in victims that they actually give up the property. *State v. Birch* (Iowa 1991) allowed a robbery conviction to stand only on proof of the defendant's intent to commit theft with a threat to the victim's life. The victim was not in fear and, in fact, had challenged the defendant to produce the gun he claimed to have, which was nonexistent. A defendant shouting, "Stop or I will shoot," sufficed for an aggravated robbery conviction in *Lowe v. State* (Ark. App. 1991). There is some difference among jurisdictions concerning whether the fear produced by the threat should be reasonable, or the actual fear felt by the victim even though that fear might be exaggerated by a particular sensitivity.

Statutes and cases are divided as to when the force must occur during the course of the robbery. Some require it to be before or contemporaneous with the taking, whereas force after the fact is treated as a separate assault. Others allow force occurring during immediate flight from the scene of larceny to constitute robbery. A defendant who stole a coin-filled container from a slot machine player was convicted of robbery because of his collisions with other casino patrons as he tried to escape [*State v. Sewell* (N.J. 1992)]. *State v. Lewis* (N.M. App. 1993), at the end of this section, clarifies the issue of the relationship necessary between the force and the theft to become robbery.

The claim of right to property targeted by robbery is increasingly being rejected as a valid defense. A defendant who tried to collect money he had left with the victim before the victim was scheduled to leave the country used threats and eventually shot and killed the victim. In affirming his robbery conviction, the court in *State v. Mejia* (N.J. 1995) stated that the claim of right is "utterly incompatible with and has no place in any ordered and orderly society such as ours, which eschews self-help through violence."

Robbery of federally chartered or insured banks is prohibited under 18 U.S.C.A. § 2113. The use of a victim's credit card in an automated teller machine, however, was not bank robbery according to the decision in *Clay v. Commonwealth* (Va. App. 1992). Can you reason why? By using threat against the victim, who had constructive possession of the money in the account, the robber took the money from her presence, so she and not the bank was the victim of robbery. Robbery of United States property, money, or mail matter is prohibited by 18 U.S.C.A. §§ 2112 and 2114. The Hobbs Act, 18 U.S.C.A. § 1951, establishes the crime of obstructing interstate commerce by robbery or extortion.

In the early 1990s an outbreak of automobile robberies from motorists on the street gave rise to the federal Anti-Car Theft Act of 1992, 18 U.S.C.A. § 2119, and corresponding state laws. The new crime of carjacking prohibits taking of a motor vehicle from another person by the use of force, violence, or intimidation with intent to cause death or serious bodily harm. Penalties are much more severe than those for simple auto theft. The federal statute survived a constitutionality challenge in *U.S. v. Cobb* (4th Cir. 1998).

 ANALYSIS PROBLEMS

5–2. What are the pros and cons of passing legislation quickly to deal with new threats in our society, such as carjacking?

5–3. If the victim is particularly timid and feels fear simply in the presence of a thief, should that person's sensitivity be protected by robbery laws?

STATE v. LEWIS
Court of Appeals of New Mexico, 1993.
867 P.2d 1231 N.M. App. 1993
[Citations omitted]

OPINION
BLACK, Judge

Defendant appeals from convictions of armed robbery and conspiracy to commit armed robbery. . . .

FACTS

The robbery victim testified that he was visiting Albuquerque to conduct business, visit friends, and see his former girl-friend. During his visit to the city, the victim met a prostitute who agreed to have sex with him. The victim and prostitute arranged to meet in a specific motel room. The victim de-scribed the motel room as having a front room that was connected to a back bedroom. There was a light on in the front room, and some of that light came into the back bedroom.

The prostitute instructed the victim to remove his clothing. The victim did so and laid his clothing on a chair in the front room and then folded his coat and placed it over his clothing. The victim testified that he had between $1500 and $1600 in his coat pocket, and that, when he laid his coat over his clothing, he did so in a manner such that he would recognize if anyone had moved it.

The victim and prostitute proceeded to the back bedroom where they engaged in sexual intercourse. While so engaged, the victim heard noises that the prostitute said were probably the neighbors. After intercourse, the prostitute went into the front room and the victim lay in bed for a few minutes. When he got up and went into the front room to get dressed, the victim noticed that his coat was not in the same position as he had left it. With his back to the prostitute, the victim looked into his wallet and noticed that his money was missing. When he turned around, the prostitute was pointing a gun at him.

The victim testified that at that point a man came out from the back bedroom and the prostitute handed the gun to the man. The couple then ordered the victim out of the motel room, but the victim demanded the return of his money. The three left the room, and, as the couple entered a vehicle, the victim grabbed hold of the vehicle and continued to demand the return of his money. The victim held onto the car as the couple, driving erratically to try to shake the victim loose, left the scene. The victim finally jumped from the car and eventually located a police officer to whom he gave an account of the incident as well as a description of the man.

ISSUE

Defendant argues that the trial court erred in denying his motion for a directed verdict because the evidence was insufficient to convict him of armed robbery. In analyzing sufficiency of the evidence issues, the inquiry is whether substantial evidence exists to support a verdict of guilty beyond a reasonable doubt with respect to each essential element of a crime charged. Specifically, defendant argues that the evidence revealed that the money was taken from the victim by stealth when the victim was not present, and that the only alleged use of force was during the escape. Defendant argues robbery can be committed only when force or intimidation is used as the method of requiring the victim to relinquish his property.

A review of the facts of this case reveals that the victim's property was removed from his clothing either during the time when he was engaging in sex or immediately thereafter when he was lying in bed. Therefore, the money already had been taken when the victim noticed it was missing. When the victim turned to confront the prostitute about the missing money, she was pointing a gun at him and only then did Defendant enter the room. These facts present the Court with the question of whether Defendant's forceful and intimidating actions with the gun, after the victim's money had already been taken through the use of stealth, are sufficient to sustain a robbery conviction. In other words, the question we are faced with is whether the use, or threatened use, of force must necessarily be concurrent with the taking of the property from the victim.

DISCUSSION

The use of force, violence, or intimidation is an essential element of robbery. Historically, the difference between larceny and robbery has turned on whether and when force was

used. Blackstone said, "if one privately steals sixpence from the person of another, and afterwards keeps it by putting him in fear, this is no robbery, for the fear is subsequent . . ." 4 William Blackstone, *Commentaries* 242.

In New Mexico, "[r]obbery consists of the theft of anything of value from the person of another or from the immediate control of another, by use or threatened use of force or violence." NMSA 1978, § 30-16-2 (Repl. Pamp. 1984). New Mexico case law makes it clear that, in order to convict for such an offense, the use or threatened use of force must be the factor by which the property is removed from the victim's possession. . . .

Under the facts of the present case, the victim's money was removed and separated from his person by stealth. Defendant clearly had control over the victim's money once it had been taken from his clothing. Defendant's use of a weapon only after the money was separated from the victim was merely an action to hold victim at bay as he escaped from the motel. For that action, it appears that defendant could have been charged with aggravated assault. However, . . . the use of force to retain property or to facilitate escape does not satisfy the force element necessary for the crime of robbery. Thus, there was insufficient evidence to support Defendant's conviction for armed robbery.

It is true, as the State argues, that other jurisdictions have interpreted different statutory language to sustain robbery convictions when the force is used after the removal of the property. The cases diverge based largely on the relevant statutory language defining robbery. Indeed, some of these jurisdictions have statutes which specifically define robbery to include the use of force to retain property immediately after it has been taken. The Model Penal Code takes this approach by defining robbery to include any violence or fear threatened or inflicted during an attempt or commission of a theft or in flight after an attempt or commission of theft.

Thus, while it may be true that "modern code" sections define robbery to allow any use of force during or after a taking of the property, it is up to the legislature, not the courts, to revise the statutory definition of robbery. . . .

We do recognize, however, that some jurisdictions have interpreted robbery statutes similar to our own to encompass situations where force is used to retain property immediately after its nonviolent taking. . . . Regardless of whether robbery is a continuing offense, New Mexico case law clearly holds that force must be the lever by which property is separated from the victim, and thus the use of force subsequent to that separation is not sufficient.

CONCLUSION

Based on the above, we hold that the trial court erred in denying Defendant's motion for a directed verdict. Accordingly, we reverse.

IT IS SO ORDERED.

I. EXTORTION

Like robbery, extortion or blackmail is a form of larceny that puts the victim in danger of harm. There is no present force in extortion, however, and the threat is of future harm rather than immediate harm. Also, the taking of property need not be from the presence of the victim. The common law offense dealt only with public officials who used their influence to force others to pay illegal fees, but the statutory offense includes anyone who intentionally and wrongfully obtains money or property as a result of the threats. A county commissioner received payment from an undercover FBI agent posing as a real estate developer seeking rezoning of a tract of land. Even though the commissioner had not demanded the payment, his extortion occurred "under color of official right," and his conviction was affirmed under the Hobbs Act [*Evans v. U.S.* (1992)].

The harm threatened may be to someone other than the possessor of the property, and does not have to be physical injury. Threatened property damage or even exposure to shame or ridicule, even if the information disclosed is the truth, is enough. A defendant who had been participating in a criminal investigation against a person who had been making harassing phone calls to him, called that person and offered to refrain from pressing criminal charges in return for payment of money. His belief that he was entitled to the money and that the victim was guilty was no defense, and his conviction for extortion was affirmed in *State v. Greenspan* (N.C. App. 1989).

Some jurisdictions require that money or property actually be obtained by the offender's threat for extortion to be complete. In others, the crime is complete when the threat is delivered with intent to carry it out. Some require that the victim actually be put in fear; others only that the offender have the intent to create fear and issue threats that would instill fear in a reasonable person, whether or not the victim is really frightened. The claim of right is recognized in some jurisdictions as a defense to extortion, but others consider threat an inappropriate way to collect debts.

Sending extortion threats through the mail is a federal offense under 18 U.S.C.A. §§ 871 to 880. Sections 891 to 896 deal with extortionate credit transactions. The Hobbs Act, 18 U.S.C.A. § 1951, controls extortion in interstate commerce.

ANALYSIS PROBLEM

5–4. How does a newspaper article revealing embarrassing facts about a political candidate differ from extortion?

J. CONSOLIDATED THEFT

Because property crimes all descended from the very severe common law crime of larceny in response to specific problems, they became a fragmented group of statutes all seeking to address the same basic offense, the misappropriation of property belonging to another. Many modern statutes have consolidated these theft crimes under one umbrella statute that avoids the sorting out of custody and possession, types of property and services subject to the crime, and time lines of intent. Robbery, forgery, and bad checks are always separate. Some states keep extortion and some false pretenses offenses separate.

Language in the consolidated statutes is often more general, "obtains" instead of "takes and carries away," for example, and accommodations are made for new means of access, products, and services that emerge from the technology explosion. Where theft is consolidated, a bill of particulars usually gives notice of specific charges to the defendant. The Model Penal Code consolidates theft in § 223. The federal comprehensive theft statute is 18 U.S.C.A. § 641. Knowledge of federal ownership is not an element. More than half the states have consolidated theft statutes.

Read *State v. Langford* (La. 1986) for an interpretation of the elements of theft and bad check offenses.

EXHIBIT 5–2
Sample Jury Instructions

THEFT OF GOVERNMENT MONEY OR PROPERTY (18 U.S.C. § 641)

Title 18, United States Code, section 641, makes it a crime for anyone to embezzle [steal] [convert] any money or other property belonging to the United States having a value of more than $100.

For you to find the defendant guilty of this crime, you must be convinced that the government has proved each of the following beyond a reasonable doubt:

First: That the money or property described in the indictment, _____ , [describe property] belonged to the United States government and had a value in excess of $100 at the time alleged;

Second: That the defendant embezzled [stole] [converted] such money [property] to the defendant's own use [to the use of another]; and

Third: That the defendant did so knowing the property was not his, and with intent to deprive the owner of the use [benefit] of the money [property].

The word "value" means the face, par, or market value, or cost price, either wholesale or retail, whichever is greater.

It is not necessary to prove that the defendant knew that the United States government owned the property at the time of the wrongful taking.

[To "embezzle" means the wrongful, intentional taking of money or property of another after the money or property has lawfully come within the possession or control of the person taking it.]

[To "steal" or "convert" means the wrongful taking of money or property belonging to another with intent to deprive the owner of its use or benefit either temporarily or permanently. Any appreciable change of the location of the property with the intent to deprive constitutes a stealing whether or not there is an actual removal of it from the owner's premises.]

No particular type of movement or carrying away is required to constitute a "taking."

Pattern Jury Instructions (Criminal Cases), 5th Circuit (St. Paul, MN: West Group, 1990), § 2.31, with permission.

STATE v. LANGFORD.
Supreme Court of Louisiana, 1986.
483 So.2d 979 La. 1986
[Citations omitted]

CALOGERO, Justice

On March 19, 1984, defendant John A. Langford was convicted of theft in excess of $500.00 from the Hibernia National Bank of New Orleans. He was sentenced to eight years' imprisonment at hard labor. The Court of Appeal affirmed. We granted writs to consider whether there was adequate proof of a non-consensual taking and/or a permanent intent to deprive the bank of its funds.

FACTS

On March 11, 1981, defendant met with a vice president in charge of lending at Hibernia to discuss borrowing $225,000 to purchase a Metairie restaurant. Two days later the vice president personally informed defendant that the loan was refused, primarily because of defendant's poor credit record. Within a week, defendant returned to the same branch of the Hibernia to open an interest-bearing checking account, known as a NOW account (negotiable orders of withdrawal). . . . Defendant exhibited a Louisiana driver's license, listed his place of employment as a company known as Furniture Distributors and deposited $5,362.21 to open the account. He neither inquired about nor requested overdraft privileges; nor was he told that he would be afforded any such privilege.

NOW checking accounts were an innovation for Hibernia. Prior to January, 1981, federal regulations did not permit banking institutions to pay interest on checking accounts. With the change in the regulations, Hibernia joined other area banks in offering interest-bearing checking accounts to their customers. To accomplish this, it was necessary for the bank to purchase, install and modify a computer program within a very short period of time. . . .

[T]he computer program came with a set of Out of Balance Processing Codes (OBPs), which instructed the computer on routing and check payment information. . . . Code "01" instructed the computer to honor the check, regardless of the amount, at no charge to the customer. In other words, an "01" code gave the customer unlimited overdraft privileges. The coding was an internal matter; individual customers would not be aware, by scrutiny of account numbers or statements, whether their accounts had been assigned to the "01," "03" or "05" codes. . . .

A former customer service representative at Hibernia's main branch testified that she placed checking account information into the computer during March of 1981. Unaware of the significance or meaning of the codes, and pursuant to instructions received from another employee, she used an "01" code on *all* new accounts. As a result, eighty-four main office checking accounts received the "01" OBP designation. The error was compounded when the bank's monitoring controls failed, notably the routing and handling of Daily and Monthly Overdraft Reports. An "01" coding indicated to the bookkeeping department that any overdraft had already been approved by an account officer. Meanwhile, the Overdraft Reports were not being delivered to the account officers but, instead, were being discarded. The officers, however, had not been told to expect the Reports and, in the absence of inquiries from bookkeeping, had no idea of the status of "01" accounts assigned to them.

Defendant began using his NOW account. After the initial deposit of $5,362.21 on March 18, 1981, defendant made no further deposits. Within two weeks, the account was overdrawn.

Defendant continued writing checks, however. He also began receiving overdraft notices from the bank. According to testimony of Hibernia officials, an overdraft notice is a computer-generated form sent one per check, "whenever there [is] activity that over[draws] the account. . . ." Such a notice did not mean that an account had been reviewed by a bank employee. In defendant's case, these notices were sent daily. By the end of September, 1981 or within about 195 days, 198 such overdraft notices were sent to the defendant, each of them reflecting the amount of a given honored but NSF check, and a correspondingly increased negative, or overdraft, balance. Bank officials conceded the notices did not contain "specific wording . . ." telling customers to come in and make a deposit but, as one witness put it, "[t]here are some things that are understood." In ever-increasing amounts over the six-and-one-half month period, defendant continued writing checks. The first of his overdraft notices showed a negative balance of $237.79; the 198th and last, $848,904.39.

Finally, on the afternoon of September 23, 1981, the bank received a call from a curious teller at Fidelity Homestead. Defendant was attempting to obtain a certificate of deposit with a large check drawn on his Hibernia NOW account. In a routine check of his account balance, officials learned that defendant was overdrawn by $848,904.39. . . .

The following day defendant and his attorney met with bank officials. Hibernia's general counsel served written demand for immediate payment of the entire sum. Defendant, and his lawyer, countered with an offer to repay the balance over a five year period, at 8% interest, with interest payments monthly and principal payments annually. Hibernia declined defendant's offer and began civil proceedings in several parishes within the state in an attempt to recover the funds. . . . The defendant was thereafter charged with theft.

At his trial the facts recited above were proven. . . .

After a bench trial, the judge found the defendant guilty as charged of theft in excess of $500.00, and sentenced him to imprisonment for eight years with the Department of Corrections, with credit for time served.

. . .

ASSIGNMENT OF ERROR NO. 1

As already noted defendant contends that there was insufficient evidence to prove that the taking was non-consensual. The state, of course, had the burden of proving that the taking of the money was without the consent of Hibernia. First of all, there was a taking. At the least that taking occurred after the NSF checks were honored and the money came into defendant's possession (if that was by virtue of a mistake rather than consent on the bank's part), when defendant diverted or used the funds, instead of returning them. With respect to the bank's non-consent the Court of Appeal found that "[t]he evidence absolutely precludes the possibility that the bank consented to defendant's conduct. The bank was a victim of it's own mistakes, one in the erroneous coding of the account when it was first opened, and the other in the destruction of the computer printouts before they could be reviewed by a responsible official. The bank's intention was to allow no overdrafts on NOW accounts but this was frustrated by its unfortunate errors. That the bank consented to the defendant's taking $848,000 as some sort of loan is not a reasonable hypothesis when its refusal to loan defendant $225,000 one week before the account was opened is considered."

With this assessment by the Court of Appeal we agree. The evidence overwhelmingly supports the fact that no human person with the bank ever made a conscious decision to honor defendant's checks notwithstanding the account's overdraft status. Equally supported, and bearing on the aspect of the taking, is the conclusion that the defendant had to have known a mistake was being made.

> "It is well settled that the recipient of the mistaken delivery who appropriates the property commits a trespass in the taking, and so is guilty of larceny, if, realizing the mistake at the moment he takes delivery, he then forms an intent to steal the property."

State v. Langford, supra, at 43, citing LaFave & Scott, Criminal Law § 85 (1972).

Defendant's argument that the record also supports the opposite conclusion, i.e., that the repeated honoring of the checks by the bank could be reasonably interpreted as consent to loan the money to the defendant, is not persuasive. . . .

The facts established by the direct evidence and inferred from the circumstantial evidence were sufficient for a rational trier of fact to conclude beyond a reasonable doubt that defendant was guilty of the essential element of the crime of theft that the taking was non-consensual.

Defendant's first assignment is without merit.

ASSIGNMENT OF ERROR NO. 2

By his second assignment of error, defendant contends that the state failed to prove that he intended to deprive the bank permanently of its money. . . .

The most favorable aspect of this case from defendant's perspective, concerning proof of intent to permanently deprive, is the manner in which defendant came by the bank's money. Because his NSF checks in ever increasing amounts were routinely being honored, and were simply prompting increasing negative balance overdraft notices (albeit up to

$848,000), any reasonable person would assume that sooner or later the mistake would be discovered and the bank would call for repayment. . . . Furthermore, the evidence which the prosecution chose to present at trial does not show any apparent effort on defendant's part to hide the greater part of the money.

On the other hand there was significant evidence that defendant intended to deprive the bank permanently of its money upon receipt, or at least some of it, for in addition to his not giving any of the money back, he spent at least $12,000 on items in the nature of support and disbursed $113,000 in large checks to various payees other than financial institutions. The greater part of the money, $724,000, comprised checks made payable to homesteads and *apparently* deposited into accounts, *possibly* in defendant's name, in the respective homesteads. The record does not show what happened to any of the money thereafter. When called upon to repay, defendant was unable, or unwilling, to do so. Rather on defendant's behalf the attorney offered defendant's promissory note.

One who takes another's property intending only to use it temporarily before restoring it unconditionally to its owner (i.e., one who normally is found not to have an intent to steal) may nevertheless be guilty of larceny if he later changes his mind and decides not to return the property after all. . . .

The facts established by the direct evidence and inferred from the circumstantial evidence was sufficient for a rational trier of fact to conclude beyond a reasonable doubt that defendant was guilty of the essential element of the crime of theft, that the defendant intended to deprive the bank permanently of more than $500.

Decree

Defendant's conviction of theft in excess of $500 and his sentence to eight years imprisonment in the custody of the Department of Corrections are affirmed.

AFFIRMED.

. . .

WATSON, Justice, dissenting.

As superficially appealing as the result is, this case represents the first time in history that a person has been jailed for overdrafting his bank account. Hibernia's negligence, and not defendant's criminality, was culpable.

I respectfully dissent.

K. CYBERCRIMES[4]

1. The Computer Crime Problem

The annual cost of computer crimes to Americans is between $500 million and $10 billion each year. Forty-two percent of respondents to a Computer Security Institute survey of Fortune 500 companies revealed that there had been an unauthorized use of their computer systems in the past year. It is not surprising that criminals have taken to computers as a new avenue of crime. Access is inexpensive, hard to trace, and, as the numbers demonstrate, very productive. Cybercrime also presents particular problems for prosecutors. Identification of offenders and the search of computer memory present evidentiary problems, and the worldwide scope of the Internet presents jurisdiction problems. Where has the crime occurred if the offender is in one state or country, the victim is in another, and the Internet service provider is in yet another? Free speech rights and access restrictions are complicated by the impossibility of determining whether a computer operator is a child or an adult.

Nevertheless, legislatures are beginning to close the gaps with new statutes. Because **cybercrime** is an area of ongoing change, continue to check statutes carefully as they affect computers as targets, as tools, and as incidental factors in crime.

cybercrime:
crime involving computers as targets, tools, and incidental factors.

2. Computers as Targets

Information stored in computers and the integrity of the computer itself are targets of some cybercrimes. Federal statute 18 U.S.C.A. § 1030 criminalizes merely accessing restricted computer information. The Virginia Computer Crimes Act passed in 1999 criminalizes as a felony, punishable in some cases by imprisonment, the malicious flooding of an e-mail address with unwanted mail ("spamming"). Other states provide civil remedies for the same actions.[5] Vandalizing Web sites and introducing viruses are also computer-damaging crimes.

German hackers gained entry to a Miami Internet service provider, captured credit card information, and threatened to crash the system unless the service provider paid a ransom. They were caught when they went to pick up the ransom money.

3. Computers as Tools

Computers are an efficient tool in the commission of a variety of traditional crimes. Telemarketing scams, transmission of child pornography, illegal electronic money transfers, and Internet gambling are just some of the old crimes that have entered the technological age.

A conviction for computer trespass was affirmed against a defendant who used a home computer to repeatedly dial a telephone company's general access number and enter random six-digit numbers to try to discover customer access codes [*State v. Riley* (Wash. 1993)]. Defendants hacked into a telephone switch to ensure that their calls to a radio station would be in the proper sequence to win promotional giveaways of two Porsche cars, $30,000, and two trips to Hawaii. Conviction for computer fraud violation of 18 U.S.C.A. § 1030 was affirmed in *U.S. v. Peterson* (9th Cir. 1996).

4. Computers Incidental to Crimes

A drug dealer's records, a prostitute's list of customers, an accountant's calculations, and other types of information that might be stored in computer memory banks can be important evidence in criminal investigations. Because access to this information differs from that on sheets of paper, there are special considerations in search and seizure. Chapter 9 discusses some of these problems.

5. No Electronic Theft (NET) Act

The No Electronic Theft Act passed in 1997 tightened United States copyright and trademark laws to target cybertheft of intellectual property. The NET Act is aimed at large-scale reproduction and distribution of copyrighted works through electronic as well as tangible means, because the Internet makes these procedures so easy. Statutes that were changed by the NET Act include 17 U.S.C.A. §§ 101, 506, and 507 and 18 U.S.C.A. §§ 2319, 2319A, and 2320.

U.S. v. LaMacchia (D. Mass. 1994) exposed the need for laws covering theft of copyrighted material where no discernible profit resulted from the theft. LaMacchia's

EXHIBIT 5–3
Sample Jury Instructions

ALTERING, DAMAGING, OR DESTROYING COMPUTER INFORMATION—USED BY OR FOR FINANCIAL INSTITUTION OR GOVERNMENT [18 U.S.C. § 1030(a)(5)]

The defendant is charged in [Count _____ of] the indictment with altering, damaging, or destroying computer information in violation of section 1030(a)(5) of Title 18 of the United States Code. In order for the defendant to be found guilty of that charge, the government must prove each of the following elements beyond a reasonable doubt:

First, the defendant intentionally accessed a computer one or more times without authorization;

Second, the computer was used by or for the [*insert name of financial institution*] [United States Government];

Third, the defendant [altered, damaged, or destroyed information in the computer] [prevented authorized use of the computer or information in it]; and

Fourth, the defendant's conduct [caused loss to one or more persons totaling $1,000 or more in a one-year period] [modified or impaired, or potentially modified or impaired, the medical examination, diagnosis, treatment or care of one or more persons.]

Ninth Circuit Criminal Jury Instructions (St. Paul, MN: West Group, 1992), § 8.22J, with permission.

charge of wire fraud for conspiring to use a computer bulletin board to copy copyrighted software was dismissed because copyrights were not covered by wire fraud, and copyright law did not cover crimes lacking a monetary motive. In 1999 the first conviction of the NET Act demonstrated that the gap had been closed. A student who posted copyrighted software programs, music recordings, entertainment software, and movies on his Web site and allowed the public to download them was convicted of a felony, even though he had not made a profit from his actions.

L.   WHITE-COLLAR CRIME

1.   Introduction

White-collar crime is a catch-all that bundles together the crimes associated with white-collar workers and businesses, the nonviolent crimes that usually have financial or regulation avoidance motives. Corporate crimes, embezzlement, extortion, computer crimes, and fraud are classic white-collar crimes that have already been discussed. Although violent crime statistics are decreasing, white-collar crime is rapidly increasing as violations previously handled in civil actions incur criminal sanctions and new forms of fraudulent crimes grow out of the explosion of business and communication networks, the technology that supports them, and the ensuing regulations. New statutes have been created to cover some new criminal methods, and old statutes have been stretched to fit others. For example, a conviction for unauthorized descrambling of satellite television signals was allowed under the federal wiretap law, 18 U.S.C.A. § 2511(1)(a), in *U.S. v. Davis* (8th Cir. 1992).

white-collar crime:
nonviolent crimes that usually have financial or regulation avoidance motives, such as embezzlement, extortion, computer crimes, and fraud.

2.   Health Care Fraud[6]

Health care fraud is a serious and growing problem in the United States. More than $20 billion in Medicare overpayments went to providers in 1997. Although some of that overpayment was the result of error, the level of fraud prompted a 14 percent increase in criminal prosecutions from 1997 to 1998 and a 22 percent increase in federal attorneys and FBI agents assigned to health care fraud cases, with funds allotted for further increases.

Health care fraud involves misrepresentations in billings to Medicare, Medicaid, and private insurers for medical services. Besides general false claims statutes, such as 18 U.S.C.A. § 287, more specific laws recently have targeted the problem directly. The Health Insurance Portability and Accountability Act of 1996 strengthens criminal prosecution of fraud through 18 U.S.C.A. § 1035, and theft and embezzlement in connection with health care through 18 U.S.C.A. § 669. The Civil Rights of Institutionalized Persons Act also protects residents of nursing homes and mental health and mental retardation facilities from providers who bill for inadequate care.

Anyone who provides health care services, medicines, or equipment, as well as scam artists posing as providers, can commit fraud in the form of billing for services not rendered or not medically necessary, double billing, kickbacks for referring patients, services by untrained personnel, distribution of unapproved drugs or devices, creation of phony insurance companies, and other means. Fraud is expected to grow in the relatively new areas of home health and hospice care.

In Illinois, Health Care Service Corporation was fined $4 million for obstructing a federal audit and making false statements. An ambulance company in Mississippi was convicted for billing for "bed confined" patients who actually had no need for ambulance transportation. The owner and president of a pharmaceutical research company was convicted of falsifying drug study data and noncompliance with testing procedures in California. In Nebraska, a man with only a high school diploma was convicted for collecting more than a million dollars for "ultramolecular medicine" purported to cure cancer, AIDS, and other diseases.

3. Trademark Infringement

Trademark infringement is a combination of unfair trade practices and counterfeiting. The Lanham Act, 15 U.S.C.A. § 1051 *et seq.*, extensively regulates trademarks as not simply a form of business advertising, but a symbol of the integrity and goodwill of the company. When such a symbol is recognized internationally, its worth to the company is enormous, so unauthorized use of trademarks can result in severe sanctions. In 1998 a computer hardware firm that sold its products in counterfeited IBM boxes was required to pay $1.1 million in restitution of profits from the sales and $2.2 million in fines.[7]

4. Economic Espionage

trade secrets:
formulas, patterns, devices, processes, or compilations of information that give companies an advantage over their competitors.

Economic espionage is the theft of **trade secrets,** those formulas, patterns, devices, processes, or compilations of information that give companies an advantage over their competitors. A trade secret must have independent economic value that derives from the fact that it is not generally known in the industry, and the owner must take steps to keep it secret. There are usually no restrictions on how the secret is stored or transmitted. "Know-how" acquired on the job does not qualify as a trade secret, nor does information discovered by "reverse engineering," taking a product apart to see how it was made. California, protective of its Silicon Valley technology companies, amended its statute to include theft of trade secrets with only potential economic value.

Computer files containing work in progress toward a design for a freonless watercooler was not a trade secret in *People v. Pribich* (Cal. App. 1994), because of uncontroverted testimony by an expert witness that the proposed watercooler would not be marketable.

Until the 1996 passage of the Economic Espionage Act, 18 U.S.C.A. §§ 1831 to 1839, there was no federal statute criminalizing theft of trade secrets. Cases were wedged under general fraud and transporting stolen goods statutes or handled in civil litigation. The first cases under the new law include prosecution of the Taiwanese-based Four Pillars Enterprise Company, Ltd., for alleged theft of formulations for self-adhesive products from Avery Dennison Corporation, and the case of *U.S. v. Hsu* (E.D. Pa. 1999) involving alleged attempted theft of anticancer drug secrets from Bristol-Meyers. *Hsu* revealed a problem in the law that may affect future prosecutions. The law contains a confidentiality section, but in order to prove that the information involved is a true trade secret, that information must be examined by the defense and then the jury, and, thus, be released to the public, which is the very thing the law was meant to prevent. In this case, the secrets were edited from 300 pages down to ten pages for use at trial.[8]

5.   Money Laundering

One who exchanges monetary instruments, knowing that they are the proceeds of crime, for other monetary instruments or equivalent property with intent to conceal the nature, location, source, ownership, or control of the proceeds or to promote criminal conduct commits the crime of money laundering. Federal law 18 U.S.C.A. § 1956 adds the alternate elements of intentionally violating the Internal Revenue Code and avoiding state or federal transaction reporting requirements. Money laundering laws give prosecutors another handle in dealing with highly lucrative crimes such as extortion, gambling, and illegal drug trafficking.

A subcontractor on a $20 million hotel renovation project told the contractor that he was a member of a crime family and would take care of labor problems on the job for payment, then threatened the contractor with death if the payments were not continued. The subcontractor brought back the $400,000 he had received as payments in $100 bills and demanded that the contractor issue checks in exchange for the cash. He also used threats to force the contractor to make a $50,000 deposit in an Irish bank in his wife's name, but because Ireland required her to establish the account in person, she never gained control of the funds. The court in *People v. Capparelli* (N.Y. Sup. 1993) ruled that the first transaction of extorted funds was money laundering, but that the second was incomplete and, therefore, attempted money laundering.

6.   Securities Fraud

After the stock market crash of 1929, state and federal laws providing for both civil and criminal sanctions were passed to promote investor confidence by ensuring honest markets. State **"blue sky laws,"** so called because they are aimed at speculative schemes hatched from thin air, and the federal Securities Act of 1933, 15 U.S.C.A. § 77a *et seq.*, require the registration of securities and criminalize making false statements in that process. Fraud in stock exchanges and trading are criminalized by the Securities Exchange Act of 1934, 15 U.S.C.A. § 78 *et seq.*, and the Uniform Securities Act adopted by most states.

blue sky laws:
state laws that criminalize making false statements in the required registration of securities.

The use of confidential knowledge about a corporation in the purchase or sale of stocks in that corporation is called **insider trading,** which violates Securities Exchange Act § 10(b) against misappropriation using deceptive devices in such transactions. In *U.S. v. O'Hagan* (1997) the Supreme Court decided whether the defendant could be convicted of a § 10(b) violation even though he was an "outsider."

insider trading:
use of confidential knowledge about a corporation in the purchase or sale of stocks in that corporation.

UNITED STATES v. O'HAGAN.
117 S.Ct. 2199 1997
[Citations omitted]

Justice GINSBURG delivered the opinion of the Court. . . .

I

Respondent James Herman O'Hagan was a partner in the law firm of Dorsey & Whitney in Minneapolis, Minnesota. In July 1988, Grand Metropolitan PLC (Grand Met), a company based in London, England, retained Dorsey & Whitney as local counsel to represent Grand Met regarding a potential tender offer for the common stock of the Pillsbury Company, headquartered in Minneapolis. Both Grand Met and Dorsey

& Whitney took precautions to protect the confidentiality of Grand Met's tender offer plans. O'Hagan did no work on the Grand Met representation. Dorsey & Whitney withdrew from representing Grand Met on September 9, 1988. Less than a month later, on October 4, 1988, Grand Met publicly announced its tender offer for Pillsbury stock.

On August 18, 1988, while Dorsey & Whitney was still representing Grand Met, O'Hagan began purchasing call options for Pillsbury stock. Each option gave him the right to purchase 100 shares of Pillsbury stock by a specified date in September 1988. Later in August and in September, O'Hagan made additional purchases of Pillsbury call options. By the end of September, he owned 2,500 unexpired Pillsbury options, apparently more than any other individual investor. O'Hagan also purchased, in September 1988, some 5,000 shares of Pillsbury common stock, at a price just under $39 per share. When Grand Met announced its tender offer in October, the price of Pillsbury stock rose to nearly $60 per share. O'Hagan then sold his Pillsbury call options and common stock, making a profit of more than $4.3 million.

The Securities and Exchange Commission (SEC or Commission) initiated an investigation into O'Hagan's transactions, culminating in a 57-count indictment. The indictment alleged that O'Hagan defrauded his law firm and its client, Grand Met, by using for his own trading purposes material, nonpublic information regarding Grand Met's planned tender offer.[1] According to the indictment, O'Hagan used the profits he gained through this trading to conceal his previous embezzlement and conversion of unrelated client trust funds.[2] O'Hagan was charged with 20 counts of mail fraud, in violation of 18 U.S.C. § 1341; 17 counts of securities fraud, in violation of § 10(b) of the Securities Exchange Act of 1934 (Exchange Act), 48 Stat. 891, 15 U.S.C. § 78j(b), and SEC Rule 10b–5, 17 CFR § 240.10b–5 (1996); 17 counts of fraudulent trading in connection with a tender offer, in violation of § 14(e) of the Exchange Act, 15 U.S.C. § 78n(e), and SEC Rule 14e–3(a), 17 CFR § 240.14e–3(a) (1996); and 3 counts of violating federal money laundering statutes, 18 U.S.C. §§ 1956(a)(1)(B)(i), 1957. . . . A jury convicted O'Hagan on all

57 counts, and he was sentenced to a 41-month term of imprisonment.

A divided panel of the Court of Appeals for the Eighth Circuit reversed all of O'Hagan's convictions. Liability under § 10(b) and Rule 10b–5, the Eighth Circuit held, may not be grounded on the "misappropriation theory" of securities fraud on which the prosecution relied. . . .

II

We address first the Court of Appeals' reversal of O'Hagan's convictions under § 10(b) and Rule 10b–5. Following the Fourth Circuit's lead, see *United States v. Bryan* 58 F.3d 933, 943–959 (1995), the Eighth Circuit rejected the misappropriation theory as a basis for § 10(b) liability. We hold, in accord with several other Courts of Appeals, that criminal liability under § 10(b) may be predicated on the misappropriation theory.

A

In pertinent part, § 10(b) of the Exchange Act . . . proscribes (1) using any deceptive device (2) in connection with the purchase or sale of securities, in contravention of rules prescribed by the Commission. The provision, as written, does not confine its coverage to deception of a purchaser or seller of securities; rather, the statute reaches any deceptive device used "in connection with the purchase or sale of any security."

Pursuant to its § 10(b) rulemaking authority, the Commission has adopted Rule 10b–5, which, as relevant here, provides:

"It shall be unlawful for any person, directly or indirectly, by the use of any means or instrumentality of interstate commerce, or of the mails or of any facility of any national securities exchange,

"(a) To employ any device, scheme, or artifice to defraud, [or]

. . .

"(c) To engage in any act, practice, or course of business which operates or would operate as a fraud or deceit upon any person,

"in connection with the purchase or sale of any security. 17 CFR § 240.10b–5 (1996)

Under the "traditional" or "classical theory" of insider trading liability, § 10(b) and Rule 10b–5 are violated when a corporate insider trades in the securities of his corporation on the basis of material, nonpublic information. Trading on such information qualifies as a "deceptive device" under § 10(b), we have affirmed, because "a relationship of trust and confidence [exists] between the shareholders of a corporation, and those insiders who have obtained confidential informa-

---

1. As evidence that O'Hagan traded on the basis of nonpublic information misappropriated from his law firm, the Government relied on a conversation between O'Hagan and the Dorsey & Whitney partner heading the firm's Grand Met representation. That conversation allegedly took place shortly before August 26, 1988. . . . O'Hagan urges that the Government's evidence does not show he traded on the basis of nonpublic information. O'Hagan points to news reports on August 18 and 22, 1988, that Grand Met was interested in acquiring Pillsbury, and to an earlier, August 12, 1988, news report that Grand Met had put up its hotel chain for auction to raise funds for an acquisition. . . . O'Hagan's challenge to the sufficiency of the evidence remains open for consideration on remand.

2. O'Hagan was convicted of theft in state court, sentenced to 30 months' imprisonment, and fined. . . . The Supreme Court of Minnesota disbarred O'Hagan from the practice of law.

tion by reason of their position with that corporation." That relationship, we recognized, "gives rise to a duty to disclose [or to abstain from trading] because of the 'necessity of preventing a corporate insider from . . . tak[ing] unfair advantage of . . . uninformed . . . stockholders.' " The classical theory applies not only to officers, directors, and other permanent insiders of a corporation, but also to attorneys, accountants, consultants, and others who temporarily become fiduciaries of a corporation.

The "misappropriation theory" holds that a person commits fraud "in connection with" a securities transaction, and thereby violates § 10(b) and Rule 10b–5, when he misappropriates confidential information for securities trading purposes, in breach of a duty owed to the source of the information. Under this theory, a fiduciary's undisclosed, self-serving use of a principal's information to purchase or sell securities, in breach of a duty of loyalty and confidentiality, defrauds the principal of the exclusive use of that information. In lieu of premising liability on a fiduciary relationship between company insider and purchaser or seller of the company's stock, the misappropriation theory premises liability on a fiduciary-turned-trader's deception of those who entrusted him with access to confidential information.

The two theories are complementary, each addressing efforts to capitalize on nonpublic information through the purchase or sale of securities. The classical theory targets a corporate insider's breach of duty to shareholders with whom the insider transacts; the misappropriation theory outlaws trading on the basis of nonpublic information by a corporate "outsider" in breach of a duty owed not to a trading party, but to the source of the information. The misappropriation theory is thus designed to "protec[t] the integrity of the securities markets against abuses by 'outsiders' to a corporation who have access to confidential information that will affect th[e] corporation's security price when revealed, but who owe no fiduciary or other duty to that corporation's shareholders."

In this case, the indictment alleged that O'Hagan, in breach of a duty of trust and confidence he owed to his law firm, Dorsey & Whitney, and to its client, Grand Met, traded on the basis of nonpublic information regarding Grand Met's planned tender offer for Pillsbury common stock. This conduct, the Government charged, constituted a fraudulent device in connection with the purchase and sale of securities.[5]

---

5.   The Government could not have prosecuted O'Hagan under the classical theory, for O'Hagan was not an "insider" of Pillsbury, the corporation in whose stock he traded. Although an "outsider" with respect to Pillsbury, O'Hagan had an intimate association with, and was found to have traded on confidential information from, Dorsey & Whitney, counsel to tender offeror Grand Met. Under the misappropriation theory, O'Hagan's securities trading does not escape Exchange Act sanction, as it would under the dissent's reasoning, simply because he was associated with, and gained nonpublic information from, the bidder, rather than the target.

B

We agree with the Government that misappropriation, as just defined, satisfies § 10(b)'s requirement that chargeable conduct involve a "deceptive device or contrivance" used "in connection with" the purchase or sale of securities. We observe, first, that misappropriators, as the Government describes them, deal in deception. A fiduciary who "[pretends] loyalty to the principal while secretly converting the principal's information for personal gain," "dupes" or defrauds the principal. . . .

A company's confidential information . . . qualifies as property to which the company has a right of exclusive use. The undisclosed misappropriation of such information, in violation of a fiduciary duty. . . . constitutes fraud akin to embezzlement—"the fraudulent appropriation to one's own use of the money or goods entrusted to one's care by another." . . .

Deception through nondisclosure is central to the theory of liability for which the Government seeks recognition. . . .

Because the deception essential to the misappropriation theory involves feigning fidelity to the source of information, if the fiduciary discloses to the source that he plans to trade on the nonpublic information, there is no "deceptive device" and thus no § 10(b) violation—although the fiduciary-turned-trader may remain liable under state law for breach of a duty of loyalty.[7]

We turn next to the § 10(b) requirement that the misappropriator's deceptive use of information be "in connection with the purchase or sale of [a] security." This element is satisfied because the fiduciary's fraud is consummated, not when the fiduciary gains the confidential information, but when, without disclosure to his principal, he uses the information to purchase or sell securities. The securities transaction and the breach of duty thus coincide. This is so even though the person or entity defrauded is not the other party to the trade, but is, instead, the source of the nonpublic information. A misappropriator who trades on the basis of material, nonpublic information, in short, gains his advantageous market position through deception; he deceives the source of the information and simultaneously harms members of the investing public.

The misappropriation theory targets information of a sort that misappropriators ordinarily capitalize upon to gain no-risk profits through the purchase or sale of securities. Should a misappropriator put such information to other use, the statute's prohibition would not be implicated. . . .

The Exchange Act was enacted in part "to insure the maintenance of fair and honest markets," 15 U.S.C. § 78b, and there is no question that fraudulent uses of confidential

---

7.   Where, however, a person trading on the basis of material, nonpublic information owes a duty of loyalty and confidentiality to two entities or persons—for example, a law firm and its client—but makes disclosure to only one, the trader may still be liable under the misappropriation theory.

information fall within § 10(b)'s prohibition if the fraud is "in connection with" a securities transaction. . . .

The judgment of the Court of Appeals for the Eighth Circuit

is reversed, and the case is remanded for further proceedings consistent with this opinion.

It is so ordered.

III. CRIMES AGAINST PUBLIC ORDER AND SAFETY

A. INTRODUCTION

This section and the two following sections cover crimes against public order and safety, public morals, and public administration. The goal of statutes and ordinances that govern these crimes is not so much to keep people from hurting each other, although that can also be a goal, but to build society along certain generally accepted norms. When public interest takes precedence over individual rights and freedoms, laws may be passed that criminalize a person's **status**—who one is rather than what one has done—or that use broad or vague language that does not give clear notice of what specific acts are prohibited and, thus, infringe on due process. Such laws are often declared unconstitutional. As societal norms shift, so do the laws, sometimes retrenching, sometimes accommodating the changes, and often creating confusion as jurisdictions move in opposite directions toward consensus.

status:
who one is rather than what one has done.

ANALYSIS PROBLEMS

5–5. Consider each crime discussed in this section. Do you think it is either primarily protective of necessary order or intrusive on civil liberties? Would other criminal statutes be sufficient to deal with the problems?

5–6. What current cases in the news reflect the attitudes of contemporary society? In these cases, are the courts attempting to hold the line against change, accepting developing patterns, or leading the way toward new attitudes?

B. DISORDERLY CONDUCT

Common law offenses of creating a public nuisance, as well as being a common scold and behaving with unneighborly conduct, evolved into the offense of disorderly conduct. Defined by statute in some jurisdictions, but more usually by ordinance, it is often considered to be a submisdemeanor offense. Elements differ widely, but always deal with actions and circumstances that are public in character. Prohibited acts, or words and acts, are specified. Intent may be included, and the lack of provocation also may be an element. Types of places where disorderly conduct laws are in effect may be designated, but need not be public if the action sets in motion a chain of events that ends in violation in a designated place.

fighting words:
speech likely to provoke violence, not protected by the Constitution.

Fighting words, not protected by the Constitution, are usually evaluated according to their likelihood of provoking actual violence. Courts tend to apply a narrower standard when the language is directed at police, because their training should make them less likely to respond violently to provocation. An airline passenger released after an illegal detention called a police officer "asshole," but because no violent response could reasonably be expected, she could not be convicted of using fighting words, *Buffkins v. City of Omaha* (8th Cir. 1990). A bumper sticker proclaiming "Shit Happens" was ruled constitutional free speech in *Cunningham v. State* (Ga. 1991). The

EXHIBIT 5–4
Sample Jury Instructions

DISORDERLY CONDUCT

You will find the Defendant guilty of Disorderly Conduct under this Instruction if, and only if, you believe from the evidence beyond a reasonable doubt all of the following:

    A. That in this county on or about _____ (date) and within 12 months before the [finding of the Indictment herein] [issuance of the warrant for his arrest], he engaged in [fighting at _____ (ID location)] [_____ (method) (describe violent, tumultuous or threatening behavior or noise)];

    B. That _____ (ID location) is a public place;

    AND

    C. That when he did so:

    (1) He intended to cause public inconvenience, annoyance or alarm [and his conduct constituted unreasonable noise];

    OR

    (2) He wantonly created a risk of public inconvenience, annoyance or alarm.

    [If you find the Defendant guilty under this Instruction, you shall fix his punishment at confinement in the county jail for a period not to exceed 90 days, at a fine not to exceed $250.00, or at both confinement and fine, in your discretion.]

William S. Cooper, *Kentucky Instructions to Juries (Criminal)*, 4th ed. § 8.31 (© Anderson Publishing, Cincinnati, Ohio, 1999), with permission.

statute prohibiting knowing display of bumper stickers "containing profane or lewd words describing sexual acts, excretory functions, or parts of the human body" was unconstitutionally overbroad and vague, and did not protect vital government interest. In Clinton Township, Michigan, however, a seventy-year-old woman pleaded guilty to disorderly conduct for using obscenities when telling children in a nearby school yard to be quiet. She was sentenced to a fine of $360 and attendance at anger management classes.[9]

More carefully worded statutes prohibit such things as fighting or tumultuous conduct, unreasonable noise, disruption of lawful assembly, and obstruction of traffic. Even here, there is latitude for interpretation. How "tumultuous" does conduct have to be to apply? When and at what level does noise become unreasonable? Loud street preaching was not considered an unreasonable noise in *Commonwealth v. Gowan* (Pa. Super. 1990), but the same volume level would be unacceptable if it were part of such unprotected activity as inciting to riot or harassing police in their law enforcement duties. In that jurisdiction the noisemaker must have intent to cause public inconvenience, annoyance, or alarm, or recklessly create a risk thereof. Police in Des Moines, Iowa, consider music audible fifty feet from a car stereo to be a noise violation.[10]

It is unlawful to willfully and knowingly impede or disrupt the conduct of the business of the federal government in or near an area where a person protected by the Secret Service will be visiting, 18 U.S.C.A. § 1752. It is also unlawful to interfere with anyone obtaining or providing reproductive health services, 18 U.S.C.A. § 248. The constitutionality of this law was upheld in *U.S. v. Wilson* (7th Cir. 1995), in agreement with two other circuit courts.

C. RIOT

Group disorderly conduct includes unlawful assembly, usually three or more people gathering for an unlawful purpose or to carry out a lawful purpose in an unlawful manner, and riot, defined in 18 U.S.C.A. § 2102 as "an act or threat of violence by one or more

"[A] municipality may not empower its licensing officials to roam essentially at will, dispensing or withholding permission to speak, assemble, picket, or parade, according to their own opinions regarding the potential effect of the activity in question on the 'welfare,' 'decency,' or 'morals' of the community."

—Potter Stewart *Shuttlesworth v. Birmingham,* 394 U.S. 147 (1969)

in an assemblage of three or more presenting clear and present danger of or actual damage or injury to other persons or property." An essential element of riot is group action. It is not necessary that the riot take place in public. Public terror may be an element, as may the requirement of a prior order to disperse—a "reading of the riot act."

The breach of peace conviction of students nonviolently protesting segregation laws was overturned in *Edwards v. South Carolina* (1963). In that decision the Supreme Court stated that "the Fourteenth Amendment does not permit a state to make criminal the peaceful expression of unpopular views." The Court's decision upholding conviction in a later protest case narrowed the *Edwards* ruling when "interest in expression, judged in light of all relevant factors, is 'miniscule' compared to a particular public interest in preventing that expression or conduct at that time and place" [*Colten v. Kentucky* (1972)].

Inciting to riot need not actually lead to riot, but it is the urging of others in a situation presenting a clear and present danger to riot. As police arrested two men at a housing project a crowd gathered. A man in the crowd told the police to leave, using profanity. When he turned to leave, an officer told him to stop, and when he turned with a clenched fist, the officer tackled him. The man asked the crowd to help him, and they moved close enough to touch the officer. The man's conviction for inciting to riot was reversed, because conduct creating a clear and present danger of immediate unlawful action was not shown [*Price v. State* (Okla. Cr. 1994)].

D. VAGRANCY AND LOITERING

Laws meant to keep serfs from wandering away from their responsibilities have survived in modern statutes against idlers, rogues, and vagabonds. Being without employment was pitiable in the weak, but able-bodied poor deserved no mercy from medieval justice that punished them without trial. Modern vagrancy statutes also deprived defendants of due process by their vagueness and broad discretion allowed to police. Although most crimes are based on acts, vagrancy is based on the status of the offender. Being unemployed, homeless, or simply out of step with the expectations of society is the actus reus of the crime, with the purpose of forcing the offender to conform or to move on out of the community. No mens rea is required.

General vagrancy laws were enforced through the 1960s in this country, until the Supreme Court decision in *Papachristou v. City of Jacksonville* (1972) set the precedent to overturn many of them for unconstitutional vagueness. Reread the Jacksonville ordinance that appears in Chapter 1. The Court ruled that statute void for vagueness because "it fails to give a person of ordinary intelligence fair notice that his contemplated conduct is forbidden by the statute," it permits arbitrary and capricious arrests, it prohibits much innocent and otherwise constitutionally protected conduct, and it provides the police with nearly unfettered discretion.

The growing problem of homelessness in the 1980s left many people living on the streets at the mercy of passersby. Annoyance at beggars grew into new statutes against suspicious loitering and aggressive panhandling. Although these crimes involve acts rather than status, they are open to police abuse. Standards are still somewhat vague, and the impact is on those who are least able to change their situation and even less able to challenge bad law. Anatole France commented in 1894 on this "majestic egalitarianism of the law, which forbids rich and poor alike to sleep under bridges, to beg in the streets, and to steal bread."

A municipal loitering ordinance was ruled an unconstitutional breach of due process. It had prohibited loitering in a manner or under enumerated circumstances, such as being underweight or exhibiting nervous behavior, that manifest a purpose to engage in drug-related activity [*City of Akron v. Rowland* (Ohio 1993)].

A Chicago loitering ordinance passed in 1992 allowed police to order groups of two or more persons gathered "with no apparent purpose" in a public place to disperse when there was a reasonable suspicion that at least one person in the group belonged to a criminal street gang. If they did not move along, they faced a six-month jail sentence. In three years, the ordinance was responsible for more than 42,000 arrests. In 1999, the Supreme Court declared the ordinance unconstitutionally vague, not giving citizens sufficient notice of what conduct was prohibited [*Chicago v. Morales* (1999)]. Defenders of the ordinance cited the dramatic decrease in street crime during the tenure of the ordinance, whereas its detractors say it punished innocent behavior and targeted racial minorities. A concurring opinion in the case suggested that an ordinance more clearly defining the purpose of the loiterers "to establish control over identifiable areas, to intimidate others from entering those areas or to conceal illegal activities" might be constitutionally acceptable.

Many cities have stepped up punitive vagrancy ordinances and their enforcement. Banned conduct includes loitering on median strips, getting food handouts in public parks, carrying open containers of alcohol, and trespassing. At least twenty-four cities send police out every night to dislodge the homeless from their streets.[11]

E. ENDANGERING PUBLIC HEALTH AND ENVIRONMENT

Industrialization, population growth, land development, and medical and technological advancements have increased the need for and availability of remedies against health and environmental problems. Regulations have proliferated in the past few decades that provide for civil actions as well as criminal sanctions for serious violations of health and environmental standards. Some health and environmental protection laws have mens rea elements, most often knowingly or negligently, but many create strict liability offenses because of the severe public consequences of violations. Public health is protected by laws governing infectious disease control; the purity of food, drugs, and cosmetics (Pure Food, Drug, and Cosmetics Act, 21 U.S.C.A. §§ 301 to 392); safe housing; pollution control; and other concerns on the state and federal levels. A physician convicted of willful violation of public health laws for failing to provide proper treatment had repeatedly used a nursing home patient's dialysis catheter as a feeding tube, then, when the error was discovered, waited ten hours before transferring the patient to a hospital. The court in *People v. Einaugler* (N.Y. 1994) ruled that the offense was not mere negligence.

The Environmental Protection Agency (EPA) works under federal law to enforce pollution control measures, and to delegate responsibility to the states for further controls, setting minimum standards for state compliance in some areas. Federal pollution control laws include the Rivers and Harbors Act of 1899 that prohibits the discharge of refuse into navigable waters (33 U.S.C.A. §§ 401 to 467); the Clean Air Act (42 U.S.C.A. §§ 7401 to 7642); the Federal Water Pollution Control Act (33 U.S.C.A. §§ 1251 to 1387); the Resource Conservation and Recovery Act, which controls transportation, storage, and disposal of hazardous waste (42 U.S.C.A. §§ 6901 to 6992); the Toxic Substances Control Act, which gives the EPA authority to test and ban dangerous chemicals (15 U.S.C.A. §§ 2601 to 2671); and the comprehensive Environmental Response, Compensation, and Liability Act, which provides funds for hazardous substance cleanups and requires factual reporting (42 U.S.C.A. §§ 9601 to 9675). The Quiet Communities Act (42 U.S.C.A. §§ 4901 to 4918) prohibits acts and products that exceed noise level standards.

As we saw in the corporate crimes section of Chapter 3, corporate officers can be held individually liable for their companies' violations of antipollution laws. In *State v. Gastown, Inc.* (Ohio 1975) the owner of a service station was convicted for an oil spill into a creek, even though the station was under the control of an independent contractor and cleanup had begun within hours of notification of the spill. The water pollution regulatory statute did not require either knowledge or intent.

States regulate hunting and fishing, but the federal Endangered Species Act (16 U.S.C.A. §§ 1531 to 1544), the Migratory Bird Act (16 U.S.C.A. §§ 703 to 712), and the Bald and Golden Eagle Protection Act (16 U.S.C.A. § 668) give further protection to specified species. Intentional and unintentional harm is covered by the laws. The migratory bird and eagle protection laws were used in their first nonhunting application against a utility company for the electrocution of seventeen birds in power lines. The utility poles were known to be a favorite roosting site in a treeless oil field, and inexpensive equipment was available to prevent harm to the birds. The utility company was sentenced to three years' probation and $100,000 in fines, and was required to install equipment to prevent further harm [*U.S. v. Moon Lake Electric Association, Inc.* (D. Colo. 1999)].

 ANALYSIS PROBLEM

5–7. Most antismoking laws carry penalties equivalent to parking tickets, but a few jurisdictions place infractions at the level of misdemeanors. At least one state has considered the criminalization of smoking by minors. Do you think such health-related conduct should be criminalized?

F. USE AND DISTRIBUTION OF FIREARMS

Gun control is a rapidly shifting area of American law. With a homicide rate ten to twenty times that of European countries[12] and mass shootings during the late 1990s, particularly in schools, most Americans favor tougher gun laws.[13] Others claim a right to bear arms based on the Second Amendment to the Constitution, so the issue is far from settled. Criminal law regarding firearms is divided in focus between the guns themselves and their possession or sale, and the connection of gun use or possession with other crimes or by those convicted of other crimes.

The United States Gun Control Act, 18 U.S.C.A. §§ 921 to 930, provides for the following:

1. Licensure for the manufacture, importation, and sale of firearms, and record keeping, background checks, and administration of sworn statements in sales.
2. Restrictions on manufacture, importation, and sales of armor-piercing ammunition, large-capacity ammunition feeding devices, destructive devices, machine guns, semiautomatic assault weapons, short-barreled shotguns or rifles, any firearm undetectable by airport security machines, and special restrictions on handguns.
3. Restrictions on delivery when knowing or having reasonable belief that the receiver is under eighteen years of age (under twenty-one if the gun is other than a rifle or shotgun), has been convicted of a crime punishable by more than one year in prison, is a fugitive from justice, is an unlawful user of a controlled substance, has been adjudicated or committed as mentally defective, is an illegal alien, has been dishonorably discharged from the Armed Forces, has renounced United States citizenship, is subject to a court order protecting an intimate partner or child, or has been convicted of a misdemeanor crime of domestic violence.
4. Restrictions on the shipping of firearms and ammunition in interstate commerce.
5. Restrictions on transportation of stolen firearms and ammunition.
6. Restriction of possession of a firearm in federal facilities.

Section 924 of the law specifies knowing or willful mens rea for most of these provisions. *Bryan v. U.S.* (1998) ruled that "willfully" selling guns without a license requires only that the seller know the sale is illegal, not that he or she knows about the licensing requirement.

After enforcement of this law began, the number of licensed gun dealers in the United States decreased from 198,848 in 1994 to 74,220 in 1999, and the FBI background check system denied more than 50,000 gun sales, not counting those denied through state systems, during that period. Violent crimes committed with handguns dropped 20 percent, and handgun homicides declined 23 percent.[14]

When combined with other crimes, the carrying of firearms, use of firearms, greater destructive power of the guns, use of a silencer, and repeated firearms offenses results in increasingly longer prison sentences, § 924(c)(1). Probation and concurrent sentences are not sentencing options when firearms are involved. In *Bailey v. U.S.* (1995), the Supreme Court narrowed the definition of "use" of a gun during the commission of a crime, requiring that active use rather than mere possession must be shown. A loaded pistol found in a bag in a locked car trunk and another gun locked in a bedroom closet were not accessible for use in the drug-related crimes for which the defendants were arrested. The court in *U.S. v. Muñoz* (2nd Cir. 1998) relied on *Bailey* in determining that a weapon was sufficiently accessible to be defined as "carried" under § 924(c)(1) when a loaded magazine clip in the pocket of a jacket the defendant was wearing fit into a handgun under the driver's seat of his vehicle. A kidnapper who drove with his hostage from Texas to New Jersey, then to New York and Maryland, was convicted in a New Jersey court of using a firearm in connection with the kidnapping, even though the possession and use of the gun occurred only in Maryland. His conviction was upheld in *U.S. v. Rodriguez-Moreno* (1999). Under Minnesota's law that includes both actual and constructive possession of a firearm in connection with a felony, a .22 revolver kept under a mattress was considered in "reasonable proximity" to the crack cocaine found in a boot three feet away [*State v. Royster* (Minn. 1999)].

Through Project Exile, federal, state, and local agencies cooperate to use the stiffer federal law at § 924 rather than the usually weaker state and local laws to prosecute the use of guns in crime.[15] In turn, federal law specifies that gun transfers must comply with state laws.

Some states issue permits to carry concealed weapons, and others ban all concealed weapons. Some states limit gun purchases to one a month per person to foil third-party purchases for buyers who would not pass a background check, and at least fifteen states and five cities have passed Child Access Prevention laws that make gun owners criminally liable for recklessly leaving guns where children can find and use them.[16]

IV. CRIMES AGAINST PUBLIC MORALS

A. INTRODUCTION

Statutes and ordinances that regulate sexual behavior of consenting adults have their origins in the canon law of the medieval church. Critics believe that moral issues concerning nonviolent sex, gambling, abortion, and drug use still ought to be left to the guidance of religion, philosophy, and conscience, with the criminal justice system dealing only with justice and not sin. Proponents argue that civilizations decay from within, so it is a public responsibility to maintain standards of decency.

"Civilization is the progress toward a society of privacy. The savage's whole existence is public, ruled by the laws of his tribe. Civilization is the process of setting man free from men."

—Ayn Rand, *The Fountainhead*, 1943

B. NONVIOLENT SEXUAL CONDUCT

1. Introduction

Current laws in many jurisdictions outlaw prostitution, incest, sodomy, adultery, fornication, indecent exposure, and obscenity. Only vaginal sexual intercourse between married heterosexuals is universally allowed. Because most sexual behavior is private, these laws go primarily unenforced, leading to loss of equal protection when violations are prosecuted. *State v. McCollum* (Wis. App. 1990) ruled that equal protection was denied when only female dancers were arrested under decency codes, and not the male patrons who fondled them. Unlike sexual conduct of consenting adults, child pornography and exploitation is universally criminalized.

2. Prostitution

Prostitution is allowed only in some counties of Nevada where it is regulated by law. The Mann Act, 18 U.S.C.A. § 2422, bans the interstate transportation of any person for the purpose of prostitution or any other illegal sexual activity. Section 2423 penalizes transportation of minors for sexual activity and travel with intent to engage in sexual activity with a minor.

Most jurisdictions include as a separate crime the procurement or transportation of prostitutes or income from prostitution. This strong prohibition has grown out of moral opposition, as well as fear of disease and corruption. There are arguments, however, that community health might be served better by the legality and regulation of prostitution. Some laws prohibit any sexual activity for hire; others define the specific activity. Some prosecute only females; others, anyone who buys or sells sexual favors. Promiscuity without the exchange of money and long-term commercial arrangements with a mistress or gigolo are not covered.

3. Sodomy

Sodomy, criminalized in eighteen states, can include oral or anal intercourse, intercourse between humans and animals (bestiality), and "deviate sexual intercourse with another individual of the same sex." The Supreme Court put its weight behind the tradition against sodomy in upholding the constitutionality of Georgia's sodomy law, even though the offense occurred in the defendant's home [*Bowers v. Hardwick* (1986)]. Some state courts have since ruled that their state constitutions provide a more extensive right to privacy and equal protection than the federal Constitution, and have struck down their sodomy laws, including Kentucky in *Commonwealth v. Wasson* (Ky. 1992) and, ironically, Georgia in *Powell v. State* (Ga. 1998). The heat of opinion in this issue is shown by the death threats sent to the Kentucky justices who voted with the majority.

4. Obscenity

"Did you ever hear anyone say 'that work had better be banned because I might read it and it might be very damaging to me'?"

—Joseph Henry Jackson, American journalist; editor, *San Francisco Chronicle,* 1894–1946

Obscenity is difficult to define. The elements of the crime are clear enough, usually distribution of obscene material knowing that it is obscene but not necessarily knowing the precise contents. Setting the standards for obscenity itself is tough, because individual sensibilities, taste, and experience vary so widely. James Joyce's novel *Ulysses* was banned in this country as obscene from its publication in 1922 to 1933 and is now regarded as one of the greatest pieces of twentieth-century literature. The rock musical *Hair* was variously banned and applauded in the late 1960s.

Roth v. U.S. (1957) established that obscenity was not protected speech and that it should be judged against "contemporary community standards" as to whether, taken as a whole, it "appeals to the prurient interest" and is "utterly without redeeming social importance." *Miller v. California* (1973) ruled that local rather than national community standards could be used and replaced "utterly without redeeming social importance" with "patently offensive" and "lacks serious literary, artistic, political, or scientific value." *Pope v. Illinois* (1987) limited community standards applications to prurient interest and patent offensiveness and disallowed community standards in the determination of "literary, artistic, political, or scientific value." The court in *State v. Groetken* (Iowa 1991) ruled that the contemporary community standard is not an element of the crime to be proven, but rather a reference for the jury to determine whether the material in question falls under the statute's definition of obscenity.

United States obscenity law is contained in 18 U.S.C.A. §§ 1460 to 1470 and covers the crimes of possession, sale, mailing, transportation, broadcasting, and transfer to minors of obscene matter. Knowingly is the mens rea element of these crimes. Items banned from the United States mails include ". . . obscene, lewd, lascivious, indecent, filthy, or vile . . . matter" as well as articles designed for producing abortion and information on where an abortion can be obtained (18 U.S.C.A. § 1461).

Because the Internet allows children easy access to information, the Communications Decency Act of 1996, 47 U.S.C.A. § 223, was passed. *Reno v. ACLU* (1997) struck down the provision in the law prohibiting on-line transmission of indecent material to children, because there was no definition of "indecent" and no requirement of lack of redeeming value. Because of the nature of the Internet, the law was believed to interfere with the rights of adults, and the transmissions it sought to control transcended geographical and identity control. The law came under further challenge in *ApolloMedia Corp. v. Reno* (N.D. Cal. 1998). The ruling, affirmed in 1999 by the Supreme Court in a summary ruling, upheld the provision criminalizing telecommunication that is "obscene, lewd, lascivious, filthy, or indecent, with intent to annoy, abuse, threaten, or harass another person." This provision was interpreted to ban only obscene material not entitled to constitutional protection.

After *Reno v. ACLU*, Congress passed the Child Online Protection Act in 1998, 47 U.S.C.A. § 231. This act makes criminal the intentional "commercial distribution of material that is harmful to minors." It applies community standards to determine prurient interest, prohibits depiction of genitals and sexual conduct "patently offensive with respect to minors," and requires lack of serious literary, artistic, political, or scientific value, but it still is under attack for being overbroad.

State laws also are changing and being challenged in response to growing computer communications capabilities. Check both federal and state statutes and decisions for changes in this area of law.

5. Child Pornography and Exploitation

Statutes punishing the sexual exploitation of children are sometimes found next to rape and abuse statutes, and sometimes next to obscenity and prostitution statutes. Using a minor to engage in sexually explicit conduct for the purpose of producing a visual depiction of that conduct, allowing a minor under one's control to engage in such conduct, buying or selling children for such use, and possessing or distributing such depictions are criminalized in state and federal law (18 U.S.C.A. §§ 2251 to 2260).

Knowing possession and knowing possession with intent to sell are the usual mens rea elements of child pornography crimes. A defendant possessing ten-year-old photos of nude boys engaged in sexual acts could not claim ignorance of the law as a defense to child pornography charges [*U.S. v. Robinson* (1st Cir. 1998)].

Use of interstate facilities to transmit information about a minor with intent to encourage criminal sexual activity is prohibited by 18 U.S.C.A. § 2425. This law was passed in 1998 in response to the Internet posting of a nine-year-old girl's name and phone number as a sexual enticement.

U.S. v. Wolf (10th Cir. 1989) upheld 18 U.S.C.A. § 2251 as further defined by § 2256, and enumerates factors used in determining whether a photo of a child is pornographic or not.

UNITED STATES v. WOLF
United States Court of Appeals, Tenth Circuit, 1989
890 F.2d 241 10th Cir. 1989
[Citations omitted]

BRORBY, Circuit Judge.

On March 8, 1988, William Joseph Wolf (Wolf) was indicted on thirteen counts of sexual exploitation of a child in violation of 18

U.S.C. § 2251 (Supp. V 1987). Counts one through twelve were based on photographs he took of a partially nude, apparently asleep or unconscious five-year-old girl. After taking the photographs, Wolf mailed the undeveloped film from Oklahoma to

Pittsburg, Pennsylvania, for processing. In the trial court Wolf challenged the constitutionality of 18 U.S.C. § 2251. After hearing evidence and argument of counsel, the trial court ruled the statute constitutional as applied. Pursuant to a plea agreement, Wolf pled guilty to count one of the indictment, reserving for appeal the issue of the constitutionality of 18 U.S.C. § 2251. On appeal Wolf contends 18 U.S.C. § 2251 is unconstitutional as applied to the photograph supporting count one. We hold 18 U.S.C. § 2251 is not unconstitutional as applied to the photograph.

FACTS

On an evening in late December 1987, Wolf went Christmas shopping with some friends who brought along their five-year-old daughter. After shopping, the girl, her parents, and her brother returned with Wolf to his apartment. Wolf asked the parents of the girl if she could spend the night with him, and they consented.

In the early morning hours of the next day, Wolf photographed his five-year-old victim as she lay on his waterbed. When he mailed the undeveloped thirty-five millimeter film to an out-of-state company for processing, Wolf sent two five-dollar bills and hand-printed instructions: "Send to W.J.W., 2421 North Sterling, Apartment 112-W, Oklahoma City, Oklahoma." The photo processing company that developed the film in Maryland recognized that the nude female was a minor and contacted the FBI. A controlled delivery of the photos was attempted by a postal inspector in a mailman's uniform. He knocked at Wolf's apartment and asked for postage due. Believing the postman was a law enforcement officer, Wolf refused to accept the package. Subsequently, the FBI obtained and executed a search warrant of Wolf's apartment. Wolf admitted to an FBI agent that he had taken the photographs of the child and mailed them interstate.

"LASCIVIOUS EXHIBITION"

Wolf contends the trial court erred by finding the provisions of 18 U.S.C. § 2251, as further defined by 18 U.S.C. § 2256(2)(E) (Supp. V 1987), were constitutional as applied to the photograph charged in count one of the indictment. 18 U.S.C. § 2251 reads in pertinent part:

> Any person . . . who employs, uses, persuades, induces, entices, or coerces any minor to engage in . . . any sexually explicit conduct for the purpose of producing any visual depiction of such conduct, shall be punished as provided under subsection (d), if such person knows or has reason to know that such visual depiction will be transported in interstate or foreign commerce or mailed, or if such visual depiction has actually been transported in interstate or foreign commerce or mailed.

The term "sexually explicit conduct" is further defined in 18 U.S.C. § 2256, which provides, in part: " '(2) sexually explicit conduct' means actual or simulated . . . (E) lascivious exhibi-

tion of the genitals or pubic area of any person. . . ." The trial court did not err in finding these provisions constitutional as applied to the photograph charged in count one.

The photograph at issue in this appeal shows the victim lying on her back. Her head is at the top of the photo, in the background of the field. Her eyes are closed, and her head is turned slightly to the right. Her mouth is open. Her left arm crosses her chest, and her right cheek rests on the back of her left hand. Her right arm extends away from her body, right palm up. She is wearing a pink and white sleep-shirt which is pulled up above her waist, exposing the lower half of her body, which is totally nude. Her left leg extends into the foreground and is cut off in the photograph just below the knee. The victim's right leg is raised up toward the ceiling, and to the right. The right knee is not bent substantially. Her right leg is supported by pillows or other bedding. Her legs are spread apart, exposing her genital region. The primary focus of light in the photograph is the victim's genitals; the victim's head and the other background is barely lit.

Wolf argues the photograph is not within the contemplation of the statute because the sleeping child is not exuding sexual suggestiveness. Therefore, he argues, the photograph is not a "lascivious exhibition of the genitals or the pubic area" under the statute.

> [T]he photograph of the sleeping, partially nude child fails to depict lust, wantonness, sexual coyness or other inappropriate precocity. In the absence of such elements, the prohibitions codified by § 2251(a), as defined in § 2256(2)(E), extend beyond constitutional limits.

Wolf misperceives the law.

Under various constitutional challenges, the term "lascivious exhibition" under the statute has been interpreted by the courts since the inception of the legislation forming the basis for the instant charge. . . .

. . . [T]he Ninth Circuit wrote *United States v. Wiegand,* 812 F.2d 1239 (9th Cir.), *cert. denied,* 484 U.S. 856, 108 S.Ct. 164, 98 L.Ed.2d 118 (1987), one of the most heavily cited cases on this issue. In *Wiegand,* the Ninth Circuit also held the statutory term "lascivious" was not unconstitutionally vague. Wiegand was indicted along with co-defendant Dost on alleged violations of 18 U.S.C. § 2251(a) and other related charges. The stipulated facts reveal that both defendants took a series of photographs of two minor females. One of the girls was fourteen years old and the other was ten years old at the time of the offenses. The defendants photographed the fourteen-year-old at Dost's residence where he had the nude girl assume various supine and sitting poses. The ten-year-old was photographed nude and sitting on a beach. *United States v. Dost,* 636 F.Supp. 828, 830 (S.D. Cal.1986), *aff'd sub nom. United States v. Wiegand,* 812 F.2d 1239 (9th Cir.), *cert. denied,* 484 U.S. 856, 108 S.Ct. 164, 98 L.Ed.2d 118 (1987), and *aff'd,* 813 F.2d 1231 (1987).

The *Dost* court found the photographs depicted "sexually explicit conduct" in that they contained a "lascivious exhibition of the genitals or pubic area" under subsection (E) of the statute. The trial court reviewed some of the legislative history of the Child Protection Act and concluded the purpose of the amendments to the act was to broaden the scope of the existing "kiddie porn" laws to protect children from the harmful effects of sexual exploitation. In finding the defendants guilty, the trial court listed what have come to be known as the *Dost* factors. These factors were enumerated "among any others that may be relevant in the particular case" in determining whether a visual depiction of a minor constitutes a "lascivious exhibition of the genitals or pubic area" under § 2255(2)(E) (now codified at § 2256(2)(E):

1. whether the focal point of the visual depiction is on the child's genitalia or pubic area;
2. whether the setting of the visual depiction is sexually suggestive, i.e., in a place or pose generally associated with sexual activity;
3. whether the child is depicted in an unnatural pose, or in inappropriate attire, considering the age of the child;
4. whether the child is fully or partially clothed, or nude;
5. whether the visual depiction suggests sexual coyness or a willingness to engage in sexual activity;[4]
6. whether the visual depiction is intended or designed to elicit a sexual response in the viewer.

In applying its factors, the trial court conceded the photo of the ten-year-old was not as graphic as that of the fourteen-year-old and also observed the girl's expression was not sexually coy, since she was squinting and looking away from the camera. The trial court described the photograph of the ten-year-old as follows:

> The . . . photograph of the 10-year-old child . . . portrays the child sitting on the beach, looking off to her right. She is leaning back, supporting her weight on her arms, hands resting on the sand. She is totally nude, and has some body painting on her chest. Her pelvic area appears to be slightly raised or hyperextended, and her legs are spread apart. Her right leg is fully extended at a slight outward angle. Her left leg is bent at the knee and extended almost perpendicularly away from the body. Her pubic area is completely exposed, not obscured by any shadow or body part.

In applying the factors, the court observed:

> As for the suggestion of a willingness to engage in sexual activity, her open legs do imply such a willingness but nothing else about the child's attitude does.

What strikes the Court most strongly, however, is the unusual pose of this girl. The average 10-year-old child sitting on the beach, especially when unclothed, does not sit with her legs positioned in such a manner. This unusual pose is one that an ordinary child would not assume but for adult coaching (as was the case here). This unnatural pose combined with the picture's emphasis on the girl's genitalia leads the Court to conclude that it too constitutes a "lascivious exhibition of the genitals."

Although Wiegand challenged on appeal the trial court's interpretation of "lascivious," the Ninth Circuit affirmed the trial court with unambiguous pronouncements.

The *Wiegand* court rejected the notion that the statute places the onus of lust on the child being photographed.

> It was a lascivious exhibition because the photographer arrayed it to suit *his* peculiar *lust.* Each of the pictures featured the child photographed as a sexual object.

> The district court noted the unlikelihood of the 10-year-old girl intending any sexual invitation by her pose. "Lascivious" does have such a connotation when applied to the conduct of adults. In the context of the statute applied to the conduct of children, *lasciviousness is not a characteristic of the child* photographed *but of the exhibition* which the photographer sets up for an audience that consists of himself or likeminded pedophiles. . . . (Emphasis added)

Thus, the Ninth Circuit clearly stated that to violate 18 U.S.C. § 2251 the photographer need not portray the victimized child as a temptress. We agree with the Ninth Circuit's interpretation of the statutory language.

Most recently, in *United States v. Villard,* 885 F.2d 117 (3rd Cir.1989), the Third Circuit adopted the *Dost* factors, stating:

> We adopt the *Dost* factors as a means of determining whether a genital exhibition is "lascivious." We do so, of course, not out of any precedential obligation, but instead because the *Dost* factors provide specific, sensible meaning to the term "lascivious," a term which is less than crystal clear. The district court in the instant case instructed the jury to consider each of the *Dost* factors, and cautioned the jury that no single factor should be given undue weight and that a depiction need not involve all the factors in order to be "lascivious." We agree with the district court's basic application of the *Dost* factors. All six factors should be presented to the jury for consideration. Although more than one factor must be present in order to establish "lasciviousness," all six factors need not be present.

Thus, the Third Circuit recognized the merit of the Dost factors when properly applied. We wholly agree with the Third

---

4. The Ninth Circuit adopted these factors only in part, stating the factors should not be applied so as to require a showing of sexual activity or willingness to engage in it. "The standard employed by the district court was over-generous to the defendant in implying as to the seventeen-year-old girl that the pictures would not be lascivious unless they showed sexual activity or willingness to engage in it." *Weigand,* 812 F.2d at 1244.

Circuit that all six factors need not be present in order to bring the depiction under the proscription of the statute.[6]

In the instant case, the trial court measured the photograph against the *Dost* factors and concluded the photograph constituted a lascivious exhibition of the genitals and the statute at issue was not unconstitutional as applied. After citing *Dost* and *Wiegand,* the trial court found five of the six *Dost* factors . . .

Although in resolving legal issues we are not called upon to write closing arguments, we echo the wisdom and the passion of Judge Noonan, who wrote:

> . . . The pornographic photographer subordinates the humanity of his subject to the sexuality of the subject. . . . But whether the person is male or female, the essential operation is the same: an assault upon the humanity of

the person pictured, making that person a mere means of serving the voyeur's purposes. . . .

Human dignity is offended by the pornographer. American law does not protect all human dignity; legally, an adult can consent to its diminishment. When a child is made the target of the pornographer-photographer, the statute will not suffer the insult to the human spirit, that the child should be treated as a thing.

We hold that 18 U.S.C. § 2251(a) as further defined by 18 U.S.C. § 2256 is constitutional as applied to count number one in the indictment against Wolf. . . . The trial court did not err in applying the *Dost* factors, and we hold that not all of the *Dost* factors need be present in order for a sexually exploitative photograph of a child to come within the constitutional reach of the statute.

AFFIRMED.

---

6. We do not hold that more than one *Dost* factor must be present to constitute a violation of 18 U.S.C. § 2251(a).

C. GAMBLING

The first federal indictments for Internet gambling were announced in March, 1998. Jurisdictional problems inherent in Internet prosecutions were overcome by use of laws prohibiting telephone use in interstate sports betting, 18 U.S.C.A. § 1084. The elements of this law require the defendant to be a professional gambler and the transmission of bets to be via wire communications, usually understood to mean by telephone, but defined in § 1081 as "all instrumentalities . . . used in the transmission of writings, signs, pictures, and sounds of all kinds by aid of wire, cable, or other like connection. . . ." Defendants in this case were charged with conspiracy to violate § 1084 by operating offshore sports betting operations using the telephone and Internet, equating the two types of transmission. *U.S. v. Blair* (10th Cir. 1995) affirms a § 1084 conviction for accepting sports bets by telephone from United States residents to the Dominican Republic.[17]

Gambling businesses also are prohibited in provisions of federal and state racketeering statutes. The elements of 18 U.S.C.A. § 1955 defines illegal gambling businesses as those that violate state law, involve five or more persons, and are in operation continuously for more than thirty days or have a single day gross revenue of more than $2,000. An operation in Georgia met these elements with opening night profits of $110,000, qualifying as sufficient "commerce" to uphold the framing of the law under the commerce clause of the Constitution [*U.S. v. Lee* (11th Cir. 1999)]. A sports wagering business accepting bets in the Caribbean and conducting related financial transactions in Texas did not violate § 1955 simply by having the opportunity to accept bets in Texas [*U.S. v. Truesdale* (5th Cir. 1998)].

States restrict gambling variously to such operations as horse racing tracks and off-track facilities, bingo and other games for charitable causes, state revenue lotteries, casinos, and riverboats. These operations are licensed and regulated.

D. DRUG OFFENSES

1. Introduction

Drug offenses are often classified as crimes against morality, but could as easily be placed with those against public order and health, because they can cause physical harm to persons and property, as well as contribute to other crimes and to economic and social problems. Therefore, unlike efforts to abolish some crimes against morality, there is no concentrated movement to allow free use of addicting or intoxicating drugs; prohibition or strict regulation are the choices. Since the prohibition of alcohol was repealed in 1933, its sale and use have been restricted to certain times of day, to adults only, and to certain places, with a few counties or precincts remaining dry. Public drunkenness statutes still exist, but are beginning to give way to an emphasis on the endangerment of others while under the influence of alcohol, such as disorderly intoxication and driving under the influence of intoxicants charges.

2. Driving Under the Influence

A DUI (driving under the influence of intoxicants), DWI (driving while intoxicated), or DUBAL (driving with unlawful blood alcohol level) prosecution must prove that the defendant was actually driving and that the defendant's blood alcohol level was at a certain level: 0.10 percent in most states, 0.08 in sixteen states and the District of Columbia. For the privilege of driving on public roads, motorists have given "implied consent" to have blood, breath, or urine tested for alcohol content. Since the Pennsylvania vehicle code designates "vehicle" rather than "motor vehicle" in its DUI provision, the drunk "driver" of a bicycle who had two previous DUI convictions could have his license suspended for five years, *Kronenbitter v. Commonwealth* (Pa. 1992).

3. Controlled Substances

Crimes involving narcotics, hallucinogens, amphetamines, anabolic steroids, and so forth do not wait until public safety is actually threatened. Interdiction comes earlier to penalize manufacture, transportation, sale, distribution, and mere possession of these drugs, or even the paraphernalia needed for their use, because their potential use is judged to be extremely detrimental to society. Violation levels depend on the harmfulness of the substance involved and the amount of that substance.

The federal Controlled Substances Act of 1970, 21 U.S.C.A. § 811 *et seq.*, was extended in the 1972 Uniform Controlled Substances Act to promote uniformity among state and federal laws. Now most states conform to the federal drug acts. The continuing criminal enterprise (CCE) statute, also known as the Drug Kingpin Act, 21 U.S.C.A. § 848, targets those who have a managing or organizing role in large illegal drug organizations. Chapter 6 discusses this statute in more detail. Some drug offenses are strict liability crimes, and others require general intent.

Possession elements usually include knowledge of the presence of contraband and the ability to exercise control over it. Constructive possession extends to control over the substance even though it is not in the defendant's presence, such as in baggage checked on a plane when the defendant has claim tickets for the baggage. Possession was ruled not to include drugs that have already been consumed by the defendant, because there was a lack of control [*State v. Thronsen* (Alaska App. 1991)]. When there is possession but no knowledge, there is no offense. Proof of knowledge is difficult when there is joint occupancy of a vehicle or dwelling.

Under the stiffer statutes, anyone who intentionally participates in bringing about the drug transaction, even if only as a translator, is a deliverer of the controlled substance, *State v. Ramirez* (Wash. App. 1991). Trafficking statutes prohibit bringing controlled substances into the state to be manufactured or delivered. Ownership or sale of the substance is not an element of the crime. Some statutes target the "narcotic vagrant," a person found where drug use is known to occur or where drugs are kept. Tossing a bag containing cocaine from a porch into a yard next door has been held to constitute "transportation," although moving drugs within a house would not qualify [*State v. Greenidge* (N.C. App. 1991)].

Many states have separate statutes for drug offenses that occur within 1,000 yards of a school. Decisions have differed about whether intent refers to general intent to deliver the substance or specific intent to deliver it in a school zone. Some states include colleges and universities as "schools," and others do not. The building housing a General Education Equivalency (GED) program was a "school" in *State v. Vasquez* (Wash. App. 1995), but not when the GED program was unrecognizable on the third floor of an office building in *State v. Becker* (Wash. 1997).

4. Drug Paraphernalia

Possession of paraphernalia, such as hypodermic needles, used in the consumption of illegal drugs is a criminal offense. The item must be designed for use with a controlled substance but need not be proven to have actually been used. The nature of the item, its proximity to drugs, and other situational facts determine the criminality of possession. Because the provision of the Anti-Drug Abuse Act, 21 U.S.C.A. § 857, that criminalized the sale of drug paraphernalia did not have a mens rea requirement and covered items that have legitimate uses, the statute was held to be unconstitutionally vague in *U.S. v. Schneiderman* (S.D.N.Y. 1991).

5. Medical and Religious Use of Drugs

Dispensing of drugs for medical purposes is allowed under careful regulation. A physician dispensing drugs outside the scope of his medical practice, even though he did not act with malicious or financial motive, was convicted of drug crimes [*U.S. v. Singh* (4th Cir. 1995)]. He exchanged drugs for sexual favors, continued to prescribe narcotics to addicted patients, and prescribed drugs inappropriate for the patients' conditions.

Seven states have legalized the medical use of marijuana. Possessors of a limited amount or numbers of plants and the recommendation of a physician are free from state prosecution under these laws, but are still subject to federal prosecution. The American Indian Religious Freedom Act of 1978, 92 U.S.C.A. § 469, and *Peyote Way Church of God v. Thornburgh* (5th Cir. 1991) allow the religious use of peyote to Native Americans under federal law. Twenty-eight states also allow such use. *Employment Division, Oregon Department of Human Resources v. Smith* (1990), however, gives states the right to deny even religious use of peyote.

Look for changes in drug laws and decisions as discussions develop about legalization, cause and effect, severity of interpretation and sentencing, and impact on society.

ANALYSIS PROBLEM

5–8. Which of the crimes against morals would you leave to religion and conscience, and which should be the province of criminal law? Why? Does the fact that law enforcement agencies and the judicial system have limited resources make a difference?

EXHIBIT 5–5
Sample Jury Instructions

CONTROLLED SUBSTANCE—POSSESSION WITH INTENT TO DISTRIBUTE [21 U.S.C. § 841(a)(1)]

The defendant is charged in [Count _____ of] the indictment with possession of [e.g., cocaine] with intent to distribute in violation of Section 841(a)(1) of Title 21 of the United States Code. In order for the defendant to be found guilty of that charge, the government must prove each of the following elements beyond a reasonable doubt:

First, the defendant knowingly possessed _____ ; and

Second, the defendant possessed it with the intent to deliver it to another person.

It does not matter whether the defendant knew that the substance was _____ . It is sufficient that the defendant knew that it was some kind of a prohibited drug.

Ninth Circuit Criminal Jury Instructions (St. Paul, MN: West Group, 1992), § 9.04A, with permission.

V. CRIMES AGAINST JUSTICE AND PUBLIC ADMINISTRATION

A. INTRODUCTION

If a criminal justice system is made unreliable by corruption, weakness, or ridicule, the basic criminal statutes become ineffective. To secure honesty, effectiveness, and dignity in the administration of government and of justice, acts that threaten those values have been criminalized.

"There are not enough jails, not enough policemen, not enough courts to enforce a law not supported by the people."

—Hubert H. Humphrey Speech, Williamsburg, Virginia, May 1, 1965

B. BRIBERY

Bribery is the ancient offense of intending to influence judges, later extended to public officials, and now into the commercial arena. A benefit, not necessarily monetary, is offered to a person in return for a favor that usually must be connected to that person's public duty. The person may not have the ability to deliver the favor, but the agreement must be made with the intent to carry it out. A government contract may be traded for money, a vote for sexual favors, a defeat in a football game for a lucrative job offer. The bribing of jurors, witnesses, and court officers is particularly damaging to the administration of justice. Those who offer and those who accept bribes are equally guilty. Giving and receiving bribes are not interdependent crimes; the conviction for one does not depend on the conviction for the other.

U.S. v. Sun-Diamond Growers (1999) established that 18 U.S.C.A. § 201 (c)(1) requires proof of "a link between a thing of value conferred upon a public official and a specific 'official act' for or because of which it was given." Such a link was not found in the gifts given the United States Agriculture Secretary Mike Espy by the agricultural trade association.

Other federal laws relating to bribery include 21 U.S.C.A. § 622 prohibiting bribery in connection with meat inspection, and the Anti-Kickback Act, 41 U.S.C.A. §§ 51-58. *U.S. v. Purdy* (2nd Cir. 1998) upheld the 41 U.S.C.A. § 53 conviction of the president of a helicopter parts company for bribing the purchasing agents of an assembly firm

EXHIBIT 5–6
Sample Jury Instructions

BRIBERY OF PUBLIC OFFICIAL [18 U.S.C. § 201(b)(1)]

Title 18, United States Code, Section 201(b)(1), makes it a crime for anyone to bribe a public official.

For you to find the defendant guilty of this crime, you must be convinced that the government has proved each of the following beyond a reasonable doubt:

First: That the defendant directly or indirectly gave [offered, promised] something of value to _____ [a public official]; and

Second: That the defendant did so corruptly with intent to:

influence an official act by the public official

or

persuade the public official to omit an act

or

persuade the public official to do an act in violation of his lawful duty.

An act is "corruptly" done if it is done intentionally with an unlawful purpose.

Pattern Jury Instructions (Criminal Cases), 5th Circuit (St. Paul, MN: West Group, 1990), § 2.12, with permission.

selling helicopters to the United States government. Intent was ruled not to be an element of the crime. Part of the federal theft statutes, 18 U.S.C.A. § 666, prohibits bribery concerning programs receiving federal funds. The bribery does not need to involve the funds themselves [*Salinas v. U.S.* (1997)]. The Travel Act, 18 U.S.C.A. § 1952, includes commercial bribery in its prohibition of travel in interstate commerce to commit a bribe in violation of state law where it occurs. The Foreign Corrupt Practices Act prohibits bribery in foreign trade.

C. PERJURY

The elements of perjury are the statement of fact, not opinion, that is both false and material to the issue at hand; that the statement is under oath; that it is made in a judicial proceeding; and that it is made with the specific criminal intent to deceive. All states and federal law, 18 U.S.C.A. § 1621, criminalize perjury. False swearing is the offense if it takes place in other than a judicial proceeding. A Washington state court ruled that if the oath was not required or authorized by law, the defendant could not be convicted of false swearing, *State v. Hovrud* (Wash. App. 1991). Subornation of perjury is the instigation of another to commit perjury, and it must include not only the inducement, but also that the perjury was actually committed by the other person. Defense to perjury charges includes proof that the testimony was truthful, and in some jurisdictions, a recantation before the same tribunal and before harm is done or the perjury is found out.

Bronston v. U.S. (1973) established that a half-truth offered by a "wily witness" is not perjury, as long as the testimony is the literal truth. When asked if he had ever had a Swiss bank account, the defendant replied that his company had had one. He did not reveal that he also had had a personal Swiss account in the past. Giving a different slant to the problem, a witness gave a factually correct answer to a question that misstated the date of a pertinent event. His perjury conviction under 18 U.S.C.A. § 1621 was affirmed in *U.S. v. DeZarn* (6th Cir. 1998), because the series of questions was based on a false premise.

Perjury is difficult to prove, so it is less often the subject of criminal charges than of sentencing enhancements and contempt sanctions.[18] Having been impeached and acquitted of perjury and obstruction of justice, President Clinton was found in civil contempt and fined for giving "intentionally false" testimony in the Lewinsky scandal.[19]

D. OBSTRUCTION OF JUSTICE

Obstruction of justice, covered in federal statute 18 U.S.C.A. §§ 1501 to 1515 and statutes in all states, prohibits a wide variety of interference with governmental proceedings and officers, and can include other crimes in this category, such as perjury and resisting arrest. Impersonating an officer, tampering with a jury or witnesses, tampering with evidence, obstructing a criminal investigation, and interrupting communication are some examples. A police officer who faked a find of cocaine near an arrestee was convicted of obstruction of justice because the arrestee's defense could have been obstructed, *People v. Hollingsead* (Ill. App. 1991).

Obstruction of justice convictions can result from conduct during civil proceedings as well as during criminal ones. *U.S. v. Lundwall* (S.D. N.Y. 1998) denied the dismissal of an indictment for the willful destruction of documents during civil litigation under 18 U.S.C.A. § 1503. Conduct that is otherwise lawful can violate § 1503 if it is done with corrupt intent to obstruct justice. The defendant in *U.S. v. Cueto* (7th Cir. 1998) was convicted of obstruction of justice for obtaining an injunction against an FBI agent investigating a gambling enterprise in which he had an interest.

E. RESISTING ARREST

Resisting arrest under common law was allowed against an illegal arrest. Recently, however, both statutes and court decisions are beginning to favor conviction for resisting any arrest by anyone appearing to be a police officer. According to the rationale behind this trend, the availability of counsel and courts makes resistance unnecessary, leading only to escalating violence. The remedy for unlawful arrest is, therefore, a civil action rather than resistance. Some statutes make resisting arrest a specific intent crime.

Using reasonable force to defend oneself from excessive force by the arresting officer is generally not a crime [*State v. Wright* (Or. 1990)]. Arrest is an ongoing process, and postcustody behavior, such as a defendant's resistance to being placed in a cell after booking and a Breathalyzer test, was found to be resistance to arrest in *State v. Dowd* (S.C. 1991).

F. ESCAPE

Escape or freeing another from lawful custody incurs more serious penalties if force is used. Lawful custody includes custody of police or institutionalization in jail, detention center, penitentiary, reformatory, or other confinement specified by law. A convict under in-house arrest in his own home could not be convicted of escape, because there was no structured or supervised confinement [*Gregory v. State* (Fla. App. 1991)]. Failure to return from temporary release also amounts to escape, although courts are divided about whether specific intent is required. If the custody is lawful, even the innocent may not lawfully escape. When prison conditions threaten harm, escape is justified only if surrender follows as soon as danger passes. Escape to obtain medical care is not usually justified. Aiding escape, rescue, and knowingly harboring a felon are also crimes.

G. CONTEMPT OF COURT

Contempt is disobedience to the court by conduct against its authority, justice, and dignity. Criminal contempt elements are misbehavior in or near the presence of the court that obstructs the administration of justice and is committed with criminal intent, 18 U.S.C.A. § 401. Criminal contempt is a generally accepted common law offense, and statutory in some states. The defendant is presumed innocent, is allowed due process, and must be proved guilty beyond a reasonable doubt.

A defendant who made a threatening gesture toward a testifying witness in a drug conspiracy trial was convicted of contempt because the proceedings had to be interrupted for an inquiry as to whether the jury saw the gesture and because of the intent to intimidate the witness [*U.S. v. McGainey* (D.C. Cir. 1994)].

Direct contempt takes place in the presence of the court, such as a disruption of proceedings. Because the judge is present at the offense, the defendant is informed of the charge, asked to give cause to preclude the judgment, and the judgment is entered summarily. Indirect contempt takes place outside the court's presence and may include violations of confidentiality by a juror or violations of a court order or other court rules. Here, the procedure is more formal, with a written order to the defendant to show cause why he or she should not be held in contempt. The defendant is allowed time to prepare a defense, seek counsel, compel witnesses, and is given access to a jury trial if the sentence is more than six months. Legislative contempt punishes interfering with legislative activities, with citations coming from the legislature for the courts to handle.

The distinction between civil and criminal contempt is not always clear-cut. If a contempt charge is used as punishment and if the act it punishes is also an indictable crime, it is more likely to be criminal. Contempt that is used to force a remedial action is more likely to be civil.

ANALYSIS PROBLEM

5–9. A judge cleared the courtroom because the gallery had gotten unruly. When people were readmitted, a man entered who had not been there before and was unaware of the problem. After the judge asked for quiet, the man popped his gum and was immediately charged and judged in contempt of court. His punishment was a night in jail.

Considering that the judge is both "victim" and trier in contempt of court cases, and also is responsible for the decorum of court proceedings, how would you balance these roles in dealing with this situation and with contempt cases in general?

VI. CONCLUSION

This chapter opened with a discussion of crimes against property. These crimes are differentiated by subtle shifts in the meaning of holding property, from custody to possession to ownership. They are further differentiated by the means with which they are accomplished, such as by force or threat, false statement or document, insider information, or computer. They can target health care funds, industrial secrets, or, again, computers.

Some crimes against the public interest in order and safety, decency, justice, and operation of government do not present a clear indication of harm done, or even require intent to harm by the offender. Vagrancy and obscenity are such crimes. Others, such as child exploitation, have specific victims. In general, these crimes are meant to protect society. As ideals and goals of the society change, so do the laws.

Rework the chart in Exhibit 5–7 to reflect your state's statutes, then use it to review the elements of the crimes covered in this chapter.

EXHIBIT 5–7
Common Elements of Crimes

CRIME	ACTUS REUS	MENS REA	GRADED BY	STATUTES
Larceny	Wrongful taking (by stealth or trick) and carrying away of property of another.	Intent to permanently deprive owner.	Value of property to owner.	
Embezzlement	Conversion rather than taking.		Value of property.	
False pretenses	Gaining title to property by false representation of past or present material fact.	Knowingly, intent to defraud.		18 U.S.C.A. §§ 1001–1035, 1341–1347, and so on.

EXHIBIT 5–7 *(Continued)*
Common Elements of Crimes

CRIME	ACTUS REUS	MENS REA	GRADED BY	STATUTES
Bad checks	Issuing insufficient funds, no-account, or forged checks.	Knowingly.	Value.	
Receiving stolen goods	Assume control of property from thief with benefit.	Knowledge (rare), belief that goods were stolen, intent to deprive owner.		
Forgery	Making false document or altering authentic document.	Intent to defraud.		18 U.S.C.A. §§ 470–514.
Uttering	Passing a forged document.	Intent to defraud.		
Robbery	Larceny in the victim's presence or from the person by force or threat of immediate force.	Intent to deprive owner.	Amount of force.	18 U.S.C.A. §§ 2111–2114.
Extortion	Larceny by threat of future harm.			18 U.S.C.A. §§ 875–79, 1951.
Consolidated theft	"Obtains" property of other.			18 U.S.C.A. § 641.
Cybercrimes	Accessing restricted computer information.	Knowingly, intentionally, maliciously.	Value of information, intent to defraud.	18 U.S.C.A. § 1030.
Electronic theft	Reproduction and distribution of copyrighted material.	Knowingly, intentionally.	Value of material.	17 U.S.C.A. §§ 101, 506, 507; 18 U.S.C.A. §§ 2319, 2319A, 2320.
Health care fraud	Misrepresentation in billings.	Knowingly, willfully.		18 U.S.C.A. § 1035.
Trademark infringement	Unauthorized use of trademarks.	Knowingly.		15 U.S.C.A. §§ 1015 *et. seq.*
Economic espionage	Theft of trade secrets.	Knowingly, intentionally for economic benefit.		18 U.S.C.A. §§ 1831–1839.

Continued

EXHIBIT 5–7 *(Continued)*
Common Elements of Crimes

CRIME	ACTUS REUS	MENS REA	GRADED BY	STATUTES
Money laundering	Exchanging monetary instruments.	Knowingly, with intent to conceal, to promote criminal conduct, or to avoid tax or reporting requirements.		18 U.S.C.A. § 1956.
Securities fraud	Fraud in stock exchanges and trading.			15 U.S.C.A. §§ 77a *et seq.*; 78 *et seq.*
Disorderly conduct	Disruption of peace.	None, or purposeful, reckless.		18 U.S.C.A. §§ 1752, 248.
Riot	Group action, public terror, prior order to disperse, clear and present danger.	With intent.		18 U.S.C.A. §§ 2101–2102.
Vagrancy, loitering	Gathering or remaining in public place.	None.		
Endangering public health and environment	Violating standards.	None, knowingly, negligently.		Many federal laws.
Illegal firearm use and distribution	Violation of restrictions on possession, sale, and transportation of firearms.	Knowing, willful.	Increased danger, type, and number of firearms.	18 U.S.C.A. §§ 921–930.
Prostitution	Sexual activity for hire.	Knowingly, with intent.		18 U.S.C.A. § 2421.
Obscenity	Possession and distribution of obscene matter, harmful to minors.	Knowingly.		18 U.S.C.A. §§ 1460–1470; 47 U.S.C.A. §§ 223, 231.
Child pornography and exploitation	Using or allowing a minor to engage in sexually explicit conduct, producing, possessing, or distributing depictions of such conduct.	Knowingly.		18 U.S.C.A. §§ 2251–2260, 2425.

EXHIBIT 5–7 *(Concluded)*
Common Elements of Crimes

CRIME	ACTUS REUS	MENS REA	GRADED BY	STATUTES
Gambling	Transmission of bets via wire communications, operating illegal gambling business.	Knowingly.		18 U.S.C.A. §§ 1081, 1084, 1955.
Drug offenses	Manufacture, transportation, distribution, possession.	Knowingly, general intent; none.	Extent of operation, value or amount of drug.	21 U.S.C.A. §§ 811 *et seq.*, 848, 853, 860.
Bribery	Offering or accepting a benefit in return for a favor connected to public duty.	Willfully.		18 U.S.C.A. §§ 201–225.
Perjury	Giving false testimony of fact under oath in judicial proceeding.	Intent to deceive.		18 U.S.C.A. § 1621.
Obstruction of justice, resisting arrest, contempt of court	Interfering with government proceedings and officers.	With intent.		18 U.S.C.A. §§ 1501–1515.

SYSTEM FOLDER ASSIGNMENTS

- Add your state's statutes to the chart in Exhibit 5–7.
- Revise the listing of elements to reflect the requirements in your state.

APPLICATION ASSIGNMENTS

1.   A defendant purchased stolen nonnegotiable savings bonds for $500. The face value of the bonds was several thousand dollars and the purchase price of the bonds was more than $100, but because they could be cashed only by the owner they were worth no more than the paper they were printed on to the thief [*People v. Dyer*, 403 N.W.2d 84 (Mich. App. 1986)]. Should his conviction for receiving stolen goods valued at more than $100 be reduced?

2.   A defendant took aluminum beams from a building site intending to sell them at a recycling center. When he found that they would not fit into his truck, he cut them into pieces. Suspecting theft, the recycling center refused to take the beams and called police. The defendant was charged with theft of the beams and criminal mischief for damage to the beams [*Coleman v. State*, 846 P.2d 141 (Alaska App. 1993)]. The defense argued that because the defendant intended to permanently deprive the owner, the damage was irrelevant. Should he be found guilty of two crimes?

3. A defendant who had left his car to be repaired was not provided with the required estimate for the costs, which he considered to be excessive. He took his car without paying for the repairs [*State v. Pike*, 826 P.2d 152 (Wash. 1992)]. Should he be charged with theft?

4. A defendant paid for cattle with a postdated check. When the seller tried to cash it, there were no funds to cover it. Should the defendant be charged with issuing a bad check?

5. If the forgery law in the state of Columbia includes only legal documents, what charges might be brought against the seller of a fake Picasso painting? If cousin Mort secretly added a paragraph praising his own good character to Aunt Bessie's will, is that forgery?

6. A Canadian national who was stopped for a traffic violation in the United States displayed a "passport" from "Elohim's Kingdom of Israel," for which he was charged with possessing falsely made documents. Considering that passports are not necessary for travel between Canada and the United States, was this traveler guilty of this forgery-related charge? Why or why not? See *U.S. v. Fox*, 776 F.Supp. 569 (N.D. Tex. 1991).

7. The defendant entered the home of an elderly couple he had worked for, killed them, then took property from their home [*Jones v. State*, 652 So.2d 346 (Fla. 1995)]. Should he be charged with robbery?

8. A man who had been on a hunting trip was turned away from purchasing beer at a store because he was already intoxicated. He went to his vehicle, returned with his shotgun, and threatened the storekeeper. When the beer was handed over, he paid for it. Should he be charged with robbery? [See *Jupiter v. State*, 616 A.2d 412 (Md. 1992)].

9. In Case III of Chapter 1, what would be the appropriate charges against Cat Bermuda? Against Lacey Rude? Why?

10. The defendant beat the victim until she gave him the bill of sale for her car. The bill of sale was not a valid one, so he did not gain title to the car [*State v. Martinez*, 884 P.2d 3 (Wash. App. 1994)]. Is this extortion in your state?

11. The defendant in *U.S. v. Starr*, 816 F.2d 94 (2nd Cir. 1987) ran a business sorting, addressing, and mailing advertising brochures. He hid higher postage mail inside bulk rate mailing sacks, only paying the lower rate while customers were billed for the higher rate. He netted $418,000. Whom did he defraud?

12. A psychiatrist sent bills through the mail to insurance companies for more than thirty-five hours of patient care per seven hour day. Besides health care fraud, what crime did he commit?

13. If you were on the defense team in Case V from Chapter 1, how would you attack possession charges against your clients? If you were with the prosecution, what would you argue?

14. The defendant in a civil rights case filed an affidavit falsely claiming not to have the money to satisfy the judgment against him [*U.S. v. Holland*, 22 F.2d 1040 (11th Cir. 1994)]. Did he commit a crime? If so, what crime?

HELPFUL WEB SITES

www.usdoj.gov/criminal/cybercrime
    Current news and federal action
www.cyber.findlaw.com
    Information and links
www.cybercrimes.net
    University of Dayton School of Law, list of computer crime statutes by state

www.jmls.edu/cyber
    John Marshall Law School, links to cases, statutes, law review articles, and pending legislation on cyberlaw
www.infowar.com
    Recent articles on cybercrime
www.loundy.com
    Resources on technology law
www.search.org
    National Consortium for Justice Information and Statistics, provides training in computer crime investigation
www.saul.com/env/
    Updates and links on developments in environmental law
http://lcweb.loc.gov.copyright.circs/circ1.html
    United States site on copyright basics
www.ipmag.com
    Intellectual Property Magazine, affiliate of National Law Journal, current cases
www.seclaw.com
    Developments in securities law

INTERNET EXERCISES

1. Go to www.cybercrimes.net; write a summary list of current "Cybercrimes in the News."
2. Go to www.ipmag.com; summarize the current issues in intellectual property law.
3. Go to www.lectlaw.com, through the Reference Room, Criminal Law and Procedure, find "Prosecuting Environmental Crime: Los Angeles County." In that article, what three elements are essential to an environmental crimes prosecution strike force?

QUESTIONS FOR STUDY AND REVIEW

1. Define and give examples of tangible and intangible property.
2. How have technological advances changed the definition of "property" in theft cases?
3. How do "possession" and "ownership" differ in theft cases?
4. What are the common law elements of larceny? List the elements of each theft crime that make it different from common law larceny by stealth.
5. What are the benefits and problems involved with consolidated theft statutes?
6. In what ways can computers be involved in crime?
7. What are the characteristics of white-collar crime?
8. Who is the victim in crimes against public order, morals, and administration? What are some of the problems with these laws?
9. What are the differences between disorderly conduct and riot?
10. What is a common problem with some ordinances against loitering?
11. What kind of laws usually are involved in health and environment offenses? What mens rea usually is required?
12. What are the major provisions of the U.S. Gun Control Act?
13. What is required for material to be considered obscene?
14. What are the *Dost* factors used in *U.S. v. Wolf* (10th Cir. 1989) to define child pornography?

15. For what purposes is the use of the otherwise illegal drugs of marijuana and peyote allowed?
16. What are the crimes against public administration? Why are they important?
17. Explain the differences between direct and indirect contempt of court.

KEY TERMS LIST

Bailee	Cybercrime	Status
Blue sky laws	Fighting words	Tangible property
Claim of right	Insider trading	Trade secrets
Conversion	Intangible property	White-collar crime

ENDNOTES

1. WAYNE R. LaFAVE AND AUSTIN W. SCOTT, JR., SUBSTANTIVE CRIMINAL LAW, vol. 2, 391 West Group, 1986.
2. MODEL PENAL CODE § 223.2, comment at 181–182 (1980).
3. LaFAVE, *supra* at 419–421.
4. Robert S. Litt, Deputy Assistant Attorney General, U.S. Dept. of Justice, Statement before Subcommittee on Technology, Terrorism and Government Information, Senate Judiciary Committee, Washington, D.C., Mar. 19, 1997.
5. Wendy R. Leibowitz, *Lawyers and Technology: Law Spanks Spammers*, NLJ, Mar. 15, 1999, A18.
6. Health Care Fraud Report, Fiscal Year 1998, Office of Deputy Attorney General, DOJ Homepage, www.usdoj.gov.
7. http://www.usdoj.gov/criminal/cybercrime/desktop.htm.
8. Efrem M. Grail, W. Thomas McGough Jr., Jeffry M. Klink, *Trade Secrets*, NLJ, Aug. 17, 1998, B5–B6; David E. Rovella, *Trial Nears for Untested Secrets Law*, NLJ, Mar. 8, 1999, B1–B2.
9. *Town Sees Red over Blue Words*, NLJ, Nov. 1, 1999, A26.
10. *Boom? To Your Room*, NLJ, Nov. 1, 1999, A26.
11. Jodie Morse, *Cracking down on the homeless*, TIME, Dec. 20, 1999, at 69–70.
12. Richard Harwood, *Huge Number of Handguns Sets U.S. Apart in the World*, LEXINGTON HERALD-LEADER, Dec. 3, 1997, at A15.
13. Associated Press, *Men, Women Differ Widely in Gun Control Poll*, THE RICHMOND REGISTER, Sept. 10, 1999 at A12.
14. Erik Larson, *Squeezing Out the Bad Guys*, TIME, Aug. 9, 1999, at 32–33, 35.
15. Elaine Shannon, *Have Gun? Will Travel*, TIME, Aug. 16, 1999, at 30.
16. John Cheves, *Vague Language, Juries Sentiments Foil Child Gun Law*, LEXINGTON HERALD-LEADER, Oct. 12, 1998, at A1, A6.
17. Kenneth A. Freeling & Donald E. Wiggins, *Internet Law*, NLJ, March 30, 1999, B7.
18. Laurie S. Levenson, *Criminal Law: Penalties for Lying*, NLJ, March 22, 1999, B23.
19. Deborah Barfield, *Judge Fines Clinton $90,000 for False Testimony*, LEXINGTON HERALD-LEADER, July 30, 1999, at A3.

INCHOATE AND ORGANIZED CRIMES

I. INTRODUCTION

What if Kate Lamb had safely escaped her attacker in Case I? What if Cat Bermuda in Case III had arrived outside Mayor Chen's home just in time to see Lacey Rude led away by police for the theft of the golden artifact? What if the homeowners of Haden Hills in Case VI had, on a day's reflection, decided to accept their new neighbors? Has a crime been committed in any of these situations?

Think back to the reasons behind criminal law. We have seen that society has adopted the right or duty to punish those who put it in danger, to deter future threat of crime, to rehabilitate offenders to live within the law. It seems only logical that those who intend to do harm, but fail, pose a danger to society that also can be considered criminal. Society does not benefit by freeing them from liability because of the stroke of luck that interrupted their criminal purpose, particularly if that fortuity was the intervention of police. It also seems reasonable to allow law enforcement intervention at an early stage to prevent completion of the crime. But to criminalize intent alone, to punish evil thoughts, has been thoroughly rejected as an undesirable goal, if not an impossible one. Therefore, some step toward completing the intended crime is necessary for prosecution. Because that step stops short of causing harm, a contrastingly high degree of intent or purpose is demanded.

Inchoate crimes are incomplete crimes; that is, crimes that are either in the beginning stages of perpetration or fail to achieve the criminal objective. In some cases the law is used to control dangerous conduct, to allow intervention where behavior is on the verge of causing harm, as in attempted murder. In other cases the law aims to control dangerous persons, such as those involved in conspiracy or organized crime. Here, the criminal intent is assumed to be strong enough to endanger society even though steps taken to complete a crime may be minimal.

Although some substantive crimes are preparatory in nature, such as burglary or assault with intent to commit another crime, inchoate crimes generally include only attempt, conspiracy, and solicitation. Each of these will be considered individually, but it may be helpful to consider them now on a scale of proximity to the completed crime. At the remotest end of the scale, Max Legrise offers Cat Bermuda a percentage of the take if she will steal the golden idol, and she refuses. He is guilty of solicitation to commit theft. If Cat Bermuda accepts the deal and buys the equipment she will need to scale the wall of the mayor's house, they are guilty of conspiracy to commit theft. If Cat is apprehended just as she reaches for the idol on its pedestal, they are guilty of attempted theft, the closest on the scale to the completed crime. A combination of two inchoate crimes is way off the remote end of the scale. Solicitation to commit conspiracy and attempted attempt, for example, are so far from the substantive crime that they are not prosecuted. The court in *State v. Sanchez* (Ariz. App. 1993) rejected attempted conspiracy to sell narcotics as a crime.

Because defenses to inchoate crimes are unique, they are discussed in this chapter rather than with the more general defenses presented in Chapter 7, which may also apply. The Model Penal Code § 5.05(2) provides for dismissal or a lower grade conviction if the conduct is "so inherently unlikely to result or culminate in the commission of a crime" that there is little public danger.

Model Penal Code § 5.05(1) gives inchoate crimes "the same grade and degree as the most serious offense which is attempted or solicited or is an object of the conspiracy." The exception is that "[a]n attempt, solicitation or conspiracy to commit a felony of the first degree is a felony of the second degree." Not all jurisdictions have adopted this guideline, however, so be sure to consult your state's statutes.

The added danger of people working together to accomplish a criminal objective, such as in conspiracy, is increased within a criminal enterprise that is ongoing and run like a business. Federal law targets drug kingpins in the Continuing Criminal Enterprise (CCE) statute and organized racketeering crimes in the Racketeer Influenced and Corrupt Organizations (RICO) Act. Some state laws also cover RICO offenses. Some states and municipalities have laws and ordinances to control criminal gangs.

"Crime and intention of crime are equal in their nature." Cicero, 106–43 B.C.

—W. Gurney Benham, *Putnam's Complete Book of Quotations, Proverbs and Household Words*, 1927

Most criminal enterprise convictions require one or more offenses in a pattern or on-going set of connecting circumstances.

II.   ATTEMPT

A.   INTRODUCTION

For all practical purposes, attempt was not formulated as a crime until 1784 in England. A servant, intending arson, left a lighted candle in his master's house, but the house did not burn. Lord Mansfield's decision in the ensuing case, *Rex v. Scofield* (Cald. 1784), criminalized a harmless act because of its harmful intent.[1] The misdemeanor crime of attempt to commit any offense was accepted doctrine in England by 1830, too late to have been brought to America in the body of common law. An 1832 United States statute criminalized attempted murder, and a generic attempt statute

"If there isn't a law there will be."

—Harold Farber *New York Times Magazine,* March 17, 1968

EXHIBIT 6–1
Sample Jury Instructions

ATTEMPT

"The defendant is charged in [Count _____ of] the indictment with attempting [e.g., to use a passport issued to another person in violation of Section 1544] of Title 18 of the United States Code. In order for the defendant to be found guilty of that charge, the government must prove each of the following elements beyond a reasonable doubt:

   First, the defendant intended to [e.g., use a passport the defendant knew had been issued to another person]; and

   Second, the defendant did something which was a substantial step toward committing the crime.

   It is a crime to [e.g., knowingly use a passport issued for the use of another person].

   [Mere preparation is not a substantial step toward the commission of the crime of _____ .]"

   Manual of Model Jury Instructions for the Ninth Circuit, Instruction No. 5.03 (1989).

"A SUBSTANTIAL STEP"—DEFINED

A defendant may be found guilty of attempting to commit a crime even though no one actually did all of the acts necessary in order to commit the crime. A defendant may not be found guilty, however, of attempting to commit any crime merely by thinking about it or even by making some plans or some preparation for the commission of a crime.

   The difference between conduct which violates the law and conduct which does not violate the law, in this regard, is what is referred to as "a substantial step" towards the commission of a crime.

   In determining whether or not the defendant took "a substantial step" towards the commission of a crime, you must consider all of the evidence admitted in the case concerning that defendant and the alleged commission of that crime.

   In order to find defendant _____ guilty of committing the crime of attempted _____ , the government must prove beyond a reasonable doubt, that the mental processes of defendant _____ passed from the stage of thinking about the crime of _____ to actually intending to commit that crime *and* that the physical process of defendant _____ went beyond and passed from the stage of mere preparation to some firm, clear, and undeniable action to accomplish that intent.

Edward DeWitt, Charles Blackmar, Kevin O'Malley, *Federal Jury Practice and Instructions, Criminal,* vol. 2 (St. Paul, MN: West Group, 1990), § 21.04, with permission.

followed in 1836.[2] Currently, there is no general federal attempt statute, but attempt is addressed in the context of specific crimes such as homicide, 18 U.S.C.A. § 1113; bank robbery, 18 U.S.C.A. § 2113; and passport offenses, 18 U.S.C.A. § 1541.

Prior to the Model Penal Code grading of attempt as equal to the completed crime, with the exception of attempted first degree felonies equal to second degree felonies, states used a variety of grading schemes. Some sentencing scales depended on the category of the completed crime; others provided for a proportion, usually half, of the sentence of the completed crime; some states fixed a maximum penalty for all attempts; and a few jurisdictions equated attempt with the completed crime. Inconsistencies abounded, with attempt sometimes being punished more severely than the completed crime. Not all modern statutes adhere to the Model Penal Code standard, but consistency has improved.[3] You will need to research the statutes in your own jurisdiction to find the grading levels used there. Also note whether your jurisdiction limits attempt to certain categories of crimes.

The elements of attempt are intent and an overt act beyond preparation toward accomplishing the intent. If the crime is indeed completed, attempt usually merges with the substantive crime and is not prosecuted separately. Even if the crime has been completed, however, prosecution and conviction for attempt rather than the substantive crime is allowed by statute in many jurisdictions. Problems arise in the balance between the two remaining elements. How far must the actor progress to demonstrate a firm intention to commit the objective offense? How soon in the progression of events leading to the crime may police intervene to prevent harm?

B. MENS REA IN ATTEMPT

The classic case for discussing mens rea in attempt is *Thacker v. Commonwealth* (Va. 1922). The defendant and his companion were walking past a tent where a woman and her child were sleeping. Intoxicated, the defendant shot a gun to put out the lantern shining through the walls of the tent, narrowly missing the woman and child. He was charged with attempted murder. Because recklessness is sufficient mens rea for the charge of murder, the death of one of the occupants of the tent would have constituted murder. There was, however, no such result. Without harm, there is a correspondingly greater emphasis on intent. It is logically impossible to intend to be or try to be reckless, so crimes committed recklessly or negligently are incompatible with attempt. Without harm and without specific intent, there was no attempted murder.

"It is worse than a crime, it is a blunder." Attributed to Talleyrand, 1754–1838

—William S. Walsh, International Encyclopedia of Prose and Poetical Quotations, 1951

Two levels of intent are at issue in *Thacker*. The defendant had the intent to shoot the gun into the tent, general intent of conduct, but not the intent to commit murder, specific intent of result. It is the specific intent to effect a criminal result that is usually required in attempt. When an act is ambiguous, such as driving slowly back and forth in front of a bank, specific intent is necessary to conclude criminal attempt.

More recent cases bolster *Thacker* by refusing to recognize depraved indifference and recklessness as sufficient mens rea for attempt. The court in *State v. Vigil* (Utah 1992) granted a motion to prevent a charge of attempted depraved indifference homicide as an alternative to second degree murder, because one cannot attempt to be depraved or indifferent. Similarly, *State v. Hemmer* (Neb. App. 1995) held that no such crime as attempted reckless assault of a police officer exists.

As we have seen, completed strict liability crimes do not require proof of intent or even knowledge. Therefore, attempt convictions for strict liability crimes are barred because they add an element of intent that the main crime lacks [*People v. Campbell* (N.Y. 1988)]. An attempted first degree robbery conviction was affirmed in *People v. Miller* (N.Y. 1995), even though the degree level was a strict liability element of aggravating circumstances, because the substantive crime of robbery requires intent.

Be careful to note that some aspects of knowledge do not affect true crimes and will not exonerate a thief who thinks she is taking a trinket when the object is actually a priceless pre–Columbian artifact. Here, specific intent applies to the taking of the object, not to its value. Usually, if the facts are enough to convict the actor of the completed crime, they also suffice for attempt.

ANALYSIS PROBLEM

6–1. *Gentry v. State* (Fla. 1983) challenged *Thacker* by allowing general intent to be sufficient for attempt. In *Gentry,* the defendant pointed a gun at his father's head and pulled the trigger several times. His conviction for attempted murder was upheld even though specific intent was not shown. Do you think the circumstances are parallel to *Thacker?* Do you think the court was justified in not requiring specific intent?

C. ACTUS REUS IN ATTEMPT

The common law elements of attempt include an act beyond preparation in furtherance of a criminal intent. Many states reiterate that mere preparation is not enough to qualify as attempt. What is often lacking is a clear description of "mere preparation," not to mention an explanation of what *is* sufficient. This lack of clarity provides a great deal of latitude in the interpretation of this element. Possession of burglary tools that might constitute no more than preparation in one state may be a substantive crime in another. A careful study of your jurisdiction's statutes and case law will help you nail down what is required in your practice. Analyze the law for comparisons to the following tests for proximity.

1. ***Res ipsa loquitur,*** a Latin phrase meaning "the thing speaks for itself," requires that the act, standing alone, reveal criminal intent. When this is the test to determine attempt, no other evidence that might corroborate the purpose is allowed. Even a confession of intent to steal a battery and radio in *Campbell & Bradley v. Ward* (N.Z.L.R. 1955) was rejected when the act of entering a parked car was determined to be insufficient to stand on its own. This test reduces the value of corroborative evidence and also raises the problem of determining whether any conduct unequivocally reveals intent.

2. The last proximate act test was used in *Regina v. Eagleton* (Cr. App. 1855) to demand that everything necessary to accomplish the target crime had been done. The gun had to go off, the payroll envelope had to be snatched, the match had to be dropped; only a defective aim, an empty envelope, a deluge of rain kept the crime from being completed. This standard was so high that it was rejected by the same court within the year and has never been widely adopted.[4]

3. Dangerous proximity is a test that can be applied to nearness in time, distance, or necessary steps to complete the crime. The defendant in *People v. Rizzo* (N.Y. 1927) planned to rob the payroll clerk of a construction company. Police observed him drive to the bank where the clerk was to pick up the money, and then to various construction sites in his search for the victim. He was stopped, found armed, and convicted of attempted robbery. The court found that his actions did not reach the New York statute requirement of being "very near to accomplishment of the crime," so his conviction was overturned. Besides "proximity," the word "dangerous" is operative in this test. The seriousness of potential harm, the certainty of suspicion, the momentum of the steps toward completion are all factors to be evaluated.

   New York's requirement of "very near" or "dangerously near" was met in *People v. Acosta* (N.Y. 1993), a case of attempted possession of a controlled substance. The defendant had ordered drugs from the supplier, admitted the seller into his home, and checked the substance. Completion of the sale was within the defendant's control. A defendant who had reached an agree-

Res ipsa loquitur:
Latin for "the thing speaks for itself"; the act, standing alone, reveals criminal intent.

ment with a cocaine dealer but found that there was not enough of the substance available or sufficient money to buy it had not gone far enough to be guilty of attempted possession [*People v. Warren* (N.Y. 1985)].

4. The indispensable step test nullifies attempt in cases where one necessary step toward the crime is left undone. Using this test, attempted computer fraud cannot be charged if the defendant has yet to gain computer system access. Potential drug kingpins who plan to distribute through street dealers are innocent until the dealers have been recruited.

5. The probable desistance test requires a prediction of whether the defendant would or would not voluntarily withdraw from the criminal enterprise if left alone. To counteract the difficulty in predicting behavior, the test is objective, asking if an average person would desist rather than asking if this particular person would desist. The defendant in *State v. Stewart* (Wis. 1988) asked the victim for money, reached into his pocket for a gun, and stopped only when his companion intervened. The court ruled that he failed the probable desistance test and affirmed his conviction for attempted robbery.

6. The Model Penal Code provides that the defendant must have committed a "substantial step in a course of conduct planned to culminate in his commission of the crime," § 5.01(1)(c), and also that the step be "strongly corroborative of the actor's criminal purpose," § 5.01(2). This standard favors control at an earlier stage than the proximity tests and, therefore, widens the net to include dangerous persons rather than only dangerous conduct. It goes beyond mere preparation, however; strong corroboration of the act with the purpose is required, which narrows the guesswork regarding intent. Activities that could qualify as that substantial step are listed in § 5.01(2)(a–g) and include the following:

   (a) *lying in wait, searching for or following the contemplated victim of the crime;*
   (b) *enticing or seeking to entice the contemplated victim of the crime to go to the place contemplated for its commission;*
   (c) *reconnoitering the place contemplated for the commission of the crime;*
   (d) *unlawful entry of a structure, vehicle or enclosure in which it is contemplated that the crime will be committed;*
   (e) *possession of materials to be employed in the commission of the crime, which are specially designed for such unlawful use or which can serve no lawful purpose of the actor under the circumstances;*
   (f) *possession, collection or fabrication of materials to be employed in the commission of the crime, at or near the place contemplated for its commission, where such possession, collection or fabrication serves no lawful purpose of the actor under the circumstances;*
   (g) *soliciting an innocent agent to engage in conduct constituting an element of the crime.*

A defendant who spent two weeks observing a bank, sketched the bank, and reconnoitered the house of the bank manager to be taken hostage had committed the substantial step required for attempted bank robbery [*U.S. v. Prichard* (10th Cir. 1986)]. Sitting in a van with the motor running 200 feet from a bank while wearing a blond wig was not considered a substantial step in *U.S. v. Still* (9th Cir. 1988).

An attempted rape was the "overt act" required in the attempted second degree murder conviction for a defendant who knew he carried HIV and neglected to use a condom [*Smallwood v. State* (Md. App. 1995)]. Read the decision in *Walters v. Maass* (9th Cir. 1995) for a discussion of the overt act as corroboration of the intent in the attempted crime.

ANALYSIS PROBLEM

6–2. Using the *res ipsa loquitur* test, can you read intent in a lighted match dropped near a highly insured tenement building? Is purpose always clear when a gun is pointed? Do you agree with the difference in the rulings of *Prichard* and *Still* using the substantial step test? What distinguishes one from the other?

WALTERS v. MAASS
United States Court of Appeals, Ninth Circuit 1993
45 F.3d 1355 9th Cir. 1995
[Citations omitted]

POOLE, Circuit Judge

Roger Matthew Walters, an Oregon state prisoner, appeals the district court's denial of his 28 U.S.C. § 2254 habeas corpus petition challenging his conviction and sentence for attempted rape, attempted sodomy, and attempted kidnapping of a thirteen-year old girl. We review de novo. We affirm in part and reverse in part and remand to the district court with instructions to grant the writ on the ground that insufficient evidence supports Walters' convictions for attempted rape and attempted sodomy.

I

Walters first contends that he was denied a fair trial when the state court admitted evidence that in 1981, he approached another thirteen-year old girl with the ploy of searching for a nonexistent white German shepherd, offered her $20, and then kidnapped her, took her to his trailer, and forcibly raped and sodomized her. Walters used the same German shepherd ploy in this case to try to lure the thirteen-year old victim into his truck. The state court admitted the prior bad acts evidence as proof of intent.

The Oregon court did not err by admitting evidence of Walters' 1981 convictions. Walters' use of the German shepherd ploy in 1981 was relevant to show his intent in using the same ploy in 1987. Moreover, the prior act was not too remote in time. Although seven years elapsed between the two crimes, Walters spent almost all of that time in jail serving his sentence for the 1981 crime. The trial court reduced the danger of unfair prejudice by giving a limiting instruction that the evidence could be used only to show "motive, opportunity, intent, preparation, plan, knowledge, or absence of mistake or accident" and could not be used to show Walters' bad character. . . .

II

Walters contends that the evidence was insufficient to support his convictions for attempted first-degree kidnapping, attempted first-degree rape, and attempted first-degree sodomy. . . .

Under Oregon law, conviction for attempt requires proof beyond a reasonable doubt that the defendant "intentionally engage[d] in conduct which constitutes a substantial step toward commission of the crime." Or.Rev.Stat. § 161.405(1).

To constitute a substantial step toward the commission of a crime, the defendant's conduct must (1) "advance the criminal purpose charged, and (2) provide some verification of the existence of that purpose." Mere preparation is insufficient to constitute a substantial step.

The difference between making preparations and taking a substantial step toward the commission of a crime is one of degree. In evaluating whether conduct constitutes a substantial step, we have stated that although behavior need not be incompatible with innocence to be punishable as an attempt, " 'it must be necessary to the consummation of the crime and be of such a nature that a reasonable observer, viewing it in context[,] could conclude beyond a reasonable doubt that it was undertaken in accordance with a design' " to commit the particular crime charged. *Scott,* 767 F.2d at 1312 (quoting with approval *United States v. Manley,* 632 F.2d 978, 987–88 (2d Cir.1980), *cert. denied,* 449 U.S. 1112, 101 S.Ct. 922, 66 L.Ed.2d 841 (1981)). Moreover, a substantial step must entail "an 'overt act adapted to, approximating, and which in the ordinary and likely course of things will result in, the commission of the particular crime.' " (quoting with approval *Manley,* 632 F.2d at 988).

Walters asserts that the evidence was insufficient to establish his intent to commit the crimes of first-degree kidnapping, rape, and sodomy and to establish that he took a substantial step toward the commission of those crimes.

Certainly Walters' intent is manifested by (1) evidence regarding his use of the German shepherd ruse in 1981 to kidnap, rape, and sodomize another thirteen-year old girl, (2) his persistent attempts to lure the victim into his truck using the same ruse, (3) his actions in following the victim home, (4) his strange speech patterns when he talked to the victim's mother, and (5) his statements to the police officer.[5] In addition, Walters' attempt to entice the victim into his truck clearly advances the criminal purpose of first-degree kidnapping and strongly corroborates the existence of his purpose to commit that crime. Thus, we agree with the Oregon Supreme Court that this conduct constitutes a substantial step toward the commission of the crime of first-degree kidnapping, and we do not disturb Walters' conviction for attempted first-degree kidnapping. *See Walters,* 804 P.2d at 1167–68. . . .

The more troubling question is whether Walters' attempt to entice the victim into his truck constitutes a substantial step toward the commission of the crimes of rape and sodomy when the only evidence of intent to rape and sodomize is Walters' 1981 conviction for kidnapping, raping, and sodomizing another thirteen-year old girl. If in 1981, Walters had committed other crimes (for example, breaking the victim's arm and stealing her wallet), it would be difficult to conclude now that enticement into the truck constituted a substantial step toward the commission of those crimes. At some point, the link between the enticement and the charged crimes becomes too attenuated: we cannot say that the enticement strongly corroborates any intent to commit those crimes such that a "reasonable observer, viewing it [the enticement] in context[,] could conclude beyond a reasonable doubt that it was undertaken in accordance with a design" to commit the crimes.

The only step Walters took toward the commission of the charged crimes was his attempt to entice the victim into his truck. It may be that this act to some extent corroborates Walters' intent to commit some sexual assault, but we cannot agree that it *strongly* corroborates his intent to commit those crimes. Moreover, attempting to entice the victim into a truck does not, in the ordinary and likely course of events, result in the crimes of rape and sodomy. . . .

In sum, where the only evidence of Walters' intent to commit the crimes of rape and sodomy is the 1981 crimes, we hold that Walters' attempt to entice the victim into his truck is not a substantial step toward the commission of the crimes of rape and sodomy. Accordingly, we direct that the writ be granted with regard to Walters' convictions for attempted rape and attempted sodomy on the ground of constitutional insufficiency of the evidence.

III

. . .

The trial court's sentencing of Walters as a dangerous offender, however, rested on its determination that he was guilty of attempted rape and attempted sodomy. Because we have invalidated these convictions, Walters is entitled to be resentenced on the sole basis of his conviction for attempted first-degree kidnapping.

IV

We affirm the district court's determinations concerning the admissibility of the prior bad acts evidence, the sufficiency of the evidence to support Walters' conviction for attempted first-degree kidnapping, and the constitutionality of Oregon's dangerous offender statute as applied to Walters. We reverse the district court's determination that the evidence was sufficient to support Walters' convictions for attempted first-degree rape and attempted first-degree sodomy. We remand the case to the district court and direct the court to grant the petition on the ground that insufficient evidence supports these convictions. Walters' dangerous offender sentence will be vacated, and the state court will conduct new sentencing proceedings to determine whether a dangerous offender sentence is appropriate on the sole basis of Walters' conviction for attempted first-degree kidnapping.

AFFIRMED in part, REVERSED in part, and REMANDED with instructions.

TANG, Senior Circuit Judge, dissenting:

I share Judge Poole's concern with this case; Oregon appears on the verge of criminalizing pure (albeit bad) thought. But in finding sufficient evidence of a "substantial step" toward rape and sodomy in Walters's efforts to have his intended victim get into his truck, the Oregon Supreme Court retains at least a vestige of the *actus reus* requirement. I therefore respectfully dissent.

. . .

Here, Oregon has declared that "enticement" constitutes one form of the "substantial step" required for an attempt conviction under state law.

Because there is sufficient evidence to support a finding of enticement under Oregon law, we should defer to state law and uphold Walters's convictions.

---

5. In response to the officer's question as to whether he had "sexual temptations" toward the victim, Walters paused and responded, "I could have found myself in an uncomfortable position today and didn't mean to." He also told the officer that his prior conviction was for first-degree rape of an adult, that he did not have prior problems with juveniles, and that he was not "a tree jumper . . . the [kind of] guy who hides behind bushes and waits for a young girl to walk down the street and jumps out of the bushes and molests them." He also told the officer that the victim was "13 going on 24" and that he thought she was "a lot older than 13."

D.   DEFENSES TO ATTEMPT

1.   Introduction

A client of your supervising attorney has been charged with attempt. The attorney asks you to look for possible defenses to the charge. Where do you start?

The general defenses discussed in Chapter 7 are most likely to be helpful. There are some defenses special to the area of attempt, however, but they apply only in very narrow circumstances. These defenses are abandonment and impossibility.

2.   Abandonment

Abandonment, giving up the criminal enterprise before its completion, is not widely accepted as a defense in attempt cases. Involuntary abandonment is particularly unacceptable. If the actor withdraws because the police arrive or the victim turns out to be especially strong and determined to hold onto her purse, the danger has not been erased. There certainly is no evidence that the intent to do harm has been abandoned.

"It ain't no sin if you crack a few laws now and then, just so long as you don't break any."

—Mae West *Every Day's a Holiday* (film), 1937

Even voluntary abandonment is rejected by many jurisdictions, just as they would reject a return of the artifact along with an apology from the Legrise gang as a defense to theft. If a crime is dangerously close to completion, attempt has already been committed and cannot be withdrawn, according to this rationale. Courts requiring a nearer proximity to the completion of the crime would be less likely to allow the abandonment defense than those following the Model Penal Code guidelines. Abandonment might still be used to show lack of intent, or could be helpful in sentence reduction.

Where the less stringent standard of actus reus, substantial step, is applied, voluntary abandonment is more likely to be accepted as a defense to attempt. The Model Penal Code makes this provision in § 5.01(4):

> *(4)* Renunciation of Criminal Purpose. *When the actor's conduct would otherwise constitute an attempt under Subsection (1)(b) or (1)(c) of this Section, it is an affirmative defense that he abandoned his effort to commit the crime or otherwise prevented its commission, under circumstances manifesting a complete and voluntary renunciation of his criminal purpose. The establishment of such defense does not, however, affect the liability of an accomplice who did not join in such abandonment or prevention.*

The abandonment must be an entirely voluntary reversal of intent, not influenced by possible failure or detection, and must be complete, not simply a tabling of plans until a better opportunity presents itself. A defendant, who was in the process of forcing his victim to disrobe at gunpoint, stopped when another victim who had been tied up broke free. The court in *Smith v. State* (Ind. 1994) ruled the abandonment was not voluntary and affirmed an attempted deviate conduct conviction. The court in *Pruitt v. State* (Miss. 1988), however, reversed an attempted rape conviction, because the defendant voluntarily and without the intervention of a third party told the victim she was free to go.

Check whether your jurisdiction accepts the defense of abandonment or renunciation.

3.   Impossibility

A defendant may claim impossibility as a defense when the crime the defendant was trying to commit was impossible to accomplish under the circumstances. Because much of the theory behind this defense depends on what the defendant believed the circumstances to be, it lies in the very uncertain realm of subjectivity. Luckily, the cases for which impossibility is a factor are rare, but you should be aware of the basic components of the doctrine.

Legal impossibility is the only impossibility defense that is generally accepted in attempt cases. Here, even if the defendant had completed the intended action believing it to be illegal, no crime would have been committed because the action is in fact legal. This defense often extends to cases in which only one factor in the circumstances makes the action legal. In *State v. Porter* (Mont. 1952) a jury tampering conviction was reversed because the bribe had been offered to a person who was not a juror. Because that scenario does not come under the statute for jury tampering, there was no illegal attempt.

Factual impossibility, however, depends on an extraneous factor being other than the actor believed it to be. Because the law is reluctant to permit luck to determine guilt, this type of impossibility is seldom accepted as a defense to attempt charges. The lack of success of a murderer who shoots an empty gun is simply a stroke of luck. The mens rea is there, the actus reus is there, and if conditions were as the actor believed them to be, a murder would have been committed. The Model Penal Code expresses this standard in § 5.01(1)(a), and *State v. Smith* (N.J. 1993) demonstrates its application. In that decision, an HIV-positive inmate could be found guilty of attempted murder by biting a corrections officer with intent to kill and belief that the bite would cause death, regardless of whether it was medically possible that the bite could have transmitted HIV.

In a sting operation police falsely led the defendant to believe that two girls were in a motel room. The defendant entered that room with the intent to molest the girls, who actually did not exist. The factual impossibility of that crime was not a defense to charges of attempted lewd acts [*People v. Keister* (Cal. App. 1996)].

Although factual impossibility is almost always rejected as a defense, when the chances of the defendant's actions actually causing harm are so remote that there is no real danger, charges for criminal attempt are not likely. A voodoo doctor's magic does not seem to approach the level of dangerous activity that would warrant criminal prosecution.

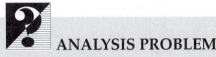

ANALYSIS PROBLEM

6–3. Compare burglary with attempted theft. Why is one a complete crime and the other inchoate?

III. CONSPIRACY

A. INTRODUCTION

Which is a greater danger to society, Cat Bermuda stealing an artifact on her own, or the Legrise gang agreeing to work together for that goal? Which is more likely to succeed? Which is more likely to continue in crime?

About 700 years ago English common law recognized the added danger of collective action to the longevity and probable success of criminal activity. Crime, like our society, has become more complex. From its rather narrow beginnings against conspiracies to bring false accusations, conspiracy law now reaches out to encompass agreements to commit any substantive crime, and is especially helpful in combatting organized crime that hides the motivating brain of the enterprise inside a web where only the outer strands are responsible for carrying out criminal actions. Federal law, 18 U.S.C.A. § 371, prohibits conspiracies to commit any federal offense, or to defraud the United States.

The elements of conspiracy always include an agreement between two or more persons and the intention to commit an unlawful act or a lawful act in an unlawful manner. The agreement is the actus reus, and the criminal purpose is the mens rea. The general federal statute and some state statutes add a third element, that an overt act furthering the purpose of the agreement must have been committed by at least one of the conspirators. Only one act needs to be proved, and that act need not be unlawful in itself, but must have been performed within the time of the conspiracy. Also, this overt act does not need to come so close to the substantive crime as the "substantial step" requirement for attempt.

Some specific federal conspiracy statutes do not require the overt act, including 18 U.S.C.A. § 241, conspiracy against rights of citizens; 18 U.S.C.A. § 286, conspiracy to defraud the government with respect to claims; 18 U.S.C.A. § 1951, interference with commerce by threats or violence; 18 U.S.C.A. § 2384, seditious conspiracy; 21 U.S.C.A. § 846, conspiracy to manufacture, possess, distribute, or dispense controlled substances; and 21 U.S.C.A. 963, conspiracy to import or export controlled substances. Some state statutes also forego the overt act element in conspiracy to commit such crimes as armed burglary and felony on the person of another.

In order to deal with the special dangers and difficulties of controlling group crime, conspiracy has taken on aspects of several other categories of crime. It is similar to complicity laws in holding one person liable for the conduct of another. Unlike the requirement of actual participation in aiding and abetting, however, conspirators only need to be involved in the agreement.

"What man was ever content with one crime?"
—Juvenal, *Satires*, c. 120

Like attempt, conspiracy is an inchoate crime and does not require the completion of the objective offense. But if the crime is accomplished, conspiracy can stand separately as a substantive crime in addition to the objective offense, unlike attempt that merges with the completed act. Sentencing for two crimes instead of one, murder as well as conspiracy to commit murder for example, makes these laws particularly effective.

A conspiracy agreement to traffic in drugs that was formed in Texas and an attempt to carry out the objective of the conspiracy in New Mexico resulted in convictions on both conspiracy and attempt charges in New Mexico [*State v. Villalobos* (N.M. App. 1995)]. The overt act, an attempted cocaine sale, in New Mexico was not an element of the conspiracy, but evidence of its continuance into the state.

Some state laws prohibit this separate conviction for conspiracy unless the conspiracy included plans to commit at least one other offense in addition to the one that was completed. Under these laws, the Legrise gang would have had to plan an additional hit, say the theft of a Daumier drawing from the art center downtown, on top of the successful theft of the idol in order to be charged with both conspiracy and theft. This approach, favored in Model Penal Code § 1.07(1)(b), is a check on possible overuse of conspiracy charges by prosecutors, as discussed in section F following.

States vary widely in their penalties. Some set conspiracies as misdemeanors regardless of the target crime, others set maximum sentences at a constant level, and still others vary the level to correspond to different types of substantive crimes.

B. MENS REA IN CONSPIRACY

The heart of the crime of conspiracy is a meeting of the minds of its participants. It is a predominantly "mental" crime, so court decisions regarding it tend to be inconsistent. In general, though, a double-pronged intent is required: the defendant must intend to agree and must intend that the substantive crime be committed with the same mens rea requirements as those for the substantive crime. Although each conspirator must have knowledge of the unlawful aims of the scheme, this does not necessarily extend to every detail of the enterprise, or even to the identity of each coconspirator.

Knowledge alone, however, is not enough to establish intent. In the case of *People v. Lauria* (Cal. 1967), the defendant whose answering service was used by prostitutes to solicit customers was acquitted of conspiracy to commit prostitution, even though he knew of that use. The decision expressed the following rule:

> [T]he intent of a supplier who knows of the criminal use to which his supplies are put to participate in the criminal activity connected with the use of his supplies may be established by (1) direct evidence that he intends to participate, or (2) through an inference that he intends to participate based on, (a) his special interest in the activity, or (b) the aggravated nature of the crime itself.

The decision gives examples of circumstantial evidence of intent based on special interest (a), as an inflated profit from the enterprise; the sale of goods with no legitimate use, such as crooked dice to gambling casinos; and sales in such volume as to be grossly disproportionate to any legitimate demand, such as the sale of narcotics to a physician in much greater amounts than the physician's legal use [*Direct Sales v. U.S.* (1943)]. The *Lauria* decision also implied that if the substantive crime is a felony, mere knowledge might suffice in establishing intent (b), but ultimately left the question open. Conversely, a defendant could not be convicted of conspiracy to sell heroin when there was no proof that he knew drugs were involved in the transaction [*U.S. v. Idowu* (3rd Cir. 1998)].

Judge Learned Hand expressed this problem of knowledge succinctly in *U.S. v. Crimmins* (2d Cir. 1941).

> While one may, for instance, be guilty of running past a traffic light of whose existence one is ignorant, one cannot be guilty of conspiring to run past such a light, for one cannot agree to run past a light unless one supposes that there is a light to run past.

This also puts to rest any possibility of conspiring to commit negligence, although conspiring to create a risk of harm is possible. When the intent of a conspiracy is to do an act that has dangerous natural consequences, there is not a sufficient level of malice for a conviction on conspiracy to commit second degree murder [*People v. Swain* (Cal. App. 1996)].

Once a conspiracy's unlawful purpose is agreed on, the acts that foreseeably follow on that agreement fall within the conspiracy's intent. Consider a variation of the situation in Case VI. The Craigs, Harveys, and Wescotts agree to harass Mason Trew and Loren Jackson. Richard Craig secretly brings along a gun, intending and succeeding in killing Trew. Are the Harveys and Wescotts guilty of conspiring to commit murder? If they had no knowledge of the gun, they could not have had the requisite intent that it be used.

In another scenario of the same case, everyone knows Craig has a gun. As the cross is lit, Trew runs from the house toward the group. Craig shoots him, then stops at the home of another neighbor who had never returned a borrowed lawnmower and shoots his car full of holes. Are the others liable for the murder? For the damage to the car? If the test of natural and probable consequences is applied, each conspirator is guilty of the murder of Trew even though it was not intended, because it is foreseeable that the gun would have been used as a consequence to the action that was intended. Because the car damage had nothing to do with the original agreement, its responsibility would rest solely with Craig. The Model Penal Code rejects the natural and probable test, restricting the liability of each conspirator to the criminal purposes that the conspirator shares or knows.

C. ACTUS REUS IN CONSPIRACY

1. Agreement

Agreement is the essence and the actus reas element of conspiracy. Conspiracy laws do not punish mere thoughts [*U.S. v. Shabani* (1994)]. Proof of the agreement is often circumstantial, but it must go beyond simple presence at the scene of the crime. Even though the defendant in *U.S. v. Cox* (8th Cir. 1991) was with companions when he sought to buy cocaine, lack of evidence that the group had agreed on what to do with the cocaine after the purchase led the court to conclude that a conspiracy had not occurred. If the circumstances are sufficiently compelling, some courts may allow an apparent singleness of purpose to indicate agreement, as in *Griffin v. State* (Ark. 1970) where a policeman was assaulted by a large group of people. A shared objective did not take the place of an agreement, however, when a defendant shot his son's wife after his son said he wanted her killed [*Rude v. State* (Wyo. 1993)].

Circumstantial evidence usually is necessary to show agreement. A conviction for conspiracy to possess and distribute marijuana was based on evidence that the co-conspirators drove similar vehicles insured by the same company and registered under the same name with similar compartments in the fuel tanks concealing more than 400 pounds of marijuana [*U.S. v. Rangel-Arreola* (10th Cir. 1993)]. Details of the agreement, such as price, do not have to be decided for the agreement to be complete [*U.S. v. Sharif* (9th Cir. 1987)]. When negotiation of the agreement is still going on, however, the conspiracy has not yet occurred. In *U.S. v. Iennaco* (D.C. Cir. 1990), "exploratory and inconclusive conversations" concerning distribution of controlled substances were not sufficient to constitute conspiracy.

An often used authority on the scope of agreement is the case of *Pinkerton v. U.S.* (1946). The defendant's conviction for substantive offenses was upheld, even though he was in prison at the time they were committed and had no knowledge of the specific crimes. Note the question of merger of conspiracy with the substantive crimes, and the distinction of conspiracy from aiding and abetting.

PINKERTON v. UNITED STATES
Supreme Court of the United States, 1946.
328 U.S. 640, 66 S.C. 1180, 90 L.td. 1489.
[Citations omitted]

Mr. Justice DOUGLAS delivered the opinion of the Court.

Walter and Daniel Pinkerton are brothers who live a short distance from each other on Daniel's farm. They were indicted for violations of the Internal Revenue Code. The indictment contained ten substantive counts and one conspiracy count. The jury found Walter guilty on nine of the substantive counts and on the conspiracy count. It found Daniel guilty on six of the substantive counts and on the conspiracy count. . . . The judgments of conviction were affirmed by the Circuit Court of Appeals. 151 F.2d 499. The case is here on a petition for a writ of certiorari, which we granted because one of the questions presented involved a conflict between the decision below and *United States v. Sall*, 116 F.2d 745, decided by the Circuit Court of Appeals for the Third Circuit.

A single conspiracy was charged and proved. Some of the overt acts charged in the conspiracy count were the same acts charged in the substantive counts. Each of the substantive offenses found was committed pursuant to the conspiracy. Petitioners therefore contend that the substantive counts

became merged in the conspiracy count, and that only a single sentence not exceeding the maximum two year penalty provided by the conspiracy statute (Criminal Code § 37, 18 U.S.C. § 88) could be imposed. Or to state the matter differently, they contend that each of the substantive counts became a separate conspiracy count but, since only a single conspiracy was charged and proved, only a single sentence for conspiracy could be imposed. They rely on *Braverman v. United States*, 317 U.S. 49.

In the *Braverman* case the indictment charged no substantive offense. Each of the several counts charged a conspiracy to violate a different statute. But only one conspiracy was proved. We held that a single conspiracy, charged under the general conspiracy statute, however diverse its objects may be, violates but a single statute and no penalty greater than the maximum provided for one conspiracy may be imposed. That case is not apposite here. For the offenses charged and proved were not only a conspiracy but substantive offenses as well.

Nor can we accept the proposition that the substantive offenses were merged in the conspiracy. There are, of course, instances where a conspiracy charge may not be added to the substantive charge. One is where the agreement of two persons is necessary for the completion of the substantive crime and there is no ingredient in the conspiracy which is not present in the completed crime. Another is where the definition of the substantive offense excludes from punishment for conspiracy one who voluntarily participates in another's crime. But those exceptions are of a limited character. The common law rule that the substantive offense, if a felony, was merged in the conspiracy, has little vitality in this country. It has been long and consistently recognized by the Court that the commission of the substantive offense and a conspiracy to commit it are separate and distinct offenses. The power of Congress to separate the two and to affix to each a different penalty is well established. . . . It has ingredients, as well as implications, distinct from the completion of the unlawful project. As stated in *United States v. Rabinowich,* 238 U.S. 78, 88:

> "For two or more to confederate and combine together to commit or cause to be committed a breach of the criminal laws, is an offense of the gravest character, sometimes quite outweighing, in injury to the public, the mere commission of the contemplated crime. It involves deliberate plotting to subvert the laws, educating and preparing the conspirators for further and habitual criminal practices. And it is characterized by secrecy, rendering it difficult of detection, requiring more time for its discovery, and adding to the importance of punishing it when discovered."

Moreover, it is not material that overt acts charged in the conspiracy counts were also charged and proved as substantive offenses. . . . The agreement to do an unlawful act is even then distinct from the doing of the act.

It is contended that there was insufficient evidence to implicate Daniel in the conspiracy. But we think there was enough evidence for submission of the issue to the jury.

There is, however, no evidence to show that Daniel participated directly in the commission of the substantive offenses on which his conviction has been sustained, although there was evidence to show that these substantive offenses were in fact committed by Walter in furtherance of the unlawful agreement or conspiracy existing between the brothers. The question was submitted to the jury on the theory that each petitioner could be found guilty of the substantive offenses, if it was found at the time those offenses were committed petitioners were parties to an unlawful conspiracy and the substantive offenses charged were in fact committed in furtherance of it.

Daniel relies on *United States v. Sall, supra.* That case held that participation in the conspiracy was not itself enough to sustain a conviction for the substantive offense even though it was committed in furtherance of the conspiracy.

The court held that, in addition to evidence that the offense was in fact committed in furtherance of the conspiracy, evidence of direct participation in the commission of the substantive offense or other evidence from which participation might fairly be inferred was necessary.

We take a different view. We have here a continuous conspiracy. There is here no evidence of the affirmative action on the part of Daniel which is necessary to establish his withdrawal from it. *Hyde v. United States,* 225 U.S. 347, 369. As stated in that case, "Having joined in an unlawful scheme, having constituted agents for its performance, scheme and agency to be continuous until full fruition be secured, until he does some act to disavow or defeat the purpose he is in no situation to claim the delay of the law. As the offense has not been terminated or accomplished he is still offending. And we think, consciously offending, offending as certainly, as we have said, as at the first moment of his confederation, and consciously through every moment of its existence." *Id.,* p. 369. And so long as the partnership in crime continues, the partners act for each other in carrying it forward. It is settled that "an overt act of one partner may be the act of all without any new agreement specifically directed to that act." *United States v. Kissel,* 218 U.S. 601, 608. Motive or intent may be proved by the acts or declarations of some of the conspirators in furtherance of the common objective. . . . The governing principle is the same when the substantive offense is committed by one of the conspirators in furtherance of the unlawful project. The criminal intent to do the act is established by the formation of the conspiracy. Each conspirator instigated the commission of the crime. The unlawful agreement contemplated precisely what was done. It was formed for the purpose. The act done was in execution of the enterprise. The rule which holds responsible one who counsels, procures, or commands another to commit a crime is founded on the same principle. That principle is recognized in the law of conspiracy when the overt act of one partner in crime is attributable to all. An overt act is an essential ingredient of the crime of conspiracy under § 37 of the Criminal Code, 18 U.S.C. § 88. If that can be supplied by the act of one conspirator, we fail to see why the same or other acts in furtherance of the conspiracy are likewise not attributable to the others for the purpose of holding them responsible for the substantive offense.

A different case would arise if the substantive offense committed by one of the conspirators was not in fact done in furtherance of the conspiracy, did not fall within the scope of the unlawful project, or was merely a part of the ramifications of the plan which could not be reasonably foreseen as a necessary or natural consequence of the unlawful agreement. But as we read this record, that is not this case.

Affirmed.

Mr. Justice RUTLEDGE, dissenting in part.

. . .

That Daniel Pinkerton had participated in an agreement and that the crimes were committed by his partner in furtherance of that agreement were sufficient means to establish his culpability.

2.   Overt Act

As we have seen, an overt act in furtherance of a conspiratorial agreement is a required part of the actus reus element in the general federal statute, 18 U.S.C.A. § 371, and some states. One act by one conspirator is sufficient. Most states and specific federal statutes such as 21 U.S.C.A. § 846 concerning controlled substance conspiracies [*U.S. v. Stassi* (7th Cir. 1992) and *U.S. v. Shabani* (1994)], however, do not require an overt act. The Model Penal Code recommends the requirement of an overt act except when the objective crime is a first or second degree felony.

Often the overt act is considered simply a procedural step in proving the existence of an agreement and the willingness of the culprits to adhere to it. The overt act does not need to be criminal. It included the lawful purchase of guns and ski masks in furtherance of a conspiracy to commit burglary in *Burk v. State* (Wyo. 1993).

3.   Number of Conspirators

Some cases hinge on the question of how many people are necessary to form a conspiracy. When the commission of a crime necessarily involves two people, such as in bribery or adultery, a doctrine called **Wharton's Rule** maintains that there is no added danger in numbers justifying a charge of conspiracy, unless a third person participates. The Wharton Rule was no defense in *People v. Laws* (Ill. 1993), where five different combinations of at least eight people conspired to participate in an enterprise of pimping and keeping a place of prostitution. When conspiracy is defined as an agreement between two or more persons, there may be a problem in prosecuting a "conspirator" whose "partner" is an undercover officer with no serious involvement in the agreement. The Model Penal Code solves the problem by defining agreement as one person agreeing with another (**unilateral conspiracy**), rather than an agreement between two or more persons. This allows for the prosecution of the single culpable conspirator [*Commonwealth v. Sego* (Ky. 1994)]. Some jurisdictions, however, require that two persons are involved in the conspiracy, neither of whom is a government agent or informer [*U.S. v. Wright* (11th Cir. 1995) based on *U.S. v. Elledge* (11th Cir. 1984) and *U.S. v. Tombrello* (11th Cir.), cert. denied (1982)]. The court in *State v. Pacheco* (Wash. 1994) required a genuine, bilateral agreement. The decision and dissent reflect the difficult issues involved.

Wharton's Rule:
there is no added danger in numbers justifying a charge of conspiracy in crimes requiring the participation of two persons, unless a third person participates.

unilateral conspiracy:
one person agreeing with another, rather than an agreement between two or more persons; allows for the prosecution of the single culpable conspirator.

STATE v. PACHECO
Supreme Court of Washington, En Banc, 1994.
882 P.2d 183 Wash. 1994
[Citations omitted]

JOHNSON, Justice.

The Defendant, Herbert Pacheco, appeals his convictions for conspiracy to commit first degree murder and conspiracy to deliver a controlled substance. He contends he did not commit conspiracy within the meaning of RCW 9A.28.040 because no genuine agreement existed between him and his sole coconspirator, an undercover police agent. We hold RCW 9A.28.040 and RCW 69.50.407 require an actual

agreement between two coconspirators, and, therefore, reverse his convictions for conspiracy to commit murder in the first degree and conspiracy to deliver a controlled substance.

FACTS

Herbert Pacheco met Thomas Dillon in 1985, when Pacheco worked about 2 months for Dillon's private investigation firm. Pacheco bragged to Dillon about his involvement in illegal activities, including enforcement, collecting debts, procuring weapons, providing protection, and performing "hits."

In 1989, Dillon learned that Pacheco was a Clark County deputy sheriff. Dillon contacted the FBI and volunteered to inform on Pacheco. The FBI began an investigation of Pacheco. The Clark County Sheriff's office joined, and later directed the investigation.

The investigation involved the recording of conversations, face-to-face and over the telephone, between Dillon and Pacheco. During these conversations Dillon asked Pacheco to perform various jobs, including collections and information checks on individuals.

On March 26, 1990, according to a plan designed by the sheriff's office and the FBI, Dillon called Pacheco and told him he would like to meet to discuss a possible deal. Dillon and Pacheco met at a restaurant. Dillon said he had ties to the "Mafia" and offered Pacheco $500 in exchange for protection during a cocaine deal. Dillon told Pacheco that a buyer (an undercover FBI agent) would arrive shortly, and Pacheco was to protect Dillon during the transaction. Pacheco agreed. The undercover agent arrived and the purported drug transaction took place. Afterward, Dillon paid Pacheco $500.

The same scenario was replayed at a second purported drug transaction on April 2, 1990. Dillon again paid Pacheco $500. Later that night Dillon called Pacheco and pretended he had been shortchanged $40,000 in that afternoon's drug transaction. Dillon said he had been given $10,000 by his superiors to take care of the situation. Dillon agreed to meet Pacheco at a convenience store. At the store, Pacheco offered to kill the drug buyer for $10,000. Pacheco indicated if he had to kill anyone else, it would cost more. Pacheco proposed he go get his gun while Dillon located the drug buyer at his motel.

Dillon and Pacheco met at a lounge near the motel. They decided Pacheco would go to the lobby of the motel, call the buyer and convince him to come down to the lobby where Pacheco would then shoot him. Pacheco went to the lobby with a loaded gun, but he did not call the buyer's room. As Pacheco left the lobby, sheriff's deputies arrested him. Pacheco contended he was collecting evidence to build a case against Dillon and he thought he was following police procedures.

Pacheco was charged with conspiracy to commit first degree murder, attempted first degree murder, two counts of unlawful delivery of a controlled substance, two counts of conspiracy to deliver a controlled substance, and official misconduct. The official misconduct charge was dismissed. The jury found Pacheco not guilty of attempted first degree murder, but convicted him on all other counts.

The Court of Appeals affirmed the convictions, 70 Wash. App. 27, 851 P.2d 734. We accepted review of the conspiracy convictions, limited to the issue of whether a conspiracy exists when the sole coconspirator is an undercover agent.

ANALYSIS

The Defendant contends he did not commit conspiracy within the meaning of RCW 9A.28.040 because his sole co-conspirator was an undercover police agent who never "agreed" to commit the crime of murder in the first degree.

The Defendant argues the statute retains the common law, bilateral approach to conspiracy, which requires an actual agreement to commit a crime between the defendant and at least one other. Therefore, a government agent feigning agreement with the defendant does not constitute a conspiracy under the common law approach because no genuine agreement is reached. The Defendant asserts Washington is among those states whose statutes are patterned after the Model Penal Code but have been interpreted as adopting only a limited form of the code's unilateral approach, and retaining the requirement of a bilateral underlying agreement.

The State contends RCW 9A.28.040 follows the code's purely unilateral approach. Under the code, actual agreement is not required as long as the defendant believes another is agreeing to commit the criminal act. Therefore, a purported agreement between a government agent and a defendant would satisfy the code's unilateral conspiratorial agreement approach.

Adopted in 1975, as a part of the overhaul of the criminal code, RCW 9A.28.040 provides in part:

(1) A person is guilty of criminal conspiracy when, with intent that conduct constituting a crime be performed, he agrees with one or more persons to engage in or cause the performance of such conduct, and any one of them takes a substantial step in pursuance of such agreement.

(2) It shall not be a defense to criminal conspiracy that the person or persons with whom the accused is alleged to have conspired:

(a) Has not been prosecuted or convicted; or

(b) Has been convicted of a different offense; or

(c) Is not amenable to justice; or

(d) Has been acquitted; or

(e) Lacked the capacity to commit an offense.

In construing a statute, our primary objective is to carry out the intent of the Legislature. When a term is not defined in a statute, the court may look to common law or a dictionary for the definition. As a general rule, we presume the Legislature intended undefined words to mean what they did at common law.

Subsection (1) of RCW 9A.28.040 expressly requires an *agreement,* but does not define the term. Black's Law Dictionary defines *agreement* as, "[a] meeting of two or more minds; a coming together in opinion or determination; the coming together in accord of two minds on a given proposition" [Black's Law Dictionary 67 (6th rev. ed. 1990)]. . . . The dictionary definitions thus support the defendant's argument.

Likewise, the common law definition of the agreement required for a conspiracy is defined not in unilateral terms but rather as a confederation or combination of minds. A conspiratorial agreement necessarily requires more than one to agree because it is impossible to conspire with oneself. We conclude that by requiring an agreement, the Legislature intended to retain the requirement of a genuine or bilateral agreement.

Subsection (2) provides the conspiratorial agreement may still be found even though the coconspirator cannot be convicted. In this sense, the statute incorporates a limited form of the code's unilateral conspiracy in that it is no longer necessary that agreement be proved against both conspirators. Thus, under subsection (2)'s unilateral approach, the failure to convict an accused's sole coconspirator will not prevent proof of the conspiratorial agreement against the accused. However, this does not indicate the Legislature intended to abandon the traditional requirement of two criminal participants reaching an underlying agreement. . . .

Additionally, the unilateral approach fails to carry out the primary purpose of the statute. The primary reason for making conspiracy a separate offense from the substantive crime is the increased danger to society posed by group criminal activity. However, the increased danger is nonexistent when a person "conspires" with a government agent who pretends agreement. In the feigned conspiracy there is no increased chance the criminal enterprise will succeed, no continuing criminal enterprise, no educating in criminal practices, and no greater difficulty of detection.

Indeed, it is questionable whether the unilateral conspiracy punishes criminal activity or merely criminal intentions. The "agreement" in a unilateral conspiracy is a legal fiction, a technical way of transforming nonconspiratorial conduct into a prohibited conspiracy. When one party merely pretends to agree, the other party, whatever he or she may believe about the pretender, is in fact not conspiring with anyone. Although the deluded party has the requisite criminal intent, there has been no criminal act.

The federal courts agree. In *Sears v. United States*, 343 F.2d 139, 142 (5th Cir. 1965), the Court of Appeals established the rule that "as it takes two to conspire, there can be no indictable conspiracy with a government informer who secretly intends to frustrate the conspiracy". Every federal court which has since considered the issue has adopted this approach.

Another concern with the unilateral approach is its potential for abuse. In a unilateral conspiracy, the State not only plays an active role in creating the offense, but also becomes the chief witness in proving the crime at trial. *Escobar de Bright*, 742 F.2d at 1199–1200. We agree with the Ninth Circuit this has the potential to put the State in the improper position of manufacturing crime. At the same time, such reaching is unnecessary because the punishable conduct in a unilateral conspiracy will almost always satisfy the elements of either solicitation or attempt. The State will still be able to thwart the activity and punish the defendant who attempts agreement with an undercover police officer.

The State argues the Legislature intended to adopt the code's purely unilateral approach, discarding the common law requirement of an actual agreement. . . .

The purpose of incorporating the unilateral approach into RCW 9A.28.040 was to obviate the prior law's implicit requirement of conviction of the coconspirators. . . .

[T]hree of the four states . . . adopting conspiracy statutes similar to ours have interpreted their statutes as retaining the requirement of a bilateral agreement. *People v. Foster*, 99 Ill.2d 48, 75 Ill.Dec. 411, 457 N.E.2d 405 (1983); *People v. Anderson*, 418 Mich. 31, 340 N.W.2d 634 (1983); *State v. Robinson*, 213 Conn. 243, 567 A.2d 1173 (1989).

In sum, the State has not persuaded us the Legislature intended to abandon the traditional requirement of an actual agreement. We hold RCW 9A.28.040 and RCW 69.50.407 require the defendant to reach a genuine agreement with at least one other coconspirator. The Defendant's convictions for conspiracy to commit murder in the first degree and conspiracy to deliver a controlled substance are reversed.

UTTER, DOLLIVER, SMITH, and MADSEN, JJ., concur.

DURHAM, Justice (dissenting).

The jury found that Herbert Pacheco, an aspiring hit man, planned a murder for money. Moreover, he took a substantial step toward that objective. Yet the majority overturns his conviction for conspiracy to commit murder solely because he conspired with a government agent rather than with another hit man. The Washington conspiracy statute does not require a co-conspirator to be a nongovernment actor. In fact, the statute explicitly envisages so-called unilateral conspiracies, as the majority admits. Because neither our case law, the statute, nor the rationale of conspiracy crimes compel the result arrived at by the majority, I dissent.

We accepted review solely to determine whether Washington's conspiracy statute countenances unilateral conspiracies. Yet the majority fails to provide even a cursory analysis of the essential differences between the bilateral and unilateral approaches to conspiracy. The bilateral approach asks whether there is an agreement between two or more persons to commit a criminal act. Its focus is on the content of the agreement and whether there is a shared understanding between the conspirators. The unilateral approach is not concerned with the content of the agreement or whether there is a meeting of minds. Its sole concern is whether the agreement, shared or not, objectively manifests the criminal intent of at least one of the conspirators. The majority does not even mention this crucial difference, and instead merely assumes that all conspiracies must be bilateral. In other words, the majority assumes precisely what it is supposed to prove; it begs the question.

The result is a tangle of inaccuracies. . . .

[T]he majority portrays the unilateral approach to conspiracy as an outdated relic from a bygone era. The Model

Penal Code endorses unilateral conspiracies, the majority admits, but "[e]very federal court, which has since considered the issue" has adopted the bilateral approach. The majority neglects to mention that all the federal courts adopting bilateral conspiracy are construing a different statute, one whose language requires bilateral conspiracies. *See* 18 U.S.C. § 371 ("If two or more persons conspire . . . to commit any offense against the United States"). In contrast, the Model Penal Code defines conspiracy "in terms of one person's agreeing *with* another, rather than in terms of an agreement *among* or *between* two or more people."

The code embodies a significant change in emphasis. In its view, the major basis of conspiratorial liability is not the group nature of the activity but the firm purpose of an individual to commit a crime which is objectively manifested in conspiring. The Washington conspiracy statute tracks the Model Penal Code's language rather than the "two or more persons" language of the general federal conspiracy statute. *Compare* RCW 9A.28.040 *with* Model Penal Code § 5.03. In any event, far from being antiquated or obsolete, the "movement toward a unilateral theory of the crime is the modern trend in conspiracy law." Patrick A. Broderick, Note, *Conditional Objectives of Conspiracies,* 94 Yale L.J. 895, 906 n. 64 (1985). *See also* Dierdre A. Burgman, *Unilateral Conspiracy: Three Critical Perspectives,* 29 DePaul L.Rev. 75, 75 n. 3 (1979) (listing 30 states that have adopted statutes conforming to Model Penal Code's unilateral approach).

A comparison of the revised Washington conspiracy statute with its predecessor is far more revealing of legislative intent than the majority's simplistic and premature resort to dictionary definitions. The predecessor statute used the phrase "[w]henever two or more persons shall conspire", which parallels the federal conspiracy statute and clearly requires bilateral conspiracy. Former RCW 9.22.010 (repealed in 1975). The revised statute, in contrast, tracks the definitional language of the Model Penal Code, which adopts unilateral conspiracy.

. . .

Next, the majority constructs a straw man by claiming that the primary purpose of conspiracy is "the increased danger to society posed by group criminal activity." Preventing group criminal activity is the rationale behind bilateral conspiracy, but that rationale was decisively rejected by the Model Penal Code. At best, controlling group criminal activity is only one rationale for conspiracy statutes.

The majority compounds its own confusion by contending that unilateral conspiracies are factually impossible and therefore presumptively invalid. This argument amounts to the truism that it is factually impossible to have a "meeting of minds" on the commission of a future crime if one of the minds is a government agent who does not intend to commit the criminal act. However, a "meeting of minds" is not a prerequisite of unilateral conspiracy. In any event, factual impossibility is not a recognized defense. The majority does nothing more than restate the discredited assumption that all conspiracies must be bilateral because conspiracy statutes attempt to target only group criminal activity.

Finally, I share the majority's concern about the potential for abuse of unilateral conspiracy. However, the majority fails to take into consideration the effect of the entrapment defense. The potential for abuse is further restricted by the statute itself, which requires not only an agreement to engage in criminal conduct but also "a substantial step in pursuance of such agreement". RCW 9A.28.040(1). (Washington's substantial step requirement provides stricter standard for overt act than majority of states adopting unilateral conspiracy). In the end, the majority succeeds only in providing a superfluous protection to criminal defendants at the price of hamstringing government attempts to nip criminal acts in the bud.

ANDERSEN, C.J., and BRACHTENBACH, and GUY, J.J., concur.

ANALYSIS PROBLEM

6–4. Do you agree with the *Pacheco* majority in its interpretation of the Washington statute? Do you more closely agree with the rationale behind the arguments of the majority or the dissent? Why?

4. Number of Conspiracies

One of the most commonly raised points on appeal is the number of conspiracies in which defendants are involved. If several substantive crimes stem from one agreement, separate charges for conspiracy will not be allowed for each of the separate crimes [*Braverman v. U.S.*(1942)]. This is also discussed in *Pinkerton.* The continuity of the conspiratorial agreement is the key.

The number of charges depends primarily on the relationship of the conspirators. If one person makes separate agreements to help two different parties commit two separate crimes, there are two separate conspiracies. Conversely, if the two coconspirators, even unknown to each other, both agree to work toward the same criminal objectives with one central person, only one conspiracy takes place; this is an example of a "wheel" conspiracy, with a "hub" person at the center and individuals or groups forming the spokes. *Kotteakos v. U.S.* (1946) is the classic example of a wheel conspiracy, where the spokes did not share objectives. The hub person was convicted of multiple conspiracies for fraudulent loan applications on behalf of several people, but neither the transactions nor the people were connected.

A "chain" conspiracy involves a linear transaction, such as from manufacturer to wholesaler to retailer to consumer. Each of the conspirators may have no knowledge of who is working two links up or down the chain, but they must have a common, interdependent objective in order to form only one conspiracy. *U.S. v. Peoni* (2nd Cir. 1938) is a classic case showing a chain conspiracy structure, but reversing conviction because of a lack of "concert of purpose." Peoni sold counterfeit bills to Regno, who sold them to Dorsey, but Peoni had no interest in the matter beyond the transaction with Regno. A common goal is reiterated as the most important factor in analyzing a chain conspiracy in *U.S. v. Tarantino* (D.C. Cir. 1988).

Some courts use the "totality of the circumstances" in determining the number of conspiracies. Interconnections among overt acts, people involved in the conspiracy, methods of operation, locations, and objectives, as well as the time period and interdependence necessary for success are considered.[5]

A change in plans as a conspiracy unfolded did not amount to a second conspiracy in *Tracy v. State* (Md. 1990). One conspirator was unable to stab the victim, so they agreed that the other would shoot the victim so they could steal his car. The court decided there was still only one continuous conspiratorial relationship.

Note that the number of conspiracies charged may be advantageous to one side or the other, so careful accuracy is required in identifying parties and counts in conspiracy complaints.

D. DEFENSES TO CONSPIRACY

Impossibility of achieving the agreed-on goal is not a defense to conspiracy, because the agreement itself is the crime. The court in *State v. Houchin* (Mont. 1988) rejected a factual impossibility defense when the intended victim of the conspiracy to commit homicide was fictitious. At the same time, it affirmed the defense of legal impossibility, saying that if a planned act is not an "offense", one element of conspiracy is missing. The court in *U.S. v. Petit* (11th Cir. 1988) rejected both legal and factual impossibility as conspiracy defenses. A defendant who conspired to receive stolen goods but actually received borrowed goods in a sting operation, making the substantive offense an impossibility, could still be convicted of conspiracy, because conspiracy depends on intent rather than conduct. See Chapter 7 for further discussion of impossibility defenses to other crimes. Similarly, many courts reject the defense of abandonment, because the agreement has already occurred. A defendant who had conspired to defraud the United States by failing to declare money at the national border gave a coconspirator last minute instructions to file a proper customs report. His conviction for conspiracy was affirmed in *U.S. v. Herron* (5th Cir. 1987), because the withdrawal came after the conspiracy agreement and overt acts had been completed. Do you think society would benefit by permitting a defense of abandonment? The drafters of the Model Penal Code seem to think so. They aver the effectiveness of renunciation in § 5.03(6).

> *It is an affirmative defense that the actor, after conspiring to commit a crime, thwarted the success of the conspiracy, under circumstances manifesting a complete and voluntary renunciation of his criminal purpose.*

The conspiracy might be considered abandoned if the defendant alerts the police, informs coconspirators that he or she is out of the agreement, tries to remedy past involvement in the conspiracy, or tries to prevent any further activities of the conspiracy.[6] In any case, withdrawal would prevent prosecution for subsequent substantive crimes by the remaining coconspirators.

The statute of limitations also can be used as a defense, giving advantage to the conspirator who abandons the enterprise. If there is agreement but no overt act, the statute of limitations begins running for all conspirators at the time of the agreement. If there are overt acts furthering the conspiracy, the running of the statute for the entire conspiracy is dated from the last act. If a conspirator abandons the enterprise before that last act, however, the statute of limitations for that conspirator is dated from the abandonment, and will run out earlier than for those who participated until the end.

Because conspiracy is a group crime, the liability of one participant is related to the liability of the others. Generally, if all other conspirators have been convicted, or even if prosecution has been suspended because of death, subsequent insanity, granting of immunity, *nolle prosequi* (the choice not to prosecute at that time), or that coconspirators are unknown to the prosecution, the issue is still alive and the last defendant may be prosecuted. *Harris v. State* (Md. App. 1990) affirmed a conspiracy conviction even though conspiracy charges were not pursued against the coconspirator.

Traditionally, if all alleged coconspirators have been acquitted or had charges against them dropped as an indication of innocence, the last defendant is also released from prosecution. One cannot conspire alone, so when all possible conspirators are eliminated, conspiracy cannot have existed. Some jurisdictions require that such an acquittal of coconspirators form a binding judicial determination of acquittal for the remaining conspirator. This **last conspirator defense** was affirmed in *State v. Robinson* (Conn. 1989). The defendant charged with conspiracy to commit murder could not be convicted after the sole coconspirator had been acquitted in a separate trial. The court in *Ydrysek v. State* (Ark. 1987) ruled that although a state statute barred the last conspirator defense when there were separate trials, inconsistent convictions in a joint trial would be set aside. *U.S. v. Bucuvalas* (1st Cir. 1990) declared the last conspirator defense no longer viable, because a jury's decision to acquit one conspirator by mistake, compromise, or lenity should have no effect on the conviction of another conspirator. *U.S. v. Zuniga-Salinas* (5th Cir. 1992) agreed with the *Bucuvalas* decision, overruling previous cases to the contrary.

last conspirator defense: if all coconspirators have been acquitted or had charges dropped, the last defendant is also released from prosecution.

ANALYSIS PROBLEM

6–5.   Do you see a relationship between the demise of the last conspirator defense and the Model Penal Code's allowance for unilateral conspiracy? What are the benefits and problems of this trend to broaden conspiracy laws?

E.   HEARSAY EXCEPTION

hearsay testimony: testimony at trial or hearing based on the account of someone other than the witness offering the testimony

Rules of evidence bar the use of **hearsay testimony** at trial or hearing, that is, testimony based on the account of someone other than the witness offering the testimony. Exceptions to this rule, however, include one specifically used in conspiracy prosecutions. Evidence of any act or declaration by one coconspirator committed during and in furtherance of a conspiracy is admissible against each coconspirator [Federal Rules of Evidence 801(d)(2)(E)]. The rationale for this rule is contained in the Federal Rule of Criminal Procedure 16(a)(1)(A), that coconspirators can be considered agents of each other, so the statements of one may be admissible against another as if it were his or her own statement. Even statements of uncharged coconspirators are admissible under the principle of agency [*Bigelow v. State* (Wyo. 1989)].

Use of hearsay evidence is usually allowed only if (1) the conspiracy has been established independently, (2) the declarant and the defendant both are shown to be involved in the conspiracy, and (3) the statements in question were made during the course of the conspiracy and in furtherance of it [*Jandro v. State* (Wyo. 1989)]. In *State v. Rivenbark* (Md. 1987) hearsay statements were not allowed because they were made during an effort to conceal the crime six months after the main objective of the conspiracy had been completed and, therefore, were not during or in furtherance of the conspiracy. If the original conspiracy had included an agreement on concealment procedures, the statements would have been in furtherance of that conspiracy and, therefore, admissible.

The time period of the conspiracy is also important in *Smith v. State* (Wyo. 1995), which illustrates the use of hearsay evidence in conspiracy cases.

SMITH v. STATE
Supreme Court of Wyoming, 1995.
902 P.2d 1271 Wyo. 1995
[Citations omitted]

THOMAS, Justice.

. . .

Smith was charged with conspiracy to intimidate a witness, in violation of Wyo. Stat. § 6–5–305(a) and Wyo. Stat. § 6–1–303(a), for his role in an assault and battery on Paul Minick (Minick), who testified at the trial of Smith's sister, Rachel Smith. In December of 1992, Minick and his friend, Mike Webb, were driving north on I-90 about 20 miles south of Sheridan when they apparently suffered a tire blowout. In fact, Rachel Smith shot the right rear tire with a rifle, and she and Tammy Higgins then robbed the two teenage boys at gunpoint. *See Higgins v. State,* 889 P.2d 964 (Wyo. 1995), and *Smith v. State,* 880 P.2d 573 (Wyo. 1994). Pursuant to a subpoena issued by the district court, Minick returned to Sheridan on July 29, 1993, and testified against Rachel Smith on July 30, 1993. He was released from the subpoena on that day, but he stayed until the jury returned a verdict of guilty at about 4:45 p.m. After the verdict was returned, Minick spent some time at the home of a deputy sheriff and, later, two deputies from the sheriff's office took Minick to dinner and then, about 8:15 p.m., to the bus depot in Sheridan to return to his home in Montana.

While Minick was at the bus depot, he was approached by David Rhoden (Rhoden), who requested assistance in jump starting his van. Minick declined at first, but then agreed to assist Rhoden. The two went into the parking lot at the bus depot and were approaching a van when Rhoden stopped to tie his shoe. When Minick turned around, Rhoden hit him in the face inflicting a bloody nose and a lip laceration that left a scar.

The conspiracy statute, WYO.STAT. § 6–1–303, provides, in pertinent part:

> (a) A person is guilty of conspiracy to commit a crime if he agrees with one (1) or more persons that they or one (1) or more of them will commit a crime and one (1) or more of them does an overt act to effect the objective of the agreement.

The crime Smith was charged with conspiring to commit, is defined in WYO.STAT. § 6–5–305(a), which provides:

> A person commits a felony punishable by imprisonment for not more than ten (10) years, a fine of not more than five thousand dollars ($5,000.00), or both, if, by force or threats, he attempts to influence, intimidate or impede a juror, witness or officer in the discharge of his duty.

Smith was tried on May 3, 1994, and Minick testified about his role as a witness in the Rachel Smith trial and about the assault and battery at the bus depot. MAG, a witness to the conspiracy, testified to the occurrence of the events on the night of July 30, 1993, including statements made by Rhoden. Following the return of the verdict in Rachel Smith's trial, MAG and Rhoden went to a bar near Rhoden's apartment to drink. Smith, Smith's mother, and another woman arrived in a car about a half hour to an hour later. Smith got out of a car where he had been sitting with the two women and approached MAG and Rhoden. The three of them had been working together for approximately two months at Carl Weissman & Sons (a supply firm for contractors), and they were friends at that time.

In an inexplicable excursion into fantasy, Smith told the other two, specifically addressing MAG, "that there was a guy that had lied in court and got the sister into trouble and convicted her, whatever, and that he wanted me to beat her up." MAG quickly corrected the reference to "her" by stating "him" in his testimony. Smith offered MAG fifteen dollars and all the beer he could drink if he would beat Minick. MAG declined the offer stating that he did not want to go to jail. Smith then asked Rhoden if he would beat Minick. Rhoden did not respond, and the five people then went to a different bar to drink and to discuss beating Minick. MAG stated, at some point, Smith's mother said, "the person that testified against the defendant's sister would be at the bus depot that night."

Around 8:00 or 8:30 p.m., Smith announced "they [Smith and Rhoden] were going to go up [to the bus station] and look things over and see if the guy was there, and he was going to point the guy out for Dave [Rhoden] and just kind of case it out and see if there was any cops there." The two left the bar and returned approximately forty-five minutes later. During that period, Rhoden lured Minick outside the bus depot and struck him in the face. When they returned to the bar, Smith and Rhoden "were all revved up and pumped up that they just did the job." When asked what that connoted, MAG explained, "They were happy. Before they parked the car then, they came down Main and were going to turn left into the bar, and they were yelling out the window and stuff, kind of yahoo and all that."

At the trial, the prosecutor and MAG then engaged in the following dialogue, punctuated by an objection:

Q: Okay. When they came back, did the defendant and Mr. Rhoden tell you what had happened?

A: Yes, Dave—Dave did.

Q: Okay.

[Defense Counsel]:   I have to object to hearsay on Mr. Rhoden's statement.

The Court: Overruled.

Q: (By [Prosecutor]) What—okay. What was explained to you when they got back? Who was doing the talking?

A: Dave was.

Q: And what happened?

A: Dave said that he kicked the guys [sic] butt. I mean, they were just revved up when they first got back. And I said, you know, what happened? We all asked what happened.

 And Dave said that Dusty had pointed him out for him and whatnot, and then he parked the car a block away or so he wouldn't be seen. And then Dave went in and told the guy—the witness that he had car problems and asked him if he would come out and hold the battery cable so he could get his car started. And I guess he said it took him awhile to get the kid

convinced he needed help with it, and then the kid finally went outside, and then that's when Dave hit him and then took off from there and then they came back.

Q: Okay. So—so the defendant—you said he pointed out Mr. Minick in the bus station?

A: Right.

Q: And he went back to the car and Mr. Rhoden carried out the plan?

A: Right.

Q: What was the defendant doing during the time that Mr. Rhoden was—

A: I guess just waiting for Dave to show back up.

Q: Okay. Now, once—when you got back to the bar and David Rhoden explained what was happening, what was the defendant doing then? Did he ever—

A: He was happy and revved up about it and just kind of, you know, going along with David's story.

Q: Did he ever interject anything into the story or—

A: Not really. He just was—he seemed real happy.

Q: Okay. Now, once you were told this happened, did you witness the payoff?

A: Yes, I did.

Q: Who paid?

A: Dusty paid, and his mom and this girl that was there with them, they all whipped it out of their pockets, or purses, or whatever.

Q: So they didn't, like, take it out of a bunch of money on the table, they actually—

A: No, no, they all pulled it out of their pockets.

Q: Did the defendant do that too?

A: Yes, he did.

Q: Took it out of his wallet?

A: Yes.

Q: Did you see actually how much was paid?

A: No, I didn't. I just saw them all throwing the money on the table to Dave.

Q: Okay. Was there anything else that was offered in the form of a payoff?

A: Just the free beer.
 Smith was found guilty by the jury.

. . .

The record demonstrates the agreement between Smith and Rhoden that Rhoden would assault Minick for the agreed consideration; the actual assault upon Minick by Rhoden; and Minick's status as a witness. The elements of the charged offense were established.

The third issue posed by Smith relates to the admissibility of MAG's testimony about Rhoden's statements. The focus is upon those statements made subsequent to the return of Smith and Rhoden from the bus depot where Minick was assaulted. Smith first argues some of the statements merely constituted a solicitation, and that does not connote an agreement for purposes of a conspiracy. He also contends Rhoden's statements were mere bragging and were not made in the course of, or in furtherance of, the conspiracy which he argues ended with the assault upon Minick. The State's position is that Rhoden's statements were not hearsay and were admissible as statements of a co-conspirator during the course of and in furtherance of the conspiracy pursuant to WYO.R.EVID. 801(d)(2)(E).

We have consistently adhered to the concept articulated in W. LAFAVE & A. SCOTT CRIMINAL LAW 460–61 (1972):

One might suppose that the agreement necessary for conspiracy is essentially like the agreement or 'meeting of the minds' which is critical to a contract, but this is not the case. Although there continues to exist some uncertainty as to the precise meaning of the word in the context of conspiracy, it is clear that the definition in this setting is somewhat more lax than elsewhere. A mere tacit understanding will suffice, and there need not be any written statement or even a speaking of words which expressly communicates agreement. * * *

"Because most conspiracies are clandestine in nature, the prosecution is seldom able to present direct evidence of the agreement. Courts have been sympathetic to this problem, and it is thus well established that the prosecution may "rely on inferences drawn from the course of conduct of the alleged conspirators."

Given the evidence at Smith's trial, we are satisfied there was ample demonstration of a tacit understanding between Smith and Rhoden.

Language in . . . cases . . . would seem to suggest the conspiracy is concluded when the object of the conspiracy, in this instance the assault upon Minick, has been accomplished. The argument of the State, however, is that this conspiracy continued until the consideration had been paid to Rhoden. That view is supported by federal precedent. *United States v. Doyle,* 771 F.2d 250 (7th Cir.1985); *United States v. Schwanke,* 598 F.2d 575 (10th Cir.1979). Both of these cases stand for the proposition that statements made in connection with payments for assistance in furthering the goals of the conspiracy are made before the last overt act of the conspiracy has taken place. . . .

We hold MAG's testimony about Rhoden's statement was not hearsay under WYO.R.EVID. 801(d)(2)(E), which is adopted from the same rule of the FEDERAL RULES OF EVIDENCE construed in *Schwanke.* . . .

This rule, now so recurrent in criminal prosecutions, had its origin, and finds its justification, in the laws of agency. . . . In *Hitchman Coal & Coke Company v. Mitchell,* 245 U.S. 229, 249, 38 S.Ct. 65, [72], 62 L.Ed. 260 (1917), the court explained:

"* * * The rule of evidence is commonly applied in criminal cases, but is of general operation; indeed, it originated in the law of partnership. It depends upon the principle that when any number of persons associate themselves together in the prosecution of a common plan or enterprise, lawful or unlawful, from the very act of association there arises a kind of partnership, each member being constituted the agent of all, so that the act or declaration of one, in furtherance of the common object, is the act of all, and is admissible as primary and original evidence against them."

Three elements must be demonstrated before a statement can be admitted as nonhearsay under Rule 801(d)(2)(E), W.R.E. There must be evidence of a conspiracy; evidence that the declarant and the defendant both were involved in the conspiracy; and a showing that the proffered statements were made during the course of, and in furtherance of, the conspiracy. The first two requirements insure that the statements were in fact made by a coconspirator, and the last introduces a measure of relevance and trustworthiness.

The record in this case demonstrates all three of the elements discussed in *Jandro* have been satisfied. There was evidence of the solicitation of MAG by Smith. There was evidence of dialogue between Smith and Rhoden with respect to beating Minick. There was evidence Smith and Rhoden left the bar together prior to the assault upon Minick, and they returned together. The record establishes evidence of a conspiracy and evidence that Smith and Rhoden were involved. We hold Rhoden's statements were made during the course of, and in furtherance of, the conspiracy because it had not been completed until he had been paid the articulated consideration. There was no error in the admission of this evidence.

An independent basis is found in the law for the admission of the testimony about Rhoden's statements. Courts have recognized statements made by a coconspirator immediately after, or close in time to, the accomplishment of a criminal purpose of the conspiracy are admissible in order to characterize the action of the party as *res gestae* of the crime charged. The evidence of Rhoden's statements was admissible under this doctrine as well as under the usual rule that it was made in the course of, and in furtherance of, the conspiracy. . . .

No error occurred in the admission of the statements of the co-conspirator, and the Judgment and Sentence must be affirmed.

LEHMAN, Justice, dissenting.

. . .

F. PROBLEMS WITH CONSPIRACY

Conspiracy has been called a "prosecutor's darling," an offense so amorphous that it can be stretched to cover a wide range of circumstances, and, therefore, is subject to abuse. It has been used interchangeably with complicity, as procedural convenience or desired aggravation of penalties dictates. Political conspiracy is an area particularly sensitive to abuse. Prosecutors can respond all too willingly to the political extremism of the day, while overlooking this country's bedrock principles of political freedom.

The decision in *Dennis v. U.S.* (1951) emerged from the first years of the Cold War to uphold the conviction of Communist organizers for conspiracy to incite the violent overthrow of the government. The "inflammable nature of world conditions" influ-

EXHIBIT 6–2
Sample Jury Instructions

CONSPIRACY—ELEMENTS

The defendant is charged in [Count _____ of] the indictment with conspiring to _____ in violation of Section _____ of Title _____ of the United States Code. In order for the defendant to be found guilty of that charge, the government must prove each of the following elements beyond a reasonable doubt:

First, [beginning on or about _____ and ending on or about_____] [starting sometime before _____] there was an agreement between two or more persons to commit at least one crime as charged in the indictment;

Second, the defendant became a member of the conspiracy knowing of at least one of its objects and intending to help accomplish it; and

Third, one of the members of the conspiracy performed at least one overt act for the purpose of carrying out the conspiracy, with all of you agreeing on a particular overt act that you find was committed.

I shall discuss with you briefly the law relating to each of these elements.

A conspiracy is a kind of criminal partnership—an agreement of two or more persons to commit one or more crimes. The crime is the agreement to do something unlawful; it does not matter whether the crime agreed upon was committed.

For a conspiracy to have existed, it is not necessary that the conspirators made a formal agreement or that they agreed on every detail of the conspiracy. It is not enough, however, that they simply met, discussed matters of common interest, acted in similar ways, or perhaps helped one another. You must find that there was a plan to commit at least one of the crimes alleged in the indictment as an object of the conspiracy.

One becomes a member of a conspiracy by willfully participating in the unlawful plan with the intent to advance or further some object or purpose of the conspiracy, even though the person does not have full knowledge of all the details of the conspiracy. Furthermore, one who willfully joins an existing conspiracy is charged with the same responsibility as if that person had been one of the originators of it. On the other hand, one who has no knowledge of a conspiracy, but happens to act in a way which furthers some object or purpose of the conspiracy, does not thereby become a conspirator. Similarly, a person does not become a member merely by associating with one or more persons who are conspirators, nor merely by knowing of the existence of a conspiracy.

An overt act does not itself have to be unlawful. A lawful act may be an element of a conspiracy if it was done for the purpose of carrying out the conspiracy. The government is not required to prove that the defendant personally did one of the overt acts. Once you have decided that the defendant was a member of a conspiracy, the defendant is responsible for what other conspirators said or did to carry out the conspiracy, whether or not the defendant knew what they said or did.

Ninth Circuit Criminal Jury Instructions (St. Paul, MN: West Group, 1992), § 8.05A, with permission.

enced the Supreme Court to soften the requirement that prohibited speech pose a "clear and present danger" to interests of the United States. In his dissent, Justice Black wrote that the doctrine behind the decision

> waters down the First Amendment so that it amounts to little more than an admonition to Congress. The Amendment as so construed is not likely to protect any but those "safe" or orthodox views which rarely need its protection. . . .
>   Public opinion being what it now is, few will protest the conviction of these Communist petitioners. There is hope, however, that in calmer times, when present pressures, passions and fears subside, this or some later Court will restore the First Amendment liberties to the high preferred place where they belong in a free society.

In another period when free speech became the crux of political conflict, Dr. Benjamin Spock was convicted of conspiracy to aid in the evasion of selective service laws after a speech against the military draft. His coconspirators were the hundreds of applauding people shown in a videotape of the speech. This time the appeals court overruled the conviction [*U.S. v. Spock* (1st Cir. 1969)], affirming the possibility of political conspiracy but determining that specific intent was lacking in this case.

IV. SOLICITATION

Like attempt, solicitation has relevance only as an inchoate crime. It is the command or inducement of another to commit a substantive crime. If that person agrees, attempts, or actually commits the crime, solicitation charges against both solicitor and solicitee usually merge with the appropriate charges of conspiracy, attempt, or substantive crime. In certain jurisdictions, however, a solicitation is regarded in itself as attempt, and more generally so when the crime would be complete on the solicitee's acceptance. For example, an offer of money to a legislator for a changed vote would be attempted bribery; an acceptance of that offer would complete the crime of bribery and make the solicitation irrelevant. In any case, in order for solicitation to stand alone, the target crime may not be committed nor attempted nor agreed on.

As one might expect with such a lack of action, the actus reus of solicitation is simply words. The words must contain an inducement to action, however, rather than simple approval or advocacy. It is not even necessary for the solicitation to reach its target. A letter that gets lost in the mail can be incriminating for its writer. Use of an intermediary party is also immaterial to the charge. In *State v. Yee* (Wis. App. 1990) the defendant who asked a second person to get a third person to commit murder was guilty of solicitation.

Because solicitation centers on the use of speech, the First Amendment can be a factor. The question comes down to specific intent, the mens rea of solicitation. There is a difference between Richard Craig saying to the Haden Hills Homeowners, "We really ought to do something about the gays in our neighborhood," and his saying, "Go at midnight tonight and shoot out their windows." The area is still fuzzy, with the line difficult to distinguish between a sincere call to action and hyperbole by a speaker on a roll. Compare this to the *Spock* conspiracy case.

Because solicitation is so far from the intended substantive crime, with an independent agent employed between the plotter and the action, it is considered by some to be the least dangerous inchoate crime. Others consider the control of the solicitor over the "hired gun" to be an insidious threat that makes the crime of solicitation much more dangerous than the crime of attempt. The Model Penal Code finds it worthy of the same punishment as the target substantive crime, unless that is a first degree felony. Some states prosecute solicitation of felonies and serious misdemeanors only; others select only certain categories, such as solicitation to riot or to commit bribery; and still others prosecute solicitation for all crimes, but allow less severe penalties than those for the target crime. Federal laws target specific situations, such

"If you think that you can think about a thing, inextricably attached to something else, without thinking of the thing it is attached to, then you have a legal mind."

—Thomas Reed Powell,
American educator,
1880–1955
Laurence J. Peter, *Peter's Quotations*, 1977

as solicitation to commit violent crime, 18 U.S.C.A. § 373; to influence voting, 18 U.S.C.A. § 597; and to obtain improper political contributions, 18 U.S.C.A. § 602.

Renunciation of the solicitation, where the offer is completely retracted from the solicitee, is usually allowed as a defense. A more problematic concern is the solicitation by law enforcement officers to determine if the solicitee is prone to commit a crime. Though the intent is to prevent crime, it can be argued that an overzealous decoy may actually encourage the commission of crime by innocent people. This topic is covered more thoroughly in the Chapter 7 discussion of the entrapment defense.

ANALYSIS PROBLEM

6–6.   What are the similarities and differences between the Model Penal Code concept of unilateral conspiracy and solicitation?

V.   RACKETEERING INFLUENCED AND CORRUPT ORGANIZATIONS (RICO)

A.   INTRODUCTION

We began the chapter with attempt offenses and the control of dangerous acts and now arrive at the opposite end of the spectrum with statutes intended to control dangerous people and organizations. A person working in established criminal enterprises in concert with other people is believed to present a greater threat to society than the lone criminal. The growing spread of organized crime into legitimate businesses and organizations led Congress to pass the Racketeer Influenced and Corrupt Organizations (RICO) Act in 1970, 18 U.S.C.A. §§ 1961 to 1968, prohibiting racketeering activity in interstate and foreign commerce. It has since been used broadly to prosecute cases not always fitting the traditional profile of organized crime.

RICO convictions impose heavy penalties. Severe sentences and forfeiture of property are assessed against RICO violators, and separate prosecution of predicate RICO acts are allowed. RICO also provides in § 1964 for civil actions by the United States and individual plaintiffs against defendants.

B.   RICO ELEMENTS

RICO crimes require the existence of (1) an "enterprise," (2) that is involved in collection of unlawful debt or a pattern of racketeering or racketeering conspiracy, and (3) the knowing participation in the enterprise by the defendant [*U.S. v. Angiulo* (1st Cir. 1988)]. An enterprise can be "any individual, partnership, corporation, association or other legal entity, or any union or group of individuals associated in fact although not a legal entity" [18 U.S.C.A. § 1961(4)]. A pattern of racketeering is established by the commission of two or more **predicate offenses** within ten years, excluding any prison time [18 U.S.C.A. §§ 1961(5 and 6)]. Predicate crimes for RICO include murder, kidnapping, gambling, arson, robbery, bribery, extortion, and dealing in obscene matter or controlled substances, which are chargeable under state law, and a long list of acts indictable under federal law, such as wire and mail fraud, obstruction of justice, money laundering, exploitation of children, payments and loans to labor organizations, and bringing in illegal aliens, among others [§ 1961(1)]. Most federal racketeering convictions are based on predicate gambling, drug, and extortion and threat offenses.[7]

Traditionally, predicate acts were those committed for the purpose of financial gain, but the social and religious reasons of antiabortion protesters were adequate in the civil RICO decision of *National Organization for Women v. Scheidler* (1994). RICO specifies four criminal violations.

predicate offenses: component crimes that are the objectives of a collective crime such as a RICO offense.

Section 1962(a) makes it a crime to invest the proceeds of a pattern of racketeering activity or collection of an unlawful debt in an enterprise affecting interstate commerce [such as investing profits from illegal drug trafficking in a legitimate business]. . . .

Section 1962(b) makes it a crime to acquire or maintain an interest in an enterprise affecting interstate commerce through a pattern of racketeering activity or collection of unlawful debt [such as an organized crime boss taking over a legitimate business through extortion]. . . .

Section 1962(c) makes it a crime to conduct the affairs of an enterprise affecting interstate commerce "through" a pattern of racketeering activity or collection of unlawful debt [such as a car dealer using the facilities of the dealership to operate a stolen car ring]. . . .

Section 1962(d) expressly makes it a crime to conspire to commit any of the three substantive RICO offenses.[8]

C. EXTENT OF CONTROL

Because the question of the extent of participation in the conduct of the enterprise is a slippery one, the most frequently litigated RICO provision is 18 U.S.C.A. § 1962(c).[9] On one hand, a RICO violator does not need to occupy the "top rung" of the ladder of control in the enterprise, but on the other hand he or she must play at least "some part in directing enterprise affairs" [*Reves v. Ernst & Young* (1993)]. Operating outside the chain of command is not enough for a RICO violation, but defendants who collected loans by extortionate means in a knowing implementation of enterprise goals were guilty of substantive RICO violations [*U.S. v. Oreto* (1st Cir. 1994), cert. denied (1995)]. The court in *U.S. v. Diaz* (2nd Cir. 1999) ruled that exercising "broad discretion" qualified for RICO, whereas simply taking directions did not. The defendants' convictions were affirmed, because they had committed murder to further the narcotics business of their street gang, then decided on their own also to kill a witness to the murder.

D. RICO CONSPIRACY

A defendant can be convicted of RICO conspiracy under § 1961(d) even if the defendant did not participate in the operation of the enterprise. Knowledge of the extent of the conspiracy, however, is necessary for a RICO conviction. A handyman for the leader of a racketeering enterprise who agreed to sell goods without knowing of the broader conspiracy was not guilty of either substantive or conspiracy RICO charges. The court in *U.S. v. Viola* (2nd Cir. 1994) said the handyman was not on the ladder of control at all, but "sweeping up the floor beneath it." RICO conspiracy also does not require that acts in furtherance of the conspiracy be committed; it is an inchoate crime. An agreement to facilitate commission of acts that would constitute a substantive RICO crime if they were completed is sufficient [*Salinas v. U.S.* (1997)].

E. STATE ORGANIZED CRIME STATUTES

Most states have RICO statutes, often following the provisions of the federal statutes. Some states have organized crime statutes requiring specific numbers of participants or predicate acts. The Texas statute VTCA Penal Code § 71.01(a) requires a group of three or more people intending to work together in a continuing course of criminal activities. The court in *Nguyen v. State* (Tex. Crim. App. 1999) reversed an organized crime conviction for a defendant who had worked with three others to commit murder, because there was no evidence of a continuing enterprise.

VI.   CONTINUING CRIMINAL ENTERPRISE (CCE)

The federal Continuing Criminal Enterprise (CCE) statute, 21 U.S.C.A. § 848, was passed in 1984 in an effort to reduce the amount of drugs on the streets. It targets the "kingpins" who run trafficking operations and provides sentences of not less than twenty years, heavy fines, and property forfeitures. A study from 1987 to 1990 concluded that CCE offenders make up less than 1 percent of all federal drug offenders, a well defined set of the most serious drug criminals.[10] To be convicted as a CCE offender, the defendant must hold an organizing, supervising, or management position in a group of at least five other persons that has undertaken a continuing series of violations of United States drug control laws, at least one of which is a felony and from which the defendant derives substantial income or resources. The number of participants and reference to income applies to the series of violations, not to each violation [*Richardson v. U.S.* (1999)].

The *Richardson* case involved a long series of predicate acts, and the jury dealt with them collectively as being sufficient to constitute the required "continuing series of violations." The Supreme Court, however, ruled that juries in CCE cases must agree on several specific violations, because each is a separate element of the crime. The Court suggested that three violations would suffice. *U.S. v. Quintana* (D. Utah 1993) extended that required jury unanimity to the five people involved with the defendant in the enterprise.

No separate, RICO-like entity is required for a CCE offense, but rather a more loosely defined operation or undertaking. Read *U.S. v. Quintana* for that definition.

UNITED STATES v. QUINTANA
United States District Court, D. Utah, C.D. 1993
839 F.Supp. 1518 D. Utah 1993
[Citations omitted]

MEMORANDUM DECISION AND ORDER RE: MOTION FOR JUDGMENT OF ACQUITTAL

J. THOMAS GREENE, District Judge.

This matter is before the court on defendant's Motion for Judgment of Acquittal as to Count 1, operating a continuing criminal enterprise, notwithstanding the jury's verdict of "Guilty" as to that count. The parties have fully briefed the issues, and the court heard extensive oral argument on November 16, 1993, after which the matter was taken under advisement. Now being fully advised, the court makes and enters the following Memorandum Decision and Order.

FACTUAL BACKGROUND

On September 10, 1993, Henry Willie Quintana, Jr., ("Quintana") was convicted of multiple counts of drug distribution as well as engaging in a continuing criminal enterprise ("CCE"). Quintana now urges this court to grant his motion for judgment of acquittal on the ground that the evidence presented at trial was insufficient to support a CCE conviction.

The evidence was unrefuted that Quintana was involved in trafficking large amounts of cocaine. The government also presented unrefuted evidence that Quintana was supplied cocaine by Juan Castanon and Richard Villanueva, and that Quintana supplied cocaine for further distribution to Randy

Mondragon, Michael Fresquez and others. Randy Mondragon, Michael Fresquez and Juan Castanon testified that Quintana had no control over them, and that they did not belong to an organization controlled or managed by Quintana. Other persons involved with Quintana in drug transactions included his father, Henry Quintana, Sr., Rodrigo "Chino" Alanis, Jose "Pepe" Lopez, Johnny Salazar, Larry Cordova, "Ruben," "Negro," an unnamed person who stored cocaine, and an unnamed person who delivered for Quintana.

Extensive evidence was presented concerning drug distribution activities of Quintana. Much of the evidence was to the effect that Quintana "organized" other persons in a continuing scheme to facilitate the distribution of cocaine. The evidence with respect to Henry Quintana, Sr. was that Quintana supplied Henry, gave him instructions concerning the distribution and price of cocaine, and orchestrated deliveries to him. The transactions with Henry provide sufficient evidence that Quintana directed some unnamed person to deliver cocaine to Henry. The transactions with Henry also provide evidence that Quintana was fronting[2] cocaine to two men, "Pat" and "Larry," for distribution. Wiretap evidence of conversations between Quintana and

_____

2. In the drug business, the term "front" merely means to supply contraband on consignment, i.e., a supplier provides a distributor with cocaine on credit and the [distributor] does not pay until he has resold the drugs, presumably for a profit.

Henry was to the effect that Jose "Pepe" Lopez delivered for Quintana, and that Lopez expected instructions from Quintana.

The evidence with respect to Juan Castanon indicated that he was one of Quintana's suppliers and that Quintana directed him concerning deliveries of cocaine. Mondragon and Fresquez were distributors who were "fronted" by Quintana. He arranged and confirmed deals with Fresquez. Both Mondragon and Fresquez testified that Quintana was their supplier. Quintana coordinated a deal between Fresquez and Mondragon, and directed them how to divide the cocaine. Quintana provided advice to Salazar about the cocaine business and arranged deliveries to Salazar through Eva Valdez. Quintana admitted in conversations with Salazar to paying an unnamed person to store cocaine for him, as well as paying "Chino" for delivering. Evidence was presented to the effect that Quintana supplied a person named "David" and that Richard Villanueva supplied Quintana.

The foregoing examples are typical of evidence presented by the government to show that Quintana played a central role in interaction with others relative to the sale and distribution of drugs.

. . .

Analysis

Quintana contests the sufficiency of the evidence to uphold his conviction for operating a continuing criminal enterprise. He contends that the evidence was insufficient to show that he was an "organizer" or "supervisor" or that he occupied a "position of management" with respect to five or more persons. At the hearing on November 16, 1993, counsel for the government conceded that its theory of liability was that Quintana was an "organizer," as distinguished from a "supervisor" or a person in a "position of management." Accordingly, the determinative issue here is whether the evidence was such that any rational trier of fact could have found Quintana to be an "organizer" within the meaning of the statute.

Counsel for the government and for the defendant disagree as to the meaning of "organizer" for purposes of the CCE statute. Quintana argues and the government disagrees that the term "organizer" necessarily requires some type of managerial responsibility or influence. The parties also disagree as to whether organizational activities must be carried on through an "enterprise" as an entity, as opposed to engaging in prohibited acts apart from a structured "enterprise." Finally, there is dispute as to whether prosecutorial reference to persons who might have been "organized" by a defendant constituted prejudicial error.

I. SCOPE AND MEANING OF THE TERM "ORGANIZER" UNDER THE CONTINUING CRIMINAL ENTERPRISE STATUTE

A person is engaged in a continuing criminal enterprise if:

(1) he violates any provision of this subchapter . . . and
(2) such violation is a part of a continuing series of violations . . .

(A) which are undertaken in concert with five or more other persons with respect to whom such person occupies a position of *organizer, a supervisory position, or any other position of management,* and
(B) from which such person obtains substantial income or resources. 21 U.S.C. § 848(c) (emphasis added)

A. The terms "organizer," "supervisor," and "position of management" are phrased in the disjunctive and each term is ascribed its separate, everyday meaning.

Defendant argues that in the context of the CCE statute an organizer must have managerial responsibilities in part because the term "organizer" is modified by the statutory language "or any *other* position of management." *Id.* § 848(c)(2)(A) (emphasis added). Counsel for defendant submits that under the statute a position of "organizer" is the equivalent of an "other position of management," hence, an organizer must possess managerial responsibilities.

In *United States v. Apodaca,* 843 F.2d 421, 426 (10th Cir.1988), *cert. denied,* 488 U.S. 932, 109 S.Ct. 325, 102 L.Ed.2d 342 (1988), the Tenth Circuit explained that "the statute is phrased in the disjunctive. The defendant must have acted as organizer, as supervisor, *or* in any other position of management" (emphasis in original). . . .

The operative terms of the CCE statute—*organize, supervise,* and *manage,* are not technical terms and are ascribed their everyday meanings. *Apodaca,* 843 F.2d at 425–26. "Organize" means to "arrange or assemble into an orderly, structured, functional whole; to manage or arrange systematically for united or harmonious action." *Webster's II New Riverside University Dictionary,* 1984. "Manage" means "to direct or control." *Id.* An organizer, from the ordinary sense of the word, is not necessarily a manager. On the other hand, an "organizer" could also be a "manager." The statute does not *require* that a person charged with CCE must be both an organizer *and* a manager, however. It is sufficient, under the disjunctive language employed, simply to be an "organizer."

B. An "organizer" need not possess managerial responsibilities for purposes of the CCE statute.

"Organizer" status under the statute requires that defendant occupy a central role in organizing the prohibited drug activities. The central role need not include control or managerial responsibility, but it must be more than a mere buyer-seller relationship.

The Tenth Circuit, in *Apodaca,* defined organizer as:

a person who puts together a number of people engaged in separate activities and arranges them in their activities in one essentially orderly operation or enterprise. . . . The ordinary meaning of the word "organizer" does not carry with it the implication that the organizer is necessarily able to control those whom he or she organizes.

Apodaca, 843 F.2d at 426.

. . .

In the case at bar, there was unrefuted evidence that Quintana supplied and fronted drugs to Mondragon and Fresquez, who were both distributors. The government also presented evidence that Juan Castanon and Richard Villanueva supplied cocaine to Quintana. There is evidence that Quintana directed Juan Castanon, "Pepe" Lopez and one other unnamed person in drug deliveries. Quintana, on a regular basis, directed Henry Quintana, Sr. as to the delivery, distribution and price of cocaine. Chino and at least one unnamed person were in the direct employment of Quintana. Evidence presented by the government was sufficient to permit the jury to find that Quintana actually controlled or managed Henry Quintana, Sr., Chino, Castanon, and an unnamed person who stored drugs for Quintana. Quintana facilitated and arranged for the supply and delivery of cocaine to all of the people discussed above and said that he needed to collect from "everybody".

The government was not obligated to present evidence that Quintana actually controlled or managed all of these people. The evidence was sufficient to convict if a reasonable jury could find that Quintana played a "sufficiently central role" in organizing at least five people in a drug distribution operation or "enterprise." The reasonable jury impanelled in the case at bar could and did so find.

II. THE CONTINUING CRIMINAL ENTERPRISE STATUTE DOES NOT REQUIRE THE EXISTENCE OF A SEPARATE ENTITY OR "ENTERPRISE"

By definition a person engages in a "continuing criminal enterprise" under the statute if he or she participates in a "continuing series of violations" in concert with five or more persons as to whom the defendant occupies a position of "organizer, a supervisory position, or any other position of management." 21 U.S.C. § 848(c). Defendant urges this court to interpret "enterprise" to require the existence of an entity, similar to the "enterprise" required for purposes of the Racketeer Influenced and Corrupt Organizations Act ("RICO"). 18 U.S.C. § 1961 *et seq.*

The court rejects defendant's conception of "enterprise." It would violate the plain meaning of the statute to define "enterprise" as requiring the existence of a separate entity. The CCE statute equates "enterprise" with activities or conduct which constitute a series of violations, not necessarily requiring the existence of a separate or distinct entity. "Enterprise" generally means an undertaking or a project. . . .

The Fifth Circuit recognized that to establish a RICO violation, there must be "proof of the existence of the enterprise itself." However, in contrast to RICO, the court noted that the CCE statute "*does not require proof of a RICO type enterprise.*"

Based upon the foregoing, this court concludes that no RICO-type "enterprise" or other separate organization or entity need exist in order for a defendant to be convicted of engaging in a continuing criminal enterprise.

III. JURY MUST UNANIMOUSLY AGREE AS TO THE IDENTITY OF AT LEAST FIVE OTHER PERSONS WHO ACTED WITH THE DEFENDANT

Quintana argues that the government's closing argument was prejudicial because the prosecutor named fifteen persons who could be regarded as having been organized by the defendant in the alleged continuing criminal enterprise without clarifying which satisfied the statutory requirement, and which did not.

The jury was given a unanimity instruction[6] which required the jury unanimously to agree upon the identity of at least five persons with whom the defendant acted in committing a series of violations. The court does not believe that the prosecutor's closing argument rose to the level of prejudicial error. . . .

Based upon the foregoing, the court finds that sufficient evidence was presented by the government to allow a reasonable jury to have convicted Quintana as an "organizer" under the continuing criminal enterprise statute. Accordingly, it is hereby

Ordered, that defendant's Motion for Judgment of Acquittal is denied.

---

6. Jury Instruction No. 48 was as follows:

> If you find, beyond a reasonable doubt, that the defendant committed a narcotics offense and that this narcotics offense was part of a continuing series of violations of the narcotics laws, then you must decide whether the defendant committed this series of violations with five or more persons.
>
> The defendant's relationships with the other persons need not have existed at the same time, the five or more persons involved need not have acted in concert at the same time or with each other, and the same type of relationship need not have existed between the defendant and each of the five or more persons. The defendant need not have had personal contact with each of the five or more persons involved. You must unanimously agree, however, on the identity of at least five persons with whom the defendant acted in committing the series of narcotics violations alleged by the government.

VII. CRIMINAL GANG CONTROL

Some states and municipalities aiming to control the criminal activities of gangs have passed statutes and ordinances that are similar to continuing criminal enterprise laws. Indiana's law is an example of this approach.

INDIANA CODE
IC 35–45–9
  Chapter 9. Criminal Gang Control

IC 35–45–9–1
Section 1. As used in this chapter, "criminal gang" means a group with at least five members that specifically:
  (1)   either:
        (A)   promotes, sponsors, or assists in; or
        (B)   participates in; or
  (2)   requires as a condition of membership or continued membership; the commission of a felony or an act that would be a felony if committed by an adult or the offense of battery (IC 35–42–2–1).

IC 35–45–9–2
Section 2. As used in this chapter, "threatens" includes a communication made with the intent to harm a person or the person's property or any other person or the property of another person.

IC 35–45–9–3
Section 3. A person who knowingly or intentionally actively participates in a criminal gang commits criminal gang activity, a Class D felony.

IC 35–45–9–4
Section 4. A person who threatens another person because the other person:
  (1)   refuses to join a criminal gang; or
  (2)   has withdrawn from a criminal gang;
        commits criminal gang intimidation, a Class C felony.

State v. Ochoa (Ariz. App. 1997) affirmed a conviction under Arizona's criminal street gang statute (A.R.S. § 13-2308) and upheld an enhanced sentence for felonies committed with the intent to promote or assist the criminal conduct of a street gang [A.R.S. §§ 13-105(7) and (8), and 13-604(T)]. At issue were seven criteria indicative of gang membership, including tattoos and clothing, that the court held not to be unconstitutionally vague because they are to be identified in conjunction with the criminal activity of the gang.

Loitering and public nuisance measures are also used to keep suspected gang members from exerting control over specific streets. Chicago's broad Anti-Gang Loitering ordinance was declared unconstitutionally vague in *Chicago v. Morales* (1999). California prosecutors, however, have successfully defended the use of evidence gathered against suspected gangs to get injunctions prohibiting specific behavior by their members, such as carrying pagers or blocking sidewalks.[11]

 ANALYSIS PROBLEM

6–7.   Research suggests that dangerous behavior is not predictable. Compare the value that our country places on freedom and presumption of innocence to the value of inchoate and organized crime law in combatting potential harm to society. Can you reconcile the two sides? Do you value one side over the other? Consider the issue of freedom of speech.

VIII. CONCLUSION

Inchoate crime laws allow for preventive law enforcement. Intervention and prosecution may occur before the target crime is committed to prevent its completion.

Inchoate crimes approach the completion of the crime in increments, as shown in the diagram in Exhibit 6–3. The chart gives you a picture of the proximity of the inchoate crimes to completion of the crime, with the furthest on the left, solicitation, to the closest on the right, attempt. Attempt statutes vary in their requirements of proximity to the completed crime from "dangerous proximity" to "substantial step"; solicitation is furthest from completion. The distance of the actus reus from the completed crime increases the importance, and sometimes difficulty, of determining mens rea. Success at any step merges into the next step toward completion. Only conspiracy can be prosecuted as a separate crime if its target is accomplished. Successful solicitation may be conspiracy, or it may jump to merge with attempt, or it may even complete the crime as in the case of bribery.

Special defenses for inchoate crimes often include abandonment or renunciation before damage is done. Others include legal impossibility and, for conspiracy, the earlier running of the statute of limitations for abandonment and the last conspirator defense. Standard defenses to substantive crimes also may apply.

Group crimes range from conspiracy, requiring an agreement with another person and sometimes an overt act, to RICO and CCE offenses that require an ongoing enterprise and specific numbers of predicate acts or persons involved. Organized crime convictions often hinge on what level defendants participate in directing the affairs of the undertaking.

Add your state statutes and elements to the charts in Exhibits 6–4 and 6–5 for a quick overview of inchoate and organized crimes.

SYSTEM FOLDER ASSIGNMENTS

Complete the following and place the documents in your system folder.

- Summary of the proximity tests for attempt, noting the tests used in your jurisdiction.
- Your state conspiracy statute requirements, including bilateral or unilateral agreement and last conspirator defense.
- Your state and municipal antigang measures.
- The chart on inchoate crimes in Exhibit 6–4 and the chart on organized crimes in Exhibit 6–5, completed with elements from your state's statutes and case law.

EXHIBIT 6–3
Increments of Inchoate Crimes

SOLICITATION	CONSPIRACY	ATTEMPT	COMPLETED
Inducement made	Agreement made	Substantial step taken	Crime
	Overt act made,	Dangerous proximity	
Failure	failure or success	Failure	Success

EXHIBIT 6–4
Inchoate Crimes

	ATTEMPT	CONSPIRACY	SOLICITATION
Statutes	MPC: § 5.01. 18 U.S.C.A. §§ 1113, 2113, 1541. *State:*	MPC: § 5.03. 18 U.S.C.A. § 371. *State:*	MPC: § 5.02. 18 U.S.C.A. §§ 373, 597, 602, and so on. *State:*
Elements	Intent to complete crime. Overt act beyond preparation. Failure. *State:*	Agreement. Intention to commit unlawful act or lawful act in unlawful manner. Often, overt act. *State:*	Specific intent. Inducement of another to commit crime. Failure. *State:*
Separate conviction	Merges with completed crime. *State:*	Does not merge, can be prosecuted as inchoate crime as well as completed crime, but separate conviction may depend on intention to commit second crime. *State:*	Merges with attempt, conspiracy, or completed crime. (May be regarded as attempt if acceptance completes the crime.) *State:*
Grading/categories. MPC: inchoate crime equal to target crimes, except first degree felonies equal to second degree felonies.	Half of target crime, or fixed maximum, or equal to target crime. Some allow for any crime, allow only certain categories, or eliminate categories. *State:*	Misdemeanors, or fixed maximum sentences, or levels correspond to target crimes. *State:*	Felonies and misdemeanors only, or only certain crimes, or all crimes but at a lesser level. *State:*
Defenses	Voluntary and complete renunciation. Legal impossibility. *State:*	Voluntary and complete renunciation. Statute of limitations. Last conspirator. *State:*	Voluntary and complete renunciation. *State:*
Problems	Defining the level of overt act. Impossibility defense. *State:*	Number of conspiracy charges. Wharton's Rule or unilateral conspiracy. Level of overt act, open to abuse. *State:*	Determination of specific intent, particularly in group situations. Entrapment. *State:*

EXHIBIT 6–5
Organized Crimes

	RICO	CCE	GANGS
Statutes	18 U.S.C.A. §§ 1961–1968.	21 U.S.C.A. § 848.	*State:* Gang control laws, public nuisance laws.
Enterprise	Individual, legal entity; nonlegal entity.	Five other persons, operation or undertaking (more loosely defined than RICO).	Group, criminal conditions for membership.
Predicate	Two specified racketeering or money laundering offenses in ten years.	Series of U.S. drug violations, at least one felony, substantial income.	Crimes promoting or assisting gang.
Control	Some part in directing affairs.	Organizing, managing, or supervising role.	

APPLICATION ASSIGNMENTS

1. If you were on the team prosecuting Thacker, who was charged with attempted murder for shooting through a tent, what charge would you recommend? Why?

2. A gun was shot from a moving car several times toward a group of people on the street. No one was injured. The shooter was charged with attempted first degree murder by creation of grave risk of death. Is this an appropriate charge? See *State v. Dunbar,* 817 P.2d 1360 (Wash. 1991).

3. A nursing director speaks with two nurses about her concern for an infant with severe birth defects in their care. She gives one of the nurses a bottle of a deadly drug. Four days later, the baby dies as a result of the administration of the drug. Should the nursing director be charged with attempted murder in your opinion? Under Model Penal Code standards? Under your state's standards? [See *Arias v. State,* 593 So. 2d 260 (Fla. App. 1992)].

4. How would the Model Penal Code standard of substantial step change the results of attempt charges in *Rizzo?* In *Campbell and Bradley?*

5. A defendant was caught walking through backyards while in possession of a pry bar, large screwdriver, two flashlights, and gloves. Does this satisfy the substantial step requirement for attempted burglary? See *Commonwealth v. Melnyczenko,* 619 A.2d 719 (Pa. Super. 1992).

6. Can Lacey Rude in Case I be charged with attempt? Why or why not?

7. A defendant completed the necessary acts for a conviction of attempted burglary, but he walked away from the scene without completing the crime. His departure was by a different route than his arrival, which allowed him to avoid an approaching police officer. Was his abandonment sufficiently voluntary to be a defense to the attempt charge? [See *Thomas v. State,* 708 S.W.2d 861 (Tex. Crim. App. 1986)].

8. A man intentionally tricked an undercover officer into paying him money for cocaine that did not exist. Should this man be charged with conspiracy to deliver cocaine? What are the issues of the case? [See *State v. Long,* 800 S.W.2d 507 (Tenn. Cr. App. 1990)].

9. In *People v. Brown,* 277 Cal. Rptr. 309 (Cal. App. 1991), a defendant who had agreed to commit robbery but whose only participation was to receive a part of the loot had his conviction overturned because the act occurred after the offense and did not fulfill the necessary "overt act" requirement. Compare and contrast this decision with the concept of overt act presented in this section of the text.

10. Your supervising attorney assigns you the task of determining appropriate charges in a new case. Facts show that the defendant transported an illegal alien, but the alien was working as a government informant immune to prosecution. What are the most appropriate charges? [See *U.S. v. Medina-Garcia,* 918 F.2d 4 (1st Cir. 1990)].

11. Three persons conspired to commit kidnapping and murder for ransom. The designated hit man became a government agent who would not carry out the objective of the conspiracy. Should the other two be charged with conspiracy? Why or why not? [See *People v. Liu,* 54 Cal. Rptr.2d 578 (Cal. App. 1996)].

12. The case of *U.S. v. Falcone,* 311 U.S. 205, 61 S. Ct. 204 (1940), is often used to illustrate required intent in conspiracy. The defendant sold sugar and yeast to known moonshiners. What did the Court need to know about the transaction to establish intent? Without further evidence of involvement by the defendant, how would you decide the case? On what case could you base your decision?

13. How would the *Peoni* and *Backun* cases (from the section on complicity in Chapter 3) be decided if those defendants had been charged with conspiracy?

14. A defendant set up a transaction for "China white" heroin. An undercover officer delivered a look-alike substance. Because the situation made it impossible for the defendant actually to purchase heroin, did she have a valid defense to an attempt to possess a controlled substance charge? [See *Grill v. State,* 651 A.2d 856 (Md. 1995)].

15. Over a period of time one person continually buys cocaine from another, then resells it on the street. They have never made a verbal agreement in the enterprise. Should they be charged with conspiracy? [See *U.S. v. Moran,* 984 F.2d 1299 (1st Cir. 1993)].

16. The defendant tells an undercover officer that he wants to get rid of his wife. That officer brings a second officer, whom the defendant pays to be the assassin. Of the three inchoate crimes, which seems to be the most appropriate charge in this case and why? [See *People v. Adami,* 111 Cal. Rptr. 544 (Cal. App. 1973)].

17. A defendant participated in a cocaine trafficking enterprise, not as the operator of the enterprise, but by deciding how much cocaine to buy and what prices and terms to charge to the lower-level distributors. Is this level of control sufficient for a substantive RICO offense? [See *U.S. v. Posada-Rios* 158 F.3d 832 (5th Cir. 1998), cert. denied, 119 S.Ct. 1792 (1999)].

HELPFUL WEB SITES

www.corrections.com
    Bulletin board for criminal gang issues and information
www.freep.com/news/local/qgang15.htm
    Article: Gang members to be indicted on racketeering charges

INTERNET EXERCISES

1. Using one of the general legal research Web sites listed in Chapter 1, find and read the text of *Kotteakos v. U.S.,* 328 U.S. 750, 66 S.Ct. 1239 (1946), and *U.S. v. Peoni,* 100 F.2d 401 (2d Cir. 1938), to understand how "wheel" conspiracy and

"chain" conspiracy theories are used to determine the number of conspiracies in which a defendant is involved.

2. Using a legal research Web site, find and read the decision in *State v. Ochoa*, 943 P.2d 814 (Ariz. App. 1997). How do the Arizona laws quoted in that decision differ from the Indiana law quoted in the text?

3. Go to www.lectlaw.com; in the "library stacks" find information about prosecuting criminal enterprises. In 1990, how many racketeering matters and how many CCE matters were investigated by United States attorneys?

QUESTIONS FOR STUDY AND REVIEW

1. Give an example of an inchoate crime law that controls dangerous conduct, and one that controls dangerous persons.
2. How is attempt graded in the Model Penal Code? In your state?
3. Name the elements of attempt.
4. Why is mens rea so important in attempt?
5. Name six tests and standards used to determine whether actus reus is sufficient for an attempt charge. Include examples of each.
6. Is voluntary abandonment more likely to be allowed as a defense to attempt where dangerous proximity is required or where Model Penal Code standards define attempt? Why?
7. What is the difference between legal impossibility and factual impossibility? Which is accepted as a defense to attempt?
8. What are the elements of conspiracy? Which element may not be present in some statutes?
9. Is conspiracy always an inchoate crime? Explain.
10. Under some state statutes and Model Penal Code § 1.07(1)(b), when does conspiracy merge with the completed crime?
11. What are the standards of conspiracy intent set forth in *Lauria?*
12. When do coconspirators have responsibility for acts committed by a fellow conspirator? According to the Model Penal Code?
13. What is Wharton's Rule? A unilateral conspiracy?
14. When there are multiple parties or multiple substantive crimes, how is the number of conspiracies determined?
15. Is impossibility a defense to conspiracy?
16. How can the statute of limitations help in the defense of one who abandons a conspiracy?
17. What is the "last conspirator defense"? Is it always accepted?
18. Why is conspiracy called a "prosecutor's darling"?
19. What conditions are necessary for the crime of solicitation to stand alone?
20. What are the elements of solicitation?
21. What is the RICO Act? What is its purpose? What is a RICO enterprise? Pattern of racketeering? What are the elements of a RICO conspiracy?
22. What is a continuing criminal enterprise? What is the purpose of the CCE statute?
23. What kinds of laws have been used to control criminal gang activity?

KEY TERMS LIST

Hearsay testimony
Last conspirator defense

Predicate offense
Res ipsa loquitur

Unilateral conspiracy
Wharton's Rule

ENDNOTES

1. JOEL SAMAHA, CRIMINAL LAW 181–82 (4th ed. 1993).
2. PETER W. LOW, JOHN CALVIN JEFFRIES, JR., & RICHARD J. BONNIE, CRIMINAL LAW, CASES AND MATERIALS 339–40 (2d ed. 1986).
3. *Id.* at 341.
4. ARNOLD H. LOEWY, CRIMINAL LAW IN A NUTSHELL 154 (1975).
5. WAYNE R. LaFAVE, AUSTIN W. SCOTT, JR., SUBSTANTIVE CRIMINAL LAW, Vol. 2 102 West Group 1986.
6. 2 DEVITT, BLACKMAR, & O'MALLEY, FEDERAL JURY PRACTICE AND INSTRUCTIONS: CRIMINAL 201 (4th ed. 1990).
7. F. Carlson P. Finn, *Prosecuting Criminal Enterprises,* www.lectlaw.com, Nov. 1993.
8. Washington Staff, Organized Crime and Racketeering Section, U.S. Department of Justice, Racketeer Influenced and Corrupt Organizations (RICO), A MANUAL FOR FEDERAL PROSECUTORS, 2–3, 2d ed. Rev. 1988.
9. Gregory P. Joseph, *Federal Practice: RICO "Conduct,"* NLJ, B11 July 26, 1999.
10. Finn, *supra* note 7.
11. Margot Hornblower, *Ending the Roundups,* TIME, June 21, 1999, at 55.

Congress OF THE United States,

begun and held at the City of New York, on

Wednesday, the fourth of March, one thousand seven hundred and eighty nine.

THE Conventions of a number of the States having at the time of their adopting the Constitution, expressed a desire, in order to prevent misconstruction or abuse of its powers, that further declaratory and restrictive clauses should be added: And as extending the ground of public confidence in the Government, will best ensure the beneficent ends of its institution.

RESOLVED, by the Senate and House of Representatives of the United States of America in Congress assembled, two thirds of both Houses concurring, that the following Articles be proposed to the Legislatures of the several States, as amendments to the Constitution of the United States, all, or any of which articles, when ratified by three fourths of the said Legislatures, to be valid to all intents and purposes, as part of the said Constitution, viz.

ARTICLES in addition to, and amendment of the Constitution of the United States of America, proposed by Congress, and ratified by the Legislatures of the several States, pursuant to the fifth Article of the original Constitution.

Article the first. After the first enumeration required by the first Article of the Constitution, there shall be one Representative for every thirty thousand, until the number shall amount to one hundred, after which the proportion shall be so regulated by Congress, that there shall be not less than one hundred Representatives, nor less than one Representative for every forty thousand persons, until the number of Representatives shall amount to two hundred, after which the proportion shall be so regulated by Congress, that there shall not be less than two hundred Representatives, nor more than one Representative for every fifty thousand persons.

Article the second. No law, varying the compensation for the services of the Senators and Representatives, shall take effect, until an election of Representatives shall have intervened.

Article the third. Congress shall make no law respecting an establishment of religion, or prohibiting the free exercise thereof; or abridging the freedom of speech, or of the press; or the right of the people peaceably to assemble, and to petition the Government for a redress of grievances.

Article the fourth. A well regulated Militia, being necessary to the security of a free State, the right of the people to keep and bear arms, shall not be infringed.

Article the fifth. No Soldier shall, in time of peace, be quartered in any house, without the consent of the owner, nor in time of war, but in a manner to be prescribed by law.

Article the sixth. The right of the people to be secure in their persons, houses, papers, and effects, against unreasonable searches and seizures, shall not be violated, and no Warrants shall issue, but upon probable cause, supported by oath or affirmation, and particularly describing the place to be searched, and the persons or things to be seized.

Article the seventh. No person shall be held to answer for a capital, or otherwise infamous crime, unless on a presentment or indictment of a grand jury, except in cases arising in the land or naval forces, or in the Militia, when in actual service in time of War or public danger; nor shall any person be subject for the same offence to be twice put in jeopardy of life or limb; nor shall be compelled in any criminal case, to be a witness against himself, nor be deprived of life, liberty, or property, without due process of law; nor shall private property be taken for public use, without just compensation.

Article the eighth. In all criminal prosecutions, the accused shall enjoy the right to a speedy and public trial, by an impartial jury of the State and district wherein the crime shall have been committed, which district shall have been previously ascertained by law, and to be informed of the nature and cause of the accusation; to be confronted with the witnesses against him; to have compulsory process for obtaining witnesses in his favor, and to have the assistance of counsel for his defence.

Article the ninth. In suits at common law, where the value in controversy shall exceed twenty dollars, the right of trial by jury shall be preserved, and no fact tried by a jury, shall be otherwise re-examined in any Court of the United States, than according to the rules of the common law.

Article the tenth. Excessive bail shall not be required, nor excessive fines imposed, nor cruel and unusual punishments inflicted.

Article the eleventh. The enumeration in the Constitution, of certain rights, shall not be construed to deny or disparage others retained by the people.

Article the twelfth. The powers not delegated to the United States by the Constitution, nor prohibited by it to the States, are reserved to the States respectively, or to the people.

Frederick Augustus Muhlenberg, Speaker of the House of Representatives.

John Adams, Vice-President of the United States, and President of the Senate.

ATTEST,

John Beckley, Clerk of the House of Representatives.

Sam. A. Otis Secretary of the Senate.

DEFENSES

I. INTRODUCTION

A. TYPES OF DEFENSES

Whether you work for prosecution or defense, it is essential for you to be aware of the possible defenses that can prevent conviction on any particular charge. The groupings of defenses presented in this chapter are not universal, but may help you in considering defenses and how they work: constitutional and statutory defenses such as statutes of limitations and protections against double jeopardy, justifications such as self-defense, excuses such as duress and insanity, proof that an essential element of the crime is missing such as alibi and intoxication, and various syndromes such as battered person syndrome and posttraumatic stress disorder.

Other defenses especially connected to inchoate crimes, such as abandonment and impossibility, are covered in Chapter 6. Be sure to review those in the context of defenses in general.

B. EFFECTIVE LEVEL OF DEFENSE

perfect defense:
one that leads to the dropping of charges or acquittal, if successful.

imperfect defense:
one that tends to allow conviction on a reduced charge.

mitigating circumstances:
favorable points about the defendant; not defenses, but possibly influencing a lighter sentence.

Even though a defense is successful, the defendant may not be free of criminal liability. Some defenses are **perfect defenses,** leading to the dropping of charges or acquittal if successful. The statute of limitations, self-defense, and duress may be among these. Others are **imperfect defenses,** tending to allow conviction on a lesser included charge. Intoxication may be used as an imperfect defense in specific intent crimes. When an element of the defense is missing, that defense may still provide some protection to the defendant. A perfect self-defense requires that the defendant responded to an unprovoked attack. If the defendant provoked the attack, then had to use deadly force to defend against an unreasonable counterattack, the defense is imperfect but effective in reducing the severity of the crime.

Mitigating circumstances are not defenses and do not affect conviction but may influence a lighter sentence. Positive points about the defendant's character, or, possibly, evidence of a deprived childhood might help the court to decide that harsh punishment is improper. Motive may be a mitigating circumstance but not a defense nor an element of crime. Instead, it is the force behind the intent, the love behind the decision to end the life of a terminally ill parent, for example. Evidence of motive may be important in establishing mens rea and, therefore, can affect conviction.

C. BURDEN OF PROOF

affirmative defense:
matter separate from the elements of the crime that is raised by the defense to counteract those elements.

The prosecution always has the burden of proving the elements of the crime beyond a reasonable doubt. When a defense tactic is to claim that a requisite element is missing, the burden remains with the prosecution to show that the element is, in fact, present. In Case V of Chapter 1 the defense for Nancy and Lisa may try to raise doubts that the requisite mens rea element for the crime was present, that the women had no knowledge of the cocaine in their apartment. A DUI defense may contend that the defendant was not the driver of the car, raising doubts about an actus reus element. To prevail, the prosecution must present sufficient evidence to overcome those doubts. The defense does not have to prove that an element is missing; the prosecution's lack of proof is determinative.

Affirmative defenses are matters, separate from the elements of the crime, that are raised by the defense to counteract those elements. These could be called "Yes, but . . ." defenses. Yes, the elements are provable, but there are circumstances that justify or excuse the conduct of the defendant. Yes, the defendant killed the victim, but did so in the execution of duties as a police officer. Yes, the defendant intended to kill the victim, but insanity prevented awareness of the nature of the act.

The **burden of production,** the responsibility to introduce an affirmative defense and the credible evidence to support it, rests with the defense. See Chapter 12 for the pretrial requirements in raising such defenses as alibi, which is not usually an affirmative defense, and insanity, which is. In some jurisdictions, the defense has the further **burden of persuasion,** the burden of proving the affirmative defense by a **preponderance of the evidence,** the greater, convincing weight of all the evidence. This is a lesser level than "beyond a reasonable doubt." Some jurisdictions require the defense to provide only "some evidence" in support of the affirmative defense claim. In other jurisdictions, once the affirmative defense has been produced by the defense, the burden of persuasion shifts to the prosecution to disprove the defense beyond a reasonable doubt. This is the same responsibility and level of proof required for the elements of the crime itself.

Many appeals on defense issues involve questions about jury instructions, whether the defendant was entitled to a desired instruction on a particular defense theory, or whether the instruction given was the proper one. Often the resolution of these questions is based on burden of proof. Did the defense raise the affirmative defense? Did the defense or prosecution meet the burden of persuasion? If the defense meets its burdens, it is entitled to an instruction on the affirmative defense. It is always the better practice for the defense to request the desired instruction, but in some cases, the court will offer the instruction *sua sponte,* on its own responsibility.

The burden of proof varies by jurisdiction and type of defense. In some cases, jurisdictions do not even agree on which defenses are affirmative defenses. In the following sections we consider the burden of proof on particular defenses. Requirements in your jurisdiction may not be the same as the examples given, so be sure to check your state's statutes and case law.

burden of production:
the responsibility to introduce an affirmative defense and the credible evidence to support it.

burden of persuasion:
responsibility to convince on all the elements of the claim.

preponderance of the evidence:
the greater weight of all the evidence.

sua sponte:
on its own responsibility, voluntarily.

II. CONSTITUTIONAL AND STATUTORY DEFENSES

A. INTRODUCTION

Constitutional and statutory defenses protect the defendant from infringements on rights guaranteed to all citizens. These are not "loopholes" to be exploited by wily criminals and their even wilier attorneys. Many of them come into play only in the context of criminal prosecution; their purpose is to ensure that the accused—which could be any of us—are not treated unfairly simply because they have been accused.

Federal and state statutes; the Constitution of the United States, primarily in the Bill of Rights; and state constitutions all provide various forms of protection for the accused. Our constitutional freedoms are normally inviolate unless there are compelling reasons for the government to regulate them, such as safety, health, or public welfare.

Procedural defenses are covered in following chapters. This section focuses on the statute of limitations and substantive defenses to criminal charges found in the First and Fifth Amendments of the Constitution.

"There is never a deed so foul that something couldn't be said for the guy; that's why there are lawyers."

—Melvin Belli *Los Angeles Times,* Dec. 18, 1981

> *AMENDMENT I*
> *Congress shall make no law respecting an establishment of religion, or prohibiting the free exercise thereof; or abridging the freedom of speech, or of the press; or the right of the people peaceably to assemble, and to petition the government for a redress of grievances.*

> *AMENDMENT V*
> *. . . [N]or shall any person be subject for the same offence to be twice put in jeopardy of life or limb; . . . nor be deprived of life, liberty, or property, without due process of law. . . .*

B. FREEDOM OF RELIGION

The First Amendment to the Constitution provides, "Congress shall make no law respecting an establishment of religion, or prohibiting the free exercise thereof. . . ." Criminal laws, however, aim to prevent harm to persons and property. When the goals of religion conflict with specific criminal laws, conflicting opinions result. Generally, the greater the harm caused by a religious practice, the weaker is the defense of religious freedom. For example, a prohibition against the handling of poisonous snakes was upheld against the claim of religious exercise in *Lawson v. Commonwealth* (Ky. 1942). A defendant claimed a Native American religious First Amendment right to take golden eagles in violation of the federal migratory bird act. The court in *U.S. v. Sandia* (10th Cir. 1999) found that because he had repeatedly sold parts of the protected birds for profit without religious purpose, the protection of the migratory birds prevailed; his conviction was affirmed. In contrast, the prosecution of an Amish driver for failure to have a slow-moving vehicle sign on a buggy was held a violation of freedom of religion, and in particular a violation of the Amish belief against the display of emblems and other symbols [*State v. Herschberger* (Minn. 1990)].

In the states that allow spiritual treatment of an ill child as an alternative to conventional medicine in an exception to child abuse laws, the treatment must be offered in good faith and must not jeopardize the child's health. That line between acceptable and unacceptable rejection of conventional medicine must be made clear in the statute, however, to avoid denial of due process, *Hermanson v. State* (Fla. 1992).

As we saw in Chapter 5, drug laws are also affected by freedom of religion. In order to preserve Native American culture, members of the Native American Church of North America are exempt in some jurisdictions from statutes prohibiting peyote possession. This exemption does not provide a defense to peyote use by members of other non–Native American churches who practice peyotist religions, *Peyote Way Church of God, Inc. v. Thornburgh* (5th Cir. 1991). Animal sacrifice was successfully defended as free exercise of religion in *Church of the Lukumi Babalu Aye, Inc. v. City of Hialeah* (1993).

Seven states have religious liberty laws that may broaden the use of freedom of religion as a defense. A similar federal law, the Religious Liberty Protection Act, is pending. The Church of Scientology is using Florida's law to defend against charges of criminal neglect regarding one of its members who died from a blood clot while in the care of church staff members. The church claims that the charges inflict undue burden and impair its right to practice religion.[1] The full impact of these laws remains to be determined.

C. FREEDOM OF EXPRESSION

Because freedom of expression runs to the very core of individual liberty and the preservation of a free thinking democratic nation, freedom of speech and press are constitutionally protected in the First Amendment. Any law that appears to abridge freedom of speech in any form will be subject to the strictest scrutiny. In defining such laws, the government has the burden of proving that a compelling state interest exists in regulating or prohibiting the speech.

"What seems fair enough against a squalid huckster of bad liquor may take on a different face, if used by a government determined to suppress political opposition under the guise of sedition."

—Learned Hand *United States v. Kirschenblatt*, 1926

A political refugee from Romania was convicted for harassment for making racist, ranting complaint calls to a government official. Because the content of the calls was primarily political, however, the expression was protected by the First Amendment, and the conviction was vacated in *U.S. v. Popa* (D.C. Cir. 1999).

There are criminal statutes and cases, however, that do regulate freedom of expression. *Schenck v. U.S.* (1919) ruled that shouting "fire" in a crowded theater created such a high risk of injury that this speech was not protected. Likewise, "fighting words" likely to provoke a violent action from the listener were not protected in *Chaplinsky v. New Hampshire* (1942). Saying "fuck you" to a police officer, however, was protected speech in *Diehl v. State* (Md. 1982; cert. denied 1983). The theft of trade secrets or defense secrets by espionage is not protected by the First Amendment, because the speech itself is the vehicle for the crime. Transmitting stolen defense secrets to the press did not activate a freedom of speech defense in *U.S. v. Morison* (4th Cir. 1988).

As we saw in Chapter 5, freedom of expression is not a defense for obscenity under *Roth v. U.S.* (1957) and *Miller v. California* (1973). In spite of the courts' attempt to establish standards for enforcement of obscenity laws, the standards themselves remain hard to fix. In 1991, Dennis Barrie, director of the Cincinnati Arts Center, was acquitted on obscenity charges for displaying the photography of Robert Mapplethorpe, including some child nudity and the depiction of homosexual acts. That the prosecutors and outspoken members of the community felt the work was obscene but twelve jurors from the same community judged it to be art, clearly demonstrates the problem with these standards and obscenity crimes in general.

Expressions of hatred also have involved free speech protections. Free speech was the successful defense to cross-burning that overturned the hate crime ordinance in *R.A.V. v. City of St. Paul* (1992), but hate speech coupled with further criminal action was allowed as grounds for an enhanced sentence in *Wisconsin v. Mitchell* (1993). See the discussion of freedom of expression as it applies to hate crimes in that decision in Chapter 4.

D.   FREEDOM OF ASSEMBLY

The First Amendment right to peaceful assembly may be a defense against some crimes against public order. Occasionally, however, the right of a group of persons to assemble and demonstrate under the First Amendment runs counter to the government's legitimate interest in order and safety. Court decisions permit limitations on such constitutional gatherings only if there is a clear and present danger, such as rioting or serious traffic congestion. Students picketing across the street from a courthouse where they had been told by a police officer in the presence of the sheriff and mayor that their activity would be permitted were still convicted of protesting near a courthouse. Their conviction was reversed in *Cox v. Louisiana* (1965). Laws regulating time, place, and manner of assembly are constitutional provided they do not defeat the purpose of the assembly, but a law denying the right of peaceful protest on the grounds of the Supreme Court building was declared unconstitutional in *U.S. v. Grace* (1983).

E.   DOUBLE JEOPARDY

Double jeopardy is prohibited by the Fifth Amendment to the Constitution and prevents the state from trying a person twice for the same criminal conduct. Absent such protection, prosecutions could conceivably become the neverending story.

> *The underlying idea [in double jeopardy] . . . is that the state with all its resources and power should not be allowed to make repeated attempts to convict an individual for an alleged offense, thereby subjecting him to embarrassment, expense and ordeal and compelling him to live in a continuing state of anxiety and insecurity. . . .*
> —Green v. U.S. (1957)

> *Multiple prosecutions also give the state an opportunity to rehearse its presentation of proof, thus increasing the risk of an erroneous conviction for one or more of the offenses. . . . Even when a state can bring multiple charges . . . a tremendous additional burden is placed on that defendant if he must face each of the charges in a separate proceeding.*
> —Grady v. Corbin (1990)

Double jeopardy is a far more complex consideration than meets the eye. Here is a summary of key principles to note that can be explored in more detail when the need arises.

jeopardy:
the danger presented by a court proceeding that may result in punishment.

1. **Jeopardy,** the danger presented by a court proceeding that may result in punishment, begins when the jury is impaneled or, in the case of a nonjury trial, when the first witness is sworn in.

2. Double jeopardy applies when a person has been tried and a subsequent charge covers the same conduct, victim, and elements as the previous charges [*Blockburger v. U.S.* (1932)].

3. Jeopardy applies to lesser included offenses and to attempted offenses that merge with the completed crime [*Brown v. Ohio* (1977) and *Harris v. Oklahoma* (1977)].

4. Jeopardy does not apply to civil cases where elements are similar to a criminal charge, such as civil damages for battery after having been convicted for criminal battery.

5. Though juvenile matters are technically civil, jeopardy occurs because of the possibility of punishment.

6. Jeopardy does not apply to convictions overturned on appeal or in the case of mistrials by the defendant's request. When mistrial is by the prosecution's motion and the defense objects, the prosecution must show the manifest necessity of a new trial, such as purposefully improper conduct by the defense.

7. Some states follow the principle that all charges, with a few exceptions, arising out of a single criminal act, episode, or transaction, must be joined.

8. Acquittal or conviction on a lesser included offense forecloses trial on the greater offense except:
   a. on postconviction discovery of new evidence supporting the additional element of the greater offense, such as a felonious assault charge on discovery that a victim's injuries were more severe than first diagnosed when the defendant entered a no contest plea to misdemeanor assault;
   b. on defendant's motion to sever (separate) the like charges; or
   c. where the lower court did not have jurisdiction to try the lesser charges. Likewise, conviction or acquittal on the greater offense prevents prosecution on the lesser included charge. A defendant acquitted as an accessory before the fact in murder by hiring someone to kill her husband, could not afterwards be tried on conspiracy to commit murder charges. The process of hiring someone necessarily includes an agreement, so the elements of the two crimes were the same [*Commonwealth v. D'Amour* (Mass. 1999)].

9. Under the dual sovereignty doctrine accepted in federal and some state courts, one criminal act may lead to a trial in a Native American tribal court, a state court, and a federal court without double jeopardy attaching.[2] Prosecution in another jurisdiction bars a second prosecution in some states, however.

The definitive case of *Grady v. Corbin* (1990) holds that a strict "technical comparison of the elements of two offenses as required in *Blockburger* does not protect defendants sufficiently from the burden of multiple trials." The crux of the matter is what conduct, as opposed to what evidence, will be proved at the second trial. If the conduct to be proven is essentially the same, double jeopardy applies. *Grady* held that a defendant's plea of guilty to a driving while intoxicated charge and failing to keep right of the median barred a subsequent prosecution for vehicular homicide and related crimes.

Double jeopardy also provides a defense against multiple punishments when two statutes have been violated by the same conduct, and when there is no legislative intent to establish two separately punishable crimes. Sentencing for conspiracy to deprive civil rights, 18 U.S.C.A. § 241, and actually depriving civil rights, 18 U.S.C.A. § 242, was allowed even though the harm was the same because Congress intended to establish two distinct and separately punishable offenses [*Fonfrias v. U.S.* (1st Cir.

1991)]. The conduct must be "unitary" for double jeopardy to occur. Because charges for intoxication manslaughter and manslaughter arising from the same traffic accident with the same victim had not been properly joined, the defendant pleaded guilty to both crimes. His conviction and sentence for one of the crimes was vacated in *Ex Parte Ervin v. State* (Tex. Crim. App. 1999).

Conduct used to increase punishment in a prior conviction may not be the target of a subsequent prosecution. A defendant's sentence for distribution of methamphetamines was increased based on an additional amount of the drug found in his home, as well as firearm possession connected to drug dealing. His subsequent prosecution for intent to distribute the drug that was in his home was double jeopardy; a charge of felon in possession of a firearm was allowed as a different offense (*U.S. v. Koonce* (10th Cir. 1991)]. In contrast, the court did not accept a double jeopardy defense in *U.S. v. Rohde* (10th Dir. 1998). The defendant, after pleading guilty to bank robbery and firearm offenses, gave false testimony at her accomplice's trial, resulting in a sentence enhancement for obstruction of justice. That was considered punishment for the underlying offenses, however, and not for perjury, so subsequent prosecution on the perjury charge was allowed.

The Supreme Court recently limited the use of the double jeopardy defense when a defendant faces criminal prosecution after having paid civil fines for the same offense. *Hudson v. U.S.* (1997) overturns a part of *U.S. v. Halper* (1989) that disallowed criminal prosecution when fines and other civil penalties were considered grossly disproportionate or punitive. The *Hudson* Court, in a case involving violations of banking and currency laws, ruled that subsequent criminal prosecution was not necessarily double jeopardy when civil fines were imposed as a deterrence, and that "only the clearest proof" will show that the fine is at the same level as criminal punishment, triggering a double jeopardy protection.

The doctrine of **collateral estoppel** prevents a retrial of a significant issue when it was determined by a previous judgment. Thus, once a defendant was acquitted because he was not present at a robbery involving one of several victims, he could not be tried for the robbery of another of the victims [*Ashe v. Swenson* (1970)].

collateral estoppel: doctrine preventing the retrial of a significant issue when it was determined by a previous judgment.

F. SUBSTANTIVE DUE PROCESS

Guarantees of due process (fair laws and procedures) were written into the English Magna Carta (1215 A.D.) to protect nobles from the power of the king. Accordingly, one could not be imprisoned or harmed "save by the lawful judgment of his peers or by the law of the land." The Fifth and Fourteenth Amendments to the United States Constitution guarantee both procedural fairness (the focus of our attention in chapters to come) and substantive fairness, also called substantive due process. Under substantive due process, statutes may not be so vague that a reasonable person must guess at what activity is prohibited, or be so broad that they give police unfettered discretion in enforcement. The likely and unfortunate result of such laws would be arbitrary or prejudicial enforcement and the invasion of legitimate and constitutionally protected activities.

Suppose that a community is suffering a serious increase in crime of a variety not previously contemplated, such as the abuse of new synthetic drugs not yet listed as controlled substances, a wave of sexually explicit computer software, mysterious pollution of air and water, or a growth in the number of uncontrollable street people. In response to these problems the community passes the following law: "Whoever commits an act which the law declares punishable or which deserves punishment according to the sound feelings of the people, will be punished."[3]

What are the advantages to this law? The disadvantages? Because this was a law passed for the convenience of the Nazi party in pre–World War II Germany, we do not have to worry about it. Such laws do not get passed in the United States, right? What about the ordinance that outlawed being "rogues and vagabonds, . . . dissolute persons

. . . common night walkers, . . . habitual loafers . . ." that was passed in Jacksonville, Florida? What about the Cincinnati law that prohibited people from congregating on the street and engaging in speech that is "annoying" to passersby? What about loitering "with no apparent purpose" in the presence of a gang member? Anything wrong with these laws? The first was declared unconstitutional in *Papachristou v. City of Jacksonville* (1972), as we saw in Chapters 1 and 5. The second was held unconstitutionally overbroad in *Coates v. City of Cincinnati* (1971). The third was ruled unconstitutionally vague in *Chicago v. Morales* (1999).

G.   RIGHT TO PRIVACY

In two landmark cases the United States Supreme Court confirmed that a right to privacy for each citizen exists even though such a right is not specifically mentioned in the Constitution or the Bill of Rights. In *Griswold v. Connecticut* (1965), a criminal law prohibiting the distribution of birth control devices or birth control information was held unconstitutional. In so holding, the Court found that "specific guarantees in the Bill of Rights have penumbras, formed by emanations from those guarantees that help give them life and substance. . . ." Included in the penumbras was the right of privacy that restricted governmental intrusion into its citizens' bedrooms and birth control practices. The source of the right, according to some justices, was the Ninth Amendment and its reserving for the people those rights and powers not specifically given to the government. Other justices found the law based in the due process concept of personal liberty found in the Fourteenth Amendment.

In *Roe v. Wade* (1973) Justice Blackmun expressed the majority's opinion that state laws prohibiting abortions were an unconstitutional invasion of the right to privacy and personal liberty anchored in the Fourteenth Amendment. The opinion finds the state without a sufficiently compelling interest to invade a woman's right to privacy and freedom of choice in the first two trimesters of pregnancy. Only when the fetus becomes viable in the third trimester does the state have a compelling interest in potential life and may regulate abortions accordingly.

More recent decisions suggest that although the Court is not interested in expanding this right of privacy, contrary to current predictions it is also not ready to forego it, at least in the case of abortion. In *Bowers v. Hardwick* (1986) the Court upheld the enforcement of sodomy laws against consenting homosexuals, but refused to dismantle *Roe* in *Planned Parenthood v. Casey* (1992), although further restrictions on abortion were allowed.

H.   STATUTE OF LIMITATIONS

State and federal laws protect suspects for most crimes from continuous threat of prosecution, especially beyond a time when evidence for their defense may become unavailable. A vehicle may be sold or junked; a letter may be lost; the mother who could have said, "She was home with me on the night of the crime," may have died. Federal statutes place a five-year limit on noncapital crimes but no limit on capital offenses (18 U.S.C.A. § 3281 *et seq.*). Limits vary by state and among felonies, misdemeanors, and violations. No state has a statute of limitation for murder, but Florida exempts only first degree murder. Kentucky, North Carolina, South Carolina, West Virginia, and Wyoming are the only states that have no time limit on any felony prosecution. Colorado has no limit for treason; and Arizona, California, Oklahoma, and Utah exempt felonies involving public money and public records.[4] Some states allow prosecution for sexual abuse of children after the victims have become adults.

Generally, the time limitation period begins when the offense is committed, not when it is discovered. As we have already seen in Chapter 6, the statute does not begin to run on a conspiracy with the commission of the first overt act, but only when the conspiracy itself has come to an end or, for a particular defendant, when that defendant abandons the conspiracy. Similarly, the statute does not begin to run on continuing offenses like receiving stolen goods until the offense ends [*State v. Lodermeier* (S.D. 1992)].

The running of the statute ends with the issue of an arrest warrant or the filing of a complaint or other charging document. The time period is interrupted, *tolled,* while the suspect is a fugitive or is concealed. The statute of limitations defense is waived if it is not raised as an affirmative defense before or during trial [*Brooks v. State* (Md. App. 1991)], or if a defendant pleads guilty to an indictment [*Acevedo-Ramos v. U.S.* (1st Cir. 1992)]. Note the effect of the tolling of the statute in *State v. Houck,* Chapter 8. In Wisconsin, DNA evidence was used to charge an unknown defendant in three rape cases just before the statute of limitations ran out.[5]

 ANALYSIS PROBLEM

7–1. What is the rationale behind longer time limits for the prosecution of more serious crimes? Do you agree with that rationale? Is deterioration of evidence less of a problem in more serious offenses?

III. JUSTIFICATION

A. INTRODUCTION

In claiming justification, the defendant admits responsibility for a harmful act but asserts that the act was the right thing to do under the circumstances. Defending the innocent against attack and carrying out public duties, such as enforcing arrest or waging war, are justifications. These defenses are used exclusively in assault and homicide cases. Note the balance that must be struck between the potential danger posed by the original wrongdoer and the acceptable level of force used by the defender or public officer.

B. SELF-DEFENSE

1. Elements

A successful claim of self-defense against a charge of homicide or assault includes several elements. First, the attack on the defendant must have been unprovoked. For a perfect defense, the defendant must not have caused or invited the attack by throwing the first punch, or even by threatening or taunting the attacker. A jury instruction on self-defense was not allowed in *U.S. v. Branch* (5th Cir. 1996), because there was only the "merest scintilla of evidence" that the gunfire from government agents, who had come to execute search and arrest warrants at the compound of a religious cult, was unprovoked. The court noted evidence that the defendants were aware of the identity of the agents and that the defendants fired the first shots, and commented that "self-defense must accommodate a citizen's duty to accede to lawful government power." It emphasized that the defense had the burden of producing enough evidence that a reasonable jury could find in its favor before the instruction on self-defense, or any other affirmative defense, could be given.

Second, the attack must be imminent, that is, in progress or obviously about to happen. Some states use the term *present* rather than imminent danger, allowing the defensive force to be used before the attack is actually begun. Self-defense is not valid against future attacks nor past attacks that can be referred to the criminal justice system, but only for the present when the protection of the state is not available.

Third, the force used is justifiable as a defense only if it is reasonably necessary to repel the attack. One may not use a shotgun to defend against a slap in the face. Homosexual advances by the victims have been held to be insufficient to support self-defense in murder cases [*State v. Flowers* (La. App. 1991) and *State v. Bell* (Wash. App. 1991)]. Deadly force is justifiable only against an attack that appears to threaten life or serious injury. Most states apply an objective test to this element. Belief in the seriousness of the attack must be reasonable, and belief in the necessity of the defensive force must be reasonable. A few states, however, use a subjective test, allowing an honest although possibly unreasonable belief in the necessity of the defensive force. Where statutes are not specific, courts must decide the reasonableness question. Factors in deciding reasonableness include relative size, age, and physical abilities of the attacker and defender, as well as whether the attacker is armed or has a reputation for violence.

If an attacker gives up the attack and withdraws in good faith, not to regroup for another attack, he or she can then justifiably defend against a subsequent attack by the original victim. If Kate Lamb sees her fleeing attacker duck into a building, waits outside three hours for him to reappear, and then tries to kill him with a pocket knife she has drawn from her purse and he retaliates with a fatal blow to her head, he may justifiably claim self-defense.

2. Imperfect Self-Defense

Self-defense, if all the previously described elements are present, is a perfect defense allowing the defendant to be acquitted. An imperfect self-defense results when one of the elements of self-defense is deficient. Perhaps the defendant precipitated the attack with an elbow to the ribs. (A felonious attack by the defendant without withdrawal negates any form of self-defense.) Perhaps the defendant honestly but unreasonably believes that deadly force is necessary in a jurisdiction where reasonable belief is required. Such an imperfect self-defense claim is used only in murder cases, where charges may be reduced to voluntary or negligent manslaughter, or in attempted murder [*Bryant v. State* (Md. App. 1990)].

3. Retreat

The Model Penal Code and many states require the victim of an attack to retreat if that can be done safely, rather than to resort to deadly force for self-protection. Where retreat is required, the attack must appear likely to cause death or serious injury, requiring self-defense of deadly force, and retreat in complete safety must be possible. If even minor injuries would result from the retreat, the person being attacked is usually allowed to stand his or her ground [*State v. Anderson* (Conn. 1993)]. Under the castle doctrine, the belief that "a man's home is his castle," defenders need not retreat in their own homes. A defendant convicted of second degree murder won a new trial on the ruling that he did not have to retreat from an intruder in his own home, particularly because he suffered from disabling arthritis that would have made his retreat hazardous [*State v. Fetzik* (R.I. 1992)]. A substantial number of states reject all "retreat to the wall" requirements, however, with the rationale that innocent people should not be forced to take a cowardly or humiliating position. In these states, a person who is attacked may defend with force anywhere.

4. People v. Goetz

As you read the case of *People v. Goetz* (N.Y. 1986), note the "triggering conditions" that allow the justification of self-defense under New York law. Also follow the discussion of "reasonable" as an objective or subjective requirement. After this decision was returned, Goetz was tried and acquitted for attempted murder and assault, but he was convicted and jailed one year on a weapons charge.

PEOPLE V. GOETZ
Supreme Court of New York 1986.
68 N.Y. 2d 96, 506 N.Y.S. 2d 18, 497 N.E. 2d 41.
Opinion of the Court
[Citations omitted]

Chief Judge WACHTLER.

A Grand Jury has indicted defendant on attempted murder, assault, and other charges for having shot and wounded four youths on a New York City subway train after one or two of the youths approached him and asked for $5. The lower courts, concluding that the prosecutor's charge to the Grand Jury on the defense of justification was erroneous, have dismissed the attempted murder, assault and weapons possession charges. We now reverse and reinstate all counts of the indictment.

I.

The precise circumstances of the incident giving rise to the charges against defendant are disputed, and ultimately it will be for a trial jury to determine what occurred. We feel it necessary, however, to provide some factual background to properly frame the legal issues before us. Accordingly, we have summarized the facts as they appear from the evidence before the Grand Jury. We stress, however, that we do not purport to reach any conclusions or holding as to exactly what transpired or whether defendant is blameworthy. The credibility of witnesses and the reasonableness of defendant's conduct are to be resolved by the trial jury.

On Saturday afternoon, December 22, 1984, Troy Canty, Darryl Cabey, James Ramseur, and Barry Allen boarded an IRT express subway train in The Bronx and headed south toward lower Manhattan. The four youths rode together in the rear portion of the seventh car of the train. Two of the four, Ramseur and Cabey, had screwdrivers inside their coats, which they said were to be used to break into the coin boxes of video machines.

Defendant Bernhard Goetz boarded this subway train at 14th Street in Manhattan and sat down on a bench towards the rear section of the same car occupied by the four youths. Goetz was carrying an unlicensed .38 caliber pistol loaded with five rounds of ammunition in a waistband holster. The train left the 14th Street station and headed towards Chambers Street.

It appears from the evidence before the Grand Jury that Canty approached Goetz, possibly with Allen beside him, and stated "give me five dollars". Neither Canty nor any of the other youths displayed a weapon. Goetz responded by standing up, pulling out his handgun and firing four shots in rapid succession. The first shot hit Canty in the chest; the

second struck Allen in the back; the third went through Ramseur's arm and into his left side; the fourth was fired at Cabey, who apparently was then standing in the corner of the car, but missed, deflecting instead off of a wall of the conductor's cab. After Goetz briefly surveyed the scene around him, he fired another shot at Cabey, who then was sitting on the end bench of the car. The bullet entered the rear of Cabey's side and severed his spinal cord.

All but two of the other passengers fled the car when, or immediately after, the shots were fired. The conductor, who had been in the next car, heard the shots and instructed the motorman to radio for emergency assistance. The conductor then went into the car where the shooting occurred and saw Goetz sitting on a bench, the injured youths lying on the floor or slumped against a seat, and two women who had apparently taken cover, also lying on the floor. Goetz told the conductor that the four youths had tried to rob him.

While the conductor was aiding the youths, Goetz headed towards the front of the car. The train had stopped just before the Chambers Street station and Goetz went between two of the cars, jumped onto the tracks and fled. Police and ambulance crews arrived at the scene shortly thereafter. Ramseur and Canty, initially listed in critical condition, have fully recovered. Cabey remains paralyzed, and has suffered some degree of brain damage.

On December 31, 1984, Goetz surrendered to police in Concord, New Hampshire, identifying himself as the gunman being sought for the subway shootings in New York nine days earlier. Later that day, after receiving *Miranda* warnings, he made two lengthy statements, both of which were tape recorded with his permission. In the statements, which are substantially similar, Goetz admitted that he had been illegally carrying a handgun in New York City for three years. He stated that he had first purchased a gun in 1981 after he had been injured in a mugging. Goetz also revealed that twice between 1981 and 1984 he had successfully warded off assailants simply by displaying the pistol.

According to Goetz's statement, the first contact he had with the four youths came when Canty, sitting or lying on the bench across from him, asked "how are you," to which he replied "fine". Shortly thereafter, Canty, followed by one of the other youths, walked over to the defendant and stood to his left, while the other two youths remained to his right, in the corner of the subway car. Canty then said "give me five dollars". Goetz stated that he knew from the smile on Canty's face that they wanted to "play with me". Although he was certain that none of the youths had a gun, he had a fear, based on prior experiences, of being "maimed".

Goetz then established "a pattern of fire," deciding specifically to fire from left to right. His stated intention at that point was to "murder [the four youths], to hurt them, to make them suffer as much as possible". When Canty again requested money, Goetz stood up, drew his weapon, and began firing, aiming for the center of the body of each of the four. Goetz recalled that the first two he shot "tried to run through the crowd [but] they had nowhere to run". Goetz then turned to his right to "go after the other two". One of these two "tried to run through the wall of the train, but * * * he had nowhere to go". The other youth (Cabey) "tried pretending that he wasn't with [the others]" by standing still, holding on to one of the subway hand straps, and not looking at Goetz. Goetz nonetheless fired his fourth shot at him. He then ran back to the first two youths to make sure they had been "taken care of". Seeing that they had both been shot, he spun back to check on the latter two. Goetz noticed that the youth who had been standing still was now sitting on a bench and seemed unhurt. As Goetz told the police, "I said '[y]ou seem to be all right, here's another'", and he then fired the shot which severed Cabey's spinal cord. Goetz added that "if I was a little more under self-control * * * I would have put the barrel against his forehead and fired." He also admitted that "if I had had more [bullets], I would have shot them again, and again, and again."

II.

After waiving extradition, Goetz was brought back to New York and arraigned on a felony complaint charging him with attempted murder and criminal possession of a weapon. The matter was presented to a Grand Jury in January 1985, with the prosecutor seeking an indictment for attempted murder, assault, reckless endangerment, and criminal possession of a weapon. Neither the defendant nor any of the wounded youths testified before this Grand Jury. On January 25, 1985, the Grand Jury indicted defendant on one count of criminal possession of a weapon in the third degree (Penal Law § 265.02), for possessing the gun used in the subway shootings, and two counts of criminal possession of a weapon in the fourth degree (Penal Law § 265.01), for possessing two other guns in his apartment building. It dismissed, however, the attempted murder and other charges stemming from the shootings themselves.

Several weeks after the Grand Jury's action, the People, asserting that they had newly available evidence, moved for an order authorizing them to resubmit the dismissed charges to a second Grand Jury. Supreme Court, Criminal Term, after conducting an in camera inquiry, granted the motion. Presentation of the case to the second Grand Jury began on March 14, 1985. Two of the four youths, Canty and Ramseur, testified. Among the other witnesses were four passengers from the seventh car of the subway who had seen some portions of the incident. Goetz again chose not to testify, though the tapes of his two statements were played for the grand jurors, as had been done with the first Grand Jury.

On March 27, 1985, the second Grand Jury filed a 10-count indictment, containing four charges of attempted murder (Penal Law §§ 110.00, 125.25[1]), four charges of assault in the first degree (Penal Law § 120.10[1]), one charge of reckless endangerment in the first degree (Penal Law § 120.25), and one charge of criminal possession of a weapon in the second degree (Penal Law § 265.03 [possession of loaded firearm with intent to use it unlawfully against another]). Goetz was arraigned on this indictment on March 28, 1985, and it was consolidated with the earlier three-count indictment.

On October 14, 1985, Goetz moved to dismiss the charges contained in the second indictment alleging, among other things, that the evidence before the second Grand Jury was not legally sufficient to establish the offenses charged (see, CPL 210.20[1][b]), and that the prosecutor's instructions to that Grand Jury on the defense of justification were erroneous and prejudicial to the defendant so as to render its proceedings defective. . . .

In an order dated January 21, 1986, Criminal Term 131 Misc.2d 1, 502 N.Y.S.2d 577, granted Goetz's motion to the extent that it dismissed all counts of the second indictment, other than the reckless endangerment charge, with leave to resubmit these charges to a third Grand Jury. The court, after inspection of the Grand Jury minutes, first rejected Goetz's contention that there was not legally sufficient evidence to support the charges. It held, however, that the prosecutor, in a supplemental charge elaborating upon the justification defense, had erroneously introduced an objective element into this defense by instructing the grand jurors to consider whether Goetz's conduct was that of a "reasonable man in [Goetz's] situation". The court, citing prior decisions from both the First and Second Departments (see, e.g., People v. Santiago, 110 A.D.2d 569, 488 N.Y.S.2d 4 [1st Dept.]; People v. Wagman, 99 A.D.2d 519, 471 N.Y.S.2d 147 [2d Dept.]), concluded that the statutory test for whether the use of deadly force is justified to protect a person should be wholly subjective, focusing entirely on the defendant's state of mind when he used such force. It concluded that dismissal was required for this error because the justification issue was at the heart of the case.[2] . . .

---

2. The court did not dismiss the reckless endangerment charge because, relying on the Appellate Division decision in People v. McManus, 108 A.D.2d 474, 489 N.Y.S.2d 561, it held that justification was not a defense to a crime containing, as an element, "depraved indifference to human life." As our reversal of the Appellate Division in McManus holds, justification is a defense to such a crime (People v. McManus, 67 N.Y.2d 541, 505 N.Y.S.2d 43, 496 N.E.2d 202). Accordingly, had the prosecutor's instructions on justification actually rendered the Grand Jury proceedings defective, dismissal of the reckless endangerment count would have been required as well.

On appeal by the People, a divided Appellate Division, 116 A.D.2d 316, 501 N.Y.S.2d 326, affirmed Criminal Term's dismissal of the charges. . . .

Justice Asch granted the People leave to appeal to this court. We agree with the dissenters that neither the prosecutor's charge to the Grand Jury on justification nor the information which came to light while the motion to dismiss was pending required dismissal of any of the charges in the second indictment.

III.

Penal Law article 35 recognizes the defense of justification, which "permits the use of force under certain circumstances." One such set of circumstances pertains to the use of force in defense of a person, encompassing both self-defense and defense of a third person (Penal Law § 35.15). Penal Law § 35.15(1) sets forth the general principles governing all such uses of force: "[a] person may * * * use physical force upon another person when and to the extent he *reasonably believes* such to be necessary to defend himself or a third person from what he *reasonably believes* to be the use or imminent use of unlawful physical force by such other person" (emphasis added).[3]

Section 35.15(2) sets forth further limitations on these general principles with respect to the use of "deadly physical force": "A person may not use deadly physical force upon another person under circumstances specified in subdivision one unless (a) He *reasonably believes* that such other person is using or about to use deadly physical force * * *[4] or (b) He *reasonably believes* that such other person is committing or attempting to commit a kidnapping, forcible rape, forcible sodomy or robbery" (emphasis added).

Thus, consistent with most justification provisions, Penal Law § 35.15 permits the use of deadly physical force only where requirements as to triggering conditions and the necessity of a particular response are met. As to the triggering conditions, the statute requires that the actor "reasonably believes" that another person either is using or about to use deadly physical force or is committing or attempting to commit one of certain enumerated felonies, including robbery. As to the need for the use of deadly physical force as a response, the statute requires that the actor "reasonably believes" that such force is necessary to avert the perceived threat.

Because the evidence before the second Grand Jury included statements by Goetz that he acted to protect himself from being maimed or to avert a robbery, the prosecutor cor-

rectly chose to charge the justification defense in section 35.15 to the Grand Jury. . . .

When the prosecutor had completed his charge, one of the grand jurors asked for clarification of the term "reasonably believes". The prosecutor responded by instructing the grand jurors that they were to consider the circumstances of the incident and determine "whether the defendant's conduct was that of a reasonable man in the defendant's situation". It is this response by the prosecutor—and specifically his use of "a reasonable man"—which is the basis for the dismissal of the charges by the lower courts. As expressed repeatedly in the Appellate Division's plurality opinion, because section 35.15 uses the term "*he* reasonably believes", the appropriate test, according to that court, is whether a defendant's beliefs and reactions were "reasonable to *him*". Under that reading of the statute, a jury which believed a defendant's testimony that he felt that his own actions were warranted and were reasonable would have to acquit him, regardless of what anyone else in defendant's situation might have concluded. Such an interpretation defies the ordinary meaning and significance of the term "reasonably" in a statute, and misconstrues the clear intent of the Legislature, in enacting section 35.15, to retain an objective element as part of any provision authorizing the use of deadly physical force. . . .

We cannot lightly impute to the Legislature an intent to fundamentally alter the principles of justification to allow the perpetrator of a serious crime to go free simply because that person believed his actions were reasonable and necessary to prevent some perceived harm. To completely exonerate such an individual, no matter how aberrational or bizarre his thought patterns, would allow citizens to set their own standards for the permissible use of force. It would also allow a legally competent defendant suffering from delusions to kill or perform acts of violence with impunity, contrary to fundamental principles of justice and criminal law.

We can only conclude that the Legislature retained a reasonableness requirement to avoid giving a license for such actions. . . .

Statutes or rules of law requiring a person to act "reasonably" or to have a "reasonable belief" uniformly prescribe conduct meeting an objective standard measured with reference to how "a reasonable person" could have acted. . . .

In *People v. Collice,* 41 N.Y.2d 906, 394 N.Y.S.2d 615, 363 N.E.2d 340, we rejected the position that section 35.15 contains a wholly subjective standard. The defendant in *Collice* asserted, on appeal, that the trial court had erred in refusing to charge the justification defense. We upheld the trial court's action because we concluded that, even if the defendant had actually believed that he was threatened with the imminent use of deadly physical force, the evidence clearly indicated that "his reactions were not those of a reasonable man acting in self-defense." Numerous decisions from other States interpreting "reasonably believes" in justification statutes enacted subsequent to the drafting of the Model Penal Code

---

3. Subdivision (1) contains certain exceptions to this general authorization to use force, such as where the actor himself was the initial aggressor.

4. Section 35.15(2)(a) further provides, however, that even under these circumstances a person ordinarily must retreat "if he knows that he can with complete safety as to himself and others avoid the necessity of [using deadly physical force] by retreating."

are consistent with *Collice,* as they hold that such language refers to what a reasonable person could have believed under the same circumstances.

The defense contends that our memorandum in *Collice* is inconsistent with our prior opinion in *People v. Miller,* 39 N.Y.2d 543, 384 N.Y.S.2d 741, 349 N.E.2d 841. In *Miller,* we held that a defendant charged with homicide could introduce, in support of a claim of self-defense, evidence of prior acts of violence committed by the deceased of which the defendant had knowledge. The defense, as well as the plurality below, place great emphasis on the statement in *Miller* that "the crucial fact at issue [is] the state of mind of the defendant." This language, however, in no way indicates that a wholly subjective test is appropriate. To begin, it is undisputed that section 35.15 does contain a subjective element, namely that the defendant believed that deadly force was necessary to avert the imminent use of deadly force or the commission of certain felonies. Evidence that the defendant knew of prior acts of violence by the deceased could help establish his requisite beliefs. Moreover, such knowledge would also be relevant on the issue of reasonableness, as the jury must consider the circumstances a defendant found himself in, which would include any relevant knowledge of the nature of persons confronting him. Finally, in *Miller,* we specifically recognized that there had to be "reasonable grounds" for the defendant's belief.

Goetz's reliance on *People v. Rodawald,* 177 N.Y. 408, 70 N.E. 1, is similarly misplaced. In *Rodawald,* decided under the 1881 Penal Code, we held that a defendant who claimed that he had acted in self-defense could introduce evidence as to the general reputation of the deceased as a violent person if this reputation was known to the defendant when he acted. We stated, as emphasized by Goetz, that such evidence, "when known to the accused, enables him to judge of the danger and aids the jury in deciding whether he acted in good faith and upon the honest belief that his life was in peril. It shows the state of his mind as to the necessity of defending himself." Again, such language is explained by the fact that the threshold question, before the reasonableness issue is addressed, is the subjective beliefs of the defendant. Nowhere in *Rodawald* did we hold that the *only* test, as urged by Goetz, is whether the defendant honestly and in good faith believed himself to be in danger. Rather, we recognized that there was also the separate question of whether the accused had "reasonable ground" for his belief, and we upheld the trial court's refusal to charge the jury that the defendant's honest belief was sufficient to establish self-defense.

Goetz also argues that the introduction of an objective element will preclude a jury from considering factors such as the prior experiences of a given actor and thus, require it to make a determination of "reasonableness" without regard to the actual circumstances of a particular incident. This argument, however, falsely presupposes that an objective standard means that the background and other relevant characteristics of a particular actor must be ignored. To the contrary, we have frequently noted that a determination of reasonableness must be based on the "circumstances" facing a defendant or his "situation." Such terms encompass more than the physical movements of the potential assailant. As just discussed, these terms include any relevant knowledge the defendant had about that person. They also necessarily bring in the physical attributes of all persons involved, including the defendant. Furthermore, the defendant's circumstances encompass any prior experiences he had which could provide a reasonable basis for a belief that another person's intentions were to injure or rob him or that the use of deadly force was necessary under the circumstances.

Accordingly, a jury should be instructed to consider this type of evidence in weighing the defendant's actions. The jury must first determine whether the defendant had the requisite beliefs under section 35.15, that is, whether he believed deadly force was necessary to avert the imminent use of deadly force or the commission of one of the felonies enumerated therein. If the People do not prove beyond a reasonable doubt that he did not have such beliefs, then the jury must also consider whether these beliefs were reasonable. The jury would have to determine, in light of all the "circumstances", as explicated above, if a reasonable person could have had these beliefs.

The prosecutor's instruction to the second Grand Jury that it had to determine whether, under the circumstances, Goetz's conduct was that of a reasonable man in his situation was thus essentially an accurate charge. It is true that the prosecutor did not elaborate on the meaning of "circumstances" or "situation" and inform the grand jurors that they could consider, for example, the prior experiences Goetz related in his statement to the police. We have held, however, that a Grand Jury need not be instructed on the law with the same degree of precision as the petit jury. This lesser standard is premised upon the different functions of the Grand Jury and the petit jury: the former determines whether sufficient evidence exists to accuse a person of a crime and thereby subject him to criminal prosecution; the latter ultimately determines the guilt or innocence of the accused, and may convict only where the People have proven his guilt beyond a reasonable doubt. . . .

Of course, as noted above, where the evidence suggests that a complete defense such as justification may be present, the prosecutor must charge the grand jurors on that defense, providing enough information to enable them to determine whether the defense, in light of the evidence, should preclude the criminal prosecution. The prosecutor more than adequately fulfilled this obligation here. . . . The Grand Jury has indicted Goetz. It will now be for the petit jury to decide whether the prosecutor can prove beyond a reasonable doubt that Goetz's reactions were unreasonable and therefore excessive.

. . . Accordingly, the order of the Appellate Division should be reversed, and the dismissed counts of the indictment reinstated.

ANALYSIS PROBLEM

7–2. Do you think the "objective" definition of "reasonable" in the *Goetz* case in New York would be different from that in a quiet, small town? Do you think Goetz was entitled to a self-defense claim? Do you think Goetz's self-defense was "premeditated?"

C. DEFENSE OF THIRD PERSONS

Self-defense logically extends to the defense of third parties. A person generally has the right to protect others whose circumstances would allow self-defense. Neither the one who is being attacked nor the defender may have provoked the attack, and the force used must be reasonable. Some states adhere to the common law rule that one may defend only members of one's own household, but most jurisdictions allow a defender to "stand in the shoes of the victim" in defending anyone who is under attack.

In *Commonwealth v. Johnson* (Mass. 1992), the victim took a gun from the defendant's companion, held it to the defendant's head, then left. The defendant and companion followed, then the victim attacked the companion, wrestling him to the ground and smashing his head repeatedly on the pavement. The defendant pried the gun from the victim's hand, tried to pull him off his companion, then shot him. His murder conviction was reversed and remanded for a new trial, because the jury instruction did not distinguish between the justification of reasonable self-defense that would relieve the defendant of all liability, and the imperfect self-defense of unreasonable force that would reduce the conviction to manslaughter.

D. DEFENSE OF PROPERTY

Reasonable force may usually be used to defend property against such crimes as trespass, theft, or destruction. The wrongdoer's life is considered more valuable than property, however, so deadly force is not usually allowed in the protection of property. Habitation, however, may be defended with deadly force under some circumstances in some states as another aspect of the castle doctrine. Usually, the defender must reasonably believe that the intruder into his or her home intends to commit a felony. *Bishop v. State* (Ga. 1987) affirmed the murder conviction of a defendant who protected his home with a trap gun that caused the death of an intruder. The defense of protection of habitation did not succeed because the defendant could not form a reasonable belief that the intruder was entering to commit a felony, because the defendant was not present at the time of the shooting. An overnight guest had the equivalent of the householder's privilege to resist unlawful police entry to the bedroom he occupied [*State v. Brosnan* (Conn. 1992)].

E. RESISTING UNLAWFUL ARREST

Dreadful prison conditions and the unavailability of bail made resisting unlawful arrest an acceptable defense to assault charges in the past. Some states still allow reasonable, nondeadly force to resist unlawful arrest, with restrictions on circumstances varying by jurisdiction. Movement seems to be in the direction of Model Penal Code § 3.04(2)(a)(i), providing no defense for force used against a known police officer. This rule quells the likely escalation of violence and encourages use of courts for redress. Because an unlawful arrest is not within the lawful performance of police duties, resistance to it may be charged with simple assault rather than aggravated assault, or a lesser degree of homicide.

An arrestee is allowed to defend against excessive force or injury by a police officer if the result would be a permanent injury that could not be rectified through the courts. An African American defendant was followed and harassed by a police officer, then stopped for failing to use a turn signal. In the ensuing arrest, the officer used a racial epithet, threw the defendant on a car, beat him with a flashlight, and put him in a chokehold so he could not breathe. At this point, the defendant resisted the arrest. *Darty v. State* (Tx. App. 1999) ruled that the defendant was entitled to a jury instruction on the necessity of his resistance.

F. EXECUTION OF PUBLIC DUTIES

Our society has authorized certain public officers to use force against people in certain situations, and even to take life. Soldiers, executioners, and police are not punished for fulfilling their prescribed roles. Restrictions do apply, though, and vary by jurisdiction. Most require care that innocent bystanders are not put in jeopardy, that deadly force is not used to apprehend a misdemeanant, and, sometimes, that deadly force is used only in response to deadly force by the arrestee. The 1993 federal conviction of two Los Angeles police officers for the beating of Rodney King, after an incendiary acquittal in state court the previous year, further underlines community intolerance of police brutality.

A teenage unarmed suspect fleeing the scene of a nonviolent crime was shot and killed by police. The resulting decision restricted the use of force by police.

> *The use of deadly force to prevent the escape of all felony suspects, whatever the circumstances, is constitutionally unreasonable. It is not better that all felony suspects die than that they escape. Where the suspect poses no immediate threat to the officer and no threat to others, the harm resulting from failing to apprehend him does not justify the use of deadly force to do so.*
>
> —Tennessee v. Garner (1985)

Most states limit the use of deadly force by police to arrests when there is substantial risk that the person to be arrested will cause death or serious bodily harm, such as when that person has committed a violent felony or is armed with a deadly weapon.

IV. EXCUSE

A. INTRODUCTION

Whereas justifications offer defenses against charges of assault and homicide, excuses offer defenses to a wide range of crimes. Excuses are affirmative defenses that assert the defendant was forced by circumstances to commit the unlawful act as the "lesser of two evils," or was otherwise not responsible under the circumstances, though all the elements of the crime are present.

B. DURESS

Threat of imminent or present great physical harm plus the demand that the defendant commit the specific offense charged amounts to duress. This defense places liability for the crime on the one who enforces the threat, not the one who performs the act. When duress seems to be clear, the actor is seldom prosecuted, but is treated as a victim.

States vary in their requirements for the defense of duress. Duress is never an excuse for intentionally taking the life of an innocent person; some states allow it to excuse only minor crimes. Some require a threat of instant death, others include less immediate threats and threats of serious bodily harm, or even threats to third parties. A threat to property or reputation is not duress. Duress is generally measured by an objective standard, that the defendant reasonably believed the seriousness of the threat. The duress defense was allowed for a defendant whose partner stashed a gun in her purse as police were arriving on the scene of a drug transaction. She was not allowed to introduce evidence of battered woman syndrome, however, to support her claims of fear of being beaten by the partner if she resisted taking possession of the weapon. Her conviction for carrying a firearm in connection with a drug trafficking crime was affirmed [*U.S. v. Willis* (5th Cir. 1994)]. A duress defense was not allowed a defendant who had imported cocaine into the United States under threat, because he had opportunities to discard the packages or to turn them in to customs officials [*U.S. v. Arthurs* (1st Cir. 1996)].

Generally, a defendant who voluntarily enters a situation where coercion is likely, such as becoming a member of a criminal gang, loses the excuse of duress [*Williams v. State* (Md. App. 1994)].

Duress has been rejected as a defense when wrongful acts are committed under superior orders. The immediacy and great danger of genuine duress are not usually present. The Nazi war crimes trials at Nuremburg and the Vietnam War trial of Lieutenant William Calley demonstrated that obedience to orders that appear illegal to an ordinary person violates the rules of war.

C. NECESSITY

Duress is often confused with necessity, which is a different type of compulsion. The defendant has not been forced by another person to commit a specific act, as in duress, but under compelling circumstances has willingly committed an illegal act to prevent even more serious consequences.

The historic case of *Regina v. Dudley & Stephens* (1884) denied the defense to two lifeboat survivors who had killed and eaten their companion to keep from starving. They claimed that their families needed them, whereas their victim had no family obligations. The prosecution asserted that one life was not more valuable than another. The law and compassion were balanced by a death sentence that was commuted to six months in prison by Queen Victoria.

The elements of a necessity defense are stated in *U.S. v. Aguilar* (9th Cir. 1989), in the affirmation of a conviction for immigration law violations. The defendants had participated in a "sanctuary movement" to bring Central American refugees into the United States without proper authorization. To claim that their actions were necessary, the defendants needed to show (1) that they faced a choice of two evils and chose the lesser one, (2) that they acted to prevent imminent harm, (3) that they reasonably anticipated that their action would cause the harm to be avoided, and (4) that there were no legal alternatives to their conduct. The defendants had no necessity defense, because their claim failed to meet these criteria. As in *Aguilar*, defendants who had obstructed activities of the Internal Revenue Service in protest against tax funds being used in the United States' involvement in the civil war of El Salvador failed to show that they had prevented immediate harm or that there was no legal alternative [*U.S. v. Schoon* (9th Cir. 1992)].

Aguilar supplies the criteria for deciding which patients could be allowed a medical necessity defense for marijuana possession in *U.S. v. Oakland Cannabis Buyers' Cooperative* (9th Cir. 1999).

A snowmobiler claimed that operating the machine in a restricted national forest wilderness area was necessary because of weather conditions that threatened his life. He was allowed to raise the necessity defense, but because the weather conditions arose before he rode into the forest, evidence did not support the defense, and he was convicted [*U.S. v. Unser* (10th Cir. 1999)].

A necessity defense is most likely to be successful under the following conditions: (1) the offense has caused relatively little social harm, (2) scientific and corroborative evidence supports the claim that there was no legal alternative to the illegal conduct, and (3) the conduct was not in protest or aimed at undermining the law.[6]

A privilege related to necessity allows a narrow defense to the strict liability charge of being a felon in possession of a firearm. Based on the decisions in *U.S. v. Gant* (5th Cir. 1982) and *U.S. v. Newcomb* (6th Cir. 1993), the defense requires (1) that the defendant reasonably believed he or she was under an imminent threat of death or serious bodily injury, (2) the defendant was not recklessly or negligently in a situation in which it was probable that he or she would be forced to possess a firearm, (3) the defendant reasonably believed there was no reasonable, legal alternative to possessing a firearm to avoid the threatened harm, (4) it could be reasonably anticipated that possession of the firearm would cause avoidance of the threatened harm, and (5) the defendant did not possess the firearm for any longer than reasonably necessary.

A defendant who was a felon was sitting in the living room when police began battering down the front door in a "no knock" search. The defendant responded by running into a bedroom to get a gun to defend himself and other occupants. The house had been robbed one month previously. The court in *State v. Coleman* (Wis. 1996) ruled that he was entitled to the privilege defense, reversed his conviction, and ordered a new trial.

D. ENTRAPMENT

In consensual crimes such as drug trafficking, prostitution, and gambling where no witness or complaining victim is likely, law enforcement officers or their paid informants often feign involvement in a crime to catch the offender. Undercover officers may let it be known that they want to buy cocaine or get in on the big stakes of a clandestine poker game to gain eyewitness knowledge of the crime. When these officers go from simply providing the opportunity for a crime that would have occurred anyway to enticing an innocent person into committing a crime he or she would never have contemplated, that innocent person can claim the defense of entrapment.

EXHIBIT 7–1
Sample Jury Instructions

ENTRAPMENT

The defendant asserts that he was a victim of entrapment.

Where a person has no previous intent or purpose to violate the law, but is induced or persuaded by law enforcement officers or their agents to commit a crime, that person is a victim of entrapment, and the law as a matter of policy forbids that person's conviction in such a case.

On the other hand, where a person already has the readiness and willingness to break the law, the mere fact that government agents provide what appears to be a favorable opportunity is not entrapment. For example, it is not entrapment for a government agent to pretend to be someone else and to offer, either directly or through an informer or other decoy, to engage in an unlawful transaction.

If, then, you should find beyond a reasonable doubt from the evidence in the case that, before anything at all occurred respecting the alleged offense involved in this case, the defendant was ready and willing to commit a crime such as charged in the indictment, whenever opportunity was afforded, and that government officers or their agents did no more than offer the opportunity, then you should find that the defendant is not a victim of entrapment.

On the other hand, if the evidence in the case should leave you with a reasonable doubt whether the defendant had the previous intent or purpose to commit an offense of the character charged, apart from the inducement or persuasion of some officer or agent of the government, then it is your duty to find the defendant not guilty.

The burden is on the government to prove beyond a reasonable doubt that the defendant was not entrapped.

You are instructed that a paid informer is an "agent" of the government for purposes of this instruction.

Pattern Jury Instructions (Criminal Cases), 5th Circuit (St. Paul, MN: West Group, 1990), § 1.28, with permission.

Entrapment also may be a defense to some white-collar crimes, such as bribery, or even street muggings where officers play the role of a vulnerable potential victim. Entrapment never excuses violent crimes. Also, entrapment is not a defense if the one enticing the defendant into the crime is a private citizen not working for the government [*U.S. v. Manzella* (7th Cir. 1986)]. This defense is designed not only to protect innocent defendants, but also to restrain overzealous law enforcement.

Jurisdictions vary in their consideration of entrapment. Most use a subjective test that focuses on whether the defendant was predisposed to commit the crime. *U.S. v. Fusko* (7th Cir. 1989) enumerated factors important in establishing predisposition: (1) the character of the defendant, (2) whether the suggestion for the crime originally came from the government, (3) whether the defendant was already involved in crime, (4) whether the defendant showed reluctance that was overcome by government persuasion, and (5) the nature of governmental enticement. Some jurisdictions refuse to permit reputation or hearsay evidence to establish predisposition, relying instead on other circumstances. In *State v. Goodroad* (S.D. 1989) predisposition was shown by a "ready response" to an offer of marijuana for sale, and an "obvious familiarity with dealing in marijuana."

A defendant had his conviction overturned in *Jacobson v. U.S.* (1992), however, because predisposition could not be shown. He had lawfully purchased a nudist magazine, was subsequently bombarded for more than two years with mailings by postal inspectors claiming to be organizations dedicated to sexual freedom, and finally purchased a child pornography magazine. The Supreme Court asserted in the decision, "When the government's quest for convictions leads to the apprehension of an otherwise law-abiding citizen who, if left to his own devices, likely would never run afoul of the law, the courts should intervene."[7]

Some jurisdictions follow Model Penal Code § 2.13 and use an objective test, allowing the defense to locate intent in the government. In these courts, the emphasis is on government misconduct, and the question to be answered is whether conduct of the officers involved would have influenced a reasonable person not disposed to crime to commit the offense. Where this test is used, the defendant's own predisposition is irrelevant. A defendant who was only a conduit of cocaine from a police informant to police officers was entrapped by improper police investigation standards, so his conviction was reversed [*Baca v. State* (N.M. 1987)]. In *U.S. v. Evans* (7th Cir. 1991), however, repeated contact by an informant leading to the defendant's purchase of marijuana was not entrapment, because profit from the crime was the only inducement, and not the "grave threats, fraud, or extraordinary promises" necessary for entrapment.

Police involvement may be so extreme as to violate the defendant's right to due process, even though the defendant's willingness to commit the crime bars the use of an entrapment defense. The court in *State v. Hohensee* (Mo. App. 1982) declared that government sponsorship of a burglary was not entrapment, but was so outrageous as to bar conviction on due process grounds. The defendant had acted as a lookout while police informants and officers carried out the burglary. Conviction on a conspiracy charge, however, was affirmed.

The burden of proof in jurisdictions using the subjective test usually requires the defendant to show government inducement. In some courts the defense has the burden of persuasion by a preponderance of the evidence; and in others, the defense merely has the burden of production of "some evidence" of inducement [*U.S. v. Pratt* (1st Cir. 1990)]. Then the burden shifts to the prosecution to establish predisposition beyond a reasonable doubt. In objective test jurisdictions, however, the defendant alone bears the burden of production and proof of impropriety of police conduct by a preponderance of the evidence [*Young v. State* (Ark. 1992)].[8]

A few jurisdictions have combined the two tests for entrapment. First, the judge decides the question of law concerning whether improper government conduct has occurred. If so, charges are dismissed. If not, the question goes to the jury to decide whether the defendant was predisposed to commit the crime. Read *Cruz v. State* (Fla. 1985) for a discussion not only of how this combined test works, but also for standards in subjective and objective tests of entrapment.

CRUZ v. STATE
Supreme Court of Florida, 1985.
465 So.2d 516 Fla. 1985
[Citations omitted]

EHRLICH, Justice.

Tampa police undertook a decoy operation in a high-crime area. An officer posed as an inebriated indigent, smelling of alcohol and pretending to drink wine from a bottle. The officer leaned against a building near an alleyway, his face to the wall. Plainly displayed from a rear pants pocket was $150 in currency, paper-clipped together. Defendant Cruz and a woman happened upon the scene as passersby some time after 10 P.M. Cruz approached the decoy officer, may have attempted to say something to him, then continued on his way. Ten to fifteen minutes later, the defendant and his companion returned to the scene and Cruz took the money from the decoy's pocket without harming him in any way. Officers then arrested Cruz as he walked from the scene. The decoy situation did not involve the same modus operandi as any of the unsolved crimes which had occurred in the area. Police were not seeking a particular individual, nor were they aware of any prior criminal acts by the defendant.

Cruz was charged by information with grand theft. Pursuant to Florida Rule of Criminal Procedure 3.190(c)(4), Cruz moved to dismiss the information, arguing that the arrest constituted entrapment as a matter of law. The trial court granted the motion to dismiss on the authority of *State v. Casper*, 417 So.2d 263 (Fla. 1st DCA), *review denied*, 418 So.2d 1280 (Fla. 1982). On appeal, the Second District Court of Appeal reversed, acknowledging its decision was in conflict with *Casper*.

The entrapment defense arises from a recognition that sometimes police activity will induce an otherwise innocent individual to commit the criminal act the police activity seeks to produce. . . .

The entrapment defense thus normally focuses on the predisposition of the defendant. . . . The First District, in *State v. Casper*, 417 So.2d 263 (Fla. 1st DCA 1982), focused on predisposition when it found the "drunken bum" decoy at issue here to constitute entrapment as a matter of law. In *Casper*, Jacksonville police set up a decoy situation legally indistinguishable from the scenario in this case. The *Casper* court held that the state must prove the defendant was predisposed to steal from the decoy and that predisposition can be found under four circumstances: (1) the defendant has

prior convictions for similar crimes; (2) the defendant has a reputation for committing similar crimes; (3) police have a reasonable suspicion the defendant was engaged in similar crimes; or (4) the defendant showed ready acquiescence to commit the crime suggested by police. . . . The question thus boiled down to whether Casper "readily acquiesced" to the criminal scenario. The *Casper* court found that an otherwise unpredisposed passerby who chose to take the money did not acquiesce, but "succumbed to temptation. . . . to the lure of the bait." The *Casper* court therefore distinguished between "succumbing to temptation" and "readily acquiescing," and found that this is a question of law: where the trial judge finds the defendant succumbed to temptation, the matter shall not be put to a jury.

The Second District, in the case now before us, rejected this position. The *Cruz* court found that such a judgment is one for the jury to make. "[W]here, as here, a defendant's intent or state of mind (i.e., predisposition) is an issue, that issue should not be decided on a motion to dismiss. . . ." 426 So.2d at 1310. Petitioner would have this court hold that where the only evidence of predisposition is the commission of the crime the police scenario was designed to elicit, there is an insufficient showing of predisposition, as a matter of law. We do not agree.

We agree with the Second District that the question of predisposition will always be a question of fact for the jury. However, we also believe that the First District's concern for entrapment scenarios in which the innocent will succumb to temptation is well founded. To protect against such abuse, we turn to another aspect of entrapment.

Entrapment is a potentially dangerous tool given to police to fight crime. "Society is at war with the criminal classes, and courts have uniformly held that in waging this warfare the forces of prevention and detection may use traps, decoys, and deception to obtain evidence of crime." *Sorrells v. United States*, 287 U.S. 435, 453–54, 53 S.Ct. 210, 216–17 (separate opinion of Roberts, J.). "The appropriate object of this permitted activity, frequently essential to the enforcement of the law, is to reveal the criminal design; to expose the illicit traffic, the prohibited publication, the fraudulent use of the mails, the illegal conspiracy, or other offenses, and thus to disclose the would-be violators of the law. A different question is presented when the criminal design originates with the officials of the Government, and they implant in the mind of an innocent person the disposition to commit the alleged offense and induce its commission in order that they may prosecute" (opinion of the Court). "Such a gross abuse of authority given for the purpose of detecting and punishing crime, and not for the making of criminals, deserves the severist condemnation, but the question whether it precludes prosecution or affords a ground of defense, and, if so, upon what theory, has given rise to conflicting opinions." These words of the United State Supreme Court, in its seminal *Sorrells* decision, outline the basis on which the entrapment practices of police are seen as a necessary evil but an evil to be controlled. The *Sorrells* Court concluded that the defense of entrapment protected against such abuse.

The entrapment defense adopted in *Sorrells,* focusing on the predisposition of the defendant, is termed the subjective view of entrapment. However, beginning with Justice Roberts' concurrence in *Sorrells,* a minority of the United States Supreme Court has favored what is termed the objective view. This view was well expressed by Justice Frankfurter, in *Sherman v. United States:*

> The crucial question, not easy of answer, to which the court must direct itself is whether the police conduct revealed in the particular case falls below standards, to which common feelings respond, for the proper use of governmental power. . . .

> . . . [A] test that looks to the character and predisposition of the defendant rather than the conduct of the police loses sight of the underlying reason for the defense of entrapment. No matter what the defendant's past record and present inclinations to criminality, or the depths to which he has sunk in the estimation of society, certain police conduct to ensnare him into further crime is not to be tolerated by an advanced society. . . . Permissible police activity does not vary according to the particular defendant concerned; surely if two suspects have been solicited at the same time in the same manner, one should not go to jail simply because he has been convicted before and is said to have a criminal disposition. No more does it vary according to the suspicion, reasonable or unreasonable, of the police concerning the defendant's activities. Appeals to sympathy, friendship, the possibility of exhorbitant gain, and so forth, can no more be tolerated when directed against a past offender than against an ordinary law-abiding citizen. A contrary view runs afoul of fundamental principles of equality under law, and would espouse the notion that when dealing with the criminal classes anything goes. The possibility that no matter what his past crimes and general disposition the defendant might not have committed the particular crime unless confronted with inordinate inducements, must not

be ignored. Past crimes do not forever outlaw the criminal and open him to police practices, aimed at securing his repeated conviction, from which the ordinary citizen is protected.

356 U.S. at 382–83, 78 S.Ct. at 825–26 (Frankfurter, J., concurring in the result).

The subjective view recognizes that innocent, unpredisposed, persons will sometimes be ensnared by otherwise permissible police behavior. However, there are times when police resort to impermissible techniques. In those cases, the subjective view allows conviction of predisposed defendants. The objective view requires that all persons so ensnared be released.

Although the United States Supreme Court implies the objective and subjective views of entrapment are mutually exclusive, we find that they are not. The objective view is a statement of judicially cognizable considerations worthy of being given as much weight as the subjective view. . . .

We do not foresee a problem in providing two independent methods of protection in entrapment cases. . . .

The subjective test is normally a jury question. The objective test is a matter of law for the trial court to decide.

The effect of a threshold objective test is to require the state to establish initially whether "police conduct revealed in the particular case falls below standards, to which common feelings respond, for the proper use of governmental power." *Sherman,* 356 U.S. at 382, 78 S.Ct. at 825 (Frankfurter, J., concurring in the result). Once the state has established the validity of the police activity, the question remains whether "the criminal design originates with the officials of the government, and they implant in the mind of an innocent person the disposition to commit the alleged offense and induce its commission in order that they may prosecute." *Sorrells,* 287 U.S. at 442, 53 S.Ct. at 212 (1932). This question is answered by deciding whether the defendant was predisposed, and is properly for the jury to decide. In other words, the court must first decide whether the police have cast their nets in permissible waters, and, if so, the jury must decide whether the particular defendant was one of the guilty the police may permissibly ensnare.

To guide the trial courts, we propound the following threshhold test of an entrapment defense: Entrapment has not occurred as a matter of law where police activity (1) has as its end the interruption of a specific ongoing criminal activity; and (2) utilizes means reasonably tailored to apprehend those involved in the ongoing criminal activity.

The first prong of this test addresses the problem of police "virtue testing," that is, police activity seeking to prosecute crime where no such crime exists but for the police activity engendering the crime. As Justice Roberts wrote in his separate opinion in *Sorrells,* "Society is at war with the criminal classes." Police must fight this war, not engage in the manufacture of new hostilities.

The second prong of the threshold test addresses the problem of inappropriate techniques. Considerations in deciding whether police activity is permissible under this prong include whether a government agent "induces or encourages another person to engage in conduct constituting such offense by either: (a) making knowingly false representations designed to induce the belief that such conduct is not prohibited; or (b) employing methods of persuasion or inducement which create a substantial risk that such an offense will be committed by persons other than those who are ready to commit it." Model Penal Code § 2.13 (1962).

Applying this test to the case before us, we find that the drunken bum decoy operation fails. In Cruz's motion to dismiss, one of the undisputed facts was that "none of the unsolved crimes occuring [sic] near this location involved the same modus operandi as the simulated situation created by the officers." The record thus implies police were apparently attempting to interrupt some kind of ongoing criminal activity. However, the record does not show what specific activity was targeted. This lack of focus is sufficient for the scenario to fail the first prong of the test. However, even if the police were seeking to catch persons who had been "rolling" drunks in the area, the criminal scenario here, with $150 (paperclipped to ensure more than $100 was taken, making the offense a felony) enticingly protruding from the back pocket of a person seemingly incapable of noticing its removal, carries with it the "substantial risk that such an offense will be committed by persons other than those who are ready to commit it." Model Penal Code § 2.13. This sufficiently addresses the *Casper* court's proper recognition that entrapment has occurred where "the decoy simply provided the opportunity to commit a crime to anyone who succumbed to the lure of the bait." 417 So.2d at 265. This test also recognizes, as the *Cruz* court did, that the considerations inherent in our threshhold test are not properly addressed in the context of the predisposition element of the second, subjective test.

For the reasons discussed, we hold that the police activity in the instant case constituted entrapment as a matter of law under the threshhold test adopted here. Accordingly, we quash the district court decision.

It is so ordered.

Boyd, C.J., and Adkins, McDonald and Shaw, J.J., concur.

Overton, J., concurs specially with an opinion.

Alderman, J., dissents with an opinion.

. . .

E. INSANITY

1. Introduction

Because the majority may believe the law reflects their own values, they might view those who break laws as deviant or abnormal. Justice overlooks individual peculiarities, however, and considers everyone sane unless shown to be otherwise under a strict definition of the law. The criminal justice system has struggled to develop a definition of insanity that will protect those defendants who truly are not responsible for their unlawful actions and who, therefore, are not responsive to punishment.

There is a distinct difference between the legal term *insanity* and the medical term *mentally ill*. Psychiatric experts may not testify in court as to whether the defendant is "insane," because that is a legal issue, but only as to the mental condition of the defendant [*Roundtree v. State* (Miss. 1990)]. The fact that a defendant can benefit from psychiatric care does not automatically provide him or her with the legal defense of insanity.

Even though enormous attention has been focused on the insanity defense by both legal scholars and the public, it is used successfully in fewer than 1 percent of all criminal cases.[9] It can hardly be called a "perfect defense," because defendants found not guilty by reason of insanity are most often committed to a maximum security psychiatric hospital, subject to the discretion of a judge or jury or commitment hearings. That may not be as harsh as it appears, because the defendant is the one who has made the claim of insanity. Once hospitalized, the burden is usually on the patient to show at periodic reviews the right to be released. Therefore, few defendants other than those facing capital or life penalties could benefit from an insanity defense.

A competent defendant may refuse to raise the insanity defense even though evidence may show that it is appropriate to do so. The court may decide voluntarily (*sua sponte*) to instruct the jury on the insanity defense if evidence suggests it is appropriate and when the defendant can make no clear choice about claiming the defense.

A verdict of guilty but mentally ill, allowed in some states, is a criminal conviction "where a defendant's mental illness does not deprive him of substantial capacity sufficient to satisfy the insanity test but does warrant treatment in addition to incarceration" [*People v. Sorna* (Mich. App. 1979)]. When mental illness is not conclusive enough to affect conviction, it may be a mitigating factor in determining the grading of the crime or in sentencing.

2. Burden of Proof of Insanity

Because there is a presumption of sanity, the defense always bears the burden of production of its contention of insanity. The level of that burden is usually to produce enough evidence to raise reasonable doubt as to the defendant's mental responsibility. A few jurisdictions require only "some evidence" of insanity [*State v. Evans* (Conn. 1987)].

Once the burden of production is met, in about half the states the burden reverts to the prosecution to prove sanity beyond a reasonable doubt. In the rest of the states, the burden stays with the defense to persuade by a preponderance of the evidence. Federal law requires the defense to show **clear and convincing evidence** of insanity, less than beyond a reasonable doubt but greater than a preponderance of the evidence. If the defense does not meet its burden, the judge may withdraw the insanity defense [*Leach v. Kolb* (7th Cir. 1990)].[10]

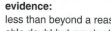

clear and convincing evidence:

less than beyond a reasonable doubt but greater than a preponderance of the evidence.

3. *M'Naghten* Test

The most enduring test of insanity came as a response to the *M'Naghten* case in 1843. M'Naghten, under a delusion that Prime Minister Sir Robert Peel was conspiring to kill him, shot and killed the prime minister's secretary Edward Drummond, believing him to be Peel. When M'Naghten was found not guilty by reason of insanity, the House of Lords answered the public outcry and Queen Victoria's request for standards with the *M'Naghten* rule.

First, this rule requires the defendant claiming insanity to suffer a disease or defect of the mind. That covers a broad range of psychoses and even retardation, but does not include neuroses or psychopathic or sociopathic disorders.

Given the disease or defect of the mind, the *M'Naghten* rule then splits into two prongs. One prong states that a person is insane when the mental defect is the cause of that person's not knowing that his or her conduct is wrong. The second prong states that a person is insane when the mental defect is the cause of that person's not understanding the nature and consequences of his or her conduct.

Wrongfulness can be legal or moral. A defendant may commit an act knowing that it is unlawful but believing that it is morally right. A defendant who claimed that God told him to stab his wife to sever their marriage bond did not believe that his action was wrong. Such a psychotic delusion qualified him for an insanity defense, because moral wrongfulness is determined by objective, "existing societal standards of morality rather than a purely subjective personal standard of morality" [*People v. Serravo* (Colo. 1992)].

The decision in *Pugh v. State* (Okl. Cr. 1989) emphasizes the differences in and the importance of the two prongs of the M'Naghten rule.

PUGH v. STATE
Court of Criminal Appeals of Oklahoma, 1989.
781 P.2d 843 Okl.Cr. 1989
[Citations omitted]

PARKS, Presiding Judge

Appellant, Roy Martin Pugh, was tried by jury and convicted of First Degree Murder. . . . We reverse and remand for a new trial.

. . . Briefly stated, the facts are as follows: Kimberly Ransome, a two-year old child, was beaten severely by seventeen (17) year old appellant, who was babysitting the child while her mother was working. Upon returning home,

Angela Rucker, Kimberly's mother, noticed bruises on Kimberly's face and realized that Kimberly was unconscious. She, along with appellant, rushed the child to the hospital. Three days later, Kimberly died as a result of her injuries. Appellant's sole defense was that of insanity. He presented expert and lay testimony, which revealed his severely troubled past. Dr. Hamilton, an expert in child psychiatry, testified that appellant had quite possibly dissociated himself from his actions, thereby not seeing his conduct as a product of his own thinking.

Appellant urges that the trial court committed reversible error by refusing to instruct the jury as to the complete definition of insanity. At trial, defense counsel presented a requested instruction which was identical to Oklahoma Uniform Jury Instruction—Criminal, Instruction Number 729:

A person is insane when that person is suffering from such a disability of reason or disease of the mind that he/she does not know that his/her acts or omissions are wrong and is unable to distinguish right from wrong with respect to his/her acts or omissions. *A person is also insane when that person is suffering from such a disability of reason or disease of the mind that he/she does not understand the nature and consequences of his/her acts or omissions.* (Emphasis added)

Both parties agreed that an instruction on insanity was required under *Broaddrick v. Oklahoma,* 706 P.2d 534, 536 (Okla.Crim.App.1985); however, the prosecution argued that the second sentence of the requested instruction was redundant and confusing. The trial court agreed, and refused to give the full and complete instruction to the jury. Instead, the trial court, omitting the second sentence, instructed the jury only that appellant could be found insane if he was suffering from such a disability or disease of the mind that he was unable to distinguish right from wrong.

Appellant claims that this omission was critical insofar as it narrowed the definition of insanity. The State agrees that the trial court could have properly given the instruction requested by appellant, but urges that it was not necessary to do so. . . .

Thus, the first issue before this Court is whether the second prong of *M'Naghten* has been abandoned by this Court. Concededly, it has long been held that *M'Naghten* is the only test used to determine criminal responsibility in Oklahoma. Furthermore, in *Jones,* 648 P.2d at 1254, this Court specifically held a defendant was legally insane if "during the commission of the crime he was suffering from a mental disease or defect rendering him unable to differentiate between right and wrong, or unable to understand the nature and consequences of his acts." This language followed explicitly the rule set forth in *M'Naghten's Case,* 8 Eng.Rep. 718 (1843), and clearly shows that both prongs of the *M'Naghten* test are applied in Oklahoma. Therefore, after full

consideration, we continue to adhere to both prongs of the *M'Naghten* test.

Having determined that both prongs are applicable, it is clear that the trial court erred by refusing to give the complete instruction requested by appellant. Our next determination is whether the trial court's error necessitates reversal. We hold that it does.

At trial, the prosecutor argued that the second sentence of Instruction Number 729 was redundant and confusing. He claimed that the language referring to the "nature and consequences" of a defendant's actions merely explained in more detail the meaning of "right from wrong" as used in the preceding sentence. Although this Court has never had the opportunity to consider this question, several other courts have confronted the issue. In *Price v. Commonwealth,* 228 Va. 452, 323 S.E.2d 106, 110 (1984), the Supreme Court of Virginia held that the two parts of *M'Naghten* are disjunctive and separate ways of determining that a defendant is legally insane:

The first portion of *M'Naghten* relates to an accused who is psychotic to an extreme degree. It assumes an accused who, because of mental disease, did not know the nature and quality of his act; he simply did not know what he was doing. For example, in crushing the skull of a human being with an iron bar, he believed that he was smashing a glass jar. The latter portion of *M'Naghten* relates to an accused who knew the nature and quality of his act. He knew what he was doing; he knew that he was crushing the skull of a human being with an iron bar. However, because of mental disease, he did not know know that what he was doing was wrong. He believed, for example, that he was carrying out a command from God. 2. C. Torcia, *Wharton's Criminal Law* § 100, at 9 (14th ed. 1979) (footnotes omitted).

As explained by the Iowa Supreme Court in *State v. Thomas,* 219 N.W.2d 3, 6 (Iowa 1974), a defendant is entitled to an acquittal "if he knew what he was doing [but] he did not know it was wrong, or vice versa." Thus, these two prongs of *M'Naghten* essentially set forth two separate and distinct ways that a defendant may be determined legally insane.

By refusing appellant's requested instruction, the trial court eliminated from the jury's consideration one distinct and separate avenue under which appellant could have been determined to be legally insane. . . . Although the State asserts such error is harmless, we believe appellant was deprived of a fair and impartial trial because the jury was not given complete instructions in conformance with the *M'Naghten* rule.

For the reasons discussed above, this cause is REVERSED and REMANDED for a NEW TRIAL.

LUMPKIN, J., concurs.

LANE, V.P.J., concurs in result.

BRETT, J., dissents.

4.   Irresistible Impulse

Critics of the *M'Naghten* rule said provision should be made for those who know what they are doing and that it is wrong, but simply cannot control their conduct. Where this volitional test is added to the cognitive test of *M'Naghten,* if an unlawful act is committed under an irresistible impulse but not necessarily an utter lack of control, the insanity defense is still valid. Only Georgia, by statute, New Mexico, and Virginia, both by court decision, have adopted this insanity standard.

5.   *Durham* or "Product" Test

Another criticism of *M'Naghten* is that it does not conform to the modern practice of psychiatry. In New Hampshire, then later in *Durham v. U.S.* (D.C. Cir. 1954), it was decided that "an accused is not criminally responsible if his unlawful act was the product of mental disease or mental defect." This much broader test considers all aspects of the mental process and brings the insanity defense closer to a medical viewpoint. When the goal of determining criminal liability rather than diagnosing mental illness was reestablished, this test was abandoned by all jurisdictions except New Hampshire where it originated.

6.   Substantial Capacity—The *Freeman* Rule

Reacting to critics of *M'Naghten* who protested that there is no clear line between sanity and insanity, the Model Penal Code set a broader standard that was reinforced in *U.S. v. Freeman* (2d Cir. 1966). It affords the insanity defense when the defendant "lacks substantial capacity either to appreciate the criminality [wrongfulness] of his conduct or to conform his conduct to the requirements of law" [Model Penal Code § 4.01(1)]. This test allows a less than absolute lack of capacity to determine wrongfulness. The word "appreciate" indicates a deeper awareness of the value of an act. The *Freeman* rule is more inclusive than *M'Naghten,* but not so broad as *Durham.* It appeared to be a good compromise and was adopted by all federal appeals courts and more than half the states by 1980. The trial of John Hinckley for the attempted assassination of President Reagan brought the substantial capacity test before the public in 1982. Besides the more relaxed definition of insanity, the prosecution had the burden of proof to show the defendant not insane beyond a reasonable doubt. The resulting verdict of not guilty by reason of insanity brought public concern and a rethinking of the insanity defense.

7.   Current Status

In response to *Hinckley,* the Insanity Defense Reform Act of 1984, 18 U.S.C.A. § 17, was passed by Congress. It shifted the burden of proof to the defense by clear and convincing evidence. Substantial capacity reverted to the *M'Naghten*-like requirement to "appreciate the nature and quality or the wrongfulness of his acts." A similar movement occurred in the states, and by 1985 about half used "know" or "appreciate" without reference to irresistible impulse; three included irresistible impulse. Twenty states kept the substantial capacity standard; New Hampshire stayed with the *Durham* product test; and Montana, Idaho, and Utah dropped the insanity defense altogether to rely on a disproof of mens rea.[11]

Compare jury instructions for the federal standard with those for the Model Penal Code standard in Exhibits 7–2 and 7–3.

EXHIBIT 7–2
Sample Jury Instructions

INSANITY

The defendant claims that he was insane at the time of the events alleged in the indictment. If you conclude that the government has proved beyond a reasonable doubt that the defendant committed the crime as charged, you must then consider whether the defendant should be found "not guilty only by reason of insanity."

The defendant was insane as the law defines that term only if, as a result of a severe mental disease or defect, the defendant was unable to appreciate the nature and quality or the wrongfulness of his acts. Mental disease or defect does not otherwise constitute a defense.

On the issue of insanity, it is the defendant who must prove his insanity by clear and convincing evidence. You should render a verdict of "not guilty only by reason of insanity" if you are persuaded by clear and convincing evidence that the defendant was insane when the crime was committed.

Remember, then, that there are three possible verdicts in this case: guilty, not guilty, and not guilty only by reason of insanity.

Pattern Jury Instructions (Criminal Cases), 5th Circuit (St. Paul, MN: West Group, 1990), 1.33, with permission.

EXHIBIT 7–3
Sample Jury Instructions

INSANITY

Even though you might otherwise find the Defendant guilty of one [or more] of the offenses mentioned in these Instructions, if you believe from the evidence that at the time he committed the offense [or offenses] (if he did so) he was insane, you shall find him not guilty and state in your verdict that you find him not guilty by reason of insanity.

A person is "insane" if as a result of mental illness, mental retardation, or other mental condition, he lacks the substantial capacity either to appreciate the criminality of his conduct or to conform his conduct to the requirements of law. [Mental illness or retardation does not include an abnormality manifested only by repeated criminal or otherwise antisocial conduct.]

[If the Defendant is found not guilty under this Instruction, he will be examined and a hearing will be held in this court to determine if he is presently mentally ill or mentally retarded; and, if so, whether he should be committed to a hospital or appropriate care facility for treatment. He will be so committed if it is found at the hearing that (1) he is presently mentally ill or retarded, (2) he presents a danger to himself, his family, or others as a result of his illness or retardation, (3) he can reasonably benefit from treatment, and (4) placement in a hospital or care facility is the least restrictive mode of treatment presently available. He will continue to be treated until the treating physicians determine that these factors no longer exist.]

William S. Cooper, *Kentucky Instructions to Juries (Criminal),* 4th ed. § 1131 (© Anderson Publishing, Cincinnati, Ohio, 1999), with permission.

8. Automatism

When somnambulism, epilepsy, or other disorders cause momentary loss of control during which an unlawful act is committed, it is difficult to ascribe responsibility to that person. At one time these cases were handled the same as insanity cases, but now automatism is likely to be treated as a separate affirmative defense without the commitment proceedings that accompany a successful insanity defense. An automatism defense may be a red flag, however, signaling the need for civil commitment proceedings.

In the trial of a woman charged with murdering her husband, the prosecution contended that she killed him because he was leaving her for another woman. Evidence showed that the defendant had been physically abused by her husband. She suffered from mental illness for twenty years, and was subject to narcolepsy, a rare sleeping disorder. The jury rejected the verdict of not guilty by reason of insanity, and acquitted her of murder on the basis of automatism caused by the disorder.[12]

9. Insanity and Mens Rea

Besides allowing insanity as an affirmative defense where the elements of the crime are admitted, most jurisdictions also accept evidence of insanity to show the defendant lacked the mens rea required for the crime. If the necessary intent is not present, of course, there is no crime, and the defense is complete. This defense is particularly effective against first degree murder charges, where evidence of insanity might not meet the standards for an affirmative defense but shows an inability to premeditate.

Some courts reject the use of insanity claims to refute elements of mens rea and require adherence to complete insanity standards for all insanity defenses. This approach is based on the belief that the insane can form the intent to commit a crime; the question is whether the defendant is a responsible moral agent. According to some, "One is a moral agent only if one is a rational agent."[13]

10. Competency to Stand Trial

A defendant deemed sane at the time of trial may have been insane at the time of the offense and, therefore, be allowed the insanity defense. If the defendant is insane at the time of the trial but was sane at the time of the offense, however, there is no insanity defense. Regardless of capability at the time of the offense, due process requires the defendant to be competent to stand trial.

Competence is determined by whether the defendant has "sufficient present ability to consult with his lawyer and whether he has a rational as well as factual understanding of the proceedings against him" [*Dusky v. U.S.* (1960)]. *People v. Medina* (Cal. 1990) allows the burden of proof of incompetency to be placed on the defendant. Most courts require the defendant to raise a bona fide doubt as to competence, then place the burden of proof on the state. If the defendant is found incompetent, necessity for institutionalization is then decided at a civil commitment hearing required in *Jackson v. Indiana* (1972). To be committed, the defendant must be found to be a danger to self or others unless he or she agrees to a voluntary commitment.

A judgment on competency has nothing to do with the merits of the charges—it is not a defense—nor is it a permanent barrier to trial. If and when the defendant regains competency, he or she is subject to trial. Many cases involving insane defendants are resolved by incompetency commitments, however, without necessity of trial. Except for the more serious offenses, charges are often dropped when the defendant is released from hospitalization, though commitment can be indefinite with periodic review if the defendant is dangerous [*U.S. v. Sahhar* (9th Cir. 1990)].

In *Riggins v. Nevada* (1992) the Supreme Court ruled that it was reversible error to administer antipsychotic drugs during trial to a murder defendant who claimed insanity. Without findings that there were no less intrusive alternatives, and that the medication was appropriate and essential for safety, the murder defendant had a right to demonstrate his true mental state.

V. MISSING ELEMENTS

A. INTRODUCTION

The defenses considered so far are raised by the defense when all the elements of the crime are present and attributable to the defendant. Another tactic of the defense is to deny that a crime was committed by the defendant, to claim that one of the essential elements is missing. The prosecution bears the entire burden of proving each of the elements, so this approach is not an affirmative defense, but rather an opportunity for the defense to show that an element is lacking. If a reasonable doubt about one of the elements of the crime can be raised by the defense, the verdict must be not guilty. In some jurisdictions, however, certain of these defenses, such as alibi and diminished capacity, are affirmative defenses and are often categorized as excuses. Always check to see how the defense you are working with is handled in your jurisdiction.

B. ACTUS REUS AS A MISSING ELEMENT

The most obvious defense, and the most definite, is to show that the alleged crime did not occur. The body cannot be found or the gems are discovered under a pillow. The DUI defendant may not have been driving the car. The burglary defendant may have walked through an open door into a public space.

Another means of casting doubt on the actus reus element is to give evidence of an alibi. If the defendant was in Chicago speaking to a roomful of stamp collectors while the burglary was taking place in Hoboken, it is reasonably doubtful that the defendant is the burglar. Of course, if most alibis were so definite, their respective cases would not be likely to go to court.

In some states alibi is treated as an affirmative defense. The majority of jurisdictions, however, treat it as a missing element, relieving the defense of any burden of proof. Not giving a jury instruction on alibi when it is requested and reasonably supported by the evidence, however, may allow the jury to assume that the defense should have proved the alibi. Such a refusal was reversible error in *State v. Rodriguez* (Ariz. 1998). In the federal system, the defendant gives notice of an alibi defense; the prosecution responds with a statement of the time, date, and place of the alleged offense; and both parties furnish information about witnesses (Fed. R. Crim. P. 12.1). See Chapter 12 for procedural requirements and check your state rules.

EXHIBIT 7–4
Sample Jury Instructions

ALIBI

Evidence has been introduced tending to establish an alibi—that the defendant was not present at the time when, or at the place where, the defendant is alleged to have committed the offense charged in the indictment.

It is, of course, the government's burden to establish beyond a reasonable doubt each of the essential elements of the offense, including the involvement of the defendant; and if, after consideration of all the evidence in the case, you have a reasonable doubt as to whether the defendant was present at the time and/or place as alleged in the indictment, you must acquit the defendant.

Pattern Jury Instructions (Criminal Cases), 5th Circuit (St. Paul, MN: West Group, 1990), 1.34, with permission.

C. MENS REA AS A MISSING ELEMENT

1. Introduction

Though diminished capacity, age, intoxication, and mistake are often seen as defenses under the heading of "excuses," they actually serve to refute the element of intent. There is a difference between intending to commit an unlawful act but not having the capacity to be responsible for that intention, as in the insanity defense, and the lack of mens rea. Here the argument is that the defendant did not have the capacity to form the intent necessary to the crime, or committed the offense by mistake. Without the requisite mens rea, there is no crime. Instead of excuse, there is innocence.

2. Diminished Capacity

"Evidence that the defendant suffered from a mental disease or defect is admissible whenever it is relevant to prove that the defendant did or did not have a state of mind which is an element of the offense" [Model Penal Code § 4.02(1)]. In courts that use this rule, evidence of diminished capacity may be used to establish innocence. Lacking mens rea does not mean that the defendant is insane, so institutionalization is not a routine consequence of this defense.

Some states reject the claim of diminished capacity, because it does not provide clear standards such as those in the *M'Naghten* rule. Others restrict it to negating specific intent only, but not general intent, usually in regard to reductions of first degree murder charges to second degree or, in some jurisdictions, to manslaughter if the mental condition was the cause of heat of passion. Because bank robbery is not a specific intent crime, the defense of diminished capacity was not allowed in *U.S. v. Gonyea* (6th Cir. 1998). Diminished capacity can give rise to verdicts of guilty but mentally ill and be a mitigating circumstance preventing death penalties in otherwise capital crimes.

The federal Insanity Defense Reform Act, 18 U.S.C.A. § 17, bars diminished capacity as an excuse, but demonstration of a mental defect can be used to negate mens rea. In contracting for the killing of his wife, a defendant did a significant amount of purposeful planning, contrary to his claim of diminished capacity. The court in *U.S. v. Pohlot* (3rd Cir. 1987) considered evidence of intent to be sufficient and affirmed his conviction.

3. Age

Common law held that those under the age of seven had no mental capacity to commit crimes, and that their mental capacity increased until age fourteen, when responsibility was assumed. Now each state has a juvenile court system that effectively eliminates the defense of age by trying juvenile defendants without juries as delinquents rather than as criminals. In most states these courts have exclusive jurisdiction up to a certain age. At the upper age range, often sixteen to eighteen years, the juvenile court can transfer or certify cases to adult criminal courts if the crime is serious and the juvenile is mature. Reaction to recent, widely publicized, violent crimes by younger children has led to a lowering of the age for trial as an adult in some jurisdictions.

In re Gault (1967) enumerated juveniles' due process rights of proper notice, assistance of counsel, and privilege against self-incrimination. The disposition of youthful offenders in the federal system is covered in 18 U.S.C.A. §§ 5001–5042.

4. Intoxication

States vary in their standards of acceptance of intoxication as a defense. Most regard voluntary intoxication only as a factor in establishing mens rea, allowing it to negate specific intent but not general intent, so it is never a perfect defense. Battery on a law enforcement officer is not a specific intent crime, so voluntary intoxication was no defense in *Frey v. State* (Fla. 1998). Likewise, voluntary intoxication was not a defense to felony murder in *State v. Campos* (N.M. 1996). It should have been allowed in a trial for depraved mind murder, however, because the defendant's mental state is an essential element of the crime [*State v. Brown* (N.M. 1996)].

Some states, however, do not allow this defense even for specific intent. The Supreme Court upheld Montana's statute denying voluntary intoxication as a factor in mens rea in *Montana v. Egelhoff* (1996). Evidence of the defendant's intoxication was admitted to show that he did not have the coordination necessary to carry out the killings, but the jury was instructed that the evidence could not be considered in deciding intent. Generally, voluntariness in consuming the intoxicant is deemed equal to voluntariness in committing the crime.

Involuntary intoxication may negate mens rea, but also can be used as an excuse for criminal behavior, similar to the insanity defense but without its consequences. This defense is rare, because it requires that the defendant did not know that he or she was taking drugs or that the defendant took drugs under extreme duress. Involuntary intoxication also may result from an unexpected physiological reaction to medications, moderate amounts of alcohol, or exposure to other chemicals (pathological intoxication). Once the involuntariness is established, the severity of the intoxication and its effect on the defendant's action are subject to the same standards as apply to insanity: determination of right and wrong, irresistible impulse, substantial capacity, and so forth. A defendant's use of anabolic steroids and claim of resulting intoxication was not sufficient to preclude specific intent for murder when other evidence showed the defendant was not acting in a wild rage and that he knew what he was doing [*State v. Knowles* (La. App. 1992)]. Intoxication resulting from addiction is not involuntary [*State v. Mash* (N.C. 1988)].

The defendant in *State v. Lohmeier* (Wis. 1996) was allowed an affirmative defense codified in Wisconsin's homicide by intoxicated use of a vehicle statute. The statute allows acquittal if the defense shows by a preponderance of the evidence that, even if the defendant had not been intoxicated and was exercising due caution, conditions were such that the victims would have died anyway.

 ANALYSIS PROBLEM

7–3. Intoxication is a factor in many crimes—the Survey of State Prison Inmates, 1991, produced by the Bureau of Justice Statistics, shows that 49 percent of the inmates in state prisons committed their crimes under the influence of drugs or alcohol. How do you think this connection affects the nonacceptance of voluntary intoxication as a perfect defense? Why do you think this is or is not fair?

5. Mistake of Fact

A golfer anxious to get back to the office after an unexcused absence for a quick nine-hole round grabs one of two identical maroon golf club bags from the rack outside the pro shop. Another golfer later takes the remaining bag, but notices that the clubs are not his expensive, custom-made ones. Later he asks that the first golfer be charged with larceny. Is the first golfer guilty?

A mistake of fact, such as taking the wrong golf bag, that negates mens rea can eliminate criminal liability for the defendant. The mistake must be honest and reasonable, although an unreasonable mistake, such as taking a green bag when yours is maroon, may also negate specific but not general intent. Mistake of fact is a mixed defense, usually used as a counterargument to mens rea elements, but also codified as an affirmative defense in some states.

Mistake is not a defense in strict liability cases when the age of a minor is in question [*State v. Oar* (Id. 1996)]. When a mistake of fact causes an element of a strict liability crime to be missing, however, the mistake can be a defense. The crime of concealing the alien status of another person, a strict liability crime, was not complete when a defendant made false citizenship documents and sold them to undercover officers, because the officers were not aliens. The case was remanded for resentencing on the lesser included crime of attempt [*People v. Rizo* (Cal. App. 1999)].

A defendant claimed that the hat he took from a store had been on the floor without a price tag and was dirty. The store security officer testified that the defendant took the hat from a rack. Even though the trial judge apparently found the defendant's claim incredible, the court should have given the jury instruction on the honest belief defense and let them decide the credibility of the testimony, according to the appellate decision [*Binnie v. State* (Md. 1991)].

6. Mistake of Law

It is much more difficult to use as a defense a mistake regarding the law. The old saying, "ignorance of the law is no excuse," is fairly true [*U.S. v. Robinson* (1st Cir. 1998)]. Difficulty in distinguishing between mistakes of fact and mistakes of law complicates matters. The case of *West v. State* (Neb. 1930) provides a good illustration of the difference. The defendant took a car, believing the owner had given it to her before he died, when in fact it belonged to the executor of the estate. The mistake could have been one of fact, that the defendant thought the owner had said he was giving her the car when he had actually said something else. Or the mistake could have been one of law, that the owner said the car would be hers, but did not write that provision into his will. Thus, her mistake of law was in misunderstanding the legal effect of his statement to her. The court reflected that, either way, the mistake negated the defendant's intent to steal the car, so her conviction was reversed. Generally, mistake of law is a defense only when it negates specific intent.

The mistake of law defense is "extremely limited and the mistake must be objectively reasonable" [*U.S. v. Moore* (7th Cir. 1980)]. Defendants charged with tax fraud were not allowed jury instructions concerning a "good faith" defense as to their interpretation of federal tax law [*U.S. v. Regan* (2d Cir. 1991)].

Although the unconstitutionality of a law may be used in a defense, belief at the time of the offense that a statute is unconstitutional is not a valid defense for breaking the law [*State v. Thorstad* (N.D. 1978)]. Even if an attorney mistakenly advises a client that an act is not unlawful or that a law is unconstitutional before the offense is committed, that mistake cannot be used as a defense [*State v. Brewer* (Tenn. Cr. App. 1996)]. Some states do permit reliance on the advice of a prosecutor.[14] Allegedly mistaken advice on fishing laws given by a state trooper did not give rise to a mistake of law defense to a strict liability offense, because the advice was not a formal interpretation of law issued by a chief enforcement official or agency [*Haggren v. State* (Alaska App. 1992)].

Entrapment-by-estoppel is an affirmative defense used narrowly when a defendant actually relies on a point of law misrepresented by a government official, and the reliance is objectively reasonable based on the identity of the official, the point of law, and the substance of the misrepresentation. A defendant convicted of being a felon in possession of a firearm was not entitled to the defense, because the advice that his right to possess a firearm resumed on his release from prison came from a state officer, whereas the crime in question is a federal crime [*U.S. v. Funches* (11th Cir. 1998)].

These decisions are based on the principle that the elements of crime are established by the state, and that individuals may not alter those definitions, whether through misunderstanding or ignorance, or by design. In *U.S. v. Berrigan* (4th Cir.

1969) for the mutilation of selective service records in the belief that the Vietnam War was illegal, the court ruled, "No civilized nation can endure where a citizen can select what law he would obey because of his moral or religious belief." Do you see a similarity to the rejection of the defense of necessity in civil disobedience cases?

ANALYSIS PROBLEM

7–4. Discuss the differences between mistake of fact and mistake of law as defenses. Should it make a difference to the case whether the mistake involved the law? Why or why not?

D. CONSENT

Consent of the victim is not a defense except for crimes that specifically include lack of consent as an element, such as rape. In other words, an individual may not negate the right of society to control violent behavior by consenting to being beaten. Thus, a husband whose alcoholic wife consented to receive a beating from him as a punishment for drinking did not have a valid defense against the charge of battery [*State v. Brown* (N.J. 1976)]. Where society has approved certain types of violent behavior, however, such as in football games, boxing matches, or beneficial treatment such as surgery, the individual's consent to participate removes criminal liability from the actor. Consent extends not only to conduct within the rules of a sport, but also to reasonably foreseeable hazards of the game. Intentionally punching an opponent in the nose was ruled not to be among the foreseeable hazards of a basketball game, however, so consent was not a defense in *State v. Shelley* (Wash. App. 1997).

When harm is slight, such as from a slap, or when the elements of the crime include "without consent," such as kidnapping or rape, the victim's consent does constitute a defense by rendering the crime incomplete. One who gives consent must do so voluntarily, be competent to do so, and not be subject to fraud or deceit. A mentally retarded person does not necessarily lack competence to give consent. *State v. Olivio* (N.J. 1991) ruled that consensual activity involving only mildly retarded persons should not be criminalized. Forgiveness or consent after the crime is not a defense [*State v. Taylor* (N.H. 1981)].

VI. SYNDROMES

Conditions that impair defendants' judgment and diminish their responsibility for their actions, or help explain and excuse their actions, are generally not accepted as defenses in themselves. Instead, various syndromes, disorders, and reactions are used to support such traditional defenses as self-defense, diminished capacity, duress, and necessity. These conditions range from the now well-accepted battered person (spouse, woman, wife, child) syndrome and posttraumatic stress disorder, to less successful claims of junk food syndrome (sugar intoxication), gay panic (reaction to a homosexual advance), and television intoxication (reaction to violent programs). Besides confusion in definitions and standards, medical and psychiatric information is not always uniform or well developed on syndromes that are only recently recognized, much less on those that have been invented as last-ditch defenses.

To be an effective defense, the syndrome must be shown to be an identifiable condition, the defendant must be shown to be suffering from that condition, and the condition must have caused sufficient impairment for the defendant to lack responsibility or mens rea for the offense.[15] Usually, syndromes are offered as proof to support more accepted defense theories. Battered woman syndrome was allowed to show a woman's vulnerability to fear in her defense of duress to drug charges [*U.S. v. Johnson* (9th Cir. 1992)]. Battered child syndrome was declared admissible to support a self-defense claim of a sixteen-year-old who killed his mother with a bow and arrow [*State v. Nemeth* (Ohio 1998)]. Testimony that the defendant, a Vietnam War veteran, suffered from posttraumatic stress disorder should have been allowed to support his self-defense claim by showing why he had failed to report the shooting of two men [*Shepard v. State* (Alaska App. 1993)]. "Television intoxication" could not be used, however, to bolster an insanity claim of an adolescent boy for the first degree murder of an elderly woman [*Zamora v. State* (Fla. App. 1978)]. Neither battered person syndrome nor cultural beliefs could be applied in the defense of a Vietnamese native who shot her husband and stepdaughter [*Nguyen v. State* (Ga. 1999)]. The defendant claimed that divorce, which her husband sought, would make her a pariah in her native culture, and that her stepdaughter had threatened and belittled her when she packed to leave. The court ruled that battered person syndrome could include verbal and emotional abuse, but only if it is extreme enough to make the defendant believe that an attack is imminent. The court also stated that strong cultural beliefs can assist the jury in understanding a defendant's action.

The battered person syndrome as a defense to the murder of the batterer combines elements of self-defense, necessity, and possibly diminished capacity. The battering creates a mental as well as physical subjugation of the person, isolating him or her from help. Courts are considering battered person syndrome as a defense to murder more seriously in the wake of recent studies and publicity. Although problems remain concerning the possibilities of escape, the motive of revenge, and gaps in time between the battering and the retaliation, expert testimony on the syndrome has been admitted in federal courts [*U.S. v. Vega-Penarete* (E.D.N.C. 1991)] and in at least thirty states [*Bechtel v. State* (Okl. Cr. 1992)]. Federal legislation, the Battered Women's Testimony Act of 1992, urges all states to accept such testimony, and calls for the State Justice Institute to develop training materials to help battered defendants and their attorneys. A study at Pace University Battered Women's Justice Center found that sentencing for women who kill their mates still averages fifteen to twenty years, whereas that of men is two to six years, but clemency is sometimes offered to spouses who were victims of batterers.[16]

Care must be taken in the use of syndromes in defense. "A superficial knowledge of stereotypes of battering and its effects will be hazardous to your client."[17] The National Clearinghouse for the Defense of Battered Women, 125 S. Ninth Street, Suite 302, Philadelphia, PA 19107, provides information and other support to battered women charged with crimes and their defense teams.

"You've got to have something to eat and a little love in your life before you can hold still for any damn body's sermon on how to behave."

—Billie Holiday, 1915–1959

ANALYSIS PROBLEM

7–5. As a member of a defense team, would you rather rely on affirmative defenses or on disproof of elements? Why? As a member of a prosecution team? Why?

VII. CONCLUSION

Criminal offenses are committed under a variety of circumstances. Some justify the defendant's action, such as self-defense or official duties; others excuse the offense as the result of duress, necessity, entrapment, or insanity that influenced the act and removed the responsibility of the actor.

In other cases the defense may argue that no crime was actually committed, at least not by the defendant. Evidence may show that one of the elements of the crime is missing. Actus reus may be challenged if the defendant has an alibi. The victim's consent may negate certain offenses. Conditions of intoxication, diminished capacity, or mistake may eliminate the intent required for the defendant's act to be criminal to a certain degree. A defendant may exhibit symptoms of a syndrome that could bolster the defense.

The process of arrest and prosecution must be in accordance with the defendant's constitutional and statutory rights, such as statutes of limitations, due process, and freedom from double jeopardy and self-incrimination. Because the strength of these rights and rules that exist to protect each of us can be measured only in the context of a criminal prosecution, it is vital that they are upheld on behalf of each defendant.

Care must be taken to determine the elements of each defense, subjective or objective tests, and the burden of proof required in your jurisdiction. You will gather evidence to prove or disprove each of these defense elements just as you do for the elements of the crimes themselves.

EXHIBIT 7–5
Defenses

DEFENSE	TYPE OF DEFENSE	PERFECT, IMPERFECT, MITIGATING	ELEMENTS AND STANDARDS; STATUTES
Statute of limitations	Statutory, affirmative. *State:*	Perfect.	Federal: 18 U.S.C.A. § 3281 *et seq.*, none on capital crimes, five years on noncapital crimes. *State:*
Freedom of religion	Constitutional. *State:*	Perfect, imperfect, mitigating.	Not allowed when significant harm is caused. *State:*
Double jeopardy	Constitutional. *State:*	Perfect.	Same criminal conduct, punitive. *State:*
Self-defense, defense of others or property	Justification, affirmative. *State:*	Perfect if reasonable, imperfect if honest or unreasonable.	Unprovoked, imminent attack, reasonable force, subjective/ objective test, retreat, habitation. *State:*
Resisting unlawful arrest	Justification, affirmative. *State:*	Perfect or imperfect.	No defense if arrest by a known officer. *State:*
Execution of public duties	Justification, affirmative. *State:*	Perfect.	Care for innocent bystanders, deadly force variously restricted. *State:*
Duress	Excuse, affirmative. *State:*	Perfect.	Coercion by another to commit crime, never murder; threat of immediate serious harm; objective or subjective; must not put self in situation where duress is likely. *State:*

EXHIBIT 7–5
Defenses

DEFENSE	TYPE OF DEFENSE	PERFECT, IMPERFECT, MITIGATING	ELEMENTS AND STANDARDS; STATUTES
Necessity	Excuse, affirmative. *State:*	Perfect.	Under compelling circumstances, chose lesser of two evils, clear and immediate danger, no legal alternative. *State:*
Entrapment	Excuse, affirmative. *State:*	Perfect.	Never violent crimes, must be by government officer or employee, subjective or objective. *State:*
Insanity	Excuse, affirmative. *State:*	Perfect, often institutionalized.	*M'Naghten* right/wrong, irresistible impulse, *Durham* product test, *Freeman* substantial capacity, lack of mens rea. Federal: 18 U.S.C.A. § 17. *State:*
Automatism	Excuse, affirmative. *State:*	Perfect.	Loss of control because of disorder. *State:*
Alibi	Missing element, sometimes affirmative. *State:*	Perfect.	Defendant was not at crime scene. *State:*
Diminished capacity	Lack of element. *State:*	Perfect, imperfect, mitigating.	Negates mens rea, sometimes specific intent only. *State:*
Age	Lack of element, juvenile court. *State:*	Imperfect, mitigating.	Age range. *State:*
Voluntary intoxication	Lack of element. *State:*	Imperfect.	Specific intent only. *State:*
Involuntary intoxication	Excuse, affirmative, *State:*	Perfect.	Drugs taken unknowingly, drugs taken under duress, pathological intoxication, then insanity standards. *State:*
Mistake of fact	Lack of element, can be affirmative. *State:*	Perfect, imperfect, never for strict liability, involving age of victim.	Reasonable and honest belief, unreasonable belief applies only to specific intent. *State:*
Mistake of law	Lack of element. *State:*	Seldom allowed, perfect.	Objectively reasonable. *State:*

Continued

EXHIBIT 7–5 *(Concluded)*
Defenses

DEFENSE	TYPE OF DEFENSE	PERFECT, IMPERFECT, MITIGATING	ELEMENTS AND STANDARDS; STATUTES
Consent	Lack of element. *State:*	Perfect.	Lack of consent is an element of crime, harm done not serious, consent voluntary by competent person. *State:*
Syndromes	Lack of element, excuse, justification. *State:*	Supports other defenses.	Identifiable condition causing impairment or excusing action. *State:*

SYSTEM FOLDER ASSIGNMENTS

Complete the following and place the documents in your system folder:

- Age limits of juvenile court jurisdiction in your state, and conditions for transferring a juvenile's case to adult criminal court.
- Use the chart in Exhibit 7–5 to organize information about defenses in your jurisdiction. The information given is general; be sure to note differences in your state codes.
- Note in the Exhibit 7–5 chart or separately:

  Your state's burden of proof requirements for each defense.
  Your state's use of objective or subjective tests for self-defense, duress, necessity, entrapment, and mistake.
  Admissibility of syndromes in your state.

APPLICATION ASSIGNMENTS

1. The Haden Hills homeowners in Case VI claim their attack on their neighbors was the free expression of their religious convictions, which condemn homosexuality. Would this defense be effective? Explain.
2. A defendant convicted of conspiracy to obstruct the IRS claimed that speech and writing urging others to file fraudulent tax documents was protected by the First Amendment [*U.S. v. Rowlee*, 899 F.2d 1275 (2nd Cir. 1990)]. Is this an effective defense?
3. A homeless man shelters himself in a packing crate under a bridge. One night as he is resting in the crate, a man runs toward him screaming, "You vermin should die!" The homeless man believes he sees a knife in the other man's hand. He could escape through the back side of the crate to the other side of the bridge where passing motorists might help him, but instead he stands and hits his attacker over the head with a metal rod and kills him. The object in the man's hand turns out to be a rolled up newspaper. What self-defense issues are involved in this case? How would you decide the case based on your state's laws and judicial decisions? What if a person were attacked in his or her car?
4. Under what conditions does *Tennessee v. Garner* allow deadly force by police?
5. A third party threatened to kill the defendant and the cashier of a store if the defendant did not participate in the armed robbery of the store. Is the defendant entitled to an affirmative defense instruction [*People v. Houser*, 712 N.E.2d 355 (Ill. App. 1999)]? If so, which defense?

6. Should the defense of necessity be allowed in the following cases? Explain.
   a. A defendant charged with driving without a license testified that his wife was in labor and he was driving her to the doctor's office at the doctor's request. She could not drive herself. See *Tarvestad v. State,* 409 S.E.2d 513 (Ga. 1991).
   b. Defendants charged with kidnapping claimed a "choice of evils" defense for removing the victim from involvement with a religious sect for "deprogramming." No evidence was offered to show impending injury or that the defendants sought alternative remedies. See *People v. Brandyberry,* 812 P.2d 674 (Colo. App. 1990).
   c. A prisoner charged with unlawful possession of a weapon claimed he had previously been cut and beaten, and had acquired the knife only after receiving a threatening note. See *People v. Ferree,* 581 N.E.2d 699 (Ill. App. 1991).
   d. A married couple ill from AIDS were charged with cultivating marijuana. Their physician could find no effective alternative to combat the nausea that otherwise threatened their lives. See *Jenks v. State,* 582 So. 2d 676 (Fla. App. 1991).
   e. A woman charged with DUI had been threatened by her boyfriend, so she left their apartment and drove under the influence of alcohol to get away from him. See *State v. Daoud,* 679 A.2d 577 (N.H. 1996).

7. A felon who had become a government informer in a murder-for-hire indictment against an alleged drug conspirator had received numerous death threats, for which he armed himself [*U.S. v. Gomez,* 81 F.3 846 (9th Cir. 1996)]. Does he have a defense to the strict liability offense of being a felon in possession of a firearm?

8. An investigator contacted a former bootlegger and urged him to go into illegal liquor production. When the bootlegger responded eagerly, the investigator supplied equipment and an operator for a still, sold him sugar at wholesale prices, and was his only customer for two and a half years. Did the bootlegger have an entrapment defense? What other defense could he claim [*Greene v. U.S.,* 454 F.2d 783 (9th Cir. 1971)]?

9. A defendant convicted of murder claimed that he acted during a disassociative state connected to posttraumatic stress disorder. As a child, he shot his abusive stepfather as he held a knife to the defendant's mother's throat. Is the defendant entitled to jury instructions on the defense of unconsciousness (automatism) [*State v. Fields,* 376 S.E.2d 740 (N.C. 1989)]?

10. A mother planned her child's death, obtained a rope, and strangled the child. Evidence showed that the mother was in an unconscious state during the act. She claimed that her Chinese cultural background was relevant to her motives and the emotional crisis that generated the act. As a paralegal on her defense team, research your state laws on the defenses of insanity, automatism, and diminished capacity, and how cultural beliefs relate to them, then write a short memo to your supervising attorney on your findings and how they might be used in this client's defense against murder charges. See *People v. Wu,* 235 3d 614, 286 Cal.Rptr. 868 (Cal. App. 1991).

11. A man who had been taking a controversial new drug to treat depression forced his way into another man's home and began beating that man with a flashlight. The victim had been dating the defendant's ex-wife, who was present in the home. The defendant was charged with burglary. Would you expect a defense of involuntary intoxication to be successful, based on this information? Why or why not?

12. a. A man in possession of a divorce decree from his first marriage remarries, then is charged with bigamy because a legal technicality has made the divorce invalid. Does he have a mistake of law defense?
   b. A woman convicted of a felony was told by her attorney that it was only a misdemeanor, which she believes. She is later charged with possession of a firearm by a felon. Does she have a mistake of law defense? See *People v. Snyder,* 186 Cal.Rptr. 485 (Cal. 1982).

13. Why is self-defense an incomplete defense in most murder trials where a battered woman is the defendant?

14. As a paralegal for either the prosecution or the defense team, you will need to consider defenses that might apply to your cases. What defenses might be

likely for the defendants from the cases in Chapter 1, and what areas would you need to investigate to determine their applicability? Be sure to review defenses for group and inchoate crimes.

DEFENDANT	DEFENSE	INVESTIGATE
Eldon Spiers		
Miguel Cordoba		
Lacey Rude		
Billy McIntire		
Nancy Stroud		
Richard Craig		

15. Research contemporary news stories about the beating of Rodney King and the riots that followed the 1992 state trials. Do they lead you to believe that King would have been justified in resisting the forceful arrest? Explain. Do you think police would have been justified in using deadly force against the rioters? Explain. What is the danger of relying on news stories in forming legal opinions?

HELPFUL WEB SITES

www.nlada.org
    National Legal Aid and Defender Association, defense resources
www.crime-times.org
    On-line journal about environmental and organic factors affecting behavior and their effect on crime and violence
www.crimelynx.com
    Links to forensic evidence resources
www.psych.org/public_info/INSANI~1.htm
    American Psychiatric Association discussion of the insanity defense
http://orion.law.pace.edu/bwjc
    Battered Women's Justice Center

INTERNET EXERCISES

1. Visit the NLADA Web site. What are the three categories of symptoms indicating posttraumatic stress disorder?
2. Visit the crime-times Web site. How are IQ and lead poisoning related to criminal behavior? How could you use this information in the defense of a client?
3. Go to the crimelynx Web site. How is the defense of "Internet intoxication" being used?

QUESTIONS FOR STUDY AND REVIEW

1. Name five types of defense.
2. What is the difference between a perfect defense and an imperfect defense?
3. What are two common burden of proof patterns in affirmative defenses?
4. Explain the differences among "beyond a reasonable doubt," "preponderance of the evidence," and "clear and convincing."
5. Name four constitutional defenses to criminal charges.
6. Under what circumstances is a second charge likely to be considered double jeopardy? Why must a prosecutor always be cognizant of the double jeopardy issue? Explain the similar concern for collateral estoppel.
7. What is the rationale behind statutes of limitations? What crimes are least likely to have such time limits?

8. What assertion is made in a justification defense?
9. What are the elements of self-defense?
10. Describe the subjective and objective tests of reasonableness in self-defense.
11. What is the castle doctrine in self-defense? In defense of habitation?
12. What restrictions does the decision in *Tennessee v. Garner* place on use of force by police?
13. How does excuse differ from justification?
14. How are duress and necessity similar? Different?
15. What are the subjective and objective tests for entrapment? Which is most widely used?
16. What is the major pitfall of the insanity defense?
17. What are the standards for insanity in the *M'Naghten* rule? The *Durham* test? The Model Penal Code substantial capacity or *Freeman* rule?
18. What is the difference between insanity as an affirmative defense and as a mens rea defense?
19. When can consent be used as a defense?
20. How does diminished capacity differ from insanity as a defense?
21. Under what conditions is voluntary intoxication a defense? Involuntary intoxication?
22. Which is generally a more effective defense, mistake of fact or mistake of law?
23. How are syndromes usually used in defense?

KEY TERMS LIST

Affirmative defense	Collateral estoppel	Perfect defense
Burden of persuasion	Imperfect defense	Preponderance of the
Burden of production	Jeopardy	evidence
Clear and convincing	Mitigating	*Sua sponte*
evidence	circumstances	

ENDNOTES

1. John Cloud, *Law on Bended Knee*, TIME, Sept. 13, 1999, at 33.
2. CHARLES H. WHITEBREAD & CHRISTOPHER SLOBOGIN, CRIMINAL PROCEDURE: AN ANALYSIS OF CASES AND CONCEPTS 721 *et seq.* (2d ed. 1986).
3. GERALD DICKLER, MAN ON TRIAL 330 (1962).
4. John Cheeves, *Kentucky Puts No Limitations on Indictment*, LEXINGTON HERALD-LEADER, July 27, 1998, at A6.
5. *ABC Evening News*, Oct. 7, 1999.
6. Laurie L. Levenson, *Criminal Law: The Necessity Defense*, NLJ, Oct. 11, 1999, at B19.
7. Aaron Epstein, *Court: Agents Illegally Caught Man with Porn*, LEXINGTON HERALD-LEADER, Apr. 7, 1992, at A1.
8. WAYNE R. LAFAVE and AUSTIN W. SCOTT, JR., SUBSTANTIVE CRIMINAL LAW, Vol. 1, 610 West Group. 1986.
9. PETER W. LOW, JOHN CALVIN JEFFRIES, JR., & RICHARD J. BONNIE, CRIMINAL LAW, CASES AND MATERIALS 733 (2d ed. 1986).
10. LAFAVE, *supra* note 8, at 499–501.
11. LOW, *supra* note 9, at 659.
12. *Covington Woman Not Guilty in Death; Sleep Disorder Cited*, LEXINGTON HERALD-LEADER, Mar. 24, 1990, at C2.
13. LOW, *supra* note 9, at 684, quoting MICHAEL MOORE, LAW AND PSYCHIATRY: RETHINKING THE RELATIONSHIP (1984).
14. JOEL SAMAHA, CRIMINAL LAW, 291 4th ed. 1993.
15. *Id.* at 322–23.
16. Nancy Gibbs, *Til Death Do Us Part*, TIME, Jan. 18, 1993, at 42–44.
17. Linda Smith, *In Defense of Abused and Battered Women*, THE ADVOCATE, July 1996, at 53.

INTAKE AND DRAFTING THE COMPLAINT

I. INTRODUCTION

intake:
(prosecutor's office) the receipt and initial evaluation of accusations to determine whether charges are appropriate and whether formal documents should be drafted and filed.

Now that you have a working knowledge of substantive criminal law (the various crimes, their respective elements, and possible defenses), you are ready to move to procedural law and conduct the first set of tasks delegated to the paralegal in the prosecutor's office. This set of tasks is centered on the process of intake. **Intake** in the prosecutor's office is the receipt and initial evaluation of accusations to determine whether charges are appropriate and whether formal documents should be drafted and filed. Related tasks include interviewing complainants, assisting and counseling victims of crime, and drafting the complaint, summons, and warrant for arrest. Intake is important to the defense, as well, but because it often occurs after charging, it will be covered later in the text.

II. INTAKE PROCEDURE

A. INTRODUCTION

Alleged criminal conduct comes to the attention of the prosecutor's office in primarily two ways: from the police or from citizens who come to or call the office. Most charges stem from police reports of crimes. When the police observe criminal conduct and make an arrest or investigate, they file reports with the prosecutor's office describing the crime. All the information needed to file charges should be included in that report. When citizens bring complaints directly to the office, it is your task to interview the **complainant,** the person swearing out the complaint, and to determine initially what, if any, charge could be brought against the accused.

complainant:
the person swearing out a complaint.

B. PREPARING FOR INTAKE

1. Introduction

Properly conducted intake can avoid some significant problems. Among these are court dockets excessively crowded with unwarranted or unprovable charges, citizens needlessly arrested and seriously inconvenienced by charges that ultimately are not sustainable, police upset because charges are not brought against defendants that they believe are guilty of crime, and citizens angered because charges are not brought against those who have hurt them. Some of these problems are inevitable, even in the best managed prosecutors' offices, but a properly prepared paralegal following intake guidelines can do much to minimize their occurrence.

Consider the consequences of improper charges in *State v. Houck* (Kan. 1986). Early attention to the necessary elements of the offenses involved could have resulted in different charges and, therefore, a different outcome of the case.

STATE v. HOUCK
Supreme Court of Kansas, 1986.
240 Kan. 130, 727 P.2d 460.

MILLER, Justice:

This is an appeal by Terrance Houck, following his conviction by jury trial in Montgomery District Court, of two counts of aggravated arson, K.S.A. 21-3718(1)(a), K.S.A. 21-3719; two counts of conspiracy to commit aggravated arson, K.S.A. 21-3302, -3718(1)(a) and -3719; one count of felony murder, K.S.A. 21-3401; and one count of felony theft, K.S.A. 21-

3701(b). The controlling issue is whether the evidence was sufficient to establish the crime of aggravated arson under K.S.A. 21-3718(1)(a) and -3719.

Briefly, these are the facts. Terrance Houck owned two houses in Independence, Kansas, one located at 1328 West Chestnut, the other at 729 South 16th Street. On June 25, 1980, the house on Chestnut was damaged by fire. Albert Hughes was the tenant; he was inside the house when the fire was discovered. The Marysville Mutual Insurance Company had a policy of insurance covering the Chestnut Street property. Houck, as owner, was the named insured. He collected $4,900 from Marysville Mutual for his loss.

On January 29, 1981, fire destroyed the 16th Street property. Carl Clay was in the house when it burned, and he was killed. The house was uninsured, but the First National Bank of Elk City held a mortgage on it.

Arson was not suspected. The fire chief concluded that both fires were caused by careless smoking. Houck, meanwhile, was charged on August 28, 1980, and was convicted on March 5, 1981, of aiding and abetting arson and theft by deception. These charges arose out of yet a third fire. On December 21, 1981, he was placed on parole, and on June 3, 1982, his parole officer granted Houck's request and authorized him to move to Arkansas. There he reported to an Arkansas parole officer upon his arrival in that state, and he remained under the supervision of that officer.

An arson investigation was initiated in April or May, 1983, when Independence authorities received anonymous letters from someone in Arkansas. Two statements were taken from the defendant. The first, taken in Arkansas on May 22, 1983, covered the Chestnut Street fire. The second, taken in Independence on May 24, 1983, covered the 16th Street fire. In regard to the Chestnut Street fire, defendant told police officers that he was buying several houses from John Briggs, and the Chestnut Street house was insured through John's son, Robert Briggs, an insurance agent. Robert Briggs called him several times and finally defendant went in to see him. Robert Briggs suggested that the Chestnut Street house was insured and a fire at that address might get the defendant out of debt. Houck said that he then talked with Michael Harris, and told Harris that if the house would accidentally burn the burning would be worth about $500. The house later burned and Houck collected on the insurance policy. Robert Briggs held out of the proceeds the money that Houck owed John Briggs (about $4,780), and Houck received a check from Robert Briggs for the balance, $120. In the May 22 statement, Houck denied ever talking to Harris about setting fire to the 16th Street house.

On the following day, May 23, Houck was returned to Kansas and on May 24, he gave a statement concerning the 16th Street fire. He stated that Suretta Beach, Carl Clay's lady friend, came to him and asked him to burn the 16th Street house so that Clay would die and she could collect on an insurance policy which she held on Clay's life. She insisted the fire occur on January 29, 1981. She promised

Houck that she would pay him after she received the insurance money. She also told him that the windows and rear door were barred and that the fire should be started on the front porch so that Clay could not escape. Houck talked to Michael Harris and paid him $500 to set the fire and promised to pay him more when the job was finished. When Harris said he had no way to carry gasoline, Houck told him that there was a five-gallon gasoline can in the back of his truck. On the morning of January 29, Houck went to a coffee shop about 6:00 o'clock and then went down to 16th Street to get Clay out of the house. When Houck arrived, the house was already on fire. Houck went on to work. After the fire, Suretta Beach stopped him on his way home and told him she would pay him as soon as she got the insurance money. She never paid him anything. Both of these statements were received in evidence.

At trial, Suretta Beach was called as a witness for the State. She testified that the windows and back door of the 16th Street house were sealed for weatherization. She denied hiring anyone to burn the house, and testified that she had no life insurance on Clay. She denied collecting any insurance money after he died. Michael Harris was killed in 1982, and John Briggs died in August 1983, before this trial, and thus neither was available as a witness. Robert Briggs, called as a witness for the State, testified as to the insurance coverage, the proof of loss, and the disbursement of the policy proceeds. He was not asked if he suggested to Houck that he burn the house.

Two other witnesses, Gary and Michael VanGilder, testified that Houck approached them about burning a house. The witnesses, however, were unsure of the location of the target properties.

The first issue is whether the evidence was sufficient to sustain the convictions of aggravated arson, as charged in the second amended information. Both charges allege the damaging of a building *in which another person has an interest,* without the consent of such other person. Count 2 charges defendant with the aggravated arson of the 16th Street property "in which another person has an interest, to-wit: The First National Bank of Elk City, Kansas, without the consent of such other person . . . ."

Count No. 5 charges defendant with the aggravated arson of the Chestnut Street property "in which another person has an interest, to-wit: Marysville Mutual, Marysville, Kansas, and Albert Hughes without the consent of such other persons. . . ." Arson is defined by K.S.A. 21-3718 as follows:

"21-3718. Arson. (1) Arson is knowingly, by means of fire or explosive:

"(a) Damaging any building or property *in which another person has any interest* without the consent of such other person; or

"(b) Damaging any building or property with intent to injure or defraud an insurer or lienholder.

"(2) Arson is a class C felony." (Emphasis added.)

Aggravated arson is defined by K.S.A. 21-3719 as follows:

"21-3719. Aggravated arson. Aggravated arson is arson, as defined in section 21-3718, and committed upon a building or property in which there is some human being.

"Aggravated arson is a class B felony."

Houck argues that neither the bank nor the insurance company had any interest in the property that burned. . . .

The information here charged that the First National Bank had an interest in the 16th Street property. It held a mortgage and was thus "interested" in the property as security for its loan. The issue here is whether the mortgagee held an interest in the building or property under the specific language of K.S.A. 21-3718(1)(a). Reading the statute in its entirety, we note that the following subsection (b) makes it an offense to knowingly, by means of fire or explosive, damage any building or property with intent to injure or defraud an insurer or lienholder. Obviously, the Bank was a lienholder and the burning of the house with intent to defraud the mortgagee would constitute a violation of subsection (b). If, as the State argues, subsection (a) prohibits destruction of mortgaged property, we fail to see why the legislature would make it a separate crime to destroy mortgaged property with intent to defraud the mortgagee by enacting subsection (b).

. . . A mortgagee has a lien, not an ownership interest in the land. Construing subsection (a) strictly, as we are required to do in the case of criminal statutes, we hold that a mortgagee does not have an interest in the property upon which it holds a mortgage, within the meaning of K.S.A. 21-3718(1)(a).

Similarly, does the "interest" of the insurance carrier, Marysville Mutual, constitute an "interest" in the Chestnut Street property within the meaning of K.S.A. 21-3718(1)(a)? Its "interest," if any, is specifically protected by subsection (b). Insurance is a matter of contract. The insurance carrier has an interest in the contract and in the premiums. It has no legal interest in the insured property. We hold that an insurer does not have an interest in the property it insures, within the meaning of K.S.A. 21-3718(1)(a).

Appellant, despite the arguments of the State to the contrary, is not challenging the information; he is challenging the sufficiency of the evidence to convict him of the specific charges of aggravated arson made against him in the information—knowingly, by means of fire or explosive, damaging a building *in which another person has an interest,* without the consent of such other person. For the reasons stated above, we hold that neither the mortgagee nor the insurance carrier had an interest under K.S.A. 21-3718(1)(a) in the property destroyed. Whether the State's evidence would or would not be sufficient to prove a charge under K.S.A. 21-3718(1)(b) is an academic question not properly before us. *The State has the responsibility to appropriately charge the accused with the crime it believes the accused has committed.* If the evidence introduced at trial does not support a conviction of the offense charged, the accused cannot be found guilty of some other offense which the State did not see fit to charge. Here, the State did not prove the charges it brought against Houck and, therefore, the convictions of aggravated arson must be reversed.

The defendant next contends that the State's failure to charge him for almost three years after the crimes occurred resulted in a delay which prejudiced him and denied him due process under the United States Constitution. He first argues that his absence from the state did not toll the running of the statute of limitations. The statute of limitations for the charges at issue is two years. K.S.A. 21-3106(2). That statute specifically provides, in subsection (3), that the period within which a prosecution must be commenced shall not include any period in which "[t]he accused is absent from the state." Thus, if the period during which Houck was in Arkansas is excluded, this prosecution was timely.

Defendant argues that he was on parole and under the joint supervision of Kansas and Arkansas parole officers during all the time that he was in Arkansas. He contends that he was in the "constructive custody" of the State of Kansas and the State could have contacted him at any time or could have returned him to Kansas if it wished. There is no dispute, however, that Houck voluntarily sought leave to move to Arkansas. He left the state of his own free will and remained out of state as a personal choice during the period in question. He was not ordered to leave the state; he was granted permission upon his request. . . .

We hold that Houck was voluntarily absent from the state and thus the two-year statute of limitations was tolled during his absence. The prosecution was timely commenced.

Houck also argues that due process requires dismissal because the preindictment delay caused substantial prejudice to his rights. We discussed a similar claim and the law applicable thereto in *State v. McCorgary,* 224 Kan. 677, 681–84, 585 P.2d 1024 (1978). In that opinion we reviewed the leading federal cases as well as our own on the point. In *McCorgary,* there was an eleven-year lapse of time between the murder and the commencement of the prosecution. Some of the principles set forth therein are as follows: (1) To prosecute a defendant following investigative delay does not deprive him of due process even if his defense might have been somewhat prejudiced by the lapse of time; (2) a due process inquiry must consider the reasons for the delay as well as the prejudice of the accused; and (3) prosecutorial delay solely to gain tactical advantage over the accused would violate due process.

In this case, as in *McCorgary,* there is not the slightest indication that the delay by the State was for the purpose of gaining tactical advantage. To the contrary, the State had no suspicion of arson until it received anonymous letters some sixty days or less prior to the time this prosecution was commenced. Once the State was alerted, its investigation moved promptly and charges were filed on May 20, 1983. Defendant contends that he was prejudiced because two witnesses, John Briggs and Michael Harris, died before the case was tried. Michael Harris, the alleged coconspirator, died of gunshot wounds approximately one year before the charges were filed. John Briggs died shortly after the charges were filed, but prior to trial. John Briggs, a former employer of the defendant, was the former owner of one of the properties and the defendant owed him money at the time the Chestnut Street property was destroyed. Briggs received a substantial portion of the insurance proceeds, as we have stated above. That evidence came in through the testimony of his son, Robert Briggs. Defendant does not allege that John Briggs had any information as to the conversations between the defendant and Robert Briggs, or that John Briggs could have disputed any of the State's evidence at trial. Michael Harris, on the other hand, allegedly conspired with the defendant and set fire to both properties at defendant's request. He was an important witness both for the State and for the defense, depending on his testimony. There is no indication, however, that the State was in any way responsible for his death or that the State deliberately delayed prosecution until after his demise. Upon the facts before us, we hold that defendant was not denied due process by the preindictment delay. . . .

Five of the offenses charged were related to or arose out of the alleged aggravated arson. All stand or fall upon the sufficiency of the proof of the aggravated arson charges. Count I charged conspiracy to commit aggravated arson, which is defined in the information in pertinent part as "knowingly by means of fire . . . damaging any building . . . in which another person has an interest without consent of such other person . . ." and describing the 16th Street residence. As we have already held, the evidence did not establish that *another person* had an interest in that property. Count II charged aggravated arson of the 16th Street residence "in which another person has an interest, to-wit: The First National Bank of Elk City . . . ." As discussed above, the evidence was insufficient to establish that offense.

Count III charged first-degree felony murder, the killing of Carl Clay "while perpetrating the felony crime of aggravated arson . . . as stated in *Count II of this Information which is hereby incorporated into this Count by reference. . . .*" The felony upon which the charge was founded was not established by the evidence.

We are not unmindful of our prior holding that one convicted of felony murder need not be charged with and convicted of the underlying felony. See *State v. Wise,* 237 Kan. 117, 122, 697 P.2d 1295 (1985). In that opinion we cited a New York case, *People v. Murray,* 92 App. Div.2d 617, 459 N.Y.S.2d 810 (1983), in which it was held that an acquittal of the underlying felony is not inconsistent with a conviction of felony murder. In the case at hand, however, there is no evidence that Houck committed, attempted to commit, or conspired to commit *the specific felony* upon which the State relied—the burning of a dwelling house in which some other person had an interest. Absent proof of this offense, the homicide conviction cannot stand.

Counts IV and V charged conspiracy to commit aggravated arson and the aggravated arson of the Chestnut Street residence in much the same manner as Counts I and II were drafted. These counts were based upon the premise that Marysville Mutual had an interest in the property, which the evidence fails to establish. Defendant's conviction of the offenses charged in those counts must likewise be reversed.

Defendant was charged in Count VI and convicted of theft by deception of the $4,900 he received from the insurance company. We find no direct interrelation between that conviction and the errors which pervade the others. The evidence was sufficient to sustain this conviction.

For the reasons stated, the convictions of conspiracy to commit aggravated arson (Counts I and IV), aggravated arson (Counts II and V), and felony murder (Count III) are reversed. The conviction of theft by deception (Count VI) is affirmed.

 ANALYSIS PROBLEM

8–1.   What should be done to prevent results such as those reached in the *Houck* case? In the second paragraph of the *Houck* opinion, the court mentions that Albert Hughes was a tenant and in the house when it was burned. Is this important to the charges? Why or why not? Why is the court not allowed to convict on a charge not brought before it by the prosecutor?

2.   Items Needed for Intake

For intake you need a statute excerpt listing the specific crimes and penalties for your jurisdiction. This excerpt allows you to pinpoint quickly the pertinent crime and assess whether the complainant has described facts that support each element of that crime. Most prosecution offices have these statutory excerpts. If the case is serious, it is better to use an updated, fully annotated set of the criminal code. A review of the annotations pertinent to each element of the crime being considered may prevent a mischarging, such as occurred in *Houck,* or similar problems.

You also need a copy of a good standardized intake form. If your office does not have one, you should create your own, similar to the one in Exhibit 8–1, page 281. Obtain the other standardized forms that you need; these usually include criminal complaints, summonses, and arrest warrants. Examples of these forms are presented in Exhibits 8–2, 8–3, and 8–4a and b, pages 282 through 288.

3.   Interview Setting

The surroundings for a complainant interview should be as comfortable as possible. Ideally, you will have your own office where you can conduct the interview one-on-one. Privacy helps convey a professionalism that instills confidence in the complainant and reduces the anxiety and intimidation that many people feel in such circumstances. Divert your phone calls to the receptionist, along with other interruptions, in order to avoid delays and give the complainant the sense of importance that is needed.

If the complainant has a particularly sensitive crime to report, such as sexual assault, child abuse, or marital rape, it may be best if the intake paralegal is of the same sex as the victim. If possible, immediate referral to the special sexual assault response team of the law enforcement agency may be the best procedure for all concerned. Police will then come back to swear out the complaint. Interviews with young children require caution and great skill. Numerous child sexual assault cases have been overturned because of improper questioning. Interviews with young children should be conducted by highly experienced individuals and should be videotaped. In most jurisdictions, matters concerning alleged criminal conduct by juveniles are referred to the juvenile authorities.

C.   The Interview

The following is an example of what might happen in an intake interview.

> *Secretary: Ms. Cordoba, our paralegal will see you now.*
> *Ms. Cordoba: Thank you.*
> *Paralegal: Please come in Ms. Cordoba and be seated. How can I help you?*
> *Ms. Cordoba: I want to know if you can get my ring back for me.*
> *Paralegal: What kind of ring?*
> *Ms. Cordoba: A diamond ring, an old one.*
> *Paralegal: What happened to your ring, Ms. Cordoba?*
> *Ms. Cordoba: Well, it all started back about five years ago when . . .*
> *Paralegal: Excuse me for interrupting, Ms. Cordoba, but what crime do you think is involved here?*

This abrupt interruption may lack tact, but it is practical and cuts to the chase.

> *Ms. Cordoba: Well, ah . . . stealing? He stole my diamond ring.*
> *Paralegal: Where did this occur?*
> *Ms. Cordoba: At my apartment.*
> *Paralegal: Is that in Legalville?*
> *Ms. Cordoba: Yes.*
> *Paralegal: What is the value of the ring?*
> *Ms. Cordoba: $10,000. We had it appraised about a year ago.*

These questions confirm the court's jurisdiction early in the interview. If the crime occurred outside the jurisdiction, the person may need to be referred to the prosecutor's office in the proper jurisdiction. The questions also establish the value of the item, which determines whether the theft is a felony.

Paralegal: Who took your ring?

Ms. Cordoba: Well, my husband, I mean ex-husband . . . actually, we are not divorced yet, and the way money is tight now I don't expect that we will get divorced for some time. We haven't lived together for about four months.

Paralegal: How did you get the ring?

Ms. Cordoba: From my husband—he gave it to me on our first anniversary.

Paralegal: When was it taken?

Ms. Cordoba: About three weeks ago. He took it from my apartment when I was gone.

Paralegal: Have you tried to get your ring back?

Ms. Cordoba: Yes, I've tried everything.

Paralegal: Well, the only means by which this office can try to get your ring back is to charge your husband with theft and bring him to court where he might get some jail time, a fine, or possibly prison time. It could be quite serious. Is that what you want to do?

Ms. Cordoba: I told him I was going to go to the police and he just laughed at me. He's left me with no choice.

Paralegal: What are the chances you two will get back together?

Ms. Cordoba: No chance. We've despised each other for three years. It's over.

Note that the paralegal has asked enough preliminary questions to determine whether this matter is appropriate for the criminal courts to pursue. It frequently falls to a paralegal to suggest alternatives to a criminal action. Criminal charges should be filed as a last resort and when it appears there is no reasonable alternative. For example, is there a mediation service for such disputes? Is there a mutually respected relative, clergy member, or other third party who could help resolve the conflict?

Recognizing that this is an unusual case, but also that Ms. Cordoba is not likely to be able to seek immediate assistance through the civil courts, the paralegal decides to go ahead. As in all cases, the ultimate decision on whether to file the charge will be made by the prosecuting attorney.

Paralegal: Okay, Ms. Cordoba, I need to record some information.

At this point the paralegal works through the intake questionnaire, recording the date of the interview and the complainant's name, address, phone number, social security number, and date of birth. The paralegal obtains several addresses and phone numbers for both the complainant and the defendant because people frequently move.[1] The paralegal records parents' names, addresses, and phone numbers, an emergency phone number, and employment phone number for both the complainant and the accused, as well as the date and approximate time of the alleged crime. Note: As a paralegal, you should develop the habit of referring to such incidents as "alleged," because doing so raises consciousness levels of the presumption of innocence.

Next, the paralegal looks up the appropriate statute in the code book, taking special note of each of the elements of the crime. The Columbia statute for theft is as follows.

COLUMBIA CRIMINAL CODE § 809.00

Any person who unlawfully takes the property of another with intent to deprive that person of its possession is guilty of theft.

a) If the property is valued at $500 or more the crime is a class D felony punishable by up to five years in prison and/or a $10,000 fine.

b) If the property is valued at less than $500 the crime is a class A misdemeanor punishable by up to six months in jail and/or a $500 fine.

The paralegal should inquire further to ensure that there are sufficient facts to support each element of the crime. A common method of covering the facts is to use the **six Ws;** Who? When? What? Why? Where? and How? These questions are generally incorporated into the intake questionnaire.

six Ws:
interview questions: Who? When? What? Why? Where? and How?

> *Paralegal: Ms. Cordoba, when did this happen?*
> *Ms. Cordoba: Easter Sunday—April 7, _____ . I had gone to visit my parents. Miguel came to my place and took some of his things—that was okay. But when I returned, the ring was gone.*
> *Paralegal: How do you know your husband took it?*
> *Ms. Cordoba: I called him and he admitted it. When I told him to give it back he just laughed and said no. He continued to refuse to give it up and, worse yet, his bimbo is wearing it!*

Ask questions to explore the possibility of other crimes, in this case, burglary.

> *Paralegal: Did he have your permission to enter your apartment?*
> *Ms. Cordoba: Yes, I told him to get the rest of his tools and some odds and ends and the rest of his clothes out of my place while I was gone. I'd been wanting him to do that for some time.*
> *Paralegal: Did he have permission to take the ring, or did you know he was going to take it?*
> *Ms. Cordoba: Of course not. It was mine.*
> *Paralegal: Did this occur at the address you have given me?*
> *Ms. Cordoba: Yes, it did.*
> *Paralegal: Was your ring given to you as a gift by your husband?*
> *Ms. Cordoba: Yes—it was his aunt's, a family heirloom. Will that make a difference?*
> *Paralegal: I'm not sure, Ms. Cordoba, and as a paralegal and not an attorney, ethical constraints prevent me from giving you an opinion. This will be taken under consideration by the prosecuting attorney and the court.*

Anticipating the need of a reasonably precise description of the ring for both a search warrant and the complaint, the paralegal will acquire such a description of the ring.

> *Ms. Cordoba: The ring is a wide gold band with a large diamond in a raised mounting at the center. Two smaller rubies are on each side, with tiny diamonds and rubies circling the larger stones. There are two small letters engraved on the inside of the band, an "A" and an "R."*
> *Paralegal: How much did you say the ring was worth?*
> *Ms. Cordoba: When I took it to the jeweler about a year ago to have the mountings checked, she said it was probably worth at least $10,000.*
> *Paralegal: Can we locate the ring at the address you gave me for your husband?*
> *Ms. Cordoba: Yes, but on the right hand of his girlfriend. They're living together.*
> *Paralegal: And what is her name?*

After all the information has been gathered that is needed to pursue filing a charge, the paralegal will explain to the complainant what will happen next and affirm, in light of that, whether he or she still wants to proceed.

> *Paralegal: Ms. Cordoba, I'll draft a complaint. In a few minutes it will be typed and will need your signature. Before I proceed, however, you should know what to expect from here. The prosecuting attorney will determine for sure whether the charge should go forward. If he rejects it, I will contact you in a day or so. Otherwise, it will be filed. The ring will be found, if possible, and your husband will be arrested or, at least, notified to appear in court. There will normally be one or more court hearings at which you will need to state what you have told me. If the case goes to trial and if your husband is convicted, he will be sentenced. Subject to any appeal, the ring will be returned to you at that time. This can take anywhere from three months to a year to resolve. Considering that your husband could go to jail or prison, are you sure you want to go ahead?*

Ms. Cordoba: Yes . . . I love that ring. It represents to me everything that did work about our marriage . . . everything that I put into the marriage. My husband stole it. He must pay the consequences.

Paralegal: I understand. Once the charges are filed, it is not necessarily easy to drop the charges. If you think there is any chance you will want to drop the charges later, it would be better not to file them now.

Ms. Cordoba: I want to go ahead.

Paralegal: Let me prepare the complaint for you to read and sign.

Prosecution offices become quite hectic, especially on Mondays following a weekend of alcohol abuse, partying, domestic problems, and a host of other possibilities. Therefore, the intake interview must be adequate but brief with as much compassion for the victim as time and reason allow. Many interviews, such as the one just given as an example, last less than fifteen minutes. More complex or sensitive cases may take an hour or more. Knowing how much time to take and what to ask, and determining how serious and delicate a matter is, comes with experience and preparation.

"Facts do not cease to exist because they are ignored."

—Aldous Huxley, 1894–1963, *A Note on Dogma*

D.   COUNSELING THE VICTIM

You will soon realize that there is more to your job than Joe Friday's "just the facts, ma'am, just the facts." The people you will be dealing with have suffered varying degrees of injury, pain, emotional trauma, fear, and anger. Part of your job is to assess quickly whether the person before you would benefit from community services. The person may need a doctor, a social worker, a spouse abuse center, or other services. Showing you care can help defuse anger and develop a bond to the office that can lead to greater cooperation on the case in days to come. More importantly, caring and acting on that caring will direct people to professionals who deal with such problems on a regular basis and who may have the resources to help people put their lives back together.

"The law is not a series of calculating machines where definitions and answers come tumbling out when the right levers are pushed."

—William O. Douglas "The Dissent, A Safeguard of Democracy," 32 *Journal of the American Judicial Society* 105 (1948)

Exhibit 8–5 page 289, at the end of this chapter, is an excerpt from a brochure on surviving sexual assault. It is the kind of resource material that can help you help the victim of a crime.

As a paralegal, you should take the time to be informed about the variety of services available in your community. Make a list of these services and a brief description of each. Include the names of contact persons. Copy the list as a resource for the people you serve.

Further inform the complainant of his or her rights under any victim compensation and rights program in your jurisdiction. Many states now compensate needy victims for physical or psychological injuries stemming from state or federal crimes. Provide the proper filing forms with adequate instructions to the victim. Inform the victim of the eligibility requirements and, possibly, some common reasons claims are denied: too high an income, inadequate or inaccurate information, lack of notification of change of address, failure to cooperate with police in prosecution, property loss only, or compensation available through other sources, to name a few.[2] If office resources permit, provide assistance in completing and filing the form. Exhibit 8–6 on page 291 is a copy of a victim impact statement. This may be referred to during any plea negotiations or at the time of sentencing. Exhibit 8–7, page 293, is a sample of a crime victim's claim form. It is representative of similar forms and defines who is eligible for compensation and under what circumstances. Some states and the federal government also provide victim and witness protection programs. Paralegals may be assigned to gather the relevant information and process the necessary forms. A list of Web site resources for assisting victims is included at the end of the chapter. Most state attorney general offices have victim assistance divisions.

ANALYSIS PROBLEM

8–2. A citizen comes in and wishes to press charges against a neighbor for threatening to kill her dog. Or a divorced woman wants to press kidnapping charges against her ex-mother-in-law for keeping the woman's son an extra day of visitation. Or someone wants to prosecute a neighbor for public drunkenness. How would you handle these situations once the prosecutor said "no way"?

III. DECISION TO CHARGE

A. AUTHORITY, LIMITS, AND IMMUNITY FROM CIVIL SUIT

Prosecutors are members of the executive branch of government and derive their authority from that branch's duty to execute the law. In that capacity, the prosecutor decides if charges should be brought and what those charges should be. Limits exist, however, on that decision. The prosecutor has the ethical duty to seek justice, protect the innocent, avoid charging for personal or political reasons, refrain from charging where evidence is insufficient, forego seeking charges greater in number or degree than evidence will support, and seek a fair penalty (ABA Standards for Criminal Justice and ABA Model Rules of Professional Conduct). When prosecutors neglect or refuse to bring warranted charges, they may be forced to do so by court order (mandamus) or by the order of a superior such as the attorney general.

Further limitations stem from constitutional concerns and center on discriminatory and vindictive prosecution. In cases where the discrimination is based on race, religion, ethnic origin, sex, age, and other traditional and obvious areas of discrimination, the courts find such prosecutions devoid of equal protection. *Yick Wo v. Hopkins* (1886) struck down the prosecution of persons for having laundry businesses in wooden as opposed to brick buildings, because only Chinese violators were prosecuted. A defendant claiming violation of equal protection, however, must establish actual and purposeful discrimination. In *Oyler v. Boles* (1962) the defendant failed to prove purposeful discrimination in his being charged as an habitual offender when five other defendants who could have been so charged were not.

More recently, five African Americans accused the government of selective prosecution by singling out the defendants, and African Americans in general, for crack cocaine violations, which have considerably higher penalties than those for powder cocaine. In finding for the government, an eight to one Supreme Court decision said that considerable deference must be given by the courts to the functions of the executive branch of government and, therefore, defendants claiming selective prosecution have a demanding burden of proof. The court said the defendants must demonstrate that the prosecutorial policy "had a discriminatory effect and was motivated by a discriminatory purpose." To establish a discriminatory effect, said the court, "the claimant must show that similarly situated individuals of a different race were not prosecuted." Despite evidence that nearly 95 percent of crack prosecutions were against African American defendants, the court found that the defendants failed to meet the burden of proof. [*U.S. v. Armstrong* (1996)].

The burden becomes more difficult when the group in question is not one of those traditionally discriminated against. The defendant in *Wayte v. U.S.* (1985) was charged with failing to register for the draft. The defense claimed that of the many violators of the law, the only ones charged were those who had protested the draft registration law by reporting their own failure to comply. The decision rejecting that claim cited the need for such "passive enforcement" to apply prosecutorial resources where they would do the most good with the least amount of effort and expense. The court found no evidence of a discriminatory purpose, and conceded that the prosecution's "broad discretion" as to whom to prosecute rests largely on the recognition that the decision to prosecute is particularly ill-suited to judicial review. This gives the defense a heavy burden of proof in nontraditional equal protection claims.

Prosecutors are also prohibited by due process considerations from vindictively increasing charges or otherwise penalizing defendants for exercising their constitutional and procedural rights. A prosecutor's attempt to raise a misdemeanor charge to a felony because a defendant exercised the right to a trial de novo (new trial) was held to be a violation of due process [*Blackledge v. Perry* (1974)]. When a court perceives that the state raises its original charge but does so in the context of plea bargaining, it generally will not find a vindictive motive. In *Bordenkircher v. Hayes* (1978), the prosecutor offered a five-year sentence if the defendant would plead, but if not, he would go to the grand jury for an indictment on an added habitual criminal charge. When the defendant refused the plea bargain and the prosecutor successfully pushed for a life sentence, the Court said this was not vindictive prosecution.

Problems akin to vindictive prosecution arise in the context of release-dismissal agreements, in which the prosecutor agrees to dismiss charges in return for the defendant's agreement not to bring a civil suit against the government (usually against the police). Although such agreements have been upheld as within the scope of prosecutorial authority [*Town of Newton v. Rumery* (1987)], it has been held to be beyond prosecutorial authority to try to protect police by adding extra charges after an accused refused to sign a release-dismissal agreement [*MacDonald v. Musick* (9th Cir. 1970).

A state statute that made it mandatory for a prosecutor to add an habitual criminal charge if a defendant had three or more felonies was held to be an unconstitutional violation of prosecutorial (executive) discretion [*State v. Pettit* (Wash. 1980)].

In *U.S. v. Goodwin* (1982) a substitute prosecutor was allowed to raise a previously filed misdemeanor to felony charges when the defendant requested a jury trial. A defendant must show "actual retaliatory motive" when the raising of the charges is equally as likely to be because of different views of different prosecutors, new evidence, or other legitimate reasons.

Once a prosecutor makes a promise to a defendant, the courts may hold the promise a binding "pledge of public faith." Thus, plea agreements are binding [*Santabello v. N.Y.* (1971)], and a promise to dismiss a charge if the accused passed a lie detector test was held binding in *People v. Reagan* (Mich. 1975). Any attempt by the prosecutor to renege may result in a reversal of the subsequent conviction.

A delay between the alleged criminal act and the actual filing of the charges may be an important factor. It can be a violation of due process if the defendant can show that the state had adequate evidence to commence the prosecution and the delay prejudiced the defendant's case. Further, it must be shown that the reasons for delay are so unjustified as to deviate from "fundamental conceptions of justice" [*U.S. v. Lovasco* (1977)].

Prosecutors could be excellent targets for lawsuits because of the tremendous discretion they exercise. They are immune, however, from civil suits for malicious prosecution and for deprivation of civil rights as long as they act within the scope of their office [*Imbler v. Pachtman* (1976)].

B. JOINDER OF OFFENSES AND DEFENDANTS

Your research and eventual experience may assist the prosecutor in deciding whether to join offenses and defendants in the charging document. Most state rules and the federal rules permit more than one charge (or count) to be filed per defendant and more than one defendant to be charged with an offense [Fed. R. Crim. P. 8(a) and (b)]. In such cases the offenses and the defendants may be joined for trial. Offenses may be joined if they are (1) the same or similar or (2) based on two or more connected acts or constituting parts of a common scheme or plan [Rule 8(a)]. Defendants may be joined "if . . . alleged to have participated in the same act or transaction or in the same series of acts or transactions constituting an offense or offenses" [Rule 8(b)]. Ordinarily this pleases both taxpayers and judges, because all the outstanding matters can be resolved before one jury and at one time, which is more efficient than holding separate trials.

The decision to join charges or defendants requires caution, however, because of possible constitutional concerns. Charges may not be joined if they result in prejudice to the defendant or the government (Fed. R. Crim. P. 14 and similar state rules). Prejudice from joinder may result for the following reasons [*Drew v. U.S.* (D.C. Cir. 1964)].

1. The defendant may need to present conflicting or inconsistent defenses to each separate charge or forego a defense on one charge because it is inconsistent.
2. Because evidence will be presented on two or more charges, the jury may think the defendant is a hard core criminal and convict accordingly.
3. The jury may convict on the basis of the cumulative evidence, and not the particular evidence that bears on each distinct charge.

Prejudice and confusion are more likely when two or more similar charges are joined, such as two or three separate robberies. It is easier for most juries to completely separate the evidence when there is joinder of offenses in one unified sequence of crime, such as terroristic threatening followed by battery followed by resisting arrest.

Double jeopardy and collateral estoppel trap the prosecution team that fails to weigh adequately the need to join charges having substantially overlapping elements and facts. Any participation on your part in drawing up charging documents or facilitating the exchange of charging information between a misdemeanor prosecutorial division and a felony prosecutorial division needs to be done with caution and more detailed knowledge of double jeopardy than this text permits. Chapter 7 summarizes some basic principles that will help you recognize danger areas. One of these pitfalls is illustrated by the *Grady v. Corbin* (1990) ruling that barred prosecution for vehicular homicide because the defendant pled guilty to a DUI charge. In such cases it is absolutely imperative for state prosecutorial teams to coordinate their charging procedures with the traffic division of local law enforcement agencies.[3]

A prosecutor may join defendants on a charging document and for trial when it is alleged that they participated in the same criminal act or transaction or a series of acts or transactions [Rule 8(b)]. This decision is subject to any Rule 14 concerns about prejudice. The burden of proving any prejudice rests on the defense, who must file a motion to sever the trials. Such a motion was granted for the two defendants in the Oklahoma bombing case, resulting in separate trials. Severance is necessary when the statement or confession of one defendant has incriminating references to the other defendant and the first defendant refuses to testify. Without severance, the second defendant is denied the Sixth Amendment right to confrontation, including cross-examination to test the truth and accuracy of the matter in the statement. A judicial instruction to the jury not to consider such evidence against the second defendant is inadequate for removing the likely prejudice [*Bruton v. U.S.* (1968)]. The prosecution may join the defendants if it agrees to delete those portions of any of the defendants' statements that refer to another defendant. This process is called redaction. Other evidentiary linkages in the first defendant's statement that raise inferences of a codefendant's guilt do not have to be deleted and can be addressed by cautionary instructions to the jury [*Richardson v. Marsh* (1987)]. Simply redacting every reference in a codefendant's confession to the name of the other defendant, submitting instead "delete" or "deletion," was inadequate, even with a cautionary instruction to the jury [*Gray v. Maryland* (1998)].

Bruton does not apply to any codefendant's statement made in the course of and in furtherance of a conspiracy [*Dutton v. Evans* (1970)]. Misjoinder will not automatically bring a reversal of conviction on appeal if prejudice is found to be minimal or harmless error [*U.S. v. Lane* (1986)].

IV. DRAFTING THE COMPLAINT

A. DRAFTING FROM THE INTAKE FORM

Once the prosecutor has made the decision regarding what charges are to be made and the number of charges and defendants, you are ready to draft the complaint. The criminal **complaint** officially starts the prosecution, provides a basis for arrest or notifies the accused to come to court, and informs the accused of the specific crime charged. Drafting the complaint is not difficult, but it is critical to the prosecution of the case. Careful drafting is essential. The intake sheet has been designed to provide necessary information for the complaint: the court, plaintiff (the people, state, commonwealth, United States, and so on), defendant, where the crime occurred (jurisdiction), when it occurred, identification of the accuser, the statute and penalty, and the date the complaint is signed. Stating the grounds for the complaint is more involved and requires some drafting precision.

> **complaint:**
> the document that officially starts the prosecution, provides a basis for arrest or notifies the accused to come to court, and informs the accused of the specific crime charged.

Using the standardized complaint form as a guide, add the elements of the crime and necessary supporting facts. The following is an example of how to draft this portion of the complaint in the *Cordoba* case.

> *EXAMPLE I*
> **The affiant,** <u>Carmen Cordoba</u>, **says that on the** <u>7th</u> **day of** <u>April,</u> _____ , **in** <u>Capitol</u> **County,** <u>Columbia</u>, **the above-named defendant unlawfully** <u>took the diamond and ruby ring belonging to the affiant valued at more than $500 with intent to deprive the affiant of its possession</u>. **This was done against the peace and dignity of the State of Columbia to wit:** <u>Theft in violation of C.R.S. 809.00 (a Class D felony)</u>.

Some jurisdictions require the statement of the maximum penalty as follows:

> <u>C.R.S. 809.00</u> **(a Class** <u>D</u> **felony) is punishable by** <u>up to five years in prison, a $10,000 fine, or both</u>.

The federal courts and some state courts require additional facts about the crime that give the defendant more notice regarding the reason for the charge and that better comply with the requirement that the criminal complaint state probable cause to believe that a crime was committed and that the defendant committed the crime. The general rule in such jurisdictions is that the restatement of the statutory language is not sufficient; facts must be alleged to support *each* element of the crime. Following the structure of the complaint used in the federal district courts and some states, a properly drafted complaint appears in Example II.

> *EXAMPLE II (ADDITIONAL FACTS)*
> **I, the undersigned complainant, being duly sworn, state the following is true and correct to the best of my knowledge and belief. On or about** <u>April 7,</u> _____ , **in** <u>Capitol</u> **County, in the state of** <u>Columbia</u>, **defendant(s) did** <u>take the diamond and ruby ring valued at more than $500 belonging to the complainant with intent to deprive the complainant of its possession</u> _____ **in violation of** <u>C.R.S. (or U.S. Code title)</u> **section** <u>809.00</u>.
>
> **I further state that this complaint is based on the following facts:** <u>that the defendant gave said ring to complainant on the date of their first anniversary, that on April 7,</u> _____ , <u>at which time defendant was separated from complainant, defendant took said</u>

ring from complainant's jewelry box and carried it away. Defendant admitted taking the ring and has refused to return it. The ring is made of gold, diamonds, and rubies and is worth more than $500.

The allegation in the complaint, and that in the indictment later, states what must be proved at trial, so draft the complaint with proof in mind. For example, note that the allegation in the sample complaints states that the ring is worth more than $500, the minimum value to comply with the statute. This statement avoids embarrassment for the prosecutor if it is impossible to prove that the ring is worth $10,000, or amendment of the document to conform with what is proved, which might not be allowed in some circumstances. Therefore, draft the complaint to describe the offense adequately, but so as not to lock the prosecutor into unprovable details. The rule of thumb is to allege enough information to support each element of the crime while keeping the details to a minimum.

In complex cases, take special care to name parties and charges accurately. Overlapping conspiracies and shared liabilities are particularly problematic. It is standard policy to run a records check on a prospective defendant. If the check reveals that the defendant has previous convictions, you may need to add a paragraph to the complaint including the relevant statute and penalties for the defendant who is a repeat offender. The check may also reveal aliases or potential danger to police officers serving a warrant, and it may be helpful at the defendant's first appearance before the judge for bail determination.

These drafting guidelines also apply to drafting an indictment or information, to be discussed later. An example of a completed multiple count criminal complaint is given in Exhibit 8–8, page 301.

When you have completed the draft of the complaint, have the secretary type your language onto the form. Then have the complainant (affiant) read the document for accuracy and sign it. If the prosecutor decides not to file the complaint, explain the reasons to the complainant. As previously discussed, prosecutors have an obligation to screen out inappropriate or unprovable charges. A citizen complainant may become upset when a complaint is rejected. How well you explain the reasons for the rejection or suggest alternative methods or resources for dealing with the matter is often the key to having an understanding citizen, as opposed to an irate one, leave the office.

B. DRAFTING FROM THE POLICE REPORT

Most frequently the complainant is a police officer. The officer should give you a copy of the written report reflecting the results of the police investigation. You will be able to draft the complaint based on the information in the report, with some occasional clarification from the officer. The officer needs to sign the complaint. Police officers generally simplify intake because they understand the process and criminal law better than the average citizen does. Getting to the point is easier. Police officers may be more resistant to being told that the charge lacks supporting evidence or that the prosecuting attorney has decided not to charge, however.

A standardized crime report is presented in Exhibit 8–9, page 302.

Once again, whether the complainant is a victim or a police officer, make sure he or she signs the complaint. This signature is vital, because the allegation in the complaint is supported on the face of the complaint by the oath of the complainant. Sound procedure requires that the complainant be sworn by a notary public, usually the paralegal or a secretary in the office. The process requires the complainant to raise his or her right hand and swear that the information in the complaint is true and correct based on information and belief. Some officers become lax in executing this procedure, making the complaint subject to attack and the prosecutor's office subject to embarrassment and ethical concerns. The correct procedure also impresses on the complainant the seriousness of the situation, which may prevent the filing of false or unsustainable charges.

After you have taken all these charging factors into consideration, and have drafted the complaint and had it reviewed and signed by the supervising attorney, then you need to file the complaint with the clerk of the appropriate court. Make copies available to the defendant. Following is a checklist for intake (prosecution).

CHECKLIST FOR INTAKE (PROSECUTION)

❑ Materials needed
- Criminal statutes (annotated)
- Intake form
- Standard complaint, summons, arrest warrant (commitment)
- Samples of completed forms (if needed)
- List of victim support services
- Victim compensation forms

❑ Setting
- Maintain privacy
- Arrange for as few interruptions as possible
- Consider comfort of complainant
- Be prepared to refer cases to juvenile authorities, sexual assault response team, and so on

❑ Interview
- Follow intake form (who, what, when, where, why, how)
- Review most applicable statutes
- Record facts in support of each element of the crime
- Determine if the accusation is likely to be sustainable based on the evidence and if it is appropriate for criminal process; consult attorney; if rejected, explain and suggest alternatives
- Obtain alternative addresses and phone numbers for complainant, accused, and witnesses
- Record address of crime scene for jurisdiction
- Record complete description of all items in question, evidence, accused, and so on

❑ Counseling
- Explain court process and possible demands on complainant
- Verify complainant's commitment to prosecution
- Discuss victim resources; provide victim with resource list
- Victim impact statement

❑ Drafting
- Draft the complaint; have it typed
- Have complainant read and confirm the accuracy of the complaint
- Administer the oath and have the complainant sign the complaint
- Date and notarize the complaint

❑ Consult the prosecuting attorney to determine whether there are any questions about filing the charge

V. THE SUMMONS AND WARRANT

A. SUMMONS

summons, criminal:
a document that, when signed by the clerk of court and served on the defendant, requires the defendant to appear before the stated court at the prescribed date and time.

If you or your supervising attorney determine that the offense is relatively minor and the defendant is likely to appear in court, draft a criminal summons. A **criminal summons** is a document that, when signed by the clerk of court and served on the defendant, requires the defendant to appear before the stated court at the prescribed date and time. The drafted summons accompanies the signed complaint for approval by the prosecuting attorney. Once approved, copies are made for the office file. The original complaint and summons are filed with the clerk of the appropriate court. Copies of the summons and complaint are sent to the police for personal service on the defendant or, in some cases, may be mailed. If delivered by personal service, the officer verifies service on the "Return of Service" portion of the summons. See Exhibit 8–3, page 284.

B. ARREST WARRANT

arrest warrant:
a document that, when signed by a judge or magistrate, authorizes the police to seek and place the defendant in custody.

If the defendant was not arrested and the charge is serious, or whenever there is a likelihood that the defendant might flee, draft a warrant for the defendant's arrest. An **arrest warrant,** when signed by a judge or magistrate, authorizes the police to seek and place the defendant in custody. Because the warrant is a serious invasion of individual liberty, use it only when necessary. The document must adequately describe the defendant. Chapter 9 provides more information on what must be alleged to produce a constitutionally valid arrest warrant. An example of a completed arrest warrant, adapted from the federal form [Exhibit 8–4(a)], page 286, is shown in Exhibit 8–10, page 304.

In some jurisdictions the arrest warrant is sufficient authorization to continue to hold a previously arrested suspect. In other jurisdictions a commitment form or other similar form must be drafted, approved by the prosecutor, and signed by the judge or magistrate.

Whether you are drafting an arrest warrant or a commitment form, check the practice in your jurisdiction to determine how detailed the language describing the offense and the defendant needs to be. In some jurisdictions including most federal jurisdictions, a brief restatement of the offense plus a sound description of the defendant (full name and address, if available) are usually adequate. In other jurisdictions a detailed probable cause statement, showing that a crime was committed and that it was this person (the defendant) that committed it, is required. If the latter is true in your jurisdiction, show facts in support of each element of the crime and give the court and the police enough information to identify the defendant adequately. To do less in such jurisdictions may subject the warrant, the arrest, and any evidence seized during the arrest, to attack.

The warrant should accompany the complaint. Once both are reviewed by the prosecuting attorney, file the complaint with the appropriate court clerk. Present a copy of the filed complaint with the arrest warrant to the judge for signature. The warrant will then be given to the police so they can lawfully make the arrest. If there is reason to suggest that the defendant may be armed or otherwise dangerous, it is important to attach a note to the warrant to that effect.

C. CHECKLIST FOR DRAFTING AND FILING THE SUMMONS AND WARRANT

Part of your job is to make your work and the work of others in the office efficient and error free. Standardized procedural checklists can be useful in that regard. Preparation of checklists can save you considerable time in the future, especially when stored in the appropriate place in your system folder. Use your experience to build on this drafting and filing checklist.

CHECKLIST FOR DRAFTING AND FILING THE SUMMONS AND WARRANT

❑ Draft Documents
- Inform and counsel complainant if the charge is rejected. Record reasons on intake form and keep in appropriate folder.
- Draft summons if arrest deemed unnecessary.
- Draft arrest warrant if deemed necessary.
- Draft commitment if required by jurisdiction to keep defendant in jail.
- Check practice in your jurisdiction for needed detail in documents.
- Have documents typed.

❑ File Documents
- Proofread all documents.
- Submit all documents to supervising attorney.
- If rejected, inform complainant.
- Have photocopies made of all documents, place in office file.
- File complaint and summons with the clerk of court.
- Take the arrest warrant (with complaint) to the judge for signature.
- File signed warrant with clerk for service by police.
- Record case file number and place in office folder.

VI. DOCKET TRACKING

One of your assigned tasks may be docket control or tracking. Each court and branch of court publishes a criminal docket for each day. The **docket** sheet sets out the name of the case, the attorneys, the charge, and the nature of the appearance (initial appearance, motion hearing, trial, and so forth). In some jurisdictions the clerk of court divides the schedule into several dockets: one for motions; one for nontrial matters (no-issue dockets) for arraignments, pleas, and other hearings; and one for trials. Many of today's dockets are computerized and accessible from a number of locations.

Check the docket each day, noting the cases that involve your supervising attorney or attorneys. Notify each of the attorneys of any scheduled appearances and the nature of the appearance, and provide the case file for the attorney's review. Upon return of the files, check to see if the result of the appearance is noted, for example, "defendant pled not guilty, trial date June 6, _____ , at 9:00 A.M." If not, obtain results from either the attorney or the clerk of court. See to it that any key dates are calendared on the office master calendar, the attorney's calendar, and your calendar. In the case of trials and other matters requiring preparation time, work back from the due date and record preparation dates allowing for adequate time to complete the work. This type of "tickler" process should keep the attorneys and the paralegal aware of what needs to be done and when.

Further, victims of crimes appreciate being informed of the regular progress of the case. Because prosecution offices are so busy, attorneys rarely have the time to do this. By assuming the responsibility of keeping victims informed, you can perform a service that is truly appreciated and is good public relations for the prosecutor's office as well.

docket:
the court schedule for each day; sets out the name of the case, the attorneys, the charge, and the nature of the appearance.

VII. CONCLUSION

Here it begins. Your painstaking study pays off when your first complainant walks through the door. You can prepare for the interview with confidence because you are familiar with the necessary forms and have references to helpful resources at hand. You know how to focus interview questions to obtain the facts you need.

Because you have code books and a working knowledge of the elements of specific crimes, you can match facts and statutes for accurate charges. Problems that are inappropriate for the criminal justice system you channel elsewhere. People coming to you can count on compassionate, knowledgeable, and truthful assistance.

You will become familiar with local practice and gain expertise with experience in drafting complaints, summons, and warrants. The process of filing documents may seem a bit daunting now, but soon will be second nature to you. As you work in the criminal justice system, you will learn the rhythms of docket tracking and deadline control.

From the point of intake on, you are no longer performing an academic exercise, you are working to deliver justice. When the first complainant walks through your door, you will not need to be reminded how important your work is to that person.

EXHIBIT 8–1
Standardized Intake Form

STANDARDIZED INTAKE FORM

No. _____   Date _____

Complainant (affiant, police officer) | Defendant | Aliases

Address | D.O.B. Sex Race | Address | D.O.B. Sex Race

Phone | Alt. Phone | Phone | Alt. Phone

Alt. Address (work, parents, other) | Alt. Address (work, parents, other)

Other Defendants   Yes _____ No _____ List on reverse side

Description of Crime (include location)

Crime   Date   Time   Fel. _____ Mis. _____   Statute/Ordinance   Penalties

---

EXHIBIT 8–1 *(Concluded)*
Standardized Intake Form

Other Counts
(this offense)
a. _____
b. _____
c. _____
Place additional counts on reverse side

Defendant's Prior Convictions   Cases Pending
1.   3.   1.
2.   4.   2

Habitual Offender Count   Statute   Penalty
Yes _____ No _____

Victim If Other Than Complainant   Injuries (damages)

Address   D.O.B. Sex Race

Phone   Alt. Phone   Alt. Address   Hospital

Police Agency   Offense Report No.   Officer   Badge No.

Defendant(s) Arrested Yes_____ No_____ Date   Time   Contraband or Evidence Seized

Defendant(s) Statement

Witnesses (If felony, check only witnesses essential for preliminary hearing)
     Address   Phone   Alt. Address   Alt. Phone
1.
2.
3.

☐ Referred to Police for Further Investigation Date, _____
☐ Rejected by Intake Officer
☐ Approved by District Attorney   ☐ Complaint Filed Date, _____
☐ Rejected by District Attorney   ☐ Summons Issued
                                         ☐ Arrest Warrant
                                   Intake Officer _____

EXHIBIT 8–2(a)
Standardized Criminal Complaint: Federal

AO 91 (Rev. 5/85) Criminal Complaint ⊕

United States District Court

———————————————— DISTRICT OF ————————————————

UNITED STATES OF AMERICA
V.

CRIMINAL COMPLAINT

CASE NUMBER:

(Name and Address of Defendant)

I, the undersigned complainant being duly sworn state the following is true and correct to the best of my knowledge and belief. On or about ————————————— in ————————————— county, in the ————————————— District of ————————————— defendant(s) did, (Track Statutory Language of Offense)

in violation of Title ——————— United States Code, Section(s) —————————————————.

I further state that I am a(n) ——————————————— and that this complaint is based on the following
                                        Official Title
facts:

Continued on the attached sheet and made a part hereof: ☐ Yes   ☐ No

_____
Signature of Complainant

Sworn to before me and subscribed in my presence,

_____ at _____
Date   City and State

_____   _____
Name & Title of Judicial Officer   Signature of Judicial Officer

EXHIBIT 8–2(b)
Standardized Criminal Complaint: State

MCA-78-1		Case No. _____
Commonwealth of Kentucky Court of Justice	**CRIMINAL COMPLAINT**	MADISON DISTRICT COURT

MADISON DISTRICT COURT

Commonwealth of Kentucky
vs.

_____

_____

(Name and Address of Defendant, if Known)

The affiant, _____ says
that on the _____ day of _____, 20_____, in
Madison County, Kentucky, the above named defendant unlawfully _____
_____
_____
_____
_____
_____ . This criminal
act was done against the peace and dignity of the Commonwealth of Kentucky to wit:
_____ KRS_____

_____
Signature of Affiant

Sworn to before me this _____ day of _____ , 20 _____

Name and Address of Affiant

_____

_____

_____

Name and Address of Other Witnesses

_____

_____

_____

_____

_____

☐ Madison County Atty.   ☐ Asst. County Atty.
☐ Paralegal, Commonwealth of Kentucky
Notary at Large. My Commission Expires _____

FOR CLERK'S INFORMATION

Bond Set At
$ _____

☐ Felony	☐ Summons for
☐ Misdeameanor	☐ Warrant
☐ Violation	☐ In Custody

EXHIBIT 8–3
Standardized Summons

AO 83 (Rev. 12/85) Summons in a Criminal Case ⊕

United States District Court

DISTRICT OF _____

UNITED STATES OF AMERICA
V.

SUMMONS IN A CRIMINAL CASE

CASE NUMBER:

(Name and Address of Defendant)

YOU ARE HEREBY SUMMONED to appear before the United States District Court at the place, date and time set forth below.

Place	Room
	Date and Time

Before:

To answer a(n)
☐ Indictment   ☐ Information   ☐ Complaint   ☐ Violation Notice   ☐ Probation Violation Petition

Charging you with a violation of Title _____ United States Code, Section(s) _____

Brief description of offense:

_____   _____
Signature of Issuing Officer   Date

_____
Name and Title of Issuing Officer

EXHIBIT 8–3 *(Concluded)*
Standardized Summons

AO 83 (Rev. 12/85) Summons in a Criminal Case

RETURN OF SERVICE

Service was made by me on:[1] Date

Check one box below to indicate appropriate method of service

☐ Served personally upon the defendant at: _____
_____

☐ Left summons at the defendant's dwelling house or usual place of abode with a person of suitable age and discretion then residing therein and mailed a copy of the summons to the defendant's last known address. Name of person with whom the summons was left: _____
_____

☐ Returned unexecuted: _____
_____
_____
_____

I declare under penalty of perjury under the laws of the United States of America that the foregoing information contained in the Return of Service is true and correct.

Returned on _____
Date

Name of United States Marshal

(by) Deputy United States Marshal

Remarks:

1) As to who may serve a summons see Rule 4 of the Federal Rules of Criminal Procedure

EXHIBIT 8–4(a)
Standardized Arrest Warrant: Federal

AO 442 (Rev. 12/85) Warrant for Arrest

United States District Court

———————————————— DISTRICT OF ————————————————

UNITED STATES OF AMERICA
V.

WARRANT FOR ARREST

CASE NUMBER:

To: The United States Marshal
and any Authorized United States Officer

YOU ARE HEREBY COMMANDED to arrest _____
Name

and bring him or her forthwith to the nearest magistrate to answer a(n)

☐ Indictment ☐ Information ☐ Complaint ☐ Order of Court ☐ Violation Notice ☐ Probation Violation Petition

charging him or her with (brief description of offense)

in violation of Title _____ United States Code, Section(s)_____

_____   _____
Name of Issuing Officer   Title of Issuing Officer

_____   _____
Signature of Issuing Officer   Date and Location

Bail fixed at $ _____   by_____
                                                  Name of Judicial Officer

RETURN
This warrant was received and executed with the arrest of the above-named defendant at _____

DATE RECEIVED	NAME AND TITLE OF ARRESTING OFFICER	SIGNATURE OF ARRESTING OFFICER
DATE OF ARREST		

EXHIBIT 8–4(a) *(Concluded)*
Standardized Arrest Warrant: Federal

THE FOLLOWING IS FURNISHED FOR INFORMATION ONLY:

DEFENDANT'S NAME: _____

ALIAS: _____

LAST KNOWN RESIDENCE: _____

LAST KNOWN EMPLOYMENT: _____

PLACE OF BIRTH: _____

DATE OF BIRTH: _____

SOCIAL SECURITY NUMBER: _____

HEIGHT: _____ WEIGHT: _____

SEX: _____ RACE: _____

HAIR: _____ EYES: _____

SCARS, TATTOOS, OTHER DISTINGUISHING MARKS: _____

_____

_____

FBI NUMBER: _____

COMPLETE DESCRIPTION OF AUTO: _____

_____

INVESTIGATIVE AGENCY AND ADDRESS: _____

_____

_____

EXHIBIT 8–4(b)
Standardized Arrest Warrant: State

MCA-78-2

Commonwealth of Kentucky
Court of Justice

**WARRANT OF ARREST
(COMPLAINT)**

Case No._____

Madison District Court

(RCr 2.04, 2.06)

COMMONWEALTH OF KENTUCKY

vs.

_____

Open Court

Date _____

Time _____

By: _____

TO ALL PEACE OFFICERS IN THE COMMONWEALTH OF KENTUCKY:

You are hereby commanded to arrest _____
(Name of Defendant)

_____

_____

and bring him forthwith before the judge of the District Court of Madison County, Kentucky (or, if he be absent or unable to act, before the nearest available magistrate), to answer a complaint made by _____

charging him with the offense of _____

_____

−BOND−

The defendant may give bail in the amount of $ _____

Issued at Richmond, Madison County, Kentucky, this _____ day of

_____, 20___.

_____
Judge, Madison District Court

RETURN

Executed this warrant by arresting _____ this the _____ day of

_____, 20___.

_____

by: _____

EXHIBIT 8–5
Assault Counseling Brochure[4]

FROM SURVIVING AND HEALING FROM SEXUAL ASSAULT
This brochure is a start in the direction of gaining knowledge to assist you in the healing.

If you have been raped or sexually assaulted, you have experienced a frightening, life threatening trauma.

It is important to remember:

You are not to blame—The rapist is solely responsible for his actions.

Rape is a violent crime.

You have probably been threatened with death, mutilation, or violence.

Survival means you have done the right thing.

No one asks or deserves to be raped.

Think of yourself not as a victim, but as a survivor.

Reactions

People who are raped or sexually assaulted may have many of the following reactions. Remember, these are normal and in most cases will be temporary.

FEARS—possibly panic, anxiety, fear of being alone or in certain places or situations.

ANGER—possibly rage, irritability, alienation from family or friends.

DEPRESSION—may include crying, withdrawal, isolation, wanting to be alone.

PHYSICAL REACTIONS—nausea, headaches, changes in eating, sleeping, or menstrual cycle.

You may feel dirty, ashamed, guilty, humiliated, or responsible.

You may experience mood swings, behavior changes, inability to concentrate or relax.

These reactions may be more difficult to handle on holidays, the anniversary date of the assault, or with an event that reminds you of the rape.

Remember, you have experienced a loss and will be grieving that loss.

What To Do If You Are Raped or Sexually Assaulted

Remember you don't have to go through this alone.

Be honest with yourself about your feelings and thoughts.

Recognize your survival and try not to punish yourself with "If only . . ."

Talk to people you trust.

Take care of yourself—get rest, plan comforting activities, avoid excessive use of alcohol or drugs.

Ask for help if necessary from family, friends, police, doctors, counselors.

Be honest with those people to whom you turn.

If the pain becomes too great or you feel you are not adjusting well, you may want to seek professional help.

Healing takes time.

FROM THE AFTERMATH OF RAPE

Police

It is your decision whether or not to file a police report, even if law enforcement has already been notified of the crime. There are advantages and disadvantages to filing this report.

Advantages:

You establish the fact that a crime has been committed and you are exercising your rights.

The rapist may be found and prosecuted, preventing further perpetration.

You may be eligible for Crime Victim Compensation funds.

Disadvantages:

It may be difficult for you to retell your story numerous times, especially those details that are necessary for investigation.

Police have the responsibility to investigate and their style of questioning may not be the most sensitive.

Continued

4. Source: Joanne Weis, M.S.W., A.C.S.W., Director of Programs, The R.A.P.E. Relief Center, 226 West Breckinridge St., Louisville, KY 40203, (502) 581-7273, reprinted with permission.

EXHIBIT 8–5 *(Continued)*
Assault Counseling Brochure

If You Do Report:

You must be truthful in each statement that you make. If you don't remember something, or recall a different detail later, present it as just that.

You may find it helpful to write down the sequence of events before being interviewed. This may help with recall.

Remember that the law enforcement agent is a professional who is discussing very delicate information for the purpose of investigation.

Expect the police officer to treat you with the respect that he/she would offer any victim of a crime.

Get the name, serial or badge number, and business telephone number of any officer with whom you have contact.

Hospital

You are strongly encouraged to go to an emergency room immediately. Again, this is your choice, but there are advantages and disadvantages. Even if you decide against the emergency room, medical follow-up to a rape is always recommended.

Advantages:

You can be assessed for physical trauma or injury and treated for this.

Available evidence will be collected and maintained for prosecution if you decide to go to court.

You will be evaluated and treated for sexually transmitted diseases and pregnancy.

You can be referred for appropriate follow-up treatments.

Disadvantages:

You will be required to tell the details of the story, possibly before you feel ready to do this.

You will be examined in a manner that may be reminiscent of the rape and may be uncomfortable.

You will not be handled as a high-risk patient and may be required to wait.

If You Go to the Emergency Room:

Don't bathe, douche, or use mouth wash. If possible, avoid using bathroom facilities prior to the examination.

Go prepared to leave your clothing for evidence.

Be as specific as possible in response to the questions asked by the nurses and doctors.

Expect to be treated as a medical patient who is requiring a medical response to trauma.

Courts

If the perpetrator is apprehended, you still have the choice regarding cooperation with prosecution. You need to be aware that even if you choose to prosecute, the prosecutors, grand jury, or judge may feel the evidence is not strong enough to proceed.

Advantages:

Unless stopped, perpetrators of sexual assault will continue.

You are exercising your right to due process of the law.

The public record may bring forward other victims of the perpetrator.

Disadvantages:

You will be telling your story numerous times, some of them in public.

The defense attorney will use all strategies available within the law to prove the defendant is innocent beyond a reasonable doubt.

You may discover some of your support systems choosing the other side.

If You Decide to Prosecute:

Be completely honest in giving information that is requested.

Write down the details of the assault so that you will have a clear memory for the trial.

Prepare yourself to see the perpetrator.

Prepare yourself for delays.

EXHIBIT 8–5 *(Concluded)*
Assault Counseling Brochure

> *Prepare yourself to be questioned publicly, dressing and using cosmetics in a manner that will not bias the jury against you.*
>
> *Be prepared for the defendant to be found not guilty or guilty of a lesser crime. This does not mean people don't believe you were raped. It means that the evidence did not convince the courts beyond a reasonable doubt.*
>
> *Remember, you are not the one on trial and you neither asked for nor deserved to be raped.*
>
> *You have rights: to an interpreter if you are deaf or are not fluent in English, to closed hearings if you are a minor, to have an attorney present for all court transactions, to be informed of reports and proceedings, to all records that are public information, to be asked only questions relative to the case, and to information on the assailant's parole or release dates if he is convicted and sentenced.*
>
> *You have a right to sue the suspect in civil court.*

EXHIBIT 8–6
Victim Impact Statement[5]

VICTIM IMPACT STATEMENT

This statement is submitted to the probation officer responsible for preparing the presentence investigation report for inclusion in the report or to the court should such a report be waived by the defendant. The victim impact statement shall be considered by the court prior to any decision on the sentencing or release, including shock probation, of the defendant. (K.R.S. 421.520)

(If you need more space to explain any of your answers, please attach additional sheets.)

Defendant: _____ Indictment #: _____

Convicted of the Following Offenses: _____

County of Indictment: _____ Date of Conviction: _____ Sentencing Date _____

Victim(s) & Date of Birth: _____

_____

Prosecutor: _____

This form was completed by: _____

If not the victim, relationship to victim: _____

Date Submitted: _____

_____

This victim impact statement should be returned to _____

by _____ in order to give the judge sufficient time to review it prior to sentencing the defendant.

Continued

5. Madison/Clark County Victim Impact Statement, 25th Judicial Circuit, Madison and Clark Counties, Kentucky, 1993.

EXHIBIT 8–6 *(Continued)*
Victim Impact Statement

1. What emotional or psychological impact or remaining effects has the crime had on you, the victim, and/or other family members? _____
_____
_____ cont.

2. Since the crime occurred, have you or any family member received, or needed professional counseling or treatment? If yes, please explain and list all expenses to date and estimate additional expenses. _____
_____
_____ cont.

3. If the crime resulted in death or physical injury, please describe the cause of death or injuries. _____
_____
_____ cont.

4. If medical treatment was received, please describe. _____
_____
_____ cont.

5. Please list medical expenses that resulted from the crime. _____
_____
_____ cont.

6. If the crime resulted in a death, were you or any members of your family financially dependent on the deceased victim? If yes, please explain. _____
_____
_____ cont.

7. If the crime resulted in a death, are you or any family members responsible for the funeral expenses or debts of the deceased victim? If yes, please list expenses. _____
_____
_____ cont.

8. Was there any damage, loss, or destruction of property? If yes, please describe the items damaged or lost and their value. _____
_____
_____ cont.

9. Were any of the items recovered? If yes, please list what was recovered. _____
_____
_____ cont.

10. Has being a crime victim affected your employment or lifestyle? If yes, please explain. _____
_____
_____ cont.

11. Have any of the professional counseling or treatment expenses; medical expenses; funeral expenses; debts; or damage, loss, or destruction of property been reimbursed through insurance, the Crime Victim's Compensation Board, or any other means? If yes, please explain. _____
_____
_____ cont.

12. What is your recommendation for an appropriate sentence of the defendant? (Optional) _____
_____
_____ cont.

EXHIBIT 8–6 *(Concluded)*
Victim Impact Statement

13.   Additional Comments _____

_____

_____ cont.

Signed: _____   Date: _____

EXHIBIT 8–7
Crime Victim Claim Form[6]

CRIME VICTIMS COMPENSATION BOARD

800-469-212-   **115 Myrtle Avenue**   502-564-2290

FRANKFORT, KENTUCKY 40601

GENERAL INFORMATION AND INSTRUCTIONS ON HOW TO FILL OUT THIS CLAIM FORM

You must use black ink or type the information. If the crime occurred before July 15, 1998, you have one year to file the claim. If the crime occurred after July 15, 1998, you have five years to file the claim. You must fill out each section completely. If you do not, the claim will be returned to you which will delay the processing time. If you need assistance in filling out the claim, please call one of the numbers above.

SECTION I.   Information about the <u>victim only.</u>

SECTION II.   If someone other than the victim is filing for assistance, this section must be completed about this person.

SECTION III.   Information about the crime may either be filled out by the victim or the claimant. **You must attach a copy of the police report or criminal complaint taken out.**

SECTION IV.   Allows the victim or the claimant to tell us in your own words what happened. Who did what, when, where and why.

SECTION V.   List the injuries that the victim received as a result of the crime.

SECTION VI.   List all of the medical bills of the victim related to the crime. **Each bill that is listed must be attached to the claim form before you send it to us. If a bill is not listed but attached, it will not be considered. If a bill is listed, but not attached, it will not be considered. Each bill must be an itemized bill and show date of service. <u>NO PERSONAL BILLS OR NOTICES FROM COLLECTION AGENCIES WILL BE ACCEPTED. IF YOU ATTACH THESE TO YOUR CLAIM FORM, THE FORM WILL BE RETURNED TO YOU AS UNACCEPTED.</u>**

SECTION VII.   What other type of benefits was the victim receiving at the time of the crime or is now receiving as a result of the crime.

SECTION VIII. Was the victim employed at the time of the crime. **If the victim is asking for lost wages, attach the Employment Verification Form that was filled out by the <u>employer</u> and the Disability Certificate that was filled out by the <u>doctor.</u>** If the victim was self-employed, attach a copy of both state and federal tax returns along with the Disability Certificate. **If these items are not attached when you send in the claim form, lost wages will not be considered.**

SECTION IX.   This section must be filled out by the person who is filing the claim.

Continued

6. Commonwealth of Kentucky, Crime Victim Claim Form and Instruction, Crime Victims Compensation Board, Frankfort, Kentucky.

EXHIBIT 8–7 *(Continued)*
Crime Victim Claim Form

SECTION X.		Fill out only if the victim is deceased. **You must attach the funeral bill showing you are the legal responsible party and the death certificate.**
SECTION XI.		Fill out only if the victim was supporting you as the surviving spouse and/or had dependent children with the victim. **You must attach all documentation showing amounts and sources of income you are receiving as a result of the death of the victim.**
SECTION XII.		This area is for statistical information only that is supplied to the Federal Government.
SECTION XIII.		Fill out about any civil lawsuit you may file or have already filed and any restitution that was ordered to be paid to you by the court or any settlement you reached with the assailant.
SECTION XIV.		**Read this section completely. ONCE YOU HAVE READ THIS SECTION AND UNDERSTAND IT, SIGN YOUR NAME, DATE THE APPLICATION AND MAIL IT TO THIS OFFICE. IF YOU HAD AN ATTORNEY ASSIST YOU IN YOUR CLAIM, YOU MUST HAVE THE ATTORNEY SIGN IT ALSO.**

**COMMONWEALTH OF KENTUCKY
CRIME VICTIMS COMPENSATION BOARD
115 MYRTLE AVENUE
FRANKFORT, KENTUCKY 40601**

800-469-2120   502-564-2290

GENERAL INFORMATION

FOR OFFICE USE ONLY

CLAIM No. _____

Fill out this form completely and accurately as possible. All claims will be thoroughly investigated and verified. You must provide the documentation necessary for your type of claim. Mail your completed form and documentation to the above address.

INVESTIGATOR: _____

SECTION I. Victim Information

Victim's Name: _____ Soc. Sec. No. _____

Date of Birth: _____ Age: _____ ( ) Male   ( ) Female
          Mo.   Day   Year   At Time of Crime

Address: _____

City: _____ State: _____ Zip Code: _____

Telephone (home): ( ) _____ (work): ( ) _____

SECTION II. Claimant Information (if someone other than victim is filing claim please complete this section)

Your Name: _____ Relationship to Victim _____

Date of Birth: _____ Soc. Sec. No. _____
          Mo.   Day   Year

Address: _____

City: _____ State: _____ Zip Code: _____

Telephone (home): ( ) _____ (work): ( ) _____

EXHIBIT 8–7 *(Continued)*
Crime Victim Claim Form

SECTION III. Crime Information (you **must** attach a copy of the police report)

Check One   Location of Crime: _____

Assault	( )	

                                                  Address   City   County

Assault ( )
Murder ( )
Sexual Assault Adult ( )
Sexual Assault Child ( )
Child Physical Abuse ( )
Domestic Assault ( )
DUI ( )
Other ( )

Date of Crime: _____ Date Reported: _____
          Mo.   Day   Year   Mo.   Day   Year

Crime Reported To: _____
                              Law Enforcement Agency

Was the crime reported within 48 hours of its discovery: ( ) Yes ( ) No
If no, please explain why: _____

Name of Offender: _____ Has offender been charged with crime: ( ) Yes ( ) No

If yes, what charge: _____

What Court: District _____ Circuit: _____ Juvenile: _____
          Case Number   Case Number   Case Number

SECTION IV. Describe what happened. (If you know the reason for the crime, please tell us)

_____
_____
_____
_____
_____
_____
_____
_____
_____

SECTION V. Describe the injuries. _____

_____
_____
_____
_____
_____
_____
_____
_____
_____

Continued

EXHIBIT 8–7 *(Continued)*
Crime Victim Claim Form

SECTION VI. Medical Expenses (You **must** list every medical bill you have that is related to the crime. You **must** attach the medical bill you listed and it must show date of service and type of service. If a bill is not listed and attached, it **will not** be considered. **Notices from collections agencies will not be accepted.**

Hospital, Doctor, Ambulance, Dentists, Counselor, and all other related medical bills	Charge	Insurance Paid	Claimant/Victim Paid	Current Balance
1. Name				
2. Name				
3. Name				
4. Name				
5. Name				

(If you need additional space, please use separate sheet of paper)

SECTION VII. Other sources of payment. (You **must** attach documentation)

Was the victim, at the time of the crime, covered by: ( ) Medicaid ( ) Workers Comp. ( ) Medicare

( ) Health Insurance ( ) Veterans Benefits ( ) Homeowner's Ins. ( ) Auto. Insurance ( ) Other

SECTION VIII. Lost wages.

What was the victim's employment status at the time of the crime? ( ) Employed ( ) Unemployed

If employed, did the victim lose time from work as a result of the injury? ( ) Yes ( ) No

If yes, is the victim applying for lost wages? ( ) Yes ( ) No

If yes, the attached Employment Verification Form **must** be filled out by the **employer** and attached to this form before returning.

If yes, the attached Disability Certificate **must** be filled out by the **doctor** and attached to this form before returning.

If the victim was self-employed, a copy of both state and federal tax returns must be attached to this claim form and the attached Disability Certificate **must** be filled out by the **doctor** and attached to this form before returning.

SECTION IX. Financial Information (This information is about the person who is filing for assistance)

What is your total monthly income? _____ What do you pay out a month? _____

List **all** sources of income: (Include every source of income including spouse's income, food stamps, welfare, child support, Social Security, pensions, Workers Compensation benefits, veterans benefits, AFDC, or any other income. List monthly amounts below)

_____ _____ _____

_____ _____ _____

EXHIBIT 8–7 *(Continued)*
Crime Victim Claim Form

SECTION X. Funeral Expenses (This section is to be filled out if the victim is deceased)

Date of Death: _____ (You **must** attach a copy of the death certificate)
        Mo.   Day   Year

Were any benefits available from any of the following sources: (List any and all amounts received or to be received)

Life Insurance $ _____ Workers Compensation $ _____

Burial Insurance $ _____ Social Security $ _____

Other $ _____ (**This includes any money received from contributions or donations.**)

Name of Funeral Home: _____

Address: _____ Telephone No. _____
       Street   City   State   Zip

Amount of Funeral Expenses $ _____ Have they been paid? ( ) Yes   ( ) No

If yes, by whom: Name _____

Address: _____ Telephone No. _____
       Street   City   State   Zip

Relationship to victim: _____ (**You must attach the funeral bill showing you are the legal responsible party for the funeral expenses of the victim**)

SECTION XI. Loss of Support (Fill this out only if you are the surviving spouse of the victim and/or had dependent children)

What was victim's employment status at time of crime? ( ) Employed   ( ) Unemployed

If employed, the attached Employment Verification Form **must** be filled out by the **employer** and attached to this form before returning.

What income are you now receiving as a result of the victim's death: (List all amounts being received)
(**You must attach all documentation showing amounts and sources**)

Social Security _____ Workers Compensation $ _____

Welfare $ _____ AFDC $ _____ Other $ _____
                                          (From where and amount received)

SECTION XII. Federal Government Information (Optional for Statistical Use Only)

Ethnic Group (Victim): ( ) White   ( ) Black   ( ) American Indian or Alaskan Native   ( ) Asian
( ) Hispanic (Mexican, Puerto Rican, Cuban, or other Spanish culture)   ( ) Multiracial

U.S. Citizen (Victim) ( ) Yes   ( ) No   Handicap (Victim): ( ) Yes   ( ) No

Federal Crime ( ) Yes   ( ) No   Kentucky Resident ( ) Yes   ( ) No

Who referred you to the compensation program? ( ) Law Enforcement Agency   ( ) Hospital

( ) Victims Advocate   ( ) Prosecutor   ( ) Other _____
                                                (Name)

Continued

EXHIBIT 8–7 *(Continued)*
Crime Victim Claim Form

SECTION XIII. Restitution and Civil Lawsuit

Have the victim and/or claimant filed a civil lawsuit against anyone relating to the injury received as a result of the crime?   (   ) Yes   (   ) No

If yes, name of attorney: _____

Address: _____ Telephone No. _____
           Street   City   State   Zip

Was the offender ordered by the court to pay any restitution? (   ) Yes   (   ) No

If yes, amount $ _____ How is it to be paid? _____

SECTION XIV. Authorization and Subrogation

VERIFICATION OF APPLICATION: I, hereby certify, subject to penalty, fine or imprisonment, that the information contained in this application for Crime Victims Compensation is true and correct to the best of my knowledge.

SUBROGATION: In consideration of the payment received from the Crime Victims Compensation Board, I agree to repay the full amount I received from the fund in the event I recover damages or compensation from the offender or from any other public or private source as a result of the injuries or death which was the basis of my claim for compensation from the fund. I understand that compensation from any other public or private source includes, but is not limited to, receipt of insurance, Medicare, Medicaid, workers compensation, disability pay, etc. I further agree and understand that no part of recovery due the Crime Victims Compensation Board may be diminished by any collection fees or for any other reason whatsoever.

Should I choose to recover damages or compensation for the injury or death from any source, I agree to promptly notify the Crime Victims Compensation Board by sending copies of any pleadings, settlement proposals and any other documents relative thereto. I further agree to fully cooperate with the Crime Victims Compensation Board should the Board decide to institute an action against any person or entity for the recovery of all or any part of the compensation I received from the fund.

MEDICAL/PSYCHIATRIC/EMPLOYMENT RELEASE: I hereby authorize any hospital, physician, funeral director, employer, insurance company, social service bureau, Social Security office, mental health counselor or facility, or any other person or firm to release any and all information requested. I understand and acknowledge that my mental health records may contain confidential remarks made by me, information regarding drug or alcohol abuse, HIV status or other personal data. I further agree and hold blameless any hospital, physician, funeral director, employer, insurance company, social service bureau, Social Security office, mental health counselor or facility or any staff person of any and all liability for the release of these records.

SIGNATURE: _____ DATE: _____

YOU ARE NOT REQUIRED TO HAVE AN ATTORNEY ASSIST IN SUBMITTING YOUR APPLICATION. IF AN ATTORNEY DOES ASSIST YOU, THE ATTORNEY MUST SIGN THIS APPLICATION.

ATTORNEY'S NAME: _____ Soc. Sec. No. Or Fed. ID _____

ADDRESS: _____ TELEPHONE NO. _____

ATTORNEY'S SIGNATURE: _____

EXHIBIT 8–7 *(Continued)*
Crime Victim Claim Form

COMMONWEALTH OF KENTUCKY
CRIME VICTIMS COMPENSATION BOARD
115 MYRTLE AVENUE, FRANKFORT, KENTUCKY 40601
EMPLOYMENT VERIFICATION
(to be completed by employer only)

Employee's Name: _____

Soc. Sec. No.: _____ Date of Crime: _____

Was victim employed at the time of crime? Yes ( )   No ( )

If yes, complete the following:

Employer's Name _____

Address _____

Telephone Number _____ Date Employed _____

Did the victim miss any time from work because of injuries from the crime? Yes ( ) No ( ).

If yes, from _____ to _____

The items listed below are to be <u>WEEKLY AMOUNTS:</u>

Gross Earnings $ _____ Federal Tax Withheld $ _____

State Tax Withheld $ _____ Social Security Withheld $ _____

Other Deductions (itemized) $ _____

Net Take Home Earning Per Week $ _____

Has the victim returned to work? Yes ( ) No ( ) Date _____

Did the victim's wage continue while off work? Yes ( ) No ( )

If yes, complete the following:

	Amount Per Week	From date to date
_____ Workers Comp.	$ _____	_____ to _____
_____ Unemployment	$ _____	_____ to _____
_____ Private or Health	$ _____	_____ to _____
_____ Vacation	$ _____	_____ to _____
_____ Sick	$ _____	_____ to _____
_____ Employers Group	$ _____	_____ to _____
_____ Disability	$ _____	_____ to _____
_____ Union or Fraternal	$ _____	_____ to _____
_____ Other, specify	$ _____	_____ to _____

_____
Signature and Title

SUBSCRIBED AND SWORN TO BEFORE ME BY _____

THIS _____ DAY OF _____ , _____ .

MY COMMISSION EXPIRES _____

_____
NOTARY PUBLIC

Continued

EXHIBIT 8–7 *(Concluded)*
Crime Victim Claim Form

COMMONWEALTH OF KENTUCKY
CRIME VICTIMS COMPENSATION BOARD
115 MYRTLE AVENUE
FRANKFORT, KY 40601

DISABILITY CERTIFICATE
(to be completed by Doctor)

Victim/Patient   Name: _____

Type of Injury: _____

Date of Injury: _____

Date(s) Victim unable to Work: From _____ to _____

Did Victim Suffer Permanent Disability? Yes ( ) No ( )

If yes, please state the victim's percentage of permanent disability to the body as a whole in accordance with the AMA Guidelines.

_____

COMMENTS:

Name of Attending Physician: _____

Address: _____

Telephone Number: _____ Federal ID Number _____

Signature _____ Date _____

EXHIBIT 8–8
Completed Criminal Complaint (*Cordoba* Case)

CRIMINAL COMPLAINT WITH MULTIPLE COUNTS

STATE OF COLUMBIA   CAPITOL DISTRICT COURT

STATE OF COLUMBIA   Criminal Complaint
                  v.   Case No._____
MIGUEL CORDOBA
1325 S. Main St.
Legalville, Columbia 00000

_____

The affiant, <u>Carmen Cordoba</u>, says that on the <u>7th</u> day of <u>April</u>, _____ , in the County of <u>Capitol</u>, <u>Columbia</u>, the above-named defendant unlawfully:

COUNT 1: Took the diamond and ruby ring valued at more than $500 belonging to the affiant and located at 935 High St. with the intent to deprive the affiant of the possession, to wit: theft in violation of C.R.S. 809.00 (a Class D felony) punishable by up to five years in prison, a $10,000 fine, or both.

COUNT 2: Intentionally destroyed an antique jewelry box belonging to affiant and valued at more than $500 located at 935 High St., to wit: criminal damage to property in violation of C.R.S. 835.00 (a Class D felony) punishable by one year in prison, a $2,000 fine, or both.

Each count against the peace and dignity of the State of Columbia.

<u>Carmen Cordoba</u>
Affiant

Sworn to before me this <u>6th</u> day of <u>June</u>, _____ .

<u>Chris Eden</u>
Name and Address of Affiant   Notary Public
<u>Carmen Cordoba</u>   My Commission Expires <u>1/1/</u>_____
<u>935 High St. Apt. 3</u>
<u>Legalville, Columbia 00000</u>

EXHIBIT 8–9
Standardized Crime Report

STANDARDIZED CRIME REPORT

Agency <u>C.S.P.</u>   Form No. <u>42-3001</u>
Fel.   **Misd.**   **Ord.**

Victim/complainant	**Soc. Sec. No.**	**Complainant if other than victim**
Kate R. Lamb	555-44-7777	Officer Timothy Grant

Age	**D.O.B.**	**Sex**	**Race**	**Phone**	**Age**	**D.O.B.**	**Sex**	**Race**	**Phone**
20	9/15/___	F	W	555-3000					555-0000

Occupation	**Phone (bus. or emer.)**	**Occupation Phone (bus. or emer.)**
student		

Address	**City**	**State**	**Address**	**City**	**State**
133 College Dr.	Legalville	CL	C.S.P. Post	Legalville	CL

Work Address (or school)	**Work Address (or school)**

Crime	**Crime Scene**	**Address**
Sexual Assault	Smiley Crk Bridge campus	College and Park

Date of Crime	**Time**	**Date Reported**	**Time**	**Nature of Report**
5/27/___	9:20 p.m.	5/27/___	9:30 p.m.	phone

Reported by	**Phone**	**Address**
Henry Peel	(111) 555-4444	1300 E. Main Legalville, CL

Report Received By	**Officer's Time of Arrival on Scene**
Dispatcher Pamela Freid	9:35 p.m.

Injuries to Victim (Emotional, Physical)
trauma, serious head injuries, broken leg, cuts and abrasions, internal injuries

Medical Treatment	**Physician**	**Hospital**
Yes _x_ **No** _____	Dr. Calvert	Good Samaritan/Legalville

Vehicle Involved	**Yr.**	**Make**	**Model**	**License**	**Yr.**	**State**	**Driven By**
Yes___ No _x_							Vict___ Sus___

Suspect One (Name or Descrip.)	**Age**	**D.O.B.**	**Sex**	**Race**	**Prior Convict.**
Eldon J. Spiers	26	2/19/_____	M	W	Poss. Drugs 6/8/_____

EXHIBIT 8–9 *(Concluded)*
Standardized Crime Report

Address (Home)	City	State	Address (Work)	City	State
4313 Southland Dr.	Legalville	CL	Maintenance Plant, Legalville College		

Phone	home	work	Other Information		Soc. Sec. No.
	none	(111) 555-2222	single, janitor for 2 yrs.		999-11-1111

Suspect Two	(Name or Descrip.)	Age	D.O.B.	Sex	Race	Prior Convict.
N/A						

Address (Home)	City	State	Address (Work)	City	State

Phone	home	work	Other Information		Soc. Sec. No.

Witness One	Best Address	Age	Best Phone	Alt. Phone
Henry Peel	1300 E. Main, Legalville CL	27	111-555-4444	555-9876

Witness Two	Best Address	Age	Best Phone	Alt. Phone

Does Victim Wish to Prosecute?   **If No, Explain**
Yes _X_ No_____

Facts to Support Charge:
Suspect attacked Ms. Lamb who was walking toward her car following her night class. Suspect grabbed victim around the arms from behind, knocked her down, sat on top of her, and began to tear away her jacket and blouse. Suspect held knife and said in low voice, "Now you're going to get what all pretty little college girls ask for." Victim screamed, knocked suspect off of her, and ran toward her car. Suspect pursued her. At bridge, victim thought male approaching from the opposite side was with suspect. She screamed and jumped over railing of bridge and landed on rocks. Suspect fled according to Henry Peel, who was approaching from car lot. Peel phoned police.

Peel said he did not get very good view of suspect but described him as medium build wearing green army jacket and camouflage trousers. He fled back toward campus and disappeared in the trees. As first officer on scene, I found victim unconscious. She was transported to hospital. Five days later after waking from a coma, she stated to Detective Smythe that even though the lighting was poor she identified the suspect as night janitor who works in the Hunt classroom building. Maintenance informed the police that the janitor on duty that evening was Eldon Spiers. Detective Smythe went to Spiers' apartment. The suspect answered the door. When the detective identified himself, Spiers said, "I thought you might come," and then refused to answer questions. He was arrested.

Victim is still in serious condition, has lapsed back into a coma and may die, according to her physician.

Include additional information on separate sheet.

Investigation Officer(s)	Reporting Officer	Date
Timothy Grant	Timothy Grant	6/10/__

Detective Robert Smythe

EXHIBIT 8–10
Arrest Warrant (Completed)

STATE OF COLUMBIA   **DISTRICT COURT**   **CAPITOL COUNTY**

STATE OF COLUMBIA

V.   **WARRANT FOR ARREST**
                                CASE NO. C.R. 92-1000

ELDON J. SPIERS
4313 Southland Dr.
Legalville, Columbia

TO: ALL PEACE OFFICERS IN THE STATE OF COLUMBIA:
    You are hereby commanded to arrest Eldon J. Spiers **and bring him or her forthwith to the judge or magistrate of the District Court of CAPITOL COUNTY, COLUMBIA, to answer a complaint charging him or her with: (brief description of offense)**

    Attempting to have sexual intercourse with Ms. Kate R. Lamb without her consent by threatening her with a knife, to wit: Attempted first degree sexual assault.

    in violation of C.R.S. 840.00(1)

Travis Marcum
Issuing Officer   June 6, Legalville, Columbia
District Attorney   **Date and Location**
Title
Travis Marcum
Signature   **Bail fixed at** $50,000   **by** _____
                                              Judge

_____

RETURN
This warrant was executed by arresting the above-named defendant this _____ day of _____ , _____ .

_____   _____   _____
Date Received   **Name of Arresting Officer**   **Signature**

[REVERSE SIDE]
The following is furnished for information only.
Defendant's Name: Eldon J. Spiers
Alias: N/A
Last Known Residence: 4313 Southland Dr., Legalville, Columbia
Last Known Employment: Janitor, Legalville College
Place of Birth: Unknown
Social Security No.: 999-11-1111

Ht: 5'10"	**Wt:** 180#	**Sex:** M	**Race:** W	**Hair:** Bl	**Eyes:** Bl

Scars, Tattoos, Other Distinguishing Marks:
FBI Number: N/A
Complete Description of Auto: N/A
Investigative Agency and Address:
    Columbia State Police, District 26
    Legalville, Columbia

SYSTEM FOLDER ASSIGNMENTS

Complete the following and place the documents in your system folder:

- Standardized intake form, criminal complaint, summons, and arrest warrant used at intake.
- Pertinent crime victim forms for your jurisdiction and information on eligibility for compensation.
- Expanded list of national resources for victims, including resources from your home jurisdiction.
- Checklist for intake.
- Checklist for drafting and filing the summons and warrant.

APPLICATION ASSIGNMENTS

1. Go to the law library and locate an excerpt of your state's criminal code and the federal criminal code to familiarize yourself with these sources and their arrangement. If the excerpts are not available, go to the state and federal code and become familiar with the location and classification scheme of the crimes.
2. Why do you think *Bruton* does not apply to conspiracy cases?
3. Based on the scenarios in Chapter 1, write a brief memorandum for your supervising attorney on whether the charges and defendants should be joined in Cases III and VI. Then draft the necessary complaint for one of the cases using the local format for such a complaint.
4. Drawing from the police report in Exhibit 8–9 and using the criminal statutes from your jurisdiction, draft the criminal complaint against Eldon Spiers in Case I. It will be up to you to determine what statutes apply. Is there a possibility of multiple counts? Habitual or repeat offender allegations?

HELPFUL WEB SITES

www.ncvc.org
    National Center for Victims of Crime
www.ncjrs.org
    National Criminal Justice Reference Service, links to victims services
www.achiever.com/freehmpg.ncas
    National Coalition Against Sexual Assault, referrals to local support services
www.nncac.org
    National Children's Alliance, goal is to ensure that children are not revictimized by the system designed to help them
www.ncadv.org
    National Coalition Against Domestic Violence
www.madd.org
    Mothers Against Drunk Driving, support services
www.naacp.org
    National Association for the Advancement of Colored People, resources for responding to hate crimes
www.cyberangels.org
    Cyberangels, assists victims of cybercrimes

INTERNET EXERCISES

Check the helpful Web sites to answer these questions.
1. What is the first thing the victim of a fraud crime should do?
2. What should be the primary goal of the victim of a stalker?
3. What victim services does MADD provide?

QUESTIONS FOR STUDY AND REVIEW

1. Discuss the various limitations and ethical considerations affecting the prosecution decision to bring criminal charges or to increase charges and penalties.
2. When can charges or defendants be joined in the charging document? What state and federal rules of procedure apply? When should charges or defendants not be joined?
3. Define intake in the context of the prosecutor's office. What are some of the tasks related to intake?
4. In what two ways, primarily, do criminal accusations come to the attention of the intake paralegal?
5. What problems may arise from poorly controlled intake? What are the social and political ramifications of an increase in each of these problems?
6. What forms are needed for intake?
7. Why is it important to provide a relatively private, undisturbed setting for intake interviewing?
8. Under what circumstances might it be best to refer a walk-in complainant to the police? To other agencies and services?
9. Why is it important to determine early in the interview if there is a crime and, if so, where it took place?
10. Why should criminal charges be filed only as a last resort?
11. What is the paralegal's role when criminal charges seem inappropriate?
12. If your office did not have a good intake form, what sections would you need to include in creating one? Beginning with "who," what standard questions should be posed by a good intake form?
13. When recording addresses, why is one address generally insufficient?
14. Why is it essential to determine if there are facts in support of each element of the crime, and to record those facts?
15. Does it make any difference in drafting the complaint whether the defendant has a prior criminal record? Explain.
16. Why is it a good practice for the paralegal to explain to the complainant what will happen if the charge is filed?
17. At what points of the intake process can a paralegal play the role of counselor to the complainant? Why is this role important?
18. Does your jurisdiction have a victim compensation program? Describe who is eligible and how it works.
19. How are victim rights and victim compensation relevant to the role of the paralegal?
20. Be able to draft the following: criminal complaint; multicount criminal complaint with habitual offender count; criminal summons; and arrest warrant (and commitment in appropriate jurisdiction).
21. What procedures are involved in seeing to it that the documents in question 20 are signed, filed, and executed by the appropriate official?
22. What is docket tracking? Explain its importance.

KEY TERMS LIST

Arrest warrant	Docket	Six *Ws*
Complainant	Intake (prosecutor's office)	Summons, criminal
Complaint		

ENDNOTES

1. Suggestion from Vickie Doolin Mills, Commonwealth Investigator (Paralegal), Commonwealth Attorney's Office, Richmond, Kentucky; in material submitted to J. McCord, Mar. 9, 1990.
2. *The Crime Victim's Compensation Board,* THE ADVOCATE, Dec. 1988, at 4.
3. *Kentucky Prosecutors Say Ruling Hinders Some DUI Cases,* LEXINGTON HERALD-LEADER, Aug. 27, 1990, at B1.
4. Joanne Weis, M.S.W., A.C.S.W., Director of Programs, The R.A.P.E. Relief Center, 226 West Breckinridge St., Louisville, KY 40203, (502) 581-7273, reprinted with permission.
5. Madison/Clark County Victim Impact Statement, 25th Judicial Circuit, Madison and Clark Counties, Kentucky, 1993.
6. Commonwealth of Kentucky, Crime Victim Claim Form and Instruction, Crime Victims Compensation Board, Frankfort, Kentucky.

SEARCH AND SEIZURE

I.   INTRODUCTION

AMENDMENT IV

The right of the people to be secure in their persons, houses, papers, and effects, against unreasonable searches and seizures, shall not be violated, and no Warrants shall issue, but upon probable cause, supported by Oath or affirmation, and particularly describing the place to be searched, and the persons or things to be seized.

[T]hese [Fourth Amendment rights], I protest, are not mere second class rights but belong in the catalog of indispensable freedoms. Among deprivation of rights, none is so effective in cowing a population, crushing the spirit of the individual and putting terror in every heart. Uncontrolled search and seizure is one of the first and most effective weapons in the arsenal of every arbitrary government.

—Justice Jackson, *Brinegar v. U.S.* (1949)

It is four in the morning in muggy late summer and you are at home with your family and all are asleep. You hear a sound, a loud knock at the door followed by a terrible crashing noise, rushing footsteps, shouting! You try in vain to discern what is being shouted, but you cannot. The sound of the footsteps gets louder, your bedroom door is thrust open and smashes against the wall. Suddenly bright lights shine painfully into your sleepy eyes. "Police! This is the police!" You cannot see, you struggle to move, but sleep-filled limbs and a growing terror leave you paralyzed. Strangers are shouting at you, "Stand up. Hands against the wall." Modesty causes you to try to cover yourself with the bedsheet, but as you grab for it, it is ripped from your hand. You hear screaming from familiar voices, more shouting from distant rooms. You are pushed against the wall and every inch of your body is searched. Drawers are being opened; your possessions are being thrown around. You are being pushed here, then there. You fall down. Someone grabs you hard and yells, "Get up!" You begin to cry and find yourself shaking uncontrollably. "Where are the drugs? WHERE ARE THE DRUGS?" You cannot believe what is happening. You close your eyes and say to yourself, "Please, please, let this be a nightmare."

"It is not only under Nazi rule that police excesses are inimical to freedom. It is easy to make light of insistence on scrupulous regard for the safeguards of civil liberties when invoked on behalf of the unworthy. . . . History bears testimony that by such disregard are the rights of liberty extinguished, heedlessly, at first, then stealthily, and brazenly in the end."

—Felix Frankfurter *Davis v. United States,* 328 U.S. 582 (1946)

Scenes similar to this have occurred regularly throughout history and will be repeated. They become graphically real on the multitude of police shows inundating prime-time television. The fear that government, through the police or military, may barge in and completely destroy a person's life and the lives of loved ones has led to constitutions like our own that restrain the reach and power of government and attempt to preserve human dignity and freedom.

Not only is the constitutional limitation of police procedure one of the most important areas of criminal law, but it also may be the most interesting. It provides fascinating conflict between the need for aggressive law enforcement and the desire to define and preserve liberties enumerated in the Constitution.

Understanding this conflict is vital to your work as a paralegal in criminal law. It comes into play when you assist the prosecutor in providing counsel to law enforcement officers, juvenile officers, probation and parole officers, and others on what is allowed in arrest, search, and seizure; when you work for the defense attorney preparing motions to suppress the evidence acquired during search and seizure; when you assist the prosecutor in responding to those motions; or when as a judicial clerk you research a judge's response to memoranda from both sides on a suppression of evidence issue. Furthermore, you will gain valuable insight into your own rights.

II. SCOPE OF THE FOURTH AMENDMENT

A. STATE ACTION

The general rule of the Fourth Amendment is that the police must obtain a warrant from a magistrate before conducting a search or seizure. The scope of the Fourth Amendment, however, is limited and does not apply in all circumstances. Therefore, efficiency dictates that warrants not be issued unless they are necessary. The police come to you and ask for a warrant to search a residence, to look into a vehicle, to place a video camera in the restroom of a business, to fly over a fenced backyard to find marijuana, to use a dog to sniff luggage on a bus, or to tap into a computer bulletin board. Should you draft a warrant in anticipation of the prosecuting attorney's approval or not?

To start, the Fourth Amendment limits the exercise of government power. It is applicable to the states through the due process clause of the Fourteenth Amendment [*Roaden v. Kentucky* (1973)] and, therefore, applies to conduct of federal and state officers and officials [*Lanza v. N.Y.* (1962) and *Burdeau v. McDowell* (1921)]. Such conduct is called **state action.** Thus, searches by the following have been held to be state action and subject to the restraints of the Fourth and Fourteenth Amendments: all law enforcement officers and officials, public school teachers [*New Jersey v. T.L.O.* (1985)], airport security personnel when acting pursuant to federal law, social workers, conservation officers, a tax appraiser and a board of dental examiners, and merchants and store security when authorized by law to detain and search suspected shoplifters, but not a licensed security guard or a prison chaplain.[1]

state action:
conduct of a state, its employees, and agents.

Generally, private persons are not subject to Fourth Amendment restraints, but they may be if they act as an agent of the government. Whether a private person's conduct becomes state action is determined by an examination of the totality of the circumstances [*Skinner v. Railway Labor Executives Association* (1989) and *State v. Buswell* (Minn. 1990) *cert. denied* (1991)] according to the following criteria: (1) whether government officials knew of or acquiesced in the search or seizure and (2) whether the private individual performing the intrusive conduct intended to assist the government or further that individual's own ends [*U.S. v. Miller* (9th Cir. 1982)]. Trash collectors, who had been contacted by police, picked up a defendant's trash, separated it from the rest of the trash, did not inspect it, and gave it to police, were held to be acting as state agents [*State v. Hauser* (N.C. App. 1994), *affirmed* (N.C. 1995)]. Bounty hunter/bail bonds officers under contract with the government, however, were held to be private, not state agents, in *Akins v. U.S.* (D.C. App. 1996). Further, the Fourth Amendment does not apply to agents of the United States outside United States borders and territories, even if the search is of a United States citizen [*U.S. v. Verdugo-Urquidez* (1990)].

B. REASONABLE EXPECTATION OF PRIVACY

Next, courts decided the need for warrants based on whether the police intrusion was directed at "persons, houses, papers, and effects," the specific language of the Fourth Amendment that focuses on location and types of property. In the landmark case of *Katz v. U.S.* (1967), however, the United States Supreme Court brought the law into the age of technology by ruling that tapping the phone line of a public telephone booth was a search under the Fourth Amendment. In its ruling the Court said that the Fourth Amendment is intended to "protect people, not places." This ruling shifted the focus from whether some type of physical trespass occurred to whether the person had a justifiable expectation of privacy.

KATZ v. UNITED STATES
Supreme Court of the United States, 1967.
389 U.S. 347, 88 S.Ct. 507.
[Citations omitted]

Mr. Justice STEWART delivered the opinion of the Court.

The petitioner was convicted in the District Court for the Southern District of California under an eight-count indictment charging him with transmitting wagering information by telephone from Los Angeles to Miami and Boston, in violation of a federal statute. At trial the Government was permitted, over the petitioner's objection, to introduce evidence of the petitioner's end of telephone conversations, overheard by FBI agents who had attached an electronic listening and recording device to the outside of the public telephone booth from which he had placed his calls. In affirming his conviction, the Court of Appeals rejected the contention that the recordings had been obtained in violation of the Fourth Amendment, because "[t]here was no physical entrance into the area occupied by [the petitioner]." We granted certiorari in order to consider the constitutional questions thus presented.

The petitioner has phrased those questions as follows:

"A. Whether a public telephone booth is a constitutionally protected area so that evidence obtained by attaching an electronic listening recording device to the top of such a booth is obtained in violation of the right to privacy of the user of the booth.

"B. Whether physical penetration of a constitutionally protected area is necessary before a search and seizure can be said to be violative of the Fourth Amendment to the United States Constitution."

We decline to adopt this formulation of the issues. In the first place, the correct solution of Fourth Amendment problems is not necessarily promoted by incantation of the phrase "constitutionally protected area." Secondly, the Fourth Amendment cannot be translated into a general constitutional "right to privacy." That Amendment protects individual privacy against certain kinds of governmental intrusion, but its protections go further, and often have nothing to do with privacy at all. Other provisions of the Constitution protect personal privacy from other forms of governmental invasion. But the protection of a person's *general* right to privacy—his right to be let alone by other people—is, like the protection of his property and of his very life, left largely to the law of the individual States.

Because of the misleading way the issues have been formulated, the parties have attached great significance to the characterization of the telephone booth from which the petitioner placed his calls. The petitioner has strenuously argued that the booth was a "constitutionally protected area." The Government has maintained with equal vigor that it was not. But this effort to decide whether or not a given "area," viewed in the abstract, is "constitutionally protected" deflects attention from the problem presented by this case. For the Fourth Amendment protects people, not places. What a person knowingly exposes to the public, even in his own home or office, is not a subject of Fourth Amendment protection. But what he seeks to preserve as private, even in an area accessible to the public, may be constitutionally protected.

The Government stresses the fact that the telephone booth from which the petitioner made his calls was constructed partly of glass, so that he was as visible after he entered it as he would have been if he had remained outside. But what he sought to exclude when he entered the booth was not the intruding eye—it was the uninvited ear. He did not shed his right to do so simply because he made his calls from a place where he might be seen. No less than an individual in a business office, in a friend's apartment, or in a taxicab, a person in a telephone booth may rely upon the protection of the Fourth Amendment. One who occupies it, shuts the door behind him, and pays the toll that permits him to place a call is surely entitled to assume that the words he utters into the mouthpiece will not be broadcast to the world. To read the Constitution more narrowly is to ignore the vital role that the public telephone has come to play in private communication.

The Government contends, however, that the activities of its agents in this case should not be tested by Fourth Amendment requirements, for the surveillance technique they employed involved no physical penetration of the telephone booth from which the petitioner placed his calls. It is true that the absence of such penetration was at one time thought to foreclose further Fourth Amendment inquiry, . . . [W]e have since departed from the narrow view on which that decision rested. Indeed, we have expressly held that the Fourth Amendment governs not only the seizure of tangible items, but extends as well to the recording of oral statements, overheard without any "technical trespass under . . . local property law." *Silverman v. United States,* 365 U.S. 505, 511. Once this much is acknowledged, and once it is recognized that the Fourth Amendment protects people—and not simply "areas"—against unreasonable searches and seizures, it becomes clear that the reach of that Amendment cannot turn upon the presence or absence of a physical intrusion into any given enclosure.

. . . The Government's activities in electronically listening to and recording the petitioner's words violated the privacy upon which he justifiably relied while using the telephone booth and thus constituted a "search and seizure" within the meaning of the Fourth Amendment. The fact that the electronic device employed to achieve that end did not happen to penetrate the wall of the booth can have no constitutional significance.

The question remaining for decision, then, is whether the search and seizure conducted in this case complied with constitutional standards. In that regard, the Government's position is that its agents acted in an entirely defensible manner: They did not begin their electronic surveillance until investigation of the petitioner's activities had established a strong probability that he was using the telephone in question to transmit gambling information to persons in other States, in violation of federal law. Moreover, the surveillance was limited, both in scope and in duration, to the specific purpose of establishing the contents of the petitioner's unlawful telephonic communications. The agents confined their surveillance to the brief periods during which he used the telephone booth, and they took great care to overhear only the conversations of the petitioner himself.

Accepting this account of the Government's actions as accurate, it is clear that this surveillance was so narrowly circumscribed that a duly authorized magistrate, properly notified of the need for such investigation, specifically informed of the basis on which it was to proceed, and clearly apprised of the precise intrusion it would entail, could constitutionally have authorized, with appropriate safeguards, the very limited search and seizure that the Government asserts in fact took place. . . .

The Government . . . urges the creation of a new exception to cover this case. It argues that surveillance of a telephone booth should be exempted from the usual requirement of advance authorization by a magistrate upon a showing of probable cause. We cannot agree. Omission of such authorization

"bypasses the safeguards provided by an objective predetermination of probable cause, and substitutes instead the far less reliable procedure of an after-the-event justification for the . . . search, too likely to be subtly influenced by the familiar shortcomings of hindsight judgment." *Beck v. Ohio,* 379 U.S. 89, 96.

And bypassing a neutral predetermination of the *scope* of a search leaves individuals secure from Fourth Amendment violations "only in the discretion of the police."

These considerations do not vanish when the search in question is transferred from the setting of a home, an office, or a hotel room to that of a telephone booth. Wherever a man may be, he is entitled to know that he will remain free from unreasonable searches and seizures. The government agents here ignored "the procedure of antecedent justification . . . that is central to the Fourth Amendment," a procedure that we hold

to be a constitutional precondition of the kind of electronic surveillance involved in this case. Because the surveillance here failed to meet that condition, and because it led to the petitioner's conviction, the judgment must be reversed.

It is so ordered.

Mr. Justice HARLAN, concurring.

. . .

As the Court's opinion states, "the Fourth Amendment protects people, not places." The question, however, is what protection it affords to those people. Generally, as here, the answer to that question requires reference to a "place." My understanding of the rule that has emerged from prior decisions is that there is a twofold requirement, first that a person have exhibited an actual (subjective) expectation of privacy and, second, that the expectation be one that society is prepared to recognize as "reasonable." Thus a man's home is, for most purposes, a place where he expects privacy, but objects, activities, or statements that he exposes to the "plain view" of outsiders are not "protected" because no intention to keep them to himself has been exhibited. On the other hand, conversations in the open would not be protected against being overheard, for the expectation of privacy under the circumstances would be unreasonable.

. . . The point is not that the booth is "accessible to the public" at other times, but that it is a temporarily private place whose momentary occupants' expectations of freedom from intrusion are recognized as reasonable.

. . .

Mr. Justice BLACK, dissenting.

. . .

My basic objection is twofold: (1) I do not believe that the words of the Amendment will bear the meaning given them by today's decision, and (2) I do not believe that it is the proper role of this Court to rewrite the Amendment in order "to bring it into harmony with the times" and thus reach a result that many people believe to be desirable.

. . .

Tapping telephone wires, of course, was an unknown possibility at the time the Fourth Amendment was adopted. But eavesdropping (and wiretapping is nothing more than eavesdropping by telephone) was, as even the majority opinion in *Berger v. New York* [388 U.S. 41] recognized, "an ancient practice which at common law was condemned as a nuisance. 4 Blackstone, Commentaries 168. In those days the eavesdropper listened by naked ear under the eaves of houses or their windows, or beyond their walls seeking out private discourse." 388 U.S., at 45. There can be no doubt that the Framers were aware of this practice, and if they had desired to outlaw or restrict the use of evidence obtained by eavesdropping, I believe that they would have used the appropriate language to do so in the Fourth Amendment. They certainly would not have left such a task to the ingenuity of language-stretching judges.

. . . By clever word juggling the Court finds it plausible to argue that language aimed specifically at searches and seizures of things that can be searched and seized may, to protect privacy, be applied to eavesdropped evidence of conversations that can neither be searched nor seized. Few things happen to an individual that do not affect his privacy in one way or another. Thus, by arbitrarily substituting the Court's language, designed to protect privacy, for the Constitution's language, designed to protect against unreasonable searches and seizures, the Court has made the Fourth Amendment its vehicle for holding all laws violative of the Constitution which offend the Court's broadest concept of privacy. As I said in *Griswold v. Connecticut*, 381 U.S. 479, "The Court talks about a constitutional 'right of privacy' as though there is some constitutional provision or provisions forbidding any law ever to be passed which might abridge the 'privacy' of individuals. But there is not." (Dissenting opinion, at 508.) I made clear

in that dissent my fear of the dangers involved when this Court uses the "broad, abstract and ambiguous concept" of "privacy" as a "comprehensive substitute for the Fourth Amendment's guarantee against 'unreasonable searches and seizures.'"

The Fourth Amendment protects privacy only to the extent that it prohibits unreasonable searches and seizures of "persons, houses, papers, and effects." No general right is created by the Amendment so as to give this Court the unlimited power to hold unconstitutional everything which affects privacy. Certainly the Framers, well acquainted as they were with the excesses of governmental power, did not intend to grant this Court such omnipotent lawmaking authority as that. The history of governments proves that it is dangerous to freedom to repose such powers in courts.

For these reasons I respectfully dissent.

Note that under *Katz* one does not have to establish a right of privacy to be protected, but simply a reasonable expectation of privacy. There is no expectation of privacy in public areas such as sidewalks, parks, or malls, so what police see or seize as evidence of illegal activity in these areas is not subject to Fourth Amendment restrictions.

The same holds true for abandoned property; any reasonable expectation of privacy is terminated at the time the property is abandoned. An abandoned residence may be searched without a warrant, as may be the satchel dropped by a person being chased by the police [*California v. Hodari D.* (1991)]. Luggage left on a bus after police questioned passengers was held to be abandoned, and a police search of a suspect's garbage was not a Fourth Amendment search, because one retains no reasonable expectation of privacy in garbage [*California v. Greenwood* (1988)]. Many of these decisions turn not on extinguished property rights, but on whether the party retains a reasonable expectation of privacy in the property [*Abel v. U.S.* (1960)].

Although police observation from common public areas such as porches, sidewalks, a neighbor's driveway, or the foyer of an apartment building does not violate a reasonable expectation of privacy, the uninvited entry of police into the front hallway of a house is a Fourth Amendment search. Our Constitution allows citizens to expect privacy behind the doors of their dwellings, extending to motel rooms, and, in *Alward v. State* (Nev. 1996), a camper's tent.

curtilage:
the area of land, enclosed or otherwise, around a house or other buildings that is used for domestic purposes.

That privacy extends to the **curtilage** of the dwelling, the area of land, enclosed or otherwise, around a house or other buildings that is used for domestic purposes. Curtilage is protected under the Fourth Amendment, except pathways for entry and exit. In *U.S. v. Dunn* (1987) the Supreme Court set out four considerations for defining the limits of curtilage: proximity of land to the house, whether it is enclosed (by a fence, for example) with the house, the nature of its use, and the existence of landscaping devices and other steps to shield that land from the view of passersby. Even if the property is defined as curtilage, however, aerial searches of that curtilage are not restricted. In *Florida v. Riley* (1989) curtilage was beyond the protection of the Fourth Amendment when searched by helicopter above the walled-in back yard and greenhouse.

We recognized that the yard was within the curtilage of the house, that a fence shielded the yard from observation from the street and that the occupant had a subjective expectation of privacy. We held, however, that such an expectation was not reasonable and not one "that society is prepared to honor." . . . "In an age where private and commercial flight in the public airways is routine, it is unreasonable for respondent to expect that his marijuana plants were constitutionally protected from being observed with the naked eye from an altitude of 1,000 feet. The Fourth Amendment simply does not require the police traveling in the public airways at this altitude to obtain a warrant in order to observe what is visible to the naked eye."

We arrive at the same conclusion in the present case. . . . [quoting from California v. Ciraolo (1986)]

Would it or should it make any difference in similar cases if the officers had to breach lawful flight clearances in order to get a sufficient look?

Offices, stores, industrial plants, and similar buildings have come under the protection of the Fourth Amendment [*See v. City of Seattle* (1967)]. Common walkways or shopping areas are not protected, but areas in which there is a reasonable expectation of privacy, such as changing rooms and restrooms, are protected. A shed used for a part-time welding business that was not locked and where the defendant did not object when another person walked out of the shed, did not hold the requisite expectation of privacy [*U.S. v. Cardoza-Hinojosa* (5th Cir. 1998)]. The enclosed land around commercial property is subject to aerial scrutiny [*Dow Chemical v. U.S.* (1986)], but courts differ on whether such fenced property is protected from surface searches. Even buildings beyond the home or office may be protected. The Court in *U.S. v. Dunn* (1987) held that a barn located well beyond the owner's curtilage line was probably protected by the reasonable expectation of privacy standard, but that officers had the right to peer into the barn from the noncurtilage or open fields land.

Open fields are the resident's lands beyond the curtilage and, therefore, are not protected by the Fourth Amendment [*Hester v. U.S.* (1924) and *Oliver v. U.S.* (1984)]. The lands may be fenced and posted with no trespassing signs, but they are still open fields [*U.S. v. Dunn* (1987)]. The open fields standard seems to have taken a back seat to the *Katz* expectation of privacy standard, as indicated by the Court's discussion of the open fields barn in *Dunn*.

open fields:
the resident's lands beyond the curtilage and, therefore, not protected by the Fourth Amendment.

Some courts have interpreted their state constitutions to be more protective of open fields than the United States Supreme Court's interpretation of the federal Constitution. Barbed wire fencing, no trespassing signs, and other clear indications of an expectation of privacy brought the fields into the warrant requirement under the states' equivalent of the Fourth Amendment [*State v. Kirchoff* (Vt. 1991) and *People v. Scott* (N.Y. 1992)].

If a vehicle is in open view, an officer may examine its exterior and look through the windows to examine its interior [*Cardwell v. Lewis* (1974) and *New York v. Class* (1986)]. Entering the vehicle is a search, unless it is clear the owner has relinquished any reasonable expectations of privacy (*Class*).

A person's effects are tangible, movable property, normally carried, worn, or stored. They bear an intimate relation to the person in possession. Articles that may contain other items, such as a suitcase, clothing, appliances, and the like, may be searched externally from a legal vantage point. Opening such items normally requires a warrant unless the possessor abandons any reasonable expectation of privacy. A detective who picked up a commuter's piece of luggage and manipulated it to determine what was inside violated the person's interest in privacy, invalidating the search [*U.S. v. Nicholson* (10th Cir. 1998)]. Use of a trained canine cop is not an unlawful search of luggage [*U.S. v. Place* (1983)], nor is the reopening of a package after a postal inspection once the package is surrendered for delivery [*Illinois v. Andreas* (1983)].

Thermal imaging devices used to detect heat emanating from buildings and used to detect cultivation of marijuana do not penetrate buildings and do not reveal "intimate activities within the building" and, therefore, do not fall within the scope of the Fourth Amendment according to most decisions [*U.S. v. Ishmael* (5th Cir. 1995), *U.S. v. Kyllo* (9th Cir. 1999)]. Similar reasoning, it would seem, will justify the use of computerized, handheld "drug sniffers," which are not only better at detecting drugs than police dogs, but also can immediately identify what type of drug has been "sniffed." There is no difference in degree of Fourth Amendment protection between property seized solely for evidence and that seized as fruit of a crime [*Warden v. Hayden* (1967)].

Based on the search cases discussed, do you think a person has a justified expectation of privacy in telephone records, bank transactions, or photo development services? A string of cases supports the principle that whenever you share information such as telephone numbers, deposit amounts, or exposed film with another such as a bank or the telephone company, that information is not protected by the Fourth Amendment [*Smith v. Maryland* (1979) and *U.S. v. Miller* (1976)].[2] Sending a computer with its stored data to a repair shop was found to eliminate any reasonable expectation of privacy and, therefore, an FBI warrantless search of the data, which revealed pornographic images of children, was upheld [*U.S. v. Hall* (7th Cir. 1998)].

Computer files, including e-mail, have required the courts to explore whether existing principles of search and seizure law apply to this relatively new focus of law. Although existing cases are mixed, a growing body of decisions, both civil and criminal, have ruled there is no reasonable expectation of privacy in either business or personal e-mail [*U.S. v. Charbonneau* (S.D. Ohio 1997) and *U.S. v. Maxwell* (C.M.A. 1996)]. Such an expectation seems reasonable, however, where data is protected by a personal password. Encrypted data, however, may be treated more like data in a foreign language; if it is open to view, then it is open to being "translated."[3]

Who is entitled to challenge a Fourth Amendment search? Anyone who has sufficient interest or an expectation of privacy in the property has the standing to challenge the search. Normally that is quite clear, but some residences are in a transitional phase that confuses the issue. For example, does a boyfriend who was thrown out of an apartment but still keeps most of his belongings there have standing to challenge the search of the apartment? Does a man who visited his fiancee and established a parental relationship with her son have standing to challenge a warrantless search of her apartment? New York said yes to both questions [*People v. Moss* (N.Y. App. 1990) and *People v. Rice* (N.Y. 1990)]. Even an overnight guest has sufficient interest to challenge the search [*Minnesota v. Olson* (1990)]. But, does a short-term guest have a reasonable expectation of privacy? This issue was addressed in *Minnesota v. Carter* (1998).

ANALYSIS PROBLEM

9–1. You are asked as a judge to decide whether an officer's "feel" search of a piece of luggage in a bus's overhead bin that reveals something that feels like a brick of drugs is illegal. What is your decision and what legal standards apply [*U.S. v. Bond,* 167 F.3d 225 (5th Cir. 1999) and *U.S. v. Nicholson,* 144 F.3d 632 (10th Cir. 1998)]? Does it make any difference regarding the legality of the search if the owner of the luggage, after the "feel" search, grants permission to the officer to search the bag? Research the subsequent judicial history of *Bond* to see what the Supreme Court said on all issues.

MINNESOTA v. CARTER
Supreme Court of the United States
525 U.S. 83, 119 S.Ct. 469 (1998)
[Citations omitted]

Chief Justice REHNQUIST delivered the opinion of the Court.

Respondents and the lessee of an apartment were sitting in one of its rooms, bagging cocaine. While so engaged they were observed by a police officer, who looked through a drawn window blind. The Supreme Court of Minnesota held that the officer's viewing was a search which violated respondents' Fourth Amendment rights. We hold that no such violation occurred. James Thielen, a police officer in the Twin

Cities' suburb of Eagan, Minnesota, went to an apartment building to investigate a tip from a confidential informant. The informant said that he had walked by the window of a ground-floor apartment and had seen people putting a white powder into bags. The officer looked in the same window through a gap in the closed blind and observed the bagging operation for several minutes. He then notified headquarters, which began preparing affidavits for a search warrant while he returned to the apartment building. When two men left the building in a previously identified Cadillac, the police stopped the car. Inside were respondents Carter and Johns. As the police opened the door of the car to let Johns out, they observed a black zippered pouch and a handgun, later determined to be loaded, on the vehicle's floor. Carter and Johns were arrested, and a later police search of the vehicle the next day discovered pagers, a scale, and 47 grams of cocaine in plastic sandwich bags.

After seizing the car, the police returned to Apartment 103 and arrested the occupant, Kimberly Thompson, who is not a party to this appeal. A search of the apartment pursuant to a warrant revealed cocaine residue on the kitchen table and plastic baggies similar to those found in the Cadillac. Thielen identified Carter, Johns, and Thompson as the three people he had observed placing the powder into baggies. The police later learned that while Thompson was the lessee of the apartment, Carter and Johns lived in Chicago and had come to the apartment for the sole purpose of packaging the cocaine. Carter and Johns had never been to the apartment before and were only in the apartment for approximately 2 1/2 hours. In return for the use of the apartment, Carter and Johns had given Thompson one-eighth of an ounce of the cocaine.

Carter and Johns were charged with conspiracy to commit controlled substance crime in the first degree and aiding and abetting in a controlled substance crime in the first degree, in violation of Minn.Stat. § 152.021, subd. 1(1), subd. 3(a) (1996); § 609.05. They moved to suppress all evidence obtained from the apartment and the Cadillac, as well as to suppress several postarrest incriminating statements they had made. They argued that Thielen's initial observation of their drug packaging activities was an unreasonable search in violation of the Fourth Amendment and that all evidence obtained as a result of this unreasonable search was inadmissible as fruit of the poisonous tree. The Minnesota trial court held that since, unlike the defendant in *Minnesota v. Olson,* 495 U.S. 91, (1990), Carter and Johns were not overnight social guests but temporary out-of-state visitors, they were not entitled to claim the protection of the Fourth Amendment against the government intrusion into the apartment. The trial court also concluded that Thielen's observation was not a search within the meaning of the Fourth Amendment. After a trial, Carter and Johns were each convicted of both offenses. The Minnesota Court of Appeals held that the respondent Carter did not have "standing" to object to Thielen's actions because his claim that he was predominantly a social guest was "inconsistent with the only evidence concerning his stay in the apartment, which indicates that he used it for a business purpose—to package drugs." *State v. Carter,* 545 N.W.2d 695, 698 (Minn.Ct.App.1996). In a separate appeal, the Court of Appeals also affirmed Johns' conviction, without addressing what it termed the "standing" issue. *State v. Johns,* No. C9-95-1765 (Minn. Ct.App., June 11, 1996), App. D-1, D-3 (unpublished).

A divided Minnesota Supreme Court reversed, holding that respondents had "standing" to claim the protection of the Fourth Amendment because they had " 'a legitimate expectation of privacy in the invaded place.' " The court noted that even though "society does not recognize as valuable the task of bagging cocaine, we conclude that society does recognize as valuable the right of property owners or leaseholders to invite persons into the privacy of their homes to conduct a common task, be it legal or illegal activity. We, therefore, hold that [respondents] had standing to bring [their] motion to suppress the evidence gathered as a result of Thielen's observations." Based upon its conclusion that the respondents had "standing" to raise their Fourth Amendment claims, the court went on to hold that Thielen's observation constituted a search of the apartment under the Fourth Amendment, and that the search was unreasonable. We granted certiorari, and now reverse.

The Minnesota courts analyzed whether respondents had a legitimate expectation of privacy under the rubric of "standing" doctrine, an analysis which this Court expressly rejected 20 years ago in *Rakas,* 439 U.S., at 139-140. In that case, we held that automobile passengers could not assert the protection of the Fourth Amendment against the seizure of incriminating evidence from a vehicle where they owned neither the vehicle nor the evidence. Central to our analysis was the idea that in determining whether a defendant is able to show the violation of his (and not someone else's) Fourth Amendment rights, the "definition of those rights is more properly placed within the purview of substantive Fourth Amendment law than within that of standing." 439 U.S., at 140. Thus, we held that in order to claim the protection of the Fourth Amendment, a defendant must demonstrate that he personally has an expectation of privacy in the place searched, and that his expectation is reasonable; i.e., one which has "a source outside of the Fourth Amendment, either by reference to concepts of real or personal property law or to understandings that are recognized and permitted by society." *Id.,* at 143-144.

The Fourth Amendment . . . protects persons against unreasonable searches of "their persons [and] houses" and thus indicates that the Fourth Amendment is a personal right that must be invoked by an individual. See *Katz v. United States,* 389 U.S. 347, 351 (1967) ("[T]he Fourth Amendment protects people, not places"). But the extent to which the Fourth Amendment protects people may depend upon where those people are. We have held that "capacity to claim the protection of the Fourth Amendment depends . . . upon whether the person who claims the protection of the Amendment has a legitimate expectation of privacy in the invaded place." *Rakas.*

The text of the Amendment suggests that its protections extend only to people in "their" houses. But we have held that in some circumstances a person may have a legitimate expectation of privacy in the house of someone else. In *Minnesota v. Olson,* for example, we decided that an overnight guest in a house had the sort of expectation of privacy that the Fourth Amendment protects. We said . . .

> "From the overnight guest's perspective, he seeks shelter in another's home precisely because it provides him with privacy, a place where he and his possessions will not be disturbed by anyone but his host and those his host allows inside. We are at our most vulnerable when we are asleep because we cannot monitor our own safety or the security of our belongings. It is for this reason that, although we may spend all day in public places, when we cannot sleep in our own home we seek out another private place to sleep, whether it be a hotel room, or the home of a friend."

In *Jones v. United States,* 362 U.S. 257 (1960), the defendant seeking to exclude evidence resulting from a search of an apartment had been given the use of the apartment by a friend. He had clothing in the apartment, had slept there "maybe a night," and at the time was the sole occupant of the apartment. But while the holding of *Jones*—that a search of the apartment violated the defendant's Fourth Amendment rights—is still valid, its statement that "anyone legitimately on the premises where a search occurs may challenge its legality," was expressly repudiated in *Rakas.* Thus an overnight guest in a home may claim the protection of the Fourth Amendment, but one who is merely present with the consent of the householder may not.

Respondents here were obviously not overnight guests, but were essentially present for a business transaction and were only in the home a matter of hours. There is no suggestion that they had a previous relationship with Thompson, or that there was any other purpose to their visit. Nor was there anything similar to the overnight guest relationship in *Olson* to suggest a degree of acceptance into the household. While the apartment was a dwelling place for Thompson, it was for these respondents simply a place to do business. . . .

Property used for commercial purposes is treated differently for Fourth Amendment purposes than residential property. "An expectation of privacy in commercial premises, however, is different from, and indeed less than, a similar expectation in an individual's home." *New York v. Burger,* 482 U.S. 691, 700. And while it was a "home" in which respondents were present, it was not their home. Similarly, the Court has held that in some circumstances a worker can claim Fourth Amendment protection over his own workplace. But there is no indication that respondents in this case had nearly as significant a connection to Thompson's apartment as the worker in *O'Connor* had to his own private office. If we regard the overnight guest in *Minnesota v. Olson* as typifying those who may claim the protection of the Fourth Amend-

ment in the home of another, and one merely "legitimately on the premises" as typifying those who may not do so, the present case is obviously somewhere in between. But the purely commercial nature of the transaction engaged in here, the relatively short period of time on the premises, and the lack of any previous connection between respondents and the householder, all lead us to conclude that respondents' situation is closer to that of one simply permitted on the premises. We therefore hold that any search which may have occurred did not violate their Fourth Amendment rights.

Because we conclude that respondents had no legitimate expectation of privacy in the apartment, we need not decide whether the police officer's observation constituted a "search." The judgment of the Supreme Court of Minnesota is accordingly reversed, and the cause is remanded for proceedings not inconsistent with this opinion.

It is so ordered.

Justice SCALIA, with whom Justice THOMAS joins, concurring. . . .

The dissent may be correct that a person invited into someone else's house to engage in a common business (even common monkey-business, so to speak) ought to be protected against government searches of the room in which that business is conducted; and that persons invited in to deliver milk or pizza (whom the dissent dismisses as "classroom hypotheticals," post, at 482, as opposed, presumably, to flesh-and-blood hypotheticals) ought not to be protected against government searches of the rooms that they occupy. I am not sure of the answer to those policy questions. But I am sure that the answer is not remotely contained in the Constitution, which means that it is left—as many, indeed most, important questions are left—to the judgment of state and federal legislators. We go beyond our proper role as judges in a democratic society when we restrict the people's power to govern themselves over the full range of policy choices that the Constitution has left available to them.

Justice KENNEDY, concurring.

I join the Court's opinion, for its reasoning is consistent with my view that almost all social guests have a legitimate expectation of privacy, and hence protection against unreasonable searches, in their host's home. . . .

The settled rule is that the requisite connection is an expectation of privacy that society recognizes as reasonable. The application of that rule involves consideration of the kind of place in which the individual claims the privacy interest and what expectations of privacy are traditional and well recognized. I would expect that most, if not all, social guests legitimately expect that, in accordance with social custom, the homeowner will exercise her discretion to include or exclude others for the guests' benefit. As we recognized in *Minnesota v. Olson,* where these social expectations exist—as in the case of an overnight guest—they are sufficient to create a legitimate expectation of privacy, even in the absence of any property right to exclude others. In this respect, the dissent must be correct that reasonable expectations of the owner are shared, to some extent, by the guest. This analysis suggests that, as a general rule, social guests will have an expectation of privacy in their host's home. That is not the case before us, however.

In this case respondents have established nothing more than a fleeting and insubstantial connection with Thompson's home. For all that appears in the record, respondents used Thompson's house simply as a convenient processing station, their purpose involving nothing more than the mechanical act of chopping and packing a substance for distribution. . . .

Respondents have made no persuasive argument that we need to fashion a per se rule of home protection, with an automatic right for all in the home to invoke the exclusionary rule, in order to protect homeowners and their guests from unlawful police intrusion. With these observations, I join the Court's opinion.

Justice BREYER, concurring in the judgment.

I agree with Justice GINSBURG that respondents can claim the Fourth Amendment's protection. Petitioner, however, raises a second question, whether under the circumstances Officer Thielen's observation made "from a public area outside the curtilage of the residence" violated respondents' Fourth Amendment rights. In my view, it did not. . . .

Officer Thielen . . . stood at a place used by the public and from which one could see through the window into the kitchen. The precautions that the apartment's dwellers took to maintain their privacy would have failed in respect to an ordinary passerby standing in that place. Given this Court's well-established case law, I cannot say that the officer engaged in what the Constitution forbids, namely, an "unreasonable search.". . .

Justice GINSBURG, with whom Justice STEVENS and Justice SOUTER join, dissenting.

The Court's decision undermines not only the security of short-term guests, but also the security of the home resident herself. In my view, when a homeowner or lessor personally invites a guest into her home to share in a common endeavor, whether it be for conversation, to engage in leisure activities, or for business purposes licit or illicit, that guest should share his host's shelter against unreasonable searches and seizures. . . .

My concern centers on an individual's choice to share her home and her associations there with persons she selects. Our decisions indicate that people have a reasonable expectation of privacy in their homes in part because they have the prerogative to exclude others. The power to exclude implies the power to include. Our Fourth Amendment decisions should reflect these complementary prerogatives. A home-dweller places her own privacy at risk, the Court's approach indicates, when she opens her home to others, uncertain whether the duration of their stay, their purpose, and their "acceptance into the household" will earn protection. It remains textbook law that "[s]earches and seizures inside a home without a warrant are presumptively unreasonable ab-

sent exigent circumstances." Karo, 468 U.S., at 714-715, 104 S.Ct. 3296. The law in practice is less secure. Human frailty suggests that today's decision will tempt police to pry into private dwellings without warrant, to find evidence incriminating guests who do not rest there through the night. Rakas tolerates that temptation with respect to automobile searches.

I see no impelling reason to extend this risk into the home. . . .

As the Solicitor General acknowledged, the illegality of the host-guest conduct, the fact that they were partners in crime, would not alter the analysis. In Olson, for example, the guest whose security this Court's decision shielded stayed overnight while the police searched for him. The Court held that the guest had Fourth Amendment protection against a warrantless arrest in his host's home despite the guest's involvement in grave crimes (first-degree murder, armed robbery, and assault). . . . If the illegality of the activity made constitutional an otherwise unconstitutional search, such Fourth Amendment protection, reserved for the innocent only, would have little force in regulating police behavior toward either the innocent or the guilty.

Our leading decision in Katz is key to my view of this case. There, we ruled that the Government violated the petitioner's Fourth Amendment rights when it electronically recorded him transmitting wagering information while he was inside a public telephone booth. We were mindful that "the Fourth Amendment protects people, not places," and held that this electronic monitoring of a business call "violated the privacy upon which [the caller] justifiably relied while using the telephone booth." Our obligation to produce coherent results in this often visited area of the law requires us to inform our current expositions by benchmarks already established. As Justice Harlan explained in his dissent in Poe v. Ullman, 367 U.S. 497:

> Each new claim to Constitutional protection must be considered against a background of Constitutional purposes, as they have been rationally perceived and historically developed. Though we exercise limited and sharply restrained judgment, yet there is no "mechanical yardstick," no "mechanical answer." The decision of an apparently novel claim must depend on grounds which follow closely on well-accepted principles and criteria. The new decision must take "its place in relation to what went before and further [cut] a channel for what is to come."

The Court's decision in this case veers sharply from the path marked in Katz. I do not agree that we have a more reasonable expectation of privacy when we place a business call to a person's home from a public telephone booth on the side of the street than when we actually enter that person's premises to engage in a common endeavor.

For the reasons stated, I dissent from the Court's judgment, and would retain judicial surveillance over the warrantless searches today's decision allows.

? **ANALYSIS PROBLEM**

9–2. Do you think it would have made any difference to the majority opinion in *Carter* if Carter had eaten and taken a short nap at the apartment? Explain.

III.   WARRANT REQUIREMENTS

A.   ISSUANCE: PROBABLE CAUSE, NEUTRALITY, PARTICULARITY

Once you determine that the Fourth Amendment applies and that a warrant is needed, certain requirements must be met to issue a legal warrant.

1.   Probable Cause

"[N]o warrant shall issue, but upon probable cause."

probable cause:
the quantum of reliable facts under the circumstances that justifies a reasonable person to believe that which is stated in a warrant.

Probable cause is an abstract Fourth Amendment standard defined as the quantum of reliable facts (evidence) under the particular circumstances that justifies a reasonable and cautious person to believe that which is stated in the warrant. Probable cause means "more than a bare suspicion" and "less than evidence that would justify . . . conviction" [*Brinegar v. U.S.* (1949)].[4] Generally, the amount of evidence required by probable cause is quite uniform, but it can be greater if the invasion of privacy is greater, as in the case of justifying a search by surgery [*Winston v. Lee* (1985)].

In any hearing to determine whether a warrant is invalid for lack of probable cause, courts should "not invalidate the warrant by interpreting the affidavit [the facts in support of probable cause] in a hypertechnical, rather than a commonsense, manner" [*U.S. v. Ventresca* (1965)]. Police testimony that they had additional evidence not stated in the supporting affidavit, however, is irrelevant [*Whiteley v. Warden* (1971)]. If evidence included in the affidavit was knowingly or recklessly false, the reviewing court must test the adequacy of the affidavit without the false information [*Franks v. Delaware* (1978)]. The fact that the affiant had given the police some false information did not undermine the credibility of the affidavit, because it was based on the affiant's overriding corroboration of key facts [*U.S. v. Burston* (11th Cir. 1998)].

"If by the mere force of numbers a majority should deprive a minority of any clearly written constitutional right, it might, in a moral point of view, justify revolution."

—Abraham Lincoln, first inaugural address, March 4, 1861

Although the level of evidence needed to support a finding that probable cause exists is generally uniform whether the warrant is for a search or an arrest, the conclusions that must be supported by that evidence are quite different. The evidence in support of a search warrant must lead to the conclusion that probable cause exists to believe: "(1) that the items sought are connected with criminal activity; and (2) that the items will be found in the place to be searched," whereas in the case of arrest it is probable cause to believe: "(1) that an offense has been committed; and (2) that the person to be arrested committed it."[5]

The type of evidence that can be included in an affidavit to support a finding of probable cause does not have to meet technical evidentiary standards. It can, for example, include hearsay [*Draper v. U.S.* (1959)] or a prior police record [*Brinegar v. U.S.* (1949)]. Information from informants may be used. The degree of reliability of such information, however, has caused considerable litigation. In *Aguilar v. Texas* (1964) the Supreme Court established a two-prong test to guide magistrates in determining whether probable cause exists when an informant is involved:

1.   Sufficient underlying circumstances must be alleged to permit a neutral and detached magistrate to determine that the informant is credible (veracity prong).

2. Sufficient underlying circumstances must be shown to permit a neutral and detached magistrate to determine the basis for the informant's conclusions (basis of knowledge prong).

With this test in mind, the *Aguilar* Court struck down a warrant based on an affidavit that stated the police received reliable information from a credible informant that narcotics would be found at a specific location. The Court's decision emphasizes that the magistrate should weigh the evidence to determine probable cause, and not base the decision on police conclusions.

In *Spinelli v. U.S.* (1969) the Court determined that probable cause could be met even if the basis of knowledge prong was not adequately alleged. The Court said the basis of knowledge prong could still be met if the tip is "in sufficient detail that the magistrate may know that he is relying on something more substantial than a casual rumor . . . or an accusation based merely on an individual's general reputation." The Court used the example of an informant who had previously given reliable information but did not say how the information had been obtained. Instead, the informant gave a detailed description of the person in question, where the person would be arriving by train, what he would be wearing, even that he would be walking fast and that he was peddling narcotics. The detail made up for the lack of knowledge about how the information was arrived at.

The *Aguilar-Spinelli* tests guided lower courts until 1983 when a more conservative Supreme Court decided *Illinois v. Gates* (1983). *Gates* gave the signal that the Court was removing the two-prong analysis from center stage and applying a less rigorous analysis of a "totality of the circumstances." Police received an anonymous letter detailing the upcoming travel plans of Gates and his wife and stating that the purpose of this activity was to ferry illegal drugs. Neither the veracity of the informant nor the underlying basis for his conclusions was provided. Based on the tip, however, the police observed Gates and his wife conforming in considerable measure with the activity described in the informant's letter, activity that the Court said is "as suggestive of a prearranged drug run, as it is of an ordinary vacation trip." After the suspects returned home, the police obtained a warrant for the search of their home and did find illegal drugs. In deciding whether probable cause existed, the Court said that the "veracity" and "basis of knowledge" prongs were useful to consider but were not tests that needed to be definitively met in a hypertechnical manner in every case; rather, the "totality of circumstances" should guide the Court in determining probable cause. It is worth noting that in relaxing the standard to an as of yet uncertain degree the Court did confirm *Aguilar* in that there must be adequate information for the magistrate to determine probable cause, not a mere ratification of either police or informant conclusions. The *Gates* standard is to be given broad interpretation by the states [*Massachusetts v. Upton* (1984)].

Some state courts in interpreting their respective constitutions have adopted the *Gates* standard, others retain the *Aguilar-Spinelli* tests, and still others have developed unique hybrid standards more protective than the *Gates* standard. Be sure to research applicable search and seizure standards in your state.

The courts have not required a showing of veracity from police or citizens who are not a part of the seamy world of criminal informants. The cases do, however, require a showing of the basis of knowledge.[6]

Whether information in the supporting affidavit is stale also can be a factor in determining probable cause to believe that the items to be seized are at the specified location. The general rule is that staleness "must be determined by the circumstances of each case" [*Sgro v. U.S.* (1932)]. In *Sgro,* the search of a hotel pursuant to a warrant was held invalid because it was based on the affiant's allegation that he had purchased illegal beer there three weeks earlier. If, however, the information pertains to an ongoing illegal enterprise rather than an isolated offense, its staleness is less likely to invalidate the warrant [*U.S. v. Spikes* (6th Cir. 1998)]. The nature of the property to be seized also can be important. For example, three-month-old information that a bank robbery suspect might have the bank's money bag at his residence was held to provide probable cause [*U.S. v. Steeves* (8th Cir. 1975)].

A growing body of court decisions upholds **anticipatory search warrants.** These warrants anticipate probable cause being present on the basis of a predictable event, such as the expected delivery of illegal drugs or other contraband to a specific location. Thus, police can be ready but, generally, may not execute the warrant until the event occurs, creating the necessary probable cause [*U.S. v. Tagbering* (8th Cir. 1993) and *U.S. v. Dornhofer* (4th Cir. 1988)]. An anticipatory search warrant issued under the condition that it could not be executed by police until arrival of the expected contraband did not need that condition to be written into the warrant when such a requirement was "logically implicit" and had been stated orally by the judge [*U.S. v. Leidner* (7th Cir. 1996)].

Because of numerous appeals on the adequacy of probable cause for warrants and warrantless searches and arrests, the Supreme Court addressed the standards for appellate courts reviewing the issue. In *Ornelus v. U.S.* (1996), the Court ruled that appellate courts should review the case *de novo,* meaning it should look at both the factual and legal basis for probable cause in the same manner that the trial court should. This would ensure more uniformity and certainty in probable cause or reasonable suspicion determinations.

Police apply for the search warrant by filling out an application for a search warrant and attaching an affidavit in support of the application. The affidavit must provide sufficient underlying evidence to demonstrate that probable cause exists for the search or arrest. The application and affidavit are normally in writing but may be made by telephone or electrical recording.

2. Neutrality

Only a neutral and detached public official, normally a judge or magistrate, can review the application for a warrant, determine from the affidavit if probable cause exists, and issue the search warrant. Judicial neutrality is essential to check the power of the police and the government, and to ensure that privacy may be invaded only when the government conforms to constitutional standards. The role of the judge, therefore, is to see to it that those constitutional standards are enforced and that the process does not deteriorate into a rubber stamp formality. For this reason an official associated with law enforcement, such as an attorney general or one who otherwise is not neutral and detached, may not issue a search warrant.

3. Particularity

A valid search warrant, according to the Fourth Amendment, must describe with particularity the place to be searched and the things to be seized. This rule embodies our founders' extreme distaste for general warrants that can be readily abused. By requiring particularity, reasonable limits are placed on what the police can seize and on how broad the search can be.

In drafting a warrant, provide sufficient detail so the officers can identify the place to be searched [*Steele v. U.S.* (1925)]. For urban areas that means a street number and possibly a specific apartment or other equally discernable criteria; for rural areas a more general but yet discriminating description is acceptable. If a vehicle is to be searched, identify one specific vehicle by license number or other clear criteria. A person to be seized must be identified by name, if possible, or a complete physical description. Minor errors in any of these descriptions will generally not affect the warrant's validity.

Leave nothing to the discretion of the officers in describing "things" to be seized. In *Marron v. U.S.* (1927) a warrant listing intoxicating liquors and articles for their manufacture did not authorize the seizure of financial records at the same location. A somewhat generic description such as "cases of whiskey" may be adequate particu-

anticipatory search warrant:
a search warrant issued on the basis of a predictable or inevitable future event, the occurrence of which is needed to form the probable cause for the warrant.

de novo:
review of both the questions of fact and the questions of law in an appellate case.

larity for seizure under prohibition or in areas today where sale of such beverages is illegal [*Steele v. U.S.* (1925)]; more precision in description is usually needed, however. When First Amendment issues are involved, such as searches for papers, books, or films, it is necessary to single out the particular book or books, and all copies or the only copy should not be seized, especially if that will interfere with public display or sale [*Andresen v. Maryland* (1976), *Stanford v. Texas* (1965), *Zurcher v. Stanford Daily* (1978), and *Heller v. New York* (1973)].

Computer searches involve special problems. Police might be able to specify and seize a particular item or document in concrete form, but it may be harder to locate and "seize" a document or data stored in a computer memory bank. Whereas a warrant directing seizure of "all records" may be too broad for traditional seizures, a warrant directing seizure of a computer and its hard drive ("all data") may be permissible because of the nature of computers [*U.S. v. Hunter* (D. Vt. 1998)]. The *Federal Guidelines for Searching and Seizing Computers* published by the Department of Justice is helpful in computer search questions. It can be requested by mail or viewed at www.usdoj.gov/criminal/cybercrime/search_docs.

Exhibit 9–1 is an example of an application and affidavit for a search warrant, and Exhibit 9–2 is an example of a search warrant and inventory.

B.   EXECUTION OF THE WARRANT

1.   Who and When

Federal and similar state rules and statutes require that warrants be executed by a police officer. The search can be rendered unreasonable regarding the expectation of privacy if the police are accompanied by persons who do not have a legitimate reason to be present to assist them. A police search of a house subject to a warrant was an unreasonable invasion of the expectation of privacy when the police were accompanied by a newspaper reporter and photographer [*Wilson v. Layne* (1999)].

A search warrant must be executed within the times specified in the warrant or in the rule or law. The Federal Rules of Criminal Procedure 41(c)(1) specify ten days. Federal and most state laws require daytime service, normally 6:00 A.M. to 10:00 P.M. [Fed. R. Crim. P. 41(c)(1)], and permit nighttime service only in justified circumstances. State laws may vary.

Under the reasonableness clause of the Fourth Amendment, police executing a warrant at a dwelling are to knock on the door, identify themselves, state that they are there to execute a warrant, and wait a reasonable period of time before breaking in [*Wilson v. Arkansas* (1995)]. How long police must wait after announcing their presence is a matter of what is reasonable under the circumstances. A five-second delay was held inadequate in *West v. U.S.* (D.C. 1998) when police thought they heard people moving around in a manner consistent with the destruction of drugs. A twelve- to fifteen-second delay was adequate, however, when police knew people were inside, had heard that they would defend themselves, and it was midmorning [*U.S. v. Spikes* (6th Cir. 1998)]. Use of subterfuge to enter is not permitted.[7]

No-knock or unannounced entries are permitted in justified circumstances, for example, when there is substantial risk that notice (knocking) will lead to destruction of evidence [*Ker v. California* (1963)] or resistance, will be likely to permit escape, will significantly increase the danger to officers, or when it becomes a useless gesture. The last applies to situations where the subjects of the search or seizure are already aware of the presence of the police. Police must have a "reasonable suspicion" that one or more of these circumstances exist before they can enter without knocking. A few jurisdictions, including New York, have enacted "no-knock" laws embodying some of these exceptions. Does your state have such a law?

An attempt by Wisconsin to make all no-knock entries reasonable in felony drug investigations was held unconstitutional in *Richards v. Wisconsin* (1997). Whether the

EXHIBIT 9–1
Application and Affidavit for Search Warrant

AO 106 (Rev. 7/87) Affidavit for Search Warrant   ⊕

United States District Court

Eastern _____ DISTRICT OF _____ Columbia _____

In the Matter of the Search of
(Name, address or brief description of person, property or premises to be searched)

504 North University Way
Apartment 3
Legalville, Columbia

APPLICATION AND AFFIDAVIT
FOR SEARCH WARRANT

CASE NUMBER:

I ____ Thomas Barger _____ being duly sworn depose and say:

I am a(n) ____ officer of the U.S. Drug Enforcement Agency _____ and have reason to believe
Official Title

that ☐ on the person of or ☒ on the property or premises known as (name, description and/or location)

504 North University Way, Legalville, Columbia, a two-story, tan brick apartment
building, with four units, specifically the second floor apartment number 3, the
front right apartment, occupied by Nancy Stroud and Lisa Munden

in the _____ Eastern _____ District of _____ Columbia _____
there is now concealed a certain person or property, namely (describe the person or property to be seized)

various plastic baggies containing controlled substances, i.e., cocaine and
marijuana

which is (state one or more bases for search and seizure set forth under Rule 41(b) of the Federal Rules of Criminal Procedure)

contraband

concerning a violation of Title ____ 21 _____ United States code, Section(s) __ 841(a)(1), 844 _____.
The facts to support a finding of Probable Cause are as follows:

Officer Harriet Malone of the U.S. Drug Enforcement Agency has informed the affiant
that they have been tracking components of a shipment of cocaine since its entry
into the United States one month ago. That federal and state agents have tracked
some of this cocaine to the above address. A DEA undercover agent, present at the
above address earlier this evening (date), reports observing some cocaine and
marijuana at the above described apartment.

Continued on the attached sheet and made a part hereof. ☐ Yes   ☐ No

_____
Signature of Affiant

Sworn to before me, and subscribed in my presence

_____ at _____
Date   City and State

_____   _____
Name and Title of Judicial Officer   Signature of Judicial Officer

EXHIBIT 9–2
Sample Warrant and Inventory

AO 93 (Rev. 5/85)   Search Warrant   ⊕

United States District Court

Eastern _____ DISTRICT OF _____ Columbia

In the Matter of the Search of

(Name, address or brief description of person or property to be searched)

504 North University Way
Apartment 3
Legalville, Columbia

SEARCH WARRANT

CASE NUMBER: XXXXXX

TO: _U.S. Drug Enforcement Agents_____ and any Authorized Officer of the United States

Affidavit(s) having been made before me by __Officer Thomas Barger_____ who has reason to
                                                        Affiant

believe that ☐ on the person of or ☒ on the premises known as (name, description and/or location)

504 North University Way, Legalville, Columbia, a two-story, tan brick apartment
building, with four units, specifically the second floor apartment number 3, the
front right apartment, occupied by Nancy Stroud and Lisa Munden

in the_____Eastern_____ District of _____Columbia_____ there is now
concealed a certain person or property, namely (describe the person or property)

Contraband, i.e., plastic baggies containing cocaine and marijuana contrary to 21
U.S.C. §§ 841(a)(1) and 844.

I am satisfied that the affidavit(s) and any recorded testimony establish probable cause to believe that the person
or property so described is now concealed on the person or premises above-described and establish grounds for
the issuance of this warrant.

                                                          (Date)
YOU ARE HEREBY COMMANDED to search on or before _____
                                                              Date

(not to exceed 10 days) the person or place named above for the person or property specified, serving this warrant
and making the search (in the daytime — 6:00 A.M. to 10:00 P.M.) (at any time in the day or night as I find
reasonable cause has been established) and if the person or property be found there to seize same, leaving a copy
of this warrant and receipt for the person or property taken, and prepare a written inventory of the person or property seized and promptly return this warrant to _____
as required by law.   U.S. Judge or Magistrate

_____   at   _____
Date and Time Issued   City and State

_____   _____
Name and Title of Judicial Officer   Signature of Judicial Officer

Continued

EXHIBIT 9–2 *(Concluded)*
Sample Warrant and Inventory

AO 93 (Rev. 3/85)   Search Warrant

RETURN		
DATE WARRANT RECEIVED (Date)	DATE AND TIME WARRANT EXECUTED (Date) 1 a.m.	COPY OF WARRANT AND RECEIPT FOR ITEMS LEFT WITH Lisa Munden
INVENTORY MADE IN THE PRESENCE OF Lisa Munden		

INVENTORY OF PERSON OR PROPERTY TAKEN PURSUANT TO THE WARRANT

4 small plastic baggies of cocaine
various amounts of loose cocaine gathered from table tops
6 small envelopes with various amounts of marijuana
1 prescription size bottle of amphetamines
1 .22 caliber pistol

CERTIFICATION

I swear that this inventory is a true and detailed account of the person or property taken by me on the warrant.

_____

Subscribed, sworn to, and returned before me this date.

_____   _____
U.S. Judge or Magistrate   Date

reasonable suspicion test has been met in no way depends on whether police had to destroy property in order to enter [*U.S. v. Ramirez* (1998)]. The degree of property destruction, however, can subject the entry to the question of whether it was a reasonable search.

2.   Detention and Search of Persons

Police may detain persons during the search. *Michigan v. Summers* (1981) spelled out three governmental interests or justifications for doing so: (1) prevents flight, (2) reduces risk of harm to police, and (3) facilitates orderly completion of the search. In *Summers* the police with a search warrant for narcotics ran into Summers, who appeared to be leaving. The police detained him, which the Court said was justified, especially because they had a warrant based on probable cause to believe that someone at Summers' house had committed a crime. The Court also mentioned that the intrusion on liberty was minimal, because it occurred in Summers' home and no public stigma attached. An interesting footnote in the case reserved judgment on the issue of whether detention is proper when the search is for mere evidence of crime, such as a search in a newspaper's file for photos of a riot that might help identify looters. In this search there is no probable cause to believe that someone at the newspaper had committed a crime. Would the *Summers* case be different in outcome if Summers had been a store owner detained openly before his customers?

Eventually, Summers was arrested because police found narcotics in the house, then, "incident to the lawful arrest," they searched Summers and found more drugs in his jacket pocket. Do police executing a warrant with probable cause to search the premises have the right to search persons present at the scene? Case law says police may not search such persons, with three exceptions: (1) the search may be made if there is separate probable cause to believe the person is in possession of contraband and there is not a reasonable amount of time for the police to obtain another warrant, although such a search cannot be based on a mere suspicion of possession [*Ybarra v. Illinois* (1979)]; (2) if there is a lawful arrest, a search may be conducted "incident to the lawful arrest," as occurred in *Summers* [*Marron v. U.S.* (1927)]; and (3) the search is legal if there is some basis for a belief that the person is armed, but then the search must be limited to a pat-down search [*Terry v. Ohio* (1968)].

3.   Seizure of Items Other Than Those Named in the Warrant

Items beyond those named in the warrant may be seized when the police *inadvertently* see contraband or evidence of a crime in "plain view" while executing the warrant [*Coolidge v. New Hampshire* (1971)]. Asking the police to wait to get a warrant or to ignore such evidence is ludicrous. Police have abused the "plain view" exception, however, to unlawfully broaden a search. Police, for example, may not open a cookie jar when the warrant calls for the search for a wide-screen television, or they may not pick up an item and look on the bottom for a serial number even if a reasonable suspicion exists that the item is contraband or evidence of a crime [*Arizona v. Hicks* (1987)]. In other words, the discovery must be a plain view discovery, and there must be probable cause to believe the item is the fruit of a crime, or an instrumentality or evidence of a crime. The concept of plain view is discussed more thoroughly in the next section of this chapter.

4.   Required Inventory

Police are required to report what they seize when executing a search warrant. This report is normally made on an inventory sheet that is attached to the return of the search warrant, which is a document or a part of the warrant that indicates that the warrant was executed, the time and place that it was executed, and any other requested information. Failure to make an inventory or to include everything that was seized is not a constitutional breach and does not invalidate the search. See Exhibit 9–2 for a sample inventory. Although seized property must be inventoried, police do not have to provide information on how the property can be recovered by the owner [*City of West Covina v. Perkins* (1999)]. Notice to owners of seizure, however, is required as a matter of due process.

C. WARRANT SUBSEQUENT TO SEARCH: INDEPENDENT SOURCE

In *Murray v. U.S.* (1988) the Court wrestled with whether a search warrant was legal after police had at an earlier time conducted an illegal search of the same place. The police had probable cause to believe that marijuana was located in a building. Before getting a warrant, they forced their way into the building and confirmed their suspicions. Hours later they received a search warrant from a magistrate without mentioning anything about the earlier search, and relying solely on the original probable cause they had prior to the illegal search. The Supreme Court said the warrant obtained after the first search would be legal if it was based on no more than the probable cause that existed for the original search. The warrant could not be based in any way on evidence gained from the first illegal search. In other words, the subsequent warrant must have an independent and untainted source of probable cause.

IV. EXCEPTIONS TO THE REQUIREMENT FOR A WARRANT

A. INTRODUCTION

The heart of the previous section is that warrants are the preferred and constitutionally mandated method for the government to conduct searches and seizures where there is a reasonable expectation of privacy on the part of a person. These warrants must be based on a proper showing of probable cause determined by a neutral magistrate. Exceptions to the warrant requirement should be rare and based on strong justification. These exceptions include the following:

- Arrest
- Stop and frisk
- Search incident to lawful arrest
- Plain view
- Motor vehicle searches
- Hot pursuit
- Evanescent evidence
- Border, regulatory, and emergency searches
- Consent searches
- Inevitable discovery
- Community caretaking function

B. ARREST

An arrest is the physical or implied seizure or taking into custody of a person by police, significantly restricting a person's freedom of movement and subjecting him or her to the authority of the officer. The Fourth Amendment applies to all police seizures of persons including those of short duration. Normally, a warrant for arrest is required if the police must go into a dwelling to make the arrest [*Payton v. New York* (1980)].

Apart from that and based on common law tradition, the Fourth Amendment does not require a warrant for the arrest of persons accused of felonies. The police must have probable cause to believe that the arrestee has committed a crime prior to making the arrest. For example, if a bank has been robbed and a police officer is informed that a person well known to the officer committed the robbery, it would be ridiculous to require a warrant to arrest the suspect if they came face to face with each other at the street corner five minutes after the bank robbery. It would be just as ridiculous, however, to permit the arrest of every person in the neighborhood if the only information police had about the robber was that the robber was wearing a light colored shirt and jeans. Any arrest without probable cause is illegal, results in the release of the suspect, and may lead to the suppression of any evidence seized as a result of the arrest. Such evidence would be "fruit of the poisonous tree" (results of an illegal arrest), the doctrine set out in *Wong Sun v. U.S.* (1963). Therefore, a determination of when an arrest has occurred has been a frequent subject of litigation.

The Supreme Court of the United States has attempted to define "arrest" in a series of cases and, thus, to establish when probable cause is necessary. There is little question that the taking of a person into a police car or into a police station is an arrest [*Davis v. Mississippi* (1969) and *Dunaway v. New York* (1979)]. An arrest can occur, as well, in a bedroom where police prevent a person from leaving and where the police consider the person to be "under arrest" [*Orozco v. Texas* (1969)]. Stopping a car is an arrest of its occupants [*Henry v. U.S.* (1959)]. A high-speed chase or other pursuit by police, however, is not an arrest [*County of Sacramento v. Lewis* (1998) and *California v. Hodari D.* (1991)]. Less intrusive seizures, which are discussed under the "stop and frisk" exception, are not arrests and, therefore, require the lesser standard of "reasonable suspicion" that criminal activity is afoot. A person is "seized" for Fourth Amendment purposes when, under the circumstances, a reasonable person would have believed he or she was not free to leave [*Michigan v. Chesternut* (1988) and *U.S. v. Mendenhall* (1980)].

Although police do not need a warrant to make an arrest for a felony, most states require a warrant for misdemeanor arrests. A warrant is not necessary if the misdemeanor is committed in the presence of the officer or, in some states, where the officer has reasonable grounds to believe a crime has been committed. Check the law of your state for essential details concerning the need for a warrant for arrest.

The Supreme Court in *U.S. v. Watson* (1976) had the opportunity to change common law and require a warrant for arrest in all cases except where exigent circumstances exist, but it declined to do so. In 1975, however, it did reiterate the principle that, even though a warrant for arrest may not be necessary, authorities must bring an individual before a judge or magistrate within a reasonable length of time to determine if probable cause exists for their detention [*Gerstein v. Pugh* (1975)]. In 1991 the Court declared that this period may be as long as forty-eight hours, but anything longer, even if it is a holiday weekend, is presumptively improper [*County of Riverside v. McLaughlin* (1991)].

Even though an arrest based on probable cause may not require a warrant, an arrest can become unreasonable under the Fourth Amendment when the means used by the officer to secure the arrest are unreasonable. The use of deadly force to secure the arrest of a felon is unreasonable unless the officer is threatened with a weapon, or probable cause exists to believe the suspect has threatened or committed serious physical harm to another [*Tennessee v. Garner* (1985)]. The United States may even invade the territory of a sovereign nation to kidnap one of its citizens based on probable cause. The Supreme Court ruled that such a seizure is a valid arrest in *U.S. v. Alvarez-Machain* (1992).

In *Whren v. U.S.* (1996) the court addressed whether an arrest is rendered unreasonable under the Fourth Amendment because officers have a pretext (ulterior motive) or depart from usual police procedure or regulation.

WHREN v. UNITED STATES
Supreme Court of the United States
517 U.S. 806, 116 S.Ct. 1769 (1996).

JUSTICE SCALIA delivered the opinion of the Court. . . .

On the evening of June 10, 1993, plainclothes vice-squad officers of the District of Columbia Metropolitan Police Department were patrolling a "high drug area" of the city in an unmarked car. Their suspicions were aroused when they passed a dark Pathfinder truck with temporary license plates and youthful occupants waiting at a stop sign, the driver looking down into the lap of the passenger at his right. The truck remained stopped at the intersection for what seemed an unusually long time—more than twenty seconds. When the police car executed a U-turn in order to head back toward the truck, the Pathfinder turned suddenly to its right, without signalling, and sped off at an "unreasonable" speed. The policemen followed, and in a short while overtook the Pathfinder when it stopped behind other traffic at a red light. They pulled up alongside, and Officer Ephraim Soto stepped out and approached the driver's door, identifying himself as a police officer and directing the driver, petitioner Brown, to put the vehicle in park. When Soto drew up to the driver's window, he immediately observed two large plastic bags of what appeared to be crack cocaine in petitioner Whren's hands. Petitioners were arrested, and quantities of several types of illegal drugs were retrieved from the vehicle.

Petitioners were charged in a four-count indictment with violating various federal drug laws. At a pretrial suppression hearing, they challenged the legality of the stop and the resulting seizure of the drugs. They argued that the stop had not been justified by probable cause to believe, or even reasonable suspicion, that petitioners were engaged in illegal drug-dealing activity; and that Officer Soto's asserted ground for approaching the vehicle—to give the driver a warning concerning traffic violations—was pretextual. The District Court denied the suppression motion. . . .

Petitioners were convicted of the counts at issue here. The Court of Appeals affirmed the convictions, holding with respect to the suppression issue that, "regardless of whether a police officer subjectively believes that the occupants of an automobile may be engaging in some other illegal behavior, a traffic stop is permissible as long as a reasonable officer in the same circumstances could have stopped the car for the suspected traffic violation."

The Fourth Amendment guarantees "[t]he right of the people to be secure in their persons, houses, papers, and effects, against unreasonable searches and seizures." Temporary detention of individuals during the stop of an automobile by the police, even if only for a brief period and for a limited purpose, constitutes a "seizure" of "persons" within the meaning of this provision. An automobile stop is thus subject to the constitutional imperative that it not be "unreasonable" under the circumstances. As a general matter, the decision to stop an automobile is reasonable where the police have probable cause to believe that a traffic violation has occurred.

Petitioners accept that Officer Soto had probable cause to believe that various provisions of the District of Columbia traffic code [regarding inattentive driving, speeding, and turning without signalling] had been violated. They argue, however, that "in the unique context of civil traffic regulations" probable cause is not enough. Since, they contend, the use of automobiles is so heavily and minutely regulated that total compliance with traffic and safety rules is nearly impossible, a police officer will almost invariably be able to catch any given motorist in a technical violation. This creates the temptation to use traffic stops as a means of investigating other law violations, as to which no probable cause or even articulable suspicion exists. Petitioners, who are both black, further contend that police officers might decide which motorists to stop based on decidedly impermissible factors, such as the race of the car's occupants. To avoid this danger, they say, the Fourth Amendment test for traffic stops should be, not the normal one (applied by the Court of Appeals) of whether probable cause existed to justify the stop; but rather, whether a police officer, acting reasonably, would have made the stop for the reason given.

Petitioners contend that the standard they propose is consistent with our past cases' disapproval of police attempts to use valid bases of action against citizens as pretexts for pursuing other investigatory agendas. . . . But only an undiscerning reader would regard these cases as endorsing the principle that ulterior motives can invalidate police conduct that is justifiable on the basis of probable cause to believe that a violation of law has occurred. In each case we were addressing the validity of a search conducted in the absence of probable cause. . . .

Not only have we never held, outside the context of inventory search or administrative inspection . . . , that an officer's motive invalidates objectively justifiable behavior under the Fourth Amendment; but we have repeatedly held and asserted the contrary [citing *U.S. v. Villamonte-Marquez,* 462 U.S. 579 (1983), *U.S. v. Robinson,* 414 U.S. 218 (1973), and *Scott v. U.S.,* 463 U.S. 128 (1978)]. . . .

We think these cases foreclose any argument that the constitutional reasonableness of traffic stops depends on the actual motivations of the individual officers involved. We of course agree with petitioners that the Constitution prohibits selective enforcement of the law based on considerations such as race. But the constitutional basis for objecting to intentionally discriminatory application of laws is the Equal Protection Clause, not the Fourth Amendment. Subjective intentions play no role in ordinary, probable-cause Fourth Amendment analysis.

Recognizing that we have been unwilling to entertain Fourth Amendment challenges based on the actual motivations of individual officers, petitioners disavow any intention to make the individual officer's subjective good faith the touchstone of "reasonableness." They insist that the standard they have put forward—whether the officer's conduct deviated materially from usual police practices, so that a reasonable officer in the same circumstances would not have made the stop for the reasons given—is an "objective" one.

But although framed in empirical terms, this approach is plainly and indisputably driven by subjective considerations. Its whole purpose is to prevent the police from doing under the guise of enforcing the traffic code what they would like to do for different reasons. Petitioners' proposed standard may not use the word "pretext," but it is designed to combat nothing other than the perceived "danger" of the pretextual stop, albeit only indirectly and over the run of cases. Instead of asking whether the individual officer had the proper state of mind, the petitioners would have us ask, in effect, whether (based on general police practices) it is plausible to believe that the officer had the proper state of mind. . . .

[It] seems to us somewhat easier to figure out the intent of an individual officer than to plumb the collective consciousness of law enforcement in order to determine whether a "reasonable officer" would have been moved to act upon the traffic violation. While police manuals and standard procedures may sometimes provide objective assistance, ordinarily one would be reduced to speculating about the hypothetical reaction of a hypothetical constable—an exercise that might be called virtual subjectivity.

Moreover, police enforcement practices, even if they could be practicably assessed by a judge, vary from place to place and from time to time. We cannot accept that the search and seizure protections of the Fourth Amendment are so variable, and can be made to turn upon such trivialities. The difficulty is illustrated by petitioners' arguments in this case. Their claim that a reasonable officer would not have made this stop is based largely on District of Columbia police regulations which permit plainclothes officers in unmarked vehicles to enforce traffic laws "only in the case of a violation that is so grave as to pose an immediate threat to the safety of others." This basis of invalidation would not apply in jurisdictions that had a different practice. And it would not have applied even in the District of Columbia, if Officer Soto had been wearing a uniform or patrolling in a marked police cruiser.

Petitioners argue that our cases support insistence upon police adherence to standard practices as an objective means of rooting out pretext. . . . But it is a long leap from the proposition that following regular procedures is some evidence of lack of pretext to the proposition that failure to follow regular procedures proves (or is an operational substitute for) pretext. . . .

In what would appear to be an elaboration on the "reasonable officer" test, petitioners argue that the balancing inherent in any Fourth Amendment inquiry requires us to weigh the governmental and individual interests implicated in a traffic stop such as we have here. That balancing, petitioners claim, does not support investigation of minor traffic infractions by plainclothes police in unmarked vehicles; such investigation only minimally advances the government's interest in traffic safety, and may indeed retard it by producing motorist confusion and alarm—a view said to be supported by the Metropolitan Police Department's own regulations generally prohibiting this practice. And as for the Fourth Amendment interests of the individuals concerned, petitioners point out that our cases acknowledge that even ordinary traffic stops entail "a possibly unsettling show of authority"; that they at best "interfere with freedom of movement, are inconvenient, and consume time" and at worst "may create substantial anxiety." That anxiety is likely to be even more pronounced when the stop is conducted by plainclothes officers in unmarked cars.

It is of course true that in principle every Fourth Amendment case, since it turns upon a "reasonableness" determination, involves a balancing of all relevant factors. With rare exceptions not applicable here, however, the result of that balancing is not in doubt where the search or seizure is based upon probable cause. . . .

Where probable cause has existed, the only cases in which we have found it necessary actually to perform the "balancing" analysis involved searches or seizures conducted in an extraordinary manner, unusually harmful to an individual's privacy or even physical interests—such as, for example, seizure by means of deadly force, see *Tennessee v. Garner;* unannounced entry into a home, see *Wilson v. Arkansas;* entry into a home without a warrant, see *Welsh v. Wisconsin;* or physical penetration of the body, see *Winston v. Lee.* The making of a traffic stop out-of-uniform does not remotely qualify as such an extreme practice, and so is governed by the usual rule that probable cause to believe the law has been broken "outbalances" private interest in avoiding police contact.

Petitioners urge as an extraordinary factor in this case that the "multitude of applicable traffic and equipment regulations" is so large and so difficult to obey perfectly that virtually everyone is guilty of violation, permitting the police to single out almost whomever they wish for a stop. But we are aware of no principle that would allow us to decide at what point a code of law becomes so expansive and so commonly violated that infraction itself can no longer be the ordinary measure of the lawfulness of enforcement. And even if we could identify such exorbitant codes, we do not know by what standard (or what right) we would decide, as petitioners would have us do, which particular provisions are sufficiently important to merit enforcement.

For the run-of-the-mine case, which this surely is, we think there is no realistic alternative to the traditional common-law rule that probable cause justifies a search and seizure.

. . .

Here the District Court found that the officers had probable cause to believe that petitioners had violated the traffic code. That rendered the stop reasonable under the Fourth Amendment, the evidence thereby discovered admissible, and the upholding of the convictions by the Court of Appeals for the District of Columbia Circuit correct.

Judgment affirmed.

C. STOP AND FRISK (INVESTIGATORY DETENTION)

stop and frisk (investigatory detention):
a brief investigatory stop occurring when a police officer confronts a suspicious looking person to ask a few questions and to "pat down" their clothing to see if they are carrying weapons.

A **stop and frisk (investigatory detention)** is a brief investigatory stop occurring when a police officer confronts a suspicious looking person to ask a few questions and to "pat down" their clothing to see if they are carrying weapons. The officer does not need a warrant and, unlike an arrest and full search that requires probable cause, a stop and frisk requires only that the officer have a reasonable, articulable, and particularized suspicion that the suspect (1) is involved in wrongdoing and (2) may be carrying a weapon [*Terry v. Ohio* (1968)]. If the pat down reveals the presence of a weaponlike object, the officer has the right to reach into a pocket to remove the weapon. If the object turns out to be a weapon or contraband, then the officer may seize the weapon or criminally tainted object.

The test in stop and frisk is not the warrant and probable cause portions of the Fourth Amendment, but its requirement of reasonableness. The balancing occurs in trying to determine how much actual evidence (objective suspicion) is required to justify the degree of intrusion, either in the form of interfering with a citizen's liberty or in the form of a search of clothing, car, or other property. The reasonable suspicion standard and the limits of *Terry* were stable law for a number of years. Recently, however, courts have been reevaluating the reasonableness test to justify expansion of the *Terry* stop and frisk. Increasingly intrusive stops and searches over longer periods of time based on less reliable and less objectively articulable evidence have been allowed. In reading through the following list of decisions on stop and frisk, keep in mind the major issues: first, what level of suspicion (evidence) is needed to make the stop reasonable; second, how long the stop can be; and third, to what or whom the stop and frisk may be applied.

Here is a sampling of cases.

"The layman's Constitutional view is that what he likes is Constitutional and that which he doesn't like is unconstitutional. That about measures up the Constitutional acumen of the average person."

—Hugo L. Black, *New York Times,* February 26, 1971

- An informant's somewhat reliable tip authorized the direct search of a suspect's pocket [*Adams v. Williams* (1972)].
- The fact that two men walked away from each other in an alley in a drug trafficking area was inadequate grounds for a stop [*Brown v. Texas* (1979)].
- A traveler's luggage could be seized on a reasonable suspicion, but for no longer than a person can be reasonably detained (ninety minutes was too long) [*U.S. v. Place* (1983)].
- The moving of an air passenger from a hall to an office for questioning, when a canine cop could have resolved the matter quietly, escalated a stop to an arrest without probable cause [*U.S. v. Sharpe* (1985)].
- Even if the person was out of a stopped car, a police officer could search the passenger compartment for weapons if there were grounds to believe the suspect was dangerous or that such a search was necessary to protect the officer [*Michigan v. Long* (1983)].
- An anonymous tip was reasonable if some details were corroborated by police before the stop [*White v. Alabama* (1990)].
- An anonymous telephone tip to police, however, that one of three young African American men (the one in plaid) was carrying a gun without addi-

tional corroboration is insufficient reasonable suspicion to stop and frisk a suspect [*Florida v. J.L.* (2000)]. The Court went on to say that an anonymous tip may be enough reasonable suspicion in the context of a school or an airport to justify a protective search.

- The confrontation by police of a bus passenger in a bus at a terminal, which led to questioning and the search of his bag, was not a seizure because a reasonable passenger would feel free to decline the questioning and search [*Florida v. Bostick* (1991)].
- Police yelling "stop" and chasing the defendant, who ran when police approached (exercising his refusal to be questioned or searched?), was not a seizure until the person was actually tackled. The officer's reasons for yelling "stop" and pursuing and tackling did not fall short of the *Terry* standard, even if the officer only had a hunch that criminal activity was afoot [*California v. Hodari D.* (1991)].

The Supreme Court stopped short of saying that running from police in and of itself comprises reasonable suspicion to justify a stop and frisk. Although the court said mere flight alone is not enough, it does not require much beyond that in *Illinois v. Wardlow* (2000). The court upheld the stop and frisk based on the defendant's running as police approached, plus the fact that it was an area known for heavy narcotics trafficking. The stop and frisk revealed a gun. Compare *Wardlow* with *Hodari D.* and *Brown v. Texas*.

It is generally understood that a person may refuse to provide identification or other information to police, and such refusal is, by itself, insufficient grounds for an investigatory detention [*Brown v. Texas* (1979)].

The use of profiling guidelines by police to stop persons suspected of drug trafficking or other crimes is controversial. Although such profiling may be helpful to law enforcement, the issue remains whether profiling alone can be a sufficient basis for a stop and frisk or, for example, the search of a vehicle. The use of a drug courier profile along with several other factors was upheld in *U.S. v. Sololow* (1989) as comprising reasonable suspicion for an investigative stop under the totality of the circumstances. Some profiling, however, targets race as an important factor, which raises serious questions about the reasonableness of searches, due process, and equal protection under the law. A 1999 study by the American Civil Liberties Union reported that along one stretch of I-95, African Americans made up 17 percent of the drivers but 73 percent of those stopped and searched. In Illinois, Hispanics made up 8 percent of the motorists, but 30 percent of those stopped.[8]

In *Minnesota v. Dickerson* (1993) the Supreme Court ruled that, in the context of a *Terry* stop and frisk, contraband does not have to be in view in order to be seized. Formerly, a police officer could seize contraband only if the pat down revealed an object that appeared to be a weapon but turned out to be contraband. In *Dickerson*, however, the Court ruled that if a pat down for weapons reveals an object that by feel is immediately identifiable as contraband, it may be seized. The officer used touch to examine a lump in the suspect's jacket and determined that "it felt to be a lump of crack cocaine in cellophane." This case broadened *Terry* to include a "plain feel" exception to the warrant requirement.

D. SEARCH INCIDENT TO LAWFUL ARREST

If police make a lawful arrest by probable cause or by arrest warrant, the area immediately accessible to the defendant may be searched without a warrant as long as the search is contemporaneous with the arrest. This rule prevents harm to police from weapons within reasonable reach of an arrestee and prevents the arrestee from destroying contraband or evidence of a crime [*Weeks v. U.S.* (1914) and *Chimel v. California* (1969)]. Four questions arise: What type of arrest justifies such a search? How close in time must the search be to the arrest? To what areas can the search be extended? What evidence can be seized?

First, what types of arrests allow "incident to arrest" searches? This exception applies to all lawful arrests and is not limited to those where the police need to protect themselves, or to arrests involving serious offenses, or where evidence needs to be protected. Pat-down searches of motorists arrested for a revoked driver's license and for not having a license were lawful [*U.S. v. Robinson* (1973) and *Gustafson v. Florida* (1973)]. The pat downs in these cases were justified on the basis that the motorists were being taken to the station, so a full custodial search was reasonable. What do you think would be reasonable for a typical highway stop for speeding or a headlight violation? Should *Robinson* apply?

Recently the Supreme Court ruled that *Robinson* does not apply to traffic stops in which a citation is issued [*Knowles v. Iowa* (1998)]. Knowles was stopped for speeding and issued a citation. Pursuant to an Iowa statute permitting a full search of driver and vehicle, the officers found marijuana and a pipe for which Knowles was charged. The need to disarm in citation cases is significantly less than in custodial arrest cases, and the need to preserve evidence for the citation had been completed. *Knowles* stands for the principle that police may not conduct full searches when incident to a citation arrest where no other grounds exist for a search.

Second, how close in time must the search be to the arrest? The search must follow the arrest and be contemporaneous with it. In *Preston v. U.S.* (1964), three men were arrested in a parked car. Later, the car was moved to a garage and searched. The Court held the search was not incident to the arrest. Exceptions are made when the police conduct a search before they make an arrest based on probable cause. Once the arrest is made, it must stand on the original probable cause, without consideration of any evidence from the related search [*Rawlings v. Kentucky* (1980)]. A search of a grocery bag, though contemporaneous with arrest, was unlawful because police lacked probable cause to arrest [*Smith v. Ohio* (1990)].

Normally, once the property in question is in the control of the police and no danger exists for the police or to the property, the time has passed for an incident search. There is no reason then why a warrant cannot be obtained [*U.S. v. Chadwick* (1977)]. A more recent decision, *Florida v. Meyers* (1984), suggests, however, that if police search property well after the arrest but could have searched it lawfully at the time of the arrest, then the subsequent search is still an incident search. This case involved the second search of a car at the police station eight hours after the arrest.

Third, what is the allowable extent of a search incident to a lawful arrest? *Chimel v. California* (1969) narrowed the range of a search by emphasizing the favored status given searches with warrants. Under *Chimel*, searches incident to arrest are limited to the immediate area of control from which the arrestee can grab a weapon or destroy evidence. A full search of a house without a warrant is not authorized. If the arrestee moves, the search may be moved to include the new immediate surrounding area. Officers may walk through a house (a protective sweep) if they reasonably believe that others who pose a threat may be present [*Maryland v. Buie* (1990)].

In some states the range of a search has expanded under the rationale that evidence may be destroyed. Generally, police may not search accomplices or other persons present unless they have probable cause specific to those persons. A *Terry* stop and frisk search may apply.

The incident to arrest exception has been applied to expand the range of search for officers in automobile cases. An officer who detected the odor of marijuana emanating from a car had the occupants get out of the car and arrested them. The officer searched the passenger area and the pocket of a jacket lying in the car. This search was upheld in *New York v. Belton* (1981) on the basis that the arrestees could still reach back into the car. In 1982 the Supreme Court expanded the exception by upholding the search of a closed container in a car on the basis that the officer had probable cause to believe the container held contraband [*U.S. v. Ross* (1982)].

Fourth, what can be seized in searches incident to arrest? The law seems clear that anything can be seized at the time of a lawful arrest if probable cause exists that the item to be seized is contraband, fruit of a crime, or evidence of a crime.

Persons arrested and taken to jail are often subjected to strip searches. Although legal in most cases, the practice of custodial strip searches is coming under greater scrutiny. They have been ruled unreasonable by some courts in the context of arrests for misdemeanors and other minor offenses unless the police have reasonable suspicion that the person is hiding something. There are increasing numbers of civil suits for unreasonable police strip searches, one of which was upheld in *Jones v. Edwards* (8th Cir. 1985).

E. PLAIN VIEW

The "plain view" exception to the warrant requirement means that police can seize items they happen to come across in the course of their duty, but this exception is not without limitations. For years the landmark case was *Coolidge v. New Hampshire* (1971). *Coolidge* permitted plain view seizures, because plain view searches arise in the field where a warrant is impractical, but attached limits. First, the police must be at the scene lawfully—for example, with a valid warrant, not necessarily for the "plain view" item; in a home but with the owner's consent; next to the passenger window of a vehicle they have stopped for a traffic violation; on a driveway or sidewalk; or other lawful presence. Second, the item to be seized must be discovered inadvertently (by accident, with no prior suspicion or probable cause to search for it). Finally, the officer must have probable cause to believe the item is contraband or evidence of a crime. By implication there is a further test: the item must be in plain view.

In 1987 the Court in *Arizona v. Hicks* (1987) strictly enforced the third prerequisite when it ruled that an officer did not have probable cause to pick up a video recorder and check the serial number on the bottom. Although the officer was suspicious that the article was stolen, the serial number was not in plain view, and the suspicion had not reached the probable cause level.

Since *Coolidge,* some courts have had to deal with whether the plain view discovery was truly inadvertent. The Supreme Court, however, threw out this second part of the three-part Coolidge test in *Horton v. California* (1990). In *Horton* the police had a warrant to search for stolen springs, but also expected to find stolen weapons. In seizing the weapons, the police had clearly violated the "inadvertent" test. In expanding this exception to the warrant requirement, the Court ruled that only two prerequisites are needed: that police are legally on the site of the seizure and that the criminal character of the object is immediately apparent.

What happens if an officer is executing a warrant to search for drugs, the lights go out, and in groping around she lays a hand on an illegal automatic rifle. Can she seize the rifle even though it is not in plain sight? Some federal and state courts have recently ruled that plain view includes the other senses, deciding several cases on the basis of plain touch.[9] As previously discussed, *Minnesota v. Dickerson* (1993) accepts the "plain feel" analogy to "plain view." This exception may eventually encompass plain smell, plain hearing, and plain taste.

The use of high technology also complicates the plain view exception. Does police use of an infrared device to check the air space immediately above a residence for telltale heat released from the growing of marijuana constitute a legal, plain view search? Yes, according to the federal district court in *U.S. v. Penny-Feeney* (D. Hawaii 1991). A "night-vision" scope used to observe the defendant in a car in the parking lot of an open tavern was not a "search," because there was no right to expect privacy. The interior light of the car was on and people regularly passed within a few feet of the car [*State v. Wacker* (Or. 1993)].

In leaving this exception, it is important to note that while a search incident to a lawful arrest is limited to the search of the area within the immediate grasp of the arrestee, under the plain view exception items at a much greater distance from the arrestee may be seized.

F.   MOTOR VEHICLE SEARCHES

The warrantless search and seizure of motor vehicles has long been permitted because of their mobility and to some extent their open use on public thoroughfares, reducing the expectation of privacy as compared to that in a home. Such a search must be based on probable cause to believe the vehicle contains an item of a criminal nature and the likelihood that the vehicle will be unavailable by the time a warrant is acquired due to exigent circumstances [*Carroll v. U.S.* (1925)]. The *Carroll* exception has been expanded to permit a search of the vehicle after its impoundment, as well as a search of a closed container in the vehicle.

In *California v. Carney* (1985) the Court decided that *Carroll* applied to a motor home, even though there might be a greater expectation of privacy surrounding it than there would be for a car and there seemed no immediate threat that the vehicle would be removed. The police did have probable cause to believe that Carney had committed a crime and that evidence of the crime would be found in the vehicle. In one state case a judge ruled that a motor-driven wheelchair was a motor vehicle.[10]

ANALYSIS PROBLEM

9–3.   Does this and should this open the way for searches of golf carts, motorized farm implements, lawn mowers, and shopping carts?

Whether the immediate area limitation of *Chimel* regarding searches incident to a lawful arrest applied to a vehicle was answered by *New York v. Belton* (1981). In *Belton* the defendant was placed under arrest and moved away from the vehicle. The arresting officer then returned to the vehicle, searched the driver's compartment, and eventually unzipped the pocket of Belton's jacket found on the back seat and retrieved a packet of cocaine. Under the rationale that police need a clearer standard than that expressed by *Chimel* in the unique situation of a motor vehicle, the Court ruled that a warrantless search incident to an arrest in the case of a vehicle extends to the entire passenger area and closed containers in that area on the basis that they may be reached for use or destruction. Note that there is no need for probable cause to search the interior or its contents if the search is incident to arrest. In the plain view exception, probable cause is required.

In *U.S. v. Ross* (1982) the Supreme Court ruled that if the police have probable cause to believe that criminal items will be found in an automobile, then the police may search the entire car including containers in it (in this case a paper bag in the trunk). Another line of cases says that personal items, such as luggage, carry with them a high expectation of privacy and, regardless of probable cause, may be searched only with a properly obtained warrant even if in a car [*U.S. v. Chadwick* (1977) and *Arkansas v. Sanders* (1979)].

In *California v. Acevedo* (1991) the Court clarified the dichotomy between *Ross* and *Chadwick* and ruled that personal containers locked in a trunk of a car may be searched without a warrant if the police have probable cause to believe they contain criminal items. Formerly, the police would have had to seize the bag and the person, and then get a warrant to search the bag. Probable cause for a specific item in a specific place (the trunk), however, does not give the police authority to search the entire vehicle. If the search yields contraband, then any occupants can be arrested, giving police the authority to search the entire vehicle as incident to the arrest (*Belton*).

If the police have probable cause to search a vehicle, can they search the personal belongings of a passenger in the vehicle? This question was raised in *Wyoming v. Houghton* (1999).

WYOMING v. HOUGHTON
Supreme Court of the United States
526 U.S. 295, 119 S.Ct. 1297 (1999)
[Citations omitted]

Justice SCALIA delivered the opinion of the Court.

This case presents the question whether police officers violate the Fourth Amendment when they search a passenger's personal belongings inside an automobile that they have probable cause to believe contains contraband.

I

In the early morning hours of July 23, 1995, a Wyoming Highway Patrol officer stopped an automobile for speeding and driving with a faulty brake light. There were three passengers in the front seat of the car: David Young (the driver), his girlfriend, and respondent. While questioning Young, the officer noticed a hypodermic syringe in Young's shirt pocket. He left the occupants under the supervision of two backup officers as he went to get gloves from his patrol car. Upon his return, he instructed Young to step out of the car and place the syringe on the hood. The officer then asked Young why he had a syringe; with refreshing candor, Young replied that he used it to take drugs. At this point, the backup officers ordered the two female passengers out of the car and asked them for identification. Respondent falsely identified herself as "Sandra James" and stated that she did not have any identification. Meanwhile, in light of Young's admission, the officer searched the passenger compartment of the car for contraband. On the back seat, he found a purse, which respondent claimed as hers. He removed from the purse a wallet containing respondent's driver's license, identifying her properly as Sandra K. Houghton. When the officer asked her why she had lied about her name, she replied: "In case things went bad." Continuing his search of the purse, the officer found a brown pouch and a black wallet-type container. Respondent denied that the former was hers, and claimed ignorance of how it came to be there; it was found to contain drug paraphernalia and a syringe with 60 ccs of methamphetamine. Respondent admitted ownership of the black container, which was also found to contain drug paraphernalia, and a syringe (which respondent acknowledged was hers) with 10 ccs of methamphetamine— an amount insufficient to support the felony conviction at issue in this case. The officer also found fresh needle-track marks on respondent's arms. He placed her under arrest.

The State of Wyoming charged respondent with felony possession of methamphetamine in a liquid amount greater than three-tenths of a gram. See Wyo. Stat. Ann. § 35-7-1031(c)(iii) (Supp.1996). After a hearing, the trial court denied her motion to suppress all evidence obtained from the purse as the fruit of a violation of the Fourth and Fourteenth Amendments. The court held that the officer had probable cause to search the car for contraband, and, by extension, any containers therein that could hold such contraband. A jury convicted respondent as charged.

The Wyoming Supreme Court, by divided vote, reversed the conviction and announced the following rule:

"Generally, once probable cause is established to search a vehicle, an officer is entitled to search all containers therein which may contain the object of the search. However, if the officer knows or should know that a container is the personal effect of a passenger who is not suspected of criminal activity, then the container is outside the scope of the search unless someone had the opportunity to conceal the contraband within the personal effect to avoid detection." 956 P.2d 363, 372 (1998). The court held that the search of respondent's purse violated the Fourth and Fourteenth Amendments because the officer "knew or should have known that the purse did not belong to the driver, but to one of the passengers," and because "there was no probable cause to search the passengers' personal effects and no reason to believe that contraband had been placed within the purse." *Ibid.*

II

The Fourth Amendment protects "[t]he right of the people to be secure in their persons, houses, papers, and effects, against unreasonable searches and seizures." In determining whether a particular governmental action violates this provision, we inquire first whether the action was regarded as an unlawful search or seizure under the common law when the Amendment was framed. See *Wilson v. Arkansas,* 514 U.S. 927 (1995); *California v. Hodari D.,* 499 U.S. 621, (1991). Where that inquiry yields no answer, we must evaluate the search or seizure under traditional standards of reasonableness by assessing, on the one hand, the degree to which it intrudes upon an individual's privacy and, on the other, the degree to which it is needed for the promotion of legitimate governmental interests....

It is uncontested in the present case that the police officers had probable cause to believe there were illegal drugs in the car. *Carroll v. United States,* 267 U.S. 132, (1925), similarly involved the warrantless search of a car that law enforcement officials had probable cause to believe contained contraband—in that case, bootleg liquor. The Court concluded that the Framers would have regarded such a search as reasonable in light of legislation enacted by Congress from 1789 through 1799—as well as subsequent legislation from the Founding era and beyond—that empowered customs officials to search any ship or vessel without a warrant if they had probable cause to believe that it contained goods subject to a duty.... See also *United States v. Ross,* 456 U.S. 798, (1982). Thus, the Court held that "contraband goods concealed and illegally transported in an automobile or other vehicle may be searched for without a warrant" where probable cause exists. *Carroll* ... We have furthermore read the historical evidence to show that the Framers would have regarded as reasonable (if there was probable cause) the warrantless search of containers within an automobile. In *Ross, supra,* we upheld as reasonable the warrantless search of a paper bag and leather pouch found in the trunk of the defendant's car by officers who had probable cause to believe that the trunk contained drugs....

To be sure, there was no passenger in *Ross,* and it was not claimed that the package in the trunk belonged to anyone other than the driver. Even so, if the rule of law that *Ross* announced were limited to contents belonging to the driver, or contents other than those belonging to passengers, one would have expected that substantial limitation to be expressed.... Finally, ... *Ross* concluded from the historical evidence that the permissible scope of a warrantless car search "is defined by the object of the search and the places in which there is probable cause to believe that it may be found." ... The same principle is reflected in an earlier case involving the constitutionality of a search warrant directed at premises belonging to one who is not suspected of any crime: "The critical element in a reasonable search is not that the owner of the property is suspected of crime but that there is reasonable cause to believe that the specific 'things' to be searched for and seized are located on the property to which entry is sought."

In sum, neither *Ross* itself nor the historical evidence it relied upon admits of a distinction among packages or containers based on ownership. When there is probable cause to search for contraband in a car, it is reasonable for police officers—like customs officials in the Founding era—to examine packages and containers without a showing of individualized probable cause for each one. A passenger's personal belongings, just like the driver's belongings or containers attached to the car like a glove compartment, are "in" the car, and the officer has probable cause to search for contraband in the car.

Even if the historical evidence, as described by *Ross,* were thought to be equivocal, we would find that the balancing of the relative interests weighs decidedly in favor of allowing searches of a passenger's belongings. Passengers, no less than drivers, possess a reduced expectation of privacy with regard to the property that they transport in cars, which "travel public thoroughfares," *Cardwell v. Lewis,* 417 U.S. 583, 590 (1974), "seldom serve as . . . the repository of personal effects," *ibid.,* are subjected to police stop and examination to enforce "pervasive" governmental controls "as an everyday occurrence," *South Dakota v. Opperman,* 428 U.S. 364 (1976), and, finally, are exposed to traffic accidents that may render all their contents open to public scrutiny.

In this regard—the degree of intrusiveness upon personal privacy and indeed even personal dignity—the two cases the Wyoming Supreme Court found dispositive differ substantially from the package search at issue here. *United States v. Di Re,* 332 U.S. 581, (1948), held that probable cause to search a car did not justify a body search of a passenger. And *Ybarra v. Illinois,* 444 U.S. 85 (1979), held that a search warrant for a tavern and its bartender did not permit body searches of all the bar's patrons. These cases turned on the unique, significantly heightened protection afforded against searches of one's person. "Even a limited search of the outer clothing . . . constitutes a severe, though brief, intrusion upon cherished personal security, and it must surely be an annoying, frightening, and perhaps humiliating experience." *Terry v. Ohio,* 392 U.S. 1, (1968). Such traumatic consequences are not to be expected when the police examine an item of personal property found in a car. . . . Effective law enforcement would be appreciably impaired without the ability to search a passenger's personal belongings when there is reason to believe contraband or evidence of criminal wrongdoing is hidden in the car. As in all car-search cases, the "ready mobility" of an automobile creates a risk that the evidence or contraband will be permanently lost while a warrant is obtained....

We hold that police officers with probable cause to search a car may inspect passengers' belongings found in the car that are capable of concealing the object of the search. The judgment of the Wyoming Supreme Court is reversed. It is so ordered.

Justice BREYER, concurring.

I join the Court's opinion with the understanding that history is meant to inform, but not automatically to determine, the answer to a Fourth Amendment question.... I also agree with the Court that when a police officer has probable cause to search a car, say, for drugs, it is reasonable for that officer also to search containers within the car. If the police must establish a container's ownership prior to the search of that container (whenever, for example, a passenger says "that's mine"), the resulting uncertainty will destroy the workability of the bright-line rule set forth in *United States v. Ross.* . . I would point out certain limitations upon the scope of the bright-line rule that the Court describes. Obviously, the rule applies only to automobile searches. Equally obviously, the rule applies only to containers found within automobiles. And it does not extend to the search of a person found in that automobile. . . .

In this case, the purse was separate from the person, and no one has claimed that, under those circumstances, the type of container makes a difference. For that reason, I join the Court's opinion.

Justice STEVENS, with whom Justice SOUTER and Justice GINSBURG join, dissenting.

. . . In light of our established preference for warrants and individualized suspicion, I would respect the result reached by the Wyoming Supreme Court and affirm its judgment.

In all of our prior cases applying the automobile exception to the Fourth Amendment's warrant requirement, either the defendant was the operator of the vehicle and in custody of the object of the search, or no question was raised as to the defendant's ownership or custody. In the only automobile case confronting the search of a passenger defendant—*United States v. Di Re,* 332 U.S. 581, (1948)—the Court held that the exception to the warrant requirement did not apply. . . . (addressing searches of the passenger's pockets and the space between his shirt and underwear, both of which uncovered counterfeit fuel rations). In *Di Re,* as here, the information prompting the search directly implicated the driver, not the passenger. Today, instead of adhering to the settled distinction between drivers and passengers, the Court fashions a new rule that is based on a distinction between property contained in clothing worn by a passenger and property contained in a passenger's briefcase or purse. . . . [U]nlike the Court, I think it quite plain that the search of a passenger's purse or briefcase involves an intrusion on privacy that may be just as serious as was the intrusion in *Di Re.* . . .

Ironically, while we concluded in *Ross* that "[p]robable cause to believe that a container placed in the trunk of a taxi contains contraband or evidence does not justify a search of the entire cab,". . . the rule the Court fashions would apparently permit a warrantless search of a passenger's briefcase if there is probable cause to believe the taxidriver had a syringe somewhere in his vehicle. Nor am I persuaded that the mere spatial association between a passenger and a driver provides an acceptable basis for presuming that they are partners in crime or for ignoring privacy interests in a purse. Whether or not the Fourth Amendment required a warrant to search Houghton's purse, . . . at the very least the trooper in this case had to have probable cause to believe that her purse contained contraband. The Wyoming Supreme Court concluded that he did not. . . .

Finally, in my view, the State's legitimate interest in effective law enforcement does not outweigh the privacy concerns at issue. I am as confident in a police officer's ability to apply a rule requiring a warrant or individualized probable cause to search belongings that are—as in this case—obviously owned by and in the custody of a passenger as is the Court in a "passenger-confederate's" ability to circumvent the rule. Certainly the ostensible clarity of the Court's rule is attractive. But that virtue is insufficient justification for its adoption. . . .

Instead of applying ordinary Fourth Amendment principles to this case, the majority extends the automobile warrant exception to allow searches of passenger belongings based on the driver's misconduct. Thankfully, the Court's automobile-centered analysis limits the scope of its holding. But it does not justify the outcome in this case.

I respectfully dissent.

Houghton is important because it continues the recent trend of opinions increasing the authority of police in warrantless car searches at the expense of privacy protections under the Fourth Amendment. It stands for the principle that police with probable cause to search a vehicle may search all containers in the vehicle that can conceal the object of the search, including personal items of the passengers. The case is significant beyond that, however, because it states the standard for analyzing warrantless searches, which emphasizes a reasonableness inquiry and deemphasizes the presumption against warrantless searches.

Maryland v. Wilson (1997) examined the competing interests of police officers to protect themselves from hidden weapons and the privacy interest of the driver or passengers to remain in the car. A person required to exit a vehicle is more likely to involuntarily expose contraband or symptoms of intoxication. When Wilson, a passenger, was ordered out of the car he dropped some cocaine on the ground. Because the police had no grounds to believe he was armed, he moved to suppress the drugs on the basis that they were the product of an unreasonable seizure. The court ruled that the government has a greater interest in protecting the officers than the occupants have in remaining in the vehicle. Therefore, police have the authority to order occupants to exit a vehicle.

A search of motor vehicles does not require a warrant when the vehicle has been impounded by the police and is being inventoried. Police are authorized to inventory the contents of an auto to protect the owner's property while in the custody of the police; to protect the government against claims of lost, stolen, or vandalized property; and to guard the police from danger [*South Dakota v. Opperman* (1976)]. The inventory must be done according to standardized procedure, and not as a subterfuge for criminal investigation.

In conducting this inventory, do police have the right to open containers, particularly personal ones? The Court said yes in *Colorado v. Bertine* (1987) where it ruled that an officer's inventory of a parked van after the owner had been arrested for drunk driving could include a search of the inside of the owner's backpack. *Opperman* protects personal items such as checkbooks and letters from intrusion in inventory searches. Some state courts, in interpreting their state constitutions or laws, require the police to show that it is necessary to impound the car and inventory it when other less intrusive means can protect the owner, the police, and the property.[11] For example, if a close family member can pick up the car, then this method should be used.

In *Florida v. White* (1999), the Court expanded the vehicle impoundment exception to a warrant. Even though the car was seized two months after White was arrested on other charges, and the police did not have probable cause to believe the car contained illegal drugs, the Court upheld the impoundment search. Applying a similar analysis to that used in *Houghton,* the Court said the police did have probable cause to believe the car had been used to deliver cocaine, that it was in a public place when seized, and that it was subject to Florida's forfeiture statute.

G. HOT PURSUIT

hot pursuit:
the chasing of a suspect or the following of "hot" leads to the suspect.

Hot pursuit consists of exigent circumstances typically involving the chasing of a suspect or the following of "hot" leads to the suspect. If probable cause exists to believe that the person being pursued committed a serious crime and is in the building to be entered, then police without a warrant may enter even a private residence to find the suspect. The underlying theory is that once police get close to the arrest of a suspect the procurement of a warrant is impractical and likely to result in the imminent escape of the suspect or the imminent loss of contraband or evidence. Once inside the dwelling, the officers may look anywhere the suspect and weapons are likely to be found. Any criminal items found in the process may be seized.

Once the suspect is arrested, however, the "search incident to arrest" rules kick in to limit the scope of the search. The leading case for these principles is *Warden v. Hayden* (1967). The period between the time probable cause arises and the entry takes place needs to be relatively brief. In *Hayden* the police arrived within minutes after the suspect entered the building. Even though more time was involved in *U.S. v. Holland* (6th Cir. 1975), the closeness in proximity of each clue to the last in a chain of clues kept the trail fairly hot (thirty minutes overall). In one federal case, entry of the suspect's residence four hours after the crime was held to be permissible because it was late at night and a magistrate was not readily available [*Dorman v. U.S.* (D.C. Cir. 1970)]. Searches conducted once the exigency evaporates generally require a warrant.

ANALYSIS PROBLEM

9–4. What are the likely issues in a motion to suppress "hot pursuit" evidence?

H. EVANESCENT EVIDENCE

Evanescent evidence is criminal evidence that will change or evaporate in a manner that will destroy its evidentiary value. For example, alcohol is detectable in the bloodstream for only a certain period of time. If it is not tested within that time, evidence of driving while under the influence will be lost. In *Schmerber v. California* (1966), Schmerber was arrested for driving while intoxicated. While at the hospital the police had Schmerber's blood withdrawn by a medical technician. Schmerber challenged his conviction on the ground that the search was without a warrant and unreasonable. The Court emphasized that bodily intrusions bring into consideration one of the highest levels of expectation of privacy and personal dignity normally necessitating warrants. When evidence is of an evanescent nature, however, a warrant is not necessary. In the case of a warrantless intrusion of the body, the Court required that there be a good indication the search will produce the evidence sought and that the search be conducted in a reasonable manner.

In *Winston v. Lee* (1985) the Court declared that surgery to remove a bullet embedded in the defendant's collarbone could not be compelled, especially because other good evidence was available and the surgery may have involved some notable risks. The ruling determined reasonableness of the intrusion to the body by the degree to which the process threatens the health or safety of the person; offends the person's dignity, personal privacy, and bodily integrity; and provides needed and accurate evidence of guilt.

The evanescent exception has been applied in contexts other than blood tests or surgery. In a California case, *People v. Bullock* (Cal. App. 1990), an officer's activation of a defendant's electronic pager display twenty times while the defendant was being booked was a search but did not require a warrant, because probable cause existed and the evidence was likely to become stale or erased.

> **evanescent evidence:** criminal evidence that will change or evaporate in a manner that will destroy its evidentiary value.

ANALYSIS PROBLEM

9–5. Based on *Schmerber,* should police be permitted to have a suspect's blood tested to determine its DNA structure without a warrant? What about a blood test for AIDS from the suspect in a rape case? Explain.

I. BORDER, REGULATORY, AND EMERGENCY SEARCHES

Warrantless searches have been approved by the Court in regulatory inspections and border situations, not on the basis of exigent circumstances, but in an attempt to balance the need of government to abate and prevent dangerous conditions and the reasonable expectation of privacy. The following principles have been established.

1. Inspection of dwellings or businesses for code or safety compliance requires a warrant. The warrant, however, requires less than a showing of probable cause. A standard that relies more heavily on surrounding conditions in the area that suggest a danger to the public exists or could develop rather than a belief that a particular dwelling is in violation is all that is needed to support the warrant [*Camara v. Municipal Court* (1967)].

   Unannounced warrantless inspections have been approved, however, in the case of businesses that have a history of significant government regulation or licensure. A warrantless search of a gun shop and seizure of unlicensed weapons [*U.S. v. Biswell* (1972)] and warrantless searches of junkyards to prevent disassembly of stolen cars [*New York v. Burger* (1987)] have been allowed. Another exception occurs where safety is an overriding factor, such as in coal mines, and the legislative or administrative regulators' scheme is reasonable with proper limits on the discretion of inspectors [*Donovan v. Dewey* (1981)].

2. Entry to fight a fire (emergency exception) and entry a short time later (five hours) to determine the cause of the fire do not require a warrant. Reentry, however, should follow advance notice to the owner [*Michigan v. Clifford* (1984)]. If the reentry to search comes considerably later (weeks), a full probable cause warrant may be necessary [*Michigan v. Tyler* (1978)].

3. Searches at national borders or international airports intrude on a low expectation of privacy, so there is no need to have a reasonable suspicion, probable cause, or a warrant to search. If the search becomes more intrusive, then the suspicion needed to conduct the search increases. A strip search requires "a real suspicion"; a search of body cavities requires "a clear indication"; and for "reasonable suspicion" a person suspected of ingesting contraband can be detained for X-rays or for Mother Nature to run her course, so to speak [*U.S. v. Montoya de Hernandez* (1985)]. In light of several civil suits alleging unreasonable racial and gender discriminatory searches, customs officials have revised and continue to study their detention and strip search policies.

   A roving stop of a car near the border to check if aliens are in the vehicle requires probable cause or a warrant [*Almeida-Sanchez v. U.S.* (1973)], but stopping a vehicle for questioning at a checkpoint reasonably close to the border does not require a warrant, probable cause, or any degree of suspicion [*U.S. v. Martinez-Fuerte* (1976)]. If a border guard routinely sticks his head into a vehicle, the act is unlawful unless it is based on consent or probable cause [*U.S. v. Pierce* (5th Cir. 1990)]. Yet, if an officer near the border reasonably suspects that aliens occupy a vehicle, the vehicle can be stopped and the occupants questioned. Any further detention, however, requires probable cause [*U.S. v. Brignoni-Ponce* (1975)].

4. International mail may be searched without probable cause or a warrant if there is "reasonable cause to suspect" it contains illegally imported goods. A warrant is needed to read correspondence [*U.S. v. Ramsey* (1977)].

5. Airport searches with the purpose of preventing hijacking and involving X-ray and magnometers to search persons and baggage have generally been upheld but on differing theories. Some courts have analogized to *Terry v. Ohio*, tending to lower the degree of suspicion needed for a stop and frisk, whereas other courts have relied on a *Camara* administration search that is neutral and limited in scope.

6. Prisoners, parolees, and probationers are generally subject to searches without a warrant and on suspicion less than probable cause.

7. Boat inspections parallel border inspections or roadblocks rather than *Carroll* car stops and, therefore, do not require a warrant, probable cause, or any degree of suspicion [*U.S. v. Villamonte-Marquez* (1983)].

8. Probable cause is not needed to search the offices of public employees when the search is for legitimate "work related" reasons, and not specifically to ferret out criminal conduct. The test is whether the intrusion is reasonable under the circumstances to achieve the limited purpose of the administrative search [*O'Connor v. Ortega* (1987)]. Drug tests may be required of public employees only when there is a reasonable suspicion of the employee, or where it can be shown that drug use among the targeted employees is widespread, or that the employees are in a position where drug use will present a serious risk to the public.[12]

Suspicionless drug tests have been upheld for railroad personnel involved in train accidents [*Skinner v. Railway Labor Executives' Association* (1989) and, on a random basis, for federal customs officers who are armed or involved in drug enforcement [*National Treasury Employees v. Von Raab* (1989)]. There was, however, no high risk or safety-sensitive justification for drug testing all candidates for public office (normally under considerable public scrutiny) under a Georgia law, which, therefore, was held by the Court to be unconstitutional in *Chandler v. Miller* (1997). See the *Vernonia School District* case principle 9 below.

In a twist on random drug tests, the Supreme Court has agreed to decide whether drug tests are constitutional when they routinely are administered by hospitals to pregnant women for medical reasons, and then the results routinely are turned over to police so women who test positive can be arrested and prosecuted.

9. School officials, though subject to the Fourth Amendment, may search the personal effects of students as long as the intrusion bears a reasonable relationship in its scope to the circumstances justifying the initial interference [*New Jersey v. T.L.O.* (1985)]. Consequently, school officials need reasonable suspicion, not probable cause in the interest of maintaining a learning environment.

In *Vernonia School District 47 v. Acton* (1995) the Court reconfirmed its opinion that public school environments are unique and that school officials will be given more latitude under the Fourth Amendment to deal with drug and other discipline problems. A random suspicionless drug testing program of middle and high school athletes was held constitutional.

A few courts have held that strip searches of students will be struck down unless there is a showing of reasonable suspicion to search a particular student, rather than a group of students [*Kennedy v. Dexter Consolidated School* (N.M. 1998), *Konop v. Northwestern School District* (D.S.D. 1998), and *Sostarecz v. Misko* (E.D. Pa. 1999)]. Further, the use of drug dogs to sniff students directly, as opposed to their lockers or containers, was held to be a search requiring reasonable suspicion in *B.C. v. Plumas Unified School District* (9th Cir. 1999) and *Horton v. Goose Creek Independent School District* (5th Cir. 1982), but not in *Doe v. Renfrow* (7th Cir. 1981).

10. Mobile road blocks and checkpoints have resulted in Fourth Amendment seizure questions because they lead to a temporary seizure of motorists and are not based on any degree of suspicion. The following case examines the issues of legality in sobriety checkpoints. What are the areas of contention between the majority and the dissent in the case?

MICHIGAN DEPARTMENT OF STATE POLICE v. SITZ
Supreme Court of the United States, 1990.
496 U.S. 444, 110 S.Ct. 2481.

Chief Justice REHNQUIST delivered the opinion of the Court.

This case poses the question whether a State's use of highway sobriety checkpoints violates the Fourth and Fourteenth Amendments to the United States Constitution. . . .

Petitioners, the Michigan Department of State Police and its Director, established a sobriety checkpoint pilot program

in early 1986. The Director appointed a Sobriety Checkpoint Advisory Committee [that] created guidelines setting forth procedures governing checkpoint operations, site selection, and publicity.

Under the guidelines, checkpoints would be set up at selected sites along state roads. All vehicles passing through a checkpoint would be stopped and their drivers briefly examined for signs of intoxication. In cases where a checkpoint officer detected signs of intoxication, the motorist would be directed to a location out of the traffic flow where an officer would check the motorist's driver's license and car registration and, if warranted, conduct further sobriety tests. Should the field tests and the officer's observations suggest that the driver was intoxicated, an arrest would be made. All other drivers would be permitted to resume their journey immediately.

The first—and to date the only—sobriety checkpoint operated under the program was conducted in Saginaw County with the assistance of the Saginaw County Sheriff's Department. During the hour-and-fifteen-minute duration of the checkpoint's operation, 126 vehicles passed through the checkpoint. The average delay for each vehicle was approximately 25 seconds. Two drivers were detained for field sobriety testing, and one of the two was arrested for driving under the influence of alcohol. A third driver who drove through without stopping was pulled over by an officer in an observation vehicle and arrested for driving under the influence.

On the day before the operation of the Saginaw County checkpoint, respondents filed a complaint in the Circuit Court of Wayne County seeking declaratory and injunctive relief from potential subjection to the checkpoints. Each of the respondents "is a licensed driver in the State of Michigan . . . who regularly travels throughout the State in his automobile." During pretrial proceedings, petitioners agreed to delay further implementation of the checkpoint program pending the outcome of this litigation.

After the trial, at which the court heard extensive testimony concerning, *inter alia,* the "effectiveness" of highway sobriety checkpoint programs, the court ruled that the Michigan program violated the Fourth Amendment and Art. 1, § 11, of the Michigan Constitution. On appeal, the Michigan Court of Appeals affirmed the holding that the program violated the Fourth Amendment and, for that reason, did not consider whether the program violated the Michigan Constitution. After the Michigan Supreme Court denied petitioners' application for leave to appeal, we granted certiorari.

To decide this case the trial court performed a balancing test derived from our opinion in *Brown v. Texas,* 443 U.S. 47. . . .

As characterized by the Court of Appeals, the trial court's findings with respect to the balancing factors were that the State has "a grave and legitimate" interest in curbing drunken driving; that sobriety checkpoint programs are generally "ineffective" and, therefore, do not significantly further that interest; and that the checkpoints' "subjective intrusion" on individual liberties is substantial. . . .

In this Court respondents seek to defend the judgment in their favor by insisting that the balancing test derived from *Brown v. Texas, supra,* was not the proper method of analysis. Respondents maintain that the analysis must proceed from a basis of probable cause or reasonable suspicion and rely for support on language from our decision last Term in *Treasury Employees v. Von Raab,* 489 U.S. 656, (1989). We said in *Von Raab:*

"Where a Fourth Amendment intrusion serves special governmental needs, beyond the normal need for law enforcement, it is necessary to balance the individual's privacy expectations against the Government's interests to determine whether it is impractical to require a warrant or some level of individualized suspicion in the particular context."

Respondents argue that there must be a showing of some special governmental need "beyond the normal need" for criminal law enforcement before a balancing analysis is appropriate, and that petitioners have demonstrated no such special need.

But it is perfectly plain from a reading of *Von Raab,* which cited and discussed with approval our earlier decision in *United States v. Martinez-Fuerte,* 428 U.S. 543 (1976), that it was in no way designed to repudiate our prior cases dealing with police stops of motorists on public highways. *Martinez-Fuerte, supra,* which utilized a balancing analysis in approving highway checkpoints for detecting illegal aliens, and *Brown v. Texas, supra,* are the relevant authorities here.

Petitioners concede, correctly in our view, that a Fourth Amendment "seizure" occurs when a vehicle is stopped at a checkpoint. . . . The question thus becomes whether such seizures are "reasonable" under the Fourth Amendment.

. . . As pursued in the lower courts, the instant action challenges only the use of sobriety checkpoints generally. We address only the initial stop of each motorist passing through a checkpoint and the associated preliminary questioning and observation by checkpoint officers. Detention of particular motorists for more extensive field sobriety testing may require satisfaction of an individualized suspicion standard.

No one can seriously dispute the magnitude of the drunken driving problem or the States' interest in eradicating it. Media reports of alcohol-related death and mutilation on the Nation's road[s] are legion. The anecdotal is confirmed by the statistical. "Drunk drivers cause an annual death toll of over 25,000 and in the same time span cause nearly one million personal injuries and more than five billion dollars in property damage." 4 W. LaFave, Search and Seizure: A Treatise on the Fourth Amendment § 10.8(d), p. 71 (2d ed. 1987). . . .

Conversely, the weight bearing on the other scale—the measure of the intrusion on motorists stopped briefly at sobriety checkpoints—is slight. We reached a similar conclusion as to the intrusion on motorists subjected to a brief stop at a highway checkpoint for detecting illegal aliens. See *Martinez-Fuerte.* We see virtually no difference between the levels of intrusion on law-abiding motorists from the brief stops necessary to the effectuation of these two types of checkpoints, which to the average motorist would seem identical save for the nature of the questions the checkpoint officers might ask. The trial court and the Court of Appeals, thus, accurately gauged the "objective" intrusion, measured by the duration of the seizure and the intensity of the investigation, as minimal.

With respect to what it perceived to be the "subjective" intrusion on motorists, however, the Court of Appeals found such intrusion substantial. The court first affirmed the trial court's finding that the guidelines governing checkpoint operation minimize the discretion of the officers on the scene. But the court also agreed with the trial court's conclusion that the checkpoints have the potential to generate fear and surprise in motorists. This was so because the record failed to demonstrate that approaching motorists would be aware of their option to make U-turns or turnoffs to avoid the checkpoints. On that basis, the court deemed the subjective intrusion from the checkpoints unreasonable.

We believe the Michigan courts misread our cases concerning the degree of "subjective intrusion" and the potential for generating fear and surprise. The "fear and surprise" to be considered are not the natural fear of one who has been drinking over the prospect of being stopped at a sobriety checkpoint but, rather, the fear and surprise engendered in law abiding motorists by the nature of the stop. This was made clear in *Martinez-Fuerte.* Comparing checkpoint stops to roving patrol stops considered in prior cases, we said,

"we view checkpoint stops in a different light because the subjective intrusion—the generating of concern or even fright on the part of lawful travelers—is appreciably less in the case of a checkpoint stop. In [*United States v.*] *Ortiz,* [422 U.S. 891 (1975),] we noted:

" '[T]he circumstances surrounding a checkpoint stop and search are far less intrusive than those attending a roving-patrol stop. Roving patrols often operate at night on seldom-traveled roads, and their approach may frighten motorists. At traffic checkpoints the motorist can see that other vehicles are being stopped, he can see visible signs of the officers' authority, and he is much less likely to be frightened or annoyed by the intrusion.' 422 U.S., at 894–895. *Martinez-Fuerte,* 428 U.S., at 558."

Here, checkpoints are selected pursuant to the guidelines, and uniformed police officers stop every approaching vehicle. The intrusion resulting from the brief stop at the sobriety checkpoint is for constitutional purposes indistinguishable from the checkpoint stops we upheld in *Martinez-Fuerte.*

The Court of Appeals went on to consider as part of the balancing analysis the "effectiveness" of the proposed checkpoint program. Based on extensive testimony in the trial record, the court concluded that the checkpoint program failed the "effectiveness" part of the test, and that this failure materially discounted petitioners' strong interest in implementing the program. We think the Court of Appeals was wrong on this point as well.

The actual language from *Brown v. Texas,* upon which the Michigan courts based their evaluation of "effectiveness," describes the balancing factor as "the degree to which the seizure advances the public interest." 443 U.S., at 51. This passage from *Brown* was not meant to transfer from politi-

cally accountable officials to the courts the decision as to which among reasonable alternative law enforcement techniques should be employed to deal with a serious public danger. Experts in police science might disagree over which of several methods of apprehending drunken drivers is preferable as an ideal. But for purposes of Fourth Amendment analysis, the choice among such reasonable alternatives remains with the governmental officials who have a unique understanding of, and a responsibility for, limited public resources, including a finite number of police officers. *Brown*'s rather general reference to "the degree to which the seizure advances the public interest" was derived, as the opinion makes clear, from the line of cases culminating in *Martinez-Fuerte.* Neither *Martinez-Fuerte* nor *Delaware v. Prouse,* 440 U.S. 648 (1979), however, the two cases cited by the Court of Appeals as providing the basis for its "effectiveness" review, supports the searching examination of "effectiveness" undertaken by the Michigan court.

In *Delaware v. Prouse,* we disapproved random stops made by Delaware highway patrol officers in an effort to apprehend unlicensed drivers and unsafe vehicles. We observed that *no* empirical evidence indicated that such stops would be an effective means of promoting roadway safety and said that "[i]t seems common sense that the percentage of all drivers on the road who are driving without a license is very small and that the number of licensed drivers who will be stopped in order to find one unlicensed operator will be large indeed." 440 U.S., at 659–660. We observed that the random stops involved the "kind of standardless and unconstrained discretion [which] is the evil the Court has discerned when in previous cases it has insisted that the discretion of the official in the field be circumscribed, at least to some extent." *Id.,* at 661. We went on to state that our holding did not "cast doubt on the permissibility of roadside truck weigh-stations and inspection checkpoints, at which some vehicles may be [more] subject to further detention for safety and regulatory inspection than are others." *Id.,* at 663, n. 26.

Unlike *Prouse,* this case involves neither a complete absence of empirical data nor a challenge to random highway stops. During the operation of the Saginaw County checkpoint, the detention of each of the 126 vehicles that entered the checkpoint resulted in the arrest of two drunken drivers. Stated as a percentage, approximately 1.5 percent of the drivers passing through the checkpoint were arrested for alcohol impairment. In addition, an expert witness testified at the trial that experience in other States demonstrated that, on the whole, sobriety checkpoints resulted in drunken driving arrests of around 1 percent of all motorists stopped. By way of comparison, the record from one of the consolidated cases in *Martinez-Fuerte,* showed that in the associated checkpoint, illegal aliens were found in only 0.12 percent of the vehicles passing through the checkpoint. See 428 U.S., at 554. The ratio of illegal aliens detected to vehicles stopped (considering that on occasion two or more illegal aliens were found in a single vehicle) was approximately 0.5 percent. We concluded that this "record . . . provides a rather complete picture of the effectiveness of the San Clemente checkpoint", and we sustained its constitutionality. We see no justification for a different conclusion here.

In sum, the balance of the State's interest in preventing drunken driving, the extent to which this system can reasonably be said to advance that interest, and the degree of intrusion upon individual motorists who are briefly stopped, weighs in favor of the state program. We therefore hold that it is consistent with the Fourth Amendment. The judgment of the Michigan Court of Appeals is accordingly reversed, and the cause is remanded for further proceedings not inconsistent with this opinion.

Reversed.

Justice BLACKMUN, concurring in the judgment.

I concur only in the judgment. . . .

Justice BRENNAN, with whom Justice MARSHALL joins, dissenting.

. . .

The majority opinion creates the impression that the Court generally engages in a balancing test in order to determine the constitutionality of all seizures, or at least those "dealing with police stops of motorists on public highways." This is not the case. In most cases, the police must possess probable cause for a seizure to be judged reasonable. See *Dunaway v. New York,* 442 U.S. 200 (1979). Only when a seizure is "*substantially* less intrusive," *id.,* at 210, than a typical arrest is the general rule replaced by a balancing test. I agree with the Court that the initial stop of a car at a roadblock under the Michigan State Police sobriety checkpoint policy is sufficiently less intrusive than an arrest so that the reasonableness of the seizure may be judged, not by the presence of probable cause, but by balancing "the gravity of the public concerns served by the seizure, the degree to which the seizure advances the public interest, and the severity of the interference with individual liberty." *Brown v. Texas,* 443 U.S. 47 (1979). But one searches the majority opinion in vain for any acknowledgment that the *reason* for employing the balancing test is that the seizure is minimally intrusive.

Indeed, the opinion reads as if the minimal nature of the seizure *ends* rather than begins the inquiry into reasonableness. Once the Court establishes that the seizure is "slight," it asserts without explanation that the balance "weighs in favor of the state program." The Court ignores the fact that in this class of minimally intrusive searches, we have generally required the Government to prove that it had reasonable suspicion for a minimally intrusive seizure to be considered reasonable. See, e.g., *Delaware v. Prouse,* 440 U.S. 648, (1979); *United States v. Brignoni-Ponce,* 422 U.S. 873, 882–883, (1975); *Terry v. Ohio,* 392 U.S. 1, 27 (1968). Some level of individualized suspicion is a core component of the protection the Fourth Amendment provides against arbitrary government action. . . . By holding that no level of suspicion is necessary before the police

may stop a car for the purpose of preventing drunken driving, the Court potentially subjects the general public to arbitrary or harassing conduct by the police. I would have hoped that before taking such a step, the Court would carefully explain how such a plan fits within our constitutional framework.

. . . I respectfully dissent.

Justice STEVENS, with whom Justice BRENNAN and Justice MARSHALL join as to Parts I and II, dissenting.

A sobriety checkpoint is usually operated at night at an unannounced location. Surprise is crucial to its method. The test operation conducted by the Michigan State Police and the Saginaw County Sheriff's Department began shortly after midnight and lasted until about 1 a.m. During that period, the 19 officers participating in the operation made two arrests and stopped and questioned 125 other unsuspecting and innocent drivers. It is, of course, not known how many arrests would have been made during that period if those officers had been engaged in normal patrol activities. However, the findings of the trial court, based on an extensive record and affirmed by the Michigan Court of Appeals, indicate that the net effect of sobriety checkpoints on traffic safety is infinitesimal and possibly negative.

. . . The Court overvalues the law enforcement interest in using sobriety checkpoints, undervalues the citizen's interest in freedom from random, unannounced investigatory seizures, and mistakenly assumes that there is "virtually no difference" between a routine stop at a permanent, fixed checkpoint and a surprise stop at a sobriety checkpoint. I believe this case is controlled by our several precedents condemning suspicionless random stops of motorists for investigatory purposes. *Delaware v. Prouse,* 440 U.S. 648 (1979); *United States v. Brignoni-Ponce,* 422 U.S. 873 (1975); *United States v. Ortiz,* 422 U.S. 891 (1975); *Almeida-Sanchez v. United States,* 413 U.S. 266 (1973); cf. *Carroll v. United States,* 267 U.S. 132 (1925).

I.

There is a critical difference between a seizure that is preceded by fair notice and one that is effected by surprise. . . . That is one reason why a border search, or indeed any search at a permanent and fixed checkpoint, is much less intrusive than a random stop. A motorist with advance notice of the location of a permanent checkpoint has an opportunity to avoid the search entirely, or at least to prepare for, and limit, the intrusion on her privacy.

No such opportunity is available in the case of a random stop or a temporary checkpoint, which both depend for their effectiveness on the element of surprise. A driver who discovers an unexpected checkpoint on a familiar local road will be startled and distressed. She may infer, correctly, that the checkpoint is not simply "business as usual," and may likewise infer, again correctly, that the police have made a discretionary decision to focus their law enforcement efforts upon her and others who pass the chosen point.

This element of surprise is the most obvious distinction between the sobriety checkpoints permitted by today's majority and the interior border checkpoints approved by this Court in *Martinez-Fuerte.* The distinction casts immediate doubt upon the majority's argument, for *Martinez-Fuerte* is the only case in which we have upheld suspicionless seizures of motorists. But the difference between notice and surprise is only one of the important reasons for distinguishing between permanent and mobile checkpoints. With respect to the former, there is no room for discretion in either the timing or the location of the stop—it is a permanent part of the landscape. In the latter case, however, although the checkpoint is most frequently employed during the hours of darkness on weekends (because that is when drivers with alcohol in their blood are most apt to be found on the road), the police have extremely broad discretion in determining the exact timing and placement of the roadblock.

There is also a significant difference between the kind of discretion that the officer exercises after the stop is made. A check for a driver's license, or for identification papers at an immigration checkpoint, is far more easily standardized than is a search for evidence of intoxication. A Michigan officer who questions a motorist at a sobriety checkpoint has virtually unlimited discretion to detain the driver on the basis of the slightest suspicion. A ruddy complexion, an unbuttoned shirt, bloodshot eyes or a speech impediment may suffice to prolong the detention. Any driver who had just consumed a glass of beer, or even a sip of wine, would almost certainly have the burden of demonstrating to the officer that her driving ability was not impaired.

Finally, it is significant that many of the stops at permanent checkpoints occur during daylight hours, whereas the sobriety checkpoints are almost invariably operated at night. A seizure followed by interrogation and even a cursory search at night is surely more offensive than a daytime stop that is almost as routine as going through a toll gate. Thus we thought it important to point out that the random stops at issue in *Ortiz* frequently occurred at night. 422 U.S., at 894, 95 S.Ct., at 2587.

These fears are not, as the Court would have it, solely the lot of the guilty. To be law abiding is not necessarily to be spotless, and even the most virtuous can be unlucky. Unwanted attention from the local police need not be less discomforting simply because one's secrets are not the stuff of criminal prosecutions. Moreover, those who have found—by reason of prejudice or misfortune—that encounters with the police may become adversarial or unpleasant without good cause will have grounds for worrying at any stop designed to elicit signs of suspicious behavior. Being stopped by the police is distressing even when it should not be terrifying, and what begins mildly may by happenstance turn severe.

For all these reasons, I do not believe that this case is analogous to *Martinez-Fuerte.* In my opinion, the sobriety checkpoints are instead similar to—and in some respects more intrusive than—the random investigative stops that the

Court held unconstitutional in *Brignoni-Ponce* and *Prouse.* In the latter case the Court explained:

"We cannot agree that stopping or detaining a vehicle on an ordinary city street is less intrusive than a roving-patrol stop on a major highway and that it bears greater resemblance to a permissible stop and secondary detention at a checkpoint near the border. In this regard, we note that *Brignoni-Ponce* was not limited to roving-patrol stops on limited-access roads, but applied to any roving-patrol stop by Border Patrol agents on any type of roadway on less than reasonable suspicion. See 422 U.S., at 882–883; *United States v. Ortiz,* 422 U.S. 891, 894 (1975). We cannot assume that the physical and psychological intrusion visited upon the occupants of a vehicle by a random stop to check documents is of any less moment than that occasioned by a stop by border agents on roving patrol. Both of these stops generally entail law enforcement officers signaling a moving automobile to pull over to the side of the roadway, by means of a possibly unsettling show of authority. Both interfere with freedom of movement, are inconvenient, and consume time. Both may create substantial anxiety." 440 U.S., at 657.

We accordingly held that the State must produce evidence comparing the challenged seizure to other means of law enforcement, so as to show that the seizure

"is a sufficiently productive mechanism to justify the intrusion upon Fourth Amendment interests which such stops entail. On the record before us, that question must be answered in the negative. Given the alternative mechanisms available, both those in use and those that might be adopted, we are unconvinced that the incremental contribution to highway safety of the random spot check justifies the practice under the Fourth Amendment." *Id.,* at 659.

II.

The Court, unable to draw any persuasive analogy to *Martinez-Fuerte,* rests its decision today on application of a more general balancing test taken from *Brown v. Texas.* In that case the appellant, a pedestrian, had been stopped for questioning in an area of El Paso, Texas, that had "a high incidence of drug traffic" because he "looked suspicious." He was then arrested and convicted for refusing to identify himself to police officers. We set aside his conviction because the officers stopped him when they lacked any reasonable suspicion that he was engaged in criminal activity. In our opinion, we stated:

"Consideration of the constitutionality of such seizures involves a weighing of the gravity of the public concerns served by the seizure, the degree to which the seizure advances the public interest, and the severity of the interference with individual liberty."

The gravity of the public concern with highway safety that is implicated by this case is, of course, undisputed. Yet, that same grave concern was implicated in *Delaware v. Prouse.* Moreover, I do not understand the Court to have placed any lesser value on the importance of the drug problem implicated in *Texas v. Brown,* or on the need to control the illegal border crossings that were at stake in *Almeida-Sanchez* and its progeny. A different result in this case must be justified by the other two factors in the *Brown* formulation.

. . . On the degree to which the sobriety checkpoint seizures advance the public interest, however, the Court's position is wholly indefensible.

The Court's analysis of this issue resembles a business decision that measures profits by counting gross receipts and ignoring expenses. The evidence in this case indicates that sobriety checkpoints result in the arrest of a fraction of one percent of the drivers who are stopped, but there is absolutely no evidence that this figure represents an increase over the number of arrests that would have been made by using the same law enforcement resources in conventional patrols. Thus, although the gross number of arrests is more than zero, there is a complete failure of proof on the question whether the wholesale seizures have produced any *net* advance in the public interest in arresting intoxicated drivers. . . .

III.

. . .

[M]y objections to random seizures or temporary checkpoints do not apply to a host of other investigatory procedures that do not depend upon surprise and are unquestionably permissible. These procedures have been used to address other threats to human life no less pressing than the threat posed by drunken drivers. It is, for example, common practice to require every prospective airline passenger, or every visitor to a public building, to pass through a metal detector that will reveal the presence of a firearm or an explosive. Permanent, nondiscretionary checkpoints could be used to control serious dangers at other publicly operated facilities. Because concealed weapons obviously represent one such substantial threat to public safety, I would suppose that all subway passengers could be required to pass through metal detectors, so long as the detectors were permanent and every passenger was subjected to the same search. Likewise, I would suppose that a State could condition access to its toll roads upon not only paying the toll but also taking a uniformly administered Breathalyzer test. That requirement might well keep all drunken drivers off the highways that serve the fastest and most dangerous traffic. This procedure would not be subject to the constitutional objections that control this case: the checkpoints would be permanently fixed, the stopping procedure would apply to all users of the toll road in precisely the same way, and police officers would not be free to make arbitrary choices about which neighborhoods should be targeted or about which individuals should be more thoroughly searched. . . .

This is a case that is driven by nothing more than symbolic state action—an insufficient justification for an otherwise unreasonable program of random seizures. Unfortunately, the Court is transfixed by the wrong symbol—the illusory prospect of punishing countless intoxicated motorists—when it should keep its eyes on the road plainly marked by the Constitution.

I respectfully dissent.

Police have moved from sobriety roadblocks to drug detection roadblocks, where police dogs are used to detect the presence of drugs in the stopped vehicles. Such methods cannot be justified on the traffic safety rationale of *Sitz,* but they have proven to be quite effective in locating illegal drugs. The Supreme Court will decide whether this expanded form of vehicle roadblock is reasonable under the Fourth Amendment or is simply an illegal dragnet search [*Edmond v. Goldsmith,* (7th Cir. 1999)].

ANALYSIS PROBLEM

9–6.   Identify the issues and interests in *Sitz,* and analyze whether the majority or the dissent has the better opinion.

J.   CONSENT SEARCHES

One of the more interesting aspects of Fourth Amendment rights is that one's expectation of privacy may be waived by oneself and others. The issues that arise where there is a consent to search are who has the authority to grant consent, whether the consent is voluntary, and what is the scope of the consent.

Who has the authority to consent? When a person's authority to consent to a search of person or property is challenged, the burden is on the government to prove by a preponderance of the evidence that the person had the necessary authority or that the police were reasonable in their belief that the consenting person had such authority. In a footnote in *Matlock v. U.S.* (1974) the Supreme Court defined the required authority:

Common authority is, of course, not to be implied from the mere property interest a third party has in the property. The authority which justifies the third-party consent does not rest upon the law of property, with its attendant historical and legal refinements, but rests rather on mutual use of the property by persons generally having joint access or control for most purposes, so that it is reasonable to recognize that any of the coinhabitants has the right to permit the inspection in his own right and that the others have assumed the risk that one of their number might permit the common area to be searched.

In general, third parties have authority to consent when they have mutual use and authority over the property, as indicated:

- A spouse (yes);
- A live-in mate (yes);
- A roommate (yes, but only to commonly used area—no to a separate bedroom, for example);
- Child (yes to enter, no to search);
- Parents (yes);
- Landlord (no to tenant's apartment, yes to common areas);
- Tenant (no to landlord's dwelling, yes to landlord's property kept in tenant's dwelling);
- Hotel manager (no to rented room, yes if the person checked out);
- Host (yes to areas occupied by a short-term visitor);
- Employer (yes to work and work storage areas, no to employees' personal storage areas at work);
- Employee (no for search of employer's business premises; yes if one is a manager with complete authority); and
- Bailee—a bailee is one who is given goods from a bailor for safekeeping or transport (yes for bailor's property offered to bailee for common use, no to locked item in bailor's goods).[13]

If the police know that a person does not have the proper authority, then the consent is invalid and evidence found as a result is suppressible. If the police reasonably believe that the consent is authorized and it is not, then the intrusion is valid and the evidence is not suppressible [*Illinois v. Rodriguez* (1990)]. In *Rodriguez* a girlfriend living elsewhere who had lived with the defendant told police the defendant's apartment was "ours" and produced a key to the apartment. It turned out the key had been taken without the defendant's permission when the couple had split up a month earlier and the girlfriend had moved out. The Court ruled that the evidence was not suppressible because police reasonably believed that the girlfriend had the proper authority to grant access to the apartment. There was a strong dissent to the majority opinion.

Is the consent voluntary? Consent must be voluntarily given to be valid. When the consent is challenged, the government has the burden of showing by a preponderance of the evidence that the consent was voluntary [*Bumper v. North Carolina* (1968)]. To determine if the consent is voluntary the court must look to all of the surrounding circumstances, the "totality of circumstances," to see that the consent was not coerced [*Schneckloth v. Bustamonte* (1973)]. This examination is parallel to the inquiry that must be made to see if confessions are made voluntarily (Chapter 10).

The following considerations are relevant to a determination of voluntariness.

- Does the person know that he or she has the right to refuse consent? (This knowledge seems to be assumed in most cases, and police are not required to inform the person of the right.)

"I know of no duty of the Court which it is more important to observe, and no powers of the Court which it is more important to enforce, than its power of keeping public bodies within their rights. The moment public bodies exceed their rights they do so to the injury and oppression of private individuals. . . ."

—Nathaniel Lindley, English jurist *Robert v. Gwyrfai District Council* (1899), L.R. 2 C.D. 614

- Is there anything particularly coercive about the circumstances—for example, the presence of several officers, drawn guns, or the person being asked is in custody?
- Is the person particularly susceptible to coercion or likely to be unaware of the right to refuse because of intelligence, education, or other personal factors? (Few if any cases turn on this issue.)
- Have the police indicated they have a warrant and do not, or have they stated they can get a warrant but in actuality know they lack probable cause? If so, any consent is invalid, because the person giving consent believes there is no right to refuse.
- Is there an overbearing show of force or authority that would deprive the person of a feeling that consent can be refused?

With these considerations in mind, an officer's statement to a suspect's wife that police were there to search for violations of revenue laws was found coercive in *Amos v. U.S.* (1921). In *U.S. v. Mendenhall* (1980), a poorly educated young woman was suddenly confronted by identified narcotics agents. She consented to further questions and even a more detailed search of purse and person while stating she needed to catch a plane. The Court considered the fact that she had been told she could refuse the searches, and found the statement about catching a plane to be a consent to a brief search, and not a refusal to any search. Her consent was held voluntary.

The opening and subsequent closing of a motel room door by an occupant on the realization that the persons knocking were police was not consent to enter and search the room [*Perkins v. State* (Md. App. 1990)]. The consent to questioning and satchel searches given to police by cornered bus passengers was voluntary, and the circumstances did not comprise an arrest [*Florida v. Bostick* (1991)].

In a similar case, police without a warrant entered a bus and informed the passengers that they were going to search all of the carry-on luggage and that each passenger could exit the bus after his or her bags were searched. Defendant Guapi, saying nothing, opened his bag, revealing illegal drugs. In overturning his conviction, the Court of Appeals ruled that a reasonable person would not feel free to ignore or decline the search request under these circumstances. Some indication to passengers that they had the choice to consent or not might have provided a more meaningful basis on which to find that Guapi's consent was voluntary [*U.S. v. Guapi* (11th Cir. 1998)].

What is the scope of the consent? Normally consent affects an area no greater than that controlled by the consenting party or the area used by the consenting party in common with the other person. If consent is granted to search for stolen rifles, police do not have consent to start looking in small paper envelopes. The search must also bear a reasonable proximity in time to when the consent is granted. Follow-up searches need a warrant or additional consent. Consent may be withdrawn, but any search up to that point is valid. Consent given to an undercover agent who is mistakenly believed to be an insider is valid, but consent is limited to the scope reasonably inferred from the circumstances [*Gouled v. U.S.* (1921)]. In *Gouled* the defendant allowed an undercover agent to enter the premises accompanied by the defendant's friend. When the defendant left and the agent searched the premises, the agent exceeded the consent to enter, which did not imply a consent to search.

The permissible scope of a consent has been further defined in several cases. In *Florida v. Jimeno* (1991) a motorist consented to a police officer's request to look for narcotics in the passenger area of a car. This consent was held to cover anything in the passenger area of the car, including a clasped container that would be a likely storage place for drugs. The permissible range of "you may search me" consent does not normally extend to the genital area when the search occurs in a public place such as an airport [*U.S. v. Blake* (11th Cir. 1989)]. When it was not clear whether genitals were "patted down," however, the consent was held to cover the crotch area, even when the search occurred in a public area [*Tognaci v. State* (Fla. App. 1990)]. Pat down of the crotch area has been held not unreasonable when it occurs on a rural highway [*State v. Valrie* (La. App. 1992)].

Police need not inform motorists that they do not have to consent to a search of their vehicle [*Ohio v. Robinette* (1996)]. States may choose to require officers to provide such information, but the Fourth Amendment does not require it.

K. INEVITABLE DISCOVERY

The inevitable discovery doctrine, like the independent source doctrine previously discussed in this chapter, allows evidence to be admitted at trial despite an illegal search or other illegal police activity, if that evidence would have been inevitably discovered had the illegal search or other illegal activity not occurred [*Nix v. Williams* (1984)]. In *Nix*, the defendant's illegally obtained statements led to the discovery of the victim's body. Although the statements were suppressed, evidence from the body was used to convict the defendant. The denial of the defendant's challenge to the evidence was upheld by the Court on the basis that the body would inevitably have been discovered by the independently deployed search party in the area where the body was located.

L. COMMUNITY CARETAKING FUNCTION

The *community caretaking function* exception to the warrant requirement has received more attention in recent years, especially in the state courts. In *Cady v. Dombrowski* (1973), the Court ruled that police could search a disabled vehicle without a warrant when they had probable cause to believe a gun was in the car and that vandals or other persons might inadvertently discover the dangerous weapon. This case recognized that police have a legitimate function, beyond criminal investigation, to protect the safety of the community. Recent state cases have expanded this concept beyond entry of vehicles to include entry into dwellings. In *People v. Ray* (Cal. 1999), the California Supreme Court upheld a warrantless entry of a house where there was no probable cause to believe a crime had occurred. An open front door and belongings and paper scattered over the floor, as well as the neighbor's concern for a possible burglary and the residents' safety, led police to enter the house. The illegal drugs found during the search were used to convict the resident, and subsequently were held to be legally found by the police under the community caretaking exception to the warrant requirement.

Exhibit 9–3 provides a capsule comparison of the exceptions to the Fourth Amendment requirement for a warrant.

EXHIBIT 9–3
Exceptions to the Fourth Amendment Requirement for a Warrant

EXCEPTION	LEVEL OF EVIDENCE	SCOPE	CIRCUMSTANCES	SAMPLE CASES
Arrest	Probable cause, felony.	Reasonable use of force.		*Wong Sun v. U.S. Michigan v. Chesternut*
State:				

Continued

EXHIBIT 9–3 *(Continued)*
Exceptions to the Fourth Amendment Requirement for a Warrant

EXCEPTION	LEVEL OF EVIDENCE	SCOPE	CIRCUMSTANCES	SAMPLE CASES
Stop and frisk (Investigatory Detention)	Reasonable, articulable, and particularized suspicion of wrongdoing, and may have weapon.	Pat down, can seize criminal object.	Not full-fledged arrest, length of detention important.	*Terry v. Ohio* *Minnesota v. Dickerson* *Illinois v. Wardlow*
State:				
Search incident to arrest	Applies to lawful arrests based on probable cause.	Area immediately accessible to suspect, any item with probable cause.	Contemporaneous with arrest.	*Chimel v. California* *U.S. v. Robinson* *Maryland v. Buie* *Knowles v. Iowa*
State:				
Plain view	Probable cause.	Anything in plain view (touch) of officer in course of duty.	Officer legally in place, apparent criminal object, plain view.	*Coolidge v. New Hampshire* *Horton v. California*
State:				
Motor vehicle searches	Probable cause.	Entire car, closed containers in car, passenger's personal items.	Search may be without probable cause if incident to arrest or if vehicle is impounded.	*Carroll v. U.S.* *New York v. Belton* *U.S. v. Ross* *California v. Acevedo* *Wyoming v. Houghten*
State:				
Hot pursuit	Probable cause.	Anywhere suspect or weapons are likely to be found, limited incident to arrest.	Proximity in time to chain of clues.	*Warden v. Hayden*
State:				
Evanescent evidence	Probable cause.	Extent to discover evidence that will disappear, even bodily intrusion.	Indication that evidence will be produced, reasonableness as to threat to health and dignity, necessity of evidence.	*Schmerber v. California* *Winston v. Lee*
State:				

EXHIBIT 9–3 *(Concluded)*
Exceptions to the Fourth Amendment Requirement for a Warrant

EXCEPTION	LEVEL OF EVIDENCE	SCOPE	CIRCUMSTANCES	SAMPLE CASES
Border, regulatory, and emergency searches	Reasonable suspicion for safety, regulation, mail, prisoners, schools; no suspicion necessary at borders (unless particularly intrusive), roadblocks, airports, boats.	Limits on time and intrusion.	Necessity, low expectation of privacy.	*Camara v. Municipal Court* *Michigan Dept. of State Police v. Sitz* *Skinner v. Railway Labor Exec. Assn.* *Chandler v. Miller* *Vernonia School Dist. 47 v. Acton*
State:				
Consent searches	No suspicion necessary.	Area controlled by consenting party, within limits of consent.	Consent must be made voluntarily and with authority.	*Illinois v. Rodriguez* *Bumper v. North Carolina* *Gouled v. U.S.*
State:				
Inevitable discovery	Probable cause independent of search or other independent and legal search.	Evidence that would legally have been discovered during a warranted search or other legal search.	Legal source for evidence independent of unlawful search.	*Nix v. Williams*
State:				
Community caretaking function	Probable cause or not, depending on circumstances.	Any evidence in plain view or otherwise legally discovered.	No probable cause to believe crime occurred; independent police function to protect.	*Cady v. Dembrowski* [line of state cases *People v. Ray* (Cal.)]
State:				

V.   ELECTRONIC SURVEILLANCE

Electronic surveillance is the use of sophisticated electronic technology for the purpose of listening to the conversations of, or observing the activities of, others. It encompasses telephone interceptions called wiretaps, "listening" transmitters placed on premises or persons called "bugs" or "bugging," tracking devices called "beepers," video cameras, night-vision scopes, and super-sensitive heat detection devices called "thermal imagers" that can penetrate the outer walls of buildings.

This section focuses primarily on the use of wiretaps and bugging devices. These devices are extremely intrusive; they expose the most private communications and acts to government observation for potentially long periods of time, encompassing much behavior not relevant to the crime being investigated.

The initial focus of our attention is Title III of the Omnibus Crime Control and Safe Streets Act of 1968 (18 U.S.C.A. §§ 2510–2522). This act preempts state law, meaning Congress intended to set the minimum legal standards for electronic surveillance for both federal and state law enforcement. State law, therefore, can be enacted to implement Title III's provisions, but not to weaken those provisions. Work in this area of law requires a thorough review of both the federal and your state law on the topic.

After *Katz* ruled that the Fourth Amendment applies whenever there is a reasonable expectation of privacy, and *Berger v. New York* (1967) held that electronic surveillance statutes must comply with the Fourth Amendment, the drafters of Title III attempted to design requirements that would pass both *Katz* and *Berger* analyses and overcome the defects in the New York electronic surveillance statute that led to its being struck down in *Berger.* These defects concerned several Fourth Amendment standards. Here is a summary of the key provisions of Title III.

A. All electronic interceptions or wiretaps are criminal and subject to $10,000 fine and five years in prison unless specifically authorized by this statute. This statute cannot authorize electronic surveillance in cases of national security, including domestic surveillance. This is now covered by the 1978 Foreign Intelligence Surveillance Act (50 U.S.C.A. §§ 1801–1811), which highly restricts any electronic surveillance of persons in the United States.

B. Application for warrants must be authorized by the United States Attorney General or other prespecified person who is responsible to the electorate; states must likewise designate such a public official to authorize applications.

C. Consistent with the Fourth Amendment, the law requires a neutral and impartial judge to grant the application for authorization.

D. An order to intercept may be issued only if:
1. there is probable cause to believe the subject is criminally involved (or about to be) in the specifically enumerated crimes; a similar provision for states specifies murder, kidnapping, gambling, robbery, bribery, extortion, dealing in dangerous drugs, and crimes dangerous to life, limb, or property and which are felonies;
2. there is probable cause to believe the interception will produce evidence concerning the specified crime;
3. there is probable cause to believe that the place to be bugged or tapped is used for the specified criminal activity (or about to be) or is listed in the name of the person who is the subject of the order; and
4. normal investigation has been tried and has been unsuccessful or is too dangerous or unlikely to succeed.

Note: The degree of probable cause required will always be an issue and can vary according to jurisdictions.

E. Consistent with the Fourth Amendment, each order must particularize:
1. the identity of the target person and details of the offense;
2. the location of the intercept;
3. the type of communication to be intercepted;
4. the name of the authorized agency and the authorizing person; and
5. the length of time authorized for the surveillance, not to exceed thirty days unless renewed on a new showing of probable cause.

F. Prior judicial permission to conduct electronic surveillance is not needed when:
1. an emergency exists (imminent danger of death or serious physical injury, a conspiracy threatening national security, a conspiracy characteristic of organized crime) requiring interception before an order can be obtained; and

    2. grounds exist for such an order. An order, however, must be obtained in forty-eight hours and the intercept terminated once the evidence is secured or the authorization is denied.

G. As in the case of the execution of a warrant, notice of the bug or tap in the form of an inventory of communication intercepted must be rendered to the targeted person and other parties to the communication no later than ninety days after denial of the authorization or its termination or the termination of an unauthorized emergency surveillance.

Title III is silent on the issue of how far government agents may go to install listening devices. *Dalia v. U.S.* (1979), however, permitted covert installation of such a device. It seems an anomaly in the law that police need a warrant to conduct a bugging but not to enter your home to place the bug.

The law provides remedies to a person who is the victim of an illegal tap or bug. In addition to invoking criminal penalties against the perpetrator, civil sanctions are available, as is the suppression of conversations illegally intercepted and any other evidence gained as a product of the interceptions. A minimal or nonsubstantive breach of the law does not result in suppression [*U.S. v. Chavez* (1974)].

"The law itself is on trial in every case as well as the cause before it."

—Harlan Stone, 1872–1946
Laurence J. Peter, *Peter's Quotations,* 1977

Some other kinds of interceptions are allowed under Title III. They include quality control checks such as would be conducted by a telephone company and "consensual" intercepts. The latter occur when one party to a conversation or a series of conversations consents to the monitoring. [*State v. Bisaccia* (N.J. 1991)]. Simple seizure of the phone numbers on a pen register or a paging device is not an intercept [*Smith v. Maryland* (1979) and *U.S. v. Meriwether* (6th Cir. 1990)]. Other interceptions are allowed if they are done by police on equipment normally used in police business. A recent state court opinion held that police using their extension phones to listen in on a suspect's conversation were not subject to the wiretap law because the suspect was using a police phone [*State v. Reyes* (Nev. 1991)].

The federal courts have upheld random and warrantless interceptions of cordless and cellular phone conversations on the basis that such devices use widely dispersed radio waves that result in a lower level of expectation of privacy [*Tyler v. Berodt* (8th Cir. 1989); *U.S. v. Smith* (5th Cir. 1992)]. Some state courts have interpreted their state constitutions as providing more privacy protection than the federal Constitution [*State v. Mozo* (Fla. 1995)].

The question of whether a court in one jurisdiction can issue an "intercept" order for a cellular phone in another jurisdiction has been raised. A line of cases says yes, because jurisdiction rests both where a call originates and where it is intercepted [*U.S. v. Ramirez* (7th Cir. 1997); *State v. McCormick* (1998)].

Encryption devices have made intercepting phone calls more difficult for law enforcement. In 1994 the Communications Assistance for Law Enforcement Act (CALEA), 47 U.S.C.A. § 1001, *et. seq.,* was passed to require telephone companies to invest in technologies that police can use to digitally intercept phone calls. In implementing the law, the government has proposed that they be permitted, with court permission, to track the location of any cell phone user, as well to use other tapping and information access procedures. Because of the threat to privacy expectations, implementation of the law was delayed until June, 2000.

Thermal imagers can penetrate behind walls to reveal heat sources, such as are used for the cultivation of marijuana and, potentially, other illegal activity. Several federal courts have ruled that the use of such devices is not a search because it is similar to high-altitude aerial photography, which does not reveal intimate activity [*U.S. v. Pinson* (8th Cir. 1994), *U.S. v. Ford* (11th Cir. 1994), and *U.S. v. Penny-Feeney* (D. Hawaii 1991)]. The Washington Supreme Court did not agree, however, in *State v. Young* (Wash. 1994), stating that Washington's constitution protected privacy against this level of intrusion.

The use of video cameras by police to record criminal activity, especially in private settings, has caused concern and raised demands for protection such as that offered in Title III of the Omnibus Crime Control and Safe Streets Act. So far, most courts have upheld the use of video equipment without prior authorization. Warrantless video surveillance of a person coming into a police agent's motel room was held legal [*Commonwealth v. Price* (Mass. 1990)]. What about covert placement of a video camera in a suspect's dwelling?

VI. SECRET AGENTS

The use of secret agents, either undercover police or friends of the suspect who carry hidden microphones hoping to record incriminating statements, does not fall under the electronic surveillance laws nor the Fourth Amendment right against unreasonable searches. The theory relied on by most courts to deflect challenges to this type of surveillance is that the suspect entered into the conversation voluntarily, "consensually," and bears the risk that the party to the conversation is disloyal or a police agent [*U.S. v. White* (1971)]. Cases in which the agent is not wired seem to fall under the same principle even though the landmark cases were decided before *Katz*. A case of interest is the Jimmy Hoffa case where on police instigation, a Teamster official visited Hoffa and overheard incriminating statements by Hoffa regarding jury tampering. The surveillance procedure was held to be free of Fourth Amendment constraints [*Hoffa v. U.S.* (1966)].

Some state supreme courts, however, have ruled that their state equivalent of the Fourth Amendment does require a warrant, even though the informant or secret agent agrees to be wired for the conversation with the suspect [*State v. Blow* (Vt. 1991), *Commonwealth v. Fini* (Mass. 1988), and *State v. Glass* (Alaska, 1978)]. Language in *U.S. v. Karo* (1984) indicates that a homeowner retains the protection of the Fourth Amendment when a guest or friend has been "bugged" without the guest's knowledge or consent. A secret recording by police of a defendant's conversation with his friend in the back of a squad car, where the two "guests" believed they had been placed for their safety and comfort was a violation of a reasonable expectation of privacy [*Barrett v. State* (Fla. App. 1993)].

VII. THE EXCLUSIONARY RULE

Reread the Fourth Amendment to the U.S. Constitution at the beginning of this chapter. If the new nation believed that the federal and state governments would adhere to these principles simply because they were stated in the Constitution, the more experienced nation realized that significant and repeated violation of these rights would occur unless some means of enforcement was established. Absent any alternative that seemed to work, the Supreme Court in *Weeks v. U.S.* (1914) ruled that any violation of the procedural safeguards of the Fourth Amendment necessitated the exclusion from the defendant's trial of all evidence produced by that illegal search or arrest. This rule was extended to the states in *Mapp v. Ohio* (1961). Every citizen's Fourth Amendment right to privacy was protected from overzealous police and government intrusion.

The exclusionary rule is premised on the belief that the police have a personal interest in the outcome of a case, so they will avoid the illegal searches and seizures that result in loss of evidence and, consequently, possible loss of the case. Police training and conduct since *Mapp* seem to bear out this premise. *Wong Sun v. U.S.* (1963) reaffirmed the exclusionary rule, calling evidence derived from an illegal arrest "fruit of the poisonous tree" and "tainted."

Other decisions prevent either the federal government or the states from using evidence illegally seized by the other [*Elkins v. U.S.* (1960), *Rea v. U.S.* (1956)]. Further, the

Supreme Court has limited the scope of the exclusionary rule, holding it does not apply to illegally obtained evidence used to secure a grand jury indictment [*U.S. v. Calandra* (1974)] and to illegally obtained evidence in parole revocation hearings [*Pennsylvania Board of Probation and Parole v. Scott* (1998)]. Although the Supreme Court had whittled at the exclusionary rule, it stayed largely intact until *U.S. v. Leon* (1984).

UNITED STATES v. LEON
Supreme Court of the United States, 1984.
468 U.S. 897, 104 S.Ct. 3405.
[Citations omitted]

Justice WHITE delivered the opinion of the Court.

This case presents the question whether the Fourth Amendment exclusionary rule should be modified so as not to bar the use in the prosecution's case in chief of evidence obtained by officers acting in reasonable reliance on a search warrant issued by a detached and neutral magistrate but ultimately found to be unsupported by probable cause. . . .

I.

. . .

A facially valid search warrant was issued in September 1981 by a State Superior Court Judge. The ensuing searches produced large quantities of drugs. . . . Respondents were indicted by a grand jury in the District Court for the Central District of California and charged with conspiracy to possess and distribute cocaine and a variety of substantive counts.

The respondents then filed motions to suppress the evidence seized pursuant to the warrant. The District Court . . . concluded that the affidavit was insufficient to establish probable cause. . . . [T]he court made clear that Officer Rombach had acted in good faith, but it rejected the Government's suggestion that the Fourth Amendment exclusionary rule should not apply where evidence is seized in reasonable, good-faith reliance on a search warrant.

The District Court denied the Government's motion for reconsideration, and a divided panel of the Court of Appeals for the Ninth Circuit affirmed. . . . In its view, the affidavit included no facts indicating the basis for the informants' statements concerning respondent Leon's criminal activities and was devoid of information establishing the informants' reliability. Because these deficiencies had not been cured by the police investigation, the District Court properly suppressed the fruits of the search. The Court of Appeals refused the Government's invitation to recognize a good-faith exception to the Fourth Amendment exclusionary rule.

The Government's petition for certiorari . . . presented only the question "[w]hether the Fourth Amendment exclusionary rule should be modified so as not to bar the admission of evidence seized in reasonable, good-faith reliance on a search warrant that is subsequently held to be defective." We granted certiorari to consider the propriety of such a modification. . . .

II.

. . .

A.

The Fourth Amendment contains no provision expressly precluding the use of evidence obtained in violation of its commands, and an examination of its origin and purposes makes clear that the use of fruits of a past unlawful search or seizure "work[s] no new Fourth Amendment wrong." *United States v. Calandra,* 414 U.S. 338, 354 (1974). The wrong condemned by the Amendment is "fully accomplished" by the unlawful search or seizure itself, *ibid.,* and the exclusionary rule is neither intended nor able to "cure the invasion of the defendant's rights which he has already suffered." *Stone v. Powell,* 428 U.S. 465, 486 (1976), at 540 (WHITE, J., dissenting). The rule thus operates as "a judicially created remedy designed to safeguard Fourth Amendment rights generally through its deterrent effect, rather than a personal constitutional right of the party aggrieved." *United States v. Calandra, supra,* at 348.

Whether the exclusionary sanction is appropriately imposed in a particular case, our decisions make clear, is "an issue separate from the question whether the Fourth Amendment rights of the party seeking to invoke the rule were violated by police conduct." *Illinois v. Gates, supra,* at 223. Only the former question is currently before us, and it must be resolved by weighing the costs and benefits of preventing the use in the prosecution's case in chief of inherently trustworthy tangible evidence obtained in reliance on a search warrant issued by a detached and neutral magistrate that ultimately is found to be defective.

The substantial social costs exacted by the exclusionary rule for the vindication of Fourth Amendment rights have long been a source of concern. "Our cases have consistently recognized that unbending application of the exclusionary sanction to enforce ideals of governmental rectitude would impede unacceptably the truth-finding functions of judge and jury." *United States v. Payner,* 447 U.S. 727, 734 (1980). An objectionable collateral consequence of this interference with the criminal justice system's truth-finding function is that some guilty defendants may go free or receive reduced sentences as a result of favorable plea bargains. Particularly when law enforcement officers have acted in objective good faith or their transgressions have been minor, the magnitude of the benefit conferred on such guilty defendants offends basic concepts of the criminal justice system. *Stone v. Powell,* 428 U.S., at 490. Indiscriminate application of the exclusionary rule, therefore, may well "generat[e] disrespect for the law and administration of justice." *Id.,* at 491. Accordingly, "[a]s with any remedial device, the application of the rule has been restricted to those areas where its remedial objectives are thought most efficaciously served." *United States v. Calandra, supra,* at 348; see *Stone v. Powell, supra,* at 486–487; *United States v. Janis,* 428 U.S. 433, 447 (1976).

B.

Close attention to those remedial objectives has characterized our recent decisions concerning the scope of the Fourth Amendment exclusionary rule. . . . [T]he balancing approach that has evolved in various contexts—including criminal trials—"forcefully suggest[s] that the exclusionary rule be more generally modified to permit the introduction of evidence obtained in the reasonable good-faith belief that a search or seizure was in accord with the Fourth Amendment." *Illinois v. Gates,* 462 U.S., at 255 (WHITE, J., concurring in judgment).

   . . .

III.

A.

Because a search warrant "provides the detached scrutiny of a neutral magistrate, which is a more reliable safeguard against improper searches than the hurried judgment of a law enforcement officer 'engaged in the often competitive enterprise of ferreting out crime,' " *United States v. Chadwick,* 433 U.S. 1, 9 (1977) (quoting *Johnson v. United States,* 333 U.S. 10, 14 (1948)), we have expressed a strong preference for warrants and declared that "in a doubtful or marginal case a search under a warrant may be sustainable where without one it would fall." *United States v. Ventresca,* 380 U.S. 102, 106 (1965). See *Aguilar v. Texas,* 378 U.S., at 111. Reasonable minds frequently may differ on the question whether a particular affidavit establishes probable cause, and we have thus concluded that the preference for warrants is most appropriately effectuated by according "great deference" to a magistrate's determination. *Spinelli v. United States,* 393

U.S., at 419. See *Illinois v. Gates,* 462 U.S., at 236; *United States v. Ventresca, supra,* at 108–109.

Deference to the magistrate, however, is not boundless. It is clear, first, that the deference accorded to a magistrate's finding of probable cause does not preclude inquiry into the knowing or reckless falsity of the affidavit on which that determination was based. *Franks v. Delaware,* 438 U.S. 154 (1978). Second, the courts must also insist that the magistrate purport to "perform his 'neutral and detached' function and not serve merely as a rubber stamp for the police." *Aguilar v. Texas, supra,* at 111. See *Illinois v. Gates, supra,* at 239. . . .

Third, reviewing courts will not defer to a warrant based on an affidavit that does not "provide the magistrate with a substantial basis for determining the existence of probable cause." *Illinois v. Gates,* 462 U.S., at 239. . . .

To the extent that proponents of exclusion rely on its behavioral effects on judges and magistrates in these areas, their reliance is misplaced. First, the exclusionary rule is designed to deter police misconduct rather than to punish the errors of judges and magistrates. Second, there exists no evidence suggesting that judges and magistrates are inclined to ignore or subvert the Fourth Amendment or that lawlessness among these actors requires application of the extreme sanction of exclusion.

Third, and most important, we discern no basis, and are offered none, for believing that exclusion of evidence seized pursuant to a warrant will have a significant deterrent effect on the issuing judge or magistrate. Many of the factors that indicate that the exclusionary rule cannot provide an effective "special" or "general" deterrent for individual offending law enforcement officers apply as well to judges or magistrates. And, to the extent that the rule is thought to operate as a "systemic" deterrent on a wider audience, it clearly can have no such effect on individuals empowered to issue search warrants. Judges and magistrates are not adjuncts to the law enforcement team; as neutral judicial officers, they have no stake in the outcome of particular criminal prosecutions. The threat of exclusion thus cannot be expected significantly to deter them. Imposition of the exclusionary sanction is not necessary meaningfully to inform judicial officers of their errors, and we cannot conclude that admitting evidence obtained pursuant to a warrant while at the same time declaring that the warrant was somehow defective will in any way reduce judicial officers' professional incentives to comply with the Fourth Amendment, encourage them to repeat their mistakes, or lead to the granting of all colorable warrant requests.

B.

If exclusion of evidence obtained pursuant to a subsequently invalidated warrant is to have any deterrent effect, therefore, it must alter the behavior of individual law enforcement officers or the policies of their departments. One could argue that applying the exclusionary rule in cases where the police failed to demonstrate probable cause in the warrant application deters future inadequate presentations or "magistrate shopping" and thus promotes the ends of the Fourth Amendment. Suppressing evidence obtained pursuant to a technically defective warrant supported by probable cause also might encourage officers to scrutinize more closely the form of the warrant and to point out suspected judicial errors. We find such arguments speculative and conclude that suppression of evidence obtained pursuant to a warrant should be ordered only on a case-by-case basis and only in those unusual cases in which exclusion will further the purposes of the exclusionary rule.

We have frequently questioned whether the exclusionary rule can have any deterrent effect when the offending officers acted in the objectively reasonable belief that their conduct did not violate the Fourth Amendment. "No empirical researcher, proponent or opponent of the rule, has yet been able to establish with any assurance whether the rule has a deterrent effect...." *United States v. Janis,* 428 U.S., at 452, n. 22. But even assuming that the rule effectively deters some police misconduct and provides incentives for the law enforcement profession as a whole to conduct itself in accord with the Fourth Amendment, it cannot be expected, and should not be applied, to deter objectively reasonable law enforcement activity....

This is particularly true, we believe, when an officer acting with objective good faith has obtained a search warrant from a judge or magistrate and acted within its scope. In most such cases, there is no police illegality and thus nothing to deter.... "[O]nce the warrant issues, there is literally nothing more the police [officer] can do in seeking to comply with the law." *Stone v. Powell,* 428 U.S., at 498 (BURGER, C. J., concurring). Penalizing the officer for the magistrate's error, rather than his own, cannot logically contribute to the deterrence of Fourth Amendment violations.

C.

We conclude that the marginal or nonexistent benefits produced by suppressing evidence obtained in objectively reasonable reliance on a subsequently invalidated search warrant cannot justify the substantial costs of exclusion. We do not suggest, however, that exclusion is always inappropriate in cases where an officer has obtained a warrant and abided by its terms. "[S]earches pursuant to a warrant will rarely require any deep inquiry into reasonableness," *Illinois v. Gates,* 462 U.S., at 267 (WHITE, J., concurring in judgment), for "a warrant issued by a magistrate normally suffices to establish" that a law enforcement officer has "acted in good faith in conducting the search." *United States v. Ross,* 456 U.S. 798, 823, n. 32 (1982). Nevertheless, the officer's reliance on the magistrate's probable-cause determination and on the technical sufficiency of the warrant he issues must be objectively reasonable, cf. *Harlow v. Fitzgerald,* 457 U.S. 800, 815–819 (1982), and it is clear that in some circumstances the officer

will have no reasonable grounds for believing that the warrant was properly issued.

Suppression therefore remains an appropriate remedy if the magistrate or judge in issuing a warrant was misled by information in an affidavit that the affiant knew was false or would have known was false except for his reckless disregard of the truth. *Franks v. Delaware,* 438 U.S. 154 (1978). The exception we recognize today will also not apply in cases where the issuing magistrate wholly abandoned his judicial role in the manner condemned in *Lo-Ji Sales, Inc. v. New York,* 442 U.S. 319 (1979); in such circumstances, no reasonably well trained officer should rely on the warrant. Nor would an officer manifest objective good faith in relying on a warrant based on an affidavit "so lacking an indicia of probable cause as to render official belief in its existence entirely unreasonable." *Brown v. Illinois,* 422 U.S., at 610–611 (POWELL, J., concurring in part); see *Illinois v. Gates, supra,* at 263–264 (WHITE, J., concurring in judgment). Finally, depending on the circumstances of the particular case, a warrant may be so facially deficient—*i.e.,* in failing to particularize the place to be searched or the things to be seized—that the executing officers cannot reasonably presume it to be valid....

IV.

. . .

In the absence of an allegation that the magistrate abandoned his detached and neutral role, suppression is appropriate only if the officers were dishonest or reckless in preparing their affidavit or could not have harbored an objectively reasonable belief in the existence of probable cause. Only respondent Leon has contended that no reasonably well trained police officer could have believed that there existed probable cause to search his house; significantly, the other respondents advance no comparable argument. Officer Rombach's application for a warrant clearly was supported by much more than a "bare bones" affidavit. The affidavit related the results of an extensive investigation and, as the opinions of the divided panel of the Court of Appeals make clear, provided evidence sufficient to create disagreement among thoughtful and competent judges as to the existence of probable cause. Under these circumstances, the officers' reliance on the magistrate's determination of probable cause was objectively reasonable, and application of the extreme sanction of exclusion is inappropriate.

Accordingly, the judgment of the Court of Appeals is
Reversed.

Justice BLACKMUN, concurring.

. . .

[It] must be stressed . . . that any empirical judgment about the effect of the exclusionary rule in a particular class of cases necessarily is a provisional one. By their very nature, the assumptions on which we proceed today cannot be cast in stone.

To the contrary, they now will be tested in the real world of state and federal law enforcement, and this Court will attend to the results. If it should emerge from experience that, contrary to our expectations, the good-faith exception to the exclusionary rule results in a material change in police compliance with the Fourth Amendment, we shall have to reconsider what we have undertaken here. The logic of a decision that rests on untested predictions about police conduct demands no less. . . .

Justice BRENNAN, with whom Justice MARSHALL joins, dissenting.

I.

. . .

A.

At bottom, the Court's decision turns on the proposition that the exclusionary rule is merely a " 'judicially created remedy designed to safeguard Fourth Amendment rights generally through its deterrent effect, rather than a personal constitutional right.' " . . .

Such a reading appears plausible, because, as critics of the exclusionary rule never tire of repeating, the Fourth Amendment makes no express provision for the exclusion of evidence secured in violation of its commands. A short answer to this claim, of course, is that many of the Constitution's most vital imperatives are stated in general terms and the task of giving meaning to these precepts is therefore left to subsequent judicial decisionmaking in the context of concrete cases. The nature of our Constitution, as Chief Justice Marshall long ago explained, "requires that only its great outlines should be marked, its important objects designated, and the minor ingredients which compose those objects be deduced from the nature of the objects themselves." *McCulloch v. Maryland,* 4 Wheat. 316, 407 (1819).

A more direct answer may be supplied by recognizing that the Amendment, like other provisions of the Bill of Rights, restrains the power of the government as a whole; it does not specify only a particular agency and exempt all others. The judiciary is responsible, no less than the executive, for ensuring that constitutional rights are respected.

When that fact is kept in mind, the role of the courts and their possible involvement in the concerns of the Fourth Amendment comes into sharper focus. Because seizures are executed principally to secure evidence, and because such evidence generally has utility in our legal system only in the context of a trial supervised by a judge, it is apparent that the admission of illegally obtained evidence implicates the same constitutional concerns as the initial seizure of that evidence. Indeed, by admitting unlawfully seized evidence, the judiciary becomes a part of what is in fact a single governmental action prohibited by the terms of the Amendment. . . . The Amendment therefore must be read to condemn not only the initial unconstitutional invasion of privacy—which is done, after all, for the purpose of securing evidence—but also the subsequent use of any evidence so obtained. . . .

Such a conception of the rights secured by the Fourth Amendment was unquestionably the original basis of what has come to be called the exclusionary rule when it was first formulated in *Weeks v. United States,* 232 U.S. 383 (1914). . . .

B.

[T]he question whether the exclusion of evidence would deter future police misconduct was never considered a relevant concern in the early cases from *Weeks* to *Olmstead.* In those formative decisions, the Court plainly understood that the exclusion of illegally obtained evidence was compelled not by judicially fashioned remedial purposes, but rather by a direct constitutional command. . . .

Despite this clear pronouncement, however, the Court since *Calandra* has gradually pressed the deterrence rationale for the rule back to center stage. See, *e.g., United States v. Peltier,* 422 U.S. 531 (1975); *United States v. Janis,* 428 U.S. 433 (1976); *Stone v. Powell,* 428 U.S. 465 (1976). The various arguments advanced by the Court in this campaign have only strengthened my conviction that the deterrence theory is both misguided and unworkable. First, the Court has frequently bewailed the "cost" of excluding reliable evidence. In large part, this criticism rests upon a refusal to acknowledge the function of the Fourth Amendment itself. If nothing else, the Amendment plainly operates to disable the government from gathering information and securing evidence in certain ways. In practical terms, of course, this restriction of official power means that some incriminating evidence inevitably will go undetected if the government obeys these constitutional restraints. It is the loss of that evidence that is the "price" our society pays for enjoying the freedom and privacy safeguarded by the Fourth Amendment. Thus, some criminals will go free . . . because official compliance with Fourth Amendment requirements makes it more difficult to catch criminals. Understood in this way, the Amendment directly contemplates that some reliable and incriminating evidence will be lost to the government; therefore, it is not the exclusionary rule, but the Amendment itself that has imposed this cost.

In addition, the Court's decisions over the past decade have made plain that the entire enterprise of attempting to assess the benefits and costs of the exclusionary rule in various contexts is a virtually impossible task for the judiciary to perform honestly or accurately. Although the Court's language in those cases suggests that some specific empirical basis may support its analyses, the reality is that the Court's opinions represent inherently unstable compounds of intuition, hunches, and occasional pieces of partial and often inconclusive data. In *Calandra,* for example, the

Court, in considering whether the exclusionary rule should apply in grand jury proceedings, had before it no concrete evidence whatever concerning the impact that application of the rule in such proceedings would have either in terms of the long-term costs or the expected benefits. To the extent empirical data are available regarding the general costs and benefits of the exclusionary rule, such data have shown, on the one hand, as the Court acknowledges today, that the costs are not as substantial as critics have asserted in the past, and, on the other hand, that while the exclusionary rule may well have certain deterrent effects, it is extremely difficult to determine with any degree of precision whether the incidence of unlawful conduct by police is now lower than it was prior to *Mapp.* See *United States v. Janis,* 428 U.S., at 449–453, and n. 22; *Stone v. Powell,* 428 U.S., at 492, n. 32. The Court has sought to turn this uncertainty to its advantage by casting the burden of proof upon proponents of the rule, see, *e.g., United States v. Janis, supra,* at 453–454. "Obviously," however, "the assignment of the burden of proof on an issue where evidence does not exist and cannot be obtained is outcome determinative. [The] assignment of the burden is merely a way of announcing a predetermined conclusion."

By remaining within its redoubt of empiricism and by basing the rule solely on the deterrence rationale, the Court has robbed the rule of legitimacy. . . . Rather than seeking to give effect to the liberties secured by the Fourth Amendment through guesswork about deterrence, the Court should restore to its proper place the principle framed 70 years ago in *Weeks* that an individual whose privacy has been invaded in violation of the Fourth Amendment has a right grounded in that Amendment to prevent the government from subsequently making use of any evidence so obtained.

II.

Application of that principle clearly requires affirmance. . . . [I]t is conceded by the Government and accepted by the Court that the affidavit filed by the police officers in support of their application for a search warrant failed to provide a sufficient basis on which a neutral and detached magistrate could conclude that there was probable cause to issue the warrant. Specifically, it is conceded that the officers' application for a warrant was based in part on information supplied by a confidential informant of unproven reliability that was over five months old by the time it was relayed to the police. Although the police conducted an independent investigation on the basis of this tip, both the District Court and the Court of Appeals concluded that the additional information gathered by the officers failed to corroborate the details of the informant's tip and was "as consistent with innocence as . . . with guilt." The warrant, therefore, should never have issued. Stripped of the authority of the warrant, the conduct of these officers was plainly unconstitutional—it amounted to nothing less than a naked invasion of the privacy of respondents'

homes without the requisite justification demanded by the Fourth Amendment. In order to restore the Government to the position it would have occupied had this unconstitutional search not occurred, therefore, it was necessary that the evidence be suppressed. As we said in *Coolidge v. New Hampshire,* 403 U.S. 443 (1971), the Warrant Clause is not "an inconvenience to be somehow 'weighed' against the claims of police efficiency. It is, or should be, an important working part of our machinery of government, operating as a matter of course to check the 'well-intentioned but mistakenly overzealous executive officers' who are part of any system of law enforcement.". . .

III.

Even if I were to accept the Court's general approach to the exclusionary rule, I could not agree with today's result. . . .

At the outset, the Court suggests that society has been asked to pay a high price—in terms either of setting guilty persons free or of impeding the proper functioning of trials—as a result of excluding relevant physical evidence in cases where the police, in conducting searches and seizing evidence, have made only an "objectively reasonable" mistake concerning the constitutionality of their actions. But what evidence is there to support such a claim?

Significantly, the Court points to none, and, indeed, as the Court acknowledges, recent studies have demonstrated that the "costs" of the exclusionary rule—calculated in terms of dropped prosecutions and lost convictions—are quite low. Contrary to the claims of the rule's critics that exclusion leads to "the release of countless guilty criminals," *Bivens v. Six Unknown Federal Narcotics Agents,* 403 U.S. 388, 416 (1971) (BURGER, C. J., dissenting), these studies have demonstrated that federal and state prosecutors very rarely drop cases because of potential search and seizure problems. For example, a 1979 study prepared at the request of Congress by the General Accounting Office reported that only 0.4% of all cases actually declined for prosecution by federal prosecutors were declined primarily because of illegal search problems. Report of the Comptroller General of the United States, Impact of the Exclusionary Rule on Federal Criminal Prosecutions 14 (1979). If the GAO data are restated as a percentage of *all* arrests, the study shows that only 0.2% of all felony arrests are declined for prosecution because of potential exclusionary rule problems. See Davies, A Hard Look at What We Know (and Still Need to Learn) About the "Costs" of the Exclusionary Rule: The NIJ Study and Other Studies of "Lost" Arrests, 1983 A. B. F. Res. J. 611, 635. . . .

What then supports the Court's insistence that this evidence be admitted? Apparently, the Court's only answer is that even though the costs of exclusion are not very substantial, the potential deterrent effect in these circumstances is so marginal that exclusion cannot be justified. The key to the Court's conclusion in this respect is its belief that the prospective deterrent effect of the exclusionary rule operates only in those situations in which police officers, when deciding whether to go forward with some particular search, have reason to know that their planned conduct will violate the requirements of the Fourth Amendment. . . .

The flaw in the Court's argument, however, is that its logic captures only one comparatively minor element of the generally acknowledged deterrent purposes of the exclusionary rule. To be sure, the rule operates to some extent to deter future misconduct by individual officers who have had evidence suppressed in their own cases. But what the Court overlooks is that the deterrence rationale for the rule is not designed to be, nor should it be thought of as, a form of "punishment" of individual police officers for their failures to obey the restraints imposed by the Fourth Amendment. See *United States v. Peltier,* 422 U.S., at 556–557 (Brennan, J., dissenting). Instead, the chief deterrent function of the rule is its tendency to promote institutional compliance with Fourth Amendment requirements on the part of law enforcement agencies generally. Thus, as the Court has previously recognized, "over the long term, [the] demonstration [provided by the exclusionary rule] that our society attaches serious consequences to violation of constitutional rights is thought to encourage those who formulate law enforcement policies, and the officers who implement them, to incorporate Fourth Amendment ideals into their value system." *Stone v. Powell,* 428 U.S., at 492. It is only through such an institutionwide mechanism that information concerning Fourth Amendment standards can be effectively communicated to rank-and-file officers.

If the overall educational effect of the exclusionary rule is considered, application of the rule to even those situations in which individual police officers have acted on the basis of a reasonable but mistaken belief that their conduct was authorized can still be expected to have a considerable long-term deterrent effect. If evidence is consistently excluded in these circumstances, police departments will surely be prompted to instruct their officers to devote greater care and attention to providing sufficient information to establish probable cause when applying for a warrant, and to review with some attention the form of the warrant that they have been issued, rather than automatically assuming that whatever document the magistrate has signed will necessarily comport with Fourth Amendment requirements.

After today's decisions, however, that institutional incentive will be lost. Indeed, the Court's "reasonable mistake" exception to the exclusionary rule will tend to put a premium on police ignorance of the law. Armed with the assurance provided by today's decisions that evidence will always be admissible whenever an officer has "reasonably" relied upon a warrant, police departments will be encouraged to train officers that if a warrant has simply been signed, it is reasonable, without more, to rely on it. Since in close cases there will no longer be any incentive to err on the side of constitutional behavior, police would have every reason to adopt a "let's-wait-until-it's-decided" approach in situations in which there is a question

about a warrant's validity or the basis for its issuance. Cf. *United States v. Johnson,* 457 U.S. 537, 561 (1982).

Although the Court brushes these concerns aside, a host of grave consequences can be expected to result from its decision to carve this new exception out of the exclusionary rule. A chief consequence of today's decisions will be to convey a clear and unambiguous message to magistrates that their decisions to issue warrants are now insulated from subsequent judicial review. Creation of this new exception for good-faith reliance upon a warrant implicitly tells magistrates that they need not take much care in reviewing warrant applications, since their mistakes will from now on have virtually no consequence: If their decision to issue a warrant was correct, the evidence will be admitted; if their decision was incorrect but the police relied in good faith on the warrant, the evidence will also be admitted. Inevitably, the care and attention devoted to such an inconsequential chore will dwindle. Although the Court is correct to note that magistrates do not share the same stake in the outcome of a criminal case as the police, they nevertheless need to appreciate that their role is of some moment in order to continue performing the important task of carefully reviewing warrant applications. Today's decisions effectively remove that incentive.

Moreover, the good-faith exception will encourage police to provide only the bare minimum of information in future warrant applications. The police will now know that if they can secure a warrant, so long as the circumstances of its issuance are not "entirely unreasonable," all police conduct pursuant to that warrant will be protected from further judicial review. The clear incentive that operated in the past to establish probable cause adequately because reviewing courts would examine the magistrate's judgment carefully, see, *e.g., Franks v. Delaware,* 438 U.S. 154, 169–170 (1978); *Jones v. United States,* 362 U.S. 257, 271–272 (1960); *Giordenello v. United States,* 357 U.S. 480, 483 (1958), has now been so completely vitiated that the police need only show that it was not "entirely unreasonable" under the circumstances of a particular case for them to believe that the warrant they were issued was valid. The long-run effect unquestionably will be to undermine the integrity of the warrant process.

Finally, even if one were to believe, as the Court apparently does, that police are hobbled by inflexible and hyper-technical warrant procedures, today's decisions cannot be justified. This is because, given the relaxed standard for assessing probable cause established just last Term in *Illinois v. Gates,* 462 U.S. 213 (1983), the Court's newly fashioned good-faith exception, when applied in the warrant context, will rarely, if ever, offer any greater flexibility for police than the *Gates* standard already supplies. . . .

IV.

When the public, as it quite properly has done in the past as well as in the present, demands that those in government increase their efforts to combat crime, it is all too easy for those government officials to seek expedient solutions. In contrast to such costly and difficult measures as building more prisons, improving law enforcement methods, or hiring more prosecutors and judges to relieve the overburdened court systems in the country's metropolitan areas, the relaxation of Fourth Amendment standards seems a tempting, costless means of meeting the public's demand for better law enforcement. In the long run, however, we as a society pay a heavy price for such expediency, because as Justice Jackson observed, the rights guaranteed in the Fourth Amendment "are not mere second-class rights but belong in the catalog of indispensable freedoms." *Brinegar v. United States,* 338 U.S. 160, 180 (1949) (dissenting opinion). Once lost, such rights are difficult to recover. There is hope, however, that in time this or some later Court will restore these precious freedoms to their rightful place as a primary protection for our citizens against overreaching officialdom.

I dissent.

Justice STEVENS, concurring in the judgment in No. 82-963, p. 981, and dissenting in No. 82-1771.

It is appropriate to begin with the plain language of the Fourth Amendment:

> "The right of the people to be secure in their persons, houses, papers, and effects, against unreasonable searches and seizures, shall not be violated; and no Warrants shall issue but upon probable cause, supported by Oath or affirmation, and particularly describing the place to be searched, and the persons or things to be seized."

The Court assumes that the searches in these cases violated the Fourth Amendment, yet refuses to apply the exclusionary rule because the Court concludes that it was "reasonable" for the police to conduct them. In my opinion an official search and seizure cannot be both "unreasonable" and "reasonable" at the same time. The doctrinal vice in the Court's holding is its failure to consider the separate purposes of the two prohibitory Clauses in the Fourth Amendment.

The first Clause prohibits unreasonable searches and seizures and the second prohibits the issuance of warrants that are not supported by probable cause or that do not particularly describe the place to be searched and the persons or things to be seized. We have, of course, repeatedly held that warrantless searches are presumptively unreasonable, and that there are only a few carefully delineated exceptions to that basic presumption. But when such an exception has been recognized, analytically we have necessarily concluded that the warrantless activity was not "unreasonable" within the meaning of the first Clause. Thus, any Fourth Amendment case may present two separate questions: whether the search was conducted pursuant to a warrant issued in accordance with the second Clause, and, if not, whether it was nevertheless "reasonable" within the meaning of the first. On these questions, the constitutional text requires that we speak with one voice. We cannot intelligibly assume, *arguendo,* that a search was constitutionally unreasonable but that the seized evidence is admissible because the same search was reasonable.

I.

In No. 82-963, the Supreme Judicial Court of Massachusetts determined that a warrant which purported to authorize a search of respondent's home had been issued in violation of the Warrant Clause. In its haste to make new law, this Court does not tarry to consider this holding. Yet, as I will demonstrate, this holding is clearly wrong; I would reverse the judgment on that ground alone.

In No. 82-1771, there is also a substantial question whether the warrant complied with the Fourth Amendment. There was a strong dissent on the probable-cause issue when *Leon* was before the Court of Appeals. . . . It is probable, though admittedly not certain, that the Court of Appeals would now conclude that the warrant in *Leon* satisfied the Fourth Amendment if it were given the opportunity to reconsider the issue in the light of *Gates.* Adherence to our normal practice following the announcement of a new rule would therefore postpone, and probably obviate, the need for the promulgation of the broad new rule the Court announces today. . . .

Judges, more than most, should understand the value of adherence to settled procedures. By adopting a set of fair procedures, and then adhering to them, courts of law ensure that justice is administered with an even hand. "These are subtle matters, for they concern the ingredients of what constitutes justice. Therefore, justice must satisfy the appearance of justice." *Offutt v. United States,* 348 U.S. 11, 14 (1954). Of course, this Court has a duty to face questions of constitutional law when necessary to the disposition of an actual case or controversy. *Marbury v. Madison,* 1 Cranch 137, 177 (1803). But when the Court goes beyond what is necessary to decide the case before it, it can only encourage the perception that it is pursuing its own notions of wise social policy, rather than adhering to its judicial role. I do not believe the Court should reach out to decide what is undoubtedly a profound question concerning the administration of criminal justice before assuring itself that this question is actually and of necessity presented by the concrete facts before the Court. Although it may appear that the Court's broad holding will serve the public interest in enforcing obedience to the rule of law, for my part, I remain firmly convinced that "the preservation of order in our communities will be best ensured by adherence to established and respected procedures." *Groppi v. Leslie,* 436 F.2d 331, 336 (CA7 1971) (en banc) (Stevens, J., dissenting), rev'd, 404 U.S. 496 (1972).

The "good faith" exception to the exclusionary rule, which applies only to a search pursuant to a warrant, is now imposed on all federal criminal courts. Some state courts follow *Leon* in the interpretation of their state constitutions. Other state courts do not. The latter hold that the state constitution contains no "good faith" exception to the protection against unreasonable searches and seizures. The state supreme court in *Commonwealth v. Edmunds* (Pa. 1991) said that the "good faith" exception did not apply because the state's constitutional provision was based on a right to privacy rather than the deterrent to police misconduct relied on by the court in *Leon*.

In 1995 the Supreme Court addressed the issue of whether evidence should be suppressed that was obtained by a police officer after an arrest based on a warrant that had been quashed (voided) seventeen days earlier. In upholding the use of the illegally obtained evidence, the Court said the exclusionary rule was intended to deter illegal police conduct and not the negligent conduct of the computer clerk who failed to note that the warrant was quashed. The Court went on to say the evidence could be used under the good faith exception in *Leon [Arizona v. Evans* (1995)].

Take special note that most of the law formulated by the courts on search and seizure, arrest, and confessions arises from the defendant's attempt to have the court enforce the exclusionary rule, to have evidence suppressed because of illegal police conduct.

ANALYSIS PROBLEM

9–7. Who do you believe has presented the stronger argument in *Leon,* the majority or the dissent? Why? Do you think the exclusionary rule should be viewed as "a judicially created remedy to safeguard Fourth Amendment Rights" as argued by the majority, or do you believe it should be viewed as included in the Fourth Amendment right of privacy through court interpretation as argued by the dissent?

VIII. CONCLUSION

It is fundamental for paralegals working in criminal law to understand that limits are imposed on criminal law and police procedures by the Constitution of the United States and the individual constitutions of each state. One constitutional right that the founders sought to protect with fervor was the right to be protected against unreasonable searches and seizures. This Fourth Amendment right protects citizens from excessive governmental action, not from private action. It has been the source of considerable litigation, largely because of the Supreme Court's exclusionary rule. This litigation, which has been covered extensively in this chapter, has created an increasingly complex set of principles and exceptions.

A basic knowledge of these principles, researched in more detail when the circumstances dictate, will give you the substantive knowledge to work effectively with law enforcement agencies, assist prosecuting attorneys in the review and possible drafting of search warrants, and assist defense attorneys in drafting motions to suppress and motions attacking any unlawful searches and seizures. Also, you will have gained a better understanding of your own rights.

SYSTEM FOLDER ASSIGNMENTS

Complete the following and place the documents in your system folder:

- Summary list of property that is protected from unwarranted searches by the Fourth Amendment, and another of property that is not protected from such searches, including case references.
- Checklist for determining when a warrant is needed.
- List of what must be included in a warrant and affidavit and what should be avoided (see *Murray*).
- Requirements for when a warrant is needed for an arrest in your state, based on your state's criminal statutes, constitution, or digest.
- Your state's application of the "good faith" exception to the exclusionary rule in *U.S. v. Leon.*
- Sample documents.
- Complete Exhibit 9–3, noting state cases that differ from Supreme Court law and their interpretations of the exceptions.

APPLICATION ASSIGNMENTS

1. Is it state action for an off-duty police officer working as a roofer to reach into an attic space to retrieve illegal drugs? What arguments are there on both sides of the issue? See *U.S. v. Paige*, 136 F.3d 1012 (5th Cir. 1998).
2. Should a person have a reasonable expectation of privacy in documents that are shredded and then placed in the person's garbage [*U.S. v. Scott*, 975 F.2d 927 (1st Cir. 1992)]?
3. Police have consent to enter the defendant's motel room after the defendant has checked out. They search the motel room's trash baskets and find incriminating evidence. Assuming the motel owners' consent was valid, should the police have had a warrant? Does the defendant have a reasonable expectation of privacy that would exclude the evidence from trial? See *Abel v. U.S.*, 362 U.S. 217, 80 S.Ct. 683 (1960).
4. Based on the cases in this section, draw analogies to resolve the following case. Police become aware that several individuals in town have ordered fifty gallons of ether from a photographic supply outlet. The police are informed that the ether will be used to extract cocaine from clothing imported into the United States. With the permission of the supply outlet, police place an electronic tracking "beeper" in the drum of ether.

   The drum is picked up by three persons and placed in their vehicle. Police track the vehicle both visually and by the beeper. Eventually the beeper tells police that the drum has been deposited at *K*'s residence where it remains, according to beeper signals, for several days.

   Eventually the police get a search warrant and find cocaine and laboratory equipment. *K* challenges the use of the cocaine and equipment as evidence on the basis that they were the fruit of an illegal search (i.e., the use of the "beeper" to locate the drum).

   You are the judge. Write an opinion on the suppressibility of the evidence. Assume that there was no other evidence or support of the police search warrant beyond that obtained by the beeper. See *U.S. v. Karo*, 468 U.S. 705, 104 S.Ct. 3296 (1984).
5. As a paralegal for the prosecuting attorney, write a memo that your supervisor can use in deciding on a response to a challenge to the warrant in this case.

A warrant specifies a search for *x* contraband in the second floor dwelling of a yellow and white house located at 315 George St. in a properly named county and city. When the police arrive, they see that the second floor of the house has been divided into two apartments instead of one. The police proceed to search both apartments. Eventually the defendant challenges the warrant and requests suppression of evidence on the basis that the description in the warrant was not specific enough (i.e., "second floor dwelling" instead of "apartment A" or "B").

On what would you base your memo? Would it make any difference if the warrant said "dwelling at 315 George St.," only for the police to find a house *and* a cottage at that address and the police searched them both? See *Maryland v. Garrison*, 480 U.S. 79, 107 S.Ct. 1013 (1987).

6. Using the documents in Exhibits 9–1 and 9–2 as a guide and using forms for your state, if available, draft a search warrant and supporting affidavit for judicial approval in the Eldon Spiers case. Use the following scenario.

Following Eldon Spiers' arrest, the Legalville police want to search his apartment for evidence of the crime. Assume that the arrest occurred yesterday, that Kate Lamb said it was the university janitor who regularly worked nights at the lecture hall, and that he was medium build, about 5'10" tall, and was wearing camouflage pants and a green army jacket; that she described the knife blade as longer than a typical pocket knife but narrow; and that she may have pulled off one of the jacket buttons. Ms. Lamb's statement was two days ago.

7. Identify the issues and points that may lead to a successful attack on the "nightmare" search at the beginning of this chapter.

8. Write a paragraph on a sample case or two from your state courts that shows whether or how far the reasonableness or stop and frisk exception to the arrest requirement has been expanded in your state.

9. Because *Sitz* is now the law, do you think the decision justifies mobile police checkpoints to search for illegal drugs? Does it make any difference if a search for licenses and registration is just a pretext to find drugs or other contraband? See *U.S. v. Ozuna-Fuentes*, 773 F. Supp. 1495 (D.N.M. 1991) and *State v. Everson*, 474 N.W.2d 695 (N.D. 1991).

10. A driver was pulled over by police for legally having his left turn signal on but failing to change lanes. Without further evidence to arouse suspicion and after ninety seconds, police got the driver's consent to search the car, which turned up illegal drugs. Is the search a reasonable investigative detention [*U.S. v. Miller*, 146 F.3d 274 (5th Cir. 1998)]?

11. Assume that you are doing an internship in your college's or school's attorney's office. The board of regents for your school has noted a significant number of illegal drug arrests on campus, and propose that before any student can participate in extracurricular activities such as the debate team, mock trial team, student judicial court, student work study programs, and similar activities, they must pass a drug test. The school attorney asks you to apply the current cases in this area of law and write a brief memo on whether the cases and legal standards will permit such a plan.

12. Write a brief memo for your supervising attorney on whether the precedent-setting ruling in *Leon* should control the following case.

Facts: Police search and seize evidence from the defendant under a state statute authorizing warrantless administrative searches of licensed automobile parts stores. Later the statute is ruled unconstitutional. Should the evidence be suppressed or should the *Leon* exception apply?

Hint: Is there any difference between a judge authorizing a search and the legislature authorizing a search? *Illinois v. Krull*, 480 U.S. 340, 107 S.Ct. 1160 (1987).

HELPFUL WEB SITES

http://members.aol.com/tcnbp/USCons1.htm
    Links to content and information on specific parts of the Constitution
http://caselaw.findlaw.com/data/Constitution/amendment04/
    Articles on specific aspects of search and seizure
http://dir.yahoo.com/Government/Law/Privacy/
    Links to sites on surveillance and privacy
www.infowar.com/class_1/class_1.shmtl
    News articles on surveillance and other privacy issues

INTERNET EXERCISE

1. Go to www.lectlaw.com, through The Reference Room, to the section on Criminal Law and Procedure, and read the analysis of DOJ computer seizure guidelines. In general, if a computer is used by more than one person, how many users need to consent to search the entire system?

QUESTIONS FOR STUDY AND REVIEW

1. What are the sources of our Bill of Rights and how have these rights become applicable to the states in a way that permits the United States and state courts to declare legislation on crime and other actions of government unconstitutional?
2. What rights in the first eight Amendments specifically relate to criminal matters?
3. Why is it important for criminal law paralegals to understand the law on search and seizure?
4. What is the significance of "state action" in the context of search and seizure? Give some examples of persons deemed to be acting under state action and those deemed not to be.
5. What is the significance of *Katz v. U.S.* in determining what areas are protected by the Fourth Amendment and what areas are not? Explain how this has been applied to specific location and property.
6. What is needed for a search warrant to be valid? Are your state provisions any different?
7. Explain probable cause and state the different probable cause conclusions that must be supported to issue an arrest warrant versus those needed to issue a search warrant.
8. What is the current standard for the use of informant information for probable cause?
9. What are some of the key principles of law regarding the relationship between probable cause and staleness of supporting information, staleness and the nature of the property to be seized, computer searches and needed specificity for a warrant, and anticipatory searches.
10. Why is a magistrate's approval for a warrant so important?
11. What is required for proper police execution of a warrant? What is the permissible scope of a warranted search?
12. Define and give the rationale for each of the exceptions to the warrant requirements. What level of evidence is needed to make the search or seizure legal? What is the permissible scope of each of these exceptions?

13. What are the significant issues that must be addressed in a consent to search case? Give a few examples to illustrate how the courts have decided these issues in specific cases.

14. What precautions are needed to make a police roadblock legal under the Fourth Amendment?

15. What law governs the use of electronic surveillance in the United States? How have the drafters of this legislation tried to meet any concerns about the constitutionality of such legislation?

16. What is the rationale for the Supreme Court's holding that secret agents do not come under the protection of the Fourth Amendment?

17. Be able to draft an affidavit in support of a search warrant and a motion to suppress evidence based on illegal search or seizure.

18. What are the issues in the following case? Police officers execute a search warrant without knocking or otherwise announcing their presence. They had received a tip seventy-two hours earlier that the person who resided at the place to be searched had a gun [*State v. Watkins* (Wis. App. 1993)].

19. Define the exclusionary rule, state its underlying justification, and explain the specific impact the holding in *U.S. v. Leon* has on it. If a state supreme court decided it did not agree with *Leon*, what can it do to avoid its ruling?

KEY TERMS LIST

Anticipatory search warrant
Curtilage
Evanescent evidence
De novo

Hot pursuit
Open fields
Probable cause
State action

Stop and frisk
(investigatory
detention)

ENDNOTES

1. 79 C.J.S. *Fourth Amendment* §§ 43–44, pp. 73–74.
2. *A Matter of Privacy*, LEXINGTON HERALD-LEADER, June 10, 1990, at F1.
3. *Keeping Secrets in Cyberspace, Establishing Fourth Amendment Protection for Internet Communication*, 110 HARV. L. REV. 1591 (1997).
4. See also *Beck v. Ohio*, 379 U.S. 89 (1964); *U.S. v. Ventresca*, 380 U.S. 102 (1965); *Jaben v. U.S.*, 381 U.S. 214 (1965).
5. JEROLD H. ISRAEL & WAYNE R. LEFAVE, CRIMINAL PROCEDURE: CONSTITUTIONAL LIMITATIONS 71–72 (1988).
6. *U.S. v. Ventresca*, 380 U.S. 102 (1965); *Jaben v. U.S.*, 381 U.S. 214 (1965).
7. ISRAEL & LEFAVE, *supra* note 5, at 87.
8. T. Drummond, *Its Not Just New Jersey*, TIME, June 14, 1999, at 61.
9. For cases on plain touch, see *State v. Washington*, 396 N.W.2d 156 (Wis. 1986); *U.S. v. Russell*, 670 F.2d 323 (D.C. Cir. 1982); *U.S. v. Ocampo*, 650 F.2d 421 (2d Cir. 1981).
10. Bob Lewis, *Judge Says DUI Laws Apply to Wheelchair Operators*, LEXINGTON HERALD-LEADER, June 26, 1992, at A1, A6.
11. *State v. Callaway*, 317 N.W.2d 428 (1982), *cert. denied*, 459 U.S. 967 (Wis. 1982).
12. ISRAEL & LEFAVE, *supra* note 5, at 133–34.
13. *Id.* at 139–44.

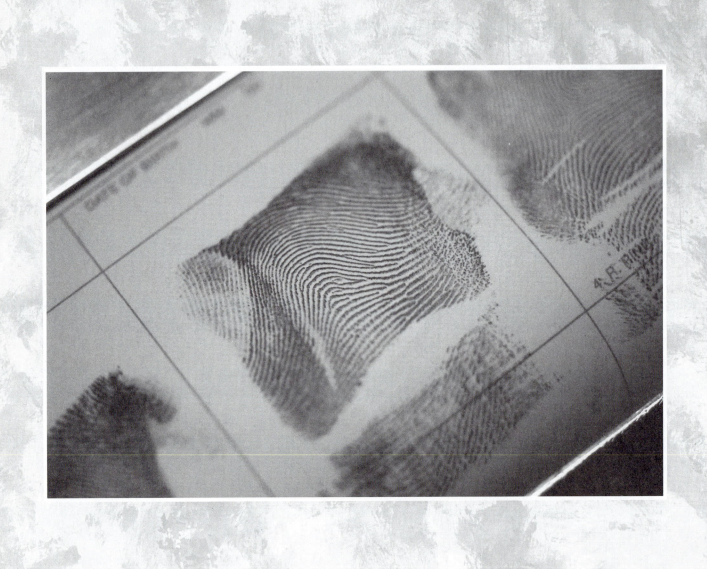

CONFESSIONS AND PRETRIAL IDENTIFICATION PROCEDURES

CHAPTER

10

I. INTRODUCTION

"It is my duty to warn you that it will be used against you," cried the inspector, with the magnificent fair-play of the British criminal law.

—Sir Arthur Conan Doyle
"The Adventure of the Dancing Men"

The need to balance aggressive law enforcement with the preservation of human dignity and freedom compete daily in our criminal justice system, as if one need were continually trying to wrest control from the other. We have seen how this struggle is joined in the area of searches and seizures. Now we will see how the law balances these societal needs in the context of other police investigatory procedures.

A number of constitutional rights and protections arise in the course of police investigation. The Fifth Amendment right against self-incrimination puts limits on police interrogation and confession. It is one of the most litigated and, possibly, the most misunderstood of our constitutional rights. The suspect is also protected by the right to due process and the right to counsel at the crucial early stages of criminal proceedings, such as lineups and other identification processes. In both the prosecution and defense of a case, numerous opportunities exist for you to employ your skills as a paralegal to either support or challenge police investigation practices.

II. THE FIFTH AMENDMENT PRIVILEGE AGAINST SELF-INCRIMINATION

A. INTRODUCTION

No person . . . shall be compelled in any criminal case to be a witness against himself. . . .

—United States Constitution, Fifth Amendment

The right against self-incrimination goes to the very heart of our criminal justice system. It is founded in the belief that the burden must rest on the state to prove that a person is guilty of a crime beyond a reasonable doubt. The proof of guilt must be sound, reliable evidence and must rely on extrinsic sources such as witnesses and scientific analysis as much as or more than it does on confessions of the accused. Our accusatory system of justice depends on the government's gathering, presenting, and testing a broad range of evidence against an aggressive defense.

The importance of this accusatory approach becomes clear when contrasted to a system that relies solely, or nearly so, on the confession, especially a confession that goes without challenge.

[A] system of criminal law enforcement which comes to depend on the "confession" will, in the long run, be less reliable and more subject to abuses than a system which depends on extrinsic evidence, independently secured through skillful investigation.

—Justice Goldberg
Escobedo v. Illinois, 1964

Emphasis on an unchallenged confession to prove guilt places tremendous power and temptation in the hands of government officials. Why spend all the extra time getting outside corroborating evidence when all police need is the simple statement, "I did it"? And, to avoid unnecessary time and expense, why not allow the police to use strong measures, yes, even torture, to assure a quick conviction? This approach was at one time the basis of the European inquisitional system of justice. The brutal Spanish Inquisition and English Star Chamber, political show trials like Stalin's Moscow trials and Hitler's Reichstag trial, and, disgracefully, a few of the trials in this country have relied on confessions that have been beaten or otherwise tortured out of people, innocent people. Torture is still a legal means to extract confessions in some countries.

Therefore, the right against self-incrimination is designed to keep the burden of proof on the state, to force the government to find a variety of reliable evidence, and substantially to reduce the temptation to use excessive means to coerce confessions. Each of these safeguards, of course, stems from the belief that protection against such abuses is consistent with finding the truth and preserving our dignity and liberty.

In practice, however, constitutional rights are only as strong as the teeth in the law that enforces their protection. Today, that protection is afforded by the exclusionary rule, which means that any confession or evidence that is obtained in violation of a defendant's Fifth Amendment rights can be excluded from use by the prosecution at trial.

The right against self-incrimination deals not only with direct confessions, but also with other kinds of self-incriminating testimony during criminal proceedings. It extends back in the process to hearings other than the criminal trial, to "any . . . proceeding, civil or criminal, formal or informal, where the answers might incriminate [the person] in future criminal proceedings" [*Lefkowitz v. Turley* (1973)]. The court must consider two questions in deciding whether to suppress the testimony of a defendant: (1) Does the testimony incriminate or tend to prove criminal conduct? and (2) Could the testimony be used in a future criminal proceeding that may lead to punishment?

"Ours is an accusatorial and not an inquisitorial system—a system in which the state must establish guilt by evidence independently and freely secured and may not by coercion prove its charge against an accused out of his own mouth."

—Felix Frankfurter, majority opinion that confessions extracted by police coercion may not be used in evidence, March 26, 1961

B. WHO IS PROTECTED BY THE RIGHT AGAINST SELF-INCRIMINATION?

Persons, and not corporations, are protected. Corporate officers may not invoke the Fifth Amendment to protect the corporation from criminal liability. They can, however, invoke the right for any personal acts, statements, or papers that may lead to their own criminal prosecution. Documents in the possession of a third party, such as tax forms held by an accountant, are subject to prosecutorial subpoena and cannot be protected except in the case of attorney-client privilege. The privilege protects criminal defendants and witnesses who, if they were forced to give incriminating testimony, might ultimately face prosecution.

The privilege does not, however, protect persons who, when responding to potentially incriminating questions from police, lie by saying "no." Such persons are subject to felony prosecution under 18 U.S.C. 1001 [*Brogan v. U.S.* (1998)]. A number of lower courts had created what was called the "exculpatory no" exception. False or perjured statements are not protected in a subsequent trial for perjury or obstruction of justice [*U.S. v. Veal* (11th Cir. 1998)]. If a witness faces prosecution only in a foreign country, the privilege against self-incrimination does not apply [*U.S. v. Balsys* (1998)].

A witness at trial must affirmatively assert the protection of the Fifth Amendment. If that assertion has been made, subsequent incriminating testimony can be found to be compelled [*U.S. v. Monia* (1943)]. At trial there is no duty to inform a witness of the right to invoke the privilege. In an interrogation setting, however, the protection is greater because the police have an affirmative duty to inform the witness or suspect of the right to remain silent [*Miranda v. Arizona* (1966)].

 ANALYSIS PROBLEM

10–1. Can you think of reasons why the courts have required informing a witness of the right to invoke the privilege against self-incrimination in an interrogation setting and not at trial?

C. IN WHAT KINDS OF HEARINGS MAY THE RIGHT BE EXERCISED?

Criminal trials and questions in proceedings that may lead to criminal trials, juvenile delinquency procedures [*In re Gault* (1967)], and death penalty sentencing hearings [*Estelle v. Smith* (1981)] are sufficiently linked to the imposition of punishment to be defined as "criminal" proceedings. Some kinds of procedures have been held to be "noncriminal" or civil in nature because they do not lead to additional convictions or penalties beyond the original conviction or sentence, or they are perceived as rehabilitative as opposed to penal. Consequently, the privilege has been held inapplicable to statements for or at psychiatric commitments [*French v. Blackburn* (M.D.N.C. 1977)], compensatory civil proceedings, probation revocations [*Minnesota v. Murphy* (1984)], and even in sexual offender commitment proceedings [*Allen v. Illinois* (1986)]. These decisions are limited to instances where the statements will not lead to or cannot be used in any new criminal prosecutions. The dissent in the *Allen* sexual offender commitment decision criticized the majority, however, for ignoring the obvious fact that such commitments are the result of criminal behavior and may result in extended incarceration in prison facilities. The privilege applies at grand jury hearings, but witnesses are not so well protected there as they are when questioned by police, as we will see in the coming discussion of the *Miranda* case.

D. WHAT IS INCRIMINATING TESTIMONY?

Testimony is **incriminating** when it "furnish[es] a link in the chain of evidence needed to prosecute" [*Hoffman v. U.S.* (1951)]. This definition is broad and may include answers to seemingly innocuous questions, such as what is your name, occupation, place of residence. The context in which the question is posed is critical in determining incrimination. To avoid being in contempt of court for not responding to a question, a witness must invoke the Fifth Amendment privilege specifically. The prosecution may object, but incurs the nearly impossible burden of proving that the information will not be incriminating (*Hoffman*).

Prosecutors often secure evidentiary documents through a **subpoena duces tecum.** These subpoenas generally withstand Fifth Amendment assertions, except where it is illegal to possess the document itself or where production of the document will verify the otherwise doubtful and incriminating existence of the document [*U.S. v. Doe* (1984)]. Once again, specific facts of the case determine whether the production of the document is incriminating to the person in possession of the document.

E. WHEN CAN INCRIMINATING TESTIMONY BE COMPELLED?

1. Under Immunity

Situations exist when an answer is incriminating and can be compelled. The first is when the statute of limitations has run on the crime, preventing the perpetrator's prosecution, and the second occurs when the witness is granted immunity from prosecution. **Immunity** is a prosecutor's or superior's binding promise that a person will not be prosecuted for certain crimes in exchange for helping to convict others with testimony that, except for the immunity, would incriminate that person of those crimes. Once immunity is granted, a witness can be compelled to testify under threat of contempt for refusal to do so.

There are two types of immunity, use and transactional. **Use immunity** is restricted to any statements or fruits from those statements that are incriminating in regard to the crime at issue. Any incidental statements that incriminate the witness regarding other crimes are not immunized. **Transactional immunity** is broader and does immunize the witness for incriminating statements about other crimes. Because

---

"Law is not justice and a trial is not a scientific inquiry into truth. A trial is the resolution of a dispute."

—Edison Haines
 Laurence J. Peter,
  Peter's Quotations, 1977

incriminating testimony: that which provides evidence needed to prosecute.

subpoena duces tecum: command to appear in court with specified documents.

immunity: a prosecutor's binding promise that a person will not be prosecuted for certain crimes in exchange for helping to convict others with testimony that, except for the immunity, would incriminate that person of those crimes.

use immunity: restricted to any statements or fruits from those statements that are incriminating in regard to the crime at issue.

transactional immunity: immunizes the witness for incriminating statements about the crime at issue as well as other crimes.

well-advised witnesses tend to protect themselves from prosecution by "confessing" all their sins while under transactional immunity, the federal government and many states now restrict immunity to use immunity.

Even if a witness may avoid conviction through immunity or the running of the statute of limitations, might the testimony be so humiliating, so damaging to the witness's reputation that it raises the testimony to the level of incrimination? What do you think? The courts have rejected such attempts to expand the legal definition of incriminating [*Ullmann v. U.S.* (1956); *Brown v. Walker* (1896)].

Once immunity is granted, it is good in other jurisdictions, including the federal system if granted in a state court and vice versa. Immunized testimony cannot be used in a later prosecution of the witness on other charges to show the witness's testimony is inconsistent with his or her protected testimony [*New Jersey v. Portash* (1979)]. An exception to this rule applies if the witness is later prosecuted for perjury while under a grant of immunity. In such cases, the immunized testimony can be entered in evidence to show its falsehood [*U.S. v. Apfelbaum* (1980)].

A recent case, which has been granted certiorari by the Supreme Court, raises the issue of when the government, under a grant of limited immunity to a defendant, can use documents discovered as a result of that grant of immunity in a prosecution against the defendant. According to the court in *U.S. v. Hubbell* (D.C. Cir. 1999), if the government had "reasonably particular knowledge" of the existence of the documents at the time immunity is granted, they cannot be used against the defendant.

2. Without Immunity

There are other circumstances when incriminating evidence can be compelled and are, for all practical purposes, true exceptions to the compulsion prohibition. Statutes occasionally require the keeping or reporting of information that may be or is incriminating. Certain kinds of administrative information or the reporting of unlawful income on an income tax form can be incriminating. Generally, the law holds that the right must be affirmatively asserted before the records are kept or before the question is answered. If not, any right against disclosure is viewed as voluntarily waived. If the reporting statute has criminal penalties for not reporting, the records may be lawfully compelled if there is an overriding public interest. That would be the case, for example, on various forms reporting securities transactions, prices under an emergency price control, or industry safety measures [*Shapiro v. U.S.* (1948)]. Compulsion is also legal when statutorily authorized, as in the case of having to stop at a traffic accident and provide one's name [*California v. Byers* (1971)].

In contrast, if the statute compels reporting and is directed at a specific group that is inherently suspect of criminal activity, and focuses on an area of law permeated with criminal statutes, then the reporting provision of such a statute is an unconstitutional violation of the right against self-incrimination [*Albertson v. Subversive Activities Control Board* (1965)]. Under *Albertson* and subsequent decisions, statutes or parts of statutes that compelled a person to register as a communist, declare earnings from gambling, and report drug possession for purposes of taxation were declared an unconstitutional violation of the right against self-incrimination. Federal and state general income tax reporting statutes are not unconstitutional under those guidelines [*U.S. v. Sullivan* (1927)].

Methods and statutes that chill the assertion of self-incrimination protection generally violate the Fifth Amendment. Police officers suspected of corruption, who were told that they would be fired if they exercised their Fifth Amendment privilege, had their convictions reversed on the basis that their incriminating statements were not voluntarily given [*Garrity v. New Jersey* (1967)]. When a defendant requests a court to instruct the jury that they are to draw no "adverse inferences" from a defendant's decision not to testify, the judge must give that instruction [*Carter v. Kentucky* (1981)]. Any mention by the prosecution of a defendant's failure to testify is grounds for immediate mistrial [*Griffin v. California* (1965)].

ANALYSIS PROBLEM

10–2. Do you think the court's instruction to the jury to draw no "adverse inferences" from a defendant's decision not to testify actually hurts the defendant by calling attention to the failure to testify?

F. HOW FAR DOES A WAIVER OF THE RIGHT EXTEND?

If a person gives incriminating evidence at a trial or a grand jury hearing on a particular crime, that person cannot subsequently refuse to answer a question on the details of that crime unless the answer to the new question will provide a link to other crimes or a connection to another independent link between the witness and the crime at hand [*Rogers v. U.S.* (1951) and *Shendal v. U.S.* (9th Cir. 1963)].

If a witness waives the right, the waiver does not extend to future hearings. A minority of federal courts have ruled, however, that a waiver at a grand jury hearing by a witness extends to the trial of the matter if the witness is not the defendant at trial.[1]

G. WHEN IS EVIDENCE TESTIMONIAL?

As a general rule evidence that is testimonial, meaning communicative in nature, is protected by the privilege. Evidence that is physical, used for identification, or is as likely to prove innocence as guilt is not protected [*Schmerber v. California* (1966)]. This rule and subsequent decisions hold that the following compelled acts are not a violation of the right against self-incrimination: giving blood and urine samples, appearing in lineups, wearing particular clothing in a lineup, giving fingerprints, giving writing or voice samples, providing one's name, stopping at an accident, being photographed, displaying tattoos or scars, and others. As we have seen, production of documents under subpoena may or may not be testimonial, depending on the circumstances.

 ANALYSIS PROBLEM

10–3. Do you think polygraph (lie detector) tests should be considered a violation of the right against self-incrimination? Why or why not?

III. CONFESSIONS AND INTERROGATION: *MIRANDA*

A. INTRODUCTION

"The great generalities of the Constitution have a content and a significance that vary from age to age."

—Benjamin N. Cardozo,
The Nature of the Judicial Process, 1921

The law on confessions has evolved in the Supreme Court's attempt to determine a workable principle of law. The task has been and still is to balance the need of law enforcement to ferret out crime while preserving a system that values voluntary as opposed to coerced confessions. This balance is a key difference between the accusatory and inquisitional systems of justice. For a while the Supreme Court relied on the Fifth Amendment's due process clause to suppress confessions that were not voluntary. Then it rested its decisions to suppress on a denial of the right to counsel in *Massiah v. U.S.* (1964) and *Escobedo v. Illinois* (1964). Fears grew, however, that reliance on the right to counsel argument could jeopardize even "volunteered" statements.[2] Thus, the Court sought still another approach that came with the landmark decision of *Miranda v. Arizona* (1966).

MIRANDA v. ARIZONA
Supreme Court of the United States, 1966.
384 U.S. 436, 86 S.Ct. 1602.

Mr. Chief Justice WARREN delivered the opinion of the Court.

The cases before us raise questions which go to the roots of our concepts of American criminal jurisprudence: the restraints society must observe consistent with the Federal Constitution in prosecuting individuals for crime. More specifically, we deal with the admissibility of statements obtained from an individual who is subjected to custodial police interrogation and the necessity for procedures which assure that the individual is accorded his privilege under the Fifth Amendment to the Constitution not to be compelled to incriminate himself.
. . .

We start here, as we did in *Escobedo,* with the premise that our holding is not an innovation in our jurisprudence, but is an application of principles long recognized and applied in other settings. We have undertaken a thorough re-examination of the *Escobedo* decision and the principles it announced, and we reaffirm it. That case was but an explication of basic rights that are enshrined in our Constitution—that "No person . . . shall be compelled in any criminal case to be a witness against himself," and that "the accused shall . . . have the Assistance of Counsel"—rights which were put in jeopardy in that case through official overbearing. These precious rights were fixed in our Constitution only after centuries of persecution and struggle. And in the words of Chief Justice Marshall, they were secured "for ages to come, and . . . designed to approach immortality as nearly as human institutions can approach it," *Cohens v. Virginia,* 6 Wheat. 264, 387 (1821).
. . .

Our holding will be spelled out with some specificity in the pages which follow but briefly stated it is this: the prosecution may not use statements, whether exculpatory or inculpatory, stemming from custodial interrogation of the defendant unless it demonstrates the use of procedural safeguards effective to secure the privilege against self-incrimination. By custodial interrogation, we mean questioning initiated by law enforcement officers after a person has been taken into custody or otherwise deprived of his freedom of action in any significant way. As for the procedural safeguards to be employed, unless other fully effective means are devised to inform accused persons of their right of silence and to assure a continuous opportunity to exercise it, the following measures are required. Prior to any questioning, the person must be warned that he has a right to remain silent, that any statement he does make may be used as evidence against him, and that he has a right to the presence of an attorney, either retained or appointed. The defendant may waive effectuation

of these rights, provided the waiver is made voluntarily, knowingly and intelligently. If, however, he indicates in any manner and at any stage of the process that he wishes to consult with an attorney before speaking there can be no questioning. Likewise, if the individual is alone and indicates in any manner that he does not wish to be interrogated, the police may not question him. The mere fact that he may have answered some questions or volunteered some statements on his own does not deprive him of the right to refrain from answering any further inquiries until he has consulted with an attorney and thereafter consents to be questioned.

I.

The constitutional issue we decide in each of these cases is the admissibility of statements obtained from a defendant questioned while in custody or otherwise deprived of his freedom of action in any significant way. In each, the defendant was questioned by police officers, detectives, or a prosecuting attorney in a room in which he was cut off from the outside world. In none of these cases was the defendant given a full and effective warning of his rights at the outset of the interrogation process. In all the cases, the questioning elicited oral admissions, and in three of them, signed statements as well which were admitted at their trials. They all thus share salient features—incommunicado interrogation of individuals in a police-dominated atmosphere, resulting in self-incriminating statements without full warnings of constitutional rights.

An understanding of the nature and setting of this in-custody interrogation is essential to our decisions today. The difficulty in depicting what transpires at such interrogations stems from the fact that in this country they have largely taken place incommunicado. From extensive factual studies undertaken in the early 1930's, including the famous Wickersham Report to Congress by a Presidential Commission, it is clear that police violence and the "third degree" flourished at that time.[5] In a series of cases

---

5. See, for example, IV National Commission on Law Observance and Enforcement, Report on Lawlessness in Law Enforcement (1931) [Wickerhsam Report]; Booth, Confessions, and Methods Employed in Procuring Them, 4 So. Calif. L. Rev. 83 (1930); Kauper, Judicial Examination of the Accused—A Remedy for the Third Degree, 30 Mich. L. Rev. 1224 (1932). It is significant that instances of third-degree treatment of prisoners almost invariably took place during the period between arrest and preliminary examination. Wickersham Report, at 169; Hall, The Law of Arrest in Relation to Contemporary Social Problems, 3 U. Chi. L. Rev. 345, 357 (1936). See also Foote, Law and Police Practice: Safeguards in the Law of Arrest, 52 Nw. U. L. Rev. 16 (1957).

decided by this Court long after these studies, the police re-
sorted to physical brutality—beating, hanging, whipping—and
to sustained and protracted questioning incommunicado in order to extort confessions.[6] The Commission on Civil Rights in
1961 found much evidence to indicate that "some policemen
still resort to physical force to obtain confessions," 1961 Com-
m'n on Civil Rights Rep., Justice, pt. 5, 17. The use of physical
brutality and violence is not, unfortunately, relegated to the past
or to any part of the country. Only recently in Kings County, New
York, the police brutally beat, kicked and placed lighted cigarette butts on the back of a potential witness under interrogation
for the purpose of securing a statement incriminating a third
party. *People v. Portelli,* 15 N.Y.2d 235, 205 N.E.2d 857, 257 N.
Y. S. 2d 931 (1965).[7]

The examples given above are undoubtedly the exception
now, but they are sufficiently widespread to be the object of
concern. Unless a proper limitation upon custodial interrogation is achieved—such as these decisions will advance—
there can be no assurance that practices of this nature will
be eradicated in the foreseeable future. The conclusion of the
Wickersham Commission Report, made over 30 years ago,
is still pertinent:

"To the contention that the third degree is necessary to
get the facts, the reporters aptly reply in the language of
the present Lord Chancellor of England (Lord Sankey):
'It is not admissible to do a great right by doing a little
wrong. . . . It is not sufficient to do justice by obtaining a
proper result by irregular or improper means.' Not only
does the use of the third degree involve a flagrant
violation of law by the officers of the law, but it involves

also the dangers of false confessions, and it tends to
make police and prosecutors less zealous in the search
for objective evidence. As the New York prosecutor
quoted in the report said, 'It is a short cut and makes the
police lazy and unenterprising.' Or, as another official
quoted remarked: 'If you use your fists, you are not so
likely to use your wits.' We agree with the conclusion
expressed in the report, that 'The third degree brutalizes
the police, hardens the prisoner against society, and
lowers the esteem in which the administration of justice
is held by the public.' " IV National Commission on Law
Observance and Enforcement, Report on Lawlessness
in Law Enforcement 5 (1931).

Again we stress that the modern practice of in-custody interrogation is psychologically rather than physically oriented.
As we have stated before, "Since *Chambers v. Florida,* 309
U.S. 227, this Court has recognized that coercion can be
mental as well as physical, and that the blood of the accused
is not the only hallmark of an unconstitutional inquisition."
Blackburn v. Alabama, 361 U.S. 199, 206 (1960). Interrogation still takes place in privacy. Privacy results in secrecy and
this in turn results in a gap in our knowledge as to what in fact
goes on in the interrogation rooms. A valuable source of information about present police practices, however, may be
found in various police manuals and texts which document
procedures employed with success in the past, and which
recommend various other effective tactics. These texts are
used by law enforcement agencies themselves as guides. It
should be noted that these texts professedly present the
most enlightened and effective means presently used to obtain statements through custodial interrogation. By considering these texts and other data, it is possible to describe procedures observed and noted around the country.

The officers are told by the manuals that the "principal psychological factor contributing to a successful interrogation is
privacy—being alone with the person under interrogation." . . .

To highlight the isolation and unfamiliar surroundings, the
manuals instruct the police to display an air of confidence in
the suspect's guilt and from outward appearance to maintain
only an interest in confirming certain details. The guilt of the
subject is to be posited as a fact. The interrogator should direct his comments toward the reasons why the subject committed the act, rather than court failure by asking the subject
whether he did it. Like other men, perhaps the subject has
had a bad family life, had an unhappy childhood, had too
much to drink, had an unrequited desire for women. The officers are instructed to minimize the moral seriousness of the
offense, to cast blame on the victim or on society. These tactics are designed to put the subject in a psychological state
where his story is but an elaboration of what the police purport to know already—that he is guilty. Explanations to the
contrary are dismissed and discouraged.

The texts thus stress that the major qualities an interrogator should possess are patience and perseverance. One

6. *Brown v. Mississippi,* 297 U.S. 278 (1936); *Chambers v. Florida,*
309 U.S. 227 (1940); *Canty v. Alabama,* 309 U.S. 629 (1940); *White
v. Texas,* 310 U.S. 530 (1940); *Vernon v. Alabama,* 313 U.S. 547
(1941); *Ward v. Texas,* 316 U.S. 547 (1942); *Ashcraft v. Tennessee,*
322 U.S. 143 (1944); *Malinski v. New York,* 324 U.S. 401 (1945);
Leyra v. Denno, 347 U.S. 556 (1954). See also *Williams v. United
States,* 341 U.S. 97 (1951).

7. In addition, see *People v. Wakat,* 415 Ill. 610, 114 N.E.2d 706
(1953); *Wakat v. Harlib,* 253 F.2d 59 (C. A. 7th Cir. 1958) (defendant
suffering from broken bones, multiple bruises and injuries sufficiently
serious to require eight months' medical treatment after being man-
handled by five policemen); *Kier v. State,* 213 Md. 556, 132 A.2d 494
(1957) (police doctor told accused, who was strapped to a chair completely nude, that he proposed to take hair and skin scrapings from
anything that looked like blood or sperm from various parts of his
body); *Bruner v. People,* 113 Colo. 194, 156 P.2d 111 (1945) (defendant held in custody over two months, deprived of food for 15 hours,
forced to submit to a lie detector test when he wanted to go to the toilet); *People v. Matlock,* 51 Cal. 2d 682, 336 P.2d 505 (1959) (defendant questioned incessantly over an evening's time, made to lie on
cold board and to answer questions whenever it appeared he was
getting sleepy). Other cases are documented in American Civil Liberties Union, Illinois Division, Secret Detention by the Chicago Police (1959); Potts, The Preliminary Examination and "The Third Degree," 2 Baylor L. Rev. 131 (1950); Sterling, Police Interrogation and
the Psychology of Confession, 14 J. Pub. L. 25 (1965).

writer describes the efficacy of these characteristics in this manner:

> In the preceding paragraphs emphasis has been placed on kindness and strategems. The investigator will, however, encounter many situations where the sheer weight of his personality will be the deciding factor. Where emotional appeals and tricks are employed to no avail, he must rely on an oppressive atmosphere of dogged persistence. He must interrogate steadily and without relent, leaving the subject no prospect of surcease. He must dominate his subject and overwhelm him with his inexorable will to obtain the truth. He should interrogate for a spell of several hours pausing only for the subject's necessities in acknowledgment of the need to avoid a charge of duress that can be technically substantiated. In a serious case, the interrogation may continue for days, with the required intervals for food and sleep, but with no respite from the atmosphere of domination. It is possible in this way to induce the subject to talk without resorting to duress or coercion. The method should be used only when the guilt of the subject appears highly probable."[14]

The manuals suggest that the suspect be offered legal excuses for his actions in order to obtain an initial admission of guilt. Where there is a suspected revenge-killing, for example, the interrogator may say:

> "Joe, you probably didn't go out looking for this fellow with the purpose of shooting him. My guess is, however, that you expected something from him and that's why you carried a gun—for your own protection. You knew him for what he was, no good. Then when you met him he probably started using foul, abusive language and he gave some indication that he was about to pull a gun on you, and that's when you had to act to save your own life. That's about it, isn't it, Joe?"

Having then obtained the admission of shooting, the interrogator is advised to refer to circumstantial evidence which negates the self-defense explanation. This should enable him to secure the entire story. One text notes that "Even if he fails to do so, the inconsistency between the subject's original denial of the shooting and his present admission of at least doing the shooting will serve to deprive him of a self-defense 'out' at the time of trial."

When the techniques described above prove unavailing, the texts recommend they be alternated with a show of some hostility. One ploy often used has been termed the "friendly-unfriendly" or the "Mutt and Jeff" act:

> ". . . In this technique, two agents are employed. Mutt, the relentless investigator, who knows the subject is

guilty and is not going to waste any time. He's sent a dozen men away for this crime and he's going to send the subject away for the full term. Jeff, on the other hand, is obviously a kindhearted man. He has a family himself. He has a brother who was involved in a little scrape like this. He disapproves of Mutt and his tactics and will arrange to get him off the case if the subject will cooperate. He can't hold Mutt off for very long. The subject would be wise to make a quick decision. The technique is applied by having both investigators present while Mutt acts out his role. Jeff may stand by quietly and demur at some of Mutt's tactics. When Jeff makes his plea for cooperation, Mutt is not present in the room."

The interrogators sometimes are instructed to induce a confession out of trickery. The technique here is quite effective in crimes which require identification or which run in series. In the identification situation, the interrogator may take a break in his questioning to place the subject among a group of men in a line-up. "The witness or complainant (previously coached, if necessary) studies the line-up and confidently points out the subject as the guilty party." Then the questioning resumes "as though there were now no doubt about the guilt of the subject." A variation on this technique is called the "reverse line-up":

> "The accused is placed in a line-up, but this time he is identified by several fictitious witnesses or victims who associated him with different offenses. It is expected that the subject will become desperate and confess to the offense under investigation in order to escape from the false accusations."

The manuals also contain instructions for police on how to handle the individual who refuses to discuss the matter entirely, or who asks for an attorney or relatives. The examiner is to concede him the right to remain silent. "This usually has a very undermining effect. First of all, he is disappointed in his expectation of an unfavorable reaction on the part of the interrogator. Secondly, a concession of this right to remain silent impresses the subject with the apparent fairness of his interrogator." After this psychological conditioning, however, the officer is told to point out the incriminating significance of the suspect's refusal to talk:

> "Joe, you have a right to remain silent. That's your privilege and I'm the last person in the world who'll try to take it away from you. If that's the way you want to leave this, O. K. But let me ask you this. Suppose you were in my shoes and I were in yours and you called me in to ask me about this and I told you, 'I don't want to answer any of your questions.' You'd think I had something to hide, and you'd probably be right in thinking that. That's exactly what I'll have to think about you, and so will everybody else. So let's sit here and talk this whole thing over."

---

14. O'Hara, at 112.

Few will persist in their initial refusal to talk, it is said, if this monologue is employed correctly.

In the event that the subject wishes to speak to a relative or an attorney, the following advice is tendered:

"[T]he interrogator should respond by suggesting that the subject first tell the truth to the interrogator himself rather than get anyone else involved in the matter. If the request is for an attorney, the interrogator may suggest that the subject save himself or his family the expense of any such professional service, particularly if he is innocent of the offense under investigation. The interrogator may also add, 'Joe, I'm only looking for the truth, and if you're telling the truth, that's it. You can handle this by yourself.'"

From these representative samples of interrogation techniques, the setting prescribed by the manuals and observed in practice becomes clear. In essence, it is this: To be alone with the subject is essential to prevent distraction and to deprive him of any outside support. The aura of confidence in his guilt undermines his will to resist. He merely confirms the preconceived story the police seek to have him describe. Patience and persistence, at times relentless questioning, are employed. To obtain a confession, the interrogator must "patiently maneuver himself or his quarry into a position from which the desired objective may be attained." When normal procedures fail to produce the needed result, the police may resort to deceptive stratagems such as giving false legal advice. It is important to keep the subject off balance, for example, by trading on his insecurity about himself or his surroundings. The police then persuade, trick, or cajole him out of exercising his constitutional rights.

Even without employing brutality, the "third degree" or the specific stratagems described above, the very fact of custodial interrogation exacts a heavy toll on individual liberty and trades on the weakness of individuals. This fact may be illustrated simply by referring to three confession cases decided by this Court in the Term immediately preceding our *Escobedo* decision. In *Townsend v. Sain,* 372 U.S. 293 (1963), the defendant was a 19-year-old heroin addict, described as a "near mental defective," *id.,* at 307–310. The defendant in *Lynumn v. Illinois,* 372 U.S. 528 (1963), was a woman who confessed to the arresting officer after being importuned to "cooperate" in order to prevent her children from being taken by relief authorities. This Court as in those cases reversed the conviction of a defendant in *Haynes v. Washington,* 373 U.S. 503 (1963), whose persistent request during his interrogation was to phone his wife or attorney. In other settings, these individuals might have exercised their constitutional rights. In the incommunicado police-dominated atmosphere, they succumbed.

In the cases before us today, given this background, we concern ourselves primarily with this interrogation atmosphere and the evils it can bring. In *Miranda v. Arizona,* the police arrested the defendant and took him to a special interrogation room where they secured a confession. In *Vignera v. New York,* the defendant made oral admissions to the police after interrogation in the afternoon, and then signed an inculpatory statement upon being questioned by an assistant district attorney later the same evening. In *Westover v. United States,* the defendant was handed over to the Federal Bureau of Investigation by local authorities after they had detained and interrogated him for a lengthy period, both at night and the following morning. After some two hours of questioning, the federal officers had obtained signed statements from the defendant. Lastly, in *California v. Stewart,* the local police held the defendant five days in the station and interrogated him on nine separate occasions before they secured his inculpatory statement.

In these cases, we might not find the defendants' statements to have been involuntary in traditional terms. Our concern for adequate safeguards to protect precious Fifth Amendment rights is, of course, not lessened in the slightest. In each of the cases, the defendant was thrust into an unfamiliar atmosphere and run through menacing police interrogation procedures. The potentiality for compulsion is forcefully apparent, for example, in *Miranda,* where the indigent Mexican defendant was a seriously disturbed individual with pronounced sexual fantasies, and in *Stewart,* in which the defendant was an indigent Los Angeles Negro who had dropped out of school in the sixth grade. To be sure, the records do not evince overt physical coercion or patent psychological ploys. The fact remains that in none of these cases did the officers undertake to afford appropriate safeguards at the outset of the interrogation to insure that the statements were truly the product of free choice.

It is obvious that such an interrogation environment is created for no purpose other than to subjugate the individual to the will of his examiner. This atmosphere carries its own badge of intimidation. To be sure, this is not physical intimidation, but it is equally destructive of human dignity. The current practice of incommunicado interrogation is at odds with one of our Nation's most cherished principles—that the individual may not be compelled to incriminate himself. Unless adequate protective devices are employed to dispel the compulsion inherent in custodial surroundings, no statement obtained from the defendant can truly be the product of his free choice.

From the foregoing, we can readily perceive an intimate connection between the privilege against self-incrimination and police custodial questioning. It is fitting to turn to history and precedent underlying the Self-Incrimination Clause to determine its applicability in this situation.

II.

We sometimes forget how long it has taken to establish the privilege against self-incrimination, the sources from which it came and the fervor with which it was defended. Its roots go back into ancient times. Perhaps the critical historical event shedding light on its origins and evolution was the trial of one John Lilburn, a vocal anti–Stuart Leveller, who was made to take the Star Chamber Oath in 1637. The oath would have bound him to answer to all questions posed to him on any subject. The Trial of John Lilburn and John Wharton, 3 How. St. Tr. 1315 (1637). He resisted the oath and declaimed the proceedings, stating:

> "Another fundamental right I then contended for, was, that no man's conscience ought to be racked by oaths imposed, to answer to questions concerning himself in matters criminal, or pretended to be so." Haller & Davies, The Leveller Tracts 1647–1653, p. 454 (1944).

On account of the Lilburn Trial, Parliament abolished the inquisitorial Court of Star Chamber and went further in giving him generous reparation. The lofty principles to which Lilburn had appealed during his trial gained popular acceptance in England. These sentiments worked their way over to the Colonies and were implanted after great struggle into the Bill of Rights. Those who framed our Constitution and the Bill of Rights were ever aware of subtle encroachments on individual liberty. They knew that "illegitimate and unconstitutional practices get their first footing . . . by silent approaches and slight deviations from legal modes of procedure." *Boyd v. United States,* 116 U.S. 616, 635 (1886). The privilege was elevated to constitutional status and has always been "as broad as the mischief against which it seeks to guard." *Counselman v. Hitchcock,* 142 U.S. 547, 562 (1892). We cannot depart from this noble heritage.

Thus we may view the historical development of the privilege as one which groped for the proper scope of governmental power over the citizen. As a "noble principle often transcends its origins," the privilege has come rightfully to be recognized in part as an individual's substantive right, a "right to a private enclave where he may lead a private life. That right is the hallmark of our democracy." *United States v. Grunewald,* 233 F.2d 556, 579, 581–582 (Frank, J., dissenting), rev'd, 353 U.S. 391 (1957). We have recently noted that the privilege against self-incrimination—the essential mainstay of our adversary system—is founded on a complex of values, *Murphy v. Waterfront Comm'n,* 378 U.S. 52, 55–57, n. 5 (1964); *Tehan v. Shott,* 382 U.S. 406, 414–415, n. 12 (1966). All these policies point to one overriding thought: the constitutional foundation underlying the privilege is the respect a government—state or federal—must accord to the dignity and integrity of its citizens. To maintain a "fair state-individual balance," to require the government "to shoulder the entire load," 8 Wigmore, Evidence 317 (McNaughton rev. 1961), to respect the inviolability of the human personality, our accusatory system of criminal justice demands that the government seeking to punish an individual produce the evidence against him by its own independent labors, rather than by the cruel, simple expedient of compelling it from his own mouth. *Chambers v. Florida,* 309 U.S. 227, 235–238 (1940). In sum, the privilege is fulfilled only when the person

is guaranteed the right "to remain silent unless he chooses to speak in the unfettered exercise of his own will." *Malloy v. Hogan,* 378 U.S. 1, 8 (1964).

The question in these cases is whether the privilege is fully applicable during a period of custodial interrogation. In this Court, the privilege has consistently been accorded a liberal construction. *Albertson v. SACB,* 382 U.S. 70, 81 (1965); *Hoffman v. United States,* 341 U.S. 479, 486 (1951); *Arndstein v. McCarthy,* 254 U.S. 71, 72–73 (1920); *Counselman v. Hitchcock,* 142 U.S. 547, 562 (1892). We are satisfied that all the principles embodied in the privilege apply to informal compulsion exerted by law-enforcement officers during in-custody questioning. An individual swept from familiar surroundings into police custody, surrounded by antagonistic forces, and subjected to the techniques of persuasion described above cannot be otherwise than under compulsion to speak. As a practical matter, the compulsion to speak in the isolated setting of the police station may well be greater than in courts or other official investigations, where there are often impartial observers to guard against intimidation or trickery.

. . . In addition to the expansive historical development of the privilege and the sound policies which have nurtured its evolution, judicial precedent thus clearly establishes its application to incommunicado interrogation. In fact, the Government concedes this point as well established in *Westover v. United States,* stating: "We have no doubt . . . that it is possible for a suspect's Fifth Amendment right to be violated during in-custody questioning by a law-enforcement officer."

Because of the adoption by Congress of Rule 5 (a) of the Federal Rules of Criminal Procedure, and this Court's effectuation of that Rule in *McNabb v. United States,* 318 U.S. 332 (1943), and *Mallory v. United States,* 354 U.S. 449 (1957), we have had little occasion in the past quarter century to reach the constitutional issues in dealing with federal interrogations. These supervisory rules, requiring production of an arrested person before a commissioner "without unnecessary delay" and excluding evidence obtained in default of that statutory obligation, were nonetheless responsive to the same considerations of Fifth Amendment policy that unavoidably face us now as to the States. In *McNabb,* 318 U.S., at 343–344, and in *Mallory,* 354 U.S., at 455–456, we recognized both the dangers of interrogation and the appropriateness of prophylaxis stemming from the very fact of interrogation itself.

Our decision in *Malloy v. Hogan,* 378 U.S. 1 (1964), necessitates an examination of the scope of the privilege in state cases as well. In *Malloy,* we squarely held the privilege applicable to the States, and held that the substantive standards underlying the privilege applied with full force to state court proceedings. There, as in *Murphy v. Waterfront Comm'n,* 378 U.S. 52 (1964), and *Griffin v. California,* 380 U.S. 609 (1965), we applied the existing Fifth Amendment standards to the case before us. Aside from the holding itself, the reasoning in *Malloy* made clear what had already become apparent—that the substantive and procedural safeguards surrounding admissibility of confessions in state cases had become exceedingly exacting, reflecting all the policies embedded in the privilege, 378 U.S., at 7–8.[33] The voluntariness doctrine in the state cases, as *Malloy* indicates, encompasses all interrogation practices which are likely to exert such pressure upon an individual as to disable him from making a free and rational choice. The implications of this proposition were elaborated in our decision in *Escobedo v. Illinois*, 378 U.S. 478, decided one week after *Malloy* applied the privilege to the States.

. . . [In *Escobedo*], as in the cases today, we sought a protective device to dispel the compelling atmosphere of the interrogation. In *Escobedo*, however, the police did not relieve the defendant of the anxieties which they had created in the interrogation rooms. Rather, they denied his request for the assistance of counsel, 378 U.S., at 481, 488, 491. This heightened his dilemma, and made his later statements the product of this compulsion. Cf. *Haynes v. Washington*, 373 U.S. 503, 514 (1963). The denial of the defendant's request for his attorney thus undermined his ability to exercise the privilege—to remain silent if he chose or to speak without any intimidation, blatant or subtle. The presence of counsel, in all the cases before us today, would be the adequate protective device necessary to make the process of police interrogation conform to the dictates of the privilege. His presence would insure that statements made in the government-established atmosphere are not the product of compulsion.

It was in this manner that *Escobedo* explicated another facet of the pretrial privilege, noted in many of the Court's prior decisions: the protection of rights at trial. That counsel is present when statements are taken from an individual during interrogation obviously enhances the integrity of the fact-finding processes in court. The presence of an attorney, and

the warnings delivered to the individual, enable the defendant under otherwise compelling circumstances to tell his story without fear, effectively, and in a way that eliminates the evils in the interrogation process. Without the protections flowing from adequate warnings and the rights of counsel, "all the careful safeguards erected around the giving of testimony, whether by an accused or any other witness, would become empty formalities in a procedure where the most compelling possible evidence of guilt, a confession, would have already been obtained at the unsupervised pleasure of the police." *Mapp v. Ohio,* 367 U.S. 643, 685 (1961) (HARLAN, J., dissenting). Cf. *Pointer v. Texas,* 380 U.S. 400 (1965).

III.

Today, then, there can be no doubt that the Fifth Amendment privilege is available outside of criminal court proceedings and serves to protect persons in all settings in which their freedom of action is curtailed in any significant way from being compelled to incriminate themselves. We have concluded that without proper safeguards the process of in-custody interrogation of persons suspected or accused of crime contains inherently compelling pressures which work to undermine the individual's will to resist and to compel him to speak where he would not otherwise do so freely. In order to combat these pressures and to permit a full opportunity to exercise the privilege against self-incrimination, the accused must be adequately and effectively apprised of his rights and the exercise of those rights must be fully honored.

It is impossible for us to foresee the potential alternatives for protecting the privilege which might be devised by Congress or the States in the exercise of their creative rule-making capacities. Therefore we cannot say that the Constitution necessarily requires adherence to any particular solution for the inherent compulsions of the interrogation process as it is presently conducted. Our decision in no way creates a constitutional straitjacket which will handicap sound efforts at reform, nor is it intended to have this effect. We encourage Congress and the States to continue their laudable search for increasingly effective ways of protecting the rights of the individual while promoting efficient enforcement of our criminal laws. However, unless we are shown other procedures which are at least as effective in apprising accused persons of their right of silence and in assuring a continuous opportunity to exercise it, the following safeguards must be observed.

At the outset, if a person in custody is to be subjected to interrogation, he must first be informed in clear and unequivocal terms that he has the right to remain silent. For those unaware of the privilege, the warning is needed simply to make them aware of it—the threshold requirement for an intelligent decision as to its exercise. More important, such a warning is an absolute prerequisite in overcoming the inherent pressures of the interrogation atmosphere. It is not just the subnormal or woefully ignorant who succumb to an interrogator's imprecations, whether implied or expressly

---

33. The decisions of this Court have guaranteed the same procedural protection for the defendant whether his confession was used in a federal or state court. It is now axiomatic that the defendant's constitutional rights have been violated if his conviction is based, in whole or in part, on an involuntary confession, regardless of its truth or falsity. *Rogers v. Richmond,* 365 U.S. 534, 544 (1961); *Wan v. United States,* 266 U.S. 1 (1924). This is so even if there is ample evidence aside from the confession to support the conviction, *e. g., Malinski v. New York,* 324 U.S. 401, 404 (1945); *Bram v. United States,* 168 U.S. 532, 540–542 (1897). Both state and federal courts now adhere to trial procedures which seek to assure a reliable and clear-cut determination of the voluntariness of the confession offered at trial, *Jackson v. Denno,* 378 U.S. 368 (1964); *United States v. Carignan,* 342 U.S. 36, 38 (1951); see also *Wilson v. United States,* 162 U.S. 613, 624 (1896). Appellate review is exacting, see *Haynes v. Washington,* 373 U.S. 503 (1963); *Blackburn v. Alabama,* 361 U.S. 199 (1960). Whether his conviction was in a federal or state court, the defendant may secure a postconviction hearing based on the alleged involuntary character of his confession, provided he meets the procedural requirements, *Fay v. Noia,* 372 U.S. 391 (1963); *Townsend v. Sain,* 372 U.S. 293 (1963). In addition, see *Murphy v. Waterfront Comm'n,* 378 U.S. 52 (1964).

stated, that the interrogation will continue until a confession is obtained or that silence in the face of accusation is itself damning and will bode ill when presented to a jury. Further, the warning will show the individual that his interrogators are prepared to recognize his privilege should he choose to exercise it.

The Fifth Amendment privilege is so fundamental to our system of constitutional rule and the expedient of giving an adequate warning as to the availability of the privilege so simple, we will not pause to inquire in individual cases whether the defendant was aware of his rights without a warning being given. Assessments of the knowledge the defendant possessed, based on information as to his age, education, intelligence, or prior contact with authorities, can never be more than speculation; a warning is a clearcut fact. More important, whatever the background of the person interrogated, a warning at the time of the interrogation is indispensable to overcome its pressures and to insure that the individual knows he is free to exercise the privilege at that point in time.

The warning of the right to remain silent must be accompanied by the explanation that anything said can and will be used against the individual in court. This warning is needed in order to make him aware not only of the privilege, but also of the consequences of forgoing it. It is only through an awareness of these consequences that there can be any assurance of real understanding and intelligent exercise of the privilege. Moreover, this warning may serve to make the individual more acutely aware that he is faced with a phase of the adversary system—that he is not in the presence of persons acting solely in his interest.

The circumstances surrounding in-custody interrogation can operate very quickly to overbear the will of one merely made aware of his privilege by his interrogators. Therefore, the right to have counsel present at the interrogation is indispensable to the protection of the Fifth Amendment privilege under the system we delineate today. Our aim is to assure that the individual's right to choose between silence and speech remains unfettered throughout the interrogation process. A once-stated warning, delivered by those who will conduct the interrogation, cannot itself suffice to that end among those who most require knowledge of their rights. A mere warning given by the interrogators is not alone sufficient to accomplish that end. Prosecutors themselves claim that the admonishment of the right to remain silent without more "will benefit only the recidivist and the professional." Brief for the National District Attorneys Association as *amicus curiae*, p. 14. Even preliminary advice given to the accused by his own attorney can be swiftly overcome by the secret interrogation process. Cf. *Escobedo v. Illinois,* 378 U.S. 478, 485, n. 5. Thus, the need for counsel to protect the Fifth Amendment privilege comprehends not merely a right to consult with counsel prior to questioning, but also to have counsel present during any questioning if the defendant so desires.

The presence of counsel at the interrogation may serve several significant subsidiary functions as well. If the accused decides to talk to his interrogators, the assistance of counsel can mitigate the dangers of untrustworthiness. With a lawyer present the likelihood that the police will practice coercion is reduced, and if coercion is nevertheless exercised the lawyer can testify to it in court. The presence of a lawyer can also help to guarantee that the accused gives a fully accurate statement to the police and that the statement is rightly reported by the prosecution at trial. See *Crooker v. California,* 357 U.S. 433, 443–448 (1958) (DOUGLAS, J., dissenting).

An individual need not make a pre-interrogation request for a lawyer. While such request affirmatively secures his right to have one, his failure to ask for a lawyer does not constitute a waiver. No effective waiver of the right to counsel during interrogation can be recognized unless specifically made after the warnings we here delineate have been given. The accused who does not know his rights and therefore does not make a request may be the person who most needs counsel. . . .

Accordingly we hold that an individual held for interrogation must be clearly informed that he has the right to consult with a lawyer and to have the lawyer with him during interrogation under the system for protecting the privilege we delineate today. As with the warnings of the right to remain silent and that anything stated can be used in evidence against him, this warning is an absolute prerequisite to interrogation. No amount of circumstantial evidence that the person may have been aware of this right will suffice to stand in its stead. Only through such a warning is there ascertainable assurance that the accused was aware of this right.

If an individual indicates that he wishes the assistance of counsel before any interrogation occurs, the authorities cannot rationally ignore or deny his request on the basis that the individual does not have or cannot afford a retained attorney. The financial ability of the individual has no relationship to the scope of the rights involved here. The privilege against self-incrimination secured by the Constitution applies to all individuals. The need for counsel in order to protect the privilege exists for the indigent as well as the affluent. In fact, were we to limit these constitutional rights to those who can retain an attorney, our decisions today would be of little significance. The cases before us as well as the vast majority of confession cases with which we have dealt in the past involve those unable to retain counsel.[40] While authorities are not required to relieve the accused of his poverty, they have the obligation not to take advantage of indigence in the administration of justice. Denial of counsel to the indigent at the time of interrogation while allowing an attorney to those who can afford one would be no more supportable by reason or

---

40. Estimates of 50–90% indigency among felony defendants have been reported. Pollock, Equal Justice in Practice, 45 Minn. L. Rev. 737, 738–739 (1961); Birzon, Kasanof & Forma, The Right to Counsel and the Indigent Accused in Courts of Criminal Jurisdiction in New York State, 14 Buffalo L. Rev. 428, 433 (1965).

logic than the similar situation at trial and on appeal struck down in *Gideon v. Wainwright,* 372 U.S. 335 (1963), and *Douglas v. California,* 372 U.S. 353 (1963).

In order fully to apprise a person interrogated of the extent of his rights under this system then, it is necessary to warn him not only that he has the right to consult with an attorney, but also that if he is indigent, a lawyer will be appointed to represent him. Without this additional warning, the admonition of the right to consult with counsel would often be understood as meaning only that he can consult with a lawyer if he has one or has the funds to obtain one. The warning of a right to counsel would be hollow if not couched in terms that would convey to the indigent—the person most often subjected to interrogation—the knowledge that he too has a right to have counsel present. As with the warnings of the right to remain silent and of the general right to counsel, only by effective and express explanation to the indigent of this right can there be assurance that he was truly in a position to exercise it.

Once warnings have been given, the subsequent procedure is clear. If the individual indicates in any manner, at any time prior to or during questioning, that he wishes to remain silent, the interrogation must cease. At this point he has shown that he intends to exercise his Fifth Amendment privilege; any statement taken after the person invokes his privilege cannot be other than the product of compulsion, subtle or otherwise. Without the right to cut off questioning, the setting of in-custody interrogation operates on the individual to overcome free choice in producing a statement after the privilege has been once invoked. If the individual states that he wants an attorney, the interrogation must cease until an attorney is present. At that time, the individual must have an opportunity to confer with the attorney and to have him present during any subsequent questioning. If the individual cannot obtain an attorney and he indicates that he wants one before speaking to police, they must respect his decision to remain silent.

This does not mean, as some have suggested, that each police station must have a "station house lawyer" present at all times to advise prisoners. It does mean, however, that if police propose to interrogate a person they must make known to him that he is entitled to a lawyer and that if he cannot afford one, a lawyer will be provided for him prior to any interrogation. If authorities conclude that they will not provide counsel during a reasonable period of time in which investigation in the field is carried out, they may refrain from doing so without violating the person's Fifth Amendment privilege so long as they do not question him during that time.

If the interrogation continues without the presence of an attorney and a statement is taken, a heavy burden rests on the government to demonstrate that the defendant knowingly and intelligently waived his privilege against self-incrimination and his right to retained or appointed counsel. *Escobedo v. Illinois,* 378 U.S. 478, 490, n. 14. This Court has always set high standards of proof for the waiver of constitutional rights, *Johnson v. Zerbst,* 304 U.S. 458 (1938), and we re-assert these standards as applied to in-custody interrogation. Since the State is responsible for establishing the isolated circumstances under which the interrogation takes place and has the only means of making available corroborated evidence of warnings given during incommunicado interrogation, the burden is rightly on its shoulders.

An express statement that the individual is willing to make a statement and does not want an attorney followed closely by a statement could constitute a waiver. But a valid waiver will not be presumed simply from the silence of the accused after warnings are given or simply from the fact that a confession was in fact eventually obtained. A statement we made in *Carnley v. Cochran,* 369 U.S. 506, 516 (1962), is applicable here:

> "Presuming waiver from a silent record is impermissible. The record must show, or there must be an allegation and evidence which show, that an accused was offered counsel but intelligently and understandingly rejected the offer. Anything less is not waiver."

See also *Glasser v. United States,* 315 U.S. 60 (1942). Moreover, where in-custody interrogation is involved, there is no room for the contention that the privilege is waived if the individual answers some questions or gives some information on his own prior to invoking his right to remain silent when interrogated.

Whatever the testimony of the authorities as to waiver of rights by an accused, the fact of lengthy interrogation or incommunicado incarceration before a statement is made is strong evidence that the accused did not validly waive his rights. In these circumstances the fact that the individual eventually made a statement is consistent with the conclusion that the compelling influence of the interrogation finally forced him to do so. It is inconsistent with any notion of a voluntary relinquishment of the privilege. Moreover, any evidence that the accused was threatened, tricked, or cajoled into a waiver will, of course, show that the defendant did not voluntarily waive his privilege. The requirement of warnings and waiver of rights is a fundamental with respect to the Fifth Amendment privilege and not simply a preliminary ritual to existing methods of interrogation.

The warnings required and the waiver necessary in accordance with our opinion today are, in the absence of a fully effective equivalent, prerequisites to the admissibility of any statement made by a defendant. No distinction can be drawn between statements which are direct confessions and statements which amount to "admissions" of part or all of an offense. The privilege against self-incrimination protects the individual from being compelled to incriminate himself in any manner; it does not distinguish degrees of incrimination. Similarly, for precisely the same reason, no distinction may be drawn between inculpatory statements and statements alleged to be merely "exculpatory." If a statement made were in fact truly exculpatory, it would, of course, never be used by the prosecution. In fact, statements merely intended to be exculpatory by the defendant are often used to impeach his testimony at trial or to demonstrate untruths in the statement given under interrogation and thus to prove guilt by implication. These statements are incriminating in any meaningful sense of the word and may not be used without the full warnings and effective waiver required for any other statement. In *Escobedo* itself, the defendant fully intended his accusation of another as the slayer to be exculpatory as to himself.

The principles announced today deal with the protection which must be given to the privilege against self-incrimination when the individual is first subjected to police interrogation while in custody at the station or otherwise deprived of his freedom of action in any significant way. It is at this point that our adversary system of criminal proceedings commences, distinguishing itself at the outset from the inquisitorial system recognized in some countries. Under the system of warnings we delineate today or under any other system which may be devised and found effective, the safeguards to be erected about the privilege must come into play at this point.

Our decision is not intended to hamper the traditional function of police officers in investigating crime. See *Escobedo v. Illinois,* 378 U.S. 478, 492. When an individual is in custody on probable cause, the police may, of course, seek out evidence in the field to be used at trial against him. Such investigation may include inquiry of persons not under restraint. General on-the-scene questioning as to facts surrounding a crime or other general questioning of citizens in the fact-finding process is not affected by our holding. It is an act of responsible citizenship for individuals to give whatever information they may have to aid in law enforcement. In such situations the compelling atmosphere inherent in the process of in-custody interrogation is not necessarily present.

In dealing with statements obtained through interrogation, we do not purport to find all confessions inadmissible. Confessions remain a proper element in law enforcement. Any statement given freely and voluntarily without any compelling influences is, of course, admissible in evidence. The fundamental import of the privilege while an individual is in custody is not whether he is allowed to talk to the police without the benefit of warnings and counsel, but whether he can be interrogated. There is no requirement that police stop a person who enters a police station and states that he wishes to confess to a crime, or a person who calls the police to offer a confession or any other statement he desires to make. Volunteered statements of any kind are not barred by the Fifth Amendment and their admissibility is not affected by our holding today.

To summarize, we hold that when an individual is taken into custody or otherwise deprived of his freedom by the authorities in any significant way and is subjected to questioning, the privilege against self-incrimination is jeopardized. Procedural safeguards must be employed to protect the privilege, and unless other fully effective means are adopted to notify the person of his right of silence and to assure that the exercise of the right will be scrupulously honored, the following measures are required. He must be warned prior to any questioning that he has the right to remain silent, that anything he says can be used against him in a court of law, that he has the right to the presence of an attorney, and that if he cannot afford an attorney one will be appointed for him prior to any questioning if he so desires. Opportunity to exercise these rights must be afforded to him throughout the interrogation. After such warnings have been given, and such opportunity afforded him, the individual may knowingly and intelligently waive these rights and agree to answer questions or make a statement. But unless and until such warnings and waiver are demonstrated by the prosecution at trial, no evidence obtained as a result of interrogation can be used against him.

IV.

. . .

If the individual desires to exercise his privilege, he has the right to do so. This is not for the authorities to decide. An attorney may advise his client not to talk to police until he has had an opportunity to investigate the case, or he may wish to be present with his client during any police questioning. In doing so an attorney is merely exercising the good professional judgment he has been taught. This is not cause for considering the attorney a menace to law enforcement. He is merely carrying out what he is sworn to do under his oath—to protect to the extent of his ability the rights of his client. In fulfilling this responsibility the attorney plays a vital role in the administration of criminal justice under our Constitution.

In announcing these principles, we are not unmindful of the burdens which law enforcement officials must bear, often under trying circumstances. We also fully recognize the obligation of all citizens to aid in enforcing the criminal laws. This Court, while protecting individual rights, has always given ample latitude to law enforcement agencies in the legitimate exercise of their duties. The limits we have placed on the interrogation process should not constitute an undue interference with a proper system of law enforcement. As we have noted, our decision does not in any way preclude police from carrying out their traditional investigatory functions. Although confessions may play an important role in some convictions, the cases before us present graphic examples of the overstatement of the "need" for confessions. In each case authorities conducted interrogations ranging up to five days in duration despite the presence, through standard investigating practices, of considerable evidence against each defendant.[51] Further examples are chronicled in our prior cases. See, *e. g., Haynes v. Washington,* 373 U.S. 503, 518–519 (1963); *Rogers v. Richmond,* 365 U.S. 534, 541 (1961); *Malinski v. New York,* 324 U.S. 401, 402 (1945).

It is also urged that an unfettered right to detention for interrogation should be allowed because it will often redound to the benefit of the person questioned. When police inquiry determines that there is no reason to believe that the person has committed any crime, it is said, he will be released without need for further formal procedures. The person who has committed no offense, however, will be better able to clear himself after warnings with counsel present than without. It can be assumed that in such circumstances a lawyer would advise his client to talk freely to police in order to clear himself.

Custodial interrogation, by contrast, does not necessarily afford the innocent an opportunity to clear themselves. A serious consequence of the present practice of the interrogation alleged to be beneficial for the innocent is that many arrests "for investigation" subject large numbers of innocent persons to detention and interrogation. In one of the cases before us, *California v. Stewart,* police held four persons, who were in the defendant's house at the time of the arrest, in jail for five days until defendant confessed. At that time they were finally released. Police stated that there was "no evidence to connect them with any crime." Available statistics on the extent of this practice where it is condoned indicate that these four are far from alone in being subjected to arrest, prolonged detention, and interrogation without the requisite probable cause.

. . .

The experience in some other countries also suggests that the danger to law enforcement in curbs on interrogation is overplayed. The English procedure since 1912 under the Judges' Rules is significant. As recently strengthened, the Rules require that a cautionary warning be given an accused by a police officer as soon as he has evidence that affords reasonable grounds for suspicion; they also require that any statement made be given by the accused without questioning by police. The right of the individual to consult with an attorney during this period is expressly recognized.

The safeguards present under Scottish law may be even greater than in England. Scottish judicial decisions bar use in evidence of most confessions obtained through police interrogation.[59] . . .

V.

Because of the nature of the problem and because of its recurrent significance in numerous cases, we have to this point discussed the relationship of the Fifth Amendment privilege to police interrogation without specific concentration on the facts of the cases before us. We turn now to these facts to consider the application to these cases of the constitutional principles discussed above. In each instance, we have concluded that statements were obtained from the defendant under circumstances that did not meet constitutional standards for protection of the privilege.

No. 759. *Miranda v. Arizona.*

On March 13, 1963, petitioner, Ernesto Miranda, was arrested at his home and taken in custody to a Phoenix police station. He was there identified by the complaining witness. The police then took him to "Interrogation Room No. 2" of the detective bureau. There he was questioned by two police officers. The officers admitted at trial that Miranda was not advised that he had a right to have an attorney present. Two hours later, the officers emerged from the interrogation room with a written confession signed by Miranda. At the top of the statement was a typed paragraph stating that the confession was made voluntarily, without threats or promises of immunity and "with full knowledge of my legal rights, understanding any statement I make may be used against me."

At his trial before a jury, the written confession was admitted into evidence over the objection of defense counsel, and the officers testified to the prior oral confession made by Miranda during the interrogation. Miranda was found guilty of kidnapping and rape. He was sentenced to 20 to 30 years' imprisonment on each count, the sentences to run concurrently. On appeal, the Supreme Court of Arizona held that Miranda's constitutional rights were not violated in obtaining the confession and affirmed the conviction. 98 Ariz. 18, 401 P. 2d 721. In reaching its decision, the court emphasized heavily the fact that Miranda did not specifically request counsel.

We reverse. From the testimony of the officers and by the admission of respondent, it is clear that Miranda was not in any way apprised of his right to consult with an attorney and to have one present during the interrogation, nor was his

---

51. Miranda, Vignera, and Westover were identified by eyewitnesses. Marked bills from the bank robbed were found in Westover's car. Articles stolen from the victim as well as from several other robbery victims were found in Stewart's home at the outset of the investigation.

59. As stated by the Lord Justice General in *Chalmers v. H. M. Advocate,* [1954] Sess. Cas. 66, 78 (J. C.):

"The theory of our law is that at the stage of initial investigation the police may question anyone with a view to acquiring information

which may lead to the detection of the criminal; but that, when the stage has been reached at which suspicion, or more than suspicion, has in their view centered upon some person as the likely perpetrator of the crime, further interrogation of that person becomes very dangerous, and, if carried too far, *e.g.,* to the point of extracting a confession by what amounts to cross-examination, the evidence of that confession will almost certainly be excluded. Once the accused has been apprehended and charged he has the statutory right to a private interview with a solicitor and to be brought before a magistrate with all convenient speed so that he may, if so advised, emit a declaration in presence of his solicitor under conditions which safeguard him against prejudice."

right not to be compelled to incriminate himself effectively protected in any other manner. Without these warnings the statements were inadmissible. The mere fact that he signed a statement which contained a typed-in clause stating that he had "full knowledge" of his "legal rights" does not approach the knowing and intelligent waiver required to relinquish constitutional rights. Cf. *Haynes v. Washington,* 373 U.S. 503, 512–513 (1963); *Haley v. Ohio,* 332 U.S. 596, 601 (1948) (opinion of MR. JUSTICE DOUGLAS).

No. 760. *Vignera v. New York.*

Petitioner, Michael Vignera, was picked up by New York police on October 14, 1960, in connection with the robbery three days earlier of a Brooklyn dress shop. They took him to the 17th Detective Squad headquarters in Manhattan. Sometime thereafter he was taken to the 66th Detective Squad. There a detective questioned Vignera with respect to the robbery. Vignera orally admitted the robbery to the detective. The detective was asked on cross-examination at trial by defense counsel whether Vignera was warned of his right to counsel before being interrogated. The prosecution objected to the question and the trial judge sustained the objection. Thus, the defense was precluded from making any showing that warnings had not been given. While at the 66th Detective Squad, Vignera was identified by the store owner and a saleslady as the man who robbed the dress shop. At about 3 P.M he was formally arrested. The police then transported him to still another station, the 70th Precinct in Brooklyn, "for detention." At 11 P.M. Vignera was questioned by an assistant district attorney in the presence of a hearing reporter who transcribed the questions and Vignera's answers. This verbatim account of these proceedings contains no statement of any warnings given by the assistant district attorney. At Vignera's trial on a charge of first degree robbery, the detective testified as to the oral confession. The transcription of the statement taken was also introduced in evidence. . . .

We reverse. The foregoing indicates that Vignera was not warned of any of his rights before the questioning by the detective and by the assistant district attorney. No other steps were taken to protect these rights. Thus he was not effectively apprised of his Fifth Amendment privilege or of his right to have counsel present and his statements are inadmissible.

No. 761. *Westover v. United States.*

At approximately 9:45 P.M. on March 20, 1963, petitioner, Carl Calvin Westover, was arrested by local police in Kansas City as a suspect in two Kansas City robberies. A report was also received from the FBI that he was wanted on a felony charge in California. The local authorities took him to a police station and placed him in a line-up on the local charges, and at about 11:45 P.M. he was booked. Kansas City police interrogated Westover on the night of his arrest. He denied any knowledge of criminal activities. The next day local officers interrogated him again throughout the morning. Shortly before noon they informed the FBI that they were through interrogating Westover and that the FBI could proceed to interrogate him. There is nothing in the record to indicate that Westover was ever given any warning as to his rights by local police. At noon, three special agents of the FBI continued the interrogation in a private interview room of the Kansas City Police Department, this time with respect to the robbery of a savings and loan association and a bank in Sacramento, California. After two or two-and-one-half hours, Westover signed separate confessions to each of these two robberies which had been prepared by one of the agents during the interrogation. At trial one of the agents testified, and a paragraph on each of the statements states, that the agents advised Westover that he did not have to make a statement, that any statement he made could be used against him, and that he had the right to see an attorney.

Westover was tried . . . and convicted. . . . His statements were introduced at trial. . . .

We reverse. On the facts of this case we cannot find that Westover knowingly and intelligently waived his right to remain silent and his right to consult with counsel prior to the time he made the statement.[69] At the time the FBI agents began questioning Westover, he had been in custody for over 14 hours and had been interrogated at length during that period. The FBI interrogation began immediately upon the conclusion of the interrogation by Kansas City police and was conducted in local police headquarters. Although the two law enforcement authorities are legally distinct and the crimes for which they interrogated Westover were different, the impact on him was that of a continuous period of questioning. There is no evidence of any warning given prior to the FBI interrogation nor is there any evidence of an articulated waiver of rights after the FBI commenced its interrogation. The record simply shows that the defendant did in fact confess a short time after being turned over to the FBI following interrogation by local police. Despite the fact that the FBI agents gave warnings at the outset of their interview, from Westover's point of view the warnings came at the end of the interrogation process. In these circumstances an intelligent waiver of constitutional rights cannot be assumed.

We do not suggest that law enforcement authorities are precluded from questioning any individual who has been held for a period of time by other authorities and interrogated by them without appropriate warnings. A different case would be presented if an accused were taken into custody by the

---

69. The failure of defense counsel to object to the introduction of the confession at trial, noted by the Court of Appeals and emphasized by the Solicitor General, does not preclude our consideration of the issue. Since the trial was held prior to our decision in *Escobedo* and, of course, prior to our decision today making the objection available, the failure to object at trial does not constitute a waiver of the claim. See, *e.g., United States ex rel. Angelet v. Fay,* 333 F.2d 12, 16 (C.A. 2d Cir. 1964), aff'd, 381 U.S. 654 (1965). Cf. *Ziffrin, Inc. v. United States,* 318 U.S. 73, 78 (1943).

second authority, removed both in time and place from his original surroundings, and then adequately advised of his rights and given an opportunity to exercise them. But here the FBI interrogation was conducted immediately following the state interrogation in the same police station—in the same compelling surroundings. Thus, in obtaining a confession from Westover the federal authorities were the beneficiaries of the pressure applied by the local in-custody interrogation. In these circumstances the giving of warnings alone was not sufficient to protect the privilege.

No. 584. *California v. Stewart.*

In the course of investigating a series of purse-snatch robberies in which one of the victims had died of injuries inflicted by her assailant, respondent, Roy Allen Stewart, was pointed out to Los Angeles police as the endorser of dividend checks taken in one of the robberies. At about 7:15 P.M., January 31, 1963, police officers went to Stewart's house and arrested him. One of the officers asked Stewart if they could search the house, to which he replied, "Go ahead." The search turned up various items taken from the five robbery victims. At the time of Stewart's arrest, police also arrested Stewart's wife and three other persons who were visiting him. These four were jailed along with Stewart and were interrogated. Stewart was taken to the University Station of the Los Angeles Police Department where he was placed in a cell. During the next five days, police interrogated Stewart on nine different occasions. Except during the first interrogation session, when he was confronted with an accusing witness, Stewart was isolated with his interrogators.

During the ninth interrogation session, Stewart admitted that he had robbed the deceased and stated that he had not meant to hurt her. Police then brought Stewart before a magistrate for the first time. Since there was no evidence to connect them with any crime, the police then released the other four persons arrested with him.

Nothing in the record specifically indicates whether Stewart was or was not advised of his right to remain silent or his right to counsel. In a number of instances, however, the interrogating officers were asked to recount everything that was said during the interrogations. None indicated that Stewart was ever advised of his rights.

Stewart was charged with kidnapping to commit robbery, rape, and murder. At his trial, transcripts of the first interrogation and the confession at the last interrogation were introduced in evidence. The jury found Stewart guilty of robbery and first degree murder and fixed the penalty as death. On appeal, the Supreme Court of California reversed. 62 Cal. 2d 571, 400 P.2d 97, 43 Cal. Rptr. 201. It held that under this Court's decision in *Escobedo*, Stewart should have been advised of his right to remain silent and of his right to counsel and that it would not presume in the face of a silent record that the police advised Stewart of his rights.

We affirm. In dealing with custodial interrogation, we will not presume that a defendant has been effectively apprised of his rights and that his privilege against self-incrimination has been adequately safeguarded on a record that does not show that any warnings have been given or that any effective alternative has been employed. Nor can a knowing and intelligent waiver of these rights be assumed on a silent record. Furthermore, Stewart's steadfast denial of the alleged offenses through eight of the nine interrogations over a period of five days is subject to no other construction than that he was compelled by persistent interrogation to forgo his Fifth Amendment privilege.

Therefore, in accordance with the foregoing, the judgments of the Supreme Court of Arizona in No. 759, of the New York Court of Appeals in No. 760, and of the Court of Appeals for the Ninth Circuit in No. 761 are reversed. The judgment of the Supreme Court of California in No. 584 is affirmed.

It is so ordered.

Mr. Justice CLARK, dissenting in Nos. 759, 760, and 761, and concurring in the result in No. 584.

. . . [I cannot] join in the Court's criticism of the present practices of police and investigatory agencies as to custodial interrogation. The materials it refers to as "police manuals" are, as I read them, merely writings in this field by professors and some police officers. Not one is shown by the record here to be the official manual of any police department, much less in universal use in crime detection. Moreover, the examples of police brutality mentioned by the Court are rare exceptions to the thousands of cases that appear every year in the law reports. . . .

I.

. . . Since there is at this time a paucity of information and an almost total lack of empirical knowledge on the practical operation of requirements truly comparable to those announced by the majority, I would be more restrained lest we go too far too fast.

II.

. . .

Rather than employing the arbitrary Fifth Amendment rule[4] which the Court lays down I would follow the more pliable dictates of the Due Process Clauses of the Fifth and Fourteenth Amendments which we are accustomed to administering and which we know from our cases are effective instruments in protecting persons in police custody. . . .

In each of those cases I find from the circumstances no warrant for reversal. . . .

---

4. In my view there is "no significant support" in our cases for the holding of the Court today that the Fifth Amendment privilege, in effect, forbids custodial interrogation. For a discussion of this point see the dissenting opinion of my BROTHER WHITE, post, pp. 526–531.

Mr. Justice HARLAN, whom Mr. Justice STEWART and Mr. Justice WHITE join, dissenting.

I believe the decision of the Court represents poor constitutional law and entails harmful consequences for the country at large. . . .

While the fine points of this scheme are far less clear than the Court admits, the tenor is quite apparent. The new rules are not designed to guard against police brutality or other unmistakably banned forms of coercion. Those who use third-degree tactics and deny them in court are equally able and destined to lie as skillfully about warnings and waivers. Rather, the thrust of the new rules is to negate all pressures, to reinforce the nervous or ignorant suspect, and ultimately to discourage any confession at all. The aim in short is toward "voluntariness" in a utopian sense, or to view it from a different angle, voluntariness with a vengeance.

To incorporate this notion into the Constitution requires a strained reading of history and precedent and a disregard of the very pragmatic concerns that alone may on occasion justify such strains. I believe that reasoned examination will show that the Due Process Clauses provide an adequate tool for coping with confessions and that, even if the Fifth Amendment privilege against self-incrimination be invoked, its precedents taken as a whole do not sustain the present rules. . . .

The Court's opinion in my view reveals no adequate basis for extending the Fifth Amendment's privilege against self-incrimination to the police station. Far more important, it fails to show that the Court's new rules are well supported, let alone compelled, by Fifth Amendment precedents. Instead, the new rules actually derive from quotation and analogy drawn from precedents under the Sixth Amendment, which should properly have no bearing on police interrogation.

. . .

Having decided that the Fifth Amendment privilege does apply in the police station, the Court reveals that the privilege imposes more exacting restrictions than does the Fourteenth Amendment's voluntariness test. It then emerges from a discussion of *Escobedo* that the Fifth Amendment requires for an admissible confession that it be given by one distinctly aware of his right not to speak and shielded from "the compelling atmosphere" of interrogation. From these key premises, the Court finally develops the safeguards of warning, counsel, and so forth. I do not believe these premises are sustained by precedents under the Fifth Amendment.

The more important premise is that pressure on the suspect must be eliminated though it be only the subtle influence of the atmosphere and surroundings. The Fifth Amendment, however, has never been thought to forbid *all* pressure to incriminate one's self in the situations covered by it. . . .

A closing word must be said about the Assistance of Counsel Clause of the Sixth Amendment, which is never expressly relied on by the Court but whose judicial precedents turn out to be linchpins of the confession rules announced today. . . .

The only attempt in this Court to carry the right to counsel into the station house occurred in *Escobedo,* the Court repeating several times that that stage was no less "critical" than trial itself. This is hardly persuasive when we consider that a grand jury inquiry, the filing of a certiorari petition, and certainly the purchase of narcotics by an undercover agent from a prospective defendant may all be equally "critical" yet provision of counsel and advice on that score have never been thought compelled by the Constitution in such cases. The sound reason why this right is so freely extended for a criminal trial is the severe injustice risked by confronting an untrained defendant with a range of technical points of law, evidence, and tactics familiar to the prosecutor but not to himself. This danger shrinks markedly in the police station where indeed the lawyer in fulfilling his professional responsibilities of necessity may become an obstacle to truthfinding. The Court's summary citation of the Sixth Amendment cases here seems to me best described as "the domino method of constitutional adjudication . . . wherein every explanatory statement in a previous opinion is made the basis for extension to a wholly different situation."

. . .

What the Court largely ignores is that its rules impair, if they will not eventually serve wholly to frustrate, an instrument of law enforcement that has long and quite reasonably been thought worth the price paid for it. There can be little doubt that the Court's new code would markedly decrease the number of confessions. To warn the suspect that he may remain silent and remind him that his confession may be used in court are minor obstructions. To require also an express waiver by the suspect and an end to questioning whenever he demurs must heavily handicap questioning. And to suggest or provide counsel for the suspect simply invites the end of the interrogation. . . .

While passing over the costs and risks of its experiment, the Court portrays the evils of normal police questioning in terms which I think are exaggerated. Albeit stringently confined by the due process standards interrogation is no doubt often inconvenient and unpleasant for the suspect. However, it is no less so for a man to be arrested and jailed, to have his house searched, or to stand trial in court, yet all this may properly happen to the most innocent given probable cause, a warrant, or an indictment. Society has always paid a stiff price for law and order, and peaceful interrogation is not one of the dark moments of the law.

This brief statement of the competing considerations seems to me ample proof that the Court's preference is highly debatable at best and therefore not to be read into the Constitution. However, it may make the analysis more graphic to consider the actual facts of one of the four cases reversed by the Court. *Miranda v. Arizona* serves best, being neither the hardest nor easiest of the four under the Court's standards.

On March 3, 1963, an 18-year-old girl was kidnapped and forcibly raped near Phoenix, Arizona. Ten days later, on the morning of March 13, petitioner Miranda was arrested and taken to the police station. At this time Miranda was 23 years old, indigent, and educated to the extent of completing half the ninth grade. He had "an emotional illness" of the schizophrenic type, according to the doctor who eventually examined him; the doctor's report also stated that Miranda was "alert and oriented as to time, place, and person," intelligent within normal limits, competent to stand trial, and sane within the legal definition. At the police station, the victim picked Miranda out of a lineup, and two officers then took him into a separate room to interrogate him, starting about 11:30 A.M. Though at first denying his guilt, within a short time Miranda gave a detailed oral confession and then wrote out in his own hand and signed a brief statement admitting and describing the crime. All this was accomplished in two hours or less without any force, threats or promises and—I will assume this though the record is uncertain—without any effective warnings at all.

Miranda's oral and written confessions are now held inadmissible under the Court's new rules. One is entitled to feel astonished that the Constitution can be read to produce this result. These confessions were obtained during brief, daytime questioning conducted by two officers and unmarked by any of the traditional indicia of coercion. They assured a conviction for a brutal and unsettling crime, for which the police had and quite possibly could obtain little evidence other than the victim's identifications, evidence which is frequently unreliable. There was, in sum, a legitimate purpose, no perceptible unfairness, and certainly little risk of injustice in the interrogation. Yet the resulting confessions, and the responsible course of police practice they represent, are to be sacrificed to the Court's own finespun conception of fairness which I seriously doubt is shared by many thinking citizens in this country.

. . .

The Court in closing its general discussion invokes the practice in federal and foreign jurisdictions as lending weight to its new curbs on confessions for all the States. A brief résumé will suffice to show that none of these jurisdictions has struck so one-sided a balance as the Court does today. . . .

In closing this necessarily truncated discussion of policy considerations attending the new confession rules, some reference must be made to their ironic untimeliness. There is now in progress in this country a massive reexamination of criminal law enforcement procedures on a scale never before witnessed. . . .

It is no secret that concern has been expressed lest long-range and lasting reforms be frustrated by this Court's too rapid departure from existing constitutional standards. . . . Of course legislative reform is rarely speedy or unanimous, though this Court has been more patient in the past. But the legislative reforms when they come would have the vast advantage of empirical data and comprehensive study, they would allow experimentation and use of solutions not open to the courts, and they would restore the initiative in criminal law reform to those forums where it truly belongs. . . .

Mr. Justice WHITE, with whom Mr. Justice HARLAN and Mr. Justice STEWART join, dissenting.

I.

The proposition that the privilege against self-incrimination forbids in-custody interrogation without the warnings specified in the majority opinion and without a clear waiver of counsel has no significant support in the history of the privilege or in the language of the Fifth Amendment. As for the English authorities and the common-law history, the privilege, firmly established in the second half of the seventeenth century, was never applied except to prohibit compelled judicial interrogations. The rule excluding coerced confessions matured about 100 years later, "[b]ut there is nothing in the reports to suggest that the theory has its roots in the privilege against self-incrimination. And so far as the cases reveal, the privilege, as such, seems to have been given effect only in judicial proceedings, including the preliminary examinations by authorized magistrates." Morgan, The Privilege Against Self-Incrimination, 34 Minn. L. Rev. 1, 18 (1949). . . .

II.

That the Court's holding today is neither compelled nor even strongly suggested by the language of the Fifth Amendment, is at odds with American and English legal history, and involves a departure from a long line of precedent does not prove either that the Court has exceeded its powers or that the Court is wrong or unwise in its present reinterpretation of the Fifth Amendment. It does, however, underscore the obvious—that the Court has not discovered or found the law in making today's decision, nor has it derived it from some irrefutable sources; what it has done is to make new law and new public policy in much the same way that it has in the course of interpreting other great clauses of the Constitution. This is what the Court historically has done. Indeed, it is what it must do and will continue to do until and unless there is some fundamental change in the constitutional distribution of governmental powers.

But if the Court is here and now to announce new and fundamental policy to govern certain aspects of our affairs, it is wholly legitimate to examine the mode of this or any other constitutional decision in this Court and to inquire into the advisability of its end product in terms of the long-range interest of the country. At the very least the Court's text and reasoning should withstand analysis and be a fair exposition of the constitutional provision which its opinion interprets. Decisions like these cannot rest alone on syllogism, metaphysics or some ill-defined notions of natural justice, although each will perhaps play its part. . . .

III.

. . . Insofar as appears from the Court's opinion, it has not examined a single transcript of any police interrogation, let alone the interrogation that took place in any one of these cases which it decides today. Judged by any of the standards for empirical investigation utilized in the social sciences the factual basis for the Court's premise is patently inadequate.

Although in the Court's view in-custody interrogation is inherently coercive, the Court says that the spontaneous product of the coercion of arrest and detention is still to be deemed voluntary. An accused, arrested on probable cause, may blurt out a confession which will be admissible despite the fact that he is alone and in custody, without any showing that he had any notion of his right to remain silent or of the consequences of his admission. Yet, under the Court's rule, if the police ask him a single question such as "Do you have anything to say?" or "Did you kill your wife?" his response, if there is one, has somehow been compelled, even if the accused has been clearly warned of his right to remain silent. Common sense informs us to the contrary. While one may say that the response was "involuntary" in the sense the question provoked or was the occasion for the response and thus the defendant was induced to speak out when he might have remained silent if not arrested and not questioned, it is patently unsound to say the response is compelled.

. . .

If the rule announced today were truly based on a conclusion that all confessions resulting from custodial interrogation are coerced, then it would simply have no rational foundation. . . . Even if one were to postulate that the Court's concern is not that all confessions induced by police interrogation are coerced but rather that some such confessions are coerced and present judicial procedures are believed to be inadequate to identify the confessions that are coerced and those that are not, it would still not be essential to impose the rule that the Court has now fashioned. Transcripts or observers could be required, specific time limits, tailored to fit the cause, could be imposed, or other devices could be utilized to reduce the chances that otherwise indiscernible coercion will produce an inadmissible confession.

On the other hand, even if one assumed that there was an adequate factual basis for the conclusion that all confessions obtained during in-custody interrogation are the product of compulsion, the rule propounded by the Court would still be irrational, for, apparently, it is only if the accused is also warned of his right to counsel and waives both that right and the right against self-incrimination that the inherent compulsiveness of interrogation disappears. But if the defendant may not answer without a warning a question such as "Where were you last night?" without having his answer be a compelled one, how can the Court ever accept his negative answer to the question of whether he wants to consult his retained counsel or counsel whom the court will appoint? And why if counsel is present and the accused nevertheless confesses, or counsel tells the accused to tell the truth, and that is what the accused does, is the situation any less coercive insofar as the accused is concerned? The Court apparently realizes its dilemma of foreclosing questioning without the necessary warnings but at the same time permitting the accused, sitting in the same chair in front of the same police-

men, to waive his right to consult an attorney. It expects, however, that the accused will not often waive the right; and if it is claimed that he has, the State faces a severe, if not impossible burden of proof.

All of this makes very little sense in terms of the compulsion which the Fifth Amendment proscribes. That amendment deals with compelling the accused himself. It is his free will that is involved. Confessions and incriminating admissions, as such, are not forbidden evidence; only those which are compelled are banned. I doubt that the Court observes these distinctions today. By considering any answers to any interrogation to be compelled regardless of the content and course of examination and by escalating the requirements to prove waiver, the Court not only prevents the use of compelled confessions but for all practical purposes forbids interrogation except in the presence of counsel. That is, instead of confining itself to protection of the right against compelled self-incrimination the Court has created a limited Fifth Amendment right to counsel—or, as the Court expresses it, a "need for counsel to protect the Fifth Amendment privilege. . . ." The focus then is not on the will of the accused but on the will of counsel and how much influence he can have on the accused. Obviously there is no warrant in the Fifth Amendment for thus installing counsel as the arbiter of the privilege.

In sum, for all the Court's expounding on the menacing atmosphere of police interrogation procedures, it has failed to supply any foundation for the conclusions it draws or the measures it adopts.

IV.

Criticism of the Court's opinion, however, cannot stop with a demonstration that the factual and textual bases for the rule it propounds are, at best, less than compelling. Equally relevant is an assessment of the rule's consequences measured against community values. . . . More than the human dignity of the accused is involved; the human personality of others in the society must also be preserved. Thus the values reflected by the privilege are not the sole desideratum; society's interest in the general security is of equal weight.

The obvious underpinning of the Court's decision is a deep-seated distrust of all confessions. As the Court declares that the accused may not be interrogated without counsel present, absent a waiver of the right to counsel, and as the Court all but admonishes the lawyer to advise the accused to remain silent, the result adds up to a judicial judgment that evidence from the accused should not be used against him in any way, whether compelled or not. This is the not so subtle overtone of the opinion—that it is inherently wrong for the police to gather evidence from the accused himself. And this is precisely the nub of this dissent. I see nothing wrong or immoral, and certainly nothing unconstitutional, in the police's asking a suspect whom they have reasonable cause to arrest whether or not he killed his wife or in confronting him with the evidence on which the arrest was based, at least where he has been plainly advised that he may remain completely silent. . . . Particularly when corroborated, as where the police have confirmed the accused's disclosure of the hiding place of implements or fruits of the crime, such confessions have the highest reliability and significantly contribute to the certitude with which we may believe the accused is guilty. Moreover, it is by no means certain that the process of confessing is injurious to the accused. To the contrary it may provide psychological relief and enhance the prospects for rehabilitation.

. . .

The rule announced today . . . is a deliberate calculus to prevent interrogations, to reduce the incidence of confessions and pleas of guilty and to increase the number of trials. Criminal trials, no matter how efficient the police are, are not sure bets for the prosecution, nor should they be if the evidence is not forthcoming. Under the present law, the prosecution fails to prove its case in about 30% of the criminal cases actually tried in the federal courts. . . . But it is something else again to remove from the ordinary criminal case all those confessions which heretofore have been held to be free and voluntary acts of the accused and to thus establish a new constitutional barrier to the ascertainment of truth by the judicial process. . . .

I have no desire whatsoever to share the responsibility for any such impact on the present criminal process.

. . .

Much of the trouble with the Court's new rule is that it will operate indiscriminately in all criminal cases, regardless of the severity of the crime or the circumstances involved. It applies to every defendant, whether the professional criminal or one committing a crime of momentary passion who is not part and parcel of organized crime. It will slow down the investigation and the apprehension of confederates in those cases where time is of the essence, such as kidnapping, . . . and some of those involving organized crime. In the latter context the lawyer who arrives may also be the lawyer for the defendant's colleagues and can be relied upon to insure that no breach of the organization's security takes place even though the accused may feel that the best thing he can do is to cooperate.

At the same time, the Court's *per se* approach may not be justified on the ground that it provides a "bright line" permitting the authorities to judge in advance whether interrogation may safely be pursued without jeopardizing the admissibility of any information obtained as a consequence. Nor can it be claimed that judicial time and effort, assuming that is a relevant consideration, will be conserved because of the ease of application of the new rule. Today's decision leaves open such questions as whether the accused was in custody, whether his statements were spontaneous or the product of interrogation, whether the accused has effectively waived his rights, and whether nontestimonial evidence introduced at trial is the fruit of statements made during a prohibited interrogation, all of which are certain to prove productive of uncertainty during investigation and litigation during prosecution. For all these reasons, if further restrictions on police interrogation are desirable at this time, a more flexible approach makes much more sense than the Court's constitutional straitjacket which forecloses more discriminating treatment by legislative or rule-making pronouncements.

Applying the traditional standards to the cases before the Court, I would hold these confessions voluntary.

B. *MIRANDA*

Understanding *Miranda* is critical because it aggressively protects a citizen's right against self-incrimination by focusing on the inherent coerciveness of police interrogation practices, and because it has been the law on confessions for more than thirty years. The decision has survived criticism, some judicial erosion, and threat of reversal, only to be reaffirmed with some continuing vitality. Cutting to its essentials, *Miranda* provides the following rules:

1. Absent equally effective safeguards, police must inform people of their continuing right to silence in order to protect the right against self-incrimination.
2. The rules apply when persons are interrogated in custody at the station or otherwise significantly deprived of their freedom of action.
3. Prior to such interrogation, persons must be informed clearly (a) of their right to remain silent, (b) that any statement can be used against them in court, (c) of their right to an attorney who can be present at questioning, and (d) if they are indigent, that the court will provide them with an attorney.
4. Interrogation must cease at any time the suspect elects to remain silent or requests an attorney.

5.   If a statement is made when there is no attorney present, the statement is presumed coerced for all practical purposes, and the state has a heavy burden of proving that any waiver to remain silent or to the presence of a lawyer was made knowingly and intelligently (voluntarily).

6.   A violation of these rules means a statement will not be admitted into evidence.

7.   Both confessions and admissions are protected. A **confession** is the defendant's acknowledgment of guilt, for example, "I did it." An **admission** is the defendant's acknowledgment of a fact that helps prove the crime but does not reach the level of a confession, for example, "I was there."

8.   Finally, because the exercise of the privilege is a right, the prosecution may not, by innuendo or otherwise, call the jury's attention to the fact that the defendant has remained silent. Such a comment raises the inference that an innocent person has nothing to hide and seriously undermines the purpose of the privilege and drains it of its strength.

confession:
the defendant's acknowledgment of guilt.

admission:
the defendant's acknowledgment of a fact that helps prove the crime but does not reach the level of a confession.

Because a large number of persons do not understand that the decision reinforces the constitutionalization of the accusatory system of justice, the decision has been heavily criticized for its purported "straitjacketing" of law enforcement. Empirical studies show, however, that the rate of useable confessions after *Miranda* is relatively unchanged from the rate of confessions before *Miranda*.[3] Other studies have shown that confessions are the key to conviction in relatively few prosecutions and, thus, are overrated in the scheme of effective law enforcement.[4] A 1968 federal law, 18 U.S.C.A. § 3501, watered down *Miranda* in determining voluntariness of confessions, but federal prosecutors have generally adhered to the stricter *Miranda* standards because of this law's likely unconstitutionality.[5]

Recently, however, the Court of Appeals for the Fourth Circuit caused quite a stir by ruling that this law is not unconstitutional, and that failure of officers to give the *Miranda* warning is just one of several factors for determining the voluntariness of a suspect's incriminating statements [*Dickerson v. U.S.* (4th Cir. 1999)]. The Supreme Court put this theory to rest, reaffirming that the *Miranda* warnings are constitutionally required and declaring 18 U.S.C.A. § 3501 unconstitutional in *Dickerson v. U.S.* (2000).

C.   ISSUES *MIRANDA* LEFT UNANSWERED

1.   In Custody

Miranda applies when persons are interrogated *in custody* or otherwise *significantly deprived* of their freedom of action. Since *Miranda,* the Court has tried to define "in custody." In *Orozco v. Texas* (1969), the suspect was confronted in his bedroom at 4:00 A.M. by several police officers who testified that they believed the suspect was under arrest when he was questioned. The Court ruled that for purposes of *Miranda* the suspect was "in custody." Toward the other end of the spectrum, the Court decided that if a suspect voluntarily responds to a written request to come into the police station and believes he or she is free to leave the station, the suspect is not "in custody," even if the intention of the officer is to arrest the suspect [*Oregon v. Mathiason* (1977)].

What is referred to as an objective standard for answering the "in custody" question was adopted in *Berkemer v. McCarty* (1984). This standard requires courts to focus on how "a reasonable [person] in the suspect's position would have understood [the] situation." In other words, how threatening, compelling, or coercive are the circumstances. This standard suggests that in each case the impact of the following may need to be assessed: timing and location of interrogation, duration, number of police present, presence of weapons, and other factors. In *Berkemer,* questioning about the use of intoxicants by a driver during a routine traffic stop was not an "in custody situation" even though the officer intended to arrest the suspect.

2. Interrogation

At what point does police conduct or speech become "interrogation" and invoke the *Miranda* rules? Walk-in, phoned-in, or even in custody statements, if "volunteered," are admissible. Once an incriminating statement is volunteered, then relevant follow-up questions are permissible. The "functional equivalent" of questioning, that is, police action that leads one to conclude that the action is intended to elicit an incriminating response, is "interrogation" [*Rhode Island v. Innis* (1980)]. Under this ruling, having a defendant look at gory photos of a murder victim or read the confession of a codefendant would be interrogation.

With this in mind, do you think it is "interrogation" for two police officers, in the presence of an arrestee, to discuss the fact that until the robbery weapon was found, it posed a threat to local schoolchildren, to which the defendant responded by showing them the gun's location? The Supreme Court said such a discussion was not interrogation in *Innis*. Permitting the wife of a murder suspect to talk with him while a tape recorder and officer were conspicuously present was not interrogation in *Arizona v. Mauro* (1987). Likewise, it was not interrogation for an undercover agent planted in a suspect's jail cell to suggest they break out and then ask, "Have you ever killed anyone before?" [*Illinois v. Perkins* (1990).] Note that the question came before any *Miranda* warnings and prior to any exercising of the right to counsel, but the Court ruled that the jail setting was not a police dominated atmosphere. Several other Supreme Court decisions address the use of undercover agents placed in cells with defendants. Though these cases seem to raise a question about interrogation, they have been decided on the issue of whether the defendant was denied the right to counsel. These cases are mentioned again later in this chapter.

"Confess and be hanged."

—Christopher Marlowe, *The Jew of Malta,* 1589

3. Incomplete Warning

The Supreme Court said in *California v. Prysock* (1981) that minor deviations in wording from the warning stated in *Miranda* are not significant. Some courts, however, find that the failure of an officer to advise an indigent defendant that the cost of an appointed attorney will be paid by the state makes the confession illegal [*Thompson v. State* (Fla. 1992)].

Police need to be careful when giving *Miranda* warnings in a foreign language. In *State v. Santiago* (Wis. 1996), the Wisconsin Supreme Court required the state to prove at a suppression hearing that the foreign language translator accurately conveyed the warnings.

It is still not entirely clear whether *Miranda* applies to a witness who can be compelled to testify at a grand jury hearing. More state and federal courts have said that it does not than have said it does. The Supreme Court has not dealt with the issue directly. In *U.S. v. Washington* (1977), however, the Court held that when a "witness" is informed of the right to remain silent, the absence of a warning that any incriminating statements can lead to indictment does not require the suppression of such statements at a subsequent trial on the charge. Also keep in mind that there is no constitutional right to counsel at a grand jury hearing, because no criminal (punitive) proceedings have been started.

A potentially significant exception to *Miranda*, called the "public safety" exception, was stated in *New York v. Quarles* (1984). A suspect was confronted in a supermarket by four police officers with drawn weapons. They searched him, discovered a shoulder holster, and handcuffed him. When an officer asked him where the gun was, he indicated, "over there." He was then formally arrested and given his *Miranda* warnings, after which he made further admissions of guilt. The Court ruled that the question about the gun was clearly "interrogation" and the defendant was clearly "in custody," but that the "public safety" concerns of the moment, in this case finding the gun, overrode any failure to give the *Miranda* warnings. Court scholars have found this decision puzzling. What is the effect of failing to give the warnings, getting an admission, then giving the *Miranda* warnings and getting further admissions? Are the subsequent admissions tainted because the suspect felt he had already confessed in what was, unknown to him, an unusable confession? The Court said when the first statement, though illegally obtained, is not given in a coercive setting, then any subsequent admissions following *Miranda* warnings are valid. The dissenting justices argued that the majority ignored the line of precedent and *Miranda* itself by finding the setting of the first questioning to be insufficiently coercive to taint any subsequent admissions [*Oregon v. Elstad* (1985)].

"Confession of our faults is the next thing to innocency."

—Publilius Syrus, Latin writer, *Sententiae*, c. 43 B.C.

4. Assertion, Waiver, and Subsequent Interrogation

A valid waiver is a prerequisite for an "in custody" statement to be admitted in court as evidence. Absent counsel,

> *[i]f the individual indicates in any manner, at any time prior to or during questioning, that he wishes to remain silent, the interrogation must cease. . . . If the interrogation continues without the presence of an attorney and a statement is taken, a* heavy burden *rests on the government to demonstrate that the defendant knowingly and intelligently waived his privilege against self-incrimination and his right to . . . counsel. . . . An express statement could constitute a waiver (emphasis added).*
>
> —(*Miranda*)

Even an express waiver can be invalid, such as one given by a youthful offender with mental deficiencies who had to stand naked during questioning [*U.S. v. Blocker* (D.C.D.C. 1973)]. *Miranda* states "a valid waiver will not be presumed simply from the silence of the accused after warnings are given or simply from the fact that a confession was . . . obtained." Quoting *Carnley v. Cochran* (1962), the *Miranda* Court said, "The record must show that an accused was offered counsel but intelligently and understandably rejected the offer. Anything less is not a waiver." Following warnings, a waiver will not be inferred simply because the defendant answered some questions [*Tague v. Louisiana* (1980)]. A voluntary waiver, however, may be inferred if a suspect's actions or words are clear [*North Carolina v. Butler* (1979)]. Police overreaching is the primary focus [*Colorado v. Connelly* (1986)] and, thus, waivers may be invalid if achieved through threats, trickery, or promises. Here is a brief taste of cases demonstrating how courts have applied these principles in specific factual contexts.

1. A confession was not rendered involuntary because police lied, telling the suspect that his cosuspect had already confessed [*Frazier v. Cupp* (1969)].
2. A suspect voluntarily waived his right by making oral statements, even though he was under the mistaken belief that only written statements could be used against him [*State v. Adams* (N.J. 1992)].
3. An officer's mention of the death penalty to a juvenile in a murder case rendered the confession involuntary [*Green v. State* (Md. App. 1992)].
4. The promise of leniency given to a suspect if the suspect passed a polygraph test was improper inducement of a confession [*U.S. v. Escamilla* (9th Cir. 1992)].
5. An "I don't know if I should have a lawyer" type of statement was not an adequate waiver in *U.S. v. Mendoza-Cecelia* (11th Cir. 1992), and, therefore, police should not have continued their questioning without a clearer waiver. In *Davis v. U.S.* (1994), a waiver was followed by the suspect's statement, "Maybe I should talk with a lawyer." The interrogator then asked, "Are you asking for a lawyer?" The suspect answered, "No." This exchange was not so clear an invocation of the right to counsel as to require the agents to stop their questioning, even though the defendant later and more clearly exercised his right to counsel. The *Davis* Court also refused to set a rule requiring interrogators to ask clarifying questions if the suspect makes an ambiguous statement regarding the right to counsel.

In *Ogle v. State* (Ind. 1998), the Indiana Supreme Court ruled that once the defendant has made a waiver, a significant interruption in the interrogation does not require new warnings.

Once the right to remain silent is invoked, a subsequent, proper waiver of that right is valid. For example, after police ended the questioning of a suspect when he invoked his right to silence, it was not a violation of the suspect's right to silence for another police officer to question the suspect several hours later about a different crime, following warnings and a clear waiver [*Michigan v. Mosley* (1975)]. A guilty plea and a court's determination that the plea is voluntary is not a waiver of the privilege against self-incrimination, because statements by the defendant about what happened could be used as a basis for a more severe sentence [*Mitchell v. U.S.* (1999)].

If an attorney tries to get in touch with a suspect who has waived rights, police have no obligation to suspend questioning or to inform the suspect that an attorney is waiting in the wings [*Moran v. Burbine* (1986)]. If the right to an attorney has been asserted, even ambiguously, however, police may not resume interrogation. An exception to this rule exists when (1) a defendant initiates a new conversation and (2) does so in a manner that suggests (note: not unequivocally) a desire to discuss the matter further [*Edwards v. Arizona* (1981) and *Mississippi v. Minnick* (1990)]. Even if a suspect is represented by a lawyer and even if they have consulted, another Supreme Court case says police may initiate questioning on a different matter without the lawyer being present [*McNeil v. Wisconsin* (1991)].

Although *Miranda* retains some vitality, it is clear that a more conservative Supreme Court has substantially limited its far-reaching protections, particularly in this area of waiver and subsequent interrogation by police.

5. *Miranda*'s Scope: Settings and Circumstances

Miranda applies to traffic, tax, and any other matter that is or may lead to criminal or punitive charges. It does not protect persons at competency, prison disciplinary, or sexual offender hearings. Statements to third-party, nonpolice persons such as school principals, private investigators, or victims are generally not protected. Statements to psychiatrists in criminal proceedings, IRS agents, and possibly probation and social workers may be protected when punitive repercussions are present.[6] As mentioned previously, *Miranda* does not allow suspects to avoid fingerprinting, writing samples, lineups, and blood tests.

6. Subsequent Use of a Suppressed Statement for Impeachment

As we have seen, a statement illegally obtained from the defendant may not be introduced at trial by the prosecution to prove the defendant's guilt. If the defendant testifies at trial and this testimony contradicts the suppressed statement, however, the prosecution may use the suppressed statement to show that the defendant is lying or, at the least, is giving testimony inconsistent with the earlier statement. This attack on a witness's credibility is called **impeachment,** and the use of a suppressed statement for this purpose is permitted under *Harris v. New York* (1971). The *Harris* Court justified its decision by reasoning that it was not the intent of *Miranda* to give a green light to defendants to testify falsely with impunity. Critics of the decision say that it chills or deters a defendant's right to testify on his or her own behalf. If the suppressed statement is seriously damaging to the defendant, the defendant's attorney may be forced to advise the defendant not to testify even on his or her legitimate view of the facts, knowing that if some inconsistency arises, the defendant will open the door to the government's use of the damaging statement.

A defendant's silence, exercised prior to *Miranda* warnings being given, or where *Miranda* warnings never were given, can be commented on for impeachment purposes [*Jenkins v. Anderson* (1980) and *Fletcher v. Weir* (1982)]. This impeachment exception, however, is restricted to the impeachment of a defendant and does not include the impeachment of other defense witnesses [*James v. Illinois* (1990)].

impeachment:
attack on a witness's credibility, showing inconsistent statements.

The impeachment exception raises the issue of whether a defendant's statements made after exercising the right to an attorney and in response to continued police questioning after exercising the right can be used for impeachment. The Supreme Court said the statements can still be used for impeachment in *Oregon v. Hass* (1975). In a more recent case, the Supreme Court of California ruled that such illegally obtained statements can be used for impeachment even when the police continue questioning for the sole purpose of gaining statements for impeachment [*People v. Peevy* (Cal. 1998)].

Keep in mind that the law on when statements can be used to impeach has some subtle complexities. If you are called on to draft a motion or perform any other task in this area, detailed research is essential. For example, not all illegally obtained statements may be used for impeachment purposes. If a statement is truly coerced, such as where immunity is granted, thus compelling testimony, any use of the testimony to impeach is a constitutional violation, and not simply a violation of the *Miranda* safeguards [*New Jersey v. Portash* (1979)].

D. EFFECT OF DENIAL OF RIGHT TO COUNSEL (*MASSIAH*) AND HARMLESS ERROR

Miranda, as we have seen, focuses on conditions that are inherently compelling, threatening a suspect's Fifth Amendment right against self-incrimination. The conditions of "in custody" and "interrogation" are essential to its invocation. *Massiah v. U.S.* (1964) focuses strictly on whether the defendant's Sixth Amendment right to counsel has been violated. It applies after a person has been indicted or arraigned, and prohibits the police from deliberately eliciting incriminating statements from the suspect. The *Massiah* doctrine, almost forgotten since *Miranda*, has been revived in the following line of cases.

In *Brewer v. Williams* (1977), an arrested and arraigned defendant had been instructed by his attorney not to answer any police questions. While being transported across the state by the police, the defendant, whom police knew to be extremely religious, revealed the location of the body of the victim in response to a deliberate appeal from the police that the murder victim be provided a "decent Christian burial." The Court ruled that the ploy was a deliberate attempt to elicit incriminating evidence outside the presence of counsel.

The *U.S. v. Henry* (1980) Court reaffirmed *Massiah* and *Williams*, ruling that the planting of a paid informant to converse with the defendant, even though the informant was instructed not to question the defendant about the alleged crime, was a deliberate attempt to elicit incriminating statements from the defendant during the conversations. Placing an informant just to overhear a defendant's statement, and not to converse with the defendant, is permissible [*Kuhlmann v. Wilson* (1986)]. It is akin to placing an electronic eavesdropping device. The clarity of this line is lost, however, when one considers that the incriminating statements in *Kuhlmann* were offered after the informant said to the defendant that his original statement "didn't sound too good."

At one time the Court held that if a conviction was obtained at trial with use of an illegal confession, the conviction had to be overturned. In *Arizona v. Fulminante* (1991), however, the Court made it clear that henceforth an illegally used confession would not bring automatic reversal if there was enough other evidence on which to base the conviction. In other words, use of the tainted confession could be "harmless error."

"A man's death-trap may be between his teeth."

—Jewish folk saying
Joseph L. Baron, *A Treasury of Jewish Quotations*, 1956

E. CHALLENGING A CONFESSION

In most jurisdictions, the judge decides whether a statement of a defendant will be suppressed following the defendant's motion for suppression and a hearing on the motion. The defendant can testify at this hearing without giving up the right to remain silent at trial. These hearings are usually held well before the trial begins. The admission of a defendant's statement can also be challenged via an objection at trial if it has not been ruled on at an earlier date.

F. THE PARALEGAL'S ROLE

Your job in attacking and responding to attacks on a defendant's statements to police is to gather the facts surrounding the defendant's statement, research the applicable law, and draft either a motion and memorandum of law attacking the use of the statement or a responsive motion and memorandum of law. When you research the law on confessions, the same rule applies as in researching search and seizure cases: you must find precedent cases as closely matched in facts to the new case at hand as possible. Because the law of interrogation and confessions has become largely a case-by-case analysis, cases that closely parallel the one on which you are working are the most persuasive. Exhibit 10–1 is an example of a defense motion to suppress a con-

EXHIBIT 10–1
Defense Motion to Suppress Confession

STATE OF COLUMBIA	CIRCUIT COURT	CAPITOL COUNTY

STATE OF COLUMBIA,
      PLAINTIFF

      v.

SHARON STRIKER,
      DEFENDANT

MOTION TO SUPPRESS STATEMENT AND TO REQUEST HEARING

The defendant by her attorney respectfully moves this court for an order suppressing evidence of all statements the defendant made to police on October 2, _____ .

AS GROUNDS FOR THIS MOTION THE DEFENDANT ARGUES THAT HER STATEMENT WAS GIVEN TO PO-LICE WHILE SHE WAS IN CUSTODY AS DEFINED BY *MIRANDA* AND SUBSEQUENT CASES, AND THAT SHE WAS NOT GIVEN THE REQUIRED *MIRANDA* WARNINGS.

At 4 A.M. on October 2, _____ , two uniformed and armed police officers entered a bus parked at the terminal in Wayland, Columbia. The police had information that one Sharon Striker had robbed a convenience store in Legalville, Columbia, and was reported to be on the bus to Wayland and beyond. The police approached the defendant, who was the only person in the bus, and positioned themselves to block any exit from the bus. (See attached police report.) Officer Mader asked and was given permission to search the defendant's purse, which revealed a driver's license in the defendant's name. Officer Riley said, "She's the one." The police moved closer to the defendant and waited briefly. The defendant began to cry and then said, "I didn't want to rob the store."

It is well established law that police must give the *Miranda* warnings in settings outside the police interrogation room when a defendant is in custody or otherwise significantly deprived of freedom. [*Miranda v. Arizona,* 384 U.S. 463 (1966) and *Orozco v. Texas,* 394 U.S. 324 (1969).] In *Orozco,* the Supreme Court ruled that a person confronted in his own bedroom by two uniformed officers in the early morning hours was "in custody" and the *Miranda* warnings were required.

Similarly, the defendant was cornered by two uniformed and armed police officers in the early morning hours, in the rear of an isolated and empty bus, and had been openly identified as the person the police wanted. Under these circumstances, it is clear that the defendant was not free to go and that the environment was coercive in nature. Therefore, the police should have given her *Miranda* warnings before inducing her to speak by stating "she's the one," followed by deliberate silence and their ominous presence.

Because the defendant, for all practical purposes, was in custody and significantly deprived of her freedom, her statement must be presumed to be involuntary and should be suppressed.

Therefore, the defendant moves this court for an order suppressing evidence of the defendant's statement, and further requests that a hearing be scheduled on the motion.

Respectfully submitted,

_____
Attorney for Defendant
(Address)
(Phone number)

Date: _____

EXHIBIT 10–2
Prosecution Response to Defense Motion to Suppress Confession

STATE OF COLUMBIA
STATE OF COLUMBIA,
  PLAINTIFF
v.
SHARON STRIKER,
  DEFENDANT
	CIRCUIT COURT	CAPITOL COUNTY
		
		RESPONSE TO DEFENDANT'S
		MOTION TO SUPPRESS
		STATEMENT

The State of Columbia requests the Court to deny the Defendant's Motion to Suppress Statement.

The defendant argues that she was in custody at the time she was questioned by the police, and was not warned of her right to an attorney and her right against self-incrimination in violation of *Miranda v. Arizona,* 384 U.S. 436 (1966).

Despite the defendant's reliance on *Orozco v. Texas,* 394 U.S. 324 (1969), the most applicable decision of the Supreme Court is the more recent case of *Berkemer v. McCarty,* 468 U.S. 420 (1984). In *Berkemer,* police questioning of the driver of a car about the use of intoxicants and absent *Miranda* warnings, even though the police were going to arrest the driver, was not a violation of *Miranda.* In establishing a more objective standard for addressing the in-custody issue, the Court focused on how "a reasonable [person] in the suspect's position would have understood [the] situation." In other words, are the circumstances such that a reasonable person would feel so isolated and restrained and so under the power of the police as to be in custody?

The facts in *Berkemer* are similar to the facts in the defendant's case. Like the suspect in *Berkemer,* the defendant was not yet under arrest, was only temporarily detained because the bus would be leaving soon, and was in a place in view and hearing of the public, particularly the bus driver who was just outside. (See the defendant's attached police report.) Also, the recent stop and frisk case of *Florida v. Bostick,* 111 S. Ct. 2382 (1991), provides guidance; in parallel circumstances the Court ruled that reasonable persons would have realized they did not have to answer questions and were free to go.

Based on the above-cited authority, the defendant's motion to suppress is without adequate grounds and should be denied.

Respectfully submitted,

_____

Date: _____   Attorney for the State of Columbia

fession and Exhibit 10–2 is an example of a prosecution's response to the defendant's motion to suppress a confession.

If you are working for a prosecutor's or other government office in either an investigatory or intake capacity, and you need to question someone whom you suspect of criminal wrongdoing about that wrongdoing, it is wise for you to give the *Miranda* warnings to the person you are questioning. Seek guidance from your supervising attorney.

IV.   LINEUPS, ONE-ON-ONE SHOW-UPS, AND PHOTO IDENTIFICATIONS

A.   INTRODUCTION

Presenting a suspect to the victim of a crime or to witnesses to a crime, whether it is at the scene, at trial, or some time in between, has always aided police in solving crimes. Unfortunately, because of weaknesses in a person's ability to observe and remember details, especially under stress, and susceptibility to the power of suggestion, such identifications are fraught with the potential for misidentification. In one famous study that parallels the results of a number of other eyewitness studies, less than 15 percent of 2,000 people who witnessed a crime simulation on television were able to identify the perpetrator correctly.[7] This is approximately the same results that could be achieved simply by guessing.

For this reason the courts have scrutinized pretrial identification procedures and have ruled that they are subject to two constitutional concerns. First, once criminal prosecution begins, a defendant has the right to counsel at such procedures, and second, the procedures must be reasonably fair to conform with the defendant's right to due process.

B.   THE RIGHT TO COUNSEL AT PRETRIAL IDENTIFICATION

The heart of the right to counsel in this context is the Sixth Amendment right to confront one's accuser, especially through cross-examination at trial. In order for a defendant to exercise the right to cross-examination fully, the defense counsel needs to be present to observe the identification procedures. The attorney's observation of any weaknesses in the procedure will give counsel a fair chance to question the person making the identification and to reveal facts, circumstances, and biases that might have produced misidentification. Without counsel at such procedures, the right of confrontation at trial and its close cousin, the right of cross-examination, are rendered powerless.

In *U.S. v. Wade* (1967) and *Gilbert v. California* (1967), the Supreme Court ruled that a lineup held after indictment requires the presence of defense counsel. This ruling was expanded to include lineups held *after criminal prosecution begins* in *Kirby v. Illinois* (1972). Criminal prosecution generally begins with an indictment, the filing of charges, or a warrant for arrest on charges. If a lineup is conducted after that initial action without the defendant's counsel being notified of its occurrence, any identification stemming from that lineup is inadmissible at trial. Should such evidence be mistakenly admitted at trial, the defendant is granted a new trial, unless enough other evidence exists to render the violation harmless error (*Gilbert*).

The right to counsel extends to the actual time the identification is made, even if that is some time after the lineup (*Wade*). It also extends to one-on-one confrontation procedures where police bring the suspect before the witness for identification, whether this occurs before trial or at trial [*Moore v. Illinois* (1977)]. The right to have counsel present at identification procedures may be waived if *Miranda*-type warnings are given to the suspect, but waiver of right to counsel for a statement does not extend to lineups and one-on-one confrontations. (*Wade*).

The right to counsel is not absolute. Exigent circumstances, such as the possible imminent death of a witness or when the identification occurs shortly after the crime, and reliable circumstances, such as when witnesses have had a good look at the suspect, outweigh other factors [*Stovall v. Denno* (1967)]. Once an identification procedure is ruled unconstitutional, any subsequent identification of the defendant by the same witness is valid only if it can be shown that the original identification has not precluded an independently based, reliable identification (*Wade*).

C.   DUE PROCESS AND PRETRIAL IDENTIFICATIONS

Identification procedures may also be found to violate the defendant's right to due process under the Fifth and Fourteenth Amendments. The court looks at the "totality of the circumstances," and if it finds that the police procedure is too suggestive and subject to "irreparable" mistake, the identification is inadmissible (*Stovall*). Suggestiveness alone is not enough to invalidate the identification, especially if all the facts reflect a reliable identification [*Neil v. Biggers* (1972), station house show-up, and *Manson v. Brathwaite* (1977), photograph]. Some factors to consider include the following:

■   The witness's opportunity to see the criminal at the time of the crime.
■   The witness's attentiveness.
■   The witness's accuracy in describing the criminal.

- The witness's certainty at the identification procedure.
- The time between the crime and the confrontation.

A procedure in which the defendant first was placed in a lineup with two others who were a half-foot shorter, with the defendant the only one wearing a jacket similar to the one worn at the crime; then he was put in a one-on-one identification; and finally he was placed in another lineup where he was the only person from the first lineup, was a violation of due process [*Foster v. California* (1969)].

In another case in which the employees of a bank had a good opportunity to view a robber, a serious felony had been committed, the felon was still at large, the FBI had not influenced the identification procedure, and five bank employees made separate and positive identifications of the defendant from six photographs, the "totality of circumstances" did not violate due process [*Simmons v. U.S.* (1968)].

The same held true for a one-on-one show-up identification where the hand-cuffed defendant was brought to the hospital bed of the dying victim, and where the defendant was the only African American person present. The court said that one-on-one confrontations are disfavored but in some circumstances are permissible (*Stovall*).

A court may permit the defense to place the defendant among other individuals in the courtroom to ensure an accurate in-court identification. Some judges use an in-court lineup. Most courts prohibit the use of decoys, or defendant stand-ins, to induce the witness or victim to misidentify.

The preferred method of pretrial identification still is the lineup, unless it is impractical. A properly conducted lineup should:

a. Include a minimum of five persons.
b. Include persons with similar physical characteristics.
c. Give the suspect a choice of place on the line.
d. Require all participants to speak, gesture, and wear certain clothing if any one of them is requested to do so.
e. Include instructions to participants to avoid any conduct that would single out the suspect.
f. Be viewed by witnesses individually, not as a group.
g. Be photographed or videotaped.[8]

A properly conducted photo identification should follow these guidelines based on the *Simmons* case.

1. More than one photograph should be shown to a witness. In the Simmons *case, six photographs were shown to several witnesses, and the Supreme Court suggested that even more than six would be preferable. "In the absence of exigent circumstances, presentation of a single photograph to the victim of a crime amounts to an unnecessarily suggestive photographic identification procedure."* U.S. v. Jones, 652 F.Supp. 1561, 1570 (S.D.N.Y. 1986).

2. The people appearing in the photographs should be of the same general age, height, weight, hair color, and skin color.

3. No group of photographs should be arranged in such a way that the photograph of a single person recurs or is in any way emphasized. Furthermore, the officer conducting the identification should do nothing to indicate which picture is that of the suspect. Cikora v. Wainwright, 661 F.Supp. 813 (S.D. Fla. 1987).

4. If there are two or more suspects, no two should appear together in a group photo.

5. Witnesses should be handled in a manner similar to that suggested in the guidelines for lineup identifications.

6. If there are several witnesses, only some of them should be shown the photographs to obtain an initial identification. Then the suspect should be displayed to the remaining witnesses in a more reliable lineup. By following this procedure, the officer helps ensure that the perceptions of the witnesses at the lineup are not influenced by a viewing of the photographs.

7. *The officer in charge should take careful notes of all remarks made by witnesses while viewing photos, and of all identifications of and failures to identify the suspect.*

8. *After the photographs have been shown to the witnesses, they should be numbered and preserved as evidence.*

9. *After a witness selects a photograph from a photographic display, that witness should not be shown the same photograph in later photographic displays. Such a procedure would tend to fix the image of the photograph in the witness's mind and blur the image actually perceived at the crime.* U.S. v. Eatherton, *519 F.2d 603 (1st Cir. 1975).*

10. *Photographs of suspects in the act of committing the crime (such as bank robbery surveillance photographs) do not present any problems of suggestiveness and mistaken identification. Courts have held that presenting such photographs to witnesses shows the actual perpetrator of the crime in the act rather than suggesting a number of possible perpetrators. The photographs refresh the witness's memory of the actual crime and thereby strengthen the reliability of the witness's in-court identification.* U.S. v. Browne, *829 F.2d 760 (9th Cir. 1987).*

11. *Mug shots should not be used together with other photographs for identification purposes. Mug shots may prejudice the pictured persons by implying that they have criminal records.*

12. *A photograph in a photographic display may be altered (to show what the person would look like with a beard or a hat, for example) so long as all other photographs in the display are altered in the same way.* U.S. v. Dunbar, *767 F.2d 72 (3d Cir. 1985).*

13. *"Once law enforcement officers obtain from a witness a photographic identification of a suspect which is both untainted and positive, they may show other pictures of that properly and positively identified suspect to the witness without implicating the concerns of* Simmons *and its progeny."* U.S. v. Jones, *652 F.Supp. 1561 (S.D.N.Y. 1986).*

14. *Photographic identification should not be used once a suspect's identity is known and the suspect is in police custody. A lineup should be used in these circumstances because lineups are more accurate than photographic identifications.* State v. Wallace, *285 So.2d 796 (La. 1973).*[9]

A recent study indicates that police and others present at an identification process can influence the degree to which an eyewitness is positive about a lineup or photo identification. Some positive reinforcement about the correctness of the identification makes the witness more sure of the identification than if no feedback is provided. Some negative feedback makes the witness less confident of the identification than if no feedback was provided.[10] A paralegal who knows this area of law can play a vital role in calling attention to such identification processes so the attorney can determine if they have met constitutional standards. This type of detailed analysis of the procedure and evidence in a case can be immensely valuable to a busy supervising attorney.

V.   CONCLUSION

The law of confessions focuses on the right against self-incrimination and the related impact of *Miranda v. Arizona.* The right against self-incrimination stems from the accusatory system of justice. It places the burden of proof on the state and deliberately deemphasizes the reliance on confessions that can so easily result in injustice and abuse of the individual. If a confession is obtained in violation of this right, it is excluded from evidence.

Persons, and not corporations, are protected. The right may be exercised in any criminal or other proceeding if testimony may lead to the punishment of the individual. If a statement can link the person to a yet-to-be-prosecuted crime, it is incriminating. Such statements can be compelled, however, when the statute of limitations has run or if immunity is granted to the person making the statement. A person must assert the right, whether in court or on documents such as tax forms, or the right is waived. An overriding public interest may require the reporting of certain kinds of information. Statutes requiring the reporting of such things as income from illegal gambling activities are unconstitutional. Any methods or statutes that restrain the exercising of the right violate the right. Once a person waives the right regarding a specific crime, it becomes more difficult to reassert the right later. The right extends only to testimonial evidence, and does not extend to nontestimonial evidence such as the taking of blood, voice samples, or other evidence for purposes of physical identification.

Miranda v. Arizona is the most significant decision in the past thirty years that protects a person's right against self-incrimination. The decision focuses on the coerciveness of police custody and interrogation and requires officers to warn suspects who are "in custody" and under "interrogation" that they have the rights to remain silent and to an attorney. Any statement made without these warnings is inadmissible; any statement made without the presence of an attorney is presumed coerced. Numerous decisions have gone beyond *Miranda* to define "in custody," determine what constitutes a waiver, and decide when a suppressed confession may be used to impeach a defendant.

A defendant's right to counsel and to due process offers protection from unduly suggestive pretrial identification procedures during lineups and photo identifications. The right to have counsel present during a lineup preserves the defendant's right to confrontation and cross-examination at trial; due process requires that the procedure not create irreparable misidentification. In both cases the rights apply only after official criminal proceedings have begun.

SYSTEM FOLDER ASSIGNMENTS

Complete the following and place the documents in your system folder:

- Summary of *Miranda* rules and other pertinent decisions on self-incrimination, including key cases from your state.
- Sample motion to suppress and response to motion to suppress.
- List of guidelines, including those used in your state, for the proper conduct of lineups and each form of pretrial identification.

APPLICATION ASSIGNMENTS

1. Using the decisions on custody discussed in the text, determine whether the suspect was "in custody" in these two cases.

   In *Minnesota v. Murphy,* 465 U.S. 420, 104 S.Ct. 1136 (1984), questioning took place at the suspect's probation officer's office. The meeting was arranged by appointment at the suspect's request and was in surroundings familiar to the suspect.

   In *New York v. Quarles,* 467 U.S. 649, 104 S.Ct. 2626 (1984), the suspect was questioned in a supermarket minutes after being confronted by four police officers with drawn guns, and then being handcuffed.

2. Assume that Eldon Spiers in Case I has been subpoenaed before a grand jury in your state. The jury is investigating Kate Lamb's death. Your boss, the prosecutor, wants to know whether the suspect must be given the *Miranda* warnings before testifying at the hearing. Research the law in your state and draft a brief memo of authorities for your supervising attorney.

   Assume that a neighboring state has jurisdiction over this matter as well. Research the law of one neighboring state to determine where it stands on the issue and, then, whether in a subsequent trial in that state, the court must adhere to a neighboring state's suppression of the suspect's grand jury testimony. Draft a brief memo of authorities.

3. Based on the principles of law set out in *Miranda* and more recent decisions, how would you decide the issue set out in Exhibits 10–1 and 10–2? Support your answer with cases, principles, and pertinent public policies.

4. Read the following summary of facts and draft a motion to suppress the defendant's statements, using the authorities cited in this section of the text. Half the class may be assigned to draft a response to the defense motion. Use the format for a motion given in the examples, or your standard state format if indicated by your instructor.

At 2 P.M. on October 6, _____ , Eldon Spiers, defendant, was asked to accompany detectives to their car. Mr. Spiers is a thirty-one-year-old college janitor with a tenth grade education. He seems unintelligent and somewhat childlike at times. He was led to an unmarked car by two plainclothes officers. Prior to getting into the police car the officers gave their weapons to a third officer. Some onlookers were nearby.

In the car one police officer said, "Eldon, you're a nice boy; you can still make this right." Then he gave Eldon the following warnings: "You have the right to remain silent; anything you say can be used against you in court. We can get you an attorney if you want, and you won't have to pay. Do you understand?"

The police report says that the defendant nodded slightly and said, "I think so."

Police: Are you ready to talk with us?
Spiers: Sure.
Police: Did you know a student named Kate Lamb?
Spiers: Yes (blushing). I used to watch her.
Police: You hurt her, didn't you?
Spiers: I need to see my mother. She's going to be real mad.
Police: Did you ever hurt Kate Lamb?

Spiers made no further response to questioning. He was arrested and taken to the police station, booked, and jailed. The next morning while a police officer delivered the defendant's morning meal, Eldon Spiers said, "Can you talk with me?" The officer said, "Sure, Eldon, I'd like to talk with you, but it better be good. I'm pretty busy."

Spiers: I did it.
Police: What did you do?
Spiers: I couldn't help myself. Uh-oh, Mother is really going to be angry.

The officer continued to question him, but Spiers retreated to the corner of his cell and said nothing more.

5. How would you rule on the admissibility of the pretrial identification procedure in the following circumstances, and why?

a. Three of five photos shown to the witness were of the suspect. See *People v. Citrino*, 90 Cal. Rptr. 80 (Cal. App. 1970).

b. Only the suspect's photo was clearly altered. See *State v. Alexander*, 503 P.2d 777 (Ariz. 1972).

c. Only one photo was shown in the identification of a rapist who told the victim he had been jailed for rape before, and where the victim had gotten a good look at the rapist. See *Chaney v. State*, 267 So.2d 65 (Fla. 1972).

d. Police conducted a lineup without counsel after the counsel left an order that the defendant not be interrogated without counsel present. See *People v. LaClere*, 564 N.E.2d 640 (N.Y. 1990).

e. A one-on-one confrontation was held months after the crime because police claimed they could not find other persons with similar physical characteristics, and where the victim had viewed the defendant for half an hour at the time of the crime. See *Neil v. Biggers*, 409 U.S. 188, 93 S.Ct. 375, (1972).

f. In the course of an investigation police asked a suspect to come to the station house. The defendant was given *Miranda* warnings, did not clearly waive counsel, then was put in a lineup. See *Kirby v. Illinois,* 406 U.S. 682, 92 S.Ct. 1877 (1972).

6. Review *Miranda v. Arizona* to determine the reasoning behind the decision. Then read the following facts and decide whether the reasoning in *Miranda* should be expanded to cover the confession in this new situation. Explain.

   A package delivery company employee was observed opening a package. He was taken by company officials to a room with no windows and led to believe that he would not be prosecuted if he confessed and returned all stolen items. He was interrogated for fifteen minutes and confessed to the observed theft. Then he was questioned for another forty minutes and confessed to other thefts. The state wants to use the confession at trial and the defense moves to suppress it because it is not voluntary. See *Commonwealth v. Cooper,* 889 S.W.2d 75 (Ky. 1995).

HELPFUL WEB SITES

www.totse.com/files/GAO19/cellmate.htm
   Cellmate Informants: A Constitutional Guide to Their Use, examines *Illinois v. Perkins* (1990)
www.vuw.ac.nz/psyc/assefiEWT/conclusions.html
   Discussion of police lineups, photo spreads, mugshots, including test photos, bibliography on eyewitness identifications

INTERNET EXERCISES

1. Go to www.lectlaw.com, through The Reference Room, to the section on Criminal Law and Procedure. In the Constitutional Guide on the Use of Cellmate Informants, find out what postcritical stage uses there are for cellmate informants once the suspect's Sixth Amendment rights have attached.
2. Go to the police lineup site in item 1 and look at the photos. Write your opinion of eyewitness identification based on those photos.

QUESTIONS FOR STUDY AND REVIEW

1. Describe how the right against self-incrimination stems from the very heart of our system of justice.
2. Who is protected by the right against self-incrimination?
3. When does the right apply?
4. What considerations determine in which hearings the right against self-incrimination applies? Give examples of hearings to which the right does apply and does not apply.
5. Define incriminating, and explain why the context of the statement, rather than the statement itself, is critical in determining whether the statement is incriminating.
6. When is a document likely to be unobtainable through a subpoena duces tecum?
7. What is the significance of the statute of limitations and immunity in regard to the exercise of the right against self-incrimination?
8. Discuss whether testimony given under a grant of immunity can be used in other courts or for purposes of impeachment.
9. Why are *Miranda* warnings necessary at police interrogation but not at trial?

10. Under what circumstances may an incriminating statement be compelled and criminal penalties be invoked for not reporting the information? Give some examples. Discuss exceptions, when the answer cannot be compelled.
11. May a prosecutor mention to a jury that the defendant did not testify?
12. To what extent is a waiver of the right against self-incrimination applicable to future hearings? To questions related to the incriminating statement?
13. Regarding the scope of the privilege against self-incrimination, why is a suspect's reply, "yes, I did it," protected when it is a response to police questions, but the statement, "I'll get you," when made by the suspect along with all other persons in a lineup is not protected?
14. Why does our system place such a high value on voluntary as opposed to coerced confessions?
15. List the essential principles of *Miranda* and give the reason or rationale behind each principle.
16. Has the *Miranda* decision been a significant "straitjacket" on law enforcement?
17. For purposes of *Miranda*, when is a person in custody? What is interrogation? Are incomplete warnings fatal?
18. What is necessary for a waiver of the *Miranda* rights to be effective? State some case examples when the waiver was valid and when it was not, and give the reason for each decision.
19. Do police need to suspend questioning when the defendant's attorney first calls to talk to the defendant? Do the police need to inform the defendant of the attorney's call?
20. Are statements to a third-party, nonpolice person ever protected under *Miranda?*
21. When can otherwise suppressible statements be used by the prosecution? Are there any exceptions?
22. Describe the normal court procedure for determining whether a statement given by a defendant will be suppressed.
23. Regarding the paralegal's work, what is the rule when researching confession cases to have a statement suppressed or to defend against a motion to suppress?
24. Be able to research and draft a motion to suppress statements and a motion in opposition to suppression.
25. Why have courts scrutinized pretrial identification procedures?
26. What does the right to counsel at lineups have to do with the right to confront one's accusers?
27. Summarize the significant points in *U.S. v. Wade.*
28. Are there exceptions to the rule that a defendant has a right to counsel at a lineup?
29. At what stage do the right to counsel and the right to due process apply in the pretrial identification setting?
30. Regarding due process, what is the standard for suppression of a pretrial identification procedure under *Stovall v. Denno?*
31. What are five to seven factors to consider in determining whether an identification procedure meets due process requirements? List cases in which the procedure was ruled adequate or inadequate.
32. What may the defense do at trial to better ensure an accurate, nonsuggestive, independent identification of the defendant?
33. List six recommended procedures for a fair lineup.

KEY TERMS LIST

Admission	Immunity	Impeachment
Confession	Transactional immunity	Incriminating testimony
	Use immunity	Subpoena duces tecum

ENDNOTES

1. CHARLES H. WHITEBREAD & CHRISTOPHER SLOBOGIN, CRIMINAL PROCEDURE 351–52 (2d ed. 1986).
2. JEROLD H. ISRAEL, YALE KAMISAR & WAYNE R. LaFAVE, CRIMINAL PROCEDURE AND THE CONSTITUTION 250–53 and 264–66 (1991).
3. Wald et al., *Interrogations in New Haven: The Impact of Miranda,* 76 YALE L.J. 1519 (1967).
4. Richard H. Seeburger, *Miranda in Pittsburg: A Statistical Study,* 29 U. PITT. L. REV. (1967) 1, 23–26; Richard J. Medalie et al., *Custodial Police Interrogation in Our Nation's Capital: The Attempt to Implement Miranda,* 66 MICH. L. REV. 1347 (1968).
5. ISRAEL et al., *Supra* note, 2, at 299–300.
6. JEROLD H. ISRAEL & WAYNE R. LaFAVE, CRIMINAL PROCEDURE AND CONSTITUTIONAL LIMITATIONS, 200–201 (1988).
7. Buckhout, *Nearly 2,000 Witnesses Can Be Wrong,* SOC. ACT. & L., May 1975, at 7.
8. WHITEBREAD, *supra* note 1, at 434, citing ARIZONA STATE UNIVERSITY & POLICE FOUNDATION, MODEL RULES FOR LAW ENFORCEMENT, EYEWITNESS IDENTIFICATION 52 (1974).
9. JOHN N. FERDICO, CRIMINAL PROCEDURE FOR THE CRIMINAL JUSTICE PROFESSIONAL, 4th Edition, 345–346, (West Group, 1989).
10. Gary L. Wells and Amy L. Bradfield, *Good, You Identified the Suspect: Feedback to Eyewitnesses Distorts Their Reports of the Witnessing Experience,* JOURNAL OF APPLIED PSYCHOLOGY, June 1998, at 360.

PRETRIAL: INITIAL APPEARANCE TO PRELIMINARY HEARING

CHAPTER

11

I. INTRODUCTION

The case enters the pretrial stage with the defendant's arrest. Initial stages in the process include the prosecutorial decision to charge and the considerations and limitations on that decision. The first section of the pretrial stage takes the case from the initial appearance through the preliminary hearing to extradition. Your tasks encompass interviewing for developing arguments on bail, learning to deal with difficult clients, and gathering information and drafting proposed questions for the preliminary hearing.

II. THE INITIAL APPEARANCE

A. INTRODUCTION

Once the defendant is arrested and booked and the charge is drafted and filed (see Chapter 8), the defendant is provided an initial appearance. The initial appearance is the first time the criminal defendant comes before a judge or magistrate to be informed of the charge and pertinent rights, and for assessment of the need for bail. In the interest of preserving liberty, an arrestee must be provided a prompt initial appearance. The maximum allowable time varies among state and federal rules. The Federal Rules of Criminal Procedure, Rule 5(a), and some state rules require the appearance "without unnecessary delays." Other states require the appearance within twenty-four hours of arrest, and still others apply a different time limit. Because of the inconsistencies among jurisdictions, the Supreme Court decided the constitutional limit in *County of Riverside v. McLaughlin* (1991). *McLaughlin* sets an outside limit of forty-eight hours including weekends and holidays. Any delay beyond forty-eight hours requires the government to prove a "bona fide emergency or extraordinary circumstances." Inadvertence, clerical error, mistake, or delay to gather enough evidence for charging is either no excuse or improper.

A state may set a limit of less than forty-eight hours for the appearance, but not longer than forty-eight hours. An unlawful delay in the initial appearance may result in the suppression of evidence, particularly confessions occurring during the time of violation [*U.S. v. Davis* (8th Cir. 1999), *McWabb v. U.S.* (1943), and *Mallory v. U.S.* (1957) on violations of Rule 5(a) and 18 U.S.C. § 3501(c)].

A judge is required to perform several tasks at the initial appearance. The judge

1. Reads the charges to provide due process notice of the pending charge to the defendant.
2. Informs the defendant of applicable rights.
3. Determines whether the defendant should be released on bail or remanded to jail.

B. NOTIFICATION OF RIGHTS AND DETERMINATION OF INDIGENCY

indigent:
not having the financial
means to hire a lawyer.

The judge informs the defendant of the right to remain silent, the right to an attorney, and the right to have an attorney appointed if the defendant is indigent. Indigency is a matter of judicial determination and discretion. An **indigent** person does not have the financial means to hire a lawyer, which means the person is either unemployed or underemployed, has no assets of significant value, and shows little potential for having such in the foreseeable future. If a defendant has income or property but it is needed for bail, a determination of indigency is likely. Seventy-five percent of felony defendants are indigent in most jurisdictions.[1]

If the judge determines that the defendant is indigent, counsel is appointed. Depending on local practice, the judge appoints a local attorney or a public defender to take the case of an indigent defendant. Appointments of local attorneys often go to new attorneys inexperienced in criminal law. These attorneys are paid by the government at exceedingly low rates that provide little incentive to remain on the prospective appointments list, resulting in little accumulation of valuable experience. Public defenders are paid low salaries, often a third to a half that of prosecuters, also resulting in frequent turnover. By and large, however, public defenders develop a sound level of expertise and, ironically, are often criticized by judges and prosecutors for adding costs and delay to the system through their zealous representation. Gross underfunding of indigent defense plagues the system, results in case overload for defenders, leads to inadequate representation, and continually jeopardizes justice for the poor. Overdue attention to indigent defense at both the national and state levels is resulting in some efforts to reestablish a critical balance in the system. State laws that require convicted indigent defendants to reimburse the government for the cost of appointed counsel are constitutional [*Fuller v. Oregon* (1974)].

A defendant, indigent or otherwise, has the right to refuse representation by an attorney [*Faretta v. California* (1975)]. Such self-representation (*pro se* or *pro per*) is said to be akin to performing one's own brain surgery. A judge may appoint standby counsel to monitor the case and assist the defendant as needed.

The court informs the defendant of the right to a preliminary (probable cause) hearing in felony cases. After determining bail, some judges simply adjourn any remaining portion of the initial appearance to provide the defendant with time to consult counsel.

Minor charges such as traffic ordinance violations and misdemeanors involve a different procedure. Normally, the defendant is summoned by citation to appear in court on a specified date. If the penalty for the crime is simply a fine or involves a jail sentence of less than six months, there is no constitutional right to a jury trial. The judge asks for a plea and briefly explores the circumstances, then renders a decision. Some minor cases may be rescheduled for trial before the judge at a later date. Indigent persons do not have the right to an appointed attorney in minor cases unless they are sentenced to jail [*Scott v. Illinois* (1979)]. In practice this means that a judge should appoint counsel for an indigent defendant even in minor cases when a jail sentence has not been ruled out. Some states require appointment of counsel in any criminal matter having a possible jail sentence.

C. BAIL

1. Conditions

At the initial appearance the judge determines whether a defendant will be released from jail and, if so, under what conditions. The Eighth Amendment states, "Excessive bail shall not be required. . . ." Most authorities presume that this provision is applicable to the states via the Fourteenth Amendment, even though the Supreme Court has not ruled on the issue [*Schilb v. Kuebel* (1971)]. The right to reasonable bail is grounded in the rationale that liberty is dear, that an accused can better assist counsel when free to locate information and witnesses, and that a person can work and better contribute to family and society when free to do so. The presumption of innocence, however, applies only at trial to delegate the burden of proof and is not applicable to bail considerations.

The two most significant cases on bail are *Stack v. Boyle* (1951) and *U.S. v. Salerno* (1987). *Stack* held that the only constitutional consideration in bail determinations is what is necessary to ensure the defendant's presence at court appearances. A judge must base that determination on standards, the most common of which are the nature and circumstances of the offense, evidence against the defendant, the financial ability of the defendant to post bail, and the history and characteristics of the person [Fed. R. Crim. P. 46, 18 U.S.C.A. § 3142(g); and similar state statutes].

"I do believe our government and my profession have a positive moral and legal duty to make sure that legal services are available to the poor on an accessible, affordable, regular, dignified basis and, if necessary, free of charge. Which means that I, as a lawyer, believe that some significant part of my money, time, thought, and energy belongs—I don't give it, it belongs—to others, not just to me.

—R. Sargent Shriver, Jr., *Washington Post*, June 6, 1982

" 'Custom is before all law.' As soon as you begin to say 'We have always done things this way—perhaps that might be a better way,' conscious law-making is beginning. As soon as you begin to say 'We do things this way—They do things that way—what is to be done about it?' men are beginning to feel towards justice, that resides between the endless jar of right and wrong."

—Helen M. Cam, English historian Lecture, Girton College, Feb. 18, 1956

Salerno holds that preventive detention, denying bail to the accused based on a determination that the accused is a threat to the community, is also a constitutionally permissible consideration [see 18 U.S.C.A. § 3142(g)(4)]. *Salerno* states that a person may not be held without bail unless there is authorizing legislation and the demonstration of a "legitimate and compelling need," following an adversarial detention hearing at which the state must show by clear and convincing evidence that the person is a danger to any person or the community. The statute upheld in *Salerno* (18 U.S.C.A. § 3141 *et seq.*) requires the judge to make a record of the justification for detention and gives the accused the right to an immediate appeal of the detention decision. Similar state laws are probably constitutional as well. Even prior to *Salerno,* state or federal court denial of pretrial release in capital (death penalty) cases had been upheld.

After considering what is necessary to ensure the defendant's presence at trial and determining whether the defendant is dangerous, the court sets the amount and conditions of bail. Some defendants are released before the initial appearance according to a predetermined bail schedule, such as the one in Exhibit 11–1, page 431.[2]

2. Types of Bail

If the defendant has not been released prior to the initial appearance, the court has the following options.

personal recognizance:
release on a promise to return to court at the next scheduled appearance.

1. **Personal recognizance** is release on a promise to return to court at the next scheduled appearance. Most courts require the defendant's signature on a bail release form that is executed in the clerk of court's office.

unsecured bond (personal bond):
release under a signed obligation to pay the court a specified sum of money in the event the defendant fails to appear.

2. **Unsecured bond,** sometimes called **personal bond,** is release under a signed obligation to pay the court a specified sum of money in the event the defendant fails to appear.

surety or cash bond:
release after surrendering to the clerk of court a specified sum of money or evidence of ownership of property sufficient to cover the amount of the bond in case of forfeiture.

3. **Surety or cash bond** is release only after surrendering to the clerk of court a specified sum of money or evidence of ownership of property sufficient to cover the amount of the bond in case of forfeiture. Typically, a family member's property can be used to secure the bond. Forfeiture results in loss of the property or a sale of the property to generate sufficient cash to pay the bond.

percent bond:
release after posting a specified percentage, usually 10 percent, of a cash bond.

4. **Percent bond** is release only after posting a specified percentage, usually 10 percent, of a cash bond. For example, if the court sets the bond at $10,000, the defendant must post $1,000. In some jurisdictions either this amount or a part of it remains with the court to cover administrative costs. Forfeiture for failure to appear, however, is for the entire $10,000.

supervised release:
release under the supervision of a probation or pretrial release officer or, in some cases, to the custody of a third party.

5. **Supervised release** is release under the supervision of a probation or pretrial release officer or, in some cases, to the custody of a third party. The third party may be a relative, a minister, or a community organization, for example, that agrees to supervise the defendant and report any violation of conditions under the bond.

Bail bondspersons are still used in some state jurisdictions. These individuals post bond for a defendant after securing the bond with the defendant's property or that of close relatives. The price paid by the defendant for such services, the premium, is often quite high. This practice took on a sleaze factor akin to loan sharking, leading to its prohibition and bail reform in many jurisdictions.

The court may also impose conditions for release that can include finding a job, restricting travel, refraining from the use of alcohol or drugs (sometimes enforced through testing), and staying away from specified persons, such as the alleged victim. Typically the court must consider the least restrictive alternative likely to ensure the defendant's presence. Exhibit 11–2, page 434 is a release order for bail for the federal system, an excellent example of one of the alternatives available for a judge to consider when imposing bail.

Release to a reliable third person who the court knows can provide more supervision than a probation or other officer and who will report any violation of conditions can be one of the most valuable conditions suggested by the defense.

3. Pretrial Release Services

Many states and the federal courts employ pretrial release services that function under the administrative arm of the court system. These services provide the court with relevant information for bail determination and supervise persons released on bail. Some paralegals work as pretrial release officers.

Initially, pretrial release officers interview persons who have been arrested and jailed. They gather information on the person's residence, ties to the community, employment or ongoing schooling, prior criminal record, drug dependency, and so forth. Exhibit 11–3, page 437, is a representative pretrial services interview form.[3]

After confirming this information, the officer evaluates the person's prospects for bail, typically by assigning a positive point value to stable community ties or a steady job, for example, and a negative point value for previous convictions or pending charges. Whether fair or not, the system favors those defendants appearing to be middle class. This evaluation is conveyed to the judge for use at the initial appearance, and it may or may not be accompanied by the officer's personal recommendation.

The officer may supervise those defendants who are released by locating community treatment programs and periodically checking on the defendant's continued residence, job status, drug tests, and other conditions imposed by the court. The officer is charged with reporting any violations of conditions and subsequent criminal conduct, and may be responsible for notifying the defendant of court dates and making sure the defendant appears, particularly if the defendant has no attorney.

There is some evidence that as many as 80 percent of all jailed arrestees meet with pretrial services.[4] The federal statutes on pretrial services are 18 U.S.C. §§ 3152–3156. Without a pretrial services evaluation, the court relies heavily on its own inquiry into the defendant's background or on information and recommendations supplied by prosecution and defense counsels. With this information, the court determines the amount of bail. Evidence suggests that 50 percent of arrestees are released without having to post any cash.[5] If a defendant is unable to make bail, some systems require a bail review hearing in twenty-four hours.

D. INITIAL APPEARANCE: THE PARALEGAL'S ROLE

1. Introduction

The more serious the case, the more important it is to be prepared for the initial appearance, regardless of which side of the case you are assigned. The prosecutor may see this as the first opportunity to place some meaningful pressure on the defendant. An incarcerated defendant is going to be more quickly demoralized, more eager to plead, and less able to assist defense counsel. Further, failure of the defense counsel to gain the release of the defendant at the initial appearance may negatively impact on the defendant's perception of the ability of the defense attorney. All these considerations, of course, must be balanced against the prosecutor's duty to fairness and justice.

Defense counsel, however, wants to demonstrate capability and preparedness to the client, prosecution, and judge. Defense counsel wants the client to have confidence in his or her work and trust counsel's judgment. Defense counsel also wants the defendant to be free to work and support family, demonstrate reliability, and assist counsel in locating information and preparing the case for trial.

Therefore, both sides need to be well prepared, and how well prepared they are may depend on your work. The foundation work that is done in preparation for the initial appearance also may have considerable value at a bail reconsideration hearing, an arraignment, or even at trial or sentencing. The amount of time and energy spent

"Lawyers: Persons who write a 10,000 word document and call it a brief."
—Popular saying

preparing for the initial appearance depends on the seriousness of the case, likelihood the defendant will remain incarcerated, availability of office resources, and other considerations. Use both the prosecution and defense checklists to provide persuasive information to your supervising attorney and to anticipate your opponent's likely position on the bail issue.

2. Obtaining the Criminal Record

Whether it is for the initial appearance or later, obtaining the criminal record of the accused is essential. Often the arresting police agency will obtain the record and pass it on to the prosecutor. Sometimes this duty falls to the prosecution paralegal. In turn the prosecution shares the record with the defense on request. To obtain as complete a record as possible, check several sources. The **National Communication Information Center (NCIC)** is an arm of the FBI that keeps criminal records on persons who have been charged with or convicted of felonies. Information in the system includes fingerprints; missing and deported persons; and stolen guns, vehicles, license plates, stocks, and other articles. Records are accumulated from all states, federal jurisdictions, and law enforcement agencies. Searches can be done by name and social security number, and fingerprints also can be matched. NCIC databanks are now computerized, facilitating nearly instantaneous searches from police stations and even squad cars and helping to prevent unwitting release of suspects who have outstanding warrants. Fingerprints and photos can be automatically matched in minutes, and mug shots can be sent electronically to improve identification of the suspect. In addition, the FBI has launched a unified, fifty-state DNA databank that will not only be able to match DNA samples, but also report whether the same DNA was found at a previous crime scene in any other state. One must be authorized and trained to do NCIC searches. Exhibit 11–4 contains a sample printout.[6]

The following is a brief translation of the printout in Exhibit 11–4. This person is probably a first offender where a reduced charge and a possible thirty-day jail sentence was dismissed following a period of time of good conduct. After an arrest on probable cause (PC) for burglary (BURG) with burglary tool (T), the defendant was released (REL). A warrant (WAR) was issued and the defendant was probably summoned to appear. A bench warrant (BW) was issued, normally for failure to appear. The burglary charge was dismissed (DISM) and reduced to loitering (LOIT), which must be deduced from the fact that loitering was not charged initially and it is a logically related but lesser crime. Apparently, the defendant pled guilty to loitering and was sentenced to a thirty-day jail sentence in a local correctional facility (ACF). Both the sentence and the charge, however, were continued (CONT), held open, pending good conduct or some other condition, such as attending alcohol abuse treatment, for a period of time. Once the condition was met, the case was dismissed (DISM LOIT). This is a form of diversion. The record comes certified for official use in court.

National Communication Information Center (NCIC): an arm of the FBI that keeps criminal records on persons that have been charged with or convicted of felonies.

EXHIBIT 11–4
Sample Printout of NCIC Search

Arrest	**Disposition**
PC BURG - T 11/30/84	REL. 11/30/84
WAR BURG 12/3/84	BW 12/5/84
	DISM BURG
	ACF 30 CONT
	DISM LOIT
	3/10/84 [sic]

In addition to the NCIC search, most states, counties, and parishes have criminal record indexes. In some cases, written requests must be submitted, taking days or weeks to get results. In other cases, research must be done on courthouse computers. A few states, such as Texas (http://records.txdps.state.tx.us), provide Internet access to their criminal data. If thorough searches are required, for example, in an attempt to discredit an important opposition witness, it may be best to employ one of a growing number of commercial agencies. If the defendant comes from a foreign jurisdiction, contact the police agency in that jurisdiction for assistance.

3. At the Hearing

If you attend the initial appearance, your task, regardless of which side of the case you are on, is to summarize the events and outcome for the file. If the defendant is not released, the defense paralegal needs to facilitate the release by contacting relatives, asking about property for bail, and performing related tasks. If the defendant is not able to gain release in the locally specified time, most courts permit a rehearing on the bail question, sometimes within twenty-four hours, or entertain a motion for reduced bail. Check local rules.

If a rehearing is denied or the bail is unreasonably high, the defense may appeal the judge's decision on bail through an immediate interlocutory appeal. An **interlocutory appeal** is an appellate court review of an issue that does not determine guilt or innocence but is necessary or useful to have decided prior to going to trial. A civil case that has been extended to the criminal arena, *Cohen v. Beneficial Industrial Loan Corp.* (1949), limits these appeals to issues (1) already finally determined by the court, (2) involving a right that would be lost if it waited for final judgment, and (3) not an ingredient of the main cause of action. Examples of interlocutory appeals issues include excessive bail and denial of a motion to dismiss on double jeopardy grounds. Most appeals issues depend on the central action of the trial, however, so they are not handled until after trial.[7]

interlocutory appeal:
an appellate court review of an issue that does not determine guilt or innocence but is necessary or useful to have decided prior to going to trial.

INITIAL APPEARANCE CHECKLIST: PROSECUTION PARALEGAL

☐ 1. Acquire a brief background on the defendant from police: nature of charge, evidence, use of aliases, lack of identification or any false identification, and other information.

☐ 2. Provide prosecutor with an early summary and request guidance on any tactical considerations that may affect the direction and extent of preparation.

☐ 3. Assess community sensitivity toward the crime.

☐ 4. Obtain criminal record through state and FBI networks: nature of crimes, penalty, and how satisfied; poor use of jail or prison time; any charges dismissed under first offender or other diversion programs; any record of escape, flight, resisting arrest, or failure to appear; any active warrants for arrest, including from other jurisdictions, or unpaid traffic tickets or violations; and whether defendant is on probation or parole and any history of violations (probation office should be able to help).

☐ 5. Any history of harassing a victim or tampering with a jury—if the current scenario is one where such is likely.

☐ 6. Any information from police, accomplices, friends, or family that indicates defendant is contemplating "skipping."

Continued

☐ 7. Residence history: any indication defendant is a transient or otherwise moves frequently; frequently travels out of jurisdiction or, more importantly, to foreign countries; is secretive about address to avoid bill collectors, child support, or other responsibilities; has no phone. If from another jurisdiction, a phone call to authorities in that jurisdiction might be informative regarding those and other matters.

☐ 8. Family and community ties: any evidence of instability in family relationships or friendships that would suggest few if any reasons to stay in area; evidence that acquaintances are gang members, felons, hoods, or other notorious types; or evidence that there are strong ties elsewhere and the nature of those ties.

☐ 9. Employment: any indication that defendant is unemployed; has history of no or brief employment stints, and reasons for this history (insubordination, incompetence, alcoholism); lacks employable skills; if migrant worker, may want to check with previous employers; if defendant is a student, any record of poor attendance or performance, failure to pay fees, or abusive or dishonest behavior toward teachers or fellow students.

☐ 10. History of chemical dependency or mental and emotional instability; previous failure to complete rehabilitation or treatment programs; abuse of medications or tendency not to take medications essential to rational conduct.

☐ 11. Any history of possession or misuse of firearms or other weapons.

☐ 12. Review statutes and rules for any special considerations regarding initial appearances and bail that give the court authority in special circumstances to invoke no bail, high bail, or place special conditions on defendant's release (see list of conditions in Exhibit 11–2).

☐ 13. Record all critical information in the file folder so that any of the office's prosecutors can pick up the file and be prepared to argue on the bail issue at the initial appearance (especially important in urban offices).

☐ 14. Temper any adversarial recommendations to the prosecutor with legitimate ethical concerns for fairness and justice.

☐ 15. If attending hearing, record results of hearing, name of defense counsel, next appearance dates, and other information.

☐ 16. Obtain a copy of any executed bail instrument from court clerk.

☐ 17. Note next appearance date on personal and office calendar system with sufficient lead time dates for adequate preparation.

INITIAL APPEARANCE CHECKLIST: DEFENSE PARALEGAL

☐ 1. Acquire a brief background on defendant through personal interview, from prosecutor's office, cooperating police agencies, family, others; nature of alleged crime; illegal police search or other factors that may show government's case is weak.

☐ 2. Provide defense attorney with an early summary and seek guidance regarding special tactical considerations; for example, is it better to leave defendant in jail for an extra day because judge rotation will give defendant a more favorable judge, or should immediate pressure be employed for appearance because today's judge will be more sympathetic.

❏ 3. Assess whether community sensitivity or politics might play a role in judge's decision, and if so, brainstorm on how to counter or take advantage of such considerations.

❏ 4. Obtain criminal record initially through client but confirm through prosecutor's office, pretrial release officer, or cooperating police agency. Caution: It is best not to rely exclusively on client's information; it will frequently be inaccurate. Look for information on punishment, escape, and so on, but seek an explanation or mitigation for unfavorable information. For example, if there is a record of escape, it may have been induced by homosexual or other abuse by inmates or a concern over serious family emergency; resisting arrest may have been self-defense in response to excessive police force or because of a particular arresting officer's propensity to provoke resistance in arrestees. Gather information to show client has appeared when requested to do so, was model prisoner, never fled when released for work with required return to jail each evening. Note if arrest came as a result of a voluntary surrender, or if client cooperated with police.

❏ 5. Consult with supervising attorney to clear up at the first opportunity any of the client's unpaid traffic fines, outstanding warrants, and other matters that will have a negative impact regarding release.

❏ 6. Check residence history: Is there a pattern of stability in residence (ownership of property) or a rational explanation for frequent change in residence or for being secretive about address; any back-up locations where client can be found frequently, such as at a relative's house, a place of employment, or a cafe; does client have a phone; client's willingness to avoid out-of-jurisdiction and out-of-country travel; and willingness to surrender passport.

❏ 7. Note family and community ties: Is there any evidence of a stable family, stable and desirable friendships, religious affiliation and regular attendance, organizational affiliations, community service projects; local bank accounts and commercial dealings; reputable persons in community that client believes might accept custody responsibilities; if from another state, any evidence of strong ties there that indicate stability and responsibility.

❏ 8. Check employment record: Is there any evidence of regular employment (vouched for by employer), or currently successful educational or vocational training endeavors; consistency and a pattern to work if a migrant worker; employable skills; leads for employment and offers of employment; rational reasons for being unemployed, such as disability, medical problems, other factors; critical and busy time at work—or for family's sake cannot afford to miss work. Because an employer's knowledge of pending criminal charges could lead to the defendant's being fired, it is best to get the defendant's permission to contact the employer.

❏ 9. Note any chemical dependency or mental or emotional illness: any evidence currently seeking treatment, any opportunity to get client into treatment program; evidence dependency is a thing of the past or treatment is showing success; good record of taking medication; strong support groups; and willingness to start or continue treatment, take drug or alcohol tests, stay away from individuals or locations that tend to encourage dependency.

❏ 10. Note any history of possession or misuse of firearms or dangerous weapons.

❏ 11. Note any medical condition or handicaps that cannot be adequately addressed if in jail (a pressing need for medical treatment may cause a judge to favor release rather than having the county pay for medical treatment).

Continued

❑ 12. Prepare client for pretrial release officer's interview and caution client to be honest but not to discuss the crime with the officer or with anyone except for attorney or paralegal.

❑ 13. Check statutes, rules, and cases for any special circumstances that require court to favor release, look to least restrictive alternative, or accommodation of special needs.

❑ 14. Contact family, supportive employer, or anyone else who could be helpful at the initial appearance or bail hearing and arrange for their presence.

❑ 15. See that client is afforded the opportunity to appear neat and clean, business clothes if possible, at the initial appearance.

❑ 16. Consider contacting pretrial release officer and see if release recommendation or evaluation can be tactfully influenced.

❑ 17. Note any inability to afford bail beyond a certain amount.

❑ 18. Prepare list of special conditions for release that may be a last resort to obtain client's freedom (see list of conditions in Exhibit 11–2).

❑ 19. Note all key factors in file so any of office's attorneys can be prepared for hearing.

❑ 20. If requested to, attend hearing, note results, get a copy of the release order, calendar next required appearance, and update file.

❑ 21. If client is not released, facilitate depositing of bail, securing bond with property, and needed preparations for any bail rehearing or interlocutory appeal "see below" of court's decision.

III. PRETRIAL DETENTION

If the defendant is jailed pending trial, issues can arise concerning the conditions of confinement. Prisoners complain to both prosecution and defense attorneys about conditions and procedures. Occasionally, it falls to the paralegal to determine if there is any legal footing for corrective action.

The crux of the matter in these cases is whether the jail conditions or procedures amount to punishment and, thus, violate due process. A person may not be punished until convicted. If the condition or procedure is related to a legitimate governmental purpose, such as security, then it is acceptable under *Bell v. Wolfish* (1979).

Bell specifically upheld restrictions on literature (except that coming directly from the publisher), packages, and contact visits. Likewise, random searches of a cell (*Bell*), strip and body cavity searches after contact visits (*Bell*), and the destruction of legal notebooks and letters in the course of a search [*Hudson v. Palmer* (1984)] have been held not to be punishment. Courts have said that juveniles must be separated from adults, and in most jurisdictions the accused must be separated from the convicted.

IV. INTERVIEWING

A. INTRODUCTION

The next major step in the process is the preliminary hearing. The preliminary hearing requires the state to prove that there is probable cause justifying continued prosecution of the defendant. Both sides must prepare for the hearing.

The prosecution must gather the police reports, talk to the victim, and ensure that enough witnesses are subpoenaed and enough physical evidence is available to prove to the satisfaction of the judge that there is probable cause to believe the defendant committed the alleged crime. The defense also must go into the hearing prepared, and this preparation begins with the interview of the client.

B. INTERVIEWING THE DEFENDANT

1. Preparing the Interview

The initial interview is a critical stage for at least three reasons. First, it will establish the nature of your relationship with the client and the client's relationship to your office. Your goal is to make the client comfortable with the relationship and confident that matters will be handled competently. Second, the interview starts the investigation stage, and that leads to the decisions to accept or reject the case and what the nature of the defense will be. Of course, if the lawyer is a public defender or otherwise appointed, there is no choice about representation. Third, the fee arrangements are frequently established at or as a result of the initial interview. Therefore, careful preparation for this step is essential. Preparation for the interview should include an examination of applicable ethical considerations, a review of information, and the development of an interview checklist or form and a checklist of items to take to the interview.

Before your first interview, good preparation includes sitting in on several interviews with your supervising attorney or another experienced paralegal in the office. Develop a sense of the difference in time and detail required in the interview for a minor offense compared to that for a more serious offense.

a. Examine Ethical Considerations   Be conscious of possible ethical and unauthorized practice of law pitfalls that apply to an interview situation. Paralegals may interview clients and are increasingly doing so, but it should be done only after you have sought clear directions from your supervising attorney. Gathering information rarely, if ever, raises questions about the unauthorized practice of law. It is in response to the client's questions or in providing information to the client that danger arises.

Describing for the client the next court steps (less any evaluation from you as to the outcome of or strategy to be used at those steps) is no problem. Providing information to the client about acceptance of representation, attorney fees, or instructions on what the client should do, such as advice not to talk to the police about the incident in question, constitutes legal advice and should be handled by the attorney directly or through a conduit, such as a preprinted form or information sheet signed by the attorney. When such a form is either inappropriate or unavailable, prior authorization from the attorney to convey specified information provides some protection against unauthorized practice of law accusations when conveyed in a manner similar to this: "Ms. Carter has authorized me to convey that you should not speak to the police or anyone else other than the attorney or me about this incident." Unanticipated questions that cannot be handled safely as described here must be referred to the attorney.

"I get paid for seeing that my clients have every break the law allows. I have knowingly defended a number of guilty men. But the guilty never escape unscathed. My fees are sufficient punishment for anyone.

—F. Lee Bailey, Los Angeles Times, Jan. 9, 1972

b. Review Information on the Case and Relevant Statutes   Newspaper articles and newscasts often provide preliminary information on the incident and likely charges, or charges may already have been filed. If you have that information, go to the relevant criminal statutes and note the statutory wording and the elements that must be proven for each charge. Look up the definitions of key words in the statute and consult case annotations and jury instruction books for judicial interpretation of the statute. This background helps in asking relevant questions and recognizing critical information. Also review materials on interviewing, ethics regarding interviewing, and good listening skills.

c. Locate or Develop a Thorough Interview Form   Most offices have developed a standardized interview form. Some of these address a brief initial interview, others go beyond that and attempt to cover as much useful information as possible. Interview forms are valuable guides that promote efficient use of time and provide reminders of what to cover. Even the most experienced interviewer will forget to gather important information without a good form. A thorough, logically developed form facilitates summarizing the interview and expedites trial preparation. A good form should cover at least the areas of information addressed in this sample defendant interview checklist. Items requiring attorney authorization are marked with a star.

DEFENDANT INTERVIEW CHECKLIST

Introductory Items

❏ *1. Introduce yourself, make your title clear, provide identification, possibly in the form of a letter from the attorney to the client explaining the paralegal's role and the need to be completely open. Find out if the client has any other attorney involved or if someone else is contacting an attorney for the client.

❏   2. Ask client for a brief introduction.

❏   3. Determine if client has any special needs, medical or otherwise, that need attention, especially if in jail.

❏ *4. Note the degree of interview confidentiality available and provide client with attorney's instruction not to talk to police, cell mates, friends, codefendants, and relatives about the charges. Make sure the client understands the significance of this warning.

❏ *5. Explain office's standardized fee arrangements and method of payment, if applicable, and have fee agreement signed.

❏ *6. Explain what client can expect from law office: confidentiality; loyalty to client tempered by exercise of independent judgment, ethical guidelines, and role as officer of the court; and clear explanation of options and importance of each decision client must make.

❏   7. Explain what office requires of client: accuracy, assistance.

❏   8. Review charging document with client.

❏   9. Obtain information about sources for bail.

❏ *10. Explain what client can expect in the way of release and future proceedings.

❏ 11. Assess client's goals for representation: acquittal, avoidance of prison, avoidance or revocation of probation on previous charge, reduced charges, rehabilitation, retention of employment, and others.

Detailed Interview

❏ 12. Obtain client's detailed version of facts regarding the charge(s):
- Who, what, when, where, why, how, with what, with whom.
- All surrounding circumstances, conversations, statements, and events.
- Address each element of offense.
- Client's knowledge of alleged victim, government's evidence, witnesses, items seized, statements made.
- Client's thinking, feeling, and state of knowledge and awareness under the circumstances.

❏ 13. Explore defenses regarding government procedures:
- Circumstances, conversations, times, places, and witnesses to any searches and seizures.
- Arrests, police stops, frisks, booking, lineups, photos, hair samples, or other identification procedures.
- Interrogations, other questions by police or agents, signed statements, rights given, conversation about crime with others, possible wiretaps and surveillance, and possible consent by client or another.

❏ 14. Explore affirmative defenses:
- Constitutional and statutory defenses: statute of limitations; freedom of speech, religion, or other civil rights; immunity; double jeopardy; equal protection.
- Justifications: (perception of threat and how imminent) self-defense, defense of others or property, resisting unlawful arrest or excessive force by police, execution of public duties.
- Excuses: (subjective/objective reasonableness) duress, necessity, entrapment, insanity, involuntary intoxication, automatism, syndromes.

❏ 15. Explore missing element defenses: alibi, physical inabilities, consent or in loco parentis acts; lack of mens rea because of age, diminished capacity (heat of passion), voluntary intoxication, or mistake.

❏ 16. Explore defenses to inchoate crimes: abandonment, impossibility.

❏ 17. Check other relevant considerations: whether client is protecting anyone; any reason for client to be framed; any reason victim or police could have made false or mistaken accusation; mistaken identity; other reasons client could not have committed crime; or any other knowledge that could be helpful.

❏ 18. Collect detailed criminal history: juvenile, adult, arrests, charges, dismissals, convictions, penalties, completion of sentence, institutions, codefendants, escapes, failures to appear, all jurisdictions, aliases, current or outstanding matters, traffic record, parking tickets, victims, previous attorneys, probation or parole, treatment programs. If client had record and facing serious charge, explore reasons for other crimes, mitigating factors, and other matters needed to defeat repeat offender penalties or to reduce penalty at sentencing.

❏ 19. Collect detailed personal history (especially detailed if capital case), including a brief life's chronology, for possible defenses, insight into crime, sentencing, or to reveal need for medical or other professional resources:
- Childhood, parents, siblings, home life growing up, discipline, disruptions, abuse, alcohol, drugs, income, living conditions, criminal activity, foster care, runaways, school, friends, accomplishments, frustrations, anger, and other matters.
- Adult family, married, divorced, children, serious disruptions, abuse, living conditions, relationships.
- Relationships with community, organizations, hobbies, employment history, why left jobs, training, education, confidants, churches, clergy, and other factors.
- Complete medical history, serious injuries, especially head injuries; epilepsy, seizures, other serious adult and childhood illnesses; mental or emotional illness; phobias, chemical dependency or abuse, institutionalizations or treatment, previous psychological workups; and other matters.

❏ 20. Collect military record and history.

❏ 21. Ascertain use or possession of weapons or other items or special skills pertinent to this or other crimes.

❏ 22. Ask for any other matters of importance that client can tell you.

❏ 23. Have client sign release forms for medical, military, employment, education, and other records.

❏ *24. Give final caution to client not to speak to anyone about this or any other crime other than you and your supervising attorney.

*If authorized by your supervising attorney, explain what the government must prove, and make client aware of possible defenses to the charges.

d. Develop a Checklist of Items to Take to the Interview   To make sure you have everything that is needed at the interview site, draft a checklist of necessary items similar to the one that follows.

CHECKLIST OF ITEMS FOR INTERVIEW

❑   1. Interview form or checklist.

❑   2. Identification or letter from attorney for admittance to jail.

❑   3. Interpreter or signer for the deaf or other special assistance (call jail to determine client's special needs).

❑   4. Standardized fee agreement as approved by attorney.

❑   5. Authorizations and releases for client to sign to access medical, military, employment, education, and other records.

❑   6. Office brochures on upcoming procedure, nature of office's representation, importance of not discussing the case with others, and other matters.

---

2.   The Interview: Tips and Considerations

Good preparation is important, and the more interviewing you do the less time preparation will take. As important as preparation is, however, it is critical to see the client as soon as possible. The client needs to be cautioned about making statements or having conversations with police, probation and parole officers, cell mates (who often are or become informants), friends, and even relatives. If applicable, explain that criminal prosecutions can place considerable strain on the client's relationships, and that it is not uncommon for significant others to appear on the prosecution's witness list. Stress that no privilege of confidentiality exists between a significant other and the client, as it does between spouses.

The client needs to know his or her rights. Further, allaying fears makes your client more comfortable and helps to avoid bizarre and irrational behavior that can damage the client's case. If you are not fully prepared, communicate this to the client in a brief meeting; you can always schedule another interview when you are adequately prepared.

Arrange for an office interview in a confidential and uninterrupted setting. If the client is in jail, go to the client with all the needed forms and documents that you have prepared. On entering the jail, be ready to present identification, be searched (possibly with a metal detector), and sign the register. Also be prepared, especially on your first visit, for those steel doors to slam shut behind you. It can be a little unnerving suddenly to realize your liberty is totally dependent on the jailer. Avoid perceiving the police or jailers as adversaries. They are there to assist you and, in general, will be courteous and respectful. They deserve the same treatment. Being relaxed yet professional, with appropriate applications of humor, can work wonders.

In jail, interviews can take place in a small interrogation room, over a phone through Plexiglas, or some other setting. Regardless, you must insist on a confidential setting. If one is not made available, consult your supervising attorney before proceeding.

Whether in your office or in jail, it is best if the supervising attorney is present to start the relationship, make introductions, and explain your role as a paralegal. With that done, the attorney can move on to other business. Many times it is impractical for the attorney to be present.

With experience you will develop ideas to add to the checklist of things to keep in mind during the interview. Review the following checklist on tips for good interviewing techniques.

CHECKLIST ON TIPS FOR BETTER INTERVIEWING

❑ 1. Establish rapport:
  Understand client's apprehensions and feelings: fears of the legal system, embarrassment, loss of job, prison, and costs; distrusts system, attorney, and you; feels alone, shamed, and angry.
  Empathize, use firm handshake and good eye contact, exude warmth and respect but not submission, be honest, be patient, and avoid being judgmental, establish a feeling that this is team effort by client and defense.

❑ 2. If it is clear the client cannot afford your office's services or does not agree to the fee, there is no need to continue unless, of course, you are working for appointed counsel.

❑ 3. Explain the interview process and all the reasons for each part of the interview.

❑ 4. Apply your office's approach to insisting on knowing whether this client actually committed the crime or not. Some attorneys demand knowing this; others do not want clients to tell them if they are guilty or not. Insisting on knowing guilt or innocence may lock the client into a position that cannot be changed later, or it may encourage self-deception. Some clients feel that if they imply they are guilty, the attorney will not be as aggressive in the defense. Explain that the determination of guilt or innocence is left to the court, but that the information the client gives you must be accurate. Here is a good example of what to say:

> *"In order to prepare the best defense for you, we need to be prepared for anything that might happen at your trial. . . .*
> *What we want to do is be thoroughly prepared—that means preparing for the worst. [W]e want everything to be ready. That's why I am going to need you to tell me everything you can. If it will not help your case, we will not use it, but I want to hear it anyway."*[8]

❑ 5. Assessing the client's goals, especially those of a client with a previous record, may give you some insight into what can be realistically achieved. Assess the client's eligibility for and interest in drug court (if available) and related programs.

❑ 6. Be positive but realistic; avoid guarantees of success and the raising of false hopes.

❑ 7. Take notes; avoid letting them become too intrusive.

❑ 8. Give the client assignments such as getting the names of alibi witnesses and gathering relevant documents. Insist on regular progress reports.

❑ 9. Give a list to the client on what is coming next and when you and the attorney will be contacting the client again. Note this date on office calendar and be sure to follow up.

❑ 10. Handle embarrassing or sensitive topics with empathy but directness.

❑ 11. Practice good listening skills:
  ■ Focus on the client's answer, the manner in which it is given, the inflection and tone, rather than on what you are going to say or your next question.
  ■ Endure pauses; let the client think.

Continued

■ It is okay for you to say "I don't know" or "Let me think about that" or "I'll have to ask the attorney about that."

■ Discriminate between fact and opinion, embellishments and understatement, and the relevant and irrelevant.

■ Discover main ideas, concerns, motivations.

■ Probe for sources, credibility, completeness.

■ Avoid evaluative feedback and being judgmental; keep an open atmosphere.

■ Use "uh-huh" and "hmmm," nods and smiles to encourage more talking.

■ Summarize and restate the client's points occasionally to ensure clear communication.

■ Be sensitive and understanding; avoid influencing the direction of responses.

■ Stay alert; use good eye contact; be attentive.

■ Sense and explore feelings.

❑ 12. Maximize your effort to get information from your client by probing for selective perception and expression. People are selective learners who may process information better through sight, sound, or feeling. If through sight, they will respond best when asked what they saw; if through sound, what they heard; and if through touch (kinesthetics), what they felt both physically and emotionally in the experience.[9] (Keep these types of learning in mind when your attorney asks you to help in drafting or evaluating opening and closing statements so you can suggest approaches for the different types of learners among the jury.)

❑ 13. Probe for mental illness or impairment if the client seems out of touch with reality, which may indicate mental illness, emotional problems, retardation, or the effects of or lack of medication. In such circumstances, ask, "Where are you? What did you do yesterday? Today? How do you feel? Are you taking medicine?"[10]

❑ 14. Do not tape record or have the client sign a statement. It may be discoverable by the prosecution.

C.   INTERVIEWING WITNESSES

Many of the tips, techniques, and considerations for defense paralegals apply to prosecution paralegals involved in working with witnesses, whether the police, victims, or third parties. Prosecution paralegals need to keep in mind that the prosecution office has many clients. It represents the general public, the victims, the police, and even victim advocacy groups. The press and its role cannot be ignored either.

In questioning and working with all types of witnesses, you must be sensitive to their perspectives, while understanding that they rarely have much insight into the role of the prosecutor, what makes a good case, the rules of evidence, the exclusionary rule, politics, and other factors. None of these people are going to come to you with an open mind. All want you to adopt their point of view and be a strident, personal advocate.

You should be sympathetic, but not to the point that you jeopardize your independence and objectivity. If necessary, explain this situation to the witness as best you can. The avenging crusader complex is fraught with problems, as is the defense paralegal's pitfall of emotionalizing the defendant's case. You need to resist these powerful seductions in order to ensure the integrity of your work and judgment. Insist on the truth and probe for all the facts, rather than settling for what the interviewee believes important. Seek the source and credibility of information. Retain control over key interviews and be cautious about delegating hearing and trial preparation interviews to other government agencies. For example, unsupervised use of psychologists and social workers in child molestation cases can result in questionable evidence built

"Who lied to me about his case,
And said we'd have an easy race,
And did it all with solemn face?
It was my client."

—Anonymous
Jacob M. Braude, *Lifetime Speaker's Encyclopedia,* 1962

on statements highly influenced and colored by the interviewers and their personal biases. Innocent lives can be destroyed if this process is not carefully controlled.

D. ETHICAL CONSIDERATIONS

You must refrain from the temptation to lead and influence the client or the witness. To do otherwise ensures altered memories at best and perjury at worst. The other side almost always questions the witness about such influence. Even if your influence was not intended to alter the truth, it undermines your case and raises questions about your integrity. In regard to working with a client or other witness, it is said that polishing is ethical but sandpapering is not. When one works with the subtleties of communication, the line between polishing and sandpapering is fine.

A prosecution paralegal may be asked to work with a defendant or participate in the process of determining whether the defendant will be a good informant and witness against a codefendant, in an effort to net bigger fish. In such circumstances and when the defendant has a lawyer, this process must be carried on in close consultation with the defense attorney. Contacting the defendant without the knowledge of the defense attorney is unethical.

E. DEALING WITH THE DIFFICULT CLIENT

You will have difficult clients and witnesses. Be ready for the common difficult types.

The abusive person rants, raves, gives orders, demeans, and usually has a volatile temper. Allowing those persons to vent their anger and express their emotions works best. When confronted by such a person, realize this is not personal and keep calm. Let them vent for a brief period of time, suggest that an appointment at another time would be better to discuss the matter, firmly excuse yourself and vacate the office to provide a cooling off period, or arrange to have a co-worker telephone you to interrupt the conversation. If the person will not calm down or gets worse, you may have no choice but to call for assistance of co-workers or the police. Often, a brief phone call made to a client prior to the initial interview can relieve some of the anxiety that leads to rude or abusive behavior and may allow you to better anticipate the types of behavior with which you will have to deal. Ask an irate telephone caller to calm down or suffer being disconnected.[11]

Deal with the compulsive drop-in and telephone caller by keeping the person focused in the first conversation. In subsequent contacts, ascertain whether there is truly a new problem or whether the goal is simply to pass the time of day by retelling their story. Identify the immediate problem, what they want to do about it, any reasonable alternatives that they can be responsible for, summarize, and terminate the conversation.[12] Some counselors end these conversations by noting that a preestablished time limit has expired or by getting up and going to the office door to usher the client out.

Some clients may be the seductive type. They have low self-esteem, appear vulnerable, and "cry out" to be cared for or nurtured. This nearly absolute dependency on the professional person feeds the counselor's or paralegal's ego and, if not guarded against, can lead to emotional and sexual attraction. Occasionally, we read newspaper reports of the attorney (and maybe the paralegal) who helps a client escape with plans to join them on Grand Cayman Island or less exotic locations. Some clients read people very well and are experienced manipulators. Once the seductive or manipulative client realizes that you are going to keep an objective and firm professionalism, they usually are discouraged easily and turn their attentions to the next victim.

Some clients are sexually aggressive. This may be because of low self-esteem and the need for positive reenforcement. Any advances need to be met with firm resolve. Office policy that prohibits dating between professional and client avoids numerous problems.[13]

Then there is the client who tempts you with gifts (often contraband), a bribe, or appealing chemical substances. Most professionals resist these inducements with ease. Given the right circumstances, such as undue stress, personal financial problems, or chemical dependency, even a person of previously strong character and considerable experience can succumb to temptation. You must anticipate that such things will happen and have firm lines drawn in your mind that you will not cross.

Frequently, the line between compassionate, professional advocacy and emotional, personal attachment becomes blurred. When this happens, seek the assistance of your supervising attorney or other people whose judgment you trust. Do this even more readily at times of particular personal vulnerability. Keep in mind that the difficult client is just as much the one who makes you feel omnipotent as the one who makes you feel inadequate.

 ANALYSIS PROBLEM

11–1. Plan your strategy for dealing with these possible situations with clients from the cases in Chapter 1.

1. Eldon Spiers seems very eager to please you. His answers to your questions vary according to what he seems to think you want to hear, and his language is childlike. He often reaches over to pat you on the arm or shoulder.

2. Carmen Cordoba calls you twice a week to ask about progress in the prosecution of Miguel Cordoba and to remind you that the ring she claims he stole is worth $10,000.

3. Max Legrise never sits down in your office; he paces constantly, occasionally hammering your desk with his fist. With a steely glare, he warns you not to make mistakes with his case or, "You and your family will regret it."

4. Billy McIntire leaves your office after asking you to hide evidence of drug possession in his home. You find that he has left a small packet of marijuana on your desk with "thanks" written across the top.

5. Mason Trew sits sullenly across from you in your office. He "knows" that the government will not prosecute his case aggressively, "because the whole community is homophobic," and refuses to cooperate.

F. INTERVIEW SUMMARIES

Once key interviews are completed, draft a summary of the information. Place the interview notes and summary into the file and ask if your supervising attorney would like a copy of the summary. A close rein on such copies is essential, for they have a way of turning up in the opposition's case file, which can lead to disaster.

V. OTHER PRELIMINARY INVESTIGATION AND PREPARATION

A. THE DEFENSE

With the approach of the preliminary hearing, the defense team needs to gather enough information to reveal initial weaknesses in the prosecution's case and to formulate a possible theory of defense. This information helps you draft questions and suggests evidence to note at the hearing. Obtain and review the charging document and any warrants and supporting affidavits. Normally, copies of warrants can be obtained from the court clerk.

The limited time before the hearing often restricts preparation to the client interview, a trip to the scene of the crime, and interviews with one or more key witnesses. Any investigation, however, should be done only with the approval of your supervisor.

A trip to the scene of the crime as early in the case as feasible is important. It is best if both you and the attorney can go. Take a camera to record various angles of the scene; video cameras are a nice plus, if available. Tape measures, graph paper for diagramming, and other materials pertinent to the type of case and location should be used. If you know the locations of witnesses at the scene, test and photograph the scene from their viewpoints to confirm witness reliability. Try to go to the scene at the time of day and day of the week the alleged crime occurred. Occasionally lighting, traffic noise, and other factors can affect the credibility of evidence presented in a case.

Efficiency can be gained by doing some screening of potential witnesses by phone. It is not necessary to conduct an interview if they do not have useful information. When you visit a witness for an interview, ideally, you should take a neutral party with you to avoid accusations of attempted bribery, threats, or other misconduct. Audiotaping or videotaping an interview can be useful, but should not be done if the prosecution's access to such can hurt the defendant. Your objectives should be clear. Many reluctant witnesses will talk when honestly faced with being subpoenaed as an alternative. Use the same techniques and cautions outlined in the section on interviewing and working with clients.

Interviewing witnesses can be a tricky business. Entire courses are taught on interviewing and investigation, and these topics are frequently covered at some length in civil litigation courses. A more detailed discussion of these subjects is beyond the scope of this text.

Your supervising attorney may ask you for suggestions on whether the defense should subpoena any witnesses for the hearing. The defense can use its right under Federal Rule of Criminal Procedure 5.1 and similar state rules to present witnesses and evidence at the preliminary hearing. Because the prosecution will limit its witnesses to as few as necessary to prove probable cause, there may be other police officers and witnesses who should be questioned. A subpoena duces tecum may be necessary to make sure that documents, photos, and other evidence are presented at the hearing, if they might not be presented otherwise. The defense needs to hear as much of the evidence as possible that is ultimately to be used against the defendant at trial.

B. THE PROSECUTION

If you are a prosecution paralegal, it will be your task to organize the proof to be presented at the preliminary hearing. Police reports need to be reviewed. The victim or a key witness may need to be interviewed. Any information suggesting the existence of a defense or that the defendant is not the right suspect should be pursued. After all, if the case has gaping holes or has been improperly brought against the defendant, this is the best time to find that out and save everyone a lot of trouble, time, and money. Note the available physical evidence, such as a weapon, seized contraband, photos of the scene, a fingerprint match, or other items.

Screen this information, summarize it, and check with your supervising attorney to verify what evidence or testimony will be needed at the hearing. Keep in mind that good prosecution tactics call for producing only enough evidence to show probable cause, while not revealing any more than is necessary at this stage.

The police need to be informed of the time of the hearing and what evidence they should bring. You can also remind them to review their reports. The key witnesses should be subpoenaed. Witnesses friendly to the prosecution and the victim should also be subpoenaed to reduce the risk of embarrassing no-shows. The subpoenas can be mentioned in court should the witness or the victim want to appear as neutral in the case as possible. The appearance of neutrality may be desirable if the witness or victim is a friend or relative of the defendant.

The victim should be informed about the hearing and what to expect. Some in-office preparation of the victim may be needed with the attorney if the case is highly significant and the victim's testimony will be subject to intense cross-examination at trial.

C. PREPARING QUESTIONS FOR THE PRELIMINARY HEARING

Enlightened supervising attorneys have learned that good paralegals do a thorough job of proposing and drafting useful questions for both direct questioning and cross-examination. If your supervising attorney is one of the enlightened, you have an interesting task ahead of you. If not, try to convince your supervisor that you can be of real assistance here. You might also try your hand at drafting some questions, then submit them to convince your supervisor of your ability to do the job.

If you are drafting questions for the prosecutor, keep these tips in mind.

1. The prosecution's burden of proof is probable cause or reasonable grounds to believe the crime has been committed and that the defendant committed the crime, a more stringent burden than that required for an arrest. It is considerably less of a burden, however, than the proof beyond a reasonable doubt required for conviction at trial.

2. Evidentiary standards are more lenient at the preliminary hearing than at trial. Evidence that might be suppressed later and hearsay evidence may be admitted.

3. Questions must elicit evidence in support of each element of the alleged crime.

4. Questions to witnesses must be direct ("What did you see?") and not leading ("You saw the knife, didn't you?"). A leading question suggests the answer.

5. The question should elicit enough evidence to meet the prosecution burden of proof, but no more. There is no need to assist the defense at this stage of the process by showing all of your cards.

If you are drafting questions for the defense, keep the following tips in mind.

1. Neither federal nor state rules permit the defense to use the preliminary hearing for unlimited discovery. In other words, the defense may not use the hearing to go on a fishing expedition by asking every conceivable question that might reveal information helpful to the defendant. Just how much the defendant may use the preliminary hearing for finding out about the prosecution's case varies. The trend seems to be to confine the hearing strictly to a determination of the burden of proof. Some state rules specifically prohibit the use of the hearing for discovery. The federal rules have been interpreted both ways, but do not specifically rule out such use. Some discovery related to exploring the prosecution's case as presented is probably permissible.

2. Your questions will be used to cross-examine the government's witnesses. The goal is to test for truth and accuracy. Because the prosecution witnesses are presumed by law to be adverse to the defense, leading questions are permitted.

3. Your questions should test the source and basis for each piece of evidence presented. Attempt to bring out evidence favorable to the client that might raise judicial doubt about probable cause, or at least reveal areas to be pursued in discovery or at trial.

4. The questions should attempt to reveal possible police misconduct, such as an illegal arrest or search, if the judge will permit such questions.

Sometimes you can draft questions that have a dual purpose—to get at the source of the evidence while also revealing police misconduct or other evidence favorable to the client.

5.   The questions should explore possible theories of defense, but not so blatantly as to tip the hand of the defense.

6.   Questions should be designed to lock the witness into a position that is favorable to the client and that, if changed, can be used at trial to show inconsistencies and inaccuracies that throw doubt on the reliability of the witness's testimony. An example of such questioning is, "Officer Johnson, the defendant made no other statements to you or anyone else in your presence, is that correct? You are unaware of any other statements made by the defendant?"

When you draft questions for hearings, review the charge and the evidence likely to be presented on each element. Make sure you thoroughly understand the definitions of each key term in the statute. Then use a tape recorder and a brainstorming process to generate every conceivable question. Have these questions entered into a computer and eliminate those you do not want. This method of generating questions has proven to be effective for most types of hearings, depositions, and trials. A prosecution paralegal must recheck the final list of questions to be sure that enough evidence will be elicited on each element of the crime.

VI.   THE PRELIMINARY HEARING

The preliminary hearing is an early step in the criminal litigation process that permits the continuation of the charge against the defendant only if the judge (or federal magistrate judge) finds that the prosecution has presented evidence showing probable cause to believe that a crime was committed and that the defendant committed the crime. It is a judicial test to provide assurance that a criminal charge is founded in reliable evidence of probable guilt. Although frequently given short shrift by the media and rarely understood by the general public, the stage is an important one demonstrating a commitment to the sensitive balance between convicting criminals and protecting personal liberty.

A preliminary hearing is not constitutionally mandated [*Lem Woon v. Oregon* (1913)]. Nearly all jurisdictions, however, require a preliminary hearing in felony cases. An exception exists in the federal system and some states if the defendant has already been indicted by a grand jury on the charge. The preliminary hearing date is set at the initial appearance. Federal Rule of Criminal Procedure 5 and similar state rules require that the preliminary hearing be held within ten days of the initial appearance if the defendant is in jail and within twenty days if not. These time limits are extended only if the defendant agrees to the extension or the state demonstrates an extraordinary reason for the delay.

The hearing is held in court before a judge or magistrate judge, and it is adversarial in nature. The prosecution presents only the witnesses necessary to meet the burden of proof. The defendant has the right to an attorney [*Coleman v. Alabama* (1970)], the right to cross-examine the prosecution's witnesses, and the right to testify and present witnesses. Normally, the defense does not present any evidence or witnesses, but may do so in those rare instances where assertion of key facts such as evidence supporting affirmative defenses is likely to lead to a permanent dismissal of the charge.

If you are asked to attend the preliminary hearing, you can head off possible misunderstanding and discontent among those in attendance. If you work for the prosecution, explain to the victim the purpose of the hearing, and why the prosecutor will not be putting in all available evidence and calling all available witnesses. If you work for the defense, explain to the client and possibly close friends or family in attendance

"[A] Judge who is both stupid and industrious is without question an unqualified disaster."

—Dana Porter, Canadian jurist; chief justice, Province of Ontario" What Once the Fleeting Hour Has Brought," 33 *New York State Bar Journal* 4 (Aug. 1961)

why the defense attorney may be calling witnesses and eliciting evidence that seems harmful to the defendant, and why the attorney is not objecting more at the hearing. Otherwise, your role is to take notes on the evidence presented, whether the court finds probable cause, and on what charge. Afterward, key testimony from the hearing needs to be highlighted and summarized. You may be asked to draft a request for a copy of the hearing tape or transcript, and to summarize it for your supervising attorney.

If the court finds that probable cause exists, the case is transferred to a district judge for trial in the federal system or the designated trial court in the state system. This process is called **binding over** when a case is transferred to the next court for the succeeding stage in the process. In some jurisdictions, a defendant is bound over to the grand jury. In others, an information is drafted by the prosecution office and presented to the defendant at the next step, which is the arraignment.

If the evidence is found to be inadequate, the judge can dismiss the case and discharge the defendant. No jeopardy attaches at this stage, so charges may be brought again if new evidence warrants it. If the government intends to recharge, most jurisdictions permit the holding of the defendant for a reasonable period of time, in some cases up to seventy-two hours. If no charges are brought by the time the statutory limit expires, the defendant is freed. Bail is often reconsidered at the conclusion of the preliminary hearing and the attorneys on either side need to be prepared for further argument on that point.

bind over:
the process of transferring a case to the next court for the succeeding stage in the process.

VII. EXTRADITION

Article Four, Section Two, of the Constitution provides for a fugitive from justice from one state to be arrested in another state and be returned to the original state for trial. This process is called **extradition** and is governed by 18 U.S.C.A. § 3182. Most states have adopted the Uniform Extradition Law, which defines the procedure. Generally, the governor of the original state signs a requisition warrant that verifies the pending charge, identifies the fugitive, and requests that the fugitive be arrested and delivered to the agents of the original state. The governor of the asylum state provides notice of the fugitive's detention. Officers from the original state then must pick up the fugitive within thirty days of the arrest.

extradition:
the process that provides for a fugitive from justice from one state to be arrested in another state and be returned to the original state for trial.

The government must prove, and the defendant can challenge, only four issues in an extradition proceeding: (1) whether the extradition documents have been properly prepared and executed, (2) whether the defendant has been charged with a crime in the demanding state, (3) whether the defendant is the person named in the documents, and (4) whether the defendant is a fugitive from the demanding state [*Michigan v. Doran* (1978)]. Even if the asylum state's court finds that the person has been treated unfairly in the demanding state and will be subject to discrimination, the asylum state court cannot refuse to return the fugitive. The Supreme Court ruled that these issues cannot be addressed by the asylum state [*New Mexico v. Reed* (1998)]. The fugitive must be returned.

Provisions are also provided for extradition from territories and foreign countries that have signed extradition treaties with the United States. Extradition is usually sought only in serious cases. Extradition may be the sole reason the defendant has been arrested; however, the issue of extradition often arises in the context of a prosecution of the defendant on charges in the asylum state.

VIII. CONCLUSION

Although overshadowed at times by popular emphasis on the trial, the pretrial stage is often where cases are won or lost. Prosecutors have the duty to bring criminal charges but must be cautious to avoid defense challenges of double jeopardy, improper joinder, and other grounds for dismissal.

Preparation must be made for the initial appearance, including investigation into the defendant's background to find reasons why he or she should be jailed or freed until trial. Forms should be gathered and checklists created to guide you through each task. Interviewing skills need to be developed, as well as methods for dealing with difficult clients. At the initial appearance, the judge determines if the charge is founded, whether the defendant should be released, and bail.

The next stage is the preliminary hearing, where the government must prove probable cause to retain the defendant. You can play a vital role in preparing questions for witnesses and evidence for presentation. Fugitives can be brought back for trial from other states by extradition.

EXHIBIT 11–1
Uniform Bail Schedule

OFFENSE, PENALTY AND BAIL SCHEDULE
(MISDEMEANORS)

SECTION	FINE Min.	FINE Max.	JAIL Min.	JAIL Max.	Other	BAIL Percentum Deposit	BAIL Bail Bond
506.010. Criminal Attempt.		$500		12 Mos.	Section 4(c)	$200	$2000
		$250		90 Days	Section 4(d)	$100	$1000
506.030. Criminal Solicitation.		$500		12 Mos.	Section 2(c)	$200	$2000
		$250		90 Days	Section 2(d)	$100	$1000
506.040. Criminal Conspiracy.		$500		12 Mos.	Section 2(c)	$200	$2000
		$250		90 Days	Section 2(d)	$100	$1000
506.050. Conspiracy—General Provisions.	X	X	X	X	X		
506.060. Criminal Solicitation or Conspiracy—Defense of Renunciation.	X	X	X	X	X		
506.080. Criminal Facilitation.		$500		12 Mos.	Section 2(b)	$200	$2000
		$250		90 Days	Section 2(c)	$100	$1000
508.030. Assault in the third degree.		$500		12 Mos.		$200	$2000
508.040. Assault under extreme emotional disturbance.		$250		90 Days	Section 2(b)	$100	$1000
508.050. Menacing.		$250		90 Days		$100	$1000
508.070. Wanton endangerment in the second degree.		$500		12 Mos.		$200	$2000
508.080. Terroristic threatening.		$500		12 Mos.		$200	$2000
509.070. Custodial Interference.		$500		12 Mos.	Section (3)	$200	$2000
510.090. Sodomy in the fourth degree.		$500		12 Mos.		$200	$2000
510.120. Sexual abuse in the second degree.		$500		12 Mos.		$200	$2000
510.130. Sexual abuse in the third degree.		$250		90 Days		$100	$1000
510.140. Sexual misconduct.		$500		12 Mos.		$200	$2000
510.150. Indecent Exposure.		$250		90 Days		$100	$1000
511.050. Possession of burglar's tools.		$500		12 Mos.		$200	$2000
511.060. Criminal trespass in the first degree.		$500		12 Mos.		$200	$2000
511.070. Criminal trespass in the second degree.		$250		90 Days		$100	$1000
511.080. Criminal trespass in the third degree.		$250				None pay full cash bond.	$50
512.030. Criminal mischief in the second degree.		$500		12 Mos.		$200	$2000
512.040. Criminal mischief in the third degree.		$250		90 Days		$100	$1000

Continued

EXHIBIT 11–1 *(Continued)*
Uniform Bail Schedule

512.050. Criminal use of noxious substance.	$250	90 Days		$100	$1000
512.060. Criminal possession of noxious substance.	$250	90 Days		$100	$1000
512.070. Criminal littering.	$250	90 Days		None pay full cash bond.	$25
512.080. Unlawfully posting advertisements.	$250			$50	$500
514.030. Theft by unlawful taking or disposition.	$500	12 Mos.	Section (2)	$50	$500
514.040. Theft by deception.	$500	12 Mos.	Section (5)	$100	$1000
514.050. Theft of property.	$500	12 Mos.	Section (2)	$100	$1000
514.060. Theft of services.	$500	12 Mos.	Section (3)	$100	$1000
514.070. Theft by failure to make required disposition of property.	$500	12 Mos.	Section (4)	$100	$1000
514.080. Theft by extortion.	$500	12 Mos.	Section (3)	$100	$1000
514.090. Theft of labor.	$500	12 Mos.	Section (3)	$100	$1000
514.100. Unauthorized use of vehicles.	$500	12 Mos.		$200	$2000
514.110. Receiving stolen property.	$500	12 Mos.	Section (3)	$200	$2000
514.120. Obscuring the identity of a machine.	$500	12 Mos.		$200	$2000
516.040. Forgery in the third degree.	$500	12 Mos.		$200	$2000
516.070. Criminal possession of forged instrument in the third degree.	$500	12 Mos.		$200	$2000
516.110. Criminal simulation.	$500	12 Mos.		$200	$2000
516.130. Using slugs in the second degree.	$250	90 Days		$100	$1000
517.020. Deceptive business practices.	$500	12 Mos.		$200	$2000
517.030. False advertising.	$500	12 Mos.		$200	$2000
517.040. Bait advertising.	$500	12 Mos.		$200	$2000
517.050. Falsifying business records.	$500	12 Mos.		$200	$2000
517.060. Defrauding secured creditors.	$500	12 Mos.		$200	$2000
517.070. Defrauding judgment creditors.	$500	12 Mos.		$200	$2000
517.080. Fraud in insolvency.	$500	12 Mos.		$200	$2000
517.090. Issuing false financial statement.	$500	12 Mos.		$200	$2000
517.110. Misapplication of entrusted property.	$500	12 Mos.		$200	$2000
518.020. Commercial bribery.	$500	12 Mos.		$200	$2000
518.030. Receiving commercial bribe.	$500	12 Mos.		$200	$2000
518.060. Tampering with or rigging sports contest.	$500	12 Mos.		$200	$2000
518.070. Ticket scalping.	$250			None pay full cash bond.	$50
519.020. Obstructing governmental operations.	$500	12 Mos.		$200	$2000
519.030. Compounding a crime.	$500	12 Mos.		$200	$2000
519.040. Falsely reporting an incident.	$500	12 Mos.		$200	$2000
519.050. Impersonating a public servant.	$500	12 Mos.		$200	$2000
519.060. Tampering with public records.	$500	12 Mos.		$200	$2000
520.040. Escape in the third degree.	$250	90 Days		$100	$1000
520.060. Promoting contraband in the second degree.	$500	12 Mos.		$200	$2000
520.080. Bail jumping in the second degree.	$500	12 Mos.		$200	$2000

EXHIBIT 11–1 *(Concluded)*
Uniform Bail Schedule

520.090. Resisting arrest.	$500		12 Mos.		$200	$2000
520.100. Resisting order to stop motor vehicle.	$500		12 Mos.		$200	$2000
520.130. Hindering prosecution or apprehension in the second degree.	$500		12 Mos.		$200	$2000
521.030. Soliciting unlawful compensation.	$250		90 Days		$100	$1000
521.040. Receiving unlawful compensation.	$500		12 Mos.		$200	$2000
522.020. Official misconduct in the first degree.	$500		12 Mos.		$200	$2000
522.030. Official misconduct in the second degree.	$250		90 Days		$100	$1000
523.030. Perjury in the second degree.	$500		12 Mos.		$200	$2000
523.040. False swearing.	$250		90 Days		$100	$1000
524.050. Tampering with a witness.	$500		12 Mos.		$200	$2000
524.090. Jury tampering.	$500		12 Mos.		$200	$2000
524.110. Simulating legal process.	$250		90 Days		$100	$1000
525.030. Riot in the second degree.	$500		12 Mos.		$200	$2000
525.040. Inciting to riot.	$500		12 Mos.		$200	$2000
525.050. Unlawful assembly.	$250		90 Days		$100	$1000
525.060. Disorderly conduct.	$250		90 Days		$100	$1000
525.070. Harassment.	$250				$30	$30
525.080. Harassing communications.	$250		90 Days		$100	$1000
525.090. Loitering.	$250				None pay full cash bond.	$50
525.100. Public intoxication.	$250		90 Days		$30	$300
525.110. Desecration of venerated objects.	$500		12 Mos.		$200	$2000
525.120. Abuse of corpse.	$500		12 Mos.		$200	$2000
525.130. Cruelty to animals.	$500		12 Mos.		$200	$2000
525.140. Obstructing a highway or other public passage.	$250		90 Days		$100	$1000
525.150. Disrupting meetings or processions.	$250		90 Days		$100	$1000
526.040. Possession of eavesdropping device.	$500		12 Mos.		$200	$2000
526.050. Tampering with private communications.	$500		12 Mos.		$200	$2000
526.060. Divulging illegally obtained information.	$500		12 Mos.		$200	$2000
527.020. Carrying a concealed deadly weapon.	$500		12 Mos.	See Section (4)	$200	$2000
527.030. Defacing a firearm.	$500		12 Mos.		$200	$2000
527.050. Possession of defaced firearm.	$500		12 Mos.		$200	$2000
528.030. Promoting gambling in the second degree.	$500		12 Mos.		$200	$2000
528.060. Possession of gambling records in the second degree.	$500		12 Mos.		$200	$2000
528.070. Permitting gambling.	$250		90 Days		$100	$1000
528.080. Possession of gambling device.	$500		12 Mos.		$200	$2000
529.020. Prostitution.	$250		90 Days		$100	$1000
529.050. Promoting prostitution in the third degree.	$500		12 Mos.		$200	$2000
529.070. Permitting prostitution.	$250		90 Days		$100	$1000
530.030. Concealing birth of infant.	$500		12 Mos.		$200	$2000
530.050. Non-support.	$500		12 Mos.		$100	$1000
530.060. Endangering welfare of minor.	$500		12 Mos.		$100	$1000
530.070. Unlawful transaction with minor.	$500		12 Mos.		$100	$1000
531.020. Distribution of obscene matter.	$500 $250		12 Mos. 90 Days	See Section (2)	$200 $100	$2000 $1000
531.030. Distribution of obscene matter to minors.	$500		12 Mos.	See Section (2)	$200	$2000
531.040. Using minors to distribute obscene material.	$500		12 Mos.	See Section (2)	$200	$2000
531.050. Advertising obscene material.	$250		90 Days		$100	$1000
531.060. Promoting sale of obscenity.	$500 $250		12 Mos. 90 Days	See Section (2)	$200 $100	$2000 $1000

EXHIBIT 11–2
U.S. District Court Release Order

EDKY FORM 241 ⊕

United States District Court
EASTERN DISTRICT OF KENTUCKY

_____

CRIMINAL NO. _____

MAGISTRATE NO. _____

UNITED STATES OF AMERICA   PLAINTIFF

VS.   **RELEASE ORDER**

_____   DEFENDANT

* * * * *

IT IS ORDERED that the release of the above-named defendant is subject to the following conditions:

(1) The defendant shall not commit any offense in violation of Federal, State, or Local Law while on release in this case and shall notify the United States Probation Office of any arrest or other contact with law enforcement officers.

(2) The defendant shall reside at his/her current address and shall notify the United States Probation Office prior to any and all changes in place of residence.

(3) Unless otherwise set forth herein, the defendant shall not leave the boundaries of the Eastern District of Kentucky unless and until ordered by the Court.

(4) The defendant shall appear at all proceedings as required and shall surrender for service of any sentence imposed as directed by the Court.

(5) The defendant shall next appear before _____ ,
                                                                          (name)

United States District Judge/Magistrate at _____ ,
                                                                                   (city)

_____ at _____ o'clock on _____ ,
          (state)   _(time)_   _(date)_

unless otherwise ordered by the Court.

PART I — Release on Unsecured Bond

It is hereby ORDERED that the above named defendant be released, provided: _(check one)_

Personal   ( )   The defendant promises to appear at all scheduled hearings as required.
Recognizance

Unsecured   ( )   The defendant will execute an unsecured appearance bond binding the defendant to the
Bond   United States the sum of $_____ in the event of a failure to appear as
                                          required or to surrender as directed for service of any sentence imposed.

— — — — — OR — — — — —

PART II — Release on Conditions

Upon finding that release by one of the above methods will not by itself reasonably assure the appearance of the defendant as required and/or the safety of any other person and the community,

IT IS HEREBY FURTHER ORDERED that the defendant be released on the condition checked below:

— — — — — BOND — — — — —

Unsecured   ( )   (1) The defendant will execute an Appearance Bond in the amount of $_____
Bond   binding himself to pay the United States such amount in the event that he fails to appear as
                                          required or to surrender as directed for service of any sentence imposed.

EXHIBIT 11–2 *(Continued)*
U.S. District Court Release Order

Surety or Cash Bond	( )	(2) The defendant will execute an Appearance Bond in the amount of $ _____ with good and sufficient surety and post with the Court such indicia of ownership of the property as required by the Court or by deposit of an equal amount of cash or other security in lieu thereof.
Percent Bond	( )	(3) The defendant will execute an Appearance Bond in the amount of $ _____ binding himself to pay the United States such amount in the event that he fails to appear as required or to surrender as directed for service of any sentence imposed, *and* will deposit with the registry of the Court the sum of $ _____ in cash representing _____ percent of the amount of said bond.

— — — — — SUPERVISED RELEASE — — — — —

Supervised Release	( )	(4) The defendant's release shall be supervised by the United States Probation Office and shall include the following conditions as checked:
Report to Probation	( )	(a) The defendant will report to the United States Probation Office in _____ *(city,* _____ *state)* on a _____ *(daily, weekly, monthly)* basis as directed by such probation office.
Remain Employed	( )	(b) The defendant remain gainfully employed in his/her current position and notify the United States Probation Office within twenty-four (24) hours of any change in employment status.
Seek Employment	( )	(c) The defendant is to actively seek gainful employment and advise the United States Probation Office as directed by them as to such efforts.
Remain in School	( )	(d) The defendant is to remain enrolled in his/her current educational institution and advise the United States Probation Office within twenty-four (24) hours of any change in his/her enrollment status.
Reside at Halfway House	( )	(e) The defendant will reside at _____ *(halfway house)* located at _____ *(street, city, state)* during the pendency of the proceedings herein and is to comply with the Rules and Regulations of the facility including curfew established by the facility or as established by the United States Probation Office.
Drug/Alcohol Testing	( )	(f) The defendant will submit to periodic drug and/or alcohol testing as required by United States Probation Office.
Third Party Custody	( )	(5) The defendant is placed in the custody of: (Name of person or Organization) _____ (Address) _____ (City and State) _____ (Telephone Number) _____ who agrees: (a) to supervise the defendant in accordance with the conditions checked herein, (b) to use every effort to assure the appearance of the defendant at all scheduled hearings before the United States Magistrate or Court, and (c) to notify the Magistrate or Court immediately in the event the defendant violates any condition of release or disappears.

Signed _____
(Custodian)

— — — — — TRAVEL — — — — —

Travel Otherwise	( )	(6) The defendant is restricted to traveling within _____ unless or until otherwise ordered by the Court
Supervised Travel	( )	(7) The defendant is restricted to traveling within _____ and shall notify the United States Probation Office prior to departure from and upon return to the district of his/her residence.
Surrender Passport	( )	(8) The defendant shall surrender his/her passport to the Clerk of the Court prior to release or within _____ hours after his/her release on the conditions herein set forth.

Continued

EXHIBIT 11–2 *(Concluded)*
U.S. District Court Release Order

— — — — — **MISCELLANEOUS** — — — — —

Avoid Alcohol   (   )   (9)   The defendant will refrain from the excessive use of alcohol, or any use of a narcotic
or Drugs   drug or other controlled substance, as defined in Section 102 of the Controlled Substances Act
(21, U.S.C., §802), without a prescription by a licensed medical practitioner.

Avoid Weapons   (   )   (10) The defendant will refrain from possessing a firearm, destructive device or any
other dangerous weapon.

Not Associate   (   )   (11) The defendant will not associate with or have any contact with any person known
With Felons   by him/her to be a convicted felon, unless such person shall be a relative by blood or marriage
living in the defendant's household.

Avoid Contact   (   )   (12) The defendant will avoid any and all contact, in person, by mail, by phone or other-
With Persons   wise, either directly or indirectly through any other person, except by his/her attorney or an
authorized representative of his/her attorney, or as otherwise ordered by the Court, with the
following persons: _____

_____

Report For   (   )   (13) The defendant will report within twenty-four (24) hours to the _____
Treatment   _____ at _____
                (institution)   *(city, state)*
for (medical) (drug dependency) (alcohol dependency) [select appropriate problem] treatment
and remain in said facility if required by the treating physician and/or report to said facility as
ordered by his/her treating physician.

Part-Time   (   )   (14) The defendant will be released from _____ .m. to _____ .m. on
Release   _____ on condition that he/she return to custody at
                  (specify days of week)
such place of confinement as the United States Marshal designates.

Other Conditions   (   )   (15) The defendant will comply with each of the following conditions: _____

_____

_____

_____

_____

PART III — FURTHER ORDERS

IT IS FURTHER ORDERED as follows:

Prior to the defendant's release, he/she shall be provided with a copy of this Order and shall execute and file the Form
captioned "Bail Reform Act of 1984 — Mandatory Advice to Defendants"

(   ) The defendant may be released after processing.

(   ) The United States Marshal is ordered to keep the defendant in custody until notified by the Clerk of Judicial
Office that the defendant has posted bond and/or complied with all other conditions for release, including any necessary
processing. The defendant shall be produced before the appropriate Judicial Officer at the time and place specified herein, if
still in custody.

On this the _____ day of _____ , 20 _____ .

_____
UNITED STATES DISTRICT JUDGE/MAGISTRATE

Distribution: U.S. Attorney
                Defendant
                Probation
                U.S. Marshal

EXHIBIT 11–3
Pretrial Services Interview Form

AOC-PT-21
Rev. 2-92   AKA: _____   Social Security Number: _____

NAME:_____   **DOB:**___/___/___ Age:____ Sex:____ Race:____
　　　　Last　　　First　　　Middle/Maiden

　　　　DATE OF ARREST: _____   **CHARGE:** _____
　　　　COURT: _____   _____
VERIFIED **COURT DATE:** _____   _____
Yes No

PRESENT ADDRESS: _____
　　　　　　　　Street/Apt. No.　　　　City　　　　State　　　Zip Code

LENGTH OF RESIDENCE: Present: Yrs.____Mos.____Area: Yrs.____Mos.____Phone: (   ) _____
　　　　　　　　□ Own □ Rent □ Other _____
ALTERNATE/PRIOR
RESIDENCE: _____
　　　　　　　Street/Apt. No.　　　　　City　　　　State　　　Zip Code
　　With Whom: _____ Phone: (   ) _____ Lgth. of Res.: Yrs. ____ Mos. ____

LIVES WITH: □ Alone□ Spouse□ Parents□ Grandparents□ Children□ Brother/Sister□ Other Relatives□ Other_____
MARITAL STATUS: □ Single □ Married □ Divorced □ Widowed □ Common Law □ Separated No. of Children: _____
SPOUSE'S　　　　　　　　　　**SPOUSE'S SOURCE**
NAME:　　　　　　　　　　　**OF INCOME:** _____
FAMILY IN AREA: Name: _____ Relationship: _____
　　　　　　Address: _____ Phone: (   ) _____

□ **EMPLOYED** □ **UNEMPLOYED** How Long Yrs. _____ Mos. _____
□ Full-time □Part-time □ Seasonal □ Welfare □ Unemployment □ Disability □ Retirement □ Other _____
EMPLOYER: _____ Job Position: _____
EMPLOYER'S ADDRESS: _____
　　　　　　　　　　Street　　　　City　　　State　　　Zip Code
　　Phone: (   ) _____ Can Contact: □ Yes □ No Who: _____
PRIOR/OTHER SOURCE
OF INCOME: Source: _____ Job Position: _____
　　　　　Address: _____
　　　　　Phone: (   ) _____ Length of Employment: _____
ATTENDS SCHOOL: □ Yes □ No　　　　　School: _____
　　　　　　　　　　　　　　　　Address _____
　GED or High School Degree: □ Yes □ No　　Can Contact: □ Yes □ No Phone: (   ) _____

PRIOR ARREST: □ Yes □ None If yes, Where: _____
PENDING CHARGES: □ Yes □ No How Released: _____ Next Court Date: _____
　　　　Where: _____ Charges: _____
ON PROBATION/PAROLE: □ Yes □ No　　Probation/Parole Officer's Name: _____
　　　　　　　　　　　　Address: _____
　　　　　　　　　　　　Phone: (   ) _____

DRIVER'S LICENSE NUMBER: _____ □ Kentucky □ None □ Other: _____

IN COURT:　　　Name　　　　Address　　　　Relationship　　　Phone
　　　　1. _____
　　　　2. _____
　　　　3. _____
　　　　4. _____

COMMENTS:

Court Dates: 1. _____	2. _____	3. _____	4. _____

ELIGIBLE INELIGIBLE	COURTS INITIAL DECISION/ JUDGE Date/Time	24 Hour Review: Yes No Courts Decision:	HOW RELEASED:
_____ Points			

Continued

EXHIBIT 11–3 *(Concluded)*
Pretrial Services Interview Form

WARNING

This interview form will be used by the Judge or Trial Commissioner to set bail. It will also be used for personal identification, future bond reviews, service of warrants, and sentencing if found guilty. The Judge may allow your attorney or probation/parole officer to review the information. Except for these situations, any information you provide will be confidential and not released without your written consent or court order. You do not have to say anything, and can stop answering questions at any time. Signing this form means you want to be interviewed.

DECLINED INTERVIEW OR REFUSED TO SIGN AFTER BEING WARNED: _____

S/Defendant

Witnessed By: _____

Date and Time: _____

Witnessed By: _____

Interviewer: _____

Date and Time: _____

Circle only one number for each category of criteria except Miscellaneous and Previous Criminal Record

RESIDENCE

+5   Has been a resident of the commonwealth for more than one year.

+3   Has been a resident of the commonwealth for less than one year but more than three months.

PERSONAL TIES

+4   Lives with spouse, grandparents, children, parents, and/or guardian.

+3   Lives with other relatives.

+2   Lives with non-related roommates.

ECONOMIC TIES   (Double length of employment if part-time)

+5   Has held present job for more than one year OR is a full-time student.

+4   Has held present job for less than one year but more than three months.

+3   Is dependent on spouse, parents, other relatives, or legal guardian, unemployment, disability, retirement, or welfare compensation.

+2   Has held present job for less than three months.

MISCELLANEOUS

+3   Owns property in the Commonwealth

+1   Has a telephone.

+1   Expects someone at arraignment.

PREVIOUS CRIMINAL RECORD (+)

+3   No convictions on record (excluding traffic violations) in last two years.

(A) _____ **TOTAL POSITIVE POINTS**

PREVIOUS CRIMINAL RECORD (-) (FTA must be verified by court records or personal knowledge)

-3   AWOL on record (current military personnel only).

-5   Probated or paroled after felony conviction in last two years.

-5   FTA on traffic citation in last two years.

-10   FTA on misdemeanor charge in last five years.

-15   FTA on felony charge at any time.

-15   Violation Conditional Release while case is pending and active.

(B) _____ **TOTAL NEGATIVE POINTS**

_____ **TOTAL PRETRIAL RELEASE POINTS** ("A" minus "B")

DATE	OFFENSE	COURT	DISPOSITION

SYSTEM FOLDER ASSIGNMENTS

Complete the following and place the documents in your system folder:

- Rule numbers and a brief summary of each rule governing pretrial release and detention in your state, including authorization of pretrial detention (no bail) and under what circumstances.
- Relevant statutes and rules on pretrial services from your state and the federal system.
- Bail schedule, United States District Court release order, and pretrial services interview form.
- List of types of bail.
- Checklists for the initial appearance.
- List of conditions for release.
- Note on methods for obtaining criminal records.
- Summary of each of your state rules regarding the preliminary hearing: requirement, time limit, discovery, bind over, and recharging.
- Revised and adapted interview checklists, including tips on dealing with difficult clients.
- Outline or checklist of tasks in preparation for the preliminary hearing, including tips for drafting questions.

APPLICATION ASSIGNMENT

1. Assume that Case I is going to a preliminary hearing. The prosecution will be calling a man who was on the other side of the bridge and who Kate Lamb thought was going to help her attacker. Also assume that the witness saw the alleged attacker. Draft ten questions on the identification of the attacker to be asked this witness by the prosecutor. Then draft ten questions on the same issue for the defense. Use the brainstorming process to generate fifteen to twenty questions, then select your best ten.

HELPFUL WEB SITES

www.search.org/nibrs/
    National Incident-Based Reporting System of the FBI
www.llrx.com
    Litigators Internet Resource Guide, links to federal, state, and local court rules
www.lawresearch.com/v2/caserulc.htm
    Federal Rules of Criminal Procedure, Federal Court Rules of Evidence, federal and state case law

INTERNET EXERCISES

1. Go to http://records.txdps.state.tx.us. Explore how the criminal data bank works and what a paralegal can find out about criminal records. Research what system for criminal record search is available in your state. Compare the two resources for ease of use, value of information that can be accessed, and safeguards regarding the proper use of the information.
2. Check to see if your state has established a Web site on sex offenders. What information is available there? Do you think making this information available is a good thing? Explain.

QUESTIONS FOR STUDY AND REVIEW

1. May a prosecutor delay charging for a significant period of time? Explain.
2. Define and give the purpose of the initial appearance. What is the significance of *County of Riverside v. McLaughlin?*
3. What must the judge or magistrate judge do at the initial appearance according to your state rules of procedure?
4. What problems exist for our appointment of counsel system, and what practical solutions would you propose?
5. What is the source of a citizen's protection against excessive bail? What is the rationale for this provision?
6. How has *Salerno* altered the law regarding the denial of bail? What procedures are required? Does your state have preventive detention?
7. Identify and define the various types of bail and describe some common non-financial conditions for release.
8. What is the function of a pretrial release officer? Why is (or is not) this position suited to paralegals?
9. Do your state rules require a review of bail if a defendant is not able to obtain release within a certain period of time?
10. What tactical and other considerations enter into an attorney's decisions on bail? Is there ever a time when the defense would delay getting the defendant into court?
11. Describe the duties of both prosecution and defense paralegals as they relate to bail.
12. How does one obtain a complete criminal record? What are your state and federal databanks involved? Be able to interpret a criminal record.
13. When does pretrial detention violate the law?
14. State three reasons why the client interview is critical.
15. List the steps for preparing a good interview. What should be covered in a good interview?
16. List at least ten tips from the interview tips checklist and explain why they are useful.
17. What concerns, realities, and ethical considerations should govern a prosecution paralegal's conduct in interviewing witnesses, police, victim advocates, possible defendant-informants, and others?
18. List suggestions for dealing with four different types of difficult clients.
19. Define preliminary hearing, explain its purpose, and state the government's burden of proof at such a hearing. What key rules of procedure and evidence govern the preliminary hearing in your state?
20. In some jurisdictions, it is not necessary to provide an accused felon with a preliminary hearing. When and why does this exception occur?
21. What must a prosecution paralegal do in preparation for the preliminary hearing? A defense paralegal?
22. Describe the methodology used to generate and prepare questions for witnesses at the preliminary hearing.
23. What is extradition? Describe the standard procedure used to extradite a person. What are the issues at the hearing?

KEY TERMS LIST

Bind over	National Communication	Supervised release
Extradition	Information Center (NCIC)	Surety or cash bond
Indigent	Percent bond	Unsecured bond
Interlocutory appeal	Personal recognizance	(personal bond)

ENDNOTES

1. *Harper's Index,* HARPER'S MAGAZINE, Aug. 1993, at 9 (Statistics from Institute for Law and Justice, Alexandria, Va.).
2. *Offense, Penalty and Bail Schedule,* KENTUCKY RULES OF COURT 303–06 (1993).
3. Pretrial Services Interview Form, KENTUCKY ADMINISTRATIVE OFFICE OF THE COURTS (1992).
4. John C. Hendricks, *Pretrial Services,* THE ADVOCATE, June 1989, at 40.
5. *Id.*
6. RICHARD T. OAKES, OAKES' CRIMINAL PRACTICE GUIDE 2–33 to 2–34 (Wiley 1991).
7. CHARLES H. WHITEBREAD & CHRISTOPHER SLOBOGIN, CRIMINAL PROCEDURE: AN ANALYSIS OF CASES AND CONCEPTS 695–97 (2d ed. 1986).
8. TRIAL FOR LIFE MANUAL, THE ALABAMA PRISON PROJECT 13.
9. L. Merrill & D. Borisoff, *Effective Listening for Lawyers,* THE CHAMPION, Mar. 1988, at 16.
10. OAKES, *supra* note 6, at 1–14.2 to 1–14.3.
11. TRIAL FOR LIFE MANUAL, *supra* note 8, at 23.
12. J. Wagner, *Maintaining Sanity in the Law Office,* LEGAL ASSISTANT TODAY, May/June 1990, at 20 and 22.
13. *Id* at 22.

PRETRIAL: GRAND JURY TO PRETRIAL CONFERENCE

CHAPTER

12

I. INTRODUCTION

The preliminary hearing has established probable cause to keep the defendant under prosecution. Now you are ready to assist in preparing the case for the significant steps that remain before trial. Your team will guide the case through the processes of grand jury, arraignment, and pretrial conference. Success depends on preparation for these appearances, as well as research, document preparation, investigation, calendaring involved in the intervening indictment and information, discovery, pretrial motions, plea bargaining, and assurance of a speedy trial. At each level, you also strengthen the case for trial.

As the case takes shape in this pretrial stage, your tasks require precision and efficiency. You have a significant role to play in translating textbooks, law codes, and rules of procedure into justice for a defendant, for a victim, and for the community at large.

II. GRAND JURY AND INDICTMENT

A. INTRODUCTION

The grand jury is a body of citizens that hears evidence regarding possible criminal activity and decides whether that evidence is sufficient to bring an accused to trial. It is designed to protect citizens from unfounded and unnecessary government charges.

The Fifth Amendment to the United States Constitution states:

No person shall be held to answer for a capital, or otherwise infamous crime, unless on a presentment or indictment of a Grand Jury. . . .

This right is not imposed on the states [*Hurtado v. California* (1884)], but many state constitutions and statutes incorporate grand jury proceedings for felonies ("infamous crime"). Some states, particularly midwestern ones, rely almost exclusively on the preliminary hearing as an intermediate step toward trial. Others employ a preliminary hearing for bind over to a grand jury. The federal system requires either one or the other, but not both. In federal practice, capital cases must be prosecuted by indictment from a grand jury. Charges with possible sentences of a year or more in prison or hard labor also must proceed by indictment or, only if the defendant waives indictment, by an information from a preliminary hearing. Other federal offenses may be prosecuted by either indictment or information.

direct submission: bypassing the preliminary hearing and submitting a case directly to the grand jury.

Even where states use the preliminary hearing to send cases to the grand jury, prosecutors have the option of bypassing the preliminary hearing and submitting a case directly to the grand jury. This is called a **direct submission.** In some jurisdictions the grand jury is required or used extensively; in others it is used rarely or has been discontinued.

The grand jury has three functions: charging, investigating, and supervising. Charging is the issuing of an indictment, the grand jury's equivalent of a criminal complaint, against a specific person targeted by the prosecutor for a specific crime. Investigating entails inquiring into an entire area of suspicious activity to see if any wrongdoing has occurred and, if so, by whom. The third function involves the grand jury's authority to oversee and issue reports on the local jail and other public offices and officials.

B. COMPOSITION

The grand jury was named for its large number of jurors. Rule 6 of the Federal Rules of Criminal Procedure requires not less than sixteen nor more than twenty-three jurors, with at least twelve members agreeing to obtain an indictment. The composition of state grand juries varies in the respective numbers, but at least a majority must agree to indict. Jurors must be selected from a cross-section of the community, and the unjustified systematic exclusion of any group (by race, sex, occupation, and other factors) may subject the grand jury process to attack on the grounds of a denial of equal protection or a violation of the Sixth Amendment guarantee of a "fair cross-section" of the community [*Taylor v. Louisiana* (1975), *Hobby v. U.S.* (1984), and *Batson v. Kentucky* (1986)]. In *Campbell v. Louisiana* (1998) the Supreme Court ruled that a white defendant had standing to allege the racially motivated exclusion of African Americans in selecting grand jury members for the purpose of challenging his indictment. Such a deficiency can lead to the overturning of any subsequent conviction, as in *Castaneda v. Partida* (1977) where the conviction of a Mexican American was overturned because Mexican Americans were grossly underrepresented on the indicting grand jury. Today, most jurors are selected at random from voter and driver's license lists through the use of computers and other objective processes. A change in Rule 6 of the Federal Rules of Criminal Procedure makes it easier for hearing and speaking impaired persons to serve on grand juries through the use of interpreters.

C.   POWERS

The powers of the grand jury make it an effective weapon for investigating crime; it has also drawn criticism for abuse of those powers. Grand juries can subpoena witnesses and documents without showing probable cause, which neither the prosecution nor the police may do on their own. This power is restricted by a somewhat vague and inconsistent standard that permits the **quashing** (voiding) of an unreasonable demand. In *U.S. v. R. Enterprises, Inc.* (1991), the Supreme Court reversed a lower court's quashing of a broadly worded subpoena for a variety of corporate books and records. The grand jury hoped to gain information about the sale of sexually explicit materials. The Court said that any challenge to a grand jury subpoena based on relevancy will be denied unless the complaining party can show that there is "no reasonable possibility" that the requested material will produce information relevant to the general subject of the investigation.

quash: void an unreasonable demand.

In contrast, a grand jury subpoena issued to an attorney requesting all documents relating to fee arrangements and trust accounts of specified clients that included a provision for *in camera,* in chambers, screening of the documents for privileged material was held to violate the attorney-client privilege and was unduly burdensome absent a good faith effort by the government to issue a more narrow subpoena [*In re Grand Jury Subpoena Issued to Horn* (9th Cir. 1992)]. Federal Rule of Criminal Procedure 17 and parallel state rules cover grand jury subpoenas.

Special terminology applies to witnesses subpoenaed by grand juries. A "witness" is simply a person who is called to provide information but is in no way suspected of wrongdoing. A "subject witness" is one who may be involved in some wrongdoing but is not the focus of the investigation. The "target witness" is the specific focus of the investigation and the person most likely to be indicted.

Grand juries can request the court to hold a witness or custodian of evidence in contempt of court for failure to appear or produce the requested evidence, for being unresponsive to questions, or for refusing to answer questions altogether. The court can impose criminal contempt with possible jail time or civil contempt requiring payment of a fine.

A grand jury witness may exercise the privilege against self-incrimination [*Lefkowitz v. Turley* (1973)]. If a witness refuses to testify, the grand jury can request that the witness be granted immunity (18 U.S.C.A. §§ 6002–6003). This request is likely only if the witness invokes his or her right against self-incrimination. As explained in Chapter 10 on interrogation and confessions, the court or the government in some jurisdictions can grant "use" or "transactional" immunity. Once immunity is granted, a recalcitrant witness is subject to contempt of court.

With these investigative powers, the grand jury can be a potent player in the criminal justice system. Its authority to question people, search for and seize evidence, and go on nearly unlimited fishing expeditions raises the concern, however, that the grand jury may be a serious threat to individual rights.

D. AUTONOMY AND SECRECY

In order to work effectively as a check on unreasonable or unfounded government charges, the grand jury is, in theory, an autonomous institution. It is to be independent of the prosecutor and other outside influences. Therefore, prosecutors are to serve only as advisors and facilitators for the grand jury, and not as adversaries for indictment. Congruently, the grand jury's meetings are closed, and all participants are instructed to keep the proceedings secret. Membership on the jury is kept secret, thus insulating the jury from public pressure, intimidation, or reprisals [*U.S. v. Proctor & Gamble Co.* (1958)]. Secrecy also protects the reputation of the unindicted and shelters witnesses from reprisal for what they might say [*Pittsburgh Plate Glass Co. v. U.S.* (1959)]. Despite these safeguards, information is often leaked to the media. Accusations of violations of the grand jury secrecy rule [6(3)(2) Fed. R. Crim. P.] clouded the efforts of the Office of Independent Counsel in its grand jury investigation of former President Clinton.

"Today, the grand jury is the total captive of the prosecutor who, if he is candid, will concede that he can indict anybody, at any time, for almost anything, before any grand jury."

—William J. Campbell, American jurist; judge, U.S. District Court *U.S. News & World Report*, June 19, 1978

Prosecutors have been known to exercise such great influence over grand juries that they may become little more than a rubber stamp of the prosecutor's objectives. In one study, the average time regularly used by the grand jury to hear evidence and deliberate was five minutes per case.[1] Consequently, some jurisdictions have turned almost exclusively to the preliminary hearing, whereas others have attempted to provide some balance by permitting the presence of defense counsel that traditionally has been excluded.

E. PROCEDURE

Once the grand jury is selected, it convenes at the time designated by the court. Jurors may serve up to six months. Special grand juries convened to hear particularly complex matters or to conduct an extensive investigation may be selected for as long as thirty-six months. The judge instructs the jurors on their duties and the secrecy of the procedure, and provides for transcription or recording of the hearing. The jury selects a foreperson and meets with the prosecutor and possibly a person in charge of recording the proceedings.

The prosecutor may present evidence and question the witnesses. The target witness or accused has no right to appear but may be subpoenaed to do so. Occasionally, a grand jury may honor the target witness's request to testify. Traditionally, the accused or other witness does not have the right to counsel or to confrontation [*In re Groban's Petition* (1957), *U.S. v. Mandujano* (1976)]. Most jurisdictions, however, permit target and other witnesses to suspend proceedings to leave the hearing room to consult counsel on a particular question. A witness's counsel may be present under Federal Rule 6(d) and similar state rules. When the prosecution has finished questioning, the jurors may ask questions. If the jurors feel they need to hear some particular evidence, they may request the prosecutor to secure the evidence through subpoena.

The normal rules of evidence do not apply to grand jury proceedings. Illegally obtained evidence [*U.S. v. Calandra* (1974)] and hearsay [*Costello v. U.S.* (1956)] are normally admissible. Privileges such as priest-penitent, husband-wife, and others, however, may not be violated [*Branzburg v. Hayes* (1972)]. The quantum of evidence needed for the return of an indictment varies. Traditionally, it is enough evidence to prove that the defendant is probably guilty of the crime. Other jurisdictions apply a **prima facie** standard. This means that enough evidence has been presented on each element of the crime, absent any evidence of refutation, to conclude that the defen-

prima facie case: enough evidence on each element of the crime, absent any evidence of refutation, to conclude that the defendant is guilty.

dant is guilty. Of the two burdens, the prima facie standard is more stringent, closer to "beyond a reasonable doubt," the burden of proof at trial. If instructed properly, a grand jury votes against indictment unless the required quantum of evidence is present, thus eliminating insubstantial or otherwise unwarranted charges. Reread *People v. Goetz* in Chapter 7 for a discussion of the differences in the level of instruction between grand jury and petit jury.

After the presentation of evidence, the jury deliberates in secret, makes a decision, and communicates that decision to the prosecutor. If the jury votes not to indict, an order of dismissal, sometimes called no bill, is entered. If the vote is to indict, the indictment is drafted by the prosecutor. The indictment must be endorsed as a true bill, be signed by the foreperson, and may need to include the names of the witnesses who testified. Once the appropriate document is presented to the judge, the jurors are dismissed.

F.   THE PARALEGAL'S ROLE: PROSECUTION[2]

If you are in a jurisdiction where a felony goes to preliminary hearing before submission to a grand jury, you probably attended the preliminary hearing as covered in Chapter 11. Information gleaned at this hearing helps the prosecutor decide which witnesses to subpoena and what questions to ask at the grand jury hearing of the same case. A tape or transcript may be obtainable if you cannot attend the preliminary hearing.

Open a file on the case and enter police reports; media reports; and copies of court documents including bond papers, the accused's criminal record, and certified copies of the judgments of felony convictions (needed for persistent felony counts or later at sentencing). If requested to do so, prepare a grand jury docket that lists pending cases, meeting dates and times, and witnesses. Cross check with the clerk of court and judge's calendar. Draft subpoenas and give them to the sheriff or other official responsible for service on the witnesses. Exhibit 12–1 presents a copy of part of a prepared grand jury docket,[3] and Exhibit 12–2 shows a copy of a grand jury subpoena.

Notify the grand jurors of the meeting or see to it that the clerk of court does. Draft any proposed indictment if requested to do so. The indictment should state each element of the crime and not simply quote the statute number. Failure to do so could result in dismissal, as it did in *U.S. v. Cabrera-Teran* (5th Cir. 1999). Some prosecutors choose not to have indictments drafted until after the grand jury has returned an indictment. You may also be asked to assist witnesses, see that any physical evidence is present, draft proposed questions, and tape (audio or video) the hearing to provide a record if it is otherwise not transcribed.

Once the grand jury makes its decision, draft the order of dismissal or the indictment. Because drafting an indictment is similar to drafting a criminal complaint, refer to that section of the text for guidance. Exhibit 12–3, page 465 presents an indictment form.

Next, notify victims, defense attorneys, witnesses, and police officers of the returned indictment. Notification may be made by letter or phone. Warrants for arrest may also have to be drafted.

"There is nothing more horrible than the murder of a beautiful theory by a brutal gang of facts."

—La Rochefoucauld, 1747–1827

G.   THE PARALEGAL'S ROLE: DEFENSE

As previously stated, a client may be subpoenaed to appear before a grand jury for a variety of reasons. Your supervising attorney may call the prosecutor to determine if your client is a "nonsuspect" witness. Some prosecutors are willing to send a letter verifying such that will put the client's mind at ease.[4] If the client has never appeared before a grand jury, you may assist by providing information to your client about the grand jury and what to expect. If such information is provided frequently, prepare a brochure or brief video for your clients' information.

EXHIBIT 12–1
Grand Jury Docket

CAPITOL COUNTY GRAND JURY
JANUARY 16, 2001

8:30–9:00	*State v. Allen W. Nunn*	Trafficking in Marijuana
	Witness:	
	1. Trp. Cole Raines, CSP	
9:00–11:30	INVESTIGATION INTO THE DEATH OF LARRY PAULUS AT JAIL	
	Witnesses:	
	1. Det. Rob Tebbit, CSP	
	2. Embry Smith, Coronor	
	3. Dr. Newman, Chief Medical Examiner	
	4. Greg Monett, Inmate at Jail	
	5. Richard Walker, Former Inmate at Jail	
	6. Trp. M. B. Miller, CSP	
	7. Betty Michaels, Sister to Larry Paulus	
	8. Other Family Members	
11:30–12:00	*State v. Michael Lawry*	Flagrant Nonsupport
	Witness:	
	1. Sonja Lawry	
	116 Westwood Drive	
12:00–1:00	LUNCH	
1:00–2:00	*State v. William McMann*	Rape
	Witnesses:	
	1. Det. Rob Tebbit, CSP	
	2. Mary Simms	
	Jefferson Street, Legalville	
	3. Patience Brown	
	Berny Lane, Legalville	
	4. Cynthia Jenn, Mother to Mary	
2:00–2:50	*State v. Danny Dernning*	Assault
	Witnesses:	
	1. Ofc. R. Jones, LPD	
	2. Roger Walters	
	Guaranteed Quick Lube	
	College Way, Legalville	
	3. Danny Dernning, REQUEST TO TESTIFY	
2:50–3:00	BREAK	
3:00–3:45	*State v. Miller Hobsen*	Wanton Endangerment
	Witnesses:	
	1. Ofc. Danny Lilly, LPD	
	2. Whitaker Johnson	
	308 N. 3rd Street	
	3. Gary Johnson	
	4. Charlie Schumacher	
	5. Miller Hobsen, REQUEST TO TESTIFY	
3:45 -	*State v. Carter Dennis*	Forgery of a Prescription, Uttering
	Witnesses:	False Prescription
	1. Ofc. Harry Sterns, LPD	
	2. Fred Lawrence	
	Legalville Pharmacy	

EXHIBIT 12–2
Grand Jury Subpoena

AO 110 (Rev. 10/82)   ⊕   SUBPOENA TO TESTIFY BEFORE GRAND JURY

United States District Court .	DISTRICT EASTERN DISTRICT OF KENTUCKY

TO:

SUBPOENA FOR

☐ Person

☐ Document or Object

YOU ARE HEREBY COMMANDED to appear in the United States District Court at the location, date, and time specified below to testify before the Grand Jury in the above entitled case.

PLACE	COURTROOM
	DATE AND TIME

YOU ARE ALSO COMMANDED to bring with you the following document(s) or object(s): [1]

☐ *Please see additional information on reverse*

This subpoena shall remain in effect until you are granted leave to depart by the court or by an officer acting on behalf of the court.

CLERK	DATE
(b)	
(BY) DEPUTY CLERK	

This subpoena is issued on application of the United States of America by:	NAME, ADDRESS AND PHONE NUMBER OF ASSISTANT U.S. ATTORNEY

1) If not applicable, enter "none."

If the subpoena is for documents, you may be asked to review the request for reasonableness or to research grounds to quash the subpoena. Generally, a subpoena duces tecum is limited to documents relevant to the investigation. It must identify the documents with reasonable particularity, and the time frame from which the documents are to be drawn must be reasonable.[5] A subpoena for all tax records for the past twenty-five years, for example, would be unreasonable. Draft the motion to quash if requested. You may be able to arrange with the prosecutor's office to surrender the documents to a person designated by the prosecutor and save your client from having to appear.[6]

Occasionally, it is in the best interest of a client to testify before a grand jury, even when the client is not subpoenaed to do so. For example, the defendant may be able to testify that the government's key witness has a criminal record and has perjured himself previously. Such evidence may cause the government to lose its zeal to prosecute. Under this circumstance, you may be asked to draft a Notice of Defendant's Request to Present Evidence Before the Grand Jury. This is submitted to the prosecutor with a copy to the clerk and the judge. It is read to the grand jury, which decides whether they want the client present.

You may be asked to assist the attorney in preparing a client for testifying. Consider the following topics to cover.

1. Have the client review copies of documents that have been produced to the jury.
2. Review likely areas of questioning.
3. Instruct the client on the importance of the oath and telling the truth.
4. Instruct the client on the right to consult the attorney outside the jury room and that consultation is accomplished by making a clear request to the foreperson.
5. Reinforce the attorney's instructions on the right against self-incrimination, including the right to refuse to produce some documents that by their very production are incriminating [See *U.S. v. Doe* (1984) and *Fisher v. U.S.* (1976)].[7]

Once your office becomes aware of a grand jury investigation, it is necessary to monitor the investigation. Monitoring is done by debriefing your client following his or her testimony. Some attorneys contact other witnesses. If you are asked to make the contact, always do so through the witness's attorney. Accusations against you for intimidation and obstruction of justice are possible.[8] The defense can start a complete, independent investigation as well.

When the indictment is issued, review it. Each element of the crime should be stated, not simply statute number. The indictment must put the defendant on notice of the charges. If it does not, it is subject to attack via the motion to dismiss. Confirm the eligibility, composition, and selection of the jurors for a possible motion to dismiss the indictment. Draft the motion consistent with the applicable rules of procedure [Fed. R. Crim. P. 6(b)(2)]. These same objections can be raised prior to the impaneling of the jurors [Fed. R. Crim. P. 6(b)(1)]. Exhibit 12–4, page 466 is an example of a motion to dismiss an indictment.

bill of particulars:
a document provided by the prosecution on request from the defense, detailing the when, where, and how of the crime charged in the indictment.

Because indictments are brief, most jurisdictions provide for a bill of particulars. A **bill of particulars** is a document provided by the prosecution on request from the defense, detailing the when, where, and how of the crime charged in the indictment [Fed. R. Crim. P. 7(f)]. A bill of particulars may be requested before or within ten days after the arraignment. It can help the defense determine what to plead; ascertain possible defenses such as double jeopardy, alibi, and statute of limitations; and otherwise prepare a defense. If requested to do so, draft a motion for a bill of particulars. An example of the motion is provided in Exhibit 12–5, page 467. Exhibit 12–6, page 468, is an example of the government's bill of particulars.

A good defense team also does everything possible to obtain a copy of the grand jury record. To do so lessens the prosecutor's advantage from being involved in the hearing and observing all the witnesses and evidence. Further, review of critical testimony may lay the groundwork for impeaching a government witness whose trial testimony is inconsistent with testimony given at the grand jury. Despite secrecy, grand jury records have become increasingly available to the defense. Federal Rule of Criminal Procedure 16(a)(3) and the Jenks Act, 18 U.S.C.A. §§ 3500(b) and 3500(e)(3), require the state to provide the defense with a copy of the grand jury testimony of any witness after direct examination of that witness at trial. Because that causes delay during the trial while the transcript is reviewed by the defense, some prosecutors and judges prefer to disclose the information sooner. A petition for disclosure can be filed under Rules 6(e)(3)(C) and (D). A defense letter requesting the record, accompanied by a blank tape or computer disk, is one method to obtain the record. Go to the custodian of the tapes and do the copying yourself, if necessary.[9]

As a matter of fairness, evidence against a target witness should be brought before a grand jury promptly. Charges against an accused will be dismissed and a conviction overturned if the defendant can show that the preindictment delay was a prosecutorial tactic to gain some advantage over the defendant and the delay caused actual prejudice to the defense. For example, a prosecutorial delay in bringing a child rape charge, which resulted in a loss of juvenile jurisdiction over the case, did prejudice the defendant in *State v. Brandt* (Wash. App. 2000). A conviction in an incest case was not reversed for a six-year preindictment delay in *Commonwealth v. Richardson* (Mass. App. 2000), however, because the defendant failed to show evidence of "dilatory tactics" or a prejudice to his defense.

 ANALYSIS PROBLEM

12-1. Which Chapter 1 cases might lead to the opening of a grand jury investigation before charges are brought? Explain.

III. THE INFORMATION

In non–grand jury jurisdictions when cases go to arraignment by bind over from the preliminary hearing, or where the defendant waives indictment, the appropriate charging document is called the information. The rules of most states parallel Federal Rule 7, requiring a document with the same essential contents as an indictment. The prosecution paralegal can draft the information using the same approach as that for drafting indictments and criminal complaints. Indictments and informations must be filed with the clerk of the appropriate trial court.

> *The court may permit an information to be amended at any time before verdict or finding if no additional or different offense is charged and if substantial rights of the defendant are not prejudiced.*
>
> —Fed. R. Crim. P. 7(e)

IV. ARRAIGNMENT

A. INTRODUCTION

Arraignment follows the issuing of the indictment or information and is an appearance of the defendant before a judge. The purpose of the arraignment is to inform the defendant of the charge, enter a plea to the charge, inform the defendant of his or her rights, address pretrial release (if not done previously), and, in some cases, set a trial date (Fed. R. Crim. P. 10 and 11). Some jurisdictions conduct arraignments of jailed defendants by closed circuit television to save time and for security reasons.

The judge reads the information or the indictment, unless that procedure is waived by the defendant. The defendant may enter one of several pleas.

Not guilty: If this plea is entered, the judge sets a trial date. The court will enter a not guilty plea for a defendant who stands mute.

Guilty: If this plea is entered, the court is obligated to question the defendant to determine whether the plea is knowingly and voluntarily given. A plea bargain is not an improper inducement to a plea of guilty. The judge also must determine that the defendant understands the nature of the charge and possible penalties and that he or she is giving up the constitutional rights to a jury trial, to cross-examine witnesses, and to testify or remain silent. If the judge is satisfied on these points, an inquiry is made of the prosecution to determine the factual basis for the charge. If the judge finds that the defendant has admitted sufficient facts to prove each element of the crime, the judge may accept the guilty plea and proceed to sentencing or to set a future date for sentencing.

No contest (*nolo contendere*): This plea essentially says, "I do not admit guilt but I am not going to challenge the charge, so treat me as if I plead guilty." The court proceeds as in the case of a guilty plea. The judge decides whether to permit a no contest plea. The purpose of this plea is to avoid a guilty plea that could prejudice a corresponding civil suit against the defendant. For example, in a vehicular homicide case, the driver is likely to face a criminal charge plus a civil suit for money damages. A no contest plea cannot be treated as an admission to liability in the civil case as a guilty plea could.

These three pleas are the only pleas accepted in the federal courts [Fed. R. Crim. P. 11(a) and (b)] and in many state courts. Twelve states have added the plea of guilty but mentally ill. When the defendant's mental illness does not meet the standard for an insanity defense, this plea permits the judge to order treatment for the defendant while any other sentence on the charge is being served. Political support for this charge arose after John Hinckley's attempted assassination of President Reagan and the subsequent finding of not guilty by reason of insanity. Few studies have been done to determine if the plea's purposes are being fulfilled: the avoidance of costly trials, improper acquittals, and punishment without rehabilitation for the mentally ill. Most prison systems lack the resources to treat the mentally ill, though there are separate facilities for the criminally insane.[10] Where the plea of guilty but mentally ill is an option, the judge will not accept the plea until the defendant has received a psychiatric diagnosis of mental illness.

Most jurisdictions also require the defense to notify the prosecution and the court of certain defenses either at the arraignment or shortly thereafter.

"In law it is a good policy never to plead what you need not, lest you oblige yourself to prove what you cannot."

—Abraham Lincoln, Letter to Usher F. Linder, Feb. 20, 1848

B.   THE PARALEGAL'S ROLE[11]

The prosecution paralegal can gather the names of all indicted defendants and their attorneys, indictment numbers, and the charges to compile an arraignment list. This list is given to the judge and the clerk of court. An arraignment list for our Chapter 1 cases in a common format appears in Exhibit 12–7, page 469.

Arraignment dates are set by the judge or clerk of court, and the attorneys are notified. Both defense and prosecution paralegals review the files to see that they are current and that the indictment, bail information, and factual summaries are readily available to the attorney.

Defense paralegals notify clients and arrange any appointments needed to prepare the client for the arraignment and to discuss possible pleas and procedure. If you know that your client will be pleading guilty or no contest, brief your client on the questions that the judge will ask to determine if the plea is knowing and voluntary.

Following the arraignment, the prosecution paralegal notifies the victim, police, and others of the trial date or checks to see that each case is placed on the clerk's trial docket and sent out. If the defendant has failed to appear, a warrant for arrest is issued. It is important to ensure that the proper police agencies are notified and that the warrant information is entered in the national computer bank (NCIC). Defense paralegals need to assist the defendant in making bail if not previously successful. Both the defense and the prosecution paralegals need to update their files.

V. DISCOVERY

A. INTRODUCTION

The next critical stage is discovery. **Discovery** is the process of requesting and disclosing information pertinent to the trial of a case. It allows attorneys to try cases on the basis of knowledge of the facts and evidence possessed by both sides in the case, and not on tactics of surprise, courtroom dramatics, or some other device intended to manipulate the jury. Discovery assists the defendant in making an informed plea, enhances the possibility of a plea bargain avoiding the necessity of a trial, and reduces delay at trial. All of that facilitates a fair resolution of the case.

discovery:
the process of requesting from and disclosing to opponents information pertinent to the trial of a case.

B. THE LAW ON DISCOVERY

Due process under the Fifth and Fourteenth Amendments requires a fair trial, and discovery is instrumental in achieving this requirement. Although discovery's importance is clear, the Supreme Court has ruled that there is no general right of discovery in criminal cases, giving states considerable flexibility in this area. [*Weatherford v. Bursey* (1977)]. Despite the absence of a mandate, all jurisdictions now provide for significant discovery. Federal Rule of Criminal Procedure 16 governs discovery practice. State rules vary as to what and when information is discoverable. In addition, judges are given some discretion to interpret the rules and to make justified exceptions in a particular case. In doing so, judges rely on case law for guidance. Discovery practice is far from an exact science, requiring knowledge of the rules, pertinent case law and forms, and some imagination and creativity.

The defense can discover a variety of information including the following:

1. The defendant's statements to police, or to others, that are relevant to the crime charged.
2. The defendant's criminal record.
3. Witnesses' names and addresses (also criminal records and inducements to testify in some jurisdictions).
4. Witnesses' statements (in some jurisdictions, statements may not be available until after witnesses testify at trial).
5. Documents, photographs, books, tangible objects, papers, and access to buildings and places if they are "*material to the preparation* of the defendant's defense or are intended for use by the government as evidence in chief at the trial, or were obtained from or belong to the defendant" [Fed. R. Crim. P. 16(a)(1)(C)].
6. Scientific tests and reports such as mental exams, drug tests, hair and clothing analysis, DNA analysis, fingerprint reports, experiments, and others.
7. Depositions in exceptional circumstances (Fed. R. Crim. P. 15).
8. Exculpatory evidence.
9. Police and other investigative reports (not available in a number of jurisdictions).

The items or information must be in the "possession, custody, or control of the government" and known or able to become known by the government through "due diligence." Normally, "known by" encompasses the entire prosecutorial staff and that of agencies closely working with the prosecutor, such as the local police.

Once the defendant submits a request for discovery to the prosecutor, Federal Rule 16(b) and similar state rules require the defendant, on request, to disclose reciprocal information to the prosecution. Neither request, however, permits discovery of the attorney's work product or otherwise privileged information. **Attorney work product** is trial preparation materials consisting of the attorney's mental impressions, conclusions, opinions, and legal theories concerning a case. Overall, the scope and means of discovery in criminal cases are not as broad as those in civil cases.

Sanctions for failure to comply with a discovery request and other disclosure obligations discussed in this chapter vary, ranging from a court order to provide the discovery to a prohibition against admission of the evidence at trial, and even a new trial in extreme circumstances [Fed. R. Crim. P. 16(d)(2)]. An overly broad or intrusive request can be defended against by a protective order by which the court denies, restricts, or defers the discovery [Fed. R. Crim. P. 16(d)(1)].

The Freedom of Information Act, 5 U.S.C.A. § 552, and state freedom of information acts may also be used to obtain relevant information. Because such searches are informal and investigatory, they are not subject to ordinary discovery rules and limitations. Although some materials are exempted from disclosure, anyone with a bona fide request has access to vast amounts of information. The FBI Web site (www.fbi.gov) has a link to the Freedom of Information Act site.

C.   EXCULPATORY EVIDENCE

Exculpatory evidence is inconsistent with guilt, raises doubt about evidence of guilt, or diminishes guilt. It is evidence favorable to the defendant or information that leads to evidence that is favorable to the defendant. The landmark decision of *Brady v. Maryland* (1963) requires the prosecution to disclose exculpatory evidence. This disclosure is mandated by constitutional due process requirements and is consistent with the prosecutor's duty to seek justice. *Brady* requires that the defendant request the exculpatory evidence and that the evidence sought be material to guilt or punishment. Failure of the defense to make the request does not necessarily relieve the government of its *Brady* duty [*U.S. v. Agurs* (1976)]. In *Agurs*, the defendant asserted self-defense, but the prosecution failed to disclose the fact that the victim had assault and weapons convictions. The standard for what was sufficiently "material," however, was unclear until the Court decided *U.S. v. Bagley* (1985). For *Brady* purposes, the *Bagley* Court set a single standard.

> [E]*vidence is material . . . if there is a reasonable probability that, had the evidence been disclosed to the defense, the result of the proceeding would have been different. A reasonable probability is a probability sufficient to undermine confidence in the outcome.*

In *Strickler v. Greene* (1999), the prosecutors violated *Brady* by failing to disclose out-of-court testimony of a witness that was arguably helpful to the defendant. The Court refused to overturn the conviction, however, because the defendant failed to show a reasonable probability that his conviction or sentence would have been different if the out-of-court testimony had been disclosed.

In *Bagley*, the defendant's somewhat general request for "any deals, promises, or inducement made to witnesses" was remanded to the trial court to determine if the actual offers made by the state to the witnesses were material under the new standard.

Other guidelines concerning or affecting disclosure have been developed. Perjured testimony may not knowingly be used by the prosecution [*Mooney v. Holohan* (1935)], and by implication, any material inconsistency in earlier testimony and what

---

attorney work product:
trial preparation materials consisting of the attorney's mental impressions, conclusions, opinions, and legal theories concerning a case.

exculpatory evidence:
evidence that is inconsistent with guilt, raises doubt about evidence of guilt, or diminishes guilt; evidence favorable to the defendant or information that leads to evidence that is favorable to the defendant.

the witness intends to say at trial should be disclosed. A court has no obligation to do an *in camera* inspection of the government's files when the defense makes a general request and the prosecution responds that there is "no exculpatory evidence" [*De-Marco v. U.S.* (1974)]. Where the defense request establishes some basis to believe that material evidence exists, however, the judge should conduct an *in camera* inspection [*Pennsylvania v. Ritchie* (1987)]. Ritchie wanted access to a child welfare agency's file on his daughter to show the daughter's accusation of rape might have been based on factors other than the truth. A recent Court of Appeals case held that the *Brady* duty to disclose includes searching the records of closely associated departments such as the police if there is sufficient prospect for finding exculpatory material [*U.S. v. Brooks* (D.C. Cir. 1992)].

What happens if the allegedly exculpatory material has been lost or destroyed by the police? In such cases the remedy has been to bar prosecution or suppress the government's best evidence. The Court said it is appropriate to do so only if the defendant shows that (1) the evidence was exculpatory and its value obvious to the custodian, (2) independent evidence to establish the point in question is not available, and (3) there is actual prejudice to the defendant even if police or the prosecutor acted in good faith [*California v. Trombetta* (1984)]. Bad faith on the part of police, however, eliminates the requirement of prejudice. In *Arizona v. Youngblood* (1988), a test of semen was inconclusive and, therefore, speculatively exculpatory, so no relief was necessary when the samples were destroyed, absent a showing of bad faith by the responsible police. Finally, the government cannot rely on negligence, poor communications between staff members, or ignorance of relevant facts to excuse a failure to disclose [*Giglio v. U.S.* (1972)].

The *Brady* doctrine is critical to both the prosecution and defense. Requests for discovery should routinely include requests for disclosure of exculpatory information that are as specific as possible. Such requests must be taken very seriously by the prosecution; a diligent effort must be made to locate the requested or other important exculpatory information. It is unethical for prosecutors to withhold such information knowingly or even recklessly.

D. DISCOVERY PROCEDURE AND THE PARALEGAL'S ROLE

Your primary tasks in discovery include drafting the necessary documents, gathering the needed items and information, and monitoring the discovery process. Discovery can start as soon as the indictment or information is filed and can continue right up to and at trial. Typically, the defendant files a motion for discovery unless there is a standing court order for discovery; in that case, follow the local practice for submitting the request. Sometimes the prosecution will simply provide all the accumulated information at the arraignment. A checklist is helpful in drafting a motion for discovery.

CHECKLIST FOR DRAFTING A MOTION FOR DISCOVERY

☐ 1. Locate a sample of a thorough discovery motion; research form books if there is no office example. Enter the form into the word processor.

☐ 2. Review the case file and note likely areas for special or particularized requests.

☐ 3. Review the latest edition of the jurisdiction's discovery rules.

Continued

❏ 4. Research the case law to support any unique or specialized requests not routinely covered by the rules of discovery (sources: rules decisions, case annotations, ABA standards on discovery, constitutional annotations, and others).

❏ 5. Meet with your supervising attorney to discuss any unique issues and to see that you are covering what is expected in the case. The more serious the case, the more thorough and imaginative the motion.

❏ 6. Check the following list of suggested items to request.[12]

■ Witnesses' names, addresses, statements.
■ Any statements of the defendant to police, jail mates, victim, others.
■ Grand jury testimony of witnesses and defendant transcribed or otherwise recorded.
■ Results of any scientific tests, related reports, and conclusions of experts, including physical or mental exams, forensic tests and analyses, drug tests, blood tests, DNA analysis, and others.
■ Notification of intent to conduct tests or experiments, especially if evidence will be destroyed in the process, so defense can be present with our expert.
■ Books, papers, documents, photos, tapes, objects, buildings, or places.
■ Criminal record of the defendant, victim, witnesses, including codefendants and informants.
■ Inducements to witnesses, codefendants, and others who will testify at trial.
■ Notice of surveillance of any form and records, tapes, or notes intended to be used at trial.
■ Exculpatory evidence pertinent to guilt or punishment under *Brady* through both routine and unique requests.
■ Copies of search and seizure warrants, supporting affidavits, inventory of seized items.
■ Notice of intent of prosecution to enter evidence of other crimes.
■ Notice of intent to use any models, diagrams, or other demonstrative exhibits or procedures.
■ Appraisals of property value, in felony theft.
■ Proposal for *in camera* review, if there is a question about discoverability or exculpatory nature.

❏ 7. Review potential grounds for supporting unique requests.[13]

■ Basic fairness, due process, alleviation of unjust advantage or imbalance.
■ Relevance, materiality.
■ Unreasonable financial or other hardship if defendant must find evidence independently.
■ Judicial efficiency in cost and time.
■ Avoidance of surprise and delay.
■ Need evidence to make informed decision on plea, severance, calling codefendant, having defendant testify, choice of defense, and others.
■ Need to impeach witness.
■ Need to confirm chain of evidence.
■ Need for independent testing by defense.

❏ 8. Draft the motion with clear and concise language, including citations of rules and cases, and even arguments to support unusual requests; include notice of the hearing on the motion if it is required.

9. Include a paragraph on the continuing obligation to provide discovery on new evidence.

10. Give the draft of the motion to your supervising attorney for additions and suggestions.

11. Revise the motion.

12. Have the attorney sign the motion.

13. File the motion with the clerk and give copies to the prosecution and judge.

Exhibit 12–8, page 469 is a routine discovery motion.[14] Exhibit 12–9, page 471, is a discovery motion in a murder case, reflecting a more detailed and particularized approach.[15]

If working for the prosecution, review the motion, note any unusual or unreasonable requests, as well as those that go beyond the bounds of the rules of discovery. Remember that attorney work product is not discoverable and information that is normally protected by the rules of evidence as privileged (doctor-patient, priest-penitent) requires sound justification for discovery, as does information that is normally confidential or highly sensitive such as national security documents.

If any item should not be disclosed, draft a motion for a protective order. This motion seeks a judge's order denying access to the information. Occasionally, the prosecution simply denies the request and leaves it to the defense to file a motion to compel discovery. In gathering the evidence and considering whether to deny access to the information, be especially sensitive to the requirements of fairness and due process, the spirit of the *Brady* and subsequent decisions, and the overriding duty of your office to seek justice. Any deliberate attempt to conceal evidence is likely to result in reversal of a conviction, subject your supervising attorney to disciplinary procedures, and cost you your job. Discovery involves critical decisions; good communication between you and your supervising attorney is essential. Also keep in mind that the defense counsel's duty is to be as zealous as the law allows.

Gather the needed information. Screen it for exculpatory evidence. Contact police and others to get all the information. Arrange for tests, get reports, establish dates for inspection and photographing.

Next, draft a written response to the motion indicating that the request is granted and either attach copies of the requested material or state at what place and time the items can be inspected or otherwise made available. Any denial of discovery should be briefly explained. The prosecutor's reciprocal request for discovery, consistent with the applicable rules, can be joined with the response to the discovery motion [Fed. R. Crim. P. 16(c)]. Some prosecutors use reciprocal discovery; others do not.

The opponent's failure to comply or an unreasonable delay in complying with a discovery request may lead your attorney to seek a sanction against the other side. Exhibit 12–10, page 478, is a motion for sanctions for failure to provide timely discovery.[16]

It is a good idea to draft an inventory of items disclosed and received for both parties to sign. The original should be filed with the clerk of court. Attorneys like to have the inventory so the opponent cannot pull any surprises at trial. The inventory also serves as a good checklist to make sure all items requested have been received. A review of the items and the request is essential. Any missed items need to be called to the attention of the opponent.

Discovered information needs to be evaluated and summarized for the attorney and placed in the file. If numerous documents are involved, you may have to catalog them and have an index or the entire set of documents computerized for easy retrieval of desired information. Keep in mind that any faxed copies may need to be photocopied, because the quality of some fax documents deteriorates quickly. The evaluated evidence may lead to additional discovery requests, pretrial motions, such as a motion to suppress, and the beginning of serious trial preparation and plea bargaining, if not started previously.

Your role in discovery is critical. Requests for discovery, responses, and fulfilling the continuing obligation to disclose must be thorough, conscientiously monitored, and timely. Being aware of any time limits in the rules or set out in pertinent court orders is essential. Also, be aware that discovery has its strategic side and, if done artfully, can help limit your opponent to only specified witnesses, evidence, and issues. Diligence and creativity in the discovery process can lead to significant dividends at trial. Despite its great usefulness, however, discovery is no substitute for thorough, independent investigation.

VI.   OTHER INVESTIGATION

Paralegals must occasionally become investigators, whether working for prosecution or defense. Investigation can involve locating and interviewing witnesses, talking with police, gathering medical and other records, visiting the scene, photographing, locating documents of various sorts, measuring, observing, and a host of other activities. Hard core investigation, however, takes specialized training and goes beyond the scope of this text. If you are interested in or find yourself faced with critical investigative tasks, consult the numerous references in your library on investigating criminal cases. Good litigation books also discuss how to interview witnesses and conduct investigation. Keep in mind that investigators often face serious ethical questions and preparation here is also important. For example, you investigate the scene of a crime for the defense after the police conclude their investigation and you find a weapon. What should you do? Take the time to be prepared in this area by reading current sources on investigation techniques and related ethical questions. Of course, the prosecution has detectives and the police, and defense offices often employ an investigator.

Some good sources on investigation that also address ethical questions are *Criminal and Civil Investigation Handbook*, McGraw-Hill; *Criminal Law Advocacy*, Vol. 1, Mathew Bender; *Investigation and Preparation of Criminal Cases*, F. Lee Bailey, Lawyers Co-operative Publishing Co.; and *Techniques of Crime Scene Investigation*, Barry A. J. Fisher, CRC Press.

VII.   PRETRIAL MOTIONS

A.   INTRODUCTION

Discovery, interviewing, and other investigation often reveals the need to file pretrial motions to resolve a variety of concerns prior to trial. These motions allow the court to decide issues to avoid delay, inefficiency, and injustice at trial. They range from the motion to suppress illegally obtained evidence, discussed in Chapter 10 (Exhibit 10–1), to motions to disqualify the judge or to change the location (venue) of the trial. The procedure used to define, research, and draft such motions and replies to them is covered in Chapter 10. This section identifies the names and purposes of some of the more common pretrial motions and pertinent rules of procedure.

B. PROCEDURE

Rule 47 of the Federal Rules of Criminal Procedure and parallel state rules require motions to be made in writing except for those made at trial, or unless the court permits otherwise. The motion states the grounds for the motion and the order or relief sought, then is served on the attorney in the manner prescribed by the Rules of Civil Procedure (Fed. R. Crim. P. 49). Some jurisdictions require certain matters to be raised by pretrial motions. In the federal system, these include defenses and objections to procedure, defenses and objections based on the indictment or information, a motion to suppress evidence, requests for discovery, and requests for severance of charges or defendants [Rule 12(b)]. In some states, judges may also require a written brief in support of the motion. Rule 12(c) Fed. R. Crim. P. directs the court at the arraignment or soon after to set a time for making pretrial motions. Local rules may be more specific.

C. COMMON PRETRIAL MOTIONS

You need to be familiar with at least the name and purpose of the following pretrial motions.

1. Motion to Dismiss

The motion to dismiss is a request to have the indictment, information, some charges, or the matter as a whole dismissed. Its purpose is to have the document or matter terminated and the defendant released. The court may permit some attacked documents to be amended and charges reissued as long as jeopardy has not attached [Rules 6(b)(2), 7(e), 12(b)(2)]. This is not true of an indictment, however, which may issue only from a grand jury. The defective indictment must be returned to the grand jury for reconsideration.

2. Motion to Suppress Evidence

The motion to suppress evidence is a request to prevent the use of evidence at trial because of an illegal search or seizure, improperly obtained confession or admission, a tainted lineup or other identification procedure, or the inflammatory or prejudicial nature of the evidence, such as a ten-foot, blow-up color photo of the victim's broken nose [Rules 12(b)(3) and 41].

3. Motion to Sever

The motion to sever is a request to have charges or defendants tried separately. Its purpose is to avoid any unfairness or prejudice to the defendant [Rules 12(b)(5) and 14].

4. Motion for Discovery

See the section on discovery in this chapter.

5. Motion for Change of Venue

When it appears the defendant cannot obtain a fair trial because of pretrial publicity or strong local feeling, a change of venue (trial location) may be requested. The purpose of the motion is to secure an impartial jury.

6. Motion for Continuance or Adjournment

The motion for continuance or adjournment is a request to postpone the trial date. The purpose is to gain more time to secure important evidence, be more prepared, change attorneys, let emotion-charged local opinion settle, or other reasons.

7. Motion to Recuse or Disqualify a Judge

The motion to recuse or disqualify a judge is a request to reassign the case to a different judge. It is not a common motion, but it is an important one. The purpose is to remove a judge because circumstances exist that might prejudice the judge, or at least appear to raise that potential. Impartiality is the goal.

"I trust that the court's indiscriminate use of the phrase 'scum of the earth' will not unduly influence the jury in reaching a decision."

Reprinted with permission from the *Saturday Evening Post* © 1985

8. Motion to Obtain Funds for Expert

If the office has been appointed to represent a defendant, it may be essential to file a motion to obtain funds to hire an expert. This is usually true if the case involves drugs and alcohol, statistics, firearms and gunshot wounds, pathology, or DNA.[17]

Ten factors must be addressed in such a motion: type of resource; nature and stage of assistance; name of the expert, qualifications and cost; reasonableness of the rate charged and cost; factual basis for the need for the expert, including case theory and relevant themes; the attorney's observations, knowledge, and insights about the case and the defendant; the legal basis for the expert in this case; the legal rationale for such resources for the defense; inadequacy or unavailability of government resources; and evidentiary documentation.[18]

A good source for additional information on the motion to obtain funds for an expert is the National Legal Aid and Defender Association (NLADA) and its publications.

9. Motion in Limine or for a Protective Order

The motion in limine or for a protective order can be a powerful tool if used thoughtfully and creatively. It is designed to get the judge to issue a protective order preventing one side or the other from using questions or arguments at trial that are irrelevant, inadmissible, or prejudicial. For example, the prosecution may want to protect a victim from cross-examination about her sexual orientation or her having had psychiatric problems years earlier, which might be only mildly relevant but likely to distract the jury from the relevance of the rest of her testimony.

The use of this motion allows the court to prevent anticipated problems or abuses. Clarifying such matters before trial is not only efficient, but also better assures a fair trial. In *U.S. v. Universal Rehabilitation Services* (3rd. Cir. 2000), the trial court had denied the defense motion in limine seeking prohibition of the introduction of the prosecution witnesses' guilty pleas to some of the same charges facing the defendants. The defense argued that evidence of the witnesses' guilty pleas would prejudice the defendants, because the jury would be more likely to convict the defendants if they knew that the witnesses' co-workers had already pleaded guilty to one of the charges. The prosecution argued that the evidence of the pleas was needed to prevent the jury from speculating that these government witnesses had been offered such a "sweet" deal to plead guilty that they were not credible witnesses. The full Court of Appeals ruled that the trial court had weighed all the factors and was correct in denying the defense motion. This case demonstrates how evidentiary issues can be anticipated and clarified through a motion in limine. It also demonstrates that a denial of such a motion can provide grounds for appeal.

Pretrial motions are frequently made not with the expectation of prevailing at the trial level, but to preserve an issue for appeal. An erroneous decision by a judge may lead to a new trial or reversal on appeal. The decision on some types of pretrial motions may be appealed before going to trial. Exhibit 12–11, page 479, is an example of a pretrial motion.

The computer age makes it imperative to (1) use discovery and pretrial motions skillfully to become aware of what kind of electronic evidence or exhibits will be used by the opposition at trial; and (2) have them viewed and, if necessary, excluded if their use will be prejudicial or if the item or exhibit is not what it purports to be. Keep in mind that digital technology increases the ease with which evidence can be fabricated.

VIII.   NOTICE OF DEFENSES

In most jurisdictions the defense has the obligation to notify the prosecution of its intention to raise specified defenses (Rules 12.1 to 12.3 Fed. R. Crim. P.). On request of a federal prosecutor, the defense has ten days to notify the government of its intention to offer an alibi defense. The notice must state the details of the alibi, including time, place, and witnesses [12.1(a) Fed. R. Crim. P.]. The prosecution must respond in ten days with the details of its rebuttal evidence [12.1(b)].

The defense has an affirmative duty under the federal rules and parallel state rules to notify the government of the insanity defense (Rule 12.3). The notice must be made during the time allowed for pretrial motions and served on the prosecution with a copy filed with the clerk [12.3(a)(1) Fed. R. Crim. P.]. As when a claim of incompetency to stand trial is made, the judge usually orders a psychiatric evaluation to help determine whether use of the insanity defense is proper.

The defendant's withdrawal of a defense under Rules 12.1 to 12.3 may not be commented on at trial. Check your state rules and statutes regarding the notification of defenses.

IX.   PLEA BARGAINING

Plea bargaining is a negotiation process between the prosecution and defense to resolve a case. The defendant gives up the significant right to a jury trial in return for a plea of guilty and a recommendation from the prosecution for reduced charges or a lighter sentence than might be recommended after trial. It is the criminal justice system equivalent to settlement in civil cases. Plea bargaining has received criticism, justifiably when plea bargains are reached pell-mell in an assembly line process without regard to constitutional defenses, the nature and certainty of the evidence,

"Those who think the information brought out at a criminal trial is the truth, the whole truth and nothing but the truth are fools. Prosecuting or defending a case is nothing more than getting to those people who will talk for your side, who will say what you want said. . . . I use the law to frustrate the law. But I didn't set up the ground rules."

—F. Lee Bailey, *New York Times Magazine,* Sept. 20, 1970

the concern of the victim and the community, and other considerations. Criticism is not justified when critics ignore the significant role plea bargaining plays in reducing expensive and costly trials and in reaching agreement in an informed, conscientious, and productive fashion. Although 90 percent of criminal cases are disposed of without a trial, there are still cases, especially misdemeanors, that could be resolved quickly and inexpensively if more formalized mediation processes were established. In short, without plea bargaining, the system would simply collapse under its own weight. With these advantages in mind, courts have officially sanctioned the once-secretive plea bargaining process [*Brady v. U.S.* (1970), *Santonella v. New York* (1971)], as have both state and federal rules of criminal procedure [Rule 11(e) Fed. R. Crim. P.].

To be upheld, however, plea bargains and the subsequent plea of guilty must conform to several standards summarized in *Bordenkircher v. Hayes* (1978).

> *We have recently had occasion to observe that "[w]hatever might be the situation in an ideal world, the fact is that the guilty plea and the often concomitant plea bargain are important components of this country's criminal justice system. Properly administered, they can benefit all concerned." The open acknowledgement of this . . . practice has led this court to recognize the importance of counsel during plea negotiations,* Brady v. United States, 397 U.S. 742, 758, *the need for a public record indicating that a plea was knowingly and voluntarily made,* Boykin v. Alabama, 395 U.S. 238, 242, *and the requirement that a prosecutor's plea-bargaining promise must be kept,* Santobello v. New York, 404 U.S. 257, 262. . . .

In *Santobello,* a guilty plea was overturned because a second prosecutor recommended the maximum sentence to the court after a previous prosecutor had promised to make no recommendation. *Bordenkircher* reiterated that pleas pursuant to a plea bargain must not be coerced by prosecutorial threats. If, however, the "threat" is an additional charge or habitual offender indictment that is supportable by the evidence, it is not impermissible for the prosecutor to use it as a bargaining chip to get the defendant to plead guilty to an existing charge.

The essentials of a valid plea include a record that reflects a knowing waiver by the defendant of three constitutional rights: the privilege against compulsory self-incrimination, the right to trial by jury, and the right to confront accusers [*Boykin v. Alabama* (1969)]; the defendant's understanding of the charge [*Henderson v. Morgan* (1976)]; and a factual basis for the plea [*North Carolina v. Alford* (1970)].

U.S. v. Gigot (10th Cir. 1998) nullified a plea bargain and the subsequent plea of guilty, because the requirement that the defendant must understand the charge and that the plea be voluntary was violated. The judge not only did not inform the defendant of the elements of the crime, but both the judge and the defendant's counsel misinformed the defendant on the maximum penalty and possible fine.

Blackledge v. Allison (1977) ruled that even if the procedure set out in pertinent rules is followed, that fact does not necessarily and automatically prohibit the defendant from trying to have the plea overturned for valid reasons.

Judges have the discretion to accept or reject a plea agreement. Rules of procedure normally require the judge to explain that to the defendant prior to a plea of guilty. The federal rules and many state rules permit the defendant to withdraw the plea of guilty if the judge rejects the plea bargain. Plea agreements have come under judicial attack as bribery, when key witnesses have been offered "deals" in return for testimony, and as excessive, when defendants have agreed to give up their rights of appeal and collateral attack of their sentences. In *U.S. v. Singleton* (10th Cir. 1999) the bribery challenge was first accepted by three judges and then rejected by the full panel. Appeal waivers, though controversial, have been upheld and are officially condoned in Rule 11(c)(6) Fed. R. Crim. P. Some prosecutors require defendants in plea agreements to waive their right to withdraw their guilty plea even if exculpatory or impeachment evidence may be found later.[19] Such agreements are likely to be challenged sometime in the future.

Jurisdictions that have mandatory sentences or strict sentencing guidelines, such as the current federal system, indirectly restrict the range of plea bargains. In such jurisdictions, bargaining is best done before the charges are filed, which is also the case where plea bargaining is not permitted. Informal plea bargains at the beginning of the process, however, often involve more speculation than information.

Your role in plea bargaining is to ensure that the attorney has the necessary information about the case to conduct informed and conscientious plea negotiations. Also, keep the victim or the victim's closest relative informed about offers of plea bargains and the agreement that is reached. Encourage the victim to attend the defendant's entry of plea and sentencing.[20] Victims are ignored too frequently in this process, and your dedication to keeping them informed makes the system more responsive and the victim more appreciative of the process.

 ANALYSIS PROBLEM

12–2.   At a family picnic, your Aunt Tildy confronts you with a tirade about how all the lawyers are in cahoots, letting criminals off through plea bargaining. How do you respond?

X.   THE RIGHT TO A SPEEDY TRIAL

You may be asked to draft a motion or a response to a motion for lack of a speedy trial. More importantly, you may recognize that speedy trial is becoming an issue in your case and point that out to your supervising attorney. The winning or losing of a case could turn on just such a suggestion.

The right to speedy trial is guaranteed in the Sixth Amendment to the Constitution and is applicable to the states through the Fourteenth Amendment [*Klopfer v. North Carolina* (1967)]. Most jurisdictions have speedy trial requirements patterned after 18 U.S.C.A. § 3161. Court rules also require the timely progression of the case. The right reduces presentencing jail time, compresses the period of emotional trauma and uncertainty associated with criminal charges, and lessens the potential for loss of evidence over time. Some argue that it curtails crime by decreasing the opportunity for defendants to commit other crimes while they are free awaiting trial.[21]

In *Barker v. Wingo* (1972), the Court ruled that a five-year delay in which the defendant failed to demand a speedy trial and demonstrate prejudice was not a violation of the Sixth Amendment. The Court established a four-item test: (1) length of the delay; (2) reason for the delay, such as whether it was caused by the defendant; (3) whether the defendant asserted the right; and (4) whether prejudice occurred, such as diminished evidence for the defense, extended incarceration, and others. The right commences on arrest and charging, and the time between a dismissal and recharging does not count if the defendant is not jailed [*U.S. v. Marion* (1971) and *U.S. v. Loud Hawk* (1986)].

The federal speedy trial statute moves a case along by requiring the filing of charges within thirty days of arrest or of summons, and trial must occur within seventy days thereafter. In contrast, a minimum of thirty days must elapse between the defendant's first appearance and trial to avoid rushed justice. Delays for mental exams, interlocutory appeals, and continuances requested by the defendant are among those periods not counted in determining a violation of the right to speedy trial.

Sanctions for violation include dismissal with or without prejudice, depending on the seriousness of the charge, the reasons for the dismissal, and administrative and fairness considerations involved in retrial (18 U.S.C.A. § 3162). Many states have a ninety-day indictment-to-trial deadline with similar exceptions for delay and sanctions for violations. Failure of a state to hold a trial within the 189-day deadline required by the Interstate Agreement on Detainer was not a denial of the right to speedy trial [*New York v. Hill* (2000)], because defense counsel agreed to the delay and, therefore, waived the right to trial within the time limit.

See *State v. Houck* in Chapter 8 for a discussion of speedy trial.

XI.   PRETRIAL CONFERENCE

pretrial conference:
a meeting of the judge with opposing parties to ensure an efficient and fair processing of the case, encourage plea negotiations, and narrow the issues to be tried.

"First settle what the case is, before you argue it."

—Lord Chief Justice Howe
Trial of the Seven Bishops
(1688, 12 How. St. Tr. 342)

Pretrial conferences may be ordered by the court under the federal and parallel state rules. A **pretrial conference** permits the judge to meet with the opposing parties to ensure an efficient and fair processing of the case, encourage plea negotiations, hear motions or schedule them for hearing, narrow the issues to be tried, and set the trial date, if not already done. The pretrial conference is often the last serious opportunity for resolving the case before trial.

A pretrial conference statement is often required, which lists the status of the case in various categories such as offenses, situation of codefendants, the finding of probable cause, trial date and estimated time required for trial, number of witnesses, discovery completed, demand for jury trial, plea bargains offered and accepted, and issues for a suppression hearing. This statement or report must be filed on the day of the conference.[22] A paralegal can help organize much of this material in a convenient form for the supervising attorney before the conference.

XII.   CONCLUSION

The grand jury process is similar to a preliminary hearing in its purpose to hear evidence and screen out unnecessary and unfounded charges. Its investigative powers often exceed those of the police and prosecutor, making it a potent weapon against crime. Preparation for the grand jury, including the drafting of information and indictments, lends itself particularly well to paralegal application. The arraignment provides the defendant with notice of the charge and is the designated time to enter one of several pleas.

Discovery is another stage that offers great opportunity for assistance by the paralegal. Effectively drafting the appropriate documents and carefully monitoring the process helps you achieve a beneficial exchange of evidence. Pretrial motions and responses, when thoroughly researched and carefully drafted, are indispensable tools for isolating and resolving pretrial issues.

Each of these pretrial processes not only guides the case toward trial, but also provides the background for informed plea bargaining, which is equivalent to settlement in the civil system. Plea bargaining is vital for reducing trial court calendars and for individualizing an increasingly crowded and mechanical system. The amount of litigation regarding plea bargaining and the subsequent plea of guilty requires the legal team to be cautious in this area and fully aware of its legal requirements.

The Sixth Amendment right to speedy trial requires the state and federal governments to ensure that an accused gets to trial in a reasonable period of time, which promotes justice by avoiding unnecessary incarceration and the loss of important evidence needed for a fair trial. Often the last step before trial is the judge's pretrial conference, which facilitates a plea agreement and, if none is reached, a fair and efficient trial of the factual issues.

EXHIBIT 12–3
Indictment Form

| CAPITOL COUNTY | CIRCUIT COURT DIVISION II | STATE OF COLUMBIA |

STATE OF COLUMBIA,
        PLAINTIFF

INDICTMENT NO. _____

v.

THEFT
CLASS D FELONY—C.R.S. 809.00

MIGUEL CORDOBA
1325 S. Main St.
Legalville, Columbia 00000,
        DEFENDANT

CRIMINAL DAMAGE TO PROPERTY
CLASS D FELONY—C.R.S. 835.00

The Grand Jury Charges:
    On or about the _____ day of _____ , _____ , in Capitol County, Columbia, the above-named defendant

COUNT I: committed the offense of Theft, a Felony, by intentionally taking a diamond and ruby ring owned by Carmen Cordoba and valued at more than $500; and

COUNT II: committed the offense of Criminal Damage to Property, a Felony, by intentionally damaging an antique jewelry box owned by Carmen Cordoba and valued at more than $500.

against the peace and dignity of the State of Columbia.

WITNESSES

Carmen Cordoba
Officer John Stern, L.P.D.

Defendant's ID: DOB: _____
        SSN: _____
Place of Birth: _____
Clerk's U.O.R. Nos: _____
_____

A TRUE BILL

_____
        FOREPERSON
Presented by the Foreperson in the presence of the Grand Jury, to the Judge in Open Court, and filed with the Clerk, this the _____ day of _____ , _____ .
_____ , Clerk
By _____ D.C.

MEMORANDUM OR ARRAIGNMENT AND PLEA

This date Defendants were formally arraigned in Open Court, being represented by
        (private)
        (court appointed)
counsel, Hon. _____ and (s)he thereupon entered a plea of _____ : whereupon Bail
    (from lower court was continued)
    (was fixed at $ _____)
This _____ day of _____ , _____ .
_____ Judge

I hereby certify that I personally handed the above-named Defendant(s) a true copy of the foregoing indictment, prior to arraignment, on this _____ day of _____ , _____ .
_____ , Clerk
By _____ D.C.

EXHIBIT 12–4
Motion to Dismiss Indictment

CAPITOL COUNTY   CIRCUIT COURT   STATE OF COLUMBIA
                                   DIVISION II

STATE OF COLUMBIA,   MOTION TO DISMISS
       PLAINTIFF   INDICTMENT NO. _____

V.

_____ ,
       DEFENDANT

_____

       Defendant, _____ , by counsel, respectfully moves this court, pursuant to Rule _____ of the Columbia Rules of Criminal Procedure, to dismiss indictment number _____ against the defendant.

       As grounds for this motion defendant states:

       (State basis for motion, such as improper paneling of jury or improper inclusion of persistent felony offender charge, defect in statement of the crime, or other basis.)

       The defendant offers the following authority in support of the motion:

       (State statutory, case law, or other legal authority and its relevance to the motion.)

       WHEREFORE, the defendant moves this court to dismiss indictment number _____ .

                                  Respectfully submitted,

                                   _____

                                   (Signature)
                                   (Address and phone number)
                                   Attorney for Defendant

                                   _____

                                   Date

EXHIBIT 12–5
Motion for Bill of Particulars

CAPITOL COUNTY   CIRCUIT COURT   STATE OF COLUMBIA
                          DIVISION II

STATE OF COLUMBIA,   INDICTMENT NO. _____
           PLAINTIFF

V.
                                       MOTION FOR BILL OF
     MIGUEL CORDOBA,   PARTICULARS
               DEFENDANT

     Defendant, Miguel Cordoba, by counsel, pursuant to C.R.Cr. P. _____ , moves the Court to require the State of Columbia to file a bill of particulars in the above-stated action as follows:

1. Count I of the indictment charges Mr. Cordoba with theft of Carmen Cordoba's ring. Mr. Cordoba requests the State to indicate:
     a. a more detailed description of the ring;
     b. the basis for the statement that the ring was owned by Carmen Cordoba and not Mr. Cordoba; and
     c. the State's basis for concluding that the ring is valued at more than $500; and

2. Count II of the indictment charges Mr. Cordoba with intentionally damaging Ms. Cordoba's antique jewelry box. Mr. Cordoba requests the State to indicate:
     a. a detailed description of the jewelry box and its alleged location at the time of the damage;
     b. a detailed description of the damage done to the box; and
     c. the basis for the conclusion that the jewelry box is an antique and that its value exceeds $500.

     Without this bill of particulars, the defendant will be deprived of his or her constitutional due process right to notice and otherwise will be unable to adequately propose a defense to the charges.
     WHEREFORE, the defendant respectfully requests this Court to order the State to file a bill of particulars on the points enumerated above.

                                         Respectfully submitted,

                                         _____

                                         (Signature)
                                         (Address and phone number)
                                         Attorney for Defendant

                                         _____

                                         Date

EXHIBIT 12–6
Bill of Particulars

STATE'S BILL OF PARTICULARS

The State of Columbia, in response to defendant's Motion for a Bill of Particulars in the above action, provides the following information:

1a. More detailed description of ring:

Ms. Cordoba's ring is a wide gold band with a large diamond in a raised center mounting. Two smaller rubies are in each side, with small diamonds and rubies encircling the larger stones. Two small letters are engraved on the inside of the gold band: an "A" and an "R."

b. Basis for Ms. Cordoba's ownership:

The ring was a gift given to Ms. Cordoba by Mr. Cordoba on their first wedding anniversary. It remained in Ms. Cordoba's possession following the couple's estrangement. The ring was kept in Ms. Cordoba's apartment of which she was the sole tenant.

c. Basis of the value of the ring:

The ring was appraised on _____ (date) _____ by Roderick Brewer, jeweler, employed by The Mother Lode Jewelers, located at 1403 N. Main Street, Legalville, Columbia, who stated it was a genuine antique with a value of approximately $8,000 to $10,000.

2a. Description of jewelry box and location at time of damage: Ms. Cordoba's jewelry box is an antique made of intricately carved mahogany wood inlaid with mother-of-pearl with brass key lock and hinges. Its size is approximately 12 inches by 8 inches by 6 inches. It was located on the top of Ms. Cordoba's dresser in her bedroom in her apartment.

b. Description of the damage done to the box:

The lock was pried from its mounting, the carved wooden top of the box was splintered, and some of the mother-of-pearl was dislodged and shattered.

c. Basis for conclusion the jewelry box had a value of more than $500:

The box was examined by Professor Adrianne Fromm of Columbia State College, Legalville, Columbia, an expert in Spanish antiquities, who assessed the box as worth approximately $1,500. She stated the box was beyond repair.

Respectfully submitted,

_____
(Signature)
(Address and phone number)
State's Attorney

_____
Date

EXHIBIT 12–7
Arraignments

DIVISION I			
No.	**Defendant**	**Attorney**	**Comments**
-CR-011	Eldon Spiers	Mason	In Jail
-CR-013	Cat Bermuda	Laurenz	Posted Bond
-CR-015	Henry Pogue	??	On the Run
and so forth			
DIVISION II			
-CR-012	Miguel Cordoba	Hernandez	Posted $10,000 Surety Bond
-CR-014	Lacey Rude	P.D.	On Bond; 10% of $2,500
-CR-016	Billy McIntire	James	In Jail, $2,500 Cash Bond Set
and so forth			

EXHIBIT 12–8
Motion for Discovery in Routine Case

STATE OF COLUMBIA
CAPITOL COUNTY CIRCUIT COURT
INDICTMENT NO. 92-CR-

STATE OF COLUMBIA   PLAINTIFF
v.   MOTION FOR DISCOVERY

                                                                            DEFENDANT
* *

Comes now the defendant, by counsel, pursuant to RCr. 7.24 and RCr. 7.26, and moves this Court to order the State to permit the defendant to inspect, copy, and or photograph the following:

1. Any relevant oral statements made by the defendant or codefendant and all written or recorded statements or confessions made by said defendant or codefendant, or copies thereof, within the possession, custody, or control of the State.

2. Any papers, documents, photographs, or tangible objects or copies or portions thereof that are within the possession, custody, or control of the State and that are intended for use by the State as evidence in chief at the trial or were obtained from or belonged to said defendant.

3. Any results or reports of physical or mental examination, and of scientific tests or experiments, made in connection with the above-styled case, or copies thereof, within the possession, custody, or control of the State, the existence of which is known by the Attorney for the State.

Continued

EXHIBIT 12–8 *(Concluded)*
Motion for Discovery in Routine Case

4. Any prior conviction(s) of the defendant that the State intends to use at the sentencing hearing must be supplied to the defendant fourteen (14) days prior to trial.

5. Written reports prepared by a witness that are signed or initialed or purport to be a substantially verbatim statement shall be made available to the defendant within a reasonable time prior to trial. *LeGrande v. State,* Cl., 494 S.W.2d 726 (1973); *Wright v. State,* Cl., 637 S.W.2d 635 (1982); *Haynes v. State,* Cl., 657 S.W.2d 948, 950 (1983).

6. Any exculpatory evidence for the defendant that may be in the possession of the State in accordance with the principles enunciated in *Brady v. Maryland,* 373 U.S. 83, S.Ct. 1194, 10 L.Ed.2d 215 (1963).

7. If the Grand Jury testimony was recorded and transcribed, then the official stenographer for the State shall provide a copy of it to the defendant at the defendant's expense, unless the defendant is an indigent defendant, in which case the stenographer shall provide the transcript free of charge.

8. Fully disclose to this defendant any agreements or understandings reached by the State, its agents, employees, attorneys, or anyone acting on behalf of or for the benefit of the State, with whereby said person or defendant has, will, or might derive any benefit, or which would cause any forbearance toward such person or defendant by the State as mandated by *Giglio v. United States,* 405 U.S. 150, 92 S.Ct. 763, 31 L.Ed.2d 104 (1972).

9. If subsequent to compliance with this order and prior to or during the trial, either party discovers additional material previously requested that is subject to discovery or inspection under RCr. 7.24 and 7.26, that party shall be under a continuing duty to promptly disclose to the other party or the other party's attorney or the Court such material.

WHEREFORE, the defendant respectfully requests this Court to order the State to permit the defendant to inspect, copy, and/or photograph the above information.

Respectfully submitted,

_____

(Name)
ATTORNEY FOR DEFENDANT
(Address and phone number)

NOTICE

Please take notice that this motion was filed in open court, Capitol County Circuit Courthouse, Legalville, Columbia, on this the 5th day of March, 2001, to be heard on the 5th day of March, 2001.

_____

CERTIFICATE OF SERVICE

I hereby certify that the foregoing motion was served by mailing a copy of same to the Hon. _____ , State Attorney, Legalville, Columbia 00000, on this the 5th day of March, 2001.

_____

EXHIBIT 12–9
Motion for Discovery in Murder Case

COMMONWEALTH OF KENTUCKY
_____ TH JUDICIAL CIRCUIT
_____ CIRCUIT COURT
INDICTMENT NO. 93-CR-000

COMMONWEALTH OF KENTUCKY   PLAINTIFF

v.

_____   DEFENDANT

FIRST MOTION FOR DISCOVERY ON BEHALF
OF DEFENDANT (NAME)—MOTION
FOR HEARING DATE CERTAIN

Introductory Statement

Comes the defendant, through counsel, and does hereby file his motions for discovery and other relief. Defendant files this pursuant to Sections 1, 2, 3, 7, 11, and 17 of the Kentucky Constitution, and Amendments 5, 6, 8, and 14 of the United States Constitution, and defendant's rights to a full and fair hearing pursuant to both the state and federal constitutions. The discovery sought is not only what is within the possession and control of the _____ County Commonwealth Attorney, but also that which is in the possession of the _____ County Sheriff's Office, the Kentucky State Police, local police agencies within and around _____ County, local coroners and/or deputy coroners, any and all other "medicolegal" investigators involved in the investigation of this case to any degree, also Federal Law Enforcement Agencies, including but not necessarily limited to the Federal Bureau of Investigation. Said Motion includes not only that which is known and possessed as set out above, but also that which can be made known or obtained through the exercise of due diligence by the _____ County Commonwealth Attorney or his agents as set out above. This demand for discovery specifically includes evidence which may reasonably be interpreted as exculpatory as to "guilt-innocence," but also as to the mitigation of punishment (mitigating evidence) which the Commonwealth intends to seek at trial or in a penalty phase presentation, or which could lead to the discovery of same. Discovery sought is as follows:

Statements Made by Defendant: Oral
and/or Written

1. All written or recorded statements or confessions of any kind made by defendant to any person. _RCr 7.24._ This request includes, but is not necessarily limited to statements made to jail companions, jailers, deputy jailers, codefendants, friends, and the like. _Hicks v. Commonwealth,_ Ky. App., 805 S.W.2d 144 (1990); _U.S. v. Atisha,_ 804 F.2d 920 (6th Cir. 1986); _Epperson v. Commonwealth,_ Ky., 809 S.W.2d 835 (1991); _Hendley v. Commonwealth,_ Ky., 573 S.W.2d 662 (1978).

2. Any oral statements known by the prosecution and/or its agents to have been made by defendant herein to any other person or persons _not_ police officers or law enforcement personnel. _Epperson, supra._

3. That defendant be permitted to obtain copies of any audio or video recordings of defendant made by or to any person. _RCr 7.24._ As an indigent, defendant will be unable to provide this for himself. Copies must be ordered produced or copied at State Police facilities.

4. The substance of any oral statements made by defendant to any person relevant to this Indictment. _RCr 7.24._ This request includes, but is not necessarily limited to, statements made to jail companions, jailers, deputy jailers, and the like.

Continued

EXHIBIT 12–9 *(Continued)*
Motion for Discovery in Murder Case

Physical Evidence: Notes,
Photographs, Writings, Etc.

5. Copies of any reports, notes, logs, photographs (slides or prints that can be reproduced at State Police Labs without need for Fiscal Court funding), or the like, including those associated with physical or scientific tests and/or experiments, medicolegal investigations, including but not limited to any videotaping and/or photographs of the alleged crime scene, both interior and exterior, and of the "victims" in this case, photos and/or videos made by the Office of the Kentucky Medical Examiner or any other local or state agency, and any and all tests performed by any medical examiners, coroners and/or deputy coroners. *James v. Commonwealth,* Ky., 482 S.W.2d 92 (1972) (right to independent test of controlled substances; right to inspect state chemist's reports); *Green v. Commonwealth,* Ky., 684 S.W.2d 13 (1984) (right to independent test of substances; right to examine chemist's work notes where evidence consumed in testing); and *Haynes v. Commonwealth,* Ky., 657 S.W.2d 948 (1983). This request also includes reports, memoranda, and the like relative to samples taken of articles and/or substances found in or around the crime scene, samples taken from defendant and/or his clothing and/or personal effects. See also *RCr 7.24.* Any scientific tests or reports thereof would be needed by counsel sufficiently in advance of trial in order that he be permitted a reasonable opportunity to defend against the results thereof, including the retaining of an expert to assist defendant in the preparation and defense of the charges. *Barnett v. Commonwealth,* Ky., 763 S.W.2d 119 (1989).

6. Copies of any notes, whether recorded or not, of any tests, examinations, and/or experiments performed by the Commonwealth, federal agencies, private labs, or the like, *RCr 7.24.*

7. Copies of any photographs, videotapes (that can be reproduced at State Police facilities), or the like associated with this action. *RCr 7.24(2).*

8. Any books, papers, documents, tape recordings, video tapes, or other tangible objects or copies thereof intended by the Commonwealth to be used as evidence in this case. *RCr 7.24.*

9. All items of evidence seized by the Commonwealth from the defendant, the defendant's home, or other places within the control or custody of the defendant, or which the prosecutor will argue were in the possession and/or control of the defendant. *RCr 7.24, RCr 7.26.*

10. Copies of any maps, diagrams, or the like that the Commonwealth intends to offer in evidence at any trial or hearing in this case. *RCr 7.24.*

Witnesses to Alleged Crimes; Persons
Having Knowledge of Events Leading to
Indictment

11. Names and addresses of any persons interviewed by the police, Kentucky State Police, coroners, and/or the _____ County Sheriff's Office, in connection with this case who have knowledge pertaining to the case *and* who were witnesses, and any person or persons who saw and/or spoke with defendant and/or the deceased prior to, during, and/or after the events which transpired that gave rise to the Indictment; persons who were witnesses to the defendant before, during, and after the events which transpired giving rise to the charges and Indictment. This request also includes any persons who may have seen defendant and the victim together prior to the time it is alleged [that the victim] died. *Burks v. Commonwealth,* Ky., 471 S.W.2d 298 (1971); *United States v. Cadet,* 727 F.2d 1453 (9th Cir. 1984). Defendant will seek appropriate funding for an investigator and/or mitigation specialist, or other experts. If the Commonwealth and/or its agents has already discovered witnesses, and if defendant has access to this information, he can conduct this investigation in a more expedient manner, with the least potential cost to the _____ Fiscal Court. See also *Wright v. Commonwealth,* Ky., 637 S.W.2d 635 (1982); *ABA Standards for Criminal Justice, Discovery and Procedure Before Trial, § 11–2.1(a)(i).*

a. If the prosecutor objects, and should the Court sustain said objection, then the defendant moves for an Order that all such reports, statements, memoranda, and the like which are sought but for which disclosure to defense counsel is not ordered be presented to the court, sealed, and made a part of the record for possible appellate review.

EXHIBIT 12–9 *(Continued)*
Motion for Discovery in Murder Case

Search Warrants/Arrest Warrants

12. Copies of any search or arrest warrants in connection with this case, including but not limited to any affidavits or other forms of sworn testimony in support thereof, and the "Returns" on said warrants, if executed. *RCr 7.24, RCr 7.26.*

Waivers, Warnings, or the Like
Executed by Defendant

13. Copies of any waivers, warnings, cautions, or instructions communicated to defendant in connection with any written or oral statements, confessions, or the like during any interview, examination, or evaluation. Defendant specifically requests the exact time, dates, and places of any such communication and the names, addresses, and phone numbers of any witnesses to the above, including witnesses who may be police officers from another state jurisdiction. *RCr 7.24; RCr 7.26.*

Disclosure by Commonwealth of Criminal
Records of Witnesses Intended to Be
Called

14. The names, addresses, and phone numbers of any persons whom the Commonwealth Attorney intends to or may call as witnesses in any trial or hearing in this case, and the local, state, and FBI arrest and conviction records of those witnesses. *Napue v. Illinois,* 360 U.S. 264 (1959); *Rolli v. Commonwealth,* Ky. App., 678 S.W.2d 800 (1984); *Moore v. Commonwealth,* Ky., 634 S.W.2d 426 (1982); *Martinez v. Wainwright,* 621 F.2d 184 (5th Cir. 1980).

Statements of Witnesses *RCr 7.26*
Generally Which Either Inculpates or
Exculpates Defendant with Reference to
Any Involvement in the Charges Within
the Indictment or Which May Exculpate
Him Relative to the Degree of
Involvement

15. That the Commonwealth provide copies of any written or oral statements of any witnesses the Commonwealth Attorney intends to call or may call as a witness in this case, or which otherwise inculpates or exculpates the defendant, including but not limited to information which would indicate that any statements by defendant are inconsistent with the objective evidence discovered by law enforcement or the Office of the Commonwealth Attorney. This request specifically includes any statements which conflict, either internally or with another statement of the same witness. *RCr 7.26. United States v. Bagley,* 473 U.S. 667 (1985), on remand 798 F.2d 667 (9th Cir. 1986); *Williams v. Commonwealth,* Ky., 569 S.W.2d 139 (1977); *Ballard v. Commonwealth,* Ky., 73 S.W.2d 21 (1988); *Stump v. Commonwealth,* Ky. App., 747 S.W.2d 607 (1988); *Rolli v. Commonwealth,* Ky. App., 678 S.W.2d 800 (1984); *Haynes v. Commonwealth,* Ky., 657 S.W.2d 948 (1983).

    a. This Motion includes any witnesses or other information from whatever source(s) that would indicate that the defendant did not participate in the offenses mentioned in the Indictment.

    b. If the Commonwealth objects, and if the Court sustains said objection, then defendant, in the alternative, moves for an *in camera* inspection by the Court to determine relevancy and preservation for possible appellate review. *RCr 7.26(12).* See *Haynes, supra; Wright v. Commonwealth,* Ky., 637 S.W.2d 635 (1982); and *LeGrande v. Commonwealth,* Ky., 494 S.W.2d 726 (1973); see also *Goldberg v. United States,* 425 U.S. 97 (1976) (notes taken by federal prosecutor during witness interview discoverable under *18 USC 3500,* "Jenks Act," as "witness statement");

Continued

EXHIBIT 12–9 *(Continued)*
Motion for Discovery in Murder Case

Lynch v. Commonwealth, Ky., 472 S.W.2d 263 (1971) (RCr 7.26(12) is "procedural equivalent" of Jenks Act); and *Haynes v. Commonwealth,* Ky., 657 So. 2d 948 (1983) (there is no generic work product exception for investigative police reports); prosecutor must comply with agreed disclosure terms, even if beyond that required by *RCr 7.24*. See also *Hendley v Commonwealth,* Ky., 573 S.W.2d 662 (1978) (court's *in camera* review of prosecutor's notes and memoranda of his investigation).

Request for Discovery Compliance
Sufficiently in Advance of Trial in
Order That Counsel Might Seek
Assistance in Any Investigation
Needed to Be Accomplished Prior to
Trial

16. Defendant seeks any orders relating to compliance by the Commonwealth to be sufficiently in advance of trial in order that defendant may conduct whatever investigation(s) are necessary in light of counsel's limited resources. *Silverburg v. Commonwealth,* Ky., 587 S.W.2d 241 (1979) (the disclosure of exculpatory evidence must be made to the defendant in time for a due investigation to be made); see also *Berry v. Commonwealth,* Ky., 782 S.W.2d 625 (1990); *Wright, supra; Hicks v. Commonwealth,* Ky. App., 805 S.W.2d 144 (1991) (error analysis when prosecutor fails to follow "open file" policy); *Epperson, supra; Barnett v. Commonwealth,* Ky., 763 S.W.2d 119 (1989) (a trial is not a "cat and mouse game").

Exculpatory Evidence Generally

17. Any items of evidence, whether real or otherwise, that are or may be exculpatory in nature. *RCr 7.24, RCr 7.26.* This request includes, but is not limited to, the following: any and all promises or consideration, or promises of consideration or inducements given to or made on behalf of prosecution witnesses, and this request includes full disclosure of all plea agreements, formal or informal, written or unwritten, with any witnesses or informants, and any and all state and/or federal presentence investigations that reflect a prosecution witness's efforts or cooperation on behalf of the Commonwealth or the federal government. This material is discoverable under the due process clause of the 14th Amendment. See *Giglio v. United States,* 405 U.S. 150 (1972); *United States v. Bagley,* 473 U.S. 667 (1985), on remand 798 F.2d 1297 (9th Cir. 1986); *Williams v. Commonwealth,* Ky., 569 S.W.2d 139 (1977). Defendant seeks an evidentiary hearing on this issue to demonstrate the lack of mere conjecture, *Key v. Commonwealth,* Ky., 633 S.W.2d 55 (1982). *See v. Commonwealth,* Ky., 746 S.W.2d 701 (1988) and *Ballard v. Commonwealth,* Ky., 743 S.W.2d 21 (1988) (entitlement upon request to exculpatory evidence in hands of prosecutor or agents of the Commonwealth); *Barnett v Commonwealth,* 828 S.W.2d 361 (1992) (right to discover exculpatory evidence which amounts to the right of defendant to present a defense).

a. In *Giglio v. United States,* 405 U.S. 150 (1972), the petitioner was convicted of passing forged money orders. He received five years. An issue arose because petitioner argued that the government's chief witness, Robert Taliento, had been made "offers" if he would testify against petitioner. Both the government and Taliento denied this; however, it was later learned that he had been made somewhat of a "promise" in exchange for his cooperation. Further evidence revealed that the chief government attorney did not actually make a "promise"; however, the witness was told that he definitely would be prosecuted if he did not testify:

> The United States Attorney, Hoey, filed an affidavit stating that he had personally consulted with Taliento and his attorney shortly before trial to emphasize that Taliento *would* definitely be prosecuted if he did not testify and that if he did testify he would be obliged to rely on the "good judgment and conscience of the Government" as to whether he would be prosecuted. (pp. 152–153) (emphasis added)

EXHIBIT 12–9 *(Continued)*
Motion for Discovery in Murder Case

b. The Supreme Court observed that there was "*at least an implication that the Government would reward the cooperation of the witness. . . .*" *Giglio v. United States, supra,* p. 153.

c. The Court went on further to hold that where the case against a defendant depends upon the testimony of witnesses who have entered into understandings and/or agreements with the government attorneys, this would be relevant to the credibility of these witnesses. This information should have been disclosed to counsel for the defense and, ultimately, to the jury.

d. It has been held to be a violation of defendant's 6th Amendment rights under the United States Constitution when a defense counsel was unable to cross-examine a witness on any understanding entered into with the governmental authorities.

Commonwealth Witnesses—Pending
Charges, Probation and Parole
Status, Etc.

18. Further, defendant seeks a listing of any and all charges, prosecutions, investigations, or possible prosecutions pending that could be brought against any prosecution witness and any probationary, parole, or deferred prosecution status of such witness, including both state and federal prosecutions, charges, or the like. *Davis v. Alaska,* 94 S. Ct. 1104 (1974).

Commonwealth Witnesses—Mental
Illnesses, Psychiatric Histories,
Psychological Problems, and the
Like, Including Drug and Alcohol
Problems

19. Defendant seeks any reports of any psychiatric, psychological, or mental evaluations of any prosecution witness or any evidence of psychiatric, psychological, or mental treatment of any prosecution witness, including but not limited to conditions of said witnesses that relate to drug or alcohol problems. See *Pennsylvania v. Ritchie,* 480 U.S. 39, 107 S. Ct. 989 (1987); *Wagner v. Commonwealth,* Ky., 581 S.W.2d 352 (1979); *Mosley v. Commonwealth,* Ky., 420 S.W.2d 679 (1967); *United States v. Lindstrom,* 698 F.2d 1154 (11th Cir. 1983).

a. In *United States v. Lindstrom, supra,* the Court cited the *Davis v. Alaska* case in commenting that

[T]he cross examiner is not only permitted to delve into the witness' story to test the witness' perceptions and memory, but the cross examiner has traditionally been allowed to impeach, i.e., discredit, the witness. . . . (p. 1160)

Certain forms of mental disorder have high probative value on the issue of credibility. . . . [Mental disorders] may tend to produce a bias in a witness' testimony. (p. 1160)

b. The Court went on to hold that broadly based assertions of confidentiality of such information (mental health records) usually argued by prosecution attorneys cannot justify denial of the defendant's right to examine and use psychiatric information to attack the credibility of a key government witness (p. 1167).

c. See also *Wagner v. Commonwealth,* Ky., 420 S.W.2d 679 (1967).

Defendant's Mental Status, Any
Evidence of Insanity, Mental
Illnesses, Drug and/or Alcohol
Involvement

Continued

EXHIBIT 12–9 *(Continued)*
Motion for Discovery in Murder Case

20. Defendant seeks any indication, whether contained in memoranda, investigative notes, or the like, that would indicate defendant was insane or suffered from mental illness or disturbance of any kind prior to, during, or after the alleged offense. Defendant seeks to discover and copy any and all records the Commonwealth and/or its agents may have regarding the mental status of the defendant, past or present, including, but not necessarily limited to, psychiatric reports, psychological evaluations and/or reports, physical exams, hospital records, or the like. See *Wagner, supra.*

Commonwealth's Evidence—Whether
Any Evidence Destroyed, Lost,
Misplaced

21. Any evidence of the destruction of any evidence by way of testing, the routine disposal of evidence, samples, or the like, and any and all other items that may have been considered in the investigation of this case but that are no longer available. Defendant specifically moves that no evidence, samples, or the like be destroyed or otherwise disposed of by the Commonwealth or its agents. *Calvert v Commonwealth,* Ky. App., 708 S.W.2d 121 (1986) (right of defendant to own evaluation of evidence); *Hendley, supra.*

Exculpatory and Impeachment
Evidence—Rewards

22. Any reward offers published concerning this case, including any claimed by any prosecution witnesses by virtue of their involvement in this case, including any rewards actually received.

Commonwealth Witnesses—Prior
History of Witnesses as
Commonwealth Informants

23. Disclosure of whether any prosecution witnesses or informants have served as informants in any other past cases, or whether such persons have testified for any prosecuting agency in exchange for their cooperation, and whether any information or testimony supplied by such persons was false.

Miscellaneous

24. All evidence not previously requested by this Motion which the Commonwealth intends to offer into evidence in this case.

25. Defendant further moves this Court to order the Commonwealth to notify defense counsel if additional material or information that is subject to discovery arises subsequent to compliance with the Order to be issued upon this Motion.

26. Defendant moves for leave to file additional Motions for Discovery for material or information that is subject to discovery that arises subsequent to compliance with the Order to be issued upon this Motion.

27. Defendant further moves for leave to file additional Motions for Discovery following the Commonwealth's Response to this Motion and Orders arising out of this Motion, some of which may require independent testing and evaluation.

28. On the issue of testing and the like, defendant moves that should there be further testing performed, then counsel for defendant and/or an expert for the defense be present, and that any samples or the like be preserved for evaluation and testing by the defense.

29. As additional argument for the discovery sought, counsel refers this court to the new Kentucky Supreme Court Rule (89–1), specifically *Rule 3.8 (SPECIAL RESPONSIBILITIES OF A PROSECUTOR) of the KENTUCKY RULES OF PROFESSIONAL CONDUCT, SCR 3.130,* which states, in part as follows:

EXHIBIT 12–9 *(Concluded)*
Motion for Discovery in Murder Case

The prosecutor at all stages of a proceeding shall: . . . (c) make timely disclosure to the defense of all evidence or information known to the prosecutor that tends to negate the guilt of the accused or mitigates the offense, and, in connection with sentencing, disclose to the defense and the tribunal all unprivileged mitigating information known to the prosecutor, except when the prosecutor is relieved of this responsibility by a protective order of the tribunal.

The "protective order" to which reference is made is clarified in *COMMENT(2)*. It refers to cases in which disclosure to the defense may result in substantial harm to an individual or to the public interest.

30. The issue for enhanced discovery in murder cases is best put in the following quotation from *Britt v. North Carolina,* 404 U.S. 239 (1971) (n. 7, p. 236):

The excessive disparity between the State and the accused in their respective investigative resources, and the common law's prohibition against discovery have been summarized by one commentator as follows:

The law enforcement agency is often at the scene of the crime shortly after its commission. While at the scene, the police have better access to witnesses with fresher recollections. They are authorized to confiscate removable evidence. In addition, the financial and investigatory resources of law enforcement agencies permit an extensive analysis of all relevant evidence.

The defendant has the option of hiring a private investigator. However, the investigator will probably get to the scene long after the occurrence of the crime and after the police have made their investigation and removed all relevant physical evidence. The defendant's investigator may have difficulty viewing the scene if it is on private property. Witnesses may be less accessible; their recollections will probably be less precise. Indeed they may choose not to cooperate at all with the defendant's investigator. However, it may all be irrelevant if, as is often the case, the defendant is unable to afford an investigator or is incarcerated pending trial.

The defendant is helpless to cope with the uncooperative witness while the prosecutor has numerous means to compel testimony. . . . [Norton, "Discovery in the Criminal Process," 61 J. Crim. L. C. & P.S. 11, 13–14 (1970)]

This defendant finds himself in just this posture, and he also is on trial for his life. It seems incongruous to strictly apply Rules that apply to all criminal cases in this Commonwealth, from "Disorderly Conduct" to "Criminal Trespass 3rd," to a death penalty proceeding. Taking this approach cannot be reconciled with the "enhanced reliability of the criminal process when death is possible." *Lockett v. Ohio,* 438 U.S. 586 (1978), and *Woodson v. North Carolina,* 428 U.S. 280 (1976).

Respectfully submitted,

_____

ATTORNEY FOR DEFENDANT
(Address and phone number)

NOTICE
This shall be heard on the 25th day of June, 2001, at 9:00 a.m.

_____

CERTIFICATE OF SERVICE
A copy of the foregoing was served upon _____ , Commonwealth Attorney, _____ , Kentucky, by mailing same this _____ day of June, 2001.

_____

EXHIBIT 12–10
Motion for Sanctions for Failure to Provide Timely Discovery

CAPITOL COUNTY	CIRCUIT COURT DIVISION II	STATE OF COLUMBIA

STATE OF COLUMBIA,
              PLAINTIFF

v.

MIGUEL CORDOBA
              DEFENDANT

INDICTMENT NO. _____

MOTION FOR SANCTION FOR
FAILURE TO PROVIDE TIMELY
DISCOVERY

The defendant, Miguel Cordoba, by counsel, pursuant to C.R.Cr.P. 337(A)(1), moves this Court for an order to sanction the State for failure to provide the defense with timely discovery. Specifically, defendant requests that the indictment charging the defendant with a violation of C.R.S. 809.00, a felony, be dismissed with prejudice. In the alternative, the defendant requests the Court for an order reducing the charge to second degree theft, C.R.S. 809.20, a misdemeanor.

As grounds for said sanction, the defendant states the following:

1. That Mr. Cordoba was indicted on the existing charge on February 12, _____ , and arraigned on February 20, _____ .

2. That Mr. Cordoba, by counsel, filed a motion for discovery on March 2, _____ , that specifically requested a copy of Roderick Brewer's grand jury testimony that addresses his basis for determining the value of the allegedly stolen ring. The motion also requested copies of any written documents stating the assessed value of the ring and the titles of any written authorities consulted by Mr. Brewer for making his assessment.

3. The Court ordered discovery on March 5, _____ .

4. Despite repeated reminders from defense counsel over a nine-month period, see Appendix A attached to this motion, the State has yet to provide this information.

5. Further, the defense has repeatedly requested the opportunity to view the ring. . . .

Because trial is scheduled in one week and any delay would now jeopardize defendant's right to speedy trial, and because defense has been prevented from having its own expert see the ring and review Mr. Brewer's basis for assessing the ring, defense has been denied the opportunity to adequately prepare for trial on the issue of the value of the ring, with the result that the defendant will be denied a fair trial.

WHEREFORE, based on Columbia's Rules of Criminal Procedure and the precedents cited in paragraphs 7–10 outlining the appropriate sanctions in these circumstances, the defendant requests that the indictment be dismissed or, in the alternative, that the charges be reduced to second degree theft, a misdemeanor.

Respectfully submitted,

_____

Attorney
(Address and phone number)
November 15, _____

Date of Service

_____

EXHIBIT 12–11
Pretrial Motion for Separate Trials

CAPITOL COUNTY   CIRCUIT COURT   STATE OF COLUMBIA
DIVISION II

STATE OF COLUMBIA,   CASE OR INDICTMENT NO. _____
       PLAINTIFF

v.   MOTION FOR SEPARATE TRIALS

_____ ,
       DEFENDANT

    Defendant, _____ , by counsel, pursuant to _____ Rules of Criminal Procedure, moves this Court for an order granting separate trials to the defendant on Counts _____ and _____ .

    As grounds for this motion, the defendant asserts the following:

    1. The defendant is charged with (state crime) _____ in Count _____ and with (state crime) _____ in Count _____ .

    2. The defendant's trial on these charges is set for (date) _____ .

    3. The defendant's right to a fair trial will be prejudiced by the joint trial of these charges because (state reasons and authority) _____

_____

_____

_____

_____

WHEREFORE, defendant moves this Court for an order separating Count _____ and Count _____ for trial.

                                            Respectfully submitted,

                                            _____

                                            Attorney

Date of Service   (Address and phone number)

_____   Date _____

SYSTEM FOLDER ASSIGNMENTS

Complete the following and place the documents in your system folder:

- Rules for federal and your jurisdiction's grand jury practice.
- Checklists of paralegal tasks for grand jury.
- Copies of the grand jury docket, grand jury subpoena, indictment, motion to dismiss indictment, motion for bill of particulars, and the bill of particulars (samples or completed class work).
- State and federal rules on arraignment.
- Checklist of paralegal tasks for arraignment.
- Summary of federal and your state's rules on discovery.
- Checklists and motions on discovery.
- Rules on pretrial motions in your jurisdiction.
- Copy of a pretrial motion.
- Your local rules regarding plea bargaining, especially on the withdrawal or change of a plea if the court rejects the agreement.

APPLICATION ASSIGNMENTS

1. Conduct a brief in-class grand jury hearing with Eldon Spiers from Case I as the target witness. Draft one or more of the following: an indictment of Eldon Spiers on an appropriate charge or charges, a motion to dismiss the indictment on any reasonable grounds, a motion for a bill of particulars, and the bill of particulars.

2. Draft a motion for discovery for the attorney defending Eldon Spiers.

3. Because your defense team failed to notify the prosecution in a timely manner of the defendant's intent to use a necessity (duress) defense in a robbery case as required by the discovery rules, the trial judge sanctioned the defense by prohibiting it from using that defense. Look at both the federal and your state rules on discovery sanctions to determine if this is an appropriate sanction. Then use an electronic research source to look up *People v. Houser*, 712 N.E.2d 355 (Ill. App. 1999). Determine if this case might be useful in preparing an appeal regarding the trial court's sanction.

4. LaVallee was tried and convicted of aggravated assault. Eventually he filed a habeas corpus action arguing that his sentence (ten to thirty years) was disproportional to the sentence awarded defendants who plea bargained on the same charge. He argued that he was being penalized for having exercised his right to a jury trial. How would you decide this case and why? Would your decision be different if records revealed that in cases where there was no plea bargain, simply a plea of guilty, defendants got seven to twenty-one years? Explain. See *LaVallee v. Perrin*, 466 A.2d 932 (N.H. 1983).

5. A defendant raised the issue of speedy trial nearly eight years after the filing of a detainer against him. Because he was illiterate, he relied on oral representation by Texas authorities that charges in Illinois had been dropped but found out they were still pending after he learned to read. Neither the defense nor state was able to show prejudice or lack of prejudice, but physical evidence against the defendant had been destroyed. Was his right to a speedy trial violated? See *People v. Prince*, 611 N.E.2d 105 (Ill. App. 1993).

HELPFUL WEB SITES

www.crimelynx.com
> Links to forensic services and witnesses, crime scene investigations

www.truth.idbsu.edu/jcawp/default.html
> Journal of Credibility Assessment and Witness Psychology, interviewing techniques, eyewitness memory, child witness issues

www.fbi.gov
> Link to Freedom of Information Act

www.bop.gov
> Bureau of Prisons, FOIA request by e-mail

www.nlada.org
> National Legal Aid and Defender Association for defense resources

www.crime-times.org
> Articles on crime and violence related to chemical imbalance, drugs, and toxic environments

INTERNET EXERCISES

1. Locate examples of the following forms using the American Jurisprudence Legal Forms 2d database (AMJUR-LF) on WESTLAW.

Motion to Quash Subpoena
Grand Jury Indictment (multiple courts)
Motion in Limine

2. Explore Freedom of Information Act accessibility through the FBI and Bureau of Prisons sites.

QUESTIONS FOR STUDY AND REVIEW

1. What are the three functions of a grand jury? How is the grand jury's autonomy protected?
2. What characteristics of grand juries lead to possible problems?
3. What is the title and focus of each type of grand jury witness?
4. How do grand jury evidentiary rules differ from those at trial?
5. What is a bill of particulars, and why is it helpful to the defense?
6. When is an information the appropriate charging document?
7. What happens at an arraignment?
8. Explain the consequences of each of the four possible pleas. Which one is used in only a few states?
9. What is the purpose of discovery?
10. What information is always protected from discovery?
11. Under what condition may the defense request an *in camera* inspection of the prosecution case file?
12. What kinds of evidence are exculpatory? What landmark decision made its disclosure mandatory?
13. What are the procedural requirements for pretrial motions?
14. List names and purposes of nine pretrial motions.
15. What is the pretrial obligation of the defense in the use of alibi and insanity defenses?
16. What is the purpose of plea bargaining?
17. To what standards must plea bargains conform, and what are the essentials of a valid plea?
18. Which amendments to the Constitution guarantee speedy trial?
19. What are the federal and state time limits ensuring speedy trial?
20. Why is speedy trial important?
21. What is the purpose of a pretrial conference?

KEY TERMS LIST

Attorney work product
Bill of particulars
Direct submission

Discovery
Exculpatory evidence
Pretrial conference

Prima facie case
Quash

ENDNOTES

1. *Studies Affirm Need to Reform Grand Jury Practices,* REPORT (National Center for State Courts, Williamsburg, Va.), citing 1973 study in Harris Co. (Houston) Texas.
2. This section drawn in part from materials submitted by Vicki Doolin Mills, Commonwealth Detective/Paralegal, Richmond, KY, Mar. 3, 1990.
3. *Id.*
4. Spencer Weber Waller, *An Introduction to Federal Grand Jury Practice,* WIS. BAR BULL., Oct. 1988, at 18.
5. JEROLD H. ISRAEL & WAYNE R. LaFAVE, CRIMINAL PROCEDURE: CONSTITUTIONAL LIMITATIONS 126 (1988).

6.   Waller, *supra* note 4, at 19, 54.

7.   *Id.*

8.   *Id.* at 55.

9.   George Sornberger, *Grand Jury Testimony: Presenting Evidence and Obtaining a Transcript,* THE ADVOCATE, Dec. 1989, at 41.

10. For an insightful discussion of the consequences of this plea, see Barbara Rankin, *The National Alliance for the Mentally Ill,* THE ADVOCATE, Oct. 1989, at 51–52.

11. Doolin Mills, *supra* note 2.

12. Drawn in part from RICHARD T. OAKES, OAKES' CRIMINAL PRACTICE GUIDE 29–36 *Wiley Law Publications* (1991).

13. *Id.*

14. David T. Eucker, Assistant Public Advocate, Office of Public Advocacy, Richmond, KY, Motion for Discovery, adapted and reprinted with permission.

15. Michael L. Williams, Department of Public Advocacy, Frankfort, KY, Defendant's Motion for Discovery and Other Relief, reprinted with permission.

16. Adapted from *Motion for Sanction for Failure to Provide Timely Discovery,* criminal law course materials, Paralegal Program, Eastern Kentucky University, author unknown.

17. Edward C. Monahan, *Effectively Obtaining Funds for Expert Help,* THE ADVOCATE, Jan. 1997, at 110.

18. *Id.*

19. David E. Rovella, *Federal Plea Bargains Draw Fire,* NLJ, Jan. 17, 2000, at A1, A8.

20. Doolin Mills, *supra* note 2.

21. NAT'L BUR. STAND. (U.S.), Tech. Note 535 (Aug. 1970), p. 161, in 4 U.S. Code Cong. & Admin. News 7407 (1974), cited in CHARLES WHITEBREAD & CHRISTOPHER SLOBOGIN, CRIMINAL PROCEDURE: AN ANALYSIS OF CASES AND CONCEPTS 552, n. 7 (2d ed. 1986).

22. RICHARD T. OAKES, OAKES' CRIMINAL PRACTICE GUIDE 17–26, 11–27 *Wiley Law Publications* (1991).

TRIAL: RIGHTS, PROCEDURE, TASKS

I. INTRODUCTION

The trial is the central test not only of the facts and points of law involved in criminal litigation, but also of the strategy, preparation, and implementation of both the prosecution and defense. The law comes alive in the courtroom, dragging all its history behind it; the evidence that you so carefully stacked in your side's favor now stands or falls under the scrutiny of judge and jury.

At each step you see your case rest on the foundation of your pretrial work, as well as on the alertness it takes to keep everything in balance throughout the shifting course of the trial. Research pays off in jury selection, as do on-the-spot impressions. Careful attention to rules of evidence is vital in preparation, in presentation, and in noting items for objection, witness impeachment, impact on jurors, and so on. Your skill at drafting pertinent questions and noting unexpected answers is tested, as is your work on motions and jury instructions. In short, two very different kinds of skills contribute to success at trial: the ability to make sometimes slow, painstaking, thorough preparations and the ability to think quickly and adjust amid the flow of events.

This chapter focuses on those aspects of trial that are particularly important or unique to criminal practice. A complete review of general litigation skills goes beyond the practical scope of this text. It is worth noting that diligent trial preparation and practice is required not only by the adversary system and, thus, the code of ethics, but also by the need to avoid costly and time-consuming appeals. This need is reflected in the statistics showing that 50 percent of death penalty cases are overturned by appellate courts, often on the basis of incompetence in representation.[1]

II. TRIAL RIGHTS

A. THE RIGHT TO A JURY TRIAL

"Jury service honorably performed is as important in the defense of our country, its Constitution and laws, and the ideals and standards for which they stand, as the service that is rendered by the soldier on the field of battle in time of war."

—George H. Boldt, American jurist *U.S. v. Beck* (1959)

The rise in religious skepticism in the twelfth and thirteenth centuries undermined reliance on the belief in divine intervention to decide criminal cases. With priests forbidden to participate in superstition-laden trials by water and fire, a trustworthy alternative was needed by the increasingly influential civil governments. Most of Europe chose the inquisitional system, whereas England developed the less oppressive jury trial. The Magna Carta (1215 A.D.) guaranteed the right to trial by peers; juries, however, were not truly independent of judicial dominance until 1670. Trial juries are rooted in the belief that a neutral body should stand between a politically motivated government and the accused citizen, and that a citizen should not be subject to punishment by the government until guilt has been proven to the satisfaction of that independent group of citizens.

These traditions and beliefs have been incorporated into our law. Article 3, Section 2, of the United States Constitution states, "The Trial of all Criminals . . . shall be by jury . . . ," and the Sixth Amendment adds, "In all criminal prosecutions, the accused shall enjoy the right to a speedy and public trial, by an impartial jury . . . to be confronted with the witnesses against him; to have compulsory process for obtaining witnesses in his favor, and to have the Assistance of Counsel for his defence." The Fifth Amendment requires that trial procedures must comport with due process. Each of these rights is applicable to the states through the Fourteenth Amendment. Juries are required in the trial of all crimes except petty offenses, juvenile cases, and military crimes. A **petty offense** is one having a maximum penalty not to exceed six months' incarceration [see *Duncan v. Louisiana* (1968) and *Codispoti v. Pennsylvania* (1974)]. No constitutional right to a jury exists, even if the defendant is facing trial on multiple petty offenses, for which the combined penalties might exceed six months in jail [*Lewis v. U.S.* (1996)]. A number of states grant jury trials in petty offenses even though

petty offense:
one having a maximum penalty not to exceed six months' incarceration.

it is not constitutionally mandated. A jury trial may be waived [Rule 23(a) Fed. R. Crim. P.], but only if the waiver is knowingly and voluntarily given. Even though a defendant may offer to waive a jury trial, neither the government nor the court is constitutionally required to acquiesce in that request, and a jury trial can still occur [*Singer v. U.S.* (1965)]. If a state has a constitutional provision that makes the defendant's waiver a constitutional right, however, then the prosecution may not be able to get a jury trial [*State v. Baker* (Ore. 1999)]. Although a statute that enhances the penalty of a person for exercising the right to a jury trial is unconstitutional [*U.S. v. Jackson* (1968)], a plea bargain that rewards an accused for giving up the right is not.

Twelve jurors are used in capital cases and most felonies. Some states use six jurors for misdemeanors. The federal rules require twelve jurors unless the accused agrees to fewer. Even without such an agreement, a federal judge can validate a verdict of eleven jurors after the jury has started its deliberations [Fed. R. Crim. P. 23(b)]. A change in Rule 24(c)(3) empowers the court to retain alternate jurors during deliberations in case one or more regular jurors has to be dismissed. There is no constitutional magic in the number twelve. Six is acceptable [*Williams v. Florida* (1970)], but not five [*Ballew v. Georgia* (1978)]. Unanimous verdicts, though commonly required, also are not constitutionally mandated; nine of twelve is acceptable [*Apodaca v. Oregon* (1972)], but a unanimous verdict is needed with six jurors [*Burch v. Louisiana* (1979)]. At least one federal court has ruled that an anonymous jury is acceptable, especially when witnesses and, therefore, jurors may be in danger [*U.S. v. Krout* (5th Cir. 1995)].

B.   THE RIGHT TO COUNSEL

The Sixth Amendment and *Gideon v. Wainwright* (1963) guarantee an accused the "assistance of counsel for his defense" at trial. Even if counsel is provided, the right is violated if (1) counsel's performance is deficient, involving errors so serious that counsel was not functioning at the level required by the Constitution, and (2) the deficient performance prejudiced the defendant, involving errors that were so serious that the defendant was deprived of a fair trial, one where the result is reliable [*Strickland v. Washington* (1984)]. The appropriate standard is reasonably effective assistance. This has been interpreted to include an adversarial testing of the government's case. Failure to comply with this standard is termed *ineffective assistance of counsel.* An attorney's decisions on strategy are generally not reviewable. The errors in question normally involve serious oversights such as the failure to present battered person syndrome evidence in a manslaughter case [*People v. Day* (Cal. App. 1992)], the failure to call police officers whose testimony clearly would have impeached that given by the state's key witnesses [*People v. Mejia* (Ill. App. 1993)], or the failure to object to the prosecution's repeated comments on the defendant's post–*Miranda* warning silence [*Pennycuff v. State* (Ind. App. 2000)]. Ineffective counsel claims also arise in conflict of interest situations—representation by an attorney of the codefendant, for example—but the defendant must show the conflict "adversely affected" the defendant's rights [*Cuyler v. Sullivan* (1980)]. Ineffective assistance is often unsuccessful on appeal, but when it is established, the remedy is reversal and remand.

Pro se (pro per) **representation** occurs when the accused elects to represent himself or herself. Self-representation is guaranteed under the Sixth Amendment [*Faretta v. California* (1975)] but must be entered into knowingly and intelligently. A court may appoint standby counsel or can end *pro se* representation if the defendant is disruptive [*Illinois v. Allen* (1970)]. A *pro se* defendant cannot later claim ineffective assistance of his or her own representation. Some experienced defendants have learned to manipulate the system to gain repeated delays and overturned convictions by waffling back and forth between *pro se* and appointed representation. Courts, however, turn a deaf ear to such defendants when they claim denial of their right to counsel [*State v. Crisafi* (N.J. 1992)]. If a defendant's mental competency is in question, *pro se* representation is

pro se (pro per)
representation:
self-representation by the
defendant.

a denial of effective counsel, unless the competency issue is resolved prior to the representation [*U.S. v. Klat* (D.C. Cir. 1998)].

C. THE RIGHTS OF PRESENCE AND CONFRONTATION

The right to be present and the right to confront one's accusers are closely tied together. The Sixth Amendment's right of confrontation gives the defendant the right to see opposing witnesses and to challenge their testimony. To achieve this, the defendant must be present. There is, however, a distinct right to be present that extends beyond the testimony phase to guarantee the defendant's presence at most aspects of the trial. Its source lies solely in procedural due process. The ruling in *U.S. v. Gagnon* (1985) restricted a court from placing unreasonable or prejudicial conditions on the right to be present and did not limit that right to testimonial stages of the trial. The court may not require the accused to wear handcuffs, shackles, or prison clothes. Such conditions violate the due process presumption of innocence [*Estelle v. Williams* (1976)]. A defendant may not be forced to take an antipsychotic drug for trial, because it effectively undermines an insanity defense [*Riggins v. Nevada* (1992)].

The right to confrontation specifically guaranteed by the Sixth Amendment is also rooted in the due process quest for fairness. It is of utmost importance, because it gives the defendant the opportunity to question each witness through cross-examination; to note and comment on a witness's inaccuracies, inconsistencies, contradictions, bias, and hostility; to observe and comment on a witness's demeanor; and to impeach or otherwise rebut witnesses [*Illinois v. Allen* (1970)]. In overturning convictions, appellate courts have said that having a witness wear a mask [*People v. Sammons* (Mich. App. 1991)], allowing a police officer to testify without the defendant present [*Commonwealth v. Rios* (Mass. 1992)], and permitting a bailiff to express an opinion to the jury [*Parker v. Gladden* (1966)] were all denials of the right to confront witnesses.

The right to confrontation is essential to fairness, so what should a court do if the witness is a young child? Should the child who is an important witness in an abuse or sexual molestation case be subject to intensive cross-examination? Is it better to protect the child or permit cross-examination in the spirit of avoiding the conviction and imprisonment of an innocent person? Because such prosecutions are numerous, the issue is a critical one. In *Maryland v. Craig* (1990), the Supreme Court ruled that a child may testify by closed circuit television out of the presence of the accused in special circumstances. In *Craig* the child was in a separate room with both the prosecutor and the defense attorney. The child's testimony was broadcast into the courtroom for the defendant, the jury, and the judge to see. The defendant could communicate electronically with the defense attorney, and the judge could rule on objections. Separating the defendant and the child-witness is permitted only if the court finds "necessity" to protect the child's physical and psychological well-being or if the trauma caused by the presence of the defendant, not simply the courtroom, would be more than minimal.

More recently the Court ruled that other persons may testify in place of the child [*White v. Illinois* (1992)]. The ruling permits doctors and nurses to testify as to what the child said out of court under a medical treatment exception to the hearsay rule, and parents and others can testify if the child's statements were "spontaneous," another hearsay exception. Recent studies provide dramatic evidence that young children are not reliable when repeatedly asked about sexual or other matters. The children in the studies fabricated elaborate stories; 70 percent of them said their genitals had been touched when they had not.[2]

Rape and other sexual assault cases also raise issues involving the right to confrontation. Most states have a rape shield law preventing a defendant in a sexual assault case from questioning the victim about or introducing evidence of the victim's past sexual conduct. This law places the focus on the relevant conduct of the defendant, rather than on irrelevant past indiscretions of the victim, and makes it easier for victims to accuse their attackers. If the accused can demonstrate the relevance of the victim's past sexual practice to the pending case, however, the court must admit the evidence or risk reversal of any conviction for denying the right to confrontation. In a sexual assault case involving alleged sexual conduct with a five-year-old girl, the rape shield law could not be used to bar testimony that the girl had experienced other sexual play with her younger brother, because this testimony revealed that the girl had knowledge relevant to the defense of fabrication [*Dixon v. State* (Fl. App. 1992)].

Occasionally a witness who testifies at a grand jury or other hearing is not available for trial or a codefendant chooses not to testify at trial. The accused may not have had an opportunity for cross-examination at the previous hearing and cannot cross-examine the witness at trial. Therefore, the transcript of previous testimony when the witness is now unavailable or unable to testify normally is not admissible [*Bruton v. U.S.* (1968)]. Simply deleting the defendant's name from a codefendant's confession when the codefendant was not available for cross-examination was a denial of the defendant's right to confrontation [*Gray v. Maryland* (1998)]. Out-of-court statements by an accomplice who was not available to testify that placed primary blame on the defendant violated the Sixth Amendment [*Lilly v. Virginia* (1999)]. The court added that the accomplice's confession did not come under the exception established in *Ohio v. Roberts* (1980), allowing such confessions when they are sufficiently reliable that cross-examination would do little to their perceived reliability. Exceptions to the admissibility of out-of-court statements include a declaration by the witness or victim in contemplation of imminent death and the instance when the defense had a chance to cross-examine the witness at a preliminary hearing but did not do so. An additional exception is found in Federal Rule of Evidence 801(d)(2)(E) and similar state rules that permit admission of out-of-court statements by one coconspirator against another, even though the coconspirator may not be available for cross-examination [*Bourjaily v. U.S.* (1987)].

Does it violate the right to confrontation and the right to be present to remove or to bind and gag a disruptive defendant? *Illinois v. Allen* (1970) ruled that "flagrant disregard . . . of proper conduct . . . cannot be tolerated." A court may hold the defendant in contempt, bind and gag the defendant, place an electrical shock belt on the defendant, or remove the defendant until he or she promises to behave. Some famous cases involving repeated disruptions by the defendant and court sanctions include the "Chicago Seven" [*U.S. v. Dellinger* (7th Cir. 1972)] and the Charles Manson murder trial. After repeated outbursts followed by repeated court warnings, Manson was confined to his cell where the trial proceedings were broadcast. In unusual circumstances, some jurisdictions allow a defendant to be tried in absentia.

ANALYSIS PROBLEM

13–1. Should Kate Lamb's statement to police before she died identifying Eldon Spiers as her assailant be allowed in evidence even though the defense does not have a chance to confront her regarding the truth and, particularly, the accuracy of the identification? Should a friend's testimony be allowed that Ms. Lamb bragged about having previously made sexually aggressive advances toward Eldon Spiers?

D. THE RIGHT TO PRESENT WITNESSES, TO TESTIFY, OR NOT TO TESTIFY

The defendant has the right to present witnesses at trial, which is guaranteed by basic due process in the Fifth and Fourteenth Amendments and the Sixth Amendment right to compel the attendance of witnesses. [*Washington v. Texas* (1967), *Chambers v. Mississippi* (1973)]. The procedure for subpoenaing witnesses is set out in Fed. R. Crim. P. 17(a-b) and similar state rules. Note that the reach of federal subpoenas in criminal cases is the entire United States and abroad (28 U.S.C.A. § 1783). Rule 17(b) allows indigents to subpoena witnesses at government expense. The right to present witnesses at trial can include providing an indigent defendant with an expert witness at public expense [*Ake v. Oklahoma* (1985)]. Under the Fifth and Fourteenth amendments, the defendant has the due process right to testify in his or her own behalf. This right is subject to reasonable limitations, but such limitations must stand up to constitutional scrutiny. Most rules of evidence designed to ensure reliability survive this scrutiny. An Arkansas rule prohibiting use of all hypnotically refreshed testimony, however, was unduly restrictive, because it ignored other factors that, in the defendant's case, might have shown the testimony to be sufficiently reliable [*Rock v. Arkansas* (1987)]. More importantly, the defendant has the right not to testify, guaranteed by the Fifth Amendment's right against self-incrimination. Any attempt by the prosecutor to raise an inference of guilt by commenting on the defendant's choice not to testify is a violation of the right sufficient to warrant a new trial or a reversal of any conviction [*Griffin v. California* (1965)].

Other considerations may raise due process questions. Permitting the courtroom audience to be 50 percent uniformed prison guards in an already inmate-hostile community deprived the defendant of a fair trial [*Woods v. Dugger* (11th Cir. 1991)], and allowing the prosecutor to designate as witnesses all of the defendant's friends so they could be removed from the courtroom was a denial of the right to a public trial [*Addy v. State* (Tex. App. 1993)].

III. FAIR TRIAL VERSUS FREE PRESS AND PUBLIC ACCESS

The defendant's right to an impartial jury under both the Fifth and Sixth amendments can run head-on into the First Amendment's guarantee of freedom of the press and public access. At least four concerns arise in this context.

1. Exposure of jurors and potential jurors to media coverage of the case may cause prejudgment or make it too difficult to find an impartial juror.
2. In-court media coverage, especially cameras and television, may increase political and community pressure on the participants; induce grandstanding by attorneys, witnesses, and the judge; and heighten jurors' fears of reprisals from the community or the defendant's sympathizers.
3. Media exposure may increase juror susceptibility to bribery and encourage other corrupt practices.
4. Extensive in-court media coverage can erode the dignity of the courtroom, which is essential to at least the appearance of a neutral and fair trial.

Because of the importance granted the freedom of the press, a judge may not forbid the press from publishing information about the case. Other remedies are available to the judge, including "gag orders" preventing attorneys, parties, witnesses, or other court officials from publicly discussing the case; isolation of both witnesses and jurors; restraints on in-court conduct of the press; and a change of venue in the case of significant pretrial publicity [*Sheppard v. Maxwell* (1966)]. Standard 8-1.1 of the American Bar Association Standards for Criminal Justice Fair Trial and Free Press is an excellent resource for what the legal team can and cannot say to the media under current ethical and judicial standards.

Press and public access extends to most other procedures, such as preliminary hearings and arraignments, but not to grand jury proceedings. No trial or procedure may be closed unless there is a compelling government need that clearly overrides the required openness [*Richmond Newspapers, Inc. v. Virginia* (1980)]. Although still prohibited by federal Rule 53, television cameras do not violate the Constitution, so criminal trials in their entirety are now televised via cable in many states [*Chandler v. Florida* (1981)]. The court has the duty to see that the coverage is unobtrusive and dignified. When done appropriately, video recording and broadcasting of local court proceedings and cases of national interest, such as the O. J. Simpson case and the impeachment trial of President Clinton, not only provide a better record of proceedings, but also enhance public understanding and scrutiny of our judicial processes.

IV. THE PARALEGAL'S ROLE IN PREPARATION FOR TRIAL

A. INTRODUCTION

The paralegal performs important tasks in preparation for trial. Critical issues regarding a defendant's trial rights may require legal research that might lead to more pretrial motions. In addition, this section explores the role of the paralegal in organizing the trial notebook, preparing the client and witnesses for court, and generally supervising trial materials and other matters.

B. THE TRIAL NOTEBOOK

The trial notebook consists of a ringed binder divided into sections for the necessary documents and materials needed at trial. A typical trial notebook for a criminal case includes the following sections.

Trial Notebook Sections

- Reference: table of contents, parties, court personnel, phone numbers, emergency resource persons and numbers, witnesses, case summaries, and chart of issues and proof.
- Pleadings and Pretrial: charging documents, any pretrial orders, and last minute motions.
- Voir Dire: notes on each juror, most wanted-least wanted, outline of voir dire questions, authorities researched on any legal issues surrounding challenges to jurors or other voir dire issues, and final jury chart.
- Opening Statement: complete text or outline.
- Order of Proof: outline of the expected order in which evidence will be presented by both sides.
- Witness Section: summary of each witness, questions to be asked, note of exhibits to be identified by witness, summary of any previous statements or testimony, cross-examination questions.
- Exhibits: exhibit log, each exhibit placed in the order likely to be presented, and demonstrative evidence log.
- Trial Motions and Supporting Legal Authority: placed chronologically as they are likely to come up at trial.
- Jury Instructions: copies of all jury instructions to be proposed to the court.
- Closing Statement: complete text or outline, any props to be used, and space to note additions that come up at trial.

- Law Section: memo of legal authorities and copy of pertinent rules of evidence or procedure likely to be in issue at trial.

Organization of a trial notebook is a lot of work, but the notebook is an invaluable trial tool for both attorney and paralegal. Most offices have a good example to use as a model.

C.   PREPARATION OF CLIENT AND WITNESSES

You can also assist by preparing witnesses and the client for trial. Taking the defendant or other key witnesses to the courtroom and letting them sit where they will testify can reduce anxiety. Assisting the lawyer in practising both direct and cross-examination and evaluating the witness's demeanor, clothing, and style can substantially improve the witness's impact at trial. Help make the witnesses comfortable at court. Let them know when they are likely to be needed. See that any witness fees, especially for expert witnesses, are ready to be paid. See to it, of course, that the witnesses are subpoenaed for the trial. Slip-ups here can be disastrous. Preparing witnesses must be done in close coordination with your supervising attorney and in accordance with long-established office guidelines.

If necessary, instruct the defendant and family or victim and family on proper courtroom demeanor. The presence of the defendant's well-behaved small children could have an impact on the jury, for example. By contrast, a rape defendant's "lewd noises" toward a female juror during recess was enough to result in a mistrial and additional charges of intimidating a juror.[3]

D.   TRIAL MATERIALS

"[Preparation] is the be-all of good trial work. Everything else—felicity of expression, improvisational brilliance—is a satellite around the sun. Thorough preparation is that sun."

—Louis Nizer, *Newsweek,*
Dec. 11, 1973

Supervise all trial materials, making sure they are present and kept secure during trial, recesses, and overnight. Observe the jurors and each witness. Take notes on key testimony, note in the exhibits log when an exhibit is presented and admitted, and record the judge's decision on juror challenges, objections, motions, and other matters. The notes are valuable not only for the closing argument, but also for posttrial motions and eventually for appeal.

Be prepared to conduct emergency research, find a witness, or call persons back at the office to assist. Being well prepared reduces the number of emergencies, but trials still retain some element of unpredictability.

V.   TRIAL PROCEDURE AND THE PARALEGAL'S ROLE

A.   VOIR DIRE

1.   Introduction

venire:
the list of eligible persons from which jurors are summoned for duty; must be a "fair cross-section" of the community.

voir dire:
to speak the truth; the in-court questioning of jurors by the judge and the attorneys to screen jurors based on the juror's bias or other reasons for inability to serve; means to attain an impartial jury.

The list of eligible persons from which jurors are summoned for duty is the **venire.** The venire must be a "fair cross-section" of the community under the Sixth Amendment right to an impartial jury. *Taylor v. Louisiana* (1975) held that the exclusion of women or other "large, distinctive groups" from the venire is unconstitutional. Equal protection under the Fourteenth Amendment is denied if the process excludes a racial or ethnic group. This protection has been broadened to cover not only the selection of the overall venire, but also the exclusion of potential jurors during voir dire. Potential jurors are selected out of the entire jury pool for that term of court. Those persons are summoned to the courtroom at the specified time and make up the in-court group from which the actual jury and possible alternates are selected.

Voir dire, meaning to speak the truth, is the in-court questioning of potential jurors by the judge and the attorneys to screen for bias or other reasons for inability to serve in order to attain an impartial jury. Impartiality is gained, in theory, when each side eliminates those persons who are most likely to be sympathetic to the other side. The potential jurors are given preliminary instructions by the court then are asked questions by the judge and each attorney. Jurisdictions vary on who asks the questions, the attorneys and the judge or only the judge, but the attorneys are generally allowed to ask questions in criminal cases. The questions attempt to elicit any information that indicates a bias, such as knowing the defendant or the victim, exposure to extensive pretrial publicity, and the like.

In an effort to screen jurors, each side can use two types of juror challenges. The first is a **challenge for cause** where an attorney requests the court to remove a potential juror on the grounds of bias or other reason. The second is a **peremptory challenge** that gives the attorney latitude to strike a potential juror without having to express any reason for the strike. Challenges for cause are unlimited; peremptory challenges are limited in number by the applicable rules of procedure. Peremptory challenges are numerous in death penalty cases (up to twenty) and progressively fewer in felony and misdemeanor cases.

The government's use of a peremptory challenge to exclude a juror on the basis of race is an unconstitutional denial of equal protection [*Batson v. Kentucky* (1986)]. The *Batson* Court eased a previously established but nearly insurmountable burden of proof for the defendant. Under *Batson,* the defendant must show only that a juror of the same race was excluded and that, considering "all relevant" circumstances, it appears as if the exclusion was based on race. Once that claim is established, the burden shifts to the prosecution to show that the peremptory challenge was for other reasons.

Batson was expanded in *Powers v. Ohio* (1991) to give a white defendant standing to challenge the prosecution's peremptory exclusion of African Americans on the basis of race. *Batson* and *Powers* were significantly weakened, however, in *Purkett v. Elem* (1995). The Court ruled that the prosecution's burden of proof to dispel accusations of racially motivated peremptory challenges was to demonstrate any facially neutral reason to exclude the juror, even if the reason were "implausible or fantastic." Further, in *U.S. v. Martinez-Salazar* (2000) the Court decided that a conviction need not be reversed when the trial judge improperly failed to remove a biased juror for cause, and the defense elected to use one of its peremptory challenges to rid the jury of apparent bias. According to the Court, had the defense refused to use one of its peremptory challenges to remove the biased juror, the judge's decision would have been reversible error as a denial of the right to a fair trial.

In *J.E.B. v. Alabama ex rel. T.B.* (1994) the Supreme Court ruled that people cannot be excluded from juries solely because of their sex. In death sentence cases, federal jurors must sign a certificate stating that their verdict was not influenced by race, color, religious belief, national origin, or sex of the defendant or the victim [18 U.S.C.A. § 3593(f)].

Jurors may not be removed by challenge for cause if they have general scruples against capital punishment [*Wainwright v. Witt* (1985)], but if they will automatically vote against the penalty, they may be dismissed [*Witherspoon v. Illinois* (1968)]. Likewise, prospective jurors may be asked if they would automatically vote for the death penalty [*Morgan v. Illinois* (1992)]. In either case, jurors must be able to place their oath and obligation to apply the law above their moral stance toward the penalty.

If a challenge for cause is successful, the juror is discharged and another is selected and questioned. Depending on local practice, it is common that once the questioning ends, each side exercises its peremptory challenges. It is necessary to place enough potential jurors in the group to be questioned so that the requisite number of jurors remain after the peremptory challenges are exercised.

After the jurors are selected, they are sworn in by the judge and instructed not to discuss the case, even with each other, until told to do so. Any objections to the jury panel or the selection process must be made before the jurors are sworn in.

challenge for cause: an attorney's request to remove a potential juror on the grounds of bias or other reason.

peremptory challenge: authority of an attorney to strike the name of a potential juror without having to express any reason for the strike; limited in number.

2. The Paralegal's Role in Voir Dire

Voir dire is an exceptionally important step in the trial process. It is here that important and often lasting first impressions are made on the jurors. In addition to providing information about each juror, the questioning process is a crucial opportunity to educate the jury on points of law, the theory of the case, or a relevant defense. It is often used to disarm arguments likely to be made by the opposition and to establish rapport with the jury. As is true of so much of legal work, good jury selection is no accident. It is the product of careful preparation and planning. Your role here is a significant one.

"The classic adversary system in the United States not only encourages, it demands that each lawyer attempt to empanel the jury most likely to understand his argument, or least likely to understand that of his opponent. You don't approach a case with the philosophy of applying abstract justice. You go in to win."

—Percy Foreman, *New York Times*, Feb. 3, 1969

Preparation for voir dire begins well in advance of the trial date. To begin, you need a clear understanding of the case and the strategies that will be applied during its presentation. A thorough planning conference with your supervising attorney is essential. Next, prepare profiles of both the defendant and the victim, highlighting age, sex, occupation, socioeconomic group, and other characteristics, then identify similar characteristics in the prospective jurors. Similar people from similar circumstances are often more sympathetic to each other than to persons of dissimilar characteristics and circumstances.

With these profiles in hand, investigate the jury panel. Obtain the questionnaires filled out by each juror for the term from the appropriate clerk of court. These forms vary, but often provide name, age, sex, race, religion, marital status, number of children, address, occupation, educational level, previous jury service, organizational memberships, whether the juror has been the victim of a crime, and more. This information is sufficient for many cases.

Unique or more serious cases require a deeper investigation. Jury selection service companies, normally found only in large cities, sell detailed juror information lists. Although no prospective juror should ever be contacted, neighbors, friends, and others can provide information. Sometimes a juror sits on more than one case in a term, and the attorneys who tried that case, or their paralegals, can provide insights on the juror. In smaller communities, those persons who seem to know about everyone else's business can also help. Public records can be searched. Some investigators even check the jurors' cars for revealing bumper stickers.[4] Some attorneys employ handwriting analysts to evaluate the jurors' writing. Legal teams are increasingly using the Internet to learn more about jurors. Search strategies encompass using prospective jurors' names or affiliations to turn up personal, work, or association Web sites; checking public records; and using on-line service message archives like DejaNews.[5] To eliminate any unnecessary work, obtain the names of jurors who have been excused.

Community surveys can be conducted to determine community attitudes, and thus juror attitudes, on matters pertinent to a case. A survey may aim to assess the impact of pretrial publicity or attitudes toward the crime involved, the theory of defense, or the death penalty, for example. Exhibit 13–1, page 508, is an example of instructions for conducting the survey and questions to be asked.[6]

Discuss the survey data with your supervising attorney. In serious cases juror selection consultants and psychologists can be employed to assist in interpreting data and recommending jury selection strategies. Locating past studies of jury attitudes in various legal periodicals and trial practice books can be useful. For example, recent studies reveal that of those polled, about 50 percent said a judge's jury instructions should be ignored to do what the person believed was the right thing; African Americans, Hispanics, and people earning less than $20,000 were highly skeptical of police testimony; 40 percent of those polled and 70 percent of African Americans said minorities are treated less fairly than others by the system; and a significant number said that they could not be a fair juror if one of the parties was a homosexual (12 percent, down from 17 percent in 1998), a computer hacker (20 percent), or a white supremacist (33 percent). The same studies indicated that previous jury experience was a modifying force in overall attitude toward the system, witnesses, and the parties.[7]

Condense the pertinent data on each juror onto a juror profile sheet to be placed into the trial binder. The binder should also contain a fill-in-the-block juror grid sheet showing the seating arrangement of the jurors. Include in the trial binder a final list of voir dire questions. Develop the questions from the office's standard set of voir dire questions, practice manuals, and other works specifically on jury selection. Tailor and supplement these canned questions according to the facts and strategies of the case at hand and according to the demands and procedures of local practice. Confer with your supervising attorney to refine the list. Here are some points to consider in educating and questioning jurors.

Educating and Questioning Jurors at Voir Dire

1. Use questions containing educational information on such matters as the burden of proof, reasonable doubt, the presumption of innocence, the role of prosecution and defense, introduction of the defendant, and like matters; and clarifying that the information or indictment is merely an accusation and not evidence, and that prejudgments are normal but need to be spoken of freely and frankly in voir dire.

2. Draft questions that get jurors talking and thinking, and that reveal their attitudes: Have you or any close relatives been a victim of a similar or other crime? Describe it. Have you been accused of a crime? Explain. This is Ms. _____the defendant or Mr. _____the victim. What impressions come to your mind about this person? Do you have any impression of the attorneys? What have you heard about the case? What are your friends and neighbors saying about the case? Do you feel any pressure to decide the case one way or the other? The defendant has a strong accent; what impression does this create? The victim was a member of a gang; does this make you value his life less? Would you be inclined to believe a police officer more than you would any other witness? What are your thoughts about the credibility of a person who has been convicted of a crime? What are your thoughts about the credibility of a spouse or friend testifying either for or against the defendant?

3. Draft questions that elicit views on race or ethnicity if pertinent to the case: How do you feel about the relationship between races in this community? What statements or comments by others in the community have you heard suggesting the existence of racism? Have you or a relative or a friend ever been the victim of a racial or ethnic slur? What is the first thing that comes to your mind when you find out a person is Italian, homosexual, an artist, and so forth, and how much stock do you place in such impressions or generalizations?

4. Consider drafting some questions for the defendant to ask, especially if that will be the only time the jurors will hear from the defendant.

5. Avoid questions that might embarrass the juror or that are too confrontational. As indicated in item 2, there are ways to get at sensitive matters more tactfully. Questions should not be condescending or seem paternalistic; jurors respond best to sincerity, respect, and empathy.

Good voir dire depends heavily on the attorney's ability to deliver well in the courtroom. Without good preparation, however, the delivery will be inadequate.

At voir dire your job is to see that the jury selection binder and any other materials are available for quick access. If jurors gather in a public area before voir dire or during breaks, go to the area and inconspicuously observe jurors who seem to be friends, and listen for revealing conversations. In the courtroom, note the jurors' clothes, jewelry, and other clues. When they answer questions, note hesitancy, tone of voice, posture, with whom they make eye contact, and how they respond to each attorney both verbally and nonverbally. Note significant points on the juror profile sheet or directly onto the juror seating grid. This information can be used by the attorney to argue challenges for cause and can be placed in the record if the challenges are denied. It is also helpful for comparing notes with the attorney in reaching peremptory challenge decisions. Record selections on the jury grid so you and the attorney will know who the final jurors are, as well as who was struck or otherwise excused. Once the jurors are selected, keep observing them for clues on which way they are leaning and to whom they are responding. Such information may assist the attorney in deciding to call that reserve witness, have the defendant testify, or adjust the closing argument.

B.   OPENING STATEMENTS

opening statement:
the initial presentation made by the attorneys to the jury, giving an overview of the case and the evidence to be presented.

Following voir dire and the swearing in of the jury, the attorneys make their opening statements to the jury. The **opening statement** is the initial presentation made by the attorneys to the jury, giving an overview of the case and the evidence to be presented. It provides the jury with a framework, and gives the attorneys the chance to state the case from their perspectives. The prosecution makes the first statement. The defense has the option to open directly following or reserve its opening remarks until after the prosecution presents its evidence and just before the defense presents its case. Opening statements provide a road map of the case for the jury and are not evidence. You may be asked to suggest approaches and items for the opening statement and to evaluate it prior to its presentation. Good opening remarks should attempt to swing the jury to your side of the case, but should never overstate the evidence. Overstatement of what would be proved at trial was held sufficient to warrant the granting of a mistrial in *Hartry v. State* (Ga. 1999). In the opening statement, the prosecutor said the state would prove that the crime was gang related, but failed to provide any such evidence. The conviction was upheld, however, because the overall evidence was overwhelming. Opening statements can be used to soften the impact of the opponent's case.

C.   THE PROSECUTION'S CASE AND THE PRESENTATION OF EVIDENCE

1.   The Prosecution's Case

The prosecution has the burden of proof and, thus, must present its case first. It must prove, beyond a reasonable doubt that a crime was committed and that the defendant committed it. Proof beyond a reasonable doubt is proof of sufficient weight to exclude any reasonable explanation other than the defendant's guilt. A reasonable doubt must be based in reason and common sense. For example, the state must prove beyond a reasonable doubt that the defendant was the person that committed the crime. If the sole evidence was a witness who was fifty feet away from the perpetrator in poor lighting, it is reasonable to doubt the identification. There is greater doubt if the defense offers alibi testimony. Conversely, if the lighting was excellent, positive identification was made by two credible witnesses, and no alibi evidence was offered, there would be no basis for doubt. The government's burden applies to each element of the alleged crime.

The prosecution's case in chief is presented through the testimony of witnesses. Witnesses may be the victim, police officers, eyewitnesses, forensic experts, physicians, and others. Either side can request the court to allow only one witness at a time in the courtroom. This procedure is called sequestering or separation of the witnesses and is done to prevent the testimony of one witness from influencing the testimony of the others, the "let's get our stories straight" syndrome. In addition to stating what they observed, witnesses identify physical evidence such as important documents, photographs, weapons, the defendant, and the like.

Witnesses are subject to direct examination from the prosecuting attorney. **Direct examination** is the questioning of a witness by the attorney for the party that called the witness. Direct examination questions must be neutral in nature, such as: What did you see? What happened next? Leading questions are prohibited. A **leading question** attempts to influence the witness by suggesting the answer: The lighting was poor, wasn't it, Mr. Witness? You're the one who fired the weapon, aren't you, Mr. Codefendant? If a witness is called on direct examination but becomes hostile to the examining attorney or is determined by the judge to be hostile to the attorney, or if the witness is a child, the judge may permit the attorney to ask leading questions.

direct examination:
the questioning of a witness by the attorney for the party that called the witness.

leading question:
one that attempts to influence the witness by suggesting the answer.

2. The Presentation of Evidence

The rules of evidence govern what and how evidence is admitted at trial. When constructed and applied evenhandedly, they are essential to a fair, reliable, and efficient fact-finding process. The Federal Rules of Evidence are used throughout the federal system and in more than thirty states. Even in those states that have not adopted the federal rules, the basic guidelines and concepts are quite similar. Despite their approximate uniformity, it is essential to research the specific rules and case law in the pertinent jurisdiction, because even the smallest difference can be significant to a case. Anticipation and diligent preparation are the means to successfully attacking or defending the admissibility of any important piece of evidence.

The rules of evidence are sufficiently complex to preclude a detailed discussion in this text. Nevertheless, here are some generalizations on the most important rules of evidence.

1. Evidence must be both **material,** topically important to a matter in issue, and **relevant,** proving or disproving a material fact. The defendant's presence at the murder scene, for example, is a material fact in issue, and the result of an analysis of fingerprints found at the scene is relevant because it helps prove or disprove the material fact of the defendant's presence.

   material:
   topically important to a matter in issue.

   relevant:
   proving or disproving a material fact.

2. Hearsay is secondhand testimony, a statement that is offered by the witness as the truth, but that was made by someone other than the witness about what that other person saw, heard, said, or did. Hearsay is inadmissible because it is basically unreliable and not subject to in-court scrutiny. Exceptions stem from circumstances that are likely to make the statement more reliable and include dying declarations, spontaneous statements, statements against one's own interest, statements made in other hearings under oath and subject to cross-examination, statements of coconspirators, and others.

3. Documents and other physical evidence must be authenticated to be admissible. A witness must have the knowledge to be able to identify the item as that which it purports to be or to establish a chain of possession to show some other item has not been substituted for the original. Some documents are authenticated by a government seal or other certification.

4. Laypersons are permitted to give opinions on matters of general knowledge such as estimates of speed or distance.

5. Expert witnesses can give opinions on scientific or similarly complex matters if their qualifications in the pertinent field are established.

6. Documents must be the original or, in some cases, an authenticated photocopy. This requirement is called the best evidence rule.

7. Otherwise admissible evidence may be excluded if its inflammatory or prejudicial nature outweighs any probative value.

8. Evidence of prior acts or crimes is inadmissable unless it shows a pattern of conduct relevant to proving the crime at hand.

9. Privileged information is inadmissable. Privileges include communication between husband-wife, clergy-penitent, attorney-client, physician-patient, and in a few jurisdictions reporter-informant. Regarding the spousal privilege, "It is a maxim that man and wife should never have it in their power to hang one another."[8]

10. Children may testify at the discretion of the court if they understand the meaning of the truth.

11. A court can take judicial notice of some evidence without testimony if it is a matter of common knowledge or public record.

12. Evidence of character to show that a person's conduct at a particular time conformed to that character trait is inadmissible except (1) evidence of general moral character or a pertinent character trait offered by the accused or by the prosecution in rebuttal, (2) evidence of a pertinent character trait of the victim of the crime offered by the accused or by the prosecution in rebuttal, or (3) evidence of peacefulness of the victim offered by the prosecution in a homicide case to counter character evidence that the victim was the aggressor [Fed. R. Evid. 404(a)(1–2)]. A proposed rule change to Rule 404(a)(1) would permit the prosecution to offer evidence of the accused's character regarding peacefulness (not just the victim's) once the issue is opened by the accused. Admissible, as well, is evidence of the character of a witness if it pertains to truthfulness.

As standards for admissibility, the rules of evidence establish that the evidence must tend to prove something of value in deciding the issues, it must by its nature and as judged by human experience be reliable, and its probative value must not be outweighed by its likely prejudicial or sensational nature. An objection to the admission of evidence must be made prior to or at the time the evidence is submitted or asked for, and the objection must normally be related to a specific rule of evidence. Improper rulings by the judge on the admissibility of evidence can be appealed only if the objection is made in a timely manner and placed in the trial record. How frequently an attorney decides to object may be based partly on strategy that takes into account the impact of the objection on the jury.

Here is a sampling of recent rulings from various jurisdictions on evidentiary matters raised at trial by objection.

"You don't have to see the lion if you see his hair."

—Jewish folk saying Joseph L. Baron, *A Treasury of Jewish Quotations*, 1956

■ Evidence of a previous sale of cannibis was held admissible in a trafficking in cocaine case [*People v. Lowry* (Ill. App. 1992)].

■ Evidence of acts subsequent to the crime charged was held admissible [*U.S. v. Bibo-Rodriquez* (9th Cir. 1991)].

■ A victim's felony conviction that was more than ten years old was admissible for purposes of impeachment [*State v. Askew* (Conn. 1998)].

■ A photograph showing a massive maggot infestation of the child-victim's body in a murder case was inadmissible [*Funk v. Commonwealth* (Ky. 1992)].

■ A computer animation of a fall off a roof was not admissible in a civil case where the plaintiff could not remember the fall, and there was no witness to confirm the accuracy of the event's portrayal [*Brown v. Boise-Cascade Corp.* (Or. App. 1997)].

direct evidence:
evidence based on a witness's firsthand knowledge that proves a fact in issue without relying on inference or other evidence.

3. Other Evidentiary Considerations

circumstantial evidence:
evidence from the situations surrounding the event that leads us to believe a person thought and acted in a manner consistent or inconsistent with the alleged wrongful act; indirect evidence proving a point by inference.

Evidence is either direct or circumstantial. **Direct evidence** is based on a witness's firsthand knowledge and proves a fact in issue without relying on inference or other evidence. A witness's testimony that the witness saw the defendant commit the crime is direct evidence. **Circumstantial evidence,** indirect evidence, proves a point by inference. Testimony by police that the defendant's baseball cap was found at the scene of the crime raises the inference that the defendant was at the scene.

Presumptions also play an important role in evidence. A **presumption** is a rule of law that requires the trier of fact to conclude on threshold evidence that an ultimate fact is true. Most presumptions are **rebuttable presumptions,** meaning that the ultimate fact can be shown not to be true by other evidence. An example of a rebuttable presumption is that a person is intoxicated if the blood-alcohol level reaches the statutory amount. Evidence that shows the testing method to be faulty rebuts the presumption of intoxication, dissolving its force. An **irrebuttable presumption** requires that the ultimate fact be treated as true once the threshold evidence has been introduced. For example, once it is proven that a child is less than seven years of age, the law says the child cannot commit a felony. Evidence to the contrary is of no consequence.

Eyewitness testimony is an important form of evidence, but deserves a healthy dose of skepticism. Witnesses to the same incident often come away with conflicting observations. Anxiety and excitement also can impair a witness's recollection.

Scientific, technical, or other specialized knowledge is often critical to a criminal case. Tests may be employed to identify and match blood and hair types, measure blood-alcohol levels, detect the presence of telltale chemicals or identify substances, analyze threads from clothing, determine the presence of semen, match a spent bullet to a specific gun (ballistics), identify a body, and a host of other purposes. The long-accepted standard for the admissibility of such evidence set out in *Frye v. U.S.* (D.C. Cir. 1923) has been superseded by Rules 702 and 703 of the Federal Rules of Evidence [*Daubert v. Merrell Dow Pharmaceuticals, Inc.* (1993)]. These rules provide a more flexible standard for admissibility of scientific and technical expert testimony. They focus on the scientific validity of the principles involved and their relevance and reliability, rather than solely on whether the methodology used is accepted in the scientific community. Factors such as the method's rate of error, whether the method lends itself to testing and peer review, and whether it has gained general acceptance in the scientific community should be considered. *Daubert* was expanded to encompass not just scientific experts, but also other experts whose testimony is based on technical or other specialized knowledge in *Kumho Tire Co. Ltd. v. Carmichael* (1999). Under *Daubert*, the trial court is given considerable discretion to determine if a witness qualifies as an expert and whether the expert testimony is admissible. Some states have adopted the new standards, and some retain the less flexible *Frye* test. Check local practice. Changes have been proposed in the language of Rules 701 to 703 that will more clearly reflect *Daubert/Kumho*.

presumption:
a rule of law that requires the trier of fact to conclude on threshold evidence that an ultimate fact is true.

rebuttable presumption:
the ultimate fact can be shown not to be true by other evidence.

irrebuttable presumption:
requires that the ultimate fact be treated as true once the threshold evidence has been introduced.

EXHIBIT 13–2
Sample Jury Instructions

DIRECT AND CIRCUMSTANTIAL EVIDENCE

Evidence may be direct or circumstantial. Direct evidence is testimony by a witness about what that witness personally saw or heard or did. Circumstantial evidence is indirect evidence, that is, it is proof of one or more facts from which one can find another fact. You are to consider both direct and circumstantial evidence. The law permits you to give equal weight to both, but it is for you to decide how much weight to give to any evidence.

It may be helpful to include an illustrative example in the instruction:

By way of example, if you wake up in the morning and see that the sidewalk is wet, you may find from that fact that it rained during the night. However, other evidence, such as a turned on garden hose, may explain the water on the sidewalk. Therefore, before you decide that a fact has been proved by circumstantial evidence, you must consider all the evidence in the light of reason, experience, and common sense.

Ninth Circuit Criminal Jury Instructions (St. Paul, MN: West Group, 1992), § 1.05, with permission.

Admission of polygraph (lie detector) evidence remains controversial. Estimates of its reliability range from 40 to 90 percent. Many states allow it if the defense and prosecution agree to its admission prior to the defendant's taking the test. In a case involving a military ban on the use of polygraph evidence, the Supreme Court ruled that it was not a denial of the defendant's Sixth Amendment rights to ban the use of such evidence [*U.S. v. Scheffer* (1998)].

Admission of expert testimony on handwriting analysis to determine authorship or authenticity of signatures can encompass opinion on unique writing styles or characteristics. Such evidence helped convict Theodore Kaczynski, the "Unibomber." Computers make such stylistic comparisons an even more powerful crime-solving device by facilitating searches of huge databanks of written materials.

Tests to match DNA (deoxyribonucleic acid) specimens gathered at a crime scene with those from a defendant are normally admissible. This genetic material found in human cells is unique to each person. Hair, saliva, semen, blood, skin, and other biological substances in amounts no larger than a pinhead can be analyzed. The chance of an erroneous match is nearly nonexistent if the analysis is done properly. FBI and state databanks consisting of DNA specimens from convicted felons and from crime scenes makes DNA an extremely powerful crime-fighting tool. It has been so effective that law enforcement agencies want to expand the DNA data pool to include all people arrested. Opponents of databank expansion express concern because of its possible misuse against innocent people in the future.

DNA evidence not only helps convict the guilty; it also exonerates the innocent. The large number of false convictions exposed by DNA analysts raises legitimate concern for how often our system convicts innocent people, especially because some of those exonerated were on death row.

Despite its unassailable reputation for reliable identification, DNA printing does not assure a conviction. Like all scientifically and technically based tests, its reliability can be attacked, as it was in the O. J. Simpson case, not as bad science, but on the basis of how the evidence was collected and stored, the competency of the forensic technicians involved, and the chance that blood specimens were planted by the police.

Scientific and technically based evidence must be scrutinized by the prosecution, the defense, and the court for reliability. Here are some lines of inquiry that are often used to test the reliability of scientific and technical evidence.

Lines of Inquiry Regarding Scientific or Technical Evidence

- Is the test or analysis based on valid scientific principles?
- Is the analysis based on valid, reliable data, and are there adequate standards for drawing the necessary conclusions?
- Are there substances other than an illegal one, such as drugs, that will cause false readings?
- Was the required procedure as directed in the operating manual followed faithfully?
- Was the machine or testing device in proper working order as proven by appropriate sample runs, periodic recalibration, cleaning, and purging of previous test materials?
- Was the lab technician properly trained and qualified to conduct the test and interpret the results? (See Fed. R. Evid. 702 and parallel state rules.)
- Were the results clear and unambiguous?
- Was the sample used for testing:
  a. unquestionably the defendant's (proper chain of custody and segregation of sample), and
  b. free of contaminants from the point of collection through actual testing?
- Could the evidence have been planted, and was there motive to do so?
- Has the expert witness reliably applied the relevant principles and methods to the facts of the case?

"If the court please, I am about to illustrate it by diagrams, and I hope to make it so plain that the audience and perhaps the court will understand it."

James T. Brown, American lawyer, addressing a circuit court judge in Indiana

—Marshall Brown, *Wit and Humor of Bench and Bar,* 1899

These questions offer important guidance in the proper collection and preservation of evidence. They are equally important for cross-examination of forensic technicians, scientific experts, and other witnesses. Keep these standards in mind as you consider evidence that should be presented or challenged at trial. These lines of inquiry have been particularly useful in cases involving drug analyses, breath tests, radar readouts, and blood and semen analyses. A useful publication is the FBI's *Scientific Aids in Criminal Investigation: Suggestions for Handling of Physical Evidence.*

Either side in a criminal case may make use of demonstrative evidence. **Demonstrative evidence** is an audiovisual aid such as a diagram, photograph, model, videotape, or computer graphic designed to enhance the jury's understanding of the evidence. The use of such evidence is subject to the judge's broad discretion based on a balancing of the item's probative value against its tendency to misrepresent, confuse, delay, or be prejudicial (Fed. R. Crim. P. 403 and parallel state rules).

demonstrative evidence: an audiovisual aid such as a diagram, photograph, model, videotape, or computer graphic designed to enhance the jury's understanding of the evidence.

Many paralegals have developed excellent skills in preparing and using demonstrative evidence and assisting at trial in its presentation. Demonstrative evidence may require no more than preparation of a simple chart, or it may involve retaining a company to prepare a detailed and dramatic computer animation. To fully assist your supervising attorney, become familiar with the rules in your area and the latitude allowed by judges for presenting demonstrative evidence. Continually look for ways such evidence can be used to better present each case. Also be aware of how evidence once perceived as reliable, such as photos, video and audiotape, and even documents, is subject to undetectable alteration in this age of digital technology. Today, this evidence should require proof of a chain of custody demonstrating that it has not been altered or fabricated.

Whether you are preparing demonstrative evidence or simply considering the most effective way to get maximum jury attention, keep the following general rules in mind.

General Rules for Maximizing Juror Attention[9]

- Attention wanes after twenty minutes, so something needs to be done to change pace or get attention at that point. This is a good time to use demonstrative evidence.
- Attention is highest at the beginning of a presentation and at the very end.
- Color gets more attention than black and white.
- The larger the display the more impact it has.
- Location of key data on a page or a chart is important; the top of the chart or page gets more attention than the bottom, and the left side more than the right.
- Variety, contrast, and movement aid attention; shifting styles in the presentation, using different attorneys at various points in the trial, and using a display or graphic where the point of desired attention moves across a stationary background can be effective.
- The number of items or points on each chart should be kept to no more than six to eleven. More items reduce attention and comprehension.
- Some repetition of key points is helpful, but too much repetition can have a negative impact.

D. DEFENSE CROSS-EXAMINATION OF PROSECUTION'S WITNESSES

Before each prosecution witness leaves the stand, the defense may conduct cross-examination. Cross-examination of key witnesses can be long and aggressive. It is a critical weapon for testing each witness and for impeachment. Relentless investigation on each witness and research into case decisions on the rules of evidence are the cornerstones to effective cross, or to anticipating cross and protecting a witness from improper cross. In one case, for example, the defense discovered that two of three victims in an alleged child molestation case had made prior false accusations against another babysitter for acts similar to those charged against the defendant. The trial court, on the prosecution's argument, denied admission of the prior accusations. The state's appellate court, however, overturned the trial court and allowed the prior false accusations to be used for impeachment [*Strickland v. State* (Ga. App. 1992)].

The O. J. Simpson case and more recent media coverage has heightened juror's awareness that some law enforcement officers and prosecutors have been implicated in hiding, altering, and planting evidence, and lying to secure convictions. Further, the government has been known to provide "rewards" to witnesses, who themselves are facing prosecution or have felony records, to testify against a defendant. In the face of public concern for the reliability of prosecutorial evidence, both prosecution and defense teams must carefully plan how best to defend and attack witnesses in the era of such public knowledge.

As previously mentioned, the attorney conducting cross-examination can use leading questions. Using the brainstorming process discussed in the section on preparing for the preliminary hearing, you can generate ideas and questions for cross-examination. Be alert for unexpected openings by the government's questioning. Suggest questions that the defense attorney might use to take advantage of any such opportunities.

redirect examination: the questioning of the witness by the party that called the witness to undo or limit any damage done during cross-examination.

Although a government witness has been through direct and cross-examination, the prosecution may conduct redirect examination. **Redirect examination** is the questioning of the witness by the party that called the witness to undo or limit any damage done during cross-examination. This is called rehabilitating the witness. Redirect examination of a witness may be followed by recross. Leading questions are not permitted on redirect examination, but they are in recross. The scope of questions in redirect is limited to material raised in the preceding cross-examination. Likewise, the scope of recross is limited to matters raised in redirect.

E. MOTION FOR JUDGMENT OF ACQUITTAL

Generally at the close of the prosecution's case, the defense submits a motion for judgment of acquittal, sometimes called a motion to dismiss or a motion for directed verdict (Fed. R. Crim. P. 29). This motion asserts the argument that the prosecution's case has failed to show sufficient proof on one or more elements of the case and, thus, the evidence is inadequate to sustain a conviction (Rule 29). In other words, the motion argues that the state has failed to prove a prima facie case. If the judge finds the evidence is lacking to meet this threshold requirement, the case is dismissed. Judges normally do not grant this motion unless the weaknesses in the evidence are quite obvious. Appellate courts tend to give trial judges considerable latitude on this point. Generally, this motion must be made at this point in order to renew the motion at the close of the defense's evidence and any rebuttal. An example of a general form for a motion for judgment of acquittal is presented in Exhibit 13–3, page 511.

F. DEFENDANT'S CASE IN CHIEF

The defendant's case in chief is next and may be preceded by defense counsel's opening statement if not given earlier. The defense occasionally chooses not to place any evidence before the court. It is not necessary, because the government has the burden of proof. If the government has established a good case, however, it is normally dangerous for the defense to choose not to counter. In presenting its case, the defense calls its witnesses and enters its exhibits and other evidence. Because this is direct examination, defense counsel must avoid leading questions.

Probably the most agonizing decision that must be made is whether the defendant should testify. The Fifth Amendment affords the right not to testify. The defendant who testifies is open to intensive cross-examination, possible impeachment by an otherwise inadmissible confession or statement, and the temptation to commit perjury. Choosing not to testify disappoints the jury, however. It may raise doubts about the defendant's innocence or concern that the defendant is hiding something, even though the jury can be instructed not to make any inferences from the defendant's decision not to testify.

Each defense witness is subject to cross-examination by the prosecution. Although the defendant can be impeached through the prosecution's use of an inadmissable but inconsistent statement made by the defendant [*Harris v. N.Y.* (1971) and *U.S. v. Havens* (1980)], a defense witness may not be impeached with inadmissible evidence [*Walder v. U.S.* (1954)]. The defense rests its case on completion of its presentation of evidence.

 ANALYSIS PROBLEM

13–2.   Consider the dilemma of placing Eldon Spiers on the stand. Despite his repeated profession of innocence, his low level of intelligence, poor education, and a sometimes childlike desire to please make him a particularly vulnerable target for being led into contradicting, incredible, and otherwise harmful statements by the prosecution on cross-examination. Attorneys may ask for your perceptions and opinions on whether the defendant should testify. Do you think Eldon Spiers should testify?

G.   PROSECUTION'S REBUTTAL AND DEFENDANT'S REJOINDER

Following the close of the defendant's case, the prosecution can call additional witnesses to rebut new matter raised by the defense. Rebuttal witnesses are restricted to this purpose. In *Tome v. U.S.* (1995) the Court limited what prosecution witnesses could testify to in rebutting the defense claim that a child alleging sexual abuse had an improper motive. The Court said the normally admissible, consistent, out-of-court statement by the child was inadmissible, because it was made after the improper motive may have arisen.

The defense may call rejoinder witnesses for the sole purpose of countering matters and evidence produced during the prosecution's rebuttal. Both rebuttal and rejoinder witnesses are subject to cross-examination.

H.   MOTION FOR JUDGMENT OF ACQUITTAL OR DIRECTED VERDICT

At the close of all evidence, the defense may again move for a judgment of acquittal. Motions for directed verdict have been abolished in the federal system, but are still used in some states. This motion is granted by the court only if it is clear, as a matter of law, that the prosecution has failed to prove its case. Judges hesitate to substitute their judgment for the jury's after the jury has heard the case for hours, days, or longer. A judge under the federal rules may reserve ruling on the motion for judgment of acquittal until after the jury has returned a verdict [Rule 29(b)].

I.   JURY INSTRUCTION CONFERENCE

The court recesses while the attorneys and the judge go into the judge's chambers to consider instructions to be given to the jury. Both sides must present any proposed jury instructions to the judge in writing with the appropriate request (Fed. R. Crim. P. 30) and the support of legal authority. The judge considers each proposed instruction and makes a decision based on the arguments presented, the apparent fairness of the instruction, the adequacy or inadequacy of the jurisdiction's set of standard or recommended jury instructions, and whether sufficient evidence was presented to warrant giving the instruction. The judge cannot give an instruction on self-defense, for example, if no evidence has been presented on this point.

You can play a vital role in preparing for the jury instruction conference. You need to research both the applicable standard instructions plus any alternative or unique instructions. An excellent source for jury instructions is *Federal Jury Practice and Instructions*, by West Group. Alternative or unique instructions can be found in criminal practice manuals, previous case files, and pertinent case law. The case law or rationale for an alternative or unique instruction must be well established before a judge is likely to substitute it for one of the standard instructions. Moreover, the legal basis for a rejected instruction should be established in order to preserve an appellate issue based on the court's rejection of the instruction or, similarly, on the court's acceptance of a flawed instruction.

Once the instructions are researched, draft the set of proposed instructions and give them to your supervising attorney for review. When approved, an original set is prepared for the judge and copies are made for the opponent and for your attorney. Place these sets in the trial notebook. The set of copies for your supervising attorney should include a checkoff box indicating "accepted" or "rejected."

 ANALYSIS PROBLEM

13–3.   Note the sample jury instructions throughout this text. Compare the two instructions on the insanity defense in Chapter 7. Which is more favorable to the prosecution and which to the defense?

J.   CLOSING ARGUMENTS

Court is reconvened and the attorneys deliver their closing arguments to the jury. Again, the government presents its statement first. Many jurisdictions permit the government to follow the defense argument with a second but usually brief rebuttal argument (Fed. R. Crim. P. 29.1 and parallel state rules). The purpose of closing arguments is to highlight key evidence and assist the jury in weighing and drawing inferences from that evidence. From the point of view of the advocates, it is a time to make one final effort to win over the jury by deflecting the impact of the opponent's evidence and increasing the impact of their own. Persuasion is the ultimate aim. The jury is instructed, however, that closing arguments are not evidence. Limits are imposed on how far the attorneys can go in trying to be persuasive. Attorneys may ask the jurors to return a verdict of guilty or not guilty but are forbidden to state their personal belief about the defendant's guilt or innocence. They may not argue any evidence at closing that was not admitted at trial, and they may not make any inflammatory or other remarks likely to mislead or prejudice the jury. Prosecutors must be particularly careful in this regard. Prosecutorial closing arguments were held to be improper in the following circumstances.

- The prosecutor commented that the defendant's nontestimonial demeanor was not that of an innocent man [*Mayberry v. State* (Tex. App. 1992)].
- The prosecutor used Bible-based arguments, saying, "the murderer shall be put to death," in a death penalty case [*Commonwealth v. Chamber* (Pa. 1991)].

Similarly, a prosecutor's use of biblical quotes to justify the death penalty improperly "urge[d] the jury to follow religious mandates . . . rather than Georgia law" [*Carruthers v. State* (Ga. 2000)].

- The prosecutor in an arson case repeatedly referred to the defendant's smokescreen [*People v. Kidd* (Ill. 1992)].
- The prosecutor told the jury that the authority to make the decision on the death penalty rested largely with the appellate court, and not with the jurors [*Clark v. Commonwealth* (Ky. 1991)].
- The prosecutor in a case involving one charge of indecent liberty told the jury to send the accused a message "that we're not gonna let him do this to the children of the community" [*Wilson v. Bruce* (D. Kan. 1993)].
- A prosecutor's comment that because the defendant could hear the testimony of all the other witnesses, he had the advantage of being able to "fit" his testimony into the evidence, however, was not an undue burden on the defendant's Sixth Amendment right to be present [*Portuondo v. Agard* (2000)].

The court may try to correct the damage of such a statement by instructing the jury to disregard it; if the likely prejudice seems too great, however, the judge may have no choice but to declare a mistrial. Can the defense, in an obviously lost cause, comment to so prejudice the jury as to necessitate a mistrial? No, the defense cannot be awarded a mistrial for its own misconduct, but contempt sanctions may be imposed, accompanied by a corrective instruction to the jury.

K. JUDGE'S INSTRUCTIONS TO THE JURY

When instructing the jury, the judge may start by reading the information or indictment and telling the jury that the document is an accusation only and is not to be considered as evidence. The duty of the jurors to adhere to the instructions is reiterated, as well as their role as sole judge of the facts. The jury is reminded that the defendant is innocent until proven guilty beyond a reasonable doubt on each element of the crime. Some jurisdictions permit an instruction for jurors to find the defendant innocent unless they believe that guilt has been proven to a moral certitude. The court instructs on direct and circumstantial evidence and any permissible inferences, credibility of witnesses and impeachment, the right of the jury to accept or reject the opinions of expert witnesses, and how to treat demonstrative evidence. The pertinent crime, its elements, and any technical terms are defined. Lesser included offenses are covered, as well as the elements, terms, and burden of proof for any applicable defenses. The court may instruct that the defendant has the right not to testify and no inference of guilt should be drawn for exercising that right. In jurisdictions where the jury determines the sentence, the jurors are instructed on the permissible range of the penalty and, in some jurisdictions, the impact of probation and parole eligibility. Some courts permit instruction on what will happen to the defendant found not guilty by insanity. The court will cover the procedure for deliberation, including the election of a foreperson, the need for unanimity, restrictions on items to be taken into the jury room, communications with the judge, and restrictions on outside conversations. Any objection to an instruction or the omission of an instruction must be made before the jury retires to deliberate (Fed. R. Crim. P. 30).

"All trial is the investigation of something doubtful."

—Samuel Johnson, 1709–1784
Eugene Brussell, *Dictionary of Quotable Definitions*, 1970

L. JURY DELIBERATION

In an attempt to develop more meaningful jury deliberation, some innovative judges, either on their own or encouraged by state projects, are allowing jurors during trial to take notes, keep juror notebooks with preliminary instructions, ask questions, listen to interim summaries by the lawyers, and hold midtrial discussions.[10] The last two procedures are used in potentially lengthy trials. All of these procedures increase jury participation and may improve the quality of jury deliberations.

When the jury adjourns to the jury room for deliberation, any alternate jurors may or may not be excused [Fed. R. Crim. P. 24(c)(3)]. In lengthy and particularly serious cases or where public feelings are likely to run high, the jury may be sequestered, which means that when the jury is not deliberating, the jurors are confined to a hotel under the close scrutiny of the bailiff. In such circumstances, jurors are denied access to media coverage of the trial. Even when not sequestered, the jury is supervised at meals and other recesses and instructed to avoid media reports or personal discussions of the case outside of the deliberations.

Jury deliberations are not public, but posttrial interviews and other sources reveal how much individual personalities and group dynamics impact on the process of reaching a verdict. It is here that the careful preparation for selection of jurors and the presentation of evidence pays off. Occasionally, that one individual you identified as having an influential personality determines the outcome.

jury nullification (jury pardon):
the right of a jury to find a defendant not guilty even though the law and evidence dictate otherwise.

Jurors are admonished to follow the judge's instructions and the law contained in them. They do, however, have the latitude of deciding a case contrary to the law. This privilege, seldom brought to the attention of the public, is called **jury nullification** (or **jury pardon**). It gives juries the right to find a defendant not guilty even though the law and evidence dictate otherwise. If juries believe that a law is being unjustly applied, is a bad law, or that the victim is more responsible for the crime than the defendant, jury nullification is proper. Judges rarely instruct juries on this privilege and are not required to do so even if asked [*U.S. v. Dougherty* (D.C. Cir. 1972)]. In any case, attorneys are not allowed to suggest to the jury that they resort to jury nullification, although they may be allowed to invite nullification by arguing that the penalty awaiting the defendant on conviction is unreasonable [*U.S. v. Datcher* (M.D. Tenn. 1993)].

Juries can become deadlocked, especially when unanimous verdicts are required. Unless the deadlock is resolved in a reasonable period of time, the judge may be forced to declare a mistrial, voiding all that has occurred at trial as though the trial were never held. To avoid a mistrial brought on by a deadlocked jury, a judge is permitted to encourage the jury to come to a decision. The *Allen* charge is an instruction for this purpose, originally telling jurors who were in the minority to pay deference to their fellow jurors and reexamine whether their own views could be reasonable in light of the majority's view [*Allen v. U.S.* (1896)]. Controversial because of its "third degree" nature, the instruction is now modified to a general request for a reexamination of the evidence and an effort to reach a verdict. The message, however, remains the same: A lot of time and expense have gone into this trial, and the court wants each juror to do everything reasonable to come to a group decision. If this instruction fails, the judge declares a mistrial, and the state must decide whether to retry the defendant at some later date.

A new trial was granted to the defendant because the trial judge failed to give the *Allen* charge, urged the jury to come to a decision in an informal instruction after the jury announced that they were deadlocked by one person, and allowed them to deliberate until 4:00 A.M. [*Thomas v. State* (Fla. 1999)]. The court said that there was a substantial risk of a coerced decision. The Supreme Court ruled that jurors deliberating on a sentence of death do not have to be told that, if they cannot agree on the death penalty, the default penalty is life in prison without parole [*Jones v. U.S.* (1999)]. Such an instruction might prevent holdouts from ultimately agreeing to the death sentence.

Other grounds for mistrial or appeal can occur during deliberations. A bailiff may improperly give an opinion of the case while transporting a jury, or the judge may erroneously allow alternate jurors to participate in deliberations or take prejudicial material into the jury room. Due process requiring a fundamental fairness and an impartial jury are the applicable legal principles at this stage. Also, a juror may become ill or otherwise unable to continue. If alternate jurors have not been retained [Rule 24(c)(3)], the federal rules [Rule 23(b)] and parallel state rules permit the case to continue with eleven jurors. Continuance with fewer than eleven jurors requires an agreement by both parties.

M. JURY VERDICT AND POLLING

When the jury notifies the judge that it has reached a verdict, court is reconvened. The written verdict is handed to the judge, who checks to see that it is in proper form, then it is usually returned to the foreperson or the clerk to be read aloud. It is common for the defense team to stand with the defendant during the reading of the verdict.

Either side may request the court for a polling of jurors [Fed. R. Crim. P. 31(d)]. The judge asks each juror if the verdict is consistent with his or her vote. If not, the jury must go back to deliberate. If all is in order and the verdict is not guilty, the defendant is discharged; if guilty, the defendant is remanded to custody or granted bail until sentencing or pending any appeal.

VI. POSTTRIAL MOTIONS

A. PURPOSE

On television or in the movies, the case seems to be over at the return of the jury's verdict. In a significant number of criminal cases, however, this is just the beginning of the important posttrial motions and possible appeal stages. Posttrial motions are essential because they isolate those things at trial that are likely to be appealed. They also give the trial court one last chance to correct any errors before the matter is appealed to a higher court.

B. TYPES OF POSTTRIAL MOTIONS

Posttrial motions come in several forms. The most common are a motion for judgment notwithstanding the verdict and a motion for a new trial. In the federal system, a motion for judgment of acquittal can be renewed or made within seven days of the discharge of the jury [Fed. R. Crim. P. 29(c)].

The motion for judgment notwithstanding the verdict (JNOV) requests the court for an order entering a judgment contrary to the verdict. Generally, a court must find that the weight of the evidence is contrary to the verdict. In some jurisdictions a motion for dismissal or directed verdict has to have been made earlier in order to move for a JNOV. For all practical purposes, this motion has been supplanted in the federal system by the motion for judgment of acquittal.

A motion for a new trial is based on alleged error at trial or new evidence that for the sake of justice requires that judgment be set aside (vacated) and a new trial be held (Fed. R. Crim. P. 33). Typical grounds for a motion for a new trial or related motions allege erroneous rulings on the admissibility of evidence, impaneling of the jury, prosecutorial misconduct, new evidence, lack of jurisdiction, improper jury instructions, and the like. The federal rules require a motion for new trial to be made within seven days after the verdict. It can be made up to three years later if its basis is the finding of new evidence. If granted, the judge may vacate the judgment of guilt and enter the taking of new evidence (Rule 33).

Some of these motions are predictable and can be drafted in advance and placed in the trial notebook for submission at the appropriate time. Notes that you have taken at trial assist in identifying other matters that are appropriate for a posttrial motion. You may be asked to draft the motion and do the necessary research to support it. Keep in mind that the time allowed for the filing of such motions is normally quite short. Most posttrial motions are denied but are still necessary to preserve issues for appeal. The case then moves on to sentencing if the defendant was found guilty. Exhibit 13–4, page 512 presents a motion for a new trial.

VII. CONCLUSION

The right to a fair trial, trial by jury, and the associated due process rights to counsel, presence, confrontation, and others are to be guarded jealously in any society. They are of such import as to be guaranteed by the Constitution of the United States and every state constitution. Occasionally these trial rights conflict with other paramount rights such as freedom of the press and the need for open and public trials. The courts have resolved such conflicts by reasonable restrictions on speech, press, and public access only when there seems to be no other reasonable alternative.

Trial consists of a sequence of steps governed by rules of procedure and evidence that assign the burden of proof, provide order and efficiency, and enhance the trier of fact's access to reliable evidence.

An effective trial presentation requires extensive planning and preparation. You can play a vital role, evaluating and organizing evidence, conducting jury research and drafting potential voir dire questions, assisting witnesses, making or obtaining demonstrative evidence, drafting questions to be asked at trial, drafting motions and doing supporting research, compiling a trial notebook, and evaluating opening and closing statements. At trial, your being well organized, exercising keen observation, and taking copious notes not only can lead to a better presentation, but also can isolate matters for posttrial motions and appeal.

EXHIBIT 13–1
Juror Attitude Survey: Instruction Sheet for Pollsters Plus Survey Questions

---

INSTRUCTION SHEET FOR POLLSTERS

1. Note the answers obtained from respondents on the questionnaire as you talk to them. Please record verbatim quotes where necessary. Put your name on all questionnaires after you complete the interview so we know who did the interview. Write legibly.

2. Do *not* suggest any answers by tone or phrasing. Answer honestly any questions by respondents.

3. Attached you will find a section of the phone book from the county in which the calls are to be made.* The phone book has been randomly divided among the pollsters. On the first page of your section of the telephone book, call the *first* name. If, for any reason, this interview cannot be completed, call the *second* name. Continue this process until an interview is completed with an individual or phone number listed on that page.

4. Turn to the next page and repeat this procedure. Do so until your assigned number of calls has been completed. If your assigned number of calls cannot be completed from the number of pages you have been provided with, begin again at the first page and call the *last* individual on the page. If, for any reason, this interview cannot be completed, go to the name directly *above*. Continue this process until an interview is completed. Continue working from the bottom up on all of the remaining pages until your assigned number of interviews has been completed.

5. It is necessary that only registered voters in the county in question be interviewed. If the first person who answers is not a registered voter in the county, inquire as to whether anyone present has these qualifications. If so, interview them. If not, politely terminate the conversation and call the number above or below, as the case may be.

6. Attached you will find a list of those individuals who may have some connection with this case. Do *not* call any of them. If you come across any of these names, simply proceed to the next one above or below, as the case may be.

7. If you have any questions or problems, see: _____
_____.

Thank you for agreeing to volunteer for this project.

Assigned Number of Calls _____
*Use pages _____ from phone book.

EXHIBIT 13–1 *(Continued)*
Juror Attitude Survey: Instruction Sheet for Pollsters Plus Survey Questions

Hello. My name is _____, and I am calling for the Kentucky Department of Public Advocacy. We are doing a survey of _____ County voters to see how they feel about our criminal justice system, certain crimes, and ways of dealing with crime in our society.

Would you mind answering a few questions? There are no right or wrong answers to these questions. We are interested in your personal opinions. All of your answers will be kept confidential. OK?

1a) First of all, are you a registered voter? (**If no, terminate call.**) Yes _____ No _____

1b) **FOR _____ COUNTY ONLY:** Have you been summoned for jury duty in _____ County for February? (**If yes, terminate call.**) Yes _____ No _____

1c) **FOR _____ COUNTY ONLY:** Are you connected in any way with _____ Circuit Court, the Commonwealth Attorney's Office, the County Attorney's Office, or the Department of Public Advocacy? (**If yes, terminate call.**) Yes _____ No _____

2) I'd like to talk a minute about different types of crimes. How serious a problem are the following types of crime in your county?

a) Burglaries and Armed Robberies. Would you say these are:

_____ Not at all serious for your county
_____ Somewhat serious for your county
_____ Very serious for your county

b) Violent Crimes—Assaults and Murders. Would you say these are:

_____ Not at all serious for your county
_____ Somewhat serious for your county
_____ Very serious for your county

3) Now, let me make some statements and see what you think.

a) The death penalty is an effective deterrent to serious violent crimes. Do you agree or disagree with that statement?

Agree _____ Disagree _____
Not sure/Don't know/No opinion _____

b) Most of what you read in the newspaper about certain crimes turns out to be pretty much the truth. Do you agree or disagree with this?

Agree _____ Disagree _____
Not sure/Don't know/No opinion _____

4) Turning now to the issue of pretrial publicity in newspapers and other sources. Do you remember ever reading or hearing anything about the shooting death of (<u>Name</u>) of the _____ community near _____ in (<u>Month/year</u>)?

Yes _____ No _____ Not sure/Don't know/No opinion _____

5) **If not sure or no opinion:** (<u>Name</u>) was sleeping in his bed when he was shot at point-blank range by a former brother-in-law with whom he had a long-standing family dispute. Do you remember reading or hearing anything about this case?

Yes _____ No _____ Not sure/Don't know/No opinion _____

6) Do you know who has been charged with murder of _____ ?

Yes _____ No _____ Not sure/Don't know/No opinion _____

7) **If yes:** What is the name of that person? _____

Continued

EXHIBIT 13–1 *(Continued)*
Juror Attitude Survey: Instruction Sheet for Pollsters Plus Survey Questions

8) Do you remember any other particulars about the case?

Yes _____ No _____ **If yes:** What? _____

9) In your mind at this time, do you think (Name), the man arrested and charged in the murder of (Name), is probably guilty or innocent?

Guilty _____ Innocent _____
Not sure/Don't know/No opinion _____

10) From what you know about this case, how much evidence is there that (Name) is guilty of murder? [**Read 4 options below.**]

_____ A lot of evidence
_____ Some evidence
_____ A little evidence
_____ No evidence
[_____ Not sure/Don't know/No opinion]

11) If a jury were to find (Name) guilty of this murder, what sentence do you think he should receive? [**Read 4 options below.**]

_____ A sentence from 20 years to life
_____ A life sentence
_____ A life sentence without the possibility of parole for 25 years
_____ The death penalty
[_____ Not sure/Don't know/No opinion]

12) Why do you think that's the appropriate sentence? _____
_____

13) **If the answer to question #11 is the death penalty:** Under what circumstances would you consider a sentence other than the death penalty in this case? _____
_____

14) How many newspaper articles about the killing of (Name) do you think you have read? _____

15) How many times have you heard stories on the T.V. or radio about this case? _____

16) Have you heard this case being discussed?

Yes _____ No _____ Not sure/Don't know/No opinion _____
If yes: How many times? _____

17) How often have you yourself discussed this case with someone? _____

18) Thinking of your own opinions about this case, what do you think has most influenced you? [**Read 4 options below.**]

_____ What you have read in the papers
_____ What you have heard on T.V. and radio
_____ Your own personal decisions
_____ Conversations you have had with others
[_____ Not sure/Don't know/No opinion]

19a) Knowing your community the way you do, do you think that _____ would receive a fair trial in your county?

Yes _____ No _____ Not sure/Don't know/No opinion _____

19b) Why or why not? _____

EXHIBIT 13–1 *(Concluded)*
Juror Attitude Survey: Instruction Sheet for Pollsters Plus Survey Questions

20) What newspapers do you regularly read? _____
_____

21) How often do you read this (these) newspaper(s)? _____

22) How often do you watch the news on T.V.? _____

23) What T.V. station do you usually watch for the news? _____
_____

24) How often do you hear the news on the radio? _____

25) What radio station do you usually listen to for the news? _____
_____

Ok, that's all the questions I have for you. Thank you very much for taking the time to talk with me. You have been very helpful.

Goodbye.

EXHIBIT 13–3
Motion for Judgment of Acquittal (at Close of State's Case)

CAPITOL COUNTY	CIRCUIT COURT DIVISION II	STATE OF COLUMBIA

STATE OF COLUMBIA,   CASE OR INDICTMENT NO. _____
                    PLAINTIFF

V.   MOTION FOR JUDGMENT
                                                                                     OF ACQUITTAL
_____
                    DEFENDANT

_____

Defendant, by counsel, requests this Court for entry of a judgment of acquittal on (state count or counts of information or indictment) _____
_____

on the grounds that the prosecution's evidence is insufficient to prove beyond a reasonable doubt that defendant is guilty of the offenses charged for the following reasons: (choose from the following or other reasons)
1. The prosecution has failed to prove a prima facie case on all of the elements of the crime of _____ , specifically (state applicable elements) _____ .
2. The prosecution has failed to establish a sufficient connection between the crime(s) and the defendant.
3. Other reasons.

A memorandum of arguments and authorities in support of this motion is attached.

WHEREFORE, defendant requests the entry of a judgment of acquittal.

                                                                          Respectfully submitted,

                                                                          _____
                                                                          Attorney
                                                                          (Address and phone number)
                                                                          Date_____

EXHIBIT 13–4
Motion for a New Trial

CAPITOL COUNTY   CIRCUIT COURT   STATE OF COLUMBIA
                                       DIVISION II

STATE OF COLUMBIA,   CASE OR INDICTMENT NO._____
       PLAINTIFF

                                      MOTION FOR NEW TRIAL

v. _____ ,
        DEFENDANT

Defendant, by counsel, moves the Court for an order for a new trial for the following reason(s): (choose from the following or state other reasons)

1. The Court erred in admitting illegally obtained evidence, specifically _____ .
2. The Court erred in refusing to permit the defendant to enter the following evidence: _____ .
3. The Court erred in admitting evidence whose probative value was outweighed by its inflammatory and prejudicial nature, specifically _____ .
4. The jury's verdict was contrary to the great weight of the evidence and to the Court's instructions to the jury, specifically _____ .
5. The Court erred in denying the defendant a separate trial on (state applicable charges or counts)_____
_____ .

6. The Court erred in denying the defendant the right to a trial separate from that of the codefendant.
7. A key witness for the prosecution has recanted his or her testimony, specifically _____ .
8. New evidence has been discovered that could not have been discovered by due diligence, specifically _____
_____ .
9. The prosecutor is responsible for misconduct, specifically _____ .
10. A juror (or the jury) is guilty of misconduct, specifically _____ .
11. The Court erred by denying defendant's motion for judgment of acquittal submitted at the close of the prosecution's case in chief.

A memorandum of arguments and authorities in support of this motion is attached.

WHEREFORE, defendant requests this Court to order a new trial.

Respectfully submitted,

_____

Date of Service   Attorney
                                          (Address and phone number)
_____   Date_____

SYSTEM FOLDER ASSIGNMENTS

Complete the following and place the documents in your system folder:

- Outline of trial notebook sections, material on preparing and assisting a witness, and trial materials supervision.
- Outline of the tips and tasks for paralegals preparing for and at voir dire. Copy of the jury attitude survey, instructions, and questions.
- List of the important general rules of evidence.
- Definitions and examples of the following terms: proof beyond a reasonable doubt, direct and circumstantial evidence, presumptions, and demonstrative evidence.
- Lines of inquiry regarding scientific and technical evidence.
- General rules for maximizing juror attention.
- Create subsections in your system folder for each trial and posttrial step identified in this chapter. In each subsection define the step and add any applicable rules, paralegal tasks, tips, and sample documents provided in the text, by your instructor, or gathered through your own research in practice manuals or other sources.

APPLICATION ASSIGNMENTS

1. Assuming that assets that are the product of or used for criminal activity may be seized by the government (as you will see in Chapter 14), is there a denial of the right to counsel in the following factual situation? Also, assume that property found to be the product of criminal activity may not be used to retain counsel. See *U.S. v. Unimex, Inc.,* 991 F.2d 546 (9th Cir. 1993).

   Keyhole, Inc., a small company, publishes adult magazines. All of the corporation's assets are seized by the government in association with a prosecution for distributing pornographic material. Keyhole goes to trial without attorney because it has no available assets with which to hire an attorney.

2. Explain whether any rights have been violated in the following factual situation. See *Young v. Callahan,* 700 F.2d 32 (1st Cir. 1983).

   At his trial for murder the defendant, like other defendants that came before this court, is restricted to a prisoner's dock. The dock is a wooden structure about four feet by four feet and open at the top so the jury can see the defendant when standing or sitting. The dock sits near the spectator area and separate from the counsel table.

3. If codefendants are being tried for bribery, is there anything wrong with admitting into evidence a codefendant's statement made before the grand jury? See *U.S. v. Flores,* 985 F.2d 770 (5th Cir. 1993).

4. You be the judge and decide whether the following facts require you to grant or deny a defendant's request for a peremptory challenge.

   A black defendant has excluded six white jurors. The prosecution challenges the defendant's strike of a seventh white juror. The defense explains that its last strike was because the juror's hair style and glasses suggested he was a conservative. See *U.S. v. Blotcher,* 142 F.3d 728 (4th Cir. 1998).

5. Assume you are part of a prosecution team with a trial soon to start involving several police officers who will testify for the state. Your boss, the prosecutor, asks your advice on what types of jurors she should exclude. What will you tell her?

6. Your supervising attorney on the defense team for Eldon Spiers, Case I, reminds you that Dr. Bernita Tucker, a specialist in head injuries, will be testifying for the state in that case. The state will be using Dr. Tucker to describe Kate

Lamb's injuries and to say that her death was due to the head trauma caused by the fall onto the rocks below the Smiley Creek bridge.

Your attorney compliments you on your medical research showing that such injuries very commonly cause confusion, lack of clarity in thought, and short-term memory loss. The doctor alluded to this at the preliminary hearing. You also have a copy of Kate Lamb's medical records. Your research is clear on this point and your attorney feels that cross-examination of the doctor can help the client and, at the very worst, not hurt the client. For those reasons, the attorney asks you to draft five to ten questions for cross-examination of the doctor for the purpose of getting testimony that can shed doubt on Kate Lamb's statement that Eldon Spiers is the perpetrator of the crime. Add any details to your questions that seem necessary to fill out the cross-examination. Once that is done, switch sides and draft redirect questions for the state that will help rehabilitate the witness, that is, undo or limit any damage done by the cross-examination.

HELPFUL WEB SITES

www.crimelynx.com
   Links to forensic expert sites
www.internetlawyer.com/facts/findpeop.html
   Person search by name or affiliation.
www.law.cornell.edu/rules/fre/overview.html
   Federal Rules of Evidence

INTERNET EXERCISES

1.   Go to the internetlawyer site and enter a name. Based on what you find only from the Internet, can you make an educated guess as to whether the person would be a good prosecution juror if the defendant is a well-educated professional? A white supremacist?
2.   Go to crimelynx; make a list of resources for forensic evidence.

QUESTIONS FOR STUDY AND REVIEW

1.   What does thorough trial preparation have to do with the adversary system, ethics, and appeals?
2.   What is the geographical reach of a subpoena in a federal criminal case?
3.   What provisions of the United States Constitution guarantee the right to jury trial in criminal cases? The right to fair procedure?
4.   Explain venire, fair cross-section, and equal protection in the context of juries.
5.   Describe voir dire and the types of and limits on juror challenges at voir dire. What is the significance of *Batson* and subsequent cases? Describe the tasks a paralegal can perform in preparing for and assisting at voir dire. How can the Internet help?
6.   What criteria are used to determine whether a defendant has been denied adequate representation by counsel under the Sixth Amendment?
7.   What is *pro se* representation? How can it be controlled by the court?
8.   What problem exists in child abuse cases in permitting doctors, parents, and others to relate to jurors what children said out of court? Does separating a child from the defendant by use of closed circuit television impact on the fairness of a trial?

9. May a prosecutor comment to the jury on the defendant's failure to testify? Are there any consequences for making such a statement?
10. Describe a trial notebook and its use.
11. Why is taking good notes during the presentation of evidence so important?
12. Define opening statements; give their purpose, and state any strategy associated with their delivery.
13. Define proof beyond a reasonable doubt, and provide examples of situations that might give rise to reasonable doubt.
14. Define direct examination, cross-examination, redirect examination, and recross. What is the difference between the types of questions that may be asked during each? Give an example of a leading question.
15. What are the general standards for admissibility established by the rules of evidence?
16. Summarize the general rules of evidence identified in this chapter.
17. What is the importance of making an objection to evidence?
18. Define and give examples of both direct and circumstantial evidence.
19. What is a presumption? Explain the difference between a rebuttable and an irrebuttable presumption.
20. What is the essence of the federal standard for admitting expert scientific and technical testimony? What rules apply?
21. If you were on the defense team, what lines of inquiry would you pursue to attack a DNA test that indicates your client is the person who committed the rape? A Breathalyzer test that says your client had a blood-alcohol level above the legal limit?
22. What is demonstrative evidence? List rules to keep in mind regarding the use of demonstrative evidence.
23. At what points in a trial may a motion for judgment of acquittal or its equivalent be made? What is the essence of the motion and what happens if it is granted?
24. Why is the decision on whether the defendant should testify such a difficult one?
25. What does the judge consider during the jury instruction conference? What role does the paralegal play in preparing for this conference?
26. What is the purpose of closing arguments from the point of view of the court? The attorneys? What are the limits on the closing argument?
27. What instructions are generally given to the jury in a criminal case?
28. What is the duty of a jury when deliberating a case? Under what circumstances may a jury depart from that duty, and what is this called?
29. What is the *Allen* charge?
30. What are some common posttrial motions called? What are the grounds for these motions?

KEY TERMS LIST

Challenge for cause
Circumstantial evidence
Demonstrative evidence
Direct evidence
Direct examination
Jury nullification (jury pardon)
Leading question
Material
Opening statement
Peremptory challenge

Petty offense
Presumption
  Irrebuttable presumption
  Rebuttable presumption
Pro se (pro per) representation
Redirect examination
Relevant
Venire
Voir dire

ENDNOTES

1. Stanley Chauvin, Jr., President ABA, *Address to Annual Public Defender Conference,* THE ADVOCATE, Aug. 1990, at 17.

2. Daniel Goleman, *Studies Cast Doubt on Truth in Children's Testimony,* LEXINGTON HERALD-LEADER, June 11, 1993, at A5, reporting studies done at Cornell University by psychologist Stephen Ceci and colleagues.

3. *Alleged Lewd Noises Lead to Mistrial in* Floyd *Rape Case,* LEXINGTON HERALD-LEADER, July 20, 1993, at B4.

4. Nancy Heller, *Jury Investigation Challenges Paralegals,* THE NATIONAL PARALEGAL REPORTER, Spring 1990, at 4.

5. Frederick S. Lane III, *Using the Web as a Jury Selection Tool,* THE INTERNET LAWYER, Sept. 1998, at 1, 11.

6. Polling Instruction and Questions from the Department of Public Advocacy, Frankfort, Kentucky, with permission.

7. See 1998 and 1999 surveys done jointly by the National Law Journal and Decision Quest, a trial consulting firm as reported in NLJ, Nov. 2, 1998, A1, A24–A25; Nov. 1, 1999, A1, A6.

8. George Farquhar, 1678–1707.

9. Donald E. Vinson, *Juries: Perception and the Decision Making Process,* TRIAL, Mar. 1982, at 52–55.

10. Elizabeth Amon, *Shaking Up Juries, State by State,* NLJ, Feb. 14, 2000, A14.

SENTENCING, PUNISHMENT, AND REVIEW

I. INTRODUCTION

A. GOALS

The stage of sentencing and punishment brings us full circle from the reasoning that forms the basis of the criminal justice system. Chapter 1 presented the concepts of retribution, deterrence, and rehabilitation as the purpose behind the effort to apprehend suspected offenders and determine their innocence or guilt. We demand that convicted offenders "pay their debt to society" in retribution, act as a deterrent to keep others from following their example and themselves from repeating their acts, or change their ways so as to be rehabilitated to take a productive place in society. Without these goals, there would be no reason to make an arrest in the first place. After the guilty plea or determination of guilt through trial, we come to the processes that carry out the goals of the criminal justice system.

B. SETTING AND SERVING THE SENTENCE

The sentence officially establishes the punishment to be meted out to the perpetrator of a particular crime. Different forms of punishment apply retribution, deterrence, and rehabilitation in differing degrees and are measured to fit the specific crime or criminal. The range in sentencing is set by federal and state statute, and more narrowly by federal and some state guidelines. In the federal system, judges always pronounce sentence, which is also true in most state systems; in Arizona, Indiana, Kentucky, and West Virginia juries recommend the sentence to be set by the judge; in Arkansas, Missouri, Oklahoma, Texas, and Virginia juries set the sentence. Juries are particularly responsible for sentencing in death penalty cases.

Legislatures do not have the freedom to set sentences randomly. The Fifth and Fourteenth amendments to the Constitution, as well as similar state provisions, prevent punishments from being enacted without due process. Procedural irregularities must be ironed out to eliminate unfair advantages or disadvantages.

The Eighth Amendment prohibition on "cruel and unusual punishment" also limits sentencing, but its interpretation by the courts provides the needed flexibility that is dictated by changing societal attitudes. The predominantly capital and corporal punishment that served as retribution gave way to the idea of reformation and the building of penitentiaries during the late eighteenth-century Enlightenment. The prison system begun in Auburn, N.Y., in 1817, where prisoners were isolated in cells at night but worked together during the day, became a model for prisons in the rest of the nation.[1] It was not until 1968, however, that corporal, or physical, punishment was officially eliminated in the United States [*Jackson v. Bishop* (8th Cir.)]. Arkansas's use of whipping, electric shock, and brutal work conditions to discipline inmates was declared unconstitutionally cruel.[2] Now penitentiaries, the intended benign alternative to corporal punishment, have been criticized as cruel. Overcrowding and lack of control frequently subject inmates to dangerous conditions. Capital punishment also continues to draw criticism.

proportionality: the attempt to balance the severity of the punishment with the severity of the crime.

A refinement of the "cruel and unusual" clause came with **proportionality** analysis, an attempt to balance the severity of the punishment with the severity of the crime, in the decision of *Weems v. U.S.* (1910). The sentence of fifteen years of hard labor in leg irons was held to be cruelly disproportionate to the crime of falsifying a minor document by a public official. Standards for proportionality analysis were set by *Solem v. Helm* (1983): (1) the gravity of the offense relative to the harshness of the penalty, (2) the sentences imposed for other crimes in the jurisdiction, and (3) the sentences imposed for the same crimes in other jurisdictions. These standards were further interpreted in *McGruder v. Puckett* (5th Cir. 1992); a court must determine that the first standard was violated by a sentence grossly disproportionate to the offense before considering the remaining two standards of the *Solem* test.

For serious crimes, sentencing procedure involves a presentence report and alternative sentencing plan leading to the hearing where the sentence is pronounced. Paralegals have important tasks in this preparation stage.

The beginning of punishment is not the end of the story, however. Problems occurring during the serving of the sentence may require continued intervention.

C. REVIEW

Conceding that errors may occur at the trial level, the criminal justice system provides for several types and levels of review where corrections can be made: trial *de novo*, appeal by right, discretionary review, habeas corpus relief, and nonjudicial remedies.

Appeals are generally made "on the record," which means that the reviewing court does not reenact the trial, but reviews the record of the trial to see if errors exist.

The United States Constitution does not provide the right to appeal a criminal conviction [*McKane v. Durston* (1894)], but federal and state statutes uniformly fill the gap. They provide for an appeal by right to the appellate court immediately higher than the trial court.

After the appeal by right, further appellate review is possible only at the discretion of the higher court. The United States Supreme Court exercises such discretion by granting a **writ of certiorari** to the lower court, ordering records of those cases it chooses to review. A denial of certiorari allows the lower court's decision to stand.

writ of certiorari: an order by the appellate court having discretion that it will hear an appeal.

Beyond appeal, relief may be sought through a writ of habeas corpus. This ancient form of remedy is the last judicial resort for those looking for release from custody they consider to be unjust.

Nonjudicial relief is still available after all other avenues have come to dead ends. An appeal to executive authority is grounded in the common law tradition of appeal to the Crown for clemency. The United States Constitution, in Article 2, Section 1, Clause 1, gives the president the "Power to grant Reprieves and Pardons for offenses against the United States, except in Cases of Impeachment." Sentences may be commuted, fines remitted, and conditional or full pardons issued; the last restores civil rights as if the crime had not been committed. Relief may be granted even before conviction, as demonstrated by President Ford's pardon of former President Nixon for offenses surrounding the Watergate scandal. State constitutions or statutes usually limit this last appeal to the governor. A few states require the governor's pardons to be approved by a state commission, and some states allow pardons only by such a commission.[3] **Amnesty** is the pardon offered to a group, such as that freeing Confederate soldiers from prosecution after the Civil War.

amnesty: pardon offered to a group.

Because appeal by right and discretion and habeas corpus review involve complicated rules and precedents, they are the remedies this chapter will emphasize. Approaches to these processes differ from those for trial, so the postconviction phase may be turned over to specialists in the field. If you work on a case from beginning to end, you have the advantage of being able to carry over information from one phase to the next. If you enter the case at the appeals level, your work begins with a review of all that has gone before. In either event, meticulous attention to detail is vital; the one overlooked bit of information may be the one necessary to convince the court.

II. FORMS OF PUNISHMENT

A. INTRODUCTION

Criminal penalties include capital punishment and incarceration, payment of fines to the state and restitution to victims, forfeiture of property, and probation that may include community control or community service as conditions. Judges, probation officers, and prosecution and defense teams sensitive to the needs of both victims and defendants are continuing to find new ways to satisfy the goals of retribution, deterrence, and rehabilitation.

 ANALYSIS PROBLEM

14–1. If a form of punishment is commonly used, can it be considered cruel and (particularly) unusual? How do you believe such a form of punishment could be attacked?

B. CAPITAL PUNISHMENT

Taking the life of one who causes harm to others is a solution that has a long tradition in history and even religion. The Massachusetts Code of 1648 provided the death penalty for idolatry, witchcraft, blasphemy, sodomy, adultery, and "man stealing," as well as for most felonies. Death provides a strong retribution and individual deterrence, but eliminates any attempt at rehabilitation and is questionable as a general deterrent. States began abandoning capital punishment with mid–nineteenth-century reform movements. The 1960s also brought strong opposition, and there were no executions in this country in the decade following 1967. Bolstering this restraint was the ruling in *Furman v. Georgia* (1972) declaring Georgia's death penalty unconstitutional.

The *Furman* Court did not consider the general question of the constitutionality of the death penalty, but it invalidated the statute because it allowed the sentence to be applied capriciously and with discrimination. There were no standards setting apart the cases whose circumstances mandated the death penalty from those that did not, leaving that to the discretion of judge or jury. Because the death penalty was invoked infrequently, its imposition was judged likely to be so uneven as to be "cruel and unusual." The defendants in the three cases considered, one murderer and two rapists, were African American with white victims.

Georgia responded to the *Furman* decision with a new capital punishment statute subsequently upheld in *Gregg v. Georgia* (1976). A total of thirty-eight states passed capital punishment statutes that enumerate aggravating and mitigating circumstances to be considered by the jury in the penalty phase of a bifurcated trial, after the defendant has been convicted. An automatic appeal to the state supreme court is an additional safeguard.

Lockett v. Ohio (1978) specified that "as a mitigating factor, any aspect of the defendant's character or record and any of the circumstances of the offense that the defendant proffers as a basis for a sentence less than death," must be allowed for consideration. Justice Scalia's concurring statement in *Walton v. Arizona* (1990), however, gives notice that he will no longer vote to uphold that decision because he finds it irreconcilable with the requirement that the sentencer's discretion be constrained by specific standards to prevent random and capricious imposition of the death penalty. Aggravating circumstances such as "utter disregard for human life" have been ruled unconstitutionally vague unless more narrowly interpreted by the courts [*Arave v.*

"Gentlemen of the jury, the charge against the prisoner is murder, and the punishment is death; and that simple statement is sufficient to suggest the awful solemnity of the occasion which brings you and me face to face."

—John Inglis, *A Complete Report of the Trial of Miss Madeline Smith,* 1857

Creech (1993)]. In *Arave*, the Idaho Supreme Court narrowed the phrase with the construction "cold-blooded, pitiless slayer" to set apart defendants worthy of the death penalty from defendants who show feeling. *Coker v. Georgia* (1977) ruled that the death penalty may not be imposed for rape.

In *Weeks v. Angelone* (2000), the Supreme Court rejected the significance of a jury's request for clarification on whether the existence of aggravating circumstances required the imposition of the death penalty. The jury was not given the defense instruction that correctly would have specified that mitigating circumstances could be used to justify a lesser sentence. The Supreme Court also ruled in *Buchanan v. Angelone* (1998) that a state may bar specific instructions on mitigating factors, as long as that does not preclude the jury from considering relevant mitigating circumstances. Studies have shown, however, that jurors often misunderstand instructions on aggravating and mitigating circumstances and when a life sentence means without parole, and they underestimate time served before a parole might begin. Therefore, they are more likely to choose a death sentence.[4]

The new statutes make imposition of the death penalty somewhat more predictable, but of course do not eliminate all discrimination. Moreover, when discrimination is claimed, it must be shown to be against the individual defendant, and not a general group to which the defendant belongs. Statistical studies showing that the death penalty is more common when defendants are African American and less common when victims are African American were rejected in *McCleskey v. Kemp* (1987).

Kentucky is unique among the states in responding to *McClesky* with a law allowing a claim of discrimination to be raised at the pretrial conference when the prosecution seeks the death penalty (KRS 532.300). At a hearing on the claim, the defendant has the burden of proving by clear and convincing evidence, including statistical evidence, that race was the basis of the decision to seek the death penalty. If that burden is met, the death penalty is barred.

Two decisions have had an impact on incompetent defendants facing execution. *Ford v. Wainwright* (1986) ruled that a defendant whose mental illness began after conviction could not be executed if he could not comprehend the reasons or implications of the sentence. *State v. Perry* (La. 1992) ruled that the forced medication of an incompetent death row prisoner with antipsychotic drugs in order to carry out his death sentence would violate the state constitutional right to privacy, as well as the prohibition against cruel and unusual punishment.

Execution by electric chair is still used in Alabama, Florida, Georgia, and Nebraska. The death penalty itself is under review after a rise in the pace of executions, ninety-eight in 1999, and at least eighty exonerations of death row inmates, about one for every seven executions since the reinstatement of the penalty in 1976. The exonerations were based on DNA testing, incompetent defense counsel at trial, and use of unreliable jailhouse informants. After having more capital inmates declared innocent than the number executed in the state, Illinois placed a moratorium on executions in 1999, and several other states are considering doing the same.

More fuel for the debate was added by a Columbia University study showing that two-thirds of death penalty cases from 1973 to 1995 were overturned on appeal primarily because of incompetent defense or withholding of evidence by police or prosecution. The error rate in other criminal cases is estimated to be less than 10 percent.[5]

Federal capital punishment statutes include air piracy with loss of life, 49 U.S.C.A. § 1472(i)(1)(B), and the "drug kingpin" statute, 21 U.S.C. § 848(e), which covers loss of life in connection with a continuing criminal enterprise.

GREGG v. GEORGIA
Supreme Court of the United States, 1976.
428 U.S. 153, 96 S. Ct. 2909.
[Citations omitted]

Judgment of the Court, and opinion of MR. JUSTICE STEWART, MR. JUSTICE POWELL, and MR. JUSTICE STEVENS, announced by MR. JUSTICE STEWART.

The issue in this case is whether the imposition of the sentence of death for the crime of murder under the law of Georgia violates the Eighth and Fourteenth Amendments.

I.

The petitioner, Troy Gregg, was charged with committing armed robbery and murder. In accordance with Georgia procedure in capital cases, the trial was in two stages, a guilt stage and a sentencing stage. The evidence at the guilt trial established that on November 21, 1973, the petitioner and a traveling companion, Floyd Allen, while hitchhiking north in Florida were picked up by Fred Simmons and Bob Moore. Their car broke down, but they continued north after Simmons purchased another vehicle with some of the cash he was carrying. While still in Florida, they picked up another hitchhiker, Dennis Weaver, who rode with them to Atlanta, where he was let out about 11 p.m. A short time later the four men interrupted their journey for a rest stop along the highway. The next morning the bodies of Simmons and Moore were discovered in a ditch nearby.

On November 23, after reading about the shootings in an Atlanta newspaper, Weaver communicated with the Gwinnett County police and related information concerning the journey with the victims, including a description of the car. The next afternoon, the petitioner and Allen, while in Simmons' car, were arrested in Asheville, N.C. In the search incident to the arrest a .25-caliber pistol, later shown to be that used to kill Simmons and Moore, was found in the petitioner's pocket. After receiving the warnings required by *Miranda v. Arizona,* 384 U.S. 436 (1966), and signing a written waiver of his rights, the petitioner signed a statement in which he admitted shooting, then robbing Simmons and Moore. He justified the slayings on grounds of self-defense. The next day, while being transferred to Lawrenceville, Ga., the petitioner and Allen were taken to the scene of the shootings. Upon arriving there, Allen recounted the events leading to the slayings. His version of these events was as follows: After Simmons and Moore left the car, the petitioner stated that he intended to rob them. The petitioner then took his pistol in hand and positioned himself on the car to improve his aim. As Simmons and Moore came up an embankment toward the car, the petitioner fired three shots and the two men fell near a ditch. The petitioner, at close range, then fired a shot into the head of each. He robbed them of valuables and drove away with Allen.

A medical examiner testified that Simmons died from a bullet wound in the eye and that Moore died from bullet wounds in the cheek and in the back of the head. He further testified that both men had several bruises and abrasions about the face and head which probably were sustained either from the fall into the ditch or from being dragged or pushed along the embankment. Although Allen did not testify, a police detective recounted the substance of Allen's statements about the slayings and indicated that directly after Allen had made these statements the petitioner had admitted that Allen's account was accurate. The petitioner testified in his own defense. He confirmed that Allen had made the statements described by the detective, but denied their truth or ever having admitted to their accuracy. He indicated that he had shot Simmons and Moore because of fear and in self-defense, testifying they had attacked Allen and him, one wielding a pipe and the other a knife.[1]

The trial judge submitted the murder charges to the jury on both felony-murder and nonfelony-murder theories. He also instructed on the issue of self-defense but declined to instruct on manslaughter. He submitted the robbery case to the jury on both an armed-robbery theory and on the lesser included offense of robbery by intimidation. The jury found the petitioner guilty of two counts of armed robbery and two counts of murder.

At the penalty stage, which took place before the same jury, neither the prosecutor nor the petitioner's lawyer offered any additional evidence. Both counsel, however, made lengthy arguments dealing generally with the propriety of capital punishment under the circumstances and with the weight of the evidence of guilt. The trial judge instructed the jury that it could recommend either a death sentence or a life prison sentence on each count. The judge further charged the jury that in determining what sentence was appropriate

---

1. On cross-examination the State introduced a letter written by the petitioner to Allen entitled, "[a] statement for you," with the instructions that Allen memorize and then burn it. The statement was consistent with the petitioner's testimony at trial.

the jury was free to consider the facts and circumstances, if any, presented by the parties in mitigation or aggravation.

Finally, the judge instructed the jury that it "would not be authorized to consider [imposing] the penalty of death" unless it first found beyond a reasonable doubt one of these aggravating circumstances:

> "One—That the offense of murder was committed while the offender was engaged in the commission of two other capital felonies, to-wit the armed robbery of [Simmons and Moore].

> "Two—That the offender committed the offense of murder for the purpose of receiving money and the automobile described in the indictment.

> "Three—The offense of murder was outrageously and wantonly vile, horrible and inhuman, in that they [sic] involved the depravity of [the] mind of the defendant." Tr. 476–477.

Finding the first and second of these circumstances, the jury returned verdicts of death on each count.

The Supreme Court of Georgia affirmed the convictions and the imposition of the death sentences for murder. After reviewing the trial transcript and the record, including the evidence, and comparing the evidence and sentence in similar cases in accordance with the requirements of Georgia law, the court concluded that, considering the nature of the crime and the defendant, the sentences of death had not resulted from prejudice or any other arbitrary factor and were not excessive or disproportionate to the penalty applied in similar cases. The death sentences imposed for armed robbery, however, were vacated on the grounds that the death penalty had rarely been imposed in Georgia for that offense and that the jury improperly considered the murders as aggravating circumstances for the robberies after having considered the armed robberies as aggravating circumstances for the murders.

We granted the petitioner's application for a writ of certiorari limited to his challenge to the imposition of the death sentences in this case as "cruel and unusual" punishment in violation of the Eighth and the Fourteenth Amendments.

II.

. . . After a verdict, finding, or plea of guilty to a capital crime, a presentence hearing is conducted before whoever made the determination of guilt. The sentencing procedures are essentially the same in both bench and jury trials. At the hearing:

> "[T]he judge [or jury] shall hear additional evidence in extenuation, mitigation, and aggravation of punishment, including the record of any prior criminal convictions and pleas of guilty or pleas of nolo contendere of the defendant, or the absence of any prior conviction and

pleas: Provided, however, that only such evidence in aggravation as the State has made known to the defendant prior to his trial shall be admissible. The judge [or jury] shall also hear argument by the defendant or his counsel and the prosecuting attorney . . . regarding the punishment to be imposed." § 27–2503 (Supp. 1975).

The defendant is accorded substantial latitude as to the types of evidence that he may introduce. Evidence considered during the guilt stage may be considered during the sentencing stage without being resubmitted.

In the assessment of the appropriate sentence to be imposed the judge is also required to consider or to include in his instructions to the jury "any mitigating circumstances or aggravating circumstances otherwise authorized by law and any of [10] statutory aggravating circumstances which may be supported by the evidence. . . ." § 27–2534.1(b) (Supp. 1975). The scope of the nonstatutory aggravating or mitigating circumstances is not delineated in the statute. Before a convicted defendant may be sentenced to death, however, except in cases of treason or aircraft hijacking, the jury, or the trial judge in cases tried without a jury, must find beyond a reasonable doubt one of the 10 aggravating circumstances specified in the statute.[9] The sentence of death may be imposed only if the jury (or judge) finds one of the statutory aggravating circumstances and then elects to impose that sentence. § 26–3102 (Supp. 1975). If the verdict is death, the jury or judge must specify the aggravating circumstance(s) found. § 27–2534.1(c) (Supp. 1975). In jury cases, the trial

---

9. The statute provides in part:

"(a) The death penalty may be imposed for the offenses of aircraft hijacking or treason, in any case.

"(b) In all cases of other offenses for which the death penalty may be authorized, the judge shall consider, or he shall include in his instructions to the jury for it to consider, any mitigating circumstances or aggravating circumstances otherwise authorized by law and any of the following statutory aggravating circumstances which may be supported by the evidence:

"(1) The offense of murder, rape, armed robbery, or kidnapping was committed by a person with a prior record of conviction for a capital felony, or the offense of murder was committed by a person who has a substantial history of serious assaultive criminal convictions.

"(2) The offense of murder, rape, armed robbery, or kidnapping was committed while the offender was engaged in the commission of another capital felony, or aggravated battery, or the offense of murder was committed while the offender was engaged in the commission of burglary or arson in the first degree.

"(3) The offender by his act of murder, armed robbery, or kidnapping knowingly created a great risk of death to more than one person in a public place by means of a weapon or device which would normally be hazardous to the lives of more than one person.

(continued)

judge is bound by the jury's recommended sentence. §§ 26–3102, 27–2514 (Supp. 1975).

In addition to the conventional appellate process available in all criminal cases, provision is made for special expedited direct review by the Supreme Court of Georgia of the appropriateness of imposing the sentence of death in the particular case. The court is directed to consider "the punishment as well as any errors enumerated by way of appeal," and to determine:

"(1) Whether the sentence of death was imposed under the influence of passion, prejudice, or any other arbitrary factor, and

"(2) Whether, in cases other than treason or aircraft hijacking, the evidence supports the jury's or judge's finding of a statutory aggravating circumstance as enumerated in section 27.2534.1(b), and

---

Concluded

"(4) The offender committed the offense of murder for himself or another, for the purpose of receiving money or any other thing of monetary value.

"(5) The murder of a judicial officer, former judicial officer, district attorney or solicitor or former district attorney or solicitor during or because of the exercise of his official duty.

"(6) The offender caused or directed another to commit murder or committed murder as an agent or employee of another person.

"(7) The offense of murder, rape, armed robbery, or kidnapping was outrageously or wantonly vile, horrible or inhuman in that it involved torture, depravity of mind, or an aggravated battery to the victim.

"(8) The offense of murder was committed against any peace officer, corrections employee or fireman while engaged in the performance of his official duties.

"(9) The offense of murder was committed by a person in, or who has escaped from, the lawful custody of a peace officer or place of lawful confinement.

"(10) The murder was committed for the purpose of avoiding, interfering with, or preventing a lawful arrest or custody in a place of lawful confinement, of himself or another.

"(c) The statutory instructions as determined by the trial judge to be warranted by the evidence shall be given in charge and in writing to the jury for its deliberation. The jury, if its verdict be a recommendation of death, shall designate in writing, signed by the foreman of the jury, the aggravating circumstance or circumstances which it found beyond a reasonable doubt. In non-jury cases the judge shall make such designation. Except in cases of treason or aircraft hijacking, unless at least one of the statutory aggravating circumstances enumerated in section 27–2534.1(b) is so found, the death penalty shall not be imposed." § 27–2534.1 (Supp. 1975).

The Supreme Court of Georgia, in *Arnold v. State,* 236 Ga. 534, 540, 224 S.E.2d 386, 391 (1976), recently held unconstitutional the portion of the first circumstance encompassing persons who have a "substantial history of serious assaultive criminal convictions" because it did not set "sufficiently 'clear and objective standards.' "

"(3) Whether the sentence of death is excessive or disproportionate to the penalty imposed in similar cases, considering both the crime and the defendant." § 27–2537 (Supp. 1975).

If the court affirms a death sentence, it is required to include in its decision reference to similar cases that it has taken into consideration. § 27–2537(e) (Supp. 1975).

A transcript and complete record of the trial, as well as a separate report by the trial judge, are transmitted to the court for its use in reviewing the sentence. § 27–2537(a) (Supp. 1975). The report is in the form of a 6 1/2-page questionnaire, designed to elicit information about the defendant, the crime, and the circumstances of the trial. It requires the trial judge to characterize the trial in several ways designed to test for arbitrariness and disproportionality of sentence. Included in the report are responses to detailed questions concerning the quality of the defendant's representation, whether race played a role in the trial, and, whether, in the trial court's judgment, there was any doubt about the defendant's guilt or the appropriateness of the sentence. A copy of the report is served upon defense counsel. Under its special review authority, the court may either affirm the death sentence or remand the case for resentencing. In cases in which the death sentence is affirmed there remains the possibility of executive clemency.

III.

We address initially the basic contention that the punishment of death for the crime of murder is, under all circumstances, "cruel and unusual" in violation of the Eighth and Fourteenth Amendments of the Constitution. . . .

A.

. . . When a form of punishment in the abstract (in this case, whether capital punishment may ever be imposed as a sanction for murder) rather than in the particular (the propriety of death as a penalty to be applied to a specific defendant for a specific crime) is under consideration, the inquiry into "excessiveness" has two aspects. First, the punishment must not involve the unnecessary and wanton infliction of pain. Second, the punishment must not be grossly out of proportion to the severity of the crime.

B.

Of course, the requirements of the Eighth Amendment must be applied with an awareness of the limited role to be played by the courts. . . .

. . . Therefore, in assessing a punishment selected by a democratically elected legislature against the constitutional measure, we presume its validity. . . .

C.

In the discussion to this point we have sought to identify the principles and considerations that guide a court in addressing an Eighth Amendment claim. We now consider specifically whether the sentence of death for the crime of murder is a *per se* violation of the Eighth and Fourteenth Amendments to the Constitution. We note first that history and precedent strongly support a negative answer to this question.

. . .

It is apparent from the text of the Constitution itself that the existence of capital punishment was accepted by the Framers. . . .

Despite the continuing debate, dating back to the 19th century, over the morality and utility of capital punishment, it is now evident that a large proportion of American society continues to regard it as an appropriate and necessary criminal sanction.

As we have seen, however, the Eighth Amendment demands more than that a challenged punishment be acceptable to contemporary society. The Court also must ask whether it comports with the basic concept of human dignity at the core of the Amendment. Although we cannot "invalidate a category of penalties because we deem less severe penalties adequate to serve the ends of penology," the sanction imposed cannot be so totally without penological justification that it results in the gratuitous infliction of suffering.

The death penalty is said to serve two principal social purposes: retribution and deterrence of capital crimes by prospective offenders.

In part, capital punishment is an expression of society's moral outrage at particularly offensive conduct. This function may be unappealing to many, but it is essential in an ordered society that asks its citizens to rely on legal processes rather than self-help to vindicate their wrongs. . . .

Statistical attempts to evaluate the worth of the death penalty as a deterrent to crimes by potential offenders have occasioned a great deal of debate. The results simply have been inconclusive. . . .

In sum, we cannot say that the judgment of the Georgia Legislature that capital punishment may be necessary in some cases is clearly wrong. Considerations of federalism, as well as respect for the ability of a legislature to evaluate, in terms of its particular State, the moral consensus concerning the death penalty and its social utility as a sanction, require us to conclude, in the absence of more convincing evidence, that the infliction of death as a punishment for murder is not without justification and thus is not unconstitutionally severe.

Finally, we must consider whether the punishment of death is disproportionate in relation to the crime for which it is imposed. . . . [W]hen a life has been taken deliberately by the offender, we cannot say that the punishment is invariably disproportionate to the crime. It is an extreme sanction, suitable to the most extreme of crimes.

. . .

IV.

We now consider whether Georgia may impose the death penalty on the petitioner in this case.

. . .

[C]oncerns expressed in *Furman* that the penalty of death not be imposed in an arbitrary or capricious manner can be met by a carefully drafted statute that ensures that the sentencing authority is given adequate information and guidance. As a general proposition these concerns are best met by a system that provides for a bifurcated proceeding at which the sentencing authority is apprised of the information relevant to the imposition of sentence and provided with standards to guide its use of the information.

We do not intend to suggest that only the above-described procedures would be permissible under *Furman* or that any sentencing system constructed along these general lines would inevitably satisfy the concerns of *Furman,* for each distinct system must be examined on an individual basis. Rather, we have embarked upon this general exposition to make clear that it is possible to construct capital-sentencing systems capable of meeting *Furman*'s constitutional concerns.

B.

We now turn to consideration of the constitutionality of Georgia's capital-sentencing procedures. . . .

Georgia's new sentencing procedures require as a prerequisite to the imposition of the death penalty, specific jury findings as to the circumstances of the crime or the character of the defendant. Moreover, to guard further against a situation comparable to that presented in *Furman,* the Supreme Court of Georgia compares each death sentence with the sentences imposed on similarly situated defendants to ensure that the sentence of death in a particular case is not disproportionate. On their face these procedures seem to satisfy the concerns of *Furman.* . . .

V.

The basic concern of *Furman* centered on those defendants who were being condemned to death capriciously and arbitrarily. Under the procedures before the Court in that case, sentencing authorities were not directed to give attention to the nature or circumstances of the crime committed or to the character or record of the defendant. Left unguided, juries imposed the death sentence in a way that could only be called freakish. The new Georgia sentencing procedures, by contrast, focus the jury's attention on the particularized nature of the crime and the particularized characteristics of the individual defendant. While the jury is permitted to consider any aggravating or mitigating circumstances, it must find and identify at least one statutory aggravating factor before it may impose a penalty of death. In this way the jury's discretion is channeled. No longer can a jury wantonly and freakishly impose the death sentence; it is always circumscribed by the legislative guidelines. In addition, the review function of the Supreme Court of Georgia affords additional assurance that the concerns that prompted our decision in *Furman* are not present to any significant degree in the Georgia procedure applied here.

For the reasons expressed in this opinion, we hold that the statutory system under which Gregg was sentenced to death does not violate the Constitution. Accordingly, the judgment of the Georgia Supreme Court is affirmed.

It is so ordered.

MR. JUSTICE WHITE, with whom THE CHIEF JUSTICE and MR. JUSTICE REHNQUIST join, concurring in the judgment.

. . .

MR. JUSTICE BRENNAN, dissenting.

. . .

MR. JUSTICE MARSHALL, dissenting.

. . .

The two purposes that sustain the death penalty as nonexcessive in the Court's view are general deterrence and retribution. In *Furman,* I canvassed the relevant data on the deterrent effect of capital punishment. The state of knowledge at that point, after literally centuries of debate, was summarized as follows by a United Nations Committee:

> "It is generally agreed between the retentionists and abolitionists, whatever their opinions about the validity of comparative studies of deterrence, that the data which now exist show no correlation between the

existence of capital punishment and lower rates of capital crime."

The available evidence, I concluded in *Furman,* was convincing that "capital punishment is not necessary as a deterrent to crime in our society."

. . .

There remains for consideration, however, what might be termed the purely retributive justification for the death penalty—that the death penalty is appropriate, not because of its beneficial effect on society, but because the taking of the murderer's life is itself morally good. . . .

Of course, it may be that these statements are intended as no more than observations as to the popular demands that it is thought must be responded to in order to prevent anarchy. But the implication of the statements appears to me to be quite different—namely, that society's judgment that the murderer "deserves" death must be respected not simply because the preservation of order requires it, but because it is appropriate that society make the judgment and carry it out. It is this latter notion, in particular, that I consider to be fundamentally at odds with the Eighth Amendment. . . . Under these standards, the taking of life "because the wrongdoer deserves it" surely must fall, for such a punishment has as its very basis the total denial of the wrongdoer's dignity and worth.

. . .

ANALYSIS PROBLEM

14–2. Does the population of death row in your state or their victims suggest a discriminatory application of the death penalty?

C. INCARCERATION

At one time prisons seemed the perfect solution to crime. Ideally, they provide retribution, deterrence, and rehabilitation in one sentence. By shutting violent offenders away from the rest of society, they represent safety and security for our population. By placing the offender in a controlled environment, they can rehabilitate that person to productive life.

"You have put me in here [jail] a cub, but I will come out roaring like a lion, and I will make all hell howl."

—Carry Nation
Carleton Beals, *Cyclone Carry,* c. 1901

Prisons, however, can be training grounds for criminals. Inmates are hardened by brutal conditions and have access to a network of expertise in crime that offers more likelihood of "success" than rehabilitation programs. These "schools for crime" cost more to house an inmate for a year than it would cost to send that person to college. Some prisoners, however, have been required to pay for the expense of their incarceration.[6]

The United States is likely to pass Russia soon with the highest per capita imprisonment rate in the world. Nearly two million Americans are behind bars, twice the number twelve years ago,[7] even though the crime rate has been dropping. Half are serving time for nonviolent crimes.[8] Of the inmate population 70 percent are illiterate, 10 percent are seriously mentally ill, and 60 to 80 percent have a history of substance abuse.[9] Some observers blame the rising prison population on mandatory sentencing levels under the United States Sentencing Guidelines and state guidelines, "truth in sentencing" laws that restrict release from prison on parole, "three strikes" laws that require up to life imprisonment after a third felony, and sentencing disparities as the result of racial factors and differences between crack and powder cocaine.[10] Federal sentences set for crack cocaine, 21 U.S.C.A. § 841(b)(1)(A and B)(iii) are the same as those for 100 times that amount of powder cocaine, § 841(b)(1)(A and B)(ii). These disparities have been upheld in *U.S. v. Armstrong* (1996) and *Graves v. U.S.* (E.D. Wash. 1999)

Sentences may be imposed in different ways.

1. A prison sentence may be pronounced then **suspended,** placing the defendant on probation—a conditional, supervised release.
2. Separate sentences must be imposed for each crime; in the case of multiple crimes, sentences may be **consecutive**—one after the other—or **concurrent**—to be served at the same time.
3. **Indeterminate sentencing** allows flexible prison terms responding to the defendant's progress toward rehabilitation. This approach led to disproportionality and is now largely abandoned.
4. **Indefinite sentences** set a maximum and minimum amount of time to be served, allowing for early release on parole if behavior goals have been reached in the minimum time. Many states use indefinite sentencing.
5. **Definite** or **determinate sentences** are fixed terms chosen from the range allowed by statute and guidelines. There is no parole. The federal system and a few states use definite sentencing.
6. **Mandatory sentences** are statutory minimum prison terms with no chance for either probation or parole.
7. **Enhancements** are automatic additions to the basic sentence for certain circumstances making the crime or the criminal more dangerous to society. Increases had been common for habitual offenders responsible for repeated felonies, for use of a firearm in the commission of the crime, and for committing the offense because of the victim's status.

    Then the Supreme Court in *Apprendi v. New Jersey* (2000) ruled that the only factor that a judge can use in the sentencing phase to increase the penalty beyond the statutory maximum is the fact of a prior conviction. Fifth and Fourteenth Amendment due process rights and Sixth Amendment rights to notice and jury trial require that other penalty enhancement facts are treated as elements of the crime, not sentencing factors. Therefore, hate crime and firearm enhancements must be submitted to a jury and proved beyond a reasonable doubt. The *Apprendi* majority did not address how the decision would impact on enhancements prescribed in the United States Sentencing Guidelines, but the dissent predicted a chaotic collision between the decision and the guidelines. The outcome remains to be seen.

suspended sentence: a sentence that is replaced by probation.

consecutive sentence: in the case of multiple crimes, sentences to be served one after the other.

concurrent sentence: in the case of multiple crimes, sentences to be served at the same time.

indeterminate sentencing: flexible prison terms responding to the defendant's progress toward rehabilitation; largely abandoned.

indefinite sentence: a maximum and minimum amount of time to be served, allowing for early release on parole if behavior goals have been reached.

definite or determinate sentence: fixed terms chosen from the range allowed by statute and guidelines; no parole.

mandatory sentence: statutory minimum prison terms with no chance for either probation or parole.

sentence enhancements: automatic additions to the basic sentence for certain circumstances making the crime or the criminal more dangerous to society.

D. FINES

Fines are the most common sentences in misdemeanor cases. They have reached the level of millions of dollars in banking and securities crimes as well as drug trafficking offenses. Fines seem particularly suited to defendants who have made large amounts of money through illegal practices and corporations, which cannot serve prison sentences.

Fines may be added to prison terms for more serious crimes, or may be an alternative to incarceration for those who can afford it. Unfortunately, the effect is that some defendants are allowed to "buy their way out of jail," whereas the poor are left to serve a more onerous incarceration for the same offense. Like prison terms, maximum and minimum amounts are set by statute. Some statutes base fines on the amount gained by committing the offense.

E. RESTITUTION

restitution:
a payment to the individual victim of the crime, a return of the value that was wrongfully taken.

As fines are a payback to society, **restitution** is a payment to the individual victim of the crime, a return of the value that was wrongfully taken. It has become more popular as victim rights movements have gained attention and is mandated by 18 U.S.C.A. § 3663.

Restitution is often a condition of probation, but also can be required in addition to incarceration. Critics point out that victims are not likely to be repaid by defendants who are in prison and not able to maintain employment, making restitution "one of the grand illusions in both sentencing reform and victim's rights. . . ."[11] Some states, recognizing the inability of many defendants to pay restitution, have established victim compensation funds to provide for victims' needs.

Restitution may also be required for damages over and above the harm for which the defendant was convicted. A defendant convicted of defrauding a federally insured bank had to pay for losses in addition to those for which he pled guilty [*U.S. v. Rice* (2d Cir. 1992)]. Restitution was affirmed in *State v. Tenerelli* (Minn. 1999) for the costs of a Hmong healing ceremony for the victim of assault after the defense failed its burden of proof that the nature of the ceremony was religious. Restitution for pain and suffering of the victim may not be included in the sentence, however, nor can restitution require the payment of the offender's entire prison income [*Southall v. U.S.* (D.C. 1998)].

F. FORFEITURE

Beyond the payment of fines and restitution, statutes provide for the forfeiture through civil proceedings of property used in crime or acquired as a result of crime, even if no criminal charges are filed. This method is increasingly popular as a way to ensure that crime does not pay. A Wisconsin law requires forfeiture of all vehicles transporting property used in the commission of a felony, even if that vehicle was not used in the crime itself. By transferring a crowbar used in a burglary from the car used in the crime to another car, the defendant subjected the second car to forfeiture [*State v. One 1971 Oldsmobile Cutlass Auto* (Wis. App. 1990)].

Forfeiture of property involved in racketeering is provided for in 18 U.S.C.A. § 1963. Empires built by drug lords became subject to forfeiture with the Comprehensive Drug Abuse Prevention and Control Act of 1970, 21 U.S.C.A. § 881. All property acquired with drug money, as well as the premises on which transactions took place, can be seized. Drug activity on a shopping center parking lot caused forfeiture of the entire center in *U.S. v. Sonny Mitchell Center* (5th Cir. 1991). The more recent decision in *Austin v. U.S.* (1993) ruled that forfeitures are subject to the Eighth Amendment restriction on excessive fines and should be limited. Forfeiture of $357,000 that a defendant tried to take out of the country was ruled grossly disproportional to the crime of not properly registering the money [*U.S. v. Bajakajian* (1998)]. A forfeiture of $15,000 was affirmed. The Court in *U.S. v. Ursery* (1996) ruled that for a double jeopardy challenge to civil forfeiture, a defendant must show legislative intent that the forfeiture is a criminal penalty and not a civil sanction, or that it is so punitive in fact that it cannot be regarded as a civil sanction.

Many state laws include provisions that the innocent owner of property may defend against a forfeiture. If property is jointly held, the innocent party must be compensated for his or her interest in the property. A Michigan law that held no such defense allowed the forfeiture of a car owned by both husband and wife, when the husband used the car for a tryst with a prostitute [*Bennis v. Michigan* (1996)]. Some states do not allow the forfeiture of a homestead, even if it has been illegally used; in other states, criminal laws prevail over homestead laws, allowing for forfeiture. Be sure to consult the laws and decisions in your jurisdiction on whether an innocent owner or homestead defense is a possibility.

An attorney may be required to investigate suspicious circumstances of property given in return for legal representation. An attorney's Porsche, given in payment by a drug defendant, was forfeited because the attorney could not show he took basic investigatory steps to determine that fees were not satisfied with a major instrumentality of his client's crime [*U.S. v. 1977 Porsche Carrera 911* (W.D. Tex. 1990)].

Only probable cause that the property was purchased with profits of crime or was used in committing a crime is necessary for the government to seize it. As a response to situations of property damage and loss to innocent owners, federal legislation has been proposed to require clear and convincing evidence of the link to crime.[12]

G. PROBATION

Nondangerous criminals may receive a sentence of probation, conditional release under the supervision of a probation officer who works within the corrections system. Probation may be combined with other forms of punishment, such as a brief imprisonment, fines, or restitution, but generally may not exceed the maximum prison term for the offense. Not surprisingly, probation is controversial. A Justice Department study including seventeen states revealed that forty-three percent of probated felons were arrested for new serious offenses within three years of the date probation was granted.[13]

The trial judge imposes the conditions for probation, often on recommendation of the probation officer. Common conditions include avoiding further illegal activity, staying away from certain people or places, maintaining or seeking employment, remaining in the area, and so forth. The court has considerable latitude in establishing these conditions, and may even curtail certain constitutional rights of the defendant. Warrantless searches of the defendant's person, vehicle, and residence for controlled substances were allowed by *People v. Hellenthal* (Mich. App. 1990), but other courts considered such conditions overboard. Conditions have other limits, too. Probation could not be revoked for a defendant who refused to enroll in a sexual therapy program, because such participation would amount to an admission of guilt to the sexual assault for which he was convicted [*State v. Imlay* (Mont. 1991)]. Also, the prohibition against the defendant's maintaining a checking account was ruled not reasonably related to the defendant's crime of coerced acquisition of the pension income of an elderly woman [*State v. Moses* (Vt. 1992)].

House arrest is a type of probation condition used for those needing stronger controls than the occasional visit with the probation officer. Extensive surveillance or electronic shackles that send radio signals identifying the wearer's location are necessary to verify that the probationer is remaining within set boundaries. House arrestees and those lodged in halfway houses may often leave the premises to go to work or carry out other conditions of probation.

Community service is seen as a sort of restitution to society. As a condition for probation, it sometimes is linked to the offense. A vehicular homicide defendant may be required to speak to youth groups about the dangers of drinking and driving; a vandal may be required to clean up a city park.

Other conditions of probation recall Hester Prynne's scarlet letter. A DUI convict's requirement to place his photo, name, and the caption, "DUI convicted" in a newspaper ad was upheld [*Lindsay v. State* (Fla. App. 1992)], but the condition that a shoplifter wear a T-shirt printed with a statement of his status as a felony theft probationer whenever he left his residence was ruled unreasonably overbroad and invalid [*People v. Hackler* (Cal. App. 1993)].

ANALYSIS PROBLEM

14–3. Which of the goals of criminal justice—retribution, deterrence, rehabilitation—do you believe are best served by each type of penalty listed in this section?

III.   SENTENCING STATUTES AND GUIDELINES

A.   SENTENCING STATUTES

Most state codes rank crimes by class for sentencing. A class C felony such as second degree burglary or first degree forgery, for example, may subject a convicted defendant to five to ten years of prison and a fine of $1,000 to $10,000. A class B misdemeanor such as false swearing or unlawful practice of law may carry a sentencing range of up to ninety days in jail and up to a $250 fine. By setting a range rather than a single term for every crime in that class, the statutes allow for factors surrounding the crime, such as aggravating and mitigating circumstances, to be considered. The **presumptive sentence** is the midway point of the sentencing range; two years would be the presumptive sentence in a one to three year range, for example. The judge must sentence within the range, and must account for deviation from the presumptive sentence by explaining for the record the mitigating or aggravating factors that affected the decision. Most sentencing statutes are indefinite, allowing for early release from prison after a portion of the sentence has been served with good behavior, or for probation rather than incarceration.

presumptive sentence: the midway point of the sentencing range.

The advantage of statutory ranges in sentencing is the flexibility afforded judges to tailor the punishment to the individual defendant and criminal conduct. The disadvantage is that the same flexibility allows two defendants convicted of the same class of offense to be given very different punishments, depending on the sympathies of their sentencers.

B.   THREE STRIKES LAWS

Federal law, 18 U.S.C.A. § 3559(c), provides for mandatory life imprisonment for a serious violent felony that follows two prior convictions for violent felonies, or convictions for one serious violent felony and one serious drug offense. The court in *U.S. v. Kaluna* (9th Cir. 1998) ruled that second degree robbery convictions did not qualify as strikes, because they did not require a weapon, and that the defendant should not bear the burden of proving the lack of a weapon as required by 18 U.S.C.A. § 3559(c)(3)(A)(i). *U.S. v. Wickes* (7th Cir. 1997) upheld the law in its entirety.

In the mid-1990s twenty-three states passed laws for long, usually mandatory sentences for second and third offenses. Most of those states have used the laws sparingly, applying them to only a handful of cases. Georgia, however, has sentenced nearly 2,000 people under its law, and California has used its law to sentence a quarter of its prison population, 40,000 people. More than one-tenth of them are serving sentences of twenty-five years to life, even for such offenses as the theft of a bottle of vitamins.[14]

A defendant convicted of burglary and assault with intent to commit murder stemming from the same incident and same victim served a prison sentence for the burglary whereas the assault sentence was stayed. His subsequent conviction for shoplifting $20 worth of cigarettes brought him under the three strikes law, resulting in a sentence of twenty-five years to life [*People v. Benson* (Cal. 1998)]. The California law allows prosecutors a second sentencing proceeding to try to convince the court to impose the three strikes sentence enhancement [*Monge v. California* (1998)].

C. SENTENCING GUIDELINES

1. Introduction

Disproportionality and judicial prejudice was the target of the Sentencing Reform Act of 1984, 18 U.S.C.A. § 3553. Through this act, Congress created the United States Sentencing Commission with the assignment to develop uniform guidelines for sentencing in federal cases. The goals of the commission were to eliminate indeterminate sentencing, and to provide uniformity and proportionality in sentencing.

For example, televangelist James Bakker was originally sentenced to forty-five years in prison and $500,000 in fines for mail fraud, wire fraud, and conspiracy, a much heavier sentence than that imposed on many violent criminals. The sentencing judge commented, "Those of us who do have a religion are ridiculed as being saps from money grubbing preachers or priests." *U.S. v. Bakker* (4th Cir. 1991) reduced the sentence to eight years.

By doing away with parole and the parole boards that determined early release, control of prison time is returned to the original sentence. Inmates may still earn 15 percent "good time" credit toward early release after the first year served, a substantial reduction from prior parole possibilities after one-third of the sentence was served. Uniformity in sentencing has improved, but differences in interpretation and calculation of the guidelines still cause unevenness. Proportionality is the continuing subject of much criticism of the guidelines; mandatory sentences in some areas seem cruelly harsh, and they are blamed for contributing to the burden of our prison system.[15] An Alabama man who bought a pound of marijuana was sentenced as a habitual offender because of several misdemeanors thirteen years before. His sentence: life without parole. Some of the states that adopted mandatory minimums and sentencing guidelines are repealing those laws or softening them by parole provisions.[16]

2. United States Sentencing Guidelines

a. Basic System   If you are working with sentencing in the federal system, it is important for you to be familiar with the guidelines. The Sentencing Commission surveys the guidelines annually, submitting recommended changes for congressional review, so keep up with current amendments. The book of guidelines contains a section on the basic offenses, including specific conduct, harm to the victim, and possible charges. Each offense is given a numerical value. Possible adjustments to the basic offense and their values are given. If the defendant "accepts responsibility" (pleads guilty), the number is adjusted downward. If the defendant obstructed the prosecution of the case, the number is adjusted upward. Characteristics of the offense, such as the value of goods stolen, carry specific numerical levels. A sentence can be based on possession of two illegal drugs, even though the conviction is based on only one, if both were part of the same course of conduct [*Edwards v. U.S.* (1998)]. Enhancements are provided for use of firearms and for career offenders, defined in United States Sentencing Guideline (U.S.S.G.) § 4B1.1 as those who were at least eighteen at the time of the current offense, whose current offense is either a violent or controlled substance offense, and who have at least two prior felony convictions of either violent or controlled substance offenses.

When the numbers are added and subtracted, the bottom line is then matched to the sentencing options available for that level. For example, sentencing for an embezzlement conviction would be calculated like this.

Basic offense level	+4	(0–6 months in prison)
amount of $10,000	+5	
	9	(4–10 months)
Pled guilty	−2	
TOTAL	7	(1–7 months)[17]

Departures from this calculation are possible, but not frequent. In a decision based on U.S.S.G. § 5.K2.0, the Supreme Court ruled that "the only circumstance in which the district court can disregard the mechanical dictates of the Guidelines is when it finds that there exists an aggravating or mitigating circumstance of a kind, or to a degree, not adequately taken into account by the Sentencing Commission in formulating the guidelines" [*Burns v. U.S.* (1991)].

Special factors allow departure from the sentencing range only if they are encouraged by the Sentencing Commission and if they are present to an exceptional degree or in a different way from an ordinary case [*Koon v. U.S.* (1996)]. Koon, one of the officers in the Rodney King police brutality case, was entitled to a five-level downward departure, because of the suspect's contributing misconduct, and further discretionary mitigation, because of his susceptibility in prison and successive state and federal prosecutions. A three-level downward departure based on his loss of employment, however, was not allowed.

Generally, a defendant may not appeal a district court's refusal to depart downward, but when the judge's decision appeared "bewildered and ambiguous" in regard to whether a defendant should be classified as a career offender, the appeal was allowed [*U.S. v. Webb* (11th Cir. 1998)].

In 1995, judges departed from federal sentencing guidelines in 29 percent of cases. Three percent of those departures were upward. Sixty-eight percent were downward departures based on "substantial assistance" of defendants to law enforcement [18 U.S.C.A. § 3553(e)].[18]

b. "Safety Valve" Provision   A 1994 "safety valve" provision of the federal law, 18 U.S.C.A. § 3553(f), allows judges to depart from mandatory minimum sentences in drug offenses if the defendant (1) has not more than one criminal history point, (2) did not use or threaten violence or possess a dangerous weapon in connection with the offense, (3) did not kill or seriously injure any person, (4) was not an organizer or leader in the offense, and (5) has truthfully provided all information and evidence the defendant has to the government not later than the time of the sentencing hearing.

Some courts deny the safety valve if the defendant lied before making a truthful disclosure at the sentencing hearing [*U.S. v. Ramunno* (7th Cir. 1998)], but others allow the departure if the full and truthful disclosure comes by the opening of the sentencing hearing [*U.S. v. Schreiber* (2d Cir. 1999)]. A refusal to testify against coconspirators does not bar the safety valve, however [*U.S. v. Carpenter* (6th Cir. 1998)]. A defendant who pleaded guilty because he was misled that he was eligible for the safety valve had his plea set aside in *Hernandez-Wilson v. U.S.* (1st Cir. 1999).

c. Calculation of Sentence Levels From the embezzlement example given, it appears that calculation of sentences is a matter of very simple arithmetic. Unfortunately, calculations are subject to the interpretation of a confusing array of characteristics, and a great deal of litigation centers on how those calculations are to be made. For example, the role of the defendant in the offense helps determine the level assigned. A defendant who was the right-hand man to the head of a large-scale heroin trafficking operation should have received a three-level enhancement because of his importance to that operation, rather than the two-level enhancement in his sentence [*U.S. v. Farah* (2d Cir. 1993)]. Other confusion arises from determining whether factors of the offense are a part of the basic crime, or should be used to enhance the sentence. When a defendant struck a pedestrian and continued driving without slowing down, his recklessness and conduct manifesting indifference to human life were elements of the basic crime of aggravated assault, and should not have been used for increasing the sentence [*State v. Mara* (N.J. 1992)].

A defendant's Fifth Amendment silence at the sentencing hearing does not warrant an enhanced sentence [*Mitchell v. U.S.* (1999)]. *U.S. v. Smith* (3rd Cir. 1999) ruled that the heartland of U.S.S.G. § 251.1 is money laundering connected with extensive drug trafficking and acknowledged a growing trend not to use it on nondrug crimes.

A felony drug conviction in the Philippines could be counted as a prior conviction for sentence enhancement, because the conviction was consistent with fundamental fairness [*U.S. v. Kole* (3rd Cir. 1998)], but the use of a gun in a crime in Mexico could not be used, because the crime was not related to the current charges [*U.S. v. Levario-Quiroz* (5th Cir. 1998)].

A police receptionist who unlawfully gave notice of an impending search and seizure did not hold a position of trust for an enhanced sentence [*U.S. v. Reccko* (1st Cir. 1998)], but a doctor convicted of Medicare fraud had abused a position of trust [*U.S. v. Ntshona* (2d Cir. 1998)]. A prison cook supervisor is not a corrections officer under the guidelines [*U.S. v. Walker* (3rd Cir. 2000)].

Help in calculating sentences based on the federal guidelines is provided by ASSYST, a computer program available from the ABA Criminal Law Section, 1800 M St. N.W., 2nd Floor, Washington D.C. 20036-8886. Although mistakes are still possible, on-screen prompts and a fill-in-the-blank format guide you through the process of calculations.

A familiarity with the guidelines will help you alert your supervising attorney to questionable sentencing calls by probation officers or judges. The specific calculation used to reach a particular sentence is classified as attorney work product, however, and as such is not discoverable by the defense [*U.S. v. Knell* (N.D. Ill. 1991)].

d. Problems with the Federal Guidelines The implementation of the United States Sentencing Guidelines brought a shift in power in the criminal justice system. Where judges had had considerable discretion in sentencing, prosecutors now wield much of that power. Because the guidelines are quite rigid, the outcome of the calculations depends heavily on what charges are brought against the defendant. Those charges provide the baseline for the sentencing calculations. This situation, of course, does not please many defense attorneys and judges.

Beyond the shift in power, harsh mandated sentences, particularly those influenced by the "war on drugs," have been frustrating for many judges. In striking down U.S.S.G. § 4B1.1 requiring a sentence of thirty years in prison without parole as an unconstitutional violation of due process in *U.S. v. Spencer* (D.D.C. 1993), Judge Harold H. Greene wrote that it is not the power to make sentencing decisions that federal judges regret losing, but the loss of the ability to do justice. By reducing the sentence for nonviolent drug charges to ten years, the court followed the federal statute rather than the guidelines, pointedly giving deference to Congress over the Sentencing Commission.

"[I]f you think only terrible people go to prison, that solves that problem."

—Alta, American poet *Untitled Poem,* 1972

Some judges support the guidelines. Gerald B. Tjoflat, chief judge of the 11th Circuit, says, "The system is constructed such that [all the parties involved] go in with their eyes wide open. The old one was just unprincipled sentencing, really. A judge never had to explain the sentence to anyone, and there was widespread disparity." But others think the guidelines go too far and are too rigid. District Judge Judith Keep of San Diego says, "Human conduct just doesn't fit into a grid." Judge Bruce M. Selya of the 1st Circuit Court of Appeals says, "The grid lends itself to low comedy. People think of it as a game, like Parcheesi."[19]

IV. SENTENCING PROCEDURE

A. INTRODUCTION

In simple cases involving lesser crimes, judges often pronounce sentence at the time of conviction. In some jurisdictions juries recommend sentences for the judge to consider, and in others sentencing is accomplished by the jury alone.

B. CAPITAL SENTENCING

States that have capital punishment statutes similar to the Georgia law upheld in *Gregg* employ a bifurcated trial. The jury first determines guilt, then considers aggravating and mitigating factors to determine whether the death penalty is warranted. A list of these factors is usually included in the statute. At least one aggravating circumstance must be found for death to be imposed.

The jury's decision must be reasonable. *Williams v. State* (Fla. 1993) upheld a Florida judge's decision to override a jury's life sentence and to impose the death penalty on a drug kingpin who directed the murder of four victims. Mitigating circumstances could not outweigh the aggravating factors.

When a death sentence has been pronounced, there is usually an automatic appeal to the state supreme court for a review of evidence supporting the sentence; proportionality with similar cases; and to discover any prejudice, passion, or other arbitrary factor that might have influenced the sentence. Subsequent appeals may take many years.

C. PRESENTENCE REPORT

In the federal system, sentencing is the province of the trial judge. In serious cases, the sentencing hearing is postponed to allow time for a probation officer to investigate the circumstances of the offense and the defendant, and to prepare a presentence report. This report is a written presentation of factors for the judge to consider in determining the sentence.

"The toughest part of this job is sentencing. I've lost all kinds of sleep over sentences. I find it dreadful."

—Malcolm Muir, American jurist; judge, U.S. District Court
San Francisco Examiner & Chronicle, Mar. 8, 1981

The presentence report is covered in Federal Rule of Criminal Procedure 32(b). This rule provides that the defendant is entitled to presence of counsel at a presentence interview. It enumerates items that must be included in the report, such as Sentencing Commission classifications, victim impact, and appropriate nonprison resources available for the defendant. Diagnostic opinions that might disrupt rehabilitation and information that is confidential or might cause harm to the defendant or others must be excluded from the report.

Rule 35(b)(6) requires the probation officer to furnish the report to the defendant, the defendant's attorney, and the prosecutor no less than thirty-five days before the sentencing hearing. The sentence recommendation may be withheld. Objections must be communicated between the parties within fourteen days, and the probation officer may revise the report.

No later than seven days before the hearing, the report and any addendum of unresolved objections must be delivered to the court and the parties. Except for unresolved objections, the court may accept the report as its findings of fact.

The presentence investigation includes interviews with family, friends, and associates of the defendant to gather information on personal background; medical, employment, criminal, and educational histories; and other factors about the defendant that might serve as mitigating or aggravating circumstances. Statements by police, prosecutors, and the victim or victim's family also are taken to provide a balanced look at the offense and its impact.

The prosecution paralegal who is aware of particular needs of the victim may bring these to the attention of the probation officer so that restitution can be considered in the report. As already noted, the primary impact of the prosecution team on sentencing in guideline jurisdictions comes with the decision of what charges to bring against the defendant. Be sure to note sentencing factors in your tasks related to determining charges. Your suggestions and observations could be helpful to the prosecutor at this stage. Exhibit 14–1 at the end of the chapter (pages 552–569) is a sample presentence report.[20]

D.   ALTERNATIVE SENTENCING PLAN

The defense should begin to prepare for sentencing before indictment by helping to shape the charges. At times, the defense team does not enter the case until after this crucial point. All is not lost, however. Defense paralegals may assist their supervising attorneys in the preparation of an alternative sentencing plan, a presentence report from the point of view of the defense. Paralegals who work as sentencing specialists become experts at this task. Some are employed by states as alternative sentencing specialists; others have become consultants, contracting out to attorneys in significant cases. To prepare an effective plan, keep these pointers in mind.[21]

1. Never underestimate the victim's plea for mercy for your client. It is best to approach the victim through the prosecutor; always have a third neutral party present, a minister, social worker, or investigator, for example. Discuss the facts of the case, then explore what the victim sees as appropriate punishment.

2. Send a letter to the prosecution, inviting comments and suggestions for the plan.

3. Submit the plan to the judge a few days or at least the day before the sentencing hearing to allow time for consideration of your recommendations.

4. Because the judge is familiar with the format of the presentence report, it is helpful to follow that format for your plan as well.

5. Get access to the presentence report as soon as possible, explaining that such access will make the hearing go more smoothly. Because the report is the "official version" of the offense and of your client's life, sift through it carefully to catch any inaccuracies or unfavorable slants that could be corrected.

6. If your client waives the presentence report, make sure it is a knowing and informed waiver. A postsentence report is more difficult to correct and may affect parole.

7. In your investigation for the alternative plan, be sure to document all your information: diagnoses, prognoses, job opportunities, availability of and a commitment for placement from social services you recommend. News clips, letters, certificates, and so forth can serve as documentation.

8. Focus on the person, not the crime. Help the judge see this person as an individual. Document the hardship a prison sentence would create for the defendant's innocent family, if possible. Point out the significant effect that

child abuse in its many forms or other family disruptions may have had on the defendant. In 1999 half the women inmates in the United States correctional system had been physically or sexually abused in their past.[22]

9. Focus on the sentencing conditions that will help this defendant succeed. Point out characteristics that will enable this person to handle employment or community service: social skills, willingness to work with the disadvantaged, job experience or know-how, and so forth. Do not identify problems you cannot solve. Help the judge find a solution for this person's problems.

10. Take into consideration the needs for retribution, deterrence, and rehabilitation.

11. If possible, document the client's exemplary conduct between the offense and sentencing. This conduct must be beyond merely lawful behavior to be effective.

12. There are no rules of procedure for presenting the sentencing plan to the judge at the hearing. It is a good idea to have witnesses and family present in case the judge has questions and to show support and demonstrate the impact of a sentence on more than just the defendant. You may summarize statements for the witnesses.

13. If the alternative sentencing plan is rejected, save it for future use at parole hearings.

Exhibit 14–2 (pages 570–575) is a sample motion for probation with an alternative sentencing plan, and Exhibit 14–3 (page 576) is a judgment of sentence of probation.[23] These exhibits are at the end of this chapter.

E. THE SENTENCING HEARING

1. Procedure

The judge must pronounce sentence in open court. This pronouncement takes place at the sentencing hearing where the judge considers trial evidence, the presentence report and any alternative sentencing plan, evidence submitted by either party, and the defendant's statement.

Federal Rule of Criminal Procedure 32(c) provides for the court to permit the parties to introduce evidence on unresolved objections to the presentence report. The defendant, defense attorney, prosecutor, and the victim of a crime of violence or sexual abuse may make statements either in open court or, by joint motion of defense and prosecution, in camera. **Allocution,** the defendant's due process right to speak in his or her own behalf, is usually limited in scope at the sentence hearing to a brief statement of mitigation or response to evidence. One who pleads guilty to a crime can still invoke the Fifth Amendment privilege not to incriminate oneself at sentencing [*Mitchell v. U.S.* (1999)]. After sentencing, the court gives notification of the right to appeal.

The defendant has the right to counsel at the sentencing hearing [*Mempa v. Rhay* (1967)], but does not have the right to confront witnesses, which prevents the sentencing hearing from turning into a minitrial.

Evidentiary rules at trial do not necessarily apply at the sentencing hearing. Courts are split over applying the exclusionary rule at sentencing. In *U.S. v. Torres* (3d Cir. 1991) a quantity of cocaine suppressed during trial was allowed to raise the sentence base level from 18 to 26 under U.S.S.G. § 2D1.1. The decision in *U.S. v. Tejada* (2d Cir. 1992) allowed evidence in violation of the exclusionary rule, absent a showing that officers obtained the evidence expressly to enhance a sentence—which raises the question of who would have the burden of proving such an intention by the police. On the other side of the issue, the exclusionary rule was applied at sentencing to a gun and additional cocaine possession suppressed at trial in *U.S. v. Cabrera* (S.D.N.Y.

allocution:
the defendant's due process right to speak on his or her own behalf.

1991). That court offered the observation that if defendants are expected to accept the requirements of the law, they are entitled to know that the courts also expect police to conform to those requirements.

2. Victim Impact

Recent focus on the impact of crime on victims has brought victims into the sentencing phase of the criminal justice system. Thirty-two states have passed victim's rights amendments since 1982. The victim impact statement presented at the sentencing hearing alerts the judge or jury to the physical, economic, and psychological harm the offense has caused for the victim and victim's family, which may influence the inclusion of restitution in the sentence or affect the harshness of the punishment in general.

Critics fear that an overuse of the victim impact statement will cause disparity in sentencing, instituting more severe sentences for offenders against victims who are well-off with close-knit families, and not penalizing so severely offenders against the homeless persons, for example, who have no one to mourn their loss. This concern was reflected in *Booth v. Maryland* (1987), which struck down a statute requiring a victim impact statement to be considered in the sentencing phase of capital cases. Subsequently, the Supreme Court reconsidered the use of victim impact evidence in sentencing in *Payne v. Tennessee* (1991).

PAYNE v. TENNESSEE
Supreme Court of the United States, 1991.
501 U.S. 808, 111 S.Ct. 2597.
[Citations omitted]

CHIEF JUSTICE REHNQUIST delivered the opinion of the court.

In this case we reconsider our holdings in *Booth v. Maryland,* 482 U.S. 496 (1987), and *South Carolina v. Gathers,* 490 U.S. 805 (1989), that the Eighth Amendment bars the admission of victim impact evidence during the penalty phase of a capital trial.

The petitioner, Pervis Tyrone Payne, was convicted by a jury on two counts of first-degree murder and one count of assault with intent to commit murder in the first degree. He was sentenced to death for each of the murders, and to 30 years in prison for the assault.

The victims of Payne's offenses were 28-year-old Charisse Christopher, her 2-year-old daughter Lacie, and her 3-year-old son Nicholas. The three lived together in an apartment in Millington, Tennessee, across the hall from Payne's girlfriend, Bobbie Thomas. On Saturday, June 27, 1987, Payne visited Thomas' apartment several times in expectation of her return from her mother's house in Arkansas, but found no one at home. On one visit, he left his overnight bag, containing clothes and other items for his weekend stay, in the hallway outside Thomas' apartment. With the bag were three cans of malt liquor.

Payne passed the morning and early afternoon injecting cocaine and drinking beer. Later, he drove around the town with a friend in the friend's car, each of them taking turns reading a pornographic magazine. Sometime around 3 p.m., Payne returned to the apartment complex, entered the Christophers' apartment, and began making sexual advances towards Charisse. Charisse resisted and Payne became violent. A neighbor who resided in the apartment directly beneath the Christophers, heard Charisse screaming, " 'Get out, get out,' as if she were telling the children to leave." The noise briefly subsided and then began, "horribly loud." The neighbor called the police after she heard a "blood curdling scream" from the Christopher apartment.

When the first police officer arrived at the scene, he immediately encountered Payne who was leaving the apartment building, so covered with blood that he appeared to be " 'sweating blood.' " The officer confronted Payne, who responded, " 'I'm the complainant.' " When the officer asked, " 'What's going on up there?' " Payne struck the officer with the overnight bag, dropped his tennis shoes, and fled.

Inside the apartment, the police encountered a horrifying scene. Blood covered the walls and floor throughout the unit. Charisse and her children were lying on the floor in the kitchen. Nicholas, despite several wounds inflicted by a butcher knife that completely penetrated through his body from front to back, was still breathing. Miraculously, he survived, but not until after undergoing seven hours of surgery and a transfusion of 1700 cc's of blood—400 to 500 cc's more than his estimated normal blood volume. Charisse and Lacie were dead.

Charisse's body was found on the kitchen floor on her back, her legs fully extended. She had sustained 42 direct knife wounds and 42 defensive wounds on her arms and hands. The wounds were caused by 41 separate thrusts of a butcher knife. None of the 84 wounds inflicted by Payne were individually fatal; rather, the cause of death was most likely bleeding from all of the wounds.

Lacie's body was on the kitchen floor near her mother. She had suffered stab wounds to the chest, abdomen, back, and head. The murder weapon, a butcher knife, was found at her feet. Payne's baseball cap was snapped on her arm near her elbow. Three cans of malt liquor bearing Payne's fingerprints were found on a table near her body, and a fourth empty one was on the landing outside the apartment door.

Payne was apprehended later that day hiding in the attic of the home of a former girlfriend. As he descended the stairs of the attic, he stated to the arresting officers, "Man, I aint [sic] killed no woman." According to one of the officers, Payne had "a wild look about him. His pupils were contracted. He was foaming at the mouth, saliva. He appeared to be very nervous. He was breathing real rapid." He had blood on his body and clothes and several scratches across his chest. It was later determined that the blood stains matched the victims' blood types. A search of his pockets revealed a packet containing cocaine residue, a hypodermic syringe wrapper, and a cap from a hypodermic syringe. His overnight bag, containing a bloody white shirt, was found in a nearby dumpster.

At trial, Payne took the stand and, despite the overwhelming and relatively uncontroverted evidence against him, testified that he had not harmed any of the Christophers. Rather, he asserted that another man had raced by him as he was walking up the stairs to the floor where the Christophers lived. He stated that he had gotten blood on himself when, after hearing moans from the Christophers' apartment, he had tried to help the victims. According to his testimony, he panicked and fled when he heard police sirens and noticed the blood on his clothes. The jury returned guilty verdicts against Payne on all counts.

During the sentencing phase of the trial, Payne presented the testimony of four witnesses: his mother and father, Bobbie Thomas, and Dr. John T. Huston, a clinical psychologist specializing in criminal court evaluation work. Bobbie Thomas testified that she met Payne at church, during a time when she was being abused by her husband. She stated that Payne was a very caring person, and that he devoted much time and attention to her three children, who were being affected by her marital difficulties. She said that the children had come to love him very much and would miss him, and that he "behaved just like a father that loved his kids." She as-

serted that he did not drink, nor did he use drugs, and that it was generally inconsistent with Payne's character to have committed these crimes.

Dr. Huston testified that based on Payne's low score on an IQ test, Payne was "mentally handicapped." Huston also said that Payne was neither psychotic nor schizophrenic, and that Payne was the most polite prisoner he had ever met. Payne's parents testified that their son had no prior criminal record and had never been arrested. They also stated that Payne had no history of alcohol or drug abuse, he worked with his father as a painter, he was good with children, and that he was a good son.

The State presented the testimony of Charisse's mother, Mary Zvolanek. When asked how Nicholas had been affected by the murders of his mother and sister, she responded:

> "He cries for his mom. He doesn't seem to understand why she doesn't come home. And he cries for his sister Lacie. He comes to me many times during the week and asks me, Grandmama, do you miss my Lacie. And I tell him yes. He says, I'm worried about my Lacie."

In arguing for the death penalty during closing argument, the prosecutor commented on the continuing effects of Nicholas' experience, stating:

> "But we do know that Nicholas was alive. And Nicholas was in the same room. Nicholas was still conscious. His eyes were open. He responded to the paramedics. He was able to follow their directions. He was able to hold his intestines in as he was carried to the ambulance. So he knew what happened to his mother and baby sister."

> "There is nothing you can do to ease the pain of any of the families involved in this case. There is nothing you can do to ease the pain of Bernice or Carl Payne, and that's a tragedy. There is nothing you can do basically to ease the pain of Mr. and Mrs. Zvolanek, and that's a tragedy. They will have to live with it the rest of their lives. There is obviously nothing you can do for Charisse and Lacie Jo. But there is something that you can do for Nicholas.

> "Somewhere down the road Nicholas is going to grow up, hopefully. He's going to want to know what happened. And he is going to know what happened to his baby sister and his mother. He is going to want to know what type of justice was done. He is going to want to know what happened. With your verdict, you will provide the answer."

In the rebuttal to Payne's closing argument, the prosecutor stated:

> "You saw the videotape this morning. You saw what Nicholas Christopher will carry in his mind forever. When you talk about cruel, when you talk about atrocious, and

when you talk about heinous, that picture will always come into your mind, probably throughout the rest of your lives.

.   .   .   .   .

". . . No one will ever know about Lacie Jo because she never had the chance to grow up. Her life was taken from her at the age of two years old. So, no there won't be a high school principal to talk about Lacie Jo Christopher, and there won't be anybody to take her to her high school prom. And there won't be anybody there—there won't be her mother there or Nicholas' mother there to kiss him at night. His mother will never kiss him good night or pat him as he goes off to bed, or hold him and sing him a lullaby.

.   .   .   .   .

"[Petitioner's attorney] wants you to think about a good reputation, people who love the defendant and things about him. He doesn't want you to think about the people who love Charisse Christopher, her mother and daddy who loved her. The people who loved little Lacie Jo, the grandparents who are still here. The brother who mourns for her every single day and wants to know where his best little playmate is. He doesn't have anybody to watch cartoons with him, a little one. These are the things that go into why it is especially cruel, heinous, and atrocious, the burden that that child will carry forever."

The jury sentenced Payne to death on each of the murder counts.

The Supreme Court of Tennessee affirmed the conviction and sentence. The court rejected Payne's contention that the admission of the grandmother's testimony and the State's closing argument constituted prejudicial violations of his rights under the Eighth Amendment as applied in *Booth v. Maryland,* 482 U.S. 496 (1987), and *South Carolina v. Gathers,* 490 U.S. 805 (1989). The court characterized the grandmother's testimony as "technically irrelevant," but concluded that it "did not create a constitutionally unacceptable risk of an arbitrary imposition of the death penalty and was harmless beyond a reasonable doubt."

The court determined that the prosecutor's comments during closing argument were "relevant to [Payne's] personal responsibility and moral guilt." The court explained that "[w]hen a person deliberately picks a butcher knife out of a kitchen drawer and proceeds to stab to death a twenty-eight-year-old mother, her two and one-half year old daughter and her three and one-half year old son, in the same room, the physical and mental condition of the boy he left for dead is surely relevant in determining his 'blameworthiness.' " The court concluded that any violation of Payne's rights under *Booth* and *Gathers* "was harmless beyond a reasonable doubt."

We granted certiorari to reconsider our holdings in *Booth* and *Gathers* that the Eighth Amendment prohibits a capital sentencing jury from considering "victim impact" evidence relating to the personal characteristics of the victim and the emotional impact of the crimes on the victim's family.

In *Booth,* the defendant robbed and murdered an elderly couple. As required by a state statute, a victim impact statement was prepared based on interviews with the victims' son, daughter, son-in-law, and granddaughter. The statement, which described the personal characteristics of the victims, the emotional impact of the crimes on the family, and set forth the family members' opinions and characterizations of the crimes and the defendant, was submitted to the jury at sentencing. The jury imposed the death penalty. The conviction and sentence were affirmed on appeal by the State's highest court.

This Court held by a 5-to-4 vote that the Eighth Amendment prohibits a jury from considering a victim impact statement at the sentencing phase of a capital trial. The Court made clear that the admissibility of victim impact evidence was not to be determined on a case-by-case basis, but that such evidence was *per se* inadmissible in the sentencing phase of a capital case except to the extent that it "relate[d] directly to the circumstances of the crime." In *Gathers,* decided two years later, the Court extended the rule announced in *Booth* to statements made by a prosecutor to the sentencing jury regarding the personal qualities of the victim.

The *Booth* Court began its analysis with the observation that the capital defendant must be treated as a "uniquely individual human bein[g]," and therefore the Constitution requires the jury to make an individualized determination as to whether the defendant should be executed based on the "character of the individual and the circumstances of the crime.". . . To the extent that victim impact evidence presents "factors about which the defendant was unaware, and that were irrelevant to the decision to kill," the Court concluded, it has nothing to do with the "blameworthiness of a particular defendant.". . . [T]he prosecution may not introduce such evidence at a capital sentencing hearing because "it creates an impermissible risk that the capital sentencing decision will be made in an arbitrary manner."

Booth and *Gathers* were based on two premises: that evidence relating to a particular victim or to the harm that a capital defendant causes a victim's family do not in general reflect on the defendant's "blameworthiness," and that only evidence relating to "blameworthiness" is relevant to the capital sentencing decision. However, the assessment of harm caused by the defendant as a result of the crime charged has understandably been an important concern of the criminal law, both in determining the elements of the offense and in determining the appropriate punishment. Thus, two equally blameworthy criminal defendants may be guilty of different offenses solely because their acts cause differing amounts of harm. "If a bank robber aims his gun at a guard, pulls the trigger, and kills his target, he may be put to death. If the gun unexpectedly misfires, he may not. His moral guilt in both cases is identical, but his responsibility in the former is greater.". . .

The Maryland statute involved in *Booth* required that the presentence report in all felony cases include a "victim impact statement" which would describe the effect of the crime on the victim and his family. *Booth, supra,* at 498. Congress and most of the States have, in recent years, enacted similar legislation to enable the sentencing authority to consider information about the harm caused by the crime committed by the defendant. The evidence involved in the present case was not admitted pursuant to any such enactment, but its purpose and effect was much the same as if it had been. While the admission of this particular kind of evidence—designed to portray for the sentencing authority the actual harm caused by a particular crime—is of recent origin, this fact hardly renders it unconstitutional. . . .

Booth reasoned that victim impact evidence must be excluded because it would be difficult, if not impossible, for the defendant to rebut such evidence without shifting the focus of the sentencing hearing away from the defendant, thus creating a " 'mini-trial' on the victim's character." In many cases the evidence relating to the victim is already before the jury at least in part because of its relevance at the guilt phase of the trial. But even as to additional evidence admitted at the sentencing phase, the mere fact that for tactical reasons it might not be prudent for the defense to rebut victim impact evidence makes the case no different than others in which a party is faced with this sort of a dilemma. . . .

Payne echoes the concern voiced in *Booth*'s case that the admission of victim impact evidence permits a jury to find that defendants whose victims were assets to their community are more deserving of punishment than those whose victims are perceived to be less worthy. As a general matter, however, victim impact evidence is not offered to encourage comparative judgments of this kind—for instance, that the killer of a hard-working, devoted parent deserves the death penalty, but that the murderer of a reprobate does not. It is designed to show instead *each* victim's "uniqueness as an individual human being," whatever the jury might think the loss to the community resulting from his death might be. . . . Courts have always taken into consideration the harm done by the defendant in imposing sentence, and the evidence adduced in this case was illustrative of the harm caused by Payne's double murder.

We are now of the view that a State may properly conclude that for the jury to assess meaningfully the defendant's moral culpability and blameworthiness, it should have before it at the sentencing phase evidence of the specific harm caused by the defendant. . . .

The present case is an example of the potential for . . . unfairness. The capital sentencing jury heard testimony from Payne's girlfriend that they met at church, that he was affectionate, caring, kind to her children, that he was not an abuser of drugs or alcohol, and that it was inconsistent with his character to have committed the murders. Payne's parents testified that he was a good son, and a clinical psychologist testified that Payne was an extremely polite prisoner and suffered from a low IQ. None of this testimony was related to the circumstances of Payne's brutal crimes. In contrast, the only evidence of the impact of Payne's offenses during the sentencing phase was Nicholas' grandmother's description—in response to a single question—that the child misses his mother and baby sister. Payne argues that the Eighth Amendment commands that the jury's death sentence must be set aside because the jury heard this testimony. But the testimony illustrated quite poignantly some of the harm that Payne's killing had caused; there is nothing unfair about allowing the jury to bear in mind that harm at the same time as it considers the mitigating evidence introduced by the defendant.

. . .

Reconsidering [*Booth* and *Gathers*] now, we conclude for the reasons heretofore stated, that they were wrongly decided and should be, and now are, overruled. We accordingly affirm the judgment of the Supreme Court of Tennessee.

Affirmed.

JUSTICE O'CONNOR, with whom JUSTICE WHITE and JUSTICE KENNEDY join, concurring.

. . .

JUSTICE MARSHALL, with whom JUSTICE BLACKMUN joins, dissenting.

. . .

II.

The overruling of one of this Court's precedents ought to be a matter of great moment and consequence. Although the doctrine of *stare decisis* is not an "inexorable command," this Court has repeatedly stressed that fidelity to precedent is fundamental to "a society governed by the rule of law," ("[I]t is indisputable that *stare decisis* is a basic self-governing principle within the Judicial Branch, which is entrusted with the sensitive and difficult task of fashioning and preserving a jurisprudential system that is not based upon 'an arbitrary discretion.' The Federalist, No. 78, p. 490 (H. Lodge ed. 1888) (A. Hamilton)").

JUSTICE STEVENS, with whom JUSTICE BLACKMUN joins, dissenting.

. . .

II.

Today's majority has obviously been moved by an argument that has strong political appeal but no proper place in a reasoned judicial opinion. Because our decision in *Lockett,* 438 U.S., at 604 (opinion of Burger, C. J.), recognizes the defendant's right to introduce all mitigating evidence that may inform the jury about his character, the Court suggests that fairness requires that the State be allowed to respond with similar evidence about the *victim.* This argument is a classic non sequitur: The victim is not on trial; her character, whether good or bad, cannot therefore constitute either an aggravating or mitigating circumstance. . . .

The premise that a criminal prosecution requires an even-handed balance between the State and the defendant is also incorrect. The Constitution grants certain rights to the criminal defendant and imposes special limitations on the State designed to protect the individual from overreaching by the disproportionately powerful State. Thus, the State must prove a defendant's guilt beyond a reasonable doubt. Rules of evidence are also weighted in the defendant's favor. For example, the prosecution generally cannot introduce evidence of the defendant's character to prove his propensity to commit a crime, but the defendant can introduce such reputation evidence to show his law-abiding nature. Even if balance were required or desirable, today's decision, by permitting both the defendant and the State to introduce irrelevant evidence for the sentencer's consideration without any guidance, surely does nothing to enhance parity in the sentencing process.

III.

Victim impact evidence, as used in this case, has two flaws, both related to the Eighth Amendment's command that the

punishment of death may not be meted out arbitrarily or capriciously. First, aspects of the character of the victim unforeseeable to the defendant at the time of his crime are irrelevant to the defendant's "personal responsibility and moral guilt" and therefore cannot justify a death sentence. . . .

Second, the quantity and quality of victim impact evidence sufficient to turn a verdict of life in prison into a verdict of death is not defined until after the crime has been committed and therefore cannot possibly be applied consistently in different cases. . . .

IV.

The majority thus does far more than validate a State's judgment that "the jury should see 'a quick glimpse of the life petitioner chose to extinguish,'" Instead, it allows a jury to hold a defendant responsible for a whole array of harms that he could not foresee and for which he is therefore not blameworthy. . . .

Payne v. Tennessee overruled most of *Booth*, allowing family evidence at sentencing. The importance of victims and their families having a voice in the criminal process is increasingly being recognized. More than revenge, they want and need community recognition of their pain and the value of the life of the victim.[24] Societal impact statements have been allowed to show how the murder of a gas station attendant affected others working in similar situations and the security measures considered for their protection [*State v. Sivak* (Id. 1990)].

 ANALYSIS PROBLEM

14–4. Compare *Booth v. Maryland* and *Payne v. Tennessee.* Which do you agree with and why?

V.   SERVING THE SENTENCE

A.   REVOCATION OF PROBATION

If conditions of probation are violated by the probationer, probation may be revoked and the probationer sent to prison to complete the term of sentence. The decision to seek revocation is exercised by the probation officer. First, a preliminary hearing is held to determine if there is probable cause for revocation, then evidence is presented at a revocation hearing for the determination of revocation. Federal Rule of Criminal Procedure 32.1(a) provides the framework for these hearings.

1.   A preliminary hearing is held to determine probable cause to hold the person for a revocation hearing. The person shall be given
   a.   notice of the hearing, purpose, and alleged violation;
   b.   an opportunity to appear and present evidence;
   c.   upon request, opportunity to question witnesses unless, for good cause, the federal magistrate judge decides that justice does not require the appearance of witnesses; and
   d.   notice of the right to be represented by counsel.

Proceedings shall be recorded. If probable cause is found, the person shall be held for a revocation hearing.

2. The revocation hearing, unless waived by the probationer, shall be held within reasonable time in the district of jurisdiction. The person shall be given

   a. written notice of the alleged violation;
   b. disclosure of evidence against the person;
   c. an opportunity to appear and to present evidence on the person's own behalf;
   d. the opportunity to question adverse witnesses; and
   e. notice of the person's right to be represented by counsel.

State rules may vary from these. Be sure to consult your rules, particularly in regard to right to counsel and confrontation of witnesses. Rules of evidence are not so stringent as those at trial. Hearsay may be allowed, but revocation may not rest solely on hearsay evidence. Also, the burden of proof is relaxed; the court may revoke probation if it is reasonably satisfied that a violation occurred. The court can exercise its discretion not to revoke probation, however, even if a violation is established.

B. PAROLE AND ITS REVOCATION

Prisoners may be released early from incarceration in many state systems if they convince the parole board that they are ready to conduct their lives within the requirements of the law. Parole is supervised by a parole officer to ensure that conditions of release are met by the parolee, much like the conditions for probation. If those conditions are violated, revocation is processed in hearings similar to those for probation revocation. A parolee who signs a parole agreement allowing unwarranted searches does not have an expectation of privacy, and the exclusionary rule does not apply to state parole proceedings [*Pennsylvania Board of Probation and Parole v. Scott* (1998)]. Twenty-seven states and the District of Columbia require violent offenders to serve at least 85 percent of their prison sentences. Fourteen states have abolished all parole releases, and six states have abolished releases of certain violent or felony offenders.[25] Check your state statutes for parole and revocation conditions and procedure.

C. RIGHTS AND RESPONSIBILITIES OF PRISONERS

Despite often wretched conditions, prisons are not "black holes" where prisoners are dumped never to be heard from again. Some constitutional rights are forfeited with conviction, such as rights to free assembly and association, as well as First Amendment rights that are "inconsistent with [the] status as a prisoner or with the legitimate penological objectives of the corrections system" [*Pell v. Procunier* (1974)]. *Pell* ruled, however, that inmates may possess religious materials and receive visits by clergy. A prison regulation forbidding Protestants from wearing religious crosses while allowing Catholics to have rosaries violated prisoners' free exercise of religion [*Sasnett v. Litscher* (7th Cir. 1999)]. Inmates have access to the mails, but letters may be censored. Censorship may not interfere with the attorney-client relationship, however [*Lee v. Tahash* (8th Cir. 1965)]. Prisoners must be allowed access to the courts [*Ex Parte Hull* (1941)] and must have access to writing materials, notarial services, law libraries, and private consultation with attorneys.

The focus on prison conditions brought an explosion of prisoners' rights cases into court following the decision in *Bounds v. Smith* (1977), which requires that the fundamental constitutional right of access to courts requires prison authorities to assist inmates in preparing and filing meaningful legal papers. Prisoner petitions constituted one-third of all appeals in 1996. Prisoner civil rights petitions doubled between 1987 and 1996. To combat the filing of lawsuits over "insufficient storage locker space, a defective haircut by a prison barber, . . . and yes, being served chunky peanut butter instead of the creamy variety," free access to the courts was limited by the Prison Litigation Reform Act (PLRA) of 1996, 28 U.S.C.A. § 1915. This law restricts *in pauperis* filing of successive, frivolous petitions and requires the inmate to exhaust administrative remedies before filing petitions [*Thomas v. McCaughtry* (7th Cir. 2000)]. The numbers of petitions dropped 20 percent the first year and another 12 percent by 1998.[26]

Lewis v. Casey (1996) further narrowed *Bounds*, giving prisoners standing to sue only when they can demonstrate actual injury from some constitutional shortcoming and providing judicial remedies only to the extent of curing the inadequacies that caused the harm. Claiming a denial of access to courts because the prison law library and legal assistance program was subpar without demonstrating that the inadequacy hindered efforts to pursue a legal claim did not reach the level of actual injury.

Actual injury was not established by the confiscation of legal materials that were passed from one inmate to another without authorization, because other materials were available [*Bass v. Singletary* (11th Cir. 1998)]. Imminent danger of serious injury from a vent emitting pollutants entitled a prisoner to file a complaint under pauper status, although three previous complaints had been dismissed as frivolous under PLRA [*Gibbs v. Cross* (3d Cir. 1998)].

Hudson v. McMillian (1992) ruled that excessive physical force against a prisoner may constitute cruel and unusual punishment even when an inmate does not suffer serious injury. The central question is whether the force occurred as a "good faith effort to maintain or restore discipline or maliciously and sadistically for the very purpose of causing harm." *De minimis* use of physical force is allowed by the Eighth Amendment, however, provided the use is not of a sort that is repugnant to the conscience of mankind, such as sexual touching.

Most frequently, prison discipline takes the form of removal of "good-time" credit for early release. Due process procedures include the rights to notice of disciplinary action, to an administrative hearing with a written record, and to produce evidence and witnesses refuting charges, but not the right to have counsel present. An HIV positive inmate who had spat on two guards was required to wear a mask that covered his entire head and was denied all outdoor exercise for nine months. Because he had not received a warning or hearing on the matter, his due process rights had been denied [*Perkins v. Kansas Department of Corrections* (10th Cir. 1999)].

VI. APPEALS

A. INTRODUCTION

The most immediate reason for appealing a case to a higher tribunal is to correct an error made at the trial court level. This function serves the due process responsibilities of the courts. When appeals reach the highest levels of the court structure, however, another function becomes primary. Here to the greatest extent, the language of the law, both constitutional and statutory, is brought into the context of actual events; the theoretical is interpreted into the practical, and adjustments are made. Laws of substance and procedure are struck down, upheld, refined, and standardized. Previous court decisions are elaborated, bolstered, or nullified. It is here that the law becomes responsive to the lives of real people. The cases you research to support your view of a case come from the body of appellate decisions whose ripple effect touches the justice system at every level.

Appeal by right is allowed, without seeking permission, to the court level just above the trial court. Appeals from federal district courts are taken by right to the United States Courts of Appeal. If granted certiorari, they may finally be heard by the Supreme Court. At the state level, appeals by right go from the trial level courts to intermediate appellate courts or, in a few states, special criminal appeals courts. In some less populous states, routine appeals may go directly to the highest court. Further

"You see a court of appeals judge has a sort of intermediate status. It is the duty of a judge of a district court to be quick, courteous and wrong, but it must not be supposed from that that the court of appeals must be slow, crapulous and right, for that would be to usurp the functions of the supreme court."

—Editorial comment, *Yearbook of the Canadian Bar Association,* 1963

appeal by right:
appeal to the court level just above the trial court; permission not necessary.

discretionary appeal:
appeal to higher-level courts; permission necessary, such as the writ of certiorari from the Supreme Court.

review may be available by the highest state courts in **discretionary appeal,** that is, at the appellate court's discretion and with its permission. As an exception, death penalty cases are automatically appealed to the highest court in many states. If a question of federal law is at issue, appeals can continue from the state high court to the United States Supreme Court through writ of certiorari.

B. BASIS FOR APPEAL

1. Conditions for Appeal

Appeals are possible usually only after final decisions on conviction and sentencing. Modification and revocation of probation may also be appealable. Exceptions to the "final decision" limit are a few collateral issues that may be subject to interlocutory appeal, allowing for resolution before trial.

Most appeals are subsequent to a plea of not guilty. Issues of jurisdiction, involuntary plea, or legality of sentence may be appealed after a guilty plea, however, if the defendant requested withdrawal of the plea and was refused by the trial court [*Counts v. State* (Fla. App. 1979)].

2. What Can Be Challenged on Appeal

plain error:
obvious error that merits appellate reversal even if not objected to at trial.

Any decision by the trial court objected to by the defense can be raised on appeal. Even if no objections were voiced, appeals may be based on improper jurisdiction or actions that could be considered **plain error,** an obvious error that merits appellate reversal even if not objected to at trial. How fundamental the error must be varies from court to court, but the seriousness of capital cases tends to lead to a more liberal consideration of error [*Fisher v. U.S.* (1946)].

A few categories encompass the most common points of appeal:[27]

a. Violation of pretrial rights, particularly those protected by the Fourth, Fifth, and Sixth amendments.

b. Admission or exclusion of evidence and other procedural matters.

c. Improper jury selection or conduct.

d. Interpretations of statutes or ordinances.

e. Prosecutorial misconduct.

f. Sufficiency of the evidence to support conviction beyond a reasonable doubt.

g. Objections to jury instructions.

h. Legality and, in some jurisdictions, the reasonableness of the sentence imposed.

3. Harmless Error

If the appellate court does determine that error occurred at the trial level, it then must determine whether the error was substantial enough to take remedial action. If the error is so blatant as to offend public standards of justice, the lower court decision is generally reversed. A less conspicuous error may be harmful enough for reversal if it substantially affected the outcome of the trial. A number of lesser errors, harmless if considered individually, may accumulate to constitute an unfair trial.

harmless error:
trivial error not prejudicial to the rights of the party; does not affect the outcome of the case.

Errors not impinging on the outcome of the trial, however, are considered **harmless errors** and, as such, are not grounds for reversal. The standards for harmlessness are somewhat more stringent for constitutional issues than for errors not involving constitutional matters. *Chapman v. California* (1967) requires appellate courts to decide harmlessness beyond a reasonable doubt in considering errors of constitutional scope.

An appellate court may not base a reversal simply on disagreement with the outcome of the trial. The fact finder, jury or judge, alone is responsible for assessing the "whodunnit" aspects of the case. Questions of law, procedural and substantive, and whether errors in these areas improperly influenced the fact finder are the issues that rise to the appellate level.

4.   Appeals by Prosecution

"Appeals by the government in criminal cases are something unusual, exceptional, and not favored" [*Carroll v. U.S.* (1957)]. Double jeopardy is a distinct danger from appeals of acquittals by the state, so appeals by the prosecution are allowed only when "plainly provided" by statute. In the federal system, 18 U.S.C.A. § 3731 permits appeals from federal district court orders that

    a.   Dismiss indictment,
    b.   Grant a new trial after judgment or verdict,
    c.   Suppress evidence prior to the time that the defendant is put in jeopardy, or
    d.   Release a defendant prior to trial or after conviction.

The government also may appeal sentences that are unreasonable or violate the law or sentencing guidelines [18 U.S.C.A. § 3742(b)]. Such statutes and those that allow appeal of sentence avoid double jeopardy concerns by entering appeal before jeopardy attaches or not challenging the acquittal itself.

C.   APPELLATE PROCEDURE

1.   Introduction

Appellate procedure is quite complex, involving exacting rules on requirements, time limits, and formats. Moreover, the rules vary in detail among jurisdictions. It is necessary to follow the pattern in your jurisdiction with great care; you do not want to be responsible for a technical error that invalidates the entire appeal. A basic progression of steps lies at the core of the appellate process; we discuss those steps briefly.

Remember that even though the defendant is not so immediately involved with the appellate process as at the trial, he or she is still intensely concerned about how the case is progressing. As a paralegal, you are in an excellent position to keep your clients informed. You need to contact them frequently, helping them understand each significant document and step of the procedure. Be honest in discussing the time required, stringency of rules, and the likelihood of success as conveyed to you by the attorney. Disgruntled defendants can do surprising things, and their angry letters to the governor, appellate court, or local newspaper will probably not help the case.

Defense attorneys are not always required to file an appeal after the defendant pleads guilty, unless the defendant specifically asks them to [*Roe v. Flores-Ortega* (2000)]. In *Martinez v. The Court of Appeals of California* (2000), the Supreme Court ruled that there is no federal constitutional right to represent oneself on appeal. States may recognize the right for the defendant to refuse counsel at the appellate level, however, under their own constitutions. The right to counsel in appeals by right was established in *Douglas v. California* (1963). After the *Douglas* decision, courts were inundated with appeals, many of them so lacking in merit that appointed counsel often attempted to withdraw. In order to ensure effective counsel, the ruling in *Anders v. California* (1967) required appointed counsel to submit a brief demonstrating that the appeal was wholly frivolous before they could withdraw. The Supreme Court ruled in *Smith v. Robbins* (2000) that *Anders* brief requirements are not obligatory as long as the state provides a procedure that adequately safeguards the defendant's right to appellate counsel.

2.   Release on Bail

Pending appeal, the defendant may be released on bail. Criteria for release are enumerated in 18 U.S.C.A. §§ 3141 to 3152 and similar state rules. Bail often depends on whether the appeal is not frivolous but based on a substantial point of law, and on whether the defendant's flight risk is low. Denial or unreasonably high bail may be appealed. Unlike bail before trial, there is no presumption in favor of postconviction release.

3. Filing the Appeal

Notice or petition of appeal is filed with the clerk of the appellate court; copies may be required for appropriate state officials and officers of the trial court. A statement of issues may be part of the notice or filed separately. A filing fee must accompany the notice; indigent appellants may move to proceed *in forma pauperis* to waive this fee and other costs of appeal.

Rule 4(b) of the Federal Rules of Appellate Procedure requires notice to be filed within ten days of entry of judgment in federal district court. A motion for expansion of time may allow an additional thirty days. When the appeal comes from the government, thirty days are allowed for notice. Appeals from state court to the United States Supreme Court must be filed within ninety days of entry of judgment. Most state courts require notice to be filed within thirty days of judgment. These time limits are strictly enforced, with late filings resulting in dismissal of the appeal.

4. Ordering the Transcript

File a designation of record with the clerk of the trial court to indicate the sections of the trial record to be sent to the appellate court. Procedures for this step vary. Make sure you order the trial transcript from the trial court reporter for your own use within the required time limit, usually thirty days or less. The delivery of the transcript starts another deadline clock giving usually sixty days to file briefs.

If you are entering the case for the first time at the appellate level, a careful digestion of the transcript is in order. Also, obtain access to the court file before it is shipped to the appellate court. This file contains more than simply the transcript of testimony; it includes a record of motions, exhibits, and physical evidence. It is also helpful to talk to the trial prosecutor and investigating police officers, and to examine the police file and other professional reports if possible. Witnesses not called and exhibits not introduced at trial may be a mine of helpful leads. Investigate all possible reasons for the appellate court to reverse the conviction of your client.[28]

5. Filing of Motions

Motions may be filed by both sides concerning matters outside the central issues of appeal. Expansion or expedition of time may be requested, multiple appeals may be consolidated or severed, or judgment or sentence may be stayed for good cause.

6. Filing of Briefs

Federal Rule of Appellate Procedure 28 and similar state rules give detailed instructions as to the form, content, and method of submission of the appellate brief. This is the document that bears the heaviest responsibility for persuading the court to decide the appeal in your client's favor. For the appeal by right, the appellant, one who is seeking relief, files the first brief containing the factual background of the case and defendant; determination of the lower court; legal position; and citations to determinative constitutional, statutory, or judicial authority supporting that position. The appellee may respond in an answer brief, then the appellant is allowed rebuttal in a reply brief.

If a petition for discretionary review is granted, all parties are ordered to submit responses. A petitioner's reply to the opposing response may be allowed. Supplemental briefs from both sides may be required by the court. In all cases, both sides send copies of briefs and other materials to the opposing side.

7.   Oral Argument

When oral argument is required, counsel for both sides present summaries of their positions to the court within time limitations. Judges then question counsel from the bench for further background or clarification.

8.   Preparation and Publication of the Opinion

After a review of the record and possibly additional legal research by counsel or the court's staff, the panel of judges meets in judicial conference to decide on the appeal. The senior judge or senior judge voting with the majority on this case usually assigns one member of the panel to write the opinion. The opinion may simply state that the trial court's judgment is affirmed, reversed, or that a new trial is ordered, or it may present elaborate arguments and precedents supporting the ruling of the court.

A *per curiam* opinion represents the decision of the entire panel. More often the opinion is signed by the writer and by others voting in the majority. Concurring opinions emphasize different arguments in support of the same conclusion. Judges voting in the minority may add their dissenting opinions. The publication of appellate decisions in reporters provides guidance for attorneys and judges in subsequent cases.

9.   Motion for Rehearing

A motion for rehearing requests the appellate court to reconsider its decision. Grounds may include misstatements of fact, or other overlooked or misunderstood matters. These motions are often denied as a last-ditch effort to throw the case on the mercy of the court.

Exhibit 14–4 (page 577) is a federal notice of appeal, and Exhibit 14–5 (page 577) is an affidavit in support of a motion to proceed on appeal *in forma pauperis.*

VII.   THE WRIT OF HABEAS CORPUS

A.   INTRODUCTION

After all rights to appeal have been exhausted and time limits have expired, review of the conviction of one in custody may still be available through the writ of habeas corpus. The federal and all state systems provide this remedy that has stood as a cornerstone for the rights of the accused since the time of the Magna Carta. The Latin phrase means "you have the body." The writ requires the person holding another in custody to show just cause for that custody.

The United States Constitution, Article 1, Section 9(2), provides that "[t]he Privilege of the Writ of Habeas Corpus shall not be suspended unless when in Cases of Rebellion or Invasion the public Safety may require it." The only suspension of the writ, during the Civil War, was subsequently declared unconstitutional. Originally applied only to federal prisoners, federal review extends to state prisoners "in custody in violation of the Constitution or laws or treaties of the United States" [28 U.S.C.A. § 2254(a)]. States provide their own collateral review on questions of state law.

The Supreme Court's expansion of the constitutional rights of the accused during the 1960s coincided with a broader access to federal habeas corpus relief, as well. As the Supreme Court became more conservative and narrowed access on the federal level, states have generally responded by providing more liberal rights and access to habeas corpus relief.

B.   CRITERIA FOR ACCESS TO HABEAS CORPUS

The petitioner for a writ of habeas corpus must be "in custody." Custody extends beyond incarceration to include parole, probation, pretrial release, or diversionary programs [28 U.S.C.A. § 1915(g)].

Defendants convicted in federal courts have rather straightforward access to habeas corpus relief in the federal system (28 U.S.C.A. § 2241). Transfers from state to federal systems, however, have numerous impediments (28 U.S.C.A. § 2254). A question of federal law must be involved and state court remedies must have been exhausted or ineffective in protecting the rights of the prisoner. The case record is presumed correct unless it is shown that the state court lacked jurisdiction; the petitioner did not receive a full and fair hearing, was denied counsel, or otherwise deprived of due process; or there was not sufficient evidence to support the factual determination in the case.

The decision in *Fay v. Noia* (1963) held that failure to meet any state procedural requirement for appeal was not a bar to federal habeas review, as long as the bypass of procedure was not deliberate. Supreme Court decisions through the 1970s gradually narrowed access to federal habeas corpus review. *Davis v. U.S.* (1973) and *Francis v. Henderson* (1976) required a show of cause and prejudice for access. *Stone v. Powell* (1976) blocks habeas relief if a full and fair litigation of a Fourth Amendment claim has been provided by the state.

In 1996 Title I of the Antiterrorism and Effective Death Penalty Act (AEDPA), 18 U.S.C.A. § 2244, restricted habeas corpus petitions. AEDPA requires permission from the court of appeals to file second or successive habeas petitions [*Greenawalt v. Stewart* (9th Cir. 1997)] and provides a one-year period of limitations for application for a writ of habeas corpus after direct review is final. Review does not become final until the Supreme Court affirms the defendant's conviction or denies certiorari. If certiorari is not sought, review is final when the time allowed for filing for certiorari expires [*Kapral v. U.S.* (3d Cir. 1999)].

A certificate of appealability must be obtained from the U.S. appellate judge before the habeas petition may be filed [§ 2253(c)(1)]. The certificate must list the specific issues on appeal [*Hiivala v. Wood* (9th Cir. 1999)]. All state remedies must be exhausted in matters pursuant to state court judgments before application can be made for a federal writ of habeas corpus [§ 2254(b)(1)]. A claim that was not raised in the state's highest court cannot be pursued in a federal habeas claim [*O'Sullivan v. Boerckel* (1999)].

Georgia and Wyoming do not provide counsel to death row inmates in habeas corpus proceedings [*Gibson v. Turpin* (Ga. 1999)]. All other states do [*Jackson v. State* (Miss. 1999)].

Most common grounds for collateral relief include the following:[29]

1. Discovery of new evidence not available at trial but possibly determinative of innocence,
2. Applicability of retroactive decisions of the United States Supreme Court or highest state court,
3. An involuntary plea or incompetence of the defendant at plea, and
4. ineffective counsel.

One of the most frequent claims in habeas corpus petitions is that counsel was ineffective. This claim is rarely subject to appeal because it is seldom an issue at trial. *Strickland v. Washington* (1984) requires ineffective counsel claims to show that counsel did not function in the capacity guaranteed by the Sixth Amendment and that that deficiency deprived the defendant of a fair trial.

A claim of ineffective counsel may be made for the first time in a habeas corpus petition, because the record may not be sufficiently developed to assess the merits of the claim at the time of direct appeal [*Woods v. State* (Ind. 1998)].

A defense attorney's failure to pursue expert opinion on the defendant's brain damage resulting from diabetes constituted ineffective assistance of counsel in *Collier v. Turpen* (11th Cir. 1998). Ineffective use of witnesses at the sentencing hearing contributed to the error, but the choice not to call certain witnesses was a tactical consideration that, though imprudent, was not in error. An attorney's failure to file notice of appeal within the time limit was enough to show constitutionally deficient assistance without a further showing of the merits of the appeal in *McHale v. U.S.* (2d Cir. 1999). Though rarely approved in a habeas case, a discovery request was granted in *Bracy v. Gramley* (1997) pursuant to a death row inmate's claim that his trial was tainted by judicial corruption. His judge was later convicted of taking bribes from defendants, and his attorney may have agreed to take his case to trial quickly to deflect suspicion from the judge in two other murder trials.

C. HABEAS CORPUS PROCEDURE

In the federal system, 28 U.S.C.A. § 2242 provides for a petition for a hearing on the writ of habeas corpus to be filed with the federal district court. Section 2243 provides that unless grounds presented in the petition are invalid, the court shall award the writ or order the respondent to show cause why the writ should not be granted. The person having custody receives the writ or order and returns the writ or cause of detention within three days, or an additional twenty days for good cause. A hearing date is set not more than five days after the return. The respondent may be required to "produce at the hearing the body of the person detained" for testimony or, if only issues of law are involved, the court may render a decision on the record. Further requirements in habeas corpus practice follow in 28 U.S.C.A. §§ 2244 to 2253. Orders granting a writ of habeas corpus are not rare; orders granting relief are. A habeas corpus claim is the last grasp for the next-to-the-last straw (executive clemency being the last), and as such, is a shaky bet. Exhibit 14–6 (pages 578–586 at the end of this chapter) is a federal application for habeas corpus.

VIII. CONCLUSION

Paralegals can accomplish some of their most significant tasks at the point where they can have the greatest effect for their client. Gathering information and planning sentencing alternatives to meet the needs of retribution, deterrence, and rehabilitation can be some of the most satisfying tasks you will accomplish. You can help give victims the opportunity to be a part of the process, to feel that their injuries are significant to society; you can help shape the rehabilitation plan to best serve needs of the defendant and to interrupt the cycle of crime. To do the work efficiently, you must know the requirements of applicable statutes and guidelines, pay attention to detail in documenting information, be intuitive as to the personalities and needs of both the victim and the defendant, and be creative in surveying possibilities for alternative sentencing. Most important is the willingness to do the hard work in pulling all these elements together.

The criminal justice system—and your work—continues after sentencing to deal with rights of convicts and postconviction review. Patience, research, creativity, and more patience are necessary to see cases through the maze. Appeals and collateral attacks on conviction and sentencing draw criticism for their seemingly endless flogging of the same issues in an attempt to avoid the inevitable. The extensive appeals processes that must be exhausted before an execution can take place make for inflammatory headlines. Accompanying costs are often cited; it is more expensive to litigate all the appeals involved in a death penalty than to house a prisoner for life. Many states have not executed a prisoner since the post–*Furman* statutes were written, so death row is crowded with petitioners, some waiting nearly twenty years for the final resolution of their cases.

However excessive the multilevel appeals process may seem to an observer, it is the best guarantee of justice that we have. We recoil at reports from repressive countries of prisoners being convicted and only minutes later taken into a courtyard and shot to death. We cry out in sympathy for those American prisoners who are released after years of incarceration when evidence finally surfaces that they are innocent. We cannot truly call ours a "justice" system without meticulous provision for the correction of error.

In a world that seems increasingly violent, there is a suspicion that crime is more successful than punishment, that the criminal justice system is slipping behind in the battle. Those who work with individual defendants and individual victims know, however, that it is not one battle. Each case presents its own problems and possibilities for justice, its own case of real people whose lives are changed at the pounding of a gavel.

EXHIBIT 14–1
Sample Presentence Report

PRESENTENCE REPORT FOR AN INDIVIDUAL DEFENDANT
Presentence Report Outline

THE FACE SHEET

PART A. THE OFFENSE

> Charge(s) and Conviction(s)
> The Offense Conduct
> Victim Impact
> Adjustment for Obstruction of Justice
> Adjustment for Acceptance of Responsibility
> Offense Level Computation
> Offense Behavior Not Part of Relevant Conduct

PART B. DEFENDANT'S CRIMINAL HISTORY

> Juvenile Adjudications
> Criminal Convictions
> Criminal History Computation
> Other Criminal Conduct
> Pending Charges
> Other Arrests

PART C. OFFENDER CHARACTERISTICS

> Personal and Family Data
> Physical Condition
> Mental and Emotional Health
> Substance Abuse
> Educational and Vocational Skills
> Employment
> Financial Condition: Ability to Pay

PART D. SENTENCING OPTIONS

> Custody
> Impact of Plea Agreement
> Supervised Release
> Probation
> Fines
> Restitution
> Denial of Federal Benefits (Drug cases only)

PART E. FACTORS THAT MAY WARRANT DEPARTURE

EXHIBIT 14–1 *(Continued)*
Sample Presentence Report

ADDENDUM TO THE PRESENTENCE REPORT

RECOMMENDATION

IN UNITED STATES DISTRICT COURT
FOR THE WESTERN DISTRICT OF ATLANTIS

UNITED STATES OF AMERICA)		
	)	
vs.	)	PRESENTENCE INVESTIGATION REPORT
	)	
Thaddeus Smith	)	Docket No. CR 91-001-01-KGG
		(INDICTMENT, INFORMATION, ETC.)

Prepared for: The Honorable Kelly G. Green
U.S. District Judge

Prepared by: Craig T. Doe
U.S. Probation Officer
Breaker Bay, Atlantis
(123) 111-1111

Assistant U.S. Attorney   Defense Counsel
Mr. Robert Prosecutor   Mr. Arthur Goodfellow   (RETAINED/APPOINTED)
United States Courthouse   737 North 7th Street
Breaker Bay, Atlantis   Breaker Bay, Atlantis
(123) 111-1212   (123) 111-1313

Sentence Date: February 8, 2001 (TIME) - at 1:00 P.M.

Offense: <u>Count one:</u> Bank Robbery (18 U.S.C. § 2113(a)) - 20 years/$308,270
fine - Class C Felony

         <u>Count two:</u> Simple Possession of Cocaine (21 U.S.C. § 844(a)) -
15 days to 2 years/$250,000 - Class E Felony

Release Status: Detained without bail since 11/21/00. 12/7/00:
Pled guilty pursuant to Rule 11(e)(1)(B) written plea agreement

Detainers: Atlantis Parole Authority - Parole violation
Breaker Bay Municipal Court - Drunk Driving misd. warrant

Codefendants: Simon Brown - CR 90-0001-02-KGG
Veronica Pond - CR 90-0001-03-KGG

Related Cases: None

Date Report Prepared: 1/15/01   Date Report Revised: 1/25/01

<u>Identifying Data:</u>

True Name: (IF DIFFERENT FROM COURT NAME)
Date of Birth: 3/15/64
Age: 35
Race: White
Sex: Male

Continued

EXHIBIT 14–1 *(Continued)*
Sample Presentence Report

S.S. #:	111-11-1111
FBI #:	444-44-44B
USM #:	11111-111
Other ID #:	Not Applicable
Education:	Vocational Degree
Dependents:	None
Citizenship:	U.S.
Legal Address:	111 Fifth St. #2B Breaker Bay, AT 99993
Aliases:	None

Optional Photograph

EXHIBIT 14–1 *(Continued)*
Sample Presentence Report

PART A. THE OFFENSE

Charge(s) and Conviction(s)

1. Thaddeus Smith and codefendants Simon Brown and Veronica Pond were named in a five-count indictment filed by a Western District of Atlantis grand jury on November 30, 2000. Count one charges that from November 1, 2000, until November 30, 2000, the above-named defendants conspired to commit bank robbery, in violation of 18 U.S.C. § 2113(a) and 18 U.S.C. § 371. Count two charges that on November 16, 2000, Smith, while armed with a revolver, robbed the Atlantis credit union, in violation of 18 U.S.C. § 2113(a). Count three charges that on November 16, 2000, Smith used a firearm in a crime of violence, in violation of 18 U.S.C. § 924(c). Count four charges that on November 21, 2000, he possessed with intent to distribute a controlled substance (cocaine), in violation of 21 U.S.C. § 841(a)(1), and Count five charges that on November 16, 2000, the defendant robbed the Williams Bank, in violation of 18 U.S.C. § 2113(a).

2. On December 7, 2000, in accordance with the terms of a written [Rule 11(e)(1)(B)] plea agreement, Thaddeus Smith, pled guilty to a two-count superseding information, charging him with armed bank robbery, in violation of 18 U.S.C. § 2113(a) and simple possession of cocaine, in violation of 21 U.S.C. § 844(a). The U.S. Attorney has filed an information charging Smith with a prior drug conviction, enhancing the penalty for this offense, in accordance with 21 U.S.C. § 851. The terms of the plea agreement call for the dismissal of the original Indictment. Codefendant Brown pled guilty to a one-count superseding information, charging robbery, in violation of 18 U.S.C. § 2113(a). Codefendant Pond pled guilty to a one-count superseding information, charging simple possession of cocaine, in violation of 21 U.S.C. § 844(a). All of the defendants are scheduled to be sentenced on February 8, 2001.

The Offense Conduct

3. On November 10, 2000, Thaddeus Smith met with Simon Brown and Brown's girlfriend, Veronica Pond at a bar in Breaker Bay. While at the bar, Smith discussed his plans of robbing the Atlantis Credit Union, located at 1948 Edgewater Street, Breaker Bay, Atlantis. Smith explained he had learned that on the following Friday, November 16, 2000, the credit union would have extra money in the safe to cash payroll checks and he planned to rob it on that date. To establish an alibi, Smith told Brown and Pond that he planned to leave the area for several days to visit relatives in a neighboring state, but would return to Breaker Bay early Friday morning, rob the credit union, and fly back to his relatives' residence before he was missed. He planned to travel using an alias to further avoid apprehension. Brown and Pond agreed to steal two getaway vehicles for Smith and to assist him in the robbery. Smith gave the couple a .357 magnum revolver, which he told them he had stolen from a friend's cabin, and asked them to leave it in the trunk of the getaway car. Smith promised to pay Brown and Pond $500 each for their help.

4. On November 14, 2000, Brown and Pond stole a 2000 sedan from a Chevrolet dealership in Surf City and, the following day, the couple stole a 1998 Ford truck from an apartment complex in Surf City. On November 16, 2000, Brown picked Smith up at the airport in the Chevrolet and drove to a nearby shopping mall where Pond was waiting in the Ford. Brown told Pond to wait while the defendant and Brown drove to the credit union.

5. At approximately 9:30 A.M., before the credit union opened, Smith, disguised with a wig and mustache, and Brown approached Patty Martinez, a teller, as she was exiting her vehicle. Armed with a revolver, Smith grabbed the teller's arm, and escorted her to the rear door of the credit union. Ordering the teller to pretend that she was alone, Brown told her to knock on the door to the credit union. The teller complied and the manager opened the door. The defendants then forced them back inside, and while pointing the revolver at two other employees, herded them into a corner near the vault.

6. Smith ordered the manager to open the vault and place five bags of cash into a duffle bag carried by Brown. Smith then directed the employees to the back of the credit union, ordered them to lie on the floor, placed his revolver inside his coat, and the two fled the credit union. Smith and Brown proceeded to the Chevrolet and immediately drove toward the shopping mall where Pond was waiting. En route, Smith threw the revolver into a vacant lot, later stating that he hoped some kid would find it, get caught, and be blamed for the robbery.

Continued

EXHIBIT 14–1 (*Continued*)
Sample Presentence Report

7. Smith and Brown abandoned the Chevrolet in the parking lot and left with Pond in the stolen Ford. While travelling to the airport, Smith changed his shirt and shoes, and threw them, along with his disguise, into a dumpster. As Smith began to count the money, Pond was shocked that over $100,000 had been stolen and demanded $5,000 for herself and Brown. Smith became angry and threatened to keep all of the money if they continued to complain. At the airport, Smith gave Brown and Pond a total of $1,000, and a small packet of cocaine as a bonus. Smith then left the couple and flew back to his relatives' residence that afternoon.

8. As Brown and Pond were driving home in the stolen Ford, they were stopped by the police for a routine traffic violation. When the police officer discovered the truck was stolen, Brown and Pond were placed under arrest. Brown and Pond each admitted their involvement in this offense and during questioning implicated Smith.

9. On November 21, 2000, Smith was arrested by Federal agents at his relatives' home. The agents seized $78,690, along with 56 grams of cocaine, from Smith's suitcase. A subsequent laboratory analysis found the seized cocaine to be 64 percent pure. The revolver, used by Smith in the robbery, has not been recovered, but was believed to be a .357 Smith & Wesson. Local police have no record of such a theft of a weapon on file. According to Smith, he purchased the weapon from an unknown individual at a gun show held at the Breaker Bay High School in October 2000.

10. Smith is the most culpable defendant in this case. Smith recruited his codefendants, Brown and Pond, and directed their activities in this offense. In addition, Smith compensated his codefendants for their participation in the offense with a small share of the bank robbery proceeds.

Victim Impact

11. The Atlantis Credit Union is the primary victim in this offense and sustained direct financial losses totalling $128,135. The credit union has recovered $78,690 seized from Smith at the time of his arrest, leaving a net loss of $49,445. According to credit union officials, Apex Insurance Company has reimbursed the credit union except for a $5,000 deductible. In addition, the credit union paid a total of $900 for Ms. Martinez to receive 12 hours of psychological counseling.

12. Three tellers and the credit union manager are also victims in this offense. The tellers and the manager were interviewed by the probation officer and provided the following information.

13. Patty Martinez was the teller approached by Smith as she left her car in the credit union parking lot. While she was not physically injured, she was reportedly emotionally traumatized by the defendant's conduct. With her consent, the credit union arranged for Martinez to receive private psychological counseling. After 12 sessions, Martinez states that she began improving, and was able to sleep at night without nightmares and felt more comfortable at work. Nevertheless, Martinez decided to resign from the credit union, due in part to the offense, and has now returned to college to pursue her education.

14. The branch manager and the other two tellers inside the credit union stated that they were not physically injured by the defendant, but each expressed anger toward Smith for assaulting them. Each employee expressed experiences of being startled by strangers who enter the credit union, but the employees do not believe they are in need of professional counseling or treatment.

15. The two stolen vehicles in this case have been recovered without damages. A representative from the Chevrolet dealership was contacted and interviewed by the probation officer and advised that he has subsequently sold the sedan for $14,000. Similarly, the owner of the Ford truck reported no losses or expenses relative to the theft of the truck.

Adjustment for Obstruction of Justice

16. The probation officer has no information to suggest that the defendant impeded or obstructed justice.

EXHIBIT 14–1 *(Continued)*
Sample Presentence Report

<u>Adjustment for Acceptance of Responsibility</u>

17. Shortly after his arrest, Smith made voluntary and candid admissions to the authorities concerning his involvement in this offense, including his recruitment of Brown and Pond to help him execute the robbery scheme. Smith also acknowledged using a weapon during the robbery, which he purchased from an unknown individual at a gun show. In addition, Smith admitted his possession of cocaine at the time of his arrest, explaining that he had purchased the narcotics with money stolen from the robbery. The defendant freely admitted his guilt in court at the time of his plea, and appears to fully accept responsibility for his conduct. During his interview with the probation officer, Smith explained that he committed this offense at the prospect of quick and easy financial gains, and expressed remorse for assaulting the credit union employees.

<u>Offense Level Computation</u>

18. The 1991 edition of the *Guidelines Manual* has been used in this case. Pursuant to the provisions found in U.S.S.G. § 3D1.1(a)(3), counts one and two are unrelated offenses and are treated separately.

<u>Count one—Armed Bank Robbery</u>

19. **Base Offense Level:** The guideline for a 21 U.S.C. § 2113(a) offense is found in U.S.S.G. § 2B3.1 which provides that robbery has a base offense level of 20. <u>20</u>

20. **Specific Offense Characteristic:** Pursuant to the provision found in U.S.S.G. § 2B3.1 because the property of a financial institution was taken, the offense level is increased by two levels. <u>+2</u>

21. **Specific Offense Characteristic:** Pursuant to the provision found in U.S.S.G. § 2B3.1(b)(2)(B) because Smith used a revolver during the commission of this offense, the offense level is increased by four. <u>+4</u>

22. **Specific Offense Characteristic:** In preparation for this offense, Smith directed Brown and Pond to steal two vehicles, valued at a total of $26,000. Smith stole $128,135 from the credit union, thus the total loss attributable to this offense is $154,135. According to the provisions in U.S.S.G. § 2B3.1(b)(6)(B), the offense level is increased by two levels in accordance with the overall loss in this offense. <u>+2</u>

23. **Victim-Related Adjustment:** None <u>0</u>

24. **Adjustment for Role in the Offense:** Smith was the organizer and leader in this offense. He provided instructions and directives to his codefendants and compensated them for their participation in this offense with a small share of the robbery proceeds. In accordance with the provisions found in U.S.S.G. § 3B1.1(c), the offense level is increased by two. <u>+2</u>

25. **Adjustment for Obstruction of Justice:** None <u>0</u>

26. **Adjusted Offense Level** (Subtotal): <u>30</u>

<u>Count two—Possession of Cocaine</u>

27. **Base Offense Level:** The guideline for a 21 U.S.C. § 844(a) offense is found in U.S.S.G. § 2D2.1(a)(2) which provides that the base offense level for the unlawful possession of cocaine is six. <u>6</u>

28. **Specific Offense Characteristics:** None <u>0</u>

29. **Victim-Related Adjustment:** None <u>0</u>

30. **Adjustment for Role in the Offense:** None <u>0</u>

31. **Adjustment for Obstruction of Justice:** None <u>0</u>

Continued

EXHIBIT 14–1 *(Continued)*
Sample Presentence Report

32. **Adjusted Offense Level** (Subtotal): <u>6</u>

Multiple-Count Adjustment (See section 3D1.4)

		<u>Units,</u>
33. Adjusted Offense Level for count one	30	1
34. Adjusted Offense Level for count two	6	0
35. Total Number of Units		1
36. Greater Adjusted Offense Level	30	
37. Increase in Offense Level	0	

38. **Combined Adjusted Offense Level:** <u>30</u>

39. **Adjustment for Acceptance of Responsibility:** The defendant has shown recognition of responsibility for his criminal conduct and a reduction of two levels for Acceptance of Responsibility is applicable under U.S.S.G. § 3E1.1. <u>−2</u>

40. **Total Offense Level:** <u>28</u>

41. **Chapter Four Enhancements:** None <u>0</u>

42. **Total Offense Level:** <u>28</u>

<u>Offense Behavior Not Part of Relevant Conduct</u>

43. Smith was also charged in an unrelated robbery on November 16, 2000, of Williams Bank in Sun City, Atlantis, as summarized in count five of the original indictment. Bank surveillance cameras show a suspect, generally resembling the defendant, as he was approaching a teller, handing her a bag, accompanied by a demand note. The suspect then left the bank with $1,375 in the bag. While the defendant has declined to discuss this robbery, at the time of his arrest, Federal agents recovered a shirt, pants, and shoes from the defendant's duffle bag, matching those of the suspect in the surveillance photographs.

PART B. DEFENDANT'S CRIMINAL HISTORY

<u>Juvenile Adjudication(s)</u>

Date of <u>Referral</u>	Charge/ <u>Court</u>	Date Sentence <u>Imposed/Dispo.</u>	Guideline/ <u>Points</u>
44. 4/15/81 (age 17)	Auto Theft, Breaker Bay Juvenile Ct., Atlantis Action #4732	5/15/81, 1 year Youth Correction Center	4A1.2(e)(3) <u>0</u>

According to court records, Smith was arrested after he stole and dismantled a 1979 Pontiac, and sold the parts. Smith was represented by counsel.

<u>Adult Criminal Conviction(s)</u>

Date of <u>Arrest</u>	Conviction/ <u>Court</u>	Date Sentence <u>Imposed/Dispo.</u>	Guideline/ <u>Points</u>
45. 4/20/82 (age 18)	Receiving Stolen Property, Continue to show felony, misd., etc. Breaker Bay Superior Court, Atlantis, Dkt. #57349	10/8/83, 2 years imprisonment; paroled 11/11/84	4A1.1(a) 4A1.2(e)(1) <u>3</u>

According to court records, Smith was arrested after he was found to be in possession of stolen automobile parts. The defendant was represented by counsel. Although Smith was arrested several times while under pa-

EXHIBIT 14–1 *(Continued)*
Sample Presentence Report

role supervision, according to his supervision record, he made satisfactory adjustment to parole supervision and was discharged from parole on April 7, 1985.

| 46. | 5/30/82 (age 18) | Petty Theft, Breaker Bay Municipal Ct. Atlantis, Dkt. #758924A | 6/15/82, 1 year probation | 4A1.2(e)(3) | <u>0</u> |

Smith was arrested after he fueled his vehicle at a service station and left without paying. The defendant waived counsel, and successfully completed probation shortly before he was convicted on the unrelated charges of his previous arrest noted above.

| 47. | 3/16/90 (age 26) | Petty Theft, Breaker Bay Municipal Ct., Dkt. #857234A | 4/10/90, 1 year probation; 10/10/90 probation revoked; 90 days jail | 4A1.1(b) 4A1.2(K)(1) | <u>2</u> |

According to court records, Smith stole two packages of frozen vegetables valued at $3.00 from a local grocery store. He waived counsel, and his probation was later revoked after he absconded from supervision.

| 48. | 8/20/90 (age 26) | Theft, Breaker Bay Municipal Ct., Dkt. #867329A | 9/10/90, Consolidated with Dkt. #867330B; 20 days jail, consecutive | 4A1.1(c) 4A1.2(a)(2) | <u>1</u> |

According to court records, Smith was arrested after he offered to sell an undercover Breaker Bay police officer stolen automobile parts as detailed in his next conviction. At the time of the defendant's arrest, police officers also recovered a vehicle stolen from a local automobile dealership. Smith admitted that on July 5, 1990 he used a false driver's license and had taken the vehicle for a test drive, but never returned it. Smith was represented by counsel. (The points assigned for this offense take into account the below-listed case which was consolidated for sentencing, in accordance with the provisions found in section 4A1.2, commentary note #3.)

| 49. | 8/20/90 (age 26) | Theft, Breaker Bay, Municipal Ct., Dkt. # 867330B | 9/10/90, Consolidated with Dkt. # 867329A; 30 days jail, consecutive | 4A1.1(c) 4A1.2(a)(2) | <u>0</u> |

According to the arrest report and court documents, Smith and a codefendant were arrested after they convinced an intoxicated acquaintance to surrender his keys to a 1989 Buick Skylark. Smith and his codefendant dismantled the vehicle and offered to sell the parts to an undercover Breaker Bay police officer. Police also recovered a stolen vehicle which had been taken from a local dealership as detailed in the above arrest. Smith was represented by counsel. (No points were assigned for this conviction because the case was consolidated with the case above and assigned one point.)

| 50. | 5/17/91 (age 27) | Reckless Driving, Breaker Bay Municipal Ct., Dkt. # 875662A | 6/9/91, 1 year probation | 4A1.1(c) 4A1.2(c)(1) | <u>1</u> |

According to court records, Smith was detained after he was observed by a Breaker Bay traffic officer driving a vehicle at 90 miles per hour in a 15-mile-per-hour school zone. Smith waived his right to counsel.

| 51. | 6/10/91 (age 27) | Insufficient Funds-Bad Checks, Breaker Bay Municipal Ct., Dkt. # 875883A | 6/30/91, 10 days jail | 4A1.2(c)(1) | <u>1</u> |

Continued

EXHIBIT 14–1 (*Continued*)
Sample Presentence Report

According to the court and bank records, Smith established a checking account in his own name and deposited $500. He then wrote personal checks payable in amounts totaling $1,000. The funds were not recovered. He was represented by counsel.

52.	5/15/92 (age 28)	Possession of Marijuana, Breaker Bay Municipal Ct., Dkt. #879322A	7/10/92, 3 years probation	4A1.1(c) 1

A Breaker Bay police officer arrested Smith after he was observed smoking marijuana at a concert. At the time of his arrest, Smith was found in possession of five grams of marijuana. According to local probation department records, Smith successfully completed probation and, as a condition of his supervision, participated in a substance abuse treatment program. The defendant was represented by counsel.

53.	3/14/95 (age 30)	Grand Theft, Breaker Bay Superior Court, Dkt. # 97456	7/15/95, 3 years probation with 59 days jail; probation terminated & deemed unsuccessful 8/30/96	4A1.1(c) 1

According to court records, on March 14, 1995, Smith stole the keys to an automobile showroom. Later that night, he returned to the showroom and stole three vehicles, valued at $56,000. Smith was apprehended as he attempted to drive the third vehicle away from the lot, and assisted in the recovery of the other two stolen vehicles. Smith was originally charged with burglary, but he was later convicted of theft. The defendant was represented by counsel. His probation was later terminated and deemed unsuccessful after he was committed to prison on an unrelated offense.

54.	12/15/95 (age 31)	Petty Theft, Breaker Bay Municipal Ct., Dkt. # 932741A	12/30/95, 20 days jail	4A1.1(c) 1

According to court records, a private store security officer arrested Smith after he stole a hat, valued at $14.00, from a local department store. Smith was represented by counsel.

55.	1/15/96 (age 31)	Robbery, Breaker Bay Superior Court, Dkt. # 65234	8/27/96, 5 years imprisonment, paroled 8/26/99	4A1.1(a) 3

According to available police reports and court records, Smith robbed a convenience store owner of $765 at gunpoint. As he attempted to leave the store, Smith was apprehended by a Breaker Bay patrol [officer]. Smith was represented by counsel. He was later committed to the Allmont Correctional Facility, and, according to institutional records, Smith was enrolled in a high school equivalency program, but did not complete the course. During his incarceration, Smith received several incident reports, including the possession and use of a weapon, fighting, and possession of marijuana. Smith also worked in the facility kitchen where he received above-average performance evaluations.

Smith was released to parole supervision on August 26, 2000, and committed the instant offense shortly thereafter. According to his parole officer, Smith reported as directed, but was unemployed and was not actively looking for work, although he had been repeatedly instructed to do so by his parole officer. The defendant has been charged with violation of his parole, based on this offense, and a warrant has been lodged as a detainer.

EXHIBIT 14–1 *(Continued)*
Sample Presentence Report

56. In addition, Smith was convicted five times, between 1982 and 1988, for public intoxication and ten times for traffic infractions. He was fined up to $150 for each traffic infraction, and for two of the intoxication convictions. Smith was jailed for up to five days for the other three intoxication convictions, and he was represented by counsel for all of the convictions which resulted in imprisonment.

Criminal History Computation

57. The criminal convictions above result in a subtotal criminal history score of 12. In accordance with the provisions found in U.S.S.G. § 4A1.1(c), only a total of 4 points have been added for the defendant's 5 prior convictions which resulted in a term of imprisonment of less than 60 days.

58. At the time that the instant offense was committed, Smith was on parole supervision for his August 27, 1996, sentence. In accordance with U.S.S.G. § 4A1.1(d), two points are added.

59. The instant offense was commited less than two years following Smith's release from custody on August 27, 2000. Pursuant to U.S.S.G. § 4A1.1(e), one point is added.

60. The total of the criminal history points is 15. According to the sentencing table (Chapter Five, Part A), 13 or more criminal history points establish a criminal history category of VI.

Other Criminal Conduct

61. During the presentence interview, Smith admitted to the probation officer that he was granted pretrial diversion in 1990 for possession of marijuana. Probation department records indicated that Smith successfully completed the diversion program.

Pending Charges

62. On August 28, 2000, the defendant was arrested for driving under the influence of alcohol. Smith has been charged with a violation in the Breaker Bay Municipal Court under docket number 945789A. An arrest warrant was issued after Smith was taken into Federal custody and failed to appear in municipal court. The warrant has been lodged as a detainer with the U.S. Marshals Service.

63. On December 1, 2000, a warrant was issued by the Atlantis Parole Authority, charging Smith with parole violations. This warrant has also been lodged as a detainer with the U.S. Marshals Service.

Other Arrests

Date of Arrest	Charge	Agency	Disposition
64. 11/14/91 (age 27)	Shoplifting	Breaker Bay Police Dept.	No charges filed

PART C. OFFENDER CHARACTERISTICS

Personal and Family Data

65. Thaddeus Smith was born on March 15, 1964, in Breaker Bay, Atlantis, to the union of Samuel and Edith Smith, nee Barker. The defendant's parents separated on numerous occasions, and Smith was often left in the care of his maternal grandmother, who has a history of severe depression. As a consequence, his childhood was chaotic. According to his juvenile record, Smith ran away from home several times and was eventually placed in his grandmother's custody. In 1978 the grandmother committed suicide and Smith discovered her body. He was returned to his mother's residence, located in a small housing project on the lower east side of Breaker Bay.

Continued

EXHIBIT 14–1 *(Continued)*
Sample Presentence Report

66. According to the defendant's mother, Smith was very respectful in the family home, although he did exhibit recurring signs of violence and temper tantrums, which she attributed to her son's inability to overcome the emotional traumatic experiences associated with the loss of his grandmother. Smith and his grandmother had been extremely close. After an episode of delinquency, Smith was committed to the Breaker Bay Youth Correctional Center.

67. Since his release from the youth center, Smith has been residing with distant relatives, with friends, or alone in a series of small apartments in Breaker Bay. His last contact with his parents was in 1994 at his brother Frederick's funeral. Since 1997, Smith has lived at 111 Fifth Street, Apartment 2B, Breaker Bay, Atlantis 99993, with his cousin, Martin Johnson. A recent home investigation found this small, sparsely furnished apartment to be located in a high-crime section in northwest Breaker Bay. According to the defendant's cousin Martin Johnson, Smith rarely stayed in the apartment and did not contribute to their monthly living expenses; however, Johnson would welcome the defendant back into his apartment upon his release because of limited housing alternatives available to the defendant at the present time.

Physical Condition

68. Thaddeus Smith is a white male who is 6'2" tall, and weighs 210 pounds. He has brown eyes and brown shoulder-length hair. Smith has a surgical scar on his abdomen, and a tattoo of a skull with the motto "Born to Lose" on his right hand.

69. The defendant describes his overall general physical health as good. He was hospitalized briefly in 1995 for the repair of a hernia he suffered while working in the Breaker Bay jail laundry.

Mental and Emotional Health

70. Smith indicated that he has never been seen by a psychiatrist and described his overall mental and emotional health as good. There is no documented evidence to suggest otherwise.

Substance Abuse

71. The defendant describes a history of alcohol and drug abuse which began when he was approximately 10 years old. According to Smith, he stole alcohol from his parents' supply, adding, ". . . they were drunk so often, they never noticed." He stated that he often attended school under the influence of alcohol, and that he has been intoxicated "too many times to count."

72. Smith stated that he began smoking marijuana when he was 12 years old. When he discovered that it was easier to attend school under the influence of marijuana without detection, than under the influence of alcohol, he became a daily marijuana smoker. The defendant reports the abuse of numerous substances, including hallucinogens, stimulants and depressants, methamphetamine, and cocaine. Smith said he never used opiates.

73. Smith reported he has often been under the influence of some substance when he had committed his crimes. Before the instant offense, he drank a pint of whisky and inhaled approximately one quarter gram of methamphetamine. Smith admitted that he used some of the proceeds from the robbery to purchase cocaine, and said he used as much as he could acquire since his most recent release from prison. Smith estimates that he has spent at least $200 each week for methamphetamine, his drug of choice, alcohol, or cocaine. The results of a urine test, administered by a pretrial services officer at the time of the defendant's arrest, were positive for methamphetamine and cocaine.

74. Smith stated that he has been referred to several alcohol and substance abuse programs as a result of his criminal conduct. In 1990, he participated in a marijuana use and education program as a condition of diversion and in 1992, he underwent drug treatment as a condition of probation. Prison records reflect that, during his most recent confinement, Smith attended Alcoholics and Narcotics Anonymous sessions regularly, but his correctional counselors noted that Smith seemed unmotivated and never selected sponsors. The defendant currently indicates that he would be willing to participate in a drug treatment program and adds that he is now motivated to address his narcotics dependency.

EXHIBIT 14–1 *(Continued)*
Sample Presentence Report

<u>Educational and Vocational Skills</u>

75. The defendant attended Kennedy High School for Boys in Breaker Bay in 1971, where he received poor grades and had a poor attendance record. After his commitment to the Breaker Bay Youth Center in 1981, Smith completed the 11th grade, but center records indicate that he reads at an 8th-grade level. He has no other formal education or identifiable skills and is in need of remedial educational or vocational training.

<u>Employment</u>

76. Since his release from State custody on August 27, 2000, Smith has been unemployed. He acknowledges he has made no attempt to actively seek employment and has relied on others for financial assistance.

77. From September 15, 1995, until December 25, 1995, Smith was employed by Sam's Super-Save Gasoline, 333 Third Avenue, Breaker Bay, as a service station attendant and cashier, earning minimum wages. In addition, from January 10, 1996, until August 26, 1996, Smith was employed as a mechanic by Al's Auto Aid, 129 5th Street, Breaker Bay, earning $10.45 per hour, until his commitment to state prison.

78. From July 10, 1991, until July 14, 1995, Smith was employed by Uriah's Cheap Heaps, 435 Ohio Street, Breaker Bay. He was first hired as a mechanic, but was later promoted to service manager at this dealership, where he earned $2,500 per month before he was terminated when the dealership learned of his arrest for stealing cars from a nearby dealership showroom. Smith's former employer, Uriah Dickens, advised that he was extremely disappointed in Smith, whom he hired despite his criminal record. Dickens described Smith as a likable employee who got along well with others. According to Dickens, hoping that a second chance would encourage Smith to reform, Dickens allowed Smith to continue in his employ, even after his 1983 conviction for petty theft.

79. From January 10, 1991, until June 9, 1991, Smith was employed by Prestigious Motors, Breaker Bay, where he worked as a mechanic, earning $9.75 per hour. According to his immediate supervisor, Smith was a knowledgeable mechanic, but was terminated after he was incarcerated for writing bad checks.

80. From October 8, 1984, until September 9, 1990, Smith was employed by the Reliable Transportation Company in Breaker Bay. He was initially employed as a mechanic, but was promoted to service manager, earning $2,100 per month. According to available employment records, Smith was terminated after a series of petty thefts which eventually resulted in his incarceration. According to a company representative, Smith would be eligible for rehire consideration.

Financial Condition: Ability to Pay—Sample

The defendant submitted a signed financial statement and accompanying documentation supporting the following financial profile:

Assets   *Indicates the defendant's half interest in assets owned jointly with his wife.
  Cash

Cash on hand	$100
Bank accounts	$11,600
Certificate of deposit	$2,000

Unencumbered Assets
  1998 Chevrolet* $6,000 (Blue Book Value)

Equity in Other Assets
  Residence*   <u>$10,000 (see Note A)</u>

TOTAL ASSETS $29,700

<u>Unsecured Debts</u>
  Personal loan from relative $ 300
  Credit cards   <u>$1,500</u>

<u>TOTAL UNSECURED DEBTS</u>   <u>$1,800</u>

Continued

EXHIBIT 14–1 *(Continued)*
Sample Presentence Report

<u>Net Worth</u>

<u>Monthly Cash Flow</u>

Income

Defendant's net salary	$1,875
Interest & dividends	$ 100
TOTAL INCOME	$1,975

<u>Necessary Living Expenses</u>

Home mortgage	$ 500	
Electricity	$ 52	
Heating Oil	$ 140	
Water	$ 15	
Telephone	$ 70	
Groceries & Supplies	$ 400	
Clothing	$ 200	
Auto insurance	$ 50	
Life insurance	$ 50	
Homeowners insurance	$ 20	
Installment payments	$ 100	(credit cards)
Gas & car maintenance	$ 125	
TOTAL EXPENSES	$1,722	

<u>Net Monthly Cash Flow</u>	$ 253

The above expenses reflect essential living expenses necessary for the defendant's continued employment and the health and welfare of his family. He has a net worth of $27,900 and liquid assets in the amount of $13,600. If the defendant is not incarcerated and can maintain employment, he will be able to make a maximum initial fine payment of $13,600 within 30 days of sentencing. He could also make payments of $100 per month. If collected for 3 years, the additional fine paid in installments would be $3,600 for a total fine of $17,200 and he could pay the interest on this amount.

If the defendant is confined within the guideline range, some of these assets should be preserved for the support of his family.

81. Overall, Smith has a sporadic work history, marked by substantial periods of employment. After his release from the Breaker Bay Youth Corrections Center, he worked sporadically as a mechanic. When unemployed, he supplemented his income by working on friends' and acquaintances' vehicles.

<u>Financial Condition: Ability To Pay</u>

82. Smith has no known identifiable assets or liabilities. While he has no sources of income, Smith claims to have spent approximately $800 per month for drugs and alcohol. Prior to his arrest in this offense, Smith was living with his cousin and the defendant provided no financial assistance to the monthly living expenses. The defendant is unemployed and upon his release, he will be dependent upon others for financial assistance. At the present time, he does not have the ability to pay a fine.

PART D. SENTENCING OPTIONS

<u>Custody</u>

83. **Statutory Provisions:** The maximum term of imprisonment for count one is 20 years, pursuant to 18 U.S.C. § 2113(a). The minimum term of imprisonment on count two is 15 days, and the maximum term of imprisonment is 2 years, pursuant to 21 U.S.C. § 844(a) since the defendant has a prior drug conviction.

EXHIBIT 14–1 *(Continued)*
Sample Presentence Report

84. **Guideline Provisions:** Based on an offense level of 28 and a criminal history category of VI, the guideline range of imprisonment is 140 to 175 months.

Impact of Plea Agreement

85. Had the defendant been convicted of all the charges in the original indictment, the guideline imprisonment range would be 120 to 150 months, plus a mandatory 60-month minimum term of imprisonment required for violations of 18 U.S.C. § 924(c)(1).

Supervised Release

86. **Statutory Provisions:** If a term of imprisonment is imposed on counts one and two, the court may impose a term of supervised release of not more than three years on count one and not more than one year on count two, pursuant to 18 U.S.C. § 3583(b)(2) and 18 U.S.C. § 3583(b)(3), since they are Class C and Class E felonies, respectively. According to 18 U.S.C. § 3624(e), the terms of supervised release shall run concurrently.

87. **Guideline Provisions:** If the defendant is sentenced to a term of imprisonment of more than one year, the court must impose a term of supervised release, pursuant to U.S.S.G. § 5D1.1. The authorized term of supervised release for count one is not less than two years nor more than three years, and the authorized term of supervised release for count two is one year, pursuant to U.S.S.G. §§ 5D1.2(b)(2) and 5D1.2(b)(3).

Probation

88. **Statutory Provisions:** The defendant is ineligible for a term of probation in this offense, pursuant to 18 U.S.C. § 3561(a)(3) since he must be sentenced to at least a 15-day term of imprisonment on count two.

89. **Guideline Provisions:** The defendant is ineligible for a term of probation since count one requires a mandatory term of imprisonment of 15 days and the minimum guideline imprisonment range exceeds ten months, pursuant to U.S.S.G. §§ 5B1.1(b)(3) and 5C1.1(f), respectively.

Fines

90. **Statutory Provisions:** The maximum fine for count one is twice the gross loss, or $308,270, pursuant to 18 U.S.C. § 3571(d). The minimum fine for count two is $2,500, plus the cost of the investigation and prosecution (unless the defendant does not have the ability to pay), pursuant to 21 U.S.C. § 844(a), and the maximum fine is $250,000, pursuant to 18 U.S.C. § 3571(b).

91. A special assessment of $50 on each count for a total of $100 is mandatory, pursuant to 18 U.S.C. § 3013.

92. **Guideline Provisions:** Pursuant to U.S.S.G. § 5E1.2(c)(3), the fine range for this offense is from $12,500 to $125,000.

93. Subject to the defendant's ability to pay, the court shall impose an additional fine amount that is at least sufficient to pay the costs to the Government of any imprisonment, probation, or supervised release, pursuant to U.S.S.G. § 5E1.2(i). The most recent advisory from the Administrative Office of the U.S. Courts suggests that a monthly cost of $1,210.05 be used for imprisonment, a monthly cost of $91.66 for supervision, and a monthly cost of $938.44 for community confinement.

Restitution

94. **Statutory Provisions:** Pursuant to 18 U.S.C. § 3663, restitution may be ordered. In this case, restitution in the amount of $5,900 is outstanding to the Atlantis Credit Union and can be forwarded to the following address:

Atlantis Credit Union
Attention: Mr. Sam Claim
1948 Edgewater Street
Breaker Bay, Atlantis 99996

Continued

EXHIBIT 14–1 *(Continued)*
Sample Presentence Report

95. In addition, restitution in the amount of $44,445 is outstanding to the Apex Insurance Company and can be forwarded to the following address:

> Apex Insurance Company
> Attention: Mrs. Cindy Claim
> 1950 Backstreet
> Breaker Bay, Atlantis 99995

96. **Guideline Provisions:** In accordance with the provisions of section U.S.S.G. § 5E1.1, restitution shall be ordered.

Denial of Federal Benefits   (DRUG CASES ONLY)

97. **Statutory Provisions:** Pursuant to 21 U.S.C. § 862, upon a second conviction for possession of a controlled substance, a defendant may be declared ineligible for any or all Federal benefits for up to five years as determined by the Court. In addition, pursuant to 21 U.S.C. § 862, the Court may require the defendant to participate and complete an approved drug treatment program which includes periodic drug testing, or to perform appropriate community service.

98. **Guideline Provisions:** Pursuant to U.S.S.G. § 5F1.6, the Court may deny eligibility for certain Federal benefits of any individual convicted of distribution or possession of a controlled substance.

PART E. FACTORS THAT MAY WARRANT DEPARTURE

99. The probation officer has no information concerning the offense or the offender which would warrant a departure from the prescribed sentencing guidelines.

Respectfully submitted,

Chief U.S. Probation Officer

by   _____

Craig T. Doe
U.S. Probation Officer

Approved:

_____

Mark T. Clark   Date
Supervising U.S. Probation Officer

EXHIBIT 14–1 *(Continued)*
Sample Presentence Report

PART E. FACTORS THAT MAY WARRANT DEPARTURE—SAMPLES

1. Presentation of information in this section does not necessarily constitute a recommendation by the probation officer for a departure.

    The results of the psychological evaluation indicating that the defendant's I.Q. tested well below the average range and close to the borderline retarded range, coupled with the psychologist's conclusion that the defendant is impressionable and easily influenced by others, suggest that the defendant is not as culpable for the offense as the average defendant. He is certainly far less culpable than his codefendants. These factors may be considered for a downward departure within the policy statement at U.S.S.C. § 5K2.13, entitled Diminished Capacity. This provision provides that if the defendant committed a nonviolent offense while suffering from significantly reduced mental capacity not resulting from the use of drugs or other intoxicants, a lower sentence may be warranted to reflect the extent to which reduced mental capacity contributed to the commission of the offense.

2. Presentation of information in this section does not necessarily constitute a recommendation by the probation officer for a departure.

    The guideline at U.S.S.G. § 2D1.8 for managing a drug establishment does not incorporate the unusual security measures employed by the defendant in managing the site where the methamphetamine laboratory was located. The elaborate electronic security system augmented with the constant monitoring of police radio transmissions at the site are factors that make the planning of this offense unusual.

3. Presentation of information in this section does not necessarily constitute a recommendation by the probation officer for a departure.

    The fact that the defendant is suffering from AIDS and is bedridden in the final stages of the disease, is a factor that the court may consider for a departure. The medical reports indicate that the defendant is near death and it is not anticipated that he will ever be ambulatory again. Treatment at the Bureau of Prisons would be extremely costly to the government. U.S.S.G. § 5H1.4 provides that physical condition is not ordinarily relevant in determining whether a sentence should be outside the guideline range. "However, an extraordinary physical impairment may be a reason to impose a sentence below the applicable guideline range; *e.g.,* in the case of a seriously infirm defendant, home detention may be as efficient as, and less costly than, imprisonment." The defendant's medical condition may be a consideration for downward departure from a sentence of custody to a sentence of community confinement with the hospice designated as the place for service of a sentence imposed within the guideline range.

4. Presentation of information in this section does not necessarily constitute a recommendation by the probation officer for a departure.

    Although two tellers were shot in the instant robbery offense, the guideline for robbery increased the offense level by 4 levels pursuant to U.S.S.G. § 2B3.1(b)(3)(B) for the serious bodily injury of only one teller. The second teller also suffered serious harm from the gunshot wound. Had the second teller been the only victim of the offense, her wounds would have also resulted in a 4 level increase.

Continued

EXHIBIT 14–1 *(Continued)*
Sample Presentence Report

SENTENCING RECOMMENDATION

UNITED STATES DISTRICT COURT FOR THE DISTRICT OF ATLANTIS
UNITED STATES V. THADDEUS SMITH, DKT. # CR 91-001-01-KGG

TOTAL OFFENSE LEVEL: 28
CRIMINAL HISTORY CATEGORY: VI

	Statutory Provisions	Guideline Provisions	Recommended Sentence
CUSTODY:	Ct.1 - 20 years Ct.2 - 15 days-2 years	104 to 175 months	160 months
PROBATION:	Ineligible	Ineligible	Not Applicable
SUPERVISED RELEASE:	Ct.1 - 3 years Ct.2 - 1 year	Ct.1 - 2 to 3 years Ct.2 - 1 year	Ct.1 -3 years Ct.2 - 1 year, cc
FINE:	Ct.1 - $308,270 Ct.2 - $2,500 to $250,000	$12,500 to $384,405	$0
RESTITUTION:	Ct.1 - $50,345 Ct.2 - N/A	Ct.1 - $50,345 Ct.2 - N/A	Ct.1 - $50,345 Ct.2 - N/A
SPECIAL ASSESSMENT:	$100	$100	$100

Justification:

The robbery of the credit union involved extensive planning in the design of the crime, as well as the recruitment of others to participate in the offense. These factors, as well as Thaddeus Smith's role in the offense, use of a gun, and the amount of loss, have been taken into account in determining the guideline range. The defendant has an extensive criminal record which is reflected in the fact that he is in the highest criminal history category. He accepts responsibility for his actions and expresses remorse for his actions in the instant case. Because the significant sentencing considerations, both aggravating and mitigating, have been factored into the application of the guidelines, a sentence near the middle of the guideline range is merited. Accordingly, a prison sentence of 160 months is recommended which would reflect the seriousness of the offense and meet the sentencing objective of just punishment.

In the past, when Smith has been subject to community supervision, his overall adjustment has been poor, as evidenced by continued conflicts with the law. He has a history of drug and alcohol abuse and could benefit from intervention and treatment. A three year period of supervised release is recommended for the protection of the public, as well as for the correctional treatment of the defendant when he is released to the community. Accordingly, a special condition for testing and substance abuse treatment is recommended.

In view of the defendant's inability to pay financial sanctions and his lack of employment stability, it is recommended that the fine be waived. However, in light of his expected lengthy jail sentence, it is recommended that the defendant be ordered to make restitution immediately to the Atlantis Credit Union in the amount of $5,900 and to the Apex Insurance Company in the amount of $44,445. The Federal Bureau of Prisons has a voluntary Inmate Financial Responsibility Program, and while incarcerated, if employed, Smith can begin immediate payment toward his restitution obligation.

EXHIBIT 14–1 *(Concluded)*
Sample Presentence Report

Although the court may deny any or all Federal benefits for up to five years because count two is the defendant's second conviction for possession of a controlled substance, denial of Federal benefits is not recommended. If the court imposes a custodial sentence within the guideline range, the period for ineligibility for benefits would expire before the defendant's release from custody.

<u>Voluntary Surrender:</u>

Smith is subject to a substantial period of incarceration in this offense and he has been detained without bail since his arrest. Although he has family members in the community, his regular contact with them has been sporadic. As a result, the defendant does not appear to be a good candidate for voluntary surrender.

Respectfully submitted,

_____

EXHIBIT 14–2
Sample Motion for Probation with Alternative Sentencing Plan

MOTION FOR PROBATION WITH AN ALTERNATIVE SENTENCE

STATE OF COLUMBIA   CAPITOL DISTRICT COURT

V.   CASE NO. _____

BILLY MCINTIRE

Comes the defendant, Billy McIntire, by his counsel, and respectfully moves that this Court grant him probation with an alternative sentence. In support of his motion, the following is noted:

1. On March 13, _____ , Billy McIntire entered pleas of guilty to the offenses of Driving Under the Influence, 4th Offense, Driving with a Suspended Operator's License, and Disregarding a Traffic Control Device. The Commonwealth is recommending a sentence of one year on the DUI charge and a concurrent 90-day sentence on the Suspended License charge.

2. This Court's decision whether or not to grant probation is obviously a critical one in the life of Billy McIntire. It is obvious that Billy has a profound and long-standing alcohol abuse problem. The most successful method of dealing with this problem is through treatment. A treatment plan to address this problem is fully outlined in the attached alternative sentencing plan, and is incorporated by reference.

3. This plan calls for Billy to spend 120 days in jail as a condition of probation. Billy has already served 14 of these days. During the remainder of his sentence, he will be able to engage in intensive alcohol counseling. He will be able to continue his military commitments to the National Guard. While he is being punished, his time will be spent productively.

4. Billy fully appreciates that this Court could take the attitude that given the community's feelings toward multiple offender drunk drivers that it would be very easy for this Court to deny probation. However, before the Court should rush to that judgment, pragmatism requires that we examine what effect this would have in reducing the likelihood of repeat offenses. Without adequate treatment there is always the possibility of another offense. Given the one-year sentence recommended by the prosecution, would denial of probation and a prison term ensure public safety? The defense submits that it would not. If Billy were to be sentenced to a one-year term, he would be eligible for parole in a period of four (4) months. Given his general lack of record, while parole is not in any sense a certainty, it is not an unreasonable expectation. Billy has already served 14 days of this 4-month term. It is reasonably anticipated he would spend around 10 to 14 days in the county jail awaiting transfer to the Correctional Center for classification. This classification process normally takes about a month. As the center is not, for these purposes, a treatment center, little if any chance is available for formal, structured alcohol treatment. It would only be upon a transfer to the general prison population that Billy could even begin to sign up for such a program, a program which would not be of the same intensive, individualized nature as that proposed by this alternative plan. Thus, Billy could be more than half way to parole eligibility before he could even sign up for treatment. It is entirely possible that Billy could be paroled without ever having had an opportunity for counseling or treatment. Counsel respectfully suggests that this method does not solve the problem; it merely delays it.

5. However, if this Court were to grant probation with alternative sentencing, Billy would serve these same 4 months while undergoing intensive, individualized treatment. If he fails at any step during these 4 months, the prison option is still there. This method not only addresses the real problem, it addresses it in a timely, responsible way.

6. If probation is denied, Billy will be released from all forms of supervision after a period of about nine months, the presumptive date of his minimum eligibility. At that point, he would be under no restraints. However, if probation is granted, Billy would be under the control and jurisdiction of this Court for up to five (5) years. As alcohol treatment and rehabilitation is a long-term process, probation with an alternative sentence would, pragmatically, seem to be the method to best secure the public safety, as well as allowing Billy to rebuild a productive life.

WHEREFORE, the defendant, Billy McIntire, by his counsel, respectfully moves this Court to grant him probation and to structure an alternative sentence.

EXHIBIT 14–2 (*Continued*)
Sample Motion for Probation with Alternative Sentencing Plan

<u>CERTIFICATE</u>

This is to certify that a copy of the foregoing was delivered to Assistant State's Attorney, on this the _____ day of _____ , _____ .

cc: Assistant Commonwealth Attorney
      Assistant District Defender
      Office of Probation and Parole
      Alternative Sentencing Unit
      Billy McIntire

**ALTERNATIVE SENTENCING PLAN
FOR BILLY MCINTIRE
Case No. _____**

<u>TABLE OF CONTENTS</u>

Continued

EXHIBIT 14–2 *(Continued)*
Sample Motion for Probation with Alternative Sentencing Plan

COUNTY PUBLIC DEFENDER CORPORATION
480 UNION PLAZA
Legalville, Columbia

PUBLIC DEFENDER

Honorable George Martin
Capitol District Court
Legalville, Columbia

SUBJECT: Billy McIntire
            Capitol District Court
            Case No. _____

Dear Judge Martin:

The following is an individualized Alternative Sentencing Plan prepared on behalf of Billy McIntire. Mr. McIntire's attorney requested the Alternative Sentencing Unit's assistance in developing a highly structured sentencing proposal for the Court's review.

As a Sentencing Specialist, I have worked with Mr. McIntire and his attorney in constructing the sentencing alternatives. In doing so, I have attempted to combine the goals of sentencing with the individual aspects of Mr. McIntire's situation. With this incorporation in mind, we believe that treatment under the guidelines of supervised probation with the attached plan, after serving a 120-day mandatory sentence, will better serve the interests of all concerned parties. Should you have any questions concerning this plan, a Sentencing Specialist will be available to the Court at the time of Mr. McIntire's sentencing.

Thank you for your consideration of this proposal.

Sincerely,

Alternative Sentencing Specialist

   I.   RECOMMENDATIONS

       A. Punishment

           1. *Incarceration:* Mr. McIntire has already served fourteen days in custody in relation to the present charges. In addition, Mr. McIntire will serve one hundred and six (106) days in a community corrections center to fulfill his one hundred and twenty day mandatory D.U.I. sentence. All fees to be paid by Mr. McIntire. (Attachment 1).

               Mr. McIntire is to report to the Court on Monday, _____ , _____ , to begin serving his sentence.

           2. *Work Release:* Mr. McIntire will be granted a Work Release in order to maintain full-time employment, college classes, and participate in one-weekend-per-month Army National Guard duty as scheduled.

           3. *Supervised Probation:* Mr. McIntire will undergo a five (5) year probation record, or for an amount of time to be determined by the Court.

       B. Treatment

           1. *Substance Abuse:* While at the community corrections center, Mr. McIntire will be attending various treatment groups in order to fulfill the requirements of an intensive, year-long treatment program. Mr. McIntire will be granted a treatment release for those meetings. Fees to be paid by Mr. McIntire. (Attachments 2a & 2b).

EXHIBIT 14–2 (*Continued*)
Sample Motion for Probation with Alternative Sentencing Plan

2. *Counseling:*

   a. While at the community corrections center, Mr. McIntire will undergo individual counseling.

   b. While at the community corrections center, Mr. McIntire will be required to attend two (2) Alcoholics Anonymous (A.A.) meetings per week. Mr. McIntire will be granted a treatment release for these meetings as scheduled. (Attachments 4a & 4b).

3. *Aftercare:* After release from the community corrections center, Mr. McIntire will attend a treatment schedule as recommended by the staff. Also, Mr. McIntire will be required to attend two (2) A.A. meetings per week at locations of his choice throughout his probation period.

C. Restitution

1. *Victim Restitution:* Victim restitution is not applicable in this case.

2. *Community Restitution:* Mr. McIntire is to perform one hundred and four (104) hours, or for an amount of hours to be determined by the Court, of community work to be completed within the probation period. After release from the community corrections center, Mr. McIntire will perform this work at the YMCA, Southeast Family Branch, if Mr. McIntire's work schedule allows him to work on weekdays. He would be under the supervision of Pat Yoder. If not, Mr. McIntire will work every Saturday that he is not on duty with the Army National Guard. His Saturday work will be with the Metropolitan Park and Recreation Department, under the supervision of Andy Wright.

D. Community Safety/Deterrence

   Mr. McIntire will be required to:

1. Continue in treatment and counseling as recommended.

2. Maintain full-time employment. If enrolled in a vocational school or college of higher education, Mr. McIntire will maintain part-time employment.

3. Donate $25.00 per year to Mothers Against Drunk Driving (M.A.D.D.). Mr. McIntire will submit receipts verifying payment to his Probation Officer.

4. At the request of his supervising Probation Officer, submit written documentation from all participants/institutions working with Mr. McIntire with this plan.

5. Submit to random alcohol and drug testing.

6. Refrain from committing any other offenses.

7. Perform any other special conditions of probation that are deemed appropriate by the Court or his Probation Officer.

E. Supervision/Modifications

1. If this plan is acceptable to the Court, it is the recommendation that Mr. McIntire be supervised by the appropriate Probation Officer in order to monitor the various components of his plan.

2. All facilities and institutions mentioned in this plan have agreed to notify the Office of Probation and Parole if Mr. McIntire does not comply with this plan in any manner.

3. Absolutely no changes or modifications in the plan will be made by Mr. McIntire without prior approval of the Court. Mr. McIntire's Probation Officer may make appropriate changes with subsequent notice to the Court.

Continued

EXHIBIT 14–2 *(Continued)*
Sample Motion for Probation with Alternative Sentencing Plan

F. Conclusion

The proposal presented here has been designed to provide the Court with an alternative to incarceration for Billy McIntire. Mr. McIntire is not a person who is habituated to a criminal lifestyle, except for a recurrent drinking and driving problem. He has no criminal charges against him except those related to alcoholism. Nevertheless, because of his abuse of alcohol, Mr. McIntire has acted in an irresponsible manner. To assist him in addressing the case at hand, we have designed the above conditions which will also meet the goals of sentencing. Several of the recommendations serve more than one goal.

The goals of punishment are accomplished by the fourteen days already served in jail, the one hundred and six days still to be served at the community corrections center, the supervised probationary period, the $25.00 per year to M.A.D.D., the hours volunteered to the community, and the inevitability of serving the rest of his sentence in prison if he fails to meet the conditions of this plan.

The goals of treatment are attained by Mr. McIntire's participation in several different classes and groups while in a chemical dependency program for at least one year, participation in A.A. meetings, abiding by the aftercare recommendations, and submitting to random alcohol and drug testing.

The goals of restitution are achieved through Mr. McIntire's payment for his treatment and counseling, his hours volunteered to the community, his payment of fees, and the $25.00 per year to M.A.D.D.

The goals of deterrence, which will help maintain community safety, are met by additional incarceration at the community corrections center, undergoing supervised probation, completing a year-long substance abuse program, paying for that program, paying for his additional incarceration, attending A.A. meetings, fulfilling his monthly National Guard Duty, volunteering time to the community, maintaining full-time employment, being randomly tested for drugs and alcohol, donating $25.00 per year to M.A.D.D., and having the knowledge that his failure to comply with any of the conditions of this plan or his probation will mean the revocation of his probation.

II. BACKGROUND DATA

Name:	Billy McIntire	
Address:	873 Old Mill Pike	
	Legalville, Columbia	
Date of Birth:	July 18, 1971	
Social Security:	555-55-5555	
Marital Status:	Married	
Education:	June 10, 1989	Graduated from Legalville High School, (Attachment 7).
	Sept. _____ to Present	Attended Capitol Community College. (Attachment 8).
Military:	Feb. 1996–Present	Army National Guard (Attachment 9).
Employment: Legalville, Columbia	May 1992–Present	Dawn Industries
		Drill Press Operator
Prior Criminal History:	Refer to Presentencing Investigation Report.	
Present Criminal Charges:	Capitol District Court Case No._____ Charges: D.U.I. IV Driving with a Suspended License Disregarding Traffic Control Device	
Attorney:	District Public Defender	

EXHIBIT 14–2 *(Concluded)*
Sample Motion for Probation with Alternative Sentencing Plan

III. SOCIAL HISTORY

Billy McIntire is before the Court on his fourth conviction of Driving Under the Influence within five years, Driving on a Suspended License, and Disregarding a Traffic Control Device.

Billy was born on July 18, 1971, to Susan and Andrew McIntire. He is the oldest of three sons born to the McIntires. Billy's early childhood was fairly normal until he was eleven, when his father was killed. Soon thereafter, Billy went to live with his grandparents.

Although Billy was not a student who made good grades in school, he did stick with it and graduated with his class in 1989 from Legalville High School. After high school, Billy got a job with Dawn Industries. Recently he was not sure what he wanted to do. Billy eventually decided upon a career in computers and enrolled at Capitol Community College in their Computer Programming course.

Billy wanted to expand his career opportunities. Therefore, he joined the Army National Guard. Not only does the Guard give Billy some job skills, it will also pay for further education. Billy realizes he needs more education and plans to finish his coursework in the computer field. In 1993 Billy married Jodie Aikens. They have three children.

Concerning the charges at hand, Billy had been partying with friends and was attempting to go home when he was pulled over. He realizes it was wrong to attempt to drive. The incident also helped Billy to see that he has a problem with alcohol abuse which he minimized before. Billy wants to get the treatment he needs so that this behavior stops before someone is injured. Billy's brothers agree that he needs help because they cannot identify with the irresponsibility of drinking and driving as they have never been in any legal trouble. In fact, if not for Billy's periodic alcohol abuse, he would not have a criminal record.

IV. VERIFICATION/AGREEMENT

The Alternative Sentencing Specialist has thoroughly discussed this Alternative Sentencing Plan with me and I am aware that contingent on this plan's acceptance, any noncompliance with the components as adopted by the Court, could result in probation revocation and a possible prison sentence.

_____
Signature

Date: _____

V. ATTACHMENTS

1. Fact sheet, community corrections center.
2. Schedule, substance abuse treatment groups.
3. State Driver Risk Inventory.
4. Information on Alcoholics Anonymous.
5. Letter to judge from Capitol Community College indicating willingness to work with Billy.
6. Selected Reserve Educational Assistance Program (G.I. Bill) eligibility.
7. High school diploma.
8. College transcript.
9. Certification and acceptance, Army National Guard.
10. Certificate of training, Army National Guard.

EXHIBIT 14–3
Judgment of Sentence of Probation

JUDGMENT OF SENTENCE OF PROBATION

STATE OF COLUMBIA   CAPITOL DISTRICT COURT

v.   Case No. _____

BILLY MCINTIRE

At a hearing held this _____ day of _____ , _____ , came the Defendant, <u>Billy McIntire,</u> who appeared with counsel, the Hon. _____ , and the Commonwealth being represented by the Hon. _____ , and this case having been called on motion of the Defendant to withhold rendition of the judgment and imposition of sentence.

The Court has considered the presentence investigation report, the nature and circumstances of the offenses, and the history and character of the Defendant, and the Court finds and is of the opinion that the imposition of the sentence herein would have a deleterious and negative effect and serve no rehabilitative purpose.

IT IS HEREBY ORDERED AND ADJUDGED that pursuant to the Judgment on Guilty Plea, the Defendant, <u>Billy McIntire,</u> is guilty of the crime admitted and the Court fixes the sentence as follows: OPERATING A MOTOR VEHICLE UNDER THE INFLUENCE OF INTOXICANTS 1 YEAR, OPERATING A MOTOR VEHICLE WHILE LICENSE IS REVOKED OR SUSPENDED FOR DRIVING UNDER THE INFLUENCE 90 DAYS, DISREGARDING A TRAFFIC CONTROL DEVICE $20.00 FINE. BOTH COUNTS TO RUN CONCURRENT WITH EACH OTHER FOR 1 YEAR.

Accordingly, IT IS HEREBY ORDERED AND ADJUDGED that the rendition of the judgment of sentence is withheld and the Defendant is placed on probation under the supervision of the Division of Probation and Parole for a period of <u>5</u> years, subject to the Defendant's compliance with the following conditions:

(1) Continued good behavior;
(2) Refrain from violating the law in any respect;
(3) Compliance with any other regulations and supervision of the Division of Probation and Parole Office and the direction of the Probation Officer;
(4) Obtain and maintain full-time employment as far as possible;
(5) Report in person or otherwise as directed by the Probation Officer;
(6) Permit the Probation Officer to visit the Defendant at home or elsewhere;
(7) Answer all reasonable inquiries by the Probation Officer and promptly notify the Probation Officer of any change in address or employment;
(8) Submit to random drug and/or alcohol urinalysis testing;
(9) Receive and successfully complete any drug, alcohol, vocational, and/or psychological counseling as recommended by the Probation Officer;
(10) Pay court costs by _____ ;
(11) DEFENDANT TO SERVE 120 DAYS (DEFENDANT HAS ALREADY SERVED 14 DAYS AND REMAINDER OF 106 DAYS TO BE SERVED AT COMMUNITY CORRECTIONS CENTER) DEFENDANT TO REPORT _____ .
(12) DEFENDANT TO HAVE WORK RELEASE IN ORDER TO MAINTAIN FULL-TIME EMPLOYMENT AND PARTICIPATE IN ONE-WEEKEND-PER MONTH ARMY NATIONAL GUARD DUTY AS SCHEDULED.
(13) DEFENDANT TO PAY MINIMUM SUPERVISION FEE.
(14) DEFENDANT TO PAY $100.00 PER YEAR TO MOTHERS AGAINST DRUNK DRIVING.
(15) DEFENDANT TO FOLLOW RECOMMENDATIONS IN ALTERNATIVE SENTENCING PLAN.

IT IS FURTHER ORDERED AND ADJUDGED that upon completion of the aforesaid probationary period the Defendant shall finally be discharged provided he/she has fully complied with the above conditions and that no warrant issued by any Court is pending against him/her and that his/her probation has not been revoked prior thereto.

DATE: _____

EXHIBIT 14–4
Federal Notice of Appeal

NOTICE OF APPEAL TO A COURT OF APPEALS FROM A JUDGMENT OR ORDER OF A DISTRICT COURT

United States District Court for the . . . .
District of . . . .

File Number . . . .

A.B., Plaintiff

v.   Notice of Appeal

C.D., Defendant
   Notice is hereby given that C. D., defendant above named, hereby appeals to the United States Court of Appeals
for the . . . .
Circuit (from the final judgment) (from the order (describing it)) entered in this action on the . . . .
day of . . . .

   . . . .

(S) . . . .

. . . .

(Address)
Attorney for C. D.

EXHIBIT 14–5
Affidavit in Support of Motion to Proceed on Appeal *in Forma Pauperis*

AFFIDAVIT TO ACCOMPANY MOTION FOR LEAVE TO APPEAL *IN FORMA PAUPERIS*

United States District Court for the . . . .
District of . . . .
United States of America . . . .
v.   No. . . . .
A. B.

Affidavit in Support of Motion to Proceed
on Appeal *in Forma Pauperis*

I, ... being first duly sworn, depose and say that I am the . . . ., in the above-entitled case; that
in support of my motion to proceed on appeal without being required to prepay fees, costs or give security there-
for, I state that because of my poverty I am unable to pay the costs of said proceeding or to give security therefor;
that I believe I am entitled to redress; and that the issues which I desire to present on appeal are the following:

   I further swear that the responses which I have made to the questions and instructions below relating to my ability to pay the cost of prosecuting the appeal are true.

1. Are you presently employed?
   a. If the answer is yes, state the amount of your salary or wages per month and give the name and address of
      your employer.
   b. If the answer is no, state the date of your last employment and the amount of the salary and wages per month
      which you received.

Continued

EXHIBIT 14–5 *(Concluded)*
Affidavit in Support of Motion to Proceed on Appeal *in Forma Pauperis*

2. Have you received within the past twelve months any income from a business, profession or other form of self-employment, or in the form of rent payments, interest, dividends, or other source?
   a. If the answer is yes, describe each source of income, and state the amount received from each during the past twelve months.
3. Do you own any cash or checking or savings account?
   a. If the answer is yes, state the total value of the items owned.
4. Do you own any real estate, stocks, bonds, notes, automobiles, or other valuable property (excluding ordinary household furnishings and clothing)?
   a. If the answer is yes, describe the property and state its approximate value.
5. List the persons who are dependent upon you for support and state your relationship to those persons.

I understand that a false statement or answer to any questions in this affidavit will subject me to penalties for perjury.

....

SUBSCRIBED AND SWORN TO before me this . . . . day of . . . . Let the applicant proceed without prepayment of costs or fees or the necessity of giving security therefor.

....

District Judge

EXHIBIT 14–6
Federal Application for Habeas Corpus

**MODEL FORM FOR USE IN APPLICATIONS FOR
HABEAS CORPUS UNDER 28 U.S.C. § 2254**

Name _____

Prison number _____

Place of confinement _____

United States District Court _____ District of _____

Case No. _____

(To be supplied by Clerk of U.S. District Court)

_____ , PETITIONER

(Full name)

v.

_____ , RESPONDENT

(Name of Warden, Superintendent, Jailor, or authorized person having custody of petitioner)

and

THE ATTORNEY GENERAL OF THE STATE OF

_____ ,

ADDITIONAL RESPONDENT.

(If petitioner is attacking a judgment which imposed a sentence to be served in the *future,* petitioner must fill in the name of the state where the judgment was entered. If petitioner has a sentence to be served in the *future* under a federal judgment which he wishes to attack, he should file a motion under 28 U.S.C. § 2255, in the federal court which entered the judgment.)

EXHIBIT 14–6 (*Continued*)

Federal Application for Habeas Corpus

PETITION FOR WRIT OF HABEAS CORPUS BY A
PERSON IN STATE CUSTODY

Instructions—Read Carefully

(1) This petition must be legibly handwritten or typewritten, and signed by the petitioner under penalty of perjury. Any false statement of a material fact may serve as the basis for prosecution and conviction for perjury. All questions must be answered concisely in the proper space on the form.

(2) Additional pages are not permitted except with respect to the *facts* which you rely upon to support your grounds for relief. No citation of authorities need be furnished. If briefs or arguments are submitted, they should be submitted in the form of a separate memorandum.

(3) Upon receipt of a fee of $5 your petition will be filed if it is in proper order.

(4) If you do not have the necessary filing fee, you may request permission to proceed *in forma pauperis,* in which event you must execute the declaration on the last page, setting forth information establishing your inability to prepay the fees and costs or give security therefor. If you wish to proceed *in forma pauperis,* you must have an authorized officer at the penal institution complete the certificate as to the amount of money and securities on deposit to your credit in any account in the institution. If your prison account exceeds $_____ , you must pay the filing fee as required by the rule of the district court.

(5) Only judgments entered by one court may be challenged in a single petition. If you seek to challenge judgments entered by different courts either in the same state or in different states, you must file separate petitions as to each court.

(6) Your attention is directed to the fact that you must include all grounds for relief and all facts supporting such grounds for relief in the petition you file seeking relief from any judgment of conviction.

(7) When the petition is fully completed, *the original and two copies* must be mailed to the Clerk of the United States District Court whose address is

_____

(8) Petitions which do not conform to these instructions will be returned with a notation as to the deficiency.

PETITION

1. Name and location of court which entered the judgment of conviction under attack _____

_____

2. Date of judgment of conviction _____

3. Length of sentence _____

4. Nature of offense involved (all counts) _____

_____

_____

_____

5. What was your plea? (Check one)
   (a) Not guilty ☐
   (b) Guilty ☐
   (c) Nolo contendere ☐
   If you entered a guilty plea to one count or indictment and a not guilty plea to another count or indictment, give details:

_____

_____

_____

6. Kind of trial: (Check one)
   (a) Jury ☐
   (b) Judge only ☐

Continued

EXHIBIT 14–6 *(Continued)*
Federal Application for Habeas Corpus

7. Did you testify at the trial?
   Yes ☐ No ☐
8. Did you appeal from the judgment of conviction?
   Yes ☐ No ☐
9. If you did appeal, answer the following:
   (a) Name of court _____
   (b) Result _____
   (c) Date of result _____
10. Other than a direct appeal from the judgment of conviction and sentence, have you previously filed any petitions, applications, or motions with respect to this judgment in any court, state or federal?
    Yes ☐ No ☐
11. If your answer to 10 was "yes," give the following information:
    (a) (1) Name of court _____
        (2) Nature of proceeding _____
            _____
        (3) Grounds raised _____
            _____
            _____
            _____
            _____

        (4) Did you receive an evidentiary hearing on your petition, application, or motion?
            Yes ☐ No ☐
        (5) Result _____
        (6) Date of result _____
    (b) As to any second petition, application, or motion give the same information:
        (1) Name of court _____
        (2) Nature of proceeding _____
            _____
        (3) Grounds raised _____
            _____
            _____
            _____
            _____

        (4) Did you receive an evidentiary hearing on your petition, application, or motion?
            Yes ☐ No ☐
        (5) Result _____
        (6) Date of result _____
    (c) As to any third petition, application, or motion, give the same information:
        (1) Name of court _____
        (2) Nature of proceeding _____
            _____
        (3) Grounds raised _____
            _____
            _____
            _____

        (4) Did you receive an evidentiary hearing on your petition, application, or motion?
            Yes ☐ No ☐
        (5) Result _____
        (6) Date of result _____

EXHIBIT 14–6 *(Continued)*
Federal Application for Habeas Corpus

(d) Did you appeal to the highest state court having jurisdiction over the result of action taken on any petition, application, or motion?
  (1) First petition, etc.   Yes ☐   No ☐
  (2) Second petition, etc.   Yes ☐   No ☐
  (3) Third petition, etc.   Yes ☐   No ☐

(e) If you did *not* appeal from the adverse action on any petition, application, or motion, explain briefly why you did not:

_____

_____

_____

12. State *concisely* every ground on which you claim that you are being held unlawfully. Summarize *briefly* the *facts* supporting each ground. If necessary, you may attach pages stating additional grounds and *facts* supporting same.

   Caution: In order to proceed in the federal court, you must ordinarily first exhaust your state court remedies as to each ground on which you request action by the federal court. If you fail to set forth all grounds in this petition, you may be barred from presenting additional grounds at a later date.

   For your information, the following is a list of the most frequently raised grounds for relief in habeas corpus proceedings. Each statement preceded by a letter constitutes a separate ground for possible relief. You may raise any grounds which you may have other than those listed if you have exhausted your state court remedies with respect to them. However, *you should raise in this petition all available grounds* (relating to this conviction) on which you base your allegations that you are being held in custody unlawfully.

   Do not check any of these listed grounds. If you select one or more of these grounds for relief, you must allege facts. The petition will be returned to you if you merely check (a) through (j) or any one of these grounds.

   (a) Conviction obtained by plea of guilty which was unlawfully induced or not made voluntarily with understanding of the nature of the charge and the consequences of the plea.
   (b) Conviction obtained by use of coerced confession.
   (c) Conviction obtained by use of evidence gained pursuant to an unconstitutional search and seizure.
   (d) Conviction obtained by use of evidence obtained pursuant to an unlawful arrest.
   (e) Conviction obtained by a violation of the privilege against self-incrimination.
   (f) Conviction obtained by the unconstitutional failure of the prosecution to disclose to the defendant evidence favorable to the defendant.
   (g) Conviction obtained by a violation of the protection against double jeopardy.
   (h) Conviction obtained by action of a grand or petit jury which was unconstitutionally selected and impaneled.
   (i) Denial of effective assistance of counsel.
   (j) Denial of right of appeal.

A. Ground one: _____

_____

   Supporting FACTS (tell your story *briefly* without citing cases or law): _____

_____

_____

B. Ground two: _____

_____

   Supporting FACTS (tell your story *briefly* without citing cases or law): _____

_____

_____

_____

_____

_____

_____

_____

_____

Continued

EXHIBIT 14–6 *(Continued)*
Federal Application for Habeas Corpus

C. Ground three: _____

_____

Supporting FACTS (tell your story *briefly* without citing cases or law): _____

_____

_____

_____

_____

_____

_____

D. Ground four: _____

_____

Supporting FACTS (tell your story *briefly* without citing cases or law): _____

_____

_____

_____

_____

_____

_____

13. If any of the grounds listed in 12A, B, C, and D were not previously presented in any other court, state or federal, state *briefly* what grounds were not so presented, and give your reasons for not presenting them:

_____

_____

_____

14. Do you have any petition or appeal now pending in any court, either state or federal, as to the judgment under attack?
Yes ☐   No ☐

15. Give the name and address, if known, of each attorney who represented you in the following stages of the judgment attacked herein:
(a) At preliminary hearing _____

(b) At arraignment and plea _____

(c) At trial _____

(d) At sentencing _____

(e) On appeal _____

(f) In any post-conviction proceeding _____

(g) On appeal from any adverse ruling in a post-conviction proceeding _____

_____

16. Were you sentenced on more than one count of an indictment, or on more than one indictment, in the same court and at the same time?
Yes ☐   No ☐

EXHIBIT 14–6 (*(Continued)*
Federal Application for Habeas Corpus

---

17. Do you have any future sentence to serve after you complete the sentence imposed by the judgment under attack?

    Yes ☐   No ☐

    (a) If so, give name and location of court which imposed sentence to be served in the future: _____
    _____

    (b) And give date and length of sentence to be served in the future: _____
    _____

    (c) Have you filed, or do you contemplate filing, any petition attacking the judgment which imposed the sentence to be served in the future?

    Yes ☐   No ☐

    Wherefore, petitioner prays that the Court grant petitioner relief to which he may be entitled in this proceeding.

    _____

    Signature of Attorney (if any)

    I declare (or certify, verify, or state) under penalty of perjury that the foregoing is true and correct. Executed

    on _____ .

         (date)

    _____

    Signature of Petitioner

IN FORMA PAUPERIS DECLARATION

_____

[Insert appropriate court]

_____

(Petitioner)

v.

_____

(Respondent(s))

DECLARATION IN
SUPPORT
OF REQUEST
TO PROCEED
IN FORMA PAUPERIS

I, _____ , declare that I am the petitioner in the above-entitled case; that in support of my motion to proceed without being required to prepay fees, costs, or give security therefor, I state that because of my poverty I am unable to pay the costs of said proceeding or to give security therefor; that I believe I am entitled to relief.

1. Are you presently employed? Yes ☐ No ☐

    a. If the answer is "yes," state the amount of your salary or wages per month, and give the name and address of your employer.

    _____

    _____

    b. If the answer if "no," state the date of last employment and the amount of the salary and wages per month which you received.

    _____

    _____

Continued

EXHIBIT 14–6 *(Continued)*
Federal Application for Habeas Corpus

2. Have you received within the past twelve months any money from any of the following sources?
   a. Business, profession, or form of self-employment?
      Yes ☐   No ☐
   b. Rent payments, interest, or dividends?
      Yes ☐   No ☐
   c. Pensions, annuities, or life insurance payments?
      Yes ☐   No ☐
   d. Gifts or inheritances?
      Yes ☐   No ☐
   e. Any other sources?
      Yes ☐   No ☐

   If the answer to any of the above is "yes," describe each source of money and state the amount received from each during the past twelve months.

   _____
   _____
   _____
   _____

3. Do you own cash, or do you have money in a checking or savings account?
   Yes ☐ No ☐ (Include any funds in prison accounts.)
   If the answer is "yes," state the total value of the items owned.

   _____
   _____
   _____

4. Do you own any real estate, stocks, bonds, notes, automobiles, or other valuable property (excluding ordinary household furnishings and clothing)?
   Yes ☐   No ☐
   If the answer is "yes," describe the property and state its approximate value.

   _____
   _____
   _____

5. List the persons who are dependent upon you for support, state your relationship to those persons, and indicate how much you contribute toward their support.

   _____
   _____

   I declare (or certify, verify, or state) under penalty of perjury that the foregoing is true and correct. Executed on _____ .
        (date)

   _____
   Signature of Petitioner

   Certificate

   I hereby certify that the petitioner herein has the sum of $ _____ on account to his credit at the _____ institution where he is confined. I further certify that petitioner likewise has the following securities to his credit according to the records of said _____ institution:

   _____
   _____
   _____
   _____

   _____
   AUTHORIZED OFFICER OF
   INSTITUTION

EXHIBIT 14–6 *(Continued)*
Federal Application for Habeas Corpus

(As amended Apr. 28, 1982, eff. Aug. 1, 1982.)

MODEL FORM FOR USE IN 28 U.S.C. § 2254 CASES
INVOLVING A RULE 9 ISSUE

Form No. 9

United States District Court,

_____ District of _____

Case No. _____

_____ , PETITIONER

v.

_____ , RESPONDENT

and

_____ , ADDITIONAL RESPONDENT

Petitioner's Response as to Why His Petition Should
Not Be Barred Under Rule 9

Explanation and Instructions—Read Carefully

(I)   Rule 9. Delayed or successive petitions

   (a) Delayed petitions. A petition may be dismissed if it appears that the state of which the respondent is an officer has been prejudiced in its ability to respond to the petition by delay in its filing unless the petitioner shows that it is based on grounds of which he could not have had knowledge by the exercise of reasonable diligence before the circumstances prejudicial to the state occurred.

   (b) Successive petitions. A second or successive petition may be dismissed if the judge finds that it fails to allege new or different grounds for relief and the prior determination was on the merits or, if new and different grounds are alleged, the judge finds that the failure of the petitioner to assert those grounds in a prior petition constituted an abuse of the writ.

(II)   Your petition for habeas corpus has been found to be subject to dismissal under rule 9( ) for the following reason(s):

   _____

   _____

   _____

   _____

(III)   This form has been sent so that you may explain why your petition contains the defect(s) noted in (II) above. It is required that you fill out this form and send it back to the court within _____ days. Failure to do so will result in the automatic dismissal of your petition.

(IV)   When you have fully completed this form, the original and two copies must be mailed to the Clerk of the United States District Court whose address is

   _____

   _____

(V)   This response must be legibly handwritten or typewritten, and signed by the petitioner, under penalty of perjury. Any false statement of a material fact may serve as the basis for prosecution and conviction for perjury. All questions must be answered concisely in the proper space on the form.

(VI)   Additional pages are not permitted except with respect to the *facts* which you rely upon in item 4 or 5 in the response. Any citation of authorities should be kept to an absolute minimum and is only appropriate if there has been a change in the law since the judgment you are attacking was rendered.

(VII) Respond to 4 *or* 5 below, not to both, unless (II) above indicates that you must answer both sections.

RESPONSE

1.   Have you had the assistance of an attorney, other law-trained personnel, or writ writers since the conviction your petition is attacking was entered?

   Yes ☐   No ☐

Continued

EXHIBIT 14–6 *(Concluded)*
Federal Application for Habeas Corpus

2. If you checked "yes," above, specify as precisely as you can the period(s) of time during which you received such assistance, up to and including the present.

_____

3. Describe the nature of the assistance, including the names of those who rendered it to you.

_____
_____
_____

4. If your petition is in jeopardy because of delay prejudicial to the state under rule 9(a), explain why you feel the delay has not been prejudicial and/or why the delay is excusable under the terms of 9(a). This should be done by relying upon FACTS, not your opinions or conclusions.

_____
_____
_____
_____

5. If your petition is in jeopardy under rule 9(b) because it asserts the same grounds as a previous petition, explain why you feel it deserves a reconsideration. If its fault under rule 9(b) is that it asserts new grounds which should have been included in a prior petition, explain why you are raising these grounds now rather than previously. Your explanation should rely on FACTS, not your opinions or conclusions.

_____
_____
_____
_____
_____
_____
_____
_____

    I declare (or certify, verify, or state) under penalty of perjury that the foregoing is true and correct. Executed on _____ .
                    (date)

                                                    _____
                                                    Signature of Petitioner

(As amended Apr. 28, 1982, eff. Aug. 1, 1982.)

SYSTEM FOLDER ASSIGNMENTS

Complete the following and place the documents in your system folder:

- If your state uses the death penalty, note the statute and list mitigating and aggravating circumstances.
- Your state's use of indefinite or definite sentencing, mandatory sentences, and enhancements.
- Property subject to forfeiture under your state laws and defenses against forfeiture.
- Expanded list of pointers for preparing an alternative sentencing plan.
- Outline of sentencing procedures.

- Sample presentence report.
- Sample alternative sentencing plan.
- Judgment of sentence of probation.
- Your state and federal law regarding probation and parole revocation and the rights of prisoners.
- Your state and federal statutes on appeals.
- General outline of appellate procedure and pertinent state and federal rules.
- Federal notice of appeal.
- Affidavit in support of motion to proceed on appeal *in forma pauperis.*
- Federal and state rules and statutes on law of habeas corpus.
- Outline of habeas procedure.
- Federal application for habeas corpus.

APPLICATION ASSIGNMENTS

1. A man shot and killed a woman he had been dating. The sentencing phase of his trial presented two aggravating circumstances: that the murder was cold, calculated, and premeditated without any pretense of justification (which was not shown beyond a reasonable doubt) and that the defendant had been convicted of violent felonies. Three mitigating circumstances were that the offense was committed while the defendant was high on cocaine, the defendant's capacity to appreciate the criminality of the offense was substantially impaired, and the defendant suffered personality changes from the drug use and severed relationship with the victim.

   How would you weigh these factors in determining the appropriateness of the death penalty for this offender? See *White v. State,* 616 So.2d 21 (Fla. 1993).

2. A defendant was not allowed to speak at his sentencing hearing to respond to the mention of a letter from the father of one of the victims. The defendant was represented by counsel. Were his rights violated? See *Boardman v. Estelle,* 957 F.2d 1523 (9th Cir. 1992).

3. Conditions of probation included that the probationer not use intoxicants to excess and that he comply with the instructions of the probation officer. The officer required the probationer to submit to urinalysis; the probationer refused. Is this refusal grounds for revocation? See *Paterson v. State,* 612 So.2d 692 (Fla. App. 1993).

HELPFUL WEB SITES

www.ussg.gov

United States Sentencing Commission, overview of guidelines, statistics

www.bop.gov

Bureau of Prisons, links to state correctional sites

www.parolewatch.org

Upcoming parole hearings, links to state corrections and parole sites

www.corrections.com

Links to correction and criminal justice Web sites

www.essential.org/dpic

Death Penalty Information Center, state information and statistics on sentencing, use of death penalty, studies on deterrence, and other issues

www.amnesty.org

Information on current activity regarding the death penalty

www.silicon-valley.com/pardonme/index.shtml

Procedure for applying for a federal pardon

INTERNET EXERCISES

1. Go to the Death Penalty Information Center site. How many death row inmates are there in Nebraska? In Texas? In New York?
2. Go to www.fbi.gov. How many hate crimes were reported in the most recent year in your city? Your state? What were the bias motivations for the crimes?
3. Your client may be ordered to pay restitution, as well as serve a prison sentence. Go to the Bureau of Prisons site to find out how much federal inmates are paid per hour.
4. Go to the United States Sentencing Commission site. What is the largest primary offense category in your state? How does that compare to national figures? For what crimes are the most departures from guidelines in your state? How does that compare to national departures for that crime?

QUESTIONS FOR STUDY AND REVIEW

1. What are the forces that influence changes in what is acceptable as punishment?
2. Why is proportionality in punishment important? What are the tests for proportionality set out in *Solem?*
3. What are the two landmark Supreme Court decisions that mark changes in capital punishment statutes? How do the new laws differ from the old ones?
4. What restrictions apply to the sentencing of a death penalty?
5. What are the advantages of incarceration as punishment? The problems?
6. List and define seven ways that sentences can be imposed.
7. What factors may incur sentence enhancements?
8. What must be the focus of a hate crime enhancement for it to be constitutional?
9. What is the most common punishment for misdemeanors?
10. What are two sources of compensation to victims of crime for their losses?
11. What property is commonly subject to forfeiture? What property may be protected? Is there a limit on the amount of forfeiture? Explain.
12. What are common conditions of probation?
13. What are the provisions of the federal three strikes law?
14. What are the advantages and disadvantages of indefinite sentencing ranges?
15. What were the goals of the United States Sentencing Commission? Have they been reached?
16. What is the "safety valve" provision regarding sentencing guidelines?
17. What are the components used to calculate sentences under the United States Sentencing Guidelines? What factors complicate calculations?
18. How are bifurcated trials used in capital punishment cases?
19. What sections are included in a presentence report?
20. List pointers that will help the defense paralegal prepare an effective alternative sentencing plan.
21. What happens at a sentencing hearing?
22. What role do victims have in sentencing?
23. What is the process of probation or parole revocation?
24. What types of postconviction review are available?
25. What are the two basic functions of appellate courts?
26. Diagram the progress of both a state and a federal case from trial to final appeal. Which courts handle appeals by right and which are discretionary?
27. What are the conditions for interlocutory appeals?
28. What types of issues can be raised on appeal? List six common grounds for appeal.
29. What is harmless error?

30. What issues may prosecutors appeal?
31. Trace the general steps of appellate procedure, including time limits.
32. What is an *Anders* brief?
33. What are the conditions required for transfer of habeas corpus cases from state to federal courts?
34. What are the most common grounds for habeas corpus relief?
35. Trace the steps of habeas procedure in the federal system, including time limits.
36. What are the PLRA and AEDPA, and how have they changed petitioning for postconviction relief?

KEY TERMS LIST

Allocution
Amnesty
Appeal by right
Discretionary appeal
Harmless error
Plain error
Proportionality
Restitution
Sentencing:
   Concurrent sentence

Consecutive sentence
Definite or determinate sentence
Sentence Enhancements
Indefinite sentence
Indeterminate sentence
Mandatory sentence
Presumptive sentence
Suspended sentence
Writ of certiorari

ENDNOTES

1. Prisons, THE NEW GROLIER MULTIMEDIA ENCYCLOPEDIA, Online Computer Systems, Inc., 1993.
2. See the film *Brubaker* for a portrayal of these conditions.
3. JOHN M. SCHEB & JOHN M. SCHEB II, CRIMINAL LAW AND PROCEDURE, 3rd ed., West/Wadsworth, 1999, p. 610.
4. David E. Rovella, *Confusing Jurors to Death*, NLJ, Feb. 14, 2000, A1.
5. Fox Butterfield, *Death-penalty Study Reveals Many Errors*, LEXINGTON HERALD-LEADER, June 12, 2000, at A1, A9.
6. Eric Gregory, *Blandford Must Pay for 64 Month Prison Stay*, LEXINGTON HERALD-LEADER, July 23, 1993, at A1.
7. Anne Gearan, *U.S. Prison Population Doubles in 12 Years*, LEXINGTON HERALD-LEADER, March 15, 1999, at A3.
8. *Ranks of Non-violent Convicts Grow*, LEXINGTON HERALD-LEADER, March 25, 1999, at A3.
9. Eric Slosser, *The Prison-industrial Complex*, THE ATLANTIC MONTHLY, Dec. 1998, at 54.
10. *The Racial Divide of Crack vs. Powder Cocaine Penalties*, THE WASHINGTON POST NATIONAL WEEKLY EDITION, Oct. 21–27, 1996, at 10.
11. The Sentencing Project, *The Thinking Advocate's List of Mitigating Factors*, at 6, KATA Criminal Law Seminar, Oct. 16, 1992.
12. David Hess, *Bill Would Curb Asset Seizures*, LEXINGTON HERALD-LEADER, June 24, 1999, at A5.
13. *Nearly Half of Felons on Probation Arrested Again in Three Years*, RICHMOND REGISTER, Feb. 10, 1992, at 7B.
14. *Justices Leave Intact California's 3-Strikes Law*, LEXINGTON HERALD-LEADER, Jan. 20, 1999, at A7.
15. *Federal Sentencing Guidelines—Are They Working & Where Are We Going?*, presented at KATA Criminal Law Seminar, Oct. 16, 1992, Louisville, KY, by Louis S. Sutherland.
16. John Cloud, *A Get-Tough Policy That Failed*, TIME, Feb. 1, 1999, at 49–51.
17. *Federal Sentencing Guidelines, supra* note 15, by Hancy Jones.

18. Joan Biskupic and Mary Pat Flaherty, *Sentencing by the Book*, THE WASHINGTON POST NATIONAL WEEKLY EDITION, Oct. 21–27, 1996, at 8.

19. *Id.,* at 8–9.

20. Model Presentence Report, Western District of Kentucky, effective Oct. 1, 1992.

21. Christopher F. Polk, *Alternative Sentencing: Theory and Practice,* at 19–25, prepared for KATA Criminal Law Seminar, Oct. 16, 1992, Louisville, KY.

22. Judy Pasternak, *Female Inmates Report More Abuse*, LEXINGTON HERALD-LEADER, April 12, 1999, at A3.

23. Adapted from Christopher F. Polk, Alternative Sentencing Plan, Office of the Jefferson District Public Defender, Inc., reprinted with permission.

24. Kevin McNally, *Capital Punishment: Present State of the Law and Trends*, KATA Criminal Law Seminar, Oct. 16, 1992, Louisville, KY.

25. Kalpana Srinivasan, *Offenders Serve More Time in Prison, Government Reports*, THE RICHMOND REGISTER, Jan. 11, 1999, at A3.

26. *Changing Trends in Prisoner Petitions Filings*, THE THIRD BRANCH, Dec. 1999, at 7.

27. SCHEB, *supra* note 3, at 586–87.

28. RICHARD T. OAKES, OAKES' CRIMINAL PRACTICE GUIDE, §§ 19–36 (1991).

29. SCHEB, *supra* note 3, at 598.

GLOSSARY

Accessory: one guilty of complicity either before or after the crime.

Accessory after the fact: one who was not present at the scene of the crime, but who knowingly gave assistance to the criminal after the crime (common law).

Accessory before the fact: one who is not present at the scene of the crime, but who provided means or advice before its commission (common law).

Accomplice: one who aids and abets the primary actor through encouragement or active involvement in the commission of a crime.

Acquit: to find not guilty of a crime.

Actus reus: wrongful or guilty act.

Admission: the defendant's acknowledgment of a fact that helps prove the crime but does not reach the level of a confession.

Adversary system: a highly competitive issue-resolving process in which two opposing sides attempt to provide the best information they can to convince the neutral tribunal of judge or jury to decide the issue in their favor.

Affirmative defense: matter separate from the elements of the crime that is raised by the defense to counteract those elements.

Allocution: the defendant's due process right to speak in his or her own behalf.

Amnesty: pardon offered to a group.

Anticipatory search warrant: a search warrant issued on the basis of a predictable or inevitable future event, the occurrence of which is needed to form the probable cause for the warrant.

Appeal by right: appeal to the court level just above the trial court; permission not necessary.

Arraignment: an appearance before the judge where the charges, as they stand after the preliminary hearing or the grand jury, are read and a plea is entered.

Arrest: the physical or implied seizure or taking into custody of a person by police, significantly restricting a person's freedom of movement and subjecting him or her to the authority of the officer.

Arrest warrant: a document that, when signed by a judge or magistrate, authorizes the police to seek and place the defendant in custody.

Asportation: the removal of the victim from a place of security to one of greater danger in kidnapping; removal of goods in theft.

Attorney General Opinions: a set of formal opinions used as persuasive authority in the argument of criminal cases in that state.

Attorney work product: trial preparation materials consisting of the attorney's mental impressions, conclusions, opinions, and legal theories concerning a case.

Bail: the amount of money or property that a defendant must post to be released; assurance to the court that the defendant will return to court when required to do so.

Bailee: an employee or agent caring for the property of another.

Beyond a reasonable doubt: the burden of proof borne by the state in a criminal trial; proof of sufficient weight to exclude any other reasonable explanation than the defendant's guilt.

Bill of particulars: a document provided by the prosecution upon request from the defense, detailing the when, where, and how of the crime charged in the indictment.

Bind over: the process of transferring a case to the next court for the succeeding stage in the process.

Blue sky laws: state laws that criminalize making false statements in the required registration of securities.

Book: to record basic information, possibly including fingerprints, from a suspect.

Burden of persuasion: the responsibility to convince on all the elements of the claim.

Burden of production: the responsibility to introduce an affirmative defense and the credible evidence to support it.

Canon law: law of the church that preserved significant aspects of Roman and other law through the Middle Ages.

Capital crime: a crime for which a person can receive the death penalty.

Causation: the link between the intent, the act, and the harm.

Challenge for cause: an attorney's request to remove a potential juror on the grounds of bias or other reason.

Circumstantial evidence: evidence from the situations surrounding the event that leads us to believe a person thought and acted in a manner consistent or inconsistent with the alleged wrongful act; indirect evidence proving a point by inference.

Civil law: law that defines the rights of individuals in their relationships with other individuals and establishes a process for righting wrongs, mainly through monetary reimbursement.

Claim of right: defense to theft; belief by the defendant that the property actually belongs to the defendant.

Clear and convincing evidence: less than beyond a reasonable doubt but greater than a preponderance of evidence.

Collateral estoppel: doctrine preventing the retrial of significant issue when it was determined by a previous judgment.

Common law: traditional law originating in England, recorded in judicial opinions rather than legislative statutes.

Complainant: the person swearing out a complaint.

Complaint: the document that officially starts the prosecution, provides a basis for arrest or notifies the accused to come to court, and informs the accused of the specific crime charged.

Concurrence: in the context of the components of a crime, the logical and consistent connection that must exist between the perpetrator's wrongful intent and the wrongful act, and between the wrongful intent and the resulting harm, for criminal liability to attach.

Confession: the defendant's acknowledgment of guilt.

Constructive possession: possession but not physical control of property.

Conversion: misappropriation for one's own use, as in embezzlement.

Corporate liability: culpability of a corporation for the criminal act of one of its representatives.

Corpus delicti: the "body of the crime"; proof that loss or injury occurred as the result of someone's criminal conduct.

Criminal law: the branch of law that identifies conduct subject to prosecution and penalty by the state, and the procedure by which it is carried out.

Curtilage: the area of land, enclosed or otherwise, around a house or other buildings that is used for domestic purposes.

Cybercrime: crime involving computers as targets, tools, and incidental factors.

Demonstrative evidence: audiovisual aid designed to enhance the jury's understanding of the evidence.

De novo: review of both the questions of fact and the questions of law in an appellate case.

Deterrence: the prevention of crime as a goal of punishment.

   General deterrence: prevention of crime in society as a whole; to bring about conformity with society's norms by identifying bad conduct.

   Individual (specific) deterrence: incapacitation or punishment to prevent criminals from repeating as offenders.

Direct evidence: evidence based on a witness's firsthand knowledge that proves a fact in issue without relying on inference or other evidence.

Direct examination: the questioning of a witness by the attorney for the party that called the witness.

Direct submission: bypassing the preliminary hearing and submitting a case directly to the grand jury.

Discovery: the process of requesting from and disclosing to opponents information pertinent to the trial of a case.

Discretionary appeal: appeal to higher-level courts; permission necessary, such as the writ of certiorari from the Supreme Court.

Docket: the court schedule for each day; sets out the name of the case, the attorneys, the charge, and the nature of the appearance.

Due process: Fifth and Fourteenth Amendment right not to be deprived of life, liberty, or property without a process that is fundamentally fair and just.

   Procedural due process:

   Substantive due process: a restraint on government prohibiting laws that are too vague, overbroad, unreasonable, arbitrary, or capricious.

Elements: those specific requirements enumerated in statutes or common law that define a particular offense.

Evanescent evidence: criminal evidence that will change or evaporate in a manner that will destroy its evidentiary value.

Ex post facto **laws:** laws that are passed after the act is committed.

Exculpatory evidence: evidence that is inconsistent with guilt, raises doubt about evidence of guilt, or diminishes guilt; evidence favorable to the defendant or information that leads to evidence that is favorable to the defendant.

Extradition: the process that provides for a fugitive from justice from one state to be arrested in another state and be returned to the original state for trial

Federalism: the relationship between the national government and each state, and the relationship among states.

Felony: the most serious crime; requires a minimum of one year in a state or federal prison (not a county jail).

Fighting words: speech likely to provoke violence, not protected by the Constitution.

General intent: intent to commit the act itself, but not necessarily to cause the results.

Grand jury: a body of citizens that hears evidence regarding possible criminal activity and decides whether that evidence is sufficient to bring an accused to trial; serves the same function as the preliminary hearing.

Habeas corpus, writ of: prevents incarceration without justification; requires law enforcement to present the individual before a judge to determine whether the person has been fairly convicted and incarcerated.

Harm: actual damage, injury, or loss that must occur as the result of the act for that act to be considered criminal.

Harmless error: trivial error not prejudicial to the rights of the party; does not affect the outcome of the case.

Hate crime: a crime motivated by bias against the victim's race, religion, sexual orientation, or other status.

Hearsay testimony: testimony at trial or hearing based on the account of someone other than the witness offering the testimony.

Hot pursuit: the chasing of a suspect or the following of "hot" leads to the suspect.

Immunity: a prosecutor's binding promise that a person will not be prosecuted for certain crimes in exchange for helping to convict others with testimony that, except for the immunity, would incriminate that person of those crimes.

    Transactional immunity: immunizes the witness for incriminating statements about the crime at issue as well as other crimes.

    Use immunity: restricted to any statements or fruits from those statements that are incriminating as to the crime at issue.

Impeachment: attack on a witness's credibility, showing inconsistent statements.

Imperfect defense: one that tends to allow conviction on a reduced charge.

Incriminating testimony: that which provides evidence needed to prosecute.

Indictment: criminal charging document produced by the grand jury.

Indigent: not having the financial means to hire a lawyer.

Information: criminal charging document produced by a preliminary hearing.

Initial appearance: first court appearance where the judge informs the accused of the charges and basic rights to an attorney and to remain silent, and sets bail.

Insider trading: use of confidential knowledge about a corporation in the purchase or sale of stocks in that corporation.

Intake (prosecutor's office): the receipt and initial evaluation of accusations to determine whether charges are appropriate and whether formal documents should be drafted and filed.

Intangible property: "choses in action"; property not valuable in itself but that conveys value, such as checks, bonds, and promissory notes.

Interlocutory appeal: an appellate court review of an issue that does not determine guilt or innocence but is necessary or useful to have decided prior to going to trial.

Jeopardy: the danger presented by a court proceeding that may result in punishment.

Judgment of guilt and sentence: the document entered by the court after sentencing from which the defendant may appeal.

Jury nullification (jury pardon): the right of a jury to find a defendant not guilty even though the law and evidence dictate otherwise.

Knowingly: to be aware that a specific type of conduct will almost certainly bring about a particular result, but without necessarily intending that or a related result; a state of awareness that a certain fact or circumstance exists.

Last conspirator defense: if all coconspirators have been acquitted or had charges dropped, the last defendant is released from prosecution.

Law: a set of formal rules enacted by government officials that governs the relationships among citizens, businesses, government, and nations for the purpose of maintaining society and preventing chaos.

Leading question: one that attempts to influence the witness by suggesting the answer.

Legal advice: independent professional judgment based on knowledge of the law and given for the benefit of a particular client; may be offered only by an attorney.

Legal precedent *(stare decisis):* a previous court decision that serves as an authority in a subsequent case with similar issues in question.

Lesser included offense (or necessarily included offense): one whose elements are all included among the elements of the more serious crime that is being charged.

Lesser related offense: one that does not meet the requirements of a lesser included offense, but bears a substantial relationship to the charged offense.

Magna Carta: English document signed in 1215 that established the principles of fair procedure and protections for the accused that are still cornerstones in our criminal justice system.

Mala in se: inherently evil or obvious wrongs generally accepted by most societies throughout time as serious crimes.

Mala prohibita: crimes not inherently evil but sufficiently bad to have been prohibited by law.

Marital exception: disallows prosecution of husbands for rape of their wives.

Material: topically important to a matter in issue.

Mens rea: a wrongful state of mind or the intent to commit a crime.

Misdemeanor: lesser crime than a felony; penalties include fines and up to one year in a county jail (as opposed to prison).

Mitigating circumstances: favorable points about the defendant; not defenses, but possibly influencing a lighter sentence.

Model Penal Code and Commentaries: a guide by the American Law Institute to reform and unify criminal law in the United States.

Motive: the reason behind the intent.

National Communication Information Center (NCIC): an arm of the FBI that keeps criminal records on persons who have been charged with or convicted of felonies.

Negligently: thoughtlessly or carelessly creating a significant unjustifiable risk of harm without realizing the risk has been created or without the intent to create the risk, yet the act is such that a reasonable person would have known that the act created such a risk.

Notice: prior warning that specified conduct is prohibited.

Omission: failure to act.

Open fields: the resident's lands beyond the curtilage and, therefore, not protected by the Fourth Amendment.

Opening statement: the initial presentation made by the attorneys to the jury, giving an overview of the case and the evidence to be presented.

Parole: release awarded to prison inmates after they serve some of their prison sentence.

Percent bond: release after posting a specified percentage, usually 10 percent, of a cash bond.

Peremptory challenge: authority of an attorney to strike the name of a potential juror without having to express any reason for the strike; limited in number.

Perfect defense: one that leads to the dropping of charges or acquittal, if successful.

Personal recognizance: release on a promise to return to court at the next scheduled appearance.

Petty offense: one having a maximum penalty not to exceed six months' incarceration.

Plain error: obvious error that merits appellate reversal even if not objected to at trial.

Plea bargain: negotiated settlement where the prosecutor reduces the charge, number of charges, or the recommended sentence in return for the defendant's plea of guilty.

Police power: the government's authority to enact laws to promote public health, safety, morals and welfare, and, pursuant thereto, to establish police departments and prevent crimes.

Possession: the acquisition of something and then the failure to get rid of it.

Actual possession: the object is on the person, under direct physical control, or within reach.

Constructive possession: knowledge of where an item is and control of that area.

Predicate offense: a component crime that is the objective of a collective crime such as a RICO or CCE offense.

Preliminary hearing: court appearance to determine if there is probable cause to believe that the defendant has committed the crime as charged.

Preponderance of the evidence: the greater weight of all the evidence.

Presumption: a rule of law that requires the trier of fact to conclude on threshold evidence that an ultimate fact is true.

Irrebuttable presumption: requires that the ultimate fact be treated as true once the threshold evidence has been introduced.

Rebuttable presumption: the ultimate fact can be shown not to be true by other evidence.

Pretrial conference: a meeting of the judge with opposing parties to ensure an efficient and fair processing of the case, encourage plea negotiations, and narrow the issues to be tried.

Prima facie case: enough evidence on each element of the crime, absent any evidence of refutation, to conclude that the defendant is guilty.

Principal: one having participation in and responsibility for a crime.

Principal in the first degree: one who committed the crime directly or caused it through the manipulation of an innocent agent (common law).

Principal in the second degree: one who was not directly involved in the crime itself but was present to give aid (common law).

Pro bono: provision of free legal services to the poor.

Pro se (pro per) **representation:** self-representation by the defendant.

Probable cause: reasonable grounds for belief; "more than a bare suspicion" and "less than evidence that would justify . . . conviction."

Probation: a judicial sentence that permits a convicted person to remain free as long as that person meets the conditions imposed by the court.

Procedural criminal law: the rules that the prosecution, the defense, and the courts must follow for the step-by-step processing of a person from accusation to sentencing and appeal.

Procedural due process: requirement that the steps in a criminal proceeding be fundamentally fair, assuring to some degree of certitude that justification exists for arrest, prosecution, and punishment.

Professional ethics: rules of conduct that govern the practice of that profession.

Proportionality: the attempt to balance the severity of the punishment with the severity of the crime.

Proximate cause: the act that is most closely and directly responsible for the injury.

Purposely: intending to accomplish a specific result.

Quash: void an unreasonable demand.

Rape shield law: statute that prevents evidence of the victim's prior sexual activity from being introduced in court, unless it is relevant to consent.

Recidivism: repeat offenses.

Recklessly: knowing that there is a substantial and unjustifiable risk that conduct might cause a particular result but not intending the harmful result.

Redirect examination: the questioning of the witness by the party that called the witness to undo or limit any damage done during cross-examination.

Rehabilitation: the objective of criminal law to reform criminals and give them the ability to compete in society.

Relevant: proving or disproving a material fact.

Res ipsa loquitur: Latin for "the thing speaks for itself"; the act, standing alone, reveals criminal intent.

Respondeat superior: the employer is responsible for the acts of the employee carrying out the employer's business.

Restitution: a payment to the individual victim of the crime, a return of the value that was wrongfully taken.

Retribution: an expressed purpose of punishment reflecting the concept of just desserts.

Rule of law: the principle that all people and organizations, both governmental and private, in a nation or state must obey the established laws rather than be above the law or conduct their lives and business any way they choose.

Sentence: assessment of penalty for a crime.

Concurrent sentence: in the case of multiple crimes, sentences to be served at the same time.

Consecutive sentence: in the case of multiple crimes, sentences to be served one after the other.

Definite or determinate sentence: fixed terms chosen from the range allowed by statute and guidelines; no parole.

Sentence enhancements: automatic additions to the basic sentence for certain circumstances making the crime or the criminal more dangerous to society.

Indefinite sentence: a maximum and minimum amount of time to be served, allowing for early release on parole if behavior goals have been reached.

Indeterminate sentence: flexible prison terms responding to the defendant's progress toward rehabilitation; largely abandoned.

Mandatory sentence: statutory minimum prison terms with no chance for either probation or parole.

Presumptive sentence: the midway point of the sentencing range.

Suspended sentence: sentence that is replaced by probation.

Six Ws: interview questions: Who? When? What? Why? Where? and How?

Specific intent: carrying out an act for the purpose of achieving the resulting harm.

Stare decisis: let the decision stand, precedent.

State action: conduct of state, its employees, and agents.

Status: who one is rather than what one has done.

Statutory rape: unforced sexual intercourse with an underage child.

Stop and frisk (investigatory detention): a brief investigatory stop occurring when a police officer confronts a suspicious looking person to ask a few questions and to "pat down" their clothing to see if they are carrying weapons.

Strict liability: requires a wrongful act only; the state of mind is irrelevant.

Sua sponte: on its own responsibility, voluntarily.

Subpoena duces tecum: command to appear in court with specified documents.

Substantive criminal law: definitions of crimes and principles governing punishment.

Summary trial: for minor charges, a brief judicial inquiry of the suspect and the police to determine guilt.

Summons, criminal: a document that, when signed by the clerk of court and served on the defendant, requires the defendant to appear before the stated court at the prescribed date and time.

Supervening or superseding cause: a new and independent act of a third person or another force that breaks the causal connection between the original wrong and the injury and that is the proximate cause of the injury.

Supervised release: release under the supervision of a probation or pretrial release officer or, in some cases, to the custody of a third party.

Surety or cash bond: release after surrendering to the clerk of court a specified sum of money or evidence of ownership of property sufficient to cover the amount of the bond in case of forfeiture.

Surreptitious remaining: entering an area lawfully but staying beyond a lawful time without permission, such as in a store after closing hours.

Tangible property: property that is valuable in itself, such as a cow or a coin.

Trade secrets: formulas, patterns, devices, processes, or compilations of information that give companies an advantage over their competitors.

Transferred intent: a legal device that holds one criminally liable for the harm to a person other than the intended victim.

Unilateral conspiracy: one person agreeing with another, rather than an agreement between two or more persons; allows for the prosecution of the single culpable conspirator.

Unsecured bond (personal bond): release under a signed obligation to pay the court a specified sum of money in the event the defendant fails to appear.

Venire: the list of eligible persons from which jurors are summoned for duty; must be a "fair cross-section" of the community.

Vicarious liability: culpability of one person for the criminal act of another.

Violation: noncriminal offense, such as traffic violations and public drunkenness, for which the city, county, or state may only fine the offender.

Voir dire: to speak the truth; the in-court questioning of jurors by the judge and the attorneys to screen jurors based on the juror's bias or other reasons for inability to serve; means to attain an impartial jury.

Wantonly: maliciously or arrogantly disregarding the known risk to the rights or safety of others.

Wharton's Rule: there is no added danger in numbers justifying a charge of conspiracy in crimes requiring the participation of two persons, unless a third person participates.

White-collar crime: nonviolent crimes that usually have financial or regulation avoidance motives, such as embezzlement, extortion, computer crimes, and fraud.

Writ of certiorari: an order by the appellate court having discretion that it will hear an appeal.

Spanish Equivalents for Important Legal Terms in English

Accessory after the fact: Quien ayuda a encubrir el delito o al criminal.

Accessory before the fact: Quien ayuda a preparar la comision del delito.

Accomplice: Complice. Una persona que provoca o facilita, con conocimiento de causa, la realizacion de un hecho o delito.

Acquit: Absolver. Exonerar. Liberar de una culpa u obligacion.

Actus reus: el acto criminal o culpable.

Admission: Admision.

Adversary system: Sistima adversario.

Affirmative defense: defensa afirmativa.

Allocution: Alocucion, discurso.

Arraignment: Acusacion, denuncia.

Arrest: Arresto.

Arrest warrant: Orden de arresto.

Asportation: Extraccion. Tomar o llevarse cosas ilegalmente.

Attorney General Opinions: Opinión solicitada del procurador o fiscal del Estado sobre la interpretación de una ley o estatuto.

Bail: Fianza.

Beyond a reasonable doubt: Mas alla de una duda razonable.

Bill of Particulars: Explicacion minuciosa de los hechos que fundan la demanda solicitada por el demandado.

Bind over: Libertad bajo fianza.

Book: Proceso de registrar en los archivos policíacos a un delincuente.

Burden of production: La obligación de presentar las pruebas suficientes para que la corte no falle contra el demandante y el caso prosiga.

Canon law: Derecho canónico.

Causation: El hacho que hace que algo ocurra o suceda.

Challenge for cause: cuando se excluye a un individuo como miembro del jurado por alguna causa.

Circumstantial evidence: Prueba o evidencia circunstancial, no basada en observaciones directas del hecho que se quiere probar.

Civil law: Derecho civil.

Claim of right: el que actúa como dueño de una propiedad, aunque no lo sea, con intensión de seguir en posesión de ella.

Clear and convincing evidence: Prueba clara y convincente.

Collateral estoppel: Prohibición de tomar una acción o posición en una corte cuando dicha acción o posición ha sido rechazada en otra corte.

Common law: derecho consuetudinario; derecho Anglosajón.

Complainant: Demandante, querellante, acusador.

Complaint: Demanda, querella.

Confession: Confesion.

Conversion: Apropiacion indebida.

Corporate liability: responsabilidad civil de una corporación algún por acto de sus empleados o de la misma corporación.

Criminal law: Ley criminal, que trata con el proceso judicial penal.

Curtilage: término que describe un área y las estructuras alrededor de una casa, normalmente definida por una cerca.

Demonstrative evidence: Evidencia demonstrativa.

Deterrence: cualquiera cosa que tiende a prevenir un crimen.

General Deterrence: algo de carácter general que tiende a prevenir un crimen; como las reglas de conducta en la sociedad.

Individual (specific) deterrence: algo de carácter especifico que tiende a prevenir un crimen—como una sentencia o castigo.

Direct evidence: Prueba directa.

Direct examination: Interrogación directa.

Direct submission: El proceder directamente a presentarle el caso a un gran jurado sin una audiencia preliminar.

Discovery: Descubrimiento.

Docket: Lista de casos que esperan juicio o audiencia.

Due process: Doctrina constitucional que proteje a cada cuidadano contra acciones arbitrarias y que requiere un proceso legal antes de despojar a alguien de algun bien o derecho.

Substantive Due Process: Restricción que se le impone al gobierno para que las leyes no sean ambiguas, generales, irrazonables, arbitrarias y caprichosas.

Evanescent evidence: evidencia criminal que cambia o se evapora al pasar el tiempo.

Exculpatory evidence: Evidencia exculpatoria.

Ex post facto **laws:** leyes que se crean después de un acto, haciendo a éste acto criminal.

Extradition: Extradición.

Felony crimen: delito grave.

General intent: una intención hacer un acto, aunque no se hay querido causar el resultado de ese acto.

Grand jury: Gran jurado.

Habeas corpus, writ of: Proceso judicial para prevenir el encarcelamiento sin justificación; normalmente requiere presentarle el caso y sus bases a un juez.

Hot pursuit: Persecucion inminente de un criminal o delincuente.

Immunity: Inmunidad.

Transactional immunity: imunidad ofrecida a un testigo por su testimonio, que se extiende a otras violaciones reveladas durante sus violaciones

Use immunity: Imunidad en el uso de cualquier información revelada cuando el testigo ha recibido un acuerdo de inmunidad.

Impeach: Impugnar.

Imperfect defense: una defensa imperfecta o defectuosa, que puede resultar en una condena por un crimen menor.

Incriminating testimony: testimonio incriminatorio que prueba un crimen.

Indictment: Encausamiento; procesamiento; sumario.

Indigent: Indigente; pobre.

Information: Acusación

Initial appearance: una apariencia inicial, donde se le informa al acusado de sus derechos de mantener silencio y a ser representado por un abogado.

Intake: el proceso del fiscal en recibir y evaluar un caso para ver si tiene mérito.

Intangible property: propiedad intangible, que no tiene valor propiamente pero que conlleva valor, como un cheque.

Interlocutory appeal: Apelación inicial, no para determinar si el acusado es culpable o no, pero para determinar puntos legales necesarios para que el caso sea juzgado.

Judgment of guilt and sentence: Documento donde se dicta el fallo de la corte y la sentencia del culpable.

Jury nullification (jury pardon): derecho del jurado de fallar a favor del acusado aunque la ley y la evidencia amerite culpabilidad.

Knowlingly: A sabiendas. Con conocimiento completo e intencional.

Law: ley; derecho.

Leading question: Una pregunta que le sugiere al testigo cómo debe contestarla.

Legal advice: consejo de un abogado a su cliente en base a la ley y para la protección del cliente.

Legal precedent (*stare decisis*): (lat.) acatar las decisiones, observar los precedentes.

Magna Carta: Carta Magna. El documento firmado por el Rey inglés en 1215 que definía y concedía derechos básicos por primera vez en Inglaterra.

Mala in se: (Lat.) Malo por su naturaleza propia. Moralmente malo.

Mala prohibita: (Lat.) crímenes comunes que han sido codificados.

Mens rea: la condición mental de uno que tiene intención de cometer un crimen.

Misdemeanor: Delito meno.

Mitigating circumstances: Circunstancias atenuantes.

Model Penal Code and Commentaries: propuesta por el American Law Institute para reformar y unificar a las leyes criminales de los Estados Unidos.

National Communication Information Center (NCIC): dependencia del FBI que mantiene récords de criminales o acusados.

Negligently: el actuar en una forma inconsecuente que crea una gran posibilidad de daño, aunque no realice ese posibilidad, pero que una persona razonable percibiría.

Notice: Noticia.

Omission: el no actuar.

Open fields: los terrenos vacíos alrededor de la casa y sus estructuras vecinas y los cuales no están protegidos por la Cuarta Enmienda de la Constitución de los Estados Unidos.

Opening statement: Exposición inicial del caso.

Parole: Libertad condicional o bajo palabra.

Percent bond: la libertad condicional después de poner un porcentaje de la fianza en efectivo.

Peremptory challenge: durante el proceso de seleccionar al jurado, derecho de excluir del jurado a uno de sus miembros sin necesidad de tener causa. Normalmente se escogen a un numero mayor de personas para después selecciona a un numero menor que forman el jurado (entre 6 y 12 personas)

Perfect defense: una defensa que resulta en un veredicto de inocente si es exitosa.

Personal recognizance: cuando una persona se libera condicionalmente y sin fianza, prometiendo aparecer en la corte en la fecha fijada.

Petty offense: una ofensa cuya sentencia no excede seis meses.

Plea bargaining: regateo por un alegato.

Possession: posesion.

> **Actual Possession:** artículos que están bajo la posesión de la persona, o accesibles.

> **Constructive Possession:** conocimiento de donde esta algo y control sobre éste.

Predicates: crímenes que forman parte de un patrón de crímenes colectivos.

Preliminary hearing: Audiencia o vista preliminar.

Preponderance of the evidence: Preponderancia de la prueba.

Presumption: Presunción, suposición, conjetura.

> **Irrebuttable presumption:** Que una vez probado un hecho, un supuesto está establecido, por ejemplo, un niño de cinco años no puede cometer un crimen.

> **Rebuttable presumption:** Suposición que puede ser refutada al probar lo contrario.

Pretrial conference: conferencia entre los abogados, las partes y el juez para determinar los puntos legales necesarios para seguir adelante con un enjuiciamiento o una resolución del caso (regateo por un alegato).

Prima facie case: cuando la evidencia, si no es negada, satisface los elementos necesarios para una condena.

Principal: Principal.

> **Principal in the first degree:** uno que comete un crimen directamente o que manipula a otros para tal efecto.

Principal in the second degree: uno que no comete el crimen directamente pero que ayuda en su ejecución.

Pro bono: (Lat.) Para el bienestar público.

Probable cause: Causa presunta; motivo fundado.

Probation: Libertad condicional.

Stop and frisk: Detener y registrar a una persona sospechosa que puede estar armada.

Strict liability: Responsabilidad ojetiva.

Subpoena duces tecum: (Lat.) Citación para comparecer y producir documentos.

Substantive criminal law: Los principios legales que rigen la ley criminal y los elementos necesarios para probar cada crimen.

Summary trial: para cargos menores, un procedimiento rápido con el acusado y la policía para determinar culpabilidad.

Summons, criminal: Convocatoria criminal.

Supervised release: la libertad condicional bajo la supervisión de un oficial judicial.

Surety or cash bond: Bono de garantía; figura de causión.

Surreptitious remaining: el entrar en una propiedad legalmente, pero el abusar de esa entrada quedándose mas tiempo de lo debido—por ejemplo, después de que cierra el negocio.

Tangible property: bienes corpóreos.

Transferred intent: doctrina legal que dice que si uno quiso causar daño a alguien y otro resulta herido, la intención criminal esta presente en ambos casos.

Unilateral conspiracy: cuando una persona esta de acuerdo con las acciones criminales de otro, en vez de un acuerdo en conspiración, esta persona puede ser culpable como conspirador.

Unsecured bond (personal bond): el acuerdo personal de un acusado con la corte de pagar una suma si no se presenta el acusado ante la corte en una fecha fija.

Venire: (Lat.) Venir; comparecer en corte.

Vicarious liability: Responsabilidad vicaria.

Violation: Violación, infracción, atropello.

Voir dire: Decir la verdad.

Wantonly: un acto caracterizado por una actitud arrogante y maliciosa hacia los derechos o la seguridad de otros.

Wharton's Rule: regla legal que no hay una conspiración si el crimen necesita a dos personas para su ejecución, a no ser que una tercera persona participe.

SYSTEM FOLDER CONTENTS

The list of system folder contents follows the text and the system folder assignments. It is a suggested list only. A good system folder has a table of contents, for which this list can be used, or a tab system for the quick location of any part of the system. Expand the system as you choose to accommodate local practice forms or alternative methods of practice. **(Practical time restraints may dictate that some or all of the summaries or outlines of the law and rules referred to in the system folder assignments be reduced to short lists of citations to applicable statutes, rules, and cases. References to pertinent pages in the text can be a useful time saver for students intending to keep the text.)**

I. Preliminary and frequently used information (Chapters 1 and 2)
    A. Important office personnel, procedures, and policies
    B. Court diagrams including criminal law jurisdiction
    C. Diagram of steps in criminal process (adapted to local practice)
    D. Key persons in applicable criminal justice system with appropriate titles and contact information.
    E. Professional development and other resources
        1. Applicable paralegal association information
        2. State prosecutor and/or criminal defense associations and other helpful resource organizations or agencies
    F. Rules of ethics summary and sources
    G. Web sites
II. Applicable principles of mens rea, actus reus, and other concepts (Chapter 3)
    A. Your state definitions (plus statute numbers) and your examples of transferred intent, general intent, specific intent, purposely, knowingly, recklessly, wanton, negligently, strict liability, and lesser included offense
    B. Summary of the applicable law regarding actus reus: acts, voluntary and involuntary; omissions, possession, and status
    C. Your state definitions (plus statute numbers) of principal, accomplice, and accessory
    D. State law governing whether and how vicarious responsibility applied

III. Crimes against persons and habitation: Chart on crimes and elements (Chapter 4)
   A. State statutes added to crimes and elements chart, Exhibit 4–3
   B. Revised listing of elements of each crime to reflect your state law
   C. Web sites

IV. Crimes against property, public order and safety, public morals, and justice and public administration: Chart on crimes and elements (Chapter 5)
   A. State statutes added to crimes and elements chart, Exhibit 5–7.
   B. Revised listing of elements of each crime to reflect your state law
   C. Web sites

V. Inchoate and organized crimes (Chapter 6)
   A. Summary of proximity tests for attempt (tests in your state and statutes)
   B. Conspiracy
      1. State statute on conspiracy requirements
      2. Requirement of bilateral or unilateral agreement
      3. Last conspirator defense in your state
   C. Inchoate crimes chart, Exhibit 6–4 with state elements, statutes, and case law added
   D. Organized crimes chart, Exhibit 6–5 with state elements, statutes, and case law added
   E. Web sites

VI. Defenses (Chapter 7)
   A. State's age limits of juvenile court jurisdiction (statutes)
   B. State's criteria for transferring a juvenile case to adult criminal court (statute)
   C. Chart on defenses, Exhibit 7–5 with the following added
      1. State's burden of proof on each defense (statutes, key case law, sample jury instructions)
      2. State's use of objective or subjective test for self-defense, duress, necessity, entrapment, and mistake (statutes, key case law, sample jury instructions)
      3. List of syndromes ruled admissible in your state (key case law, sample jury instructions)
   D. Web sites

VII. Intake and drafting of the complaint (Chapter 8)
   A. Standardized and/or office intake form
   B. Forms and eligibility information on state compensation of crime victims
   C. List of state and national resources for crime victims
   D. Checklist for intake (prosecution)
   E. Developed checklist or guidelines for drafting a complaint
      1. Sample complaint form
      2. Sample completed complaint form
   F. Checklist for drafting and filing the summons and warrant
      1. Sample completed summons
      2. Sample completed warrant
   G. Web sites

VIII. Search and seizure (Chapter 9)
   A. Summary of property protected from unwarranted searches and key cases
   B. Summary of property not protected from unwarranted searches and key cases
   C. Checklist: when a warrant is needed

D. List of elements needed for legal search warrant and supporting affidavit and what must be avoided (*Murray*)

E. Summary of requirements for when a warrant is needed for an arrest in your state (relevant state statutes, state constitutional provisions, and digest cases)

F. Sample forms: search warrant and affidavit, and completed search warrant and affidavit

G. Summary of your state law and key cases on application of "good faith" exception to the exclusionary rule

H. Chart on exceptions to warrant requirement, Exhibit 9–3 with added state cases that differ from United States Supreme Court decisions

I. Web sites

IX. Confessions and pretrial identification (Chapter 10)

A. Summary of *Miranda* rules and subsequent pertinent decisions on self-incrimination and the right to an attorney at interrogation plus key decisions from your state

B. Sample documents: motion to suppress and response to motion to suppress, including any motions drafted for class

C. List of guidelines for proper lineups and other forms of pretrial identification, including key cases (state and Supreme Court).

D. Web sites

X. Pretrial procedure (Chapter 11)

A. Pretrial release (bail)
1. Key federal and state rules on pretrial release and detention, including when the court can deny bail (key cases)
2. Key federal and state rules and statutes on pretrial release services
3. Summary of types of bail available in your jurisdiction (key statutes)
4. Bail forms: current state bail schedule, United States District Court release order, and relevant pretrial interview form

B. Initial appearance
1. Key rule, and/or statute and case law on when it must be held
2. Checklist for initial appearance
3. List of conditions for release for use at initial appearance
4. Note on how to obtain criminal records

C. Preliminary hearing
1. Key federal and state rules and/or statutes on the preliminary hearing: requirement of, when it must be held (time limits), use for discovery, burden of proof, bind over, and recharging
2. Interview checklists with your own additions and tips on dealing with difficult clients
3. Checklist of tasks to prepare for the preliminary hearing, including question-drafting tips

D. Web sites

XI. Grand jury to pretrial conference (Chapter 12)

A. Grand jury
1. Key federal and state rules of procedure on grand jury practice
2. Checklist: paralegal tasks for grand jury
3. Forms and documents: sample local grand jury docket, grand jury subpoena, indictment, motion for bill of particulars, motion to dismiss indictment, and forms completed for class

B. Arraignment

        1. Key federal and state rules of procedure on arraignment

        2. Checklist: paralegal tasks for arraignment

    C. Discovery

        1. Summary of federal and state rules of procedure on discovery (key cases)

        2. Checklist: discovery

        3. Forms: motion for discovery and response to motion for discovery

    D. Pretrial motions

        1. Key federal and state rules, including time limits, on pretrial motion practice

        2. Forms: pretrial motion(s), response

    E. Plea bargaining: key rules regarding plea bargaining, especially any rules or case law on withdrawal or change of plea if court rejects plea agreement

    F. Web sites

XII. Trial (Chapter 13)

    A. Outline of trial notebook sections

    B. Outline of preparing, assisting, and supervising witnesses

    C. Voir dire

        1. Outline of tips and tasks for paralegal preparing for and at voir dire

        2. Forms: jury attitude survey, instructions, and questions

    D. Evidence

        1. Outline of most significant federal and state rules of evidence

        2. Definitions (jury instructions) and key cases on proof beyond a reasonable doubt, direct evidence, circumstantial evidence, presumptions, privileges, and other significant evidentiary concepts

        3. Federal and state rules regarding admissibility of scientific and expert testimony and suggested lines of inquiry

    E. Suggestions for maximizing juror attention

    F. Trial steps reference guide: subsections in this part of system folder for each trial and posttrial step. For each subsection: define the step, add key federal and state rules of procedure, list paralegal tasks and tips, and insert relevant sample documents

    G. Web sites

XIII. Sentencing, punishment, and review (Chapter 14)

    A. Sentencing and punishment

        1. Death penalty statute(s) for your state, if applicable, with list of mitigating and aggravating circumstances

        2. Summary of sentencing procedure in your state (key rules and statutes): indefinite or definite sentencing, mandatory sentences, and enhancements

        3. List of property subject to forfeiture in your state, defenses to forfeiture (statutes)

        4. Pointers for preparing an alternative sentencing plan

        5. Outline of sentencing procedure, key rules, and statutes

        6. Forms: sample presentence report, alternative sentencing plan, and judgment of sentence of probation

        7. Summary of state and federal law regarding probation and parole revocation

        8. Summary of law on prisoner rights

B. Review
   1. Summary of federal and your state law and rules of procedure on appeals
   2. Outline of steps in appellate procedure
   3. Forms: federal and state notice of appeal, affidavit in support of motion to proceed on appeal *in forma pauperis,* application for writ of habeas corpus
   4. Outline of steps in habeas corpus procedure
C. Web sites

EXCERPTS FROM THE CONSTITUTION OF THE UNITED STATES OF AMERICA

We the People of the United States, in Order to form a more perfect Union, establish Justice, insure domestic Tranquility, provide for the common defence, promote the general Welfare, and secure the Blessings of Liberty to ourselves and our Posterity, do ordain and establish this Constitution for the United States of America.

ARTICLE I

Section 1 All legislative Powers herein granted shall be vested in a Congress of the United States, which shall consist of a Senate and House of Representatives.

. . .

Section 8 (1) The Congress shall have Power To lay and collect Taxes, Duties, Imposts and Excises, to pay the Debts and provide for the common Defence and general Welfare of the United States; but all Duties, Imposts and Excises shall be uniform throughout the United States;

(2) To borrow Money on the credit of the United States;

(3) To regulate Commerce with foreign Nations, and among the several States, and with the Indian Tribes;

(4) To establish an uniform Rule of Naturalization, and uniform Laws on the subject of Bankruptcies throughout the United States;

(5) To coin Money, regulate the Value thereof, and of foreign Coin, and to fix the Standard of Weights and Measures;

(6) To provide for the Punishment of counterfeiting the Securities and current Coin of the United States;

(7) To establish Post Offices and post Roads;

(8) To promote the Progress of Science and useful Arts, by securing for limited Times to Authors and Inventors the exclusive Right to their respective Writings and Discoveries;

(9) To constitute Tribunals inferior to the supreme Court;

(10) To define and punish Piracies and Felonies committed on the high Seas, and Offenses against the Law of Nations;

(11) To declare War, grant Letters of Marque and Reprisal, and make Rules concerning Captures on Land and Water;

(12) To raise and support Armies, but no Appropriation of Money to that Use shall be for a longer Term than two Years;

(13) To provide and maintain a Navy;

(14) To make Rules for the Government and Regulation of the land and naval Forces;

(15) To provide for calling forth the Militia to execute the Laws of the Union, suppress Insurrections and repel Invasions;

(16) To provide for organizing, arming, and disciplining, the Militia, and for governing such Part of them as may be employed in the Service of the United States, reserving to the States respectively, the Appointment of the Officers, and the Authority of training the Militia according to the discipline prescribed by Congress;

(17) To exercise exclusive Legislation in all Cases whatsoever, over such District (not exceeding ten Miles square) as may, by Cession of particular States, and the Acceptance of Congress, become the Seat of the Government of the United States, and to exercise like Authority over all Places purchased by the Consent of the Legislature of the State in which the Same shall be, for the Erection of Forts, Magazines, Arsenals, dock-Yards, and other needful Buildings;—And

(18) To make all Laws which shall be necessary and proper for carrying into Execution the foregoing Powers, and all other Powers vested by this Constitution in the Government of the United States, or in any Department or Officer thereof.

Section 9　(1) The Migration or Importation of such Persons as any of the States now existing shall think proper to admit, shall not be prohibited by the Congress prior to the Year one thousand eight hundred and eight, but a Tax or Duty may be imposed on such Importation, not exceeding ten dollars for each Person.

(2) The Privilege of the Writ of Habeas Corpus shall not be suspended unless when in Cases of Rebellion or Invasion the public Safety may require it.

(3) No Bill of Attainder or ex post facto Law shall be passed.

(4) No Capitation, or other direct, Tax shall be laid, unless in Proportion to the Census or Enumeration herein before directed to be taken.

(5) No Tax or Duty shall be laid on Articles exported from any State.

(6) No Preference shall be given by any Regulation of Commerce or Revenue to the Ports of one State over those of another; nor shall Vessels bound to, or from, one State, be obliged to enter, clear or pay Duties in another.

(7) No Money shall be drawn from the Treasury, but in Consequence of Appropriations made by Law; and a regular Statement and Account of the Receipts and Expenditures of all public Money shall be published from time to time.

(8) No Title of Nobility shall be granted by the United States: And no Person holding any Office of Profit or Trust under them, shall, without the Consent of the Congress, accept of any present, Emolument, Office, or Title, of any kind whatever, from any King, Prince or foreign State.

Section 10　(1) No State shall enter into any Treaty, Alliance, or Confederation; grant Letters of Marque and Reprisal; coin Money; emit Bills of Credit; make any Thing but gold and silver Coin a Tender in Payment of Debts; pass any Bill of Attainder, ex post facto Law, or Law impairing the Obligation of Contracts, or grant any Title of Nobility.

(2) No State shall, without the Consent of Congress, lay any Imposts or Duties on Imports or Exports, except what may be absolutely necessary for executing its inspection Laws: and the net Produce of all Duties and Imposts, laid by any State on Imports or Exports, shall be for the Use of the Treasury of the United States; and all such Laws shall be subject to the Revision and Control of the Congress.

(3) No State shall, without the Consent of Congress, lay any Duty of Tonnage, keep Troops, or Ships of War in time of Peace, enter into any Agreement or Compact with another State, or with a foreign Power, or engage in War, unless actually invaded, or in such imminent Danger as will not admit of Delay.

ARTICLE II

Section 1 (1) The executive Power shall be vested in a President of the United States of America. . . .

ARTICLE III

Section 1 The judicial Power of the United States, shall be vested in one supreme Court, and in such inferior Courts as the Congress may from time to time ordain and establish. The Judges, both of the supreme and inferior Courts, shall hold their Offices during good Behaviour, and shall, at stated Times, receive for their Services, a Compensation, which shall not be diminished during their Continuance in Office.

Section 2 (1) The judicial Power shall extend to all Cases, in Law and Equity, arising under this Constitution, the Laws of the United States, and Treaties made, or which shall be made, under their Authority;—to all Cases affecting Ambassadors, other public Ministers and Consuls;—to all Cases of admiralty and maritime Jurisdiction;—to Controversies to which the United States shall be a party;—to Controversies between two or more States;—between a State and Citizens of another State;—between Citizens of different States;—between Citizens of the same State claiming Lands under Grants of different States, and between a State, or the Citizens thereof, and foreign States, Citizens or Subjects.

. . .

(3) The Trial of all Crimes, except in Cases of Impeachment, shall be by Jury; and such Trial shall be held in the State where the said Crimes shall have been committed; but when not committed within any State, the Trial shall be at such Place or Places as the Congress may by Law have directed.

Section 3 (1) Treason against the United States, shall consist only in levying War against them, or in adhering to their Enemies, giving them Aid and Comfort. No Person shall be convicted of Treason unless on the Testimony of two Witnesses to the same overt Act, or on Confession in open Court.

(2) The Congress shall have Power to declare the Punishment of Treason, but no Attainder of Treason shall work Corruption of Blood, or Forfeiture except during the Life of the Person attainted.

ARTICLE IV

Section 1 Full Faith and Credit shall be given in each State to the public Acts, Records, and judicial Proceedings of every other State. And the Congress may by general Laws prescribe the Manner in which such Acts, Records and Proceedings shall be proved, and the Effect thereof.

Section 2 (1) The Citizens of each State shall be entitled to all privileges and Immunities of Citizens in the several States.

(2) A Person charged in any State with Treason, Felony, or other Crime, who shall flee from Justice, and be found in another State, shall on Demand of the executive Authority of the State from which he fled, be delivered up, to be removed to the State having Jurisdiction of the Crime.

. . .

ARTICLE VI

. . .

(2) This Constitution, and the Laws of the United States which shall be made in Pursuance thereof; and all Treaties made, or which shall be made, under the Authority of

the United States, shall be the supreme Law of the Land; and the Judges in every State shall be bound thereby, any Thing in the Constitution or Laws of any State to the Contrary notwithstanding.

. . .

AMENDMENT I (1791)

Congress shall make no law respecting an establishment of religion, or prohibiting the free exercise thereof; or abridging the freedom of speech, or of the press; or the right of the people peaceably to assemble, and to petition the Government for a redress of grievances.

AMENDMENT II (1791)

A well regulated Militia, being necessary to the security of a free state, the right of the people to keep and bear Arms, shall not be infringed.

AMENDMENT III (1791)

No Soldier shall, in time of peace be quartered in any house, without the consent of the Owner, nor in time of war, but in a manner to be prescribed by law.

AMENDMENT IV (1791)

The right of the people to be secure in their persons, houses, papers, and effects, against unreasonable searches and seizures, shall not be violated, and no Warrants shall issue, but upon probable cause, supported by Oath or affirmation, and particularly describing the place to be searched, and the persons or things to be seized.

AMENDMENT V (1791)

No person shall be held to answer for a capital, or otherwise infamous crime, unless on a presentment or indictment of a Grand Jury, except in cases arising in the land or naval forces, or in the Militia, when in actual service in time of War or public danger; nor shall any person be subject for the same offence to be twice put in jeopardy of life or limb; nor shall be compelled in any criminal case to be a witness against himself, nor be deprived of life, liberty, or property, without due process of law; nor shall private property be taken for public use, without just compensation.

AMENDMENT VI (1791)

In all criminal prosecutions, the accused shall enjoy the right to a speedy and public trial, by an impartial jury of the State and district wherein the crime shall have been committed, which district shall have been previously ascertained by law, and to be informed of the nature and cause of the accusation; to be confronted with the witnesses against him; to have compulsory process for obtaining witnesses in his favor, and to have the Assistance of Counsel for his defence.

AMENDMENT VII (1791)

In Suits at common law, where the value in controversy shall exceed twenty dollars, the right of trial by jury shall be preserved, and no fact tried by a jury, shall be otherwise re-examined in any Court of the United States, than according to the rules of the common law.

AMENDMENT VIII (1791)

Excessive bail shall not be required, nor excessive fines imposed, nor cruel and unusual punishments inflicted.

AMENDMENT IX (1791)

The enumeration in the Constitution, of certain rights, shall not be construed to deny or disparage others retained by the people.

AMENDMENT X (1791)

The powers not delegated to the United States by the Constitution, nor prohibited by it to the States, are reserved to the States respectively, or to the people.

. . .

AMENDMENT XIII (1865)

Section 1 Neither slavery nor involuntary servitude, except as a punishment for crime whereof the party shall have been duly convicted, shall exist within the United States, or any place subject to their jurisdiction.

Section 2 Congress shall have power to enforce this article by appropriate legislation.

AMENDMENT XIV (1868)

Section 1 All persons born or naturalized in the United States and subject to the jurisdiction thereof, are citizens of the United States and of the State wherein they reside. No State shall make or enforce any law which shall abridge the privileges or immunities of citizens of the United States; nor shall any State deprive any person of life, liberty, or property, without due process of law; nor deny to any person within its jurisdiction the equal protection of the laws.

. . .

AMENDMENT XV (1870)

Section 1 The right of citizens of the United States to vote shall not be denied or abridged by the United States or by any State on account of race, color, or previous condition of servitude.

. . .

AMENDMENT XVIII (1919)

Section 1 After one year from the ratification of this article the manufacture, sale, or transportation of intoxicating liquors within, the importation thereof into, or the exportation thereof from the United States and all territory subject to the jurisdiction thereof for beverage purposes is hereby prohibited.

Section 2 The Congress and the several States shall have concurrent power to enforce this article by appropriate legislation.

. . .

AMENDMENT XXI (1933)

Section 1 The eighteenth article of amendment to the Constitution of the United States is hereby repealed.

INDEX